Syllabus (in English) of the Documents Relating to England and Other Kingdoms Contained in the Collection Known as "Rymer's Foedera." Volume 1

SYLLABUS

(IN ENGLISH)

OF THE DOCUMENTS

RELATING TO

ENGLAND AND OTHER KINGDOMS

CONTAINED IN THE COLLECTION KNOWN AS

"RYMER'S FŒDERA."

BY

THOMAS DUFFUS HARDY,

DEPUTY KEEPER OF THE PUBLIC RECORDS

UNDER THE DIRECTION OF THE MASTER OF THE ROLLS, AND WITH THE SANCTION OF THE
LORDS COMMISSIONERS OF HER MAJESTY'S TREASURY

VOL. I.
1066—1377.

LONDON:
LONGMANS, GREEN, & Co.
1869.

A. 100789

CONTENTS.

a 2

PREFACE.

THIS Syllabus of "Rymer's Fœdera" has been undertaken by the direction of the Lords Commissioners of Her Majesty's Treasury, at the recommendation of Lord Romilly, Master of the Rolls

Before explaining the nature of the work, it will be expedient to lay before the reader a brief relation of the causes which led to the publication of the "Fœdera" itself.[1]

Anterior to the Restoration of Charles the Second, the transactions between England and Foreign Princes were deemed to be of too secret a nature to be revealed to the public   Though "they ought " to be of record and enrolled in the Chancery, to the end the sub- " ject may know, who be in amity with the King and who be not ; " who be enemies and can have no action here, and who in league " and may have actions personal here,[2] but letters and writings " concerning matters of State, which were not fit to be made " vulgar, were enrolled in the Wardrobe and not in the Chancery, " as leagues were and ought to be ,"[3] the mysteries of State were nevertheless strictly preserved and guarded with watchful jealousy. Even the offices in which they were deposited were viewed with some degree of awe, and the imposing name of "Treasuries" was conferred upon them, as if the documents themselves were a portion of the national wealth, which it would have been impolitic to exhibit to the eyes of the world. To have committed the secrets of government to the press without royal authority would have

The publication of State documents anciently regarded with great jealousy by the Executive.

---

[1] Fœdera, Conventiones, Litteræ, et cujuscunque generis acta publica, inter Reges Angliæ et alios quosvis Impera-tores, Reges, Pontifices, Principes vel Com-munitates , ab ineunte sæculo duodecimo viz ab anno 1101 ad nostra usque tempora habita aut tractata ; ex autographis, infra secretiores archivorum regiorum thesau-rarias, per multa sæcula reconditis fideliter exscripta in lucem missa de mandato Reginæ accurante Thoma Rymer ejusdem Serenissimæ Reginæ Historiographo

[2] 4 Inst 152

[3] 4 Inst. 132.

entailed severe punishment upon the offending person[1] Information relating to such transactions could only be communicated to the people by the special authority of the Crown.[2] Hence partly arose the restrictions formerly placed upon consulting the public muniments

The first treaty printed in England by authority

The practice of publishing treaties by authority seems to have been introduced by James the First The treaty with Spain, bearing date the 18th of August 1604, is perhaps the earliest that was committed to the Press[3] It was followed by the commercial treaty with France dated 24th of February 1605-6 ;[4] but the innovation thus begun does not appear to have been fully carried out, as the old system of proclamation was also occasionally continued,[5] and such reasons we find assigned for the publication of treaties, as indicate that they were printed only as a special favour[6]

Alteration in the feelings of people on this subject, consequent on the Civil War

During the Civil War a great alteration occurred in the feelings of the people with respect to this subject The two parties into which the nation was divided treated with each other like independent states, and by printed declarations, answers, proposals, and addresses, appealed by turns to the people as the judges and arbiters of their disputes. Thus the people were taught to take part in political questions of the highest moment, and the exclusive character

---

[1] In the suit of the Stationers' Company against Seymour, in the 29th year of the reign of Charles II, the Court held that " matters of State and things which con- " cern the Government were never left to " any man's liberty to print that would " —(1, Modern Reports 256-258.)

[2] Before the invention of printing, whenever the Crown had occasion to notify a fact to the public, it was proclaimed *vivâ voce* in the several counties by the sheriffs or others of the King's officers, who had written authority for their guidance. The proclamation was made according to the form determined upon by the Privy Council, and annexed to the Royal Commission —Fœd II 537. O E. The right of ordering proclamation was one of the *flores coronæ*, which no private individual could invade with impunity Even as late as the reign of Henry VIII, a gentleman of Northumberland was punished for announcing by proclamation that he was the executor of a person deceased, and was ready to pay his debts —Archæolog XXV 381.

Although the introduction of printing promoted the communication of information, yet it did not confer the right of publishing " State transactions ' The " new art " was taken under the care of the Government, and frequently used as a substitute for the ancient commission, but nothing short of royal authority could set the press in motion to proclaim matters of State —Mod. Reports, I 256

[3] Printed by Robert Barker Lond 4to n. d See " A Collection of Treaties by G Chambers " Pref p v

[4] Printed by Robert Barker, Lond 4to 1606

[5] Fœd XIX. 211.

[6] In a preface to the treaty of the 5th of November 1630, between England and Spain, it is stated that because the benefit of the reconciliation with Spain would consist in the renewal of commerce, therefore his Majesty had thought it expedient, " for the better encouragement and direc- " tion of merchants, that the articles of the " treaty should be published " —Lond. 1630 4to pref.

of matters of State was of necessity destroyed: in addition to which the Government was then too much occupied with domestic affairs to trouble itself with giving to the world its transactions with foreign powers.

Between the Restoration and the Revolution of 1688 all the public treaties to which Great Britain was a party were published by authority, both separately and in small collections, but no attempt was made towards the publication of any *general* collection, unless, indeed, something of the kind was contemplated when Joseph Williamson was empowered, by a Royal Warrant,[1] in 1669, to peruse and copy all treaties, leagues, or public acts which he should deem fit for the King's service. By virtue of this authority, Williamson formed a collection of such documents from the reign of Henry VIII. to that of Charles II; but there is no evidence to show what was the immediate purpose of his work; probably nothing more was intended by it than a repertory of precedents. By the direction of Lord Burleigh,[2] an earlier compilation had been made by Arthur Agarde in the sixteenth century, and Sir Julius Cæsar, when he was Chancellor of the Exchequer, ordered a treaty-book to be drawn up for his own use[3] It would therefore seem that these collections were formed solely for official purposes.[4]

Publication of treaties between the Restoration and the Revolution.

Williamson's and Agarde's compilations.

The four treaties of Breda[5] were printed by order of Charles II. in 1667, and proclamations were also made for publishing the peace on the same occasion. A collection, comprehending seventeen trea-

---

[1] The warrant, dated 5th March 1669, directs the Master of the Rolls to permit Mr. Williamson and any one employed by him to peruse and copy whatever treaties, leagues, commissions conducing thereto, or public grants, he or they should deem fit for the King's service The result was a Collection of Copies of Treaties from the reign of Henry VIII to that of Charles II, and of State Papers during the reign of the latter monarch Williamson's Collections are still preserved in the Public Record Office.

[2] It appears in the Proceedings of the Record Commission (printed, but not published), pp 278–279, that an original MS of Agarde's "Compendium Recordorum," dedicated to the first Earl of Salisbury, has been found at Hatfield House In the preface, Agarde states that it was commenced under the directions of Lord Burleigh in 1570, and that it had occupied him from that time to 1610.

[3] MS. Lansdown, No 137, contains an account and Catalogue of the Records in the King's Treasury at Westminster, dedicated to Sir Julius Cæsar in 1610 In the same Collection, No. 799, is a Catalogue of Treaties between 1286 and 1551, also drawn up by Agarde in 1612.

[4] Perhaps the earliest attempt to form a collection of treaties was in the compilation of the "Black Book" of the Exchequer, at the beginning of which are entered five Charters of Convention and four Papal Bulls. With a similar design, *Liber A.* and *Liber B.* (Muniment Books of the Exchequer) were evidently compiled.

[5] With reference to the treaties of Breda, there is extant in the Public Record Office a holograph letter of Matthew Prior, the poet, dated from the Hague, 15th October 1697, when he was secretary to the embassy at the treaty of Ryswick. It will be found in Appendix I

ties, beginning with the commercial treaty with Spain in 1667 and ending with the Algerine treaty in 1685, was printed by direction of Secretary Lord Sunderland in March 1685.

Publication of diplomatic instruments on the Continent Goldast's collections.

Although England had not as yet published any general collection of treaties, works of that nature were springing up on the Continent. The indefatigable Melchior Goldast has the credit of having led the way in the publication of ancient diplomatic instruments for Germany His multifarious compilations, printed principally at Frankfort, between the years 1607 and 1614, contain many State documents, mixed up with ecclesiastical constitutions and other papers of a more miscellaneous nature

Chifflet's collection.

In 1644, a small collection of diplomatic documents, confined exclusively to treaties between France and Spain, was compiled primarily for the use of the Spanish Plenipotentiaries at Munster, by Jean Jacques Chifflet, physician to Philip IV. of Spain, under the direction of the Spanish Governor of the Low Countries [1]

A French collection.

Another small collection, extending to treaties of all kinds to which France had been a party, was published at Amsterdam in 1650, and again in 1672

Leonard's Recueil.

A more important work, however, was in preparation. Frederic Leonard, whose name is creditably remembered as the printer of the Delphin Classics, was employed by the French Government, as " premier Imprimeur du Roi," to print the Treaty of Aix-la-Chapelle in 1668, and afterwards that of Nimeguen in 1678. Leonard, in consequence, formed the notion of publishing all the treaties made by France during that century. They appeared at different times as separate pamphlets in various types, and were sold singly or in a collected form, as his customers required   In this way he brought together as many treaties as sufficed to fill four quarto volumes, which were published at Paris in 1683. As his collections increased, Leonard became more alive to their practical importance, and, observing in what manner one treaty depended upon another, he determined to carry back his researches to the Treaty of Arras in 1435 , and to publish all the treaties between that year and the

---

[1] The treaties in the first edition, published at Antwerp in 1644, are ten in number, and range from A D 1526 to A D. 1611. A second edition was published in 1650 In the third edition, published in 1664, there is added the treaty between France and Spain, made in the Isle of Faisans on the 7th of November 1659 and commonly known as the Pyre-

nean treaty Copies of the third edition are found with the treaty of Aix la Chapelle of the 12th of May 1668, added at the end This little work is entitled to the honorable distinction of being the first direct collection of treaties , the precursor of a long series of useful, and some of them very magnificent volumes.

seventeenth century, to which his four volumes, already compiled, were confined. In ten years he had collected nearly three hundred treaties concluded between France and various European governments during the fifteenth and sixteenth centuries These were added to his previous collections, which now amounted to nearly six hundred documents. The whole was published in six quarto volumes at Paris in 1693, and a seventh was added in 1697[1] A dissertation, upon the uses of the collection, drawn up by Amelot de la Houssaie, was prefixed to the work.

Contemporaneous with Leonard's " *Recueil*," another work of the same character was published in two volumes quarto at Nuremberg in the year 1685, under the title of "Theatrum Pacis." The seventy treaties, ranging between 1647 and 1660, of which this collection is composed, are translated into German. A second edition appeared in 1702. *The "Theatrum Pacis."*

The spirit diffused by these publications extended itself into other countries. M. de Nessel, librarian to the Emperor Leopold at Vienna, meditated the idea of publishing the treaties of all nations from A D. 1400 to A D 1685. Failing, however, to attain that completeness at which he aimed, he published at Vienna in 1690 a catalogue of the documents intended to be included in his work, inviting the attention and aid of the literary world. It contains the titles of more than fifty treaties between England and various foreign states. *Nessel's Catalogue of Treaties.*

The diplomatic collection which immediately preceded "Rymer's Fœdera," and may almost be said to be its prototype, was the "Codex Juris Gentium Diplomaticus," of Godefrid William Leibnitz.[2] It was   ublished at Hanover in March 1693, only *Leibnitz's ' Codex Juris Gentium Diplomaticus" and his "Mantissa"*

---

[1] It may be stated here that Leonard's collection contains many documents relating to England, which do not occur in the "Fœdera." A list of them will be found in the Appendix to the next volume. With all its imperfections, Leonard's *Recueil* deserves to be regarded as a work of great importance in the history of diplomatic literature, and especially as a most honourable proof of the indefatigable diligence of its compiler.

[2] In his letter dated 1 March 1693, prefixed to his preface of the "Codex " Juris Gentium Diplomaticus," he writes, " Cæterum Codex iste non Germanicis tan- " tum aut alterius populi rebus astringitur, " sed pleraque Europæa attingit nec tan-

" tum pacificationum tabulas et fœdera, " aliave, quæ vulgo Tractatuum nomine " censentur , sed et contractus matrimo- " niales Principum, testamenta, adoptiones, " varias obligationes, pacta, conventa et " alienationes ; uniones territoriorum, li- " mitum designationes , commerciorum, " navigationum, et in eam rem initarum " societatum articulos , recessus conven- " tuum publicorum, edicta rem publicam " afficientia ac leges fundamentales ; at- " que etiam nonnulla Conciliorum gene- " ralium acta singularia, concordata natio- " num, aliaque ad rem publicam Christiana- " rum gentium pertinentia , tum arbitraria " vel lauda, et res judicatas ; belli denun- " ciationes vel diffidationes, protestationes,

a few months before the "Fœdera" was projected. The influence it exercised over the English editor will be noticed hereafter. The compilation of Leibnitz, taken in conjunction with the "Mantissa,"[1] which he subsequently published, comprehends treaties and other "*Acta publica*" from the end of the eleventh to the end of the fifteenth century. Leibnitz, like De Nessel, regarded his collections as a contribution to that literature from which the science of the diplomatist and the law of nations were to be gathered, rather than as furnishing materials for history. He has, however, in his preface to the "Mantissa,"[2] dwelt upon the use of diplomatic instruments for the latter purpose, in a manner which proves that he was fully alive to the subject, never forgetting, however, that its prime use was as a "Codex Juris Gentium," for the statesman and practical lawyer.

Moetjens'Dutch collection.

Simultaneously with the appearance of the "Codex Juris Gentium," if not before its actual publication, Adrian Moetjens, a bookseller at the Hague, in conjunction with other publishers, projected a Dutch Collection of Treaties, in which he designed to incorporate such diplomatic documents as had ever been published in any part of Europe.[3]

" expostulationes, rerum repitationes et
" fecialia manifesta , confiscationes, des-
" titutiones, depositiones , et contra elec-
" tiones, hominia, investituras, cæremonia-
" rum solennia, dispensationes, privilegia
" majora, aureasque et plumbeas bullas
" ad rem facientes , creationes quoque
" novarum dignitatum ac principatuum
" quin et regnorum erectiones, aliaque id
" genus plura continebit "

[1] Mantissa Codicis Juris Gentium Diplomatici Godefridi Guilielmi Leibnitii —(Ed 1747. præf p 14.)

[2] In his preface to the "Mantissa," Leibnitz gives the following account of the success of the "Codex Juris Gentium " Diplomaticus "—" Anni sunt septem, " quod specimen edidi majoris operis, quo " *Acta publica juris Gentium* selecta, et ut " verbo dicam, *Diplomata majora* collige- " rentur . unde *Codicem Juris Gentium*, " eumque *Diplomaticum* appellavi Cum " enim Gehtes nulla superiore in terris " potestate contineantur, sunt illis pro " legibus, quas ipsi dixere , vel tabulis " vel moribus introductis, qui sæpe scrip- " turis istis comprobantur Gratenter " accepta est passim voluntas bene merendi " mea à viris doctis et in republica ver-

" satis, ipsisque etiam prohata Regibus,
" Principibus, et rerum administris Itaque,
" ex Archivo Angliæ Regio, Septentrione
" etiam et Gallia, Italiaque submissa sunt
" non pauca , et in Germania potissimum,
" Serenissimus ac Potentissimus Princeps
" Elector Brandenburgicus instituto favit "

[3] We learn, from the very interesting preface to this work, that the community of booksellers derived considerable assistance, and procured copies of scarce diplomatic instruments, from various persons engaged in what appears to have been at that time a favourite occupation—collecting and indexing treaties. The "Recueil " of Leonard, the "Codex" of Leibnitz, and upwards of fifty other publications, were examined, and after many years of preparation the booksellers obtained the materials for their comprehensive work It was published at Amsterdam and the Hague in 1700, in four folio volumes. The arrangement of the articles, the titles, and the preface, were the work of Jaques Bernard, a French Protestant exile, who had edited several works connected with diplomatic literature He afterwards held a professorship at Leyden, and was for a time editor of the " Nouvelles de la republique des Lettres '

The great avidity with which collections of this kind were sought for at the close of the seventeenth century, and the popularity of such publications, undoubtedly had a share in the production of the English "Fœdera." In one year Leonard published his *Recueil* at Paris, Leibnitz his *Codex* at Hanover, Moetjens had issued his prospectus, and De Nessel was forming his collections at Vienna. Such being the condition of diplomatic literature upon the Continent in 1693, it was scarcely possible for England, with her vast stores of muniments, to have remained uninfluenced by such examples. She did not continue long passive, but took steps to place herself on a par at least with the other kingdoms of Europe

The diplomatic collections on the continent led to the publication of the Fœdera.

Before I inquire what were the measures adopted by England to place herself in this position by the publication of the "Fœdera," it is essential to notice an error on the subject into which Dr Adam Clarke, the principal editor of the latest edition of the "Fœdera," has been led by Sir Joseph Ayloffe [1]

Origin of the Fœdera erroneously attributed to Harley by Ayloffe.

According to Ayloffe's statement, attributed by Dr. Clarke to Thomas Astle, keeper of the Tower Records,[2] it appears "that "Mr Harley, afterwards Earl of Oxford, soon after the accession of

---

The materials, however, of this new "Re-"cueil," were collected solely by the book-sellers, and Bernard's name did not appear upon it The work professes to range from the Nativity to the period of publication, but no treaty occurs earlier than A D. 536 The first volume contains documents be-tween that period and A.D. 1500 The second, to which is prefixed the introduction written by Amelot de la Houssaie for Leo-nard's "Recueil," extends from A.D 1500 to 1600 The third volume comes down to A D. 1660, and the fourth to A D 1700 This work, which unquestionably excels its predecessors, as well in completeness as in style and manner of its execution, sold rapidly, and within a few years became so scarce that copies of it which occurred at auctions produced as much as 150 florins The booksellers, consequently, soon began to prepare for a new edition They procured the editorial assistance of M Dumont, the Imperial Historiographer, who was enabled to incorporate many new documents from the Imperial Archives, the Royal Library at Berlin, and his own col-lections during fifteen years He also took advantage of the various diplomatic works which had appeared since the publication of the Dutch "Recueil," and "*surtout des*

"*actes de Rymer*" Thus was laid the foundation of the "Corps Universal Diplo-matique du droit des gens," published at Amsterdam and the Hague in 14 volumes folio, afterwards increased by six supple-mentary volumes edited by Barbeyrac, and continued by the "Recueil" of Rousset in 21 volumes 8vo These works were all published subsequently to the appearance of the Fœdera, but they had their origin in undertakings conceived, if not commenced, about the same period as our own collection

[1] The "Introduction" to the Calendars of the Ancient Charters, &c, published anonymously in 1772, and under the name of Ayloffe in 1774, is said to have been written by Thomas Astle.

[2] Although Astle has the credit of having written the Introduction to the Calendars of the Ancient Charters, pub-lished anonymously in 1772, and after-wards under the name of Sir Joseph Ayloffe in 1774, yet in Astle's letter to a select committee of the House of Lords, dated 1st December 1788, he makes no allusion to the statement about Harley He writes thus, "My Lords, your Lordships "having been pleased on the 12th inst. to "ask my opinion concerning the accuracy "of the Fœdera by Rymer and Sanderson,

" King William and Queen Mary to the throne, formed a plan for
" printing, at the public expense, all the leagues, treaties, alliances,
" capitulations, and confederacies which had at any time been made
" between the Crown of England and other kingdoms, princes, and
" states, intermixed with such instruments and papers of State as
" either more immediately related to them, or were curious and
" useful in illustrating the English History.   He communicated
" this design to the Earl of Halifax,[1] who laid the same before the
" Queen (the King being then with his army in Flanders), who
" was pleased to approve of it, and to appoint Mr Rymer,
" Historiographer Royal, to carry the design into execution."
Mr. Harley's interference in this matter may be questioned, for no
evidence of it exists, except Ayloffe's allegation, made nearly a
century after the publication of the " Fœdera " was first projected.

But there is other evidence for supposing that Ayloffe was mistaken

Halifax and
Somers the
originators of
the Fœdera.

Madox, the author of the "History of the Exchequer," in his
Epistolary Dissertation, written in the year 1708, and prefixed to
the "Ancient Dialogue on the Exchequer," enumerated among the
reasons which induced him to dedicate his work to Lord Halifax

---

" and conceiving it to be my duty to pay
" attention to any question coming from
" your Lordships, I desire permission to lay
" before the committee what has since oc-
" curred to me, and what I have been able
" to collect concerning the reputation of the
" editors of this work, as well as the work
" itself   I find that in the year 1692
" Mr Rymer was appointed Historiogra-
" pher to King William , his first warrant,
" empowering him to search the Public
" Records for the materials which compose
" the Fœdera, is dated 26 August 1693
" His authorities were renewed by warrant
" from Queen Anne, dated May 3rd, 1707,
" when Mr Sanderson was joined with
" him in the undertaking   Mr Rymer
" died Dec 14th, 1713   He was esteemed
" a man of considerable learning, and is
" generally allowed to have been an
" excellent antiquary and historian   After
" his death, Mr Sanderson continued to
" add to the collection, &c.
    " I beg leave to acquaint your Lordships
" that for a course of twenty-five years
" and upwards I have had frequent
" occasion to consult the Fœdera, which I
" have considered as a work of authority "
    There is not, it will be observed, the

slightest reference here to "Harley's Plan,"
nor any allusion to the want of correctness
of the Fœdera, both of which points are
brought prominently forward in the Introduction to the " Calendars of the Ancient
Charters" ascribed to Astle
    [1] Astle has here committed a slight
anachronism, Charles Montague was not
created Baron Halifax until 13th Dec.
1700, and Earl of Halifax on the 19th of
Oct 1714
    Charles Montague, born on the 16th of
April 1661, was the son of the Honorable
George Montague   He was educated at
Westminster, and chosen King's scholar in
1677.   At school he contracted a more
than ordinary degree of friendship with
Mr George Stepney, whose name is connected with Rymer and Leibnitz.   The
two friends went to Trinity College, Cambridge, together, where they encouraged
each other in their love of poetry   Montague was a fellow of Trinity in 1684, and
his verses on the death of Charles the
Second attracted the attention of the
Earl of Dorset, who invited him to
London   George Stepney, who had also
written on the same subject, was also invited, but declined the invitation out of

the part taken by his Lordship in promoting the publication of the
" Fœdera." [1]

This statement of Madox is confirmed by Dr. White Kennet,
afterwards Bishop of Peterborough [2]

A third witness to the origin of the work is Dr Edmund Calamy,
author of the " Lives of the Nonconformists," and who, mixing a
great deal with the literary men of the period, had ample opportunities of knowing the truth. [3]

---

love of a retired life In 1688 Montague
signed the invitation to the Prince of
Orange to come over to England. He purchased the place of one of the clerks of the
Council, and not long afterwards the Earl of
Dorset, who had been made Lord Chamberlain, introduced him to the King, with
whom he soon became a favorite In
1688–9 he was made one of the commissioners of the Treasury, and during his
Majesty's absence from the Kingdom in
1698, being then first commissioner, he
was appointed one of the Lords Justices
of England. He was created a Peer on
the 13th of December 1700, by the title of
Baron of Halifax, and Earl of Halifax on
the accession of George the First He died
on the 15th of May 1715 There is a portrait of Montague in the Combination Room
of Trinity College, Cambridge.

[1] Speciatim vero, hoc potissimum nomine
a me celebrandus es, quod nempe Histo-
ricen Scientiamque Antiquariam promovere
curasti Baro Somers ac Turpse, pro ea
qua apud Dominos Wilhelmum et Mariam
pridem Regem et Reginam Angliæ felicis
memoriæ valuistis gratia, auctores fuistis
ut jussu Regio inchoaretur præclarum illud
opus colligendi et in lucem emittendi
Fœdera, Conventa et Acta Publica, quot-
quot uspiam in Archivis reperiri poterant,
quæ inter Anglorum Reges et Exteros Reges
atque Respublicas, per aliquot præterita
secula intercesserunt Quod quidem opus
gratia Serenissimæ Reginæ Annæ etiam
num ut cunque pergit.

[2] In his second letter to Nicolson,
Bishop of Carlisle, ' on the subject of
Bishop Merks (8vo. Lond 1716), he
there notices a charge brought against
Rymer of having suppressed certain documents to suit party purposes. He says—
" My blood was a little quick at this para-
" graph Surely thought I, if the writer
" could not spare the Times, nor the
" adverse party, yet he might have spared

" Mr Thomas Rymer, and not have made
" the honest man such a tool as to pick
" out the instruments that made for the
" present Civil Government to be published,
" while he suppressed the most material
" relating to the interest of the church and
" clergy Your Lordship has had great
" opportunities to know the truth of that
" matter, and I think you can better relate
" it to this effect, that in the happy and
" victorious part of the Queen's reign
" some of the prime ministers, especially
" the Lords Somers and Halifax, assisted
" by the Bishops of Canterbury, Sarum,
" and Norwich, (nor was your Lordship
" wanting,) did consult of a better way to
" preserve the records in the Tower, did
" move it in the House of Peers, and had
" a standing committee appointed for it,
" who from time to time came to several
" resolutions for searching out and digest-
" ing the original rolls and papers, for
" providing and framing a better repository
" for them, for committing them to a safer
" custody, and for securing an easier access
" to them It was under the influence of
" this public spirit that it was thought it
" would be a benefit and credit to the
" nation to print and publish a collection
" (in order of time) of authentic copies
" of the original instruments more espe-
" cially relating to peace and war treaties,
" articles and other intercourse with foreign
" states and princes Mr Rymer, as
" Historiographer Royal, was appointed
" to collect them, and Mr Churchill to
" print them, upon the public account, and
" (which was pity) in too small a number
" of copies, for presents only and public
" respect, not for common sale Mr Rymer
" was obliged to trust to other hands, not
" only in the transcribing, but in the
" selecting of materials for them. When
" he came to review them in the single
" sheets he threw by several of them "

[3] In his historical account of his own

But the testimony of Leibnitz, whose connexion with the House of Hanover and with many Englishmen gave him means of accurate information on such a subject as this, puts the question beyond dispute. He was a literary friend and correspondent of Rymer, was personally acquainted with Lord Halifax, was intimate with his most familiar friend Stepney,[1] and took, as will hereafter appear, great interest in Rymer's work. Among some of his memoranda upon literary subjects we find the following. "Promovit " quidem editionem actorum publicorum Anglicanorum Rymeri " Halifax, primus Gazophylacii commissarius; sumtus autem ex " ærario publico facti sunt."[2]

In another place Leibnitz writes to the effect that Lord Halifax, first Commissioner of the Treasury, certainly forwarded Rymer's " Acta Publica Anglicana," but the cost was defrayed by the public.[3]

The testimony of these writers may be thought to go no farther than that Lord Somers[4] and Lord Halifax were great promoters of

---

life he writes, 'At this troublesome time " was a foundation laid for the noble col- " lection of Rymer's Fœdera, a work so " useful to the English History, containing " a collection of all the leagues, treaties, " alliances, capitulations, and confederacies " at any time made between the Crown " of England and any other kingdoms, " princes, and states, &c For the per- " fecting which Queen Mary signed an " order, bearing date August 26th, 1693, " which gave him free access to search " the Records in the Tower, the Rolls, " the Augmentation Office, the Exchequer, " the Journals of Parliament, and the " Paper Office, and to transcribe what " was for his purpose, without paying any ' fees, &c Of this noble work, as well " as that of digesting the Records and " Archives of the Kingdom, that would " otherwise have lain in dust and oblivion, " into a proper order, the first promoter " was Charles Earl of Halifax Upon " that account, as well as several others, " his name is to be mentioned with " honour ' Dr Calamy's History of his Life and Times, i 319

[1] Speaking of those who had assisted him, Leibnitz thus mentions Rymer, who had been introduced to him by George Stepney " Hoc autem præstitit imprimis conciliata " mihi benevolentia V Cl. Thomæ Rymeri " in lucem proferendis Angliæ tabulis Regio " jussu destinati, de quo mox plura dicam ' Again, speaking of Rymer, he says that

he had printed the title of his intended work . "Sed et Th Rymerus supra laudatus " Pandectis Anglicanarum Tabularum jam " titulum in typos præire jussit "

[2] Opera Omnia Edit 1786, v 191.

[3] Es hat my Lord Halifax, erster commissarius von der Schatzkammer zwar des Herrn Rymers Acta Publica Anglicana befordert, die Kosten aber sind auch Publico dazu hergeschossen worden Es wird auch das werk nach Herrn Rymers Tode fortgesetzet (Leibnitz Deutsche Schriften Guhrauer, Berlin 1838, vol ii , p 487.)

[4] John Somers was born at Worcester about the year 1651 The exact date cannot be ascertained, as no register of his birth has been discovered He was the son of John Somers, a successful attorney in that city, and Catherine Ceavern, of a respectable family in Shropshire. He received the earlier part of his education under Dr Bright at the college school at Worcester, and was matriculated and admitted at Trinity College, Oxford, on the 23rd March 1667-8, when he was only sixteen years of age He left the University without taking a degree, and became clerk to his father He continued in that capacity up to 24th May 1669, when he was entered as a student of the Middle Temple, and became a pupil of Sir Francis Winnington Feeling dissatisfied with his defective education, he returned to Oxford in the year 1674, being then in the 24th year of his age, but still keeping his

the work, leaving untouched the question of its having originated with them or with any other person. The next statement bears directly upon that point. It proceeds from Le Clerc, a man thoroughly conversant with the European literature of his time.

Le Clerc received from Lord Halifax copies of the volumes of the Fœdera as they were published;[1] and by a series of articles in his "Bibliotheques" made known the value of the work. The first of these articles, written by himself, and published at Amsterdam in the 16th volume of the "Bibliotheque Choisie," contains information of importance to the present purpose. After praising highly the enlarged views of the Government which had carried out an undertaking of such magnitude, under the pressure of an expensive war, he acknowledges his obligations to Lord Halifax, " dont le merite est connu de tout le monde, non seulement " en Angleterre, mais encore deça la mer" Then, cursorily commenting on the contents of the first volume, he finds himself, at the close of his remarks, on the verge of a metaphysical discussion, and suddenly breaks off thus: "Je ne veux pas m'engager dans ce " sujet, qui est da plus grande étendere que bien des gens ne " pensent, en finissant cet extrait. Il vaut mieux avertir le public, " qu'il a l'obligation du prémier dessein de ce Recueil à my lord " Halifax et à my lord Sommers, qui l'ont aussi soutenu depuis."[2]

---

terms at the Middle Temple On the 5th of May 1676 he was called to the bar Having mastered the common law under Winnington, he devoted himself to the civil law and the study of modern languages In the beginning of May 1689 he was made Solicitor General, and on the 2nd of May 1692 Attorney General On the 23rd March following he became Lord Keeper of the Great Seal, and on the 22nd April 1697 was created Lord Chancellor, and called to the Peerage by the title of Lord Somers, Baron of Evesham. That he omitted no opportunity of continuing and improving his acquaintance with constitutional studies may be inferred from his expending the large sum of 700l. in procuring records and precedents upon which to found his judgment in the celebrated Bankers case In this judgment he stated "that he had " caused the 'Liberate' Rolls and the " bundles of petitions at the Tower to be " searched from the beginning of King " John's time as low as the records there " go, and had some extracts made from " them " The whole judgment shows a most intimate acquaintance with Records.

His private papers, which would probably have thrown light upon the origin of the Fœdera as well as upon many other important transactions, were unfortunately lost to the world in the year 1752, having been destroyed in the fire which consumed the Chambers of the Honorable Charles Yorke, No 10, New Square, Lincoln's Inn, and out of sixty volumes quarto a few mutilated fragments only being saved Lord Somers was removed from the Chancellorship in April 1700, impeached by the House of Commons in 1701, and acquitted by the Lords. He died on the 26th of April 1716, and was buried in the parish church of North Mymms Lord Campbell does not seem to have been aware of the active interest taken by Lord Somers in the Fœdera

[1] In the Appendix XXV will be found a list of the several persons to whom the Government presented copies of the Fœdera Lord Halifax had thirteen copies, a fact which certainly adds to the probability of his being the instigator of the work.

[2] Bibl Choisie, xvi. p. 60, Edit 1726.

To these testimonies may be added that of a writer whose means of information were not less accurate than those of the persons already mentioned, Peter des Maizeaux, the friend and correspondent of Bayle, who was in London during the whole period of the publication of the " Fœdera," and entertained a design of compiling an Historical Dictionary after the manner of Bayle. Among his collections, now in the British Museum, is an unfinished life of Rymer, in which the following passage is found in allusion to the "Fœdera"; "Ce Recueil, qui fait tant d'honneur à l'Angleterre, " avoit eté projetté par deux des plus grands hommes de nostre " siecle, my Lord Somers et my Lord Halifax   Le Public leur " en est redevable "[1]

Thus, with some few discrepancies, Madox, Kennet, Le Clerc, and Des Maizeaux concur in attributing the publication to Lord Somers and Lord Halifax jointly , and the words of Calamy and Leibnitz by no means exclude the subsequent co-operation of Lord Somers. They merely seem to attribute the original notion to Lord Halifax [2]

That these facts were unknown to Sir Joseph Ayloffe or Thomas Astle is not surprising, because much of the evidence that is now extant was not at that time to be obtained. The like excuse, however, cannot be extended to Dr Adam Clark. He was especially directed to inquire into the origin of the "Fœdera," and he wrote two or three elaborate reports on the subject; in each of which he gives the whole credit of the design to Robert Harley, by whom, he states, it was communicated to Lord Halifax. It is difficult to account for Harley's supposed connexion with the work; but the proof is ample that he is not entitled to this honour.[3]   We have the direct assertion of Madox in the year 1708,—while Harley

[1] The sketch of the life of Rymer is to be found in the volume of Biographical Collections of Dr. Thomas Birch, now in the British Museum (MS Addit No 4423, f 161) It is proved to be the handwriting of Des Maizeaux by comparison with some of his letters in one of the Harleian MSS

[2] Another testimony, though not quite contemporaneous, yet earlier than the allegation which occurs in Sir Joseph Ayloffe's Preface, may be added to the foregoing It is that of Tindal, the translator of Rapin's History of England, in 1743   In his preface he says, " However, when he " came to the reign of Henry II , he was " on the point of relinquishing his work, " of which the beginning gave him no

" encouragement, when an unexpected " assistance not only induced him to " continue it, but also to form the project " of a much larger history than what he " at first intended This assistance was " Rymer's Fœdera, communicated to our " author by the famous Le Clerc, to whom, " being then publishing at the Government " charge, the volumes were sent by the " Lord Halifax, a great promoter of that " noble work "

[3] The origin of attributing the scheme to Harley may have arisen from the fact that he was Lord Treasurer of Great Britain when Rymer died, and nominated Sanderson to continue the work

was Speaker of the House of Commons, and at the same time one of the Principal Secretaries of State, and when Rymer was in the plenitude of his reputation, having published six volumes of his work,—that Halifax and Somers were the authors of the scheme for collecting and publishing the national Acts of this Realm. If Harley, then, had had any connexion with the first suggestion of the publication or of projecting the plan, surely Madox would have made some allusion to him; Rymer too, who was intimately acquainted with Madox, would not have remained silent

Other circumstances tend to show that Harley was not in any way a party to this publication.

(I.) At the time the "Fœdera" was first undertaken he was a member of the House of Commons, in direct opposition to the Government, of which Somers and Montague were members: Somers being then Attorney-General and Montague one of the Commissioners of the Treasury.

(II) No contemporary writer, so far as it is at present known, ever asserted that Harley had a share in the origin of that work, nor is it claimed for him in any published biography, or in the one written by Dr. Zachary Gray which remains in manuscript;[1] nor has anything been found respecting it among the Harleian MSS. in the British Museum.

(III.) In the Biography of Montague, printed in the year 1715, it is positively stated that he was the first promoter of "Rymer's Fœdera,"[2] and, as far as Somers is more immediately concerned, a personal dislike appears to have existed between him and Harley[3]

Under all these circumstances, it is clear that the assertion of Ayloffe, made eighty years after the event, is not sufficient to outweigh the previous statement of contemporary persons.

Whether or not Rymer suggested the "Fœdera" to Somers

---

[1] See Nichols's Literary Anecdotes, ii. 547. This book is now in the possession of Mr John Gough Nichols, and was carefully examined by my friend Mr. John Bruce, who assures me of the fact

[2] The Works and Life of the Right Honourable Charles late Earl of Halifax, including the History of his Lordship's Times London, 1715.

In the dedication to George Earl of Halifax, the author says of Earl Charles —
"His singular goodwill to posterity, "in being the first promoter of Rymer's "Fœdera, and of digesting the records and "archives of the kingdom, that would "otherwise have lain in dust and oblivion, "into a proper order"

[3] In the Life of Somers, 8vo, 1716, p. 119, is mentioned the very rough answer which is reported to have been given by Lord Somers to a person who advised him to be upon friendly terms with Harley. In the additional MSS. in the British Museum (No 4244, p 84), in a paper containing various characters founded upon original letters of Somers and others, it is stated that Harley was the restless and avowed enemy of Somers

and Montague there is no evidence to prove; but there is no reason to suppose that the work was designed by Rymer. Neither his social position nor his reputation as an author would have given any weight to a proposition of such magnitude and importance coming from him. The character of the " Fœdera " very much increases the probability of its having originated with some one of great power and influence An extensive publication of the national records for purposes principally historical, the open promulgation of many thousands of documents previously kept under close and jealous guardianship, was a project so directly opposed to what had been the practice of the Government of England, as to be extremely unlikely to be contemplated by any one whose official or personal authority could not be brought to bear upon the difficulties with which it was surrounded. In every point of view in which the work can be regarded, whether in its origin or the royal manner in which it was published and circulated, it seems to have been entirely an undertaking of the Government, brought about by persons of great influence at Court, and possessing a thorough knowledge of history and love of literature; in both of which essentials Somers and Montague were conspicuous

The new work entrusted to Rymer, then Historiographer Royal

The first step taken, after the work was determined upon, was to select an editor   The office of Historiographer Royal, which had been filled successively by James Howell, Sir William Davenant, John Dryden, and Thomas Shadwell, was then held by Thomas Rymer The duties of that office have never been very clearly defined , but when a work of the character of the Fœdera was to be undertaken at the public expense, the materials for which were to be obtained from among those documents which constitute the most important part of historical literature, the Historiographer Royal seemed to possess something like an official right to have its execution confided to him   This was doubtless the reason for the selection of Rymer, and we do not find that he hesitated to undertake the work. It may be interesting to my readers to learn what were the motives that first directed Rymer's attention to a subject so diametrically opposite to that which had engaged his thoughts in the earlier part of his career   His contemporaries suffered him to pass away without any biographical memorial[1] Neither Sanderson, who con-

---

[1] MS Lansd No 987 professes to contain a memoir of Rymer by White Kennett, but the article is nothing more than a few memoranda relating to him, excerpted from the Life of Mr John Kettlewell by Dr George Hickes, which will be more fully noticed presently

tinued his work, nor Holmes, who edited the second edition of the Fœdera, threw any light upon his character or history, and later writers of English Biography, prejudiced against him for his daring dramatic criticisms, have made no attempts to repair this neglect

Thomas Rymer was a younger son of Mr Ralph Rymer,[1] a man of considerable substance and of some notoriety in his day   Lord Clarendon[2] describes him " as possessed of a good estate," and " of " the quality of the better sort of grand jury men , he was esteemed " a wise man, and was known to be trusted by the greatest men " who had been in rebellion"   He was lord of the manor of Brafferton in Yorkshire, and possessor of other property in the same county.   Being a Roundhead of inflexible pertinacity, he enjoyed the confidence of the ruling powers of the Commonwealth, by whom he was appointed treasurer of the district in which he resided.   Before the commencement of the royal troubles, he held an estate in Yafforth and Wickmore in Yorkshire of Sir Edward Osborne, Bart , at an annual rent of 200*l*   Sir Edward, being a determined royalist, had his estates sequestrated, and Ralph Rymer became proprietor of the lands which he had previously occupied as tenant

Some account of Rymer and his family

At the Restoration he was compelled to give up, not only this property, but also a great deal more, which it was alleged he wrongfully enjoyed.

Sir Thomas Osborne, son of Sir Edward, petitioned the King on the 21st April 1663 to have his lands restored, which had been sequestrated and were in the possession of Ralph Rymer[3]   The petition was referred to the Lord High Treasurer, who thereupon reported to the King " that the petitioner and his father had been " eminently loyal in the service of the Crown, and that Mr. Rymer " deserves a very contrary character"   Thus compelled to make restoration, Rymer entered into a conspiracy, and joined the " Presbyterian Rising" in the autumn of 1663.

The professed object of the conspiracy was to get rid of the payment of subsidies and excise ; to re-establish a gospel magistracy and ministry ; to restore the Long Parliament , and to curb the

---

[1] In all probability Ralph Rymer was the son of John Rymer, and was baptised at Northallerton on the 9th of September 1601.

[2] See Life of Edward, Earl of Clarendon, Oxford 1759   Continuation, p 416
[3] See Appendix II

gentry, lawyers, and clergy. The night of the 12th of October witnessed the commencement and termination of this ill-devised plot The insurgents were vigorously attacked and completely routed and the ringleaders captured.

On the 7th of January 1664 a commission[1] was issued to try the conspirators for high treason, and twenty-two[2] were condemned to be drawn, hanged, and quartered at York

Ralph Rymer,[3] senior, was among the number[4] and ended his life on the scaffold Many others were kept in prison. One of these was Ralph Rymer, his eldest son, who, on the 25th of July following, was sentenced to imprisonment for his life in York Castle, with forfeiture of all his goods and lands. By a long and close durance he was reduced to such a weak condition that he excited the compassion of the high sheriff and deputy lieutenants of the county, who forwarded his petition to the King that he might be liberated on bail On the 15th of May 1666, after nearly three years of ignominious confinement, the high sheriff and three of the deputy lieutenants of Yorkshire certify to the King "that Ralph " Rymer, now a prisoner in the castle of York, is weak in body, " being both hydropical and consumptive, and that they cannot " apprehend him to be a man able to continue long in that air and " durance "[5]

His Majesty compassionated the prisoner, and allowed him to go at large upon bond on the 16th of July following,[6] Sir Robert Strickland, Sir Thomas Strickland, Sir Jordan Crosland, and Sir Richard Graham, being his sureties

Educated at Northallerton. But to return to Thomas Rymer He was born probably at the house called "The Hall" in the little village of Yafforth,[7] and was

---

[1] The commissioners were Sir Christopher Turnor, Baron of the Exchequer, Sir John Kelyng, Justice of the King's Bench, and Sir John Archer, Justice of the Common Pleas

[2] Mr Secretary Bennet, in a letter to the Duke of Ormond, dated 20th of January 1664, writes, "Our letters from York tell " us the judges have found fifteen guilty, " and this, by the proof of two witnesses " against each of them, as well as their " own confessions, so that by the next, I " suppose, we shall send your Grace the " sentence and execution of at least so " many" The Rev James Raine of York has, however, discovered and printed in Vol 40 of the Surtees Society, a very

curious document, giving the names of twenty-two, not fifteen, persons who suffered at York for this conspiracy.

[3] See Appendix III.

[4] See Appendix IV.

[5] See Appendix V.

[6] See Appendix VI

[7] The "Diary of Ralph Thoresby," edited by the late Mr Joseph Hunter, vol. ii., p 24, gives Yafforth Hall as the place of Thomas Rymer's birth, but Mr. Ingledew, in his History of Northallerton, p. 288, states that Rymer was born at Appleton-upon-Wisk in 1638. I have not been able to settle this disputed point, as the baptismal registers for Yafforth do not commence until 1673, and those of Great Smeaton

educated at a private school kept by Thomas Smelt, at Danby Wisk. One of his schoolfellows was the celebrated Dr. George Hickes, who states that Rymer was "a great favorite of his master," and, at the time when he wrote, was very learned and ingenious, "and " well known for his great critical skill in human learning, especially " in poetry and history." Thomas Burnet, Master of the Charter House, and Dr Radcliffe, the celebrated physician, also were pupils of Mr. Smelt.

Smelt was a loyalist; and although he endeavoured during the civil war and the usurpation to conceal his principles, there were occasions upon which they would discover themselves even in the school. "North Allerton," remarks Dr Hickes, "is a " noted thoroughfare on the northern road, through which part of " the army of those times, both horse and foot, did often march ; " and we observed that as soon as he heard the sound of drum " or trumpet his countenance did always fall, and it usually " was a good while before he could recollect himself and reform " his disordered looks The officers of the army would some- " times come to beg play-days, but he would never grant it ; " and once, one of Cromwell's great commanders, whose name I " have forgot, lying in the town, he sent one of his officers in his " name to beg a play-day, but as I remember he would not grant " it, and this coming to the knowledge of the boys who went to " petition the major-general to make that request unto him, he " chastised them in a most severe manner, and had like to have " turned them out of the school. I remember when we read " Justin's History he made many reflections upon Agathocles, which " he intended we should understand of the Protector, insomuch " that, being a young scholar at Oxford when the life of Agatho- " cles came out, without the author's name, I could not but think " it had been written by some that had been his scholar before my " time. When we came to read Homer, he would take occasion

---

(in which parish Appleton-upon-Wisk is situate) until 1650. The date of 1636, however, must be incorrect, inasmuch as the entry in the Sidney College book shows that Thomas Rymer was 17 years old in 1658, and therefore must have been born early in 1641 I am informed, through the medium of Mr. W T Jefferson, of Northal- lerton, that, " the first Thomas Rymer that

" occurs in the book of baptisms of Apple- " ton Wisk was baptized in 1679, and " was the youngest son of John Rymer. " After that date there are several Thomas " Rymers " I think it therefore quite clear that the Rymers of Appleton Wisk are only collaterally connected with Thomas Rymer the historiographer.

" from the many passages in that poet which the learned know
" are written for the honour of kings, to read us a lecture against
" rebels and regicides, whom he compared to the giants that fought
" against the gods. And I do here offer all humble thanks to God
" that by his means I first received that light which made me first
" discern the iniquity of the times in which I was born and hitherto
" bred "[1]   The contrast between Rymer's paternal politics and
those which he himself advocated upon his first entrance into the
world, leads to the inference that he, as well as Hickes, had felt
the influence of Mr Smelt's lectures against rebels and regicides
Under his tuition Rymer remained eight years

Sent to Cambridge

On quitting Northallerton he went to Cambridge, and was ad-
mitted on the 29th of April 1658 as a "pensionarius minor" at
Sidney College, being then in the seventeenth year of his age.[2]
He quitted the University without taking his degree.[3]   His father's

---

[1] Memoirs of the Life of Mr John Kettlewell, 8 vo , 1718, pp 10-14

[2] Thomas Rymer filius Radulphi Rymer de Brafferton in comitatu Eboracensi generosi Lit Gram per octo annos a Thoma Smelt apud oppidum Northallerton dictum institutus, annos agens septemdecem, admissus est pensionarius minor, tutore et fidejussore Johanne Luke in artibus magistro 29 Ap 1658   The foregoing is from the Admission Book of Sidney College, Cambridge, and was kindly communicated to me by the Master of Sidney, through my friend the Rev. H R Luard, Registrary of the University of Cambridge.

[3] With the object of preventing persons falling into error, I may mention that about this period, or rather a little later, another Thomas Rymer was a member of the University of Cambridge , he was admitted a pensioner of Queens' College on the 25th of January 1697, and elected a fellow of that society on the 6th November 1709   I am indebted for this information to the President of Queens' College, also conveyed to me through my friend Mr Luard   Queen Anne's letter to the President and Fellows of Queens' College, dated 3rd November 1702, is registered among the State Papers in the Public Record Office, in the volume entitled "Domestic, Various, No 60, King's " Letters, 1689–1710 "   It states that " Thomas Rymer, Bachelor of Arts and " Scholar of our College, is for his virtues,

" learning, and good behaviour fitly qualified to be chosen a Fellow thereof, and that you the Master and Fellows are willing to choose him into a fellowship; but that in regard of a local statute of the said College, whereby there can be but two Fellows at the same time of one county or diocese, he is therefore incapable of being elected a Fellow without our Royal dispensation in that behalf, we are graciously pleased to dispense with the said Statute according to the power therein reserved to us, and we do hereby signify unto you that it is our will and pleasure that his being of the same county or diocese with other Fellows be no impediment to his being elected , but on the contrary we recommend him to you to be chosen a Fellow of the College "

I am inclined to think that this Thomas Rymer belonged to the family of the Rymers at Appleton-upon-Wisk, and only collaterally connected with the Historiographer   I may here mention that I have received a great deal of information relating to the Rymers of Appleton from Mr W T Jefferson, High Bailiff of Northallerton, and I avail myself of this opportunity to record my obligations to that gentleman for his very kind assistance, as also to Mr. J Horner, Head Master of the Northallerton Grammar School, for his polite attention to my requests.

troubles and those of his family cast a dark shadow over the life of
Rymer, and reduced him to great extremities   He struggled hard
against misfortune, but though he lived to a venerable age yet he
never obtained independence, or was able to surmount the "res
angusta domi."

On the 2nd of May 1666,[1] he became a member of the Honourable
Society of Gray's Inn, but was not called to the bar until the
16th of June 1673[2]

Becomes a
Member of
Gray's Inn.

As early as 1668 he made his first appearance as an author, and
became a candidate for public fame by publishing a translation of
a Latin Treatise that had been compiled for Prince Henry, entitled
" Cicero's Prince.   The reasons and councels for settlement and
" good government of a kingdom, collected out of Cicero's works."
This work he dedicated to the Duke of Monmouth   He did not
appear again as an author until September 1677.   This time he
produced a tragedy called " Edgar, or the English Monarch,"[3]
dedicated to the King.   It is written in rhyme, and evidently
alludes throughout to the recent political struggles of England.
" This," he says, "I call an Heroic Tragedy, having in it chiefly
" sought occasions to extoll the English Monarchy; and having
" writ it in that verse which, with Cowley, Denham, and Waller,
" I take to be the most proper for epic poetry."   The extracts given

His early
works

---

[1] Sol 3ˡⁱ· 6ˢ 8ᵈ. Thomas Rymer geñ
fillius Radolphi Rymer de Brafforton in
Com' Eboÿ geñ defunct admissus est in
Societatem hujus hospitii secundo die Maii
Anᵒ Dñi 1666
                              Willm Ellys.

[2] Gray's Inn :
   At a sitting held June 16, 25 Car 2.
1673,—
" It is ordered that Mr Thomas Rymer
attend the next pencion to take the oaths
of supremacy and allegianc and in he
meantime to give good security for payment of all commons and duties, and to
pay his caution money."
   At the sitting of the next day,—
" Ordered, that Mr. Rymer, having paid
his duties, be permitted to take the oaths of
allegiance and supremacy at this next

reading, and after the taken the said oaths
to be called to the bar and published
accordingly "

[3] Edgar, or the English Monarch; an
Heroick Tragedy. By Thomas Rymer of
Gray's Inne, Esq. Licensed Sept. 13, 1677.
Roger L'Estrange, London. Printed for
Richard Tonson, at his shop under Gray's
Inne Gate, next Gray's Inne Lane,
MDCLXXVIII

   A second edition of this piece appeared
in 1693, with the same dedication, "By
" Thomas Rymer, servant of their Ma-
" jesties " Printed for James Knapton at
the Crown in St. Paul's Church Yard,
1693 Though this is called the second
edition, another had appeared in 1691
without any dedication, also published by
James Knapton

in the note[1] exemplify its political character and poetical pretensions.[2]
It met with no success, though it went through three editions, or
rather the same impression appeared with new title-pages in 1691
and 1693. Rymer, however, was not discouraged, immediately
afterwards, he issued, in a letter to Fleetwood Shepheard, Esq,[3]
" The Tragedies of the last Age considered and examined by the
" practice of the ancients and by the common sense of all ages."
In this work he was unmerciful on three of Fletcher's plays, and

---

[1] The death of Cromwell is thus pictured in that of the usurper of France:—
> *Lew —*   "Is Rudolph dead?
> *2nd Statesm.*—And (to the just reproach of Heav'n) in bed
>   Yet his black soul did th' air and Heav'n deform,
>   And dying Breath did bluster to a storm,
>   As if the Troubles (since he ceas'd to live)
>   Which to the Earth he could no longer give,
>   He still would through the aery Regions drive"   *Act. IV., Sc 2*
The following is clearly a scene at home —
> *Edi —*   "A curst usurper's bed
>   Whom conscience with a silent scourge shall tear,
>   And pale fac'd Ghosts from my embraces scare;
>   Whose Throne by bloody scaffolds is upheld,
>   And by slaves guarded who their Master kill'd.
> *Lew —*His throne is fix'd and the Foundation good
>   'Tis not less firm if cemented with Blood.
>   Right is a notion may the simple sting,
>   But with the wise, possession is the King
> *Edi —*Your speech a strange and insolent Doctrine bears,
>   And maximes yet unknown to English ears.
>   Rather to the true Prince (did he survive)
>   'Midst his distress, I would my person give,
>   With him partake his indigence and Toil,
>   Lurking in Holes or wand'ring in Exile;
>   How 'ere from Land to Land, from Coast to Coast,
>   By restless storms of adverse Fortune tost,
>   I'd rather with him all disgraces bear
>   Than guilty pomps with your usurper share."   *Act 3, Sc 5*

[2] The reader interested about the criticisms and dramatic powers of Rymer will peruse with pleasure " An Essay on the Drama" by Sir Walter Scott, first published in the "Encyclopedia Britannica," and afterwards in his Collected Prose works, vol 6, p 366, and will come to the conclusion "that it was possible for a " Drama to be extremely regular, and, at " the same time, intolerably dull " The fate of Rymer's Tragedy has been illustrated by the inimitable humour of Addison in No 692 of " The Spectator " Describing different theatrical properties, he says—"They are provided with above " a dozen showers of snow, which, as I am " informed, are the plays of many unsuccessful poets artificially cut and shredded " for that use Mr Rymer's *Edgar* is to " fall in snow at the next acting of *King* " *Lear*, in order to heighten, or rather " alleviate, the distress of that unfortunate " prince, or to serve by way of decoration " to a piece which that great critic has " written against."

[3] Fleetwood Shepheard or Sheppard was a great friend of Matthew Prior, the poet, and to whom Prior addressed the celebrated epistle, asking for a place at Court, and for an introduction to the Earl of Dorset.

exhibited himself as a strenuous advocate for the Aristotelian principles in the drama, and laid down those canons of dramatic
criticism which have exposed him to so much censure, and which
he afterwards so unhappily applied to some of the noblest works
of Shakespeare.[1]

Whatever may have been Rymer's learning, he certainly had
few qualifications for a critic. Lord Macaulay, speaking of him,
remarks, "Rymer we take to have been the worst critic that ever
"lived." The liberties he took with Shakespeare exposed him to
the wrath of that poet's admirers, who naturally contrasted the
dramatic talents of the critic with those of the person whose
writings he has with so much rigour attacked. His failure in this
walk of literature perhaps induced him to turn his thoughts to
graver subjects, and in which his talents were better adapted to
shine, and his profession to illustrate

In 1683, Rymer translated "The Life of Nicias by Plutarch,"
included in the general collection of the Lives by Plutarch, Englished
by Dryden and other scholars of the time.

---

[1] Dryden, having received from Rymer a copy of his work, wrote those remarkable observations on it on the blank leaves of the volume which Dr. Johnson has preserved in his Life of Dryden (pp 128–138).

On the whole Dryden thought well of it, though he dissents from many of Rymer's conclusions and prejudices, and sums up the evidence against him in the following words "My judgment on the piece is "this, that it is extremely learned, but "that the author of it is better read in the "Greek than in the English poets; that "all writers ought to study this cri"tique, as the best account I have ever "seen of the ancients, that the model of "tragedy he has here given is excellent "and extremely correct, but that is not "the only model of all tragedy, because it "is too much circumscribed in plot, cha"racters, &c ; and lastly, that we may be "taught here justly to admire and imitate "the ancients without giving them the "preference with this author in prejudice "to our country"

Dr Johnson, in comparing the criticisms of Rymer with those of Dryden, says, "The different manner and effect with "which critical knowledge may be con"veyed was perhaps never more clearly "exemplified than in the performances of

"Rymer and Dryden. It was said of a "dispute between two mathematicians "'malim cum Scaligero errare, quam cum "Clavio recte sapere;' that it was more "eligible to go wrong with one than right "with the other A tendency of the same "kind every mind must feel at the perusal "of Dryden's prefaces and Rymer's dis"courses With Dryden we are wander"ing in quest of truth, whom we find, if "we find her at all, drest in the graces of "elegance, and if we miss her, the labour "of the pursuit rewards itself, we are led "only through fragrance and flowers "Rymer, without taking a nearer, takes a "rougher way, every step is to be made "through thorns and brambles, and truth, "if we meet her, appears repulsive by her "mien, and ungraceful by her habit Dry"den's criticism has the majesty of a "queen, Rymer's has the ferocity of a "tyrant"

Disraeli, in his "Amenities of Literature" (vol. 2, p. 187, Ed 1859), states that Rymer translated the "Reflections on Aristotle's Treatise of Poetry" by Père Rapin, to which he prefixed an ingenious critical preface on comparative poetry. Disraeli's very pertinent and interesting remarks on Rymer and his Shakesperian criticisms are well worthy of the reader's attention.

In 1684 he published a tract "Of the Antiquity, Power, and Decay
" of Parliaments, being a general view of Government and Civil
" Policy in Europe, with other Historical and Political observations
" relating thereunto." It is in the form of a letter to a person of
eminence,[1] and, like all Rymer's publications, shows extensive
reading; but is rather to be regarded as a party pamphlet than
as a philosophical investigation. He commences thus: "Sir,—See
" the effect of your commands. The want of time, of books, and
" assistance, in this my retirement, make me very uncapable of the'
" undertaking But my obedience and performance with a kid
" will, I hope, be accepted, when I cannot sacrifice an hundred
" bulls."

It is amusing to find him at this time reflecting in the following
style upon the worth of that office, to which he was afterwards
nominated: "You are not to expect truth from an historiographer
" royal; it may drop from their pen by chance, but the general
" herd understand not their business, they fill us with story, acci-
" dental, incoherent, without end or side, and never know the
" *government* or *policy* where they write Even the *Records*
" themselves are not always accurately worded."

Preface to
Hobbes'
"Historia
Ecclesiastica"

In 1688 he is said by Des Maizeaux and Aubrey[2] to have written
the Preface to the "Historia Ecclesiastica carmine Elegiaco concin-
" nata; authore Thoma Hobbes Malmesburiensi Opus posthumum."
This may have given rise to the report that Rymer wrote the Life
of Hobbes, but as to which there seems to be some question; there
can, however, be but little doubt that Richard Blackbourne, M.A,
of Trinity College, Cambridge, contributed the Preface, which Rymer
would scarcely have permitted had he written the Life. The editor
states that the Life was written "a docto quodam, summo ejus
" amico," and came to him through J. A., initials which are understood to mean "John Aubrey" The Life is attributed to Rymer by
Des Maizeaux in the incomplete French Life of Rymer already
referred to, and also by the writer of the Life of Hobbes in the
" Biographia Britannica" (IV 2,615).

Poems on
Waller's
memory and

In the same year (1688), Rymer wrote three pieces in the collection of "Poems to the Memory of Edmund Waller;" one strictly

---

[1] There is some reason for believing that
the "person of eminence" was John Somers
(afterwards Lord Somers), who at that
time was devoting his attention to parliamentary and constitutional history, and
afterwards became one of Rymer's patrons.
This tract was reprinted in 1689, and
again in 1714

[2] Letters and Lives of Eminent Men.
II. 631

elegiacal, a translation of some lines by St. Evremont, and a third other poetical productions of Rymer. addressed to John Riley, on drawing a portrait of Waller. They were all afterwards reprinted in Dryden's "Miscellany Poems." To Rymer also is attributed the inscription on the monument erected to Waller at Beaconsfield. I give it in the Appendix as a specimen of his monumental latinity.[1]

In 1689 he published a poem on the arrival of Queen Mary February 12th, 1688–9. It appeared three days after that event.

In 1692 appeared his translation of the sixth Elegy of the Third Book of Ovid's "Tristia." This is included among the "Miscellany Poems" published by Dryden, 2nd edition, 1692, p. 148.

On the death of Thomas Shadwell in 1692, either Rymer's necessities, or the gratitude of his party, procured for him the office of Historiographer Royal. Shadwell had held this post in conjunction with the Laureateship, as Dryden had done before him, but on his death the offices were divided. Tate was appointed Poet Laureate, and Rymer Historiographer Royal,[2] on the same day, at a salary of 200*l.* per annum.

Rymer appointed Historiographer Royal

Immediately after his appointment he published, under the following title, "A Short View of Tragedy ; its original Excellency and "Corruption. With some reflections on Shakespeare and other "practitioners for the stage, by Mr. Rymer, servant to their Majes-"ties." This work he dedicated to the Earl of Dorset,[3] Lord Chamberlain, to whom, in all probability, he was indebted for his office. It is clear that Rymer had been known to this nobleman

His "A short View of Tragedy."

---

[1] See Appendix VII.

[2] Dryden, perhaps nettled at one of Rymer's criticisms upon him, hints at the difference the public was likely to experience between the present Royal Historiographer and him whose place he occupied, and wrote these humorous lines to Tate given by Scott in his Life of Dryden, section vii

[3] Charles Sackville, Earl of Dorset and Middlesex, was born on the 24th of January 1637–8. He sat, as Lord Buckhurst, as member for East Grinstead He went with the Duke of York as a volunteer during the Dutch war in 1665, and the night before the battle of Solebay is said to have composed the song beginning, "To all you ladies now at land we men at sea indite," which is generally esteemed the happiest of his poetical productions. Upon

the death of his uncle, James Cranfield, Earl of Middlesex, the estates devolved upon him, and he obtained the title in 1675 He succeeded his father as Earl of Dorset in August 1677. He openly espoused the interest of the Prince of Orange, and was selected to convey the Princess Anne, afterwards Queen, out of the reach of danger from her father's displeasure King William the Third appointed him Lord Chamberlain of the Household, and made him a Privy Councillor The Garter was conferred upon him in February 1691, and he attended the King to the congress at the Hague in the year following He retired on account of delicate health from active political life about the year 1698, and died on the 19th of January 1705–6.

for some time, for he professes that his countenance had supported him against the public indignation excited by his former work upon the drama, or, as he expresses it, "supported a righteous cause " against the prejudice and corruption then reigning."

At the conclusion of his previous work upon tragedy he had promised that upon some future occasion he would resume the subject, with an examination of the Othello and Julius Cæsar of Shakespeare, and the Catiline of Ben Jonson. At the same time he had stated that he should append "some reflections on that Paradise Lost of Milton's, which some are pleased to call a poem ," but either public indignation, or his engagement upon the " Fœdera," prevented him from executing his design.

Bitter feeling against him.

As a specimen of the bitter feeling exhibited against Rymer, the reader will find in the note below a scurrilous satire which appeared under the title of " Garreteer Poet," in a print representing Rymer and his distressed family in a miserable attic.[1]

His qualifications as editor of the Fœdera.

It may be thought, upon a cursory glance at the literary labours of Rymer at the time of his appointment as " Historiographer Royal," that they afford but little indication of fitness for the important work that was about to be entrusted to him. We might conclude that it was unfortunate that the office of Historiographer Royal, by virtue of which he obtained the appointment of editor of the Fœdera, was not at that time filled by Tyrrell, Brady, or Madox,

---

[1] "In one corner of this poetical apartment stood a flock bed, and underneath it a green jordan presented itself to the eye, which had collected the nocturnal urine of the whole family, consisting of Mr Rymer, his wife, and two daughters, three rotten chairs and a half seemed to stand like traps in various parts of the room, threatening downfall to unwary strangers; and one solitary table in the middle of this aerial apartment served to hold the different treasures of the whole family there was now lying upon it, the first act of a comedy, a pair of yellow stays, two political pamphlets, a plate of bread and butter, three dirty night caps, and a volume of miscellaneous poems. The lady of the house was drowning a neck of mutton in meagre soup, and their two daughters sat in the windows mending their father's brown stockings with blue worsted Such was the mansion of Mr. Rymer, the poet, and to complete his misfortunes, instead of an expected reward for his works from a nobleman, he brought home as a present little Pompey. This so exasperated his wife, that with savage hands she seized his works on the table, and was going to commit them to the flames, but her husband's voice interrupted her, crying out,—'See! see! 'see! my dear, the pot boils over, and 'the broth is all running into the fire' This, luckily, put an end to their debate, they sat down to dinner without a table-cloth, envying one another every morsel that escaped their own mouths "—See Caulfield's Portraits, Memoirs and Characters of Remarkable Persons, &c., 1819, Vol I., p. 50. Rymer appears with a cocked hat and long flapped coat and breeches; no sword, but under his arm a King Charles spaniel, evidently the Pompey alluded to in the description.

or some other person avowedly acquainted with the historical if not
with the record literature of the country. A political play, party
pamphlets, and absurd dramatic criticisms, do not seem to be a very
fitting preparation for so important a task If, however, we
examine Rymer's publications more closely, we shall find reason to
moderate our opinion That he was a man of sound learning is
indisputable. The references scattered throughout his books give
evidence of reading far removed from that of an ordinary student,
and in his researches into the history of poetry and the drama he
exhibits an acquaintance with the English monastic chronicles and
antiquarian writers, and some knowledge also of the Cottonian and
Bodleian libraries, which in his time was not common. His defi-
ciency in the knowledge of the actual forms and characters of
records, was perhaps more than counterbalanced by a greater com-
petency to judge of their general value.

Within eight months after his appointment as Historiographer *Appointed editor of the Fœdera* Royal, fresh honours awaited Rymer. He was directed to carry
out the great national work which Montague and Somers had
recommended It was probably the friendship of George Stepney[1]
that procured him the honourable distinction which has placed his
name on the roll of fame, and rendered it familiar to all scholars
from one end of Europe to the other

Of Rymer's personal character and the circumstances of his life *His position at the time.* at the time of his appointment to this important post, we know
comparatively nothing That he lived in an honourable intimacy
with Hobbes and Waller there is no doubt, and that he addressed
Bishop Nicolson as his "old acquaintance" is equally clear.
Familiar allusions to various members of several noble families
are scattered throughout his writings, and John Dunton styles him
the "orthodox and modest Rymer" Dr. Smith thought well of
him, and George Stepney numbered him amongst his friends. In
Thoresby's Diary he is alluded to, some years later, as "good
old Mr Rymer;" and Bishop Kennett, writing after his death,
mentions him with respect. Until this period of his life he

---

[1] George Stepney, descended from the
ancient family of Prendergast, was born in
Westminster in 1663, and educated at the
public school there. Having been chosen
King's scholar in 1676, he went to Trinity
College, Cambridge, in 1682 He was
appointed a Commissioner of Trade in 1697,
and was constantly employed in foreign
missions and embassies from May 1691 to
his death in 1707. Several of his poetical
pieces are preserved in the collection
entitled "The Works of the minor Poets."
He was buried in Westminster Abbey, and
a marble monument, with a Latin inscription, was erected to his memory.

appears to have spent his time in the country, probably in Essex, as might be inferred from various allusions in his poetical works. He certainly wrote his treatise on Parliaments "in retirement," for in his letter to Fleetwood Shepheard he mentions that he had several times come to London to see that gentleman at St. James's. What were his pecuniary means at this period is equally unknown. He could not have inherited any property from his father, as all his possessions, goods, and chattels had been forfeited to the Crown on his attainder. Previously to his conviction he had assigned to his son a mortgage from a Mr. Wood of certain lands in Kirkby Wisk. Probably this mortgage was all that Rymer had for his support, except the small precarious income he may have derived from his publications, for literary labour at that time was so badly paid, that authors even of reputation and undoubted merit probably could not derive more than a pittance from the exercise of their pens. If the genius of Dryden was so ill requited, we may easily infer that the press was no fertile source of emolument to Rymer, who had little genius and no popularity. The salary attached to his office of 200*l*. per annum, equal to about 333*l*. 6*s* 8*d*. of our present money, must have been a great boon to a man who, if the scurrilous attacks upon him may be trusted, was then living in abject penury and distress.

History of the Foedera

The history of the rise and progress of the " Foedera " is of so much interest in a literary point of view, that I feel no hesitation in entering fully upon the subject, especially as I have obtained, through the kindness of many friends, ample materials for the purpose. I may be forgiven, in tracing the history of a great national work, the first and in some respects the most important of the kind ever undertaken at the public expense, if I lay before my readers the materials I have been able to collect with no little assiduity. Probably such details do not exist for the history of any other literary work of a similar nature.

Rymer received his appointment on the 26th of August 1693, under the Sign Manual of Queen Mary, who possibly may not have forgotten his complimentary poem on her arrival in England a few years before. The order directs him " to transcribe and publish " all the leagues, treaties, alliances, capitulations, and confederacies, " which have at any time been made between the Crown of " England and any other kingdoms, princes, and states, as a work " highly conducing to our service and the honour of this our realm." The better to enable him to carry out the work " he is empowered

" to have free liberty and access from time to time to search
" into the records in our Tower of London, in the Rolls, in
" the Augmentation Office, our Exchequer, the Journals of both
" Houses of Parliament, or any other places where records are kept,[1]
" for such records as we have or shall direct, and the same to tran-
" scribe: And that he also have access from time to time to our
" library at St. James's, and our Paper Office, upon such matters
" as we have or shall appoint for our service, without paying any
" fees; whereof the respective officers and all other persons whom
" it may concern are to take notice and yield due obedience to our
" pleasure herein declared"

Unfortunately Rymer has not left behind him any papers or memoranda from which it can be gleaned what assistance he received
in the way of digests, tables, or calendars, to facilitate his researches.
There, however, can be no doubt that he took the " Codex Juris
Gentium Diplomaticus " of Leibnitz as his model; at least, this is,
I think, the natural interpretation to be put on the words of Leibnitz himself, when speaking on the subject. " Professus est nostro

He adopts the " Codex Juris Gentium Diplomaticus" as his model

---

[1] Several warrants and orders of Council for access to the public records, differing in form according to the several purposes for which they were granted, are in existence. One, granted to Joseph Williamson, has been already noticed Another, granted to Sir Edward Dering, for his encouragement in the study of anti-quities, has been printed among Hearne's additions to Leland's Collectanea, I 653, in the Archæologia, VIII 439, and in Cooper on the Public Records, II 426. Similar favours were conceded to Ferdinando Pul-ton, editor of the Collection of Statutes published in 1618 (vide Authentic Edition, Introd. I xxii. xxvii), to Dr. Plot, who had very extensive powers of research Gilbert Burnet received permission " to " search the Paper Office, in order to fur-" nishing the History of the Reformation of " this Church " His holograph letter on the subject, dated 24th July [1679], and directed to Sir Joseph Williamson, is still extant in the Public Record Office

There is also a letter from Prince Rupert to Williamson, stating, " Mr. Roger Le " Strange is about writinge a History of " of the Civill Wares of England whoe " desires to serch in the Paper Office to " find out there some passages which may " be very convenient for that purpose I " have already spoken to his Ma[te] whoe " hath granted me this request My " desire to you therefore is that you admitt " the said Mr Le Strange to looke into " those papers in the said office accord-" ingly, and for so doeing you will oblige " your assured friend, Rupert." On the 24th of June 1700 Vernon informs Sir Joseph Williamson that " Mr John Strype " having humbly represented to his Ma[te] " that he intends to publish a History of " the Ecclesiastical State of the Kingdome " in the last Age and prayed he might have " access to the Paper Office to peruse there " as well Civill as Ecclesiasticall papers in " the reigns of Henry VIII Edward VI " R Mary & Q Elizabeth, & to take " notes or copies of such papers & " matters as he shall judge usefull to his " purpose His Ma[te] commands me to " signifie his pleasure to you that the said " Mr. John Strype have admittance to the " said office according to his desire." On the 7th June 1768, David Hume, having applied for permission to inspect papers and books in the Paper Office and elsewhere, Lord Shelburne desired Sir Joseph Ayloffe, Dr. Ducarel, and Mr. Astle to allow Mr. David Hume to inspect any of the papers in their several offices

" se exemplo excitatum, eosdemque sibi limites præscripsit, à quibus
" Tomus noster primus cœpit, annum æræ Christianæ 1101."
Moreover, in a letter to Leibnitz, Rymer says, ' I am most obliged
" in many ways to you, who have shone with such great praise as
" my guide and predecessor in this province I feel the greatest pos-
" sible gratitude to you on that account. Your kindness touches
" me still more keenly respecting the treaty you intend to send me
" as a present, although I already possess it, and indeed almost
" everything relating to us which has a place in your ' Codex
" Diplomaticus'." In another letter, undated, Rymer writes to
Leibnitz, " ut videas qualiter labores quos, te hortante, te laudante,
" te præeunte, susceperam " Besides having Leibnitz's Collection as
the prototype of his work, he had the benefit of Agarde's Collection
of Treaties for his guidance; a fact that cannot be disputed, for in
the first receipt given by him to the Chamberlains of the Exchequer
for documents entrusted to him to copy, he acknowledges having
received, " A Book of Abbreviations of Leagues by Arthur Agarde."[1]
It is therefore clear that Rymer had determined to follow the
plan[2] adopted by Leibnitz, and availed himself of such tables, digests,
and calendars, as came within his reach, this, indeed, was his duty,
and he could not have had a better guide than Agarde's collection.
It is also clear that he made his researches personally. He appears
to have commenced his labours within the first month after his
appointment, for I find him working at the Chapter House,
Westminster, and giving a receipt to the Auditor and Under-Cham-
berlains of the Exchequer for certain documents entrusted to his care
as early as the 18th of September 1693

*Probable prin-
ciples adopted
for his guid-
ance.* Neither in his dedications to Queen Anne, nor in his General
Preface to the reader, has Rymer pointed out the plan he followed
in forming his collection. I have therefore endeavoured to discover
what were the leading principles he laid down for his own guidance.

---

[1] Anthony Wood, in his Athenæ
(1 444), thus describes these abbreviations "A collection of all leagues, and
" treaties of peace, entercourses and
" marriages with foreign nations, which
" book was three years' labour and was
" very carefully preserved for the King's
" service The writer and collector there-
" of took order that it should be preserved
" in his Majesty's Court of Receipt, under
" the charge and custody of the officers
" there, and to be delivered to them by
" inventory, because it is very necessary
" for the King's use, good of the subject,
" and readiness and light to the officers."

[2] Leibnitz intimates that he had seen
two title-pages by Rymer for the Fœdera,
the larger one of which he prints, at
least so I understand his words " Sed
" Rymerianı operis editam inscriptionem,
· posteriorem scilicet, eamque priore am-
" pliorem, (nemo enim intelligens hic pro-
' lixitatem tituli culpabit) qualis autoris
" missu ad nos pervenit."

His object appears to have been two-fold; first, to publish all records of alliances or other transactions in which England was concerned with foreign powers from the year 1101 down to his own times;[1] secondly, to limit his collection to the originals preserved in the Royal Archives, adding thereto such documents from the Cottonian, Lambeth, and the Universities' Libraries as might serve to supply the links required in the chain of evidence.

Either through jealousy, or perhaps necessary strictness, Rymer seems to have experienced some little difficulty at the Exchequer in obtaining the documents required for his work, although the Queen's warrant had given him free access to all the public muniments of the kingdom. At all events, he was compelled to apply to the King in Council for relief. On the 12th of April 1694, the Lord Keeper of the Great Seal was directed by an order in Council to issue a writ to the Lords Commissioners of his Majesty's Treasury and to the Chamberlains of the Exchequer, "authorising and "desiring them to deliver to Thomas Rymer, from time to time, all

Difficulties in carrying on his work.

---

[1] This was in one respect a more extensive plan than that of Leibnitz, inasmuch as Rymer intended to bring down his collections two centuries later than that of the "Codex Diplomaticus" In another point it was more limited, as he confined himself to the transactions of England with other states, whereas Leibnitz had extended his to the affairs of Europe generally On the subject of the difference between the plans of Leibnitz and Rymer the following letter from Dr Thomas Smith to Humphrey Wanley will be interesting to the reader.—

"Mr. Rymer's designe (about which he is now employed, and for the carrying on which hee has the encouragement of the Government, with an ample pension, under the title and qualification of Historiographer Regius), tho' highly and truly laudable, does not fully come up to what I propose and wish were done, for hee only will take in the Diplomata of our Kings and Princes, their contemporaryes and allyes, with the bulls of Popes, for those four or five hundred yeares last past, being such a worke as the 'Codex Juris Gentium Diplomaticus' published by my excellently learned friend Monsieur Leibnitz, chiefly out of the archives of the famous Library of Wolfenbuttel about four yeares since, and as the six volumes of Publick Acts and

Charters relating to the kingdom of France not long since printed at Paris . . . .
"London, 3 July 1697.
"For Mr Humfrey Wanley, at University College in Oxford.
"MS. Harl 3782, p 251."
H Wanley's answer, dated 5 July 1697, is printed in the Letters from the Bodleian Library, vol. 1, pp. 83–87

When Rymer commenced, he does not appear to have meditated the introduction into the Fœdera of any documents preserved in foreign Archives, but he seems to have extended his plan in a few instances. In his second volume, pp 226–230 and pp 230–234, he published two documents concerning the duel proposed between the Kings of Arragon and Sicily in 1282, with these references: "Ex Archivo Reg Palensi" and "Ex Archivo Episcopi Albiensis" There is in his first volume a convention between Henry III and Louis IX, dated 1259; the French text of which is accompanied with a Latin translation, in parallel columns, thus headed —
"Ex quodam transcripto Archiepiscopi "Burdegal inter alia, hanc conventionem "habemus Latine redditam, hisce verbis," but it does not appear whether the transcript was procured from Bordeaux, or how Rymer obtained it.

" Leagues, Treaties, Alliances, Capitulations, and Confederacies, with
" all other records relating thereunto, remaining in the several Trea-
" suries of the Exchequer which he shall have occasion of and desire,
" to be delivered back by him unto the said Treasurer." Accordingly, on the 6th of June following, a writ was sent to the
Commissioners of the Treasury and to the Chamberlains of the
Exchequer, directing them to permit Rymer to have any and what
leagues, treaties, &c. he might require, on an undertaking by indenture to be given by him that he would safely return the
same into the Treasury Afterwards, on the 11th of July, he was
informed by one of the Deputy Chamberlains, that the Lords of the
Treasury had directed that the writ should be executed with the
restrictions and limitations following, viz · that the Deputy Chamberlains should not suffer Mr Rymer to carry any records out of the
Treasury, but that a place should be separated in one Treasury, by
boards, doors, and locks, from the other part of the Treasury ; in
which separated place no records should be left, and that they were
to deliver to Mr Rymer so many records only and no more at a
time (and that by indenture) that he could get copied out in that
separated place in a week's time, and to deliver him no more till
those were returned, and that he should not carry any away to any
other place. To this message Mr Rymer agreed, and also that the
place should be at the entrance and going into the Chapter House
in the Abbey before coming into the round building I have been
particular in mentioning these facts, because it has been reported
and commonly believed that Rymer had unlimited access to the
documents in the Chapter House, with power to remove them to
his own house,[1] and that several very important instruments were
never returned. It is, however, true that many documents which
can be proved to have passed through Rymer's hands are not now
forthcoming, but there is no ground for charging him with their loss,
as the receipts of the officers of the Exchequer for nearly all that
he used at the Chapter House are still extant

His receipts for the documents he used.

Of Rymer's method of proceeding we know but little. Many of
the receipts that he gave to the officers of the Chapter House for
the records which passed through his hands are still extant in
the Public Record Office, but it would be impossible to divine from
them his plan of operations In Appendix IX will be found a copy
of the first receipt given by him, dated 18th September 1693

---

[1] Appendix X.

by which it appears that all the documents he then received belonged to the fourteenth and fifteenth centuries His next receipt, dated the 1st of August 1694, is for documents of a very miscellaneous character of the reigns of Henry III., Edward I., Edward III, Richard II, Henry IV, Henry V., Henry VI, and Edward IV. His third receipt is dated 11th August 1694, and refers only to documents of the same period, except one styled "a deed in Henry "the 1st time of Flanders," and which in all probability is the instrument with which the "Fœdera" commences.

We catch some interesting glimpses of Rymer at work through Thoresby in his "Diary and Correspondence"[1] He states "that he "walked with Mr Churchill to Westminster, and there visited the "industrious antiquary and ingenious poet, Mr Rymer, whom we "found amongst the musty records, supervising his amanuensis "transcribing" These facts and other evidences which exist on the same subject prove that Rymer gave his personal attention to the searches, selections, and transcription of the various instruments for the "Fœdera."

About this time, that is, in 1694, Rymer commenced his acquaintance with Leibnitz, and was materially influenced by him in the plan and formation of the "Fœdera" A correspondence between the two scholars was brought about by George Stepney, the poet. As both were engaged in the publication of diplomatic collections, they were naturally drawn together, and a friendly interchange of letters continued between them for many years.

On the 5–15 October 1694, Leibnitz wrote as follows to George Stepney ; "Dr. Smith, a very learned man, and author of several "excellent books, has very obligingly written to me, and informed "me that Mr Rymer, a learned man, who has hitherto devoted "himself to poetry and 'belles lettres,' is now working at a collec- "tion of monuments of English history, and has obtained permis-

Marginal notes: Rymer at work. His first acquaintance with Leibnitz Correspondence between Rymer and Leibnitz

---

[1] (Vol. 1. p 296) "On the 18th of January 1709 visited the ingenious Mr Madox (son of my late dear friend Mr Madox), the author of Formulare Anglicanum, and who is now upon a noble design, the History of the Exchequer I afterwards visited our countryman, good old Mr. Rymer, her Majesty's Historiographer, who was born at Yafforth Hall near North-allerton, who has published seven or eight volumes, in folio, of the public Leagues and Treaties of Foreign States, &c " (Vol. II, p 24.) "On the 22nd of January 1709, in returning " (from Soho Square), "called at Mr Rymer's, who presented me with his *three* letters to the Bishop of Carlisle " (Ibid, p 27) I have been able to find only *two* of the letters to which Thoresby alludes "On the 13th of August 1712 visited the learned Mr Anstis, and in the same court our countryman, Mr Rymer, the Historiographer Royal, who would needs engage me to visit him again to show me more curiosities " (Ibid, p. 156)

" sion to examine the archives , as the History of Brunswick (with
" which I sometimes occupy myself) has a great connexion with
" that of England, at certain periods, especially during the 12th
" and 13th centuries, I hope Mr Rymer will be able to favour us
" with many things, and we should not be ungrateful. If we could
" have, by his means, catalogues of documents and manuscripts, we
" should be much obliged, for then a selection might be made from
" them. One of my friends has a Latin history of the church of
" Ely, very old, which might throw light on the history of England,
" and I could furnish many other documents of that nature. As to
" Dr. Smith, I will write direct to him, but not having the honour
" of Mr Rymer's acquaintance I hope that your interposition may be
" useful to me."[1]

There can be no doubt that the formal introduction of Rymer to
Leibnitz was effected by Stepney, for Leibnitz writes as follows
" Ex Anglia misit aliqua Gilbertus Burnetus, reverendissimus
" Sarisberiensium episcopus , in quo pro meritis provehendo 1es
" publica literariaque certavere, et qui tot aliis doctrinis laudibusque
" etiam actorum publicorum perquisitionem conjunxit Præterea
" Stepneius, Ablegatus Regius, non minus gerendis principum
" negotiis quam eorum gestis prosa versaque eloquentia ornandis
" aptus, obtinuit nobis insignia ex publicis tabulariis monumenta,
" quæ cum pleraque historiam Brunsvicensem aliquando illustrare
" possint, nonnulla tamen etiam hinc præsenti operi convenire sunt
" visa Hoc autem præstitit inprimis conciliata mihi benevolentia
" V. Cl. Thomæ Rymeri in lucem proferendis Angliæ tabulis Regio
" jussu destinati, de quo mox plura dicam." Shortly afterwards
he states that Rymei had printed the title of his intended work:
" Sed et Th Rymerus supra laudatus pandectis Anglicarum tabu-
" larum jam titulum in typos præire jussit."

A rough draft of one of Rymer's letters in Latin to Leibnitz[2] is
still in existence ; it bears no date, but it must have been written
shortly after Stepney had made the two scholars acquainted with
each other , probably in 1695 He writes, " When I first heard,
" from the most learned Dr Smith, that you were engaged upon
" the antiquities of Brunswick, I immediately arranged for copying
" whatever came in my way, and afterwards for sending them to you
" through our friend Stepney. If they are at all useful to you, I
" shall rejoice, and desire nothing further, as I know how greatly

---

[1] See Appendix XI   [2] See Appendix XII

" I am obliged in many ways to you, who have shone with such
" great praise, as my guide and predecessor in this province. I
" feel the greatest possible gratitude to you on that account Your
" kindness touches me more keenly respecting the treaty you
" intend to send me as a present, although I possess it already, and
" indeed almost everything relating to us, which has a place in
" your 'Codex Diplomaticus' I am eagerly expecting a second
" volume from you, and, if I hear that you are desirous of anything
" in particular, I promise most willingly, as far as lies in my power,
" to send it to you. For your second volume I have selected a
" treaty embellished with a golden seal, which has been copied for a
" long time It is the treaty between Henry VIII and Francis I.
" King of France, of which Spelman, in his Glossary, under the
" word 'Bulla,' and Du Cange also under the word 'Bulla,' say
" that a duplicate (that is the other part of the ratification) is
" preserved in the French Archives. With it I send an impression
" of the gold seal. My letters to you have been delayed, because
" I have been waiting for a visit from Mr. Berry, by whom, as I am
" informed, your letters to me were brought over But it is not easy
' to find him, as he is always employed in the affairs of princes
" and upon business, while I am kept at hard work in the Royal
" Archives, hidden from the eyes of men, and where I grub and dig
" daily among decaying parchments covered with dirt and mildew.
" Here the autographs of princes, which have long time lain in dark-
" ness and decay, nay even buried, at length arise and see the light,
" by the favour of King William, under whose auspices we hope
" for light and liberty. Much remains to be done, but in a short
" time I shall make a truce, and prepare my first volume for the
" press I will send you the first pages Be gracious to my at-
" tempts, and may God preserve you."

We have here a faithful view of Rymer at work in the wooden
partition in the Chapter House, Westminster, where Thoresby visited
him several times, amid dirt and mildew, to which he more than once
touchingly alludes in his memorials to the Treasury.

A letter in Latin addressed to him by Leibnitz, dated 16–26
July 1695, runs thus .[1] " I have already shown my appreciation of
" your gifts by my many expressions of thanks. There are some
" among them which have enlightened me, especially the charter of
" Otto, which he granted to the people of Oleron. I did not know

---

[1] See Appendix XIII.

c

" that our countryman Otto bore the title of Duke of Aquitain. If
" anything else occurs, do not forget us   Your friend Stepney, an
" excellent man, and deserving not less of the whole community than
" of your King, sent me an advertisement of yours in the London
" Newspaper,[1] inviting the assistance of those who can contribute
" to your project of collecting the documents of the kingdom   I
" consider it the same as if you had sent it to me   That there are
" some documents in my hands you will judge from what I have
" inserted in my 'Codex Diplomaticus,' I did not use all of them,
" as I announced that I should content myself with the more select.
" I confess that I have not now all I once had , but I hope to be
" able to recover them when I hear that they will be of service
" to you, although I should think that you wanted but little—the
" Archives of the kingdom being at your disposal. I send you now
" a specimen of my good will. I found among my documents a
" treaty between Philip King of France and Edward King of
" England, confirming the treaty, edited by me, between their
" fathers St. Louis and Henry the Third   As to the rest, let me
" know more fully about your magnificent plans. I see that Thomas
" Gale, a most famous man, in the preface to the Authors of your
" Country, edited by him, wished for some one to illustrate the
" history of your country in such a way that he would seem to
" have foretold you   Farewell. Hanover, 16/26 July 1695."

On the 13–23 of January 1696, Leibnitz wrote again to
Rymer[2] He says, "While expressing to my friend the accus-
" tomed good wishes for the new year, I also wish to pray that
" everything may be fortunate and happy for you, that you may
" duly complete what has been so gloriously begun for the good
" of the community. I have obtained the most profitable fruit
" of my labours on the Codex Diplomaticus, as I hear that my
" attempts have instigated you to a useful examination of the

---

[1] (Copy of Advertisement)
His Majesty having been pleased to
appoint Thomas Rymer, Esq , Historiographer Royal, to transcribe and make publick the Ancient Leagues and Transactions
between the Crown of England and other
Nations , And it being now intended that
an History or Annals of the Kings of
England, digested and supported by the
said Originals, and the other Records,
Manuscripts, and Memorials in the King's
Archives at Westminster, the Tower, and

elsewhere, shall be published with all
convenient speed , these are to desire all
Gentlemen, in whose hands are any Manuscripts or Memorials, that may help or be
of use in this Work, to give notice thereof
to A and J. Churchhill at the Black Swan
in Paternoster Row, where the same will
be gratefully received
(London Gazette, No 3069. From
Monday, April 8, to Thursday,
April 11, 1695.)
[2] See Appendix XIV.

" records of the kingdom. The treaty between Henry VIII and
" Francis I King of France, with the impression of the gold seal
" appended, is most acceptable. I should wish to obtain the will
" of Henry VIII, unless you think it is one of those things which
" cannot be easily communicated. Coke, unless I am mistaken,
" asserted in the action against Garnet, that the Pope of Rome
" promised his sanction of the English Liturgy and other such things
" for the purpose of enticing Queen Elizabeth. It would be worth
" while to have these letters of the Pope, as well as the aliena-
" tion of the goods of the church, confirmed in the reign of Mary
" by the authority of Cardinal Pole, that the nobility might not
" suspect a change. Moreover, the suppression of the monasteries
" by Wolsey, under the authority of the Bishop of Rome, while
" Henry was still attached to that party, is also worthy of remem-
" brance, and it would be well to have the Papal Bull concerning it.
" I would not dare to ask all these of you, but if any of them
" can be conveniently granted, I will add it to the number of your
" kindnesses. You have caused me great joy by informing me of
" your plan for hastening the publication of the first fruits of your
" great work, about which I hope to learn more as soon as possible
" Thomas Gale, your countryman, a most learned man, in his pre-
" face to the " Scriptores Britannici xv ," says that Magna Charta,
" the mother of your laws, is not now extant in its original form ;
" but I suppose that search had not then been made, and that you
" may have seen it. Some persons, it is said, are intending to
" build up the whole body of your history. They will be wonder-
" fully assisted by your work, though I doubt not that the rest of
" Europe will owe very much to you from the connexion of Euro-
" pean history with that of England. Farewell. Hanover, 13–23
" January 1696."

Several other letters passed between these two friends on the
subject of their similar pursuits, but unfortunately they are not
to be found. Two or three others, which, I believe, have never
been printed, appear in the Appendix, but the one the most
to be desired has not occurred. It relates to the second title-
page issued by Rymer, which Leibnitz translated into Latin
and printed in his " Mantissa Codicis Juris Gentium Diplomatici," to which I have already alluded. After acknowledging
there his obligations to his English correspondents, Bishop
Burnet, George Stepney, Dr Thomas Smith, and Rymer, Leibnitz
says, " We are now looking forward to the appearance of the

" great and important work of Thomas Rymer, who will deserve
" the gratitude of the political and literary world for bringing to
" light out of the obscure recesses of the Archives, to which they
" have until now been condemned, so many of the ancient monu-
" ments of England   Engravings will also appear of the seals and
" signatures appended or subjoined to the ancient charters   Moved
" as he himself confesses by our example, he has also prescribed to
" himself the same limit of date as that with which our first volume
" begins, so the year 1101 of the Christian era   But he has enjoyed
" one most important advantage denied to us , that of access to
" original documents   And thus, while we are generally compelled
" to content ourselves with transcripts, and have frequently been
" left in utter doubt, he has been able to pronounce with perfect
" certainty on the true readings of the documents with which he
" has dealt   We trust other nations will be excited by the
" example of England to publish their manuscript treasures for
" the use of history and international law.   Thus innumerable
" facts will become known, some illustrating the chronology and
" causation of events, the origin and vicissitudes of families, which
" are now erroneously narrated , others again geography ; and in
" fact every kind of literature at present utterly unknown.   But
" we will here present the published title of Rymer's work, in the
" later and fuller form (and no intelligent person will find fault
" with its fulness), which by the kindness of the author has reached
" our hands."

It is unfortunate that the letter conveying this title-page
cannot be found, as it would probably have contained other information relating to the Fœdera not generally known   A thorough
search has been made at the British Museum and elsewhere for
a copy of the title-page, but without success.   I am, therefore,
compelled to give an English translation of the Latin version of
Leibnitz [1]   It shows Rymer's intention respecting the plan of the
Fœdera, and how far he had departed from it, when he began to
print his work.   It runs thus :—

" Pandects of leagues, conventions, alliances, letters, appoint-
" ments, obligations, grants, renunciations, and treaties whatsoever,

---

[1] Leibnitz writes " Pandectæ Fœderum, Conventionum, Alligantiarum, literarum, appunctuamentorum, obligationum, concessionum, renunciationum, et tractatuum quorumcunque, inter Reges Angliæ, *ex una parte*, et Imperatores, Reges, Pontifices, communitates, aliosve quosvis principes sive potestates, *ex altera*, ab ineunte sæculo duodecimo, vidz ab Anno Domini 1101, ad nostra usque tempora, secundum temporum seriem digestæ ; instrumenta omnimoda, chirographata indentata, per alphabetum

" between the Kings of England of the one part, and Emperors,
" Kings, Pontiffs, Communities, or any other princes or powers, on
" the other, from the beginning of the twelfth century, viz , from the
" year of the Lord 1101, to our own times, chronologically digested;
" comprising indented instruments of all kinds, chirographed or
" cut through the alphabet; authentic writings or authenticated
" transcripts of writings, and diplomas sealed with wax, or con-
" firmed with leaden and even with golden bulls; concerning
" peace, amity, marriage, war, mutual aid, captures, hostages, hom-
" ages, truces, or intercourses, (of which some of the more important
" and most notable have the great seal of the nation to which they
" refer engraved on copper, and appended in the proper place), like-
" wise the charters of the liberties of Scotland, which Edward I,
" having subdued that kingdom, brought with him into England
" among the regalia, as it is believed , all faithfully transcribed
" from the originals within the more secret treasuries of the royal
" archives, through many ages hidden and inaccessible, now at
" length brought to light and drawn forth, and are published
" by the King's command By the labour and study of Thomas
" Rymer, historiographer royal To which are added from divers
" manuscript books of the Exchequer, from the Records of Public
" Acts in the Tower of London, and from the Cottonian library,
" whatsoever instruments have seemed fit to supply, continue, or
" perfect the same. A work whereby to distinguish the laws,
" manners, and character of each nation and age; to illustrate the
" antiquities, dignities, and genealogies of families , to reform,
" amend, and correct the chronologies of histories and annals , and

divisa transumta , transcripta seu scripta authentica, aut authenticata, et diplomata, cera sigillata, vel plumbo roborata, vel etiam auro bullata pacem, amicitiam, matrimonium, bellum, mutuum auxilium, captiones, hostagiamenta, homagia, treugas aut intercursus, concernentia , (quorum insigniora nonnulla ut etiam cujusque Gentis insigniora magna sigilla æri incisa, appositis tabellis, suis quæque locis, sunt inserta), insimul et chartas libertatum Scotiæ quas Edw. I. subacto regno, secum inter regalia in Angliam adportasse creditur ex autographis, infra secretiores archivorum regiorum thesaurarias, per multa sæcula, latentibus et inaccessis, jam tandem erutis et eruderatis, fideliter exscripta, complectentes in lucem prodeunt de mandato Regis Opera et studio. T. R. Historiographi Regii Quibus addita sunt ex diversis libris MSS Scaccarii, ex actorum publicorum tabulis in Turri London et ex Bibliotheca Cotoniano, quæcunque ad prædicta supplenda, continuanda, aut perficienda, idonea visa sunt Opus ad jura moresque et ingenium cujusque gentis et sæculi dignoscendum , ad familiarum antiquitates, dignitates et genealogias illustrandum ; ad historias et annalium calculationes reformandum, emendandum et corrigendum accuratum. Ac denique ad rancores inter gentes emolliendos, ad pacem ubique terrarum conciliandam et ad antiquata amicitiæ Fœdera, intelligentias et commercia, renovanda, stabilienda et firmanda efficacissimum."

" lastly, most efficacious to soften rancours between nations, to con-
" ciliate peace everywhere, and to renew, establish, and strengthen
" ancient leagues of amity, good understanding, and commerce "

The reputation of Leibnitz was thus made available in spreading throughout Europe a knowledge of the contents of the forthcoming work, and in keeping alive the interest which had already been excited respecting it in England and on the continent   Still, however, the work itself did not appear. Rymer was busy in his collections, and continued to amass materials.[1] That fact was universally known; why then was the work so long delayed? However necessary it may have been at that time to hide the cause of the procrastination, the reason for concealment no longer exists, and the truth may now be told without disguise. Want of funds to carry it on was the undoubted cause of the delay   In the Appendix XXVI will be found an extraordinary document, which shows the state of insolvency of the Royal Treasury at that time. There was scarcely a public functionary whose salary was not in arrear, some for nearly three years; but when work was to be paid for out of funds arising from contingencies, the difficulty was greatly increased. The payment for the publication of the "Fœdera" was in this predicament. When the work was undertaken, no funds were specially appropriated to its cost; hence arose, not only delay in printing the work, but also injury and wrong to the unfortunate editor, who frequently had not only to find money for the payment of his assistants, but was himself allowed to remain unpaid for more than a year; in addition to which, during the whole time before he commenced printing, nearly eleven years, he never received one farthing for himself by way of remuneration.

His mistake in engraving a forged charter.

During the period that Rymer was collecting his materials, and before he commenced printing, his course was disturbed by an incident which threw some doubt upon his qualification for conducting so great a work as that which had been placed in his hands. He stumbled, in fact, at the very threshold of his record career.

It is well known to those who are conversant either with Scottish history or with the muniments in the Public Record Office, that there is a document formerly belonging to the Chapter House collection, which purports to be Letters Patent by which Malcolm Canmore, King of Scotland and of all the circum-

---

[1] See Appendix XV

jacent islands, and his eldest son, Edward Earl of Carrick and Rothesay, acknowledge that they hold the whole kingdom of Scotland and the adjacent islands of Edward the Confessor by liege homage and fealty, as their predecessors had done, and as appeared by ancient records of the Scottish crown; and therefore, says the document " we become your men, O liege Lord, most serene Edward, " son of Ethelred, King of England, our Lord of the kingdom of " Scotland and of all the circumjacent islands, during our lives, with " you and against all men to live and die, as your liege and faithful " subjects, and liege fealty will we bear to you and your heirs. In " witness whereof we have caused our seal to be affixed to these " presents for ourself and our son, at York, the fifth day of June " in the ninth year of our reign, in the Parliament of our said Lord " superior there held: by the consent and advice of Margaret our " consort, the daughter of Edward the son of Edmund Ironside " and of Edgar Atheling, the brother of our said consort, and of " many other magnates of our said kingdom." A fragment of a seal is pendant; it is in brown wax, and impressed on one side with the lion within the double tressure, the modern arms of Scotland; on the reverse there is no impression No one now entertains the slightest doubts that this is an ancient forgery; but Rymer happened to discover this document; he unwisely, perhaps unwittingly, gave it an importance to which it was by no means entitled, by causing it to be engraved in fac-simile. The Scottish antiquaries, alarmed at this attack upon their national independence, at the time when the question of the Union was under discussion, took instant advantage of Rymer's indiscretion A Latin treatise by Sir Thomas Craig upon the independence of the Scottish crown, which had hitherto remained in manuscript, was translated by Mr George Ridpath, and published under the title of " Scotland's Sovereignty Asserted." [1] In a preface to this work the claims of the pretended charter were entirely demolished, and Rymer was convicted of having ignorantly engraved as the precursor of his collections an undoubted and palpable forgery.[2]

---

[1] 8vo Lond 1695.

[2] Hickes, Rymer's old schoolfellow, thus speaks of this charter, and of Rymer's acquaintance with Anglo-Saxon literature, " Denique agmen claudat ingemo excellens " et humaniorum literarum, præsertim dra-" maticæ poesios, scientia clarus Thomas " Rymer, qui literaturæ Saxonicæ prorsus " ignarus, commentitium instrumentum " ante ducentos circiter annos fictum, " sigilloque Malcolmi R Scotorum muni-" tum esse simulatum, quo rex ille S Ead-" wardo II Anglorum regi, tanquam " Scotiæ superiori domino, homagium,

The subject was further alluded to in the following manner by Bishop Nicolson, in his "Scottish Historical Library," published in 1702 After mentioning Sir Thomas Craig's disquisition, he adds, that "Mr Rymer lately occasioned its being translated into " English" He then proceeds, "Our English historiographer had " unluckily printed a pretended form of homage said to have been " done by King Malcolm the Third to our Edward the Confessor ; " and to take off all objections that might be started about the " intent of the publication, 'twas alleged that this was only a fore- " runner of some volumes of public treaties which would shortly be " sent abroad. 'Twas an unlucky stumble on the threshold to begin " the work with such a counterfeit monument as this ; which Mr. " Ridpath (the translator of Mr. Craig's book) has deservedly exposed, " and convicted of several notorious and undeniable marks of " forgery"[1]

Some other subjects, which had been commented upon in the "Scottish Historical Library," induced Rymer shortly after this time to address several letters to Bishop Nicolson He took advantage of the opportunity thus afforded him of departing from the discreet silence he had hitherto maintained, and referring to the charter of King Malcolm, he notices his own indiscretion in the following words : " Give me leave to warn you of a misrepresentation " your Lordship has somewhere met withall, touching my pub- " lishing a charter of homage by King Malcolm My Lord, the " fact is I never did publish it, nor ever saw it in print, save in a " book by Mr. Ridpath. True it is I found such a thing in the " archives, and had it engraved, but had no design to publish it, ' unless it should be in company with that famous league betwixt " Charlemagne and King Archaicus, the seals of them both being " exactly the same "[2]

While on the subject of Rymer's letter to Bishop Nicolson, it may be as well to allude to others connected with this subject. The first two were published about the same time, if not together,

---

" lignum & fidelitatem spopondisse et " professus esse dicitur, cælatura splen- " dide expressum, quasi ad pompam, " edidit. Quod tamen, non dicam si " linguam, antiquitates et solennia verba, " sed si vel literas manusque Saxonicas " typorumque scatariorum originem cog- " novisset, adeo tanquam genuinum et " verum edere noluisset, ut id plane uti

" figmentum primo intuitu, & omni procul " dubio damnasset" (Hickesii Thesaurus " præfat. p. xxv.)
[1] Scottish Historical Library, 8vo, 1702, p 277.
[2] Letters to the Bishop of Carlisle, 8vo, 1702, p. 18. printed for James Knapton at the Crown in St. Paul's Churchyard.

and are usually found under one cover. Their titles are in the following words :—

"Letters to the Right Reverend the Lord Bishop of Carlisle, " occasioned by some passages in his late book of the Scotch Library. " Wherein Robert the Third is beyond all dispute freed from the " imputation of bastardy A particular account is given of King " David's ransom, and of the hostages for the payment of the same. " With several original papers relating to the Scotch affairs and a " grant of the liberties of Scotland. Letter I. London, printed " for James Knapton, at the Crown in St. Paul's Church Yard, " 1702." (pp. 52)

"To the Right Reverend the Ld Bishop of Carlisle, containing " an Historical Deduction of the Alliances between France and " Scotland. Whereby the pretended Old League with Charle- " magne is disproved , and the true Old League is produced and " asserted. To which is added, A notable piece of Church-History " from Her Majesty's Archives, never before published. Letter II. " London : Printed for Thomas Hodgson, over-against Gray's Inn " Gate in Holborn , and sold by J Nutt, near Stationers-Hall." (pp. 101, without date).

"To the Right Reverend the Ld Bishop of Carlisle, containing " a Vindication of Edward the Third . Letter III "

This last letter is not easily found; no copy of it is known to exist in England, but the fact of its publication is indisputable.[1] Thoresby states in 1709 that Rymer presented him with his "three " letters to the Bishop of Carlisle."[2] Leibnitz[3] mentions having received a copy of it from Rymer, and describes it as in the foot-note. Des Maizeaux[4] details the subject of the letter more fully, but substantially in the same manner as Leibnitz, adding that the point of Rymer's argument was "que ce Seaton n'etoit " pas Gouverneur de la place, mais le Chevalier Guillaume Keith," and he proved this fact " par les Archives"[5]

---

[1] There is no entry of it in the books of the Stationers Company, permission to search which was given to me by the courteous master of the Company, Mr. Hodgson.

[2] Thoresby's Diary, II 27.

[3] Opera, VI 280

[4] MS. Addit 4223, f 162ᵃ.

[5] Leibnitz in a letter to Thomas Burnet, (MS Addit 5104, f. 20,) writes, "Mons " Rymer m'envoyant son 4ᵐᵉ volume des " Actes Publics de l'Angleterre m'a envoyé " de meme temps une lettre imprimée to " the Right Reverend the Lord Bishop of " Carlisle, containing a vindication of

" Edward the Third touchant ce que les " historiens Ecossois Buchanan et Hector " Boèthius lui imputent comme s'il avoit " fait pendre deux fils d'Alexandre " Seaton, Gouverneur du Chasteau de " Berwic, qui estoient ses ostages, parce- " que le pere ne volut point rendre le " Chastean. On pretend que cette histoire " est fausse "

In the catalogue of the library of Thomas Madox, p 21, are "Rymer's three " letters to Bishop Nicolson, and Du " Fresnoy's New Method of Studying His- " tory, ii 478. Edit 1728

It was about this time that Rymer published " An Essay
" concerning critical and curious learning, in which are contained
" some short reflexions on the Controversie betwixt Sir William
" Temple and Mr Wotton and that betwixt Dr Bentley and
" Mr Boyle. By T R., Esq "

Some very interesting matter, connected with the remuneration
Rymer received for his labours, has lately been brought to light.
It was anything but encouraging · but I leave Rymer to tell his
own story, or rather, the public documents which are still extant to
tell it for him.

The first pay-
ment for the
work

It will be observed that in Queen Mary's warrant[1] no reference
is made to the payment Rymer was to receive for his labours.
Having commenced his work without any agreement with the Government as to his remuneration, he was now constantly compelled
to petition the Crown for money to carry it on.

As early as the 23rd of April 1694 (eight months after his
appointment) he was obliged to apply to the King for money. His
letter on the subject is still extant   It is curious, as showing how
straitened the Government then was, and to what shifts the Treasury was driven in order to satisfy his just demands. Here was
a scholar, assiduously devoting nine months to a great national
work, and obliged to point out to his Sovereign the mode by which
he might be remunerated for his labour   His petition to the King
is thus curtly expressed: "To the King's most Excellent Majesty,
" the petition of Thomas Rymer humbly sheweth that about 3 or 4
" years ago, upon the conviction of Gervas Cartwright, a Romish
" priest, at Leicester, there was seized in money 200*l*. for your
" Majesty's use by Mr. Will. Bentley, then mayor of Leicester, in
" whose hands it still remains   And whereas your Majesty has
" been graciously pleased to order that your petitioner transcribe and
" publish the ancient leagues and treaties betwixt the Crown of
" England and other nations, which will be a work of great charge,
" it is therefore humbly prayed that your Majesty towards the
" defraying of that charge may be pleased to grant the above men-
" tioned 200*l*. to your petitioner."

Rymer's petition was solemnly read before the King in his Court
at Whitehall, and "his Majesty being graciously disposed to gratify
" the petitioner in his request, is pleased to refer this petition to
" the Right Honorable the Lords Commissioners of the Treasury, to
" consider thereof and report their opinion what his Majesty may

---

[1] See Appendix VIII.

" fitly do therein, whereupon his Majesty will declare his farther
" pleasure." The facts, as stated in Rymer's petition, were duly
reported to the Treasury on the 25th of May following, and the
first payment to the editor of the " Fœdera," towards his expenses,
amounting to 100*l.* (for he only obtained half of what he applied
for), was ordered to be made out of the estate of the ill-fated
Gervas Cartwright of Belgrave in the county of Leicester, who
was indicted, convicted, and attainted of the crime of being a
Romish Priest.[1]

It will thus be seen that the first payment to carry on the
" Fœdera " was derived from the forfeiture of a Romish priest. In
the same year the Lords of the Treasury added another hundred
pounds, making in all 200*l* ; no part of which, however, was appropriated to Rymer himself, as appears by the accounts which he
rendered to the Treasury.[2]

*Rymer's diffi-
culties in ob-
taining money
to carry on
the Fœdera.*

In the next year, having expended 250*l.* for the Government and
received nothing, not even the balance of 133*l.* due to him for
money out of pocket, he was again compelled to petition, and
to point out a mode by which he might be paid. His petition runs thus :—" To their Excellencies the Lords Justices. The
" humble petition of Thomas Rymer, sheweth, That it is now (this
" present month of August) three years since your petitioner was
" employed to see transcribed and published the ancient Leagues
" and public acts between the Crown of England and Foreign

---

[1] The following letter from Aaron Smith, Solicitor to the Treasury for Law Affairs, relative to the forfeiture of Gervas Cartwright in connexion with the payment to Rymer, will not be out of place It will be seen that although the Treasury had ordered the money to be paid, yet there was still a chance of its not finding its way to Rymer.

" Sir,

" Yesterday in Westminster Hall,
" Mr. Serjeant Wright Recorder of Lei-
" cester askt mee what was intended to
" bee done about the money forfeited to
" their Maj^ties upon the attainder of Gervas
" Cartwright att Leicester I told him
" their Maj^ties had disposed of it to you,
" He replyed you would doe well to looke
" speedily after it, for tho it might be secure
" now, yet in case of death of the person
" in whose hands it now is, hee would not
" undertake for it This I thought fitt to
" informe you of, being satisfyed that in
" case of death it may bee all hazardous.

" I am y^r most humble serv^t,
" 26 June 1694   AARON SMITH.
" For Thomas Rymer, Esq—These."

[2] " An Account of Mr. Rymer's expenses in the year 1694 ,—

	£	s.	d.
A warrant under the sign manual and signet, order of council, writ under the great seal, with other fees and preliminaries - - -	30	0	0
To 4 writers and 2 engravers, each 40*l* per annum -	240	0	0
To seats, desks, copper paper and other necessaries - -	13	0	0
To coaches and boat betwixt Westminster and the Tower, and other casualties	50	0	0
Making a total of - -	333	0	0"

" Powers from the Originals, then in a great measure putrified and
" hardly legible ; that the charge in carrying on this work doth
" amount to upwards of 200l. per annum, yet hath not your Peti-
" tioner effectually hitherto received more than 200l. in all this
" three years ; the 300l. granted on this occasion the last year out
" of the late teller Mr. Villar's debt being litigated and uncertain
" when it may be paid   Now whereas Mr. James Grahme by a
" Bond dated 6th of February 1691, became obliged to pay to His
" Majesty on the 1st of April 1693 the sum of 2,364l 9s , for the
" recovery of which debt process has since been issued out and
" 500l thereupon in October 1694 paid into the Exchequer, may it
" please your Excellencies that the above said Bond entered into by
" Mr. Grahme be assigned to the use of your Petitioner in con-
" sideration of the premises, for the service, and to defray the
" charge specified "   The Lords Justices recommended the Treasury
to pay the same, but Rymer was not benefitted by their recommendation   He, moreover, had now (1696) expended another
250l, making a total of 633l. This item in his account sent
into the Treasury tells a lamentable tale   " For the year 1696.
" Conceal'd money in the Teller's hand, sayed to be 300l, wch occa-
" sioned a suit wth Squib's Executors   This was granted to me
" and to the 2 Chamberlayns, in consideration of their extra-
" ordinary attendance, of wch came not clear to my share more
" than about 140l. 0s. 0d."

On the 30th of June 1697, the Lords of the Treasury directed
that he should be paid 200l. by tally on malt to carry on his
work ; but he seems to have been again disappointed, for we find
him complaining to the Lords Justices in October 1697   This is
evident from their letter of the 4th of October 1697 to the Lords
of the Treasury, enclosing a petition from Rymer,[1] which the
Lords Justices think very fit to be considered, and that he should
be encouraged to proceed in so laborious and useful a work, as he
is engaged on, by his Majesty's special command, and since he hath
been disappointed in what was formerly proposed, their Excellencies hope he may be gratified out of the forfeiture[2] he now
petitions for, and accordingly they refer and recommend it to their
lordships' consideration.

There is still extant a debtor and creditor account, showing the
different sums expended and received by Rymer on account of the

---

[1] This petition is not extant.   [2] It probably refers to Sir John Freend's estate.

"Fœdera," by which it appears that he had spent the sum of 1,253*l*. during the years 1694, 1695, 1696, 1697, and 1698, and had received only 500*l*. The accounts of his receipts are curious, and reveal a sad story of the way in which literary men employed by the government were paid in those days In 1697 he spent 210*l* for the government, and received from the Lords of the Treasury " 200*l* in lottery tickets, of which I made about 160*l*."

In the year 1698 he expended for the government 210*l*., and received nothing He again states that up to August 1698 he had expended 1,253*l* [1] and had received only 500*l*., so that there remained due to him 753*l*. He also states that " here are now two " volumes ready for the press, as now set forth in a memorial [2] " to the Lords of the Treasury about two months since." The Lords of the Treasury thereupon order, on the 19th of August 1698, a sum of 200*l*. in part payment of his expenses.

It does not appear whether Rymer received the 200*l* which the Lords of the Treasury had ordered in part payment of the 753*l* due to him, but in all probability he was once more doomed to disappointment, for he was compelled to memorialize His Majesty on the 9th of January in the following terms.—"Something of a " Memorial being required of me, I crave leave to repeat that " I was employed by the King in Council to see transcribed the " old Leagues and Treaties, that no provision being made to defray " the charges, it lay upon me to provide the money, and I gave " account from time to time to the Lords of the Treasury in order " to be reimbursed, and from them had several sums, but in such " proportion, that by an account I stated this last Midsummer " there appeared to be laid out by me more than received 563*l* , " upon a representation then of my very great necessities, an order " for 150*l*. was granted me, which no way answering my neces- " sities and the charge still growing upon me, I humbly beg a " further consideration may be had of me, the rather in that " I ask no reward for my time, and seven years continual appli- " cation and attendance in this service."

Notwithstanding that he was labouring gratuitously, Rymer could not obtain money from the Treasury to replace the sums he had disbursed out of his own resources, and he was again compelled to

Parsimony of the government.

---

[1] His friend Charles Montague had, however, procured warrants for him to the amount of 1,130*l*., but these, like many other warrants for the payment of money at that period, were disregarded, on account of the impecuniosity of the Treasury.

[2] Not now forthcoming.

petition for money. The Lords of the Treasury, on the 15th of November 1700, summoned him to appear before them, and after hearing his grievances, "order him a warrant for 250*l.* towards his charges, " but do determine this expense shall end at Midsummer next." He does not, however, appear to have received the money assigned him, for on the 10th of January following "a warrant for 250*l.* " was to be issued to Mr. Rymer on his order;" and on the 18th of June 1701 a further sum of 200*l.* was awarded to him, " in part of 383*l* due to him to discharge his clerks," and he is again reminded that this charge for clerks, &c is to cease from Midsummer 1701. On the 6th of March 1702, Rymer was again compelled to write to the Treasury a letter, which cannot be read without deep emotion by every literary man:—" No allowance " from the Treasury on account of the old Leagues and Treaties " hath been made me since Midsummer 1701, yet from that time " and still the same charge in Clerks and Lodgings continues upon " me , because to part with them would be to put it out of my " power to print and publish as the Order of Council had directed. " By this means a debt is brought and grows upon me, which " of necessity I must sink under (unless relieved by the Treasury), " which I may the rather expect in regard that hitherto no " manner of consideration hath been had of my almost ten years " constant attendance in that service. Let me also remind you " that old age comes so fast upon me, that I cannot expect to be " much longer in a condition to do anything. I beg your favour " in representing this to my Lord Treasurer " This letter was laid before Queen Anne, but it does not appear to have received any attention from Her Majesty.

On the 17th of June 1702, Rymer addressed Queen Anne in the following words —" To the Queen's most Excellent Majesty The " petition of Thomas Rymer, humbly sheweth that your petitioner " in the fourth year of the reign of King William and Queen " Mary was constituted Historiographer Royal, and was then also " employed to see transcribed and published the ancient Leagues, " Treaties, and Public Acts of State from the Originals, then in a " great measure rotten and defaced, which service your petitioner " from that time constantly has attended , but hitherto has not " published any part of the premisses. May it please your Majesty " to grant the like patent of Historiographer to your petitioner " during your Majesty's most gracious pleasure , and in order to " the publishing of the above-mentioned Leagues, Treaties, and

" Public Acts of State, to direct your Majesty's Lord High Treasurer
" of England to allow the like encouragement as heretofore has
" been granted by your Majesty's most noble progenitors and
" predecessors Kings of England, on the like occasion And your
" petitioner," &c

On the 18th of June ,1702, it appears by a Treasury Minute
" that Mr. Rymer prays to renew his Patent of Historiographer
" Royal, and to have such encouragement for transcribing and
" publishing ancient Leagues, Treaties, and Public Acts of State as
" heretofore hath been made." This encouragement was at the
rate of 200l. per annum for copying clerks , but no order seems to
have been made. By an abstract of papers laid before the Queen
it was recommended that his salary as Historiographer should in
future be only 160l per annum ; by another minute it was further
proposed to reduce it to 100l. per annum ; but neither recommendation was carried out, and his former salary of 200l. per annum
was continued up to the day of his death. *Prays for a renewal of his patent as Historiographer Royal*

Such continual petitions and disappointments were sufficient to
have overwhelmed the strongest and most hopeful man, and it is a
matter of surprise that Rymer did not sink under them , few could
have borne up so manfully, and laboured so indefatigably and zealously amidst a life of such trials and misfortunes Probably no other
man would have had the energy and perseverance to have carried
the Fœdera to its conclusion, but he struggled bravely through all
discouragements to the end of his most laborious and arduous
task. Light was now beginning to dawn upon him. His patron,
Montague, had been raised to the peerage at the recommendation
of the House of Commons, with the title of Baron Halifax, and
had acquired additional favour at Court. He induced the Queen to
take an active interest in the Fœdera, and to promise to be at the
charge of printing it.[1] *His continual disappointments*

Her Majesty kept her word, and on the 19th of May 1703
ordered under sign manual the sum of 500l. to be paid to " Peter
" Hume, Esq , without account, the same being intended to be by
" him paid over unto our trusty and well-beloved Thomas Rymer,
" our Historiographer, and Awnsham Churchill, bookseller, at such
" times and in such proportions as are mentioned in certain articles
" of agreement made the 16th of April last between the said Peter
" Hume for and on our behalf of the first part, the said Thomas *The work ordered to be printed.*

---

[1] Treasury Minute Book, vol. XII. p. 54.

" Rymer of the second part, and the said Awnsham Churchill
" of the third part, for transcribing a volume of Leagues and
" Treaties extracted from ancient records by the said Thomas
" Rymer, and printing 250 volumes thereof, to be disposed of as
" in the said Articles are also contained." Thus the publication'
of this great national work was ordered after Rymer had been
engaged upon it upwards of ten years, and without having received
any remuneration whatever.   Before the printing of the first
volume of the work was finished, Rymer was again compelled to
apply for money ; he thus addressed the Lord High Treasurer .—
" The case of Tho. Rymer, humbly presented   May it please your
" Lordship, that there is due to him, on his usuall allowance of
" 210l. per ann for Clerks (without whome He could never print)
" and other necessary charges relating to his Collections, 2 yeares
" from Midsum.r 1701 to ye time He began to print his first volume.
" Which arreare has run him into so great a debt that He is not
" able to disengage himselfe unlesse your Lordship of your great
" Goodnesse will be pleased to order payement thereof."

It was not, however, until the volume was finished at press, that
the Treasury entertained Rymer's petition.   On the 6th of June
1704 he was paid " £200 in full of all services of himselfe & his
" clerks till Lady-day 1703, from wch time [he] has allowance for
" printing his books "   He was thus mulcted of 400l of his just
demand.

Publication
of the first
volume

The printing of the first volume was finished at the end of
February 1704,[1] and it was published on the 20th of November
1704[2]   It commences with a turgid and eulogistic dedication to
Queen Anne, in Latin, which is so perfectly characteristic of its
author that I give an English translation of it

Dedication to
Queen Anne

" To the Queen —To relieve the wretched and feed the poor
" by bestowing gold and silver on those even who do not ask it, what
" you are doing daily and continually   And now you give out
" of the more sacred vaults of your archives a treasure to be used
" and enjoyed by the world of letters , whence may be every-
" where fed the hunger for learning.   A gift to an erudite people
" such as no Emperors, yea such as no other King has to give
" Hence you diffuse a light to surrounding nations.   Hence Danes,
" Norwegians, Flemings, Germans, Italians, may seek that light

---

[1] See Appendix XVI.

[2] The printing cost only 500l, exclusive
of course of the expense of transcripts

" by which every one may see and discover his own affairs, long
" obscured by darkness To the Spaniards is given many a wise
" Alfonso ; to the French is given a Saint, (I say a Saint) Louis,
" with Blanch his mother and Margaret his consort, who through
" many folios occupy each page.

" Lest anything should be wanting to adorn ecclesiastical affairs,
" here may be abundantly seen Popes' bulls, monitions, menaces,
" and fulminations, and ancient disputes everywhere shining and
" glittering

" Truly the beautiful face of England is everywhere and at all
" times apparent, and without stain, now glad, sometimes sad,
" often disturbed, often doubtful ; but certainly never unless after
" many revolving ages do we, glad and rejoicing, see it so vivid,
" smiling, florid, and full of blood and sap as under your reign,
" most serene Queen.

" Henry, the first of that name, King of England, your pro-
" genitor, opens this first volume A.D. 1101, the first year of his
" reign, the very same year in which Matilda the Scot (on account
" of the excellence and sweetness of her manners, called the Good)
" was joined to him in conjugal compact, which Matilda the Good
" was the daughter of the blessed Margaret and mother of the
" Empress Matilda. Oh chance and vicissitudes of birth ! This
" Henry, most skilled in civil prudence and warlike valour, lan-
" guished in his great grandson King John, and almost expired in
" his great great grandson Henry the third ; but conquered Wales
" and captive Kings showed him resuscitated in Edward the First,
" and born again in Edward the Third.

" In like manner, they who through the courses of so many
" years have disappeared, who for so many ages have lain hid,
" Margaret the Holy, Matilda the Good, Matilda the Empress,
" your noble ancestresses, who does not see, acknowledge, and
" venerate resuscitated in you, most holy, most good, and most
" august Queen ? in you reborn, in you revived refulgent with
" new rays of virtues, and new endowments of divine favour.
" What immaculate purity of life ! What unwearied anxiety for
" the reformation of morals ! What goodness, what holiness !
" When I speak of these, I speak of private things , however
" great the praises of your noble ancestors may be they never
" adequately rise to your height, not even if British Helena herself, a
" name celebrated through so many nations, your kinswoman in
" blood and holiness, be borne in mind.

d

" For you, most Christian Queen, for you greater things remain;
" through what climes (unheard of in former ages) and lands and
" countries, does your name resound with joy, is your sacred
" command obeyed, and your august person venerated !

" You, beloved of God, and the especial daughter of Divine
" Providence, are destined for the safeguard of the human race,
" against the wicked and invaders, you are the only bulwark and
" public security, you, the ornament and defence of Europe.

" There was a Queen who governed the realms of England and
" Ireland firmly and happily ; but you are the first to whom it has
" been given to rule the whole of Britain—England and Scotland,
" with Ireland—as one empire.

" Henry the son of the Empress Matilda, your progenitor, was
" esteemed in his time by far the most powerful of Kings, because
" he extended his dominion from the borders of Scotland to the
" Pyrenees. But truly, most potent Queen, neither the confines
" of Scotland hem you in, nor does your labour stop short at the
" Pyrenees Unhappy Europe ! if the eye of your providence did
" not look beyond the Pyrenees, yea, if the arm of your power
" did not thunder beyond the Alps may I not refer the victorious
" fleet of your ships to the traversed ocean, and to the subjugated
" pillars of Hercules; a fleet with which you there impose laws on
" Africa, while here by threatened war, you hold the minds of Italians
" captive and given over to the pleasure of your will. It is the set
" task of your prowess everywhere to repulse the oppressors and the
" wicked You take up arms for justice, for the right of nations:
" for liberty, for public faith. You who care for the things of God
" are God's care ; the God of Hosts wages your wars, shines every-
" where on your banners, animates and thunders over your
" squadrons Hence it is, most invincible Queen, that a nation
" never goes to war more successfully than when under your
" auspices ; but not victory, not spoils, not triumphal cars are dear
" to your heart, to you peace only, the most lovely of things, peace
" is dear

" If you look to the Danube, if you survey the Rhine, or tread
" the Ligurian shores, peace you seek, peace you ask, peace you
" command That a joyful peace may soon shine on mortals is
" (with God's help) your work , if there be any tranquillity, any
" safety, any happiness of the age, it is of your making , which
" peace and happiness, it might be hoped, would be lasting and
" perpetual, if you, pitying the travail of your people, in an

" earthly throne, and in the glory of good works, would, with
" God's favour, deign to reign on earth for ever

" There was a custom among the ancients, a votive song of accla-
" mation for a good Prince ' May Jupiter encrease your years out
" ' of ours.' You, oh most blessed Queen ! who are the life of all
" and the public health, what may not we vow for your dearest
" life ? What may we not ask of God for your most precious
" health ? That which your most sacred Majesty's most devoted
" servant does with a grateful mind and most ready heart."

Rymer's Address to the Reader, which especially relates to the first
volume, will be found in Appendix XXIV. It contains little or no
reference to the general plan of the "Fœdera." After stating that
the work is drawn for the most part from authentic sources, and
contains matter which may be searched for in vain among historians
and contemporary writers, he hastens to a description of some
of the principal documents to be found in the volume In one
place he speaks in slightly apologetic terms of his collection. If
some matters, he says, are inserted which appear of minor
importance and unworthy of being printed, before you rashly
conclude that they should have been rejected, think of Æsop's
fable "The Cock." In another place, he says that it is not
his intention to waste many words in proving what valuable
information genealogists may gather from his book. Again,
The observant reader may see, wherever he searches, very many
germs budding forth ; but how many more of the same sort which
ought to be brought under notice we must defer to some other
time.

The earliest document is a convention between King Henry the
First and Robert Earl of Flanders, dated the 17th of May 1101 ([1]),

General con-
tents of the
first volume.

---

[1] Rymer has been condemned by Dr
Clarke for commencing his work in 1101,
on the ground "that neither that year, nor
" the accession of Henry I., constitute any
" remarkable era in our annals or history ,
" he should," continues Dr. Clarke, "at
" least have gone back as far as the Nor-
" man Conquest in 1066. This is a
" remarkable era , none, indeed, more so,
" previously to the Revolution ; it brought
" about changes, the influence of which has
" been felt through every period of our
" history, from that time to the present
" day" Dr Clarke says a great deal
more on this subject, which it is unneces-

sary to repeat, but, without justifying
Rymer, it may be remarked that Rymer
commenced his work with the earliest
political document found in this country,
Doomsday Book of course excepted , and
yet Dr Clarke states that "Mr Rymer
" greatly departed from the principle laid
" down by Mr Harley, in beginning the
" work with the accession of Henry I.
" A.D 1101, when he might have carried
" it much farther back ; and leaving be-
" hind many important instruments in the
" same sources from which he had derived
" others " If we examine what was done
by Dr Clarke to supply these omissions of

upon which the editor makes some especial remarks in his preface—I am now speaking of Rymer's own work, and not of the additions to it by Dᵣ Clarke in the Record Commission Edition, to which I shall presently allude,—and the volume ends with two bulls from the Pope, ordering the prosecution of Guy de Montfort, dated on the Calends and Nones of March 1273. It contains 900 pages, embracing a period of one hundred and seventy-two years, from A D 1101 to A D 1273.

Opinions on the work

Of the great value of the volume there cannot be a doubt. Rapin the historian, who minutely analysed its contents, speaks of it in unqualified terms of approbation, and he is only able to discover one fault in its execution, viz, that Rymer has not inserted any of the Acts relating to the re-establishment of the laws, and in particular of "Magna Charta" Immediately on its publication the "Fœdera" attracted the attention of the whole of the literary world, as well in England (¹) as on the Continent The work was regarded as the most important contribution which had yet been made to the history of this or any other nation. The learned Bréquigny commends it in the following terms: "Un peuple dont les annales se confondent " souvent avec les nôtres, et que nous aimons à imiter par estime " et par rivalité, nous donna le modèle de l'execution et la preuve " de l'utilité d'un pareil ouvrage. L'histoire d'Angleterre etoit " demeurée dans le même état d'imperfection où semble encore " languir la nôtre, lorsque le fameux ' Recueil de tous les Actes ' " relatifs à cette histoire fut publié au commencement de ce siècle, " par les ordres de la reine Anne, et par les soins du savant Rymer " dont une si grande entreprise a rendu le nom immortel. La " vaste collection de ces Actes important ranima le courage de " Rapin Thoyras Aidée ce nouveau secours, en peu d'années il fut " en état de publier son histoire d'Angleterre, qu'il avoit été sur le " point d'abandonner, et dont le mérite non seulement effaça toutes " celles qui avoient précédé, mais se soutient encore, malgré les

---

Rymer, it will be found that for the reign of William I he prints *fourteen* articles, only one of which comes within the proper scope of the Fœdera, and that is derived from a doubtful source, viz, a transcript made by Archbishop Parker from an old "Passionale" formerly belonging to Canterbury Cathedral, and in private hands. For the Reign of William II. he prints only *four* documents,

none of which ought to have been inserted. Thus he was not able to supply a single treaty or convention earlier than given by Rymer

¹ Bishop Nicolson, speaking of it, said, " this great work we have from Thomas " Rymer, Historiographer Royal, com- " manded and supported by Her Majesty, " and it may justly be reckoned one of the " many glories of her reign."

" talens et les recherches des écrivains qui ont glané depuis dans
" les champs où Rymer avoit moissoné."

I have already stated that only two hundred and fifty copies were ordered to be printed; nearly all these were disposed of as presents among the nobility and chief persons about the court; a list of whom will be found in Appendix XXV. A correspondent of the "Nouvelles " de la Republique des Lettres," who there is every reason to believe was Des Maizeaux, writing to that journal in 1705, states, " Il (the ' Fœdera') est imprimé aux depens de la Reine, et ne se " trouve point chez les Libraires. On en a fait present aux pairs " du royaume, aux barons de l'Echiquier, et aux avocats que " servent la cour." The "Journal des Savans" confirms these statements. There are several announcements relative to the "Fœdera" in that work, but no review until 1709. (1709. Supplement, p. 245.) In the volume for that year, the editor states, " Comme ce " livre s'imprime aux depens de la Reine Anne, il ne s'en vend " aucun exemplaire; ils sont tous destinés pour des presens." In a subsequent part of the same volume, after having given a highly flattering review of the volumes then published, the writer adds, " Il y a long temps que nous aurions dû rendre compte de cet " ouvrage, mais il n'a pas été possible d'en faire venir plutôt un " exemplaire." The difficulty of purchasing copies, and the exclusive character of the distribution of the work, may be inferred from the circumstance that no copy of it is found in the libraries of Madox, Thomas Rawlinson, or any other of the celebrated collectors of that day, whose catalogues have been examined.

In the distribution of the volumes as they appeared we again trace Lord Halifax's connexion with the "Fœdera" He had *thirteen* copies presented to him The fact is important upon this account: Mr. Harley had now become Speaker of the House of Commons and one of the Secretaries of State, and it may therefore be presumed that, if the "Fœdera" had originally been projected by him, he would have vindicated his claim to the work by an active ·interference in it; of the earlier volumes no copies were presented to Harley, and it was not until he became Chancellor of the Exchequer in 1710 that any copies were assigned to him, and then only *two*; while the Earl of Halifax was still receiving thirteen. The following passages from contemporary writers also show that Lord Halifax had the management of the distribution. Nicolson, Bishop of Carlisle, writing to the Archbishop of Canterbury, May 19th, 1709, says, "I ought at our last meeting to have acquainted you

" that Lord Halifax was under some difficulty to procure for your
" Lordship the fifth volume of " Rymer's Fœdera," the two following
" and even the eighth, which his Lordship kindly sent to me the
" day before I left town, being at your service. He can hardly be
" persuaded but that you as well as his other customers must
" already have had that volume   If not, it will be retrieved." (*M.S.
Addit. No.* 6116, p 17). Again, March 23rd, 1709–10, " Mr Rymer
" by this time may perhaps have published a ninth (if *not a* tenth)
" volume of his ' Fœdera.' If your behaviour has demanded it, I
" doubt not but my Lord Halifax will continue his benefaction to
" us both ; and I beg your making suit for your poor brother,
" together with yourself. I shall direct my brother to wait on you
" for tidings of this matter "—(*Ibid.* p. 35) Menckenius, the
editor of the "Acta Eruditorum," acknowledges that he had
received a copy of the work through the liberality of Lord Halifax,
" non est tacenda nobis perillustris viri Caroli Halifaxii munifi-
" centia, cui librum in publicis officinis nequaquam prostantem
" debemus." (Acta Eruditorum, anno 1709, p. 529) Le Clerc also,
as before remarked, had a copy from Lord Halifax. He lent it to
Rapin, who was at that time on the point of relinquishing his
History of England, after he had proceeded as far as the reign of
Henry II No one perhaps ever studied the "Fœdera" more deeply,
and no one ever found it more valuable By its assistance he
was enabled not merely to continue his history but to enlarge
it far beyond his original plan. Rapin's work may indeed be
considered as the firstfruits of that abundant harvest which historians have since reaped from Rymer's labours.

When the publication was once begun it proceeded with great
rapidity. Fifteen volumes were published by Rymer in nine
years.

The second volume was published in 1705 ([1]) It begins with
the public acts which were completed before King Edward's return
from the Holy Land, and it embraces all the acts of this King's
reign from 1272 to 1307 The principal matters contained in it are
the Welsh wars, which ended with the conquest of that country by
Edward the First, the differences between the royal families of

The second
volume.

---

[1] On the 24th of May 1704, Rymer's
petition was read before the Queen at her
Court of St James' He prays Her Majesty
to order him some money to enable him to
proceed to the printing of the second
volume of ancient Leagues and Treaties
He was ordered to proceed in his work,
and to be allowed as last year. (Treasury
Minute Book, XII 259) The second
volume cost 650*l* printing, exclusive of
transcripts.

Arragon and Anjou, of which King Edward was chosen the mediator, the war in Scotland, the disputes of Edward with the King of France, affairs which immediately concern England, Edward's controversies with the Pope, acts relating to King Edward in particular, and matters of a miscellaneous nature. This brief description will suffice to show of what use the "Fœdera" must be to all who are engaged in writing English History. In his dedication in English, to Queen Anne he says, " This second " volume gives a view of what passed worthy of memory during " the reign of your most noble progenitor, King Edward the First, a " prince, the most renowned for arms in that age , and that was an " age of much war and action and of many famous captains , Albert " the Great, Duke of Brunswick , William the Great, Marquess of " Montferrat ; Amadeus the Great, Count of Savoy ; three of King " Edward's nearest kindred, and his familiars ; each of whom by " their signal conduct and bravery had the title of *Great* added for " their surname

"These were great captains in that age ; but many ages, " many achievements, toils, and traverses of war pass, many " new stars rise and disappear, many comets blaze and vanish, and " a long course of years is run, before the world behold anything " so transcendent as, *most dread Sovereign*, is reserved for the glory " of your auspicious reign ; I mean so important a battle, so signal " a victory, and so distinguished a captain.

" Germany, one may reckon, has twice been saved by the " English.

"To that nation, about a thousand years ago, from your county " of Devon, on a spiritual expedition, marched St. Winifrid (whom " they call the Apostle of Germany) and from their idolatry " converted them to the Christian faith.

"And now your most excellent Majesty (the same divine grace " assisting) has rescued them from the French, and brought them' " to their allegiance He instructed them to fear God, and you " have taught them to obey Cæsar

"Thus you provide for the peace and felicity of your people, and " of your neighbour princes ; for the present time and for futurity.

"But your noble unbounded piety looks back also upon ages by- " past ; your archives are the magazine from whence you give out " arms to rescue from oblivion the acts and monuments of your " royal ancestors, and secure them from the injury and enterprises " of time.

" Some, whose memory was doubtful, some desperate, and
" eclipsed totally, you bring again to light, and adorn with a new
" lustre.

" One of these here, under your conduct, makes his entry into
" the world. You show him in his public acts of state, and
" attended, as becomes a king, with his lords spiritual and tem-
" poral, his bishops and his barons.

" Yet this crowned head, dropt as it were, and lost in the dark,
" not known in history, was son-in-law to King Alexander the
" Third, and father to a sovereign Queen of Scotland.

" A queen whose life was the most precious, and who was
" designed for a band of *union* betwixt your two kingdoms,
" England and Scotland; but this, most gracious sovereign, is a
" blessing also reserved to be accomplished in your most glorious
" reign, which God long continue "

The third
volume

The third volume was commenced on the 4th of July 1705,
and appeared in August 1706, being ushered in by the following
English dedication to Queen Anne.—" May it please your Majesty.
" In this volume you present the world with the acts of state in
" the reign of King Edward the Second, in a very nice juncture
" a time of great struggling and difficulty, of great trouble and
" disorder all Europe over   Your three kingdoms had each their
" share, and drank deep of the bitter cup.

" Who look so far back into ages by-past, must be sensible of the
" great felicity we now enjoy under a most gracious sovereign,
" ruling with a gentle rein, a willing people, and may compare
" the hardships, heretofore undergone, to the passage of the
" Israelites through the Red Sea and the Wilderness, in their
" way to the Land of Promise, especially your clergy, delivered from
" the bondage, from the vexations, exactions, and oppressions
" (which they laboured under) by a foreign, tyrannical supremacy,
" may now in full ease and security, sitting under their own
" vines, bless God, who has set over them a pious Queen, your
" most sacred Majesty, their head and governor

" In this, the darkest period of time, from your royal archives,
" you set up, as it were, a *pillar of fire* for the direction of
" travellers in their way to truth ; and with an unparalleled bounty
" give out, and make such provision, that in this uncultivated,
" in this so barren tract, in this very desert, the curious want
" not for the entertainment, not to say their quails and their
" manna.

" Amongst the negotiations, in the book published, may be
" noted, that during the most unprosperous and disastrous admi-
" nistration, amidst the greatest confusion and dismal jumble of
" affairs (so it pleased Almighty Providence) that, with William
" the Third, surnamed the Good, Count of Holland, was contracted
" an alliance, whereby those measures were concerted which, in
" the next succeeding reign, carried the English arms into France,
" to Cressy and to Poictiers ; and thence brought the French King
" from the field of battle into this your kingdom captive.

" These were noble exploits of former days, but the business
" of war may be reckoned, as it were, then in its infancy, the
" achievements of those times manly essays, and a prelude of the
" English valour, then a training-up, to be exerted in its perfect
" and consummate vigour in the most important war, and in this
" your Majesty's most glorious reign, which that God long con-
" tinue," &c.

The volume embraces the period from 1307 to 1323, and relates to the domestic troubles of England brought on through
the Spensers and Gaveston, the affairs of Scotland, in continuation of those in the second volume, ecclesiastical matters,
disputes with Rome, and the affairs of the Knights Templars,
whose Order was abolished in this reign. Rapin, speaking of
this volume, says, " Before I had duly considered this advantage
" (giving the dates of place as well as time of the several
" documents, whereby one is enabled to trace the prince from
" one place to another throughout his reign), I believed that
" Mr Rymer was a little to blame, and wondered at his swelling
" his collection with a great number of things which at first sight
" appear of little consequence, if not altogether unnecessary , but
" after matuier reflection I am convinced that there is not one
" piece in the 'Fœdera' but what may be of use, especially to those
" who would write a history of England   The history of France
" is capable likewise of receiving great lights from it, by reason
" of its connexion with the history of England, on account of the
" affairs that have been frequently transacted between these two
" kingdoms in particular. For my own part, I have discovered
" that the best histories of France may be often improved by the
" help of this collection " Again he writes, " We need not look
" back to the first and second volumes of this collection to be
" convinced how the history of Sicily may be illustrated with a
" great number of particulars there mentioned, of which one does

" not see the least trace in the historians of Sicily or Naples. The
" histories of Castille, Arragon, and Portugal may also be furnished
" from this collection with certain facts that were not known to
" their best historians, or else were never explained. . . .
" 'Tis plain, therefore, that this collection is of vast use to those
" who affect the study of history, and particularly that of England,
" for which reason such can never sufficiently extol the bounty
" of that august queen who made them so royal a present, or the
" generosity of those noblemen who procured it. If all other
" nations would follow this example, one might have a history
" of the several states of Europe, at least as to what relates to the
" last seven centuries, as perfect as could be wished"

Sanderson
appointed as
Rymer's
assistant.

For some reason which does not appear, a fresh warrant, dated
3rd May 1707, was granted for access to the Record Offices, in
which the name of Robert Sanderson was joined with that of
Thomas Rymer. It will be seen, however, that Sanderson is not
nominated a co-editor of the work. The privilege of consulting
the records is conceded to him no otherwise than as Rymer's
assistant

The fourth
volume

The fourth volume was commenced on the 10th of April 1706;
it was finished on the 23rd of November following, and published
in 1707 It extends from 1323 to 1338. The chief transactions of
the fourth volume (which embraces the last four years of the reign
of Edward II. and the first eleven years of that of Edward III)
may be reduced to four principal heads, 1 domestic affairs;
2 affairs common to England and Scotland; 3. the King's quarrel
with France, 4. ecclesiastical affairs generally. In his dedication
to Queen Anne, the editor gives the following account of this
volume, comparing the times to which it relates with those in
which he was writing "This book, may it please your Majesty,
" gives a prospect into the reign of your most noble progenitor,
" King Edward the Third, a time of great war, and great successes.
" Some years from the beginning of his reign, he wrote himself
" King of France, and before the end of his reign he saw his
" younger son (that was born at Gaunt) saluted King of Spain.
" His confederates, the Counts of Holland and Zealand, the
" Marquesses of Cleves and Juliers, the Dukes of Brabant and
" Gelder, of the Nassau family, the then Emperor, and other
" German Princes, names (till now, from your archives revived and
" raised to light) long buried in oblivion; these his confederates,
" seem much-what of the same mould with your Majesty's allies

" But, most redoubted sovereign, how much faster run your
" chariot wheels ? How much swifter your course of glory ? In
" half the time that he consumed in labouring and twisting
" alliances, you bring your allies into the field , fight battles, and
" sing Te Deum for your victories.

" In the 20th year of his reign was the battle of Cressy.

" In the 30th was the battle of Poictiers

" In the one and 40th year of his reign was that total rout
" given to the united forces of France and Spain whereby King
" Pedro was set upon the throne, his rival forced to quit the
" kingdom, and flee into France for shelter.

" When we reflect on what has been achieved, and the wonderful
" progress of your Majesty's arms this first five years, what may
" your people expect by the 20th year of your reign ?

" What will Almighty Providence bring about for the good of
" human kind by the 30th year of your Majesty's reign ?

" And what can remain for the 40th year unless that happy
" state of the thousand years which some great divines have
" promised before the end of the world ?

" But what may He not do in five years, who made the world
" in six days ?

" It is not from the strong outstretched arm , it is most gracious
" sovereign, it is from your uplifted devotions, and to your
" sincere and singular piety, that we owe this unparalleled pro-
" sperity of your arms.

" When a war is not to be avoided, when a war is necessary,
" and that there must be fighting, you resort to the Lord of Hosts,
" you sue to Him for victory, and your prayers are heard.

" It is from that retirement, it is from your closet that He
" presents you in public in your triumphant proceeding to St. Paul's,
" where in a grateful return, with hymns and hallelujahs, you
" give Him the praise who had given you the glory, whilst your
" people all rejoice, and say amen," &c.

The fifth volume was commenced on the 3rd of November *The fifth*
1706, was finished on the 27th of October 1707, and published in *volume*
1708 ; it serves as a continuation to the reign of Edward the Third,
and extends from the year 1338 to 1357 inclusive In his dedication to Queen Anne, Rymer does not forget to compare Crecy with
Blenheim and Poictiers with Ramillies. He writes, "This Volume
" is a continuation of the public acts and treaties in the most active
" and prosperous reign of King Edward the Third

"In course of time it brings to that memorable day, the battle
"of Poictiers, where Edward of Woodstock (otherwise called the
"Black Prince) took the French king prisoner

"The battle of Cressy, in the 20th, and this of Poictiers in the
"30th year of his reign, were two of the most famous actions (of
"any ages by-past) that have the honour to live in story.

"But, most tremendous sovereign, the God of Battles goes along
"with your armies, and the beginning of your reign is crowned
"with the most exalted, the most dazzling rays of military
"glory

"The fight of Cressy brought into English hands the fair town
"of Calais.

"How many towns, territories, and countries rescued from the
"enemy were the consequence of your victory at Blenheim ?

"From Poictiers, besides the French king, were brought over
"into England (what prisoners, what hostages) the Duke of
"Orleans, the Duke of Anjou, the Duke of Berry, the Duke of
"Vendôme, the Duke of Bourbon, and James of Bourbon, pro-
"genitor of your Majesty's now adversary of France.

"Those were times of triumph ! those were shining days !

"Yet add 20 great names more, and throw in the obligations of
"three millions for the French king's ransom, all together will
"not tantamount, will not weigh against the town of Bruges, the
"town of Gaunt, the town of Brussels, Louvain, Antwerp, and the
"many good towns more, which followed your victory at Ramil-
"lies, and were the fruit of that glorious labour.

"To this success in war, may I add how, to complete the felicity
"of your people, Almighty Providence hath distinguished your
"Majesty, above all your most noble predecessors, by this especial
"prerogative favour, *The Union of your Two Kingdoms*

"From these marvellous beginnings, what may not your people
"hope, for theirs, and for the good of human kind, in the perpetual
"successive futurity of your reign ?"

The sixth
volume.

The sixth volume [1] was commenced on the 17th of October 1707,
was finished the 31st May 1708, and published in 1708. It contains

---

[1] This volume cost 605*l* for printing, but of this sum Rymer received 42*l*, "the same "being in satisfaction of his trouble and "charges in correcting and transcribing "forty-two supernumerary sheets (over "and above his contracts) which were "added to the fourth and fifth volumes of "Leagues and Treaties extracted from "ancient Records, and 63*l* to Awnsham "Churchill, Bookseller, in satisfaction of "his charges for printing the said super- "numerary sheets" (Treasury Chambers Accounts, Vol 16, p 279)

16 years of the reign of Edward the Third, beginning with 1357 and ending with 1373. In his dedication to Queen Anne, Rymer says, "After the many leagues and alliances in former volumes, in " the last (that was presented to your Majesty) appeared the " operations of war, and a wonderful success in battles.

"In this book two captive kings (which God had given into the " hands of your most noble progenitor Edward the Third) are " ransomed, and set at liberty.

"Thereupon ensued (that commonly called) The Great Peace ; " a treaty the most solemn and the most memorable that ever " had been formed between two contending nations.

"This furthermore contains, besides the peace with France, one " exploit of war on the other side of the Pyreneans, one decisive " blow at Nazara.

"In short, your Majesty, with this volume, gives to the world a " partition of France and the conquest of Spain.

"This shining period of time, most redoubted sovereign, brings " our thoughts home, and makes us reflect as if it did, in some " measure, shadow and give a semblance of these our days, under " your Majesty's most auspicious government.

"In course of time that of Azencourt (Agincourt) will be the " next great battle that comes in our way.

"And now the rumours and ostentation of princes unusual, so " many glittering names, fleurs de lises, and powdered coats, " drawing to the field, seem to make a sort of portending blaze, as " if your Majesty's arms were now not many days march off from " another Azencourt

"Edward the Third, unless in conjunction with Henry the Fifth, " will not be sufficient to represent your much more important " victories.

"Oppressed nations cry aloud to Heaven, and the Almighty, " knowing your pious heart, hath trusted the sword in your hand, " to make you their deliverer, and distinguish you in the most " especial manner, beyond all your predecessors and ancestors, of " immortal memory, for the instrument of His glory.

"Your already so early successes shew that His blessing goes " along with your armies;" &c

The seventh volume[1] was commenced in June 1708, and finished

The seventh volume

---

[1] The indenture for printing the seventh volume, dated 20th of June 1708, is witnessed by Leatitia Wicksted and Anné Parnell, the latter was the sole executrix of Rymer's last will.

on the 5th of November following, but it was not published till
1709; it extends over a period of 25 years, viz, from 1373 to
1397. In the dedication of this volume to Queen Anne, Rymer
proceeds in the usual eulogistic strain,"—This volume shews the
" transactions and state of affairs in these and the neighbouring
" kingdoms, such as it was, during the course of twenty-four years;
" which tract of time affords but little matter that may shine in
" history, and has very little resemblance to these our days, when
" the British sceptre is swayed by your most excellent Majesty.

" This long train of twenty-four years cannot boast of any one
" great and distinguished captain, any one memorable battle, nor
" one important siege, no proceeding to St Paul's, no *Te Deum*
" for victory.

" Beyond the Pyreneans, John Duke of Lancaster, without
" fighting, made a composition with his adversary, and took an
" equivalent for the crown of Spain

" Beyond the Alps, Sir John Hawkwood gave law to the Italian
" princes, and taught them the mystery of commanding armies

" But on this side the mountains continued a wavering, hazy,
" undetermined face of things, neither peace nor war

" Prorogations of truces, abstinences, sufferances, patiences,
" tolerances were the language and the amusement of the times; and
" all the while were kept on foot treaties for a perpetual peace:

" Treaties hitherto fruitless, illusory, and unpracticable

" Who knows (most gracious sovereign) what blessing God, from
" His unsearchable magazines, hath ordained, in regard to your
" singular piety and zeal for His service? what untrodden path for
" your chariots and yet undiscovered way to glory.

" Something more bright than victory, more magnificent than
" triumph

" Who knows (most redoubted sovereign) what may be the
" result of His blessing upon your pious arms, which that He
" continue is the prayer of your servant " &c [1]

___

[1] Rapin, in commenting on the Seventh volume of the "Fœdera," makes the following flattering and pertinent remarks upon the work generally.—" Avant que le " finir cet extrait, je crois devoir avertir, " que bien que je n'aye consideré ce Re- " cueil que par rapport à l'Histoire, parce " que c'est apparemment le but principal " de ceux qui ont pris soin de le donner " au Public, on peut pourtant en tirer " divers autres usages. Par exemple, pour " les Traités de Paix ou de Trève, qui s'y " trouvent en fort grand nombre, les " Ministres publics peuvent en tirer quelque " utilité, tant par raport à la forme de ces " Traités, qu'au choix des termes, aux " précautions qu'on a prises pour les bien " expliquer, et à diverses autres choses de " cette nature Si quel qu'on faisoit des " recherches sur les progres de la Langue

The eighth volume was commenced on the 5th of November The eighth
volume. 1708, and finished on the 22nd of March following, and was also published in 1709 ; it is devoted to the reign of Henry the Fourth, with the exception of the 'last two years of that of Richard the Second.

Rymer, in a very characteristic dedication of it to Queen Anne, makes several very pointed and what may be considered illiberal allusions to the Pretender, who was at that time publicly supported. He thus expresses himself. " This, the eighth volume which you " give the world, contains within a small compass of time a " wonderful variety and vicissitude of affairs. The beginning gives " some glimpses of a change to ensue in England, and towards the " end it discovers the likely prospect of a revolution in France

" That people, whose humour it has always been to be trouble- " some to their neighbours, now that Henry the Fourth, your " Majesty's most noble progenitor, is upon the throne, make their " usual efforts to annoy and give disturbance in all parts of his " dominions.

" And, to perform some feats of an extraordinary figure, they hit " upon a new device, of forging kings and making counterfeit " princes.

" In North Britain is idolized that phantom of a king, Thomas " of Trumpyngton

" And Owen Glendourdy, that impostor of a prince, is set up to " play the mimic in Wales

" And so it was that this Pretender had the honour to enter into " a league offensive and defensive with the then French king, a " league transacted with all the solemnity and equipage of their " reciprocal ambassadors and credentials

" And, undoubtedly, the French were not wanting on occasion " to support this their new confederate, their trusty ally Owen " Glendourdy.

" But so far from success were those machinations of the enemy, " that, not long after, we see the most eminent amongst them sue " to this very King Henry the Fourth for his protection.

" Of which number are the Duke of Berry, the Duke of Orleans,

---

" Francoise, il pouroit trouver ici quelque " secours, dans une infinité de Pieces écrites " en cette Langue, depuis le Regne de " Henry I Enfin, il y a dans ce Recueil " une si grande variété d'Actes de toute " espece qu'il ne faut pas douter que des " gens habiles n'en puissent tirer du fruit, " selon les diverses vues dans lesquelles ils " voudront les examiner "

" and the Duke of Bourbon , they own this Henry the Fourth fo
" their lord and sovereign, do him homage, and become his vassals

" And now it is, most redoubted sovereign, now it is that the
" English troops pell mell enter France ; and but one battle remains
" betwixt them and Paris.

" For now indeed were the dispositions made and operations
" concerted which afterwards are accomplished, and have effect
" under Henry the Fifth, in the eighth year of his reign.

" Besides the traverses of war, which are very extraordinary,

" Treaties of marriage, may it please your most excellent
" Majesty, make the most shining part of this volume.

" Philippe of Lancaster is married to Ericus, King of Denmark,
" Sweden, and Norway, and Duke of Pomerania; and this is done
" more than ten years before that this King Ericus is discovered
" or brought to appear in history.

" Here also is negotiated, by the Emperor Rupert, that Palatine
" match betwixt his son Lewis and Blanch our king's daughter,
" with a noble train of German princes attending the ceremony.

" From which marriage are descended the Palatine families, to
" this day so much the support and ornament of the German
" nation.

" God's providence, hitherto so manifest in your preservation,
" hath still the same eye on your piety and zeal for His service ;
" who shall say what yet farther blessings are in store, ordained
" for your Majesty's glory, the good of your people, and the
" common benefit of human kind ?" &c.

The ninth volume[1] was commenced on the 9th of April 1709,
and finished the 15th of September ; it also appeared in 1709   It
commences with the acts of King Henry the Fifth on the 21st of
March 1413, the day of his father's death, the narrative being
brought down to the peace of Troyes, signed on the 21st of May
1420. The last document in the volume is dated 7th of July of that
year.   It contains 923 pages   Rapin, who had studied the contents
of the Fœdera more carefully than most persons, and laid its pages
under contribution for his History of England, commenting on this
ninth volume, writes,—" Parmi ceux dont on a déja vu les
" extraits, il n'y en a point de si abondant que celui-ci en pieces
" importantes, secrétes et utiles pour l'eclaircissement des Histoires

The ninth volume

---

[1] It appears by Mr. Bowyer's affidavit, | cancelled three sheets of this volume, which
dated 28th September 1709, that Rymer | were reprinted by his direction.

" de France et d'Angleterre. J'ose même dire qu'il s'y en trouve
" de si necessaires, que pour les avoir ignorées, les Historiens
" François et Anglois n'ont donné qu'une connoissance trés im-
" parfaite de ce temps là."

In dedicating the ninth volume to Queen Anne, Rymer writes:—
" With this volume, in order of time, you raise to life, and set
" forth the acts and achievements of that most victorious prince,
" your royal progenitor, King Henry the Fifth.

" From whence the world may observe how well you trace,
" how justly you parallel, how far you surpass, the most surprising
" actions of former ages

" Armies, and battles, and victories, and glory, are become
" familiar, and an every-day entertainment, in the proceeding of
" your Majesty's most auspicious reign.

" For some hundreds of years a long train of quarrels, enter-
" prises, and hostilities ; yet no memorable battle ensued, till the
" time of Edward the Third.

" His long (more than fifty years) reign was famous for Cressy
" and Poictiers

" And now, in the time of King Henry the Fifth, for ever
" renowned is the Field of Agincourt.

" And to blazon it the more, after the mode of the times, an
" herald is created by the name of Agincourt

" Would your Majesty, after so noble a precedent, go into that
" fashion, and create a Blenheim herald, a Ramilies herald, an
" Audenard herald, a Blaregnies herald, where might you stop ?
" but go on to Paris, and there erect a new college for your
" heralds, in the Place of Victoire

" Thus, most redoubted sovereign, thus you set out, thus you
" begin your reign , these are the dawn, the morning glimpses,
" and first tokens of your rising sun ; what must the world expect
" from your meridian splendour ?

" Yet fortune has no share in your successes , God Almighty
" is manifest in all you undertake, in all you do

" And what may we not promise from the superior steady
" conduct of your general, and the determined bravery of your
" troops, supported by your Majesty's uplifted heart. your firm
" devotion, and pious zeal for God's service ?

" After various adventures, treaties of peace, and operations of
" war, this volume ends with a peace and a marriage.

" In the eighth year of King Henry the Fifth, the French are
" brought to an agreement with him on his own terms.

e

" In this the eighth year of his reign the great peace, as they
" called it, and a royal marriage, are concluded and solemnized.

" Whatsoever yet remains, which may add to the felicity and
" glory of your Majesty, that God grant," &c.

The principal subjects to which the ninth volume relates are
the pretensions of Henry the Fifth to the crown of Franne, the
negotiations for that purpose; the war which was consequently
renewed; and the peace which terminated the war; domestic
affairs, and ecclesiastical matters.[1]

The tenth volume was commenced on the 15th of September
1709, and finished on the 18th of March following. It was published in 1710, and contains the acts relating to the last two years
of the reign of Henry the Fifth, and to the first nineteen years of
Henry the Sixth's reign, that is from the 1st of September 1422 to
the last day of October 1441. In the dedication to Queen Anne,
Rymer is still highly eulogistic, and takes an opportunity of paying
various compliments to Her Majesty at the expense of posterity;
the different topics illustrated by the volume being made subservient
to enhancing the glories of his royal patron —" This is the tenth
" volume of your royal bounty in this kind to the world.

" It contains what passed most memorable within the compass
" of one and twenty years, from 1420 to 1441, a period of great
" variety in the turn of affairs, and of great curiosity.

" A time wherein lived no writer of note to describe or transmit
" the transactions to posterity.

" It begins when all the talk and all the business in Europe was
" the great peace concluded betwixt England and France.

" The emperor and princes of any figure at that time in Europe
" send their ambassadors to give their laud and approbation of this
" peace, and to be comprehended in it.

" The French king, with his lords spiritual and temporal, citizens
" and burgesses, representing the three estates of France in Par-
" liament, assembled at Paris in the palace of St. Paul, make this
" peace a public law, and enact that every subject swear to
" observe and maintain it, and take an oath of allegiance to King
" Henry, regent and heir of the kingdom of France.

" Pursuant thereunto we see King Henry, by virtue of his

The tenth volume

---

[1] It is somewhat remarkable that Rymer has not inserted in the ninth volume, which is devoted to the time of John Huss and Jerome of Prague, any piece which makes mention of their affair.

" regency, according to emergencies, settling both Church and
" State.

" Bishops, abbots, deans, and priors, with the subaltern digni-
" taries, all strive who the foremost to take the oaths.

" And what a dust make the parsons, with all the flock their
" parishioners at their heels, showing their zeal and forwardness in
" this point of swearing?

" No abbey, convent, or religious house is easy till King Henry
" does confirm their charters; nor is any corporation pleased till
" they see their franchises under the broad seal of King Henry.

" This, the invincible, your most noble progenitor, King Henry
" the Fifth, a Bois le Vincennes, on a day well known in those
" parts by the name of St. Fiacres[1] (not of a disease called
" St. Fiacres, as histories have reported) yielded to death, leaving
" his son King Henry the Sixth, not then nine months old, to
" succeed him.

" Which Henry the Sixth, in the eighth year of his reign, was
" crowned at St. Peter's, Westminster, and soon after embarked
" for France, where he in Notre Dame at Paris, with the like
" ceremonies and solemnity, was crowned King of France.

" But why do I commemorate the successes of former ages?
" Your reign, most redoubted sovereign, your reign is all along a
" reign of wonders; and now the eyes of Europe are all fixed upon
" you, all big with expectation what shining superlative blessing
" your God, who is the God of wonders, reserves for you in this
" critical juncture, in this the ninth year of your glorious reign;
" with assurance that He will thereby complete their deliverance
" from the impending yoke, and from the oppression under which
" they labour," &c.

The eleventh volume[2], also made its appearance in 1710. It *The eleventh*
embraces the period from November 1441 to 27th of February 1475. *volume.*
As no description of mine can convey to the reader so good an
idea of the contents of this volume as Rymer's dedication to Queen
Anne, I make no scruple to transcribe it here.

---

[1] The disease of St Fiacre is a flux accompanied with hemorrhoids. He died on the 31st of August 1422, and not on the 28th of that month, as it is sometimes alleged

[2] The indenture for this volume is dated 30th March 1710, and John Anstis certifies to the Lords Commissioners of the Treasury, on the 16th September 1710, that the eleventh volume was printed.

The eleventh volume contains 52 pages beyond the contract for 500 sheets, besides three sheets and a half for the dedication and chronological table of contents Two sheets were cancelled and reprinted.

" In this eleventh volume you give the transactions from 1440
" to 1474

" Besides, what in common you give to other nations, your allies
" in the north receive a great light, and, in a more especial manner,
" your ancient kingdom, by this your royal bounty, is pulled out
" of the dark, and brought to a new life and lustre, you give them
" their share in the public treaties, even their language you
" authenticate and give it a currency.

" Whether peace, war, marriages or commerce is to be negotiated,
" who make a more goodly appearance, who shew a more numerous
" train and equipage, than the ambassadors of Scotland ?

" Within this compass of time, negotiations were always upon
" the carpet: England and France were much what about the
" same distance as they are at this day ; no wind could blow, no
" ship pass without some plenipotentiary.

" The burthen of the song was peace, a final peace, a perpetual
peace.

" In those days also rose up great plenty of philosophers ; no
" lord chancellor or keeper of the great seal but did pass some
" patent out of the King's special grace, granting a licence to
" exercise their skill, to make elixir of life, or to transubstantiate
" metals, to turn copper and iron into gold and silver, any act,
" law, or statute to the contrary notwithstanding.

" But (most invincible sovereign) there was shewn no miracles
" in those days ; splendid embassies, negotiations, communication
" and appunctuations without end, but no solid peace, nor yet any
" memorable achievement of war.

" No Blenheim, no Ramillies, no Audenarde, no Blaregnies,
" battles and victories ; by the Divine Providence appropriated to
" crown with glory the beginning of your so happy and auspicious
" reign.

" This book ends with the fourteenth year of your most noble
" progenitor, King Edward the Fourth, when,

" He, tired with tedious and fruitless treaties, carries a royal
" army into France against Lewis, Lewis the XI., who being a
" very wise prince and philosopher above the common sort, imme-
" diately capitulates, and without much of preliminaries 'tis agreed
" that King Lewis pay costs and defray the charges of the
" expedition, King Edward is to abstain from war and to carry
" back into England his army and his navy

" And, as for his hereditary right to the crown of France, King

" Lewis offers an equivalent in gold, and gives security to pay the
" sum agreed upon in London yearly during the lives of the two
" kings and the longest liver of them, and to his successors kings
" of England for an hundred years after.

" Whatever God hath ordained, most gracious sovereign, what-
" ever is in reserve, your people, sensible of the blessing they enjoy,
" and in zeal for their country, will continually pray for your
" length of days, and count it an happiness that, when they die,
" you live, and such is the prayer of your sacred Majesty's servant,
" &c."

The twelfth volume[1] was commenced on the 2nd of October The twelfth
volume
1710, and finished on the 3rd of July 1711, being published in that
year It relates to the last Acts of Edward the Fourth, and also
takes in those of Richard the Third and Henry the Seventh as far
as the year 1502.   In his dedication to Queen Anne, Rymer
addresses her Majesty in a more sober strain than usual, and con-
descends to a more prosaic analysis of the valuable results of his
useful labours : " Most excellent sovereign.

" This book affords not much variety in the business and adven-
" tures of war ; the language is changed, and peace now is become
" the word in fashion.

" Our neighbour, for so many generations called our adversary of
" France, now in this your twelfth volume is our most dear cousin
" of France, or Lewis of France our most dear cousin.

" Twice indeed armies are raised, and we find on the muster roll
" archers on horseback, archers on foot, bills, halberds, demi-lances,
" spears, and men of arms with their custrells

---

[1] There are four pages in this volume beyond the 200 sheets contracted for, besides three sheets and a half for the dedication and index. One sheet was cancelled and reprinted.

There were only 250 copies printed of all the previous volumes, but this, and all the succeeding ones, were augmented by nine additional copies, pursuant to the Act of Parliament, 8 Anne, c. xxi § v, which directs " That Nine Copies of each Book " or Books upon the best Paper that from " and after the said Tenth Day of April " One thousand seven hundred and ten " shall be printed and published as afore- " said, or reprinted and published with " Additions, shall, by the Printer and " Printers thereof, be delivered to the

" Warehouse-Keeper of the Company of " Stationers for the Time being at the " Hall of the said Company before such " Publication made, for the Use of the " Royal Library, the Libraries of the " Universities of Oxford and Cambridge, " the Libraries of the Four Universities in " Scotland, the Library of Sion College in " London, and the Library commonly " called the Library belonging to the " Faculty of Advocates at Edinburgh, " respectively."

It appears by the letter of Anstis to the Lord High Treasurer (26 June 1711) that the binding of the nine additional copies, printed in pursuance of the above-mentioned Act of Parliament, cost forty-five shillings.

" These are carried into France, but no fighting.

" They bring home French gold ; so many hundred thousand
" scutes, which was money in those days, decide the controversy,
" and make an end of the quarrel.

" Lewis the Eleventh, that wise prince, struck the bargain with
" our King Edward IV. And the bargain was renewed, the
" payments continued, and the arrearages accounted for by him
" during life, by his son Charles the Eighth, and by their successors,
" with our King Henry VII. your Majesty's most noble progenitor.

" But this reign, beside the old trade of war, was more especially
" distinguished on account of adventures of quite another nature ;
" now it is that new schemes of navigation are devised, new
" searches made, new land, new seas, another world, another Indies
" are found out, till then not known nor before discovered to
" mankind that inhabit on this side the globe.

" Thus traffic and commerce had a new countenance, and the
" Northern America successfully cultivated by our merchants and
" planters ever since, down to our times ; but the Mar del Zur
" was not yet rendered English ; the South Sea, navigation,
" discoveries and trade, seem as a particular blessing by the
" Divine Providence reserved for your Majesty's most auspicious
" reign, that with the benefits of civil life our true religion might
" be communicated and carried to the extremities of the earth ;
" and the light of the Holy Gospel shine forth in the most remote
" and darkest region.

" This book, most gracious sovereign, ends with a treaty, of all
" treaties the most memorable and most important ; the effects
" of which make the ornament and security, the joy and felicity
" of these our times ; for the which, your kingdoms and even all
" Europe at this day have cause to bless God : I mean the
" marriage treaty of your most noble progenitors, Margaret of
" England with James the Fourth of Scotland, from which your
" most sacred person is descended to the imperial seat, and so
" happily fills the throne of Great Britain at this day.

" Whereon that God long continue your most glorious reign,
" is the prayer of all good people, and your Majesty's most devoted
" servant"

The thirteenth
volume

The year 1712 saw the publication of the thirteenth[1] and four-

---

[1] The thirteenth volume has four pages   contents. Two sheets were cancelled and
beyond the contract for 200 sheets, besides   reprinted
3 sheets for the dedication and table of

teenth volumes of the Fœdera. The first of these embraces the period of one and twenty years, from 1502 to 1523. It was commenced on the 10th of July 1711, and finished on the 19th of January following Rymer's dedication to Queen Anne runs as follows :

" This volume, most excellent sovereign, contains, in course of time " the period of one and twenty years, seven years the last in the " reign of your most noble progenitor King Henry the Seventh, " and twice seven which next follow in the beginning of that most " victorious reign of his son and successor King Henry the Eighth.

" We see the annuities and the stipulated payments duly made " and accounted for, and when Christendom is invaded by the " infidels, confederacies are made with the Emperor, and with the " King of Hungary and Bohemia, for the defence of Christendom. " The enemy being in remote and so far distant countries, King " Henry the Seventh would not harras his English armies with so " long a march ; but that wise prince did freely contribute his " quota in money ; he sends his nobles, his angles, and the " sovereigns of gold for his auxiliary troops against the Turk and " Mahometans.

" No sooner did your most redoubted predecessor King Henry " the Eighth ascend the throne but he is solicited for aid against " the Moors, and his first operations of war are on that side, in " conjunction with King Ferdinand the Catholic. Soon after this, " enemies nearer home gave umbrage to the Church, and now it " is that our civil negotiations and our warlike preparations are " all in order to defend the Church. Commissions issue out for " admirals and vice-admirals, generals and lieutenant-generals, for " the defence of the Church, and the proclamations tells us that " the King hath now, by God's grace, decreed and fully deter- " mined, in his own most noble person to pass over the sea with " his armies royal, against his ancient enemy Lewis, the French " King, and his adherents.

" Our next news is that famous action, the memorable day, " ever since called La Journé d'Esperons, the Battle of Spurs

" Then followed the besieging and taking of towns, Theroan, " Tournay, and other places in that territory, which make some " part of your Majesty's late conquests.

" Thence forward this reign proceeded in great prosperity and " magnificence, and by reason of his more particular care and " readiness to protect the Church, it is now in most solemn " manner decreed that in testimony of their gratitude and ac-

" knowledgment the title *Defender of the Faith* should be a title
" for King Henry VIII and his successors

" Which title, how well it suits with the so eminent zeal, the
" so distinguished piety, in your Majesty's most sacred person, and
" your Majesty's invincible armies abundantly demonstrate, so
" that the title might be taken for a prophetical designation to be
" accomplished and fulfilled in these our days, in this your Majesty's
" most triumphant reign

" Hence it is that all who profess our holy faith bless God, and
" for a life so precious continually pray," &c.

This thirteenth volume contains most important documents,
illustrative not only of the history of England and Scotland, but
of France, Spain, and Italy

The fourteenth volume[1] was published, as already stated, in 1712.
It was commenced on the 14th of January 1711–12, and finished on
the 2nd of August 1712   It contains instruments for a period of
twenty years between July 1523 and July 1543.   I will again
content myself with describing this volume in Rymer's own words,
as they appear in his Dedication to Queen Anne.   " Most excellent
" sovereign, in this volume you give the world a view of what was
" transacted within the compass of twenty years, from the fifteenth
" to the five and thirtieth of Henry the Eighth, your Majesty's
" predecessor of most noble memory.

" Nothing of public affairs in Europe, ecclesiastical or civil,
" were transacted without his countenance or direction.   His title
" *Defender of the Faith* is repeated and confirmed to him with
" the highest applause and in a most solemn manner   And now
" it is that he casts a particular eye on his two universities,
" Cambridge and Oxford   Schools and colleges are every where,
" for the advancement of learning, founded and endowed , and
" with the utmost application they proceed to improve and cul-
" tivate the liberal sciences and good literature.

" Now it is that we hear of the Hebrew lectures, and the
" Linacre lectures ; now is our holy Bible printed in English, as
" are also the grayle, the antiphoner, the hymptual, the portans,
" and the other books for divine service of the use of Sarum ; and
" to set the church in a clearer light, instead of the ill-digested
" rude economy of former times, instead of White Friars, Black

The fourteenth volume.

---

[1] The fourteenth volume contains 16 pages beyond the 200 sheets contracted for, including the dedication and table of contents

" Friars, and Grey Friars, now have our clergy an uniform decent
" garb, wear a new face, grow refined, and act a more polite part
" in conversation.

" And now for their greater dignity, lustre, and authority, new
" churches, cathedral churches, are appointed all over the realm,
" and we have so many bishop suffragans, together with their
" deans, archdeacons, prebendaries, and their other subalterns.

" Now it is that we have a Bishop of Oxford, a Bishop of Bristol,
" Bishops of Peterborough, Taunton, Colchester, Ipswich, Glou-
" cester, Shaftesbury, Hull, Bedford, Penrith, Thetford, Chester,
" suffragan bishops up from Berwick-upon-Tweed to the Bishop
" of Westminster.

" Furthermore, if a deserving person came in the way when
" no cathedral vacant, there wanted not for him pluralities and
" incompatibilities that mount to an equivalent.

" Nor was the building of churches his only glory , he had his
" share in the secular occurrences of his time , he held the balance
" of power in his hand, and the scale turned according to his
" direction. He was declared Protector of Leagues, and no con-
" federacy was firm without him. His contemporaries, Francis,
" the French King, and Charles the Fifth, two ambitious, unquiet,
" enterprising princes, in their turns never failed to cut out work
" for him ; one while they court him for their ally, or make him
" umpire, and submit their quarrel to his arbitration

" To whichsoever party he joins, success and victory go along
" with them. If he sides with the French, the imperial armies are
" defeated , when he sides with the emperor, King Francis in the
" field of battle is made prisoner In other expeditions some good
" French towns and territory remain to the English.

" Thus proceeded the reign of King Henry the Eighth, as appears
" in the course of this volume, which ends with the most joyful
" prospect of uniting your two kingdoms, England and Scotland,
" by the means of a marriage for the king's only son, Prince
" Edward, with the young Queen of Scotland This marriage
" was negotiated, concerted, and concluded ; but this union was
" a blessing reserved for your Majesty to be accomplished in
" our time, in this your most auspicious and glorious reign, which
" that God, the author of all blessings, may long continue over
" us," &c.

The fifteenth volume was commenced about the middle of February 1712-13, and the printing of it was finished on the 25th of

August 1713, about four months before the death of Rymer. One
hundred and twenty sheets of it were destroyed in the fire which
broke out in the house of William Bowyer, the printer, in White
Friars, on the 30th of January 1712–13, immediately on the eve
of the publication[1] It commences in July 1543, and comes
down to July 1586. In addressing Queen Anne he says; "Most
" gracious sovereign, this is the fifteenth volume drawn forth from
" your most sacred treasuries for a bounty to the world.

" It comprehends a period somewhat more than forty years, in
" which so long space, achievements of war, battles, victories, and
" triumph are not so much in vogue.

" 'Tis now matters of the Church, the operations of religion, the
" reformation and application to cultivate true piety, and give our
" holy faith a new light and lustre.

" As to civil affairs, it begins with a ratification of a treaty
" concluded for her Majesty the Queen of Scotland, to marry
" Prince Edward, apparent and undoubted heir of King Henry
" the Eighth, your Majesty's predecessor of most glorious memory;
" and it ends with an account of the States General,—Guelders,
" Zutphen, Flanders, Holland, West Friesland, Zealand, and
" Utrecht, and other the United Provinces of the Netherlands,—
" who declare themselves discharged from all ties to the King
" of Spain, and therefore resolved to provide themselves with
" another master, capable to defend and protect them against the
" tyranny of the aforesaid King of Spain, and against the Spanish
" most barbarous Inquisition, introduced for no other end but the
" extirpation of the true religion.

" Hereupon they sue to Queen Elizabeth to take them under
" her care and protection, which readily she grants.

" And now it is that Escluse, the Brill, with Flushing, and the
" Rammakins are delivered into the hands of English governors
" and garrisons.

" This done, the queen despatches away her ambassadors to
" Scotland for a closer friendship, and a league offensive and
" defensive, in order to support the reformed religion against all
" enemies and opposition, and for the king to be a partner with
" her, and effectually to have his share in being a defender of the
" faith, which seasonable confederacy cleared the way to a Pro-

---

[1] See Appendix XX

" testant succession in the person of King James, your Majesty's
" progenitor, of ever blessed memory

"He was a peace-maker, and he was a king fifty-five years.

"Long was the reign of his contemporary and confederate, Queen
" Elizabeth.

"That, with the other so many superlative and distinguishing
" blessings, God grant your precious life and reign over us long
" may continue," &c.

The dedication to the fifteenth volume is the last it was Rymer's Reason for
fate to compose I have considered it but just to the man to allow printing
Rymer's
him to describe his work in his own mode; but it must be, I think, various
dedications
apparent to the reader that these dedications are by no means
calculated to exalt Rymer either as an historian or English scholar.
They do not exhibit any critical skill, or show that he appreciated
the value of the important materials upon which he was engaged.
He seems to have had little or no other object beyond eulogizing
his royal patron.

Though Rymer died shortly after the publication of the fifteenth
volume of the Fœdera, yet he had prepared some materials for
bringing down his collection to the end of the reign of James the
First. These were placed in the hands of Robert Sanderson, who
had been assisting him in his great work [1]

During the period of this rapid progress of his work, Rymer's Return to
personal history is still involved in obscurity. Whenever the Rymer's per-
sonal history
clouds clear away for a moment, the scene presented to us is indeed
pitiable. I have already submitted to my readers his memorials to
the Lords of the Treasury, complaining of his indigence and of their
neglect. I have called particular attention to his petition of the 6th
of March 1702, which cannot be perused by any sensible person without feelings of regret and shame. He there speaks of the neglect to
which he had been exposed, of his unrequited labour of ten years,
and his constant attendance in the service on which he was employed
by the Government. "Let me also," he says, "remind you that old
" age comes so fast upon me, that I cannot expect to be much
" longer in a condition to do anything." These expressions occur
before he commenced printing the "Fœdera" We shall presently
see what sums he received during the progress of the work through

---

[1] In Queen Anne's warrant, dated 3rd
May 1707, these words occur, which prove
that Sanderson had been some years
Rymer's assistant, "Our will and pleasure
" is, that the said Thomas Rymer and
" Robert Sanderson, who has hitherto been
" employed by him as his assistant, have
" free liberty of access, &c."

His poverty.

the press, and what reason there was for his selling his collection of books. We know too little of Rymer's situation in life to judge accurately of the following letter, but certainly the state of things it exhibits is as lamentable as it is extraordinary. The man whose labours during a period of twenty years had produced the noblest collection of acts and monuments ever yet seen, a work, which to use the words of Bishop Nicolson, "may justly be reckoned one of " the many glories of perhaps the brightest period of English " history," had been forced in old age to sell his books for bread The relief was but temporary; and we here find him, when incapacitated probably by illness from writing himself, employing a friendly hand to lay his distresses before the Earl of Oxford He offers for sale his manuscript collections , and such, it is stated, is his pressing need, that, if they are not purchased for the royal library, he must dispose of them to the highest bidder. The causes of this destitution, during a period which is often represented as the golden age of literary patronage, are stated to be that no one had yet indented [1] with him for a new volume, and that his salary as a servant of the crown was then two years in arrear

Le Neve's letter to the Earl of Oxford relative to Rymer's destitution.

The letter to which I refer is here subjoined: "My Lord, I am " desired by Mr. Rymer, historiographer (who cant doe it himself) " to lay before your lordship the circumstances of his affairs. " He was forct some years since to part with all his choice printed " books to subsist himself by reason of his salary being so much " in arrear, and now he says he must be forct for subsistence to " sell all his manuscript collections to the best bidder, without " your Lordship will be pleased to buy them for the Queen's " library. The parcel are 50 (59 ?) volumes in folio of public affairs " which he hath collected and are not printed The price he asks " is 500l. Whether they are of that value I cant say, having not " seen them. The reason of his being in such want of money, as " he tells me, is because nobody hath yet indented with him for " a new volume, and that he is two years or thereabout behind " in his salary [2] I beg your Lordship would be pleased to consider

[1] The meaning of this expression is not very clear, but it seems to show that Rymer was obliged to find a publisher for each volume, although the Queen was at the charge of printing it.

[2] It is difficult to test the truth of this allegation, as the Treasury pay-book from Mich 1709 to Mich. 1710 is missing, but there is evidence, derived from another source, which is almost conclusive, that the Treasury did not owe Rymer anything on

the score of salary as Historiographer ; moreover the first payment in the book from Mich 1710 to Mich. 1711 makes no mention of money being in arrear, and all the other payments before 1709, and after Mich 1710, were regularly made to him. Le Neve therefore must have been misinformed, so far as Rymer's salary of Historiographer is concerned Nor was any money due to him at this time as editor of the Fœdera.

" his condition as to your great wisdom shall be thought fit. I
" am, my Lord, your Lordship's most humble and obedient servant,
" Peter le Neve, Norroy, College of Arms, 13 February 1711.

" Addressed to the Right Honourable Robert Earl of Oxford
" and Earl Mortimer, Lord High Treasurer of Great Britain."
(Ms Harl. 7525).

This letter seems to have been written in a very cautious manner,
but it does not appear whether out of respect to the person to whom
it is addressed, or out of any feeling of distrust of Rymer Probably there was a great deal more respecting him than it was
prudent to communicate to Lord Oxford ; but no one can fail to
pity and regret the misery it discloses What ensued is not
known, but it will be presently seen that the MSS were not
then sold.

Within twelve months after the date of this letter an event *Destruction by
fire of a portion
of the fifteenth
volume.*
happened, to which I have already alluded, and which must have
greatly increased the labours of poor Rymer, now in his 73rd year.
The greater portion of the fifteenth volume of the " Fœdera " was
destroyed in the fire which consumed the premises of Bowyer the
printer.

Rymer died in Arundel Street, in the Strand, on the 14th of *Death of
Rymer.*
December 1713, and was interred in the church of St Clement Danes,
on the third day after his decease It does not appear that any
monument was erected to his memory He made his will on the 10th
of July 1713. It contains a general bequest of all his property to
Mrs. Anne Parnell, of the parish of St. Clements Danes, spinster, with
an appointment of the same person as his executrix She proved
the will in the Prerogative Court at Canterbury, on the very day of
his death The haste with which the probate was granted, would
seem to imply that it was necessary to sell some of his effects in
order to defray the expenses of the funeral. I have not been able
to discover who Mrs. Anne Parnell, spinster, was, but in all probability she was his housekeeper. I find her attesting one of his
indentures, together with Leatitia Wicksted. The name of the last
person appears as a witness to four other indentures

Some pains have been taken to ascertain whether Rymer died
a bachelor. The general belief is that he was never married : but
the scurrilous print, to which allusion has been already made,
mentions a Mistress Rymer and two daughters. A careful search
for evidence on that point has been made in all available quarters,
but without success There is one point in favour of the statement

that Rymer had been a married man: had he been living in a discreditable state of concubinage, the lampooner would probably have barbed his satire by declaring the fact.

Rymer's remuneration.

I have frequently mentioned Rymer's remuneration in these pages, as well as his poverty. It will only be just to the government whose servant he was, as well as to the memory of his friends, to take a retrospective glance at his pecuniary resources from the earliest trace we have of him; for the purpose of shewing that his means, had they been properly applied, were sufficient to have maintained him respectably, and that the state of indigence into which he had fallen must have arisen from unthriftiness rather than neglect.

It has been shewn that the father possessed sufficient wealth to give his son an University education, and previously to his conviction had assigned to him a mortgage from a Mr. Wood of certain lands in Kirkby Wisk, and that the son left the University without taking his degree, owing in all probability to the father's fate.

As there is no proof to the contrary, I think it may be assumed that the mortgage was sufficient to have supported him at Cambridge had he thought proper to remain there. I attribute his leaving the University without taking his degree, not so much to want of means as to the misfortunes which had overtaken his father and his family. This mortgage was his chief support through life, enabling him to enter himself as a student at Gray's Inn, and maintaining him there until he was called to the bar. At the bar he gained no distinction, so far as I am able to ascertain: had it procured him rank or emolument, it is not likely that he would have abandoned it for dramatic writing and criticism, at all times a meagre subsistence, except for the most favoured and successful[1] Moreover, in his letter addressed to a friend on the subject of Parliament, he speaks of his retirement, his distance from books, &c, expressions wholly inconsistent with the occupations of a successful barrister practising in London. It was impossible that he could have derived any considerable profits from his publications, and as he had no other ostensible means of support, I am driven to

[1] Macaulay, speaking of the literature of this period, especially the drama, that department of polite literature in which a poet had the best chance of obtaining a subsistence, remarks that 'the sale of "books was so small that a man of the "greatest name could hardly expect more "than a pittance for the copyright of the "best performance"

the conclusion that up to the time of his appointment as Historiographer Royal this mortgage was the sole means of Rymer's subsistence He seems to have received regularly the salary of his office up to the day of his death , at least, most of the orders for paying him are extant, and there is no complaint of his salary being in arrear, except the allusion made to the circumstance in Le Neve's letter to the Earl of Oxford[1] His salary of 200*l* a year, added to the produce of his mortgage, enabled him, not only to support himself, but to advance money to pay a staff of clerks and engravers engaged upon the "Fœdera"[2] when the government had not sufficient funds at their command In some years he received nothing on account of the "Fœdera" from the government, although they were indebted to him in a large sum It is, however, true that he constantly complains of being kept out of his money, and of his obligation to keep up a staff of clerks.

As his complaints cease about the year 1701, it is probable that the government had then paid up all arrears Be this, however, as it may, it is clear that from the month of May 1703, when the printing of the "Fœdera" commenced, up to the time of his death, he had received of public money 400*l* annually, viz , 200*l*. as Historiographer and 200*l*. as editor of the "Fœdera." In addition to which, he also had twenty-five copies of each volume of the work, which may be valued at about 83*l*. of the money of the period, making a total of 483*l*. a year, and equal to about 805*l*. of our present money Besides this, he likewise received 1*l*. a sheet for correcting the press, when the sheets extended beyond what he had agreed for by indenture.

The various sums received by Rymer before he commenced printing, amounting to 2,263*l*., appear to have been employed exclusively in the payment of his clerks and engravers,[3] and the other expenses incurred for transcribing the instruments printed in the "Fœdera;" but I cannot find that he ever received any recompense for his labours as editor during the time he was collecting his materials , indeed, he more than once expressly states that he never was allowed any remuneration on that score

He left behind him a large collection of papers, evidently intended to be used in a second edition , for he well knew the scarceness of Plea for continuing the work

[1] See note ¹, p. lxxvi.

[2] Without entering into long and tedious details, I think it may be safely assumed that after the Restoration, until about the Accession of Queen Anne, and perhaps a little later, six shillings went as far as ten now , in other words, money is now two-fifths less in value than it was then

[3] The clerks received 40*l*. per annum and the engravers 40*l*. per annum, equal of present money to about 67*l* a year each

the first impression, and the defects and errors inseparable from a work of such magnitude. Up to a short time before his death he was actively engaged in collecting materials. The result of his diligence amounted, when bound, to fifty-nine[1] volumes, embracing the period between 1115 and 1698 It is this collection which his friend Le Neve offered for sale to the Earl of Oxford, and for which the Treasury paid to his executrix 215*l* The volumes were ordered to be placed among the manuscripts in the Cottonian collection, but somehow or other they fell into the hands of Awnsham Churchill, the publisher of the Fœdera; and the interference of the House of Lords was required before they could be rescued from Churchill's hands It appears that the Lords Committee on the Public Records received information that several unprinted transcripts of records had been left by the late Mr. Rymer, and were in the hands of Awnsham Churchill, a bookseller. Upon this information Churchill was sent for and examined He acknowledged that the transcripts were in his custody, but he had been accustomed to consider them as of no value, being only papers which Rymer had thrown aside as not fit to print. He added "that "Rymer's executors had procured them to be bound, and they "were paid for by the Treasury, and were to be applied for the "public inspection." He further informed the committee that the transcripts were ready to be delivered in accordance with their directions. They were, in consequence, placed for the present under the custody of Mr Incledon, then Lordships' housekeeper Several orders upon the subject will be found in the Journals of the House of Lords. According to one of them, the transcripts, when delivered up by Churchill, were to be deposited in the Chapter House of Westminster, there to be digested and put in order [2]

These brief and imperfect notices contain all that I have been able to discover concerning the life of a man who has been cursorily passed over by writers of English biography. It seemed due to his

---

[1] Fifty-eight of these volumes now form the Additional MSS in the British Museum, from No 4573 to No 4630 inclusive The 59th vol was not given up to the Museum with the other fifty-eight volumes, but it is now No 18,911 of the Additional Manuscripts. Various opinions have been expressed as to the value of these materials, they have been condemned as worthless by some, and extolled for their great importance by others There is no doubt that

many of the transcripts are incorrectly copied, and abound with errors ; nevertheless a very extensive use has been made of them, in one work alone no less than 171 documents have been printed.

[2] See "Journals of the House of Lords," Vol. XXI p 143, and Vol. XXIII. p 282 A catalogue of Rymer's Collectanea is given in the 17th volume of Tonson's edition, and an index of the contents of each volume

memory to bring together as much as could be collected; but after the lapse of more than a century of comparative forgetfulness, little can be gathered respecting the fate of a writer whose name has been rescued from oblivion solely from its connexion with a work which, though of great national importance, of necessity keeps the author's personal history altogether out of view His name is imperishably bound up with the reputation of his country; for "those fifteen " volumes of public acts are the best monument of the past glories " of a nation that ever yet appeared since the beginning of nations"[1]

The death of Rymer occasioned no interruption in the progress of the "Fœdera."[2] Robert Sanderson, who has been mentioned before as Rymer's assistant, at once stepped into the vacant place of editor. Rymer, it will be borne in mind, had edited and published fifteen volumes. He had also very nearly completed the arrangements for the sixteenth This fact has been misrepresented by Dr. Clarke in his Introduction to the new edition of the "Fœdera" At p. 1 he states, that "the first fourteen volumes were published in " Rymer's lifetime; the fifteenth and sixteenth, which he had " prepared for the press, were published after his death by Robert " Sanderson." The same mis-statement is repeated at p 3 , whereas the fifteenth volume not only bears Rymer's name on the title-page, but the dedication is signed by him The sixteenth is the only volume stated to have been compiled from the papers of Rymer.

Sanderson's qualifications for the task

The sixteenth volume contains the acts of 30 years, viz, from 2nd of November 1586 to the 4th of November 1616. It was published in 1715. In the title page the new editor thus acknowledges his obligation to his predecessor: "Ex schedis Thomæ Rymer potissimum edidit Robertus Sanderson."

A brief and meagre dedication to George I, contrasting strongly with the diffuse and ornate style of Rymer on such occasions, is all that the new editor deems necessary for ushering his new volume into the world. It is in the following words: "Serenissimo

---

[1] Bishop Kennett's Second Letter to the Bishop of Carlisle, p. 32

[2] Shortly after Rymer's death, the following remark on his work was written in a letter by Thomas Hearne to his friend Anstis, dated at Oxford, 11 July 1714 (Letters by Eminent Persons, London, 1813, i. 289) "I should be glad to know " whether Rymer's Fœdera will be con- tinued He intended to have published " a separate volume of Critical Observa- " tions ; but how well he was qualified for " that I know not. It is certain such a " performance would be acceptable, and " whoever does it will have thereby an " opportunity of showing his learning and " judgment, both as a critic and an anti " quary."

" celsissimo augustissimoque Georgio Dei gratia Magnæ Britanniæ
" Gallæque et Hiberniæ monarcho fidei defensori Robertus San-
" derson majestatis ejus humillimus et devotissimus subditus tomum
" hunc decimum sextum D. D. D."

The seventeenth volume was published in 1717, with a dedication
to the same King, as terse as its predecessor It extends from the
30th of March 1617 to the 21st of June 1625. This volume is
much more miscellaneous in its character than any of those that
preceded it. Several of the papers in it were collected by Rymer.
The incapacity of Sanderson[1] and his want of judgment are very
perceptible in the volumes entrusted to his care; they contain
documents of a nature unfit for the " Fœdera " in the proportion of
three to one. To the seventeenth volume Sanderson appended
various indexes to the whole work, and also a catalogue or syllabus
of the contents of Rymer's 59 volumes of Manuscript Collections.[2]
This syllabus was published at the time as a separate work, with the
following title : " Syllabus, seu index actorum manuscriptorum quæ
" lix. voluminibus compacta (præter xvii. tomas typis vulgatas)
" collegit ac descripsit Thomas Rymer. Quæ in his voluminibus in
" Bibliotheca Cottoniana nunc reservatis, continentur versa pagina
" monstrabit Londini, per A. and J. Churchill, 1717."[3] For his
labours on the seventeenth volume Sanderson was paid on the
7th of March 1714 the sum of 200l.

These seventeen volumes constitute what is generally understood
to be the first London edition. The first sixteen volumes were

[1] Menckenius, under whose care the
Leipzig edition of Du Fresnoy's new
method of studying History appeared, entertained a different opinion of Sanderson;
he states that Sanderson's character is
much superior to his predecessor in the
undertaking (Du Fresnoy translated by
Rawlinson, vol ii , p 464)

[2] See note at p. lxxx Rymer's Collectanea may be thus divided —

Three volumes embrace the materials from
1115 to the end of the reign of Edward I. The
reign of Edward II. occupies 4 volumes ,
those of Edward the Third, 11 volumes,
Richard II., 5 volumes , Henry IV , 4
volumes , Henry V , 4 volumes , Henry IV ,
9 volumes , Edward IV , 3 volumes,
Edward V. and Richard III , 1 volume ,
Henry VII , 2 volumes , Henry VIII , 5
volumes , Edward VI and Mary, 1 volume ,
Elizabeth, 3 volumes; Miscellaneous matter, 4 volumes.

[3] Fol pp 129 A copy of the Syllabus
as a separate publication occurs in Madox's
Catalogue, p 28. The cost of this volume
is thus recorded in the Treasury accounts
300l to Awnsham Churchill, bookseller, for
paper and printing 250 volumes of the seventeenth volume of the book called Rymer's
Fœdera, and 74l 15s more for binding the
said volumes, and for paper, printing, and
binding of nine supernumerary books for the
Universities, according to the Act of Parliament in that behalf, and the sum of 200l.
more to be paid to Robert Sanderson, Esq ,
for collecting together the instruments
which completed the said seventeenth
volume, and for making the index of that
and the preceding volumes, and 24l 7s. 6d.
to satisfy fees, charges, &c., making a total
of 599l 2s 6d

published by A. and J Churchill, and the seventeenth by
W. Churchill The addition of indexes would lead to the inference
that the work was then thought to be complete, and it has consequently been supposed that the 18th, 19th, and 20th volumes
were undertaken at private expense, by the permission and not
at the cost of the government. I am not inclined to think that
this surmise is correct, though I have not been able to trace in the
public accounts any indications of money having been furnished by
the government for the compilation and printing of these three
volumes. Their publication was conducted by Jacob Tonson, who
was licensed to reprint and publish the first seventeen volumes
In his licence no mention is made of any intended continuation.

The first edition of the "Fœdera" (that is, Churchill's seventeen
volumes,) was, as already stated, limited to two hundred and fifty
copies (to which nine additional copies were added by Act of Parliament for the universities and other privileged places); twenty-five
were presented to Rymer as part payment for his labour; one hundred
and eighty-five were given away,[1] and the forty-five copies which
remained were not allowed to be sold, but were kept in store
for the use of the government. No wonder, then, that the value
of a single copy rose as high as one hundred guineas, whenever
one was submitted to sale. The cost price of a single copy to the
government, when one was required for a special purpose, was
eighty pounds. The charge for printing the seventeen volumes (exclusive of the sums paid for editing and transcripts) amounted to
10,255l. 2s. 6d. to which must be added 115l. for 17 sheets printed
in the 15th, 16th, and 17th volumes beyond the number of sheets
contracted for; 95l. for composing the several tables in the
17th volume, consisting of 95 sheets; 50l for making the Index
Nominum to the several volumes, and arranging them in one Index,
and 100l for making and composing the Index Locorum et Rerum
added to the 17 volumes, making in all a total of 10,615l. 12s. 6d.

In taking an unprejudiced view of the contents of the first
fifteen volumes, it must not be supposed that no blame attaches
to Rymer for their miscellaneous character; the original rules which
seem to have guided him in making his selection having been
widely departed from as he proceeded with his work. From the
commencement of the "Fœdera" down to the end of the reign of

General obser-
vations on the
Fœdera Its
merits and
defects

---

[1] A list of the names of the persons to whom copies were presented will be found in
the Appendix XXV.

Richard I (about ninety-eight years) he has only printed eighty-six documents[1] Of these, sixty-one are either conventions, letters of state, or other documents of intercourse between English princes and those of foreign countries. Sixteen relating to England refer to Papal privileges of a private or local character, and nine do not fall within the scope of the original design of the work With the reign of John the enrolments of the Chancery commence, and as the Chancellor at that time was the Chief Secretary of State both for Home and Foreign Affairs, all documents, both domestic and public, were enrolled in his office. Such a plethora of information would naturally puzzle a man in Rymer's position. There was scarcely a document which came before him from which he could not extract some fact useful either to the statesman or the lawyer, the churchman or topographer, the biographer or critic; hence he was induced gradually to introduce documents referring to domestic affairs much more liberally than he had done in the first instance, and altogether inconsistently with a strict adherence to the purposes of a work devoted to "Acta Publica" or "Fœdera," from the title of which the student will be lead to expect nothing but public acts These additions were probably an afterthought, as Rymer makes no allusion to them in his title-page.

While mentioning this departure of the editor from the real purpose of his work, it is right also that I should correct an assertion, which has sometimes been made with greater positiveness than accuracy, that Rymer has omitted nothing from his collections which would properly fall within the description of his title-page I notice this subject because it is stated in the Introduction to the "Acta Regia" that there is not one important act omitted by Rymer in any of the reigns over which the "Fœdera" extends: whereas, in reality, his omissions are numerous.

These remarks, however, must be applied to the collection as it appeared at the death of Rymer, and not to the additions for supplying its defects made by the Record Commissioners, which will presently be brought under notice.

There is no doubt that a considerable mass of materials exists to which Rymer had not access, but which, in all probability,

---

[1] Of these eighty-six documents the sources of only thirty have been alluded to by Rymer The remaining 56 are without any reference as to the place of their deposit. Indeed the larger number of the thirty are merely designated as "Ex ong " or "Ex Autogr." without mentioning where they are kept.

he would have used had he been aware of them ;[1] there are others, again, of which he certainly was aware, and yet he did not use. This is clear from the contents of the " Collectanea Rymeri," but the reasons for his omissions cannot be conjectured.

I must now allude to some of the anachronisms, merely as a warning to the reader Rymer, for instance, has placed under the year 1174 a charter belonging to the year 1236, being 62 years out of date. Again, he has printed a Commission of James IV. of Scotland, dated 19th of July, in the 32nd year of his reign, under the year 1427 instead of 1509, a misplacement of no less than 82 years before its proper time. These wrong dates and several others have been corrected in the " Syllabus."

While exposing the shortcomings of Rymer,[2] I ought not to pass over the fact that he has, without acknowledgment, inserted docu-

---

[1] It has been already stated (p v note[1]) that Leonard's *Recueil*, published in 1693, contains many documents relating to this country which are omitted in the *Fœdera*, for instance, between the years 1485 and 1644 Leonard has printed *eighty-three* instruments which concern Great Britain , of these Rymer has only given *eighteen*, thus leaving *sixty-five* unnoticed It seems scarcely credible that Rymer was unacquainted with Leonard's Collection, the whole of which was published before the Fœdera was contemplated, or at any rate before Rymer was appointed its editor I am at a loss for a reasonable excuse for this great omission, but I fear others equally great could be indicated In the Appendix will be found a list of 65 omitted documents

[2] The historian, Thomas Carte, has made a most unfounded charge against Rymer In his letter to Swift, dated 11th August 1736, and printed in Nichol's Literary Anecdotes, vol 2, p 477, he states, " that " Rymer's collection contains only such " treaties as were enrolled in the Tower or " in the Rolls of Chancery He knew " nothing of such as were enrolled in the " Exchequer, and of the public treaties " with foreign princes enrolled in the latter " office I have now a list of above four " hundred by me. Rymer never made use " of that vast collection of materials for an " English History which is preserved in " the Cotton Library, nor ever consulted ' any journal of our Privy Council , when- " ever he refers to any, still quoting Bishop

" Burnet for his author He never read " the Rolls of Parliament, nor any journal " of either House, where the chief affairs " within the nation are transacted , and " did not so much as know there was " such a place as the Paper Office, where " all the letters of the English ambas- " sadors abroad, and all the despatches of " our secretaries of state at home, from " the time of Edward the Fourth to the " Revolution (since which the secretaries " have generally carried away their papers), " are kept in a good method and with " great regularity; so that he wanted like- " wise the best materials for an account of " our foreign affairs These defects have " made several of our nobility and gentry " desire a new history to be wrote, in " which the above-mentioned, and other " materials as authentic as they, may be " made use of."
When Carte published his general account of the necessary materials for the History of England, he repeated this charge in the following words " Rymer has printed " several volumes of records, enrolled in " Chancery, but not one out of the Exche- " quer, where are many of much greater " importance to the subject than most in " his collection, and where likewise are " abundance of treaties with foreign " princes , that being the court in which " most kings of Europe used anciently to " enroll such treaties Powel, in his ' Reper- " tory of Records,' gives us a list of the " contracting powers, dates, &c of above " 400 treaties of our kings with foreign

ments in the "Fœdera" obtained from printed sources[1] instead of
from manuscripts. This is the less excusable, as Leibnitz had
pointed out the advantage that Rymer possessed over himself. He
writes, "Sed hoc illi præ nobis eximium contigit, quod ad ipsa
" authentica originalia admissus de veris lectionibus tuto pronun-
" tiare potest, dum nos plerumque apographis contenti esse cogimur,
" sæpeque in incerto versamur." In some instances, and with
less pardonable grounds, he has positively taken matter from
Leibnitz, and printed it as "ex originali" and "ex autograph"
I do not here bring into the account against Rymer those pieces
which he derived from ancient chronicles and histories that had
been already printed, because he does not in those reprints profess to have derived them from manuscripts, but simply leaves his
reader in ignorance as to their source or place of deposit.[2]

It will not be necessary to make more than a passing allusion
to the numerous errors which are to be found in the "Fœdera," as

---

" princes, which are not in Rymer Ano-
" ther very considerable body of materials,
" very proper, if not necessary, must be
" sought in foreign parts There is always
" a continual intercourse of friendly or
" hostile transactions between adjoining
" countries , for which reasons the records
" of all nations furnish abundance of mate-
" rials for the history of their neighbours
" This I have observed particularly in
" France, where, in my searches for some
" years together after records relating to
" England, I took notes or made abstracts
" of above a thousand instruments of
" treaties and transactions between the
" two kingdoms, scarce any of which
" appear in Rymer "
    Nearly all of Carte's assertions are false,
as may be tested by any one who will
take the trouble to examine Rymer's Collection. References to treaties, and other
materials deposited in the Treasury of the
Exchequer, are constantly made. Moreover, there is still extant a book containing
a list of all the documents belonging to the
Exchequer which passed through Rymer's
hands, each receipt signed by himself
That the Cottonian manuscripts were
frequently used and quoted is beyond
doubt, as may be seen by numberless
marginal notations. Indeed the whole
of Carte's accusation betrays both ignorance and malice. He was getting up a
case for himself, to fill a subscription list

for his History of England. Rymer, who
edited the Fœdera, and Rapin, who popu-
larized it, are both condemned as sciolists
and ignoramuses, in order to exalt himself
at their expense
[1] From a passage in the preface of the
General History of England by Tyrrell,
who was contemporary with Rymer, it
would seem that the fact of Rymer employing *printed* materials was well known at
the time He says, "I am very well in-
" formed that the learned and ingenious
" Mr Rymer, his Majesty's Historiographer,
" designs to give the world a large collec-
" tion of leagues, treaties, and articles of
" peace between the Kings of England
" and other foreign princes, collected not
" only from *printed authors* but also from
" that hidden treasure of originals and
" records at this day deposited in the old
" Chapter House of the Abbey of West-
" minster "
    As this is a grave charge it ought to
be fully proved. The convention in 1198
between Philip II King of France and
John Count of Mortain is taken by Rymer
from the Codex Diplomaticus, with all the
errors of that copy. The original, from
whence Leibnitz printed, is in the public
archives of France Rymer derived four
other documents from the same Codex
Diplomaticus without acknowledgment.
[2] See Appendix XXVII

Rymer seems to have been fully aware of them, and makes some apology for, or rather ₊allusion to, them. In his note on the ".Errata," at the end of his preface, he says, " In ipsis autographis " aliquando deficiunt, 'aliquando redundant nonnulla vocabula, et " etiam aliquando, vel ipsæ Grammaticorum conculcantur leges, " sed hæc quovis modo tangere, prophanum duximus Si quando " leges *preminere, iminere, consumare,* in pontificum Litteris ; vel " *orribile, ortus, erba, ylariter, anelare,* ubi desit litteraaut aspiratio; " vel quando legas *hodium, hirasci, cohoperante,* ubi respiratio " additur ; hæc pro more fiunt, et minime typographo imputanda."

That Rymer's work created some disappointment on its first *Contemporary criticism.* appearance must not be concealed. At least Ayloffe states[1] that the public had formed high ideas of this proposed collection of records, long before its publication ; but their expectations were greatly disappointed. They could not, he says, without injustice to Rymer, neglect to applaud his labours, but at the same time they regretted his want of correctness, and that he had not more maturely considered the merits as well of several of those instruments which he printed as of many others which he rejected. This opinion of Ayloffe has been urged several times by Dr Clarke in condemnation of Rymer; and yet he has felt himself compelled to admit that ' perhaps there are few (if any) men in his day who could have " executed a design with so much accuracy and success, at once as " difficult and complex as it was important and useful "

For myself, I am inclined to think that Ayloffe has magnified the number as well as the importance of the censures to which he refers He has mistaken the voice of a few like himself, who may have read the " Fœdera " with attention and compared it on some occasions with the originals, for the voice of the public, who neither could nor would do the one or the other. Considering the extent of his task, the difficulties and the intricacies against which Rymer had to contend single-handed, his work is by no means amenable to the censures that were thus insinuated by Ayloffe. Many of his supposed errors are nothing more than typographical inaccuracies ; some are the obvious misreadings of his scribes—palpable enough, and pardonable in transcribing from faded parchments, often closely generally obscurely, written ; and from the enormous size of the documents themselves, and their involved and perplexed Latinity, wearisome in the extreme.

---

[1] Introduction, p. xxxviii.

But to return to the 18th, 19th, and 20th volumes, which were wholly entrusted to the editorship of Sanderson [1] These volumes are quite different in their nature from those that preceded them. Sanderson either mistook his instructions, or wilfully perverted them. Instead of a "Fœdera" he has rather produced a new work in the shape of materials for our domestic history, in which foreign affairs are slightly intermingled. The reader's attention to this fact is particularly desired, as Rymer has been frequently undeservedly blamed for the miscellaneous character of these volumes, in which he had no hand whatever It is true that in the 15 volumes edited by himself he frequently enlarged his plan, but Sanderson entirely changed it. It was his object to spare himself labour. He seems to have contented himself with making selections from those muniments which came easily to hand, and he seldom prosecuted his researches beyond the precincts of the Rolls Chapel, of which he was one of the chief clerks. It was less trouble to print the Patent Rolls entire than to make researches at the Chapter House.

The eighteenth volume of the "Fœdera" made its first appearance in 1726, but it was recalled for the reason which will be presently given, and did not finally appear until 1731. It embraces the period from 28th March 1625 to 10th of October 1628. It bears upon it every appearance of a continuation issued under the same authority as the preceding seventeen volumes, and accompanied by the same immediate sanction of the crown. The descriptive portion of the title-page agrees verbatim with the previous volumes, the royal warrant, dated the 17th February 1718, is prefixed as a frontispiece. The volume is dedicated to the king, and is stated to be "in lucem missa de mandato regio," an assertion which it is difficult to suppose any one would have hazarded who was merely acting with the royal permission and not by royal command In all these particulars there appear to be positive indications that the "Fœdera" still preserved its original distinction as a publication issued by the government and not as private speculation. In his dedication to King George the First, Sanderson follows in the steps of Rymer; but is less florid, and his compliments are less laboured. He says, "I must " esteem it as a very particular felicity in having had the honour

---

[1] I have already stated that the 16th volume, though edited by Sanderson, was principally taken from Rymer's papers.   The seventeenth volume also contains a portion of Rymer's collection

" of serving three crowned heads (I mean King William, Queen
" Anne, and your royal Majesty) for more than thirty years, in a
" work declared by the greatest potentates in the world as a
" work highly conducing to their service and the honour of their
" crowns. This is the eighteenth tome of that work, wherein
" your Majesty may please to observe a certain prophetic care
" and regard, by your royal predecessor King Charles the First,
" for that illustrious family from which hath been derived unto
" us the choicest blessing that Heaven could bestow upon a loyal
" people, the greatest king and best of men, who hath made us
" greater by your excellent power and better by your royal
" example. Your Majesty will please to indulge me here the
" liberty of making the most dutiful profession of an unalter-
" able zeal and affection to both your Majesty's person and your
" government, and these, I think, I can't declare in a better, I am
" certain in a more agreeable manner, to your Majesty's eminent
" piety, than by my constant wishes and ardent prayers for your
" sacred Majesty's long, very long and prosperous reign over a
" contented people; and that there never may want a person
" issuing from your sacred loins to sway the sceptres of these
" your kingdoms, so long as the sun and moon endure. These
" are the wishes and these are the continued prayers, may it
" please your Majesty, &c "

In this volume Sanderson was guilty of a great indiscretion
and committed a grave breach of the privilege of Parliament,
by printing the Journals of the first Parliament of Charles I,
contrary to the standing orders of both houses. He was summoned
before the House on the 7th of May 1729,[1] and obliged to withdraw

---

[1] The Lord Delawarr reported from the Lords Committees appointed to inspect Public Records, "That their Lordships, in " pursuing the Directions of the House for " inspecting Records, thought proper to " send for and examine Mr Sanderson, " Clerk of the Rolls, who informed the " Committee, that he had prepared an " Eighteenth Volume of Records, of the " Nature of the late Mr. Rymer's Fœdera, " and that the same was printed by J Ton- " son, which the Committee, upon in- " specting, observed, that in the said " Eighteenth Volume, One of the Journals " of this House, of the First year of King " Charles the First, is inserted And the " Committee think proper further to " acquaint your Lordships, that the said " Tonson has deposited, with the Clerk " Assistant, in the House belonging to the " Parliament Office, such Part of the Im- " pression of the said Eighteenth Volume " as remained undisposed of at the Time " the Committee took Notice of the print- " ing the said Journal " Which Report being read by the clerk. It is ordered, that such Part of the said Books as is a Copy of the said Journal of this House be taken out of each respective Volume, and that the Clerk Assistant do take care the same be burnt or destroyed, which when done, the said Mr Tonson may have the remaining Part of the said Books delivered to him (Journals of the House of Lords, vol. 23, p 422)

the volume; he cancelled 230 printed folio pages, with the following advertisement :[1] "The reader will be pleased to observe that the " pages between 334 and 566, which were transcripts of the " Journals of both Houses of Parliament, and, through ignorance, ' printed contrary to the standing orders of both houses, were " therefore (in all dutiful obedience to the same) laid aside after " they were printed, and are now supplied at the end of this " volume, with proper collections from the records, which follow in " due course of chronology, by Mr. Robert Sanderson. N.B.—The " 19th and 20th volumes of the Fœdera are compiled, and will be " published in due time by J Tonson."

The amended volume received its full complement of 1060 pages, but did not make its appearance until the year 1731.

The nineteenth volume was published in 1732, and was dedicated to King George the Second. It embraces the period of 1628–1636. Speaking of this volume in his dedication to the King, Sanderson says, "I take this first opportunity of laying " myself at your Majesty's royal feet, together with an offering " that best becomes me to make, and is the fittest for your Majesty " to receive, it is the nineteenth tome of the Fœdera, &c., a " collection containing so vast and rich a fund of useful and " instructive learning, in all transactions, whether foreign or " domestic, as I will adventure to say no other nation ever did " nor indeed is able to produce the like. The collection is drawn " from the pure and unadulterate fountain of your Majesty's " sacra scrinia, which give the firmest sanction to the veracity " and the surest proof to the authority. This inestimable trea- " sure the learned world owes to three of your royal predecessors " and to your own beneficence. I might, on this occasion, say " a thousand things which duty and affection to your sacred Majesty do very naturally   spire, but that profound awe and " reverence which I shall always profess for your royal person do " command a dutiful silence; concluding with my sincerest wishes " that all your Majesty's subjects may by their stedfast duty and

---

[1] It ought, however, to be stated, in justification of Sanderson, that in the warrant of George I., dated 17th Feb 1717–8, he was permitted to have access to the Journals of both Houses of Parliament. Probably the houses considered that only access was intended, and not the privilege of printing It does not appear that the subject was ever noticed in Parliament, as Sanderson recalled his work immediately he became aware of his indiscretion. Several copies of it, however, must have been circulated One I have myself consulted, and another fell into the hands of Rapin, who made an abridgment of it in the xxxiv number of the Acta Regia, and which may be seen in the folio edition of that work.

" fidelity make it appear to all the world that they are not
" altogether unworthy of the favour and protection of so good
" and gracious a prince."

The twentieth volume made its appearance in 1735, and is also
dedicated to George the Second It extends from 28th of March
1636 to 29th of April 1654.

The dedication to King George the Second, which is dated
21st August 1735, is conceived in the same spirit, and written
in the same tone, as those that preceded it. " May it please
" your Majesty, this is the twentieth volume of the Fœdera,
" &c., which I humbly presume to lay now at your Majesty's
" feet. It contains the last twelve years of the reign of King
" Charles the First, and the first six years of King Charles the
" Second, your royal progenitors; a very small number of years
" indeed, but filled with innumerable instances of rage, distraction,
" madness, confusion, unreasonable dissensions, and unchristian
" quarrels, under the pretence of supporting religion (which very
" few practised), and of asserting regal power (which fewer valued).
" This was the melancholy face of affairs in those unhappy days.
" It would ill become my duty to interrupt your Majesty with
" a tedious relation of the various turns and changes in both
" church and state, but a serious reflection upon them naturally
" leads me to express my joy for falling into times under your
" sacred Majesty's auspicious reign, wherein we are sufficiently
" guarded from all fears and apprehensions of such dreadful vicis-
" situdes. May your Majesty live long to preserve to us those
" blessings which by your consummate wisdom and unwearied
" pains and labour you have procured for us May the true
" sense of such inestimable blessings inspire every honest heart
" with an active becoming zeal for the sole service and interests
" of the excellent author of them, for it is to you (great king)
" we truly owe the full enjoyment of them. May just Heaven
" (whose care you are) ever protect and guard your Majesty, your
" royal consort, and all your royal family, for the glory and support
" of all your subjects in particular, and for the general good and
" benefit of mankind, &c."

These three volumes edited by Sanderson were published by
Jacob Tonson This circumstance, added to the fact that Tonson
was the real and responsible publisher of the second edition, has
probably given occasion to the supposition that the volumes were
published at Tonson's risk

Sanderson does not appear to have satisfied either the government or the public in his capacity of editor of the Fœdera, as he was not employed to continue it. He died on the 25th of December 1741 The little that is known of his personal history appears in the note below[1] It would be unjust to his memory not to state that the text of his three volumes, which he had taken from the records with which he was most conversant, is generally printed with care , but certain letters which he had borrowed from the papers of Secretary Thurloe are disfigured with gross inaccuracies. This statement is made on the authority of Birch, the editor of the Thurloe Papers, who says, " the reader will be· convinced of the " necessity of reprinting them in this collection, when he is assured " that the whole are most incorrectly transcribed, the dates often " mistaken, and the names of persons and places generally dis- " guised in such a manner as to be quite unintelligible."

Holmes's labours.

The large sum of money at which the seventeen volumes of Rymer's "Fœdera" were valued, one hundred guineas being paid for a single copy, the very great estimation in which it was held abroad, the high encomiums passed upon it by Bishop Nicol-

---

[1] The following facts of his personal history will, it is hoped, be of some interest to the reader Robert Sanderson, a younger son of Christopher Sanderson, a justice of the peace for Durham, who suffered for his attachment to the royal cause, was born at Eccleston Hall in Durham, on the 27th of July 1660 He was entered as a student of St John's College, Cambridge, under Dr Baker, on the 7th of July 1683, and continued several years at the University, being contemporary there with Matthew Prior From the year 1696 to 1707 he was employed by Rymer In 1704 he published a translation of original letters from William to Charles the Second He wrote also a History of Henry the Fifth, part of which is lost and part remains in manuscript On the 3d of May 1707 he was named in the Royal Warrant as Rymer's assistant On the death of Rymer he applied for the place of Historiographer Royal, and was offered assistance by Prior, but was defeated by the change of ministry on the Queen's death in 1714 In 1715 he edited the 16th volume of the Fœdera ex schedis Thomæ Rymer On the 15th February 1717 he was appointed by Royal Warrant editor in Rymer's place. On the 28th of November 1726 he was made usher of the Court of Chancery by Sir Joseph Jekyll, Master of the Rolls, and afterwards clerk or keeper of the Records in the Rolls Chapel. The dates of the publication of the later volumes of the Fœdera have already been given In 1727 he succeeded to considerable property in Cumberland, the North Riding of Yorkshire, and Durham, on the death of an elder brother, and he afterwards occasionally resided at his seat, Armathwaite Castle, on the banks of the Eden, 10 miles from Carlisle, but his chief residence was in London. He died at his town residence in Chancery Lane, and was buried in Red Lion Fields. Sanderson was married four times , the last time in his 70th year to Elizabeth Hickes of London He was considered as a learned man, and was acquainted with many languages He had a choice collection of books and manuscripts, and is said to have kept a journal, in which he noted down the minutest actions. On the death of his wife, in 1753, his estates descended to the family of his eldest sister, Margaret, the wife of Henry Milburne, of Newcastle.

son, M Rapin, and M. le Clerc,[1] and, above all, its scarcity,
naturally attracted the attention of English publishers, and the
celebrated Jacob Tonson determined to produce a second edition,
or rather a reprint of the seventeen volumes, by subscription [2]
He obtained a royal licence for the exclusive publication of the
work for a period of fourteen years from the 24th of May 1723
In the licence the work is treated as complete in 17 volumes
folio, and Tonson is authorized to publish those volumes, without
any mention of an intended continuation. With so little care was
it at first conducted that many of the errors rectified by Rymer
at the end of his preface were repeated without correction George
Holmes,[3] then deputy keeper of the records in the Tower of
London, and a man of considerable merit as an antiquary, was
employed as editor. The work, however, had proceeded as far as
p. 113 before Holmes's services were secured, at least from that

[1] Speaking of the "Fœdera," the celebrated Le Clerc, in his "Bibliotheque
Choisie," says, "On trouvera ici des maté-
"riaux très considerables, pour l'embel-
"lissement et pour l'éclaircissement de
"l'Histoire d'Angleterre, des Etats voisins,
"et en géneral de tous ceux avec qui elle
"a eu quelque chose a traiter, depuis le
"commencement du douzieme Siecle. On
"decouvrira par la quantité des fautes des
"Historiens, qui ont ecrit ce qui s'est passé
"depuis ce tems-la, et pour les faits et
"pour les dates, on suppliera des vuides
"considerable, par le moyen des actes
"secrets que l'on n'avoit pas encore
"publiés, et qui n'etoient pas venus à la
"connoissance des Historiens contem-
"porains, ni meme de siecles suivans;
"enfin on etablira tout sur des actes
"authentiques de tems mêmes et sur des
"Originaux dignes de foi."

[2] Kennet relates an anecdote which
sufficiently proves the difficulty of obtaining a copy "His Majesty (George I)
"within his dominions in Germany had a
"late occasion to enquire for them (the
"seventeen volumes), and could not have
"been supplied with them at any mart in
"Europe, nor indeed at any place or rate
"in Great Britain, had not the worthy
"comptroller signified so much to a
"noble peer in England, who by the next
"return presented his Majesty with his
"own set of them curiously bound"
(Second Letter to the Bishop of Carlisle,
1716, p 36)

[3] George Holmes was born at Skipton
in Craven in the year 1662 He became, in
1685, the clerk of William Petyt, keeper of
the Records in the Tower of London, and
upon his death (9th Oct 1707) was appointed by Lord Halifax to methodize and
digest the records in that repository, at a
salary of 200l per annum He had been
previously appointed (28 Sept. 1704)
chief clerk, for the arranging and calendaring
the undigested records in the Tower, at an
annual salary of one hundred pounds He
was for nearly 60 years deputy to Petyt,
Topham, and Polhill, successively keepers of
the Tower Records, and was one of the original members of the Society of Antiquaries
of London, undertaking to describe the
Saxon coins in the account projected by
that Society He re-edited, in 1727, the
seventeen volumes of Tonson's edition of
the Fœdera, and died on the 16th of February 1748-9 in the 87th year of his age,
and was buried in the Tower Chapel The
Society of Antiquaries engraved his portrait with an inscription on it By his
wife (a daughter of Mr Marshall, a sword
cutler in Fleet Street,) he had an only son,
George, who was educated at Eton, and was
clerk under his father, but died aged 25,
many years before him Mrs Holmes
survived her husband, and received from
Government 200l for his manuscripts
relative to the Tower Records His
books, prints, and coins, were sold by
auction.

page his superintendence becomes apparent; but the errors pointed out in the foot note[1] below seem to have escaped observation

Of Tonson's edition, volumes I. to VIII, and also volumes X, XI, XII., XIII, XVI., and XVII, appear from their title-pages to have been published in 1727. Volumes XIV. and XV. bear date 1728, and volume IX, which was strangely delayed, completed the series of reprints in 1729 These dates upon the title-pages are in some degree at variance with a paper preserved in Nichols' Literary Anecdotes, i. 386,[2] which is evidently genuine, and details the particulars respecting the mode of Tonson's publication

Only the first twelve volumes, which contained the records derived from the Tower, were edited by Holmes, the name of the editor of the others does not appear His corrections exhibit the nature of the errors which had escaped Rymer They are more numerous in the earlier volumes.

Tonson published in 1730 the result of George Holmes' collation in a thin volume, with the title of "The emendations " in the new edition of Mr Rymer's Fœdera are all printed in " these sheets, for the use of those gentlemen who are possessed of " the former edition, the pages of which are exactly referred to in " such a manner that the reader may easily mark those altera- " tions with his pen which are made in the new edition.

The two editions of the "Fœdera" having become scarce and expensive, a third edition, embodying Holmes' collation and Sanderson's additional volumes, was commenced at the Hague in the year 1737, and completed in 1745. It is in smaller type than the other two editions, and is compressed into ten volumes. The work appears to have been undertaken by the Dutch book-sellers as a private speculation, we are not informed of the name the editor they selected, though there is some reason to suppose that it was John Neaulme, the publisher.

---

[1] Rymer's notes of three grave errors are reprinted in the same place, though one of them, if heeded, would have caused the transposition of a document ten years later in the subsequent editions, p 374, col 1, l 23, "Pro node quedam, *leg* nodo " quondam Isabellam Sic corrigendum " ex codice Cottomano, unde patet hanc " Epistolam, post mortem Isabellæ, scrip- " tam, ac proinde ad annum 1247 de- " ferendam, ut in Chronologico Indice " emendatur" Accordingly, in the index it is placed, together with a correlative document, among the Omissa, not under 1237, but at 1247, to follow page 442, yet in the new edition they are both absurdly separated, so as to follow Rymer's erro-neous marginal date—p 456 ad calcem. in marg pro *ex Autogr.*, leg. *Pat* 34 *H* 3,— p 512, col 2, l. 29, pro 14 *Martii* leg. *pridie nonas Martii.*

[2] See Appendix XXII

This new edition was published at the Hague "Hagæ comitis, " apud Joannem Neaulme. " It is somewhat inaccurately described in the title-page, as "Editio Tertia, ad originales Chartas in Turri ' Londinehsi denuo summa fide collata et emendata, studio Georgii " Holmes."

Volume I., which includes the whole of volumes I. and II. of the London editions, and 312 pages of volume III., bears date 1739.

Volume II. contains the remainder of volume III., the whole of volume IV., and 535 pages of volume V., and is also dated 1739.

Volume III. finishes at the 187th page of volume VIII., and bears date 1740.

Volume IV, also dated in 1740, brings the reprint down to the 565th page of volume X.

Volume V. ends with the 247th page of volume XIII., and was published in 1741.

Volume VI., dated in the same year, comes down to the end of volume XV. of the London editions.

Volume VII. concludes volume XVII. of the London editions, and is dated 1742.

Volume VIII. was published in 1743, and ends with the 658th page of volume XIX. of Sanderson's edition.

Volume IX., published in 1744, includes the remainder of Sanderson's portion; also 107 letters attributed to Queen Mary I. of England, a translation into French of an English treatise "de " l'Estat et Gouvernement du royaume d'Angleterre," said to have been written by Sir Thomas Smith, and the Syllabus to Rymer's manuscript collections.

Volume X. contains an "Abrege Historique" of the documents contained in the "Fœdera," and an Index rerum præcipuarum to the nine preceding volumes. It was published in 1745.

Prefixed to the tenth volume is sometimes found an advertisement from John Neaulme, the publisher, in which he states the account between himself and the subscribers according to the terms contained in his proposals. The whole cost to the subscribers was 134 florins and 3 sols for each copy. Neaulme also submits to his subscribers an account of various unanticipated expenses which he had necessarily incurred with a view of rendering the edition more complete, the result of which is that in his opinion each subscriber ought to pay him 13 florins and 3 sols

beyond the stipulated price He makes no demand for the amount,
but states the circumstances, and adds "ceux que voudront me les
" payer me feront plaisir, et me rendront justice."

It may be inferred from the statements in this advertisement
that John Neaulme was himself the editor as well as the publisher
of the Hague edition

Comparison of
the various
editions of the
Fœdera
A few words on the comparative advantages of the three
editions of the " Fœdera " will not be out of place here

There is very little difference in the *appearance* of the editions
printed by Churchill and by Tonson , perhaps the latter has a slight
advantage , but if either be compared with the Dutch edition it
will at once be seen how superior is either of the former to the
foreign reprint in clearness of type, in the texture of the paper,
and the disposition of the printed matter In the English editions,
consisting of twenty handsome volumes, the printer has done
everything in his power to assist the reader. In the Dutch edition, on the other hand, the documents are crowded together, with
an evident view to abridge space , the type is less clean, and the
paper less firm ; indeed the work throughout has something of a
niggardly and stinted look. So far, therefore, as regards *appearance*, the English editions are certainly to be preferred.

Putting aside appearance, and limiting the comparison to accuracy, Tonson's edition is undoubtedly superior to Churchill's,
inasmuch as it contains George Holmes' corrections, the exact
nature of which will be presently explained To equalize the
editions as far as possible in respect to accuracy, Tonson issued, as
already stated, a thin volume, entitled "The Emendations in the
" new edition of Mr. Rymer's Fœdera, ... published for the use
" of those gentlemen who are possessed of the former edition, &c
" London, 1730 " These emendations are sometimes bound up
with copies of the first edition, but cannot be thought to supply
adequately the place of the corrections themselves In other
respects Tonson's edition is a mere reprint page by page of
Churchill's Even the documents which Rymer inserted at the
end of the first and second volumes under the title of " Omissa "
are retained in the same places in Tonson's edition, although
they ought to have been inserted in their proper places according
to the order of their dates.

The Dutch edition has many peculiarities and some improvements. Among the former, certainly no advantage, is the awkward
division of the volumes into four parts , each separately paged ;

which not only needlessly burthens the memory in using the Index, but produces great inconvenience, as there are four pages with the same number in each volume. Among the improvements may be reckoned, the diminished size of the work and its general index,[1] but which, however, is very defective, and can never be depended upon   The marginal references to the paging of the English editions, beginning at p. 26 of the first volume, and carried on from thence to the end of the work, are also of considerable use.   In typographical accuracy the Dutch edition is far superior to either of the preceding [2]

The Dutch edition also contains additional matter of three kinds: (I.) Original documents ;   (II) A translation from the English ; and (III) a French abridgment, or synopsis of the work.

The original documents consist of one hundred and seven letters of Queen Mary I, "desumptæ ex manuscripto originali in Biblio-" theca Ducis Kantiæ" Some of these are merely complimentary letters, containing few allusions to public affairs , but others, as, for instance, those to the King of Denmark in reply to his applications on behalf of Miles Coverdale, are interesting and valuable   All of them were worthy of publication.   Dr. Clarke, in his General Intro-duction to the "Fœdera," p. vi , has remarked that these letters were probably written by Roger Ascham , and this is not unlikely, as Ascham was Latin Secretary during the period in which these letters were written (Fœd xv 388).   The Duke of Kent, from whose library the original manuscript was derived, was Henry Grey de Ruthyn, who enjoyed that title from the 28th of April 1710 until his death in 1740.

The translation from the English is of a little treatise of great merit in its day, and even yet worthy of notice, ascribed to Sir Thomas Smith, and entitled "De republica Anglorum."   In this work, after a general view of the several kinds of government, the author explains the peculiarities of the institutions of England, and

---

[1] In Churchill's edition, at the end of the seventeenth volume, is an Index nominum, referring to the whole of the seventeen volumes; also seventeen different "Indices locorum Omnium et rerum præcipuarum," corresponding with each volume   Nothing can well be more inconvenient   The three volumes under Sanderson's editorship, viz. the 18th. 19th, and 20th, have no indexes whatever.   Tonson's edition gives precisely the same array of indexes as Churchill's

[2] In the *Avertissement* prefixed to the first volume the editor says —" Je ne m'éten-" drai point sur ce qui la rend préférable " aux deux premières, par rapport à l'ex-" actitude j'avoue même qu'on auroit pu " pousser les corrections beaucoup plus " loin encore qu'on n'a fait, s'il avoit été " permis de donner quelque chose à la con-" jecture, dans des pieces ou tout est " sacré "

briefly describes the different classes of the people and the various natures of the Courts of Justice. It was first published in London in 1583, and has been many times reprinted both in Latin and in English in various sizes. The author is well known, not only as a statesman of some celebrity, but as the learned coadjutor of Sir John Cheke in the revival of classical learning in the sixteenth century. The nature of the work, and the hands through which it came to the editor of the Dutch edition of the "Fœdera," are explained by him in the following title prefixed to the treatise, "De l'estat et " Gouvernment du Royaume d'Angleterre, avec une nouvelle " addition des principales Cours du dit Royaume et des officiers " d'icelles Cours. Faict a la Main le 28 Mars l'an de Salut 1565 " pendant le Reyne de la Serenissime et Excellentissime princesse " la Reine Elizabeth, par un Gentilhomme, Ambassadeur en France " pour sa Majesté a pres le Roy Charles IX. de ce nom. N B.—Le " Manuscrit a été donne par feu Monseigneur le Prince de Condé à " M la Comte de Bethune "

The *Abrégé Historique,* perhaps the most remarkable feature in this edition, occupies nearly six hundred pages of the tenth volume This *Abrégé* is so intimately connected with the "Fœdera," and indeed has so nearly become a component part of it, that its history deserves some attention.

At the time when Le Clerc received the volumes of the "Fœdera" through the medium of Lord Halifax, he was the editor of a literary review, entitled "Bibliotheque Choisie," published at Amsterdam in 12mo. Desirous of doing honour to Lord Halifax for his valuable gift, and, at the same time of giving his review all the superiority over its competitors which could be derived from the possession of these important volumes, he proposed to insert in the "Bibliotheque Choisie" a series of articles which should illustrate and explain the contents of the "Fœdera." The first of these articles appeared in the 16th volume of the "Bibliotheque Choisie," and, besides a brief account of the history of the work, contained an abstract of the contents of the first volume.

Le Clerc's numerous occupations prevented him from fulfilling his intention of continuing these articles, and for several years after the publication of the first of them the design was dropped. In the meantime the subject was taken up in another quarter. Le Clerc, as before mentioned, lent the volumes of the "Fœdera" to Rapin, who was then employed upon his English History Upon returning the second volume, Rapin acknowledged his obligation for the loan, accompanying it with an abstract or abridgment of its contents, written in French, and arranged under the heads of the principal historical transactions to which the documents contained in the volume related. This was exactly what Le Clerc wanted, and it was probably written with more knowledge of the subject than was possessed by Le Clerc himself. Rapin's abstract of the second volume was immediately published in the "Bibliotheque Choisie," and he was invited by Le Clerc to write a series of similar articles upon the remaining volumes He did so, and the papers which he thus contributed were from time to time inserted in the "Bibliotheque Choisie," and, after its relinquishment, in the "Bibliotheque Ancienne et Moderne," another review of the same kind established by Le Clerc as a successor to the Bibliotheque Choisie This long series of articles comprised abstracts made by Rapin of the whole seventeen volumes of the "Fœdera," and were highly and justly esteemed as a useful abridgment of an extremely scarce and exclusive work Rapin's papers were considered to be of such value that, by the direction of Pensionary Fagel, the States printer at the Hague was employed to reprint them in one volume, with the addition of an article upon the first volume written by Rapin, in conformity with the plan upon which he had composed the rest Only thirty copies of this work were printed, one of which found its way into the library of Martin Folkes, Esquire, President of the Royal Society

Abridgments of the remaining volumes edited by Sanderson were shortly afterwards made by some other person, but whether they were included in the Pensionary Fagel's reprint I have not been able to discover , they are, however, to be found in the last volume of the Hague edition.

A work relating principally to English history, and which had attracted so much attention upon the continent, was soon thought worthy of publication in England. Mr. Stephen Whatley, a person employed by the London booksellers in making translations from the French, was encouraged to undertake a translation of it by William Benson, to whom the nation is indebted for the monument to Milton in Westminster Abbey, and Martin Folkes lent Whatley his copy of Pensionary Fagel's reprint. The translation was first published in the years 1726 and 1727 in twenty-five numbers, which form four volumes 8vo, and besides the article by Le Clerc upon the first volume, and Rapin's articles upon the volumes from II. to XVII., it also contains Rapin's supplementary article upon volume I. The full title of Whatley's book will be seen in the foot note.[1]

An edition of Whatley's translation was published in 42 numbers, in folio in 1732, and in 1733 the translator prefixed a dedication to William Prince of Orange, although his old patron, Benson, to whom the octavo edition was dedicated, was still alive. The folio edition does not comprise Le Clerc's article upon vol. I., but, on the other hand, it contains a translation of the abridgments of volumes XVIII.[2] and XIX., which were not included in the octavo edition. In neither of them is there any abridgment of volume XX.[3]

The publication of the "Acta Regia" seems to have been an infringement of Tonson's licence of the 24th of May 1723, but probably evaded its literal meaning.

In the Dutch edition of the "Fœdera" we find the abstract of vol. I by Le Clerc, all Rapin's papers, and also a continuation,[4] which embraces the documents in volumes XVIII., XIX., and XX.

---

[1] "Acta Regia, or an Account of the "Treaties, Letters, and Instruments be-"tween the Monarchs of England and "Foreign Powers, published in Rymer's "Fœdera, which are the basis of the Eng-"lish History, and contain those authorities "which rectify the mistakes that most of "our writers have committed for want of "such a collection of Records Translated "from the French of M. Rapin, as pub-"lished by M. Le Clerc To be published "monthly"

[2] A large portion of the 18th volume was cancelled, but the Folio Edition of the "Acta Regia" contains an analysis of the cancelled printed sheets, a circumstance which adds greatly to the value of that edition.

[3] The Hague edition, however, contains an abridgment in French of the 20th volume. In mentioning it the editor says :—"Il y a "sept ans que ce nouveau Tome a paru, "sans que l'Abréviateur Anglois ait "rempli sa promesse Pour suppléer à ce "défaut, le Libraire J Neaulme en donne "ici en François un Extrait Historique, "qui, quoique travaillé moins à loisir que "ceux des dix-neuf autres Tomes, ne "laissera pas de mettre le Lecteur au fait, "tant des évenemens les plus remarqua-"bles de dernieres années du Regne de "Charles I., &c "

[4] This continuation is epitomized in an alphabetical order, and has been condemned

by Dr Clarke as "destitute of lucid ar-"rangement and distinguishing leading "principles" (See Dr Clarke's Second Report in the General Reports of the Com-missioners of Public Records, 1819, i, p 127, also the General Introduction to the Fœdera, p vii.) Rapin, however, differed essentially from Dr Clarke on this subject He states :—"Puisque nous voici parvenus "à la fin de cette année, qui doit faire "aussi la conclusion du XVIII. Tome des "Actes Publics d'Angleterre, je vais don-"ner l'Extrait que j'ai promis des pieces "qu'il contient, et qui ne se rapportent "par seulement à l'Histoire des années "précédentes, mais encore à plusieurs "autres matieres qui intéressent des per-"sonnes de tous les rangs et de toutes "les conditions J'ai pris soin de ranger "ces Extraits par ordre alphabétique, "comptant que le Lecteur aimera mieux "trouver chaque sujet traité à part et sous "son propre chef, sur tout les dates ayant "été très fidelement marquées, que de voir "une multitude d'articles, qui n'ont aucun "rapport entre eux, assemblés pêlemêle, "sans autre avantage que de garder l'ordre "chronologique D'ailleurs, ce Tome "XVIII. contient si peu de pieces propres "à être incorporées dans le tissu de l'His-"toire, que le Lecteur sentira bien la "nécessité qu'il y avoit de ne pas suivre "la methode qu'on a observée dans les "Extraits des Tomes précédens."

All these papers are classed together under the general title "Abrege
" Historique des Actes Publiés d'Angleterre recueilles par Thomas
" Rymer "

On the score of greater convenience, more portable size, a better
index and increased comprehensiveness, the third or Hague edition
of the " Fœdera " is preferable to the others.

The Hague edition, like its two predecessors, soon became difficult to obtain, and was much in demand.   These facts and other circumstances determined the late Commissioners on Public Records to
undertake a new edition, and on a more extensive and magnificent
scale.   Their resolution arose out of the following circumstance
A Select Committee of the House of Commons was appointed in the
year 1800 to inquire into the state of the public records of the
realm, and, among other things, it reported to the house that the
state papers published together in " Rymer's Fœdera" formed a most
valuable collection   As the work did not come down lower in date
than the first six years of Charles the Second during the usurpation, they recommended a supplementary selection of such other
important papers as had been omitted by the original compiler,
and they deemed it advisable to have it continued to the Revolution,
or even to the accession of the House of Hanover.

Latest edition
under the
superintend-
ence of the
Record
Commission

The Record Commissioners, who were appointed by George the
Third to carry out the measures recommended by the House of
Commons, gave their early attention to the " Fœdera ; " but, unfortunately, they possessed little acquaintance with the literature of
records and ancient diplomacy   They had not sufficiently weighed
the difficulties they would have to encounter in following out
the suggestion of the Committee of the House of Commons
However, they directed their secretary, Mr. Topham, to write to
the several keepers of the records in the Tower of London, the
Rolls Chapel, the Chapter House, Westminster, the State Paper
Office, the Privy Council Office, and to the Clerks of the Signet,
to consider and submit to the Board a proper selection of records,
instruments, and state papers in their custody, for the purpose of
forming a supplement to Rymer's Fœdera during the period of time
comprehended in that work, and also with a view to its continuation to the accession of George the Second

Steps taken by
the Record
Commissioners.

No time was lost in replying to the Commissioners by the several
gentlemen having the custody of the public records   Mr Astle reported to the Board on the 24th of March 1802, that he had caused
selections to be made from the records in his charge at the Tower
from the reign of John to that of Edward the Fourth, both included.

Mr Kipling stated that he had prepared selections from the muniments at the Rolls Chapel down to the time of George the Second, and Mr. Planta was requested to examine the collection of Rymer's manuscripts in the British Museum, to compare them with the printed work, and to report how far the same had been already included in it.

The next step taken by the Record Commissioners was that which they ought to have taken in the first instance, namely, to secure the services of a person duly qualified to undertake the examination and arrangement of the returns made from the State Paper Office, the Tower, Chapter House, and British Museum. Mr Kipling was ordered to revise his selections from the Rolls Chapel, and the Master of the Rolls was requested to inspect the catalogue proposed by Mr. Kipling, and to note such as he judged unfit to be included in the supplement to and continuation of Rymer's work Mr. Kipling was further ordered to prepare his work for press, and submit his manuscript to the Record Commissioners

Mr. Samuel Lysons (who had succeeded Mr Astle as keeper of the Tower records) was requested to report on the documents which had been selected at the Tower under the superintendence of his predecessor ; that conscientious and erudite scholar, however, finding such a work incompatible with his official duties, respectfully declined the task. After he had commenced an examination of the extracts from the calendars to the patent and close rolls, with a view to a report on a proper selection of the Tower records for the continuation and supplement of the Fœdera, Mr Lysons remarks, "As a general report on a proper selection from the " records in my office, which appears to be desired by his Majesty's " Commissioners, it would have given me much pleasure to have " been able to comply with this request, but what I consider as " the positive duties of my office occupying so much of my time " at present, that I could not undertake a work of such magni- " tude and nicety, even if I were confident in the sufficiency of my " judgment for it."

Their difficulty in finding an editor

The office of chief editor was then offered to Mr. Lysons, but he felt it his duty to decline it

The Commissioners were greatly embarrassed to find a fit person to undertake the editorship of the new "Fœdera," and they had the mortification of recording their failure on three[1] other occasions

---

[1] Record Minutes, 16 December 1805, 23 March 1806, 21 July 1806, 16 December 1807

Chance at last threw in their way a gentleman who was distinguished for his biblical learning and oriental scholarship, though quite unskilled in diplomacy and palæography, and without any profound acquaintance with English historical and antiquarian literature.

On the 25th March the secretary reported to the Board that Dr. Adam Clarke, LL.D., who had been recommended as a fit person to undertake the editorship of the Fœdera, on account of his extensive learning and indefatigable industry, having been desired to prepare "an essay on the best mode of carrying into "effect a compilation to form a supplement and continuation of "Rymer's Fœdera," had complied with the request   Dr. Clarke's essay was read at the Board, and the Commissioners having signified their approbation of the method suggested by Dr Clarke for executing the work, it was ordered that the synopsis[1] subjoined to his essay should be returned to him, to be filled up as he had proposed, for the purpose of completing the specimen from the Conquest to the end of the reign of John   The secretary was also directed to obtain admission for him to the several public offices and libraries which it might be necessary for him to consult   He was further ordered to prepare a scheme for the first volume of a supplement, and the first volume of a continuation, specifying, in the same manner as sketched out in his synopsis, all the articles or instruments he proposed to insert, and to lay the same before the Board with all convenient despatch.

Dr. Adam Clarke appointed to complete the "Fœdera"

The essay referred to bears date the 18th of March, and is published in the General Reports of the Commissioners on Public Records. It is not necessary here to do more than remark, that it is evidently the production of a person unskilled in records, and who wrote from the information of others rather than from his own experience. About fourteen months after Dr. Clarke had issued this essay, he appears to have entirely changed the opinions he then expressed, and recommended the Record Board to alter the supplement and continuation which had been suggested by the House of Commons into a new edition of the whole work, with a

He recommends a new edition of the "Fœdera"

---

[1] "A Synopsis of the Contents and Defi- "ciencies of the first 100 years of Rymer's "Fœdera." Dr Clarke designed it as an appendix to his essay. It will be found in a MS. volume of "Orders, Reports, &c. on the Fœdera, from 1808 to 1811," now preserved in the Public Record Office   It consists of a table divided into spaces for all the years from 1066 to 1202, those spaces only being filled when a document occurs in Rymer. All the rest are left blank.

more scientific and methodical arrangement. Some of the reasons pressed by Dr. Clarke for this total change of purpose, if not convincing were at least specious, and were calculated to mislead a body of gentlemen little acquainted with matters of this nature. He pointed out the importance of the Fœdera as a great national work, the scarcity and value of copies of it, the fact that many of the originals had been either lost or rendered useless by an injurious application of a solution of galls. He pressed upon the Commissioners the necessity of having the whole body of its contents corrected, methodized, and arranged, in conjunction with the new materials which had been discovered since Rymer first formed his collection. In direct opposition to the House of Commons, he condemned "supplements," as being of comparatively little use, and in support of his censure he brought forward the fact that when George Holmes was employed to examine and collate the articles in Rymer with the originals in the Tower, the fruit of his labour was a volume of corrections and emendations, which were printed separately, and yet this was not judged sufficient; consequently, a new edition of the work had been recommended and executed, in which the corrections and emendations were inserted in their proper places. Either for the purpose of undervaluing the services of Holmes, or for some other object not apparent on the face of his censure, Dr. Clarke asserted that he had sufficient proof that Holmes did not collate the papers at the Tower with any tolerable degree of care, and that many omissions had been discovered on recollation, not of single words only, but of whole sentences.

Dr Clarke's censure ordered to be examined

For the purpose of ascertaining the correctness of Dr. Clarke's accusation, I was employed in the year 1834 by the Commissioners on Public Records to make a careful examination into this subject. From my report to the Commissioners, as it has never been printed, I have no hesitation in selecting the following extracts

Extracts from a Report on subject.

here. I observed that "it is only necessary to consider the emendations really effected by Holmes in his edition, and to oppose "them to the variations from the original records to be found, as ' well in the new as in the old edition of Rymer, to make it "evident that so severe a censure upon Holmes had better have "been spared, for, notwithstanding this charge of errors ascribed "to the neglect of the latter, I have not been fortunate enough to "discover any instance of the correction of such errors in the *new* "*edition*. In justice to the memory of Holmes, it is but fair to "state that he certainly did collate most of the articles in the 1st

" edition with their corresponding documents in the Tower, dis-
" covering and correcting many errors, and that those he allowed
" to remain in the 2nd edition are but few in number, of very
" trifling importance, and scarcely, if at all, affecting the sense of .
" the passages to which they belong. It is likewise clear that of
" the instruments in which such errors are to be found he had not
" compared a single one with its original, probably owing to his
" being unable to lay his hand upon such original at the time.
" What were his reasons for not collating any of the documents
" prior to the reign of King John, it would perhaps be difficult
" at this time to say ; but that he began no earlier is fairly to be
" concluded from his emendations commencing *with the first*
" *instrument in that reign*"

To return to the new edition. "I felt it my duty to state, that   Clarke's in-
" my researches had not enabled me to find therein any emendation justice to
" of importance beyond those actually made by Holmes. This con-   Holmes.
" clusion, founded upon the examination of only a very limited
" number of the instruments, is, however, by no means intended to
" convey an impression that *no corrections* have been made in the
" *new edition*. Possibly there may be many, and very valuable
" emendations may have been effected with regard to those instru-
" ments, which it has not occurred to me to compare with the
" originals ; but in those which I have *collated*, the alterations
" appear to be merely such as would readily suggest themselves to
" any person possessing a competent knowledge of the Latin
" language when collating the original record. The only example
" of gross inaccuracy amended in the new edition seems to me to
" be merely the particular one selected for notice in the preface to
" the same; and even in this instance it is observable, that the
" correction occurs in a portion of the work relative to a period
" long preceding that at which Holmes appears to have commenced
" his labours, that is, before the first year of the reign of John,
" which was probably owing to the fact that the *regular series* of
" the Chancery rolls in the Tower does not begin at an earlier period.

" It is somewhat remarkable that Holmes should have been
" accused, in such unqualified terms, of a general want of care,
" since it is admitted in the General Introduction to the new
" edition (page 10) that 'as the work had been printed from the
" ' 2nd edition, collated by Holmes with the originals in the
" ' Tower, it was not thought necessary to recollate all the papers
" ' in that repository.' That the new editor should thus follow in
" the steps of a man whom he charged with having so unsteadily

" trod the path of duty was assuredly not to have been expected
" in a work where accuracy was a desideratum of great if not of
" the very first importance ; more especially as it had been pre-
" viously stated that ' the papers from the Tower were in a more
" ' incorrect state than those taken from any other office ,' and that
" ' many had been copied with a most reprehensible neglect ' It
" is also difficult to conceive for what reason the recollation of
" documents in the new edition began *no sooner* than the reign
" of Edward I , and still more incomprehensible that, after the
" beneficial results of such recollation had become strikingly ap-
" parent, this most important part of the editor's duty was
" totally abandoned.

Remarks on the advantages and disadvantages of Dr Clarke's edition

" It would lead me into a discussion of too great length to enter
" here into a detail of the particulars in which the *new edition* of
" the Fœdera may be considered as an improvement upon its pre-
" decessors, or to enumerate the many points in regard to which
" the just expectation of those who have had occasion to consult
" it have been disappointed. Many have complained of negligence
" and inconsistency in its orthography and punctuation ; others, of
" great inaccuracy as to dates, and in the arrangement of its instru-
" ments , and, on the other side, some few have been found to
" speak of it in terms of unqualified approbation. Opposite
" opinions of its faults and its advantages may doubtless continue
" to be entertained. For myself, I am wholly unconscious of any
" disposition to view the *new edition* of the Fœdera through a
" medium of hypercriticism , but, called upon for a statement of
" facts, it has imperatively become my duty to make you no other
" than a faithful return to your inquiries regarding its accuracy ;
" and though some of the errors noticed in Appendix A.[1] may be
" considered but of a trifling nature, and others may be found to
" have in no way acted as impediments to a complete or sufficient
" understanding of the instruments to which they respectively
" belong, yet it cannot be denied that, insignificant or not, they
" could scarcely have been overlooked in the course of a careful
" collation with the original records, had such been the practice
" adopted and strictly adhered to "

The Record Board did not at first accede to the advice given by
Dr. Clarke , but he was not to be defeated   At the end of twelve
months he again brought forward his project, and endeavoured to
show that a new edition was the only course likely to meet the
wishes or demands of the public. In an evil hour the counsels of

---

[1] Appendix to the Report

Dr. Clarke prevailed, and the Commissioners gave way, in hope that the work would thus be made more complete and more useful. We must lament the step thus taken by the Commissioners. The determination to reprint 20 folio volumes, in an extravagant and unwieldy form, whilst whole classes of important records remained unpublished, was, to say the least of it, a proceeding of lavish impropriety, and of which no persons who had to employ their own means and substance would have been guilty. The determination was opposed to the recommendation of the House of Commons; but what was to be expected from an irresponsible Board, the several members of which had probably never consulted the Fœdera, and only knew its nature from the reports of Dr. Clarke? Be this, however, as it may, Dr Clarke was on the 24th of March 1810 authorized to undertake a new edition of the Fœdera. That the Fœdera is a most important national publication is conceded by everyone whose opinion is worth regarding, but its scarceness was very much exaggerated by Dr Clarke, and his allegation that many of the original documents had been lost, and many destroyed by galls, was most illogical and absurd. Had such been the case, how could they have been of any use in a new edition? Documents lost or destroyed were no longer available for examination or collation, whereas the press had already perpetuated them, and given them all the publicity and permanency within its power. The only valid argument, brought forward by Dr Clarke in favour of the new edition, was the convenience of having the supplementary documents inserted in chronological order with those previously printed, an advantage that no one will deny, but which it was possible to purchase too dearly.

I propose in my preface to the next volume of this Syllabus to examine critically the materials added to the work by Dr. Clarke, and which he has condemned Rymer for omitting.

It now only remains for me to explain the object and plan of the present work. Its object is to give, in English, a condensed notice of each instrument, printed in the several editions of the "Fœdera," arranged in chronological order, as a sort of precursor of the Calendars of State Papers now in progress, under the direction of the Master of the Rolls, and thus supply the student, who may not have the means of procuring the ponderous and expensive volumes of the "Fœdera," with a synopsis of state papers anterior to the time of the Tudors when the Calendars commence. It is not intended to supersede the "Fœdera," but to bring it more under the notice of the statesman and historical scholar than it has

The Syllabus explained. Its object

lately occupied. It is true that the " Fœdera" does not exhaust
the subject to which it is devoted, as I shall presently show ; but
it is, nevertheless, a vast magazine of state papers, protocols, and
memorials, which ought to be gravely studied, not only for the
history of England, but for that of Europe generally.

Its plan.

It has already been stated that Le Clerc and Rapin both
published abstracts or abridgments of the Fœdera, the former
confining his task to the first volume, the latter extending his
to the seventeen volumes which had appeared during his time ;
a third (unknown person) abridged the 18th, 19th, and 20th
volumes. The present Syllabus does not resemble either of its
three predecessors

Le Clerc's object.

Le Clerc's object was to give a comprehensive idea of the use
that might be made of the " Fœdera," first, by general remarks
on the importance of its materials, and secondly, by making selections from it in illustration of his comment   This plan was
certainly justified in explaining to foreigners the speciality of a
work, so unlike anything that had hitherto been published on the
continent. His selections, however, were few in comparison with
the instruments with which he had to deal

Rapin's

Rapin's intention was to show the relation which the acts in the
Fœdera stand to the events which occurred, and to illustrate the
one by the other   To use his own words, he considered the
' Fœdera" as a body without a soul, which required the thread
of history to illustrate and support it.   He therefore undertook
to show the relation of the acts in the Fœdera to the History of
England, and their importance in illustrating the public and private
transactions of each reign ; but as he proceeded, his materials
became too diversified for his project, and he found it impossible
to reduce his plan to general heads, and consequently was under
the necessity of varying the course of his design, and was compelled, as it were, to cut up the History of England into strips
and classify his subjects under different heads ; for instance, he
divides the events of the reign of Edward the First into eight
sections, bringing under each the various instruments especially
pertaining to each topic from the beginning to the end of the reign ;
thus, all the acts relative to Scotland are brought together ; as are
all ecclesiastical affairs relating as well to England alone as to
the King's controversies with Rome ; the disputes between England and France ; the war in Wales ; the affairs concerning
England in particular , the differences between the two families
of Aragon and Anjou, of which Edward I. was the mediator,

special acts relating to the King and his family; and, lastly, distinct acts which could not be arranged under either of the other sections. It should also be stated that Rapin did not include in his abridgment all the documents printed in the Fœdera; he omitted those which were not important for the object he had in view. This mode of proceeding might have been well enough for Rapin's purpose, but it is surely not the way to study history as a science.

The Syllabus aims at none of these distinctions, its object, as I The Syllabus. have already stated, is simply to give a synopsis of the *whole* of the Fœdera in the fewest words possible and in strictly chronological sequence, pointing out the pages where each act occurs in the several editions; and with this view it has been found necessary to depart from the order in which several of the acts have been placed by Rymer and the editors who followed him, either through carelessness or ignorance; for instance, under the year 1101 Rymer has printed three documents—one of which belongs to the year 1249, another to 1177, and a third to 1174. Under the year 1162 he has given a papal bull belonging to the year 1257, under the year 1200 another bull is found appertaining to 1245. Under 1174 he has placed a charter of the year 1236, and under 1427 a document belonging to 1509 But it is needless to continue this subject, inasmuch as a list of all the transpositions will appear in the Appendix to the next volume.

That the Syllabus might have been given in greater detail there can be no doubt, but a fuller abstract would have greatly increased the size of the work without effecting any positive advantage, and in fact would have deprived it of its chief recommendation, as affording a compact and lucid outline of the leading wants of our national history If it had been an analysis of unpublished materials, which could not be readily consulted, then a more ample abridgment would have been required; but in a synopsis of a printed work, usually found in every public library and in many private collections, it would seem to be a superfluous task to do more than call attention to each piece in as brief a manner as is compatible with clearness. Each article has been condensed into the fewest words, and it is hoped that the arrangement will satisfy the requirements of those for whose service it has been compiled.

The Syllabus may also be used as a general index to the several editions, chronologically arranged, and if read continuously it will afford the student a skeleton of English History, and give him a much more faithful picture of the events of any particular period than can be gathered from the pages of the writers of the age to which those events relate. For instance, secrets of state quite unknown to contemporary annalists are brought to light; chasms in history are filled up from undoubted sources; the causes and consequences of things are made clear by tracing their beginning, their progress, and their end, for it must be remembered that every event in history arose from some preceding transaction, and became in its turn the parent of others A contemptible squabble between the masters of two trading vessels has more than once brought two friendly nations into a collision which has only been repaired after years of sanguinary conflict and ruinous expense

A general index of the names of persons and places which occur in the Syllabus will be found at the end of the second volume

A third volume will be wholly devoted to a general index of the names of persons and places, including also matters which appear in all the editions of the Fœdera, and so arranged as to suit each edition.

It is, however, necessary to state that, except under special circumstances, the orthography of the proper names, as they occur in the Fœdera, though not always correct, has been adopted both in the Syllabus and the indexes. To have altered the spelling from what it appears in the printed volumes would have been productive of much inconvenience to those consulting the work

I have already intimated that, although the Fœdera supplies a vast amount of historical information in the character of State Papers and diplomatic instruments anterior to the reign of Henry VIII, when the Calendars to those documents commence, yet it does not, by any means, exhaust those subjects: much more remain unpublished than have already appeared Any work, therefore, which should indicate these inedited materials would be of the highest importance to the student; and no one can doubt that the nation ought to possess some uniform work of the kind, in which all articles of real importance should be noticed, necessary for the illustration of English history from the earliest period down to the Revolution of 1688. I do not now allude to topographical or local history, but to a public or political history in the widest sense of the term. In such a work should be found (those printed in the Fœdera, of course, always excepted) all conventions and treaties between foreign princes and the sovereigns of England; letters and other documents illustrative of such treaties; conventions and treaties between foreign princes and powers having reference to English interests, or illustrative of English history; conventions between foreign princes and potentates and the subjects of Kings of England; public and private acts of foreign princes illustrative of English history, papal bulls, briefs, and other ecclesiastical documents manifesting the exercise of papal authority over the subjects or institutions of this kingdom; correspondence of the Kings of England with their own subjects, illustrative of general history; correspondence of Kings of England with foreign communities, noblemen, merchants, and others, correspondence between foreign potentates and British subjects; acknowledgments of allegiance and service of rights belonging to the Kings of England from foreign princes and their subjects, letters of safe conduct, credence, and protection, and letters, though neither royal, nor proceeding from any constituted authorities, yet illustrative of English history. Specimens of the whole of these here enumerated may be seen in the Fœdera. Such a work as I have suggested should be a Supplement to the Fœdera, and should contain a brief but complete Calendar of all authentic documents to be found amongst English Records, necessary for the verification and illustration of the political, ecclesiastical, civil, and military history of Great Britain.

In the Appendix to the Second Volume of the Syllabus will be found a specimen of the work to which I have called the reader's attention

I cannot close these pages without referring to the assistance I have received in collecting the materials which form the basis of this preface. I should indeed be ungrateful did I not acknowledge, with very many thanks, the valuable and ready aid I have received from several members of the Public Record Office who have helped me in every way in their power, to mention their names would look like a parade of friendship; there is one of them, however, to whom I would tender my especial thanks—I mean my valued friend, Mr. John Bruce, who, having travelled over the same ground as myself in a Memoir of Rymer, placed the whole of his materials in my hand. Although I found much that I already possessed, yet Mr. Bruce's papers gave me information that had escaped my research.

Unconnected with the Public Record Office, I gladly record my obligations to the Rev. H. R. Luard, of Cambridge, the President of Queens' College, Cambridge, the Master of Sydney College, Cambridge, the Rev. James Raine, of York, Mr. N. E. S. A. Hamilton, of the British Museum, Mr W T. Jefferson, of Northallerton, and to Mr. J. Horner, of the same town

APPENDIX.

I.

Sir,—By my last you knew that the French had received our ratification under the signett, and putt it collationed into the mediatour's hands : so that I thought the difficulty over . but on Saturday, when they understood that the Instrument under the great seal was come from England, they informed my Lords Ambassad^{rs} by the mediat^r that they excepted ag^t the stile of *rex Franciæ*, and after some arguing upon that point they came to this, that they would be satisfied provided we would declare that we would change it if it were found otherwise in the ratification of the treaty of Breda, *and of other treaties made since.* It would be long to tell you the expedients wch have been proposed and the messages wch have been sent and returned upon this subject. Their Excell^{ces} stick to the treaty of Breda for their precedent, but do not think it proper to stick to such loose terms as, *and the treaties made since,* or *and all other treaties,* for they do not know but that the style of *rex Franciæ* may have been omitted in those negligent times, when France had but too much influence upon our negociations : their Excell^{ces} will have a conference with the French Ambass^{rs} too-morrow on this subject, of which in my next I shall send you the result. I do not question but that the thing will go as we desire it, the ratification having already been effectually exchanged. It is not proper that our Jacobites have the least air of it, for they turn everything to an ill use, tho' I think the French themselves mean no more in it then to be assured that this is the usual stile, and to have made a little shuffle in yielding : this is my present thought of this matter. I have yours of the 28th past and 1st of this month, with the old records of Mr. Rymer. There will be no difficulty about the language then to know if the part of the Instrument which the French took away with them were in Latin or (as they pretend) in French : and as to this point of *rex Franciæ,* tho' surely that style was never omitted in any act of ratification that passed the great seal, yett their Excell^{ces} would not be ensnared (at the latter end of a negociation) by either their tout les traites faits depuis celuy de Breda or tous les traites en general, if Mr Rymer would give us an acc^t of the ratifications that have been made these 30 years (with reference to this point) he would oblige us.—I am, Sir, your most ob^{dt} and most humble ser^t,—M. Prior.

The original of the American treaty wh^{ch} you have in yor keeping does not determine the question as to the language, for that is our part of the treaty, in which you will find (I suppose) that we signed first, but the other part in which vice versâ they signed first, and which Barillon took to France, would clear the doubt ; the Latin instrument would tell us if *rex Franciæ* be expressed : of which a word   .   .   .

Hag. 15 Oct. 1697.

II.

To the King's most Excellent Majesty.

The humble petition of Sir Thomas Osborne, Baronet.

Sheweth,

That Ralph Rymer, gentleman, at the beginning of the late troubles was tenant unto Sir Edward Osborne, your petitioner's late father, deceased, of certain lands in Yafford and Wickmore, in the county of York, under the yearly rent of 200*l.* And your petitioner's father being enaged in the serving of your Majesty's late royal father during the war, and sequestered for his pretended delinquencies, the said Ralph Rymer received the profits of the said lands, and also seized upon several of his goods, all which he converted to his own use, without giving any account for the same till your petitioner commenced suit against him.

That, now being questioned for the said rent and goods, the said Rymer, being a treasurer under the late usurped authority, hath charged himself in his account given in before an auditor with the sum of 346*l.* received out of the said lands and for the said goods not accounted for, which, according to the late Act [12 Car. II (1660) c. 11. § 10. (Stat. of Realm, vol. 5. p. 228–9] is due unto your Majesty.

He therefore humbly prays that your Majesty would be graciously pleased to grant unto him the said sum appearing to be due for the profits of his said father's lands and for his goods, which were sequestered and seized only for his loyalty.

And your petitioner shall ever pray, &c.

At the Court at Whitehall, April the 21st 1663.

His Majesty being sensible of the petitioner's good affection and loyalty, is graciously inclined to grant to the petitioner's suit, and refers it to the Right Honourable the Lord High Treasurer of England to examine the truth of what is alleged in the petition, and that appearing, to certify his opinion thereupon to his Majesty; who will then declare his further pleasure.

HENRY BENNETT.

Endorsed.—Sir Ed. Osborne.
Sir Tho. Osborne
Intr.

Southton House,
May the 5th 1663

May it please your Majesty,

This petitioner and his father having been eminently loyal in the service of the crown, one Mr. Rymer (who deserves a very contrary character), and who being tenant to Sir Edward Osborne and sequestrator of all your Majesty's good subjects in those parts, discharges his own rent (being now sued for it) upon that receipt, I cannot (who find your Majesty inclined otherwise) think fit to divert the grant of your Majesty's interest to what was received of Sir Edward Osborne's, which I find by he petition amounts to three hundred forty-six pounds. And therefore humbly submit it to your Majesty.

T. SOUTHAMPTON.

III.

To be hanged, drawn and quartered   Captain Thomas Oates of Morley, Samuel Ellis, John Ellis of Morley, John Nettleton, sen. and jun. of Dunningley, Robert Scott of Alverthorp, Wm. Tolson, John Fossard, Robert Oldroyd of Dewsbury, Joshua Askwith *alias* Sparling of Morley, Peregrine Corney, John Lowden, John Smith, Wm. Ash, John Errington, exequendus apud Leeds, Robert Atkins, exequendus apud Leeds, Wm. Cotton, George Denham, Henry Watson, exequendus apud Leeds, Richard Wilson, Ralph Rymer, sen.

IV.

A Special Commission issued on the 15th of September 1664, stating that Ralph Rymer, late of Brafferton, in the county of York, having been attainted of high treason at the gaol delivery held in York Castle on Thursday, the 7th of January in the 15th year of the reign of King Charles II., was hanged, and an inquisition was thereupon directed to be made of his landed and personal property. By the inquisition it appears (inter alia) that the said Ralph Rymer before his conviction disposed of a mortgage from one Mr. Wood of certain lands in Kirkby Wisk unto Thomas Rymer, his son, but it was not known what sum there was yet due upon the said mortgage

V.

To the King's most excellent Majestie.

The humble petition of Ralph Rymer, prisoner in the castle of York :

Sheweth,

That whereas your petitioner, by his long and close durance, is reduced into such a weak condition that he cannot expect to continue for any time, as is well known to the high sheriff and several of your Majesty's Deputy Lieutenants, as may appear by this certificate hereto annexed :

Doth therefore pray your most sacred Majesty that, in your great compassion and clemency, you would be pleased to grant your warrant to authorize the high sheriff of the county of York to take sufficient bail of your petitioner for his return to the castle of York upon summons.

And your petitioner will ever pray for the long life and prosperous reign of your most sacred Majesty.

RA. RYMER.

Domestic State Papers, Charles II., Vol. CLVI, No. 37

These are to certify that Mr Ralph Rymer, now a prisoner in the castle of York, as we are informed by persons worthy of credit, is weak in body, being both hydropical and consumptive : And that we cannot apprehend him a man able to continue long in that air and durance.

Witness our hands this 15th day of May 1666.

THO. GOWER.
THO STRICKLAND.
J. CROSLAND.
ED. JENINGS.

Endorsed :—Mr. Ralph Rimer.

Treasury Warrant Book, vol 23, p. 216.

VI.

Rimer to go out upon bond

Warrant for   Rimer to have his liberty upon sufficient bond to be entered into by the said Rimer, Sir Robert Strickland, Sir Thomas Strickland, Sir Jordan Crosland, Sir Richard Graham, or any of them, and some other third person, for his rendering himself a prisoner. Dated July 16, 1666.

One of the Deputy Lieutenants who signed the certificate was Sir Jordan Crosland, of Haramhaugh, in Yorkshire, Bart., to whom the King, on the 8th of February 1664–5, under his sign manual, granted the manor of Brafferton and the estate of Helperby, which Ralph Rymer, senior, attainted of high treason, and Ralph Rymer, junior, attainted of misprision of treason, held under a lease for 99 years of the Archbishop of York.

VII.

In the churchyard of Beaconsfield, on a large sarcophagus of white marble, having four urns, with a pyramid in the centre, is the following inscription, on the south side :—

Heus Viator, tumulatum vides Edmundum Waller,
Qui tanti nominis Poeta et idem avitis opibus
Inter primos spectabilis : Musis se dedit et Patriæ ,
Nondum octodecenarius, inter ardua regni tractantes
Sedem habuit, à Burgo Amersham missus.
Hic vitæ cursus : nec oneri defuit senex, vixitque semper
Populo charus, Principibus in deliciis, admiratione
omnibus.
Hic conditur, tumulo sub eodem,
Rarâ virtute et multâ prole nobilis
Uxor MARIA ex Bressyorum familiâ
Cum EDMUNDO WALLER conjuge charissimo,
Quem ter et decies lætum fecit patrem
V Filiis & Filiabus VIII.
Quos mundo dedit, et in cœlum rediit.

On the west side .—

Edmundi Waller hic jacet id quantum morti cessit ;
Qui inter Poetas sui temporis facile princeps,
Lauream quem meruit Adolescens,
Octogenarius haud abdicavit.
Huic debet patria lingua, quod credas,
Si Græcè, Latinèque, intermitterent Musæ
Loqui, amarent Anglicè.

h 2

On the north side :—

Hoc marmore Edmundo Waller,
Mariæque ex secundis nuptiis conjugi,
Pientissimis parentibus, pientissimé parentavit
Edmundus Filius
Honores bené merentibus extremos dedit,
Quo ipse fugit.
E. L. W. I F. III. G. ex testamento H. M. P. mense Julii 1700.

On the east side :—

Edmundus Waller, cui hoc marmor sacrum est,
Colshill nascendi locum habuit, Cantabrigiam studendi,
Patrem Robertum, ex Hamdenâ stirpe matrem.
Cœpit vivere 3° Martii A. D. 1605
Prima uxor Anna Edwardi Banks filia unica et hæres ;
Ex primâ bis pater factus; ex secundâ tredecies,
Cui et duo lustra superstes. Obiit 21 Octob. A.D. 1687

VIII.

Marie R.

Whereas we have directed our trusty and welbeloved Thomas Rymer. Esq., Historiographer Royall, to transcribe and publish all the leagues, treaties, alliances, capitulations, and confederacies which have at any time been made between the crown of England, and any other kingdoms, princes, and states, as a work highly conducing to our service and the honour of this our realm, for the better enabling him therefore to carry on the said work our will and pleasure is that he the said Thomas Rymer have free liberty and accesse from time to time to search into the Records in our Tower of London, in the Rolls, the Augmentation Office, our Excheqer, the Journalls of both houses of Parliament, or any other place where Records are kept, for such Records as we have or shall direct, and the same to transcribe And that he also have accesse from time to time to our library at St. James's and our paper office, upon such matters as we have or shall appoynt for our service without paying any fees, whereof the respective officers and all other persons whom it may concern are to take notice, and to yield due obedience to our pleasure herein declared. Given at our Court at Whitehall the 26 day of August 1693, in the fifth year of our reign.

By Her Majty's comand,
J. Trenchard.

In dorso.   26 August 1693.

         A copy of the Queen's warant for Mr. Rymer to serch Records and have copies, and in particular he began with the Leagues.

IX.

Received this 18th of September 1693 of the Honourable Sr Robert Howard, Kt., Auditor of the Court of the Receipt of Exchequer, John Lowe and Peter Le Neve, gentlemen, under chamberlains of the said Receipt, these severall instruments and leagues following, by virtue of an order directed to us.

* Imp̄s Relaxatio Regis Castiliæ with a golden seale.

* 2. Littera obligatoria petri Rg Castiliæ, 6 May 1367.   42 E. 3.

* 20 Nov. 1430.   9 H. 6.

* Al dat 6 Feb. 1411.

* Obligatio 6 May 1367.

* A deed very much worn of Peter King of Castile, several instruments tyed together with pack thread, some of them numbered 2*, 4*, 5*, 6*, 7*, 10*, 11*, 12*, 14*, and three others not marked, dated 1366*.

Another parcel tyed up together, numbered 7, of the dates of 1362–3*; of them, 1 dated 1363*, another 1364*, another 1369*, another 1399

16 delivered, wants 2. { A box written upon it Castillia Querimoniæ hominum de Bilboa de Piracys, markt with a castle, containing 13 instruments of Piracys and 5 others, tot 18.

Another box marked Castilia, with a fifth containing 5 instruments, with 2 or 3 leaden seals loose.

Also a book of abbreviations of leagues by Arthur Agard, and a book of Receipt of Leagues.

T. RYMER.

Witness, Fra. Shuter.

In dorso.   Sept. 18 1693.

Mr. Rymer's Receipt for Leagues.

X.

The following letter from the Bishop of Carlisle to the Rev. G. Ridley, dated March 14, 1756, bears upon this point. It is in the handwriting of Dr. Thomas Birch, and is in the British Museum (MSS. Birch 4297, f. 69):—

" Old Burlington Street,

"Rev^d. Sir,   March 14, 1756.

"A continual hurry of business & a good deal of illness, for these five weeks past, prevented my visiting the Chapter-house at Westminster till lately, agreeable to my promise, when I had the pleasure of seeing you in Burlington Street, else you had sooner heard from me. I got a sight of the Cromwell Collection of Letters, but found it impossible, without spending more time than I could afford, to make myself sufficiently acquainted with their contents so far to form a proper judgement how far they might be usefull to you or Dr Neve in your intended answer to Phillips. Mr. Farley, who is the chief clerk under Mr. Morley, Keeper of the Records here, told me he did not doubt of your having free access to these papers on a proper application to Mr. Morley, and you might transcribe whatever you chose out of them, as the office is open certain hours every day. I doubt indeed a daily attendance here would not well suit either with you or Dr. Neve's situation. I would, therefore, advise you to engage Dr. Birch, who grudges no trouble where he can serve the public in a literary way, to spend some mornings in looking over the collection, and if he finds much to your purpose, it may be worth while to apply to the Crown, or perhaps to Mr. Grenville only, for permission to borrow them out of the office, as

XIII.

Leibnitz to Rymer.

Thomæ Rymero viro insigni.

1695
14 July
Harl MS 4718 f 14
B M.

Godefridus Gulielmus Leibnitius, S.P.D.

Quanti muneia tua faciam jam tum multa gratiarum actione significare memini. Sunt in iis quæ aliquam mihi lucem accendunt, et
præsertim Ottonianum diploma placuit, Oleronis incolis datum, neque
enim Ottonem nostratem, Aquitaniæ ducis nomen gessisse sciebamus.
Si qua porro offerant sese, rogo ut nostri meminisse velis. Stepneius
vester, vir plane eximius, et de Republica omni non minus quam Rege
vestro præclare merens, misit ad me programma quoddam tuum, novellis
publicis Londinensibus insertum, quo invitantur qui habent quod
instituto tuo prodesse possit, colligendorum regni monumentorum. Ego
id perinde habeo ac si mihi nominatim scriptum esset. Nam aliqua
mihi fuisse in manibus, judicabis ex his quæ Codice meo Diplomatico
sunt inserta, neque omnia dedi quod tum selectioribus contentum me
futurum essem professus. Fateor non omnia nunc ad manus esse, quæ
tunc habebam. Speiem tamen recuperare aliquando ubi intellexero
posse me tibi vicem reddere, quamquam putem tibi regni Archiva in
potestate habenti, pauca deesse. Mitto tamen nunc specimen voluntatis
meæ. Reperi enim inter Schedas tractatum inter Philippum Regem
Galliæ et Eduardum Regem Angliæ, quo declarant ac prosequuntur quæ
inter genitores ipsorum, Ludovicum Sanctum et Henricum III. Reges
tractatu a me edito erant constituta. Quod superest fac quæso ut de
præclaris consiliis tuis edocear paulo uberius. Video Th. Gale, virum
clarissimum in præfatione editorum a se scriptoium vestratium voto
aliquem vestris rebus illustrandis ita designare ut tua animo præsagiisse
videatur. Vale. Dabam Hanoveiæ 14/24 Julii, 1695.

Hol.

XIV.

Leibnitz to Rymer.

V. Clmo.

1696
13 Jan
Harl MS 4713 f 12.
B.M.

Thomæ Rymero

Godefridus Gulielmus Leibnitius S.P.D.

Ineuntis anni solennia vota pro amicis nuncupans tibi quoque fausta
omnia et felicia apprecari volui ut præclare cœpta in usum reipublicæ
rite perficias. Uberrimum laboris in Codicem Diplomaticum a me
impensi fructum vel ex eo cepi, quod qualiacunque tentamenta nostra
tibi animos addidisse intelligo, ad utilissimam tabularum regni eruderationem. Gratissimus erit tractatus inter Henricum VIII. vestrum et
Franciscum I. Galliarum Regem, una cum appensæ bullæ aureæ
expressione.

Hujus Henrici VIII. testamentum nancisci optem nisi ex earum rerum
numero esse putas quæ non facile communicantui.

Cocus, ni fallor, in actione contra Garnetum asseveravit Romanum
pontificem Elisabetæ Reginæ pelliciendæ causa, Liturgiæ Anglicanæ
comprobationem aliaque id genus pollicitum fuisse. Literas pontificis
habere opeiæ pietium foret, quemadmodum et Cardinalis Poli autoritate
sub Maria confirmatam bonorum Ecclesiæ alienationem ne nobilitas in
suspicionem rerum novandarum adduceietui. Sed et suppiessio monasteriorum quam Romani Episcopi autoritate, Henrico adhuc partibus obnoxio

aggressus est Wolsæus Cardinalis, memoratu digna est et e re foret ipsam bullam Pontificis eam in rem haberi.

Non ausim hæc a te flagitare omnia ; si quid tamen commode indulgeri possit, tuis beneficiis addam.

Imprimis exhilarasti me, nuntiato consilio tuo de primitiarum magni operis tui editione maturanda, qua de ic plura quam primum discere spero.

Thomas Gale, vestras, vir doctissimus, præfatione in Scriptores Britannicos XV. negat legum vestrarum matrem Magnam Chartam apud vos hodie comparere genuinam, sed credo tunc nondum fuisse explorata, quæ tu interim videre potuisti.

Ajunt esse qui integrum Historiæ Vestræ corpus condere aggrediantur Hi tuis laboribus mirifice juvabuntur, quamquam non dubitem et reliquam Europam plurimum tibi ipsa rerum connexione debituram. Vale, Dabam Hanoveræ. ⅓⅓ Januar. 1696.

Hol.

The address separate at f. 11. A Monsieur Monsieur Rymer, Historiographe de la Reine de la Grande Bretagne. Londres.

XV.

In addition to the information afforded by Rymer's receipts for documents which passed through his hands at the Chapter House, and the knowledge we possess of his visits to the Tower of London, to search and copy the records there, there are extant several letters which prove that he diligently sought for information in the public libraries of our Universities. The following letters from the Tanner MSS., which have never been printed, will be interesting to the reader, as they show how diligent Rymer was in his researches —

Tanner MSS., vol. xxiv., 43.

"15 June 1695.

"In your letter some while ago to Mr Churchill, you were pleas'd to impart some notes, wᶜʰ did very much oblige me, And I shall not be unmindful of your kindness, the [1] I had formerly noted in your Catalogues, when I was once at Oxford, And had it copyed out the last sum'er, but the title (as they sent it) was.—*Pacta conventa inter* H. 1 *Angl regem et Ludovicum* le gross *Galliæ regem*. And upon reading it I saw amongst the *testes* Hen regis, Hen. filii, &c., wᶜʰ showd it to be of H 2 his reign, & I reckoned it for the counterpart to that in Hoveden, fol. 388 b. Lond. edit.

"The [2] is it not the same wᵗʰ that in Hoveden fol. 311.

"The [3] I suppose the same wᶜʰ in Hoveden fol. 419 b, dated at Northampton 12 Apl 1194, that wᵗʰ you is dated 7 Apl. the original wᵗʰ me is 17 Apilis wᵗʰ some other differences from Hoveden.

"The [4] is entered in a book wᵗʰ me from the Archives wᶜʰ is also printed Acherii Spicilegio tom. 12. p 58 b.

"The 5 & 6 I desire Mr. Churchill to get transcrib'd, but in the first place we are to be inform'd from what sort of Codex our copy is taken, what marcks of its antiquity or reputation. I have not yet searched for what is more modern but I keep your papers in view that I may profit thereby . . . . ion. That memorial concerning W. the Conqueror (in your second letter) pleased me extremely, but we want to know how

XIII.

Leibnitz to Rymer.

1695
½⁴ July
Harl MS 4713 f 14
B M

Thomæ Rymero viro insigni.

Godefridus Gulielmus Leibnitius, S.P D.

Quanti munera tua faciam jam tum multa gratiarum actione significare memini. Sunt in iis quæ aliquam mihi lucem accendunt, et præsertim Ottonianum diploma placuit, Oleronis incolis datum, neque enim Ottonem nostratem, Aquitaniæ ducis nomen gessisse sciebamus. Si qua porro offerant sese, rogo ut nostri meminisse velis. Stepneius vester, vir plane eximius, et de Republica omni non minus quam Rege vestro præclare merens, misit ad me programma quoddam tuum, novellis publicis Londinensibus insertum, quo invitantur qui habent quod instituto tuo prodesse possit, colligendorum regni monumentorum Ego id perinde habeo ac si mihi nominatim scriptum esset. Nam aliqua mihi fuisse in manibus, judicabis ex his quæ Codice meo Diplomatico sunt inserta, neque omnia dedi quod tum selectioribus contentum me futurum essem professus Fateor non omnia nunc ad manus esse, quæ tunc habebam. Sperem tamen recuperare aliquando ubi intellexero posse me tibi vicem reddere, quamquam putem tibi regni Archiva in potestate habenti, pauca deesse. Mitto tamen nunc specimen voluntatis meæ. Reperi enim inter Schedas tractatum inter Philippum Regem Galliæ et Eduardum Regem Angliæ, quo declarant ac prosequuntur quæ inter genitores ipsorum, Ludovicum Sanctum et Henricum III. Reges tractatu a me edito erant constituta Quod superest fac quæso ut de præclaris consiliis tuis edocear paulo uberius. Video Th Gale, virum clarissimum in præfatione editorum a se scriptorum vestratium voto aliquem vestris rebus illustrandis ita designare ut tua animo præsagiisse videatur. Vale. Dabam Hanoveræ ½⁸ Julii, 1695.

Hol.

XIV.

Leibnitz to Rymer.

V. Cℓmo.

1696
½² Jan
Harl MS 4713 f 12.
B M.

Thomæ Rymero.

Godefridus Gulielmus Leibnitius S.P.D.

Ineuntis anni solennia vota pro amicis nuncupans tibi quoque fausta omnia et felicia apprecari volui ut præclare cœpta in usum reipublicæ rite perficias. Uberrimum laboris in Codicem Diplomaticum a me impensi fructum vel ex eo cepi, quod qualiacunque tentamenta nostra tibi animos addidisse intelligo, ad utilissimam tabularum regni eruderationem. Gratissimus erit tractatus inter Henricum VIII. vestrum et Franciscum I. Galliarum Regem, una cum appensæ bullæ aureæ expressione

Hujus Henrici VIII. testamentum nancisci optem nisi ex earum rerum numero esse putas quæ non facile communicantur.

Cocus, ni fallor, in actione contra Garnetum asseveravit Romanum pontificem Elisabetæ Reginæ pelliciendæ causa, Liturgiæ Anglicanæ comprobationem aliaque id genus pollicitum fuisse. Literas pontificis habere operæ pretium foret, quemadmodum et Cardinalis Poli autoritate sub Maria confirmatam bonorum Ecclesiæ alienationem ne nobilitas in suspicionem rerum novandarum adduceretur Sed et suppressio monasteriorum quam Romani Episcopi autoritate, Henrico adhuc partibus obnoxio aggressus est Wolsæus Cardinalis, memoratu digna est et e re foret ipsam bullam Pontificis eam in rem haberi.

Non ausim hæc a te flagitare omnia , si quid tamen commode indulgeri possit, tuis beneficiis addam.

Imprimis exhilarasti me, nuntiato consilio tuo de primitiarum magni operis tui editione maturanda, qua de re plura quam primum discere spero.

Thomas Gale, vestras, vir doctissimus, prefatione in Scriptores Britannicos XV. negat legum vestrarum matrem Magnam Chartam apud vos hodie comparere genuinam, sed credo tunc nondum fuisse explorata, quæ tu interim videre potuisti.

Ajunt esse qui integrum Historiæ Vestræ corpus condere aggrediantur Hi tuis laboribus mirifice juvabuntur, quamquam non dubitem et reliquam Europam plurimum tibi ipsa rerum connexione debituram. Vale, Dabam Hanoveræ. $\frac{13}{23}$ Januar. 1696

Hol.

The address separate at f. 11. A Monsieur Monsieur Rymer, Historiographe de la Reine de la Grande Bretagne. Londres.

XV.

In addition to the information afforded by Rymer's receipts for documents which passed through his hands at the Chapter House, and the knowledge we possess of his visits to the Tower of London, to search and copy the records there, there are extant several letters which prove that he diligently sought for information in the public libraries of our Universities. The following letters from the Tanner MSS., which have never been printed, will be interesting to the reader, as they show how diligent Rymer was in his researches —

Tanner MSS., vol xxiv., 43.

"15 June 1695.

"In your letter some while ago to Mr Churchill, you were pleas'd to impart some notes, wch did very much oblige me, And I shall not be unmindful of your kindness, the [1] I had formerly noted in your Catalogues, when I was once at Oxford, And had it copyed out the last sum'er, but the title (as they sent it) was:—*Pacta conventa inter* H 1 *Angl regem et Ludovicum* le gross *Galliæ regem*. And upon reading it I saw amongst the *testes* Hen. regis, Hen. filii, &c., wch showd it to be of H. 2 his reign, & I reckoned it for the counterpart to that in Hoveden, fol. 388 b. Lond. edit.

"The [2] is it not the same wth that in Hoveden fol. 311.

"The [3] I suppose the same wch in Hoveden fol. 419 b, dated at Northampton 12 Apl. 1194, that wth you is dated 7 Apl. the original wth me is 17 Apilis wth some other differences from Hoveden.

"The [4] is entered in a book wth me from the Archives wch is also printed Acherii Spicilegio tom. 12. p 58 b.

"The 5 & 6 I desire Mr. Churchill to get transcrib'd, but in the first place we are to be inform'd from what sort of Codex our copy is taken, what marcks of its antiquity or reputation. I have not yet searched for what is more modern but I keep your papers in view that I may profit thereby . . . . ion. That memorial concerning W. the Conqueror (in your second letter) pleased me extremely, but we want to know how

authentick or of what credit the book may be whence it is taken, no doubt
but the Conqueror was principally assisted by his bro.-in-law, the Count of
Flanders, the Count of Britanæ and the other princes along the sea coasts.

"I could wish to be inform'd something concerning the books in
Ashmoles Library marckt H. K. M. 2 & Q. but you must not think I am
willing to lay so much farther trouble on you beeing already so much your
debtor and

"Y^r most humble
"servant,
"T. RYMER."

Tanner MSS., vol. xxii., fol. 129.

"S^r   Circa Nov. 1. 1698.

"That singular favour of yours in lending me your loose sheets of
the Catalogue must never be forgotten, but hitherto you have only thereby
put me in the way to run more immoderately in your debt. The ill
weather comes on so fast that I have dropt my hopes of seeing Oxford
this season, so that all my dependance must rest upon your kindness for
what I want.

Codex 954   Nota de H. 5. rege Angl. Laud E. 31.

NE B 11. 14 1979   Epistola ad Hen. Wint.

NE. D. II. 1. 2159.   Acta rs. H. 5.

NE. F. VII. 8. 2436.   l'ie inter PP. Martini' et Tho. Waldens.

D. 1. Art. 14 2653.   Judiciu' Nativitatis H. 5.

Arch. B. 44. 3033.   A brief account of Liber regalis.

James 34 3871   Legend and defence of St. Jo. Oldcastle (the same I
suppose with fol. 263 n. 34. is sayd to be written by R. James).

Hatton. 94 4119.   A ballad sent to H. 5.

Dodow. 28 4170.   Registru' Hen

New Coll fol. 34.

1125 Propositio Ambaxiatorum rs. Angl. contra Gallicum &c.

Corpus Xti Coll p. 53. 1650.

Lre' oxon ad H. 5.

"All the particulars aboue noted I desire to be written and charged
upon Mr. Churchill. And I beg of you especially to look with your own
eyes in Cod. 1797, Bodviff Cronicon R. 2. H 4. H 5. et H. 6. And let
me be inform'd if he does not say that H 5. was crowned ix° die mensis
Aprilis dominica in passione domini.

"I shall not be satisfyde that you will pardon me all this trouble till you
lay some commands on me   And make tryall of my readiness in beeing

"S^r
"Y^r most faithfull
"humble servant,
"T. RYMER."

Tanner MSS. vol. xxii. fol. 156.

"S^r   Jan. 10 [1698–9].

"I have looked upon all business as becalm'd these holidays, but
now take leave to put you in mind of those matters wch you were so kind

to promiss me that you would get transcribed for me, the Fortefour I sent you was in order to have it Collated and amended by your Oxford Copy, wch I reckon is more correct and perfect than this of Cotton's Library, I did think you might have remembered what we talked together at my Lodgings concerning the printing of it There is N. 7354 and (the same I suppose) 7984. *Serjeantyes of sundry kinds in Coronatione H. 5 Autog. Ashmole.* And N. 7440, *Nomina eorum qui in Azencourt.* These also I want to be transcribed. But S^r be pleased to understand that my request goes always with a Proviso that you can set somebody to work, and oblige me w^thout entrenching upon your time wch you know so well to employ another way.

"I am

"Sir

"Y^r most obliged serv^nt

"T. RYMER."

Tanner MSS., vol. xxi. fol. 150.
"S^r.   Sep. [16]99.

"A long time ago Mr. Churchill procur'd one to write out for me at the Mæu' Ashmol' a list of them that were at the battle of Azencourt wch I rec^d, and find it agrees with that, wch by your means I had from the Stillingfleet MSS but is in the original French, and free from the gross mistakes in the other. What I want is to know whence Ashmole took his copy, doubtless he had it from a Roll called Rot. Rob'ti. Babthorp but where that Roll is lodged I cannot learn The same hand should also write for me the clayms at the coronation of H. 5. he likes not, I believe, the writing of old French however I must have it. And the transcriber must not be discouraged. I want also to know whence Mr. Ashmole had these claims, pray be so kind to examine his book's title, preface, margent, & everywhere to satisfye me in that matter Because I would find the originals, And not rest on authority at second hand. Pray desire the same person to write out for me in New Colledge Cod 1125, Propositio Ambasciatoru' regis Angliæ contra Gallicum & *Libri Theolog.* 61.

"Thus you for what answer I make to your kindness, and letters of ceremony trouble is my element and that is what you may expect from y^r acquaintance

"w^th

"S^r

"Y^r most faithful & most humble servant,

"T. RYMER"

Ballard MSS. vol. vi. fol. 57 :

"Lambeth,
"Honor'd S^r,   March 24, 170$\frac{4}{5}$

"Mr. Rymer, who has already publisht two volumes of the English Leagues and now is drawing near the reign of Edward the third, has been inform'd that Dr. Hudson has a Manuscript in his hands containing many memorable Transactions of the reign. Some days since, he desir'd me to ask the favour of Dr. Hudson, to lend him the Manuscript to London, for the completing of his 3rd Volume, wch he is now upon ; imagining that I had more interest in the Doctor, than any man who belongs to Lambeth, is to reckon upon, after the War declar'd in his Preface to Dionysius. However being very desirous to serve Mr. Rymer, and to see his Collection as complete as it can be made; I would beg the favour of you, to ask Dr Hudson whether he have such a manuscript, and whether he will be pleas'd to favour the publick by communicating it to Mr. Rymer, for the Design I have mention'd. I doubt not Dr. Hudson's readiness to help forward soe good a work, but am afraid that he may have made it a part of the Bodleian Library, so far as to bring it under the Statute. If he have not, Mr Rymer will think it a great obligation to have the favour of perusing it in London, and having serv'd the design he has in hand, will faithfully return it

"We are told that Dr Hudson is upon a new Catalogue of the printed books in the publick Library. I was going to make references to the Libraries of Lambeth and St Martin in the Catalogue already publisht, but if we may expect Dr Hudson's in any reasonable time, I will hold my hand.

"Dr Wake is sure of the Bishoprick of Lincoln, but I believe it is still a moot point between Dr Atterbury and Dr Younger which shall succeed him at Exeter; the first making a powerful applic[a] by Mr. Harley (who, everybody says and believes, is to be Lord Keeper) and the second pleading the merit of above 20 years attendance, enforc'd by his disappointm[t] of the Deanery of Canterbury.

"I made my application formerly for my Lord Clarendons History in the Royal Paper; and now the work is finisht, should be extremely thankful, if by your interest I might be furnisht with it in the best paper; tho' it must be own'd, the common is very good. I believe it has been seldom known, that a whole Impression was printed in such a splended and honorable way, as that and Dr. Hickes's.

"It was a great pleasure to me, to receive from my kinsman of Queens College, the other day, an undeniable Evidence that Dr. Potter was not Actual Fellow when he was chosen Provost; because I wisht well to my Tutors titles and alway reckon'd the Statute upon w[ch] it has been controversed, extremely prejudicial to the College, in any other sense

"E. GIBSON.

"For
     "The Reverend Dr Charlett,
          "Master of University College in Oxford."

"Dr Gibson 170$\frac{4}{5}$ In a manuscript Dr Hudson has in his hands containing many memorable transactions of Edward 3rd's reign for Rymer's 3 vol. of English Leagues, about Lindgon declaring war ag[st] Gibson in his preface to Dionysius. Dr Hudson about a new Catalogue of the Bodleian Library. Dr. Wake Bp of Lincoln.

"Mr. Gibson March 25"

Ballard MSS. vol xii. fol. 123.

In a letter from Dr Geo. Hicks to Dr. Charlett. Nov. 10, 1711:—

"A friend of mine hath 22 vol of Mr. Rymer's Collections bound, w[ch] he will part wth for £33[libb]. If any Coll' have a mind to them they may have them at that price, and the rest of the volumes as they come out."

XVI.

William Bowyer maketh oath, That on or about May 1703 Mr. Awnsham Churchill agreed with him the said W. Bowyer for the printing of Two hundred and fifty and no more of a book to be set forth by Mr. Rymer which was entituled Conventiones Literæ et cujuscunque generis Acta Publica, inter Reges Angliæ, et alios quosvis Imperatores, Reges, Pontifices, Principes vel Communitates ab ineunte Sæculo duodecimo viz. Anno 1101 ad nostra usque tempora habita aut tractata, &c. Which book the said W. Bowyer did accordingly print and finish ready for delivery by the end of February following, that is to say, Two hundred and fifty copies of each sheet thereof, only allowing about a dozen sheets upon every sheet for casualties in the time of printing as is usual, it being impossible to print to a precise number, or without wasting and spoiling many sheets. But to prevent a greater number being clandestinely printed or fraudulently dispersed under pretence of copies which by custom the journeymen of the trade of printing claim a title to, he the said W. Bowyer did agree for and pay to every of his journeymen a weekly stipend in money in lieu of the said copies. And farther, that he the said W. Bowyer is now printing a second volume of the same work, of the same number, and in every respect under the same conditions as the former.

W. BOWYER.

Jurat. hoc. 1° die Novembr.
Anno Dñi 1704, Coram
Rⁱ. Levett.

These are to certifie That on this Twentyeth day of November 1704 was entred in the Register Booke of the Company of Stac'on^rs London and for Awnsham Churchill, Citizen and Stac'on^r of London, In trust for Her p'sent Maj^tie Queene Anne her heires and successors under the hand of Mr. Warden Hodgkin a Booke or Copy Entituled Fœdera Conventiones Literæ et cujuscunque generis acta publica, inter Reges Angliæ, et alios quosvis Imperatores, Reges, Pontifices, Principes, vel Communitates, ab ineuente sæculo Duodecimo, vizt. ab Anno 1101 ad nostra usque tempora habita aut tractata, ex autographis, infra Secretiores Archivorum Regiorum Thesaurariis per multa sæcula reconditis, fideliter ex scripta in Lucem missa de mandato Reginæ aucuranta Thoma Rymer Ejusdem Serenissimæ Reginæ Historographo, in severall volumes. As witness my hand the Twentieth Day of November Anno Dñi. 1704.

SIM. BECKLEY
Clerke to the said Comp^ie of Stac'oners.

XVII.

I venture to give here a document, the *earliest* I have found relative to the printing of the Fœdera, and Rymer's remuneration :—

" Articles of Agreement indented Tripartite, between Peter Hume on Behalf of Her Majesty of the first part, Thomas Rymer of the second part, and Awnsham Churchill of the third part

" Whereas Her Majesty has been graciously pleased to grant 500*l.* for printing a third volume of Leagues and Treaties, &c., extracted from ancient records by Tho. Rymer, Esq. Historiographer to Her Majesty

" Impiimis it is agreed between Peter Hume and Awnsham Churchill, bookseller of London, that he the said Awnsham Churchill shall and will undertake the printing of the third volume aforesaid.

" 2ndly It is agreed that the said Awnsham Churchill shall print or cause to be printed 250 volumes of the said third book only, each consisting of about 200 sheets more or less, and that the said Awnsham Churchill, nor any person employed by or under him, shall not presume to print any more than the said 250 volumes, for any person, or on any pretence whatsoever . But that the right of copy shall be reserved to Her Majesty, entry whereof shall be made in the Register of the Company of Booksellers London.

" 3rdly. It is agreed, that the said Awnsham Churchill shall print off the said 250 volumes, on good demy paper, and in such a fair and clear letter as shall be conformable to the specimen hereunto annexed.

" 4thly. It is agreed that for printing the said 250 volumes in manner aforesaid the said Peter Hume will pay or cause to be paid unto the said Awnsham Churchill the sum of three hundred pounds (usual fees deducted), that is to say 200l., part of the said sum, within one month after signing and sealing these articles (or sooner if it may be) and the remaining 100l. upon delivery of 200 of the said volumes in sheets, to the said Peter Hume, for the use of Her Majesty, and also on delivery of 25 of the said volumes in sheets to Tho Rymer, (the other 25 being to remain to himself the said Awnsham Churchill) fairly printed, without any other demand for paper, plates, printing, engraving, correcting, or any other charges whatsoever

" 5thly. It is agreed that the said Awnsham Churchill will print off the said 250 volumes within the space of 12 months next ensuing the date hereof, provided the said Tho Rymer do and shall from time to time deliver sufficient copy fairly written of the same, so that the press, for want thereof, may not be hindered or delayed.

" Lastly it is agreed between Peter Hume and Thomas Rymer aforesaid, that he the said Tho Rymer shall and will transcribe, or cause fairly to be transcribed, the said copy intended to be printed, with such constant care and in such due time that the press may not be delayed for want thereof, and the said Peter Hume doth promise to pay unto the said Tho Rymer one hundred pounds (usual fees deducted) within one month's time as aforesaid, as also the sum of one hundred pounds more, as soon as he the said Tho. Rymer shall have delivered to Awnsham Churchill aforesaid, well and fairly transcribed, which with 25 volumes fairly printed off, and delivered to him the said Thomas Rymer by the said Awnsham Churchill, shall and is to be in full recompense and satisfaction of all his charges, pains, and care in transcribing, examining, and correcting thereof.

" In witness whereof, the parties above-named to these present Articles have mutually set their hands and seals this 14th day of June in the fourth year of the reign of our Sovereign Lady Queen Anne, Anno Domini, 1705. [Peter Hume.]

" Signed and sealed in the presence of Fran. Aston. Jo. Hutton."

The printing of this volume cost only 500l. The following paper will be interesting to the reader :—

"To the Right Honourable the Lord High Treasurer of England. The humble memorial of Francis Aston and Peter Hume. May it please your Lordship, Mr. Rymer and Mr. Churchill complaining that they are hardly dealt with, in the allowances made them, for the surplusage of sheets, printed over and above their contract, in the preceding volumes, we crave leave to lay before your Lordship—

	£	s.	d.
"That there is due to Mr. Rymer for 53 sheets in former volumes (over and above what has been allowed him) and for 64 sheets in this now printed off, at the rate of his contract - - - - - -	117	0	0
"There is also due to Mr. Churchill for the same number of sheets at the rate of his contract - -	175	10	0
In all -	292	10	0
"We also beg leave to move your Lordship for 500*l.*, the contract for the next volume being ready to be sealed -	500	0	0
	792	10	0

"PETER HUME.   "FRAN. ASTON."

The indenture for printing the 10th volume is dated 1st September 1709.

XVIII.

"May it please your Lordship, the tenth volume of the Leagues and Treaties being finished; if it be your Lordship's pleasure that I shall enter into articles for printing another volume according to the method of the former agreements, I humbly desire money may be ordered to perform the contract.

"5th April 1710.   JOHN ANSTIS."

To the Right Honourable Sidney Earl of Godolphin, Lord High Treasurer of Great Britain. The memorial of Thomas Rymer and Awnsⁿ Churchill showeth—

		Sheets.
"That Mr. Rymer's 6th vol. of Fœdera was - - -		201
7 - - - - -		220
8 - - - - -		199
9 vol. 3 sheets being twice printed -		240
10 - - - - - - -		218
Sheets - -		1078

"For which seventy-eight sheets printed more than their contract, they humbly crave from your Lordship an allowance of one hundred ninety-five pounds; when you shall be pleased to give direction for contracting for the eleventh volume of the said *Fœdera*, which is now in the press.

"T. RYMER.

"April 4th, 1710.   A. J. CHURCHILL."

XIX.

The following letter from John Anstis, with an inclosure, is valuable as a connecting link in the history of the Fœdera :—

" My Lord.—The fourteenth volume of the Leagues being now finished, if it be your Lordships' pleasure that I shall enter into articles for printing another volume, I humbly desire that there may be an order for payment of the money for the same.

" By Mr Churchill's desire, I have hereunto annexed his demands for sheets printed beyond those contained in the contract, and the nine volumes according to the late Act of Parliament for the Universities and other Libraries, as also for two sets of these volumes in quires.

" Your Lordship's most obedient Servant,

" 6th August 1712.   JOHN ANSTIS.

			Sheets			
" For overplus sheets in Mr Rymer's 11th vol		-	19			
"	"	12th vol.	-	5		
"	"	13th vol.	-	6		
"	"	14th vol.	-	7		
			37	= £92	10	0
" For overplus books in 12th vol.	-	-	-	9		
"	" 13th vol.	-	-	-	9	
"	" 14th vol	-	-	-	9	
			27	= £67	10	0

		£	s.	d.
" March 1711.				
" 2 Mr Rymer settled in 13th vol. &c. - - - -		65	0	0
2. " 14th vol. in quires -		5	0	0
For binding 9 of the 14th volumes - - -		2	5	0
		£232	5	0

" The XIth Vol hath 52 pages beyond the Contract, besides three sheets and half for the Dedication and Index, and the Printer informs me that two sheets were twice printed.

" The XIIth Vol. hath four pages beyond the Contract, besides three sheets and half for the Dedication and Index, and the Printer informs me that one sheet was reprinted.

" The XIIIth Vol hath four pages beyond the contract, besides three sheets for the Dedication and Index, and the Printer informs me there were two sheets twice printed.

" The XIVth Vol. hath (as I am informed) 16 pages beyond the contract, including the Dedication and Index therein, and three copper cuts.

" JOHN ANSTIS.

" (Endorsed :)

" Memorial from Mr. Anstis about printing the XVth Vol. of Leagues.

		£	s.	d.
Warrant prepared for - - -		832	5	0 vizt.

£	s.	d.	
522	10	0	" For transcribing and printing 259 vol of the 15th Tom of Rymer's Fœdera
52	5	0	" For binding at 5s. each.
92	10	0	" For transcribing and printing 37 overplus sheets beyond the contracts in the 11th, 12th, 13th, and 14th volumes.
67	10	0	" For 27 overplus books above the 250, contracted for in the 12th, 13th, and 14th volumes being for the Universities and other libraries pursuant to Act of Parliament
70	0	0	" For two sets of the fourteen volumes in quires provided and deducted for our service.
27	10	0	" For the fees and charges."
835	5	0	

XX.

A long account of this fire will be found in Nichols's "Literary Anecdotes of the Eighteenth Century," i. pp. 50–68. The following documents add to the literary history of the Fœdera :—

" William Bowyer maketh oath that on the 30th of January last past, when a fire happened in his printing office in Whitefriars, he was then printing by Mr. Churchill's order the fifteenth volume or Tome of a book set forth by Mr. Rymer, entitled Conventiones Literæ, &c., and that he had then proceeded in the printing about one hundred and twenty sheets thereof as he verily believes, all which said sheets were burnt and destroyed by the said fire, together with all the copy he had received from Mr Rymer towards the finishing of the same, and also a great quantity of paper he received from Mr. Churchill for the printing the said work, and likewise all his goods and printing materials with his books of accounts and workmen's bills, &c , which is the reason he cannot be punctual as to the number of sheets printed, but is very certain he is herein within three or four sheets at most under or over of the sheets of Mr. Rymer's book so destroyed by the said fire.

                                                " William Bowyer.

" Jurat 4to die Aprilis
" Anno 1713, coram me,
" Richard Hoare, Mayor."

" To the most Honourable Robert Earl of Oxford, &c., Lord High Treasurer of Great Britain, the humble memorial of Tho. Rymer, Esq , and Awnsham and John Churchill, whereas there was 120 sheets of Mr. Rymer's 15th volume burnt in the house of Mr. Bowyer, the printer in Whitefriars, being six tenths of the impression, which amounts to 300l.

" Also the manuscript copy to finish the said volume and a great quantity of paper for carrying on the said work.

" Thomas Rymer, A. and John Churchill, humbly pray that the said 300l. may be allowed them : 100l. of which to be paid Mr Rymer toward making good the copy

" 100l. to A. and John Churchill toward their loss for the paper.

" 100l. to Wm. Bowyer, the printer, whose house was burnt."

ι

" To the most Honourable the Earl of Oxford and Mortimer, Lord High Treasurer of Great Britain.—In obedience to your Lordship's commands, I have considered the within petition, and for my better information as to the facts therein alleged, required that the same should be ascertained in the best manner that could be ; whereupon Mr. Churchill produced the annexed affidavit of Mr Bowyer, the printer, and I am humbly of opinion it may be reasonable (if her Majesty shall be so graciously pleased) to make to the Petitioners the allowance prayed by them for their respective losses, paper and expenses mentioned in their said petition, since the bare printing of 120 sheets is the six tenths of the impression, and amounts to 300*l.*

" All which is most humbly submitted to your Lordship's great wisdom.
" 12 May 1713   JOHN ANSTIS."

" To the most Noble the Earl of Oxford and Mortimer, Lord High Treasurer of Great Britain —The memorial of Mr. Anstis about printing the XVIth Vol. of Fœdera, &c. showeth that the XVth volume being printed and bound according to the articles, so if it be your Lordship's pleasure that another volume he printed, according to the former contracts, that your Lordship would please to give directions for an order and warrant for the money.

" *Nov.* 17, 1713	*John Anstis.*		
	£.	s.	d.
For the 16th vol. of Rymer - - -	500	0	0
—— 9 supernumerary books of that volume -	22	10	0
—— binding 259 of 16th vol. - - -	52	5	0
—— binding 9 of a former 15th vol. unpaid -	2	5	0
—— 8 odd vol d'd. bound - - -	22	0	0
—— 2 of the 15th vol. in quires - - -	5	0	0
—— fees of 300*l.* given for that volume which was burnt -	15	7	0
—— fees of the above - - - -	23	10	0
	£642	17	0

" JOHN CHURCHILL."

XXI.

The impropriety of inserting instruments only found in printed books in such a work as the Fœdera, professing to contain only original instruments preserved in the royal archives, cannot be wholly defended. Though Rymer has printed no less than 118 of such instruments, and very seldom mentions the source from which he had derived them, some plea may be advanced in his vindication, so far as monastic chronicles are concerned. It must be remembered that in ancient times, when the king travelled, he was always accompanyed by his chancellor, and generally held his court at those monasteries which were of royal foundation.   At these places public instruments of every description were executed with the same solemnity as in the royal palace, and the archives of such religious houses were used for the temporary repository of these royal evidences. This is evident from the fact that on the 23rd of March, in the 19th year of his reign, Edward I. issued his writs under the Privy Seal to various religious

houses, commanding them "to cause their chronicles and other secrets to
" be diligently searched under the direction of the king's messenger, and
" to transcribe and certify in open letters, sealed with their common seal,
" whatever they should find relating to the kingdom, kings or presidents of
" Scotland." Various certificates were consequently sent to the king, from
which an abstract was drawn up, and inserted in the public instrument
known as the Great Roll of Scotland, by John Erturi of Caen, and entitled,
" Hæc sunt quæ in antiquis cronicis, de quibus supra in principio fit mentio,
" in diversis Angliæ et Scotiæ monasteriis, inter alia fuerunt inventa ; per
" quæ evidenter apparet, quod Reges Angliæ, ab antiquo, habuerunt
" subjectionem, homagium, et fidelitatem, ac superius et directum dominium
" regni Scotiæ, sicut plenius infra patet." The historians named in this
instrument are Marianus Scotus (i.e. Florence of Worcester), Roger of
Hoveden, William of Malmesbury, Henry of Huntingdon, Ralph de Diceto,
the "Cronica Sancti Albani," and a book of the Life and Miracles of St.
John of Beverley. As bearing strongly on the question under consideration, it is necessary to cite a passage extracted from Hoveden's Annals,
under the year 1175, containing a complete copy of the convention
between William King of Scotland and Henry II , executed at St Peter's
Church at York, when the Scottish monarch and his subjects swore allegiance to the King of England. It is introduced thus : " Anno Domini
" millesimo centesimo septuagesimo quinto, decimo quinto Kal Martii,
" Willelmus Rex Scotorum liber abire permissus est. postea vero, apud
" Eboracum, eodem anno, tertiâ die post Assumptionem beatæ Mariæ,
" scilicet decimo septimo Kalendas Septembris, facta fuit conventio et finis
" inter prædictum Henricum Regem Angliæ, et præfatum Willelmum
" regem Scotiæ. Cujus tenor talis est."

    *   *   *   *   *

    "Huis itaque recitatis, in ecclesia Sancti Petri Eboracensis, coram præ-
" dictis regibus Angliæ et coram Rege Scotiæ et David fratre suo, et
" universo populo, episcopi, comites, barones, et milites de terrâ Regis
" Scotiæ, juraverunt domino regi Angliæ et Henrico filio suo, et hæredibus
" eorum, fidelitatem contra omnem hominem, sicut ligiis dominis suis."

    It is a curious fact that Hoveden's recital of this important public instru-
ment,—the proof of England's sovereignty in deciding the claims of the
competitors for the Scottish crown,—was used as evidence in a matter
of the most critical moment, in preference to the public record of the
homage recorded in the black book of the Exchequer, and which is fuller
and apparently more trustworthy than Hoveden's text.

    In addition to these facts, it may be mentioned that Edward I. issued
his writs, dated 26th September 1300, to forty-six abbeys, priories, and
cathedrals, requiring them diligently to search all the chronicles, archives,
and secrets of their houses, and to transmit whatsoever they could find
touching the right and dominion of the Kings of England (the sovereignty
of which had been claimed by the Pope) by the most trusty and skilful of
their societies respectively, to the King at his Parliament, appointed to
meet at Lincoln.

    The reader's attention must also be directed to the fact that in 1207 the
letters testimonial of Adelheid, Countess of Holland, certifying to the King
the marriage of her daughter with Louis Count of Los, and the letters of
Thomas Bishop of Utrecht, and Count Odo, were placed in the custody of

the Abbot of Reading, "Quæ omnes litteræ patentes missæ sunt abbati de "Rading ad custodiendum." There is further proof that instruments of great national importance, such as Magna Charta, the Charta de Forestis, &c , were sent to the principal monastic houses, to be recorded in their archives.

The foregoing instances are sufficient to exculpate Rymer from the charge which has been brought against him of printing instruments from monastic chronicles in preference to the originals in the public archives. In those cases where the instrument is clearly within the scope of the Fœdera, and about the authenticity of which there can be no doubt, and which cannot be found among the public muniments, it seems permissible to supply them from contemporary chronicles; but where there is any doubt of the verity of the documents, such, for instance, as the letter of the Old Man of the Mountain, this licence must be withheld. Great blame, however, rests upon Rymer for concealing the sources whence he obtained his documents. His omission naturally awakens doubts as to his candour, and has the appearance of a desire to conceal a proceeding which he could not justify.

XXII.

Jacob Tonson's proposals appeared on the 28th January 1728-9 , they were " for completing the subscription to a new edition of Rymer's Fœdera " in 17 volumes folio, of which 15 volumes are already printed, and the " remaining 2 volumes will be finished before the 25th day of March next : " I. The number printed are only 200 copies, of which 150 are already " subscribed for   II. This work is printed with the utmost care ; and to " make it as exact as the nature of it requires and the importance of it " deserves, it hath been collated anew with the records in the Tower by " Mr. Holmes ; by which means many paragraphs and lines omitted in the " former edition are with due care supplied and corrected in this, which is " printed page for page with the first   III. The price to the subscribers of " the remaining 50 sets is 50 guineas for each set in sheets, 10 guineas of " which is to be paid at the time of subscribing, and the remaining 40 " guineas upon delivery of the 17 volumes in sheets.   The subscrip- " tions are taken in by J Tonson in the Strand , and will be closed the " 10th day of March next at farthest, or sooner if completed before."

Tonson thus announced his new edition in the " Daily Post Boy," October 6, 1730 : "Now published, the new edition of seventeen volumes in " folio, of ' Fœdera,' Conventiones, Literæ, et cujuscunque generis Acta Pub- " lica, inter Reges Angliæ, et alios quosvis Imperatores, Reges, Pontifices, " Principes, vel Communitates, ab inuente Sæculo Duodecimo, viz. ab anno " 1101, ad nostra usque Tempora, habita aut tractata , ex Autographis " infra secretiores archivorum Regiorum Thesaurarais, per multa secula " reconditis, fideliter exscripta   In lucem missa de mandato nuperæ " Reginæ.   Accurante Thomâ Rymer, ejusdem serenissimæ Reginæ " Historiographo. Editio Secunda, ad originales chartas in Turri Londinensi " denus summâ fide collata et emendata, studio Georgii Holmes, Londini, " Impensis Jacob Tonson." The second, or Tonson's Edition, first appeared in 1725, and was finished in 1730. It also contains the three volumes which were added by Robert Sanderson, 1726-1735, bringing the collection down to the year 16   .

XXIII.

The undertaking was thus announced in the literary news of the day .
" De la Haye.—On voit ici un projet du souscription pour réimprimer
" seulement en dix volumes, les Acts Publics d'Angleterre, recueillis et
" publiés par Rymer. dont les deux Editions précedentes sont si rares et si
" cheres. It seroit inutile de faire ici l'eloge de cette utile et importante
" collection qui consiste à present en vingt volumes in folio. Voici les
" avantages que l'Edition qu'on annonce aura sur les deux autres. 1°. Il y
" aura une Table generale des Matiers pour tout le Recueil . au lieu que
" dans les autres il n'y en a qu'une particuliére pour chaque volume   2°
" Les Pieces qui sont en Anglois seront traduites en Francois . mais afin
" qu'on ne coupçonne cette Traduction d'infidelité, et pour mettre le Lecteur
" en etat de corriger les fautes s'il s'y en trouve, l'original et la traduction
" seront imprimés a côté l'un de l'autre sur deux colonnes. Les dix
" volumes in folio de cette nouvelle edition doivent faire environ 2,000
" feuilles et coûteront aux souscripteurs 112 florins 10 sols de Hollande ,
" dont en payera dix florins en souscrivant, dix florins à chaque volume
" que l'on retirera, jusqu'au neuvieme et 12 florins dix sols en retirant le
" dernier volume. Les exemplaires en grand papier coûteront comme a
" l'ordinaire un tiers de plus. S'il y a plus ou moins de 2,000 feuilles
" les Souscripteurs payeront à proportion et ou leur tiendra compte de
" cette différence sur le dernier payement   On promet de plus de ne tirer
" que 550 exemplaires à moins qu'il ne se trouve un plus grand nombre de
" Souscriptions.   On peut souscrire chez les principaux Libraires de
" l'Europe jusqu'au premier Juin de cette année 1737." (Journal des
," Savans pour l'an. 1737, p. 317.)

XXIV.

To the Reader

In this collection there is before you, and for the most part from
authentic sources, much information, which you would expect to learn, but
will search for in vain in the pages of our historians. You will here find
abundantly unfolded to your view those ancient memorials which were
concealed from the knowledge of the writers of contemporary history.

Eadmer, writing of the arrival of the Earl of Flanders at Dover, says
in express words, that as regards the negotiation of the matter of his visit,
it is known that nothing was done " nihil fuisse agnitum est" Here,
however, you will see the very conventions themselves, made and written
at Dover, transcribed from the autographs ; from them we learn, and
posterity will also know, what was the object of his coming over, p 6, 7

Now we ought not to be surprised at the ignorance of the monk Eadmer,
who cannot be supposed to have taken much interest in secular matters,
but what must we think of our own Matthew Paris, in whom you would not
expect such an imperfect knowledge of events , for he is regarded as a
man of most careful observation, and is believed to have known everything
that could be ascertained. Yet Matthew Paris himself frequently declares
that he knew nothing of the mission on which messengers (afterwards
called ambassadors) either came or were despatched.

Thus he writes under the year 1255 "The elect of Toledo came into
England, but for what cause it was not known." Now here we have

(pp. 325, 328, 331, 340) not only notices of his coming, but the cause of his coming.

Under the year 1256 he writes "The Lord Abbot of Westminster and "Master Rustan, and the elect of Sarum, at the desire of the King, went "abroad on the King's affairs, but nobody knows what was the secret "business they went on, and we must trust that it may be good!" Here (pp. 350, 351, 355) you may fully learn from autograph bulls, what was the King's business, and the secret causes which made our monk so anxious and doubtful. Thus the mystery will no longer be concealed from the eyes of the curious.

The Archbishop of Messina was sent from the Lord the Pope, but nobody knows why, says Matthew Paris, under the year 1257. Now the matters the Archbishop came to treat upon, and the letters of credence from Pope Alexander, together with the King's letter to Alexander, are fully set out at p. 350, 351, 355.

But let us return to our old friends and the Flemish conventions, and while we ourselves are in darkness, let us see whether the historians of that country possessed greater light.

A D 1066. It is certain that a sum of money for some ages was annually paid to the Counts of Flanders by the Kings of England. It is thus the historians of Flanders relate the matter. The Count of Flanders promised his co-operation and his aid to his son-in-law, William the First, on the condition that he and all the Kings of England after him should pay annually to the Counts of Flanders 300 marks of silver for ever.

A.D. 1098. Robert [Friso] died : he had resolved to wage war on England, to enforce the payment of 300 marks of silver, as we have mentioned above, but being prevented by death he was unable to accomplish this.

A.D. 1111. It is alleged by the Flemings) the annalist is speaking of Henry and Robert, between whom the present convention was made), that upon the tribute being demanded, Henry made answer, "It is not "consistent with the dignity of England that the realm should pay a subsidy "to Flanders" It happened not long afterwards, during a war with England, that Robert being in the retinue of the King of France, fell from his wounded horse, was crushed, and the third day afterwards died.

A.D. 1119 Baldwin, Count of Flanders, was incited against the English, by the memory of his father slain in the English war, and the denial to himself of the above-mentioned tribute.

The like statements Mezery, and I know not how many other minor historians, inculcate and repeat again and again. They were probably led into this error by our William of Malmesbury, who thus mentions the subject from the beginning :

Baldwin had powerfully assisted William when going to England, by the wisdom of his counsels and by a supply of soldiers. William had frequently made splendid returns for this, giving every year, as they report, three hundred marks of silver to his father-in-law on account of his fidelity and affinity. This munificence was not diminished towards his son Baldwin, but it was suspended in the case of Robert Friso. This Robert, the son of Friso, easily obtained the omitted largess from William the Second. But Henry, examining the business more deeply, as a man who nevei desired to obtain money improperly, nor ever wantonly exhausted it when acquired, gave the following reply to Robert on his return from Jerusalem, when imperiously making a demand, as it were, of three hundred marks of silver. He said that the Kings of England were not accustomed to pay tribute to the men of Flanders.

In this way little stories are made up from vulgar rumours and conjectures, which are supported by no authentic memorials But how different do the facts appear ! If any one will consult the chirographs of those acts he will find that no tribute or subsidy was ever paid to Flanders at all, but that an annual fee was granted to the Count of Flanders by his friend and superior lord the King of England, for homage done, fealty sworn, and service to be rendered These facts we learn from the first convention, and from those which follow for some ages afterwards :

(*Of the first chirograph.*) 1. We gather from the words, "salva fidelitate Lodovici regis Francorum," that the Counts of Flanders from ancient times were vassals and men of the Kings of France.

Pierre Dupuy, treating of this matter in his book, *Des Droits du Roy,* cites the first instance from Pierre d' Oudegreest under the year 1192, when Baldwin VII. did homage to Philip Augustus, but the authority given by us here is undoubtedly a noble and unimpeachable testimony almost a century earlier, and is derived from Robert of Jerusalem [1]

(2) Ecclesiastical writers may see what these five words, "salva fidelitate Lodovici regis Francorum," make for the authority of the church and the power of the Pope ; for it must be known that when these things were being done, Philip, the father of Louis, was still alive, but being excommunicated by the Papal authority, was put aside, and all fealty, with the title of King, was transferred to his son Louis.

David Blondel, in his large work, *De Formula, Regnante Christo,* denies that Philip was in reality injured by this anathema, or in any way affected by the Papal thunderbolt. He says : " The royal title was never conferred upon Louis, during the lifetime of his father Philip ;—in the charters, which conclude with these words, 'facta an. ab incarnatione Domini 1100, Lodovico rege Francorum regnante ;" and he asserts that the year 1100 is falsely written for 1108, and he wrongly condemns our Hoveden for writing that "Louis King of the French was present, in 1101, at the court of " King Henry, in London, on Christmas Day." But why more on the subject ? In our chirograph the name of *King Louis* occurs so often that it speaks volumes against the contrary hypothesis, and serves to show how vain is Blondel, and futile his labours.

The date of this convention I gather thus A D. 1099, July 14, Jerusalem is taken. A.D. 1100, Robert, the brother of the King of England, Robert count of Flanders, and Eustace Count of Boulogne, return home. On his way, Robert, the King's brother, stops at Apulia to celebrate his nuptials with Sibylla, daughter of the Count of Conversana. Aug. 2 (in the same year), William II , King of England, died. Aug 5, on Sunday, Henry I. was crowned. And in the year following (May 7, 1101), which was the first year of the reign of Henry I, this convention was made. In the

---

[1] He was called Robert of Jerusalem from his being present at the capture of   that city from the Saracens by Godfrey of Bouillon

month of August following, Robert, the King's brother, with Sibylla his wife, returned to Normandy, prepared arms, and having got together his forces invaded England, to vindicate his right to that kingdom as the eldest son of William I. Robert de Belesme deserted Henry and gave in his adhesion to Robert. This is the same Robert de Belesme who was at Dover in the month of May to execute, on the part of King Henry, the chirograph between the King and the Count of Flanders.

It appears, from the incision and a sort of label at the foot of the parchment, that the count's seal, which has been destroyed by age, was attached to it, in the Norman fashion, although that custom had not at the period obtained in Flanders

This first specimen shows the style of writing employed at the time, and also what was anciently understood by the term chirograph, and what by the expression " Charter divided after the manner of a chirograph "

Mabillon (lib v., *De Re Diplomatica*) gives the date 1167 to a chirograph of this sort engraven on copper from an autograph of Louis VII, King of the French, and could discover no earlier document of the kind amongst the royal muniments   But the chirograph given by us is more than half a century earlier, and may be seen also engraven on copper.

We have another chirograph of the same character in the reign of Henry II, A D 1163, and a chirograph indented under Richard I, A.D. 1197. From such instruments without the majuscule letters, simple and letterless indentures, similar to those now in use, took their origin.

The last-named specimen exhibits the very elegant and beautiful diploma of Alfonso, corroborated with a golden seal, to which Matthew Paris refers,[1] when he says : " The ambassadors aforesaid brought back " both favour and friendship, together with a certain noble charter, the " golden bull of which weighed one mark of silver." From which we infer that our Matthew Paris had both seen and handled it

This instrument is one of those called *Privilleios Radados*, from the " Rueda del Signo," the wheel or cipher of the royal signature, called by us the " sign manual" or " royal signature ; " the form of which is described in the laws of Alfonso, written in a wheel   In the centre are a cross and the royal arms ; in the next circle the name of the King from whom the privilege emanates , and in the larger circle the confirmation of the Alferiz and majordomo.   In this one of ours the " Alferizia " is not given

Many persons who happen to have seen only bullaria and short apographs have no means of knowing what is the signature of the Pope, and what is a monogram ; and some persons can scarcely distinguish between the Pope's monogram, his signature, and his seal. Papebroch is of opinion that the custom of dating bulls and pontifical rescripts from the incarnation of our Lord was introduced by Eugenius IV., and that the bulls anterior to that period bearing the year of the incarnation are either false or corrupt. This Mabillon fully refutes , that no one in our days may fall unawares into similar errors, we have given three specimens of the more remarkable of such Papal bulls

(*Of the second chirograph.*) The capital letters at the top of this parchment, cut in two, shew that this instrument of convention is also a

---

[1] Under the year 1253, p. 873

chirograph ; the lower part of the membrane has suffered from decay, so that no remains of the sealing are to be seen.

Eadmer seems to point out the date when this treaty was made in the following passage : [1] —." In the year of our Lord's incarnation, 1102, in the " fourth year of the Popedom of Paschal, the Supreme Pontiff, the third " of the reign of Henry, the glorious king of the English, he himself " consenting, a council is celebrated at the Church of St Peter, in the " west part, near London. . . . . . The king about Mid-lent went to " Canterbury to treat with the Count of Flanders, at Dover, on certain " matters (so people said) respecting the kingdom "

This same council (says Florence of Worcester) was celebrated on the Feast of St Michael, in the year 1102, Indiction x , & 3 of Pope Paschal.

Now Mid-lent in the year 1103 fell on the 8th of March, and this convention was made on the 10th of March, *i e.* on the second day after Mid-lent. And the William who, at the beginning of this diploma on the 10th of March, is called "William Giffard, the chancellor," went the very next month, that is, April 27, to Rome under the name of "William elect of Winchester" in the train of Abp Anselm, to oppose King Henry on the subject of investitures. This convention is nearly of the same tenour as the previous one, having been amended only in some few points

In the first we read " salva fidelitate Lodovici regis ," in the second "salva fidelitate Philippi regis." The fealties and the name of the King, which the Papal thunderbolt had shattered in the year 1100, were now in the year 1103 restored to Philip, peace having been made with the Pope.

Baronius and his epitomisers—Spondanus, Zovius, &c.—make out that Philip was liberated from the bonds of his anathema in the year 1104 ; but this charter of convention, more favourable to Philip King of the French, indicates that he was absolved at least a year sooner But it is not necessary to dwell any longer on these matters.

I had prepared many other prefatory remarks and some matters to be added in appendices (which, though not "public acts," yet conduce materially to our knowledge of the genius and customs of the times), which must be deferred to some other opportunity.

In the meantime you may compare the documents here with coeval historians, or (which comes to the same thing) you may examine Matthew Paris, and see what documents in this collection add to, illustrate, or correct that author

For example, you may see what writers upon Sicilian and Italian affairs, or, indeed, other historians, say concerning the transactions in Sicily between 1250 and 1265, and you will find what very little information you can gather from them which they have not borrowed from our Matthew Paris.

You may read here [a] about the grants made to Bertold Marquis of Hoemburg or Hohemburg, probably the same person who, in the bull of Alexander IV , recited by Matthew Paris, is called "Bertold Marchio de Cambrigia."

---

[1] Eadmer Hist. Nov , lib. iii p. 67-67. ed. 1623.

[a] Matt. Paris, under 1256, p. 933 or 628 Ed. Franf

Here, too, you may read of a Marquis of Herebrok (as the name is spelt in our instruments), of whom King Henry says to the cardinals :—
" A terrible rumour has spread abroad of the hurt and losses incurred by
" the Roman church from the treason of the Marquises of Herebrok, falsely
" calling themselves the faithful and devoted sons of the Church, in con-
" sequence of which the Sicilian business is damnably marred."

Would you know the nature of this treason ? Our Paris thus relates the affair :—

" About the same time Pope Alexander, by following the footsteps of
" Innocent, his predecessor, in the Sicilian and Apulian business, appointed
" Cardinal Octavian, with an army of 60,000 men, to destroy the city of
" Nocera, with all its inhabitants, and Manfred, who lay concealed there.

" The Emperor Frederick had mustered in the city more than 60,000
" Saracens, and to these infidels, exposed as they were to all the hazards of
" war, had given permission to take up their abode there, and the city then
" opened its bosom of refuge to Manfred and the other partisans of the
" emperor.

" When Octavian had arrayed his troops for battle, with the aid and
" counsel of Marchio, a skilful and puissant warrior (on whose advice and
" help the Papal army fully relied), he felt sure of success, and that the
" army of the Pope was invincible , but when he had advanced to within a
" few miles of the city a panic seized both the invaders and the invaded,
" insomuch that the former durst by no means advance further to attack the
" city, and the citizens were equally afraid to make a sortie against the
" army ; so both parties remained inactive for several days. and the time
" was lost in useless delay

" The Papal army was, however, very numerous and formidable, receiving
" large daily stipends from the coffers of the King of England, and being
" under expectation of more from the Papal promises ; for Pope Innocent,
" lately deceased, had promised them. It was with him that the present
" war originated, but the continuation thereof was by the cardinals.

' When both sides had continued in this inert state for some considerable
" time, Marchio, the traitor, who had in the army a large number of par-
" tisans, came to Octavian and said, 'My lord, why stand we here so long
" in idleness ? We are consuming large sums of money ; let a third of the
" army return home   As for Manfred and his men, they dare not issue
" from the town in which they are shut up and beleaguered ; a very small
" number of men will suffice to terrify and repress them.'

" The citizens, still declining to come forth, Marchio again reduced the
" Papal army, so that scarcely ten or twelve thousand remained with them

" Having accomplished this part of his project. the traitor, one night,
" rode post-haste on one of his swiftest horses to the city of Nocera, and
" said to Manfred, 'O ' my dearest friend, you have been induced to believe
" that I have injured you, and am prepared to do so again. I wonder that
" you listen to or put faith in such reports. You know how faithfully
" I served your father, the Emperor Frederick, in his wavering fortunes ;
" and how could I persecute the son of so beloved a lord and so revered a
" father ? Now may you make trial of my devotion and fidelity towards
" you. The Papal army has, by my advice, been so much reduced that
" scarcely 10,000 men, of whom the greater part are my partisans, remain
" with Octavian. Away, then, with delay ' Let all your vassals in the

" city arm and follow where I will lead, and you shall take Octavian and
" all his men captive.'   •

" So Manfred sallied forth, and all the citizens with him, and all his
" vassals and retainers, armed to the very teeth, and rushed like a whirl-
" wind upon the Papal army ; but when, as they thought, they had entrapped
" them all like birds in a net, Octavian, warned by some friend, made his
" escape. The rest, however, except indeed the retainers of Marchio, were
" either slain, routed, or made prisoners."[1]

Thus was the Italian cardinal circumvented, deceived, and cajoled by a
German.

A charter, granted by Frederick II to the Dukes of Styria, is cited by
Wolfgang Lazius (A.D. 1248), to which the witnesses are Henry King of
Sicily (that is, the son of Isabel of England), Manfred the marquis, and
Berthold, a count from Hohemberg, and many others of the family of
Hohemberg.

But in Sicilian or Italian authors I do not recollect to have found a
word about these marquises They say, indeed, that Octavian was recalled because he had mismanaged the expedition ; but they never even
touch upon the particulars of the failure. Even Sigonius, who occasionally is very glad to borrow from Matthew Paris, and who, on his authority,
has made famous a certain Duke Stollius,[2] has nevertheless chosen to
compress very briefly this very important narrative.

But what I think worse is that neither Sigonius, nor any of the host
of historians, mention one word about the nuptials of the emperor with
Isabel, or of Isabel's son, whom Matthew thus eulogises . "Henry the
" hope and glory of the English, the delight of men, a youth of marvellous
" beauty " (*Matt. Par.*, 1254). And that Matthew Paris may not stand
alone, I quote the words of three others who bear testimony to our
Henry :—

" He left the kingdom of Sicily to Henry, who was a child, but of
" supreme attraction and beauty " (*Tarchagnota*).

" He was a most excellent and prepossessing young man, and of greater
" promise than any other of the children of Frederick " (*Collenutio*).

" This was the handsomest and most talented of all the children of
" Frederick " (*Summonte*)

These testimonies, reader, I produce because you may feel surprised
that the kingdom of Sicily, the patrimony of this Henry, was in his life-
time offered by the Supreme Pontiff to Richard Earl of Cornwall, or Henry
King of England. Earl Richard refused it " because it would seem dis-
" honourable in him to supplant his own nephew." And King Henry
did not accept it because, in the words of Pope Innocent, " there was still
" surviving in the same kingdom your only nephew ; and lest you might
" seem to thirst for your own blood, and covet the spoils of your own
" nearest relatives, you have hitherto deferred to accept this great honour

---

[1] Matt. Paris under 1255, p 906.

[2] Matt Paris had read in one of Frederick's letters these words. *victoriosum Gale-
arum stollium*, and being unacquainted with
the Italian language, thought *stollium* was
the captain or leader of the galleys. His
words are, "In prima fronte, quibus pri-
" moerius praeerat stollius, pyratarum
" peritissimus." Whereas " Stollius " is
simply a Latin form of the Italian word
stuolo, meaning a *fleet* of ships

[3] Matt. Paris under 1252.

" and advantage." These were the words of Pope Innocent IV. to Henry III., King of England, in the bull notifying the death of this often-mentioned Henry, and continuing, and he being dead, the Pope goes on immediately to propose a successor for the kingdom of Sicily (p 302).

In the month of May (according to Matthew Paris) this Henry died; the bull is dated "The Ides of May," from which and numberless other documents the reader may see how just and strictly true is the judgment of Cardinal Baronius on the historical credit of our Matthew Paris . ' You " might term it a golden commentary, as whatever can be found in public " muniments is there admirably woven and joined together in just so " many words."[1]

But before we finally leave the kingdom of Sicily you must be reminded, reader, that this renunciation of the kingdom of Sicily is not to be ascribed to King Henry, nor yet to his son Edmund, but to Simon de Mont-fort, who had usurped the name and seal of the King, at that time his prisoner Simon de Montfort did it to gratify the Count of Anjou, and please the Pope; but we have been careful to distinguish, both in the text of the Fœdera and also in the chronological tables, all the acts of Simon, because by not observing this precaution the greatest confusion and disputes amongst scholars have arisen.

A D. 1265, 29 Hen III. In reference to what is called " The summons to parliament," what disputes have arisen, and even yet to this day continue among the most learned men, under a dreamy impression that some new sort of parliament was devised by King Henry to curb his turbulent barons, and suppress their daily increasing and encroaching power, whereas, you see only the abbots with certain accomplices and partisans who were con-voked by Simon de Montfort for his own aggrandisement and the deposi-tion of the king.

Through how many volumes is not this mooted by William Prynne, and is it not still a vexed question? But here I hope to have given sufficient to prevent the republic of letters from being hereafter torn to pieces on this subject.

If some matters are here inserted which appear of minor importance and unworthy of print, before you rashly reject them remember the cock of Esop Take, for example, the safeconduct of Henry Duke of Limburg I consider that worthy of mention, because he was the last of the Dukes of Limburg, and although Limburg at present be of no great moment, yet Pontus Heuter informs us that " before the names of Brabant, " Holland, Zeeland, Flanders, and Namur were known Limburg was " illustrious and noted " Elsewhere we read that Limburg was impreg-nable to Charlemagne

Perhaps, again, the oft-named Louis Count of Loss, liegeman of John King of England, may not impress you more, but stay awhile, reader; you must have heard, if you have heard of anything, of Holger the Dane, the paladin so famous in song, who they say was the first invested by Charlemagne with the county of Loss. Well, this Louis Count of Loss was his successor by hereditary right. This we learn from the testimony of Louis Guicciardini, Pontanus, Desselius, Bartholinus, Scriverius, and a host of other historians, topographers, and genealogists.

---

[1] Annal under 996

You may consider as trifles those documents which we have brought together respecting the marriage of Isabel and Margaret, sisters of Alexander King of the Scots (p. 178) ; but read what Buchanan says in his *Rerum Scoticarum, libro vii.* : " Before the same Pandulph, the King " [Henry III.] solemnly swore that he would provide for the two sisters " of Alexander in dignity according to their rank, as Henry's father had " previously promised. He purveyed only for one, and sent the other home " unmarried." Buchanan casts the stigma of perjury on two Kings of England, but here they are exonerated and cleared of every stain.

So again, by similar small documents, it is demonstrated that Robert III. King of Scotland was not the son of a concubine, but was born in lawful wedlock , but you must wait for this in our second volume

It is not my intention to point out what valuable information genealogists may gather from this book.

Albert Duke of Brunswick, who merited for his deeds the name of " Great," the great-grandson of Henry II. of England, married Alexia (some say Alexina), daughter of Aldrovandin Marquis d'Este So say Bertius, Ritterhusius, Reusner, Buzelinus, Baptista Pigna, Albizius, and Morerus ; but Meibomius and Winckelman (as I learn from Imhoff) assert that the wife of Albert the Great was Adelheid, daughter of Otho Marquis of Monferrat. You stand, reader, in this cross road, undetermined whether to take your direction from the more or fewer authorities. Our own monarch King Henry shall serve you for a Mercury, from whom you may, with the few, learn the real truth

The words of King Henry are " The illustrious man Albert Duke of " Brunswick, our beloved kinsman, married by our advice Alaisia de Mont- " ferrat, niece of our consort Queen Aleanor " (p. 470). From this alliance you see the most serene princes of Brunswick, Luneburg, and Hanover, who are now living, derive their origin.

Here, too, you have the great Italian names of Baglioni, Visconte, Ubaldino, Valori, Brancaleone, which the stemmatologists may see, and prepare to trace out

Here, too, may you see deacons who have become cardinals, and chaplains who have risen to the papacy, fulminating their decrees from the Pontifical pinnacle From what a little spark bursts forth suddenly a mighty blaze !

Here you may often note some Hercules mewling in his cradle ; some root or first germ of most important events.

How often in this work are repeated the names of Balliol, Bruce, Stuart and Tudor, destined to the sceptre, and to be immortalized in the Book of Kings ?

Nor can I be silent concerning the Lords of Lebreton, always the most faithful of the vassals of the Kings of England, from whose blood we have seen that the Kings of Navarre and subsequently of France were elevated

The observant reader may see, wherever he searches, many germs budding forth ; but very many more of the same sort, which ought to be brought under notice, we must defer to some other time

XXV.

The Disposičon of the Sets of Rymer's Fœdera wᶜʰ belonged
to her late Maᵗʸ.

A.	
Mʳ Addison - - - -	1
Mʳ Aislabie - - -	1
Admiralty Office - - -	1
Mʳ Anstis - - -	1
Mʳ Ashton - -	2

B	
Mʳ Bromley - - -	1
Lᵈ Bingley - -	1
Mˢ Battle -	1
Mʳ Baillie - - -	1
Mʳ Blathwaite - -	1
Mʳ Bowen - -	1
Mʳ Borret - -	1

C.	
Duke Chandois - - -	1
Mʳ Clayton - - -	1
Mʳ Conyors - - -	1
Lᵈ Conyngsby - - -	1
Lᵈ Cobham - - -	1
Lᵈ Cowper - - -	1
Arch Biᵖ of Canterbury	1
Chamberlains of the Excheqʳ -	1
House of Commons - -	2
Four Courts - - -	4
Mʳ Clark - -	1
Lᵈ Carleton - - -	6
Mʳ Compton - -	1
Lᵈ Cholmondly - - -	1
Mʳ Congreve - -	1
Mʳ Cooke - - -	1
Councill Office - - -	1
Lᵈ Clarendon - -	1

D.	
Mʳ Duncomb - -	1
Lᵈ Dartmouth - - -	1
Duke of Devonshire - -	2

E.	
Lᵈ Chief Baron Eyre - -	1
Lᵈ Essex - - - -	1
Mʳ Ellis - - -	1
Sʳ John Eden - - -	1

F.	
Mr. Farrer - - -	1
Lᵈ Findlater - - -	1
Sʳ Thoˢ Franklin - -	1
Sʳ Robᵗ Furneis - - -	1

G	
Lᵈ Godolphin - - -	8
Sʳ Samˡ Garth - - -	1
Mʳ Glanville - -	1
Mʳ Gwyn - -	1
Doʳ Godolphin - - -	1
Mʳ Graham - -	1
Mʳ Gale - -	1

H.	
Mʳ Hopkins - -	1
Lᵈ Halifax - - -	13
Mʳ Thoˢ Harley - -	1
Mʳ Andʳ Harley - - -	1
Sʳ John Holland - -	1
Lᵈ Hay - -	1
Sʳ Thoˢ Hanmere - -	1
Lᵈ Harcourt - -	1
Mʳ Hungerford - -	1
Mʳ Hill - -	1
Sʳ Chaˢ Hedger - -	1
Herald's Office - -	1
Dʳ Harnsnot - -	1

I.	
Mʳ Jett - - -	1
Sʳ Joseph Jekyll - -	1

K.	
Lᵈ Chief Justice King -	1
Duke of Kent -	1

L.	
Mʳ Lowndes - - -	7
Mʳ Lechmere - - -	1
King's Library - - -	1
House of Lords - -	1
Inner Temple Lib - -	1
Mʳ Le Neve - - -	1
Mʳ Lewis - - -	1
Mʳ Lowndes Jun. - -	1
Librarys in Scotland - -	4
Lᵈ Limington - - -	1
Lᵈ Loudoun - - -	1

M.	**S.**

L⁴ Mansell	1	Mʳ Smith	4
Sʳ Jamˢ Montague	1	L⁴ Sunderland	2
Duke of Montagu	1	Mʳ Stanyan	1
Dr. Moore late Bp, Ely	1	Mʳ Scrope	1
Mʳ Micklethwaite	1	L⁴ Stairs	1
Duke of Montross	1	L⁴ Somers	1
		Duke of Somerset	2
		Mʳ Southwell	1
		Dʳ Sharp late Archbp. York	1
N		Dʳ Sprat late Bp. Rochester	1
		Dʳ Swift	1
Sʳ Edwᵈ Northey	1	Dʳ Sloane	1
L⁴ Nottingham	1	3 Secrys of State	3
Mʳ Naylor	1	Mʳ Stanhope	1
Mʳ Nicholas	1	Sʳ Richᵈ Steel	1
Sʳ Davᵈ Nairne	4		
Duke Newcastle	1		

		T.	
O.		Mʳ Townshend	2
		Mʳ Tilson	1
L⁴ Oxford	2	Mʳ Taylour	1
L⁴ Onslow	1	L⁴ Townshend	1
		Mʳ Tucker	1
		Sʳ Chaˢ Turnei	1
		Tower Records	1
P.		Mʳ Topham	1
Mʳ Pulteney	1		
Mʳ John Pulteney	2		
Sʳ Thoˢ Powys	1	**V.**	
Mʳ Powys	1		
L⁴ Paulet	1	L⁴ Uxbridge	1
L⁴ Pembroke	1		
Paper Office	1		
Mʳ Pryor	1	**W.**	

		Mʳ Walpole	1
		Sʳ Marmaduke Wyvill	1
Q.		Mʳ Winnington	1
		L⁴ Weymouth	1
		Mʳ Warr	1
		Mʳ Wekett	1
R.		Sʳ Wm. Whitlock	5
		L⁴ Wharton	1
Dʳ Radcliff	1	Sʳ Xtopher Wren	1

PREFACE.

XXIII.

An Acco^r of Fees & Salarys Payable by His Late Majesty with the Sumes due thereupon at Xmas 1701, viz.

Salarys ℔ Ann			To whom Payable.	Sumes due at Xmas 1701		
£	s.	d.		£	s.	d.
8000	–	–	To Lords Comm^{rs}. Treáry. - -	–	–	–
1500	–	–	To Ea. Pembroke Lord President One year & half - - - -	2250	–	–
1460	–	–	To Lord Privy Seal now in Comission 181 days - - -	724	–	–
365	–	–	To Ditto more - -	181	–	–
1850	–	–	To Mr Secretary Vernon -	–	–	–
100	–	–	To Ditto more Three Quarters - -	75	–	–
1850	–	–	To the other Secretary - -	–	–	–
100	–	–	To Ditto more - -	–	–	–
600	–	–	To Mr Vice-Chamberlain One year & half - - - -	900	–	–
1825	–	–	To Mr Harley Speaker of the House of Commons - - -	–	–	–
12,000	–	–	To 12 Judges - - -	–	–	–
500	–	–	To Sr Joseph Jekyll Chief Justice of Chester	–	–	–
200	–	–	To Sr Salathiell Lovell Second Judge there - -	–	–	–
1100	–	–	To 11 Masters in Chancery -	–	–	–
81	6	8	To Mr Attorney Generall One Quarter -	20	6	8
70	–	–	To Mr Sollicitor Generall -	–	–	–
40	–	–	To Mr Conyers as King's Councill Two years - - -	80	–	–
40	–	–	To M^r. Cooper as Ditto One year -	40	–	–
2000	–	–	To Earl of Romney First Gent Bed-chamber One year & a Qua^r.	2500	–	–
1000	–	–	To Duke of Queensborough One year & half - - -	1500	–	–
1000	–	–	To Earl of Oxford Do. -	1500	–	–
1000	–	–	To Earl of Essex - Do. -	1500	–	–
1000	–	–	To Earl of Burlington Do. -	1500	–	–
1000	–	–	To Earl of Scharborough Do	1500	–	–
1000	–	–	To Earl of Selkirk - Do. -	1500	–	–
1000	–	–	To Lord Lexington - Do. -	1500	–	–
1000	–	–	To Earl of Arran - Do. -	1500	–	–
1000	–	–	To Earl of Carlisle One year	1000	–	–
500	–	–	To Hatton Compton Esq. One of the Grooms One year & half -	750	–	–
500	–	–	To Lord Windsor One year & half -	750	–	–
500	–	–	To Mr Cholmondeley Do. -	750	–	–
500	–	–	To Lord Raby - Do -	750	–	–
500	–	–	To Mr Borcelas Do. -	750	–	–
500	–	–	To Mr Sayers - Do. -	750	–	–
500	–	–	To Mr How - Do. -	750	–	–
500	–	–	To Mr Stanley - Do. -	750	–	–
8000	–	–	To 8 Comm^{rs}. for Trade One year & three quarters - - -	14,000	–	–

Salarys ℔ Ann.			To whom Payable.	Sumes due at Xmas 1701.		
£	s.	d.		£	s.	d.
1090	–	–	To the Secretary and Clerks One year & a Quarter - - -	1262	10	–
400	–	–	To 4 Clerks Councill for the business of Trade One year and a quarter - -	500	–	–
250	–	–	To Sr John Nicholas One Clerk Councill One year & ¼ - - -	437	10	–
250	–	–	To Mr. Blathwaite One year & three quarters - - -	437	10	–
250	–	–	To Mr Povey - Do. -	437	10	–
250	–	–	To Mr Southwell - Do. -	437	10	–
45	12	6	To Mr. Coling one of ye Keepers Councill Chamber Two years - -	91	5	–
45	12	6	To John Cox the other Keeper -	–	–	–
200	–	–	To Sr Charles Cotterell Mar Ceremonys One year & half - -	300	–	–
100	–	–	To Ditto more in lieu of Bills One year & half - -	150	–	–
121	13	4	To Charles Cotterell Esqr. his assistant Do.	182	10	0
100	–	–	To Mr Le Bass Marshall - Do.	150	–	–
175	18	4	To Earl of Romney Mar Ordnance One year	175	18	4
66	13	4	To Sr Henry Goodrick, Leivt. - Do. -	66	13	4
36	10	–	To Mr Charlton Surveyor - Do. -	36	10	–
54	15	–	To the Storekeeper - Do. -	54	15	–
36	10	–	To Mr Musgrave Clerk of the Ordnance - - Do.	36	10	–
18	5	–	To Mr Lowther Clerk of the Deliveries - - Do.	18	5	–
40	–	–	To Mr Mordaunt Trea'rer - Do	40	–	–
120	–	–	To Mr Fitch Workmar - Do.	120	–	–
36	10	–	To Mr Brown Mar Gunner - Do.	36	10	–
15	4	2	To Mr Gardner Keeper of Small Arms - - Do.	15	4	2
100	–	–	To Sr Thomas St George Garter Principall Two years & half -	250	0	0
40	–	–	To Sr Henry St George Clarencieux Do.	100	–	–
40	–	–	To Sr John Dugdale Norroy Do.	100	–	–
26	13	4	To Mr Devenish York Herald Do. -	72	13	4
26	13	4	To Mr Dethick Richmond Herald Do. -	72	13	4
26	13	4	To Mr Burghill Somerset Herald Do. -	72	13	4
26	13	4	To Mr King Lancaster Herald Do	72	13	4
26	13	4	To Mr Mawson Chester Herald Do. -	72	13	4
26	13	4	To Mr Mawditt Windsor Herald Do. -	72	13	4
20	–	–	To Mr Gibbons Blewmantle Pursuivant Do.	50	–	–
20	–	–	To Mr Cromp Portcullis Do. -	50	–	–
20	–	–	To Mr Le Neve Rouge Croix Do.	50	–	–
20	–	–	To Mr Clopton Ronge Dragon Do. -	50	–	–
100	7	6	To Mr Serjt Temple Two years -	200	15	–
100	7	6	To Mr Serjt Lawson Do. -	200	15	–
100	7	6	To Mr Serjt Gregg Do. -	200	15	–
100	7	6	To Mr Serjt Turst Do. -	200	15	–
100	7	6	To Mr Serjt Williamson Do. -	200	15	–
100	7	6	To Mr Serjt Powell Do. -	200	15	–
100	7	6	To Mr Serjt Charnock One year & ½	150	11	3
100	7	6	To Mr Serjt Ryley Do. -	150	11	3

k

Salarys ⅌ Ann.			To whom Payable.	Sumes due at Xmas 1701.		
£	s.	d.		£	s.	d.
100	7	6	To Mr Serjt Gardner Do. -	150	11	3
100	7	6	To Mr Serjt Hutton Half a year -	50	3	9
45	12	6	To Sr Xpher Wrenn Survr Genl Maty Works Two years & half -	114	1	3
27	7	6	To Mr Talman Comptroller Two years & ½	68	8	9
36	10	-	To Mr Lloyd Paymar Do. -	91	5	0
18	5	-	To the Mar Mason Do. -	45	12	6
66	13	4	To Mr Dickenson Clerk Engrosser Do. -	166	13	4
19	9	-	To Mr Ireland Mar Glasier Do.	48	12	6
18	5	-	To Mr Stacey Mar Bricklayer Do. -	45	12	6
18	5	-	To Mr Atherton Serjt Plumber Do. -	45	12	6
52	12	6	To Mr Fort Mar Joyner Do. -	131	11	3
18	5	-	To Mr Grove Mar Plasterer Do.	45	12	6
27	7	6	To Mr Gibbons Mar Carver Do. -	68	8	9
18	5	-	To Mr Roberts Plumber at Windsor Do. -	45	12	6
19	11	8	To Mr Norris Joyner Privy Chamber Do.	48	19	2
18	5	-	To Mr Banks Master Carpenter Do. -	45	12	6
12	3	4	To Mr Hobson Purveyr Do. -	30	8	4
80	-	-	To the Housekeeper at St. James's Three years - - -	240	-	-
200	-	-	To Mr Walker Housekeeper at New Market Two years - -	400	-	-
36	10	-	To Mr Ford Keeper of the Gardens there Two years & ½ - -	91	5	-
9	2	6	To Mr Whynyard Housekeeper at Westmr Two years - -	18	5	-
300	-	-	To the Housekeeper at Kensington One year - - -	300	-	-
160	-	-	To the Keeper of the Paper Office	-	-	-
200	-	-	To Dor Bentley Library Keeper St. James Two years - -	400	-	-
132	3	4	To Mr Moor Keeper of the Tennis Court Two years & ½ -	330	8	4
200	-	-	To Mr Kien Closset Keeper at Kensington	-	-	-
100	-	-	To Lord Fitzharding Keeper of the Mall One year & a quarter -	125	-	-
380	-	-	To Mr Beaubuisson Keeper of the Setting Dogs One year -	380	-	-
97	6	8	To Capt Studholme Keeper and Guide of the Roads Two years -	194	13	4
60	-	-	To the Keeper of St. James's Park, Two years & half - - -	150	-	-
200	-	-	To the Earl of Jersey Keeper of Hyde Park Two years & ½ - -	500	-	-
109	10	-	To the Earl of Rochester Keeper of New Park Do. - -	237	15	-
50	-	-	To Mr. Branch Bailiff Battles Walk Two years - - -	100	-	-
210	-	-	To the Conservator & Keepers of Dean Forrest Do. - - -	420	-	-
233	10	-	To the Keepers of Waltham Forrest Six years & a quarter -	1459	7	6
25	-	-	To the Woodward of Windsor Forrest Half a year - - -	12	10	-

Salarys ⅌ Ann.	To whom Payable.	Sumes due at Xmas 1701
£ s. d.		£ s. d.
30 – –	For Hay for the Deer Do. - -	15 – –
60 – –	To Underkeepers Sandhurst Walks Do. -	30 – –
20 – –	To the Constable of Windsor Do.	10 – –
10 – –	To the Lieut of the Forrest Do. -	5 – –
9 2 6	To the Vermin Killer Do. -	4 11 3
6 1 8	To Housekeeper New Lodge Do. -	3 – 10
20 – –	To the Underkeeper of the Forrest Do. -	10 – –
5 6 5½	To the Riding Forrester Do. -	2 13 2
40 – –	To the Keeper of the Water Engine Two years - - -	80 – –
– – –	To Underkeepers of Windsor Little Park -	– – –
182 10 –	To the Constable of Windsor at 10s. per Diem 87 days - - -	43 10 –
150 – –	To the Keeper Alice Holt Forrest One year & a quarter - -	187 10 –
344 13 –	To Officers of Hampton Court Two years & ¼ - -	772 9 3
100 – –	To the Duke of Devon Justice in Eyre Trent South Two years & ½ -	250 – –
166 13 4	To Lord Wharton ditto Trent North Two years & ¾ - -	458 6 8
200 – –	To Earl of Portland Superintendant Gardens Two years & half -	500 – –
80 – –	To Mr Hill Latine Secretary Two years -	160 – –
66 13 4	To Mar of the Horse Two years & ½ -	169 13 4
1372 10 0	To Mar of the Hawkes One year -	1372 10 –
200 – –	To Mr Pullein Mar of the Studd Two years & ½ - -	500 – –
30 – –	To Mr Warner the Mar of the Barges Do.	75 – –
10 – –	To Charles Killigrew Mar of the Revells Two years & half - -	25 – –
12 3 4	To Mr Simes Comptroller of the Revells Do.	30 8 4
9 2 6	To Mr Harris Yeoman of the Revells Do. - -	22 16 3
53 6 8	To Mr Jones Apothecary to the House-hold Do.	133 6 8
115 – –	To Mr Chase Apothecary to the King's Pson. Do.	287 10 –
195 16 8	To Sr Lambert Blackwell Knt Harbinger Two years - -	391 13 4
200 – –	To Sr David Mitchell Black-Rod One year & a quarter -	250 – –
100 – –	To Dor Oxenden Judge of the Admiralty a year & quarter - -	125 – –
200 – –	To Mr Walton for Repairing Pictures Two years & ½ - -	500 – –
18 5 –	To Mr Lawrence Surveyor of the Ways Do. - -	45 12 6
100 – –	To Mr Tate Poet Laureat - -	– – –
200 – –	To Mr Rimer Historiographer - -	– – –
50 – –	To Mr Wintour Clerk of the Crown Office 2 years & ½ - -	125 – –

Salarys ⅌ Ann			To whom Payable.	Sumes due at Xmas 1701.		
£	s.	d.		£	s.	d.
60	–	–	To Mr Stephens, Messenger of the Press Do.	150	–	–
50	–	–	To Mr Harris Chief Graver of Seals Do	125	–	–
200	–	–	To Mr Baker Sollicitor at the Trea'ry One quarter	50	–	–
400	–	–	To Mr Borret the other Sollicitor there Do.	100	–	–
240	–	–	To Capt Bennet Governor Bermudas Do.	60	–	–
69	–	–	To the Keepers of Richmond Park 3 years	207	–	–
20	–	–	To Mr Dolben & Cann Clerks Fines at Ludlow 7 years	140	–	–
50	–	–	To Mr Ryley Surveyr Woods Trent South 2 years & ½	125	–	–
300	–	–	To Mr Atwood Chief Justice New York One quarter	75	–	–
150	–	–	To Mr Broughton Attorney Generall there Do.	37	10	–
20	–	–	To Mr East Clerk of the Estreats 2 years & ¾	55	–	–
260	3	4	To Lord Halifax Audr of the Receipt One quarter	65	10	–
200	–	–	To Ditto for Extra Service	–	–	–
90	13	4	To Mr Pelham Clerk of the Pells One quarter	42	13	4
20	–	–	To Ditto for a Clerk Do.	5	–	–
61	13	4	To Ditto more Do.	15	8	4
100	–	–	Ditto more for his attendance in Vacacõns a year	100	–	–
45	8	4	Ditto more formerly paid ⅌ assignmt on Customs a year	45	8	4
50	–	–	Ditto more for Locking up Treasure	50	–	–
33	6	8	To Lord Fitzharding 1st Teller One quarter	8	6	8
31	13	4	To Guy Palmes a 2d Teller Do	7	18	4
31	13	4	To Mr Godolphin a 3d Teller Do.	7	18	4
31	13	4	To Sr John Stanley a 4th Teller Do.	7	18	4
52	3	4	To Sr Nicholas Steward One of the Chamberlains Do.	13	–	10
52	3	4	To Charles Cole Esqr the other Do.	13	–	10
10	–	–	To Mr Low Senr Deputy Chamberlain for Striking Tallys Do.	2	10	–
40	–	–	To Ditto for Sorting Records Do.	10	–	–
40	–	–	To Ditto for Locking up the Treasure	–	–	–
10	–	–	To Mr Le Neve the other Deputy-Chamberlain Do.	2	10	–
40	–	–	To Ditto for Sorting Records Do.	10	–	–
5	–	–	To Mr Smith one of the Deputy Chamberlains for Joyning Tallys Do.	1	5	–
5	–	–	To Mr Ballow the other Do	1	5	–
36	10	–	To Mr Clayton the Auditors Clerk in the Tally-Court Do.	9	2	6
20	–	–	To Mr Fox another Clerk there Do.	5	–	–
5	–	–	To Clerk Pells Clerk there Do.	1	5	–

Salarys ℔ Ann.			To whom Payable.	Sumes due at Xmas 1701.		
£	s.	d.		£	s.	d.
35	–	–	Clicis & Ministris 3 quarters - -	26	5	–
27	7	4	To 4 Messengers of the Rec^t 4d$\frac{1}{2}$ ℔ Diem One quarter - - -	6	16	10
208	–	–	Ditto for their Extra Attendance Do. -	52	–	–
2	–	–	To Garčonibus Recepte Do. - -	0	10	–
20	–	–	To Exchequer Porter - - -	–	–	–
400	–	–	To Mr Crompton Payma^r Malt Ticq^{ts} Half a year - - -	200	–	–
200	–	–	To Mr Wiseman Comptroller Do. Do. - - -	100	–	–
20	–	–	To Mr Farra a Messenger for Extra Service - - -	–	–	–
60	16	8	To Mr Thorowkettle a Messenger -	–	–	–
200	–	–	To Mr Boyle Chancellour of the Exchequer One Qua^r - -	50	–	–
163	6	8	To Sr William Simpson Cursitor Baron Do - - - -	40	16	8
55	17	4	To the King's Remembrancer 11 years -	613	10	8
8	–	–	To 2 Secondarys there 3 years & $\frac{1}{2}$ -	28	–	–
7	13	4	To y^e Clerks on a Fee of 15l 6s 8d. payable every 2^d year 4 years -	30	13	4
64	2	1	To the Trea'rers Remembrancer -	–	–	–
5	–	–	To the 1st Secondary in that Office One quarter - - -	1	5	–
26	13	4	To the 2^d Secondary - - Do.	6	13	4
11	5	–	To Clerks in y^t Office on a Fee of 22. 10. 0. every 2^d year - -	22	10	–
107	4	2	To Clerk of the Pipe One quarter -	26	16	–$\frac{1}{2}$
40	–	–	To Mr Pottinger Comp^r of the Pipe 2 years & $\frac{1}{4}$ - - -	90	–	–
20	–	–	To Mr Wallinger & Mr Cole Secondarys there 2 years & $\frac{1}{2}$ - -	50	–	–
4	11	8	To Clerks in that Office upon a Fee of 9l 3s 4d. in every 2^d year -	–	–	–
96	13	4	To Mr Hastings Clerk of Foreign Estreats One year & $\frac{3}{4}$ - -	169	3	4
40	–	–	To Mr Whitaker Foreign Apposer -	–	–	–
20	–	–	To Mr Squibb Clerk of the Nitchells Half a year - - -	10	–	–
66	13	4	To Mr Bridges one of the Aud^{rs} of Imprests 3 quarters - -	50	–	–
66	13	4	To Mr Done the other Aud^r Do. -	50	–	–
250	–	–	To Mr Booth Survey^r of the Greenwax 2 years & $\frac{3}{4}$ - -	687	10	–
73	–	–	To 2 Messengers attending Chancell^r Exchequer - - -	–	–	–

Salarys ⅌ Ann			To whom Payable	Sumes due at Xmas 1701.		
£	s.	d.		£	s.	d.
900	–	–	To the Agents for Taxes - - -	–	–	–
60	–	–	To Mʳ Millart their Clerk - - -	–	–	–
20	–	–	To Mʳ Brudenall their Messenger -	–	–	–
5	–	–	To Clerk Pleas in the Excheqʳ 2 years -	10	–	
20	–	–	To the Judge Advocate Sʳ John Cook Half a year - - - -	10	–	–
10	–	–	To Clerk of the House of Commons 2 years & ½ - - - -	25	–	–
249	3	4	To Mʳ Wm. Young in lieu of Offices & other Profits One quarter - -	62	5	10
73,760	**12**	**8½**		**64,504**	**18**	**6¼**
			By Tallys of Assignmᵗ			
500	–	–	To Keeper Records in the Tower - -	–	–	–
27	4	7	To Maʳ of Rolls for keeping yᵉ Hᵒ of converted Jews a year - - -	27	4	7
10	–	–	To Ditto for Examining Estreats Do. -	10	–	–
74,297	**17**	**3½**		**64,542**	**3**	**1¼**
			Others in Arrear whose Salarys by Death or Removall determined before Xmas 1701.			
			To Sʳ Joseph Williamson late Keeper of the Paper Office at 160l. ⅌ ann 2 years & ¾ to Michas 1701 - -	440	–	–
			To Mʳ Tancred late Maʳ Harriers on 500l. ⅌ ann. 2 years to Midsʳ 1701 -	1000	–	–
			To Do. E. Pinfold deceᵈ late his Maᵗˢ Advocate 20l. ⅌ ann. Nine years to Lady Day 1701 - - -	180	–	–
				66,162	3	1¼
			Undercast page 2ᵈ -	–	12	6
				66,162	**15**	**7¼**

•

CHRONOLOGICAL TABLE

REGNAL YEARS of the KINGS of ENGLAND from the NORMAN CONQUEST to the END of the REIGN of EDWARD THE THIRD, corresponding with the Dominical Years, both Historical and Legal.

THE written acts of the Sovereigns of Europe generally bear the date of the Regnal year of the potentate to which they severally belong; but as such dates would have been very inconvenient for reference, and no useful purpose would have been effected by retaining them in the Syllabus, they have all been reduced to the Dominical Era, as being the more useful and common computation. To assist the Historical student, for whose especial benefit the Syllabus has been compiled, the following table is offered to show at once the correspondence between the Regnal year of each King of England and the Dominical year, whether it be historical or legal, civil or ecclesiastical. It has not been deemed necessary to construct tables of the Regnal years of Foreign Sovereigns, as not more than one-sixth of the documents in the Foedera originated out of this country, and such tables would have required five times the space now filled. A Table of Contemporary Sovereigns will, however, be useful, and is given immediately after the Regnal years of the Kings of England. Each date has been reckoned according to the historical or common era commencing on the 1st of January, and not according to the Civil, Ecclesiastical, and Legal Era commencing on the 25th of March. By this latter computation all dates between the 1st of January and 25th of March are one year earlier than the historical or common year; for instance, the period between the 1st of January and the 24th of March 1371 in the Legal year is in the year 1372 of the historical era. Again, King Edward the Third came to the throne on the 25th of January 1326 of the Legal, Civil, and Ecclesiastical Era, while according to the historical or common era it was the 25th of January 1327. Queen Elizabeth died on the 24th of March 1602 of the Legal, Civil, and Ecclesiastical year, but according to the historical or common era on the 24th of March 1603.

WILLIAM I.

His reign is reckoned from his Coronation.

Historical	Day of Month	Legal, Civil, and Ecclesiastical	Regnal	Historical	Day of Month	Legal, Civil, and Ecclesiastical	Regnal
1066	25 Dec	1066		1077	25 Dec.	1077	
1067	1 Jan	,,	1.	1078	1 Jan.	,,	12.
,,	25 Mar	1067		,,	25 Mar.	1078	
,,	24 Dec.	,,		,,	24 Dec	,,	
1067	25 Dec.	1067		1078	25 Dec	1078	
1068	1 Jan	,,	2	1079	1 Jan	,,	13.
,,	25 Mar	1068		,,	25 Mar.	1079	
,,	24 Dec	,,		,,	24 Dec.	,,	
1068	25 Dec	1068		1079	25 Dec	1079	
1069	1 Jan	,,	3.	1080	1 Jan	,,	14.
,,	25 Mar.	1069		,,	25 Mar	1080	
,,	24 Dec.	,,		,,	24 Dec	,,	
1069	25 Dec.	1069		1080	25 Dec	1080	
1070	1 Jan	,,	4	1081	1 Jan.	,,	15.
,,	25 Mar.	1070		,,	25 Mar.	1081	
,,	24 Dec	,,		,,	24 Dec.	,,	
1070	25 Dec.	1070		1081	25 Dec.	1081	
1071	1 Jan	,,	5.	1082	1 Jan	,,	16.
,,	25 Mar	1071		,,	25 Mar.	1082	
,,	24 Dec.	,,		,,	24 Dec.	,,	
1071	25 Dec.	1071		1082	25 Dec.	1082	
1072	1 Jan	,,	6.	1083	1 Jan	,,	17.
,,	25 Mar	1072		,,	25 Mar.	1083	
,,	24 Dec	,,		,,	24 Dec.	,,	
1072	25 Dec	1072		1083	25 Dec.	1083	
1073	1 Jan	,,	7.	1084	1 Jan	,,	18.
,,	25 Mar.	1073		,,	25 Mar.	1084	
,,	24 Dec.	,,		,,	24 Dec.	,,	
1073	25 Dec.	1073		1084	25 Dec.	1084	
1074	1 Jan	,,	8.	1085	1 Jan.	,,	19.
,,	25 Mar	1074		,,	25 Mar.	1085	
,,	24 Dec	,,		,,	24 Dec	,,	
1074	25 Dec.	1074		1085	25 Dec.	1085	
1075	1 Jan.	,,	9.	1086	1 Jan	,,	20.
,,	25 Mar.	1075		,,	25 Mar	1086	
,,	24 Dec.	,,		,,	24 Dec.	,,	
1075	25 Dec	1075		1086	25 Dec.	1086	
1076	1 Jan	,,	10.	1087	1 Jan.	,,	21.
,,	25 Mar.	1076		,,	25 Mar.	1087	
,,	24 Dec.	,,		,,	9 Sept	,,	
1076	25 Dec	1076					
1077	1 Jan.	,,	11.				
,,	25 Mar.	1077					
,,	24 Dec.	,,					

WILLIAM II.

His reign is reckoned from his Coronation

Historical	Day of Month	Legal, Civil, and Ecclesiastical	Regnal	Historical	Day of Month	Legal, Civil, and Ecclesiastical	Regnal
1087	26 Sept.	1087		1089	26 Sept	1089	
1088	1 Jan	,,	1	1090	1 Jan.	,,	3
,,	25 Mar.	1088		,,	25 Mar	1090	
,,	25 Sept	,,		,,	25 Sept	,,	
1088	26 Sept	1088		1090	26 Sept	1090	
1089	1 Jan	,,	2	1091	1 Jan	,,	4.
,,	25 Mar.	1089		,,	25 Mar	1091	
,,	25 Sept	,,		,,	25 Sept.	,,	

Historical.	Day of Month.	Legal, Civil, and Ecclesiastical	Regnal		Historical.	Day of Month	Legal, Civil, and Ecclesiastical	Regnal.
1091	26 Sept.	1091			1096	26 Sept.	1096	
1092	1 Jan.	"	} 5.		1097	1 Jan.	"	} 10.
"	25 Mar.	1092			"	25 Mar	1097	
"	25 Sept.	"			"	25 Sept.	"	
1092	26 Sept.	1092			1097	26 Sept.	1097	
1093	1 Jan	"	} 6.		1098	1 Jan.	"	} 11.
"	25 Mar.	1093			"	25 Mar.	1098	
"	25 Sept.	"			"	25 Sept	"	
1093	26 Sept.	1093			1098	26 Sept.	1098	
1094	1 Jan	"	} 7.		1099	1 Jan.	"	} 12.
"	25 Mar.	1094			"	25 Mar	1099	
"	25 Sept.	"			"	25 Sept.	"	
1094	26 Sept.	1094			1099	26 Sept	1099	
1095	1 Jan.	"	} 8		1100	1 Jan.	"	} 13.
"	25 Mar	1095			"	25 Mar	1100	
"	25 Sept.	"			"	2 Aug	"	
1095	26 Sept.	1095						
1096	1 Jan	"	} 9					
"	25 Mar.	1096						
"	25 Sept	"						

HENRY I.

His reign is reckoned from his Coronation.

Historical.	Day of Month.	Legal, Civil, and Ecclesiastical	Regnal		Historical.	Day of Month	Legal, Civil, and Ecclesiastical	Regnal.
1100	5 Aug	1100			1108	5 Aug	1108	
1101	1 Jan.	"	} 1.		1109	1 Jan	"	} 9.
"	25 Mar.	1101			"	25 Mar.	1109	
"	4 Aug.	"			"	4 Aug	"	
1101	5 Aug.	1101			1109	5 Aug.	1109	
1102	1 Jan	"	} 2		1110	1 Jan.	"	} 10.
"	25 Mar.	1102			"	25 Mar.	1110	
"	4 Aug	"			"	4 Aug.	"	
1102	5 Aug.	1102			1110	5 Aug.	1110	
1103	1 Jan	"	} 3.		1111	1 Jan.	"	} 11.
"	25 Mar.	1103			"	25 Mar.	1111	
"	4 Aug.	"			"	4 Aug.	"	
1103	5 Aug.	1103			1111	5 Aug.	1111	
1104	1 Jan.	"	} 4		1112	1 Jan	"	} 12
"	25 Mar.	1104			"	25 Mar	1112	
"	4 Aug.	"			"	4 Aug.	"	
1104	5 Aug.	1104			1112	5 Aug.	1112	
1105	1 Jan	"	} 5.		1113	1 Jan.	"	} 13
"	25 Mar.	1105			"	25 Mar	1113	
"	4 Aug.	"			"	4 Aug.	"	
1105	5 Aug.	1105			1113	5 Aug.	1113	
1106	1 Jan	"	} 6.		1114	1 Jan	"	} 14.
"	25 Mar.	1106			"	25 Mar	1114	
"	4 Aug.	"			"	4 Aug	"	
1106	5 Aug.	1106			1114	5 Aug	1114	
1107	1 Jan.	"	} 7.		1115	1 Jan	"	} 15
"	25 Mar.	1107			"	25 Mar	1115	
"	4 Aug.	"			"	4 Aug	"	
1107	5 Aug.	1107			1115	5 Aug.	1115	
1108	1 Jan	"	} 8.		1116	1 Jan.	"	} 16.
"	25 Mar.	1108			"	25 Mar	1116	
"	4 Aug.	"			"	4 Aug.	"	

Historical	Day of Month	Legal, Civil, and Ecclesiastical	Regnal	Historical	Day of Month	Legal, Civil, and Ecclesiastical	Regnal
1116	5 Aug	1116		1126	5 Aug	1126	
1117	1 Jan	,,	17	1127	1 Jan.	,,	27.
,,	25 Mar	1117		,,	25 Mar.	1127	
,,	4 Aug	,,		,,	4 Aug	,,	
1117	5 Aug	1117		1127	5 Aug	1127	
1118	1 Jan.	,,	18	1128	1 Jan	,,	.28
,,	25 Mar.	1118		,,	25 Mar	1128	
,,	4 Aug	,,		,,	4 Aug	,,	
1118	5 Aug	1118		1128	5 Ang.	1128	
1119	1 Jan	,,	19	1129	1 Jan	,,	29
,,	25 Mar	1119		,,	25 Mar	1129	
,,	4 Aug	,,		,,	4 Aug.	,,	
1119	5 Aug.	1119		1129	5 Aug.	1129	
1120	1 Jan	,,	20	1130	1 Jan	,,	30
,,	25 Mar	1120		,,	25 Mar	1130	
,,	4 Aug	,,		,,	4 Aug.	,,	
1120	5 Aug	1120		1130	5 Aug	1130	
1121	1 Jan	,,	21.	1131	1 Jan	,,	31.
,,	2 Mar	1121		,,	25 Mar	1131	
,,	4 Aug	,,		,,	4 Aug	,,	
1121	5 Aug	1121		1131	5 Aug.	1131	
1122	1 Jan	,,	22	1132	1 Jan	,,	32.
,,	25 Mar	1122		,,	25 Mar	1132	
,,	4 Aug	,,		,,	4 Aug.	,,	
1122	5 Aug.	1122		1132	5 Aug	1132	
1123	1 Jan	,,	23	1133	1 Jan.	,,	33.
,,	25 Mar	1123		,,	25 Mar.	1133	
,,	4 Aug.	,,		,,	4 Aug.	,,	
1123	5 Aug	1123		1133	5 Aug.	1133	
1124	1 Jan	,,	24.	1134	1 Jan	,,	34.
,,	25 Mar.	1124		,,	25 Mar	1134	
,,	4 Aug	,,		,,	4 Aug	,,	
1124	5 Aug	1124		1134	5 Aug	1134	
1125	1 Jan.	,,	25.	1135	1 Jan.	,,	35
,,	25 Mar.	1125		,,	25 Mar	1135	
,,	4 Aug	,,		,,	4 Aug	,,	
1125	5 Aug	1125		1135	5 Aug	1135	
1126	1 Jan	,,	26.	,,	1 Dec.	,,	36
,,	25 Mar.	1126					
,,	4 Aug	,,					

STEPHEN.

His reign is reckoned from his Coronation

Historical	Day of Month	Legal, Civil, and Ecclesiastical	Regnal	Historical	Day of Month	Legal, Civil, and Ecclesiastical	Regnal
1135	26 Dec	1135		1137	26 Dec	1137	
1136	1 Jan	,,	1.	1138	1 Jan.	,,	3.
,,	25 Mar	1136		,,	25 Mar	1138	
,,	25 Dec.	,,		,,	25 Dec.	,,	
1136	26 Dec.	1136		1138	26 Dec.	1138	
1137	1 Jan.	,,	2	1139	1 Jan	,,	4.
,,	25 Mar	1137		,,	25 Mar.	1139	
,,	25 Dec	,,		,,	25 Dec	,,	

Historical.	Day of Month	Legal, Civil, and Ecclesiastical.	Regnal	Historical	Day of Month	Legal, Civil, and Ecclesiastical	Regnal
1139 1140 ,, ,,	26 Dec. 1 Jan 25 Mar. 25 Dec	1139 ,, 1140 ,,	} 5.	1147 1148 ,, ,,	26 Dec. 1 Jan 25 Mar. 25 Dec	1147 ,, 1148 ,,	} 13.
1140 1141 ,, ,,	26 Dec. 1 Jan. 25 Mar. 25 Dec	1140 ,, 1141 ,,	} 6	1148 1149 ,, ,,	26 Dec 1 Jan 25 Mar 25 Dec.	1148 ,, 1149 ,,	} 14.
1141 1142 ,, ,,	26 Dec. 1 Jan 25 Mar. 25 Dec.	1141 ,, 1142 ,,	} 7	1149 1150 ,, ,,	25 Dec. 1 Jan 25 Mar 25 Dec	1149 ,, 1150 ,,	} 15.
1142 1143 ,, ,,	26 Dec 1 Jan 25 Mar. 25 Dec.	1142 ,, 1143 ,,	} 8.	1150 1151 ,, ,,	26 Dec 1 Jan 25 Mar 25 Dec	1150 ,, 1151 ,,	} 16.
1143 1144 ,, ,,	26 Dec. 1 Jan 25 Mar. 25 Dec.	1143 ,, 1144 ,,	} 9.	1151 1152 ,, ,,	26 Dec 1 Jan 25 Mar 25 Dec	1151 ,, 1152 ,,	} 17.
1144 1145 ,, ,,	26 Dec 1 Jan. 25 Mar. 25 Dec	1144 ,, 1145 ,,	} 10	1152 1153 ,, ,,	26 Dec. 1 Jan 25 Mar 25 Dec	1152 ,, 1153 ,,	} 18.
1145 1146 ,, ,,	26 Dec 1 Jan. 25 Mar. 25 Dec	1145 ,, 1146 ,,	} 11	1153 1154 ,, ,,	26 Dec. 1 Jan. 25 Mar. 25 Oct.	1153 ,, 1154 ,,	} 19
1146 1147 ,, ,,	26 Dec. 1 Jan 25 Mar. 25 Dec.	1146 ,, 1147 ,,	} 12				

HENRY II.

His reign is reckoned from his Coronation.

Historical.	Day of Month	Legal, Civil, and Ecclesiastical.	Regnal	Historical	Day of Month	Legal, Civil, and Ecclesiastical	Regnal
1154 1155 ,, ,,	19 Dec. 1 Jan. 25 Mar. 18 Dec	1154 ,, 1155 ,,	} 1	1158 1159 ,, ,,	19 Dec 1 Jan 25 Mar. 18 Dec	1158 ,, 1159 ,,	} 5.
1155 1156 ,, ,,	19 Dec. 1 Jan. 25 Mar. 18 Dec.	1155 ,, 1156 ,,	} 2.	1159 1160 ,, ,,	19 Dec 1 Jan 25 Mar. 18 Dec.	1159 ,, 1160 ,,	} 6.
1156 1157 ,, ,,	19 Dec. 1 Jan. 25 Mar. 18 Dec.	1156 ,, 1157 ,,	} 3.	1160 1161 ,, ,,	19 Dec. 1 Jan 25 Mar. 18 Dec.	1160 ,, 1161 ,,	} 7.
1157 1158 ,, ,,	19 Dec. 1 Jan. 25 Mar. 18 Dec.	1157 ,, 1158 ,,	} 4.	1161 1162 ,, ,,	19 Dec. 1 Jan. 25 Mar. 18 Dec.	1161 ,, 1162 ,,	} 8.

Historical	Day of Month	Legal, Civil, and Ecclesiastical	Regnal	Historical	Day of Month	Legal, Civil, and Ecclesiastical	Regnal
1162	19 Dec.	1162		1175	19 Dec	1175	
1163	1 Jan	"	} 9	1176	1 Jan	"	} 22.
"	25 Mar.	1163		"	25 Mar.	1176	
"	18 Dec.	"		"	18 Dec.	"	
1163	19 Dec	1163		1176	19 Dec	1176	
1164	1 Jan	"	} 10	1177	1 Jan.	"	} 23.
"	25 Mar.	1164		"	25 Mar.	1177	
"	18 Dec.	"		"	18 Dec	"	
1164	19 Dec	1164		1177	19 Dec.	1177	
1165	1 Jan	"	} 11.	1178	1 Jan	"	} 24.
"	25 Mar	1165		"	25 Mar	1178	
"	18 Dec	"		"	18 Dec	"	
1165	19 Dec	1165		1178	19 Dec.	1178	
1166	1 Jan	"	} 12.	1179	1 Jan	"	} 25.
"	25 Mar	1166		"	25 Mar	1179	
"	18 Dec.	"		"	18 Dec.	"	
1166	19 Dec	1166		1179	19 Dec	1179	
1167	1 Jan	"	} 13	1180	1 Jan.	"	} 26.
"	25 Mar	1167		"	25 Mar	1180	
"	18 Dec	"		"	18 Dec	"	
1167	19 Dec.	1167		1180	19 Dec	1180	
1168	1 Jan.	"	} 14.	1181	1 Jan.	"	} 27.
"	25 Mar	1168		"	25 Mar.	1181	
"	18 Dec	"		"	18 Dec	"	
1168	19 Dec	1168		1181	19 Dec	1181	
1169	1 Jan	"	} 15	1182	1 Jan.	"	} 28
"	25 Mar.	1169		"	25 Mar.	1182	
"	18 Dec.	"		"	18 Dec	"	
1169	19 Dec	1169		1182	19 Dec.	1182	
1170	1 Jan	"	} 16.	1183	1 Jan.	"	} 29.
"	25 Mar	1170		"	25 Mar	1183	
"	18 Dec	"		"	18 Dec.	"	
1170	19 Dec.	1170		1183	19 Dec	1183	
1171	1 Jan	"	} 17.	1184	1 Jan	"	} 30
"	25 Mar.	1171		"	25 Mar	1184	
"	18 Dec	"		"	18 Dec	"	
1171	19 Dec.	1171		1184	19 Dec.	1184	
1172	1 Jan	"	} 18.	1185	1 Jan	"	} 31.
"	25 Mar	1172		"	25 Mar.	1185	
"	18 Dec	"		"	18 Dec.	"	
1172	19 Dec	1172		1185	19 Dec.	1185	
1173	1 Jan	"	} 19	1186	1 Jan	"	} 32
"	25 Mar.	1173		"	25 Mar	1186	
"	18 Dec.	"		"	18 Dec	"	
1173	19 Dec.	1173		1186	19 Dec	1186	
1174	1 Jan	"	} 20	1187	1 Jan	"	} 33.
"	25 Mar	1174		"	25 Mar	1187	
"	18 Dec.	"		"	18 Dec	"	
1174	19 Dec.	1174		1187	19 Dec.	1187	
1175	1 Jan	"	} 21	1188	1 Jan.	"	} 34.
"	25 Mar	1175		"	25 Mar	1188	
"	18 Dec	"		"	18 Dec	"	
				1188	19 Dec	1188	
				1189	1 Jan.	"	} 35
				"	25 Mar	1189	
				"	6 July	"	

RICHARD I.

His reign is reckoned from his Coronation

Historical.	Day of Month	Legal, Civil, and Ecclesiastical	Regnal.	Historical	Day of Month	Legal, Civil, and Ecclesiastical	Regnal
1189	3 Sept	1189		1194	3 Sept	1194	
1190	1 Jan.	„	1.	1195	1 Jan	• „	6
„	25 Mar.	1190		„	25 Mar	1195	
„	2 Sept.	„		„	2 Sept	„	
1190	3 Sept.	1190		1195	3 Sept	1195	
1191	1 Jan	„	2.	1196	1 Jan	„	7
„	25 Mar.	1191		„	25 Mar	1196	
„	2 Sept.	„		„	2 Sept	„	
1191	3 Sept.	1191		1196	3 Sept	1196	
1192	1 Jan	„	3.	1197	1 Jan	„	8.
„	25 Mar	1192		„	25 Mar	1197	
„	2 Sept.	„		„	2 Sept	„	
1192	3 Sept	1192		1197	3 Sept	1197	
1193	1 Jan.	„	4	1198	1 Jan	„	9
„	25 Mar.	1193		„	25 Mar.	1198	
„	2 Sept.	„		„	2 Sept	„	
1193	3 Sept.	1193		1198	3 Sept	1198	
1194	1 Jan	„	5.	1199	1 Jan	„	10.
„	25 Mar.	1194		„	25 Mar	1199	
„	2 Sept	„		„	6 Apr.	„	

JOHN.

His reign is reckoned from Ascension Day to Ascension Day

Historical	Day of Month	Legal, Civil, and Ecclesiastical	Regnal.	Historical	Day of Month	Legal, Civil, and Ecclesiastical	Regnal
1199	27 May.	1199		1206	11 May.	1206	
1200	1 Jan.	„	1.	1207	1 Jan.	„	8.
„	25 Mar.	1200		„	25 Mar.	1207	
„	17 May.	„		„	30 May.	„	
1200	18 May	1200		1207	31 May	1207	
1201	1 Jan.	„	2	1208	1 Jan	„	9
„	25 Mar.	1201		„	25 Mar.	1208	
„	2 May.	„		„	14 May.	„	
1201	3 May.	1201		1208	15 May	1208	
1202	1 Jan	„	3.	1209	1 Jan.	„	10
„	25 Mar	1202		„	25 Mar	1209	
„	22 May.	„		„	6 May.	„	
1202	23 May	1202		1209	7 May	1209	
1203	1 Jan	„	4.	1210	1 Jan	„	11
„	25 Mar	1203		„	25 Mar.	1210	
„	14 May.	„		„	26 May	„	
1203	15 May.	1203		1210	27 May	1210	
1204	1 Jan	„	5.	1211	1 Jan	„	12.
„	25 Mar	1204		„	25 Mar.	1211	
„	2 June	„		„	11 May	„	
1204	3 June	1204		1211	12 May	1211	
1205	1 Jan.	„	6	1212	1 Jan	„	13
„	25 Mar.	1205		„	25 Mar	1212	
„	18 May	„		„	2 May	„	
1205	19 May.	1205		1212	3 May	1212	
1206	1 Jan	„	7.	1213	1 Jan.	„	14
„	25 Mar.	1206		„	25 Mar	1213	
„	10 May.	„		„	22 May	„	

Historical.	Day of Month	Legal, Civil, and Ecclesiastical	Regnal	Historical	Day of Month.	Legal, Civil, and Ecclesiastical.	Regnal.
1213	28 May.	1213		1215	28 May.	1215	
1214	1 Jan.	,,	15	1216	1 Jan.	,,	17.
,,	25 Mar.	1214		,,	25 Mar.	1216	
,,	7 May.	,,		,,	18 May.	,,	
1214	8 May.	1214		1216	19 May.	1216	
1215	1 Jan.	,,	16.	,,	19 Oct.	,,	18
,,	25 Mar	1215					
,,	27 May	,,					

HENRY III.

His reign is reckoned from his Coronation

Historical.	Day of Month	Legal, Civil, and Ecclesiastical	Regnal	Historical	Day of Month.	Legal, Civil, and Ecclesiastical.	Regnal.
1216	28 Oct	1216		1226	28 Oct.	1226	
1217	1 Jan.	,,	1	1227	1 Jan	,,	11
,,	25 Mar	1217		,,	25 Mar.	1227	
,,	27 Oct.	,,		,,	27 Oct.	,,	
1217	28 Oct.	1217		1227	28 Oct.	1227	
1218	1 Jan.	,,	2.	1228	1 Jan.	,,	12.
,,	25 Mar.	1218		,,	25 Mar.	1228	
,,	27 Oct.	,,		,,	27 Oct.	,,	
1218	28 Oct.	1218		1228	28 Oct.	1228	
1219	1 Jan	,,	3	1229	1 Jan.	,,	13.
,,	25 Mar	1219		,,	25 Mar	1229	
,,	27 Oct	,,		,,	27 Oct.	,,	
1219	28 Oct	1219		1229	28 Oct.	1229	
1220	1 Jan	,,	4	1230	1 Jan	,,	14.
,,	25 Mar	1220		,,	25 Mar	1230	
,,	27 Oct	,,		,,	27 Oct.	,,	
1220	28 Oct.	1220		1230	28 Oct.	1230	
1221	1 Jan	,,	5.	1231	1 Jan.	,,	15
,,	25 Mar.	1221		,,	25 Mar	1231	
,,	27 Oct	,,		,,	27 Oct.	,,	
1221	28 Oct	1221		1231	28 Oct.	1231	
1222	1 Jan	,,	6.	1232	1 Jan.	,,	16.
,,	25 Mar.	1222		,,	25 Mar	1232	
,,	27 Oct	,,		,,	27 Oct.	,,	
1222	28 Oct.	1222		1232	28 Oct.	1232	
1223	1 Jan	,,	7.	1233	1 Jan	,,	17.
,,	25 Mar.	1223		,,	25 Mar.	1233	
,,	27 Oct	,,		,,	27 Oct.	,,	
1223	28 Oct	1223		1233	28 Oct.	1233	
1224	1 Jan.	,,	8	1234	1 Jan.	,,	18.
,,	25 Mar.	1224		,,	25 Mar	1234	
,,	27 Oct	,,		,,	27 Oct.	,,	
1224	28 Oct	1224		1234	28 Oct.	1234	
1225	1 Jan.	,,	9.	1235	1 Jan	,,	19.
,,	25 Mar.	1225		,,	25 Mar	1235	
,,	27 Oct	,,		,,	27 Oct	,,	
1225	28 Oct	1225		1235	28 Oct.	1235	
1226	1 Jan.	,,	10	1236	1 Jan.	,,	20.
,,	25 Mar.	1226		,,	25 Mar.	1236	
,,	27 Oct.	,,		,,	27 Oct.	,,	

Historical.	Day of Month.	Legal, Civil, and Ecclesiastical.	Regnal.	Historical.	Day of Month.	Legal, Civil, and Ecclesiastical.	Regnal.
1236	28 Oct.	1236	} 21.	1249	28 Oct.	1249	} 34
1237	1 Jan.	„		1250	1 Jan.	„	
„	25 Mar	1237		„	25 Mar.	1250	
„	27 Oct.	„		„	27 Oct.	„	
1237	28 Oct	1237	} 22	1250	28 Oct.	1250	} 35.
1238	1 Jan	„		1251	1 Jan.	„	
„	25 Mar	1238		„	25 Mar.	1251	
„	27 Oct	„		„	27 Oct.	„	
1238	28 Oct.	1238	} 23.	1251	28 Oct	1251	} 36.
1239	1 Jan.	„		1252	1 Jan.	„	
„	25 Mar.	1239		„	25 Mar.	1252	
„	27 Oct.	„		„	27 Oct.	„	
1239	28 Oct.	1239	} 24	1252	28 Oct	1252	} 37.
1240	1 Jan	„		1253	1 Jan	„	
„	25 Mar	1240		„	25 Mar.	1253	
„	27 Oct	„		„	27 Oct.	„	
1240	28 Oct	1240	} 25	1253	28 Oct	1253	} 38
1241	1 Jan.	„		1254	1 Jan.	„	
„	25 Mar.	1241		„	25 Mar	1254	
„	27 Oct.	„		„	27 Oct.	„	
1241	28 Oct.	1241	} 26	1254	28 Oct.	1254	} 39.
1242	1 Jan.	„		1255	1 Jan	„	
„	25 Mar.	1242		„	25 Mar	1255	
„	27 Oct	„		„	27 Oct.	„	
1242	28 Oct.	1242	} 27.	..1255	28 Oct	1255	} 40
1243	1 Jan]	„		1256	1 Jan	„	
„	25 Mar.	1243		„	25 Mar	1256	
„	27 Oct.	„		„	27 Oct.	„	
1243	28 Oct.	1243	} 28.	1256	28 Oct	1256	} 41
1244	1 Jan.	„		1257	1 Jan	„	
„	25 Mar.	1244		„	25 Mar	1257	
„	27 Oct	„		„	27 Oct	„	
1244	28 Oct	1244	} 29.	1257	28 Oct	1257	} 42
1245	1 Jan	„		1258	1 Jan.	„	
„	25 Mar.	1245		„	25 Mar.	1258	
„	27 Oct.	„		„	27 Oct.	„	
1245	28 Oct.	1245	} 30	1258	28 Oct.	1258	} 43
1246	1 Jan.	„		1259	1 Jan	„	
„	25 Mar.	1246		„	25 Mar	1259	
„ ●	27 Oct.	„		„	27 Oct	„	
1246	28 Oct	1246	} 31	1259	28 Oct	1259	} 44
1247	1 Jan.	„		1260	1 Jan	„	
„	25 Mar.	1247		„	25 Mar	1260	
„	27 Oct.	„		„	27 Oct	„	
1247	28 Oct.	1247	} 32.	1260	28 Oct.	1260	} 45
1248	1 Jan.	„		1261	1 Jan.	„	
„	25 Mar.	1248		„	25 Mar	1261	
„	27 Oct.	„		„	27 Oct.	„	
1248	26 Oct.	1248	} 33.	1261	28 Oct.	1261	} 46.
1249	1 Jan.	„		1262	1 Jan	„	
„	25 Mar.	1249		„	25 Mar	1262	
„	27 Oct	„		„	27 Oct.	„	

Historical.	Day of Month.	Legal, Civil, and Ecclesiastical	Regnal.	Historical	Day of Month.	Legal, Civil, and Ecclesiastical	Regnal
1262	28 Oct.	1262		1268	28 Oct.	1268	
1263	1 Jan.	"	47.	1269	1 Jan.	"	53
"	25 Mar.	1263		"	25 Mar	1269	
"	27 Oct.	"		"	27 Oct.	"	
1263	28 Oct	1263		1269	28 Oct	1269	
1264	1 Jan	"	48	1270	1 Jan.	"	54.
"	25 Mar.	1264		"	25 Mar.	1270	
"	27 Oct	"		"	27 Oct	"	
1264	28 Oct.	1264		1270	28 Oct	1270	
1265	1 Jan.	"	49.	1271	1 Jan	"	55.
"	25 Mar	1265		"	25 Mar.	1271	
"	27 Oct	"		"	27 Oct	"	
1265	28 Oct.	1265		1271	28 Oct.	1271	
1266	1 Jan	"	50	1272	1 Jan.	"	56.
"	25 Mar.	1266		"	25 Mar.	1272	
"	27 Oct	"		"	27 Oct	"	
1266	28 Oct.	1266		1272	28 Oct	1272	
1267	1 Jan	"	51.	"	16 Nov.	"	57.
"	25 Mar	1267					
"	27 Oct	"					
1267	28 Oct.	1267					
1268	1 Jan	"	52.				
"	25 Mar.	1268					
"	27 Oct.	"					

EDWARD I.

His reign is reckoned from his Proclamation

Historical	Day of Month	Legal, Civil, and Ecclesiastical	Regnal	Historical	Day of Month	Legal, Civil, and Ecclesiastical	Regnal
1272	20 Nov	1272		1278	20 Nov.	1278	
1273	1 Jan.	"	1	1279	1 Jan	"	7.
"	25 Mar.	1273		"	25 Mar.	1279	
"	20 Nov	"		"	20 Nov.	"	
1273	20 Nov	1273		1279	20 Nov	1279	
1274	1 Jan.	"	2	1280	1 Jan	"	8.
"	25 Mar	1274		"	25 Mar	1280	
"	20 Nov.	"		"	20 Nov	"	
1274	20 Nov.	1274		1280	20 Nov.	1280	
1275	1 Jan	"	3.	1281	1 Jan.	"	9.
"	25 Mar	1275		"	25 Mar.	1281	
"	20 Nov	"		"	20 Nov.	"	
1275	20 Nov	1275		1281	20 Nov.	1281	
1276	1 Jan	"	4	1282	1 Jan	"	10.
"	25 Mar.	1276		"	25 Mar.	1282	
"	20 Nov.	"		"	20 Nov	"	
1276	20 Nov	1276		1282	20 Nov.	1282	
1277	1 Jan	"	5.	1283	1 Jan.	"	11.
"	25 Mai	1277		"	25 Mar.	1283	
"	20 Nov	"		"	20 Nov.	"	
1277	20 Nov	1277		1283	20 Nov.	1283	
1278	1 Jan.	"	6	1284	1 Jan.	"	12
"	25 Mar	1278		"	25 Mar.	1284	
"	20 Nov.	"		"	20 Nov	"	

Historical.	Day of Month.	Legal, Civil, and Ecclesiastical	Regnal.	Historical.	Day of Month	Legal, Civil, and Ecclesiastical	Regnal.
1284	20 Nov.	1284		1296	20 Nov.	1296	
1285	1 Jan.	„	13.	1297	1 Jan	„	25.
„	25 Mar.	1285		„	25 Mar.	1297	
„	20 Nov.	„		„	20 Nov.	„	
1285	20 Nov.	1285		1297	20 Nov	1297	
1286	1 Jan	„	14.	1298	1 Jan	„	26.
„	25 Mar.	1286		„	25 Mar.	1298	
„	20 Nov.	„		„	20 Nov	„	
1286	20 Nov.	1286		1298	20 Nov	1298	
1287	1 Jan.	„	15.	1299	1 Jan.	„	27
„	25 Mar.	1287		„	25 Mar.	1299	
„	20 Nov.	„		„	20 Nov	„	
1287	20 Nov.	1287		1299	20 Nov.	1299	
1288	1 Jan.	„	16.	1300	1 Jan.	„	28.
„	25 Mar.	1288		„	25 Mar.	1300	
„	20 Nov.	„		„	20 Nov	„	
1288	20 Nov.	1288		1300	20 Nov.	1300	
1289	1 Jan	„	17	1301	1 Jan	„	29.
„	25 Mar	1289		„	25 Mar	1301	
„	20 Nov.	„		„	20 Nov.	„	
1289	20 Nov.	1289		1301	20 Nov.	1301	
1290	1 Jan.	„	18.	1302	1 Jan.	„	30.
„	25 Mar	1290		„	25 Mar.	1302	
„	20 Nov.	„		„	20 Nov.	„	
1290	20 Nov.	1290		1302	20 Nov	1302	
1291	1 Jan.	„	19	1303	1 Jan	„	31.
„	25 Mar.	1291		„	25 Mar.	1303	
„	20 Nov.	„		„	20 Nov.	„	
1291	20 Nov.	1291		1303	20 Nov.	1303	
1292	1 Jan.	„	20.	1304	1 Jan.	„	32.
„	25 Mar.	1292		„	25 Mar	1304	
„	20 Nov.	„		„	20 Nov.	„	
1292	20 Nov.	1292		1304	20 Nov	1304	
1293	1 Jan.	„	21.	1305	1 Jan.	„	33.
„	25 Mar.	1293		„	25 Mar	1305	
„	20 Nov.	„		„	20 Nov.	„	
1293	20 Nov.	1293		1305	20 Nov.	1305	
1294	1 Jan.	„	22	1306	1 Jan.	„	34.
„	25 Mar.	1294		„	25 Mar.	1306	
„	20 Nov.	„		„	20 Nov	„	
1294	20 Nov.	1294		1306	20 Nov	1306	
1295	1 Jan.	„	23.	1307	1 Jan.	„	35.
„	25 Mar.	1295		„	25 Mar.	1307	
„	20 Nov	„		„	7 July	„	
1295	20 Nov.	1295					
1296	1 Jan.	„	24.				
„	25 Mar.	1296					
„	20 Nov.	„					

EDWARD II.

His reign is reckoned from his Recognition

Historical	Day of Month.	Legal, Civil, and Ecclesiastical	Regnal.	Historical.	Day of Month.	Legal, Civil, and Ecclesiastical.	Regnal
1307	8 July	1307		1317	8 July	1317	
1308	1 Jan	,,	1	1318	1 Jan	,,	11
,,	25 Mar	1308		,,	25 Mar	1318	
,,	7 July	,,		,,	7 July.	,,	
1308	8 July	1308		1318	8 July.	1318	
1309	1 Jan.	,,	2	1319	1 Jan.	,,	12.
,,	25 Mar.	1309		,,	25 Mar.	1319	
,,	7 July	,,		,,	7 July	,,	
1309	8 July	1309		1319	8 July	1319	
1310	1 Jan	,,	3	1320	1 Jan	,,	13.
,,	25 Mar	1310		,,	25 Mar	1320	
,,	7 July	,,		,,	7 July	,,	
1310	8 July.	1310		1320	8 July	1320	
1311	1 Jan.	,,	4.	1321	1 Jan	,,	14.
,,	25 Mar.	1311		,,	25 Mar	1321	
,,	7 July.	,,		,,	7 July	,,	
1311	8 July.	1311		1321	8 July.	1321	
1312	1 Jan	,,	5.	1322	1 Jan.	,,	15
,,	25 Mar.	1312		,,	25 Mar	1322	
,,	7 July	,,		,,	7 July	,,	
1312	8 July.	1312		1322	8 July	1322	
1313	1 Jan	,,	6.	1323	1 Jan	,,	16.
,,	25 Mar	1313		,,	25 Mar	1323	
,,	7 July	,,		,,	7 July	,,	
1313	8 July.	1313		1323	8 July.	1323	
1314	1 Jan	,,	7	1324	1 Jan.	,,	17.
,,	25 Mar	1314		,,	25 Mar.	1324	
,,	7 July.	,,		,,	7 July.	,,	
1314	8 July.	1314		1324	8 July.	1324	
1315	1 Jan	,,	8.	1325	1 Jan	,,	18
,,	25 Mar	1315		,,	25 Mar.	1325	
,,	7 July	,,		,,	7 July	,,	
1315	8 July	1315		1325	8 July.	1325	
1316	1 Jan.	,,	9	1326	1 Jan	,,	19
,,	25 Mar.	1316		,,	25 Mar.	1326	
,,	7 July	,,		,,	7 July.	,,	
1316	8 July	1316		1326	8 July.	1326	
1317	1 Jan	,,	10	1327	1 Jan.	,,	20
,,	25 Mar.	1317		,,	20 Jan.	,,	
,,	7 July	,,					

EDWARD III.

His reign is reckoned from the day after his Peace was proclaimed.

Historical	Day of Month	Legal, Civil, and Ecclesiastical	Regnal.	Historical	Day of Month	Legal, Civil, and Ecclesiastical	Regnal
1327	25 Jan	1326		1329	25 Jan.	1328	
,,	25 Mar.	1327	1.	,,	25 Mar	1329	3.
1328	1 Jan	,,		1330	1 Jan	,,	
,,	24 Jan.	,,		,,	24 Jan	,,	
1328	25 Jan.	1327		1330	25 Jan.	1329	
,,	25 Mar.	1328	2.	,,	25 Mar.	1330	4.
1329	1 Jan	,,		1331	1 Jan	,,	
,,	24 Jan.	,,		,,	24 Jan.	,,	

Historical	Day of Month.	Legal, Civil, and Ecclesiastical	Regnal	Historical.	Day of Month.	Legal, Civil, and Ecclesiastical	Regnal.
1331	25 Jan.	1330		1344	25 Jan.	1343	
„	25 Mar	1331	5	„	25 Mar.	1344	18.
1332	1 Jan.	„		1345	1 Jan.	„	
„	24 Jan.	„		„	24 Jan.	„	
1332	25 Jan.	1331		1345	25 Jan	1344	
„	25 Mar	1332	6.	„	25 Mar.	1345	19
1333	1 Jan.	„		1346	1 Jan.	„	
„	24 Jan.	„		„	24 Jan.	„	
1333	25 Jan.	1332		1346	25 Jan	1345	
„	25 Mar.	1333	7.	„	25 Mar	1346	20
1334	1 Jan.	„		1347	1 Jan	„	
„	24 Jan.	„		„	24 Jan.	„	
1334	25 Jan.	1333		1347	25 Jan	1346	
„	25 Mar	1334	8.	„	25 Mar.	1347	21.
1335	1 Jan.	„		1348	1 Jan	„	
„	24 Jan.	„		„	24 Jan.	„	
1335	25 Jan.	1334		1348	25 Jan.	1347	
„	25 Mar	1335	9.	„	25 Mar.	1348	22
1336	1 Jan.	„		1349	1 Jan.	„	
„	24 Jan.	„		„	24 Jan.	„	
1336	25 Jan.	1335		1349	25 Jan.	1348	
„	25 Mar.	1336	10.	„	25 Mar	1349	23.
1337	1 Jan.	„		1350	1 Jan.	„	
„	24 Jan.	„		„	24 Jan.	„	
1337	25 Jan	1336		1350	25 Jan	1349	
„	25 Mar.	1337	11.	„	25 Mar.	1350	24
1338	1 Jan.	„		1351	1 Jan	„	
„	24 Jan.	„		„	24 Jan.	„	
1338	25 Jan.	1337		1351	25 Jan.	1350	
„	25 Mar.	1338	12.	„	25 Mar.	1351	25
1339	1 Jan.	„		1352	1 Jan.	„	
„	24 Jan.	„		„	24 Jan.	„	
1339	25 Jan.	1338		1352	25 Jan.	1351	
„	25 Mar.	1339	13.	„	25 Mar.	1352	26
1340	1 Jan.	„		1353	1 Jan.	„	
„	24 Jan.	„		„	24 Jan	„	
1340	25 Jan	1339		1353	25 Jan	1352	
„	25 Mar.	1340	14.	„	25 Mar.	1353	27
1341	1 Jan.	„		1354	1 Jan	„	
„	24 Jan	„		„	24 Jan.	„	
1341	25 Jan.	1340		1354	25 Jan.	1353	
„	25 Mar.	1341	15	„	25 Mar.	1354	28
1342	1 Jan.	„		1355	1 Jan	„	
„	24 Jan	„		„	24 Jan.	„	
1342	25 Jan.	1341		1355	25 Jan	1354	
„	25 Mar.	1342	16.	„	25 Mar.	1355	29
1343	1 Jan.	„		1356	1 Jan.	„	
„	24 Jan.	„		„	24 Jan	„	
1343	25 Jan.	1342		1356	25 Jan	1355	
„	25 Mar.	1343	17	„	25 Mar.	1356	30
1344	1 Jan	„		1357	1 Jan	„	
„	24 Jan.	„		„	24 Jan	„	

Historical	Day of Month	Legal, Civil, and Ecclesiastical	Regnal	Historical	Day of Month	Legal, Civil, and Ecclesiastical	Regnal
1357	25 Jan	1356		1368	25 Jan.	1367	
„	25 Mar.	1357	31	„	25 Mar	1368	42
1358	1 Jan	„		1369	1 Jan.	„	
„	24 Jan	„		„	24 Jan.	„	
1358	25 Jan	1357		1369	25 Jan.	1368	
„	25 Mar.	1358	32.	„	25 Mar.	1369	43
1359	1 Jan	„		1370	1 Jan.	„	
„	24 Jan.	„		„	24 Jan.	„	
1359	25 Jan	1358		1370	25 Jan.	1369	
„	25 Mar	1359	33.	„	25 Mar.	1370	44
1360	1 Jan	„		1371	1 Jan.	„	
„	24 Jan	„		„	24 Jan.	„	
1360	25 Jan	1359		1371	25 Jan.	1370	
„	25 Mar.	1360	34.	„	25 Mar.	1371	45.
1361	1 Jan.	„		1372	1 Jan.	„	
„	24 Jan	„		„	24 Jan.	„	
1361	25 Jan	1360		1372	25 Jan.	1371	
„	25 Mar.	1361	35.	„	25 Mar.	1372	46.
1362	1 Jan.	„		1373	1 Jan.	„	
„	24 Jan.	„		„	24 Jan.	„	
1362	25 Jan	1361		1373	25 Jan.	1372	
„	25 Mar.	1362	36.	„	25 Mar.	1373	47.
1363	1 Jan.	„		1374	1 Jan.	„	
„	24 Jan.	„		„	24 Jan.	„	
1363	25 Jan	1362		1374	25 Jan	1373	
„	25 Mar.	1363	37.	„	25 Mar.	1374	48.
1364	1 Jan.	„		1375	1 Jan.	„	
„	24 Jan.	„		„	24 Jan.	„	
1364	25 Jan	1363		1375	25 Jan.	1374	
„	25 Mar.	1364	38.	„	25 Mar.	1375	49.
1365	1 Jan	„		1376	1 Jan.	„	
„	24 Jan	„		„	24 Jan.	„	
1365	25 Jan.	1364		1376	25 Jan.	1375	
„	25 Mar.	1365	39.	„	25 Mar.	1376	50.
1366	1 Jan	„		1377	1 Jan.	„	
„	24 Jan	„		„	24 Jan.	„	
1366	25 Jan	1365		1377	25 Jan.	1376	
„	25 Mar.	1366	40.	„	25 Mar.	1377	51.
1367	1 Jan	„		„	21 June	„	
„	24 Jan	„					
1367	25 Jan	1366					
„	25 Mar.	1367	41.				
1368	1 Jan	„					
„	24 Jan	„					

These tables, from the first year of the reign of Richard II to the year 1654, when the Syllabus ends, will be continued in the Second Volume.

TABLE OF CONTEMPORARY SOVEREIGNS.

From the Reign of William I. to Edward III. inclusive.

A.D	England.	Scotland.	France.	Germany	Spain				Papal States.
					Leon.	Castile.	Navarre.	Aragon.	
1056				Henry IV.					
1057		Malcolm III		..					
1060		..	Philip I.	..					
1061		..	..	..					Alexander II
1063		..	..	..				Sancho-Ramirez	..
1065		..	..	..	Alphonso VI.	Sancho II		..	..
1066	William I.	..	..	..	..	..		..	..
1072	..	..	..	..	..	..		..	..
1073	..	..	..	..	..	..		..	Gregory VII.
1076	..	..	..	..	..	..	Sancho-Ramirez.	Sancho-Ramirez.	..
1086	..	..	..	..	..	..	—	.	Victor III
1087	William II	..	..	..	..	..	..	..	..
1088	..	..	..	..	..	..	..	..	Urban II
1093	..	Donald VI.	..	..	..	..	..	..	.
1094	..	Duncan II.	..	..	..	..	Pedro I.	Pedro I.	..
1095	..	Donald VI. restored.	..	..	..	..	..	..	..
1098	..	Edgar.	..	..	..	..	..	..	..
1099	..	..	..	..	..	..	..	..	Pascal II.
1100	Henry I.	..	..	..	.	..	..	..	..
1104	..	..	..	..	..	..	..	Alphonso I the Warrior.	..
1106	..	..	..	Henry V.	..	..	.	..	..
1107	..	Alexander I	..	..	..	..	..	..	..
1108	..	..	Louis VI	..	..	..	..	.	..
1109	..	..	..	..	Urraca, and Alphonso VII.	Urraca, and Alphonso VII	.	..	..
1118	..	.	.	..	..	.	..	..	Gelasius II.
1119	..	..		..	..	..	..	..	Calixtus II.
1124	..	David I	..	..	..	..	..	..	Honorius II.
1125	..	..	..	Lothair II.	..	..	..	..	..
1128	..	..	..	..	Alphonso VIII.	Alphonso VIII.	..	.	..
1130	..	..	..	..	..	..	..	..	Innocent II.
1134	..	..	..	..	..	..	Ramirez IV.	Ramirez II.	..
1135	Stephen	.	..	..	..	.	..		..

D	ENGLAND	SCOTLAND.	FRANCE	GERMANY	SPAIN				P⌐ St⌐
					Leon	Castile	Navarre	Aragon.	
137		..	Louis VII.				..	..	..	
38		..	..	Conrad III			.	.	..	
43	.	..	.	..			.		..	Celes⌐
44	.	.	..		.	..	.	.	Luci⌐
45	.		..	.	..	.		.	Euge⌐
50			.		..		Sancho VI.	..	
52	.		.	Frederic I	.		..	..	
53	.	Malcolm IV	.	..			..	.	Anasta⌐
54	Henry II		..	.		.		.	Adria⌐
55	..		.	.	.			.	
57	..	.		.	Ferdinand II	Sancho III		Petronilla and Raymond Beranger	
58	..	..	.	.	Alphonso VIII	..	..	.	
59	.		.	..	.	.	.	.	Alexan⌐
62	.		.	.	.	.	.	Alphonso II.	
65	..	William I	.	..	.	.	..	.	.
80	..		Philip II	..	.	..	..	.	
81	.	..	.	.	.	.		.	Luci⌐
85	.	..	..	..	..		..	.	Urba⌐
87		.	.	.	..		..	.	Gregor⌐
"		..	.	.	..	.	..	..	Cleme⌐
88	..		.	.	Alphonso IX	.	..	..	.
89	Richard I.		.	.	.	.	..	..	.
90	..	.	..	Henry VI	.	.	..	.	
91	..	.	..	.	.	.		.	Celest⌐
94	.		..	..	.	.		Sancho VII	
96	.	.		.		.		Pedro II.	•
98	..	.		Philip	..	.	.		Innoce⌐
,		.		Otho IV	.	.	..	..	.
,	..		.	Frederic II		..	..	..	.
99	John	..	..		.	.	.	..	
13	.	..	.	.	.	.	..	Jayme I	
14	..	Alexander II.			Henry I.	Henry I	.	..	
16	Henry III		.	..	..	..	.	.	Honor⌐
17			.	Ferdinand III	..	.	..	
23			Louis VIII	..	..	..	..	..	
26	..	..	Louis IX.	..	.		..	.
27	.	..		.	.	..	..	..	Grego⌐
30	.			.	.	Ferdinand III	..	..	
34	..		..	..	.	.	Theobald I.	..	.
41	..	..	.	..	..	. .	.	.	Celest⌐
43	..		.	.	.	..	..	..	Innoce⌐
49	.	Alexander III.	.	.	..	..	.	..	

| A.D | ENGLAND | SCOTLAND. | FRANCE | GERMANY. | SPAIN | | | | PAPAL STATES |
					Leon.	Castile	Navarre.	Aragon.	
1250	..	..	.	Conrad IV.	..	..	..	.	.
1252	..	..	..	..	Alphonso X.	..	..	..	
1254	..	..	..	William of Holland.	..	..	.	..	Alexander IV.
1257	..	..	..	Richard duke of Cornwall.	..	..	.	..	..
1261	.	..	..	..	..	..	..	..	Urban IV
1265		..	..	..	..	..	..	..	Clement IV
1270	.	..	Philip III.	..	..	..	Henry I.	..	.
1271	.	..	..	..	..	..	..	..	Gregory X
1272	Edward I	..	..	..	..	..	..	..	..
1273	.	..	..	Rodolph of Hapsburgh.	..	..	..	..	.
1274	.	..	..	..	.	.	John I	..	..
1276	..	..	..	..	..	..	.	Pedro III.	Innocent V.
"	..	..	..	..	..	..	..	..	Adrian V.
"	..	..	..	..	..	..	..	..	John XXI
1277	..	..	..	..	..	..	..	.	Nicolas III
1281	..	.	..	..	..	.	..	..	Martin IV
1284	.	.	..	..	Sancho the Great	Sancho the Great	John L. and Philip Le Bel.	.	..
1285	.	.	Philip IV., Augustus	..	..	..	.	Alphonso III	Honorius IV.
1286		Margaret.	..	..	..	..	..	.	..
1288	.	..	..	..	..	..	..	..	Nicolas IV.
1290	..	Interregnum.	..	..	..	..	..	..	..
1291		.	..	..	..	..	..	Jayme II.	.
1292		John Bahol	..	Adolphus of Nassau.	..	..	..	..	.
1294	..	..	..	..	..	..	..	.	Celestine V
"		..	..	..	..	..	..	..	Boniface VIII
1295	..	..	..	..	Ferdinand IV.	Ferdinand IV.	.	..	.
1296	.	Interregnum	..	..	..	..	..	..	..
1298		..	..	Albert of Austria.	..	..	..	..	..
1303	..	..	..	..	..	..	..	..	Benedict XI.
1305	..	..	..	..	..	..	Louis Hutin	..	Clement V.
1306	..	Robert I.	..	..	..	..	..	..	..
1307	Edward II.	..	..	..	..	..	..	..	.
1308	..	..	..	Henry VII	..	..	..	..	.
1312	.	.	..	.	Alphonso XI.	Alphonso XI.	- ..	..	..
1314	.	..	Louis X King of Navarre	Louis V. and Frederic III.	..	..	..	..	..
1316	..	..	John I.	..	.	..	Philip Le Long.	..	John XXII
"	..	..	Philip V.	..	..	..	..	..	..
1322	..		Charles IV.	.	..	..	Charles I. Le Bel	..	

D	ENGLAND.	SCOTLAND.	FRANCE	GERMANY	SPAIN.				P. ST.
					Leon.	Castile.	Navarre.	Aragon.	
27	Edward III	..	..	..	..	..	..	Alphonso IV	
28	..	..	Philip VI. de Valois.	..	..	..	John and Philip d'Evreux.	..	
29	..	David II	..	..	..	..	.	..	Bened
34	..	..	..	.	..	..	..	..	
36	..	..	..	..	..	..	..	Pedro IV.	
42	..	..	..	..	..	..	..	..	Cleme
46	.	.	..	Charles IV	..	..	..	..	.
49	..	..	..	.	..	..	Charles II	.	.
50	.	..	John II.	.	Pedro IV	Pedro IV.	..	..	.
52	.	..	..	..	..	..	..	..	Innoc
62	..	..	..	..	..	.	..	..	Urb
64	..	.	Charles V.	..	..	..	..	..	.
66	.	..	..	..	Henry II	Henry II.	..	..	
70	..	..	..	..	..	..	..	..	Grego
71	..	Robert II	..	.	..	.	..	..	.
77	..	.	.	.	.	..	..	..	.
87	.	..	..	..	..	..	Charles III.	John I.	.

The table from the reign of Richard II. will be continued in the next volume.

Explanation of certain Abbreviations relative to the several Editions of the Fœdera.

R Signifies The Record Edition

O „ The Original Edition published in Rymer's life-time.

H. „ The Hague Edition.

SYLLABUS

OF

RYMER'S FŒDERA.

WILLIAM I.

Dec. 25, 1066—*Sept* 9, 1087.*

DATE.	SUBJECT
[1069.]	The K. orders the observance of certain laws, here set forth. R. 1. 1.
[1070]	The K. settles the terms upon which wager of battle shall take place between his French and English subjects R 1 2
[1071]	Pope Alexander II exhorts the K to favour abp Lanfrank, to whom he has committed the case of Alfric, the deposed bp. of Chichester, and the dispute between the abp. of York and the bp of Dorchester R. 1 1
[1072.]	The K to Lanfrank and others To cause the restitution of property withheld from the church R. 1 3
[1081-7.]	The K (at the request of abbot Ingulf) confirms the charter of K Edred to the abbey of Crowland. R 1 2
	The K. confirms K. Ethelbert's grant of 24 hides of land to the ch. of S Paul's, London. R. 1. 3.
[1081–7]	The K. confirms to the monastery of S. Pancras, Lewes, the mansion of Walton, co. Norfolk R 1 3.
[1083–7]	The K confirms to Hugh de Coleham and his heirs the grant (by abbot Gilbert) of the office of dapifer and procurator of Westminster Abbey. R 1 2
1084.	The K confirms all the dignities, honours, liberties, and possessions of the monks of S. Cuthbert [Durham]. *Westm* R 1 3
[1085]	The K orders that bps. shall not plead in the hundred court, and that spiritual causes shall be heard where the bp directs. R 1 3
1087.	Foundation Charter of Battle Abbey, granting the manors of Wye, Alsistone, Limenesfield, Hone, Cranmareis, and Bristwoldintone , with the churches of St. Martin, Reading, Culinton, and St Olave, Exeter R, 1. 4.
[1087]	Grants to the abbot of Chertsey of certain liberties and privileges by the K. R 1 2
[1087]	Grant by the K. of eight hides of land at Puriford, in Windsor Forest, to S. Peter's, Westminster. R 1. 4.
1087. Sept 9.	Testament of William I. R. 1. 4.

* The duration of each king's reign, from the Norman Conquest down to the reign of Henry III , is reckoned from his coronation to his death , after that reign from his proclamation to his death.

A

DATE	SUBJECT

WILLIAM II

Sept. 26, 1087—Aug 2, 1100.

[1087–9]	The K grants to S Andrew's, Rochester, the manor of Haddenham (co Bucks), the ch of S Mary, Lambeth, with the vill, and confirms all privileges Confirmed by abp Lanfranc R. 1 5.
[1093]	The K grants to abp Anselm, the abprick of Canterbury, with its liberties and dignities confirms all their liberties to the monks of Ch Ch Cant, and grants the port of Sandwich, with its issues and customs R 1 5
[1093 ?]	The K to Osmond, bp of Salisbury, and the men of Wiltshire. Grant of the manor of Bornham to Battle Abbey *Winchester* R. 1. 5.
[1100]	The K grants to William bp of Durham certain liberties in Clacheston, Olveston, Cilton. Stannncton, Richenehall, Woden, Acle, Hewarde, Presteton, Bradfortun, Esmidehroc, Cul verdeby, Cathon, Wineston, Newchus, Westewic, and in other lands of S Cuthbert, which had been in dispute between the bp. and Robert earl of Northumberland. R. 1 5.

HENRY I.

Aug 5, 1100—Dec. 1, 1135.

[1100]	The K confirms to the monks of S Pancras, Lewes, all previous freedoms and privileges R 1 12.
1101 May 17	Agreement whereby the K undertakes to pay Robert count of Flanders 400 marks of silver annually, in fee, for which the count is bound to defend the person of the K and the realm of England with 500 knights against all persons. *Dover.* R. 1. 6 O. 1 H. 1
[1101.]	The K to pope Paschal [II] Rejoices to hear of his promotion to the papacy, sends the usual present, as his ancestors have done, will continue to render the obedience which his father did, and hopes that he shall not be compelled to withdraw his obedience. R. 1. 8.
[1101]	The K grants a charter of liberties and privileges to his citizens of London *Westm* R 1. 11.
[1101]	The K commands that abp Anselm's men in London have same exemption from customs as they had under Lanfrank. *Westm* R 1 12 The same in Anglo-Saxon
[1101–7]	The K commands that Otho Juvenis shall enjoy the office of the mint, and all other offices, lands, and privileges held by his father in Lisleston. *Arundel* R 1. 9.
	Grant to Richard bp of Rochester R 1 8 *See* A.D. 1249
	The K to the church of Rochester R. 1 9 *See* A D 1177
	The K. to Roger de Flamenville R 1 9 *See* A.D 1174, Dec 25
[1102]	Pope Paschal [II] to the K. Congratulates him on forsaking the impiety of his brother, which has had a terrible punishment, and advises him to abstain from investitures, from which he interdicts all laymen R 1 13
Nov. 23.	Pope Paschal [II] to the K Is glad to hear of the birth of his son William, but cannot consent to his request in regard to investitures, which would be dangerous to both. Exhorts him to recall Anselm *Lateran.* R 1 13
[1103] March 10.	Agreement whereby the K undertakes to pay Robert count of Flanders 400 marks of silver annually, in fee, for which the count is bound to defend the person of the K and the realm with 1,000 knights *Dover* R. 1 7. O 1 4 H 1. 2.
March 12.	The K grants to bp Gundulf and the monks of Rochester certain churches and tithes, viz, Tarenteford, Eilesford, and Mideltun *Rochester.* R 1 10
Dec. 25.	The K. to the bp and barons of Worcestershire Orders for the punishment of coiners and those who pass had money *Westm.* R 1 12
[1106 Sept 28.]	The K to abp Anselm Announces the capture of Robert count of Normandy and 400 knights at Tinchebray R 1 9
[1107]	The K. restores to the church of S Mary and S. Peter, Exeter, the churches of S Petroc, S Stephen, Plinton, Brancton, S. Stephen Exeter, and Culiton, of which it had been deprived by his predecessors R 1 11
[1107–8]	The K confirms all the lands and liberties held by the monks of Ch. Ch. Cant., in the days of Ks Edward and William I. R. 1. 9.

DATE	SUBJECT
[1108]	The K to the bp , dean, and canons of S. Paul's, London Regulations concerning burial of deceased citizens *Farnham* R 1 10
	The K grants to the canons regular of the H. Trinity, London (founded by his Queen Matilda) the rents and privileges herein named *Northampton* R 1 12.
	The K to the sheriff and barons of London Grants to the canons of the H Trinity, London, to hold their men and land of the English knightengild as under Ks. Wilham I. and II. and bp. Leostan. *Westm* R 1 11
	The K to the bp and barons of Worcestershire. That the county and hundred courts should sit as in the time of K Edward. *Reading* R 1. 12
[1108–18]	The K confirms to the ch of the H Trinity at Norwich the grant made to it by Ralph FitzGodric of land in Newton R 1. 11.
[1108–21]	The K (in atonement for the injuries done by his father to the monastery of the H Trinity at Winchester) grants to it a liberty beyond the north gate of the city R 1 10
1111 Aug 8	The K confirms the removal of the see of Somerset from Wells to S Peter's in Bath, to which he gives the hidage of 20 hides of land. *Bishop's Waltham* R. 1. 8.
[1117.] April 5	Pope Paschal [II.] to the K [Thurstan] abp. elect of York, who has been driven from his church, should be restored, and all disputes respecting the two primacies should be referred to the writer. *Benevento* R 1 9
[1124–7]	The K. to Richard bp of London, &c That the canons of the H Trinity, London, hold their soc of the English knightengild, with the land, as under Ks Edward and William I. and II *Woodstock* R 1 11
[1124–6]	The K to the bp of London and men of Essex. Has granted to his goldsmith, Otho, the land of Benfleet with Chilcendic R 1 10
[1100–1125]	The K to Ralph bp of Chichester Has exempted the manor of Alciston (given by his father to Battle Abbey) from all customs, specially for aid for the building of London Bridge and Pevensey Castle. *Burn'.* R 1. 8
1127.	The K confirms the statutes of the council of Westminster *London* R 1. 8
[1130]	Thurstan, abp of York, grants to the men of Beverley all the liberties, &c. which the men of York enjoy R 1 10
[1134]	The K takes under his protection friar Algar and the monks of S. Cuthbert [Durham], with all their possessions, they having sustained injuries from the late bp Ralph [Flambard] *Rouen.* R 1. 11
[?]	The K. confirms to Ralph Peche and his heirs the manor of Chaveley, the gift of Roger FitzRichard *Fecamp*
1135. Dec 11.	Death of Henry I. R 1. 13.

STEPHEN.

Dec 26, 1135—Oct. 25, 1154.

[1136.] March 22.	The K grants the see of Bath to Robert 'its bp , if canonically elected and afterwards approved by those present *Westm* R 1 16
[1136]	The K certifies that he has created Geoffrey de Mandeville hereditary earl of Essex. *Westm* R. 1 18.
	The K to the bp of London The canons of the Holy Trinity to hold, free of all customs, &c., what they have in London by the gift of himself and of Matilda, wife of Henry I *Westm* R 1 17.
[1137]	Pope Innocent [II.] to Norman, prior of Ch Ch within London Takes their possessions in Exeter, Lectun, and the churches of Bix and Tottenham, under his protection. R 1 14 O 17 H 1. 3
1137	The K. to the bp., sheriffs, and barons of London. Has restored to the canons of Trinity Church, London, their land of Smithfield, which Geoffrey earl [of Essex] had converted into vineyard. *London* R 1 17
[1138]	Osbert de Clare, provost of Westminster, to Henry bp of Winchester To promote the canonization of Edward K. and Confessor, whose miracles are notorious R 1. 16
	The K. to Pope Innocent [II.] Solicits the canonization of K Edward, for which purpose he sends Osbert (who has been five years friar of Westminster) with a life of the holy king R. 1. 17.

DATE	SUBJECT
Dec 9	Pope Innocent [II] to the prior and convent of Westminster Prior Osbert has been with him and has urged the canonisation of K Edward, which, however, he is compelled to delay *Lateran* R 1 17.
[1141] July 25	The empress Matilda notifies that she has created Milo of Gloucester earl of Hereford, with various lands and privileges, for services rendered at the battle of Lincoln on 2 Feb. last *Oxford* R 1 14 O 1 8 H 1 3
1144	Bull of Pope Lucius. R 1 14 O. 1 9 H 1 3 *See* A D 1182, June.
1146 March 8	Pope Eugenius [III] confirms to Gervase abbot of Westminster, and his successors, all their possessions and liberties R 1 14
1147 Oct 26	Pope Eugenius [III] to Ralph prior of Ch Ch within London Confirms their possessions and takes them under his protection R 1 15 O 1 11 H 1 4
1148 April 12	Pope Eugenius [III] confirms to William prior of S Giles's, Canwell, their lands, &c. at Canwell, Stikesley, Drayton, Dunton, and Elleford. *Rheims* R 1 15 O 1. 11. H 1. 4
[1153]	Grant by Henry duke of Normandy and count of Anjou to Ralph earl of Chester of various honors, fees, castles, &c in Normandy and England (specified). *Devizes.* R 1 16. O 1 13 H 1 4
1154	Treaty between K Stephen and Henry duke of Normandy respecting the terms on which the latter shall succeed to the crown of England *Westm* R 1 18 O 1. 13 H 1 7.

HENRY II.

Dec 19, 1154—July 6, 1189

[1154] Dec 1	The K grants to William earl of Arundel the castle and honor of Arundel, to be held in fee, with the third penny of the pleas in Sussex whereof he is earl *Westm* R 1 41
Dec 2	The K grants to William son of Robert of Windresor all the lands held in capite of K Henry I by his father *Westm* R 1 46
[1155] Dec]	Pope Adrian [IV] to the K Approves his design of subjugating Ireland, and of paying one penny to S Peter from each house R 1 19 O 1 15 H 1 5
[1157.]	The K intimates that he has made Hugh Bigot earl of Norfolk, with various privileges, and the four manors of Eresham, Walsham, Alvergate, and Ackly R 1 42
	The K confirms and extends their privilege to the citizens of Lincoln and merchants of the county *Nottingham* R 1 40
	The K. confirms the liberties of the burgesses of Nottingham R 1 41.
[1159]	The K confirms to the canons of the H Trinity, London, the soc of the English knight-engild and the land thereto belonging *London* R 1 41
	The K grants to Aubrey de Vere and his heirs the third penny of the pleas of the county of Oxford whereof he is earl *Dover* R 1 41
	The K grants to Ralph son of Solomon three halfpence a day for keeping his garden and embankment in the park of Havering R 1 42.
	The K notifies that he has granted to Roger de Warenguefort the office of usher of his exchequer *Pontaudemer* R 1 42
Sept.	The K. confirms to Robert de Insula and Galliena, his wife, daughter of William Blund, the land in Ixning given by Geoffrey Ridel, archd of Canterb, by the service of one sparrow hawk at Michaelmas *Argentan* R 1 42
Oct 28.	The Emperor Frederic [I] to the K On the death of pope A[drian IV] a double election having taken place, a general council is about to be held at Pavia to settle these disputes, to which the K is invited to send some of his bps *Siege of Crema* R 1 19
[1161 March]	John of Salisbury reports to pope Alexander [III] the facts of the suit between Richard de Ainstey (nephew of Richard de Sacville) and Mabel de Francheville, in which Richard had appealed to the Apostolic See R 1 20. O 1 17 H 1 6
April 16.	Pope Alex [III] to the bp of Chichester &c. To adjudicate in the suit last mentioned. *Anagni* R 1. 19 O 1 18 H 1 6
[1162 May]	Charter to the abp of Canterbury and his successors, that no one shall hunt in the lands of the archbp and church of Canterbury without permission. *Winchester.* R 1. 40.

DATE	SUBJECT
[June]	Tho Becket abp. of Cant. to the K Asks to be allowed to return to his see in peace. R 1 24
1162. July 13	Bulls of Pope Alexander; see A D 1257, July 15, Sept 18, Oct 10 R 1 21.
[1162?]	The K. certifies that he has granted to Ralph Purcell, his usher, the lands of his uncle, Rob Burnell, in England and Normandy. R. 1. 42.
[1163] March 18.	Pope Alex [III] to the K Thanks for promising that his abps, bps, and barons shall attend the approaching conference Paris R 1 44
March 19.	Convention by which Thierri count of Flanders and his son Philip bind themselves (on payment of 500 marks) to aid the K and his son Henry with 1,000 knights, the latter parties finding ships Dover. R 1 22 O 1 23 H 1 8
[1164]	Recognisance of service due to the K by the barons, &c of the count of Flanders Dover R. 1 24 O 1 27 H 1 9
May 26	Pope Alex. [III] confirms to the prior and convent of Snape, the churches of Freston and Bedingfield [co Suffolk] with Brostanhay Tours R. 1 23 O 1 28 H 1 9
June 9.	Pope Alex [III.] to Tho [Becket] abp. of Cant. To proceed to the canonization of his predecessor Anselm Tours R 1 42. •
[1164?]	Tho [Becket] abp of Canterb to the K, urging him to grant liberty to the church R 1 24
1165.	The archbp of Canterbury to the K, asking for an interview R 1 24.
[1165] July 14	Bull of Pope Alex [III] on the perilous condition of the Holy Land, the capture of Antioch, and the danger of Jerusalem, to the rescue of which the faithful are exhorted to hasten Montpellier R 1 21
[1166.]	The K to Pope Alex [III], complaining of his conduct in the dispute between the writer and Becket, and asking him to absolve the persons whom the abp. had excommunicated. R 1. 24 O 1 28. H 1 9.
Dec. 20.	Pope Alex [III] to the K Will dispatch next January plenipotentiaries to decide all ecclesiastical disputes between him and Becket, in the meantime no sentence pronounced by the abp shall be considered valid R 1 25
1169. Nov 4.	Pope Alex to the archbp of Canterbury R 1 26 See A.D 1175, Nov 4
[1170] Feb. 26.	Bull of Pope Alex [III] forbidding [Roger abp of York] to crown [Henry] the K's son, while Becket is in exile. Cisvinarum [?] R 1 25
	Pope Alex [III] to the abp of York, to the same effect as the preceding bull R. 1. 25.
Sept. 26	Pope Alex [III] to Roger abp of York and Hogh bp. of Durham, censuring them for aiding in the coronation of prince [Henry], to the prejudice of the abp of Canterbury, and suspending the abp. of York from his episcopal functions Ferentino R 1 26.
	Pope Alex [III] to the bps of London, Salisbury, Exeter, Chester (Coventry), Rochester, S Asaph, and Llandaff, suspending them from their episcopal dignity for having assisted in the coronation of prince Henry R. 1. 26
[Oct. 12.]	The K to his son Henry Announces his reconciliation with Becket, to whom restoration of his property is to be made Chinon R 1 26
[1171 Jan]	Louis [VII] K of France to pope Alex. [III] Asking for vengeance on the murderers of Becket R. 1 27.
Feb. 7.	Pope Alex. [III.] confirms to Robert parson of Cheddleworth [Bucks] the chapel of Vuelera Frascati R 1 43 O 1 59 H. 1 19
[1172] Sept 20.	Pope Alex [III] to the K Is informed by Christian bp. of Lismore, and others, of the abominable practices which prevail in Ireland, which the K. is exhorted to remove Frascati. R. 1 45.
Sept. 20.	Pope Alex. [III] exhorts the kings and princes of Ireland to persevere in their fealty to the K. Frascati R 1 45
Sept. 20.	Pope Alex [III] exhorting Christian bp of Lismore, papal legate, and the abps. and bps. of Ireland to co-operate with the K. in reducing the Irish to better usages Frascati. R 1 45.
[Sept 28]	The papal legates accept the purgation made by the K (upon certain conditions here specified) from the murder of abp. Becket R 1 27
[1173] March 15.	Pope [Alex III], upon the report of the papal legates, has canonized Becket, and decides that the anniversary of his passion shall be celebrated. Segni. R. 1. 29

DATE	SUBJECT
1173	The K to pope Alex [III] Asks his advice and assistance against his rebellious sons R 1 29　O 1 33　H 1 12
[1173.]	William [II] K. of Sicily to the K Condoles with him on the rebellion of his sons. R 1 29
	Agreement between the K. and Humbert count of Maurienne respecting the marriage of the count's daughter Aalis with prince John　R 1 28.　O 1 33　H 1 11
Oct 26.	Pope Alex [III.] grants to the Knights Templars various privileges　Anagni　R. 1 27 O 1 30　H 1 10
[1174 Sept. 30]	Treaty of peace between the K and his sons Henry, Richard, and Geoffrey. Falaise R 1 30　O 1 37　H 1 12
[1174.]	Notification by the K that he has made peace with the K of France and his own sons R 1 31
[1174]	The K grants to Richard de Lacy and his heirs the hundred of Ongar Beauvoir super Mouram　R 1 46
[1174 Dec 8]	Convention by which William K of Scotland becomes liegeman to K Henry for Scotland and all his other territories　Falaise　R 1 30　O 1 39　H 1 13
[Dec 25]	The K confirms to Roger de Flamenville and his heirs the land which belonged to Utred the son of Gamel, in Wytingham, Troventon, Barton, and Glantedon　Argentan R 1 9
[1175 April]	Reginald bp elect of Bath to the K Intimates the consecration of [Richard] abp. of Canterbury.　R 1 31
1175. [April 1]	The K notifies that he has received his son, the young K Henry, into his favour. Bures　R 1 32
[July]	The K notifies that he has permitted William, the son of Durand the dwarf, (who is about to become a monk,) to convey to his kinswoman, Margaret, wife of Alexander de Barentine, the land of Warnborough and Odiham　Woodstock　R 1 45
[July]	The K notifies that he has confirmed to Roger FitzRomfrid the soc in London given him by Simon earl of Huntingdon　Woodstock　R 1 46
[1175 Oct 6]	Agreement by which Roderic K of Connaught, being permitted to retain his kingdom, consents to become liegeman and to pay tribute to the K　R. 1 31　O 1 41　H. 1 13.
[1176. Jan 25]	The K grants 40 marks a year to the lepers of S Lazarus of Jerusalem. Northampton. R. 1. 40
[1176. March]	The K grants to Richard Ruffus, his chamberlain, Immemere and Immedon, and the wood of Sende　Winchester　R 1 41
[1176 Aug 23]	William [II] K of Sicily to the K on the interchange of oaths for the marriage of Henry's daughter with the writer　Palermo　R 1 32　O 1 42　H 1 14
Aug 25	Covenant between Alphonso K of Castile and Garcia K Navarre to refer their disputes to K Henry　R 1 32　O 1 43　H 1 14
Nov. 4.	Pope Alex [III] to Richard abp of Canterbury. Restricting to the abps of Canterbury the right of crowning and anointing the Ks. of England　Anagni　R 1 26
[1176.]	The K notifies to his subjects in Ireland that he has sent William Fitz Adem to them as his lieutenant, and that he will himself speedily attend to their affairs.　Valognes　R. 1. 36.
[1177] Jan. 27.	Pope Alex [III] takes under his protection the prior and convent of S Margaret of Elenfordesmer, and confirms the grants made to them by Ralph de Cheddlesworth Anagni　R 1 43　O 1 59　H 1 19
Jan 27	Pope Alex [III] confirms to Rob de Chaddlesworth, clerk, the four hides of land in Cheddleworth granted to him by the monks of Abingdon　Anagni　R 1. 43　O 1 60 H 1 20
Feb 2	The K confirms and augments the possessions and privileges of Ch. Ch, Canterbury. Marlborough　R 1 40
Feb.	Settlement of lands, &c, by William K of Sicily, on his queen Joanna, daughter of the K of England　R 1 35　O. 1 52　H 1 17
[March]	Peter of Blois to the K Has been detained by illness at Newport, the K's messengers have returned from Rome, and also those sent by the K of Spain for the settlement of the disputes　R 1 33　O 1 45　H 1. 15
[March]	The allegations and requests of Alfonso K. of Castille　R 1. 33　O. 1 46　H 1 15
[March.]	The allegations and requests of Sancho K of Navarre　R 1. 34　O 1 47　H 1. 15

DATE.	SUBJECT
[1177.]	The K's sentence of adjudication between the Ks. of Castille and Navarre R 1 34. O. 1. 48. H. 1. 15.
	Treaty of peace for ten years between the Ks. of Castille and Navarre. R. 1 34. O 1. 48 H. 1 15
[Sept. 21.]	Convention between the Ks of England and France, by which they pledge themselves to go to the Crusades and mutually to protect each other's dominions. R. 1 35. O 1. 50. H 1. 16.
[1177]	The K requests that favour may be shown to such preachers as collect contributions for the restoration of Rochester Cathedral, lately damaged by fire R. 1 9
[1178] Feb 22.	Pope Alex [III] grants privileges to the clergy of the archdeaconry of Berkshire *Lateran.* R. 1. 43. O. 1 60 H 1 20
[April]	Louis [VII.] K of France notifies that he has taken under his protection all the K's foreign dominions. *Vincennes* R 1 35.
[1179] Aug. 2.	Pope Alex [III.] confirms the peace between the orders of the Knights Templars and Hospitalers *Signi* R 1 44 O. 1. 61. H. 1. 20.
[Dec 25]	The K confirms and augments the possessions and privileges of S Andrew's, Rochester. *Nottingham* R 1 46
[1180] June 28.	Renewal of the treaty of peace between the Ks of England and France. Between *Gisors and Trie.* R 1 36. O 1 53. H. 1 17.
[1180]	The K confirms to William de Humez and his heirs the office of constable, with the lands of Stamford, Leten, Dudintone, Risinberga, Siringeham, Waddon, Wichendon in Norf and in Normandy Meisi, Lalutemire, and Appelgard, held by his father Richard. *Caen* R. 1 43
[1181. Jan 16]	Pope Alex [III], urges the clergy to exhort the faithful to succour the Holy Land. R 1 37.
[1181]	Assize of arms in England R 1 37
[1181?]	The K confirms the privileges of the burgesses of Beverley *Arundel.* R. 1. 40.
[1182 Jan. 6]	Geoffrey, bp elect of Lincoln, [natural] son of the K, to Richard, abp of Canterbury. Resigning the see of Lincoln, at the advice of his father and brothers. R. 1. 37.
[March]	Will of Henry II *Waltham* R 1 47 O. 1 57. H. 1. 19.
[June.]	Pope Lucius [III.] to the friar and monks of St Pancras [Lewes]. Abrogating the usage of the hereditary transmission of churches from father to son *Veletri* R. 1. 14 O 1. 9. H 1 3
1183. May 4.	Pope Lucius [III] to Arnald, master of the Knights Templars Confirming the privileges, &c already granted *Veletri.* R 1 37. O 1 54 H 1 18
[1184. Dec]	Pope Lucius [III] exhorts the K to assist the Holy Land, the desolate condition of which will be reported to him by Heraclius, patriarch of Jerusalem, and the master of the Temple R 1. 38.
[1185]	The convent of Ch Ch, Canterb, to the K. Abp [Baldwin] having wrongfully stated that they hold their lands of him, they trace their tenure from abps Theodore and Dunstan. R 1 44
[1187. Sept]	Aimeric, patriarch of Antioch, reports to the K the siege of Jerusalem, and solicits assistance. R. 1 39
[1188]	The K promises aid to the patriarchs of Antioch and Jerusalem, and Ramund prince of Antioch, he and his son will speedily set out to visit them R. 1. 39
[1188 Jan]	Terric, preceptor of the temple of Jerusalem, to the K. Jerusalem has surrendered to Saladin R. 1. 39.

RICHARD I.

Sept 3, 1189—*April* 6, 1199

1189. Oct 6	The K confirms the possessions and privileges of the Knights Templars throughout his lands. *Westm.* R. 1. 49.
Oct. 10	The K confirms to the lepers of S Lazarus of Jerusalem their annual grant of 40 marks. *Westm.* R. 1. 49.

DATE	SUBJECT
Oct.	Philip [II.] K of France to the K Being about to proceed to Jerusalem, would be glad to know the K's intention in the matter R 1 49. O 1 63. H. 1 20
[1189.] Nov 8	The K grants certain privileges to the Knights Templars. *Westm.* R. 1 74
1189 Nov 25.	The K creates Roger Bigod earl of Norfolk, as Hugh his father was, with various privileges. *Westm.* R 1. 49.
1189 Nov 26.	The K confirms to Rainer bp. of Bath, and his successors, the right of hunting in all Somerset *Canterbury* R 1. 49
1189. Nov. 30.	The K grants to Osbert, brother to Wilham de Longchamp, chancellor and bp elect of Ely, the custody of the K.'s houses in Westminster, and of the gaol of London. *Canterbury* R 1 50
Dec 5	The K restores to Wilham K. of Scotland his castles of Roxburgh and Berwick, and frees him from all obligations extorted from him by Henry II. The boundaries of the two realms are restored to their former condition, and Wilham has restitution of his demesnes in Huntingdon. *Canterbury* R 1 50. O 1 64 H 1 21
Dec. 30.	Articles of agreement between the Ks of France and England preparatory to their expedition to the Holy Land *Nonancourt* R 1 50 O 1 63 H 1 20
[1190 Jan]	Ordinances by the K for the punishment of crimes committed on shipboard during the voyage to Jerusalem *Chinon* R 1 52. O. 1. 65. H 1. 21
[1190 Feb]	Notification by A[ymar] count of Limoges and his son Guy, that they have placed themselves under the protection of the K of France R 1 52
1190 March 14	The K confirms the privileges of the citizens of Winchester *Nonancourt* R 1. 50
March 20	The K ratifies the exchange by which the abp of Canterbury receives from the prior of Rochester certain lands at Lambeth, on which the K. permits him to erect a church in honour of the martyrs SS. Stephen and Thomas *Rouen* R 1 51
March 22	Confirmation by the K of all the privileges granted by his father to the Jews in England and Normandy *Rouen* R 1 51
1190 March 24	Protection for the canons of the ch. of S Bartholomew, London, in the exercise of their fair, as also for those who attend it *Rouen* R 1 51
March 27	The K confirms to Ric Ruffus, his chamberlain, and his heirs, Ymmemere and Ymmedon, and Yarmsden, with their wood of Sendes *Lions* R 1 51
June 24	The K confirms to David, brother of the K. of Scotland, and to the men of the honor of Huntingdon, all the liberties, &c enjoyed by K David, his grandfather, and Malcolm, his brother, in the time of K Henry I *Tours* R 1 48
June 25	The K. confirms to Wm de Humez and his heirs the office of constable, with certain lands, &c. (as at p 7). *Tours.* R 1 48
June 27	The K notifies that he has confirmed to Wm earl of Arundel and his heirs the castle and honor of Arundel, with the third penny of the pleas of Sussex, of which he is earl *Montrichard* R 1 48
July 1.	The K. quitclaims for himself and his heirs the payage hitherto levied on the crusaders in the town of Rochester *Donzy* R 1 48
[July.]	The K. orders his subjects in England to be obedient, during his absence, to his chancellor [W de Longchamp], bp of Ely. R 1 52
[Nov]	Treaty of friendship between the K. and Tancred K of Sicily, preliminary to a marriage between Arthur duke of Brittany and Tancred's daughter. R 1 52 O. 1 66 H 1. 21.
[Nov]	Oath for the observance of the above treaty R 1 53. O 1 67. H. 1. 22
Nov. 11.	The K to Pope Clement [III.] Has executed the above treaty. *Messina* R 1. 53 O 1. 68 H 1 22
1191 [March]	Convention between the K and Philip [II] K of France respecting the marriage of the latter and the settlement of his issue, he undertaking to pay 10,000 marks *Messina.* R 1 54 O 1 69 H 1 22
March 27.	The K confirms to the men of Rye and Winchelsea their privileges as under Hen. II , they finding two ships to complete the 20 ships of Hastings *Messina* R 1. 53.
Oct. 1.	The K to N[icolas, his chaplain]. Narrates his exploits since the base departure of the K of France, his expedition to Joppa, the defeat of Saladin, his own wound, and his advance on Jerusalem *Joppa* R. 54.

DATE	SUBJECT
Oct. 1.	The K to [Henry] abbot of Clairvaux. Narrates his exploits since his arrival in the Holy Land, in which he cannot continue longer than next Easter, unless aided by the preaching of the abbot *Joppa.* R 1 54
1192 May 14.	John lord of Ireland and count of Mortain grants to the citizens of Dublin certain metes and liberties *London* R 1 55
Dec. 28.	The emperor Henry [VI] to Philip [II] K of France. Narrating the shipwreck, pursuit, and capture of K Richard. *Rithenca* [?]. R 1. 55 O 1 70 H 1 23.
1193 Jan. 11	Pope Celestine [III] to the abps and bps of England. Exhorting to unity and forbidding tournaments during the calamities of the Holy Land. *Rome.* R 1 56
Jan	Agreement by which John earl of Mortain surrenders to his lord, Philip [II] K of France, certain lands in Normandy and France, without whose leave he promises that he will not make peace with his brother K Richard *Paris* R 1 57 O 1 85. H 1 27.
	Q Eleanor to Pope Celestine [III] Praying him to procure the release of her son K. Richard R 1 56 O. 1 72 H 1 23
	Q Eleanor to Pope Celestine [III] Censures his delay, and recounts the evil deeds of the emperor R. 1 58 O 1 76 H 1 25
	Q Eleanor to Pope Celestine [III] Renews her complaints, and can no longer trust the promises of his cardinals R 1 57 O 1 74. H 1 24
1193	Walter abp of Rouen to Hugh bp of Durham It is too true that the K is prisoner, as will appear by the letters of the emperor to the K of France, a copy of which he encloses Asks for a meeting at Oxford to deliberate on the K's release, about which the bp of Bath has already had an interview with the emperor R 1 59
	Peter of Blois to the abp of Mentz. To use his influence for the deliverance of the K R. 1. 59 O 1 78 H 1 25.
April 19	The K to the Q his mother, and his subjects Gives directions how the money necessary for his ransom (70,000 marks) is to be raised and transmitted *Hagenau.* R 1 60. O 1 80 H. 1 26
April 19.	The emperor Henry [VI] to the English nobles. The K. and he are on good terms. *Hagenau.* R 1 60
[June 25]	Contract between the K and the emperor respecting the terms of the payment of the ransom of the former R 1 62 O 1 84 H 1. 27
1193 July 8	Treaty of peace between the K. and Philip [II.] K. of France. *Meduana.* R. 1. 61. O 1 81 H 1 26
Sept 15	The Old Man of the Mountain to Leopold duke of Austria. Vindicating K Richard from the murder of the Marquess of Montferrat *Castle of Messiat* R 1 61. O 1 71 H 1 23
[Sept 15]	The Old Man of the Mountain certifies to Christendom that K Richard is guiltless of the murder of the Marquess of Montferrat R 1 62
Sept 22.	The K to Hubert abp of Canterbury The emperor has fixed a day for his liberation, and another for his coronation as K of Provence *Spires* R 1 62 O 1 83 H. 1 27
Dec 20	The emperor Henry [VI.] to the nobles of England To the same effect as the last instrument *Theallusa* [?] R 1 62. O. 1 83 H 1 27.
1194. April 17.	The K. renews to William K of Scotland and his heirs the allowances and privileges enjoyed by his ancestors on visiting the English court *Winchester* R 1 62. O 1. 87. H 1 28
April 20	The K confirms to Adam and his heirs (cook to Elianor, his mother) all his land at Old Saleshild. *Winchester* R 1 63
[April]	Charter of liberties to the citizens of Lincoln on the payment of 180l. per ann. Lincoln tale *Winchester* R 1 52
May 2	Charter of liberties to the burgesses of Portsmouth *Portsmouth* R 1 63
May 5.	Charter of liberties to the citizens of Norwich, on the payment of 108l. per ann Norwich tale. *Portsmouth* R 1 63
June 6	Pope Celestine [III] to the bp of Verona To cause the duke of Austria to send home the English hostages, to restore the money received as the K's ransom, to command the duke to remain in the holy war as long as the K was in captivity, and in case of refusal to pronounce excommunication *Rome* R 1 64 O 1 88 H 1 28
July 22	The K to Hubert abp of Canterbury Has taken Taillebourg, Marsillac, the city of Angouleme, &c , 300 knights, and 40,000 men-at-arms *Angoulême* R 1 64
July 23.	Truce for one year between the Ks. of France and England Between *Verneuil and Tilliers* R 1 64

DATE	SUBJECT
Aug 22	The K to the abp of Canterbury Fixes the localities within which tournaments may be held in England, and the fees and regulations for the same ap *Villam Episopi* R 1 65
1195	Hubert abp of Canterbury receives from the prior and convent of Rochester the manor of Lambeth in exchange for that of Darent, &c R 1 65
April 7	The K. confirms the above exchange *Isle of Andely.* R. 1 65
Sept. 28.	Convention of Iscoudan between the Ks of France and England *Between Gaillon and Vaudreuil.* R 1 66 O 1 91. H 1 29
1196 [March.]	Hubert abp of Cant to the officials of the abp of York. Has received a bull from Pope Celestine [III] requiring that all who have vowed to join the crusades either do so immediately or provide substitutes. R. 1 66
April 27.	Pope Celestine [III] forbids the prior of S Pancras, Lewes, to promise any benefice before it is actually vacant *Lateran* R 1 66
1197. July 14	The K orders the removal of all kidels and wears from the Thames *Isle of Andely* R 1 67.
Sept. 30.	The K to Philip bp of Durham Has defeated [Philip II] K of France, near Gisors. *Dangu* R 1 68 O 1. 96 H 1 31
[Oct]	League, offensive and defensive, between the K and Baldwin count of Flanders against the K of France R 1 67 O 1 94 H 1. 30
Oct 17	Exchange of lands, towns, &c in Normandy between K Richard and Walter abp. of Rouen *Rouen* R 1 68 O 1 96 H 1 31
1198 May 30.	Pope Innocent [III] informs the duke of Austria that he shall be excommunicated, and his land placed under interdict, unless he refunds the sums extorted by his father from K Richard for his ransom R 1. 69 O 1 102 H 1 32.
May 31	Pope Innocent [III.] directs the abp of Magdeburg to compel the duke of Swabia (the late emperor's heir) to make a like restitution to that last mentioned, and under similar penalties *Rome* R 1 69 O 1 102 H. 1 33.
May 31	Pope Innocent [III.] to the K Refers to the orders given in the previous letter, and to the kings of Navarre and France, all in the K's favour *Rome* R 1 69. O 1 98. H 1. 33
1198 June 3	Pope Innocent [III.] encourages Walter abp of Rouen to depend upon his protection while supporting his ecclesiastical jurisdiction against the Ks of France and England. *Rome.* R 1 70 O 1 103 H 1 33
June 29	Treaty, offensive and defensive, between Philip K of the Romans, and Philip [II] K. of France, against the K and his allies *Worms.* R. 1 70 O. 1. 107 H 1 34.
July 11.	The K notifies that he has accepted the resignation of Hubert abp of Canterbury as guardian of the realm, and appoints in his stead Geoffrey FitzPeter [*Château Gaillard*]. R 1 71
[July 12]	The nobles of Germany certify to Pope Innocent [III] that they have appointed Otho to the rule of the empire, whose coronation they solicit R 1 71. O 1 105. H 1 34.
Aug. 22	The K. confirms his charter (dated 12 Dec in the 6 year of his reign) to Alan Basset and his heirs of the gift, by Walter de Dunstanville, of the manor of Winterburn *Roche Aurival.* R 1 67
[Sept]	Pope Innocent [III] exhorts the Ks of France and England to make peace, and to embark for the Holy Land. R 1 72 O 1 100 H 1 32.
[Sept]	Pope Innocent [III] commissions Peter, cardinal and apostolic legate, to arrange a peace, or at least a truce for five years, between the Ks of France and England R 1 72. O. 1 103 H 1 33.
Sept. 17.	Pope Innocent [III.] recites and confirms the K's assurance that the money advanced by his subjects for his ransom shall not be held as a precedent *Perugia* R. 1. 71. O 1 104 H 1 33
Nov 20.	Pope Innocent [III] solicits the K to aid the monks of Canterbury in the matter of the chapel at Lambeth *Lateran* R 1. 73. O. 1 108 H. 1. 35.
[Nov]	Oath of [Odo] duke of Burgundy that he will not aid the K, nor any of his blood, against the K of France *Vincennes.* R 1. 71
Dec 29	Charter of privileges granted by Otho duke of Aquitain to the men of Oleron, with the consent of the K his uncle *Benaon* R 1 71 O. 1 103 H 1 34
1199 March 26.	The Pope [Innocent III] confirms the truce between the Ks of France and England *Lateran* R. 1 73 O 1 109 H 1. 35

DATE	SUBJECT
March 30.	[Pope Innocent III. to the Papal Legate]. Notifies that he has confirmed the above truce. *Lateran.* R 1 73 O. 1. 109 H 1 35.
April 1.	The same to the same Praises him for having arranged the above truce, and asks him to urge forward sluggish crusaders *Lateran* R 1 73 O. 1. 110. H. 1 35
April 6.	Testament of K. Richard. R. 1. 74.

JOHN.

May 27, 1199—Oct 19, 1216 *

1199 June 7	The K notifies that he has granted to Wm de Ferrers earl of Derby and his heirs the third penny of all the pleas in the county of Derby. *Northampton* R 1 75.
June 7.	The K settles what fees shall henceforth be payable to the great seal upon charters of new feoffment of land, simple confirmation and simple protection *Northampton* R 1.75.
June 17	Charter of Liberties to the city of London *Shoreham.* R. 1. 76 H 1. 36.
July.	Eleanor, the Q Mother, confirms a charter of liberties to the men of Oleron. *Andely.* R 1 75 O 1 111 H 1 36
July.	Eleanor, the Q Mother, confirms a charter of liberties to the commoners of Oleron. *Andely.* R. 1.'75 O 1 111. H. 1 36
July 23.	The K confirms the above charters granted by the Q Mother to Oleron. *Verneul.* R 1 77 O. 1 112 H 1 36
Aug 18	Treaty by the K. and Reginald count of Boulogne against France. *Roche Andelys.* R 1 77 O. 1 114 H. 1 36
[Aug.]	Treaty by the K and [Baldwin] count of Flanders against France. R. 1 77 O. 1 114 H 1 36
Aug 25	The K promises to pay to certain merchants of Placentia 2,125 marks, lent by them, at the request of K. Richard, to promote the interests of K Otho in the court of Rome *Rouen* R. 1 78 O 1 115 H 1 37
Aug 30.	The K confirms all the possessions and liberties of the knights hospitallers. *Roche Andely* R 1 71.
1199 Aug 30	The K confirms the testament of [Hubert] abp of Canterbury *Rouen* R. 1. 78
[Aug]	The K grants to the Q Mother the whole of Poitou for life. R. 1 77. O 1. 113. H 1 78
Sept. 29	The K. confirms to the abp of Canterbury and his successors three moneyers and three mints in Canterbury. *Le Mans.* R 1 78
Dec 28	The K confirms to Walter Bustard the serjeantry of the royal chapel, &c *Caen.* R 1 79
1200 Jan 28.	Notification by Hugh Brun count of Marche and Ralph count of Eu that they have become the K.'s liegemen *Caen.* R 1 79 O. 1 116. H. 1. 37.
Jan. 28.	The K notifies that he accepts the above proffer of allegiance. *Caen.* R. 1 79. O 1 116 H 1. 37
[Jan]	The K. notifies the proffer of allegiance by Amaury viscount of Thouars. R 1 79. O 1 117. H 1 37
Jan. 30.	The K. to the envoys of Castille and Toledo Credence for three persons. *Carentan* R 1 76 O 1 113 H 1. 36
Jan 30	The K orders that the envoys of the K. of Portugal be well treated by his clergy. *Carentan.* R. 1. 76. O 1 113 H. 1. 36.
Jan 30.	Mandate to the same effect addressed to his bailiffs *Carentan* R 1 76 O 1 113. H 1 36.
May [16]	Treaty between the Ks of England and France respecting the settlement of their allies, boundaries, &c. *Guleton.* R. 1. 79. O. 1. 117 H 1. 37.
1200 June 22.	Bull of Innocent [III] R 1. 80. O 1 119 H 1 38 *See* A D 1245, June 22.
June 25	Safe-conduct for the viscount of Limoges to come to the K. *Chinon* R 1 80

* King John's regnal years are calculated from Ascension Day to Ascension Day.

DATE	SUBJECT
1200 Aug 3	Bulls of Innocent [III] R 1 80 O 1 120. H. 1. 38. *See* A D 1245, Aug 3.
Aug. 16.	The K grants to William Marshall earl of Pembroke the privilege of giving the pastoral staff of Nutley Abbey, within his fee *La Reole.* R. 1 81
Oct 23.	Safe-conduct for Griffin, son of Rees, coming to the K *Chelsworth.* R 1.81. O 1.120 H 1 39
Oct. 30.	Safe-conduct for [William] K. of Scotland, coming to the K. *Gloucester.* R. 1. 81 O 1 112 H. 1. 39
Nov 7	Confirmation of metes and liberties formerly granted to the citizens of Dublin. *Upton.* R. 1 82
1201 Jan 12	Pope Innocent [III] confirms to the canons of H Trinity, London, their possessions and privileges R 1 82 O 1 122 H 1 39
Jan. 12.	The K confirms to William de Braose the honor of Limeric, to be held by the service of 60 knights *Lincoln* R 1 83.
March 17	The K confirms to William de Ferrers earl of Derby the service of William de Gresley of the land of Drakelaw, held of the King *Barnwell* R 1 83.
[March 19]	Amaury count of Thouars to the K Q. Eleanor is ill at Fontevrault, and desires to see him speedily R 1 81 O. 1 121. H 1 39.
[March 19]	Q Eleanor to the K Amaury count of Thouars having visited her in her sickness, she has gained him to the K's party, which he will join on his arrival here *Fontevrault.* R 1 81 O. 1. 122 H 1 39
July 11	Form of peace between the K and Lewelin ap Jorweth and his nobles. R 1 84. O 1 123 H 1 39
Aug 2.	Assignment of dower by the K to Q Berengaria, widow of K Richard, viz, 1,000 marks per ann *Chinon* R 1. 84 O 1 128 H 1 40
Aug 16	The K grants Andrew de Montfort, burgess of Rochelle, and his heirs, to Aymar count of Angoulême, his father in-law *Verneuil* R 1 84. O 1. 125 H 1 40
Sept. 26	The K directs W Ornald, master of the Knights Templars of Aquitaine, to send to the count of Angoulême certain letters of agreement between the count and the writer *Verneuil* R 1 84 O 1 125 H 1 40
Oct 14.	Johel of Mayenne notifies that he has taken the oath of fealty to the K. *Chinon.* R 1. 84. H 1 125 H 1 40
[Oct]	Similar notification by Gui de Châtillon. R 1 85. O 1 126 H 1 140
Oct 14	Saucho [VII] K of Navarre notifies that he will aid the K against all persons, the K. of Morocco alone excepted *Chinon* R 1 85 O 1 126 H 1 40
Oct. 29	Charter of liberties for the stannaries of Cornwall and Devon *Bonnerville-sur-Touques.* R 1 85.
1201. Nov 4.	The K (being in confederacy with the K of Navarre) forbids the citizens of Bayonne to hold intercourse with the subjects of the K of Castile *Seez* R 1 85 O 1 127. H 1 41.
1202 Jan 30	The K orders that the barons of Brittany shall suffer the will of the late countess Constance to be carried out *Loches* R 1 85 O 1 127 H 1 41
Feb 5	Treaty between the K and Sancho K. of Navarre against the Ks of Castile and Anjou. *Angoulême* R 1 86
Feb 18	Safe-conduct for Ysmael, the messenger of the infanta Constance, sister of the K. of Navarre *Chinon* R 1 86 O 1 128 H 1 41
March 27.	The K summons his nephew Arthur to be at Argentan in the octaves of Easter to do homage. *Andely* R 1 86. O. 1 128 H 1. 41
March 27	Mandate that master Andrew (clerk to the K's nephew Lewis) may enjoy his rents in Dieppe *Andely.* R 1 86. O 1 128 H 1 41
April 18.	The K to the mayor and citizens of London. Recommending that Isenbert, master of the schools at Saintes (who has lately built bridges at Saintes and Rochelle) be employed to erect London Bridge *Molineux.* R 1 83
May 4	Licence for Hubert abp of Canterbury and his successors to hold great assizes concerning their gravelkind lands in their court *Roche Aurival* R 1 83
May 4.	Licence to the above to convert into knight's fees all the lands held in gavelkind by the men of the see of the church of Canterbury *Roche-Aurival* R 1 83
May 11.	The K. notifies that the abp of Canterbury, &c will report to the English the proud conduct of the K of France, and how he has broken the peace. *Pont de l'Arche* R. 1. 84 O 1 128 H 1 39

DATE.	SUBJECT
1202. May 27	The K. summons the knights of Flanders, Hainault, and Brabant to enter his service, and to give credence to the report of Simon de Haveret *Gournay* R 1 86, O. 1. 129. H. 1. 41
July 7.	The K asks a loan of money from the Cistercian abbots of the province of York, to be employed against the K of France *Bonport.* R. 1. 86. O. 1. 129. H. 1 41.
July 22	The K permits his mother Q Eleanor to make a will *Rouen* R 1 86
Sept. 8.	The K asks a subvention from the clergy of the province of Canterbury to aid the appointment of his nephew Otho as emperor *La Suse* R 1 87 O 1 130 H. 1. 41.
Nov. 2.	Truce between the K and the viscount of Thouars *Chinon.* R. 1. 87 O 1. 131. H 1 42.
Nov. 6.	The K notifies that he has received the viscount of Beaumont into his favour *Saumur.* R. 1. 87 O 1 131. H 1 42
Dec 11.	The K asks a contribution from the English Cistercians to be employed against the K. of France *Argentan* R 1 87 O 1 132 H 1 42
Dec 26.	Credence by the K for the traders about to arrange a meeting between him and the K of France *Caen.* R. 1 87 O 1 32 H 1. 42.
1203. July.	Odo duke of Burgundy notifies that he has counselled his lord the K of France to make neither peace nor truce with the K of England *Vaudreul.* R 1 89
July 29.	The K to the mayor and barons of London. Is surprised that they permit the Jews in London to be injured, as they are under the K's protection. Throughout the rest of England they are well used. Henceforth the K will require their blood at the hands of the mayor. *Montfort* R 1 89
Aug. 13	The K directs that all who have rents and tenements in Jersey and Guernsey shall give one fifth thereof for one year to support the soldiers sent for their defence. *Alençon* R 1 89.
Nov. 27.	The K requires the barons of Gascony and Perigord to hold themselves in readiness for military service *Morfaruille* R 1 89
1204 Jan. 10.	The K to his brother Geoffrey abp of York At the request of the pope has granted the bpk of Carlisle to the abp of Ragusa. *Marlborough* R 1 90. O. 1 135 H. 1. 43
Feb 10	The K requests aid from the clergy of Ireland against the K of France *Nottingham* R 1 90 O 1. 16 H 1 43
[Feb]	Otho K of the Romans to the K his uncle In order to assist him against his enemies, will make a truce for one or two years with his relative the duke of Swabia R 1 88 O 1 133 H 1 42
March 18	The K (at the petition of Albrida de Rumenel, who was the wife of Wm de Jarpunville) grants to Thos FitzBernard the marshalsea of the royal birds *Woodstock* R 1 90
1204 April 11.	The K requests the citizens of Cologne to continue their aid towards his nephew Otho, and has taken them under his protection. *Winchester.* R. 1. 88. O 1 133. H 1. 42.
April 15.	Assize of bread at Winchester, regulations as to weight, price, &c *Freemantle* R. 1 88
April 15	General pardon for all prisoners, excepting prisoners of war, prisoners sent from Normandy into England, and Jews imprisoned by the K *Freemantle* R 1 90
1204 April 30.	Bull of Pope Innocent [III] R 1 91 O 1 137. H 1 42 *See* A D 1250, April 30
May 5.	Assignment of dower to Q. Isabella in England and Normandy for life. *Porchester.* R. 1. 88. O 1 134 H. 1. 43.
May 18	The K disafforests the whole of Devonshire, excepting Dartmouth and Exmoor *Winchester* R 1 89
Aug 31	The K gives directions as to the settlement of two parts of Connaught, which have been ceded to him by the K. thereof, who will also pay 100 marks per ann. for the other third. *Geddington.* R. 1. 91
Nov 24.	The K. to Pope Innocent [III], requesting that the justiciary of England, Geoffrey FitzPeter, may delay his pilgrimage to Jerusalem for four or five years. *Winchester.* R. 1 91 O. 1. 137 H 1 44.
1205 Jan. 13.	The K permits Alice countess of Warwick to remain a widow as long as she pleases, and to have the custody of her children and a reasonable dower *Bishop's Sutton.* R. 1 91.
Feb 8.	The K takes into his protection Reginald K of Man, his lands and men *Woodstock* R 1 91.

DATE.	SUBJECT.
1205 Feb 28	The K. confirms the privileges of the men of Oleron. *Lexington* R 1. 92. O. 1. 138. H. 1 44
April 3	The K to the sheriff of Rutland, &c Arrangements as to the finding and payment of troops for the defence of the realm against invasion *Winchester* R 1 92
[April]	The K to Hugh Constable of Chester and the others of the garrison of Andely. To hold the castle to the uttermost R 1 90 O 1 136. H 1 43
May 2.	The K notifies to the barons of Ireland that he has granted the land of Ulster to Hugh de Lacy *Windsor.* R. 1. 91.
May 29	The K notifies that he has granted to Geoffrey FitzPeter earl of Essex the honor and castle of Berkhamstead *Winchester* R 1 93
May 29	Pope Innocent III sends to the K a gift of four rings set with precious stones, the emblematical meaning of which is here stated *Roma.* R 1 93 O 1 139 H 1 44
June 23	The K notifies that he has given to his salter two messuages in Lincoln and London, formerly belonging to Jews *Dorchester* R 1 93
Oct 7	The K notifies that he has granted to Walter de Gray his chancery for life *Nottingham.* R 1 93
Dec 27	The K (at the request of his nephew Otho) pardons Hugh de Burnay, who may pass through England either to Jersey or Rochelle on the K's service. *Marlborough* R 1 93. O 1 139 H 1 44
Dec 28	The K appoints Michael Beleth to be his hereditary butler, and confirms his lands. *Marlborough* R. 1. 93.
1206 Feb 8	Safe-conduct for R[eginald] K of the Isles, coming to the K *Salisbury* [?] R. 1. 94. O 1 140 H 1 44
March 25.	The K to Saher de Mauleon To see that the monks of S Mary de Charron shall have the 50*l* rent in Poitou given them by his nephew Otho *Lambeth.* R 1 94. O 1 140 H 1 45
March 27	Safe-conduct for Q Berengaria to come to the K in England *Otford* R 1 94 O 1. 140 H 1 45
April 20	The K grants to Richard Flamenge the custody of the lands and the wardship and marriage of the heirs of Richard de Grenville, and the marriage of their mother Gundreda *Winchester* R 1 92
May 8	The K. requests the bps of S Asaph, &c to affix their seals to four letters already sealed by the bps of London, &c *Porchester* R 1 92 O. 1. 138. H 1 44.
[Sept]	Safe-conduct for Eleanor Q of Castile, the K's sister, coming to him. R. 1. 94. O 1 141 H 1 45
Oct. 26	Terms of the truce for two years between the K. and the K of France. *Thouars* R. 1 95 O 1 141 H 1 45
Dec 21.]	Pope Innocent [III] confirms the right of the monks of Canterbury to elect an abp. without the K's interference. *Rome* O 1 95
1207 Jan 5.	The K confirms to Josce, a priest of the Jews of London, the priesthood of all the Jews in England for life *Canterbury.* R 1 95.
Feb. 17	Regulations respecting the rate at which all lay fees throughout England are to be taxed (according to the decision of the council of Oxford) for the defence of the realm. *Northampton* R 1 96
Feb 20]	The K pledges himself to repay (on the production of these letters) the 500 marks lent to his messengers going to the court of Rome *Rockingham* R. 1. 95
March 10.	The K confirms the partition between Simon de Montford earl of Leicester and Saher de Quency earl of Winchester of the lands and honours in England and Normandy lately belonging to Robert earl of Leicester. *Hallingbury.* R 1 96.
May 8	The K confirms to the burgesses of Cambridge their ancient possessions and privileges. *Lambeth* R 1 94
May 26.	The K forbids the clergy to meet in council at S Albans, nor shall they impose Rome-scot, nor hold any assembly until they have discussed matters with the K. *York* R. 1. 94.
Aug 7.	The K thanks Alfonso K of Leon for having entered into a treaty with him *Woodstock* R. 1 96 O 1 142 H 1. 45
Sept 3	Pope Innocent [III] requires the K to show cause why he has not paid the dower of Q Berengaria *Viterbo* R. 1 97 O 1 142 H. 1 45.
Sept. 6.	The K. fixes the ransom of Amphulsus Tilhs at 10,000 marks and 10 horses worth 30 marks each *Holwell-in-Blachmore* R 1. 98 O 1 146. H. 1. 47.

DATE.	SUBJECT.
1207. Nov 8	The K confirms to Wm de Barry the cantreds of Cork given to his father Philip by Robert FitzStephen. *Woodstock.* R 1 97.
[Nov]	Pope Innocent [III] censures the K for his obstinate rejection of Stephen [Langton] abp elect of Canterbury *Lateran* R 1. 97. O 1 143 H 1 46
[Nov]	Adelaide countess of Holland entreats the K to procure the liberation of her daughter, the countess of Los R 1 97 O 1 144. H 1. 46.
[Nov.]	Tho bp of Utrecht and count Odo de Benethen certify the marriage of the daughter of the countess of Holland R. 1 98 O 1. 145 H 1 46
[Nov]	Louis count de Los certifies that he has become the K's liegeman, and will defend him and his nephew Otho K of the Romans. R 1 98. O. 1. 145 H 1. 46
[Nov]	Walter Birtan certifies that he has become surety for the fidelity of Louis count de Los towards the K. R 1 98 O 1 146 H 1 46
Dec 9	The K notifies that he has received from Germany a great crown, a sceptre, a golden rod with a dove at the top, &c, for the coronation R 1. 99
1208 [Jan]	The Pope exhorts the nobles of England to induce the K to act with prudence in the matter of the abp. of Canterbury R 1. 99 O 1 147 H 1 47.
Jan. 21.	The K notifies that he is ready to obey the Pope in the matter of the church of Canterbury, saving the royal right, dignity, and liberties. *Lambeth.* R. 1. 99.
Jan 23.	The K notifies that he has committed the custody of Ch. Ch, Canterbury, with its manors, &c, to certain persons here named *Westm* R 1 99
March 6	Safe-conduct for Peter Girard coming into England from Henry emperor of Constantinople. *Bristol* R. 1 99. O 1 148 H 1 47
March 8	Safe-conduct for the chancellor of the K of Castille coming into England *Devizes* R 1. 100 O 1 149 H 1. 47
March 14	The K requires the men of Kent to give credence to what Reginald de Cornhul will tell them respecting the terms upon which Stephen de Langton has been received as abp. of Canterbury *Winchester* R 1 100
March 18	The K confirms to the burgesses of Yarmouth their ancient rights and liberties *Marlborough* R 1 100
March 18.	The K notifies that he has made arrangements for seizing the lands and possessions of such of the clergy in the bprick of Lincoln as refuse to celebrate divine service after the Monday after Palm Sunday *Clarendon* R 1 100
April 5.	The K orders that the bprick of Winchester, &c, taken from Peter de Rupibus, bp thereof, by reason of the late interdict, be restored to him. *Waverley* R. 1. 100.
[April 5]	Similar writ for the bp of Norwich, in regard to the royalty of his see, but earl Roger shall have the rents, &c of the clerks and religious houses for the K's use R 1 100
April 8.	The K requests his mariners and merchants to aid the barons of the Cinque Ports in arresting all ships found on the seas, and conveying them to England *Ludgarshal.* R. 1 96
April 11	The K has caused proclamation to be made that if any one injure religious persons or clerks, he shall be hung on the nearest oak *Marlborough* R. 1. 100.
May 27.	Eleanor countess of Brittany requests the bp of Nantes, &c to proceed into England to her uncle the K, as their visit will be much to her advantage *Salisbury* R 1 101. O. 1. 149 H 1. 48
May 29.	Safe-conduct for the envoys of the countess of Brittany aforesaid. *Southampton* R 1 101 O 1. 149 H 1 48
May 31.	Pope Innocent [III.] grants an indulgence to those who attend annually on the feast of S. Edward at the church at Westminster *Assisi* R 1 101 O 1. 150. H 1 48.
[June 19]	Letters of credence for the bp of Ferns, &c. going from the K to the kings and nobles of Ireland R 1 101. O 1 150 H 1 48.
Sept. 11.	The K grants to Geoffrey FitzPeter earl of Essex, Queenhithe, London, paying yearly 30l to the K., and 60s to the lepers of S. Giles, London. *Aston* R. 1. 102
Sept 23.	The K grants to the men of Kingston the vill thereof in fee farm, paying yearly 50l. of silver *Taunton* R 1. 102
Oct. 8.	Agreement between the K. and Wenhuwen, the son of Owen de Keveliac, respecting the liberation of the said Wenhuwen *Shrewsbury* R 1 101 O 1 150 H 1. 48.
Dec. 25.	The K. has pardoned Lewellin [prince of Wales] the injuries by him committed on Wenhuwen while in the K's custody, and will regard him as his son[-in law] *Bristol.* R. 1. 102. O. 1 151. H. 1. 48.

DATE	SUBJECT.
1209. [Jan.]	Otho K of the Romans asks his uncle the K. to accept Stephen [Langton] as abp. of Canterbury. R. 1 103
Jan 21	Pope Innocent [III] to the K To pay her dower, withheld for more than eight years, to Q Berengaria *Lateran* R 1 102 O. 1. 152 H 1. 49
March 24.	The K to the nobles of Germany The bearers will signify the decision of the council in England, which he will send to their lord, his nephew Otho *London* R. 1 103 O 1 153. H 1 49
March 24.	The K notifies that he has paid (among other sums) 1,000 marks to the duke of Saxony. *Lambeth* R 1. 103 O. 1. 154. H. 1. 49.
March 24	Letters of protection for Conrad de Wilra, seneschal of K Otho, and all his lands, &c , in England *London* R 1 103 O 1. 154 H 1 49
Aug 7	William K. of Scotland engages to pay to the K 15,000 marks within two years. *Northampton* R. 1. 103. O 1 155 H. 1 50
1212	William K. of Scotland gives the marriage of his son Alexander, within the next six years, to the K , and promises that in the event of the K.'s death they both will be loyal to prince Henry R 1. 104.
April	Louis, eldest son of the K of France, declares that if he is crowned K. of England he will take an oath from all who do homage to him that they will do no harm to the realm of France *Soissons* R 1 104
May 4	The K will lend 3,000 marks for a year to Margaret countess of Flanders *Lambeth*. R 1 105 O 1. 157 H 1 50
May 4	The K informs [Amaury] viscount of Thouars that the emperor [Otho] has sent the count of Boulogne into England, whose homage the K will receive on Ascension Day, in London *Lambeth* R 1 104 O 1. 156 H 1 56
	Reginald count of Boulogne notifies that he had done homage to the K , and that he will make neither peace nor truce with the K of France nor his son Louis R 1. 104. O 1 156 H 1 150
May 4	The K promises that he will make neither peace nor truce with the K of France nor his son Louis without the count of Boulogne *Lambeth* R 1 105 O 1. 158 H 1 59.
May 4.	The K will gladly arrange the terms upon which a league may be effected between himself and Ferrand count of Flanders *London* R 1 105 O 1 152 H 1 50
May 16	Reginald K of the Isles notifies that he has become the K's liegeman *Lambeth* R 1 105 O 1 159. H 1 51
May 23	To the mayor of Angoulême and others Encloses copy of a letter from the emperor Otho , will soon have good news to forward *Lambeth* R 1. 105 O 1 159 H 1. 51
May 24	The K to the duke of Limberg Accepting his suggestion , will restore to him the fee granted by the late K Richard, and will, in return, accept the duke's homage. *London*. R 1. 106 O 1 159 H 1 51
May 24	The K to Theobald count of Bar Will restore the lands and fees which he formerly gave him, with the arrears, and will accept his homage *Lambeth* R 1. 106 O 1 160 H 1 51
[May 24]	The K willingly accepts the service and homage of Henry, son of the count of Bar, whom he invites into England. R 1 106 O 1 160 H 1 51
May 24	The K. summons Waleran, son of the duke of Limberg, into England with nine knights. *Lambeth* R 1 106 O 1 160 H 1 51
[May]	The K to the emperor Otho Has received his letters and messengers, and despatched others in reply. R 1 104 O 1. 156 H. 1. 50
[May]	The K thanks Henry duke of Louvaine for having assisted in the promotion of his nephew [Otho], whom he asks to visit along with an embassy from England R 1 106 O 1. 160 H 1 51
[May]	The K. requests that the troops furnished by the duke of Louvaine may join those of the count of Boulogne R 1 106 O 1. 161 H. 1 52.
[May.]	The K requests the seneschal of the duke of Louvaine to come into England, ready for military service R 1 107 O 1 161 H 1 52
July 20	The K asks the count of Flanders whether he can meet him at Dover, for which purpose he has sent the earl of Salisbury with the count's safeconduct R. 1 107 O 1. 161. H 1 52.
	The K narrates various acts of misconduct on the part of William de Breose, Matilda de Heya, his wife, and his nephew W earl of Ferrers, &c. R 1 107. O 1. 162. H 1 52

DATE.	SUBJECT
1212. Oct. 30.	The K. orders Wm. Marshall earl of Pembroke to swear fealty to prince Henry, saving that due to himself, during life *New Temple, London.* R. 1. 108
Nov 2.	The K. exhorts the viscount of Thouars, to hold out, and promises speedy help *Windsor.* R 1 108 O 1 164 H 1 53
1213. Jan 28.	The K. to the emperor Otho, gives information respecting some money transactions, and will speedily meet the messengers who are coming to him. *Bamburgh.* R. 1. 108 O. 1 164 H. 1. 53.
Feb 5.	Grant of the town of Newcastle-upon-Tyne to the good men thereof, saving to the K his rents, &c. in the port *Stockton* R 1 108
[March 1.]	Pope Innocent [III] to the K The many injuries which he has inflicted on the Ch of England deserve excommunication, which shall be issued unless he pledges himself to observe the conditions mentioned in the letter R. 1 108. O. 1. 165 H 1 53.
March 1	The conditions of reconciliation referred to in the previous letter *Lateran* R 1 109. O. 1 166 H 1 53.
[March 1]	The instructions given to the legate in the above matter R. 1. 109. O 1. 167. H 1 54
[March 1]	Innocent [III] annuls the conditions enforced upon the clergy by the king R 1 110 O 1 168 H 1 54
March 3	The K orders the whole shipping from every port in England to be at Portsmouth by Mid-lent R 1 110
[March 3]	The K. summons the whole of his military power to meet him at Dover at the close of Easter to defend England R 1 110
March 29.	Wm count of Holland gives the K his homage and service for a yearly fee of 400 marks *London* R 1 110 O 1 168 H 1 54
March 29	Publication of the previous agreement London R. 111 O 1 169 H. 1 55
[May 13]	The K.'s submission to Innocent [III] *Dover* R 111
[May 15]	The K resigns his kingdom to the Pope R 1 111
May 15	Homage done by the K. to the Pope before Pandulph *Dover.* R 1 112
[May 15]	Absolution granted by Pandulph to the K upon the above submission. R 1. 112.
May 24.	The K admits Stephen abp of Canterbury and other bps. to his peace. *Temple Ewell.* R 1 112 O 1. 171. H. 1. 55
[May 24.]	Certain nobles warrant the observance by the K of the above arrangements. R 1. 112 O 1 172 H 1 56
May 25.	The K. sends certain messengers with credence to Ferrand count of Flanders *Temple Ewell.* R. 1. 113. O 1. 172. H 1 56.
[May ?]	The K. sends messengers to Peter K. of Aragon for more accurate information. R 1 113. O 1 173. H 1. 56
June 13.	The K. publishes the removal of the outlawry against ecclesiastics *Battle* R 1 113 O. 1. 174. H. 1. 56.
. June 13	The K. orders that the hostages of the K of Scots should come to him at Portsmouth. *Battle.* R 1 113 O 1 174. H 1. 57
June 22.	The K. directs that 20,000 marks, in the custody of the Master of the Temple, be delivered to his order *Corfe.* R 1 113 O 1 173 H 1 56.
. June 26.	Credence for messengers from the K. to Ferrand count of Flanders. [*Beer Regis ?*] R 1 113. O 1. 173 H 1. 56.
July 5.	Pope Innocent [III] advises the K of France to accept the advice of the bp of Frascati in the settlement of his dispute with K. John *Lateran* R. 1. 113. O 1. 174. H. 1. 56.
July 6.	Pope Innocent [III] exhorts the English barons to accept the arrangements to be proposed by the bp. of Frascati *Lateran* R. 1 113. O 1. 174 H 1. 57
July 25.	Credence for messengers sent by the K. to the emperor Otho. *Corfe.* R 1 114 O 1 174. H. 1. 57.
Aug. 17.	The K to Raymond duke of Narbonne; has been prevented by contrary winds from coming with a large force to help him. *Ludgershall.* R 1 114 O 1 175 H 1 57
. Aug. 17.	The K. to count Gui of Auvergne, to the same effect as the previous letter *Ludgershall.* R. 1. 114. O. 1. 175. H. 1. 57.

B

DATE	SUBJECT.
1213 Aug. 22	The K to Savary de Mauleon , if he wishes to return to the K's service, the K. will act by the advice of his men of Rochelle *Bishop's Clere.* R 1. 114 O 1 175. H. 1. 57.
Aug. 31.	The K directs that inquiry be made respecting the losses sustained by the clergy during their late disputes with him *Northampton* R. 1. 114.
Sept 21.	The K to Ferrand count of Flanders; will send him money and men by Michaelmas. *Stretton* R I 114 O. 1. 176 H 1 57. Similar letters to Johanna countess of Flanders, and R count of Boulogne.
Oct. 3.	Charter (with golden bull), by which the K. resigns his realm and crown to pope Innocent [III.,] with the form of homage appended. *London* R. 1. 115. O. 1. 176. H 1 57.
Oct. 5.	The K permits the Knights Templars to export their own wool for sale. *London.* R. 1. 115.
Oct. 22.	Pope Innocent [III] provides that the K's submission shall not be turned to his prejudice. *Lateran* R 115. O. 1. 177. H 1. 58.
Oct 22	The pope admonishes the K how to conduct himself for the future. *Lateran.* R. 1. 116. O. 179 H. 58
Oct 22.	The pope to the bp of Frascati , to burn the papal letters formerly obtained against the K *Lateran.* R 1 116 O 180 H 59.
Oct. 22	The pope to the same , to dissolve all associations formed during the late disputes. *Lateran.* R 1 116 O 180 H 59.
Oct. 28.	The pope to the English nation and to the K. of Scotland , to exhibit fealty and devotion to the K R 1 116 O 1. 178. H 58.
Oct 28.	The pope to the Irish nation , to the same effect as the above. *Lateran.* R. 1. 116. O 1 179. H 1 58
Nov 1.	The pope to the papal legate , to fill vacant sees and abbeys in England. *Lateran.* R 1. 117
Nov 4	The pope, in virtue of the K's resignation of his realm, takes him under his protection. *Lateran* R 1 117.
Nov 7	Summons to the Parliament at Oxford *Witney* R 1 117.
Dec. 10	Licence to the friars of S Maria in Saxia, at Rome, to preach and collect alms in England *Reading.* R 1 117
Dec. 28	Summons for the shipping to meet the K at Portsmouth on 14 Jan. *London.* R. 1, 117. O 1 180 H 1 59.
1214. Jan 28.	Pope Innocent [III.] orders the collection of Peter's pence in England *Lateran.* R 1 118 O 1. 182. H. 1 60.
Feb. 1.	The K about to sail for Poitou, places his realm under the protection of the pope, and appoints the bp. of Winchester his lieutenant *Portsmouth* R 1. 118. O. 1. 18]. H 1 59
Feb. 1	The K appoints the bp of Winchester to be guardian of the realm during his absence. *Portsmouth.* R 1. 118. O. 1 181 H 1 59
Feb. 1	The K grants to his clerk Thomas de Neville the houses in Lothbury, near Walbrook, belonging to Aaron the Jew of Lincoln *Portsmouth* R 1 118
[March 8]	The pope announces that he has relaxed the interdict upon England *Lateran.* R. 1. 122.
March 8	The K to Wm earl Marshall and other magnates of England ; details his proceedings in Poitou since 15 Feb , and sends the suspension of the interdict of England received from the Pope *Rochelle.* R 1. 118. O 1. 181 H 1. 59
March 8	The K. to the citizens of Canterbury and others , to the same effect as above, and soliciting a loan. *Rochelle* R 1 118. O 1. 182. H 1 60
April 8.	Appointment of Henry de Ver as the King's proctor. R 1. 119. See April 8, 1215. O 1 183 H 1 60
April 15.	Pope Innocent [III] decrees that the K's. person shall not be excommunicated, nor his chapel interdicted, without the pope's special mandate *Rome.* R. 1 119.
April 21.	The pope takes England under his protection by gift of the K.'s golden bull. *Rome.* R 1 119.

DATE	SUBJECT.
April 22.	Bull of pope Innocent [III] R 1 120 O 1 183 H 1 60 See April 22, 1215
April 26	Credence for messengers R 1 120 O 1 184 H 1 60 See April 26, 1215
April 28.	The K. acknowledges that he has received the Scottish hostages. R 1. 120. O 1. 184. H. 1 60 See April 28, 1215
May 2	Safe conduct for P de Jomy R 1 120 O 1. 184 H 1 60 See May 2, 1215
May 13.	Safe conduct for Henry de Bailloel, coming to the K. into England. *Wallingford.* R 1 119
May 16.	The K.'s authority to the abp. of Canterbury R. 1. 121. O 1 185 H 1 61. See May 16, 1215
May 17	Credence for the bp of Coventry R. 1 121 See May 17, 1215.
May 18.	The K. to Rowland Bloet R 1 121. See May 18, 1215
May 20	The citizens of London having revolted from the K., damage may be done to them or their property. *Winchester* R 1. 121
May 24.	All persons coming into England to assist the K., shall obey the directions of Hubert de Burgh or Philip de Albiniaco *Odiham* R 1 106
May 25.	The K. to the abp of Cant R 1 121. See May 25, 1215
June 17	The K promises that he will pay 12,000 marks yearly until he shall have made full restitution to the abp of Canterbury and others *Angers* R. 1 122 O. 1. 187. H 1. 61
June 17.	Wm earl of Ferrers becomes one of the K.'s securities for the above payment *Rochefort.* R. 1. 123 O 1 183 H. 1 63
June 26	The papal legate states that the K will obey the pope's orders about the towns in Agen and Cahors *Bordeaux* R 1 123 O 1 188 H 1 62
July 15.	The K exhorts his English barons to join him in Poitou *Rochelle* R. 1. 123 O 1 188 H. 1 62
July 15.	The K requests that the men of S Junien may be properly treated *Niort* R 1. 123.
Aug 23	The K takes Kathel, K of Connaught, under his protection *S. Maixent* R 1 123 O 1 189 H 1. 62
[Aug 31.]	The K informs his justiciaries in England of his successes in Poitou *Partenai* R 1 123 O 1 189 H 1 63
Aug 31	The K has granted a truce for 15 days to the K of France, at the instance of the papal legate *Partenai* R 1. 124. O 1 190. H 1. 62
Aug 31	The K. to the legate of France, respecting an interview *Partenai* R 1 124. O. 1 190 H 1 63
Aug 31	The K requests the papal legate to provide that the K. of France does no injury to the count de Enevers *Partenai* R 1 124. O. 1 190. H. 1 63
Sept 6.	The K orders 2,500*l* Poitou, to be paid to the countess of Angoulême *S Maixent* R 1. 124 O 1 190 H 1 63
Sept 6.	Proposal for the exchange of Wm earl of Salisbury, prisoner in France, for Robert, son of Robert count of Dreux, prisoner in England *S Maixent* R 1. 124 O 1 191. H. 1 63
Sept. 13	The K promises to observe the truce made by his agents with the K of France. *Partenai* R 1 24 O 1 191. H 1 63
Sept. 18	Truce between the Ks of England and France for five years from next Easter *Chinon.* R 1 125 O 1 192 H. 1. 63.
Nov. 1	The K. to Queen Berengaria ; refers her for information to her own messengers. *Havering* R 1 126 O 1 194. H. 1. 64.
Nov. 5	Pope Innocent [III] warns Eustace de Vescy not to trouble the K by reason of his previous disputes with the barons *Lateran* R 1 126 O 1 195 H. 1 64
Nov. 20.	The K requests his seneschal of Gascony to repress the heretics of that country *New Temple, London* R 1 126 O 1. 195 H 1 64
Nov. 22.	The K. has restored to the abp of Canterbury his right of patronage of the see of Rochester. *London.* R. 1 126
Dec. 18.	The K has restored to Lewellin (at the petition of his wife, the K.'s daughter), Lewellin's hostages. *Monmouth.* R. 1. 126 O. 1. 195 H. 1 65

DATE.	SUBJECT
1215. Jan 15.	The K. grants that the elections of prelates of all cathedrals and convents in England shall be free, permission to elect having been first obtained *New Temple, London* R. 1. 126
[Feb 12.]	W Mauclerc to the K , details his proceedings at Rome with the pope in the K 's behalf, in which he has been hindered by the agents of the northern barons. R. 1 120. O 1 184. H 1 60
March 2.	The K asks Lewellin to fix a meeting with his commissioners. *Tower of London.* R. 1. 127. O 1 196 H. 1 65
March 19.	Pope Innocent [III] urges the K to deal gently with the barons, and admit their just requests *Lateran* R 1 127 O 1 196 H 1 65.
March 19.	The pope to the English barons, urging moderation in their dealings with the K. *Lateran* R 1 127. O 1 197 H 1 65
March 30.	The pope confirms the K 's charter of free elections in churches R. 1. 127. O. 1. 197. H. 1 65
April 1.	The pope directs that the English nobles and knights shall pay accustomed scutage to the K *Lateran* R 1 128 O. 1 199 H. 1 66
April 8.	The K has appointed a proctor to treat respecting the union of the churches of Bath and Glastonbury, *Oxford* R 1. 119.
April 22.	Pope Innocent [III] mediates between the Ks of England and France. *Rome.* R 1. 120. O 1. 183 H 1 61
April 26.	Credence for messengers sent by the K to Philip K. of France *Clarendon.* R 1 120. O 1. 184 H 1 60
April 28	The K acknowledges that he has received the hostages of the K of Scots and others *Corfe* R 1 120 O 1 184. H 1. 60
May 2.	Safe conduct for Peter de Joiny, coming from the K of France *Reading.* R. 1. 120. O 1 184 H 1 60.
May 8.	The K. promises that he will pay the troops which Gerard de Graveling is bringing to him in England *New Temple, London* R 1 128
May 10.	The K will not proceed against his barons until the dispute between them and him is debated by commissioners *Windsor* R 1 128
May 13.	Safe conduct for H de Bailloel R 1 119 See May 13, 1214
May 16.	The K authorizes the abp of Canterbury and others to make a truce with his barons *Marlborough* R 1 121 O 1 185. H 1 61
May 17.	Credence for the bp of Coventry and Hubert de Burgh to treat (on behalf of the K) with the earl of Salisbury and the citizens of London. *Marlborough* R 1 121.
May 18	The citizens having surrendered London to the K,'s enemies, Rowland Bloet shall destroy Knapp and establish his force at Bramble *Freemantle.* R 1 121.
May 26.	The K requests that the abp. of Cant will cause Rochester Castle to be delivered to him. *Farnham* R 1 121
May 29.	The K to pope [Innocent III] , is prevented from going to the Holy Land by the insurrection of the barons *Odiham.* R. 1 129 O 1 200 H. 1. 66.
[May ?]	The papal legate invites the K to attend a council to be held at Bordeaux R 1. 121.
[May ?]	The Statutes enacted in the council in Bordeaux R 1 122
[May ?]	Settlement for the marriage of Joan, the K's daughter, with Geoffrey, son of the count de la Marche R 1. 125
June 8.	Safe conduct for all who will come from the towns to treat with the K at Stames. *Merton.* R. 1. 129.
June 10.	Extension of the length of the truce mentioned in the last document *Windsor.* R. 1. 129.
[June]	The articles of the Great Charter demanded by the barons, and granted by the K. R. 1. 29.
June 15	The Great Charter of K. John. *Runimede* R 1 131.
[June]	The charter of forest liberties granted by the K R. 1. 133.
[June]	Agreement between the K and his barons as to the holding of the city and tower of London, *etc* R. 1 133 O 1. 201 H 1 67
June 18.	The K tells Stephen Harengod that he has made peace with his barons *Runimede.* R. 1 133 O 1. 202 H 1 67.
[June 18]	The abps of Canterbury and Dublin, *etc.,* explain the meaning of a clause in the charter of forest liberties. R. 1. 134.

DATE	SUBJECT
1215 June 19.	The K orders that 12 knights be chosen from each shire to inquire about unlawful customs, as provided in the royal charter *Runnmead* R. 1 134
[June 19]	Protestation by the abp of Canterbury and other bps., that the barons refused to execute a charter demanded of them by the K, for the observance of peace R. 1. 134.
June 23.	The K directs that all troops at Dover be allowed to return to their own county. *Runnmead* R 1 134
June 27.	The lands, &c. of such persons as will not swear to the 25 barons appointed by the charter of liberties shall be seized. *Winchester* R 1 134
[June ?]	Robert FitzWalter invites Wm de Album to the tournament near Staines and Hounslow; the prize to be a bear given by a lady R 1 134
[June?]	The K, much troubled by the disobedience of the English prelates, sends Pandulph, elect of Norwich, to the pope for advice. R. 1. 135.
July 3.	Charter of liberties and privileges granted to the city of Dublin. *Marlborough.* R 1 135.
July 7.	Alexander [II] K of Scotland sends his agents to confer with K. John. *Calth'.* R. 1 135 O. 1. 203 H. 1 67
July 20,	The K to Philip K of France, has permitted the French merchants to remove their goods from London. *Oxford.* R 1. 135. O 1. 203. H 1. 67
Aug. 25.	Pope Innocent [III] absolves the K from his oath to the barons *Anagni.* R 1 135.
Aug 25.	The pope exhorts the barons of England to renounce the composition made between them and the K *Anagni* R 1 136 O 1 205 H 1 68
[Aug?]	Gilbert FitzReymfrid pledges his fealty to the K, and surrenders his castles of Mirhulle and Kirkeby. R. 1 136. O. 1. 206. H. 1. 68.
[Aug. ?]	John constable of Chester pledges his fealty to the K R 1 137 O 1 206. H 1. 69.
Sept 4	The K sends to the pope the copy of his agreement with Q Berengaria, (dat 2 Sept), as to the payment of her dower. *Dover.* R. 1. 137. O 1. 207 H 1. 69
Sept 4.	The K sends to the pope the copy of another agreement with Q Berengaria as to property to be held by her from him. *Dover* R. 1 137 O 1. 210 H 1. 70
Sept. 13	The K, sending messengers to the K of France, informs him that French merchants may trade with England. *Dover.* R. 1 137. O. 1. 207 H 1 69.
[Sept 13]	The K. informs prince Louis of France that all injuries done to him shall be amended R 1 138 O 1 207 H 1 69
Sept 13	The K. sends messengers to the pope, soliciting aid against the barons, who have risen against him. *Dover.* R. 1. 138. O. 1. 207. H 1. 69.
[Sept]	Pope Innocent [III.] directs the abp of Cant to pronounce the sentence of excommunication against the barons R. 1. 138
Sept. 25.	Q. Berengaria states the arrangements which she has made with the K. about her dower. *Le Mans.* R. 1. 138 O. 1. 208. H. 1. 69.
[Sept?]	The K appoints proctors for his causes in the papal court. R 1 139.
Nov. 4.	Pope Innocent [III] enforces the observance of the sentence of suspension against the abp. of Cant *Lateran.* R. 1. 139.
Dec. 16.	Special excommunication against the barons (mentioned by name) *Lateran.* R 1. 139. O. 1. 211. H 1 70
[Dec. 16]	The pope orders that the above sentence be publicly pronounced in the churches throughout England on Sundays and festivals. R. 1 139
1216. Jan. 27.	The K grants certain lands and liberties in Ireland to Tho de Galway *Winchester.* R. 1. 140.
[March ?]	Prince Louis of France to the barons of England; will be at Calais by Easter Sunday on his way to help them R 1 140
March 29.	The K acknowledges the receipt of certain jewels (enumerated) from Walerandus Teutonicus and Hugo de Baltronia *Canfield* R 1 140
[April?]	Prince Louis of France explains the origin of his right to the crown of England. R. 1. 140
April 28.	The K appoints his proxies to arrange the terms of the truce with the K. of France. *Dover.* R. 1 128 O 1. 199 H 1 66
[May ?]	The K to Otho K of the Romans, to assist the count of Los in his claim upon Holland, count Wilikin having invaded England with Louis R. 1. 141 O. 1. 212. H. 1. 71.

DATE	SUBJECT
1216 [May ?]	Protest by Walter Bertrand respecting the terms upon which he will deliver the above letters to the count of Los R 1 141 O. 1. 213 H. 1 71.
June 2.	The K. requests the jurates of Bayonne to employ their galleys in annoying his enemies, *Winchester* R. 1 141
June 5.	The K orders the earl of Chester to destroy the castle of Richmond, if he cannot hold it. *Winchester* R 1 141.
June 7.	The K orders that all persons faithful to him be received by the mayor of Lyn within that town *Devizes* R 1 141
June 8.	The K asks Queen Berengaria to excuse the non-payment of his debt to her, all his ready money having been spent on the invasion of England by Louis. *Devizes*, 8 June R. 1. 140. O. 1. 213. H. 1. 71.
June 9.	The K permits the barons of Winchelsea to ransom their town by the payment of 200 marks to Louis *Devizes* R 1 142
June 21	The K orders Brian de Insula to surrender Peek Castle to the earl of Ferrers. [*Wareham?*]. R 1 142.
Aug. 8	The K permits Walter de Beauchamp to go to G[ualo] the papal legate in order to be absolved by him *Whitchurch.* R. 1. 142 O 1 213. H 1. 71.
Aug. 19	John Marshal is permitted by the K. not to enter the castle of Worcester if it be besieged by Louis, the same permission to Walter de Lacy for the castle of Hereford *Berkley.* R 1 141 O 1 214 H 1 71
[Sept 2]	The K. exhorts the barons of Hastings to return to him, notwithstanding the oath which they have made to Louis of France [*Taynton*] R 1 143.
Sept 3	The K exhorts the men of Sussex, Kent, Surrey, and Southampton to remain firm to him, notwithstanding their oath to Louis *Oxford.* R 1 142. O 1 214 H. 1. 71.
Sept 3	The K. thanks the men of Safford for their constancy towards him *Oxford.* R. 1. 142
Sept. 4	The K will receive into his favour all the men of the co. of Lincoln who will return to their fealty to him. *Oxford* R 1 143
Sept. 27.	Gualterus, the papal legate, intimates that he has absolved Louis from the sentence of the pope for having invaded England. *Dover* R. 1. 143
Sept 28	The K has granted to Oliver de Albini the land which belonged to Wm. de Landa (the K's enemy) in Coleby *Lincoln* R 1 143
Oct 11.	The K has granted to John de Pavilly, his clerk, the land of Rob de Crimplesham. *Lynn* R 1 143
Oct 11	The K has received from Agatha Trusbert 100 marks for the deliverance of her husband Wm de Albini. *Lynn* R 1 143
Oct 15	The K takes under his protection the abbey of S. Edward's of Shaftesbury. [*Sleaford.*] R. 1 144
Oct. 17	The K. orders that Walter de Montgomery, earl of Ferrers, shall have restitution of his land of Hondesdon *Newark.* R. 1 144
Oct 18	The K asks Hervey Belet to give credence to what Savarie de Mauleon and others shall state on his part *Newark* R. 1 144
[1216?]	Names of knights and others in Rutland and Leicester who bore arms against the K. R. 1 144
1216.	The testament of K. John R 1 144.

HENRY III.

28 *Oct* 1216—16 *Nov.* 1272.

1216.	The K informs the justiciary of Ireland of his father's death and his own coronation. R. 1 145 O. 1 215. H. 1. 72.
Nov. 18	The K promises Hugh de Lacy that if he returns to his fealty, his rights shall be restored. R 1. 145
Dec. 22	The K exhorts the people of Poitou and others to continue in their fealty to him. *Gloucester.* R. 1 145. O. 1. 216. H 1 72
[Dec.]	The earl of Pembroke and others promise that they will procure the absolution of the earl of Salisbury and such as return to the King. R. 1. 145 O 1. 216. H. 1. 72.

DATE.	SUBJECT
1217. Feb. 6.	The K. sends to the people of Ireland a sealed copy of the liberties granted by his father and confirmed by himself and his council. *Gloucester.* R. 1. 146.
March 28	The K commits to the abp of Bordeaux the custody of Gascony and Poitou *Winchester* R 1 146 O. 1 216 H 1 72
March 28.	The K orders his seneschal of Poitou and Gascony to deliver them to the abp. of Bordeaux *Winchester* R 1. 146 O. 1 217 H. 1 72
[April.]	The earl of Chester has abandoned his intention of going on the crusade at the request of Gualo, the papal legate, to the great advantage of the K R 1. 146 O 1 217 H 1 73
April 16.	The K approves of the truce between his council and the earl of Warren *Winchester.* R 1. 146 O 1 217. H 1 72
April 16.	The K orders the barons of Ireland to obey the abp of Dublin, whom he sends back to Ireland *Winchester* R 1 146 O 1 218 H 1 73
April 26.	The K complains to pope Honorius [III] that the canons of Carlisle adhere to the Scotch *Winchester.* R 1 147 O 1 218 H 1 73
June 12.	Safe conduct for certain of the council of Louis about to confer with the K's council. *Chertsey.* R. 1. 147 O 1 219 H. 1 73
June 23	The K orders the sheriffs to read to the county the charters of liberties granted by the K and confirmed by the legate *Chertsey* R 1. 147
[June.]	The K's council inform Louis of France and his council that they will observe the truce. R 1 147. O. 1 219. H. 1. 73
July 14.	Pope Honorius [III] directing Gualo, the papal legate, to inquire into and punish the misconduct of the canons of Carlisle *Anagni* R 1 147 O 1 219 H 1 73
July 24.	The K. asks the people of Poitou and others to give an honourable reception to his mother, who proposes to visit her native country *Oxford* R 1 148 O. 1. 220. H. 1. 74
Sept 11.	Treaty of peace between the K and Louis son of the K of France *Lambeth.* R 1 148 O. 1. 221. H 1 74
Sept. 14.	Letters of peace and protection for Louis of France *Kingston.* R 1. 148. O 1. 222. H 1 74.
Sept. 19.	The K. orders that no injury be done to the men of Norfolk, Suffolk, Essex, and Hereford, peace being established with Louis of France *Merton* R 1 148 O 1 222 H. 1 74
Oct 2.	The K orders the deliverance from prison of Osbert FitzNigel, peace being established with Louis of France *Lambeth* R 1 149 O 1 223 H 1 75
Oct 10	The K to the K. of Norway, will gladly promote commercial intercourse with that realm *Lambeth* R. 1 149 H 1 223. O 1 74
Oct. 10	Letters of safe conduct for Gilbert FitzRainfrid and others, to treat for peace. *Lambeth.* R 1 149. O 1. 223. H 1. 75.
Nov 3	Letters of safe conduct for Alex [II] K of Scotland and Rob de Ros, coming to the earl marshal. *Westm.* R. 1 149. O 1 224 H 1 75.
Nov. 7.	The constable of Chester shall conduct the K of Scotland and Rob. de Ros from Berwick, to the K. *London.* R. 1. 149. O. 1. 224 H 1 75.
Nov. 18.	H. de Mortimer shall conduct Lewellin and others from Hereford to Northampton, there to do their homage to the K *Gloucester* R. 1. 149. O. 1 224. H 1. 75
1218. Jan. 13.	Pope Honorius [III] confirms the peace between the K and Louis of France. *Lateran.* R. 1. 149
Jan. 16.	Safe conduct for the K of the Isles, coming to do his homage to the K *Winchester.* R 1. 150. O 1 224 H. 1 75
Feb. 12.	The K. fixes a time to receive the homage of Lewellin, prince of N Wales *Exeter.* R 1. 150 O 1 225. H 1. 75
Feb. 18.	All clerks excommunicated for their adherence to Louis of France, and yet unabsolved, shall leave the realm before Mid-Lent *Stoke* R 1 150
Feb. 22.	The K. orders that the charters of liberties be publicly read by the sheriffs, and that the "adulterine" castles be destroyed *Sturminster* R 1. 150.
March 15.	The K has given safe conducts to the nobles of N and S Wales to come to do their homage to him at Worcester. *Worcester* R 1 151 O 1 226 H. 1 76.
[March.]	Lewellin, prince of N Wales, records the promises made by him to the K. at Worcester. R. 1. 150. O 1 225. H 1. 75

DATE.	SUBJECT.
1218 [March]	Lewellin, prince of N Wales, certifies that he takes the protection of the lands belonging to Wenhunwen in Wales and Montgomery R 1 150. O 1. 226. H 1 75.
March 30	The K orders that all Jews shall wear two white tablets upon their breasts, to distinguish them from Christians *Oxford* R 2. 151
May 6	Peter count of Brittany protests that he will claim only such lands of the house of Brittany beyond the Humber as shall be awarded to him by the K's council. *Westm* R 1.151. O 1 226 H 1 76
May 25	Lewellin prince of N Wales is ordered to restore their lands to certain persons who have come to the K's service *Woodstock* R 1 151 O 1 227 H 1 76.
June 19	The K grants to the Jews in Hereford, &c the liberties which they enjoyed in the time of his father *London* R. 1. 151.
July 24.	The K orders that the forests be perambulated and regulated according to the charter of Forests *Leicester* R 1 151.
Sept 2.	Gualo, the papal legate, to the earl of Pembroke, complaining that Louis of France still keeps in prison the hostages of the barons of the Cinque Ports *Chichester* R 1 152
Oct. 10	The K orders the sheriff of Warwick to give seisin of the vill of Budiford to Lewellin, prince of N Wales *Westm* R. 1 152 O 1 227 H 1 76.
Nov 13	Regulations as to the treatment of the Jews coming into England from abroad. *Westm.* R 1 152
[Nov ?]	Provision, by the common council of the realm, that no charter or letters patent be sealed with the great seal before the K comes to full age R 1 152
Nov 21	Pope Honorius [III] grants certain liberties to the church and realm of Scotland *Lateran* R 1 152
1219 Jan 16	The K orders seisin of the honour of Richmond and of other lands in England to be given to Peter count of Brittany, with the exception of certain knights' fees, which he retains *Westm* R 1 153
Jan 25.	Pope Honorius [III] sanctions the intended translation of the body of Thomas abp. of Canterbury *Lateran* R 1 153
Jan 26.	Pope Honorius [III] gives an indulgence of 40 days to those who assist at the translation of S. Thomas of Canterbury *Lateran* R 1. 154.
Jan 26.	The K informs his justices itinerant how they shall punish certain criminals; judgment by fire and water having been forbidden by the church of Rome. *Westm.* R 1 154 O 1 228 H 1 76
July 21.	The K. appoints commissioners to settle disputes with the K. of Scotland. *Westm.* R 1 154 O 1 229 H 1 77
July 24.	The K requests of the papal legate that his lands be protected from injuries inflicted by the crusaders against the Albigenses *Westm* R 1 154 O 1 229 H 1 77.
[July 24]	The K complains to the pope and cardinals of the misconduct of Robert who styles himself the bp. elect of Ely R 1 155 O 1 229 H 1 77
July 24.	The K informs the mayor of Bordeaux respecting various matters of detail, and gives directions about the same *Westm* R 1 155 O 1 230 H 1 77
July 24	The K asks Wm Mayngo to act with Hugh de Lusignan in defending his territories from the crusaders against the Albigenses *Westm* R 1.155. O 1. 231 H. 1. 77.
July 24	The K. informs Hugh de Lusignan that he can have, if necessary, certain sums of money and troops for the protection of the K's lands *Westm* R 1 155. O 1. 231. H. 1. 78
July 24.	The King is prepared to extend the duration of the truce with the K of France. *Westm* R 1 156 O 1 232. H 1 78
Sept 2	Safe conduct for the messengers of the K of France to treat about the truce *Norwich.* R 1 156 O 1 233 H 1 78
[Sept ?]	Pope Honorius [III] to the bp of Angoulême, to cause the castle "de Merpus" to be restored to the K *Rome* R 1 156 O 1 233 H 1 78
Sept 21	Reginald K of the Isles surrenders the Isle of Man to the pope to be held of him in fee. *London.* R. 1 156 O 1 234. H. 1 78
Sept 24	Safe conduct for Reginald K. of Man returning to Man *London.* R. 1. 157. O. 1. 234. H 1. 79.
Sept. 24.	Letters of protection for Reginald K of Man, he having done homage to the K. R. 1. 157. O 1. 234 H. 1. 79.

DATE	SUBJECT
1219. Nov. 10.	Pope Honorius [III ?] directs Pandulph, the papal legate, to confirm or annul the treaty between Wm. K. of Scotland and John K. of England. *Lateran.* R. 1 157 O 1. 235. H. 1. 79.
[1219]	Letters [of Pandulph] on the affairs of Scotland. R. 1. 157. O. 1. 235 H. 1 79. See [Aug 2] 1220
[1219.]	Letter of Pandulph on the affairs of Scotland. R. 1. 157. O 1 235. H. 1 79. See Aug. 8, 1220
[1220] Jan. 10.	Pandulph, the papal legate, to Hubert de Burgh, on the truce with the K of France *Bath.* R. 1. 157. O. 1. 236. H. 1 79
[1220?] Jan. 25	Pandulph, the papal legate, to Hubert de Burgh, on the indiscreet conduct of P de Hulcote in the matter of Roger Bertram *Malmesbury.* R 1. 158 O 1 236. H. 1. 79
[1220?]	Pandulph, the papal legate, to Hubert de Burgh ; is returning from Wales to London. *Cirencester.* R 1 158. O 1. 237. H. 1 80
[1220?]	The K. to the K. of France, is willing to extend the truce. R. 1. 158 O 1. 237. H. 1. 80.
[1220?]	The K to Peter de Collemedio, to proceed in the K's business with the K. of France. R 1 158. O 1 237 H 1 80
March 3	The King has extended for four years the truce with the K of France *London.* R. 1 158.
March 7.	The King has confirmed the truce, and begs the K of France to do the same *Westm* R. 1 159. O 1. 238 H 1 80
March.	W earl of Warren swears that the K. will observe the truce with the K. of France. R 1. 159. O. 1. 238. H 1 80
March 10.	The K to H. de Lezignan, count of March, on various matters connected with the count's affairs in France *Westm* R 1 159 O 1 238 H 1 80
1220 May 1.	The K to Lewellin, prince of N Wales, appointing an interview at Shrewsbury on May 4 *Campedene.* R 1. 159. O. 1. 239 H. 1 81
May 5.	The K. has taken into his protection his nephew David, son of Lewellin, prince of N Wales. *Shrewsbury* R. 1 159 O 1 239 H 1 81
May 7.	The K. summons Peter de Maulay to attend him at London on his coronation [on May 16]. *Shrewsbury* R. 1 160 O. 1. 240. H 1 81
[May.]	Wm earl of Warren, prevented by illness from attending the coronation, petitions that his right of bearing the K's sword be not impaired by his absence R. 1 160
May 22.	The K congratulates the earl of March upon his marriage with the K's mother. R 1 160.
May 28.	Pope Honorius [III] desires that no one person shall have the custody of more than two of the K's castles at the same time. *Viterbo* R 1 160 O. 1. 240 H. 1. 81.
June 15.	The K promises to give his sister Johanna, in marriage to Alex. K. of Scotland. *York.* R. 1. 161. O. 1. 240 H 1. 81
June 15.*	Alex K of Scotland promises to marry Johanna or Isabella, sister of the K of England. *York.* R 1. 161. O 1. 241 H 1 81.
June 20.	The K entreats the pope to compel Hugh de Lezignan to restore to him his sister Johanna. *Nottingham.* R. 1. 161. O. 1. 241. H 1. 81.
June 20.	The K. to the cardinals, to the same effect as the previous letter. *Nottingham* R 1. 161. O 1 242 H 1. 81.
July.	Agreement between the K. and Q. Berengaria respecting the payment of her dower. *London.* R 1 161 O 1. 242. H. 1. 83.
[Aug. 2.]	Notification by the papal legate respecting the progress of his business with the K. of Scotland. R. 1 157. O 1. 235. H. 1. 79
[Aug. 8]	The papal legate, having finished his business with the K of Scotland, is hastening to join the bp of Winchester R 1 157 O. 1. 235. H 1 79.
[Aug. 11]	Agreement between the K and Geoffrey de Marisco, justiciary of Ireland, respecting the government of Ireland. *Oxford.* R 1. 162 O 1 244 H 1. 82.
Aug. 13.	Safe conduct for the K. of Scotland to treat with the K at York *London* R 1. 162. O 1. 244 H 1 82
Aug. 25.	Pandulph, the papal legate, to Hubert de Burgh , has no faith in Philip de Ulecot ; has forbidden tournaments this year , and expects him to come into Dorset. *Cery.* R. 1 162. O. 1. 245. H. 1. 83
[Aug.]	The bp. of Winchester to Pandulph, on the affairs of Poitou and on tournaments, which have been forbidden. R. 1. 162. O 1. 245. H. 1. 83.

DATE	SUBJECT.
1220 Sept 3	The K to A son of A. viscount of Limoges, on the claim made by him to the county of Cornwall *Exeter* R 1. 163 O 1 246 H 1 83
Sept 16	The K has committed Gascony to the custody of Philip de Ulecot *Winchester.* R 1. 163 O 1 246 H 1 83
Sept 16	The men of Bordeaux shall pay the usual taxes to Philip de Ulecot, seneschal of Gascony R 1 163 O 1 247 H 1 83.
Sept. 16.	The K to the keepers of his castles in Poitou and Gascony, to deliver them to Philip de Ulecote. R 1. 163 O 1 247 H 1 83
Sept 16	The K. to the citizens of Poitiers, &c , to deliver the towns of Poitou and Gascony to Philip de Ulcote R. 1. 163 O 1 247 H 1. 84.
Sept 16.	The K repeats his request that Hugh count of March will deliver up his sister at Rochelle R. 1. 163 O. 1. 248 H 1. 84
[Sept ?]	Peter bp of Winchester announces to Hubert de Burgh the death of the abp of Bordeaux. R. 1 164. O. 1 248 H. 1 84
Oct. 5.	The K disclaims any participation in the inroad made by Lewellin, prince of N. Wales, upon the lands of Wm earl Marshall. *Westm.* R. 1 164 O. 1 248. H 1. 84.
Oct 5.	The K to Lewellin, prince of N Wales, to make compensation for the injuries committed on Wm earl Marshall and the barons of the Marsh *Westm* R 1 164 O 1 249. H. 1 84
[1220?]	The convent of S Patrick of Down request the K to give them a settlement in England. R 1 164 O 1 250. H. 1 85
Dec 2	The barons of the Cinque Ports are summoned to answer the complaint of the men of Calais *Canterbury* R. 1 165 O 1 250 H 1 85
[Dec ?]	H de Viven undertakes to serve the K as his seneschal of Poitou, Aquitaine, and Gascony R 1 165 O 1 251 H 1 85.
1221 Feb 17.	Pope Honorius [III] announces that he has canonized Hugh bp of Lincoln *Viterbo* R 1 165. O. 1 251 H 1 85
March 12	The K of Scotland has given the custody of the honor of Huntingdon to R. earl of Chester *Newark* R 1. 165
June 18.	Assignation of dower by the K of Scotland on his marriage with Johanna, sister of the K of England *York* R 1 165. O 1 252. H. 1. 85.
[1221?]	Henry duke of Saxony to R de Neville, vice chancellor , credence for the bearer. R. 1 166
Dec 15	The K. to the duke of Austria, credence for the bearer *Tower of London.* R 1 166. O 1 252 H 1 85
1222 April 16	The K notifies that he has surrendered to his mother, and her husband Hugh count of March, all the dower of his said mother, queen Isabella *Westm.* R 1. 166. O. 1. 253. H 1 86
April 16	The K. orders Richard de Rivers to surrender to the count and countess of March the castle of Berkhampstead R 1 166 O 1 253 H. 1. 86.
April 29	The pope directs the bp. of Winchester and others to cause the wards and escheats to be restored to the K. *Lateran.* R 1 167. O. 1 254 H 1 86
April 29	The pope directs the abp of York and his suffragans to secure the quiet of the realm. *Lateran* R 1 167 O 1. 254 H 1. 86.
April 30.	The K orders Lewellin, prince of N Wales, to extend till Easter next the truce with Wm earl Marshall R 1. 66. O 1 253 H. 1. 86
[1222 ?]	Cardinal Rayner petitions for a pension for services done to the K and his father. R 1. 167. O 1 255 H 1 86
June 23	Pope Honorius [III] against the annoyances occasioned to the K. by the knights templars in Rochelle *Lateran* R. 1. 169. O. 1 258 H L 88
June 25	Pope Honorius [III] admonishes the count and countess of Lusignan to surrender certain possessions unjustly withheld from the K. *Lateran* R. 1. 169 O. 1. 259 H. 1 88.
July 5	Pope Honorius [III] threatens to excommunicate the abp of Poitiers unless he satisfies the K for injuries inflicted on him *Lateran.* R 1 169 O 1 259 H 1 88
July 18	The K grants (until his majority) the land of Thomond to Donald K of Thomond. *Tower of London* R 1 167 O 1 255 H 1. 87.
Aug. 13.	Safe conduct for Alexander K of Scotland going to Canterbury. *Tower of London.* R 1 167. O 1. 256 H 1 87.

DATE.	SUBJECT
1222 Aug. 27.	The K. is happy to have come to an agreement with the count of March, for whose reception in Guernsey he wishes arrangements *Havering* R 1 167 O 1 256 H 1 87.
Nov 9	The K to the bps. of Saintes and Limoges, the papal sentence against the count of March shall be suspended till 1 Aug in hope of peace. *Westm.* R 1 168 O 1 257. H. 1. 87
Nov 9	The K. to the count and countess of March, hopes that peace will be established. *Westm.* R. 1. 168. O 1 257 H 1 87
1223 Jan. 29.	The K grants to Wm Jonner, his " chamberlaria ' of London, for two years, at 100l. per ann *Westm* R. 1. 168.
Jan 30.	The K orders an inquisition to be made as to the customs and liberties enjoyed by K John before the war with his barons *Westm* R 1 167.
June 22.	Safe conduct for Lewellin, prince of N. Wales, to meet the K at Worcester *Woodstock.* R. 1 168 O 1 258 H 1 87
June 23	Bull of pope Honorius [III] R 1 169 O 1 258 H. 1 88 See June 23, 1222.
June 25	Bull of pope Honorius [III.] R 1 169 O 1 259 H 1 88 See June 25, 1222
July 5	Bull of pope Honorius [III.] R 1 169 O 1 259 H 1 88 See July 5, 1222
July 11.	The sheriff of Devon shall take care that no victuals are conveyed into the land of Lewellin or his adherents *Worcester* R 1 169 O 1 260 H 1 88
July 23.	The K promises the barons of Normandy that if they return to their fealty to him he will restore to them the lands they lost in England when K John lost Normandy *Cricklade* R. 1. 170 O 1 260 H 1 88
Aug 29	Safe conduct for the messengers of Lewellin returning home. *Westm* R 1. 170. O. 1. 261 H. 1 89.
Sept. 12	Writ of summons for the tenants by military service to meet the K at Gloucester, Lewellin having besieged the castle of Buelt *Westm* R 1 170 O 1 261 H 1 89
Sept. 12	Similar summons for the barons. R. 1. 170 O. 1. 261 H 1 89.
[Oct. 9]	Lewellin and others swear to satisfy the K. for the injuries done to him by them R 1 170. O 1 261 H 1 89
Nov 8	The K cites Lewellin to produce before him the hostages for S Wales. *Westm.* R. 1. 170. O 1 262 H 1 89
Dec. 19.	The King informs the pope of the present state of affairs in England. *London* R 1. 171 O 1 263 H 1 89
Dec. 19	The K writes to the same effect to [cardinal] Gualo R 1 171. O. 1 264 H 1 90.
[Dec]	Hubert de Burgh and others request that the pope will not allow certain mischiefmakers, now at Rome, to return into England R 1 171 O 1 264 H 1 90
1224	The K grants his peace to the merchants of France trading into England *S Alban's.* R 1 172 O 1 265. H. 1 90
Feb. 24.	The K. desires inquiry to be made as to the damages inflicted on his subjects by those of the K of France *Westm.* R. 1 172 O 1 266. H 1 90.
March 25.	The K has appointed commissioners to enquire into the injuries inflicted on the French by the English during the late truce *Westm.* R 1 172 O 1 266 H 1 90.
March 27.	The K will hold the abp of Canterbury free from a bond given by him, on the K.'s behalf, to the count of March *Westm.* R 1 172 O 1 266. H. 1. 91.
April 24.	The K postpones his meeting with Lewellin, prince of N Wales. *Westm* R. 1 172. O 1 267 H 1 91.
April 27.	The pope exhorts the K to accompany the emperor F[rederic] in the crusade. *Lateran.* R 1 172 O 1 267 H 1 91
April 27.	The pope requests that the K will exempt the crusaders from the payment of tolls. *Lateran* R 1 173.
[1224.]	The mayor of Bayonne informs the K of the surrender of Rochelle to the K of France R 1 173 O 1 269 H 1 91
April 28.	Credence for messengers treating with the K. of France about the extension of the truce *New Temple, London* R 1 174 O 1 270 H. 1 92
April 28.	The K to the bp of Sens, on the extension of the truce with France *Westm.* R. 1. 174. O 1 270 H 1 92

DATE	SUBJECT
[1224 ?]	The bp of Lichfield to the bp of Chichester, on his proceedings in the papal court for the marriage of the K. with the daughter of the count of Brittany R. 1. 174 O. 1 271. H 1 92
May 15.	The K warns the barons of the Cinque Ports and others to prepare their shipping for his service, the truce with the K of France having expired Westm. R 1 174. O 1 272 H 1 93
[1224?]	The bp of Coventry informs the K. that he has excommunicated Falkasius de Breante. R 1 175 O 1 272 H. 1. 93
Aug 2	The K does not hold Cohn de Breaute, clerk, answerable for the misdeeds of his brother Bedford R 1 175
Aug 18	The K will not cite as a precedent the aid given him by the clergy against Falkasius de Breaute Bedford R 1 175.
Aug 25	Falkasius de Breaute specifies the process of his satisfaction made to the K London. R 1 175 O 1 273 H 1 93
[19 Dec ?]	G de Craucumbe informs the K. of the details of his proceedings in the papal court. R 1 175. O 1 273 H 1 93
[Dec]	The legate to the Pope, on the capture of Falkasius de Breante in Burgundy R 1 176 O 1 274 H. 1. 94
[Dec]	Letter to master T to the same effect as the above R 1 176 O 1 275 H 1 94.
[1224?]	The duke of Austria on the proposed marriage of his daughter with the K R 1 176
1225 Jan 3	The K to the duke of Austria, &c , on his proposed marriage with the duke's daughter. Westm R 1 176 O 1 275 H 1 94
Feb 15.	Commissioners appointed for the collection of a fifteenth on all moveables throughout England Westm. R 1 177
March 14	The pope cautions the K. to carry himself with prudence and moderation towards his subjects Lateran R 1 177 O 1 276 H 1 94
March 23.	The K sends his brother Richard to assist his faithful subjects in Gascony and Poitou. Sunvich R 1 177 O 1 277. H 1 94.
April 11	The K congratulates the count of Flanders upon his delivery from captivity Westm. R 1 177 O 1 277 H 1 95
April 14.	The K further prorogues the meeting with Lewellin prince of N Wales Westm R 1 178 O 1 277 H 1 95
[May 2]	Richard earl of Cornwall informs the K of his success in Gascony. S Masaure R 1 178
May 14	Mandate on the marriage of Roger son of the earl of Norfolk with Isabella sister of the the K of Scotland Westm R 1 178 O 1 278 H 1 95
[May 7]	Agreement between the K and the countess of Eu, as to the delivery of the castle of Hastings Westm R 1 180
[May ?]	The archbp of Bordeaux to the K on the affairs of France R. 1. 178 O. 1 278. H. 1 95.
June 30.	The K further prorogues the meeting with Lewellin, prince of N Wales. Westm. R 1 179 O 1. 280. H. 1 96
[June?]	The K to the Pope in favour of the bearer, master John of Bayonne R. 1. 179. O 1 280. H 1. 96
July 7	The K informs the bp of Carlisle that he must patiently await the answer of the Emperor and the duke of Austria. Westm R. 1 179 O 1 280. H 1 96.
Aug. 14.	The K to the duke of Narbonne on the treaty proposed between them Westm. R 1 179 O. 1 281 H 1 196
Aug 14.	The K to his brother Richard, on the interchange of writings relative to the above treaty. R. 1 179
Aug 27.	The K. praises the bishop of Carlisle for the pains taken in his service. Westm. R. 1 180
Oct 5.	Pope Honorius [III] to the K on the threatened excommunication of Lewellin prince of N Wales and the interdict of his lands Anagni. R 1 180
Oct. 19.	The K to the mayor of Bordeaux. R. 1 182. O. 1 287 H 1. 98 See Oct. 19, 1226

DATE.	SUBJECT
1226. Jan. 9.	Pope Honorius [III*] censures Geoffrey de Lezigniaco for having broken faith with the K *Reati.* R 1 181
Jan. 29.	Pope Honorius [III] exhorts the clergy of Ireland to tax themselves in order to support the K.'s expenses. R 1. 181
March 22.	The K consults the papal legate as to the form in which he shall resume the treaty of peace with the K of France. *Westm* R 1 181
May 15.	Pope Honorius [III] exempts the K and his brother Richard from sentences of excommunication and interdict. *Lateran.* R 1 185 O 1 293. H. 1 100
May 15.	The pope to Romanus cardinal of S Angelo; instructions in accordance with the above. *Lateran* R. 1 185 O 1 293. H 1 101
May 30.	The pope exempts the abbot of Begham from serving upon papal commissions *Lateran.* R. 1 185 O 1. 294 H 1. 101
July 3.	The K to the legate of France concerning the above treaty. *Westm.* R 1. 181
July 3.	On the interchange of messengers between the Ks of England and Bohemia *Westm* R 1 182 O 1 286 H 1 98
July 4.	Grant of an annual fee of 580*l* to Geoffrey de Marisco, justiciary of Ireland, for the custody of Ireland. *Westm.* R. 1 182.
July 10	The K reminds the earl of Pembroke how he affirmed that he was going on a pilgrimage to S Andrew's, whereas it appears that he is going to Ireland, to which intention if he adheres he must surrender to the K. the castles of Carmarthen and Cardigan *Huntingdon.* R 1 182 O 1 286. H. 1 98
July 26	Safe conduct of Lewellin prince of N Wales, and his wife and son, coming to the K at Shrewsbury *Worcester* R 1 182 O 1 287. H 1 98
Oct 19	The K having appointed Hy de Trubleville seneschal of Gascony, recommends him to the mayor, &c. of Bordeaux. *Westm* R 1. 182. O 1 287 H 1. 98
Nov 5.	The K directs that ships from France, laden with corn, wine, and victuals, may enter English ports R 1 182 O 1 287 H 1 98
Dec. 18.	The K restores to his mother Q. Isabella all her dower in England, as it was held by his grandmother Eleanor *Westm* R 1 182. O 1 288 H. 1 99
Dec. 18.	Grant of various lands and privileges in Saintes, &c to Hugh count of March and his heirs by Isabella the K's mother *Westm.* R. 1. 183. O 1 288 H 1 99
Dec. 18.	Agreement by which the K undertakes to support Hugh viscount of Thouars against the K of France. *Westm.* R 1. 183 O. 1. 290 H 1 99
Dec. 18.	Grant by the K of the castle of Lodun, &c to Hugh viscount of Thouars. *Westm.* R 1 183 O 1 289 H 1 99
Dec. 20.	The archbp of Canterbury and other bishops pledge themselves to promote the above conventions. *London* R 1. 184 O. 1. 290 H 1 99
1227. Jan 13.	The K to Peter count of Brittany , has followed his advice and will continue to do so. *Reading* R 1 184. O 1 291 H 1 100
Jan 13	The K. has sent the archbp of York, &c to complete the business which he has in hand with the count of March and others *Reading* R 1 184. O. 1 291. H 1 100
Jan. 13.	The K. requests the count of Poitou to confer with the messengers to the count of March and to be guided by their advice *Reading* R 1 184 O 1 291. H 1 100
Feb. 20.	Pope Honorius [III] exempts the prior of the H Trinity of London from serving on papal commissions *Lateran* R 1 184. O 1 291. H 1 100
April 13	The K grants tallage to his sister Johanna, lady of N Wales, from the manors of Ralegh and Cunedour. *Westm* R 1 184 O 1 292 H. 1 100
April 13	The K has received the messengers of the K of the Romans and the duke of Bavaria, who have come to promote a confederacy between the empire and England, and in return has despatched to the K and duke his own messengers. *Westm.* R. 1. 184. O. 1. 292 H 1 100.
April 13.	The K to the K of the Romans. To the same effect as the preceding *Westm* R. 1 185 O 1. 292 H 1 100.
April 13.	The K. to the archbp of Cologne on the proposed confederacy with the princes of the empire and on his willingness to marry the daughter of the K. of Bohemia, as recommended *Westm* R 1 185 O 1 293 H 1. 100
May 15.	The pope to Romanus. R. 1 185. O. 1. 293. H. 1. 101 *See May 15, 1226.*
May 30.	Exemption for the abbot of Begham. R. 1. 185. O. 1. 294. H. 1 101

DATE	SUBJECT
1227. June 4	Safe conduct for Baldwin count of Gisnes coming to the K.　R. 1. 185.　O. I. 294 H 1 101
July 17	The K to R earl of Chester. Having received good news from France the K. will not proceed to Winchester　*Westm*　R 1 185　O 1 294.　H 1. 101
July 17	A truce having been concluded with the King of France, K Henry will not proceed to Gascony, as intended　*Westm.*　R 1. 186　O 1 294　H 1 101
July 18.	Charter of liberties for Hubert de Burgh earl of Kent and Margaret his wife.　*Westm.* R 1 186
July 19	Notification that K Henry has sworn to observe the truce with the K of France　*Westm.* R 1 186　O 1 295　H 1. 101
[July]	Richard earl [of Cornwall] announces conditions of the truce which he has made with France　R. 1 186
July 24	Romanus, the papal legate, informs the K. that he has received his letters, and has sent back messengers with an answer thereto　*Paris*　R 1 187　O 1 295　H 1 101
Sept 4.	Credence for the English commissioners sent to meet the envoys from the princes of the empire at Antwerp to treat about a treaty between the empire and England.　*Windsor.* R 1. 187.　O 1. 295　H 1 101
Sept 16	The K renews to F count of Flanders the fee granted him by K John, and gives him letters of safe conduct to come into England　*Windsor*　R 1 187　O 1 296.　H 1. 101
Oct 10.	The K complains to the K of France of injuries done to Savary de Mauleon after the date of the late truce　*Westm*　R 1 187　O 1 296.　H 1 101.
[Nov ?]	The K. thanks Coradin, soldan of Damascus, for presents sent, and asks for the release of Christian captives　*Westm*　R. 1 187.　O 1 296　H. 1. 102.
Nov 9	Pope Gregory [IX] orders the yearly observation of the festival of S Edward　*Lateran.* R 1 188　O 1 297　H. 1. 102
1228. Jan 11.	Pope Gregory [IX] confirms the bull of Innocent III (30 March 1215) on the election of prelates in England　*Lateran*　R 1 183
Feb 12	Pope Gregory [IX] orders the abbot of Tichfield to excommunicate those who plunder the property of the monastery of Quarraria　*Lateran*　R. 1 183.　O 1. 297.　H 1 102.
Feb. 12.	Pope Gregory [IX] permits the Knights Templars to be produced as witnesses in suits affecting their own order　*Lateran.*　R 1 188　O. 1 298.　H 1 102
Feb 18	Falkes de Breaute having made over to the K all that he possesses, the K requests the precentor of Treves not to proceed against his widow Margaret　*Westm*　R. 1. 188 O 1 298　H 1 102
Feb. 20.	The K has received the pope's account of the failure of the expedition to the Holy Land through the fault of the emperor, for whom the K. apologises and intercedes　*Westm* R 1 189　O 1 299　H 1 102
Feb 20	The K. exhorts the emperor to sue for a relaxation of the papal sentence　*Westm* R 1 189　O 1 299　H 1 103
Feb 22.	The pope orders that the privileges of the Knights Templars be not infringed.　*Lateran.* R 1 189　O 1 300　H 1 103
Feb 27	The pope exempts the K , the queen, and the royal princes from excommunication and the royal chapel from interdict.　*Lateran.*　R 1 189.　O 1 300.　H. 1. 103.
Feb 27	The Pope orders the bp of Norwich, &c. to excommunicate those who attend tourna- ments, they being mere pretences for conspiracies.　R 1 189　O. 1 301　H. 1 303.
March 11.	The K. orders Hy de Trubleville to rectify the violations of the treaty with France. *Lambeth*　R. 1. 190.　O 1 301　H 1 103.
March 11	The K asks the K of France to grant letters of safe conduct to his commissioners em- ployed in rectifying the violations referred to above　R 1 190　O 1 301.　H 1 103.
April 13.	Pope Gregory [IX.] decrees that the K , though a minor, be permitted to administer his own realm　*Lateran.*　R. 1 190
April 22	Safe conduct for Olave K. of Man coming to the K.　*Westm*　R 1. 190.　O. 1 303. H. 1 104.
May 6	The K sends commissioners to the K. of France to confirm the truce between the realms. *Westm.*　R 1 190　O 1 302.　H 1 104.
May 6.	The K informs the archbp. of Sens and others that he has sent the commissioners for the settlement of the truce　R. 1. 190.　O. 1. 302.　H 1 104

DATE.	SUBJECT.
1228.	
May 6.	General announcement by the K. to the same effect R 1. 190 O 1 302 H. 1 104.
May 6.	The K to Hy. de Trubleville, seneschal of Gascony, &c., ordering them to observe the above truce. R 1 191. O 1 302. H. 1. 104
June 8	The K. to the K. and Queen of France ; in obedience to the pope, will observe the truce *Windsor.* R 1 191 O 1. 303 H 1 104.
June 8.	The K. to the archbp. of Sens and others, to the same effect. R. 1. 191 O 1 303. H. 1 104.
June 8.	The K. to Hy de Trubleville, seneschal of Gascony ; to the same effect R 1 191 O 1 304 H. 1 104
June 24.	The K, to G. [?] k. of Bohemia , on the interchange of messengers. *Westm.* R 1 191 O. 1. 304. H. 1 105
June 26.	Pope Gregory [IX.] informs the K. that the K of France, in his war against the Albigenses, is not authorized to molest the subjects of K. Henry *Lateran* R 1 192 O 1. 304 H 1 105
June.	Truce between France and England for one year. *Nogent.* R. 1. 192.
July 6.	Notification of the above truce *Canterbury* R 1 192. O 1. 305. H. 1 105
[July ?]	The K. asks permission from the pope to remove the body of K. John to the house which he had founded at Beaulieu. R. 1 192
July 13.	Pope Gregory [IX.] announces to the K that he has confirmed the election of Nicholas, archbp. of Armagh. R. 1. 192. O 1. 305 H 1 105.
Aug. 2	The K orders that the money of Bordeaux be made according to the law and weight of that of Tours *Reading.* R 1 192 O. 1. 306 H 1 105
Nov 16.	The K. grants to Ralph bp. of Chichester, his chancellor, and his assigns, a piece of ground in Newstreet *Westm* R. 1 193
1229. Jan. 21	The K. to J constable of Chester and others, to conduct the K. of Scotland from Berwick to York, there to meet the King. *Westm* R 1. 193 O 1 306. H. 1 105
Jan. 22.	Safe conduct for Alexander [II] k of Scotland coming to meet the K. at York. *Westm* R. 1. 193. O. 1. 306. H 1 105.
Feb.	Alexander K of Scotland to the K of England R 1. 193 See Feb 1262
Feb 6.	The K to Cardinal Romanus , requests to be informed whether the K of France has accepted the truce *Westm.* R. 1. 193. O 1. 309 H. 1 105
March 4	The K to the K. of France , again requests him to make amends for the infringements of the truce. *Westm* R. 1 193 O 1 310 H 1. 106
March 7	Credence for master Philip de Ardern to the count of Toulouse. *Mortlake.* R. 1. 194 O 1. 307. H 1 106.
March 7	Credence for Wm Riem' Columb', citizen of Bordeaux, to the count of Toulouse *Farnham.* R 1 194. O 1 307 H 1. 106
March 7	The K. congratulates O duke of Brunswick on his delivery from his enemies. *Guilford.* R 1. 194 O. 1. 308. H. 1. 106.
April 4.	The K to O duke of Brunswick ; has written to the pope on his behalf *Marlborough* R. 1 194 O 1 308. H 1. 106
April 4.	The K to the pope, in favour of O. duke of Brunswick R 1 194. O. 1. 309. H 1. 106.
April 5.	The K to Romanus, the papal legate , has sent certain plenipotentiaries to conclude a peace with the K of France. *Hampstead.* R. 1. 194. O 1. 309 H. 1. 106
April 5.	The K to the same. The same commissioners have power to conclude a truce R 1 195. O 1. 309 H. 1. 106.
April 5.	The K to the K of France. The same commissioners have power to conclude a peace. R. 1 195 O 1 310 H 1. 106.
April 5.	The K. to the same The same commissioners have power to conclude a truce R. 1 195. O. 1 310 H 1 107.
April 5.	The K to Q Blanche of France. Has sent the above commissioners to conclude a peace R 1 195. O 1. 310 H 1. 107
April 5.	The K. to the same. Has sent the same commissioners to conclude a, truce. R 1. 195. O. 1 310. H 1 107.

DATE	SUBJECT.
1229 April 19	Safe conduct for Baldwin count of Gisnes and Rob de Becum to come to the K. *Guilford* R 1. 195 O. 1 310 H 1 307
July 16.	The K promises the masters and scholars of the university of Paris certain advantages if they will transfer themselves into England *Reading.* R. 1. 195.
July 22.	Safe conduct for Baldwin count of Gisnes to come to the K *Westm* R 1. 195. O 1 311 H 1. 107
Oct 3,	The K notifies that he has received the homage of his nephew David, son of Lewelin, prince of N Wales *Westm* R 1 196 O 1. 311. H. 1 107.
Dec. 9	The K. orders the payment of his fee of 500 marks to Ferrand count of Flanders *Clyne.* R. 1 196 O. 1 311 H 1 107
Dec 29.	Safe conduct for the duke of Lorraine and Brabant and his son coming to the K. *Westm.* R. 1. 196 O 1 311 H. 1 107
1230. March 16.	The men of Savary de Mauleon are not to be prevented from plundering those of Rochelle *Nantes* R 1 196 O 1. 312 H 1 107
April 5.	Bull of protection by Pope Gregory [IX] in favour of the prior and convent of H Trinity, London *Perugia* R 1 197 O 1. 314. H. 1. 108
July 21.	The K. restores certain liberties to the men of Oleron *Myrebel* R 1 197. O 1 314 H 1 108
July 30	The K grants a truce, during his pleasure, to Gerard viscount of Brusc'. *Mirabel* R 1 197. O. 1 315. H 1 108
Aug 26	Extension of the truce with France *Luscun* R 198 O 1 315 H 1 108
Sept 6.	The K appoints commissioners to treat with the K of France respecting the truce. *Luscun.* R 1 198. O 1 315 H 1 109
Sept 23	The K promises to assist Peter duke of Brittany as long as the war lasts with the K of France *Nantes* R 1 198 O 1 315 H 1 10⁹
Sept. 23.	The K. informs Gerard viscount of Brusc' that the truce with him shall end on Wednesday (?) the vigil of Michaelmas. *Nantes* R 1 198 O 1 316 H 1 109
Sept 26.	The K promises to pay, on his arrival in England, 6,000 marks to Peter duke of Brittany *Redon* R 1 198 O 1 216 H 1 109
Sept. 27.	Commission to Peter duke of Brittany and others to induce as many as they think necessary to join the K 's service *Redon* R 1 198 O 1. 316 H 8 109
[Oct]	Emericus de Tuarcio pledges himself that Emericus de Lezyniaco shall faithfully serve the K R 1 196 O.1.312. H 1. 107.
[Oct]	Emericus de Toarcio notifies his fealty to the K. R 1 196 O 1 312 H. 1. 108.
[Oct]	Notification of the terms upon which the K delivered from prison Galfridus de Lezyniaco and his knights. R 1 197. O. 1 313 H 1 108
[Oct]	Herveus de Volurio announces that he has done fealty to the K R 1. 197 O. 1 314. H 1 108
[Nov. 10]	The K has paid his annual fee to Ferrand count of Flanders, whose merchants may trade into England *Westm* R 1 198 O 1 316 H 1 109
[Nov 10]	The K has taken under his protection the men of Otho duke of Brunswick. *Westm.* R 1 199 O 1 317 H 1 109
1231 Jan 20	Bull of Gregory [IX] exempting the K. from excommunication and his chapel from interdict *Lateran* R 1 199 O 1 317 H 1 109
April 11.	The K to the constables of various castles in Ireland, to deliver them to Walerand Teuton', to whom the K has granted the custody of the castles and lands in Ireland lately held by Wm Marshall earl of Pembroke, decd *Westm* R 1 199.
April 27.	Pope Gregory [IX] rebukes the K of Scotland for not observing his oath to the K of England. *Viterbo.* R 1 199.
May 25	The K notifies that he has seized the lands, &c in Ireland lately held by Wm. Marshall earl of Pembroke, whose brother Richard has become the liegeman of the K of France. R 1 199
May 27.	Safe conduct for the messengers of Lewelin prince of Aberfraw, coming to the K. at Worcester. *Worcester.* R 1. 200. O. 1 317. H 1 109.
June 25.	The K invites the Irish to seize whatever lands they can in Wales, Lewelin having injured the K. *Windsor.* R. 1. 200. O. 1. 318. H. 1 110.

DATE	SUBJECT
1231. July 16	The K orders the sheriff of Gloucester to cause men at arms and carpenters to join the army *Hereford* R 1 200
July 20	Pope Gregory [IX] forbids the excommunication, without urgent cause, of the K's justiciaries, &c *Rieti.* R. 1. 200 O 1 318. H 1 110.
July 20.	Pope Gregory [IX] authorizes the bp of Ely and the archdeacon of Norwich to excommunicate such laymen as disturb the peace of the realm *Rieti* R. 1 201
July 20	Pope Gregory [IX.] grants that the English nobles shall not be summoned to judgment out of England by apostolical letters *Rieti.* R 1. 201.
Nov. 30	Extension of the truce with Lewelin prince of Aberfraw. *Westm* R. 1 201 O 1 319 H 1 110
1232 Jan 16	The K invites Peter duke of Brittany to come into England, and will bear his expenses during his stay *Lambeth.* R 1. 201 O 1 320 H 1 110.
Jan. 16.	The K orders the sheriffs of Devon, &c to provide the duke of Brittany with provisions free of charge, should he land within their jurisdiction R 1 201 O 1 320 H 1 110
Jan 16	The K. endows with 700 marks per annum the house in New Street, in the suburbs of London, which he had founded for converts from Judaism R. 1. 201
Feb 11	The K. grants certain privileges to the men of Kent holding lands in gavelkind *Westm* R 1 202
Feb 20.	The K will meet Lewelin prince of Aberfraw as soon as the visit of Peter duke of Brittany shall have ended, and will settle about the truce *Geldof* R 1 202. O 1 320 H 1 110.
Feb	Amaury count of Montfort and Leicester requests the K to restore him his lands in England, or if he will not do this, to grant them to his brother Simon, who holds nothing from the K of France *Paris* R 1. 202
April 20	The K. to the Count of Savoy, apologizing for the losses which the count's son had sustained in England *Westm* R 1. 203 O 1 321 H 1 111
April 20.	Almeric count de Montfort grants to his brother Simon and his heirs all his portion of the honor of Leicester *Westm* R 1 203.
May 27.	The K notifies that at the petition of Almeric count of Montfort he has restored to Simon de Montfort the lands held in England by his father Simon *Shrewsbury* R 1 203
June 7	Pope Gregory [IX] complains that his ministers are ill used and his bulls disregarded in England. *Spoleto* R 1 203 O 1 322 H 1 111.
June 10	The K grants to the citizens of Gloucester, for the enclosure of their town, certain tolls for three years *Winchcomb* R 1. 204
June 10	The K orders the sale of certain underwood for the building of a great hall in Winchester castle *Ottinton.* R 1 204
June 16	The K. grants certain dues to the men of Bristol and Carlisle for the enclosure of their towns R 1. 205
June 16.	The K grants certain liberties to the men, women, boys, and girls of Conteshale, co. Norf *Woodstock* R 1 204
June 25	Safe conduct for S duke of Norway, coming to visit the shrine of S Thomas the Martyr *Ely* R 1 205 O 1 324 H 1 112
June	Safe conduct for Henry duke of Lemburg, coming to visit the shrine of S Thomas the Martyr R 1. 205. O 1. 324 H 1 112
June	Amaleric count of Montfort grants to his brother Simon earl of Leicester, all his lands in England which belonged to his father Simon *Paris* R 1 205
July 20	The K forbids the holding of the Round Table, he being about to meet Lewelin prince of Aberfraw at Shrewsbury *Westm* R. 1 205 O 1 324 H 1 112
Aug.	Almeric count of Montfort informs the K of England that he has granted to his brother Simon all his lands and rights in England *Paris* R 1 206
[Aug 4]	Safe conduct for Lewlin prince of Aberfraw coming to the K at Shrewsbury R 1 206 O. 1 326. H. 1. 112.
[Sept 14]	Instructions for the assessing and collecting of a fortieth granted to the K. R 1 207
Sept 19	The K to the emperor Frederic, on his campaign against the K of France. R 1 206 O 1 325. H. 1. 112 See A D. 1242, Sept 19
Sept 28	Proclamation against exchanging of money, save at the K.'s exchanges. *Lambeth* R 1 207

C

DATE	SUBJECT
1232 Oct 8	Safe conduct for the K of Navarre, passing to his own parts through the K.'s lands. *Bordeaux* R. 1 207 O. 1 327 H 1 113
[Oct 13]	Settlement respecting the imprisonment of Hubert de Burgh in the castle of Devizes R 1. 207
[Nov 12]	Safe conduct for Margaret, wife of Hubert de Burgh, sister of the K. of Scotland, and Magota her daughter, going to the lands of her husband. *Westm.* R. 1 207. O. 1 327 H 1 113
Dec 7	The K pledges himself to adhere to the arrangement to be made with Lewelin prince of Aberfraw *Shrewsbury* R. 1 208 O 1 227 H 1. 113
1233 April 19	The K. grants to the house founded for the conversion of Jews in New Street, certain houses and lands forfeited in London *Westm.* R. 1 208
May 4	The K appoints Ralph bp of Chichester to be keeper of the K's seal during life *Westm* R 1 208
May 4	The K grants to Ralph bp of Chichester his chancery of England during life R 1 209
May 4	The K grants to Ralph bp of Chichester his chancery of Ireland during life R 1 209
May 6	The K notifies the appeal about to be made by W archbp of York against the coronation of Alexander K. of Scotland R 1 209. O 1 328 H. 1. 113
May 28	Safe conduct for F , son of the late K of Connaught, coming to the K *Tewksbury* R 1 209 O 1 328 H 1 113
June 1	Regulations for the preservation of the public safety by day and night. *Fecham* R. 1 209
June 2	The K orders the keepers of H de Burgh to admit into the castle of Devizes certain knights whom they had refused to admit *Walingford* R. 1 210
July 13	The K to Louis K of France ; has sent his commissioners to Abbeville to await those of France to treat of peace *Westm* R. 1. 210.
Sept 2	The K asks Lewelin prince of Aberfraw to send his council to Colewent, there to treat of peace *Haya* R 1 210 O 1 328 H 1 114.
[Sept]	Lewelin prince of Aberfraw promises that he will observe peace with the English R 1 210 O 1 329 H 1 114
Oct. 9	Safe conduct for P duke of Brittany, coming to the K *Westm* R. 1 210 O 1 329 H. 1 114
Oct. 15.	The K has appointed justiciaries to receive the abjuration of the realm by Hubert de Burgh, and gives instructions how to proceed if he refuse *Westm* R 1 211.
1234 March 2	The K grants certain privileges to Stephen de Segrave respecting his wood at Alemundebir'. *Fodergeye* R 1 211.
April 20	Writ of military summons to meet at Portsmouth to proceed to Brittany *Westm* R 1 211. O 1 329 H. 1 114
May 3	Pope Gregory [IX] intercedes with the K. for H. de Burgh and his wife *Lateran* R. 1 211 O 1 330 H 1 114.
May 10	The K. to the bps of Paris and Sens , is ready to obey the Pope in the matter of a peace or truce with France, and will send them safe conducts *Woodstock* R 1. 211. O. 1. 330 H 1 114
May. 10.	The K forwards to the bps of Paris and Sens the letters of safe conduct mentioned above R 1 212 O 1 330 H 1 114
May. 15.	The K to Roger la Zuche (and 26 others), to send each a knight to serve, at the King's cost, with the count of Brittany *Gloucester* R 1 212 O 1 331 H 1 115.
May 21	The K notifies the appointment of G de Turville, archdeacon of Dublin, to be vice-chancellor of Ireland *Gloucester* R 1 212
June 16.	The K. assigns priority of payment to the debts of his sister Alianor countess of Pembroke to Ralph abbot of Tintern, and Ralph parson of Chelefend, over her other debts due at her death *Tewkesbury* R 1 212. O 1 332 H. 1 114.
[June.]	The K. certifies to Lewelin prince of Aberfraw that he has taken into his favour Gilbert Marshall and his followers R 1. 212 O. 1 332 H 1. 114
June 30.	The K certifies to Richard earl of Cornwall the terms of the truce with Lewelin prince of Aberfraw. *Westm.* R. 1. 213
July 2	The K. confirms to the men of Newcastle-on-Tyne their town, with certain liberties. *Westm.* R 1. 213.

DATE	SUBJECT
1234. Oct 7	The K grants to Richard de Burgo (for a fine of 3,000 marks and an annual rent of 500 marks) his lands in Connaught, with certain exceptions. *Westm.* R. 1 213
Nov 3	The K to the sheriff of Dorset, to prevent the tournament [buhurdicium] about to be held at Shirburn *Reading* R 1 213 O 1 332 H 1 115
Nov 15	The emperor Frederic [II], narrating the proceedings in his intended marriage with Isabella, the sister of the K. of England *Foge* R 1 220 O 1. 346 H. 1. 120
Nov 18	Safe conduct for the councillors of Lewellin prince of Aberfraw, coming to the K. *Westm* R 1 214 O 1 332 H 1. 115
Nov 22	The K appoints Reginald de Ponte and Neodrat 'de la Ramad' to settle the truce between himself and Louis K. of France *Westm* R 1. 214 O 1 332 H 1 115.
Nov 22	The K. notifies the above appointment *Westm.* R 1 214 O 1 333 H 1 115
Nov 22	The K. certifies that he has appointed Simon de Langton archdeacon of Cant. and the abbot of S Radegund's, to make oath for him respecting the truce with France. *Westm.* R 1 214 O 1 333. H. 1. 115
Nov 22.	The K. to B queen of France, announcing the appointment of the persons named in the last article *Westm.* R 1 214 O 1 333 H 1 115
Dec 5	Gregory [IX] to the K, recommending the proposal of marriage by the emperor Frederic [II.] for the K.'s sister, Isabella *Perugia.* R. 1. 220. O 1 348. H. 1 121
[Dec]	The K. to the emperor Frederic [II.], acknowledging the receipt of his letters, brought by master Peter de Vinea, who is sent to treat about the marriage of the K.'s sister with the emperor R 1 221 O 1 349 H. 1. 121
Dec 6	The K orders Henry de Trubleville, his seneschal in Gascony, to take care that the truce with France be observed R. 1. 214 O 1. 333. H. 1 115.
1235 Jan 3	The K to the K of Navarre; will observe the truce with him until Easter 19 Hen. III *Waverley* R 1 214 O 1 334 H 1 115
Jan 4	Gregory [IX] to the abp. of York and bp of Carlisle, requesting them to admonish the K. of Scotland to perform the conditions of the treaty between Henry [II.] and K. William of Scotland *Perugia.* R. 1. 214 O 1 334. H. 1 116
Jan 4	Gregory [IX] to the K of Scotland, exhorting him to observe the above treaty *Perugia.* R. 1 215 O 1 335 H 1 116
Feb 22	Marriage contract between the emperor Frederic [II] and Isabella sister of K. Hen [III] *Westm* R. 1. 223 O. 1. 353 H 1 123
Feb. 22.	Peter de Vinea notifies the completion of the above treaty of marriage *London* R 1 224 O 1 353 H. 1 123
Feb. 24.	The K. has gladly received the emperor's messenger. *Windsor.* R. 1 224 O 1 353 H. 1 123
Feb 24	The K to his sister, Johanna queen of Scotland, the K of Scotland, L abp of Dublin, Lewellin, and the justiciary of Ireland, announcing the marriage of his sister Isabella *Westm* R 1 224 O 1. 356 H 1 124.
[Feb 24]	The K. to H. abp of Cologne, recommending the princess Isabella to the abp's protection R. 1 225. O 1 357 H 1 124
Feb. 25.	The K complains of the continued misconduct of Peter count of Brittany, and asks the assistance of his Holiness. *Westm.* R 1 215 O 1. 335 H 1 116
Feb 25	The K informs the pope that the count de la Marche has hindered the truce between England and France. *Westm* R 1 315 O 1 332 H. 1 116
Feb. 25.	The K. explains to the cardinals why he has not paid the yearly sum of 500 marks claimed by them from England *Westm* R 1. 216. O 1. 337 H. 1. 117
Feb 26	The K. asks credence for the abbot of Beaulieu and Henry chancellor of S Paul's, London, sent by him to Blanche queen of France and her son K. Louis *Westm* R. 1 216. O 1. 337 H 1 117
March 17.	Pope Gregory [IX] takes the hospital of Alverton, in the dioc of York, under his protection *Viterbo* R 1 225 O. 1 358. H 1. 124.
March 24.	The K. orders his bailiffs in the ports of Norfolk and Suffolk to provide ten ships for the use of his sister Isabella. *Hetham* R 1 225 O 1. 358 H. 1 125
[March 24]	The K to Thomas de Emmenenegrave, sheriff of Norfolk and Suffolk, instructions respecting the above-mentioned shipping R 1 225 O. 1 358. H. 1. 125.
April 8.	The K specifies the terms upon which he will marry the daughter of S count of Ponthieu. *Reading* R 1 216. O 1 338 H 1. 117

DATE	SUBJECT
1235 April 8	The K to S. count of Ponthieu, repeating the conteuts of the previous document *Reading* R 1 216 O 1 338 H 1. 117
April 8	The K to Johanna, daughter of the count [of Ponthieu], enclosing the form of a letter to be by her sent to the pope to expedite the marriage mentioned above *Reading*. R. 1. 216. O 1 338 H 1 117
April 8	The letter referred to in the last document *Reading* R 1 216 O 1 339 H 1 117
April 13.	The K, notifies that he has granted letters of safe conduct to Olaf K of Man, coming to speak with the K *Windsor* R 1 217 O 1 339. H 1 117
April 25	The K to the pope on the marriage of the princess Isabella with the emperor. *Westm* R. 1 225 O 1 359 H 1 125
April 25	The K to the cardinals, on the same subject *Westm* R 1 226 O 1 360. H 1 125
May 1	The K has appointed proctors to assist in compelling the count de la Marche to assent to the truce between England and France. *Westm* R 1 217 O 1 339 H 1 118
May 1	The K intimates to the archdeacon of Canterbury and others, in France, the appoint-ment of the proctors mentioned above *Westm* R 1 217 O 1 340 H 1 118
May 3	Henry duke of Brabant notifies that he has received authority from the emperor Frederic [II] to remove the princess Isabella, and to convey her to the emperor *Westm* R 1 226 O 1 360, H 1 125
[May 3]	Henry abp of Cologne notifies that he has received authority as above *Westm.* R 1 226 O 1 361 H 1 126
May 3.	The K pledges himself to the pope to pay 30,000 marks to the emperor Frederic [II] as the dowry of the princess Isabella R 1 226
May 3	The K asks the pope to become security for the payment of the above sum to the emperor. R 1 226. O 1 362 H 1 126
May 7	The K promises to give to Henry duke of Lorraine the honour of Eye upon certain conditions *Sandwich* R 1 217 O 1 340 H 1 118
June 2	The K undertakes to protect Theobald K. of Navarre his men and goods, while they are in England, Gascony, and Poitou *Merton* R 1 217 O 1 340 H 1 118
June 22	The K to A count of Savoy, proposing a marriage with Eleanor daughter of Raymond count of Provence, the count of Savoy's niece *Woodstock* R 1 217 O 1 341 H 1 118
June 22	Letters of safe conduct for the duke of Norway, coming into England on his way to the Holy Land *Woodstock.* R 1 218 O 1 341 H 1. 118
June	Pope Gregory [IX] annuls certain acts by which the K has alienated from the crown some of its prerogatives *Perugia* R. 1 229 O. 1. 368 H 1 128.
June 11	The K orders M FitzGerold, justiciary of Ireland, to pay annually 40 marks, 100 cran-nocks of wheat, and 5 casks of wine to Olaf K of Man, for protecting certain parts of the coast of England and Ireland *Westm* R 1 218 O 1 341 H 1 118
July 16	The K suspends the application to the pope for a dispensation for the K's marriage with the eldest daughter of the count of Ponthieu *Westm* R 1 218 O 1. 342 H 1 118
Aug 25	The K to Louis K of France, has appointed certain persons to receive the oath of Louis for observing the truce between France and England *Waltham* R 1 218 O 1 342 H 1 119
[Aug]	The K undertakes to pay 800l Tournois, due by him to the count de la Marche for the island of Oleron, held by the K R 1 218 O 1 342 H 1 119.
Oct 10.	The K asks Raymond count of Provence to proceed with the arrangements for the marriage of his daughter Eleanor with the K *Windsor* R 1 218 O 1 343 H 1 119.
[Oct 10]	The K. to Beatrix countess of Provence, to the same effect as the above R 1 219 O 1 343 H 1 119.
Oct 14	The K orders that the suit between Hugh count de la Marche and his wife Isabella queen of England, the K's mother, should be set aside for the present *Westm.* R 1. 219 O 1. 344 H 1. 119.
Oct 15.	Marriage contract between the K and Eleanor, daughter of Raymond count of Provence *Westm.* R. 1. 219
[Oct 15]	Credence for the messengers sent by the K to Raymond count of Provence and Beatrix his wife to treat of the above marriage R 1 219 O 1. 345 H. 1. 120
Oct 15	Commission to the proctors appointed by the K to arrange his marriage with Elianor, daughter of Raymond count of Provence, to receive 20,000 marks with the said Elianor *Windsor.* R. 1 220. O 1 346. H 1 120.
Oct 15.	Similar letters authorizing the said proctors to receive 15,000, 10,000, 7,000, 5,000, or 3,000 marks, as above. R 1 220 O 1 346 H. 1. 120.

DATE.	SUBJECT
1235. Oct. 19	The K authorizes the commissioners appointed to treat of his marriage, if they cannot obtain Eleanor of Provence according to the terms expressed in their letters, to bring her with them into England without the payment of any money to the K. *Westm.* R. 1 220. O. 1 346. H 1 120.
Nov. 15.	The emperor Frederic [II] respecting his marriage with Isabella the K.'s sister. R. 1. 221. *See* Nov. 15, 1234
Dec. 5.	Gregory [IX] to the K respecting the marriage of his sister Isabella R 1 220 *See* Dec 5, 1234.
Dec. 8.	Safe conduct for Alexander [II] K. of Scotland, and Johanna his wife, coming to London to speak with the K. *Brunmore* R. 221. O. 1. 348. H 1, 121
Dec 12	The K requests William, abp of York, to join with others, whose names are specified, in conducting Alexander K of Scotland to London *Clarendon* R 1. 221 O 1 348 H 1 121
[Dec.]	The K. to the emperor, relative to the advent of Peter de Vinea. R 1. 221. O. 1. 349 H 1 121. *See* [Dec.] 1234.
1236. Jan 16.	Safe conduct for the prior of Beaumont and master William de Sens, coming into England respecting the truce with France *Canterbury* R. 1 221 O 1 349 H 1. 121
Feb. 3	Truce with France for five years *Winchester.* R. 1. 221. O 1. 349. H 1. 121.
Feb 3.	Richard earl Cornwall and others, certify that they have sworn to induce the K to observe the truce with France *Winchester* R 1 222 O 1. 351. H 1 122
Feb 7	The K. informs the abp of Auch that he has married, at Canterbury, Alianor, daughter of the count of Provence, and has made a truce with France *Winchester* R 1 222 O. 1. 351 H 1 122
Feb. 7.	The K to the count of Bigorre, to the same effect as the above. R 1 222 O 1 351. H 1 122
Feb. 7	The K promises to give to Henry duke of Lorraine the honour of Eye upon certain conditions *Winchester* R 1. 222 O 1 352 H 1 122
Feb 10	The K requests that Henry duke of Lorraine would do homage for the lands which he holds in England within a month from Michaelmas next *Winchester* R. 1 223 O 1 352. H 1 122
Feb. 18.	The K. cites Lewellin prince of Aberfraw to make satisfaction for injuries done by him to the earl marshal. *Marlborough* R 1 223. O 1 353 H 1 123
Feb 22	Marriage contract of the emperor Frederic with Isabella, the K.'s sister R 1 223 O 1 353 H 1 123. *See* Feb 22, 1235.
Feb. 22.	Notification of the above. R 1 224 O. 1 353. H 1. 123 *See* Feb 22, 1235
Feb. 24.	The K to the emperor, gladly receives his messenger R. 1 224. O 1. 353 H 1 123 *See* Feb 24, 1235
Feb. 24.	The K to Johanna queen of Scotland on the marriage of his sister R. 1 224 O 1 356 H 1 124 *See* Feb. 24, 1235
[Feb 24.]	The K to the abp of Cologne, on the same subject. R. 1 225 O. 1 357 H. 1 124 *See* Feb 24, 1235
March 12.	The K to the constable of Dover; if any subject of France shall henceforth land in his bailiwick without the K's permission, he shall be sent back by the constable, with similar mandate to the abp of Canterbury *S Edmunds* R 1 225. O 1. 357. H 1 124
March 17	Bull of Gregory [IX], relative to the hospital of Alverton. R 1 225. O. 1 356 H 1. 124 *See* March 17, 1235
March 24.	The K to the bailiffs of Norfolk and Suffolk, relative to ships for his sister Isabella R 1 225 O 1 358 H. 1 125 *See* March 24, 1235
[March 24]	The K to Tho de Emmenegrave, on the same subject R 1. 225 O. 1 358. H 1 125 *See* March 24, 1235
April 25	The K to pope [Gregory IX.], on the marriage of his sister Isabella R. 1. 225 O 1 359 H 1. 125. *See* April 25, 1235.
April 25.	The K to the cardinals, on the same subject R 1 226 O 1 360 H 1. 125 *See* April 25, 1235
April 27.	Bull by which Gregory [IX] absolves the K from marrying Johanna, daughter of the count of Ponthieu *Viterbo* R 1 231 O 1 371 H 1. 129.
May 3	Notification by Henry duke of Brabant, relative to Isabella, the K.'s sister R 1. 226 O 1 360 H 1. 125 *See* May 3, 1235.
[May 3]	Notification by Henry abp. of Cologne, on the same subject R. 1. 226. O. 1. 361 H 1 126. *See* [May 3], 1235.

DATE.	SUBJECT
1236 May 3	The K to the pope, asking him to be security for the payment of his sister's dower. R. 1. 226. *See* May 3, 1235
May 3	The K to the pope, pledging himself to pay his sister's dower R 1 226. O 1. 362 H 1 126 *See* May 3, 1235
May 19.	Safe conduct for master Walter de Ocra, messenger to the K from the emperor Frederic [II.] *Winchester.* R 1 227 O 1 362 H 1. 126.
May 24	Protection for Olaf K of Man and the Isles going into Norway by command of the K of Norway *Merewell* R. 1. 227 O 1 363 H 1 126
May 26	Proclamation respecting the goods of persons escaping from shipwreck on the coasts of England, Poitou, Gascony, and Oleron *Merewell* R 1 227. O. 1 36. H. 1. 12
May 29	The K to J count of Flanders, has made compensation for injuries sustained by the count of Flanders, and sends an emerald in token of amity R. 1 227. O. 1 362. H. 1. 126
May 30	The pope Gregory [IX] absolves the K from his oath to marry Johanna, daughter of the count of Ponthieu. *Tern:* R 1 231 O 1. 371 H. 1 129
[June.]	The K to the emperor Frederic [II] on the insurrection of the Lombards, and asking a delay in paying the money due and shortly to become due R 1 223. O. 1 364. H. 1. 127.
[June 29]	The K to the emperor Frederic [II], has sent messengers to the pope in the matters of the Lombards, and will send 5,000 marks to the emperor for the term of Easter last past *Bristol.* R 1 228 O 1 364 H 1 127
[June 29]	The K informs the emperor of the reasons which prevent him from sending to him R. earl of Cornwall, the K.'s brother R 1 228 O 1 365 H. 1 127
[June 29]	The K. asks the emperor to send a safe conduct for Richard, earl of Cornwall, about to visit the emperor R 1. 228 O. 1 366 H. 1. 127
June 30	The K to the empress [Isabella], would be glad to know how she is. R. 1 229 O 1. 366 H 1 128.
June 30	The K asks the pope to assist the emperor against the rebellious Lombards *Bristol* R. 1 229 O 1. 367 H 1 128
[June 29.]	The K to the cardinals , to the same effect as the letter to the pope *Bristol* R. 1. 229 O 1 367. H 1. 128
June	Bull of pope Gregory [IX], annulling certain of the K.'s acts. R. 1. 229. O 1. 368. H 1 128 *See* June, 1235
July 11.	Truce with Lewellin prince of Aberfraw, for one year *Tewkesbury* R 1 229 O 1 368 H. 1 128.
July 12	Safe conduct for the convoys of Lewellin coming to Shrewsbury and Wenlock, to swear to the truce mentioned above *Tewkesbury* R. 1 230 O 1 369 H. 1 128.
July 26	The K announces to Lewellin the names of the persons selected by him for the settlement of the truce *Pars'* R. 1 230 O. 1. 369. H 1 128
July 26	The K. appoints the bp of Hereford and others to settle the truce with Lewellin *Pars'* R 1. 230 O. 1 369 H 1 129
Sept. 20	The K grants the manor of Driffield to Johanna queen of Scotland *York* R. 1 230 O. 1 370. H. 1 129
Sept 24	The K. to Alexander [II] K of Scotland, respecting the apprehension of Richard Siward *Sharburn* R 1. 231 O 1. 370 H. 1. 129.
1237 March 20	The K grants to the merchants of Gutlandt freedom to trade with England *Westm* R 1 231
April 8	Letters of protection for Olaf K of Man going to Norway *Kenton* R. 1. 231. O 1 371 H 1 129.
April 27	Bull of pope Gregory [IX.], absolving the K from marrying the daughter of the count of Ponthieu R 1. 231. O 1 371 H. 1 129 *See* April 27, 1236
May 30.	Bull of pope Gregory [IX.] on the same subject. R. 1 231 O 1 371. H. 1 129. *See* May 30, 1236
June 3	The K pledges himself for the safety of his nephew David, son of Lewellin, and of all coming with him, to meet the K at Worcester *Westm.* R 1 232 O. 1. 372. H. 1 130
June 14	Extension of the truce with Lewellin for one year. *Westm.* R 1 232 O. 1. 373 H 1 130
June 26.	Writ to pay 10,000 marks to the emperor, in full discharge of the marriage portion of 30,000 marks paid by the K as his sister's portion. *Woodstock.* R 1. 232 O 1 373 H. 1. 130.
June 27.	The K expresses his wish for peace and concord between the barons of the Cinque Ports and the citizens of Bayonne. *Woodstock* R 1 232 O 1 373 H 1 130

DATE.	SUBJECT
July 2	Mandate for the collecting of a thirtieth granted to the K by the synod lately held at Westminster *Westm.* R 1 232
[July]	The emperor [Frederic II.] informs the K. of the birth of a son, whom he has named Henry R 1 233. O 1 374. H 1 130.
July 9	The pope Gregory [IX] requests that the K will pay the annual tribute of 1,000 marks still due. *Risti.* R. 1. 233. O 1 374. H 1 130
Sept 25	Settlement of all disputes between the K and Alexander K of Scotland. *York* R. 1. 233. O. 1. 374. H. 1. 131
[Sept.]	Alexander K of Scotland informs the pope that he has sworn to observe the above settlement R. 1. 234 O. 1 377 H 1 132
Nov 3	Attestation that William Talbot has delivered up to the K the castle of Gloucester, together with the princess Eleanor, the K.'s cousin *Woodstock.* R. 1 234. O. 1 379. H. 1. 132.
Dec 11	Pope Gregory [IX] requests that Theodin, son of Oddo Branchaleon, be restored to the rectory of South Elmham, from which he had been ousted *Lateran* R. 1 234. O 1 378. H 1 132
1238 Feb 20.	Pope Gregory [IX.] requests that the K will revoke the prodigal gifts made by him to the prelates, churches, and nobles of England *Lateran* R. 1 234 O 1 378 H 1 132.
Feb 21.	The K permits his sister Johanna Q of Scotland to dispose, by her will, of the issues of the manors of Staunton and Driffield, for two years *Westm* R. 1 235. O 1 379 H 1 132
March 8.	The K summons Wm. de Stateville and 12 others to meet him at Oxford to confer respecting the truce with Lewellin, prince of Aberfraw *Tewksbury* R 1 235 O 1 379. H 1 132
[March 8]	The K. orders prince Lewellin to prevent his son David from receiving the homage of the nobles of North Wales and Powys *Tewksbury* R. 1. 235. O. 1. 379. H. 1 132
[March 8]	The K. to his nephew David, forbidding him to receive the homages above mentioned *Tewksbury* R 1 235 O 1 380. H 1 132.
May 1	The K orders the payment of 500l as a gift to the emperor of Constantinople. *Reading.* R 1 235 O 1 380 H 1 133
June 12	The K. orders that the Saracen, whom he sends with this writ, be permitted to reside in Canterbury castle, but that no one be allowed to confer with him *Ditton.* R 1 235. O 1 380 H 1 133
July 8	The K prolongs the truce with Lewellin for another year *Reading.* R. 1. 235. O. 1 380 H 1. 133
July 8	The K orders Lewellin to observe the above truce *Reading* R 1 236. O 1 381 H 1 133
[July]	Lewellin prince of Aberfraw pledges himself to observe the said truce. R 1 236. O 1 381 H 1 133
July 15	Letters of protection for Richard of S Alban's, messenger of the K of Norway *Windsor* R 1 236. O 1 382 H 1 133
July 20	The K. to Tath', messenger from "the Old Man of Mussa;" will be glad to see him in England, provided he bring with him the treaty into which his master has entered with the K of France *Kenynton* R 1 236 O 1 382 H 1 133
[Sept]	The Emperor to the K , complains of the pope having joined against him with the Lombards, to aid whom he has summonded a council If any of the English prelates attend it, they must do so at their peril R. 1. 236 O 1 382. H. 1. 133
[Oct 29]	The Emperor to the K , whom he blames for permitting the sentence of excommunication against him to be published in the churches of England, and for allowing money to be raised in England for the use of the court of Rome R 1 237 O. 1. 383. H 1. 134.
Oct 29	The Emperor to the barons of England , expostulates with them for aiding the pope against the empire *The camp before Piacenza* R 1 237 O 1 385 H 1 134
[Nov]	The Emperor to the K., warmly censuring the pope and his legate, whose obnoxious proceedings he details R 1. 238 O. 1 386 H 1 135
1239 Jan 12	Bull of pope Gregory [IX] relative to the see of Winchester. R 1. 238 O 1 387 H 1 135 See Jan 12, 1240.
Feb 8	Bull of pope Gregory [IX.] on the same subject R 1. 238. O 1. 138. H. 1. 135. See Feb 8, 1240
Oct. 21	Bull of Pope Gregory [IX]; nothing shall be done prejudicial to the interests of the crown during the present vacancy of the see of Durham *Anagni* R 1. 239. O 1 388. H 1 136

DATE	SUBJECT
1239 Dec 8	The K to his proctors in the court of Rome , to promote the interests of his uncle, Thomas count of Flanders, in the court of Rome *Clarendon* R 1 239 O 1 388 H. 1 136
1240 Jan 12.	Bull of Gregory [IX], informing the K that, although he cannot remove from the papal letters a clause objectionable to the K , yet he has directed his legate to take care that no one suspected by the K shall be appointed to the see of Winchester. *Lateran* R 1 238 O 1 387 H 1. 135
Jan 22	Inspeximus and confirmation of a charter by which Odo, the son of John the smelter, quit-claims to Edward, son of Odo the goldsmith, and his heirs, all his rights in the K's smelting office in the exchequer *Westm* R 1 239
Feb 8	The pope Gregory [IX] to the earl of Cornwall and others , has already settled the business connected with the church of Winchester, about which they had written to him *Lateran* R. 1. 238 O 1. 388 H 1. 135
May 15	Convention by which David, son of Lewellin, formerly prince of N Wales, consents to do homage to the K for his land of N Wales and elsewhere. *Gloucester* R. 1 239 O 1 389 H 1 136
July 4	Bull of Gregory [IX], confirming to the convent of the H Trinity, London, the chapels of S. Catherine and S Michael, London, and the tithes of Walmer *Lateran.* R. 1 240 O 1 390 H 1 136
[July]	Letter of Fedlin, K of Connaught, thanking the K for assistance R 1 241 O 1 391 H 1 136 See [Aug.] 1261
Nov 31	The K summons David, son of Lewellin, to come to London to proceed in the matters in dispute between them *Windsor* 31 Nov R 1 240 O 1 391 H 1 137.
[April 21]	Statement of the proceedings of the arbitrators of David, son of Lewellin, on the one part, and the lords marchers of Wales, on the other , a meeting appointed at Maneford Bridge, near Shrewsbury R. 1 241 O 1 392 H 1 137
April 23	The K requests the prelates of the two provinces to collect the sums arising from the redemption of the vows of crusaders, and to pay over the same for the Holy Land. *Windsor*. R. 1. 241. O 1 393 H 1 137
1241 Feb 19	The K complains to David, son of Lewellin, of having failed to attend the meeting at Worcester, and cites him to appear at Shrewsbury *Woodstock* R 1 240. O 1 392 H 1 137
[May.]	The emperor Frederic [II] informs the K of the taking of the city of Faenza, and that three legates and above 100 prelates had fallen into his hands *Faenza* R 1 241 O 1 393 H 1 137
June 33	Commission to Peter of Savoy, the K's uncle, to secure the services of the count of Châlons and others *Marlboro'* R 1 242 O 1 395 H 1 138
July 14	The K orders David, son of Lewellin, late prince of N Wales, to make amends for the injuries lately done to the K's subjects *Marlboro'* R 1 242 O. 1 395 H. 1 138.
Aug. 29.	David, son of Lewellin, recites the promises which he has engaged to perform to the K. *Alney* R 1 242. O 1 396 H 1 138
Aug 31.	David, son of Lewellin, undertakes to perform the promises contained in the previous article In the King's tent at *Rhyddian* R 1 242 · O 1 397 H 1 139
[Aug 31]	David, son of Lewellin, promises that he will observe the compacts made with the K. respecting the land held by his father, and other matters R 1 243 O 1 397 H 1 139.
Sept 25	The K. has granted to Peter de Savoy the lands of John de Warren in Surrey and Sussex, during the K's pleasure *Westm* R 1. 243 O 1 399 H. 1 139
Oct 25.	Walter Marshall has licence to perform homage to Louis [IX] K of France for his rights in Normandy *Westm* R 1 240 O 1 391 H 1 137
1242. Jan 30.	The emperor Frederic [II] announces to the K the death of the empress, his sister Isabella, which occurred on Dec 1, 1241. *Coronutum* R 1. 243. O 1. 399 H. 1 140
Feb 16	The K empowers N bishop of Durham to assign to Alexander K of Scotland lands in England to the annual value of 200*l* *Reading* R 1 244 O 1 400 H 1 140
March 8.	The K promises that he will observe the truce entered into by him with Louis [IX] K of France, who, if the K violate it, may invade England. *Westm* R 1 244. O. 1. 400 H 1 140
May 5	The K (being about to sail for Gascony), by the advice of all his earls and barons, intrusts the regency of his realm to W. abp. of York *Portsmouth*. R 1 244 O 1 400 H 1 140
May 24	The K appoints commissioners to settle the infringement of the truce with the commissioners of Louis [IX] K. of France *Pons* R 1 244 O 1 401. H 1. 140.

DATE	SUBJECT
1242. May 25	Military summons to the men of Gascony, the mayor of Bordeaux, and others, to meet the K at Pons *Pons* R 1 244 O 1. 401. H 1 140
May 31	The K appoints commissioners to settle the infringement of the truce with the commissioners of Louis [IX] K. of France. *Pons.* R 1. 245. O. 1 403 H 1 141.
May 31.	The K authorizes the above commissioners to treat with the French commissioners respecting certain affairs here specified *Pons* R 1 245 O 1 403 H 1 141
May 31.	The K informs the above commissioners that Louis [IX] K. of France has now openly violated the terms of the truce *Pons.* R 1 245. O 1. 403. H. 1 141.
June 8	The K informs Hugh bp of Ely that the truce with France having been openly violated by [Louis IX] K of France, war is imminent, for which more men and money are required *Saintes* R 1 245 O 1 243 H. 1 141
June 8	The K, being in pressing want of men and money, requests that he be immediately furnished with the same from England. *Saintes* R 1. 246 O 1 404. H 1 142
June 8.	Writ of military summons to W de Cantilupe the younger, to serve the K against the French *Saintes* R 1 246 O 1 405 H 1 142
June 8	The K to the barons of the Cinque Ports and the men of Dunwich, to fit out shipping to ravage the coasts of France. *Saintes* R 1 246 O 1 406 H 1. 142.
June 15	Writ of military summons to Vitalis Engayne and 50 others to serve the K against the French *Saintes* R 1 246 O 1 405 H 1 142.
June 15.	The K to the garrison of Parteney, to harass the K of France in every way possible *Saintes* R 1 247 O. 1 406 H 1 142
June 17.	Credence from the K for certain persons sent to treat with the emperor on matters already discussed between them *Saintes* R 1 247. O 1 406 H 1 142
June 28.	The K. permits the inhabitants of the isle of Ré to have a mayor, jurates, and commune, while they are in fealty with him *Taunay* R 1 247 O 1 407 H 1. 143
June 30	The K promises that he will promote a marriage between R count of Toulouse and Margaret, the K's sister *Taillebourg.* R 1 247 O. 1. 407. H. 1 143.
July 5	Commission to Peter de Bordeaux and Bartholomew Peche to conclude a treaty of mutual aid between K Henry and the emperor *Saintes.* R 1 247 O 1. 407 H 1 143
July 7.	Mandate to the town of Marsan to send 100 cross-bowmen to the K. *Saintes.* R. 1. 247. O 1 407. H. 1. 143
July 7	The K directs that the gallies of Bristol shall harass the coasts of France *Saintes* R 1 247 O 1 407. H. 1 143
July 7.	The K orders the employment of all the gallies of Ireland in the above service. *Saintes.* R 1 247 O 1 408 H. 1 143
July 7	The K orders the payment of the wages of Peter Alard, knt *Saintes* R. 1. 247 O 1. 408 H 1 143
July 7	The K orders the mayor of Bordeaux to send him 300 cross-bowmen, and to fortify the bridge at Taunay. R 1 247 O 1. 408 H 1 143
July 21.	Writ of military summons to Geoffrey de la Laund and two others, to join the K at Pons. *Saintes* R. 1 247 O 1. 408. H. 1. 143
Aug 4	The K. grants to the men of Bayonne the first 1,000 marks which they may take from the K. of France, and one half of the remainder of the plunder *At the camp on the Gironde.* R 1. 248 O 1 408 H 1 143
Aug 14	Agreement by which Raymond vicount of Fronsac undertakes to serve K Henry against France. *At the camp on the Gironde.* R 1 248 O. 1 408 H 1 143
Aug 20.	The K orders Arnold de Blankeford to keep the peace with the vicount of Fronsac. *Silva* R. 1 248 O 1 409 H 1 144.
Aug 28	The abp of York (regent of the realm) appoints constables and leaders of the knight sent to the K in Poitou *Winchester* R 1 248. O. 1 410 H. 1 144.
Aug 28	Notification by the K that he has entered into a treaty with Raymond count of Toulouse against the K of France *Bordeaux* R 1 248 O 1 410 H 1 144
Sept 3	Notification of Raymond count of Toulouse, that he has entered into a treaty with the K against the K of France. R 1 249 O 1 411 H. 1 144
Sept 5.	The K certifies that he has procured an agreement between the count of Toulouse and Arnold de Tantalon' and the vicount of Fronsac *Bordeaux* R 1 249 O 1 412 H 1 144.

DATE	SUBJECT
1242 Sept 11	Writ of military summons to Aquenville del Sparre and others, to join the K. at Ste Basille *Bordeaux.* R. 1 249 O 1 412 H 1. 145.
Sept 15	Writ of military summons to the men of Langun and S Macaire to join the K at Ste. Basille *Bordeaux* R 1 249 O 1 413 H 1 145.
Sept 15	Similar writ to Amamun de Varens to join the K. at S Emilion R 1 249 O 1. 413. H 1 145
Sept. 19	The K informs the emperor of the details of his campaign against the K. of France, and attributes his want of success to the treachery of the nobles of Poitou. *Bordeaux* R. 1 206 O 1 325 H 1 112
Sept 25	Writ of military summons to Girard de Bleyne to join the K at S Emilion *Bordeaux* R 1 249 O. 1 413 H 1 145
Oct. 18	Writ of military summons to Robert de Rauncever, and others, to join the K *Bordeaux.* R 1 249 O. 1. 413. H 1 145
Oct 29,	Bull of pope Innocent [IV.] for Geoffrey Ledespris R 1 250 O 1 413. H 1 145 *See* Oct 29, 1243
[Oct]	For the barons of the Cinque Ports , that their liberties shall not be prejudiced R 1 250 *See* Jan 23, 1243
Nov 10.	The K to John duke of Brittany , is unable at this time to aid him in recovering the county of Richmond. *La Reole* R 1 250 O 1 413 H 1 145
1243. Jan 8.	The K informs the emperor of the treachery of R count of Toulouse, (who has joined the French,) and of the men of Poitou *Bordeaux* R 1 250. O 1 414 H. 1 145.
Jan 8	The K to Peter de Vinea, on the treachery of the count of Toulouse *Bordeaux* R 1 250 O 1 414 H 1 145
Jan 8	The K reminds Eyma de Gumpers of their conversation in the presence of P of Savoy, and asks to be informed of what has been done herein with the emperor *Bordeaux* R 1 251 O 1 415 H 1 146
[Jan. 23.]	The barons of the Cinque Ports are assured that what they have done at their own charges against the French shall not prejudice their liberties R 1 250
Jan. 25	The K requests R Berenger count of Provence not to go into France, and not to send his daughter Senchia into England, under the safe conduct of the K of France *Bordeaux* R 1 251
March 26	Agreement between the K and Sicard de Mundgroum, respecting the tenure of the castle de la Clotere *Bordeaux* R 1 251 O 1 415 H 1 146
April 7	Truce for five years between Henry K of England and Louis K. of France *Bordeaux* R 1 251 O 1 416 H. 1 146
April 25	Bull of pope Innocent [IV] for the Queen of England to enter any monastery. R 1 252 O 1 417 H 1 146 *See* April 25, 1244
April 25	Bull of pope Innocent [IV] to B elect of Canterbury. R 1 252. O. 1 417 H 1 147 *See* April 25, 1244
April 29	Safe conduct for David, son of Lewellin, late prince of N Wales, coming to London *Fulham.* R 1 252. O 1 418 H 1 147
May 29	Bull of pope Innocent [IV] on the festival of S Edward R. 1. 252 O. 1 418 H 1 147 *See* May 29, 1244
[May]	The K. (being on his way to Bayonne) invites the K. of Navarre to meet him at Erbroe, to settle disputes R 1 252. O 1 419. H 1 147
June 30.	Will of K Henry III , dated on Tuesday next after the feast of Ss. Peter and Paul, 1253 R 1. 496.
July 12	The K directs that the men of the Cinque Ports shall make reprisals upon John Duke of Brittany, who has broken his truce with England. *Bordeaux* R 1 253. O 1 219. H 1 147
[July]	Protestation by Pontius de Agtuac and others that they have done homage to the K at Saintes R 1. 253 O 1 419 H. 1 147
Aug 7	Commission to Ralph FitzNicolas and others to enter into a treaty on behalf of the K with Geoffrey de Moretaigne and others *Bordeaux* R 1 253 O 1 420 H 1 147
Aug. 17	Assignment of dower for Eleanor queen of England, in the event of the death of the K. *Bordeaux* R 1 253. O 1 420 H 1 147
Aug. 28	The K to W de Lungespe and Nicholas de Molis, seneschal of Gascony , will not for the present besiege the castle of Aigremont *Bordeaux* R 1 253 O 1 420 H 1 148
Oct 29	Pope Innocent [IV] permits Geoffrey Ledespris to build a chapel in the diocese of Lincoln *Lateran* R 1 250 O 1 413 H 1. 145

DATE	SUBJECT
1243 Dec. 1.	Settlement of the property awarded by the K to his brother Richard earl of Cornwall, upon his marriage with Senchia *Westm* R 1 258 O 1 421 H 1 148
Dec 15	Safe conduct for Fedlin Oconcanir, son of the K of Connaught, coming into England to confer with the K. *Windsor.* R 1 254. O. 1. 422. H. 1 148
Dec 15	Certificate by the K that the service in the butlery rendered by the barons of London at the marriage of R earl of Cornwall was gratuitously done by them. *Windsor.* R. 1 254 O 1 422 H 1 148
1244. Jan 10.	The K. lends 4,000 marks to R Berenger count of Provence on the security of five castles *Westm* R 1 254 O 1 423 H. 1. 148.
Jan 23.	Pope Innocent [IV] expects the K to undertake a crusade for the help of the Holy Land *Lyons* R 1 254 O 1 423 H. 1 147.
March 27	The K asks Akenwill de la Sparre and the rest of the barons of Gascony to aid Nicholas de Molis, seneschal of Gascony, against the K. of Navarre *Westm* R. 1. 255. O 1 424 H 1 149
April 7	Bull of Innocent [IV] for the K's ecclesiastical rights R 1 255 O 1 425. H. 1 149 *See* April 7, 1245.
April 8.	Bull of Innocent [IV] relative to David prince of N. Wales. R 1 255 O 1 425 *See* H. 1. 149 April 8, 1245
April 10	Bull of Innocent [IV] on the K's right of patronage R. 1. 256. O. 1. 426 H 1 149 *See* April 10, 1245
April 25	Pope Innocent [IV] permits the Q of England, and ten honest women with her, to enter certain Cistercian and other monasteries in England, for the purpose of prayer *Lateran* R 1 252 O 1 417. H 1 146.
April 25	Pope Innocent [IV] permits B elect of Canterbury to absolve the K, excepting in certain reserved cases *Lateran* R. 1. 252 O. 1. 417. H. 1. 147.
April 30.	The K. certifies that the misfortune which befel Grifin, late prince of Wales, in attempting to escape from the Tower of London, is not to be an occasion of trouble to W abp of York *Westm* R 1 256
May 29.	Bull of Innocent [IV.] ordering that the festivals of the nativity and translation of S. Edward be observed *Lateran* R 1 252 O 1 418 H 1 147.
July 7.	The K summons Donald K of Terchenull and 22 others (whose names are specified) to aid him against the K of Scotland *Stamford* R 1 256 O 1 426 H 1 150
July 15	Commission to settle a truce with David, son of Lewellin, late prince of Wales *Nottingham* R 1 256 O 1 427 H 1 150
July 22.	Pope Innocent [IV.] assures the K that the royal privileges shall not be impaired in any matters connected with the churches of Winchester, Norwich, and Bath. *Genoa.* R 1. 256 O 1. 427 H 1. 150.
July 29	Pope Innocent [IV.] exhorts the clergy of England to grant a subsidy to the K. *Genoa.* R 1 257 O 1 427 H 1 150
Aug 13	The K to G Prendergast, a treaty having been executed at Newcastle upon Tyne with the K of Scotland, he may return home *Newcastle* R 1 257 O 1 429 H. 1 151.
Aug 13	The K ratifies the treaty with Scotland made in his name. *Newcastle* R 1 257 O 1. 429 H 1. 151.
[Sept]	Alexander [II] K of Scotland promises that he will keep good faith with the K R 1 257 O 1 428
Oct. 21	Protection for Fethel K of Connaught *Gournay.* R 1 257 O 1 429 H 1 151
Nov 29.	The K requests W bp of Winchester to excommunicate David, son of Lewellin, formerly prince of N Wales, for having violated the truce *Marlborough.* R 1 258 O 1 430 H 1 151
1245. Jan 6	The K. desires J Le Strange, Justice of Chester, to summon David, son of Lewellin, and 23 others, to appear before the K, to answer the charge of having broken the truce R. 1 258 O 1 430 H 1 251.
Jan 10	The K orders M FitzGerard, justiciary of Ireland, to bring troops in Ireland against David, son of Lewellin. *Westm* R 1 258 O 1 431 H 1 251
Jan. 30	Pope Innocent [IV] exhorts the abbots and priors of England to attend the council about to be held at Lyons *Lyons* R. 1. 258
March 6.	Commission to John Lestrange, Justice of Chester, and Henry de Audley, to treat respecting a truce with the envoys of David, son of Lewellin *Westm.* R. 1. 259 O 1 432 H. 1 152

DATE	SUBJECT
1245 April 7	Bull of Innocent [IV] to the K, confirming his ecclesiastical rights and privileges. *Lyons* R 1 255 O 1 425 H 1 149
April 8	Bull of Innocent [IV], by which he annuls certain letters granted by him to David, prince of N Wales, upon false information *Lyons* R 1 255 O 1 425 H 1 149
April 10	Pope Innocent [IV.] assures the K that he has no wish to interfere with his right of patronage *Lyons* R 1 256. O 1 426 H 1 149
[April 12]	Margaret countess of Flanders to the K, asking that he will cause 50*l* to be restored to John Baderel, burgess of Ypres, of which he had been robbed in England R 1 259 O. 1 432 H 1 152
April 21	The K. directs G Rydell and Peter de Bordeaux to receive amends for the infringement of the truce with France *Windsor.* R 1 259 O 1 432 H 1 152
[April 26]	Margaret countess of Flanders requests the K to send the arrears of her fees of Flanders and Hainault *Lille* R 1 259 O 1 432 H 1 152.
May 20.	Pope Innocent [IV]. excuses the attendance of certain English prelates at the council of Lyons. *Lyons.* R 1 259.
May 31	Pope Innocent [IV] permits Philip Basset, his wife and family, to attend divine service in interdicted churches and chapels *Lyons* R 1 260 O 1 433 H 1 152.
June 7	The K directs that preparations of horses, arms, and troops be made for the war against David son of Lewellin *Westm* R 1 260 O 1 433 H 1 152
June 8.	The K. asks the emperor to give a kindly hearing to the messengers whom he sends to the council of Lyons *Westm* R 1 260 O 1 434 H 1 152
June 8	The K asks pope Innocent [IV] to suspend the discussion in the council of Lyons of the affairs of England until the arrival of the English messengers *Westm* R 1 260 O. 1 434 H. 1 153
[June 11]	The K requests the bps of England, Ireland, and Gascony to be watchful over the rights of his crown in the council at Lyons R 1 260 O 1 434 H. 1 153.
June 17	The K grants to John eldest son of the duke of Brittany 2,000 marks a year for the county of Richmond *Vyldeford.* R 1 260
June 22.	Pope Innocent [IV] forbids the English prelates from receiving money on relaxing the sentence of excommunication. *Lyons* R 1. 261 (80) O 1 435 (110) H 1 143. (38)
July 21.	Pope Innocent [IV.] confirms every privilege hitherto granted by the apostolic see to the K over the churches of England and Ireland *Lyons.* R 1. 261 O 1 435 H 1. 153
July 21	Pope Innocent [IV] cancels the election of R Passalewe to the see of Chichester. *Lyons.* R. 1. 261 O 1 436 H 1 153
July 21.	Pope Innocent [IV] exempts the K's royal chapels from all sentences of excommunication *Lyons.* R 1 261 O 1 436 H 1 153
July 27	Pope Innocent [IV] authorizes the chancellor of Oxford to determine a claim of jurisdiction made by the archdeacon of Stafford over the K's exempt chapel of "Bruges" [Bridgenorth] *Lyons* R 1. 261 O 1 436 H 1 153
[July]	The nobility and commonalty of England complain to pope [Innocent IV] of the extortions and aggressions of the court of Rome. R 1 262
Aug 3	Pope Innocent [IV] to the prelates of England, dispensing with the strict rule against plurality of benefices *Lyons* R 1 262 O 1 437 H 1 154
Aug 3	Pope Innocent [IV] grants to the prelates of England the right of presenting to benefices. *Lyons* R 1 262 (80) O 1 437 (120) H 1 154 (38).
Aug. 3.	Pope Innocent [IV] to the prelates of England, to the same effect as the preceding *Lyons* R 1 80 O 1 120 H 1 38.
Aug. 3	Pope Innocent [IV] informs the K that crusaders are bound to observe the customs of his realm. *Lyons.* R. 1 263 O 1 438 H 1 154.
Aug 20	The K assigns to B. de Mastok count of Bigorre 250 librates land during life, and 100*l*. (Paris) payable at the Exchequer *Chester* R. 1 263 O. 1. 438 H 1 154
Sept 11	Pope Innocent [IV] directs that his delegates for trying Scottish ecclesiastical causes shall hold their sittings either within Scotland or in the dioceses of Carlisle or Durham, but not in that of York. R 1 263 O 1 438 H 1 154
Sept. 11.	Pope Innocent [IV] directs that the bp of London shall see that the papal licence granted to Philip Basset be not violated *Lyons* R 1 263 O. 1. 439 H 1 154.

DATE	SUBJECT
1245 [Sept 24]	Odo abp of Rouen excuses his inability to appear before the K , and delegates master J de Flavylla for that purpose. *Demill.* R 1 263 O 1 439 H 1 155
Oct. 12	Pope Innocent [IV] explains to the abps and bps of England his meaning in regard to papal provisions. *Lyons* R 1 263. O 1 440. H. 1 155.
Nov 10	The K forbids the sale of food, cloth, iron, &c to the Welsh, the K 's enemies *Worcester* R. 1 264 O 1 440 H 1 155
Dec 4	The K appoints commissioners for the extension of the truce with France. *Windsor* R 1 264 O. 1. 440 H. 1 155.
Dec 29	Pope Innocent [IV] to his chaplain Marinus, on the proceeds of ecclesiastical benefices R 1 264 *See* Dec 29 1246
1246. Jan 9	Safe conduct for Harold K of Man coming to the K. *Westm* R. 1 264 O. 1. 441 H. 1. 155
Jan 16.	The K. grants to Amadeus count of Savoy a fee of 1,000*l* per an for homage done to the K for lands, &c here specified, and a further fee of 200 marks *Westm* R 1 264. O 1 441 H 1 155
Jan. 16	The K promises that he will give in marriage to one of the daughters of Amadeus count of Savoy either John de Warren (who will be earl of Warren) or Edmund de Lacy (who will be earl of Lincoln) *Westm* R 1 264. O 1 441 H 1 155
March 20	The K intimates that his messengers have brought with them from the council of Lyons a bull of privileges for the royal chapels *Westm* R 1. 265
[March].	The K requests the pope [Innocent IV] to give ear to the complaints of the clergy and people of England, and to remedy the same R 1 265
[April]	The complaints of the clergy and people of England presented to pope [Innocent IV] R 1 265
[April]	Similar petitition sent by the abbots and priors of England to the pope [Innocent IV] R 1 265
June 12	Pope Innocent [IV] apologises to the K for demanding a subsidy for the Holy Land *Lyons* R 1 266 O 1 441. H 1 155
Sept. 9.	The K orders that the laws and customs of England shall prevail in Ireland *Woodstock* R 1 266 O 1 442 H 1 155
Oct 5.	Pope Innocent [IV] requests the K to make the annual payment of 1,000 marks *Lyons* R 1 266 O 1. 442 H. 1 156
Dec 29.	Pope Innocent [IV] to Marinus, his chaplain , desires that one half of the proceeds of such ecclesiastical benefices as have been for six months without a resident parson shall oe applied to certain other pious uses here specified *Lyons* R 1 264
1247 Feb 10.	The K confirms to Adam de Bassing, citizen of London, the lands, advowsons, &c in London late belonging to his father Gervase and his ancestor Reyner de Aldremannesbury *Westm.* R 1 266.
[March ?]	Henry son of the emperor informs the K that he has been appointed lieutenant of Sicily during the emperor's absence in Italy. R 1. 267 O 1 893 H. 1 part ii 126
April 30	Convention by which the K pardons the rebellion of Owen and Lewellin, sons of Griffin prince of Wales, on the terms here specified *Woodstock* R 1 267 O 1 443 H 1 156
Aug 27.	Pope Innocent [IV] requests the K to pay the 1,000 marks due annually *Lyons.* R 1 267 O. 1 444 H 1 156.
Oct 12	Pope Innocent [IV] requests the bp of Lincoln to compel all the clergy of his diocese, having cure of souls, to reside on their cures, excepting such as have special exemptions *Lyons* R 1 268. O 1 444 H 1 156
Nov. 12	The K grants to Peter of Savoy the manor of Aldebury, in Richmondshire, saving certain knights' fees to Roald FitzAlan the younger *Windsor* R 1 268
1248 Feb 1	The K. directs that if Margaret countess of Flanders do not pay the annuity due by her to Thomas de Savoy before Michaelmas next, the men and merchandise of Flanders shall be arrested for the same. *Westm* R 1 268 O. 1 444 H 1 156
Feb 15	The K permits Thomas count of Savoy to receive in the K 's name at the Exchequer the homage of Margaret countess of Flanders for the fee due by her *Westm* R 1 268. O 1. 445. H. 1 156
Feb 15	The K promises that he will provide his uncle Thomas count of Savoy with lands to the value of 500 marks *Westm* R. 1. 268 O 1. 445. H. 1. 157.

DATE	SUBJECT
1248. Feb 20	The K undertakes to pay to Thomas count of Savoy 500 marks out of the 700 marks payable annually by Hugh le Bigod at the Exchequer *Westm.* R 1. 269. O. 1 445 H 1 157
Feb 20.	The K undertakes to pay to his uncle Amadeus count of Savoy 200 marks out of the 700 marks payable annually by Hugh le Bigod at the Exchequer R 1 269. O 1 445 H 1 157
Aug 20	Pope Innocent [IV.] permits Wm. de Valence to confess to any priest, and to receive penance from him *Lyons.* R. 1 269 O 1 146 H 1. 157.
Sept. 11.	The K authorises Drogo de Barentine, governor of Jersey and Guernsey, to inquire into the customs and services of these islands. *Marlborough* R 1 269
[Sept 20]	Simon earl of Leicester notifies that he has extended the truce between England and France *Lorris* R 1. 269.
Nov 22.	The K grants to Richard bp of Rochester free warren in the manor of Frekenham *Clippenham.* R 1 8
1249 Feb 6	The K accepts the terms of the agreement between Theobald K of Navarre and Simon de Montfort. *Clarendon.* R 1 168 O 1 446 H 1 157
Feb 7	Commission to Simon de Montfort to act in the above business *Clarendon* R 1 270. O 1 447. H 1 157.
June 27	Protection for Robert de Ver going to Jerusalem *Westm* R 1 270 O. 1. 447. H 1 157.
June 27	Protection for Wm Lungespee going to Jerusalem *Westm* R 1 270 O 1 147 H 1 157
Oct 2	The K. authorizes Geoffroy de Grandi Monte to swear that the K will observe the truce with France *Windsor* R 1 270 O 1 447. H. 1 157
Oct 2	The K authorizes Peter de Savoy, the bp of Hereford, and P Chaceporc to swear as before *Windsor* R 1 270 O 1 448 R 1 157
Oct 27	Pope Innocent [IV] directs inquiry to be made confirmatory of the validity of the marriage of the K. with the daughter of the count of Provence. *Lyons* R. 1. 270. O 1 448. H. 1 158
Nov 30	The K directs Simon de Montfort earl of Leicester and seneschal of Gascony to inquire into the truth of certain statements made by Amalrinus de Varens to the K. *Clarendon* R 1 271 O 1 449 H 1 158
Dec 7	Pope Innocent [IV] acknowledges the receipt of 500 out of the 1,000 marks to be paid by the K *Lyons.* R 1 271 O 1 450 H. 1. 158.
[Dec. 18]	The K requires Simon de Montfort to demand the land of Agen from the executors of the count of Toulouse *Clarendon* R 1. 271 O 1 450 H 1 159
Dec 18	Pope Innocent [IV] exempts the convent of Holy Cross, Waltham, from papal provisions. *Lyons* R. 1 271. O 1 450 H 1 158
Dec 28	Licence to Artald K. of Man to come into England to confer with the K. *Winchester* R 1 272 O 1 451 H. 1. 159
1250. [March 8]	Commission to Philip, elect of Lyons, and others, to extend the truce with France for 16 years. *Cancelled* *Westm* R. 1 272 O 1 451 H 1. 159
April 6	Pope Innocent [IV] dissuades the K. from going at present to the Holy Land. *Lyons* R 1 272
April 26	Pope Innocent [IV] commands the preaching in England of a crusade to the Holy Land, and specifies the indulgences to be given for the same. *Lyons* R 1. 272 O 1 |452 H 1 159
April 30	Pope Innocent [IV] desires that, as the K is about to undertake the crusade, certain ecclesiastical grants shall be made to him for the purpose *Lyons* R 1 274 O. 1 456. H 1 161
April 30	Pope Innocent [IV] permits the friars preachers and minors to ride on horseback while they attend the K to the parts beyond the sea *Lyons* R 1. 274 (91). O 459 (137) H 61 (44).
June 13	To the abps of Dublin, Cassel, and Armagh, and others, to preach the crusade in Ireland. *Woodstock* R 1 274. O 1 456 H 1 161.
July 18	The K gives licence to the masters of the law of the Jews in London to excommunicate such Jews as having promised money for the support of their cemetery have not paid the same *Clarendon* R 1 274
Sept. 24.	Pope Innocent [IV] commands the abps , bps., and chapters of Ireland to revoke, within one month, that statute of theirs which ordains that no Englishman shall be collated to a canonry in Ireland. *Lyons.* R 1. 274 O 1. 457. G 1 161

DATE	SUBJECT
1250 Sept. 24.	Pope Innocent [IV] to the abps of Dublin and the bp of Ossory, to enforce the execution of the previous bull *Lyons* R. 1. 274. O 1 161. H 1 437
Oct 1	Pope Innocent [IV] orders that if the K does not go to the Holy Land the money raised for the expedition shall still be employed towards that object *Lyons* R 1 275. O 1. 458 H. 1. 161.
Oct 7	The K orders the religious in Normandy to insert the obit of his mother in their martyrologies, and to say masses for her on her anniversary *Westm* R 1 274. O 1. 458 H 1 161.
Oct 11	Pope Innocent [IV] removes from the prior and convent of H Trinity, London, the excommunication pronounced against them by the abp of Canterbury. *Lyons* R 1 275 O 1 458. H 1 162
Oct 11	Pope Innocent [IV] announces to the convent of H Trinity, London, the import of the previous bull. *Lyons* R 1 275 O 1 458 H 1 163
[Nov 27.]	Peace between the citizens expelled from Bordeaux by order of Simon de Montfort, the K's seneschal in Gascony, and those within the city *Bordeaux* R 1 275. O 1. 459 H. 1. 162
1251 Jan 18	Confirmation of the above by the K *Windsor*. R 1 276 O 1 461 H 1 162
Jan 18	The K. promises that no crusader shall be required to pay for the redemption of his vow more than he undertook to do when he assumed the cross *Windsor* R 1 276 O 1 461. H 1 163
Jan 21	The K. proposes that the discussion on the marriage of the duke of Brabant be postponed for the present *Windsor* R 1 276 O 1 461 H 1 163
Feb 26	Pope Innocent [IV] informs the K that John de Frusinon will answer him about the money collected in Ireland for the crusade *Lyons* R 1 276 O 1. 462 H 1 163.
March 1	The K appoints new commissions to settle the truce with France in the place of certain persons lately deceased *Westm* R 1 277 O 1 462 H 1. 163
March 5	Pope Innocent [IV] exempts the K's clerks from the payment of first fruits due to the abp of Canterbury for the debts of his cathedral *Lyons* R 1 277 O 1 462 H 1 163.
March 29	Pope Innocent [IV] directs inquiry to be made whether the convent of the H Trinity, London, have abused the papal letters *Lyons* R 1 277 O 1 463 H 1 163
[April 3]	Judicial sentence annulling the contract of marriage between the K and Joanna daughter of the count of Ponthieu. *Sens* R 1 277 O 1 464 R 1 164
April 6	Pope Innocent [IV] refuses to grant the requests made by the K to the disadvantage of the K and realm of Scotland. *Woodstock* R 1 277 O 1 463 H. 1. 163
July 10	The K has granted to his sister Isabella, who was the wife of Maurice de Croun, an annuity for life of 100 marks *Woodstock* R 1 278 O 1 465 H. 1 164
Sept 4.	Pope Innocent [IV] permits the Scottish crusaders to redeem their vows *Milan* R 1 278 O 1 464 H 1 164.
Sept. 24	Safe conduct for Mary queen of Scotland and her attendants coming into England *Windsor*. R 1 278 O 1 466 H 1 164
Oct. 18	Safe conduct for Alexander K of Scotland and his retinue coming to K. at York. *Westm.* R 1. 278 O. 1. 466 H 1 165
Dec 27	The K is bound to pay to Alexander K of Scotland 5,000 marks of silver as the portion of his queen Margaret, K Henry's eldest daughter *York* R 1 279 O 1 467 H. 1 165
1252. Jan 2.	The K pledges himself to ratify the truce with the K of Navarre *Thorp* R 1 279 O 1 467 H. 1 165
Feb. 20.	Pope Innocent [IV] asks the K to protect two merchants of Sienna, about to settle in England. *Perugia* R 1 279 O 1 467 H 1 165
Feb 22	The K exempts Matilda, widow of Wm de Cantilupe, (who has gone with the queen of Scotland into Scotland) from the payment of various taxes *Westm* R 1 279 O. 1 467 H 1 165
[Feb]	Pope Innocent [IV] to all the faithful , regulations how to conduct themselves during the crusade R 1 279 O 1 468 H 1 165
March 7	Pope Innocent [IV] to the abp. of Bordeaux and the bp of Bazas, that the excess of the money paid by crusaders for the redemption of their vows be given to the K of England *Perugia* R 1. 280. O. 1. 470. H 1 166
March 13	Bull of pope Innocent [IV] relative to the tenths given by the clergy R 1 280 O. 1 471 H 1. 166 *See March 13, 1253*

DATE.	SUBJECT
1252 May 20	Regulations addressed to the sheriffs throughout England by the K and council for the serenity and peace of the realm *Westm* R 1 281.
May 22	Pope Innocent [IV] replies to the complaints laid before him by the clergy of the church of England *Assisi* R 1 281. O 1. 471. H 1 166
May 26	Safe conduct for Alfonso count of Eu coming as a pilgrim to Canterbury *Reading* R 1. 282 O 1 473 II 1 167.
June 6	The K to R. patriarch of Jerusalem, and others, announcing his resolution to set out for the Holy Land within four years, and asking to be assisted with shipping *Westm* R 1. 282 O. 1. 473. II 1 467
June 8	The K. asks Louis [IX.] K of France to restore the lands of England seized by him and his ancestors, as thereby the writer's journey to the Holy Land would be accelerated *Westm* R 1 282 O 1 474 H 1 167
June 8	The K to M[argaret] queen of France, to the same effect as the preceding *Westm* R 1 282 O 1 474 H 1 167
June 13	The K (hearing that disagreements have arisen in Gascony) sends certain regulations which are to be observed until either he himself or his son Edward can go thither in person for the settlement of these disputes. *Windsor* R 1 283 O 1 474 H 1 168
July 9	Pope Innocent [IV] in favour of the bp of S David's, to whom he exhorts the K to make satisfaction for the violation of his rights *Perugia* R 1 283 O 1. 176 H 1. 168.
July 20	Pope Innocent [IV] admonishes the abp of Canterbury to restore to the convent of H Trinity, London, the church of Bexley, which he has seized *Perugia* R 1 283 O 1 477 H 1 169
Aug 3	Pope Innocent [IV] prays the K to accept the throne of Sicily for his brother R[ichard] earl of Cornwall *Perugia* R 1 284 O 1. 476. H 1. 168.
Aug 29	Pope Innocent [IV.] ratifies the K's marriage with Eleanor of Provence, and annuls his contract with Joanna of Ponthieu *Perugia* R 1 284 O 1 478 H 1 169
Aug 31	Pope Innocent [IV] directs the abp of Canterbury and the bp of Chichester to publish the nullity of the K's contract of marriage with Joanna of Ponthieu *Perugia* R 1 284 O 1 479 H 1 169
Sept. 1.	Pope Innocent [IV] directs the abp. of Canterbury and others to see that the money collected for the Holy Land be laid up in safe places for the use of the K. when he begins his journey. *Perugia* R. 1 285 O 1. 480. H 1 170
Sept 26	Pope Innocent [IV] grants certain privileges to the clergy and laity who are going to the Holy Land to make arrangements for the K's journey thither *Perugia* R. 1 285 O. 1 480 H 1 170
Sept. 27.	Pope Innocent [IV.] extends the period of the licence of non-residence to the clerks employed in the King's affairs. *Perugia.* R 1 285 O 1 481 H 1 170
Sept 27	Pope Innocent [IV] directs the abbot of Westm to give authority to the above privilege *Perugia* R 1 285 O 1 481 H 1 170.
Sept 29.	Pope Innocent [IV] regulates the acts of devotion to be performed for the K when he has set out for the Holy Land *Perugia.* R. 1 286 O 481 H. 1. 170
Oct. 14.	Pope Innocent [IV] takes under his protection the K, the queen, his family, and his realm, while the King is in the Holy Land *Perugia* R 1 286 O 1 483 H 1 171.
Oct 14.	Pope Innocent [IV] authorizes the abbot and prior of Westm to excommunicate such as withhold or neglect to pay the tenths granted to the K. for the aid of the Holy Land. *Perugia* R 1 286 O 1.483 H 1 171
Oct 14.	Pope Innocent [IV] directs that in all cases where the legacies of deceased persons are not specifically left to some definite object they should be applied to the furtherance of the crusade *Perugia.* R 1. 286. O 1. 483 H. 1 171.
Oct 15	Pope Innocent [IV] directs that all sums restored by usurers and by conscience-stricken penitents, if not specifically appropriated, shall be given to the K for the Holy Land. *Perugia* R 1. 287 O 1 484 H 1. 171
Oct 19	Pope Innocent [IV] directs that prayers be offered up for the K and his company as soon as he embarks for the Holy Land. *Perugia* R. 1 287 O 1 481 H 1 171
Nov 5	Pope Innocent [IV] directs that all who trouble the provinces of Bordeaux and Auch during the K's absence in the Holy Land shall be excommunicated *Perugia* R 1 287. O 1 485. H. 1. 172
Nov. 5.	Bull of Pope Innocent [IV] to the same effect as the preceding. *Perugia* R. 1. 287. O 1. 486 H. 1. 172.

DATE	SUBJECT
1252. Nov. 13	The K requests the abps to aid the bp of Chichester in his office of preaching the crusade *Marlbro'* R. 1 288 O 1 486. H. 1 172.
1253 Jan 28	The K informs pope Innocent [IV] that he will set out for the Holy Land on the nativity of S John the Baptist three years hence *Westm* R 1 288 O 1 486. H. 1 172.
Jan 28	The K thanks pope Innocent [IV] for having offered the crown of Sicily to his brother Richard earl of Cornwall. *Westm* R 1 288 O 1. 893 H 1 p u. 126
March 13	Pope Innocent [IV] requires the collectors of the tenths assigned to the K for the Holy Land to see that this grant be not evaded by ecclesiastics who claim exemption for their manors *Perugia* R. 1 280 O 1 471 H 1 166
April 18	The K recites the letters of Peter de Savoy, by which he promises that he will accompany the K to the Holy Land *London* R. 1. 288 O 1 487 H 1 172
April 18	The K. promises to give to Peter of Savoy (who has promised to accompany him to the Holy Land) 10,000 marks at Marseilles, and a ship, and 20 war horses on their arrival in the Holy Land. *Westm* R 1 288 O 1 488 H 1 173
April 18	The K recites the gifts and grants made by him to Peter of Savoy to facilitate his expedition to the Holy Land *Westm* R 1 289 O 1 488 H 1 173
April 30	Safe conduct for M, heir of Man and the Isles, going to Norway *Merton* R. 1. 289. O 1 489 H 1. 173
April 30.	The K exhorts the abp of Auch and others to make amends to Arnold Octon', vicount of Lomagne, for injuries done to him [*Merton*] R 1 289 O 1. 487. H. 1. 172.
May 9.	The K requests the Irish crusaders to meet him at a place to be specified when he is on his way to the Holy Land *Westm* R 1 289 O 1 489. H 1 173
May 13.	Excommunication upon such as violate Magna Carta and the Carta de Foresta granted by K. John *Westminster Hall* R 1 289
[May 13]	Notification of the above sentence of excommunication R 1 290 O 1 489 H 1 173
May 15.	The K to A King of Castile, relative to the formation of a treaty of marriage *London* R 1. 290. O 1. 490 H 1. 173.
May 24.	Commission to the persons mentioned above to treat of a marriage between Beatrice the K.'s daughter and the eldest son of the K of Aragon *London* R 1 290 O 1 490 H 1 174
May 24	Commission to the same persons to treat of a marriage between prince Edward and Eleanor, sister to the K of Castille *London* R 1 290 O 1 491. H 1 174
[June 12]	The K orders the annual payment of 500 marks to Thomas of Savoy *Windsor* R 1 291 O 1 492. H 1. 174.
June 22	The K, about to go into Gascony, commits the keeping of the great seal to the queen. *Winchester*. R 1 290 O 1 491 H 1 174
July 2.	The K, on going into Gascony, appoints queen Eleanor to be regent during his absence *Suwic.* R 1 291 O 1 491 H. 1 174
July 2	The K arranges certain details respecting such vacancies of ecclesiastical sees as may occur during his absence in Gascony R 1 291 O 1 491 H 1 174
July 7.	Proclamation that the regency is intrusted to the queen by the K during his absence in Gascony *Portsmouth* R 1 291 O 1 492 H 1 174
[July 7]	Safe conduct for David, son of Griffith, and his family, coming to do his homage. *Portsmouth* R 1 291 O. 1. 492 H 1 174
July 12.	The K orders the annual payment of 500 marks to Thomas of Savoy R 1 291 O 1 492 H 1 174 *See* June 12, 1253
July 18	Writ of military summons for the knights, free tenants, and others of Essex and Hertford, to perform what shall be required of them by the K *Portsmouth.* R 1 291
July 20.	The K directs Henry de Colville to explain to the men of Cambridge, Huntingdon, Hertford, and Essex certain articles (here embodied) relating to the watching of towns, the harbouring of strangers and suspicious characters, &c *Portsmouth* R. 1 292
July 20.	The K. commands Bertram de Criol, constable of the castle of Dover, not to deliver that castle (in the event of the K's death) to prince Edward before he is of age, without the consent of the queen *Portsmouth* R 1 292 O 1 493 H 174
July 21.	The K empowers the queen and R earl of Cornwall to remove from their offices offending sheriffs and to appoint others during his absence *Portsmouth* R 1 292.
July 30.	Pope Innocent [IV] authorizes the bp of Bath and Wells and the dean of Bordeaux to excommunicate all who disturb the peace after the K's departure for the Holy Land *Assisi* R 1 292 O. 1 493 H 1 175

D

DATE	SUBJECT
1253 Sept 5	Pope Innocent [IV] notifies that he has taken the royal family and the realm of England under his protection *Assist.* R 1 293 O 1 494 H 1 175
Sept. 30.	Pope Innocent [IV] recites and confirms the statute passed in Westminster Hall, 13 May 1253 *Anagni* R 1 293
[Oct]	The K. notifies to the justices of the Jews, certain regulations which he has made respecting the Jews R 1 293
Nov 3	Pope Innocent [IV] recites and confirms the statute lately made by him respecting papal provisions *Lateran* R 1 294 O 1 496 H 1 176
Dec 18	Pope Innocent [IV] (in reply to a playful observation in the K's letter in regard to their respective ages) assures him that he, the pope, is the elder He would be delighted to see the K *Lateran* R 1 294 O 1 494 H 1 175
[Dec 21]	The dean of Bordeaux, having excommunicated various persons who had invaded the K.'s territory, intimates the same to the bp of Adour *Bazas* R. 1 294 O 1 496 H. 1. 176
Dec 29	The K requires the prelates of Ireland to meet his justiciary at Dublin next Mid Lent, to hear from him of the intended invasion of England and Ireland by the K of Castille and the Saracens, to oppose whom in Gascony a subsidy is required *Westm.* R 1 295 O 1. 497 H 1 176
1254 Jan. 30	The K requires the barons of the Cinque Ports and other parts to provide shipping to be at Portsmouth to convey the queen, prince Edward, and others into Gascony *Westm* R 1 295
[Jan 28]	The queen and Richard earl of Cornwall to the King The barons will sail from Portsmouth by the end of May, to protect Gascony from the K of Castille, and the bps and abbots will contribute money. R 1 296 O. 1 499 H 1 177
Feb 5.	Certain nobles being promised to join the K in Gascony to resist its invasion by the K of Castille, Wm de Oddinggeselles and Wm de Beauchamp are invited to join the expedition *Westm* R. 1 295. O 1 498 H 1 176
Feb 5	The K directs the sheriff of Wiltshire to see that all who hold of the K in capite in his bailiwick meet at Portsmouth to embark for Gascony *Westm* R 1 295. O 1 493 H 1. 176
Feb 8.	The K appoints commissioners to treat of peace with the K of Castile *Bazas* R. 1 295 O. 1 498 H 1 177
Feb 11	The K has received a loan of 300 marks sterling from the abbot and convent of . Bordeaux *Bazas* R 1 296 O 1 500 H 1 177
Feb 14	The K promises that the yearly value of the lands settled on prince Edward in Gascony, Ireland, and England, shall not fall short of 15,000 marks *Bazas* R 1 296 O 1 500 H 1 177
Feb 14	The K grants to his son Edward all the lands, &c which have at any time been taken from the K or his predecessors by the Kings of France, in addition to Gascony, which he has already granted to prince Edward *Bazas* R 1 296 O 1 500 H 1 177
Feb 14	The K orders Richard de Grey to surrender to prince Edward the islands which he holds for the K *Bazas* R 1 296 O 1 501 H 1 177
Feb. 14	The K grants to prince Edward all Ireland, the earldom of Chester, the K.'s conquests in Wales, certain castles and lands, and the isles of Jersey and Guernsey ; and renews the grant of all Gascony and the isle of Oleron *Bazas* R 1 297 O 1 501 H 1 178
Feb 14.	The K. directs Peter of Savoy to give seisin to prince Edward of the lands in England which belonged to the countess of Eu *Bazas* R 1 297 O 1 502 H. 1 178
March 7	Albert, the papal notary, conveys to Edmund, the K's son, the realm of Sicily. *Vendôme* R 1 297 O 1 502 H. 1. 178
April 1	Treaty of alliance between Alfonso K of Castile and the King of England *Toledo* R 1 297 O 1 503 H 1 178
April 1	Counterpart of the above treaty on the part of K Henry *Toledo* R. 1 298 O. 1. 504 H 1 179
April 1.	Alfonso K of Castile promises to furnish prince Edward with letters of safe conduct on going into Spain *Toledo* R 1 298 O 1 504 H 1 179
[April 1]	Copy of the safe conduct promised in the above letter R 1 298 O 1 504 H 1 179
April 18	The K grants to prince Edward all the profits of the lands lately belonging to Sabina de Orciato, deceased *Milan.* R 1 299 O 1 504 H 1 179
April 20	The English commissioners promise that they will procure the sealed ratification of the treaty of alliance between Alfonso K of Castile and the K of England *Toledo* R. 1 299. O 1 504 H 1 179
April 20	The K confirms the above convention R. 1. 299 O 1. 506 H. 1 180.

DATE.	SUBJECT
1254. April 22.	Alfonso K. of Castile transfers to prince Edward all his rights in Gascony *Toledo* R. 1 300. O, 1 509. H. 1 181.
April 22.	K. Alfonso reforms the barons of Gascony that he has transferred to K Henry and prince Edward all his rights in Gascony *Toledo* R 1 300 O 1 509. H 1. 181
April 22	K. Alfonso confirms to the K. and his successors the lands, &c. seized by the Ks of Navarre *Toledo*. R 1 300. O 1 520 H 1. 181.
April 22	K Alfonso agrees to divide with the K whatever lands they may conquer in Africa, if the K will join him in an expedition thither *Toledo* R. 1 301. O. 1 510. H 1 181
May 14	Pope Innocent [IV] authorizes the abp of Canterbury and the bp. of Winchester to borrow money in England for the prosecution of the rights of prince Edmund in Sicily *Assisi.* R 1 301. O 1 511 H. 1 181
May 14	Pope Innocent [IV.] to Edmund K of Sicily confirming the grant of that realm made to him by the papal legate. *Assisi* R 1. 301 O 1 512 H 1 182
May 14.	Pope Innocent [IV.] desires his legate to expedite the departure of K Edmund to Sicily, *Assisi* R 1 301. O 1. 512 H 1 182
May 14	Pope Innocent [IV] informs the K of the death of his nephew, son of the emperor, which leaves the realm of Sicily open to Edmund, the K's son *Assisi* R 1 302 O. 1 513. H 1 182
[May]	[The Emperor Conrad] to K Henry announcing the death of the writer's brother Henry R 1 302. O 1 514 H 1 182
May 22	Pope Innocent [IV.] exhorts the K. to avoid unnecessary expenses, so as to be able to proceed with energy in the affairs of Sicily *Assisi* R 1. 302. O 1 515 H 1 183
May 22	Pope Innocent [IV] to the queen, to the same effect as the preceding *Assisi* R 1. 302 O 1 515 H 1 183
May 22.	Pope Innocent [IV] to Peter of Savoy, to the same effect as the preceding *Assisi* R. 1. 302 O 1 515 H 1 183
May 22	Pope Innocent [IV] promises that he will make the K two payments, each of 50,000*l* tournois, and will aid him with men, &c, in the matter of Sicily. *Assisi*. R. 1 303 O 1. 516 H 1 183
May 23	Pope Innocent [IV.] extends the period of the grant to the K in aid of the Holy Land, and gives directions for the safe custody of the money so collected. *Assisi* R. 1 303 O 1 516. H 1 183.
May 23	Pope Innocent [IV] directs John de Frusmon, his chaplain in Scotland, to collect a twentieth in Scotland for the use of K Henry's crusade *Assisi* R. 1 303 O 1 517 H 1. 183
May 25	Pope Innocent [IV] desires that the K. will cause a great seal to be engraved for the use of his son Edmund as K. of Sicily, will send his final resolution in the matter of Sicily before Michaelmas, and will style him "king" in his letters patent *Assisi* R. 1 303 O 1 513 H 1 182
May 31	Pope Innocent [IV] permits the K to undertake the conquest of Sicily instead of his vow to go to the Holy Land *Assisi.* R. 1. 304 O 1 517. H. 1 184
June 9	Pope Innocent [IV] assures the K. of the death of Conrad, son of the late emperor Frederic, and urges activity in the affairs of Sicily *Anagni.* R. 1. 304 O 1 518 H 1 184
July 18	The K notifies the intended marriage of his heir Edward with Eleanor, sister of Alfonso K. of Castile. *S Macaire.* R 1. 304. O. 1 518. H. 1 184.
July 20	Assignment by prince Edward of dower in England for Eleanor of Castile. *S. Macaire* R 1 304 O 1. 519. H. 1. 184
July 23.	Prince Edward notifies his assent to his marriage with Eleanor of Castile. *S Macaire.* R. 1 304. O. 1 519. H. 1. 184
July 23.	Prince Edward makes oath that he will observe the terms of his contract of marriage *S Macaire* R 1 305 O 1 520 H 1 185
Aug 22.	The K. assents to the marriage of prince Edward with Eleanor of Castile. *Bordeaux* R. 1. 306. O. 1. 522 H. 1 185.
Aug 22.	The K promises that he will confirm under his great seal all the grants made by him to his son Edward *Bordeaux*. R 1 306 O 1 523 H 1 186
Aug 25	The K sends Simon de Montfort earl of Leicester on secret business to the K of Scotland *Bordeaux* R 1 306. , O 1 523 H 1 186.
Aug 26	The K undertakes to give Eleanor lands to the yearly value of 1,000*l* if she is not satisfied with those already assigned in dower *Bordeaux*. R. 1. 306. O. 1. 523 H 1. 186.

D 2

DATE	SUBJECT
1254 [Aug 28]	The K undertakes to provide prince Edward with wardships to the yearly value of 3,000 marks *Bordeaux* R 1 305. O 1 520 H 1 185
[Aug]	The K appoints commissions to settle disputes arising out of the truce with the count of Toulouse R 1 305 O 1 521 H 1 185
Aug	Settlement of the losses sustained by the men of La Réole on the part of the K of Castile *Bordeaux* R 1. 305. O 1 521 H 1 185
Sept 4	Pope Innocent [IV] appoints commissioners to act in favour of the prior of H Trinity, London *Assisi* R 1 306 O 1 511 H 1 181
Sept. 9	The K orders the mayor of Bayonne to arrest all the goods and chattels of Gaston de Bearn "*In castris de Kepal*" R 1 306 O 1 523 H 1 186
Sept 9	Pope Innocent [IV] orders the excommunication of the bp and chapter of Cassel unless, within two months, they repay the money borrowed from certain merchants of Sienna. *Anagni* R 1 307 O 1 524 H 1 186
Sept 15	Girald de Armignac admits that his uncle Girold did homage to K John for the comtés of Armignac and Fesenzac, and that he has renewed the same R 1 307. O 1 525 H 1 186
Sept. 15	Girald de Armignac promises that he will search for the homage to K John mentioned in the above document *Bordeaux* R 1 007 O 1 525 H 1 186
Sept 18.	The K promises to grant to prince Edward all debts in Ireland due to the crown *Bordeaux* R 1 308 O 1 526 H 1 186
Sept. 18.	The K informs pope Innocent [IV] of the treaty which he has made with the K of Castile, and asks to be allowed to exchange his expedition to the Holy Land to one into Africa *Bordeaux*, R. 1 308 O 1 527 H 1 187
Sept	The prelates, nobles, and people of Jerusalem entreat the K to hasten his expedition to the Holy Land, the miseries of which they describe *Acres* R 1 308
Oct 3	The K ratifies the gift of the principality of Capua made to his uncle Thomas of Savoy by Edmund K of Sicily *Bordeaux* R 1 308 O 1 527 II 1 187
Oct 11	Confirmation by the K under the great seal of the grant of Ireland made to prince Edward under the seal used in Gascony *Bordeaux* R 1 309 O 1 528 H 1 187
Oct 11	Similar confirmation of the grant of lands not within the realm of England *Bordeaux* R 1 309 O 1 528 H 1 188
Oct 11	Similar confirmation of the grant of 15,000 marks *Bordeaux* R 1 309 O 1 529. H 1 188
Oct 11	Similar confirmation of the grant from the lands of Sabina de Orciato *Bordeaux*. R 1 309. O 1 529 H 1 188
Oct 11	Similar confirmation of the grant of wardships *Bordeaux* R. 1 309 O 1 530 H 1 188
Oct 14	The K commands the men of Sicily to do what they are directed by the bearers of this letter *Bordeaux* R 1 310 O 1 530 H 1 188
Nov 1.	Alfonso K of Castile conveys to prince Edward (whom he has knighted) whatever rights he may have in Gascony *Burgos* R 1 310 O 1 531 H 1 188
Nov	Prince Edward, "now reigning in Gascony as prince and lord," orders the citizens of Bayonne to swear to preserve peace with each other, according to the form of the oath which he encloses *Bayonne* R. 1 310 O 1 531 H 1 189
Nov 3	Pope Innocent [IV] grants to Berthold marquis of Hohemburch the office of seneschal of Sicily for life *Naples* R 1 311 O 1 532 H 1 189
Nov 3	Pope Innocent [IV] confirms certain grants of lands, &c in Sicily made by C[onrad] to Berthold marquis of Hohemburch *Naples* R 1 311 O. 1 533. H 1 189
Nov 3	Pope Innocent [IV] confirms to Berthold marquis of Hohemburch the annual grant made by [Conrad] of 1,500 ounces of gold *Naples* R 1 311 O 1 534 H 1 189
Nov 3	Pope Innocent [IV] confirms to Louis, brother of the marquis Berthold, the grant of the comté of Crotona made by Conrad *Naples* R 1 311 O 1 534 H 1 190
Nov 17	Pope Innocent [IV] informs the K that the "arduous and difficult business" cannot longer be postponed, and that unless the K moves herein the writer must provide for it elsewhere *Naples* R 1 312 O 1 535 H 1 190
Dec 3	Pope Innocent [IV] confirms to Oddo, brother of the marquis Berthold, the comté of Chieti, granted to him by Conrad *Naples* R 1 312 O 1 534 H 1 190

DATE	SUBJECT
1254 Dec 22	Pope Alexander [IV] announces the death of his predecessor, Innocent [IV], and his own election to the papacy *Naples* R 1 312 O 1 536 H 1 190
1255 Jan. 13.	Pope Alexander [IV] cautions the K against believing the detractors of the abp of Armagh. *Naples.* R. 1. 313 O. 1 538 H 1 191
Jan 31	Pope Alexander [IV] directs that the church of Bexley be restored to the convent of H Trinity, London R 1 313 O 1 539 H 1 191
Feb 9	Pope Alexander [IV.] grants the duchy of Amalfi to the marquis Berthold and his brothers Oddo and Louis *Naples.* R 1. 314 O 1 540 H 1. 192.
Feb. 10	Pope Alexander [IV] confirms all the grants made by pope Innocent [IV] to the marquis Berthold and his brothers Oddo and Louis *Naples* R. 1 314 O 1 541 H 1 192
Feb 11.	The K. thanks the barons of the Cinque Ports for their present of jewels on occasion of his return home *Westm* R 1 314
Feb 15	Pope Alexander [IV] undertakes to establish peace between the marquis of Hohemburch and Manfred prince of Tarente *Naples* R 1 315 O 1 542 H 1 192
Feb 15	Pope Alexander [IV] promises that he will protect the marquis of Hohemburch against Manfred prince of Tarente *Naples.* R 1. 315. O. 1. 542. H. 1. 193.
Feb 15	Bull of Pope Alexander [IV], granting that, on the death of the marquis of Hohemburch or either of his brothers, the survivors shall succeed to the property of the deceased *Naples.* R 1 315 O 1 543 H 1 193
Feb 24	The K assigns to his brother Richard earl of Cornwall all the Jews in England, in security for money advanced by the earl to the K *Westm* R. 1 315. O. 1 543 H 1 193.
March 11.	The K gives his bond for the payment of his debts to certain merchants of Lucca. *S Alban's* R 1 316 O 1 544 H 1 193
March 12	Safe conduct for Hugh duke of Burgundy passing through Gascony on pilgrimage to St James's. *Seauve Mayeu* R. 1 316 O 1. 545 H 1 194
March 15.	Pope Alexander [IV.] states that he cannot consent to the K's request to be allowed to go to Africa instead of the Holy Land *Naples.* R 1 316. O. 1. 545. H. 1. 194.
April 9.	Pope Alexander [IV.] specifies the terms upon which pope Innocent [IV.] granted Sicily to prince Edmund. *Naples* R 1 316 O 1 893 H 1. p. ii, 126
April 19.	Pope Alexander [IV.] notifies to the K. that he has confirmed all the privileges granted by pope Innocent [IV] to Berthold, Oddo, and Louis, marquises of Hohemburch *Naples.* R 1 319 O 1 546 H 1 194
April 21	Pope Alexander [IV] values at 8,000 ounces of gold the damages sustained by the marquises of Hohemburch, which he requests the K to pay *Naples.* R 1 319 O 1 547 H 1 194
April 30	Pope Alexander [IV] requests the K to repay 4,000*l* Turon to the bp of Bologna for expenses incurred in the affairs of Sicily *Naples* R 1 319 O 1 547 H 1 194
May 3	Pope Alexander [IV] permits the K to commute his vow to go to the Holy Land for the expedition into Sicily *Naples* R 1 319 O 1 547 H 1 195
May 7	Pope Alexander [IV] allows the abp of Canterbury to absolve the K from his vow to go to the Holy Land, that he may engage in the expedition to Sicily against Manfred late prince of Tarente, who formerly had allied himself with the Saracens against the Christians *Naples* R 1 320 O 1.549 H 1 195
May 8	Record of the production of Domesday Roll called "Domesday Cestr," as evidence in a suit at law. *Reading* R. 1 320
[May 12]	Pope Alexander [IV.], directs that the K of Norway and his nobles, having been absolved from their vows to go to the Holy Land, shall join K Henry in his descent upon Sicily *Naples* R 1 320 O 1. 549 H 1 195.
May 12.	Bull of Alexander [IV] to the same effect as the preceding *Naples* R 1 320. O 1 549 H 1 195
May 13.	Credence for the bp of Bologna, sent by pope Alexander [IV] to the K, for the settlement of the affairs of Sicily, granted to prince Edmund *Naples* R. 1. 321. O 1 550 H 1 196.
May 13.	Duplicate of the above, sent to prince Edmund *Naples* R 1 321 O 1 550. H. 1 196.
May 14.	B prince of Antioch solicits aid from the K for the relief of his afflicted realm *Tripoli* R 1. 321.

DATE	SUBJECT
1255 May 15.	Pope Alexander [IV] sanctions the transfer to the K, for the expedition to Sicily, of the money contributed for the Holy Land. *Naples* R 1 322 O. 1 551 H 1 196
May 16	Pope Alexander [IV] sanctions the exchange of the vow for the Holy Land for that of the expedition into Sicily *Naples* R. 1 322 O 1 552 H 1 196
May 16	Pope Alexander [IV] extends for three years longer the grant of a twentieth made to the K of the subsidy from Scotland for the Holy Land *Naples*. R 1. 322 O 1 552 H 1 196
May 16	Pope Alexander [IV] directs that the sums arising from the redemption of the vows of the Scottish crusaders be given to K Henry for the relief of the Holy Land *Naples* R 1 322 O 1 553 H 1 197
May 21	Pope Alexander [IV] requires the K to make an oath of fealty to him and his successors, and to do liege homage in the name of his son Edmund for the realm of Sicily *Naples* R 1 322 O 1 553 H. 1 197
May 25	The K. forbids the holding of a tournament at Blythe, having heard that prince Edward is in great danger in Gascony. *Clarendon* R 1. 323 O 1 554 H 1 197
May 25	Pope Alexander [IV] exempts the English Cistercians from the payment of the tenths in aid of the Holy Land *Naples* R 1 323 O 1 554 H 1 197
June 14.	The K grants an annuity for life of 100 marks sterling to the countess of Thouars, his sister *Woodstock.* R 1 323. O 1 555 H. 1 197.
June 18	The K grants certain liberties to the scholars and burgesses of Oxford, and issues regulations for the government of the town. *Woodstock* R 1. 323.
June 24.	The K authorizes Edmund K of Sicily to make provision for Matthew Hanybald, proconsul of Rome *Woodstock* R 1 324 O 1 558 H 1 197
June	Commission for the propagation of the truce between England and France *Paris* R 1 324
[July 12]	Thalesia, lady of March, notifies the terms on which she delivers the castle of Blankfort to prince Edward for five years R 1 330 O 569 H 1 p n. 6
[July 29.]	Prorogation for five years of the truce with France *Nottingham* R 1 324 O 1 555 H 1 p n 1
July 22	Credence for two messengers sent from the K to B duke of Sweden. *Nottingham*. R 1 325
July 25.	The K sends four casks of wine to the New Temple, London, for the use of the envoys of the K of Castile *Nottingham* R 1. 325 O 1 557 H. 1 p n 1
July 25	The K sends ten bucks to the New Temple, London, for the same purpose *Nottingham* R 1 325 O 1 557 H 1 p n 2
July 26.	The K directs that the envoys of Castile shall be courteously treated in London *Nottingham* R 1 325 O 1 557. H 1 p n 2.
July 28.	Pope Alexander [IV] directs that the privileges granted to the K. by pope Innocent [IV] in respect to payments made for the redemptions of the vows of crusaders shall remain in force *Anagni* R. 1 325. O. 1 558 H. 1 p n 2
Aug 10	Credence for Richard earl of Gloucester, and others, about to confer with the envoys of the K of Scotland *Cawood* R 1 325 O 1 558 H 1 p n. 2.
Aug. 10	Commission to the earl of Gloucester and others to receive under the K's protection such Scotchmen as will aid the K and Q of Scotland against certain Scottish rebels. *Cawood*. R 1. 326. O 1 559 H 1 p u 2
Aug. 10.	The K grants his protection to such of the Scottish barons as will aid the K. and Q. of Scotland against the rebels *Cawood* R 1 326 O 1. 558 H 1 p n. 2
Aug 16.	Writ of military summons by the K. to assist the K and Q of Scotland *York*. R 1. 326 O. 1. 560. H 1 p n 2
Aug 17.	The K advises prince Edward (the affairs of Gascony being now settled) to spend next winter in Ireland, the condition of which requires reform. *York*. R 1 326 O 1. 560. H. 1 p. n 3
Aug 17	The K asks Peter of Savoy to arrange the departure of prince Edward from Gascony into Ireland, and then himself to hasten into England. *York* R. 1. 326 O 1 561 H. 1 p n. 3.
Aug. 25.	The K protests that he has no desire to prejudice the liberties of the realm of Scotland. *Newcastle-on-Tyne* R 1 327 O 1. 561. H 1. p n. 3
Aug. 28.	Commission to settle injuries arising from the infringement of the truce with France. *Newcastle-on-Tyne* R 1 327 O. 1 561 H 1 p n 3

DATE	SUBJECT
1255 Aug 29	Commission to act in the settlement of the above damages *Newcastle-on-Tyne* R 1 327 O 1 562 H. 1. p II 3
Sept. 2	The K appoints certain noblemen to conduct the K. and Q of Scotland into his presence *Alnwick* R. 1 327 O 1 562 H 1 p II 3
Sept. 5	Safe conduct for the K and Q of Scotland coming to the K. at Wark *Chinelung* R 1 327 O 1 562. H 1 p II 3
Sept 13	The K , being unable to be present at the approaching feast of S Edward at Westminster, directs how it shall be celebrated *Wark* R 1. 328 O 1 593. H 1. p II 4
Sept 15	The K. gives directions as to the reception and treatment of the messengers of the K of Castile *Wark* R 1 328. O 1 563 H 1 p II. 4
Sept 18	Credence for John de Dya, sent by pope Alexander [IV] to urge the K. to expedite the affairs of Sicily. *Anagn*. R. 1. 328. O. 1 564 H. 1. p. II. 4.
Sept 20	The K promises to restore to her husband Margaret Q of Scotland, remaining with the Q of England who is sick *Wark* R 1 328 O 1 565 H 1 p II 4
Sept 20	The K recites letters of Alexander [III.] K of Scotland, detailing changes made by him in the government of his realm, which K Henry promises shall not be prejudicial to the liberties of Scotland. *Sprouistone* R 1 329. O 1 561 H 1 p II 4
Sept. 21	The K undertakes to protect certain nobles of Scotland, and not to make peace or truce with the rebellious barons *Wark* R 1 329 O 1. 567 H 1 p II 5
Sept 23	The K. appoints two commissioners to act for him with certain persons of Scotland *Alnwick* R 1. 330 O 1 568. H. 1. p II 5
Sept 26	Pope Alexander [IV] asks that Gervase de Londonus, canon of Lichfield, banished from England, may be restored to the K.'s favour *Anagm* R 1 330 O 1 568. H 1 p II 5
Oct 12	Pope Alexander [IV] to his nuncio in England, concerning the application of various sums of money contributed by English ecclesiastics *Anagm* R 1 330 O 1 568. H. 1. p II 6
Oct 13	Protestation of Ebulo de Montibus and Stephen Bauzan respecting the surrender of the castle of Agramont to prince Edward *Bordeaux* R 1 330 O 1 569 H 1 p II 6
[Oct.]	Notification by Thalasia, lady of March, of the terms of the delivery of the castle of Blank-fort R 1 330. O 1 569 H 1 p. II 6 *See July 12, 1255*
Oct. 18	Mandate to receive the kingdom of Apulia for the K. and prince Edmund. *Westm.* R 1 331 O 1 570 H 1. p. II 6
[Oct]	Letters of the bps of S Andrew's and Glasgow to Walter de Merton, chancellor of England, in favour of Nicholas Corbet, cousin of the K. of Scotland. R 1 331 O 1 570 H 1. p II 6.
[Oct]	Instructions sent to John Mansel respecting his intended conference with the K of Castile *Oxford* R 1 331 O 1. 570. H 1 p II 6
Oct. 27	Arnold Wilhelmi de Agramont pledges himself to be faithful to prince Edward *Acristis* R. 1 331 O. 1 572. H 1 p II 7.
Nov 18	Robert de Baro is appointed the K's proctor in the papal court for the affairs of Edmund K of Sicily *Windsor* R. 1 332 O 1 572 H 1 p II. 7.
Nov 18	Master Finatus is appointed the K's proctor in the papal court *Windsor* R 1 332 O. 1 573. H 1 p II. 7.
Nov 19.	The K permits prince Edward to pledge himself for his brother Edmund in the affairs of Sicily. *Windsor* R 1 332 O 1 573 H 1 p II 7
[Nov. 21]	Memorandum respecting the sealing by the K of the privileges respecting the affairs of Apulia. R 1 332. O 1 573 H 1 p. II 7
Dec 2	Safe conduct for Arnold count of Gunes coming on a pilgrimage into England. *Windsor* R 1 332. O 1 574 H 1 p II. 8
Dec 5	Pope Alexander [IV] confirms to the Knights Templars their right of sanctuary in their churches. *Lateran*. R 1 333. O 1. 574. H 1 p II 8
Dec. 7	Pope Alexander [IV] confirms their privileges to the Knights Templars *Lateran* R 1. 333 O 1 575 H 1 p II. 8
Dec 7	Pope Alexander [IV] orders that no one injure, annoy, or insult the Knights Templars *Lateran* R 1 333 O. 1 575. H 1 p. II. 8
Dec. 8	Pope Alexander [IV] orders the prelates of England to see that the Knights Templars be not injured *Lateran* R. 1 333. O 1 576 H 1 p II. 8.
Dec. 9.	Pope Alexander [IV] orders that such persons as strike or wound the Knights Templars shall be held as excommunicate *Lateran* R 1 334 O 1 576 H 1. p. II. 9

DATE.	SUBJECT
1255 Dec 29	The K asks the abbot, prior, and convent of Westminster, to become security for the payment of 4,000*l* Tournois for the matter of Sicily. *Clarendon* R 1 344 O 1 577 H. 1 p n 9
1256 Jan 3	Pope Alexander [IV] orders that the usual collection made once a year for the Knights Templars shall be strictly applied to that object *Lateran* R. 1 334 O 1. 577. H 1 p. n. 9
Jan 10	Pardon for John the Convert for the death of the boy who was crucified by the Jews at Lincoln while the said John was a Jew *Westm* R 1 335
[Jan. 10]	Pardon for Benedict son of Mosseus of London, a Jew, for the death of the boy Hugh, who was crucified by the Jews at Lincoln *Windsor.* R 1. 335.
Jan 13	Edmund K of Sicily grants an annual rent of 100 ounces of gold to Bartholomew de Florentino *London.* R. 1 335 O 1 579 H 1 p n 10
Jan 18	Pope Alexander [IV] permits the Knights Templars in England to revive such of their privileges as had fallen into desuetude *Lateran* R 1 335 O 1 579 H 1 p n 10
Jan 20	Commission for Peter de Montfort to rectify and complete the terms respecting the violation of the truce between England and France *Windsor* R 1 335 O 1 580 H 1 p n. 10
Jan 24	The K authorizes the extension of the truce with France *Windsor* R 1 335 O 1 580 H 1 p n 10
[Jan]	L, son of Griffin prince of Wales, asks the K to alter the time and place of meeting respecting the truce R 1 336 O 1 580 H 1 p n 10.
Feb 5	Pope Alexander [IV] urges the immediate payment of the money due for the affairs of Sicily, and the more active prosecution of the whole business by the K *Lateran* R 1. 336 O. 1 581. H 1 p n 10.
Feb 8	Pope Alexander [IV] orders that no prelate shall demand hospitality from the houses of the Knights Templars as of right *Lateran* R. 1 336 O 1 582 H 1 p n, 11
Feb 10	The K certifies that the grant made to him by the pope of a twentieth from the benefices of Scotland shall not be prejudicial to the liberties of that realm *Woodstock.* R 1 336. O 1 582 H 1 p n 11
Feb 16	The K orders that neither Angus, son of Donald, nor his Scottish followers, shall be harboured in Ireland *Woodstock* R. 1 336 O 1 582 H 1 p n 11
Feb 15	The K orders that all clerks leaving the Cinque Ports for Rome shall swear not to interfere in the affairs of Sicily *Woodstock* R 1 337 O 1 583 H. 1 p n 11
Feb 17	The K certifies that the abbot of Westminster has paid 1,075*l* 17*s* 8*d* sterling on his account for the affairs of Sicily. *Woodstock* R 1 337 O 1 583 H 1 p n 11.
[Feb]	The K sends Wm Bonquer to obtain information as to the most eligible person to be elected King of Germany, and to procure from the pope a delay in the payment of various sums Letters are sent to the pope and the papal notary on the same subject R. 1 337. O. 1. 588 H. 1. p. n 11.
[Feb]	The K to the cardinal of S Angelo and others, asking for a modification of the terms on which Sicily is granted to prince Edmund R 1 339 O 1 587 H 1 p n 12
March 1	The K authorizes his brother the earl of Cornwall to search the coffers of the Jews in London, and to enroll their debts *Ditton* R. 1 337
March 27	The K to the pope, is unable to meet the expenses connected with the affairs of Sicily, and asks delay *Norwich* R 1 337 O 1 584 H 1 p n 11
March 31	Pope Alexander [IV] to the K in favour of the archbp. of Armagh. *Lateran.* R. 1. 338. O 1 585 H 1 p n 12
April 17	The K grants to his sister Isabella, lady of Croun, 1,000 marks for her marriage with the duke of Burgundy. *Westm* R. 1 388 O 1 585 H 1 p n 12
April 21	The K gives letters of protection for Magnus king of Man (whom he has knighted), and directs his bailiffs not to harbour Harold son of Guthred, and others, who had murdered Magnus's brother *Westm* R 1 338 O 1 586 H 1 p n 12
[April]	Prince Edward ratifies on behalf of his brother Edmund the conditions required by the pope in the affairs of Sicily R 1 238
[April.]	Oath of prince Edward to the above ratification R 1 338 O 1 586. H 1 p n 12
[April]	The K to the cardinal of S Angelo and others, asking for a modification of the terms respecting Sicily R 1 339 O 1 587 H. 1 p n 12. *See* [Febr] 1255
[April]	L prince of Wales complains to the K. of aggressions committed on the lands of Griffin de Bromfeud by the English R 1 339 O 1 588 H 1 p n 13
[April]	Letters of Peter de Montfort relative to the Welsh insurgents R 1. 339 O. 1. 588 H 1 p. n. 13. *See* [Oct. 2, 1256]

DATE	SUBJECT
1256 [April]	K Henry proposes to the K of Castile a marriage between the K of Castile's brother and a daughter of the writer *Oxford* R 1 340. O 1 589 H 1 p 11 14
[April]	Lewelin prince of Wales will cause inquiry to be made respecting the invasions said to have been made by his subjects in England R 1 340 O 1 590 H 1 p 11 14
[April]	L prince of Wales complains to the K of the conduct of Roger de Mortimer and others, who have invaded his territories R 1 340 O 1 591 H 1 p 11 14
[April]	L prince of Wales assures the K that he has not violated the truce R 1. 340 O. 1 590 H 1 p 11 14
	P de Montfort to the K. on the disturbed state of the Welsh borders. R 1 341 O 1 590 H 1 p 11 14
[April]	The K to the bp of Bethlehem and cardinal Albus on the marriage of prince Edmund with the Q of Cyprus R 1 341 O 1 592 H 1 p 11 14
[May 16]	Fulk lord "de Mastacio" asks prince Edward to accept the fealty of Geoffrey Martelli for certain land in the isle of Oleron *Mornac* R 1 341 O 1 593 H 1 p 11 15
May 16	The K desires that the seal of his son prince Edward shall be of force in Ireland *Reading.* R 1 341.
June 11	Pope Alexander [IV] urges prompt payment of the money promised by the K for the use of Sicily *Anagni* R 1 342 O 1 593 H 1 p 11 15
June 11	Pope Alexander [IV] permits the K and his guests to eat meat on the feast of S Edward, though it falls on Saturday, notwithstanding his vow to the contrary *Anagni.* R 1 342. O 1 594. H. 1. p 11 15
June 12	Credence for Richard de Clare earl of Gloucester, and others, sent by the K. to the princes of Germany *Westm* R 1 342 O 1 595 H 1 p 11 15
June 13	Pope Alexander [IV] decrees that the manors belonging to the bps of England shall pay tithes to the K. for a certain time *Anagni* R 1 342 O 1 595. H. 1 p 11. 15
June 13	Pope Alexander [IV] directs the K how to act in regard to disputes which have arisen as to priority of payment of sums advanced for the affairs of Sicily *Anagni* R 1 343 O 1 595 H 1 p 11 16
June 13	The K notifies to the K of Castile that he has sent to him William bp of Ely and John de Gatesden, to treat of a composition between them *Winchester* R 1 343 O 1 595. H 1 p 11 16
July 10.	Letter of credence for the bp of Ely and John of Gatesden going to the king of Castile. *Winchester* R 1 343 O 1 596 H 1 p 11 16
July 10.	Commission for the bp of Ely and John de Gatesden to proceed to the K of Castile *Clarendon* R 1 343 O 1 595 H 1 p 11 16
July 10	Instructions to the above to inform the K of Castile that K Henry will endeavour to induce the pope to favour the expedition to Africa *Clarendon* R 1.343 O 1 598 H 1 p 11 16
July 12	Pope Alexander [IV] asks the K to interpose in a dispute between two clerks as to the church of Stodintone in the diocese of Hereford *Anagni* R 1 344 O 1 595 H 1 p 11 16.
July 20.	Richard de Crokesley, abbot of Westminster, going to Rome, swears that he will not solicit anything prejudicial to the convent *Gloucester.* R. 1 344 O. 1 596 H 1 p 11 17
Aug 20	The K orders the sale of the houses of the Jews of Lincoln hanged for crucifying the boy *Woodstock* R 1 344
Aug 21	Pope Alexander [IV] orders that the fruits of vacant benefices be applied to the crusade *Anagni* R 1 344 O. 1 597. H 1 p 11 17
Aug 21.	Pope Alexander [IV] makes a like order in regard to the fruits of the benefices of non-residents. *Anagni* R 1 344 O 1 597 H 1 p 11 17
Aug 23.	Pope Alexander [IV] gives to the furtherance of the crusade the fruits of all benefices vacant for one year *Anagni* R 1 345 O 1 598 H 1 p 11 17
Aug 23	Pope Alexander [IV] gives to the K the tenths of all the church revenues in England for the same purpose. *Anagni* R 1 345 O 1 598 H 1 p 11 17
Aug 23	Pope Alexander [IV] orders that the tenths of the churches of the archdeaconry of Richmond be applied to the purposes of the crusade. *Anagni* R 1. 345. O 1 601. H 1 p 11 17
Aug 25	Pope Alexander [IV] orders that the goods of persons dying intestate in England be applied to the same purpose *Anagni* R 1 345 O 1 601 H. 1 p 11 18
Sept. [2]	Pope Alexander [IV] orders that the goods of the abps and bps of England be taxed for the same purpose *Anagni* R 1 345 O 1 602 H 1 p 11 16

DATE	SUBJECT
1256 Sept. 2	Pope Alexander [IV] orders that the above regulation be strictly enforced　*Anagni.* R 1 346　O 1. 602.　H 1 p ii 18
Sept. 2	Pope Alexander [IV] orders that the above sums be collected and handed over to the abp of Canterbury for the use of the crusade　*Anagni*　R 1 346　O. 1. 603.　H 1 p ii. 18.
Sept. 2	Pope Alexander [IV] orders that the above sums be employed in paying his debts due to the K　*Anagni.*　R 1 346　O 1 603　H 1 p ii 18
Sept 2	Pope Alexander [IV] assures the K that the above proceedings shall not be prejudicial to his rights　*Anagni*　R 1 346　O 1 604　H 1 p ii 19
Sept 2	Pope Alexander [IV] orders the collectors of the subsidies for the crusade to render an account of their receipts　*Anagni*　R. 1 347　O 1 604.　H 1 p ii 19
Sept. 2	Pope Alexander [IV] orders that a day be fixed for the king to embark for the crusade. *Anagni*　R 1 347　O 1 605　H 1 p ii 19
Sept 13	The K provides aid for the K. of Scotland against his rebels　*Westm*　R 1 347. O 1 605　H 1 p ii 19
[Sept. 13]	Commission to John Mansell to arrange the business of Alexander K. of Scotland. *Westm*　R 1 347　O 1 605　H 1 p. ii 19
[Sept 13]	Commission to John Mansel to treat with Alexander K of Scotland　*Westm.*　R 1 347　O 1 606　H 1 p ii 19
Sept 13	Pope Alexander [IV] authorizes collections to be made for the priory of the leprous women of S. Mary de Pratis　*Anagni*　R. 1. 347.　O. 1. 606　H 1 606　H 1 p ii 19
Sept 17	Gaillard de Solaris, citizen of Bordeaux, undertakes to support prince Edward in Gascony　*Windsor*　R 1 348　O 1 606　H 1 p ii 20
Sept 22	Pope Alexander [IV] excommunicates all prelates and ecclesiastics who have not paid the tenth for the Holy Land.　*Anagni*　R 1 348.　O. 1 607　H 1 p ii 20
Sept 22	Pope Alexander [IV] permits the celebration of low mass at the monastery of Pochele in the dioc of Salisbury, during periods of excommunication.　*Anagni*　R 1 348　O 1 670　H 1 p ii 20
Sept 27	Pope Alexander [IV] extends the time within which the K must send men and money for the aid of Sicily　*Anagni*　R 1 348　O. 1 608　H. 1 p ii 20
Sept. 27	Pope Alexander [IV] orders a twentieth to be paid by all Scottish benefices for the aid of Sicily　*Anagni*　R 1. 348　O 1 608　H. 1 p ii 20.
Sept 27	Pope Alexander [IV] orders the collection of various subsidies in Scotland in aid of the Holy Land　*Anagni*　R 1 349　O 1 609　H 1 p ii 21
Sept 27	Papal bull for the protection of the monks of Pochele, in the dioc. of Salisbury　*Anagni* R 1 349　O 1 610　H 1 p ii 21
Sept 30	Pope Alexander [IV] permits John le Despenser to build a private chapel and to keep a chaplain　*Anagni*　R. 1 349　O 1 610　H 1 p ii 21.
[Oct 2]	Letter from Peter de Montford and Roger le Bigod and others, describing his progress against the Welsh insurgents　R 1 339　O 1 588　H 1 p ii 18
Oct. 4	Pope Alexander [IV] renews his licence to John le Despencer to build a chapel　*Anagni*　R 1 349　O 1. 610　H 1 p ii 21
Oct 4	Pope Alexander [IV] extends the time within which the K must send men and money in aid of Sicily　*Anagni*　R 1 350　O 1 611　H 1 p ii 21
Oct. 6	Pope Alexander [IV] takes measures for enforcing the prosecution by the K of the affairs of Sicily　*Anagni*　R 1 350　O 1 611　H 1 p ii 21
Oct 7	Pope Alexander [IV] gives an indulgence to those who contribute tenths to the Holy Land　*Anagni*　R 1 350　O 1 612　H 1 p ii. 22
Nov 8	Pope Alexander [IV] urges the K. to rectify ecclesiastical abuses, of which previous complaints have been made to him by the bp. of Rochester　*Anagni*　R 1 350
Nov 9	Pope Alexander [IV] urges the K. to expedite the affairs of Sicily.　*Anagni.*　R. 1 351　O 1 612　H 1 p ii 22
Dec 11	Pope Alexander [IV], in favour of penitents going to the monastery of S Mary de Pratis, near S Alban's　*Lateran*　R 1 351　O 1 614　H 1 p. ii 22
Dec 13	Pope Alexander [IV] recommends Roger Fimett de Lentino and his adherents to the K for services rendered by them to his cause in Sicily　*Viterbo*　R 1 366　O. 1 646　H 1 p ii 34
Dec 13	Pope Alexander [IV] to the K in favour of the abp of Armagh　*Viterbo.*　R. 1. 366.　O. 1. 647.　H. 1. p. ii. 35.

DATE	SUBJECT
1256 Dec 15	Pope Alexander [IV] appoints Huguitio called Matze, a Florentine merchant, to receive moneys paid in England in the affair of the crusade *Lateran* R 1 352 O 1 614 H 1 p ii 23
Dec 16.	Pope Alexander [IV] to the K. in favour of G bp of S Andrews, banished by the K of Scotland *Lateran* R 1 352 O 1 615 H 1 p ii. 23
Dec 23	Bull for the restoration of the monastery of S Mary de Pratis, near S Alban's *Lateran* R 1. 352. O 1. 616. H. 1 p ii. 23
1257 Jan 1	The K. to the countess of Provence, agrees to the peace between her and Charles count of Provence. *Merton* R 1. 352 O 1 616 H 1 p ii 28
[Jan 1]	The K condoles with the countess of Provence on the injuries which she has sustained from the count of Provence. *Merton* R. 1 352 O 1 616 H. 1 p ii 23
Jan. 17.	The K thanks the bp of Hereford for his negotiations in Castile, and informs him of the election of Richard earl of Cornwall to be K of Almain *Windsor* R. 1 353 O 1 617 H 1 p ii 24
Jan 22	Richard, K elect of the Romans, reports his election to John abp of Messina. *Wallingford* R 1 353 O 1 618. H 1 p ii, 24.
Feb 4	Credence from Alexander K of Scotland to the K of England, in lieu of messengers sent to consult him on some points in which the writer is in discussion with his barons *Roxburgh* R 1 353 O. 1 618 H. 1 p ii 24
Feb 3	The K assigns to Peter of Savoy the 4,000 marks due by Raymond late count of Provence and his wife Beatrice *Westm* R. 1 354 O 1 619 H 1 p. ii 24
[Feb 10]	Safe conduct for the messengers of Lewellin son of Griffin, coming to Richard, King elect of the Romans R 1 354 O 1 619 H 1 p ii 24
Feb. 12	The K requests the abbot of Burton to attend a conference to be held at London before R. earl of Cornwall leaves England for Germany *Westm.* R 1 354
March 30.	The K. complains to P cardinal of S. George, that the monks of Ely have elected a bp of Ely without his licence *Westm* R 1 354
[March 30]	The K will permit collections to be made in England for the rebuilding of Cologne cathedral, destroyed by fire R 1 363 O 1 640. H. 1 p ii 32
April 1	The K informs pope Alexander [IV] that he has appointed proctors in the papal court *Westm* R. 1 354 O 1. 619. H. 1 p. ii 25
April 13	Appointment of English Commissioners to treat respecting the violations of the truce with France *Westm* R 1. 355. O 1 620 H 1 p ii 25
April 13.	Appointment by the K. of dictators to act in the above matter. *Westm.* R 1 355. O. 1 620 H 1 p ii 25.
May 10	The K. to pope Alexander [IV], has appointed a captain for the expedition to Sicily. whom he has furnished with money *Merton* R 1 355 O 1 620 H 1 p ii 25
[May 10]	The K to the pope and cardinals, is ready to make peace with France in furtherance of the interests of Sicily R 1 355 O 1 621 H 1. p ii 25
[June 2]	Protection for 47 persons (here named) accompanying Richard K of the Romans into Germany. R. 1. 355 O 1 621 H 1 p ii 25
May 18	Richard K of the Romans informs his nephew prince Edward of his coronation at Aix-la-Chapelle, on the feast of the Ascension *Aix-la-Chapelle* R. 1 356 O 1. 622 H 1 p ii 25
May 20	Cresse and Hagen, Jews, are free from aids for five years for the help they gave Richard the K's brother in gaining the crown of the Romans *Westm* R 1 356 O 1 623 H 1 p ii 26
June 3	Pope Alexander [IV] to the papal nuncio, as to the application of the sums collected in England in aid of Sicily *Viterbo.* R. 1 356 O 1. 624. H 1 p. ii. 26
June 6	The K. informs John, son of the K. of Jerusalem, that he and his wife the Q. of Scotland may have a passport for Scotland under certain conditions *Westm* R 1 357 O. 1 625. H 1 p ii 27
June 7	The K. objects to restore certain lands and castles to the K of Castile *Westm* R 1 357 O 1 625 H 1 p ii. 27
June 7	The K. objects to restore certain lands and castles to the K of Aragon *Westm* R 1. 357 O 1 626 H 1 p ii 27
June 8	Safe conduct for the messenger of the K. of Castile passing through Germany. *Westm.* R. 1 357 O 1 626 H. 1 p. ii. 27.

DATE	SUBJECT
1257 June 18	Safe conduct for John de Acre, son of the K of Jerusalem, and the Q of Scotland his wife, passing through England into Scotland *Westm* R 1 358. O 1 627. H 1 p ii. 27.
June 22.	Commission to treat for peace with France *Westm* R 1 358 O 1 627 H 1 p ii 27
June 22	Another commission for the same purpose *Westm* R 1 358 O 1 627 H 1 p ii. 27.
[June 22]	The K asks his brother Richard K of the Romans to advise the above commissioners in the matter of France *Westm* R 1 358 O 1 628 H 1 p ii 28
[June]	Pope Alexander [IV] will send his notary, master Ailott, into England to remodel the affairs of Sicily R 1 358 O 1 628 H 1 p ii 28
June 26	Edmund K of Sicily asks pope Alexander [IV] to revise the conditions by which he holds Sicily *Windsor.* R 1 359 O 1. 359 H 1 p ii 28
June 26.	The K sends commissioners to settle the affairs of Sicily *Windsor* R 1 359 O 1 629 H 1 p ii 28
June 26	Credence for the commissioners to treat in the affairs of Sicily. *Windsor* R 1 359 O 1 630 H 1. p ii 28.
June 28.	The K informs the pope [Alexander IV] and cardinals that he will make peace with France *Windsor* R 1 358, 359 O 1 621, 630 H 1. p ii 25, 28
[June 28]	The K informs the pope and cardinals that he has renounced Sicily on the part of prince Edmund *Westm* R 1 359 O 1 630 H 1 p ii 28
[June 28]	The K. explains to the pope his conduct in regard to Sicily, the decision respecting which he leaves to the pope *Windsor* R 1 359 O 1 630 H 1 p ii 29
[June 28]	Instructions for the earl of Leicester and Peter of Savoy as to the management of the affairs of Sicily R 1 360 O 1 632 H 1 p ii 29
June 28	The K intrusts Simon de Montfort and Peter de Savoy with various blank letters, sealed, to be used by them in the affairs of Sicily *Reading* R 1 360 O 1 633 H 1 p ii 29
July 5	The K sends to Simon de Montfort and Peter de Savoy, by master Rostand and Arthald de S Romain, the grant of Sicily formerly given by pope Innocent IV *Woodstock* R 1 361 O. 1 634 H 1 p ii 30
July 8	The K asks pope Alexander [IV] to furnish him with letters vindicating his honor from certain calumnies *Woodstock* R 1 361 O 1 634 H 1 p ii 30
July 8	Master Rostand acknowledges the receipt of the papal writ about Sicily *Rochester* R 1 361 O 1 634 H 1. p ii. 30
[July 13]	Pope Alexander [IV] permits the prior of the Holy Trinity, London, to punish the excesses of his inferiors *Viterbo* R 1 21. O 1 20 H 1 7
July 18	Writ of military summons to 51 persons (here named) to be at Bristol to serve against the Welsh *Woodstock* R 1 361 O 1 635. H 1. p ii 30
July 19.	The K inhibits the clergy from meeting in convocation until the war with Wales has ended, and orders their attendance with his army *Woodstock* R 1 362 O 1 636 H 1 p ii 30
July 20	The K grants the community of the Jews free liberty to choose their own high priest. *Woodstock* R 1 362 O 1 636 H 1 p ii 30
July 20	The K. sends commissioners to Stirling, to settle disputes between Alexander K of Scotland and his subjects *Woodstock* R 1. 362 O 1 637 H 1 p ii 31
Sept 9.	Settlement of the disputes connected with the church of Bexley *Viterbo.* R 1 362 O 1 637 H 1 p ii 31
Sept 11	The K to the K of Spain, the Welsh wars have caused his silence. *In the camp at Dissard* R 1. 363 O 1 638 H 1 p ii 31
Sept. 11	The K informs the K of Spain that messengers have been detained by sickness in France *In the camp at Dissard* R 1 363 O 1. 639 H 1. p. ii 32
Sept 11	The K to the K of Castile, to the same effect. *In the camp at Dissard* R. 1 363 O 1. 639. H 1 p ii 32
———	The K to the abp of Canterbury, on the rebuilding of Cologne Cathedral R 1. 363 O 1 640 H. 1 p ii 32 *See* March 30, 1257
Sept 13	Pope Alexander [IV] recommends to the K friar Mansuetus, a Minorite, sent to make peace between England and France *Viterbo* R 1 21. O 1. 21 H 1 7
Oct.	Pope Alexander [IV] orders that the tenths be collected for the execution of the K's vow *Viterbo.* R 1. 363. O 1 640 H. 1 p ii 32

DATE.	SUBJECT
1257 Oct 10	Pope Alexander [IV] confirms the taxations made for the priory of the Holy Trinity, London. *Viterbo* R 1 21 O 1 22 H 1 7
Oct 11	Pope Alexander [IV] confirms the church of Bexley to the convent of the H Trinity, London. *Viterbo.* R. 1. 364 O 1 640 H 1 p n 32.
Oct 15	Pope Alexander [IV] insists upon the payment of the annual pension due by the convent of the H Trinity, London, to Ubaldinus, his agent *Viterbo* R 1 364 O 1 641 H 1 p n 32.
Oct 15	Pope Alexander [IV] wishes to make provision for Stephen de Ponte from the church of Biston, in the dioc of Norwich *Viterbo.* R 1 364 O 1. 642. H 1 p n 33
Oct 26	The K encourages the men of Oleron to resist the orders of Guy de Lezegnan, to whom prince Edward has unadvisedly granted the island *Westm* R. 1 365 O 1. 643 H 1 p n 33
Nov. 5	The K's agents acknowledge the receipt of 540 marks stg. from certain Italian merchants for the affairs of Sicily *Viterbo* R 1 365 O 1 643 H 1 p n 33
Nov 7	Pope Alexander [IV], relative to the provision for Ubaldinus in the church of Bisle, in the dioc of Rochester *Viterbo* R 1 365 O. 1 644 H 1 p n 34
Nov 21.	Pope Alexander [IV], in favour of the convent of the H Trinity, London, against the provision of Ubaldinus in the church of Bixle *Viterbo* R 1 366 O 1 645 H 1 p n 34
Dec. 12	Pope Alexander [IV] places the affairs of Sicily on a new footing in regard to the K and his son Edmund *Viterbo* R. 1 366 O. 1 646 H 1 p n 34
Dec. 13	Bull for Roger Finett, for his services in the cause of Sicily. R 1 366 O 1 646 H 1 p n 34 *See* Dec 13, 1256
Dec 13.	Bull in favour of the abp of Armagh R 1 366 O 1 647 H 1 p n 35 *See* Dec 13, 1256
Dec 14.	The K informs the K of Castile of his success against the Moors and the coronation of his brother as the K of the Romans *Westm* R 1 367 O 1 657 H 1 p n 38.
Dec 18.	Pope Alexander [IV] to the K, in favour of Abraham abp of Armagh. *Viterbo.* R 1 367
Dec. 24.	Pope Alexander [IV] orders that various dues, &c should be paid to the K. in aid of the crusade *Viterbo* R. 1 367 O 1 649 H 1 p n 35.
Dec. 26.	Pope Alexander [IV] arranges certain new proceedings in regard to Sicily, contingent upon the K's consent *Viterbo* R 1 368 O 1. 649 H 1 p n 36
1258 Jan 1	Pope Alexander [IV] begs the K to repay 4,500 marks sterling, borrowed from merchants of Sienna for the affairs of Sicily *Viterbo.* R 1 368. O 1 650 H 1 p n 36
Jan 2	Pope Alexander [IV] to the K, in favour of Abraham abp of Armagh R 1 368 O 1 651 H 1 p n 36.
Jan 7	Credence from the K for the abbot of Shrewsbury and John de Castello sent to the K of Castile *Merton* R. 1 368 O. 1 651 H 1 p n 36
[Jan 7]	The K sends the 50 marks to the above messengers for their expenses going to Castile *Merton* R 1 369. O 1 651 H. 1 p n 36.
Jan 19.	Pope Alexander [IV] suspends the penalties threatened against the K and prince Edmund for their delay in the matter of Sicily *Viterbo* R 1 369 O 1 652 H. 1 p n 36
Jan. 22	The K orders the barons of the Cinque Ports to arrest Gomelin bp of S Andrew's, who has brought from Rome a bull disinheriting K. Alexander *Windsor* R. 1. 369. O 1. 652. H 1 p n. 37.
[Jan]	The K. orders Richard earl of Gloucester to lay hold of Margaret, sister of Lewellin, son of Griffin, and keep her safe, as a marriage which is being planned for her might be dangerous to the K R 1 369 O 1 653 H 1 p n 37
March 6	Pope Alexander [IV.] confirms various charters by which the ecclesiastical liberties of England had been secured at different times *Viterbo* R 1 369
March 18	Treaty by which the nobles of Scotland and Wales mutually pledge themselves never to make peace with the K of England without the consent of both R 1 370 O. 1 653 H 1 p n 37
May 2.	The K notifies that, by the approval of the great council of the realm, his son Edmund may again engage in the affairs of Sicily *Westm* R 1 370 O 1 654. H 1 p n 37
May 2	The K notifies that he has consented to a meeting at Oxford for the reform of the state of the realm. R 1 371 O 1 655 H 1 p n 37

DATE	SUBJECT
1258 May 6.	Malise earl of Stratherne to K Henry, will attend on the queen of Scotland, the K's daughter, and obey K Henry's instructions regarding her place of residence *S Andrew's* R 1 371
May 8	The King appoints commissioners to settle a truce with France. *Westm* R 1 371 O 1 655 H 1 p II 38
May 30	Pope Alexander [IV] urges the K to settle his debts for the affairs of Sicily with the merchants of Sienna *Viterbo* R 1 371 O 1 656 H 1 p II 38
June 2	Safe conduct for the messengers of Lewellin, son of Griffin, coming to the parliament at Oxford *Marlborough* R 1 372 O 1 657 H 1 p II 38
June 17	Truce for one year with Lewellin, son of Griffin *Oxford* R 1 372 O. 1 658 H. 1 p II 39
June 25	The K to Alfonso K of Castile, relative to the affairs of Africa, his brother, K of the Romans, and to a proposed marriage between the daughter of the K of England with a brother of the K of Castile *Oxford* R 1 372 O 1 657 H 1 p II 38
June 28	The K charges the clergy and laity of Ireland not to obey any justiciary or keeper of any castle in Ireland who may be appointed by prince Edward *Oxford.* R 1 373
[June]	The barons of England (in the name of the commonalty) to the pope, complaining of the K, the bp elect of Winchester, and his brothers, in the matter of Sicily, and of their violation of the liberties of the realm R 1 373 O 1 660 H 1 p II 39
July 5	Safe conduct for Aymer bp elect of Winchester and his brothers going into France *Winchester* R 1 374 O. 1 662 H 1 p II 40
July 8	The K. demands from Lewellin, son of Griffin, amends for the violation of the truce *Westm* R 1 374 O 1 662 H 1 p II 40
July 10	The K sends 3,000 marks to Dover for the use of his brother Wm de Valence. *Winchester* R 1 374 O 1 663 H 1 p II 40
July 11.	The K advises the men of Oleron not to permit the island to be sold by prince Edward, or separated from the crown *Winchester* R. 1 374 O 1 663 H 1 p II 41
July 12.	Prince Edward revokes the appointment of his uncle, Geoffrey of Lesignan, as seneschal of Gascony. *Winchester* R. 1 374 O 1 663 H 1 p II 41
July 27	The K asks the pope to extend the period for the final settlement of the affairs of Sicily *Westm* R. 1 375 O 1 664 H 1 p II 41
July 28	The K solicits the abp of Tarente to join the embassy which he is about to send to Rome on the affairs of Sicily *Westm* R 1 375 O 1 604 H 1 p. II 41
July 28	The K will send passports for Theobald K of Navarre and others to visit in pilgrimage the shrine of S Thomas at Canterbury *Westm.* R. 1 375 O 1 665 H 1 p II 41
July 28.	Passport referred to in the previous letter *Westm* R 1 375 O 1. 665 H. 1 p II 41
July 28	Writ for the appointment of four knights of the shire for the correction of injuries, according to the provisions of the parliament at Oxford R 1 375
Aug 1	The K informs pope Alexander [IV] that if the conditions for Sicily were abated he could proceed with the matter *Westm* R 1 376 O 1 606 H 1 p II 41
Aug 1	The K. informs pope Alexander [IV] that he will accept the terms of peace with France proposed by the pope's chaplain *Westm* R 1 376. O. 1 606 H 1 p II. 42
Aug 1	The K asks the cardinals at Rome to promote the peace with France *Westm* R. 1 376 O 1 667 H 1 p II 42
Aug 4	The K appoints commissioners to settle peace between the rival parties in Scotland *Westm.* R. 1 376 O 1 668 H 1 p II 42
[Aug]	The K to the K of Scotland, apologies for delay and irregularity in his money matters, and will arrange about the liberty of Penrath and the manor of Wheteley. R. 1 377 O 1. 668 H 1 p. II. 42
Aug 18	The K appoints commissioners to settle the infractions of the truce with Lewellin, son of Griffin *Woodstock* R. 1 377 O 1 669 H 1 p II 43
Aug 18.	The K directs inquiry to be made about the large sums of money carried out of the realm by his brothers *Woodstock* R 1 377
[Aug]	For the K of the Romans, on the levying of a tallage R 1. 377 O 1 669 H 1 p II p 43 *See* Oct. 29, 1259
[Aug.]	For the K. of the Romans, on the same subject R 1 377 O 1 669 H. 1 p II 43 *See* Oct 29, 1259

DATE	SUBJECT
1258 Oct. 18	The K. pledges himself henceforth to rule the realm by the advice of the council elected by himself and the commonalty, which shall be accepted by all persons *London* R 1 377
Oct. 18	The K.'s charter in early English, on the reformation of the state of the realm. *London* R 1 378.
Nov. 4	Prince Edward revokes the grant made of the island of Oleron which he had unadvisedly made to his uncle, Guy de Lesignan *Southwerk* R. 1 678 O 1 669 H 1 p ii 43
Nov. 6.	The K. sanctions the government of Scotland by the nobles who have taken it in hand. *Westm.* R. 1 378 O 1 671 H. 1 p. ii. 43.
Dec. 3.	Pope Alexander [IV] excommunicates all who do not, within two months, pay their debts to certain merchants of Florence *Anagni* R 1 378 O 1 670 H 1 p ii 43
Dec. 18.	Pope Alexander [IV] rescinds the grant of Sicily to prince Edmund, unless the conditions are fully carried out *Anagni* R 1 379
1259 Jan 23	The K requests his brother Richard K. of the Romans to swear to observe the statutes made for the reformation of the state of the realm *Canterbury* R 1 380 O 1 671 H 1 p ii 44
Feb 17.	Letter of Alexander K of Scotland relative to the payment of money. R 1 380 O 1 671 H 1 p ii 43 *See* Feb 17, 1262
Feb 20	The K notifies that the K of France is not bound to deliver up certain lands until he (Henry) has done liege homage to him *Westm* R 1 380 O 1 685 H. 1 p ii 49
Feb 24	The K surrenders Normandy, Anjou, Touraine, Le Mans, and Poitou to the K of France, according to the terms of the peace *Westm* R 1 380 O 1 684 H 1 p ii 48
March 16	The K requests the cardinals to induce the pope to tolerate the delay in the matter of Sicily *Windsor* R 1 381 O 1. 673 H 1. p. ii. 44
March 23.	Pope Alexander [IV] to the K in favour of the bp of Elphin, now made abp of Tuam *Anagni* R 1 381 O 1 672 H. 1 p ii 44
March 28	The K sends to each county in England the ordinances made for the government of the realm by his council *Westm* R 1 381
April 21	Pope Alexander [IV] congratulates Richard K of the Romans upon his coronation *Anagni* R 1 382 O 1 673 H 1 p ii 44
April 22	Pope Alexander [IV] requests that the K. will permit the bp of Rochester, resident in the papal court, to appoint an attorney *Anagni*. R 1. 382 O. 1. 674 H 1 p ii 45
May 10	Commission to settle a contract of marriage between Beatrice, the K's daughter, and John, eldest son of the duke of Brittany *Windsor* R 1 382 O 1 675 H 1 p ii 45
May 20	Treaty of peace between the K of England and the K of France *Westm.* R 1 383 O. 1 675 H 1 p ii 45.
[May 20]	Declaration of Simon de Montfort. R 1 384 *See* May 27, 1259.
May 20.	Commission to inquire concerning the tenure of certain lands in France *Westm* R 1 384 O. 1 678 H 1 p ii 46
May 20.	Commission to Simon de Montfort to complete the peace with France *Westm* R 1 384 O 1 678 H 1 p ii 46
May 20	Commission to settle the terms for the pay of 500 soldiers for 2 years, according to the treaty of peace with France *Westm.* R 1 384. O. 1. 679 H 1 p. ii. 46
May 20	Commission to appoint arbitrators in the above matter *Westm* R 1 385 O 1. 679 H. 1 p ii 47
May 20	Commission to John Mansel and Rob Waleran to arbitrate as above *Westm* R 1. 385 O 1 679 H 1 p ii 47.
May 20	Commission for five arbitrators in the above matter *Westm* R 1. 385 O 1 680 H 1. p ii 47
May 20	Commission to value the country of Agen for the payment to be made to England by France *Westm* R 1 385 O 1 680 H 1 p ii 47.
May 20	Commission for new arbitrators to settle the value of Agen. *Westm.* R. 1. 385 O 1 680. H. 1 p ii 47.
May 20	The K promises to hold the K of France free from the claims of the countess of Leicester in regard to lands in France *Westm* R 1 385 O 1. 681 H. 1 p ii. 47
May 20.	Commission to indemnify the K of France in the above matter *Westm* R. 1 385 O 1 681 H 1 p ii 47
May 20.	Credence to pope Alexander [IV.] for Wm Bonquer on the affairs of Sicily and of the bprick. of Winchester. *Westm* R. 1. 386. O. 1 681. H 1 p. ii. 47.

DATE	SUBJECT
1259 May 20	Credence to several cardinals for Wm Bouquer in the above matters. *Westm* R 1 386 O 1 682 H 1 p ii 47
May 20.	Commission to treat of a marriage between Beatrix, the K 's daughter, and John, eldest son of the Duke of Brittany *Windsor*. R 1 386 O 1 682 H 1 p ii 47.
May 24	Credence for certain clerks sent from the K to the abp of Embrun on the affairs of Sicily *Windsor* R 1 386 O 1 682 H 1 p ii 48
May 24	Credence for Wm Bouquer sent to the abps of Embrun and Tarante, &c , on the affairs of Sicily *Windsor* R 1 386 O 1 683 O 1 p ii 48
[May 27]	Notification by Simon de Montfort and others, proctors of the K of England, that the K. of France has made certain reservations in the treaty of peace with England R 1 384
June 13	Pope Alexander [IV] asks the K to promote the election of John de Cheyam as bp of Glasgow *Anagni* R 1 387. O 1 683 H 1 p ii 48
June 27	Pope Alexander [IV] grants certain privileges to the priory of the H Trinity, London *Anagni* R 1 387 O 1 684 H 1 p ii 48
July 26	Ratification by the K. of the truce with Wales *Westm* R 1. 387 O 1 684 H 1 p ii 48
July 26	Ratification by prince Edward of the peace with France *Westm* R. 1 387. O 1 685. H 1 p ii 49
July 26	Ratification by prince Edmund of the peace with France *London*. R 1 387 O 1 686 H 1 p ii 49
[July 27]	Henry of Castile, brother to the K of Castile, pledges himself to the K of England that when going from Bayonne into Africa he will not make war upon the K of Castile *Westm* R 1 388. O 1 686 H 1 p ii 49
July 28.	The K consents that certain bonds for money due to him may remain with Louis [IX] K. of France *Westm* R 1 388 O 1 686 H 1 p ii 49
July 28	Credence for Simon de Montfort and others sent to the K of France *Westm* R 1 388. O. 1 686 H 1 p ii 49.
July 28	Commission for the exchange of writings between the kings of England and France. *Westm* R 1 388. O 1 686 H 1 p ii 49
[July]	The K permits Henry of Castile to engage ships at Bordeaux and Bayonne for his expedition into Africa *Westm* R 1 388 O 1 687 H 1 p ii 49
Aug 2	Commission appointing certain persons to negotiate with the pope for the appointment of a legate to England, there to settle the affairs of Sicily *Westm* R 1 388. O 1 687 H 1 p ii 49
Sept 3	The K gives the island of Oleron to prince Edward, who, however, must not alienate it from the crown of England *Westm* R 1 388 O 1 688 H 1. p ii 50
Oct	Composition between the kings of France and England respecting Limoges, Cahors, and Périgord *Paris* R 1 389 O 1 688. H 1 p ii 50.
[Oct 13]	Ratification of the above composition by the prelates and barons of England *London* R. 1 390
Oct 18	The K. to John duke of Brittany respecting the restitution of the earldom of Richmond *Westm* R. 1 391 O 1 693. H 1 p ii 52
Oct. 18.	Proclamation by the K. respecting the terms of the marriage between his daughter Beatrice and John, son of the duke of Brittany R 1 391 O 1 693 H 1 p ii 52
Oct 21	The K. to Louis [IX] K. of France , will proceed to Paris to complete the peace *Westm* R 1 391 O 1. 694 H 1 p ii 52
Oct. 29	The K permits his brother Richard K of the Romans to levy a tallage upon his boroughs and manors, usually exempt *Westm* R 1 377 391 O 1 669 694 H 1 p ii 43 52
Oct. 29.	The K. begs that the above tallage may be paid *Westm* R. 377 391. O 1 669 694 H 1 p ii 43 52
[Nov. 27]	Simon de Montfort earl of Leicester and Eleanor countess of Leicester consent to the treaty of peace between England and France *Paris* R 1 392
Dec 19	The K to the pope and certain cardinals , excuses his delay in sending the promised envoys to Rome *Paris*. R 1 392. O 1 695 H 1 p ii 52
Dec 28	The K to the pope and certain cardinals , after much delay, peace with France was concluded before Christmas. *Paris*. R 1 392 O 1 695 H 1 p ii. 52

DATE	SUBJECT
1260 [Jan 5]	Louis [IX] K of France to the K; does not think he is bound to pay 1,000 marks to John of Brittany, about to marry Beatrix, K Henry's daughter, in compensation for the land of Agen *Compiègne* R 1 392 O 1 696 H 1 p ii 52
[Jan]	Pope Alexander [IV] assures the nobility of England that he will inquire into the truth of the complaints respecting the state of their country which they have addressed to him R 1. 393
Jan 23	Pope Alexander [IV] urges the K to restore the castle of Rochester to the abp of Canterbury *Anagni* R 1 393 O. 1 696 H 1 p ii 53
Feb. 5.	Credence for messengers sent by the K to transact business in France *Westm* R 1 394 O. 1. 704 H 1 p ii 56
Feb 5	The K asks the queen of France to aid the furtherance of the peace *Westm* R. 1 394. O 1 705. H. 1. p. ii 56
[Feb]	Blanch duchess of Brittany informs the K that her son John is on his way to England R. 1 394 O. 1. 696 H 1 p ii 53.
Feb 25.	Commission appointing arbitrators to settle the violations of the truce with Wales *Westm* R 1 394 O 1 697 H. 1 p ii 53
Feb 25	Safeconduct for the Welsh commissioners on the above business. *Westm* R 1 394 O. 1. 697. H. 1. p ii 53
March 6	The K to the K of Scotland and others in Scotland, in favor of John de Cheyham, bp. elect of Glasgow *S Omer* R 1 394 O 1 697 H 1 p ii 53
March 9	The K. asks John duke of Brittany to permit him to knight his [the duke's] son at the feast of S. Edward next. *S Omer* R 1 395 O 1 698 H 1 p ii 53
March 10	The K complains to Louis [IX] K of France of certain unruly persons in the sees of Limoges, Cahors, and Périgord R 1 395
April 1.	The Masters of the Hospitalers and Templars and others to the K upon the occupation of the Holy Land by the Tartars *Acre* R 1 395 O 1 699 H 1 p ii 54
April 5	Thomas Berardi, Master of the Knights Templars, to the K, asking for aid for the Holy Land *Acre* R 1 396 O 1 698 H 1 p ii 54.
April 17.	Pope Alexander [IV.] to prince Edward, asks protection for Keran dean of Cashel against the abp of Cashel *Anagni* R 1 396. O 1. 700. H 1 p ii 54
April 18	The K asks his brother Richard K of the Romans to prevent certain troops from France landing in Cornwall, in which he, the K of the Romans, has jurisdiction *Boulogne* R 1. 396 O 1 701 H 1 p ii 54
April 28	The K to Louis [IX.] K of France, complaining of the levies of troops mentioned above *Uissant* R. 1 396 O 1 701 H 1 p ii 55
May 3	Inspeximus of a letter of Louis [IX] K of France, by which he receives the homage of Eblo viscount de Ventedore *Dels Glotos* R 1 397 O 1 702 H 1 p ii 55.
May 21.	Pope Alexander [IV] orders the revocation of all sentences against Scotland, in compliance with the provision for the bp of Glasgow. *Anagni* R 1 397 O 1 703 H 1 p. ii. 55
May 30.	The K begs the loan of 5,000 marks sterling from Louis [IX] K of France *Westm.* R. 1 397. O 1 702 H 1 p ii 55
May 30.	The K authorizes the pledging of certain jewels as security for the above loan *Westm* R. 1. 397. O 1 703 H 1 p ii 55
May 30.	The K. to Alfonso K of Castile, Gascony has long been given to prince Edward, the writer will do his best in regard to the subsidy against the K. of the Romans *Westm* R 1 397. O 1 704 R 1 p ii 56
June 15	Confirmation to the merchants of the Guildhall of the Teutons of their ancient privileges. *Westm* R 398
[July 5]	Receipt by the K. for 14,580*l* 66*s* 8*d* Tournois lent by Louis [IX] K. of France. *Westm.* R 1 398 O 1. 705 H 1 p ii 56
July 30	The K acquits Roger de Mortimer of blame in having lost the castle of Buelth to the Welsh *Westm* R 1 398 O 1 705 H 1 p ii 56
Aug. 1	Writs of military summons to appear at Shrewsbury to serve against the Welsh *Westm.* R 1. 398. O 1 700 H 1 p ii 56.
Aug 1.	Writs of military summons to appear at Chester *Westm* R 1 399 O 1 708 H 1 p. ii. 57.

E

DATE	SUBJECT
1260 Aug 1	The abp of Canterbury will excommunicate Llewellin son of Griffin and his adherents, unless they make restitution for injuries done to the K of England *Lambeth* R 1 399 O 1 708 H. 1 p ii 57
Aug 10	Commission to treat of a peace between the K. and Edward his son on the one part and Llewellin son of Griffin on the other *Windsor* R 1 400 O 1 709 H 1 p ii 58
Aug 10	Commission to extend the truce with Llewellin son of Griffin *Windsor* R 1 400 O 1 710 H 1 p ii 58
Aug 10	Commission to enter upon a new truce with Llewellin son of Griffin *Windsor* R 1 400 O 1 710 H 1 p ii 58
Aug 10.	Separate commission to each of the commissioners to treat of the above matters *Windsor.* R 1 400 O 1 710 H 1 p ii. 58.
Sept 14	The K urges prince Edward to interest himself in the affairs of Gascony, and to send commissioners thither forthwith *Marlborough* R 1 410 O 1 711 H 1 p ii 58.
Sept 20	The K to the bp of Bazas and Bertram de Cardilac upon the affairs of prince Edward in Gascony *Marlborough* R 1 401 O 1 711 H 1 p ii 58
Sept 20	The K. to Drogo de Barentine, seneschal of Gascony, upon the same subject. *Marlborough* R 1 401 O 1 712 H 1 p ii 59
Sept 20	The K requests the mayor, &c of Bordeaux to aid his commissioners in the above matter. *Marlborough* R 1 401 O. 1. 712 H 1 p ii 59
Sept 20	Commission to the bp of Bazas and others to treat in the above matter *Marlborough* R 1 401 O 1 712 H 1 p ii 59
Sept 30	Safe conduct for Alexander K of Scotland and his queen coming into England. *Windsor* R 1 402 O 1 713 H 1 p ii 59
Sept 30	Arrangements respecting the possible case of the Q of Scotland giving birth to a child while in England *Windsor* R 1 402 O 1 714 H 1 p ii 59
Sept 30	Arrangements as to the honors to be shown to the K and Q of Scotland in their journey through England *Windsor* R 1 402 O 1 714 H 1 p ii 59
[Oct]	Arrangement that Henry son of the K of Germany shall discharge the office of seneschal at the approaching festival of S Edward R 1 402 O 1 715 H 1 p ii 60
Nov 16	Arrangements respecting the *accouchement* of the Q of Scotland in England *Westm.* R 1 402 O 1 715 H. 1 p ii 60
Nov 17	Pope Alexander [IV] urges prince Edward to deliberate with his father how best to resist the incursions of the Tartars *Lateran* R 1 403 O 1 716 H 1 p ii 60
1261 Feb 1	Protection for the masters and scholars about to open a school in Northampton *Windsor.* R 1 403
Feb 8	The K. orders the commune of the isle of Oleron to see that it is not severed from the crown of England. *Tower of London.* R 1 404 O 1 717. H 1. p ii 61
March 12	The K confirms the truce with Llewellin son of Griffin at Montgomery *Tower of London* R 1 404 O 1 718 H 1 p ii 61
March 14	The K orders the arrest of persons throughout the realm who had reported that he was about to impose new taxes *Tower of London* R 1 404 O 1 720 H 1 p ii. 62.
March 20	Edmund K. of Sicily desires his subjects to prepare for his reception *Windsor* R 1. 405. O 1 720 H 1 p ii 62
March 20	Edmund K of Sicily appoints proctors to receive possession of that realm *Windsor* R 1 405 O 1 721. H. 1 p if 62.
March 21	Edmund K of Sicily asks the aid of the pope in the above matter *Windsor* R. 1 405. O 1 721 H. 1 p ii. 62
April 13	Pope Alex [IV] absolves the K of England from an oath made to his nobles to the injury of the liberties of the crown *Lateran* R 1 405
April 29	Pope Alex [IV] absolves the clergy and laity of England from an oath prejudicial to the liberties of the realm *S Peter's, Rome* R 1 406 O 1 722 H. 1 p ii 62
May 7	Pope Alex [IV], on the above absolution, and on the duty of obedience to the K. *Viterbo* R 1 406 O 1 722 H 1 p ii 62
May 18	The K orders the barons of the Cinque Ports to prevent the landing of troops sent by Simon de Montfort *S Paul's, London* R 1 406
June 17	The K orders the payment of various sums of money to John eldest son of the duke of Brittany *Guilford* R. 1 406 O 1 723 H 1 p ii. 63
July 17.	The K. orders that an inventory be made of all debts due to the Jews *Tower of London.* R 1 407.

DATE	SUBJECT.
1261 July 20	The K submits to the Q of France the arbitration of his disputes with the earl and countess of Leicester *Tower of London* R. 1 407. O 1 724 H 1 p 11 63
July 20	The K. informs Louis [IX] K of France of the import of the preceding letter relative to the earl and countess of Leicester. *Tower of London* R. 1. 407 O 1 724 H 1. p. 11 63
July 20.	The K leaves to the decision of the K of France [Louis IX] the settlement of the value of the land of Agen *Tower of London* R 1 407 O 1 724. H. 1. p 11 63
July 30	The K cautions the men of Kent against giving heed to disquieting reports *Tower of London* R. 1. 407
Aug 5	Ratification of three treaties between the Ks of England and Castile *Windsor.* R 1 408 O 1 725 H 1 p 11 63
[Aug]	Fedlimid O'Connor thanks the K for the assistance rendered to him by Wm de Dene, justiciary of Ireland, against the aggressions of Walter de Burgh R. 1 241 O 1 391 H. 1. 136
Aug 8	B abp of Canterbury sends a copy of a bull of pope Alex [IV] by which he excommunicates Hugh le Bigod, unless he gives up the castles of Scarbro' and Pickering. *Windsor* R 1 408 O 1 726 H 1 p 11 64
Aug 16	The K vindicates himself from the slanders circulated against him by his barons *Windsor* R 1 408
Aug 30	J Maunsel announces to the abp of Canterbury the refusal of Hugh le Bigod to surrender the castles of Scarbro' and Pickering R 1 409 O 1 726 H 1 p 11. 64
Sept. 2	The K cautions Louis [IX] K of France against encouraging or sheltering Simon de Montfort *Windsor.* R 1. 409. O 1. 728 H 1 p 11 64
Sept 12	Agreement between the Ks of England and France as to the value of the land of Agen. *Windsor* R 1 409 O. 1. 728 H. 1 p 11 65
[Sept.]	J cardinal of S Lawrence asks the K. to induce his brother Richard to repay sums advanced by the writer in obtaining for him [Richard] the dignity of a senator *Viterbo* R 1 410 O L. 728 H 1 p 11 65
[Sept]	Geoffrey de Lezignan to his brother the K in favor of Wm. de Sancto Hermite R 1. 410 O 1 729 H 1. p. 11 65
[Sept.]	Geoffrey de Lezignan to the K on the same subject R 1. 410. O 1 729 H 1 p 11. 65 *See* March 2, 1262
Oct 6	The K to pope Urban [IV], appointing proctors in the court of Rome *London* R 1 410 O 1. 729 H 1. p 11 65
Nov. 6.	Inspeximus by the K. of a letter by which Margaret Q of France acknowledges the receipt from him of certain jewels to be deposited in the Temple of Paris *Tower of London* R 1 410. O 1 730 H 1 p 11 65.
[Nov]	The K. to the K and Q of France and the K. and Q of Navarre to intercede with the pope and cardinals to preserve the rights of his son Edmund to the throne of Sicily R 1 410 O. 1 730 H 1 p 11 65
Nov 12	Pope Urban [IV.] complains to the K of the injuries inflicted by his ministers upon the clergy of Ireland *Viterbo* R. 1 400 O 1 731 H 1 p 11 66
Dec. 7	The K certifies that all disputes between himself and his barons respecting the conventions at Westminster and Oxford are now settled *Tower of London* R. 1 411
Dec 7	The K requires the above-mentioned fact to be proclaimed throughout England. *London.* R 1. 412
Dec. 11	The K congratulates pope [Urban IV] upon his accession *Westm* R 1 412. O 1 732 H 1 p 11 66
Dec 11	Angerius de Ganeretto, citizen of Bayonne, swears fealty to prince Edward. *Bordeaux* R 1 412 O 1 733 H 1 p 11 67
Dec. 12.	The K acknowledges the receipt of 10,416l. 13s 4d tournois, in part payment of the sum due by Louis [IX.] for military expenses *Westm.* R 1 412 O 1 733. H 1. p 11 66
Dec 13.	Pope Urban [IV] asks the K. to send to Rome 2,000 marks sterling, the arrears of the annual tribute *Viterbo* R 1 413 O 1. 734 H 1. p. 11 67.
Dec. 15	The K undertakes to pay the value of the earldom of Richmond to John duke of Brittany until he receives the land of Agen *Paris* R 1 413
Dec. 28.	The K. asks the K. of France to pay to the duke of Brittany the 1,000 marks annually due from the Agenois. *Westm* R 1 413 O 1. 734. H. 1 p. 11 67.

DATE	SUBJECT
1261 Dec 28	The K asks the Q of France to aid the above arrangement *Westm.* R 1 413 O 1 735 H 1 p ii 67
Dec 28	The K, informs the duke of Brittany of certain offers which he has made as to the payment of the value of the earldom of Richmond and land of the Agenois. *Westm* R 1 413. O 1 735 H 1 p ii 67
Dec. 28	The K to John, eldest son of the duke of Brittany, to the same purport as the preceding *Westm* R 1 413 O 1, 735 H 1 p ii 67.
Dec 31.	Pope Urban [IV] asks the King to allow certain merchants of Sienna to settle and trade in London *Viterbo* R 1 414 O 1 736 H 1, p ii. 68.
1262 Jan 1	The K. asks pope [Urban IV] to exempt him from his oath to observe certain ordinances prejudicial to the royal power *Westm* R 1 414 O 1 736 H 1 p ii 68
Jan 1	The K to cardinal Ottoboni, to the same effect as the preceding *Westm.* R 1 414. O 1 737 H 1 p ii 68
Jan. 1.	The K to the college of cardinals, vindicating John Mansel, treasurer of York, from certain false charges *Westm* R 1 414 O 1 737 H 1 p ii 68
Jan 8	The K cannot treat with Llewellin son of Griffin respecting peace until the return of prince Edward into England *Westm* R 1 144 O 1 739 H 1 p ii 69
Jan 29	Philip Basset, justiciary of the realm, and others refer to the arbitration of Richard K of the Romans a question in dispute between the K and the barons *London.*
[..]	Decision of the above question by Richard K of the Romans in favour of the K. R. 1. 415 O 1 738 H 1 p ii 69
[.]	Margaret viscountess of Thouars asks the K to continue her allowance to her R 1 415 O 1. 739 H 1 p ii 69
[Feb]	Alex K of Scotland to the K respecting the payment of a portion of the sum due to the writer from the K of England R 1. 193
Feb 6	Letter to the K upon the promotion of several cardinals , and the canonization of Richard bp of Chichester , and on the occupation of Sicily by Manfred *Viterbo* R 1 415 O 1 740 H 1 p ii 69
Feb 17	Alexander K of Scotland to the K on the payment of a portion of the sum due by the K of England to the writer *Sna* R 1 380 O 1 671 H 1 p ii 43
[Feb 23]	J de Chyshull and another to the K on an interview with the K and Q of France respecting a treaty *Paris* R 1 416. O 1 741 H 1 p ii 69
[ ]	K Louis [IX] to the K respecting the K's message as above *Paris* R 1 416 O 1 742 H 1 p ii 70
Feb 25	Pope Urban [IV] absolves the K , Q , and the princes Edward and Edmund from their oaths for the observance of certain obnoxious statutes. *Viterbo* R 1 416 O 1 742 H. 1. p ii. 70
[March 2]	Geoffrey de Lesignan asks the K. to give credence to Wm de Sancto Hermete *Beamont- sur-Oise* R 1 410 O 1 729 H 1 p ii 65
[March 16]	Louis [IX.] K of France asks the K to make arrangements respecting certain matters of business in Gascony. R 1 418 O 1 744 H 1 p ii 17.
March 23.	The K to the K of Scotland , answers in detail the matters submitted to him by John de Londors, the clerk and messenger of the K of Scotland *Windsor* R 1 417 O. 1. 743 H. 1 p ii 70
March 25	The K permits his uncle, Peter of Savoy, to bequeath his lands in England by will *Windsor* R 1 417
March 31	Prince Edward to the K , will be with him at Easter *Bristol* R 1 417 O 1 743 H. 1 p ii 70
April	"B, Minister of Seauve Majeur," prays that this monastery may be placed under the protection of prince Edward, governor of Gascony *"Remis "* R 1 418 O 1 744 H 1 p ii 71
[April 16]	Louis [IX] to the K , credence for Nicholas de Senooz, citizen of Rouen *Gisors* R 1 418 O 1 745 H 1 p ii 71
April 22	The K asks the K of France to discuss the terms of peace at a personal interview *Westm* R. 1 418 O 1 748 H 1 p ii 72
[April 25]	Isabella, lady of Craon, the K sister, asks the K to restore her pension. R 1 418. O 1. 745. H 1. p ii 71
[.]	Geoffrey de Lesignan asks his brother the K to expedite the above matter R 1 419. O 1 745 H 1 p ii 71.

DATE	SUBJECT.
1262 [April]	Beatrice, wife of John of Brittany, to her father the K , asking for the restitution of the above pension R 1 419
May 2	The K orders the sheriffs of England to proclaim that pope Urban [IV] has sanctioned the abrogation of the ordinances of Oxford *Westm* R. 1 419 O 1 746 H 1 p ii 71
May 6	Pope Urban [IV] forbids the monks of Waltham Cross from getting into debt *Viterbo* R 1 419 O 1 747 H 1 p ii 72
[May 7]	Louis [IX] K of France asks K Henry to cause the heirs of John Flaming to pay what is due to Nicholas Le Ber *Vincennes* R. 1 418 O 1 745 H 1 p ii 71
[May 7.]	The K asks Louis [IX] to pay to John of Brittany the annual sum of 3,720*l* 8*s* 6*d*. tournois, due from Agen *London* R. 1. 419
May 11	Richard K of the Romans to the K ; is compelled to hasten back to Germany, and cannot meet the K at Chippenham *Wallingford.* R 1 420 O 1 747. H 1. p ii 72
June 8	The K asks Llewellin son of Griffin to settle with his commissioners respecting the violation of the truce *Westm* R 1 420 O 1 747 H 1 p ii 72.
June 24	The K informs K. Louis [IX] that on his visit to France he should prefer to reside at S Maur -des-Fossez rather than at Poissy *Westm* R 1. 420 O 1 748 H 1 p ii 72
July 22	The K. (on the reported death of Llewellin, son of Griffin) orders Philip Bassett, justiciary of England, to summon his army to meet at Shrewsbury *Amiens* R 1 420 O 1 748 H 1 p ii 72
Aug 16	The K to Alfonso K of the Romans, on the affairs of Wales, Germany, Gascony, and Africa *S Germain-des-Prés* R 1 420 O 1 749 H 1. p ii 73
Aug 25	The K appoints commissioners to settle violations of the truce with Llewellin, son of Griffin. *Banbury* R 1 421 O 1 750 H 1 p ii 73
Sept 30	The K. to Richard K of the Romans , has had a smart attack of fever , when he returns to England he will attend to Richard's affairs *S Germain des-Prés* R 1 421 O 1 750 H. 1 p ii 73
Oct. 1.	Pope Urban [IV] instructs the abp. of Canterbury as to the application of the offerings made at the relics of Thomas the Martyr, and for the rebuilding of Lambeth Palace *Verona* R. 1 421
Oct. 6.	The K orders the duke of Brunswick to come to London to take home with him his bride, the sister of the marquis of Montferrat *S Germain-des-Prés* R 1 421 O 1 751 H 1 p ii. 73
Oct. 8.	The K. orders that the rolls of Chancery be searched for the writ for the annual fee of the abp of " Carent" *S Germain-des-Prés* R 1 421 O 1 751 H 1 p ii 73.
Oct 8.	The K orders defensive measures to be adopted for the safety of the realm, which has been entered by the earl of Leicester. *S Germain-des-Prés* R 1 422
Oct 12	The K orders the annual payment of 1,000 marks to Philip bp elect of Lyons, executor and brother of Amadeus count of Savoy and Tho. count of Flanders *S Maurice-des Fosses* R 1 422 O 1 751 H 1 p ii 73
[Oct.]	J Mansell to W de Merton, treasurer of England , news respecting his own movements and those of the K , who is going to Rheims R 1 422 O 1 752 H 1 p ii 74
Nov. 7.	Bull of pope Urban [IV] exempting the K and Q from sentence of excommunication for five years *Orvieto* R 1 422 O 1 752 H 1 p ii 74
Nov 15	The K to H King of Norway, on the disputes between Norway and Scotland, now happily ended *Rheims* R. 1. 422 O 1 753 H 1 p ii 74
Dec. 18	The K informs the duke of Brunswick of his proceedings and advice in regard to his [the duke's] proposed marriage with the sister of the marquis of Montferrat *Wytsand* R. 1. 423 O 1 753 H 1 p ii 74
[Dec 24]	J bp of Winchester laments that he cannot be with the K at Canterbury on Christmas Day on his return to England *Winchester* R 1 423 O 1 754 H. 1. p. n. 74.
1263 [Jan]	The bp of Hereford informs the K of the inroad by Llewellin into the lands of Roger de Mortimer, and asks for help R. 1 423 O 1 754 H 1 p ii 74
[Jan]	The K informs prince Edward of his return into England and of the invasion of the Welsh, and begs him to return immediately to expel them R 1 423 O 1. 755 H 1 p ii 75.
Jan 30	Pope Urban [IV] exhorts the K to respect the ecclesiastical liberties of his realm, and not to confirm the statutes made by the abp of Canterbury and his suffragans without the King's assent *Orvieto* R 1 424 O 1 755 H 1 p ii 75
[ ]	Basso lord of Bordelais complains to the K of the destruction of his town of Paussac by the viscount of Limoges, the K's subject. R 1 424 O 1 756 H 1 p ii 75
[...]	Guy de Ratis asks the K to pay his fee and its arrears R. 1. 424 O. 1 757 H 1 p ii 75

DATE	SUBJECT
1263 [Feb]	Joanna Q of Castile to the K in favour of the bp of Elphin R 1 424 O 1 757. H 1 p ii 75
[Feb 14]	Louis [IX.] K. of France to the K. in favour of the same bishop R. 1 424 O. 1. 757. H 1 p ii 75
Feb 20	H de Sandwich bp elect of London to the K , is sorry to hear of the ruin of the K.'s houses at Westm by fire *Langstow* R 1 424
March 6	Margaret Q of France to the K , wishes to be informed how he is *S. Germain-en-Laye* R. 1 425 O 1 757 H 1. p ii. 76
[March 9]	W bp of Exeter to W de Merton, the K's chancellor, they have received the final answer of the K of France to the three questions submitted to his council *Paris* R 1 425 O 1 758 H 1 p. ii 76
[ ]	Margaret Q of France to the K ; is happy to hear of his improved health R. 1. 425. O 1 758 H. 1 p ii 76
March 22	The K. orders that all his subjects shall make oath before prince Edward that they will be loyal to the K and him *Westm* R. 1 425
April 15	Prince Edward asks the K to issue certain orders for the defence of the Welsh marches *Shrewsbury* R 1 425 O 1 759 H 1 p ii 76
April 22	Convention between the K and Raymond viscount of Touraine respecting the allegiance of the latter to the crown of England. *London* R 1 425 O 1 759 H 1 p ii 76
April 22	Convention between the K. and Pontius de Gordon respecting the allegiance of the latter to the crown of England. *London* R 1 426 O 1 760 H 1 p ii 77
June 15	The K requires the barons of the Cinque Ports to make their fealty to prince Edward *S Paul's, London* R 1 427 O 1 768 H 1 p ii 79
June 28	Richard K of the Romans to the K , has had a conference with the barons, whom prince Edward would not attack for the present. *Itelbord* R 1 427 O 1 768. H 1 p ii 80
June 29	W bp of Worcester advises W de Merton, the K's chancellor, to urge the K to accept the proposals submitted to him by the barons R 1 427 O 1. 768 H 1 p ii. 80
July 10	Richard K of the Romans thanks the K for the liberation of his eldest son Henry. *Berkhampstead* R 1 427 O 1 769 H 1 p ii 80
July 18	The K orders his son prince Edmund and the constable of Dover Castle to deliver the said castle to H bp of London *Westm* H 1 427.
July 26	Prince Edmund and Rob de Glaston, constable of Dover Castle, inform the K. why they scruple to deliver the said castle to the bp of London *Dover* R 1 427
July 28	Pope Urban [IV] informs the K and prince Edmund that as they have not kept their engagements he has resolved to give the kingdom of Sicily to another *Orvieto* R 1 428 O 1 769 H 1 p ii 80
[.]	R de Neville urges the K to make arrangements for the preservation of peace to the north of the Trent. R 1 429 O 1 772 H 1 p ii 81
[.]	R. de Neville asks W de Merton, his chancellor, for money to defend the northern counties, and informs him that the Ks of Denmark and Norway are cruising off the islands of Scotland R. 1 429. O 1 772 H 1 p ii 81.
[.]	Ralph Russel to the K , asks for help to defend Salisbury Castle, about to be attacked by the barons R 1 429 O 1. 772 H 1 p. ii 81
Aug 16	The K informs Louis [IX] K of France that he is unable to meet him as he intended to deliberate upon the affairs of England *Westm* R 1 420. O 1 773. H 1. p ii 81.
Aug. 16	The K to the K. of France upon the same subject *Westm.* R. 1 429 O 1 773 H 1 p. ii 82
Aug 18	Prince Edward and certain barons agree to refer their disputes to the arbitration of two referees *Lambeth.* R 1 430 O 1 773. H 1 p ii. 82
Aug. 22	Commission to make peace with Llewellin, son of Griffin *Westm* R 1 430. O. 1 774 H 1 p ii 82
Aug 31	Citation of Richard, brother of K. Hen. III , and Alfonso K. of Castile, to appear before pope Urban [IV] to settle their claims to the title of K of the Romans *Orvieto* R. 1 430 O 1 762 H. 1 p ii 77.
Sept. 9	Pope Urban [IV.] confirms the election of Roger de Norton as abbot of S. Alban's. *Orvieto* R 1 432. O 1 774 H. 1 p ii 82
Sept. 15	The K promises that if he attends the French parliament at Boulogne-sur-Mer he will return into England before 6 Oct *Westm* R 1 432 O 1 755. H. 1 p ii 82

DATE	SUBJECT.
1263 Sept 18	The K confirms the truce with Llewellin, son of Griffin *Westm* R 1 433. O 1. 775 H. l. p. ii 82
Sept 18	Safe conduct for the messengers of Llewellin coming to the K's parliament *Westm* R 1. 433 O 1 775 H 1 p ii 82
Sept 18	Memorandum that the K. left Westm. for foreign parts on 18 Sept , leaving his seal in the custody of Nicholas archdeacon of Ely. R 1 433 O 1 775 H. l. p. ii 82
Dec. 20	The K disclaims the intention of introducing foreigners into his realm, to the injury of his subjects. *Windsor.* R 1 433
1264 Jan 1	Protections for various persons going with the K into foreign parts *Dover* R 1 433 O. 1. 776 H. l. p ii 82
Jan. 12	The K orders that the issues of the lands, &c of Peter of Savoy be paid to the said Peter *Amiens* R 1 433 O 1 776 H 1 p ii 83
Jan 23.	Arbitration by Louis [IX] K of France upon the questions in dispute between the K and his barons upon the provisions of Oxford *Amiens* R. 1 433 O 1 776 H 1 p ii 83
Jan 25	The K. arranges with John, eldest son of the duke of Brittany, for the payment of money due to him *Amiens* R 1 434 O 1 778 H 1 p ii 84
Jan 30	The K announces that he has arranged for the payment to the K of France stipulated for at the peace *Amiens* R 1. 434 O 1 779 H 1 p ii 84
Feb 7	The K settles the mode of payment of the money due to Raymond viscount of Touraine *Bouiogne sur-mer* R 1 435. O 1. 779 H 1 p. ii 84
Feb. 8	Commission to Margaret Q of France to settle the affair of Brigeriac *Whitsand* R 1 435 O 1 780 H 1 p ii 84
Feb 14	The K appoints commissioners to receive the money due by Louis [IX] *Whitsand.* R 1 435 O 1 780 H 1 p ii 84
Feb 14	The K. appoints commissioners to bring back his jewels deposited in the Temple at Paris. *Whitsand* R 1 435 O 1 780 H 1 p ii 84
March 12	The K desires that the scholars be removed from Oxford during the time that he is to reside there. *Oxford* R 1 435
March 12	The K appoints commissioners to treat with Simon de Montfort in the presence of the nuncios of France *Oxford.* R 1 436 O 1 780. H 1 p ii 84
March 16	Pope Urban [IV] confirms the arbitration of Louis [IX] between the K and the barons upon the provisions of Oxford *Orvieto* R 1 436 O 1 780 H 1 p ii 84
March 17	Pope Urban [IV] will punish the opponents of the above arbitration. *Orvieto* R. 1 436 O 1 782 H l. p ii 85.
March 18	Safe conduct for the delegates of the barons coming to treat with the K at Brackley. *Oxford* R. 1 437
March 20	Commission from the K to treat with the barons at Brackley *Oxford* R 1 437 O 1 784 H 1 p ii 86
March 20	The K summons the men of Hampshire to meet him at Oxford with all their force *Oxford.* R 1 437
March 21	Pope Urban [IV] dissolves all confederacies formed against the K *Orvieto* R 1 438 O 1. 785 H. 1 p ii. 36
March.	Note of the conditions under which the abp of Canterbury may return into England R 1 438 O 1 785 H 1 p ii. 86
March 23	Pope Urban [IV] sets aside the provisions made at Oxford *Orvieto* R 1 438 O 1 786 H 1 p ii 86
March 25.	Pope Urban [IV.] orders all ecclesiastics to consider the provisions of Oxford to be repealed. *Orvieto* R 1 438
March 28	Pope Urban [IV] orders that the hospital of S Catherine near the Tower be restored to the convent of the H Trinity, London *Orvieto* R 1 439 O 1 787 H. l p ii 87
April 1	Pope Urban [IV.] asks the Q of England to promote the restitution of the above hospital to the convent of the H. Trinity. *Orvieto.* R. 1. 439 O. 1 787 H. 1 p ii 87
April 1	Pope Urban [IV] permits the prior and convent of the H Trinity, London, to bear witness for themselves in their own suits *Orvieto.* R 1 439 O 1 788 H 1 p. ii 87
[May]	The barons to the K., will respect himself personally, but will proceed against the enemies of the nation R 1. 440.
May 12	The K informs the barons, in answer to the above, that he distrusts and defies them. *Lewes* R 1 440

DATE	SUBJECT
1264 May 12	Richard K of the Romans, prince Edward and others, inform the adherents of Simon de Montford that they will treat them as enemies *Lewes* R. 1 440
May 14	Receipt by the K of 134,000 marks Tournois, paid by Louis K of France *Lewes* R 1. 440 O 1 789 H 1. p 11. 87.
	The acts of Simon de Montfort, the King being in captivity, under the name and seal of the King *
May 17	The K orders the liberation of certain prisoners of the family of Montfort, taken at the battle of Northampton. *Battle* R. 1 441 O 1. 790. H 1 p 11. 78.
May 25	The K orders that his peace be proclaimed *Rochester* R 1 441
May 28	The K appoints Henry de Montfort, son of the earl of Leicester, to be constable of Dover castle *Westm* R 1 441 O 1. 790. H. 1 p 11 88
June 2	The K orders the Jews to evacuate the castle of Northampton, into which they had fled, and to return into the town *S Paul's, London* R 1 441
June 4	The K forbids the carrying of arms, and orders that the prisoners taken at Northampton be liberated *S Paul's, London* R 1. 442 O 1 791 H. 1. p 11 88
June 4	Similar mandate addressed to the constables of the castles of Nottingham, Windsor, Norwich, and others *S Paul's, London* R 1 442 O 1 791 H 1 p 11. 88.
June 4	The K appoints certain persons to keep the peace in various counties *S Paul's, London* R 1. 442 O 1 792 H 1 p. 11. 88
June 11	The K orders it to be proclaimed that peace has been established between himself and his barons, and that he has taken the Jews under his protection. *S Paul's, London* R 8 443.
June 18	The K orders that the wife and family of prince Edward remove from Windsor castle to Westminster *S Paul's, London* R 1 443
June	The form of the peace agreed to by the K, prince Edward, and the barons after the battle of Lewes. *London* R 1 443 O 1 793 H 1 p 11 89
June	Provisions made by the K, prelates, and nobles respecting the affairs of the church R 1 443
June 23	Commission to Simon de Montfort and others to nominate a council of 9 prelates and 9 laymen for the government of the realm *S Paul's, London* R 1 444
June 25	The K warns the abp of Canterbury against violating the prerogatives of the crown *S Paul's, London* R 1. 444.
July 8	The K summons the commonalty of Cambridge to be ready, under arms, to defend the realm *S Paul's, London* R 1 444
July 16	The K forbids anyone, saving Simon de Montfort, to carry arms *S Paul's, London* R. 1 445. O 1 795 H 1 p 11 90
Aug 23	Commission for Simon de Montfort to treat with Robert de Ferrers *Canterbury.* R 1. 445
Sept. 1	Mandate for the bp of Norwich to send all tenths to Simon de Montfort *Canterbury* R. 1 445 O 1 795 H 1 p 11 90
Sept 1	Grant to Hugh le Despenser, justiciary of England, of 1,000 marks annually, to sustain his office *Canterbury* R 1 445
Sept. 3	The K orders the abp of York to levy the tenths of his province without delay. *Canterbury* R 1 445
Sept. 4	Permission for Henry, son of Richard K of the Romans, to proceed into France to negociate a peace by the aid of K. Louis [IX] *Canterbury.* R 1. 446. O 1 796. H 1. p 11 90.
[Sept. 11]	The K promises to accept the peace with S de Montfort and his adherents, according to the form to be drawn up by the bp of London and others *Canterbury* R. 1. 446. O 1 796 H 1 p 11 90
[Sept 11]	Commission appointing proctors to treat, in the K's name, before Louis [IX] on the reform of the government of England *Canterbury* R. 1 446. O 1. 797 H 1 p 11. 90
Sept 13.	Commission, as above, in the names of three new proctors *Canterbury* R 1 447. O 1 797 H 1 p 11 91
Sept 21	Commission to buy 300 qrs of corn for the use of the ships protecting the south coast of England against invasion *Canterbury* R 1 447

* The documents, as far as 7 Aug 1265, were issued under the dictation of Simon de Montfort, the K. being in captivity during this period

DATE	SUBJECT.
1264 Sept 24.	The K asks the papal legate to send to him letters of protection for Peter de Montfort going to treat with him *Canterbury* R. 1 447 O 1 798 H 1 p 11 91
Oct. 20.	Guido, papal legate, publishes excommunication and interdict against Simon de Montfort and his adherents *Hesdin* R. 1. 447 O 1. 799. H 1. p. 11 91.
Nov. 18.	Safe conduct for messengers going from the K to the K of France and Eleanor, Q of England *Windsor* R 1 448 O 1. 800 H 1 p 11 92
Nov. 18.	The K informs his wife Q Eleanor that he and prince Edward are well, and that a good peace may be expected. *Windsor.* R. 1 448. O 1. 800. H 1. p 11 92
Nov 18	The K. urges the K and Q of France not to consent to the proposed sale or alienation of K Henry's possessions or rights in France *Windsor* R 1. 448. O 1 800 H. 1 p. 11 92
Nov. 18	The K to Peter count of Savoy, to the same effect as the preceding *Windsor* R 1 448. O. 1 801 H 1 p 11 92.
Dec 13	The K requires the men of Devon to aid Simon de Montfort against the tenants of Richard K of the Romans in Devon, he having the custody of Richard's lands *Worcester.* R 1 448 O 1. 801 H 1 p 11 92
Dec 14.	Writs of summons by the K to consult as to the restoration of peace addressed to various ecclesiastics, earls, barons, and others *Worcester* R 1 449 O 1 802 H 1 p 11. 92.
Dec 15	The K. enjoins the marchers of Wales to cease from their co-operation with prince Edward. *Worcester* R 1. 449. O 1. 804 H 1 p 11 93.
1265 Jan 9.	The K. orders the liberation of prisoners taken at Northampton *Westm.* R. 1 450.
Jan 17	Safe conduct for John de Balliol and others here named coming to the K from the north. *Westm.* R 1 450 O 1 804 H 1 p 11 93
Feb 13	Q. Eleanor acknowledges the receipt of 124*l* (Poitou) from the mayor and others of Oleron *S Macaire* R 1 450 O 1 805 H 1 p 11 93
Feb 14	Q Eleanor undertakes that the gift of 390*l* (Poitou) made by the mayor of Oleron to prince Edward shall not be used as a precedent *S Macaire* R 1 450 O 1. 805 H 1. p 11 93.
Feb. 16	The K summons Gilbert de Clare and S de Montfort to a meeting for the liberation of prince Edward *Westm* R 1. 450.
Feb 16	The K. forbids the holding of a tournament at Dunstable. *Westm* R 1. 450. O 1. 906. H 1 p 11 94.
March 8	Form of peace between the K, prince Edward, and Henry son of the K of Germany, on the one part, and Simon de Montfort and the barons on the other *In the parliament of London* R 1 451
March 10.	Attestation by the K that prince Edward and Henry, son of the K of Germany, have been surrendered *London.* R 1 452
March 10	Oath by prince Edward for the observance of the Charter of Liberties *London* R 1 452
March 14	The K. permits Peter de Montfort to occupy the houses which belonged to Edward of Westminster in Westminster *Westm* R 1 453 O. 1 806 H 1 p 11 94
March 14	Charter by the K for the observance of the terms of peace with the barons *Westm* R. 1 453
March 15	Safe conduct for the eldest son of the duke of Brittany coming to the K. *Westm.* R 1 453. O 1 807 H 1 p. 11 94
March 15.	Safe conduct for the messengers of the K of France coming to the K *Westm* R. 1 453 O 1 807 H 1 p. 11. 94
March 17	The K (for the preservation of peace) gives up to prince Edward the castles of Dover, Scarbro', Bambro', Nottingham, and Corfe for 5 years *Westm* R 1 454
March 19.	Summons to parliament for Peter de Savoy, John de Warren, and Hugh le Bigod, for the county of Sussex. *Westm* R 1 449 O 1 804 H 1 p 11 94
March 20	Grant to Simon de Montfort of the county, castle, and honor of Chester, the castle and honor of Peak, and the vill and castle of Newcastle-under-Lyme *Westm* R. 1 454 O 1. 807 H. 1 p. 11. 94.
April 2	The K repeats his orders to Adam FitzPhilip, constable of the castle of Montgomery, to deliver up to John Lestrange the castle of Montgomery *Westm* R 1 454 R 1 808 H 1 p 11 94
April 11	Robert Aguilun is required by the K. to take the oath presented by the council before Thomas FitzThomas, mayor of London *Northampton* R 1. 454 O. 1 808. H 1 p 11. 94.

DATE	SUBJECT
1265 April 16.	The K orders that the son and heir of John FitzAlan be given as a security to Simon de Montfort, son of the earl of Leicester *Winchcomb* R 1 454. O 1. 809 H 1 p ıı 95
April 16.	The K orders John FitzAlan to deliver up to Simon de Montfort, the younger, his son, or the castle of Arundel. *Winchcomb* R 1 455 O 1. 809 H. 1 p ıı 95
May 18	The K urges the K of France to expedite the matters for which Henry, son of the K. of the Romans, was sent into France *Hereford* R 1 455 O 1. 810 H 1 p. ıı 95
May 20	The K contradicts the false reports to the effect that disagreements had arisen between him and Simon de Montfort, and censures the proceedings of those who foment discord between them *Hereford* R 1 455
May 22	Safe conduct for the messengers of Alexander K of Scotland coming to the K. *Hereford* R. 1 455 O 1 810 H 1 p ıı 95
May 30.	The K orders the assembling of troops against prince Edward, who escaped from his keepers at Hereford on 28 May *Hereford* R 1 455 O 1 810 H 1 p ıı 95
June 7	The K orders the arrest of all the adherents of prince Edward, as breakers of the peace *Hereford* R 1 456 O 1 811 H 1 p ıı 96
June 8	The K orders the bps of the province of Canterbury to excommunicate prince Edward and his adherents *Hereford* R 1 456 O 1 812 H 1 p ıı 96
June 9	The K orders that the castle and town of Bristol be defended for Simon de Montfort against prince Edward *Hereford* R 1 457. O 1 813 H. 1. p ıı. 96.
June 22	The K. restores various possessions and remits various fines to Llewellin son of Griffin *Hereford* H 1 457 O 1 814 H 1 p ıı 97
June 28	Letters to the keepers of the peace in various counties to harass and injure prince Edward and his adherents *Monmouth* R 1 457 O 1. 814 H. 1 p ıı. 97
[June]	The K. to the Pope, on the renunciation of Sicily R 1 457 O.1 815 H 1 p ıı 97 *See* [June 28], 1257
	The following documents were issued by the K after his restoration to liberty upon the death of Simon de Montfort at the battle of Evesham
Aug 7	The K cancels the extorted appointment of Almaric de Montfort to the treasurership of York *Worcester* R 1 458 O 1. 816 H 1 p ıı 97
Aug 24	The K requires the citizens of Hereford to pay a fine of 560 marks for pardon for their late rebellion *Gloucester* R 1 458
Sept 10	Peter count of Savoy is put in possession of his lands, of which he had been ousted by the late insurrection *Winchester* R 1 458 O 1 817 H 1 p. ıı 97
Sept 13	Pope Clement [IV] orders that the money collected in England be employed in the defence of the realm *Perugia* R. 1 458 O 1 817 H 1 p ıı 97
Sept. 13	Pope Clement [IV] to the prelates in England, to the same effect as the preceding. *Perugia*. R 1 459 O 1. 818. H. 1 p ıı 98
Sept 13	Pope Clement [IV] annuls all conventions between the K and the rebellious barons. *Perugia* R. 1 459. O 1 818 H 1 p ıı 98
Sept 13	Pope Clement [IV] urges prince Edward to liberate his father from the rebellious barons *Perugia* R 1 459 O 1 819 H 1 p ıı 98
Sept 13	Pope Clement [IV] orders the rebellious barons to be excommunicated, and that aid should be given to prince Edward by the English clergy *Perugia* R 1 460 O 1 821 H 1 p ıı 99
Sept 13	Pope Clement [IV] warns the English clergy to abandon the cause of Simon de Montfort, and to aid prince Edward *Perugia* R 1 461 O 1 823 H 1 p ıı 100
Sept 13	Pope Clement [IV] warns Llewellin prince of Wales to restore the castles he has seized, to abandon S de Montfort, and to aid prince Edward *Perugia*. R 1 461 O 1. 823 H 1 p ıı 100
Sept 17	The K grants to Edmund de Mortimer the treasurership of York *Winchester* R. 1 461 O 1 824 H 1 p ıı 100
Sept 21	Commissions to take possession of the lands of those who were rebels in the late insurrection *Winchester* R 1 462
Sept 24	Pope Clement [IV] orders the absolution of Gilbert de Clare, who left the party of Simon de Montfort, and joined that of prince Edward *Perugia*. R. 1 462 O 1. 825 H 1. p ıı. 100.

DATE	SUBJECT.
1265 Sept 24	Pope Clement [IV] directs that the tenth ordered to be collected by Simon de Montfort be given to the K. for the defence of the realm *Perugia* R 1 462 O. 1 825. H 1 p. ii 101
Oct 1	The K repeals all discharges of debt sealed with his seal, extorted from him by Simon de Montfort *Windsor* R 1 463 O 1 826 H 1 p ii 101
Oct 4	Pope Clement [IV] congratulates the K. on his victory, and advises him to use it with moderation and clemency *Perugia* R 1 463 O 1 827. H 1. p ii 101
Oct 6.	Pope Clement [IV] removes from Gilbert earl of Gloucester the sentence of excommunication pronounced against him for adhering to the insurgents. *Perugia* R 1 463. O 1 827 H 1 p ii 101
Oct 6.	The K grants to his son prince Edward the lands and tenements of certain citizens of London *Windsor* R 1 464
Oct 6	The K pardons Gilbert de Clare earl of Gloucester and others their adhesion to S de Montfort at Lewes, out of regard to their good service at Evesham. *Windsor*. R 1 464.
Oct 8	Pope Clement [IV] congratulates prince Edward upon his victory, and asks him to use it with clemency *Perugia* R 1 464 O 1 829 H 1 p ii 102
[ ]	Odo Okonchubyr K of Connaught asks the K's permission for the dean and chapter "Akaden" to appoint a bishop R 1 464 O 1 829 H 1 p ii. 102
[ ]	Blanche duchess of Brittany informs the K that his daughter Beatrix is ill of a fever R 1 464 O 1 830 H 1 p ii 101
[ ]	Beatrix, wife of John of Brittany, informs the K that she is still ill, and that her son Arthur is a handsome boy R 1 465 O 1 830 H 1 p ii 101
Oct 26	The K grants to prince Edward the earldom and honor of Leicester, and all the lands and tenements formerly belonging to Simon de Montfort and Nicholas de Segrave *Canterbury* R 1 465 O 1 830 H 1 p ii 101
Oct. 29	Grant to Henry son of the K of Almain of the manor of Gringelay, forfeited by Wm de Furnival, a rebel. *Canterbury* R 1 465 O 1 831 H 1 p ii 103
Oct. 29	The K asks for a subsidy for Richard K. of Almain, who was taken prisoner at the battle of Lewes, and his lands forfeited *Canterbury* R. 1 466 O 1 832 H 1 p ii. 103
Nov 4	Pope Clement [IV.] grants his protection to the prior and brethren of Heveringlande, in the dioc of Norwich *Perugia* R. 1 466. O 1 833 O 1 p ii 103
Nov. 18	Commission to make a truce with Llewellin son of Griffin *Westm* R 1 466 O 1 834 H 1 p ii 104
Dec 10	Summons to assist the K against the rebels who hold the castle of Kenilworth against him *Windsor*. R 1. 467
Dec 14	Safe conduct for the messengers of Llewellin son of Griffin, going to the papal legate. *Windsor* R 1 467 O 1. 834 H 1. p ii 104
Dec 26	Commission to Osbert Giffard and Reginald FitzPeter to storm the castle of Kenilworth with the men of Oxfordshire and Warwickshire *Northampton* R 1 467
1266 Jan 8	Writ to arrest those who circulate false reports against the K and prince Edward *Northampton*. R. 1 467
Feb 12	Pardon for Robert Paignell, rebel *Westm* R 1. 467 O 1 835 H 1 p ii 104
April 2.	The K ordains that no foreign merchant shall come into England to trade without the licence of prince Edward *Westm* R. 1 468
May 6	Commission to deliver to John duke of Brittany the earldom and honor of Richmond, obtained by the K. from Peter of Savoy *Northampton* R. 1 468 O 1 835 H 1 p ii. 104
May 12.	The K asks M. countess of Flanders to consign to prince Edward the goods arrested in Flanders belonging to the English merchants who favoured the late rebellion. *Northampton*. R 1 468
May 18	The K. orders that the ports be watched to prevent the arrival from France of S de Montfort and his followers *Northampton* R 1 465
May 23.	Certificate by the K that certain northern barons had performed their military service of 40 days. *Northampton* R. 1, 468 O 1 835 H 1 p ii 104
June 10	Mandate to deliver the earldom and honor of Richmond to the duke of Brittany *Northampton* R 1 469
[July 18.]	Certificate of the delivery of the K's "curtina" to the keeper of the royal tents R 1 469 O 1 837. H p ii 105.

DATE.	SUBJECT
1266 Aug 20	The K (at the request of the K of France), enters into a truce for three years with the K of Navarre *Kenilworth.* R 1 469 O 1 836 H 1 p 11 104
Sept 3	The K orders the payment of 900 marks to Frederic de Frisco, count of Lovaine, of which 500 are for the count's expenses in besieging Kenilworth castle. *Kenilworth.* R. 1 469 O. 1. 837 H 1 p 11 105
Sept 15	Pope Clement [IV] removes the sentence of excommunication from Simon de Montfort and his adherents *Viterbo* R 1 469 O 1 837 H 1 p 11 105.
Oct 7.	Commission to Philip Marmiun and others to make terms of peace with the K's rebels *Kenilworth.* R 1 470
Nov 4	The K undertakes to pay an annual sum of money (according to his power) to Albert duke of Brunswick *Kenilworth* R 1 470 O 1 838 H 1 p 11 105.
Nov. 7.	Writ to pay 1,000 marks to Albert duke of Brunswick for his expenses in coming into England with his wife Alice, the niece of Q Eleanor *Kenilworth* R 1 470. O 1 838 H 1 p 11 105
Nov 10	Credence for the lords commissioners authorized to make a truce with the K of Navarre. *Kenilworth* R 1 470 O 1 838 H 1 p. 11. 105
Nov 10	Second credence for the same persons for the same purpose *Kenilworth* R 1 470 O 1 639 H 1 p 11. 106
Nov 10	Notification by the K that he has issued the above commission *Kenilworth* R. 1 471. O 1 839 H 1 p 11. 106.
Nov. 10	Second notification to the same effect *Kenilworth* R 1 471 O 1 839 H 1. p 11 106
1267. Jan. 5.	The K grants certain privileges to the burgesses and merchants of Lubeck *Westm* R 1 471 O. 1. 839 H 1 p. 11 106
Jan 10.	Inspeximus and confirmation of the charter granted by K Henry [II] to the burgesses of Wallingford *Westm* R 1 471
Feb. 21.	Commission to Rob Waleraud to make truce for three years with Llewelhn son of Griffin *S Edmunds* R 1 472 O 1 840 H 1 p 11 106
Feb 21	Warrant to associate prince Edmund in the above commission *S Edmunds* R. 1 472. O 1 840 H 1 p 11 106
May 28	The K. exonerates the abbot of Westminster from blame in having sold the gold, &c. of the shrine of S Edward for the K's use, and pledges himself to restore it *Stratford.* R 1 472 O 1 841 H 1 p 11 106.
June 16.	The K and Gilbert earl of Clare submit to the decision of the pope the sufficiency of the earl's bond to the K of 20,000 marks for his future allegiance *Stratford* R 1 472 O 1 841. H 1 p 11 106
June 25	Decision of the dispute between the K and prince Edward on the one part, and Reginald de Pontibus and Margaret his wife on the other, respecting the castle of Brageriac *London* R 1 472. O 1 842 H 1 p 11 107
July 15	Pope Clement [IV] grants to the Q. 60,000*l* tournois arising from the tenth to be collected for the K *Viterbo* R 1 473 O 1 842 H. 1 p 11 107.
July 26	Writ to pay to pope [Clement IV] 7,000 marks of the arrears of the annual grant. *S Paul's, London* R 1 473
Sept 21.	Commission to Ottoboni, the papal legate, to make a truce, upon his own terms, between the K and Llewelhn son of Griffin *Shrewsbury* R 1 473 O 1 843 H 1 p 11 107
Sept. 21	Commission to Geoffrey de Geneville and Rob Wallerand to swear to the above truce on the K's part *Shrewsbury* R 1 473 O 1 843 H 1 p 11 107
Sept 25	Safe conduct for Llewelhn, son of Griffin, to come to the K. at Montgomery, to do homage. *Shrewsbury* R. 1 473 O 1 843 H 1 p 11 107
Sept 29	The K arranges the details necessary for the carrying out of the peace with Wales. *Montgomery* R 1 473 O. 1 844 H 1 p 11 107
Sept 29	Treaty by which the K grants to Llewelhn son of Griffin the principality of Wales, to be held of the English crown by homage *Montgomery* R 1 474 O 1 844 H 1. p 11 108
1268. [Feb 3.]	The K appoints proctors to appear in the court of France in the dispute about Gascony between the K. and Theobald K of Navarre R 1 478 O 1 852 H 1 p 11 110.
May 10	The K grants 500 marks to the daughter of Thomas late count of Savoy *Westm.* R. 1 475 O 1 847 H 1 p. 11 108

DATE	SUBJECT
1268. June 19	The K confirms to the widows of London their accustomed exemptions from taillages, &c *Woodstock* R 1 475
[ ]	Protection for the K of Almain and his suite going into Germany R.1 475 O 1 847 H. 1. p 11 109
July 15.	Peter count of Savoy grants to Eleanor Q of England the honor of Aquila and Richmond, and other lands and rents *Woodstock* R 1 475 O 1 848 H 1 p 11 109
July 16	The K directs prince Edward to order the knights, &c of the earldom of Richmond to be obedient to John duke of Brittany *Woodstock* R 1.476. O 1.847. H 1 p 11. 109
July 16	The K (at the request of prince Edward) remits to Gilbert de Clare, earl of Gloucester, the security which the pope decided should be given by him to the K *Woodstock* R 1 476 O 1 849 H 1 p 11 109.
July 16	John son of the duke of Brittany resigns to the K. all claim to the district of Agen *Woodstock* R 1 476
July 20	Writ to Guischard de Charron to deliver the castle of Richmond to John son of the duke of Brittany *Northampton* R 1 476
July 28	Inspeximus and confirmation of the lease of lands at Gaytinton granted by Beatrix, wife of John of Brittany, to Richard Gruscet *Gaytinton.* R. 1 477 O 1. 850. H 1 p 11 110.
Aug 2	Safe conduct for the K and Q of Scotland coming to the K *Gaitintone* R 1 477 O 1 851 H 1 p 11 110
Aug 17	The K appoints commissioners to settle the peace with Wales. *Lincoln* R 1 477 O 1 550 H 1 p 11 110
Aug. 17.	Commission to the same effect, but in a different form. *Lincoln* R 1 477 O 1 851 H 1 p 11 110
Sept. 12.	Charles K of Sicily informs Louis [IX.] K of France of his successes *Guazant.* R 1 477. O 1 851 H 1 p 11 110
Dec 10	Commission to proceed with the assessing of the tallage arising from all cities, boroughs, and demesne lands not already assessed *Clarendon* R 1 478
1269 [.]	Proctors appointed in the court of France. R. 1. 478. O. 1 852 H. 1 p 11 110 *See* [Feb 9], 1268
Jan 27.	The K grants leave to John of Brittany (going to the H Land) to let to farm the honor of Richmond, to the value of 2,000 marks. *Westm* R 1 478
1269 [Jan]	The K sanctions the exchange of the honor of Richmond (bequeathed to the Q by Peter of Savoy) with payments to the annual value of 500 marks arising from certain lands, &c. here specified, to be made to the Q R 1 482
March 6	The K confirms the terms of the marriage agreed upon between his nephew Henry son of the K of Almain and Constance daughter of Gaston viscount of Bearn *Westm* R 1 478 O 1 852 H 1 p 11 111.
May 4	Prince Edward orders his seneschals of Limoasin, Perigord, and Cahors to protect Bernard de Burdell *Chippenham* R.1 478 O 1 852 H 1 p 11 111
[May 20]	Commission to John de Graelly and others to act as the K's proctors in all suits in the court of the K of France R 1 479 O 1 853. H 1 p 11 111
May 20	The K notifies the same to the K of France *Windsor* R. 1 479. O. 1. 854 H 1 p 11. 111
May 21.	Commission to prince Edward to settle the peace with Llewellin prince of Wales *Windsor.* R. 1 479. O 1 855 H 1 p 11 111
[June 14]	Notification by P bp. of Agen that he has received the homage and fealty of Henry son of the K of Germany, and his wife Constance, for the church of Agen R 1. 580 O 1 855 H. 1. p 11 112
July 5	The K arranges respecting the oath to be taken in the settlement of the peace with France *Westm* R. 1 480 O 1 856. H 1 p 11 112
Aug 9.	Commission to perform fealty in the K's name to the K of France for the Agenois *Sutwyk* R. 1 480 O 1 856 H 1 p 11 112
[Aug 21]	Confederation of amity and commerce between the K and Magnus K of Norway. *Winchester.* R 1 480 O 1 857 H 1 p 11 112
[Aug. 27]	Prince Edward enters into an agreement to go to the H Land with Louis [IX] K of France. *Paris* R. 1. 481. O. 1 858. H. 1. p 11 113.

DATE	SUBJECT
1269 [Sept 24]	Confirmation by the K of the above *Winchester* R. 1. 481 O 1 859 H 1 p ii 113
[Sept 24]	The K and prince Edward (at the instance of K Louis [IX]) grant a truce of five years to Theobald K. of Navarre *Winchester* R 1 482
[.]	The K sanctions certain grants made to Q. Eleanor R 1 482 See [Jan] 1269
Oct. 19	Protection for five years for prince Edmund and others, about to proceed to the H Land *Westm.* R 1 482. O 1 861 H 1 p ii 114
1270 Feb 12	Regulations for the guidance of treasurer and barons of the Exchequer as to the form henceforward to be pursued in framing the rolls of the Exchequer *Westm* R 1 483
May 20	The K. and his sons being about to proceed to the H Land, the K summons certain bps to assist him to arrange for the government of the realm during his absence *Westm* R 1 483
July 13	Protection for 80 persons proceeding with the K and prince Edward to the Holy Land *Westm* R 1 483. O. 1 861. H 1 p ii 114.
Aug 2	Prince Edward commits the charge of his children, castles, lands, and lordships in England, Wales, Ireland, and Gascony, to his uncle, Richard K of the Romans *Winchester* R 1 484 O 1. 862 H 1 p ii 114
Aug 2	The K permits Stephen de Penacestre to buy from two Jews the debt due to them by John de Pekeham *Winchester* R 1 484.
Aug 4	It being considered inexpedient that the K and prince Edward should both leave England, the K entrusts the crusade to the prince *Winchester* R 1 485
Aug 4	Pardon for John de Warren, earl of Surrey, and his men, for having struck Alan la Zouche and his son Roger in the Hall at Westminster *Winchester* R 1 485
Aug 18	Licence to prince Edward to pledge, or let out to farm, the customs of Bordeaux for four years *Clarendon* R 1 485 O 1 864 H 1 p ii 115.
Sept 5	The K requires the clergy of Ireland to aid in collecting the tenths in Ireland, assigned by the pope to Q Eleanor *Brampton* R 1 485 O 1 864 H 1 p ii 115
Sept. 7.	Charles K of Sicily arranges for the honorable reception of prince Edward in Sicily *Trapani* R 1. 485. O 1 868 H 1 p ii 117.
Oct 16	The K informs Llewellin son of Griffin prince of Wales that he is sending commissioners to treat of peace with him *Westm* R 1 486. O 1 865 H 1 p ii 118
Nov 2	The K grants to Thomas of Savoy and his brothers an annuity of 100 marks *Windsor* R 1 486 O 1 866 H 1 p ii 116
Nov 18	Charles K of Sicily grants safe conduct through Sicily to prince Edward *The camp near Carthage* R. 1 486 O 1 866 H 1 p ii 116
Nov 18	Translation into French of the same safe conduct *Carthage.* R 1 486 O 1 687 H 1 p ii 116
Nov 28	Charles K of Sicily grants to prince Edward the privilege of judging his own men while in Sicily. *The camp near Carthage* R 1 487 O 1. 867 H 1 p ii 116
Nov 18	Translation into French of the same privilege *Carthage* R. 1. 487. O. 1 868 H. 1 p ii 117
Dec 20	Charles King of Sicily orders his subjects to show all honour to prince Edward "*Partona*" R. 1 487 O 1 869 H 1 p ii 117
1271 Feb 6	The K (conscious of his own infirm health) urges his son prince Edward to return home without delay *Westm* R 1 487 O 1 869 H 1 p ii 817
March 10	The K notifies that he has caused inquiry to be made as to the disputes between the baroness Matilda Longespee and John Giffard of Brimmesfelde *Westm* R. 1 488 O 1. 870 H 1 p ii 117
March 13	Charles K of Sicily informs prince Edward of the murder at Viterbo of his cousin Henry, son of Richard K of Germany, by Simon and Guy de Montfort *Viterbo* R. 1 488 O 1 870 H 1 p ii 118
April 16	The K having recovered from a grievous malady, out of gratitude to God assumes the cross *Westm* R. 1 488 O 1 871 H 1 p ii 118
May 16	Safe conduct for the messengers of Margaret countess of Flanders coming to the K. *Westm* R 1 489 O 1 872 H 1. p ii 118.
June 20	The K grants to Richard K of Germany the Jewry in England, for the repayment of the 2,000 marks advanced by K Richard to prince Edward *Westm* R 1. 489 O 1 872 H 1 p ii 118

DATE.	SUBJECT
1271 June 25	The K orders certain regulations to be observed by the Jews in England, and directs how they are to be treated *Westm* R 1 489
Oct. 25.	Commission for the abbot of Westminster and John de la Lynde to receive from Philip K of France the districts of Agen and Saintes *Westm.* R. 1 490 O 1 873. H 1. p n 119.
[Oct 25]	Commission to the above persons to do fealty for the same districts *Westm* R. 1. 490 O 1 874 H 1 p n 119
Oct 28	Commission to the above persons to receive all that ought to be restored by the K of France. *Westm.* R. 1 490. O 1 874. H 1. p. n. 119
Oct 28	The K notifies the grant to Q Eleanor of the district of Agen *Westm* R 1 490 O 1 874 H 1 p n 119
1272. Jan 28.	The K to the K. of France, on the oath of fealty for the castle of Limoges. *Tower of London* R 1 490 O 1 875. H 1 p n 119.
Jan 28	Commission for proctors appointed to settle the peace between the K. and the King of France *Tower of London* R 1 491 O 1 876 H 1 p n 19
Jan 28.	The K to Philip [III] K. of France, respecting the treaty of peace between the K and Louis [IX.] *Tower of London* R 1 491. O 1 877 H 1 p n 120
Feb 20	Acquittance by the K to Giles de Andenard, on the delivery of jewels pledged to various creditors, and now restored to the K *Westm* R 1 492 O 1 878 H 1 p n 120
March 29	Pope Gregory [X] announces to the K his elevation to the papacy *Lateran* R 1 492 O 1 879 H 1 p n 121
March 31	Pope Gregory [X] invites the K to attend a general council about to be held on the affairs of the H Land *Lateran.* R 1 493 O 1 881 H, 1 p n 121
May 20	The K excuses himself from rendering personal homage to the K of France by reason of his ill health *Westm* R 1 494
May 31	Pope Gregory [X] confirms the privileges of the Knights Templars *Lateran* R. 1 494 O 1 883 H 1 p n 122
June 5	The K and prince Edward appoint Luke de Tany their seneschal of Gascony *Westm* R. 1 494 O 1 884. H 1 p n 123
June 5	The K requires Hugh de Turberville to deliver the custody of Gascony to his successor, Luke de Tany *Westm* R 1 494 O 1 884 H 1 p n 123
June 5	The K complains to the K of France that his rights in Gascony have been violated *Westm.* R 1 494 O 1 884 H 1 p n 123
June 18	Will of prince Edward *Acre* R 1. 495 O 1 885 H 1 p n 123
July 21.	Pope Gregory [X.] takes under his protection prince Edward, his family, lands, &c *Orvieto* R 1. 495 O 1. 886 H 1 p n 123
Aug. 10.	The K makes arrangements for the repayment of certain sums advanced to him for his expenses in going into France to do homage for the duchy of Aquitaine and other lands in France *Westm* R 1 495 O. 1. 886. H 1 p n 124
Oct 1	Pope Gregory [X], at the K's requests, exempts six clerks from residence on their livings, provided they employ vicars in the same *Orvieto* R 1 496 O 1 887 H 1 p n 124
Nov 4	The K, to keep his Christmas at Winchester, orders 100 oxen to be sent thither *Westm* R 1 496 O 1 887. H 1 p n 124
[. .]	Will of K Henry III , dated at Suwick on Tuesday next after the feast of SS Peter and Paul, A.D. 1253 R. 1 496 *See* June 30, 1243

EDWARD I.

(20 *Nov* 1272—7 *July* 1307)

Nov 20	Notice of the death of K Henry III. R 1 497 O 1 888 H 1 p n 124
Nov 22	Pope Gregory [X] congratulates prince Edward on his safe arrival at the port of Trapani *Orvieto* R. 1 497 O 1 888 H 1, p. n 124
Nov 23	The K orders his peace to be proclaimed *Westm* R 1 497 O n 1 H 1. p n 129
Nov 23	The bishops and nobles of England inform the K of the death and burial of h father, and of their loyalty to himself. *New Temple.* R 1. 497 O 1. 888 H 1 p. n. 124.

DATE	SUBJECT
1272. Nov 29	Commission to receive the oath of fealty of L prince of Wales *New Temple, London* R 1 498 O ıı 2 H 1 p ıı 129
Nov. 29	The K cites L prince of Wales to do his fealty *New Temple, London* R 1 498
Dec 2	The K requests L prince of Wales to pay 3,000 due at Christmas. *Westm* R 1 498
Dec 7	The K orders his peace to be proclaimed throughout Ireland *Westm* R 1 498 O ıı 2 H 1 p ıı 129.
Dec 7.	The K requires the people of Ireland to take the oath of fealty to him *Westm* R. 1 498 O ıı 2. H 1. p. ıı 129
1273 Jan 9	Pope Gregory [X] asks A queen of England to induce the K to visit him *Orvieto* R 1 499 O 1 889 H 1 p ıı 124
Jan 14	Gasto vicomte of Bearn promises that he will conform to the pleasure of the K *Orvıesıum* R 1 499 O ıı 3 H 1. p ıı 129
[ ]	The abbots of Dore and Haghem inform the chancellor that L prince of Wales had not appeared to take his oath of homage to the K R 1 499 O ıı 3 H 1 p ıı 129
[··]	The constable of Montgomery to the chancellor, to the same effect as the preceding R 1 499 O ıı. 4 H 1 p ıı 130
March 1	Bull of pope Gregory [X], on the citation of Gui de Montfort for the murder of Henry of Almaine *Orvieto* R 1 499 O 1 890 R 1 p ıı 125
March 6.	Pope Gregory [X] directs that information should be collected on the circumstances of the above-mentioned murder *Orvieto* R. 1 500. O 1 891 H 1 p ıı 125.
March 26	F bishop of Adour excuses his non-appearance at Bordeaux to enquire into the state of Gascony *"Planum"* R 1 500 O ıı 4 H 1 p ıı 130
April 1.	Judicial process of pope Gregory [X] against Gui de Montfort for the murder of Henry of Almaine R. 1 501 O ıı 4 H 1 p ıı 130
April 13	Pope Gregory [X] asks the K to assist at the General Council about to be held at Lyons *Orvieto* R 1 503 O ıı 10 H 1 p ıı 132
April 28	The K forbids the holding of a tournament at Blythe *Westm* R 1 503
June 10	The K forbids the holding of a tournament at Kingston *Westm.* R 1 503
June 18	The K orders the expulsion of the jews from Winchelsea *Westm* R 1. 503.
June 22	Wm de Toınon submits himself to the K , who forgives the injuries committed on him as he was going to the Holy Land *Castle of S George* R 1 504 O ıı 11 H 1 p ıı 132
June 23	Alfonso K of Castile asks the K. to give credence to his sister A queen of England *Sıbıl* R 1 503 O ıı 11 H 1 p ıı 132
June 23	The K forbids L, son of Griffin prince of Wales, to build a castle near that of Montgomery *Westm* R 1. 504
June 25	Homage of Philip count of Savoy to the K. *S. George de Sperenche* R 1 504 O ıı 12 H 1 p ıı 133
July 4	The K. orders Stephen de Penecestre constable of Dover, to provide shipping for his return into England *Westm* R 1 504
Aug 9	The K thanks Walter de Merton for his diligence in the affairs of the kingdom *Melun* R 1 505 O ıı 13 H 1 p ıı 133
Aug 10	Receipt by Philip K of France for 1,000*l* sterling paid by K Edward *Melun* R 1 505 O ıı 13 H 1 p ıı 133
Aug 23	The K permits the merchants of Ireland to trade in England *S Martın the Great, London* R 1 505
Sept 2.	L prince of Wales to R de Grei Cannot at present decide whether he will be present at the K's coronation *Ryd Gastell* R. 1 505
Oct 1	Gasto de Bearn promises that he will not leave the court without the K's leave *"Saltum"* R 1 505 O ıı 13 H 1 p ıı 13.
Oct. 1.	Gasto de Bearn promises that he will give up the castle and men of Ortes to the K *"Saltum"* R 1 506. O ıı. 14. H. 1 p. ıı 133
Oct. 8.	Agreement for a marriage between the K's eldest daughter and the eldest son of Peter infant of Aragon *"Serdua"* R 1 506 O. ıı 14 H p ıı 134
Oct. 11.	The K notifies that he has given the Isle of Oleron in dower to his mother. R. 1. 506. O. ıı. 15. H. 1 p. ıı. 134.

DATE.	SUBJECT
1273 Nov 11	Certificate by the abbot of St Severe and others of the citation of Gaston de Bearn to appear before the K *S Severe* R 1 506 O ʼʼ 16 H 1 p ʼʼ. 134
Nov. 28	Credence for Reynald de Sulimiaco, messenger from the community of Limoges, coming to the K R 1 507 O ʼʼ 16 H 1 p ʼʼ 134
Nov 29	Pope Gregory [X] informs the K of the repentance and imprisonment of Guy de Montfort [for the death of Henry de Alemannia] *Lyons* R 1 507 O ʼʼ 17 H 1 p ʼʼ 134
Nov 30.	Pope Gregory [X.] exhorts the K to deal liberally and kindly with his brother Edmund earl of Leicester and his mother *Lyons.* R 1. 507. O. ʼʼ 17. H. ı. p. ʼʼ. 155.
Nov 30	Agreement for a marriage between Henry, the K's eldest son, and Joanna, daughter and heiress of Henry K. of Navarre *"Hospitale de Bono Loco"* R 1 508 O ʼʼ 18 H 1 p ʼʼ 135
Dec. 1.	Pope Gregory [X] advises the K to postpone his coronation that it may not interfere with the council at Lyons. *Lyons* R 1. 508 O ʼʼ 20. H 1 p ʼʼ 136
[Dec 21 ?]	Certain persons intercede with the K for the liberation of Gulielmus Vigeri R 1 508 O ʼʼ 20 H 1 p ʼʼ 136
1274 Feb 10	Writs to various sheriffs to send to Windsor certain provisions for the K.'s coronation *Westm.* R. 1 509 O ʼʼ 21 H 1 p. ʼʼ 136.
March 8	The clergy of Auxonne complain to the K of the oppression of the seneschal of Gascony R. 1 509 O ʼʼ 22 H 1 p ʼʼ 136
March 15	Pope Gregory [X] takes under his protection the convent of the H Trinity, London. *Lyons* R 1. 509 O. ʼʼ. 23 H 1. p ʼʼ 137
April 9	The K informs pope Gregory [X] of proctors being sent by the English clergy to the council at Lyons *London* R 1 510 O ʼʼ 23 H 1 p ʼʼ 137
April 10.	The K forbids the exportation of wool to Scotland, Ireland, Wales, or any place whatever out of the realm *Westm* R 1 510 O ʼʼ 24 H. 1. p ʼʼ 137
April 14	The K. summons a meeting at Montgomery to settle disputes about the truce with Wales *Westm* R. 1 510 O ʼʼ 25 H 1 p ʼʼ 137
April 15	Ralph, prior of Mont S Michael, complains to the K of the oppressions of his bailiff of Guernsey and Jersey R 1 510 O ʼʼ 24 H 1 p ʼʼ 137
May 24	Notarial copy of the process (before the K) between the seneschal of Gascony and Gaston de Bearn, Francis Accursius professor at Bologna being present *Limoges* R 1 511 O ʼʼ 25 H 1 p ʼʼ 138.
May 24	Further proceedings in the above process *Limoges* R 1 512. O ʼʼ 28 H 1 p ʼʼ 139
May 15	Pope Gregory [X] dissuades the K from attending a tournament about to be held in France *Lyons* R 1 512 O ʼʼ 29 H 1. p ʼʼ 139.
May 18.	Postscript to the above letter, enforcing the same caution *Lyons* R 1 512 O ʼʼ 30 H. 1 p ʼʼ 139
May 20	John de Montfort in a letter in French urges the constable of France and others to contribute money towards the liberation of Guy de Montfort. *Naples* R 1 512 O ʼʼ 30 H 1 p ʼʼ 139
May 20.	The same letter translated into Latin *Naples.* R. 1. 513. O. ʼʼ 31 H 1 p ʼʼ 140
June 27.	The K orders that his purveyors be aided in preparing for his coronation *Westm* R 1 513 O ʼʼ 31 H 1 p ʼʼ 140
June 28	Treaty of peace between the K and Guy count of Flanders. *Montreuil-sur-Mer.* R. 1 513. O ʼʼ 32. H. 1. p ʼʼ 140
June 29.	Guy count of Flanders complains of the injuries done to his subjects. *Montreuil-sur-Mer* R. 1 514 O ʼʼ 33 H 1 p ʼʼ 141.
Aug 11.	Receipt by Gulielmus de Bello loco, Master of the Temple, for money repaid by the K which he had borrowed while in the Holy Land *London* R. 1 514 O ʼʼ. 34. H 1 p ʼʼ 141.
Aug 18.	Pope Gregory [X] directs that prince Lewelin shall not be cited to appear anywhere out of Wales *Lyons* R 1. 515 O ʼʼ 35 H 1 p ʼʼ. 141
Aug. 18.	Pope Gregory [X] confirms an agreement made between Lewelin prince of Wales and his brother David *Lyons* R 1. 515 O ʼʼ 36 H 1 p ʼʼ 141
Aug 19	Memorandum of the K's arrival at Dover and coronation at Westm R 1 514 O. ʼʼ 34 H. 1 p. ʼʼ 141
Aug. 20.	Notification that prince Edmund claims the office of seneschal of England for his own life only *Westm* R. 1 515. O. ʼʼ 35. H. 1 p. ʼʼ. 141.

F

DATE	SUBJECT
1274 Aug 23.	Pope Gregory [X] cautions the K. against interfering in ecclesiastical matters in Gascony during the vacancy of cathedral churches *Lyons* R 1 515 O ii 36 H. 1. p ii 142
Sept 2	The K orders the payment of 200*l* or 300*l* tournois to his messengers sent to the parliament at Paris *Odyham* R. 1 516 O ii 37 H. 1 p ii 142
Sept 7	Margaret countess of Flanders intercedes with the K for the liberation of certain Flemish sailors imprisoned at Northampton R. 1 516 O ii 37 H 1 p ii. 142
Sept 10	Wm de Valence authorizes the payment to the K of 350 marks sterling by the executor of Henry of Almain *Windsor* R 1 516 O ii 38 H 1. p ii 142
Sept 11	The K confirms to John of Brittany the honor and rape of Hastings *Windsor* R 1 516 O ii 38 H 1 p. ii. 142.
Sept 12.	The K pardons the outlawry against Walter de Baskerville for the murder of Henry of Almain *Windsor* R 1 516 O ii 39 H 1. p. ii 143
Oct 7.	Pope Gregory [X] in favor of the abp of Cashel going to the H Land. *Lyons* R 1 517 O ii 39 H 1 p ii 143.
Oct 11	The K. directs inquiry to be made throughout England relative to certain liberties belonging to the crown and the state, with the articles of inquiry *Tower of London.* R. 1 517.
Oct 16	Commission to inquire as to disputes between the merchants of England and Flanders *Westm* R 1. 518 O ii 39 H 1 p ii. 143.
Oct 20	Commission to collect the arrears of the tallages due by the Jews *Westm* R 1. 518 O ii 40 H 1 p ii 143
Oct 21	The K appoints Robert Bagod chief justiciary of Ireland *Westm* R 1 518 O. ii 40 H 1. p. ii 143
Nov 3	Mandate to Lewelin prince of Wales to do his homage to the K. at Shrewsbury *Northamp.* R 1 518 O ii 41 H 1. p ii 143
[ ]	The K acknowledges the loan of 2,000 marks from Edmund earl of Cornwall *Northamp* R. 1 519 O ii 41 H 1 p. ii 143
Nov 11	Restitution of his annuity to Philip count of Savoy, who has performed his homage to the K *Northamp* R 1 519. O. ii 41. H 1 p. ii 143
Nov. 22	The K urges Lewelin prince of Wales to pay 6,000 marks due by him *Clyve* R 1 519 O ii 41 H 1 p ii 144
Dec 20	Pope Gregory [X] enjoins the restitution of certain property alienated from the chapel of Pomfret Castle *Lyons* R 1 519. O. ii 42 H. 1 p ii 144
Dec 28	Writ for the payment of the expenses of Alexander K of Scotland on coming to the K's coronation *Woodstock* R 1. 520 O ii 42 H. 1 p ii 144
Dec 30	The K requires the abps and bps of England and Ireland to assist the foundation of a chaplaincy in the church of S. Mary at Oxford *Woodstock* R 1 519 O ii 43 H 1 p ii 144
1275 Jan 26	The K to Abaga-Chaan prince of the Magali; rejoices to hear of his affection to the Christian faith and of his aid to the Holy Land *Beaulieu* R 1 520 O ii 43 H 1 p ii 144
Feb 9.	Protection for Wm le Provencal, physician to queen Eleanor the K's mother, going abroad with her *Windsor* R 1 520 O. ii 44 H 1 p ii 144
[ ]	The mayor and commonalty of Carrigfergus, in Ulster, inform the K of the rebellion which has broken out there R 1 520 O ii 1060 H 1 p. iv. 76
[.]	N O'Nel K of Yncheun and five other Irish kings ask the K's aid in the above-mentioned rebellion R 1 520 O ii 1061 H 1 p iv 76
March 4	John duke of Brittany asks the K's aid for the convent of Marmoutier at Tours *Paris* R 1 521 O. ii 44. H 1 p ii 145
March 17.	Credence for a messenger treating on a double marriage between the royal families of England and Aragon. *Milton* R 1 521
April 22	The K issues regulations respecting the custody and preservation of the charters and records of the realm. *Wallingford* R 1. 521
April 27	The K. directs his men of Saintes to make oath to the K of France according to the late treaty *Westm* R 1 522 O ii 45 H 1 p ii 145
May 4.	The K. cannot inform Alfonso K of the Romans and Castile whether he will be able to resume the war against the Saracens. *Westm.* R. 1. 522. O ii 45. H 1 p. ii. 145.

DATE	SUBJECT
1275 May 4	The K. entreats pope Gregory [X] to preserve the rights of Alfonso K. of the Romans and Castile *Westm* R 1 522 O u 46 H 1 p u 145
May 5	The K asks Alfonso K of the Romans and Castile to preserve his rights in the affairs of Navarre *Westm* R 1 522 O u 46 H 1 p u 145
May 5.	The K promises that he will aid Alfonso K of the Romans and Castile against Rodolf of Hapsburg *Westm* R. 1 523 O u 47 H 1 p u 146
May 18	Jacobus Amarotus Lanceavegia reminds the K of his promise to confer knighthood on him when he was at Bologna, and wishes to come to him for the purpose *Milan.* R. 523. O u 1062 H 1 p iv. 77
May 23	The K. desires that the Jews in Gascony be exempted from taillage this year *Westm* R 1. 523 O u 49 H. 1 p u 146
[. .]	John de Bohun and Johanna his wife remit to the K the sergeancy of his chapel, and the office of spigurnel R 1 523 O u 49 H 1 p u 146
May 30	The K. pardons certain acts of misconduct committed by the merchants of Flanders *Westm* R 1 524 O u 50 H 1 p u 147
June 8.	Commision to Francis Accursius of Bologna and others sent from the K. to the parliament of the K of France *Westm.* R. 1 524 O u 50. H. 1 p u 147
June 8	The K notifies to the K of France that he has appointed the aforesaid procters *Westm* R. 1 524 O u 52 H 1 p u 147.
June 9	Pope Gregory [X] provides Anthony Bek with an archdeaconery and prebend in the church of Salisbury, void by the resignation of Gerard de Grandison "*Belhcadri*" R 1 525 O u 47 H 1 p ii 146
June 9	Pope Gregory [X] to the bps of Bath and Rochester, for the promotion of Anthony Bek "*Belhcadri*" R 1 525 O u 48 H 1 p u 146
June 13	The K requests the K of France to deliver the comté of Agen to Q Eleanor, widow of K. Hen III *Westm* R 1 523 O u 52 H 1 p u 148
June 20	The K cautions Bogo de Knoville, sheriff of Shropshire and Stafford, relative to his dealings with Lewellin prince of Wales *Westm* R 1 526 O u 53 H 1 p. u 148
July 11	Pope Gregory [X] gives a canonry in Salisbury cathedral to Matthew Caraculus. "*Belhcadri*" R. 1 526 O u 53. H. 1 p u 148
July 11	Pope Gregory [X] grants another bull for a similar purpose to Matthew Caraculus "*Belhcadri*" R 1 526 O u 54 H 1 p u 148
July 15	Pope Gregory [X] grants a dispensation for a marriage between Isabella de Valentia and John de Hastings "*Belhcadri*" R. 1 527 O u 55 H 1 p u 149
July 19.	Pope Gregory [X] permits three of the K's clerks to be provided with benefices "*Belhcadri*" R. 1 527 O u 55 H 1 p u 149
July 28	The K orders that one of his horses shall be given to Wm de Rupe Canardi, who is about to fight a duel at Limoges *Brehul* R. 1 527 O u 56 H 1. p. u 149
Aug 9	The K releases Philip count of Savoy from the payment of 1,000 marks due to the late K Henry *Oxford* R. 1 527 O u 56 H. 1 p u 149
Aug 12	The K asks the bps and people of Ireland to exert themselves for the quieting of Ireland, impoverished by wars and discord *Woodstock* R 1 527 O u 56 H 1 p u 149
Aug 30	H. de Bohun earl of Hereford (worn out with old age) asks the K to permit his nephew Humphrey to perform the office of constable of England. *Wocheseye* R 1 528 O u 57 H 1 p u 149
Sept. 10.	The K again commands Lewelin prince of Wales to perform his homage and fealty *Chester.* R 1 528 O u. 57 H. 1 p u 150
Sept. 11	L prince of Wales asks pope Gregory [X] to take no proceedings against him during the war between Wales and England *Treschyn* R 1 528 O u 57 H 1 p u 150
Sept 20.	The K to the pope relative to the bps of S Andrew and Glasgow. *Thirlwall.* R 1 528 *See* Sept 20, 1306.
Sept 23	The K instructs Stephen de Penecester constable of Dover relative to the contentions between the merchants of London and Seland *Acheston* R 1 529 O. u 59 H 1 p. u 150
Oct. 15.	Jacobus Amarotus Lanzavigia informs the K. that he will come into England to receive knighthood from him "*At the seige of Oran*" R 1 529 O ii 1063 H 1. p. iv 77
Oct 19	The chapter of Dax in Gascony complains to Philip K of France of the conduct of the bailiffs of the K of England *Dax.* R 1 529 O u 59 H 1 p u 150

DATE	SUBJECT
1275 [ ]	The K. appoints commissioners to receive the land of Agen R 1 529 O. ii 60. H 1 p ii 151
Nov 5	The K grants 500 marks sterling to Robert count of Boulogne *Westm* R. 1. 530. O ii 60 H 1 p ii 151
Nov 11	The K (being unable to attend personally) requests the K of France to excuse his absence in his parliament, in relation to the suit between Robert duke of Burgundy and Robert count of Nyvers and Yolenda his wife, concerning the duchy of Burgundy. *Westm.* R. 1 530 O ii 60 H 1 p ii 161
[. . . .]	A duchess of Brunswick, in congratulating the K on various subjects, asks him to send her some portion of the pension promised her by the late K on her marriage R. 1 30. O ii 1063 H 1 p iv 77
Nov 11	The count of Savoy informs the K that he is at war with the K of Almain *Aquian'.* R. 1 530 O ii 61 H 1 p ii 151
	Louis of Savoy recommends Grimund or Grimoard de Altisvineis to the K R 1. 530 O ii. 61 H 1 p ii 77
[Nov 13]	Margaret Q of France asks the K to be favourable to the suit of Grimoard de Altis Vineis *Matisc* R 1 537 O ii 72 H 1 p ii 155
Nov 15	The K. repeats his orders to the barons of Limoges, &c, to take the oath required by the K of France *Westm* R 1 531 O ii 61 H 1 p ii 151
Dec	The chapter of Dax complain to the K of the exactions of his seneschal of Gascony. R. 1 531. O ii 62 H 1 p ii 151
1276 Jan 7.	The K asks the men of Bayonne to aid the K of Castille, about to be attacked by the Saracens *Caneford* R 1 531 O ii 62 H 1 p ii 151
March 26	Alexander K of Scotland complains to the K. of the conduct of his bailiffs upon the Marches *Edinbro' Castle.* R. 1 531 O ii. 1004 H 1 p iv 77
March 29	Florence count of Holland grants leave to the English to trade in Holland for two years R 1 531 O ii 62 H 1 p ii 152
[. .]	The K congratulates Pope Innocent [V] upon his promotion to the papacy. R. 1. 532. O ii 63. H 1 p ii 152
April 18.	The dean and chapter of Bangor complain to the abp of Canterbury of a conspiracy against Lewelin prince of Wales *Bangor* R 1 532 O. ii 64 H 1 p ii 152
April 26	Sifrid abp of Cologne asks credence for Wynemars de Gynenick, the bearer *Aix la Chapelle* R 1 533 O ii 1064 H 1 p iv. 77.
May 10	Magnus K of Norway, sends a present of falcons, a silver cup, some furs, and the head of a whale, &c to the K *Bergen* R 1 533.
May 25	Alexander K of Scotland asks the K to see that his liberties are not violated. *Selkirk* R 1 533 O ii 1054 H 1 p iv 77
June 5	The K submits to the arbitration of Philip K of France a dispute which has been carried into his court between himself and Reymund vicomte de Fronzac R 1 533 O ii 65 H 1 p ii 153
June 1.	Garsio de Marchin undertakes to serve the K. R 1 533 O ii 66 H 1 p ii 153
June 10	Albert duke of Brunswick asks the K to promote amity between the citizens of Bremen and London *Verde* R 1 534 O ii 1065 H 1 p iv 78.
June 10	Albert duke of Brunswick asks for letters of safe conduct for his messengers coming into England R 1 534 O ii 1065 H 1 p ii 78
[ ]	The citizens of Bremen ask of the K justice from the citizens of London. R. 1 534 O ii 1011 H 1 p iv 78
July 22	John de Bohun and Joan his wife certify that they have sold to the K the sergeancy of the chapel royal and the office of spigurnel *London* R 1 534.
Oct. 7	Pope John [XXI] notifies his promotion to the K *Viterbo.* R. 1 534 O ii 66 H 1 p ii 153.
Oct. 29.	The K confirms the grant of dower made to Blanch Q. of Navarre, wife of his brother Edmund *Westm* R. 1. 535. O ii 67 H. 1 p ii. 153
[.]	War declared against L prince of Wales *Westm.* R 1 535 O ii 68 H 1 p ii. 154.
Nov. 12.	The K thanks the bp of Bâle for a present *Westm* R 1 536 O ii 69 H. 1. p ii 154
[. .]	Opinion of the English Council on the marriage proposed between the K.'s daughter [Joan] and Hartman son of the K of Almain. R. 1. 536. O. ii 70 H. 1 p. ii 154.

DATE	SUBJECT
1276 [.]	Instructions to the messengers going into Germany to treat of the above-mentioned marriage R 1 536 O ii 70 H 1 p ii 154
[Nov 13]	Margaret Q of France to the K relative to Grimoard de Altis Vineis. R. 1. 537. *See* [13 Nov] 1275
Nov 13	The English prelates advise Lewelin prince of Wales to cease from his inroads upon the English *Westm* R 1 537 O ii 71 H 1 p ii 155
Nov 15	The K. appoints Roger Mortimer as his captain against the Welsh. *Westm.* R. 1. 537. O ii 71 H 1. p ii. 155.
Nov 16	Commission to Wm de Beauchamp earl of Warwick to receive the Welsh into the K.'s peace. *Westm.* R 1 537 O ii 72 H 1 p ii 155
Dec. 12.	The K pledges himself to pope John [XXI] that either he or his brother Edmund earl of Lancaster will join the crusade. *Windsor* R. 1 537. O. ii. 72. H. 1 p ii 155.
Dec 12	Writ of military summons to Edmund earl of Lancaster and 177 others to meet at Worcester to proceed against Lewelin prince of Wales *Windsor* R 1 537 O ii. 73 H 1 p ii 155
Dec. 12	Writ of summons for the abps and bps to send their military service for the same purpose. *Windsor.* R 1 538 O. ii 74 H 1 p. ii. 156.
Dec 12	Military summons to all tenants in capite to meet for the same purpose *Windsor* R. 1 538 O ii 75. H 1 p ii. 156.
Dec 12	Military summons to all abbots, abbesses, and others, to send their service as above *Windsor* R 1. 538 O ii 75 H. 1. p ii. 156.
Dec. 13	Commission to inquire about Judaizing Christians who extort illicit usury *Windsor* R 1 539
Dec 13	Commission to inquire about certain Jews and Christians who clip the coin *Windsor.* R. 1 539.
Dec. 13.	Pope John [XXI] asks the K to protect the Cardinal de Sancto Martino in holding the churches Wistanestea, Frondingham, and Archexea, assigned to him by the pope his predecessor *Viterbo* R. 1 539 O ii 76 H 1 p ii. 157
Dec 18	Pope John [XXI] asks the K. to pay the annual papal tribute now in arrear for 7 years. *Viterbo.* R 1 540 O ii 157. H. 1 p ii 156.
Dec. 26.	Safe-conduct for M Q. of Scotland, going abroad on a pilgrimage. *Cirencester* R. 1. 540. O ii 78. H. 1 p ii 157
[.]	The K directs Robert de Ufford, justiciary of Ireland, to endeavour to introduce English laws into Ireland. R. 1. 540 O. ii 78. H 1. p ii. 157.
1277. Jan 8	The K replies in detail to various questions and requests addressed to him by the K of Castille *Windsor* R. 1 541. O ii 78 H. 1 p ii 57.
Jan 14	Safe-conduct for the messengers of Lewelin son of Griffin, coming to the K. *La Bruere.* R. 1 541. O. ii 84. H 1 p ii 159.
Jan 25	The K of Aragon to the K ; professions of amity. *Saragossa* R 1 541. O ii 79. H 1 p ii 158
Feb 27	The abp of Cant orders the abp. of York to excommunicate Lewelin prince of Wales *Northstock* R. 1. 541. O ii 79 H. 1. p. ii 158.
April 4.	Treaty of peace between the K. and Res son of Mereduc *Caermendyn.* R 1 542. O ii 81 H 1 p ii 158
May 1	Certificate by the K to the pope that Ebolo vicomte de Ventodoro will join the next crusade *Westm.* R 1 542. O ii 82 H 1 p ii. 159.
May 1	The K desires his proctor to forward the affairs of Ebolo de Ventodoro. *Westm.* R. 1. 542 O ii 182 H 1 p. ii 159
May 15.	Notification of the conclusion of peace between the men of Bayonne and the barons of the Cinq Ports. *Westm* R 1 542 O ii 82 H 1 p ii 159
[. . .]	Manuel Saladini and others ask to be informed of the K's prosperity R 1 542. O ii 83. H. 1 p. ii 159.
May 24.	The K desires that inquiries be made as to the conduct of the Jews on various points here specified *Windsor* R 1 543 O ii. 83 H 1 p ii 159
[July 10]	K. Alexander to the K in favour of certain persons here mentioned R 1 543. O. ii. 84 H. 1 p ii. 160 *See* July 10, 1278
Aug 1.	Notarial copy of letters between Henry III K of England and Alfonso K. of Castile, sent to K. Edward *Burgos.* R. 1 543 O ii 84 H 1 p ii. 160.

DATE	SUBJECT
1277 [Aug 1]	Notice of the settlement of a dispute between the K of Scotland and the bp of Durham *Birkenhead* R 1 544 O ii 86 H. 1 p ii 160.
Aug 8	The K asks the troops of prince Edmund to remain where they are in S Wales *Walrescote* R 1 544
[Aug 23]	Agreement as to the lands here mentioned to be given by the K to David son of Griffin, on the overthrow of Lewelin prince of Wales *In the camp at Flint, near Basingwerk.* R 1 544 O ii 86 H 1 p ii 160.
Sept 4	The K interposes in the suit instituted by Beatrix Q of Alman against Edmund earl of Cornwall *Woodstock* R 1 544 O ii 87 H 1 p ii 161
Sept 25	Commission by Rudolph K. of the Romans for the marriage of his son Hartman with Joanna, the K's daughter *Vienna* R. 1 545. O ii 88 H 1 p ii 161
Nov 9	Lewelin prince of Wales undertakes to observe the peace with the King *Aberconway* R 1 545 O ii 88 H 1 p ii 161
Nov 9	Lewelin prince of Wales quits claim to four cantreds in Wales to the K *Aberconway* R 1 546 O ii 89 H 1 p ii 162.
Nov 9	Lewelin prince of Wales consents that the K shall award 1,000 marks to Roderick, Lewelin's brother *Aberconway* R 1 546 O ii. 91 H 1 p ii 162
Nov 9	Lewelin prince of Wales undertakes to pay to the K 500 marks by the year for Anglesey, in discharge of his debt to K. Henry *Aberconway* R 1 546 O. ii 91 H 1 p. ii 162
Nov 10	The K remits to Lewelin the annual payment of 1,000 marks for Anglesey *Rothelan.* R. 1 546 O ii 91. H 1 p. ii. 162
Nov 10	The K ratifies the peace with Lewelin prince of Wales *Rotheland* R 1. 546. O ii 91 H 1 p ii 162
Nov 11	The K remits the fine of 50,000*l* sterling payable by Lewelin prince of Wales for having peace *Rothelan* R 1 547 O. ii 92 H 1 p ii 163
Nov 15	Commission by the K to his proctors to proceed in certain causes in the court of the French K. *Rothelan* R 1 547 O ii 93 H 1 p ii 163
Nov 15	The K appoints proctors in the suit in the court of the K. of France respecting Gaston de Bearn and Constance his daughter *Rothelan* R. 1 547 O ii 93 H 1 p ii 163
Nov 15	The K informs the K of France that Gaston de Bearn submits himself to his [Edward's] decision, and is coming into England *Rothelan* R 1 547 O. ii 95. H. 1 p. ii 163
Nov 16	Lewelin prince of Wales conveys all his right in Anglesey to the K if he dies without heirs *Aberconway* R 1 548 O ii. 95 H 1 p ii 164
Nov 23	The K. appoints proctors to appear for him in the French court *Newmarket.* R 1 548. O ii 95. H. 1 p ii. 164
Dec 6.	Safe conduct for Lewelin prince of Wales coming to the K at London. *Worcester.* R 1 548. O ii 96 H 1 p ii 164
1278. Jan 2	Oath by the messengers of the K of the Romans, as to the marriage between Hartman his son and the K's daughter Joanna *London* R. 1 548 O ii 96 H 1 p ii 164
Jan 4	The K orders that the messengers sent by prince Lewelin to Eleanor daughter of Simon de Montfort shall be well treated *Tower of London.* R. 1 548 O ii 97 H 1 p. ii 164
Jan. 4.	The K appoints commissioners to receive the oaths and hostages of the Welsh, and for other matters connected therewith *Westm.* R. 1 549. O ii 97 H 1. p ii 165
Jan 6	Commission from John duke of Lorraine and Brabant to treat of the marriage of his son with the K's daughter R 1 549 O ii. 97 H 1 p ii. 165
Jan 15	Pope Nicolas [III.] certifies his election to the K *Rome* R. 1. 549. O ii 98 H. 1 p ii 165
[Jan 24]	John duke of Lorraine and Brabant binds himself to observe the agreements on the marriage between John his eldest son and the K's daughter Margaret *London* R. 1 550 O ii 100 H 1 p ii 166
Jan 24	Several of the nobility of Brabant bind themselves to the same purpose. *London* R 1.550 O ii 101 H 1 p ii 166
Feb 1	John duke of Lorraine and Brabant ratifies the act of his nobility *Compiegne* R. 1 550 O ii 101 H 1 p ii 166
Feb 1	Oath of Godefroys son of the duke Brabant and others to accept the same agreement *Compiegne* R 1. 551 O ii 102 H 1 p ii 166

DATE	SUBJECT
1278 Feb 6	Oath of John duke Lorraine and of Brabant to the same effect *Compiegne* R 1 551. O. ii 102 H 1 p ii 167.
[Feb. 6.]	Assignment of dower to the princess Margaret by John duke Lorraine and of Brabant R. 1. 551. O. ii 103 H 1 p. ii 167
Feb 6	The K sanctions the building of galleys at Bayonne for service of the K of Castille against the Moors *Dover* R 1 552 O ii 105 H. 1 p ii 168
Feb 8.	Commission to treat with the K. of France as to the land of Agen, and to complete the articles of peace commenced by K Henry III *Dover* R 1 552 O ii 106 H 1 p. ii 168.
Feb 8	The K asks the K of France not to proceed to extremities against Gaston de Bearn. *Dover* R 1. 553 O ii 106 H 1 p ii 168
Feb. 8	The K intercedes with the K of France in favour of Gaston de Bearn *Dover*. R 1 553 O ii 107 H. 1 p ii 168.
Feb 23.	The pope acknowledges the receipt of 8,000 marks at Rome for the tribute of eight years *Rome* R 1 553 O ii 107 H 1 p ii 169
March	Margaret duchess of Lorraine and Brabant assents to the arrangements made with the K respecting the marriage between their children R 1 553 O ii 108 H 1 p ii 169.
March	Bond by the mayors of Louvaine, Brussels, Auniers, Thyelemont, and Lywes, to pay to the K. 40,000*l* tournois, if the duke of Brabant fail to perform his agreement respecting the marriage of his son with the princess Margaret "*In Brabant*." R. 1 553. O. ii. 108. H. 1. p. ii 169
March 21.	The K informs his chancellor and Oto de Grandison of the state of affairs in Gascony, and of matters connected with the prince of Wales and K of Scotland. *Donameneye*. R. 1. 554 O ii 109. H. 1 p. ii 169.
[April 1]	Robert duke of Burgundy asks the K to help the monks of Citeaux, whose church at Scardebour is impoverished through the friars preachers *Berne*. R 1 555. O ii 110. H 1 p ii 170
April 25.	Rudolph K. of the Romans promises that he will try to secure the election of Hartman count of Hapsburg as K of the Romans R 1 554 O ii 110 H 1 p ii 169
April 25	Rudolph K of the Romans promises to try and secure the election of Hartman count of Hapsburg as K. of Arles. R. 1 554 O. ii 110 H 1 p ii. 170
April 25	Rudolph K of the Romans promises that the marriage portion of the princess Joanna shall be augmented proportionably with the income of count Hartman *Vienna*. R. 1 554.
May 3	Assignment by K Rudolph of dower to the K's daughter Joanna, on her marriage with Hartman count of Hapsburg. *Vienna* R 1 555 O ii 112 H. 1. p. ii 170.
May 3	Rudolph K of the Romans confirms the proceedings of his nuncios respecting the above marriage *Vienna* R 1 557 O ii 113 H. 1 p ii 171
May 3	Rudolph K of the Romans makes oath to the observance of the above agreement. *Vienna* R 1 556. O ii 113 H 1 p ii 171
May 3	Anna Q. of the Romans promises that the above marriage shall take place about the feast of the Nativity of the Virgin next *Vienna* R 1 556
May 3	Rudolph K of the Romans gives the K power to contract a peace between himself and the count of Savoy *Vienna* R. 1 p ii 556 O ii. 114 H 1 p ii 171
[May 26]	Certain of the nobility of Flanders pledge their liberty for the payment of the sums promised on the settlement of the peace at Montreul between the K and Guy count of Flanders. *Alost*. R. 1 555. O. ii 111. H. 1. p. ii. 170.
[May 26]	Guy count of Flanders pledges his liberty for the payment of the sums promised on the settlement of the peace at Montreul *Alost* R 1 555 O ii 111 H 1. p. ii 170.
May 4	Notification by K Rudolph as to the application of the 10,000 marks given by K Edward as his daughter Joanna's dower *Vienna* R 1 557 O ii 115. H 1. p ii 171
[May]	K. Edward's notification of the omission of the word "marks" in the assignment of dower of the princess Joanna R 1 557 O ii 115 H 1 p ii 172
[May]	Corrected copy of the letter referred to above R 1 557 O ii 115 H. 1 p ii 172.
[May]	The K's peace secured to Henry, a converted Jew, (created a knight by K Henry III.,) who had bought the clippings of the silver coin R. 1 557 O ii 116 H 1 p p ii 172
June 4.	The K to Lewelin prince of Wales, as to the holding of pleas in Wales and regarding fugitives from Wales into England. R. 1. 557. O ii 116 H 1. p. ii 172

DATE	SUBJECT.
1278 June 12	Safe conduct for Alexander K of Scotland coming to the K R. 1 558 O n 117. H 1 p n. 172
June 17	Charter of liberties for the barons of the Cinque Ports *Westm* R 1 558
June 17	Brumisan, wife of Ugolin de Fusco, entreats the K. to continue to her son Rimund the pension enjoyed by his uncle Ottobon, papal legate in England " *Clauri.*" R. 1. 559. O n 1066 H. 1. p iv 79
June 26	The K thanks the queen of Castile for her careful education of his daughter Joanna. *London* R 1 559 O n 1067 H 1 p iv 78
July 10.	The K asks pope [Nicholas III] to confirm the election of Robert bp of Bath and Wells to the abprick of Canterbury *Windsor.* R 1 559. O n 118 H 1 p n 173.
July 10	Alexander K of Scotland asks the K to give credence to the bearers of his letter. R 1 543 O n 84 H 1 p n. 160.
July 14.	The K to Lewellin prince of Wales, relative to the bp of Bangor, the abbot of Basingwerk, and other matters in debate respecting Wales and the Welsh borders *Windsor.* R 1 559 O n. 119 H 1. p n 172
July 15	Commission for assessing the tallage to be paid by the Jews *Windsor* R 1 560.
Aug 1	Pope Nicolas [III] informs the K as to the terms on which he may have a tenth from the ecclesiastical revenues of England *Viterbo* R. 1 560. O. n 119 H. 1. p n 173
[Aug 5]	Pope Nicolas [III] rejects the K 's offer to give certain abbeys in England instead of the annual tribute of 1,000 marks sterling *Viterbo* R 1 560 O n 121 H 1 p n 174
[Aug 5]	Joanna queen of Castile asks the K to receive by proxy the homage of Wm. abp of Rouen R 1 561 O n 121 H 1 p n 174
[Aug 5.]	Joanna countess of Alençon to the K , with the same petition *Etampes.* R. 1. 561 O n 121 H 1 p n 174
Aug 12	Pope Nicolas [III] states the conditions on which he will grant a tenth to the K. *Viterbo* R 1 561 O. n 122 H 1 p n. 174
[Aug 19.]	Matthew abbot of S Denis asks the K to receive by proxy the oath of fealty of Wm abp of Rouen *Rouen* R 1 561. O n 123 H. 1 p n 175
Aug 24	Wm abp of Rouen asks permission to perform his fealty by proxy. R. 1. 562. O n 124 H 1 p n 175
Sept 15	The K orders that the price of provisions, &c , be not enhanced on the visit to England of K Alexander of Scotland *Shotwick* R 1 562 O n 124 H 1 p n 175.
Sept 17	The K restores to Lewelin prince of Wales ten Welsh hostages *Shotwick* R 1 562 O n 125 H 1 p n 175
Sept 17.	Mandate from the K to pay the expenses of Francis Accursius employed on the K 's business *Shotwick* R 1 562 O n 125 H 1 p n. 175
Sept 20	Names and oath of the ten Welsh hostages restored by the K. R 1 562 O n. 125. H 1 p n 175
Sept 29	Homage and fealty rendered to the K by Alex K. of Scotland. R. 1 563 O. n 126. H 1 p n 176
Nov 1.	Giles de Neville asks leave to do battle with Gaston de Bearn, who has insulted the K. at the court of France. *Nuevill* R 1 563 O n 127 H 1 p n 175
Nov 8	The K asks G bp of Verdun to accompany Hartman of Hapsburg into England on his marriage *Westm* R 1 563 O n 1067 H 1 p. iv 78.
Nov. 8.	The K informs G bp of Verdun of the victory of the K of the Romans, of the affairs of the duke of Brabant, and of his daughter's intended marriage *Westm.* R.1 563. O n 1068 H 1 p iv 79.
Dec 17	The K forbids the exportation of silver plate, or coin, or broken metal *Windsor.* R 1 p n. 564
[Dec 18]	Philip K. of France to the K , in favour of certain men of Rouen whose goods were seized Southampton *Paris* R. 1 564. O n 127 H 1 p. n 176.
[.]	Charles prince of Salerno asks the K to grant a benefice to Nicolas Boncelli. *Paris.* R 1 564 O n 128 H 1 p n 176
1279 Jan 4	The K requires R bp of Durham to punish John de Grendone, burgess of Durham, for an assault on one of the men of Alexander K of Scotland, passing through Durham. *Windsor* R 1 565
[Jan 27]	Alfonso K of Castile to the K in favour of Henry Barleti, who had been to Tartary. *Bruges* R 1 564 O n 128 H 1 p n 177

DATE.	SUBJECT
1279 Feb. 4.	The abp of Auch and others complain of the plunder of the church of Auch by the seneschal of Gascony *Auch* R 1 565 O u 129 H 1 p u 177
Feb. 4.	Commission to the bp of Norwich and others to hear the disputes between Alexander K. of Scotland and R. bp of Durham *Woodstock.* R 1 565 O u 129 H 1 p u 177.
Feb. 7.	The K entreats pope [Nicholas III] not to meddle with the privileges of the realm. *Woodstock* R 1 565 O u. 13 H. 1 p u 177
Feb. 12.	Commission to conclude the treaty of marriage between John duke of Brabant and the princess Margaret *Woodstock* R 1 266 O u 131 H 1 p u 177
Feb. 16.	Commission to enquire into the custom between England and Scotland respecting fugitives across the border *Woodstock* R 1. 566.
[Feb 27]	Charles prince of Salerno intercedes with the K for Guy de Montfort *Paris* R 1 566 O u 1068 H 1 p iv 79
[Feb 27]	Hugh bp. of Bazas appoints the K his arbitrator in certain disputes with Bernardus de Ladils and others "*Hingonium*" R 1 566. O u 131. H 1 p u 178
March 11	The K orders the people of Fezenzac to do homage to their count Gerard *Woodstock* R 1 567 O u. 131 H 1 p. u. 178
March 12	Commission to enquire who are or ought to have been knighted. *Woodstock* R 1 567
March 12	Commission to examine (by oath here given) into the knights' fees and other liberties throughout England *Woodstock* R 1 567.
April 1	Credence by Alfonso K of Castile for master Jofre, his notary, going to the K *Toledo.* R. 1 567 O ii 1066 H 1. p iv. 79
April 11	The K informs Charles prince of Salerno that he will lay his petition in favour of Guy de Montfort before the nobles of England, and will send the harriers he asks for *Brehull* R 1 568 O u 1069 H 1 p iv 79
April 11	The K to R king of the Romans, is satisfied with the reasons assigned for the delay of the journey of Hartman, for whom he will send ships to Holland *Brehull.* R 1 568. O u 1070. H 1. p iv. 79
April 11.	The K. asks the count of Guelders to grant a free passage through his territories to Hartman, son of the K of the Romans *Brehull* R 1 568 O u 1070 H 1 p iv 80
April 27	The K. appoints lieutenants to govern the realm during his absence in France *Westm.* R 1 568 O u 132 H 1 p u 178
April 28.	The K arranges for the honorable reception of Hartman, son of the K of the Romans *Westm* R 1 568 O u. 132 H 1 p u 178
April 28	The K. assigns in dower to Constance, widow of Henry of Almain, 300*l* sterling annually from the customs of Bordeaux *Westm* R. 1 569 O u 132 H 1 p u 178
April 28	The K notifies that he has pardoned and restored to Gaston viscount of Bearn all his lands, castles, &c *Westm.* R. 1. 569. O u 133 H 1 p u 178
April 28	The K orders John de Greilly, seneschal of Gascony, to restore to Gaston de Bearn his lands, &c *Westm* R 1 569 O. u 133 H 1 178.
April 28.	The K orders the restoration of certain possessions herein specified to Gaston de Bearn *Westm* R 1 569 O u 133 H 1 p u 178
May 4.	Magnus K of Norway sends to the K. certain girfalcons *Bergen* R 1 569. O u 1071. H 1 p iv 80
May 7	The K orders Stephen de Penchester and others not to molest those Jews who were indicted for clipping coin, provided they pay a fine *Canterbury* R 1 570
May 7	The K issues certain orders respecting the conduct and treatment of the Jews *Canterbury* R 1 570
May 10	Don Sancho, eldest son of Alfonso K. of Castile, to the K , credence for master Jaffre, his father's notary. *Toledo.* R 1 569 O u 1071. H 1 p iv 80.
May 12	Credence by Alfonso K. of Castile for his notary, master Jaffre, going to the K. of England. *La Real.* R 1. 570.
[May 19,]	The K advises Constance (widow of Henry of Almain) to marry Edmund Genenne, nephew of the bp of Langres. *Monstroul* R 1 569 O u 133 H 1 p u 178
May 23.	Confirmation of the peace between K Henry III and Louis K of France relative to claims in the district of Agenois *Amiens.* R. 1 571 O u 134 H 1 p r 179
May 23.	The K acknowledges that he is bound to pay to Philip [III] K of France 6,000*l* Paris " ex Rachetto " of the comté of Ponthieu *Amiens.* R 1 572 O. u. 137 H 1 p. u 180.

DATE	SUBJECT
1279 May 24	J. abp of Cant informs pope Nicholas that he was present at the renewal of the treaty of peace between the Ks of England and France at Amiens. *Amiens.* R 1 579 O 11 1072 H 1 p 1v 80
June 2.	Settlement of disputes between the counts of Bearn and Bigorre on the one part and the K on the other *Abbeville* R 1. 572 O 11 137. H 1. p 11 180
[June]	Eleanor Q [dowager] asks the K to write in her favour to the K of Germany respecting her matters in Provence. R 1 573 O 11 1073 H 1. p 1v. 81
June 4	The K sends Wm de Valence to the K of France to receive the land of the Agenois *Abbeville* R 1 573 O 11 138 H 1 p 11 180
June 4	Commission to Wm de Valence for the above purpose *Abbeville.* R 1. 573. O 11. 139 H 1 p 11. 180
June 4	The K requests the bp of Agen to receive from the seneschal of Agen the oath which ought to be made by the K in person *Abbeville* R 1 573 O 11 139 H 1 p 11 181.
June 4	The K. grants to John count of Brittany exemption from military service for 5 years during his absence in the H Land *Westm* R 1 573. O 11 139 H. 1 p. 11 181
June 6	The K and Q notify that the land of Ponthieu having fallen to them by the death of Joanna Q of Castile, they have taken possession of it *Abbeville* R 1 574. O 11 139 H 1 p 11 181
[June 6]	The form of the oath made by the K and Q to the men of Ponthieu, and of that made by them to the K and Q R 1 574 O 11 140 H 1 p 11 181
June	The K and Q notify that the mayor, &c of Rue and the other communes of Ponthieu here specified have taken the oath to their proctor *Logard.* R 1 574 O 11 140 H 1 p 11 181
June 8	The K asks the K of France to deliver to Wm de Valence whatever ought to be delivered to the K. in Limoges, Cahors, &c *Logard* R 1 574 O 11. 141. H. 1 p. 11 181
June 13	The K notifies that he will pay half the debts of John late count of Ponthieu *Valoilles* R 1 574 O 11 141 H. 1 p 11 182.
June 19	Memorandum of the K.'s arrival at Dover, and of the delivery of the great seal to the chancellor R 1. 575
June 21	The K permits his mint-master of Canterbury to receive, for a time, the coins minted at the mint of the abp *Canterbury* R 1 575
July 8	Those who circulate false reports about the K. to be arrested. *Westm* R 1 575.
[July 13]	Letter relative to the interview between the Ks of France and Spain at Beaucaire R 1 575 O 11 1073 H 1 p 1v 81
Sept 5	The K to W. de Valence, on the marriage of Sancho, son of Alfonso K of Castile, with the daughter of Gaston of Bearn " *Sliptos* " R 1 575 O. 11. 1073 H. 1. p 1v 81
Sept 23	The K sends to Magnus K of Norway certain relics, at his request *Westm* R. 1. 575 O 11 1074 H 1 p 1v 81
Oct. 10	Eleanor princess of Wales asks the K. to arrange with her as to her portion left by the will of Q Eleanor, the K's aunt *Aberden* R 1 576. O 11. 1074 H 1 p 1v 81
Nov 10	Edmund earl of Lancaster exchanges the counties and castles of Caermarthen and Kardigan with the K for the manors, &c. of Wirks, Worth, and Essehurn *London* R. 1 576. O 11 142 H 1 p 11 182.
Nov 10	The K orders the payment of the balance of her annuity due to Constance, widow of Henry of Almain *Westm* R 1 576 O 11 142 H 1 p 11 182.
Nov. 28	Letters patent of Alfonso [X] K. of Castile agreeing to a truce with the K of France at the request of Edw I *Seville* R 1 576
1280 Jan 2	The K orders that the converted Jews be induced to attend the discourses of the provincial of the Friars Preachers *Winchester* R. 1 576
Jan. 13	Agreement with the barons of Norway for the capture of Guy de Montfort in Norway. R 1 577 O 11 143 H 1 p 11 182
[Jan]	Augustine, seneschal of the K. of Norway, to the K, on the capture, in Norway, of a knight supposed to be Guy de Montfort R 1 577 O 11 143 H 1 p 11. 182
Feb 17	Pope Nicholas [III] prays the K to liberate Almaric de Montfort. *S Peter's, Rome* R 1 577 O 11 144 H 1 p 11 182
Feb. 17.	Pope Nicholas [III] requests master Raymond to go to England, concerning the liberation of Almeric de Montfort *S Peter's, Rome* R 1. 578. O 11 145 H. 1. p 11 183.
Feb. 17.	The K orders that certain jewels, which had been removed from the shrine of S Richard of Chichester, should be restored. *Clarendon* R. 1 578 O 11 146. H. 1. p 11. 183.

DATE	SUBJECT
1280 March 3	Warrant for the payment of the annuity of 40 marks to Ordeonius bp. of Frascati *Dounamony* R 1 578 O ii 146 H 1 p ii. 183
March 16.	Attestation of the homage done by Jordan de Insula for his lands in Agen *Dunamony* R 1 578 O. ii. 146. H. 1. p. ii. 183
April 9.	Pope Nicholas [III] exhorts the K to restore the bp of Carlisle to his favour *S Peter's, Rome* R 1 579 O ii 148 H 1 p ii 184
April 24.	Writ for the payment of 80 marks to Berard de Neapoli, papal notary. *Bristol* R 1 579. O. ii. 148. H. 1 p ii 184
May 6	Magnus K of Norway, on the approach of death, recommends his son Eric to the K.'s protection *Bergen* R 1 579 O ii 1074 H 1 p iv 81
May 17	Eric K of Norway announces the death of his father K Magnus *Bergen* R 1 580 O ii. 1075. H. 1. p. iv. 81.
May 18	The K orders that Alfonso K of Castile may be allowed to buy materials at Bayonne for building galleys against the Saracens *Westm* R 1 580. O ii 149 H 1 p ii 184
May 23.	Alfonso [X] K of Castile authorizes the K to make a truce, in his name, with the K of France *Seville* R 1 580 O ii 149 H 1 p ii 184
[May]	Adelheidis duchess of Brunswick informs the K of the death of her husband. R 1 580 O ii 1076 H 1 p iv 83
[May 25]	Henry duke of Brunswick to the K , professions of devotion *Brunswick.* R 1 581 O ii. 1076 H 1 p iv 82.
[May]	Form of truce between the Kings of France and Castile R 1 581 O ii 150 H 1. p ii 185.
June 1	Alfonso [X] K of Castile notifies that he has made a truce with the K of France *Seville* R 1 581 O. ii. 151 H. 1 p. ii. 185.
June 3	Regulations for the management of the house of the converted Jews in London *Westm* R. 1 582
June 10.	Writ for the payment of 100 marks to Cardinal Jacobus Sabellus, being part of his annual fee *Westm* R 1 582 O ii 152 H 1. p. ii. 185.
June 10.	The K orders the English inhabitants of Ireland to discuss the expediency of introducing the English laws into Ireland, and inform him of the result *Westm* R 1 582
[June 29]	Philip K. of France will be glad to know how the K is *Paris* R 1 585. O ii 158 H 1 p ii 188
[July 2]	Philip [III] K of France asks the K. to order that the K. of Castile be honourably received at Bayonne. *Paris* R 1 582 O ii 152 H 1 p ii 186
July 3	Maurice lord of Creon informs the K. of the proceedings of the Kings of France and Castile as to a truce between them *Paris.* R 1 583 O ii 153 H 1. p. ii. 186.
July 3.	Maurice lord of Creon and Sir Geoffrey de Greinvile to the K on the mediation of the prince of Salerno in the treaty of truce R 1 583 O ii 153 H 1. p ii 186
July 5.	Geoffrey de Greinvile and John de Greilh inform the K. that the conference is to be at Bayonne between the Kings of France and Castile *Paris* R 1 583. O. ii 154. H. 1 p ii 186
July 8	Eleanor princess of Wales asked the K. not to credit reports raised against her husband *Launmaes* R 1 584 O ii 1076 H 1 p iv 82
July 11	Philip [III] K of France urges the K to be present at a conference to be held at Mont de Marsan between the Kings of France and Castile *Paris* R. 1 583 O ii 155 H 1 p. ii 187
July 15.	The K directs the seneschal of Gascony to give an honorable reception at Bayonne to the K of Castile *Langley* R 1 584 O ii 155 H 1 p ii 187
July 15	The K. informs Philip K of France of the directions he has given in the previous letter. *Langley* R. 1 584. O ii 155. H. 1. p ii. 187
[July 15]	The K to the prince of Salerno, relative Guy de Montfort, of the reception of the K of Castile at Bayonne, and of his request in favour of Peres de Cotim R 1 584 O ii 156 H 1 p ii 187
July 17.	Writ of protection for the merchants of Seiland trading with England *Langley* R. 1 484 O ii 156 H 1 p ii 187
July 17	The K advises the people of Bayonne how to proceed in their dispute with their bp *Langley* R 1 585. O. ii 157. H. 1. p. ii 187
July 18.	The K. to the bailiffs of Gascony relative to the duel about to be fought at Bordeaux in the court of Lucas de Tany. *Langley* R. 1 585 O ii 157 H 1. p ii 188

DATE	SUBJECT
1280 July 21	The K informs Philip K of France that he cannot be present at the meeting at Mont de Marsan *Langley* R 1.585 O ii 158. H 1 p ii 188.
[Aug 5]	Philip K of France as to the K.'s health R 1 585 O ii 158 H 1 p ii 188 *See* June 29
Aug 17	The K appoints John de Greilly seneschal of Gascony *York.* R. 1. 585. O. ii. 158. H 1 p ii 188
Aug 19	The K forwards to the K of France some information lately received about the peace with the K of Castile *York* R 1 586 O ii 159 H 1 p ii 188.
Aug 27	The K informs the K of Castile that he will meet him at Bayonne about next Easter. *Richmond* R 1 586. O ii 159 H 1. p ii 188
[Sept 20?]	Charles prince of Salerno to the K, in behalf of Guy de Montfort. R. 1 586 O. ii 159. H 1 p ii 188
Sept 20	The K to Margaret Q of France, on the help he will give her in supporting her rights. *Sooton* R 1 586 O ii 159. H 1. p ii. 188
Oct 5	Geoffrey bp of Evreux informs the K of the miserable state of the Christians in the Holy Land *Arles* R 1 586 O ii 160 H 1 p ii 188.
Oct 18	Eleanor princess of Wales in favour of her brother Amalric de Montfort. *St. Annœr.* R 1 587 O ii 1077, H 1 p iv 82
Oct. 28	The mayor, &c of Bayonne appoint proctors in their disputes with the bp of Bayonne R 1. 587 O ii 161 H 1 p ii 189
Nov 6	Licence to John Giffard of Brumpsfield to hunt wolves *Westm* R 1 587
[Nov]	The K asks Eric K of Norway to send to him the knight arrested in Norway on suspicion of being Guy de Montfort R 1 587 O ii 1078 H 1 p. iv 83
Nov 17	The K renews to the merchants of Germany the grant of their Guildhall in London *Westm.* R 1 588 O ii 161 H 1 p ii 189
Nov 22	The K licenses the bp of Agen and Berald Delgot his brother to build a fortified house in the fief of Laranus *Westm* R 1 588 O ii 1078 H 1 p iv. 83.
[Dec]	Adelheydis late duchess of Brunswick, now lady of Hertesberge, asks credence for the bearer, who will tell him how vilely she and her children have been used by her brother As her messenger does not understand French, she prays that he may be put into communication with some clerk who understands Latin R 1 588 O ii 1079 H 1 p iv 83.
Dec 23	John de Greilh informs the K of the movements of the K. of France, the prince of Salerno, and himself *Bayonne* R 1 588 O ii 162 H 1. p ii 189.
1281. Jan	Otho count palatine of Burgundy enumerates the lands, &c for which he has done homage to the K *Lyons* R 1 588 O ii. 162 H 1 p ii 189
Feb. 15.	Philip K of France inquires after the health of K Edw *Montargis* R. 1. 589 O ii. 163 H 1 p ii 190
Feb 18	Commission for a peace, or truce, between R K of the Romans and Philip count of Savoy. *Shirburn* R 1 589 O ii 163. H 1. p ii 190
Feb 18	Mandate to Otho de Grandeson appointed to act in the above matter R. 1. 589. O ii. 164 H 1 p ii 190
Feb 18	Mandate to Thomas de Savoy appointed to act in the above matter R. 1. 589 O ii 163 H 1. p ii 190.
Feb. 18	The K asks the K of Germany to accept the mediation of those persons whom he has sent to bring about a peace with Philip of Savoy. *Shirburn* R 1. 589. O. ii 164 H 1 p ii 190
Feb 22	The K purposes [to the K. of Castile?] to meet him after Easter on the borders of Gascony and Spain *Windsor* R 1 589 O. ii 164 H. 1 p ii 190
Feb 22	[The K] sends messengers [to the K. of Castile], and hopes to meet him about June 24. R 1 590 O ii 165 H 1 p ii 190
[March 16]	Settlement of matters in dispute between the K and the communalty of Abbeville. R. 1 590 O ii 165 H. 1 p ii 190
March 25	Pope Martin [IV] announces his promotion to the K *Orvieto.* R 1. 590 .O ii 166. H 1 p ii 191
March 27	The K begs the K of France not to change the customs of Gascony without his consent. *Clarendon* R 1 591. O ii 167 H 1 p ii 191
May 1	The nobles of Gascony entreat the K not to subject the supreme jurisdiction of their lands to any person of mean condition, for they will not bear it R 1 591. O. ii 168. H 1 p ii. 192.

DATE	SUBJECT.
1281. May 5	The K accepts the attornies appointed to plead in his courts by Alexander K. of Scotland *Kenynton* R 1 591. O. 11 168. III p 11. 192.
May 5	The K.'s bailiffs and others are ordered to aid Peter Corbet in destroying all wolves within certain shires here named *Westm* R 1 591 O 11 168 H 1 p 11 192
May 5	The K appoints Hagin son of Deulacres to be high priest of the Jews for life *Westm.* R 1 591 O. 11. 169 H 1 p 11 192.
June 3.	The K adjudicates in the dispute between the commonalty of Bayoune and their bishop *Domme In the K's palace* R 1 591 O 11 169 H 1 p 11 192
June 5	Letter of Dom mo bp of Bayonne by which he approves of the above arbitration *London* R 1 592 O 11 170. II. 1 p 11 192
June 5.	Letter of the proctors of the mayor of Bayonne by which they approve of the above arbitration. *London* R 1 592 O 11 170 H 1 p 11 192
June 6	The mayor of Abbeville accepts and confirms the treaty made with the K of England *Abbeville* R 1 592 O 11 171 H 1 p 11 193
June 6.	The K informs Lewelin prince of Wales that the laws hitherto observed in Wales and the marches are still to be used *Westm* R 1. 593 O 11 172 H 1 p 11 193
June 8	Jordan de Podyo notifies that he has done homage to the K for lands in the diocese of Bazas. *Westm.* R 1 593 O 11 172 H 1 p 11 193
June 19.	Instructions from the K to John de Vescy and Anthony Bek how to proceed in the settlement of the marriage between his daughter and the son of the K of Aragon *Chester* R 1 593 O 11 173 H 1 p 11 193
June 21	The K asks the K of France to complete the terms required by the peace between his father Louis and He 1 III ' *Chester* R. 1 593. O 11 173 II. 1 p 11 193.
July 1	The K informs the bp of Chichester that the K 's clerks are exempt from residence upon their benefices *Westm* R 1 593
July 3.	The K informs Alfonso [X.] K of Castile that he will be in Gascony in Sept , relative to the truce, when he hopes they will meet *Westm* R 1 594 O 11 174 H 1 p. 11 194
July 3.	The K informs Philip K of France that he is authorized by K Alfonso to extend the truce between France and Spain *Westm* R 1 594 O 11 174 H 1 194
July 3.	Credence for Anthony Bek and L de Tany going to Philip K. of France *Westm.* R 1 594. O 11 174. II. 1. p 11. 194
[July]	Instructions to the messengers sent by the K to the K of France relative to the truce between France and Castile R. 1 594 O 11 175 H 1 p 11 195
July 5.	The K to the seneschal of Aquitain , that the Q of England is not to receive from Agen a smaller sum of money than the wives of previous lords. *Westm* R. 1 594. O. 11 175 II 1. p 11 194
July 5.	Proposals made by Florence count of Holland on the projected marriage of his daughter Margaret with Alfonso, son of K Edward *Westm* R 1 594 O 11 175 H 1 p 11 194
July 25	Marriage contract between Eric K of Norway and Margaret daughter of Alex. K of Scotland *Berwick* R. 1. 575 O 11 1079 II. 1 p 1v 63
Aug. 10.	Commission to end disputes between the K 's subjects and those of Florence count of Holland *Ospring* R 1 596 O 11. 177 H 1 p 11 195
Aug 21.	Pope Martin [IV] asks the K to pay the annual tribute for England to Rome, now in arrear for three years *Orvieto* R 1 597 O 11 177 H 1 p 11 195
Sept 10.	The K requests the loan (on his security) of 40l from two merchants of Lucca for Robert de Brus, earl of Carrick *Windsor* R 1 597 O 11 171. H 1 p 11 195
Sept 20	Pope Martin [IV] urges the K to grant liberty to Almaric de Montfort, whom he holds in prison *Orvieto* R. 1 597. O. 11 178 H 1 p 11 195.
Sept. 29	The K enjoins the clergy, about to meet in council at Lambeth, to attempt nothing prejudicial of his crown *Lyndhaist* R. 1 598.
Oct. 1.	Francis Accursius of Bologna notifies that he has taken an oath of fealty to the K for an annuity of 40 marks. *Lyndhurst.* R. 1. 598. O 11 180 H 1 p 11 196
Oct. 4.	The K. orders the seneschal of Gascony to see that the Jews there be not unjustly oppressed. *Lyndhurst* R 1 598 O 11 180 H 1 p 11 196.
Oct. 4	The K orders the seneschal of Gascony to see that the Jews there be not made to pay oppressive talliages *Lyndhurst* R 1 598 O. 11. 180 H 1 p 11 196
Oct. 10.	The K. to the Q [dowager] of France , has much pleasure in permitting John de Greilly to prolong his stay with her *Winchester* R 1 599 O 11 181 H 1 p 11 196.

DATE	SUBJECT
1281 Nov 13	The K desires the justices itinerant in Lincoln and Devon to pay to the House of the Converts in London all deodands received by them *Westm* R 1 599
Nov 26	The K informs the Q [dowager] of France that he is about to send troops to Lyons to help her in the matter of Provence *Westm* R 1 599 O ii 191 H 1 p ii 196
Dec 1	The K issues regulations to be observed by all Jews and Jewesses throughout England. *Westm* R 1 590
[Dec]	The K advises Charles K of Sicily to settle amicably his disputes about Provence with Margaret Q of France R 1 599 O ii 181 H 1 p ii 196
[Dec]	The K asks the pope [Martin IV] to interfere for the amicable settlement of the above-mentioned disputes R 1 600 O ii 182. H 1 p ii. 197
[Dec]	The K informs Charles prince of Salerno of what he has done to promote an amicable settlement of the above-mentioned disputes R 1 600 O ii 183 H 1 p. ii 197
Dec 20	The K informs the K of France that he will not intermeddle in the dispute between him and the K of Castile "*Swell*" R 1 600 O ii 183 H 1 p ii 197
[Dec 20]	The K's message to the K of France having been misreported by the messengers of the latter, the K now sends his own messengers with a correct statement R 1 600 O ii 184 H 1 p ii 197
Dec 27	The K directs the seneschal of Aquitaine as to the steps which are to be taken in regard to a certain duel which was to have been fought in Aquitain *Kemsey*. R 1 600 O ii 184 H 1 p ii 197
1282 Jan 28	Pope Martin [IV] informs the K that he has written to Charles prince of Salerno, and to Philip K of France and Q Margaret, counselling peace *Orvieto* R 1 601. O ii 184 H ii 197
Feb 4	The K to the K of France in favour of the suit of the community of Lectour *Cirencester*. R 1 601 O ii 185 H 1 p ii 198
Feb 7.	The abp of Canterbury entreats the K for the liberation of Almaric de Montfort *Mortlake* R 1 601. O ii 185 H 1. p ii. 198
Feb 9	Pope Martin [IV] to the abbot of Westminster in favour of John prior of Lewes *Orvieto* R 1 602 O ii 187 H 1 p ii 198
Feb 10	Commission to John de Vescy and A Bek to contract a marriage between the K's eldest daughter and the eldest son of P King of Arragon *Cirencester* R 1 602 O ii. 187. H 1 p ii 198
[Feb 14]	The bp of London informs the abp of Canterbury of the K's decision as to the liberation of Almaric de Montfort *Peyreford* R 1 602 O ii 188 H 1 p ii 199
[Feb 19]	John de Greilh informs the K of the debates which have arisen in the court of France on the formula used by the K in his charters in Gascony, "Regnante Edwardo, rege Angliæ," which has now been altered *S Germain-en-Laye* R 1 602 O ii 1088 H. 1 p iv. 85
March 28	The K requests the abps of Canterbury, York, and Dublin to excommunicate those who are breaking the peace in Wales. *Devizes* R 1 603 O ii 188 H 1 p ii 199
April 2	The bp of Bath and Wells informs the abp of Canterbury that he may, by the K's leave, bring Almaric de Montfort with him to London *Peulesholte* R 1 603 O. ii 189 H 1 p. ii 199
April 6	Writs of military summons, 158 nobles and others to be at Worcester, on Whitsunday, for an expedition against the Welsh *Devizes* R 1 603. O ii 189. H 1 p ii 199
[April]	The barons of the Exchequer to the K, relative to the fees of the constable of England R 1 604 O ii. 191 H 1 p ii 200 *See* [Sept 7] 1282
[April]	The abbot of S Edmund's informs the K that while the Welsh war lasts certain masses &c shall be said for him and the royal family R 1 604 O ii 191 H 1. p ii 200.
April 13	The K orders that 4,000 quarrels be made for the Welsh expedition *Devizes* R 1 604.
April 21.	Notarial process upon the liberation of Almaric de Montfort *New Temple, London* R 1 605 O ii 192. H 1 p ii. 200
April 23	The abp of Canterbury and his suffragans inform pope Martin [IV] of the liberation of Almaric de Montfort *London* R. 1 605 O ii 193 H 1 p ii 201
April 27	Bull of pope Martin [IV] to the prior of Crucerois [? Royston], to impose the payment of the tithes of the parishes of Lesenes and Bixele *Orvieto* R. 1 606 O ii 194 H. i p ii 201
April 30	Alfonso infant of Aragon to the K., is glad to receive his letter and to hear of his health *Value* R 1 606. O ii 195 H. 1 p. ii 201.

DATE.	SUBJECT
1282 April 30.	The K notifies that he has appointed Edmund earl of Cornwall to be conservator of the peace in certain counties in England *Gloucester* R 1 606 O 11 195 H 1 p 11 201
May 1	P King of Aragon informs the K. that the commissioners sent to treat of a marriage are returning to England for more definite instructions *Valuc* R 1 606 O ii 196 H 1 p. 11. 202
[May]	The K informs the K of Castile that in consequence of the insurrection of the Welsh he cannot render any help against the Saracens. R 1 606 O 11 196 H 1 p 11 202.
[May]	The K informs the K of France that in consequence of the outbreaks in Wales and Ireland he cannot help him in his war against the K of Spain, with whom he advises him to make peace R 1 607 O. 11 197. H 1 p 11 202.
May 6	Statement of the pledge given by Almaric de Montfort, at Arras, that he will not return to England *Arras* R 1 607 O 11 197 H 1 p 11 202
[May]	Notification that the K has restored the jewels removed from the shrine of S. Edward at Westminster R 1 607. O. ii 198 H. 1 p 11 202
May 20.	Military summons for the clergy to send their service to meet at Rhyddlan against the Welsh *Worcester* R 1. 607 O 11 198 H 1 p 11 202
May 24	Military summons for the barons to meet at Rhyddlan to serve against the Welsh *Hartlebury* R 1 608 O 11 199. H 1 p 11 203
May 24	The K forbids the exportation out of the realm of the money collected from the clergy for the H Land *Hartlebury* R 1 608 O 11 201 H 1 p 11 203
May 26	Ferrand, son of the late K of Aragon, informs the K that 5 cities of Sicily have lately revolted, and massacred the French *Paris* R 1 609 O 11 201. H 1 p 11 204
May 27.	Pope Martin [IV] permits the convent of the H Trinity of London to celebrate divine service during times of interdict *Orvieto* R 1 609 O 11. 203 H 1 p 11 204
June 3	Pope Martin [IV] orders the laity to pay their rents, &c to the convent of the H. Trinity, London. *Orvieto* R 1 609 O 11 203 H 1 p 11 204
June 4.	Pope Martin [IV] orders certain parishioners of London to pay their rents, &c to the convent of the H Trinity, London *Orvieto* R 1 609 O 11 203 H 1 p 11 204
June 8	The K gives power to the K of France to settle all disputes in his courts between the men of Aquitain and the bp of Bazas *Chester* R. 1 609 O 11 203 H 1 p 11 204
June 10	The K sends to pope [Martin IV] messengers with a reply to his letters about assuming the cross. *Chester* R 1 610 O 11 203 H. 1, p 11 204
June 25	Pope Martin [IV.] informs the K of the election and confirmation of John bp of Winchester *Orvieto* R. 1 610 O 11 204 H 1 p 11. 205
July 1	Alexander K of Scotland begs the K to excuse the absence of Alexander Comyn earl of Buchan *Scone* R 1 610 O 11 205 H 1 p 11 205
[July 1]	Alexander Comyn earl of Buchan begs the K. to excuse his absence from the expedition into Wales. R 1 611 O 11 205 H 1. p. 11 205
[July 3.]	Gaston de Bearn informs the K of the injuries committed by the bailiffs of John de Greilli in Gascony. R 1 611 O 11 206 H 1 p 11 205
July 3	Alex prince of Scotland asks the K to obtain longer leave of absence for Adam de Kercadbricht, the physician of the writer *Scone*. R 1 611 O 11 206 H. 1 p 11. 206.
July 8	Eleanor Q (dowager) of England asks the K to forward and enforce her letters about Provence to the K of France *Waltham*. R 1 611 O 11 207 H 1 p 11 206
July 15	The K orders pioneers to be provided for clearing away the timber in Wales. *Rhuadlan* R 1 611 O 11 207 H. 1 p 11 206
July 15	Certain citizens of Bordeaux inform the K that, wishing to come into England to serve him, their journey through France was forbidden by the K. of France. *Bordeaux* R. 1 612 O 11 208 H 1. p. 11. 206
[July ?]	P King of Arragon to the K , has been solicited to accept the crown of Sicily, to which he will assent. *Altoyll.* R 1 612 O. 11 208 H 1 p 11 206
July 21	The K replies in detail to certain questions respecting the affairs of Gascony on which he has been consulted *Rhuddlan*. R. 1 612. O 11 1078. H 1 p 1v 85
[Aug]	Guy count of Flanders asks for a safe conduct for his daughter to pass through England to marry Alexander prince of Scotland R. 1 613 O 11 209 H 1 p. 11 207
Aug 11.	Safe conduct for the daughter of Guy count of Flanders *Rhuddlan* R 1. 613 O 11 209 H 1 p. 11 207.

DATE	SUBJECT
1282. Aug 15	Letters of procuration by Peter K of Arragon for the marriage of his son Alfonso with Eleanor K Edward's daughter *Osca* R. 1, 613. O 11 210 H 1 p 11 207
Aug 15	Letters of procuration by K Edw for the same marriage *Osca.* R 1 614 O 11 213 H 1 p. 11. 208
Aug 15.	Contract of marriage between Alfonso and Eleanor, by her proxy John de Vescy *Osca* R 1 615 O 11. 211 H 1 p 11 209
Aug 17	Rudolf K of the Romans informs the K of the death of his son Hartman, and recommends Grimoard de Altis Vineis *Aure Sanegye* R 1 615 O 11 215 H 1 p 11 209
Sept. 8	The K wishes to be informed by the barons of the Exchequer as to the fees of the constable of England *Rhuddlan* R 1 615
[Sept.]	The barons of the Exchequer inform the K as to the fees of the constable of England R 1 604. O 11 191 H 1. p 11. 200.
Sept 29	Memorandum, as to certain papal bulls and muniments and writings touching England, Norway, Flanders, &c , seen in the treasury at Edinburgh R 1 615 O 11 215 H 1 p 11 209
Oct 2	Commission to Tho de Clare to borrow money from the clergy and others of Ireland for the K's use in the Welsh war *Thlangernon* R 1 617 O 11 220 H 1 p 11 211.
Oct 8	Eleanor Q dowager of England requests the K to permit Nicholas de Stapleton to act as attorney of John duke of Brittany *Leiergetsele* R 1. 617 O 11. 221 H 1. p 11 211
[Oct]	Peter prior general of the Carmelites asks the K to intercede with the pope in favour of the order R. 1 618. O. 11 221. H 1 p. 11 211.
Oct 16	The K orders letters to be written to several of the cardinals in favour of the order of the Carmelites *Rhuddlan* R 1. 618 O 11 222 H 1 p 11 212
Oct 28.	Rudolf K of the Romans to the K in favour of Henry de Hameisten. *Maints.* R 1. 618 O 11 222 H 1 p 1 212
[Oct.]	Florence count of Holand informs the K that he has defeated the Frisians in four battles R 1 618 O. 11 223 H 1 p 11. 212
[Nov]	The K desires the barons of the Exchequer to dismiss all pleas which do not refer to himself or his exchequer officers R 1 618
Nov 12	Writ of military summons to Oliver de Dyneham and 38 others to serve the K. at his pay in the Welsh war. *Rhuddlan* R.1 619 O 11 223 H. 1 p 11 212
[Dec 17]	The abp of Cant informs the K of the death of Lewelin prince of Wales, and of a letter (in obscure words and fictitious names) found on him by Edward Mortimer at his death *Pembridge* R 1 619 O 11 224 H 1 p 11 212
[Dec]	The abp of Cant informs the bp of Bath and Wells of the contents of the letter found on the body of Lewellin by Edmund Mortimer, and on other matters connected with the Welsh outbreak R 1 619 O 11 224 H 1. p 11 212
Dec 22	The K authorizes Gaston de Bearn to employ 100 horsemen at the K's expense in aid of the K of Castile *Rhuddlan.* R 1 620 O 11 1085 H 1 p 1v 85
[Dec]	Piero K of Aragon and Sicily orders Charles K of Jerusalem to depart from Sicily R 1 620 O 11 225 H 1 p 11 213
[Dec]	Charles K of Jerusalem and Sicily to Piero K of Aragon, refusing to leave Sicily R 1 620 O. 11. 225 H 1 p 11 213.
Dec. 26.	The K informs Alfonso K of Castile of the assistance to be provided by Gaston de Bearn *Rhuddlan* R. 1 621. O 11. 1086 H. 1 p 1v 86
[Dec]	The K sends his uncle, Wm de Valence, to the K of Castile, to explain the meaning of the interview with the K of France at Am ens R 1 620 O 11 1086 H 1 p 1v 86
Dec 30.	Conditions (on the part of the K of Aragon) of the duel to be fought between the Ks of Aragon and Sicily at Bordeaux in the K Edward's presence *Messina* R. 1 621 O 11. 226 H 1 p 11 213
Dec 30.	Counterpart (on the part of the K of Sicily) of the conditions of the said duel. *Reggio* R 1 622. O 11. 230 H 1 p 11 215
1283. Jan 5	Bull of pope Martin [IV] in favour of the prioress and convent of Wilkes, dioc London *Orvieto* R 1 624 O 11 234. H 1 p 11. 216.
Jan 8	Pope Martin [IV] regrets that the K will not proceed in person to the Holy Land, and will not accept his brother Edmund as his substitute *Orvieto* R 1. 624 O 11. 235 H 1 p 11 216

DATE	SUBJECT
1283 Jan 12	The K informs Constance Q. of Aragon that he cannot go to war with France on her account, but that he will write to the pope on her behalf. *Rhuddlan.* R. 1 625. O. ii. 1087 H 1. p iv. 86
[Jan. 14 ?]	The K authorizes the levying of a subsidy from the clergy north of the Trent for the Welsh war *Rhuddlan.* R. 1 625. O ii 237. H 1 p ii 217
[Jan 18]	Receipt, by Gaston de Bearn, for money sent by the K. to pay the troops for the service of the K of Castile *Pampeluna* R 1 625 O. ii 236 H 1 p. ii. 217
[Jan. 25.]	Voucher, by Gaston de Bearn, for the payment by the K. of the value of certain horses killed in his service *Pampeluna* R 1 625 O ii 237 H 1 p ii 217, and R 1 638 O ii 265 H 1 p ii 228
[Jan. 25]	Receipt, by Gaston de Bearn, for 2,270l. Tournois for the pay of 41 knights. *Pampeluna* R. 1. 638 O ii 265. H. 1. p ii 228.
Feb. 1.	Commission to order and dispose of the services granted by the meeting at York for the benefit of the K *Rhuddlan* R 1 625 O ii 237 H 1 p ii 217
Feb 1	Pope Martin [IV] recommends the order of the Clumacs to the K. *Orvieto* R. 1. 626 O ii 238 H 1 p ii 217
Feb 12.	The K. grants to John de Brittania the liberty of the honor of Richmond at 20l a year *Rhuddlan* R 1 626 O ii 238 H. 1 p ii 218.
Feb. 13	Bull of pope Martin [IV] in favour of the prioress and convent of Wikes, dioc. London. *Viterbo* R 1 626 O ii 238 H 1 p ii 218
[March.]	The K to Charles of Anjou K of Sicily , has received his letters relative to the duel, and will answer them speedily R 1 626 O ii 239 H 1 p ii 218
March 25	The K to Charles of Anjou K of Sicily, refuses to be present at the duel at Bordeaux. on 1 June *Aberconway* R 1 626. O ii 239. H 1 p ii 218
March 25	The K informs Charles prince of Salerno that he has refused to be present at the duel at Bordeaux *Aberconway* R. 1 627. O ii 240 H 1 p ii 218.
March 26	The K to Peter, son of the K of France , thanks him for his letters, and is in good health *Aberconway* R 1 627 O. ii 241 H 1 p ii 219
April 4	The K. to the K of Aragon Credentials for the bearers, with list of letters sent by them *Aberconway* R 1 627 O ii 241 H 1 p ii 219
April 4	The K thanks the men of Bordeaux and other towns in Gascony for their subsidy against the Welsh *Aberconway.* R 1 627. O ii. 241. H i. p. ii. 219
April 4.	Letters of credence for messengers sent to John de Grailey, seneschal of Gascony, and others, in Gascony *Aberconway* R 1 627 O ii 242 H 1 p ii. 219
April 5	Additional letters of credence for the same messengers *Aberconway* R 1 628 O ii 240 H 1 p ii 218.
April 9.	Pope Martin [IV] asks the K not to sanction the duel between the Ks of Sicily and Aragon, but to discourage it to the utmost of his power *Orvieto* R 1 628 O ii 242 O 1 p ii 219
May.	The K sanctions the treaty of marriage of his daughter Joanna with Gilbert de Clare earl of Gloucester *Dohnthelen in Snowdon.* R 1 628 O ii 244 H 1 p. ii. 220.
May 1.	Pope Martin [IV] asks the K to favour Tho de Fyndon, whom he has appointed abbot of S Augustine's, Canterbury, in the stead of Nicholas *Orvieto* R 1 629. O. ii. 245 H 1 p ii 220
[May]	The K. to Cardinal . . recommending that the see of S Asaph he translated to *Rhuddlan* R. 1. 629. O ii. 245. H. 1. p ii 220.
June 6	Gaston de Bearn notifies that he accepts the terms proposed to him by the K. as to engaging troops for the K. of Castile *Bordeaux* R 1 629 O ii 246 H 1 p ii 220
June 25.	The K grants to Avian, son of Ynor, and others, exemption from certain military services, they having brought to him a portion of the true cross. *Rhuddlan.* R 1 630 O. ii 247. H 1. p ii 221.
June 28	Summons to Gilbert de Clare and 109 others to meet the K at Shrewsbury on 30 Sept to confer on the affairs of Wales *Rhuddlan* R 1 630. O ii 247 H 1 p ii 220.
June 28.	Writ to various mayors and sheriffs to elect citizens and burgesses to meet the K in conference at Shrewsbury on 30 Sept. *Rhyddlan.* R 1 630 O. ii. 249 H 1 p ii 222
July 5.	Pope Martin [IV.] requires the K. to restore the money collected for the Holy Land, of which he has obtained possession by violence. *Orvieto.* R. 1. 631 O ii. 250. H 1. p. ii. 222.

G

DATE	SUBJECT
1283 [July 20]	Prince Edmund to his brother the K on the affairs of Bordeaux and Provence, of Raulin de Kemiller, John de Vaus, and Otes de Granzon *Paris* R 1 631. O. ii. 1087 H 1 p iv 86
Aug 9	Pope Martin [IV] asks the K. to endeavour to settle the quarrels between Alfonso K. of Castile and his children *Orvieto* R 1 631 O ii 251. H. 1. p ii 222
Aug 27	Bull of pope Martin [IV], by which he excommunicates Peter K. of Aragon, and gives the kingdom of Sicily to Charles, son of Philip K. of France *Orvieto* R. 1 632 O ii 252 H 1. p ii 223
Sept 2	Writ for the payment of his annual fee of 60 marks to Matthew, cardinal of S Maria in Porticu. *Brumburgh* R 1 634 O ii 257 H 1 p ii. 225
Oct. 3	Receipt by Gaston de Bearn for the money sent by the K. for the service of the K. of Castile *Bazas* R. 1. 634. O ii 257. H 1 p ii 225
Oct 13	The K orders the removal of all Jews from the town of Windsor. *Acton Burnell* R 1 634
Oct. 20	The K restores to Res, son of Mereduc, his lands in Mechlaen Kayo, Meb Weneo, and Gwenonuch, which he had placed in the K's hands *Acton Burnell* R 1 634 O ii 258. H 1, p, ii, 225.
Oct 20	The K to cardinal O Protests against the election by the pope of Nicholas Mayglyn to the see of Tuam, and requests that another be chosen *Acton Burnell.* R 1. 635
Dec 1	Rudulf K of the Romans recommends to the K. the brothers De Raperch coming into England "*Hageri*" R 1 635 O ii 259 H 1 p ii 325
Dec	Letter of the bp of S David's relative to the marriage of Res, son of Mereduc. R 1 635. O ii 259 H 1 p ii 225 *See* June 26, 1284
Dec 28.	Charter of liberties and privileges granted by the K to the new fortress of Valentia, in the dioc of Agen *Chester* H 1 635 O. ii 260 H 1 p ii 226
1284 Jan 10	Pope Martin [IV] authorizes the cardinal of S Cecilia to proceed in the business of the settlement of the kingdom of Aragon on the son of the K. of France. *Orvieto* R 1. 637. O ii 263 H. 1 p ii 227.
Jan 10	Pope Martin [IV] explains a passage in one of his letters] respecting the above settlement *Orvieto* R 1 637 O ii 263 H 1 p ii 227
Jan 10	Pope Martin [IV] explains another passage relative to the above settlement *Orvieto.* R. 1. 637. O, ii 264 H 1 p ii 227
Jan 12	The K to the abbot of S Denis in France, asks him to endeavour to settle the disputes between the Ks of France, Sicily, and Aragon *York* R 1 637 O ii 264 H 1. p ii 227
[Jan 25]	Voucher, by Gaston de Bearn, for the payment for horses. R 1 638. O. ii. 265 H. 1 p ii 228 *See* [Jan. 25,] 1283
[Jan 25]	Voucher by Gaston de Bearn for the payment of knights R 1 638. O. ii 265 H 1 p ii. 228. *See* [Jan 25,] 1283
Feb 5	The nobles of Scotland bind themselves to receive as heiress to the throne Margaret, daughter of Eric K of Norway, and Margaret, daughter of Alexander K. of Scotland *Scone.* R. 1 638 O ii 266 H 1 p ii 228
Feb 13.	Pope Martin [IV] asks for the payment of the annual tribute of 1,000 marks, now in arrear for two years *Orvieto.* R 1 638 O ii 267 H 1 p ii 228
Feb 13	Pope Martin [IV] authorizes master Giffard to give a receipt on the payment of the above annual tribute *Orvieto* R 1 639 O. ii 267 H 1 p ii 228
March 1	Bull of pope Martin [IV], by which he deprives Peter of the realm of Aragon, and transfers it to Charles son of the K of France R 1 639 O ii. 267 H 1 p ii. 229
March 23	Alfonso K of Castile informs the pope of his reconciliation with his son Sancho *Seville.* R 1 640 O ii 271 H 1 p ii 230
April 26	Eric K of Norway asks the K to renew the treaty made between K Hen [III.] and Magnus [IV] of Norway *Bergen* R 1 640 O ii, 272 H. 1. p. ii. 230
[April 27]	Letter of credence from Philip count of Savoy, in favour of Gregory, the bearer of the letter R 1 641. O. ii 1089 H 1. p ii 87 *See* June 16, 1284
May 26	Pope Martin [IV] absolves the K from all crimes committed by him in the wars with Simon de Montfort and more recently against the Welsh *Orvieto* R 1. 641. O. ii. 272. H 1 p ii 230.
May 26.	Pope Martin [IV.] congratulates the K. on his determination to go to the Holy Land. *Orvieto.* R. 1 641. O. ii 273 H. 1. p. ii. 231.

DATE	SUBJECT.
1284. May 26	Pope Martin [IV] replies in detail to the petitions of the K respecting the tenths collected for the Holy Land *Orvieto* R 1 642 O n 274 H 1 p n 231
June 15	Ordinance by the K's council relative to the restoration of the temporalities taken from the Welsh churches during the late war *Baladeuchn* R 1 642 O. n 273. H 1 p n 232.
[June 16.]	Philip count of Savoy to the K in favour of the bearer Gregory. *Mont Mel* R 1 641. O n 1089. H. 1 p iv. 87
June 20	The K mediates in the disputes between the duke of Brabant and the count of Guelders. *Baladeuchlyn* R. 1. 643. O n 276 H 1 p iv 232
June 25	The abp of Canterbury expresses to the K his opinion as to the best mode of making compensation for injuries done to church property during the war in Wales *Bangor*. R 1. 643 O n 279. H. 1 p n 232
June 25	The abp of Canterbury appoints commissioners to enquire as to the injuries mentioned above, and to report thereon to the K *Bangor* R 1. 644. O n. 279 H 1 p n 233
[June 26]	Thomas bp of S. David's notifies that he has received letters from the pope on the marriage of Res, son of Mereduc, and Auda de Hastings *Landegoue*. R. 1 635 O n 259. H 1 p n 225
June 29	Constance de Bearn submits herself to the K for all acts of disobedience done in Gascony *Carnarvon* R 1. 644 O n. 279 H 1 p n 233
July.	Certain merchants of Lucca send 3,000*l.* to the K for his army, and will send more on a written order R 1. 644 O n 279 H 1. p n 233
July 7.	Writ to pay 2,000*l* to the pope for the tribute for two years *Carnarvon* R 1. 644. O n 280 H 1 p n 233
July 12.	Alex [III] K. of Scotland begs the K to excuse the personal attendance of Alex. de Balliol of Cavers *Kinross*. R 1 644 O. n 280 H. 1 p n. 233
July 19	The proctors of K Eric of Norway promise to observe the conditions of the treaty with K Edward *Carnarvon* R 1 645 O n 281 H. 1. p n 234.
July 20	Treaty between the Ks. of England and Norway *Carnarvon*. R. 1. 645, O. n. 281. H 1 p. n. 234
[Aug 9]	Treaty of peace between Florence count of Holland and Reginald count of Guilders made in the presence of the English envoys R 1 645 O n 281 H 1. p n 234
Aug 12.	Recognizance of Florence count of Holland as to the terms of the marriage between his daughter Margaret and the K.'s son Alfonsus *Hague* R. 1. 645 O n 283 H 1 p n 234
[Aug]	Guy count of Flanders thanks the K for his courteous reply relative to the affair which the count has against his nephew of Hainault R. 1. 646 O n 284 H 1. p n. 235
[Aug]	Florence count of Holland asks the K to restore to him silver to the value of 960*l* st which had been seized on its way to the coast to be shipped for being coined in Holland. R 1 646 O n 284. H. 1. p n 235
[Aug]	The K. quit claims S bp of Cadiz of 5,000 marks returned by him to the K. R 1 646 O ii 285 H 1 p n 235
[Aug]	The K orders the mayor of Rochelle to arrest the 6,000 marks mentioned in the previous document R. 1. 647 O n 285 H 1 p 11 235
[Sept 10]	Gaston de Bearn vindicates himself from the charges brought against him and his daughter Constance by the seneschal of Gascony *Paris* R 1. 647 O n 285 H 1 p. 11 235.
Sept 14.	Recital of the terms upon which the K constituted Reginald de Grey justiciary of Chester R 1 647
Sept 22	Pope Martin [IV] asks the K to preserve to the hospital of the Holy Ghost at Rome the church of Wyntel, given to it by K John "*Castrum plebis*." R 1. 648 O n 287 H 1. p n 236
[Oct.]	Receipt by Anian bp of Bangor for 250*l* given by the K in compensation for injuries done to church property in the late war in Wales R. 1 648 O n 287 H 1 p n 236.
Oct. 4.	The K. asks Peter de Petrisgrossis, vice-chancellor of Rome, to continue to act for him in the court of Rome "*Hopa*," in *Wales* R 1 648 O n 287 H 1 p n 236.
Oct. 5.	The K. asks M cardinal of S Maria in Portico to inform him of the reports current in the court of Rome. "*Mons Altus*" R 1 648 O. n. 288 H 1 p ii 236

DATE	SUBJECT
1284. Oct 5	The K ratifies the appointment of Percival de Lovania as his clerk "*Mont Alt*," in *Wales*. R 1 648 O. ii 288 H 1 p. ii 236
Oct 10	Inspeximus by the Infant John of Castile of the letter of reconciliation of K. Alfonso with his son Sancho *Samore* R 1. 649. O ii 289 H 1 p ii 237
Oct 22	Writ for the payment of 60 marks, the annual pension to Matthew cardinal of S Maria in Portieu *Carnarvon* R 1 649 O ii 289 H 1 p ii 237
Oct 22	Writ for the payment of 40 marks, the annual pension to James cardinal of S Maria in Cosmedin. *Carnarvon* R 1 649 O ii 289 H 1 p ii 237
Oct 22	Writ for the payment of 20 marks, the annual pension to master Angelo, the pope's notary *Carnarvon* R 1 649 O ii. 290 H 1 p ii 237
[Oct. 23]	Philip count of Savoy authorizes the K and his mother to nominate the said count's successor in Savoy *Rousillon.* R 1 649 O 11 290 H 1 p ii 237
[Nov 2]	Receipt by the dean and chapter of S Asaph for 100*l* given by the K. in compensation for injuries done to their churches in the Welsh War *Chester* R 1 650 O ii 291 H 1 p ii, 238.
Nov 3	Receipt for 78*l* given by the K in compensation for injuries done to the house of Strata Florida during the war in Wales *Chester* R 1 650 O ii 292. H 1 p ii 238
[Nov.]	Receipt by A abbot of Strata Florida for the above-mentioned sum of 78*l* R 1 650 O ii 292 H 1 p ii 238
[Nov 5]	Receipt for 17*l* paid to the Friars Preachers of Rhuddlan by the K for their losses in the Welsh wars *Chester* R 1 650 O ii 292 H 1. p ii 238
[Nov]	Margaret abbess of Fontevrault asks Q. Eleanor to make a gift to the nunnery on the occasion of her daughter becoming a nun R 1 651
Dec 28	The K asks H. cardinal of S Laurence in Lucina to cause the sentence obtained by Almaric de Montfort against Edmund earl of Lancaster to be remitted to the English court. *Bristol* R 1 651 O ii 293 H 1 p ii 238
1285 Jan 1	Exemplification (the seal being suspiciously affixed) of a charter of Henry III. to Edmund earl of Cornwall, of the honor of Walingford and manor of Watlinton *Bristol* R 1 651
Jan. 2.	Charter of exemption from toll throughout the whole of the realm for the burgesses of Rhuddlan, Aberconway, and Carnarvon. *Bristol* R. 1. 651. O ii. 293 H 1 p ii. 238
[March 10]	Pope Honorius [IV] authorizes a licence of marriage between John Giffard Lord of Clifford and Margaret de Neville *S Sabina, Rome* R 1 663. O ii. 315. H. 1 p iii. 6.
March 27	Safe conduct from Philip K of France for the K, on going through France. *Dax.* R 1 652. O ii 294 H 1 p ii 238
April 10	Commission by Florence count of Holland to settle the acts of the marriage between his son and the K of England's daughter R 1 652 O ii 294 H 1 p ii 239
April 10	Commission by Florence count of Holland to settle (by the decision of the K) his dispute with Reginald count of Guelders. R 1. 652 O ii 294. H 1 p ii 239
April 21	Bull of Honorius [IV] (elected pope, but not consecrated,) to the K in answer to his inquiries as to the tenths granted for the Holy Land. *Perugia* R 1. 652. O ii. 295. H. 1. p. ii 239
April 21	Honorius [IV], elected to be pope, grants to the K's envoys licence to visit Charles, son of Charles late K of Sicily, now a prisoner *Perugia* R 1. 653. O. ii 296 H 1. p. ii 239
April 26.	Honorius [IV] informs the K of his election to the papacy *Perugia.* R 1 653 O ii 297. H. 1 p ii. 240
May 5	Honorius [IV], in answer as to the K's letters about the affairs of Aragon, refers him to the report of Otho de Grandison *Sancta Subina* R. 1 652. O. ii. 208. H 1. p. ii 240
May 6	The K announces that the standard for the obligation to be knighted is raised from the holding of 20 librates of land to 100 librates of land *Westm* R. 1 653.
May 10.	Eric K of Norway asks the K. to see that the Germans [Teutonici] do not plunder the Norse merchants while within K Edw's jurisdiction *Bergen* R 1. 654 O. ii 1088 H 1 p iv 87
May 10	The K grants licence to Avian bp of Bangor to make his will *Westm.* R 1. 654
May 15.	Regulations by the K and his council as to the compulsory unloading of ships in the Cinque Ports in time of danger *Westm.* R. 1. 654. O ii. 298. H. 1. p ii, 240

DATE	SUBJECT
1285 May 16	Agreement as to the lands assigned by Gilbert de Clare earl of Gloucester to Alice de March on his being divorced from her *London* R 1 654 O ii 299 H. 1 p ii 240
May 18.	Writ for the payment out of the issues of the port of Dover to Stephen de Penecestre, of his salary as constable of Dover Castle *Westm* R. 1 655.
May 30.	Pope Honorius [IV] recommends to the K John de Sanford as abp of Dublin, who has been confirmed at Rome *S Peter's, Rome* R. 1 655 O ii 299 H 1 p ii 241
June 1.	The K confirms and augments the charter of privileges granted by K Hen III to the burgesses of S. Omer's *Westm* R 1. 655 O ii. 301 H. 1 p iii 1.
June 4	The K appoints Aymer de Valence earl of Pembroke to be lieutenant of England during his own absence abroad. *Westm* R 1 656 O ii 301 H i p iii 1
June 4.	The K orders the seneschal of Gascony to restore to Amanenus de Labret certain lands in Gascony *Westm.* R. 1 656. O ii. 302. H. 1. p iii. 1
June 4.	The K orders the seneschal of Gascony to cease from annoying Constance viscountess of Marcian *Westm* R 1 656 O ii 302 H 1 p iii 1.
June 4.	The K again orders the seneschal of Gascony to make amends for injuries done to Gaston de Bearn and his daughter Constance *Westm* R 1 656 O ii. 302. H. 1. p. m. 1.
June 5	Inspeximus by the K of an instrument relative to certain transactions between Gaston de Bearn and his wife Beatrice *Westm* R 1 656 O ii 303 H 1 p iii 1
June 5	Composition between the K and the abbot of S Giosse ou Bois in Ponthieu *Westm.* R. 1. 657. O ii 205 H. 1 p.. iii. 3.
June 6	The K orders the seneschal of Gascony to revoke any injustice done to Gaston de Bearn in the barony of Ganardon *Westm.* R 1 658 O ii 306 H 1 p iii. 3.
June 6	Writ to allow certain sums of money to John de Burne, late warden of the port of Dover, for the customs of the passage at Dover. *Westm.* R 1 659 O ii 309 H 1 p. iii 4
June 11.	Commission to John de Vescy, Thomas de Sodinton, and John de Lovetot to conclude a marriage between [John] son of the count of Holland and the K's daughter *Westm* R. 1 658. O ii 306 H 1 p iii 3
[June]	Contract of marriage between Elizabeth the K.'s daughter and the son of the count of Holland R 1. 658 O ii 307 H 1 p iii. 3
June 18.	Proffer of homage to the K for the comté of Bigorre by Philip, son of the count of Flanders *Westm.* R 1 659 O. ii 309 H 1 p iii 4
June 20.	The K ratifies the composition made by Q. Eleanor with Wm. Amanenus viscount of Fronsac *Westm.* R. 1 659 O ii 309 H. 1 p iii 4
June 22	Writ to the seneschal of Bordeaux to pay 1,812*l* 10*s* (Tourns.) to Wm Amanenus viscount of Fronsac *Westm* R 1 659 O ii 309. II 1. p. iii 4
June 24.	The K summonses six men of Flanders to surrender themselves at Mustroil, according to the treaty between the K. and Guy count of Flanders *Westm* R. 1. 659. O ii 310 II 1 p. iii 4
June 24.	The K appoints proctors to act for him in all suits in the court of France. *Westm.* R 1 660 O.. ii 310 H 1 p iii. 5.
July 11.	Pope Honorius [IV] recommends certain merchants of Florence to the K *Tivoli* R 1 660 O ii 311 H 1 p iii. 5.
July 27	Maria princess of Salerno, daur of the K of Hungary, acknowledges the receipt of 800 ounces of gold as a present from the K. "*Novum Castrum prope Neapolim*" R 1 660 O ii 311. H 1 p. iii. 5.
July 28.	Pope Honorius [IV] extends the period at which the K must take the cross *Tivoli.* R. 1 660 O.. ii 312 H 1 p iii 5.
Aug 5	Pope Honorius [IV] thanks the K for a present of jewels. *Tivoli* R. 1 664. O ii 312. H 1 p iii. 5
Aug. 10.	Philip count of Savoy, being sick, appoints as his executors the K and Q of England. "*Rupec?*" R 1. 660 O ii. 312. H 1 p iii 5
[Sept 14]	The general chapter of the Cistercians complain to the K. of the conduct of the Friars Preachers and minors at Scarborough. *Citeaux* R. 1 661. O ii 313 H 1 p iii 6
Oct. 2	Florence count of Holland swears to observe the conditions of the marriage contract between John his son and Elizabeth the K's daughter R 1 661 O ii. 314. H 1 p iii 6.
[Oct.]	Inspeximus of the charters granted by Hen III to the citizens of Dublin. R. 1 661.

DATE	SUBJECT
1285 Dec 5	Pope Honorius [IV] orders a cause to be heard between the prior of the H Trinity, London, and Robert de Horsele, rector of the church of S Edmund, Gracechurch Street. *S· Sabina, Rome*. R 1 662 O u 314 H 1 p m 6
[Dec]	The K. asks Sancho K. of Castile to be at peace with the K of France, and to promote peace between the Kings of Aragon, France, and Sicily R 1 662 O u 315 H 1. p. m. 6.
1286 March 7	Eric K of Norway complains that the Teutonic pirates injure his trade and threaten to invade his realm *Bergen* R 1 602 O u 1089 H. 1 p iv. 87.
[March 10]	Bull of Pope Honorius [IV.] relative to the marriage of John Giffard. R 1. 663 O u 315. H 1 p m 6 *See* March 10, 1285
March 11	The K. orders that 120 lbs of silver be given to William de Farndon, his goldsmith, to make silver vessels for himself and the Q *Woodstock* R 1 663.
[March 22]	Amadeus de Savoy thanks the K for his kindness in reference to the affairs of Savoy *Belois.* R 1 663 O u 1089 H 1 p iv 87
April 1	Pope Honorius [IV] extends the time within which the K must take the cross *S Sabina, Rome* R 1 663 O u. 316. H l. p m 6
April 1.	Anianus bp of Bangor asks alms for the rebuilding of the priory of the Valley of S Mary, in Snowdon, accidentally destroyed by fire, he has seen certain charters granted to that house by divers princes of Wales *Maesyllan* R 1 664 O u 316 H 1 p m 7
May 2	The sons of Charles prince of Salerno entreat the K to cause their father to be delivered from prison "*Sistanti.*" R. 1. 664 O u 317 H. 1 p m 7
May 2.	Certain prelates and nobles of Provence supplicate the K for the liberation of Charles prince of Salerno "*Sistanti.*" R 1 664 O u 318 H 1 p m 7
May 13.	Proctors appointed by Alfonso K of Aragon to conclude a truce and peace in his name with the K of France *Osta* R 1 664 O u 318 H 1 p m 8
May 13	Alfonso K of Aragon empowers the K of England to make a truce in his name with the K of France *Osta* R 1 665. O u 319 H 1 p m 8
[May 13]	Memorandum : that the K crossed from Dover into France R 1 665
May 27	Pope Honorius [IV] does not mean that the dispensation for the marriage of the K 's children should apply to a union with the family of the late K. of Aragon *S Sabina, Rome*. R. 1 665 O u 320 H. 1. p. m. 8.
[June 5]	Homage of K Edw to the K. of France at Paris R. 1 665. O u 320 H. 1. p m 8.
[June 15]	Charter by which Philip K of France grants certain privileges to K Edward in the lands of Gascony and the parts adjacent. *Paris* R. 1 665. O u. 321 H 1. p. m. 8
June 17	Pope Honorius [IV] replies in detail to the K 's request relative to the affairs of the Holy Land *S Sabina, Rome.* R 1. 666. O u 323 H 1 p m 9.
June 17.	Pope Honorius [IV.] grants the K unprecedented privileges as to the marriages of is children *S. Sabina, Rome* R 1 666 O u 323 H 1. p m 9.
June 22.	The K. to Edmund earl of Cornwall, on the murder of the late K of Denmark, grandfather of the K. of Norway. *Paris* R 1 667 O. n 323. H 1. p. m 9
June 26.	The K lends 2,000 marks to Eric K. of Norway *Paris* R 1. 667. O u 324 H 1 p m 9
June 29.	The K informs the bps. and nobles of Provence that he will endeavour to procure the liberty of the prince of Salerno *Paris* R 1 667. O u 324 H 1 p m 10
July 5.	Receipt by Amadeus count of Savoy for 400 marks paid to him by the K *Paris* R. 1 667 O u 325. H 1. p. m 10
July 12	Pope Honorius [IV.] asks the K to restore the royalties of the bishopric of Meath to Tho de S Leodegario, the bp elect. *Tivoli.* R. 1 667 O u 325 H 1 p m 10
July 15.	Philip K. of France, authorizes K Edw to make a truce for him with Alfonso K of Aragon *Paris.* R. 1 668. O. u. 326. H 1 p. m 10
July 15	The K tells the princes of Salerno that he hopes to obtain the release of their father *Paris* R. 1 668 O u 327. H 1. p m 11.
July 20.	Receipt of Oliver de Monte Spine count of Saresburg for 2,000 marks lent by the K to the K of Norway *London.* R. 1. 668. O u. 327 H 1 p m 11
July 22.	Alfonso K. of Aragon authorizes his proctors to request K Edward to make a truce for him with the K of France. *Paris.* R 1. 669. O. n 328 H 1 p m 11.

DATE	SUBJECT
1286 July 23.	The proctors of the K of Aragon authorize the K to act in behalf of their master. *Paris.* R. 1. 669 O ii 328 H 1 p. iii 11.
[July 25]	Safe conduct by Philip K of France for the K of England coming into France *Paris.* R. 1 669 O ii 329 H 1. p iii 11
July 25	The K. thanks Alfonso K of Aragon for what has been done in the business and interview referred to by Alfonso's proctors *Paris* R 1 669 O ii 329 H 1. p iii 12
July 25.	Truce by the mediation of the K of England between the Kings of France and Aragon *Paris* R. 1. 670. O. ii. 330. H. 1. p. iii 12.
July 25	Counterpart of the above truce on the part of the K of Aragon. *Paris* R 1. 670. O ii 331 H 1 p iii 12.
July 25.	The K. informs the K of Aragon as to the period when the above truce shall come into operation *Paris* R 1 670. O. ii. 332 H. 1. p iii. 13.
[July 26]	Philip K of France tells the K that he has prorogued the truce with the K of Aragon at the request of the pope *Paris* R 1 671 O ii 332. H 1 p. iii 13
[July 27]	The K. of England informs the K of France when the truce shall come into operation. *Paris.* R 1. 671. O ii 333 H. 1. p. iii. 13
July 27.	The K asks pope Honorius [IV] to sanction the above-mentioned truce. *Paris.* R. 1. 671. O. ii. 334. H. 1 p iii 13
July 27.	K. Edward's letters to the cardinals to sanction the above-mentioned truce. *Paris.* R. 1. 672 O. ii. 334. H. 1. p. iii. 13.
[July 29]	Receipt by John duke of Lorraine and Brabant for 50,000*l.* (*Turon'*) given by the K as a marriage gift with his daughter Margaret R. 1 672. O ii 336 H 1 p iii 14
[Aug.]	Revision by the Kings of England and France of the treaties of peace between the two realms *Paris* R. 1 672 O ii 336 H 1 p ii 14.
[Aug.]	Letters of Philip K. of France relative to an exchange of lands between himself and K. Edward *Paris* R 1 673 O ii 338 H 1 p iii 15
Aug. 8	The K asks the clergy of the province of York to pay the contributions which they promised during the late war in Wales. *Semoys* R 1 673 O ii. 338 H 1. p iii. 15.
[Aug. 21]	James K of Majorca to the K., assenting to the truce between the Kings of France and Aragon. "*In Castris de Podio de Faro*" R 1. 673 O ii 339 H 1 p iii 15.
Sept. 29.	Eric K. of Norway accepts the bond given in his name by Oliver de Monte Spine. *Bergesem'.* R 1 673 O. ii 339 H 1 p iii. 15
Oct 3	The K exhorts the sheriffs of England to be more diligent in causing the peace to be kept *Westm* R 1. 674.
Nov 6.	Pope Honorius [IV] sends messengers to the K. to promote peace between the Kings of France and Aragon. *S. Sabina, Rome* R. 1 674. O. ii 340. H 1 p. iii. 15.
1287 March 1	Pope Honorius [IV] sends messengers to the K to assist in promoting peace *S Sabina, Rome* R 1 674 O ii. 340 H 1 p iii 16.
March 1.	Pope Honorius [IV] to the K on the same subject *S. Sabina, Rome.* R. 1. 674. O. ii 341 H. 1. p iii 16.
March 15	Pope Honorius [IV.] to the K. in answer to his propositions as to the expedition to the Holy Land. *Rome, S. Sabina.* R 1 674 O. ii. 341 H 1 p iii. 16
June 14.	Summons to Robert Peche and 117 others to meet at Gloucester with horses and arms to assist Edmund earl of Cornwall, the lieutenant of the realm during the K's absence *Westm* R 1 675 O ii 343 H 1 p iii 17.
July 16.	Writs to provide horse and foot soldiers to proceed against Res son of Mereduc and the rebellious Welsh. *Gloucester* R. 1. 676. O. ii 344 H. 1. p. iii 17
July 23	Writs of military summons to march under the earl of Gloucester against the rebellious Welsh *Hereford* R 1. 676 O ii 345 H 1 p iii. 17.
July 25	Conditions under which Charles prince of Salerno is to be released from prison. *Oleron.* *in Bearn* R 1 677 O ii. 346 H 1. p. iii 18.
July 28.	The K promises to send Alianor his daughter into Aragon when the pope has consented to the proposed marriage between her and K. Alfonso. *Oleron.* R 1 678 O. ii 349. H. 1 p. iii. 19
July 28	Alfonso K of Aragon asks the K. to extend the truce between Aragon and France. *Oleron* R 1 678 O ii 350 H 1. p iii 20.
July 28.	Alfonso K. of Aragon empowers the K to extend the truce with France. *Oleron.* R. 1. 678. O ii 351 H 1. p. iii. 20

DATE	SUBJECT
1287. Aug 1	The K extends the duration of the truce between the Kings of France and Aragon *Oleron.* R 1 679 O ıı 352 H 1 p ııı 20
Aug. 4.	Alfonso K of Aragon informs the K that he accepts the above truce without any limitation *Jacca.* R 1. 679 O ıı 352. H 1 p ııı 20
Sept 12.	The K directs that measures be taken to stop the dissension between the abp of York and the dean and chapter of York *"Aquis"* R. 1 679 O ıı 353 H 1 p iıı 20
Sept 17.	The K promises that the office of marshal of England shall not be prejudiced by the earl of Norfolk serving under the earl of Cornwall ın the Welsh war. *Westm* R. 1 679. O ıı 353 H 1 p ııı 2I
Nov 4	The Roman cardinals (the see being vacant) urge upon the K the liberation of the prince of Salerno *Rome, S Sabına* R 1 679 O. ıı 353 H 1 p ııı 21
Nov. 14.	Writs to Edmund de Mortimer and 26 others to reside on their estates on the marches of Wales during the insurrection of Res son of Mereduc *Westm* R 1 680. O. ii. 354. H 1 p ııı 21
1288. Feb 19	Philip K of France orders his seneschal at Perigord to cease from annoying the English at Libourne *Paris* R 1 680. O ıı 355. H 1 p. ıı 21
Feb 23	Pope Nicholas [IV] announces his election to the K *Lateran* R. 1 680 O. iı. 357 H 1 p ııı 22
March 15.	Pope Nicholas [IV] asks the K. to exhort Alfonso K. of Aragon to liberate Charles son of Charles K of Sicily. *S Peter's, Rome* R 1 681 O ıı 358. H 1. p ııı 22
March 15.	Pope Nicholas [IV] informs the K. that he will not assent to the conditions proposed for the liberation of Charles prince of Salerno *S Peter's, Rome* R. 1. 681. O ıı. 358. H 1 p ııı 23
March 20	Philip K of France complains to K Edw that K Alfonso does not observe the truce. *" Bellum Lectum"* R 1 681 O ıı. 357 H 1 p ııı 22
April 3	Alfonso K. of Aragon notifies the conditions on which he will liberate Charles prince of Salerno *Saragossa* R 1 683. O ıı 362 H 1. p ııı. 24
April 20	The university of Bologna ask the K to restore to Boniface de Langlano his pension of 30 marks *Bologna* R 1 683 O ıı 363 H 1 p ııı 24
April 28.	Pope Nicholas [IV] asks the K. to pay the tribute of 1,000 marks, now three years in arrear *S. Peter's, Rome* R 1 683 O. ıı. 364. H. 1 p ııı 25
May 1	The K to Edmund earl of Cornwall forwarding the petition of Matthew cardinal of St Mary for Neapoleon canon of Lincoln *"Burgum Reginæ"* R 1 684 O ıı 364 H. 1 p. ııı 25
May 1.	Pope Nicholas [IV] asks the K to continue his efforts for the liberation of Charles son of Charles K of Sicily *S Peter's, Rome* R 1. 684 O ıı 364 H 1 p ııı 25
May 15.	Safe conduct for the K travelling in France *Orleans* R 1 684 O ıı 365. H 1. p ııı 25
May 26	Pope Nicholas [IV] exhorts the K to persevere in his efforts for the liberation of Charles son of Charles K of Sicily. *Rieti.* R 1. 684 O ıı 365 H 1 p ııı. 25
Aug 13	Pope Nicholas [IV] to the K in favor of Alfonso son of Valasco Gomez, of Portugal, now a Friar Mınoı. *Rieti* R. 1. 685. O ıı 366 H 1 p ııı 26
Aug 22	The K desires various noblemen in England to take care that the peace is not endangered by their travelling with horses and arms *Westm* R 1 685.
Aug 25	The K to the sheriffs throughout England, to the same effect as the preceding. *Westm* R 1 685
Sept 15	Protestation by K. Edward that he does not acknowledge James (son of Peter K. of Aragon) to be K of Sicily *Jacca ın Aragon* R 1 685 O ıı 366 H 1 p ııı. 26
Sept. 18	The citizens of Jacca swear to use their best efforts to procure the liberation of Charles prince of Salerno. R 1 686 O. ıı. 367. H 1 p ııı. 26.
Oct 19.	Hugh bp of Saragossa announces his voluntary return into prison, and demands from Charles K of Jerusalem the liberation of his hostages *"Monte Sono"* R. 1. 686. O ıı 368 H 1 p ııı. 26
Oct 21.	Alfonso K. of Aragon to Charles K. of Jerusalem, on the above transaction *" Monte Seno"* R 1 686 O ıı 368. H. 1. p ııı 26
Oct 21	Pledge given by Alfonso K of Aragon that K Edward may safely come to the conference *" Campo Francho"* R 1. 686 O ıı 369 H 1 p ııı 27.
Oct. 26.	Pledge given by K Alfonso to the same effect for the K. and the hostages to be delivered at Campo Francho " *" Campo Francho"* R 1 687. O. ıı. 370 **H. I.** p. iii. 27.

DATE	SUBJECT
1288 Oct. 27.	The approval given by the citizens of Saragossa and Jacca to the above pledges. " *Campo Francho* " R 1 687 O 11 370. H 1 p. 111 27
Oct. 27.	Treaty by the Kings of England and Aragon for the delivery of Charles prince of Salerno. " *Campo Francho* " R 1 687 O 11 371 H 1 p 111. 27
Oct. 27	The K becomes bound (in 20,000 marks and 50,000 marks) for the good faith of Charles prince of Salerno towards Alfonso K of Aragon " *Campo Francho* " R 1 689 O 11 375 H 1 p 111 29
Oct 27	Alfonso K of Aragon acknowledges that he has received the hostages of the K. of England. " *Campo Francho* " R 1 690 O 11 378 H 1 p 111 30
Oct. 27	The K and the prince of Salerno agree to the alteration of a date in the treaty of Campo Francho R 1 690 O 11 380 H 1 p 111 31
Oct. 27	Alfonso K. of Aragon acknowledges the receipt of 23,000 marks from K Edward on behalf of Charles prince of Salerno " *Campo Francho.* " R 1 691 O. 11. 383 H 1. p 111 31
Oct 27.	Bond of Alfonso K of Aragon to repay to Charles prince of Salerno the 30,000 marks advanced by K Edward. " *Campo Francho* " R 1 691 O 11 381. H 1 p 11 32
Oct 28.	Proxy given by K Alfonso to receive the hostages provided by K. Edward " *Campo Francho* " R 1 922 O 11 385 H 1 p 111 32
Oct. 28.	Oath required by K Alfonso from the syndics of Saragossa and other cities on the liberation of prince Charles " *Campo Francho* " R 1 692 O 11 385 H. 1 p 111 33
Oct. 29.	Proxy of Alfonso K of Aragon to receive the oaths of the towns of Bordeaux, Bayonne, Dax, and five other towns, on the delivery of prince Charles " *Campo Francho* " R. 1. 693. O 11 386 H 1 p 111 33
Oct 29	Alfonso K. of Aragon acknowledges that he has received as hostages Louis and Robert, sons of Charles prince of Salerno. " *Campo Francho* " R 1 693. O 11. 386 H 1 p. 111 33.
Oct. 29	Alfonso K of Aragon permits John de Vescy and Arnold lord of Gerund, two of the English hostages given to him by K Edward to have leave of absence for three months " *Campo Francho* " R 1 693 O 11 386 H. 1 p 111 33.
Oct. 29	Ordinance as to the mode in which the 76 barons, &c, given as hostages by K. Edward to the K of Aragon, shall be guarded *Canfrank.* R 1 694 O. 11. 387 H. 1. p 111 34
Nov 3	Receipt by Charles prince of Salerno on the loan of 10,000 marks advanced by K Edward *Oleron* R 1 694 O 11 388 H 1 p. 111 34.
Nov. 3.	Recognizance by Charles prince of Salerno that he is delivered from prison by the mediation of K Edward *Oleron* R 1 694 O 11 389 H 1 p 111 34.
Nov 3	Recognizance by Charles prince of Salerno that certain hostages have been delivered for his benefit by K Edward to the K of Aragon *Oleron* R. 1 695 O 11. 391 H. 1. p 111. 35
Nov 3.	Recognizance by Charles prince of Salerno that K Edward has bound himself in various sums (here specified) to the K of Aragon *Oleron* R 1 696 O. 11 392 H. 1. p 111 36.
[Nov]	The city of Bordeaux appoints proctors to swear to the conditions for the liberation of Charles prince of Salerno. R. 1 697 O 11. 396. H. 1. p. 111 37
Nov 18.	Peter prior of S Eutropius in Saintes promises to say certain masses and prayers for K Edward and the English hostages *Saintes* R. 1 697 O 11 396 H 1. p. 111 37
Nov 19	The town of Marmande appoints proctors to swear to the conditions for the liberation of prince Charles. *Marmande.* R 1 697 O 11. 396 H 1 p 111. 38.
Nov. 21.	The town of Condom appoints proctors for the same purpose *Condom.* R. 1. 698. O. 11 398 H 1 p 111 38.
Nov. 23.	The town of Lectour appoints proctors for the same purpose *Lectour.* R 1 698. O. 11. 398 H. 1. p 111 38
Nov. 25.	The city of Saragossa appoints proctors to swear that they will influence K Alfonso to keep the treaty of Oleron. *Saragossa* R 1 698 O 11 398 H 1 p 111 38
Nov. 25.	Certificate that the proctors of Saragossa have taken the oath above mentioned *Saragossa* R. 1. 699. O 11 400 H 1 p 111 38
Nov 27.	The city of Osca appoints proctors to swear to the conditions for the liberation of prince Charles. R 1. 699 O. 11 400. H. 1. p 111 39.

DATE	SUBJECT.
1288 Nov 28	The city of Dax appoints proctors for the same purpose *Dax* R 1 399. O ii 471. H. 1 p iii 39
Nov 30	Notification that Eximinus de Urrea refuses to take the oath for the liberation of Charles prince of Salerno *Carayuca* R 1 699 O ii 401. H 1 p. iii 39
Nov 30	The city of Bayonne appoints proctors to swear to the conditions for the liberation of prince Charles *Bayonne.* R 1 700 O ii 402 H 1 p iii 39
Dec. 6.	Notification that Artaldus de Luna and Lupus Ferrench de Luna refused to take the oath for the liberation of Charles prince of Salerno *Castro de Erle* R. 1. 700. O. ii. 403. H 1 p iii 40
Dec 9.	Certificate that the proctors of the city of Osca have taken the oath. R. 1. 700 O ii 403 H 1 p iii 40.
Dec 10	Certificate that the oath was taken by Acho de Focibus *Ortus* R. 1. 701. O ii. 404 H 1. p iii 40
Dec 11	Certificate that the oath was taken by Santius de Antihone *Arneles* R. 1 701 O ii 404. H 1. p iii 40
Dec 19	Certificate that the oath was taken by Gerald de Capraria *Menarges* R 1 701. O ii. 405 H 1 p iii 40
Dec. 21.	The city of Lerida appoints proctors to swear to the conditions for the liberation of prince Charles R 1 701. O ii 405 H 1 p iii 41
Dec. 21	Notification that the oath was taken by Ermingand count of Urgel *Albesia* R 1 702. O ii 406 H 1 p iii 41
Dec 23	The city of Cervaria appoints proctors to take the oath, as above R. 1. 702. O ii 406 H. 1 p iii 41.
Dec 30	The city of Montauban appoints proctors to take the oath, as above R. 1 702 O. ii. 407 H 1 p iii 41
1289 Jan 4	Certificate that the oath was taken by Wm de Anglaria. *S Matheu* R 1 702 O ii 407 H. 1 p iii. 41
Jan 10	Certificate that the oath was taken by Raymond Fulk vicomte of Cordona *Merle* R 1 703 O ii 408 H 1 p iii 42
Jan. 12.	The K. grants to Arnold de Marmand certain land in the parish of St Martin d'Artrus *Bona Garda* R 1 703. O ii 408 H 1 p iii 42.
Jan 22.	The town of Villefranche appoints proctors to take the oath for the liberation of the prince of Salerno *Villefranche* R 1 703 O ii 409 H 1 p. iii 42
Jan 24	Certificate that the oath was taken by Gerald de Cervilione *Zecours.* R 1 703. O ii 410. H 1. p. iii. 42
Jan. 28	The city of Barcelona appoints proctors to take the oath, as above. *Barcelona* R 1 704 O ii 410 H 1 p iii 42
Jan 30	The city of Gerunda appoints proctors to take the oath, as above *Gerunda* R. 1 704 O ii 410 H 1 p iii 43
Jan 30	Certificate of the oath being taken by Pontius viscount of Empuries *Empuries* R 1 704 O ii 412 H 1 p iii 43
Feb 1.	Pope Nicholas [IV] asks the K to restore the castle of Blankfort in the diocess of Bordeaux to Arnold, son of Peter Bertrand *Rome, S Maria Maggiora* R. 1 704. O ii 412 H 1 p iii 43
Feb 3	The K assents to the conditions required by pope [Nicholas IV] as to the crusade *Westm* R 1 705. O ii 413 H 1 p iii 43
Feb 3	The K promises to restore the tenths collected for the Holy Land if he fails to go thither *Westm* R 1 705 O ii 413 H 1 p iii 44
Feb 20	Pope Nicholas [IV] asks the K to favor the suit (for Bigorre) of Philip son of the count of Flanders *Rome, S. Maria Maggiore* R 1 705 O ii 414 H 1 p. iii 44.
[Feb]	Memorandum as to the descent of the comtés of Armagnac and Fezenzac, for which homage was done to the K of England R 1 705. O ii. 414. H 1 p iii 44
March 9.	K Alfonso notifies that K Edward has surrendered the 20 hostages of Marseilles *Petra Nigra* R 1 706 O ii 415 H 1 p iii 44.
March 9.	K Alfonso notifies that K Edward has surrendered the 36 nobles and the 40 other hostages *Petra Nigra* R 1 706 O ii 415 H 1 p iii 44
March 9.	K Alfonso notifies that he has received the 7,000 marks due to him by Gaston de Bearn. *Petra Nigra* R. 1 706. O ii. 416. H. 1. p iii. 45.

DATE	SUBJECT
1289. April 1.	Eric K of Norway appoints proctors to treat with K. Edward on matters touching Margaret Q. of Scotland *Bergen* R 1 706 O ii 416 H l p iii. 85
April 1.	Pope Nicholas [IV] censures the clergy of Scotland for objecting to promote foreigners to ecclesiastical dignities in Scotland *Rome, S. Maria Maggiore* R 1 707. O. ii 417 H l p iii 45.
April 7	Notification of the terms on which the K granted a pension of 100*l*. to Bernard count of Armignac *Condom*. R. 1. 707. O. ii. 417. H. l p iii. 45.
April 23	Pope Nicholas [IV] complains of the injuries caused to Bernard canon of York by John de Caen *Rome, S Maria Maggiore* R 1 707. O ii. 418. H. 1 p. iii 45.
April 24	The K grants to Amanenus de Lebret certain lands in Gascony and Aquitain. *Condom*. R. 1 708. O ii 419 H. l p iii 46
April 24	The K grants to Amanenus de Lebret possession of the jurisdiction of the parish of Dargelose, &c *Condom* R 1. 708 O ii 420 H l p iii 46
April 25.	The K appoints as his proctor John de Reda to settle certain accounts with the K. of France. *Condom* R. 1. 708. O. ii. 420 H. l. p iii 46
May 4.	Grant by the K. of lands to Arnald, moneyer of Bordeaux, a hostage for Charles prince of Salerno *Condom* R 1. 708 O ii 421 H l p iii 46.
May 8.	Credence for Otho de Grandison and brother Wm de Hotham, sent by the K. to the pope *Lauerdake* R 1 708 O ii 421 H 1 p iii. 47
May 8	Credence for the same two persons sent from the K. to the cardinals *Lauerdake* R 1 709 O ii 421 H l. p iii 47.
May 8.	Credence for the same to Charles K. of Jerusalem. R. 1 709 O ii 422 H 1 p iii 47
May 8	Credence for the same to Charles K of Jerusalem and Q Mary R 1 709 O ii 422 H. 1 p iii 47
May 8	Credence for the same to the bp of Ravenna and others R 1 709 O ii 422 H l. p iii 47
May 15.	Alfonso K of Aragon submits himself to the K in the matter of Charles prince of Salerno *Terrer* R 1 709 O ii 423 H 1 p iii. 47.
May 27.	The K repeats the proclamation [of the 22 Aug] against journeying with horses and arms *Westm* R 1 709
May 27.	Inspeximus and confirmation of charters granted to the convent of Font William *Cundat, near Libourne* R. 1 710 O ii 423 H 1 p iii. 47.
June 2	Grant by the K of the castle of Lados to Gaston de Bearn *Condat, near Libourne* R 1. 710 O ii 424. H 1 p iii 48
June 26	The K orders Gilbert de Clare to discontinue assembling armed men, to the danger of the peace of the realm *Westm*. R. 1 710
July 1.	Grant by the K. of lands, &c to Bernard Dantes, citizen of Dax. "*Metulum*" R 1 710 O ii 424 H l p iii. 48
July 24	The K. defines the emoluments and jurisdiction of the bp of Agen. "*Gundamium*" R. 1 711. O ii 425. H 1 p. iii 48
July 28.	The K. pardons John duke of Brittany, earl of Richmond, for his absence from the three expeditions against the Welsh *Amiens* R. 1 711. O ii 427 H 1 p. iii 49.
Aug. 12	Memorandum that the K. landed this day at Dover. R 1 711. O. ii. 427 H 1 p iii. 49.
Aug. 13	Pope Nicholas [IV] informs the K of the miserable condition of the Holy Land and urges him to aid it *Rieti* R 1 712 O ii 428 H 1 p iii 49
Aug 21.	The sheriffs throughout England are to send in the names of the persons who go about with horses and arms in despite of the proclamation of the 25 Aug. *Ledes*. R 1 711
Aug 21	Pope Nicholas [IV] ratifies the letters of pope Honorius [IV.] for the translation of the abbey of Aberconway. *Reati* R 1 712 O ii 427 H 1 p iii 49.
Aug 31.	The K. confirms (with one exception) the conditions agreed to for the liberation of Charles prince of Salerno. *Rayleigh*. R 1. 712. O ii. 428. H 1 p iii 49
Sept 2	The K. orders Thomas de Normanville to ascertain the condition of the daughters of Lewelin son of Griffin and his brother David, nuns of the order of Sempringham *Rayleigh*. R 1 712 O ii. 429 H 1 p iii. 50
Sept. 5.	The cp of Saragossa informs Charles K of Jerusalem that the K of Aragon has accepted the treaty of peace *Barcelona* R. 1. 713. O ii. 429 H 1 p iii 50

DATE.	SUBJECT
1289 Sept. 7	Letter from Alfonso K. of Aragon to Charles K. of Sicily on the treaty of peace *Barcelona* R 1 713 O ii 430. H 1 p iii 50
Sept 7	K Alfonso extends the period for the completion of the treaty from Nov 1, 1289, to May 1, 1290 *Barcelona* R 1 713 O ii 431 H 1 p iii 50
Sept 30.	Pope Nicholas [IV] tells the K that Argonus K. of Tartary is ready to march to the aid of the Holy Land. *Reati* R 1 713. O ii 429. H. 1. p iii 50
Oct 3	The guardians of Scotland appoint agents to treat with those of Norway respecting the affairs of Scotland *Melrose* R 1 712. O ii 421 H 1 p iii 50
Oct 7.	Pope Nicholas [IV] replies in detail to eight requests relative to the tenths granted for the Holy Land, &c, presented to him by his envoys. *Rieti.* R 1 714 O ii 432. H 1 p. iii 51
Oct. 13	Writs to all the sheriffs for the appearance at Westminster of all persons who have been aggrieved by the K's ministers during his absence *Westm* R 1 715
Oct 31	Certificate by Charles K of Jerusalem that he was ready to return to the prison of the K of Aragon R 1 715 O ii 435 H. 1 p iii 52
Nov 1	Certificate, as above, renewed on 1 Nov R 1 716 O ii 438. H. 1 p iii 53
[Nov]	Certificate that James K of Majorca has become security for Alfonso K of Aragon R 1 717 O ii 440. H 1 p iii 54
Nov 1	Charles K. of Sicily informs Alfonso K of Aragon of what he had done since his liberation from prison R 1 717 O ii 441 H 1 p iii 54.
Nov 2.	Rastaynus bp of Ailes and William de Vilareto, prior of the hospital of St Giles of Jerusalem, in Provence, certify that Charles K of Jerusalem was present at the meeting "inter collem de Paniczarus et Junkeriam." R 1 719 O ii 444 H 1 p iii. 55
Nov. 4.	Receipt by Pope Nicholas [IV.] for the payment of 6,000 marks, the annual tribute from England for six years. *Rome S Maria Maggiore* R 1 p ii. 719 O. ii. 445. H. 1 p iii 56
Nov 6.	The K trusts that the people of Scotland will be obedient to the guardians of that realm. *Clarendon* R 1 719 O ii 445 H 1 p iii 56
Nov 6.	Treaty of Salisbury, relative to the return of Q. Margaret from Norway into Scotland. *Salisbury* R 1 719 O. ii 446. H. 1 p iii 56
Nov 6	Form of the above treaty, in French *Salisbury* R 1 720. O ii 447 H 1 p iii 56
Nov 6	Covenant as to the terms upon which K Edward and the commissioners of Scotland mutually promise to act towards Margaret Q of Scotland. *Clarendon.* R. 1 721. O ii 448 H 1 p iii 57
Nov 16	Dispensation by which pope Nicholas [IV] permits Gilbert earl of Gloucester to marry Joan, the K's daughter *Rome. S Maria Maggiore* R 1 721 O ii 449 H. 1. p iii 57
Nov 16	Dispensation by which pope Nicholas [IV] permits prince Edward to marry Margaret Q of Scotland *Rome S Maria Maggiore* R 1 721 O ii 450 H 1 p iii. 57.
Nov 24	K Alfonso complains to K. Edward of the insincerity and bad faith of Charles prince of Salerno *Lerida* R 1 722 O ii 450. H. 1. p. iii 58
Dec 11.	Pope Nicholas [IV.] to the K in favor of Peter de Siviriaco, prior of Lenton. *Rome. S Maria Maggiore* R 1 723 O ii 453 H 1 p iii 59
1290 Jan 2.	K Alfonso complains to the K. of the injuries which he has sustained from his uncle James. *Truchon* R 1. 723 O ii 454 H. 1 p iii 59.
Jan. 10	K Alfonso complains to the K. of the want of faith of Charles prince of Salerno. *Terraema* R 1 723. O ii 455 H 1 p iii 59
Jan 10	Pope Nicholas [IV] informs the K. how the tenths collected for the Holy Land are to be valued and by whom collected *Rome. S Maria Maggiore.* R. 1. 725 O ii 459 H 1 p iii 61
Jan. 10.	P infant son of Pedro K of Aragon desires to hear of the health of K. Edward *Osca.* R. 1 725 O ii 459 H 1. p iii 61
Jan. 10	Pope Nicholas [IV] grants that the benefices to be taxed for the Holy Land shall be rated at their true value *Rome S Maria Maggiore* R. 1 725. O. ii. 460. H. 1. p. iii 61
Jar. 18	Alfonso K. of Aragon excuses himself to K Edward for not having sent messengers to Perpignan *Alcala* R 1 726 O ii 460 H 1 p iii 61
Jan 18	Alfonso K of Aragon excuses himself to Anthony Bek bp. of Durham for not having sent messengers to Perpignan. *Alcala.* R 1 726 O ii 461. H 1 p iii 62.

DATE.	SUBJECT.
1290. Feb 3.	The K. asks certain cardinals to expedite the business of the bearers of these letters, relative to the subsidy of the Holy Land. *Westm.* R 1. 726 O II 462 H 1 p III 62
Feb. 3.	Damages awarded at Perpignan for the injuries committed during the truce between France and Aragon R. 1 726. O II 426 H 1 p III 62
Feb. 15.	The K to the mayor of the port of Sandwich, relative to the wardship of the orphans of that town. *Westm.* R 1. p II 730
March 17.	The clergy, nobles, and community of Scotland request Eric K of Norway to send his daughter Margaret Q of Scotland to be married to prince Edward of England *Brigham.* R 1 731 O II 472. H 1 p III 66
March 18	The clergy, nobles, and community of Scotland to K Edward on the proposed marriage of prince Edward with Q. Margaret. *Brigham* R 1. 730. O II 471 H 1. p III 66
March 28	John duke of Brabant settles lands to the value of 6,000*l* on Margaret, daughter of K Edw and wife of John, the duke's eldest son R 1 731 O II 473 H 1 p III 66
April 10	The K grants full and special powers to Anthony bp of Durham to treat with the K of Norway on the affairs of Scotland. *Woodstock.* R. 1. 731. O II 474 H 1 p III 67.
[April 17]	Gilbert de Clare earl of Gloucester swears that he will not hinder the succession of prince Edward to the throne *Amesbury* R 1 742 O II 497 H 1. p III 75
[April 17]	Settlement of the disputes between the K. and Gilbert de Clare respecting the bishoprick of Landaff *Amesbury.* R. 1 742.
April 17.	The K, having obtained a papal dispensation for the marriage of Margaret Q of Scotland with prince Edward, begs K Eric to send his daughter to England without delay *Amesbury* R 1 731 O II 474 H 1 p III 67.
April 18.	The K. allows to Sir Reimond de Campania the expenses of the late duel in the Agenois. *Amesbury.* R. 1 732. O. II 475 H 1 p. III 67
[April?]	Eric K. of Norway asks the K to procure for him payment of his annuity of 700 marks from Scotland, now four years in arrear R 1 732 O II 1090 H 1 p IV 87
May 11.	Roger Bernardi count of Foix to the K., on the homage of the viscomté of Bearn *Morlan* R. 1. 732. O. II 475 H 1 p III 67
May 14	Pope Nicholas [IV] to the K as to the mode in which the tenths for the Holy Land should be collected *Rome* R 1. 732 O II 475 H 1 p III 67.
May 15	Bond of the K to pay to the Scottish ambassadors 3,000 marks in case of the non-arrival of the Q of Scotland within the promised period. *Westm* R. 1 734. O II. 479 H 1 p III 69.
June 20.	The K. appoints commissioners to treat with the commissioners of Scotland *London* R. 1. 734 O II 480 H 1 p III 69
July 2.	Assignment of dower to Margaret the K.'s daughter on her marriage with John son of the duke of Brabant *London.* R 1 734 O. II 480. H. 1. p III. 69.
July 8.	Pope Nicholas [IV] recommends the bearer, Labrus Vulpelli of Lucca, to the K.'s favourable notice. *Orvieto.* R 1. 735 O. II 481 H. 1 p III 70
July 13	The K assigns to Robert Tybetot the custody of the castles and lands forfeited by Res son of Mereduc. *Westm* R 1 735 O II .
July 18	Marriage contract between prince Edward and Margaret Q. of Scotland. *Brigham.* R. 1. 735 O II 482 H II p III. 70.
July 18	Notification by the guardians of Scotland of the completion of the above treaty. *Brigham.* R 1 736 O II 485. H. 1. p II 71.
July 27	Safe conduct for the Jews commanded by the K to leave the realm with their wives, children, and property *Westm* R 1 736
July 28	Charles K of Jerusalem to the K of England; regrets that he cannot at present accept his invitation to come to England R 1. 736. O II 485 H 1 p III 71
July 31.	The guardians of Scotland appoint plenipotentiaries to treat with K Edward on the marriage of Q Margaret and prince Edward *Kelso.* R. 1. 737 O II 485 H 1. p III 71.
Aug. 8	The K. appoints Anthony bp of Durham to act as lieutenant of Scotland for Q. Margaret *Northampton* R. 1 737. O. II. 487 H 1 p III 71
Aug 28	K Edward appoints proctors to treat with the proctors of K Eric on the aforesaid marriage. *Northampton* R 1 737. O II 488. H 1 p III 72
Aug. 28	Prince Edward appoints proctors to act for him in regard to his marriage with Q. Margaret. *Northampton* R. 1 737. O. II 487. H 1 p III 72

DATE	SUBJECT
1290 Aug 28	The Scottish commissioners promise (under certain conditions) to deliver all the fortresses of Scotland to the K of England *Northampton* R 1 737 O ıı 488. H 1. p ııı 72.
Aug 28	The K ratifies the marriage contract aforesaid. *Northampton* R 1 738 O ıı 489 H 1 p ıı 72
Aug	The K approves of the marriage contract of Thomas son of Edmund, son of Hen III , and Beatrice of Burgundy. *Northampton* R 1 738 O ıı 489 H 1 p. ıı 73
Sept 1	The K authorizes Anthony bp of Durham to protect the proctors of K Eric coming into England *Geddington* R 1 739 O ıı 391 H 1 p ıı 73
Sept 8	The K to the duke of Brabant, respecting the lands assigned ın dower to the princess Margaret *Torpel* R. 1. 739 O ıı 491 H 1 p ıı 73
Sept. 8	The K appoints proctors ın the matter of the above assignment of dower *Torpel.* R 1 739 O ıı 491 H 1 p ıı 74
Sept 8	John of Brabant and his wife Margaret appoint the same proctors ın the above business. *Torpel* R 1. 739 O. ıı 492. H 1 p ıiı. 74.
[Sept]	The ınhabitants of the Isle of Man pledge their fidelity to the K under a bond of 2,000*l* *Abbey of Russyn* R 1 739 O ıı 492 H 1 p ıı 74
[Sept]	The R complains to pope Nicholas [IV] of certain ecclesiastical abuses ın the matter of " collations and executions," respecting prebends ın the churches of York and Lincoln. R 1 740 O ıı 493 H 1 p ıı 74
[Sept]	The nobility of England to pope Nicholas [IV] on the same subject. R 1 740 O ıı 493. H 1 p ıı 74
Sept. 17	Pope Nicholas [IV] to the K ın answer to the above complaints. *Orvieto* R. 1 740 O ıı 494 H 1 p ıı 75
Oct 7	W. bp of S Andrew's, having heard a report of the death of the Q of Scotland, urges the K. to hasten to the borders of Scotland. *Leuchars.* R 1. 741. O ıı. 1090. H. 1. p ıv 87
Oct 14	The K protests that he ıntends to go to the Holy Land, and accepts the tenths granted for that object *King's Clıpston* R 1 741 O ıı 495 H 1 p ıı 75
Oct 23.	Writ for the payment of the annual fee of Francıs Accursıus. *King's Clıpston* R 1. 741 O ıı 496 H 1 p ıı 75
[Oct 30].	Oath of Gılbert de Clare as to the succession of prince Edward to the throne R. 1. 742. O ıı 497 H 1 p ıı 75 *See* [April 17,] 1290
[Oct 30]	Settlement of the disputes between the K and Gılbert de Clare R 1 742. *See* [April 17,] 1290
Dec 2	Pope Nicholas [IV] ıntroduces to the K the ambassadors of Argo K of the Tartars. *Orvieto* R 1 742 O. ıı 498 H 1 p ıı 76
Dec 31.	Pope Nicholas [IV.] ıntroduces to the K another ambassador of Argo K of the Tartars *Orvieto* R 1 743 O ıı 498 H 1 p ıı 76
1291 Jan 4	The K asks the abbot of Cluny to cause masses to be sung for the soul of Q Eleanor *Ashrıdge* R 1 743 O ıı. 491. H 1. p ıı 76
Feb. 12	Pope Nicholas [IV] answers ın detail the requests of the K. ın reference to the tenths and other matters connected with the Holy Land *Rome* R 1 743 O ıı. 499. H. 1 p ıı 76
Feb 12	Pope Nicholas [IV] cautions the K. against delay ın the expedition to the Holy Land. *Rome.* R 1 744. O ıı 501 H 1 p ıı 77
Feb 19	Treaty between the Kings of Aragon and Sicily on various matters ın dispute between them, agreed upon ın the presence of the K of England's commissioners. *Brignon.* R 1 745 O ıı 501 H 1 p ıı 77
Feb 20	The proctors of the K of Aragon and the comıssioners of K Edward accept the above treaty *Brignon* R. 1 745. O. ıı. 504 R 1 p ıı 78
Feb 28	Pope Nicholas [IV] asks the K to procure the liberation of Wm marquıs of Montferrat *Orvieto* R 1 745 O ıı 504 H 1 p. ıı 79
March 13	Pope Nicholas [IV.] recommends John de Berkhamstede, elected abbot of S Albans, to the K *Orvieto* R 1. 745 O ıı 505 H. 1 p ıı 79.
March 16	Pope Nicholas [IV.] replies ın detail to various letters sent to him by the K relative to the crusade *Orvieto* R. 1 746 O ıı 505 H 1 p ıı 79.
March 18.	Pope Nicholas [IV] grants the tenths of England, Scotland, Wales, and Ireland to the K for six years, ın order that he may go to the Holy Land *Orvieto.* R. 1 747 O ıı 509 H 1 p ıı 80

DATE	SUBJECT
1291 March 18.	Pope Nicholas [IV] ratifies the K.'s acceptance of the crusade, and grants the usual indulgences to him and the other crusaders. *Orvieto* R 1 747 O ii. 511 H. 1 p iii 81
March 18	Pope Nicholas [IV] exhorts the bps of Scotland to preach the crusade throughout that realm *Orvieto* R 1. 747. O ii 512 H 1 p iii 81
March 18	Pope Nicholas [IV.] grants privileges and indulgences to those who join or assist the crusade *Orvieto.* R 1 749 O. ii 513. H. 1. p iii 82
March 18	Pope Nicholas [IV] arranges as to the payment to the K of the tenths collected for the crusade *Orvieto* R 1. 750 O ii. 516 H 1 p iii. 83.
March 18.	Pope Nicholas [IV.] gives directions to certain ecclesiastics to carry out the previous arrangement *Orvieto.* R. 1. 750. O. ii 517 H 1 p iii 83
March 18.	Pope Nicholas [IV] exhorts the whole of the clergy of Scotland to give their tenths in aid of the Holy Land *Orvieto.* R 1 750 O ii 518 H 1 p iii 84.
March 18.	Pope Nicholas [IV] exhorts the whole of the clergy of Ireland to the same effect *Orvieto* R 1 751. O ii 519. H 1 p iii. 84
[March 18]	Pope Nicholas [IV] to the bps of Carlisle and Caithness, on the exercise of their authority in collecting the above-mentioned tenths in England and Scotland R 1 752 O ii 521 H 1. p. iii 85
March 25.	Pope Nicholas [IV] thanks the K for presents sent by Labrus Vulpelli of Lucca. *Orvieto* R 1. 752 O ii 521 H 1 p iii 85
March 29	Pope Nicholas [IV.] grants to the K. additional aid towards his crusade. *Orvieto* R 1 753. O ii. 522 H 1 p iii 85
March 29	Pope Nicholas [IV] orders the bps of Winton and Lincoln to assign to the K the aid referred to in the bull before mentioned *Orvieto* R 1 752 O ii 523 H 1 p iii 86
April 12.	Charles K of Jerusalem to the K of England on the treaty respecting the kingdom of Majorca *Montpelier* R 1 753 O ii 523. H 1 p iii 86
April 16	Writs of military summons to the barons, &c of the north to meet the K at Norham on 3 June *Darlington* R 1 753 O ii 525 H 1 p iii 86
April 23.	The K. informs Philip K of France that he has appointed commissioners to do homage and fealty for the land of Ponthieu *Newcastle-on-Tyne* R 1. 754 O ii 525 H 1 p iii. 87.
April 23	Commission to Geoffrey de Geneville to deliver the land of Ponthieu to Edmund the K's brother, to hold until the K's son Edward comes of age *Newcastle-on-Tyne* R 1 754 O ii 526 H 1. p iii 87
May 10.	Notarial instrument containing the proceedings upon K Edward's adjudication of the crown of Scotland R. 1 762–784 O ii 542 H 1 p iii 93
May 10	Pope Nicholas [IV] to the K on granting to Rome certain prebends in the churches in York and Lincoln. *Orvieto* R 1 754 O ii 526 H 1 p iii 87
May 24	The K confirms to the lord de Sparra that portion of the sea coast in Gascony granted to his predecessor by K John *Norham* R 1 754 O ii 527 H 1 p iii 87,
May 31	Safe conduct for the Scottish bps and nobles coming to treat with the K of England at Norham *Norham* R 1. 755 O. ii 528 H 1 p iii 87
May 31	Notification that the fact of the Scottish nobles and commons coming to the K. at Norham should not turn to their prejudice *Norham* R 1 755 O ii 528 H 1 p iii. 88
June 5	The K. orders the justiciary of Ireland to take care that the French merchants trading to Ireland be not molested *Norham* R 1 755 O ii 528. H 1 p iii 88
June 5.	The competitors for the crown of Scotland acknowledge K. Edward as superior lord of that realm, *Norham* R. 1. 755. O ii 529 H. 1. p iii 88
June 6.	The above competitors grant possession of Scotland to the K of England until the decision of the question relative to the right to the crown *Norham* R 1 755 O ii 529 H 1 p ii 88
June 7.	The K acquits John duke of Brabant of his debt of 6,000*l* assigned by him to his son on his marriage with the princess Margaret *Norham* R 1 756 O ii 530. H 1. p iii 88
June 8	Pope Nicholas [IV] admonishes the K not to invade the liberties and rights of the church *Orvieto.* R 1 756. O ii 530 H 1. p iii. 89.
June 10	The K undertakes to indemnify Gilbert de Umfraville for the surrender of the castles of Dundee and Forfar *Norham* R 1 756 O ii 531 H 1. p. iii 89
June 12	The K. agrees to settle the question in dispute relative to the crown within the realm of Scotland *Norham* R 1 756 O ii 532 H 1 p iii 89
June 21	The K grants to his brother Edmund the land of Poitou until prince Edward comes of age *Berwick-upon-Tweed* R. 1. 757.

DATE	SUBJECT.
1291 June 29	The K orders a monthly allowance to be made to the chancellor of Scotland and a clerk for the expenses of their office *Berwick-upon-Tweed* R 1 757 O ii 532 O. ii. p iii. 39.
July 1	Pope Nicholas [IV.] grants the use of an altar "portatile" to the chaplain of Wm. de Valence, earl of Pembroke *Orvieto* R. 1. 757. O. ii. 533. H. 1. p. iii. 89.
July 3	The K directs that as England and Scotland are now united, the K.'s writs shall run in both realms *Berwick-on-Tweed* R 1 757 O ii 533 H 1 p. m 90
Sept. 27.	The K grants to the executors of the will of his mother, Q. Eleanor, the proceeds of all her lands and tenements from 25 June till 29 Sept 1291 *Devizes* R 1 757.
[Dec]	Memorandum as to a chest in the New Temple, London, being broken open in the Chancery, and two rolls taken thence and sent to the K then in Scotland R 1 757
Dec 3	The K orders that Michael Scot, who went for the Q. of Scotland into Norway, should have a part of some competent wardship or marriage by way of recompense *London* R 1 758 O ii. 533 H. 1 p iii 90.
Dec 3	The K notifies that the heart of his father, Henry III , had been delivered to the abbess of Fontevrault to be buried there *London* R 1 758. O ii 533 H 1 p m 90
Dec.	The K renews to the abbess and convent of Fontevrault the right of free passage through his realm granted by his predecessors *Stubenhethe* R. 1 758 O ii 534 H 1. p iii. 90
1292 Jan 2.	The K grants to the princess Mary, nun of Fontevrault, dwelling at Amesbury, 40 oaks annually for firewood and 20 casks of wine. *Westm.* R 1 758 O ii 534 H 1 p. m. 90
Feb 6	Mandate that all persons having 40 librates of land shall be knighted before Christmas next *Westm* R 1 758
Feb. 18.	The K orders that those knights who have commuted for their scutage shall be acquitted of all distraints for the same *Chautone* R. 1. 758.
March 26	Grant that M bp of Ossory may receive compensation for injuries done by the Irish. *Westm* R 1 759 O ii 535 H 1 p m 90
April 6.	Safe conduct for Guy count of Flanders coming into England. *Westm* R 1. 759 O. ii 535 H. 1 p. iii 90.
April 27	The K orders that certain privileges of the university of Cambridge are not to be violated *S Edmunds* R 1 759 O ii 535 H 1 p iii 90
May 6.	Protection to be given to the subjects of Guy count of Flanders *Culford.* R 1 759 O ii 536 H. 1 p m 91
May.	The K orders the bailiffs of Law to restore the ships which they have taken from the subjects of the count of Flanders *Culford* R 1 759 O ii 537 H 1 p m. 91
May 8.	Treaty of peace between Guy count of Flanders and the K.'s subjects in Gascony, Bayonne, &c R 1. 760 O ii 536 H 1 p m 91
June 6	The K orders John de Havering, seneschal of Aquitain, to restore to the K certain perquisites which he had wrongfully appropriated. *Berwick-on-Tweed* R 1. 760 O ii 532 H. 1 p m 91
June 23	K Edward thanks Andrew K of Hungary for his aid for the Holy Land. *Berwick-on-Tweed* R 1 760 O ii 538 H 1 p m 92
July 5	Declaration by certain nobles of England and Scotland that the K may exercise in England his rights over Scotland if he so please *Berwick-on-Tweed* R. 1. 760 O ii 539 H 1 p m 92
July 7.	" Alisaundre de Ergaithl " lord of Lorne, promises to keep the peace in the Isles of Scotland *Berwick-upon-Tweed* R 1 761 O ii 540 H 1 p m 92.
[July 7]	Similar promise by Alexander of the Isles, son of Angus, son of Donald *Berwick-upon-Tweed.* R 1 761 O. ii 521 R 1 p m 92.
[July 7.]	Similar promise by Angus son of Donald of the Isles and Alexander his son. *Berwick-upon Tweed.* R. 1. 761 O ii 541 H 1. p m 93
July 15	Grant to the town of Libourne of power to erect a toll-bar *Berwick-on-Tweed.* R 1. 761. O ii 93 H 1 p m. 541.
Aug 16	Mandate to the chancellor of Scotland to pay the fees of the guardians of Scotland. *Alnwick.* R. 1 561. O ii. 541. H 1 p m 93.
Oct 22	Mandate to the council of Ireland to admit Tho bp of Meath as one of their number. *Berwick-on-Tweed* R 1. 762 O ii 542 H. 1 p iii 93
Oct. 27.	Memorandum of the death, upon this day, of Robert Burnell, chancellor of England, and of the delivery of the K.'s great seal into the wardrobe. R 1 762.

DATE	SUBJECT
1292. [Oct.]	Notarial instrument on the adjudication of the crown of Scotland R. 1, 762–784. O ii 542 H 1 p. iii 93. *See* May 10, 1291
Nov.	The K settles what fee shall be paid by John K of Scotland on making his homage to the K of England R. 1 784 O ii 600 H 1 p iii. 115
Nov 21	Mandate to John de St John to place John K of Scotland on his royal seat at Scone *Norham.* R. 1. 785. O ii 600 H 1 p iii 115
Dec. 28.	Mandate to certain sheriffs, &c. of Scotland to pay money due to Eric K of Norway. *Newcastle-on-Tyne* R. 1 785 O ii 600 H 1 p iii 116.
1293 Jan. 4	The K reasserts the article by which he pledged himself to demand nothing but homage in Scotland *Newcastle-on-Tyne* R 1 785 O. ii 602 H 1. p iii 116
Jan 4	The K. orders the late guardians of Scotland to deliver to John K of Scotland the rolls in their custody *Newcastle-upon-Tyne* R 1 785 O ii 602 H 1. p iii 116
Jan 5.	The K orders Walter de Huntercombe to give seisin of the Isle of Man to John K of Scotland *Newcastle-upon-Tyne* R 1 785 O ii 602. H 1 p iii 116
Jan 6	The K. exempts the bp of Agen from the payment of "pedage" *Newcastle-upon-Tyne* R 1 786 O ii. 602 H 1. p. iii. 116.
Feb 8	The K. of England to K. Eric, relative to the money he owes to Peter Algot. R. 1 786. O ii. 603 H 1 p iii 116 *See* Feb 8, 1294
[Feb 8]	The K of England to the K of Scotland, relative to money due to Peter Algot. R 1 786 O ii 603 H 1 p iii 117 *See* 8 Feb 1294
[Feb 8]	The K to Peter Algot, thanks him for his presents R. 1 786 O ii 603 H. 1 p iii 117 *See* 8 Feb 1294
Feb. 9.	Pleadings at Scone before the K of Scotland and his council, relative to certain tenements claimed by Macduf, son of Malcolm earl of Fife. R 1 786 O ii 604 H 1. p iii 117
Feb 21.	John K of Scotland summons Angus, son of Donald Lawemund MacEreghere, and Auneesius, son of Duncan McEregere, to do homage. *Dundee* R 1 787. O ii. 604. H. 1 p. iii 117
[March 5]	Peter Martini de Luna in Aragon offers to serve the K of England with 100 knights in the Holy Land. *Saragossa* R 1 787 O ii. 605. H. 1. p. iii. 117
March 8	John K of Scotland is summoned to appear at Westm, to answer the appeal of John Mason, merchant of Gascony, for a denial of justice in Scotland *Kirkby* R 1 787 O ii. 605 H 1 p. iii 117
[March]	Florence count of Holland asks the K to give credence to Arnold de Raust R. 1. 787. O ii 606 H 1 p iii. 118.
[March 22]	Haco duke of Norway recommends to the K a clerk named Geoffrey, a clerk in Yorkshire, who wishes to join the crusade. *Hamar* R 1 787 O ii 1091 H. 1 p iv 88
March 25.	John K of Scotland is summoned to answer the appeal of Macduff, son of Malcolm earl of Fife, for a denial of justice. *Cambridge* R. 1 788 O. ii 606 H 1 p iii 118
May 6.	Indemnity to certain Florentine merchants who had become security for 10,000*l* borrowed for Gascony affairs by the K from the tenths *Westm* R 1 788 O. ii 607 H 1 p iii 118
May 6	Credence by Guy count of Flanders for messengers sent to relate the quarrels between the Flemings and the English. *Malea, near Bruges* R. 1. 788. O. ii. 607. H. 1. p iii 118
[May 14.]	Petitions addressed by John K of Scotland to K Edward, with the K.'s answers thereto *London* R 1 800 O ii 635 H 1 p iii 129
May 19	Eric K of Norway recommends to the K his clerk Geoffrey, son of John, who wishes to join the crusade *Bergen* R 1 788 O ii 1091 H 1 p iv 88
June 15	John K of Scotland is cited to answer the appeal of Aufrica, heiress of Magnus K. of the Isle of Man *Westm* R 1 789 O ii. 608. H 1 p iii 118
June 18	The K. permits the nuns of the order of S. Francis to build a house and settle in the parish of S. Botulph without Aldgate. *Westm* R. 1 789. O. ii. 608 H 1 p iii 119
June 21	Licence to Edmund the K's brother to fortify his house called the Sauvoy in the parish of S Clement Danes *Westm* R. 1 789 O ii 609. H 1. p iii 119
July 15.	The K to Dionisius K of Portugal relative to the quarrel between the merchants of Bayonne and the citizens of Lisbon *Canterbury* R 1 789 O ii 609 H 1 p iii 119
July 15.	The K ratifies the peace between Sancho K of Castile and the men of Bayonne *Canterbury*. R 1 789 O ii. 610 H 1 p iii. 119.

H

DATE	SUBJECT
1293 July 18	John de St John appointed to receive and make the oaths of fealty, &c between the K and Bertrand bp of Agen. *Canterbury* R. 1. 790 O ii 612 H. 1 p iii 120
July 19	John de St John appointed to receive what ought to be done to the K by Bertrand bp. of Agen *Canterbury* R. 1 790 O ii 612 H 1 p iii 120.
July 24.	Safe conduct for Robert de Brus earl of Carrick going into Norway *Canterbury.* R. 1. 790 O ii 612 H 1 p iii 120
July 25.	The K orders that 16 stags be sent from Windsor forest to the abbot of Westminster *Canterbury* R 1 791
Aug. 2	Record of pleas held before John K. of Scotland and his council at Stirling. R. 1 791. O. ii. 613 H 1 p iii 120
Sept. 2	The K cites John King of Scotland to appear before him on the appeal of the abbot of Reading *Dunton* R 1 792 O ii 615 H 1 p iii 121
Nov. 16.	K Edward orders John K. of Scotland to pay the money due to Eric K. of Norway. *Westm.* R. 1 792 O ii 616 H. 1. p iii 121.
Nov 26	Commission to inquire into the injuries done by the men of Norfolk to the men of Florence count of Holland. *Westm* R 1 792 O ii 916 H 1 p iii 122
Dec. 2	The escheator north of the Trent is ordered to deliver to John K of Scotland his lands in England, viz, Tyndale, Soureby, and Penreth. *Westm* R 1 792 O ii 616 H. 1 p iii 122
Dec 6.	Philip de Castro, a baron of Aragon, offers to serve the K. with 200 or 300 horsemen *Paris* R 1 793 O. ii 617. H. 1. p iii 122.
[Dec]	Philip K of France cites K Edw to appear personally at Paris, to answer the complaints against him as duke of Aquitain by the Normans *Paris* R 1 793 O ii 617. H 1. p iii 122
1294 Feb 3	Edmund, the K's brother, orders John de St John, seneschal of Guyenne, and others, to deliver the seisin of all Guyenne to the K. of France. *Paris* R 1 793 O. ii 617. H. 1 p iii 123
Feb 3	Prince Edmund forwards to John de St John, lieutenant of Aquitain, copies of letters from the K, and a statement of the treachery of Philip K of France in regard to that province *Paris* R. 1 794. O ii 620 H 1 p iii. 153.
Feb	Treaty of marriage between the K of England and Margaret, sister of Philip K. of France *Paris* R. 1 795 O ii. 622 H 1 p iii 124
[Feb 8]	The K informs Eric K of Norway that he will aid him in the matter referred to in the letters brought by Peter Algot. *Hundeslowe* R 1 786. O ii 603. H. 1. p iii. 116.
[Feb 8]	The K asks John K of Scotland to pay to Peter Algot the money due to the K of Norway *Hundeslowe* R 1 786 O ii 603 H. 1 p iii 116
[Feb 8]	The K to Peter Algot, has written to the K of Scotland on the above debt. *Hundeslowe.* R 1 786 O ii 603 H 1 p. iii 117
Feb 14	The K's letters to the prelates, asking for the prayers of the clergy during his approaching absence from England. R 1 796 O ii 626 H. 1 p iii 126.
Feb. 17.	The K. orders letters of safe conduct to be prepared for the merchants of Spain and Portugal trading with the K's subjects *S Albans* R 1 797 O. ii. 627. H. 1 p iii 126
March 13	Alvarus count of Agen asks the K to give credence to the bearer "*Corbius*" R 1 797 O. ii 627. H. 1. p iii. 126
March 13	Hinardus de Ceteyles offers his services to the K in the war with France. "*Bellipodium.*' R 1 797 O ii 628 H 1 p iii 126
March 13	Bernard Petracissa, and various others, offer their services to the K in the war with France. "*Bellipodium*" R 1. 797 O ii 628 H 1 p iii 126
April 2.	Artaldus de Alagone offers his services to the K in the war with France. *Saragossa.* R. 1. 797. O ii. 628 H 1. p iii 126
[April 4]	Eximinus de Urreya, a baron of Aragon, offers to serve the K in the Holy Land with 200 horsemen. *Saragossa.* R. 1. 798 O ii 629 H. 1 p iii 127
April 5	Hugh bp of Saragossa to the K, in favour of Arnaldus de Alagone *Sarogossa.* R 1 798 O ii 629 H 1 p iii 127
April 5.	Hugh bp of Saragossa to the K, in favour of Wm de Fluviano and others. *Saragossa.* R 1. 798 O. ii 630 H 1 p iii 127.
April 15.	Commission to Guy Ferre and others to see to the assignment of the dower of Eleanor countess of Bar, the K.'s daughter *Canterbury*. R 1. 798. O ii 630 H. 1. p. iii 127.

DATE	SUBJECT
1294 April 15	Letters patent of the K in furtherance of the above-mentioned commission. *Canterbury* R 1. 798 O n. 631 H 1 p m 127
April 19	Writ for the payment of 100*l* to Mary the K.'s daughter, nun of Amesbury. *Canterbury.* R. 1 799 O n 631 H 1 p m. 127
April 21	The K orders the adjournment of the duel between William de Vescy and John Fitz-Thomas, and makes certain arrangements relative to Ireland during his absence abroad. *Canterbury* R. 1 799 O n 631 H 1 p m 127
April 22	The K cites John K of Scotland to answer before him on the appeal of Anthony bp. of Durham relative to Berwick and Hadington *Canterbury* R. 1 799. O n 632. H. 1. p. m 128
April 23	The K. approves and enforces the agreement between the men of Bayonne and Portugal *Canterbury* R. 1 799 O n 632 H 1 p. m 128
[April 28]	Letter of the princess Blanche, relative to the Friars Minors R 1 800. O ii 633 H. 1 p m. 128. *See* [Dec], 1293.
[April 28]	Citation by K Philip for K Edward to appear before him. R. 1. 800. O. n. 634. H. 1. p m 128 *See* May 5, 1292
[May 5.]	K. Philip renews the citation to K. Edward to appear at Paris *Paris.* R. 1. 800 O n 634 H. 1 p m 128
[May 7]	The princess Blanche of France asks K. Edw to favour the Friars Minors of Paris, executors of the will of John Peschan [Peckham], late abp of Canterbury. *Poissy* R. 1 800 O n 623 H 1 p m 128
[May 14.]	Petitions of John K of Scotland to K. Edward. R 1. 800. O n 635 H 1 p m. 129. *See* May 14, 1293
May 28	The K informs the count of Flanders that he has revoked the safe conduct which he had granted to the Flemish merchants *Guilford* R 1 801 O n 636 H 1 p m 129
June 2.	The K directs John K of Scotland to forbid the departure, from his ports, of any man or vessel going to foreign parts *Westm* R 1 801 O n 636 H 1 p m 129
June 14.	Writs summoning all persons owing military service to meet the K at Portsmouth, to go with him into Gascony *Westm.* R. 1 801 O n 637 H 1 p m. 130.
June 15.	The K sends to Haco duke of Norway safe conduct to come to England to take an English wife. *Westm* R 1 802 O n 638 H 1 p. m 130.
June 18	The K going into Gascony asks the prayers of the clergy. *Westm,* R. 1. 802 O. n. 639. H. 1 p m 130
June 18.	Letters of safe conduct for John duke of Brabant, the K's son, going into Brabant. *Westm.* R 1 802 O n 639 H 1 p m 130
June 20	Credence for J abp. of Dublin and others going from the K. of England to A. King of the Romans *Westm* R 1 802 O n 640 H 1 p m 131
June 20.	Credence for the same, going to S. abp. of Cologne *Westm* R 1 803. O n 640. H 1 p m 131.
June 20.	The K grants full powers to the same to conclude a treaty of alliance with A. King of the Romans against all persons excepting the pope *Westm* R. 1. 803. O. n 640. H 1. p m 131
June 20	Commission to the bp of Durham to settle a marriage between prince Edward and Philippa, daughter of Guy count of Flanders *Westm* R 1 803
June 26	The K requests John K of Scotland to give John de Insula possession of lands which he has bought at Whitesuyn in Scotland. *Brunbelshete.* R. 1. 803 O. n. 641. H. 1. p m 131.
June 26	Writ to Geoffrey de Genevill and 58 others to meet the K. at Portsmouth, to serve in Gascony *Westm.* R. 1. 803. O n 641. H. 1. p m 131.
June 29	The K requires John K of Scotland to send his service to meet the K. at London, to proceed with the K. into Gascony. *Portsmouth.* R. 1. 804 O. n. 642. H. 1. p m 132.
June 29	Military summons to Robert de Brus, lord of Annandale, to meet the K at London, and go with him into Gascony *Portsmouth.* R. 1. 804 O n 643. H. 1. p m. 132.
June 29.	Military summons to John Comyn earl of Buchan and others to meet the K. at London for the same purpose. *Portsmouth.* R. 1. 804 O n. 643 H 1 p m. 132.
June 29.	Military summons to Patrick de Dunbar, earl of March and 16 others to serve the K (personally, if possible), as above mentioned. *Portsmouth.* R. 1. 804. O. n. 643 H 1 p. m. 132.

H 2

DATE.	SUBJECT
1294 June 29	Military summons to certain of the nobility of Ireland to serve the K personally, as above mentioned *Portsmouth* R 1 805 O ɪɪ 664 II. 1 p ɪɪɪ 132
July 1	The K to the prelates and barons of Gascony; he has been over-reached by the K of France in regard to Gascony, but he is coming in person thither *Portsmouth* R 1 805. O ɪɪ 644 H. 1 p ɪɪɪ 132
July 1	The K appoints John de St. John to be seneschal of Gascony *Portsmouth* R 1 805. O ɪɪ 645 H 1 p ɪɪɪ 133
July 1	The K appoints John de Britannia to be his lieutenant in Gascony *Portsmouth* R 1 805 O ɪɪ 645 H. 1 p ɪɪɪ 133
July 3.	The K gives John de Britannia and others power to treat of a league between the Kings of England and Castile *Crevecoeur* R 1 805 O ɪɪ 646. H 1 p ɪɪɪ 133
July 9	The K. gives John de Britannia power to treat with all who will enter into a league with him the K *Portsmouth* R 1 806 O ɪɪ 646 H 1 p ɪɪɪ 133
July 9	The K gives John de Britannia power to form a league with the count de Foix. *Portsmouth* R. 1. 806 O ɪɪ 646 H 1 p ɪɪɪ 133
July 10	The K asks the aid of the abp of Auch and other bps in recovering Gascony *Portsmouth* R 1. 806 O ɪɪ 647 H 1 p ɪɪɪ 133
July 12.	The K. asks Arnald de Blanquafort and the other nobles of Gascony to aid him in recovering Gascony *Portsmouth* R. 1 806. O ɪɪ 647 H p ɪɪɪ. 133.
July 16	The K appoints commissioners to receive the fines applicable to the expedition into Gascony *Portsmouth* R 1 807 O ɪɪ 650. H 1 p ɪɪɪ 134
July 24	The K to James K of Aragon, credence for John de Britannia going to Gascony. *Funtele* R 1 807 O ɪɪ 650 H 1 p ɪɪɪ 135
[July]	Instructions by the K as to what his messengers shall say to the K of France on resigning his homage. R 1 807 O ɪɪ 650 H 1 p ɪɪ 135
Aug 13	Writ to John duke of Lorraine to pay 22,000*l* to the men of Savoy and Burgundy who have promised to help the K. against the K of France *Portsmouth* R 1 808 O ɪɪ 651. H 1 p ɪɪɪ 135
Aug 13	Writ to Robert de Segre to pay 22,000*l* as above mentioned. *Portsmouth*. R 1 808. O. ɪɪ. 651 H. 1 p ɪɪɪ 135.
Aug 17	Prorogation of the departure of the expedition into Gascony from 1 Sept. to 30 Sept. *Portsmouth* R 1 808 O ɪɪ 651 H 1 p ɪɪɪ 135
Aug 19	Writ of summons to the clergy to be present at Westminster on 21 Sept to deliberate with the K on the affairs of Gascony *Portsmouth* R 1 808 O ɪɪ 652 H 1 p ɪɪɪ 135
Aug 30	Writ to the men of the counties of Caernarvon, &c , to give credence to what the justiciaries of Chester and N Wales shall tell them from the K relative to the affairs of Gascony *Donameny* R 1. 809 O ɪɪ 654 H 1 p ɪɪɪ 136
Sept 3.	The K orders the barons of the Cinque Ports and others to provide shipping for the transit of his brother Edmund to Gascony *Pershore* R. 1 809 O ɪɪ 654 H 1 p ɪɪɪ. 136
Sept 3	Pope Celestine [V.] announces his election to the K *Aquilea* R 1 809 O ɪɪ 654 H 1. p. ɪɪɪ 136
Sept 24	Pope Celestine [V] asks the K to restore the temporalities of the see of Canterbury to Robert de Winchelsea. *Aquilea* R 1 810
Sept 27.	The K takes under his protection all the bps and clergy of the realm *Westm*. R. 1 810
Oct. 2.	Pope Celestine [V] advises the K to be at peace with France *Aquilea*. R 1. 810 O ɪɪ 657 H 1 p ɪɪɪ 137
[Oct. 5]	Credence and recommendation from Florence count of Holland for Adulf de Waldogge, archdeacon of Utrecht R 1. 811. O. ɪɪ. 658. H 1 p ɪɪɪ 138.
Oct 8 and 9	The K orders the sheriffs of England to elect four knights from each county to be present at the parliament at Westm on Nov 12 *Westm* R 1 811
Oct. 16	Writ to arrest and sell all the goods of French merchants in Ireland *Westm* R 1 811 O ɪɪ 659 H 1 p ɪɪɪ 138
Oct. 22	Confederation between the K of England and Adolph K of the Romans. *Westm* R 1 812 O ɪɪ 659. H 1 p ɪɪɪ 139
Oct 22.	Notification by the K of England as to the observance by himself and his nobles of the above-mentioned confederation *Westm*. R. 1 812 O ɪɪ 661. H. 1. p. ɪɪɪ. 139

DATE	SUBJECT
1294 Nov 5	Safe conduct for Reginald count of Guelders coming into England *Tower of London* R 1 812 O ii 661 H 1. p. iii 139
Nov 6	The K. thanks Herstrad lord of Merenbergh for his services. *London.* R 1. 813 O ii 661. H. 1 p iii 139
Nov 6	The K to the abp of Cologne relative to the time for meeting the army of the K of the Romans. *London* R 1 813 O ii 662 H 1 p iii 139
Nov 6	The K thanks Wychbold dean of Cologne for his services *London* R 1. 813. O ii. 662 H 1. p iii, 139
Nov 7	The K. appoints Wychbold to be his secretary *London.* R. 1 813 O ii 662. H. 1. p iii 139
Nov 7	Commission for Eustace de Pomerio to receive for the K of England the homage of Eberhard count of Kazinlugbogin *Tower of London* R 1 813 O ii 663 H 1 p iii 139.
Nov. 7.	Eberhard count of Kazinlugbogin admits that he owes homage to the K. of England. *Tower of London* R 1 813 O ii 663 H 1 p iii, 139
Nov 8	Notification by the K of the understanding upon which he holds an instrument of Florence count of Holland *Tower of London* R 1 814 O ii 661 H. 1. p ii 139
Nov 8	The K. confirms certain grants made by various persons to the Franciscan sisters of the order of S. Clare in Aldgate. *Tower of London.* R 1 814. O ii 664. H. 1. p iii. 140
Nov 9	The K swears to observe the convention made with the K of the Romans *London* R. 1 814 O ii 664 H 1 p iii. 140
Nov 9	The K. to the K of the Romans The bearer will tell him of the day and place fixed for the meeting of the armies. *London.* R 1 814 O ii 665. H. 1 p iii 140
Nov 12	The K. informs Eberhard count of Kazinelugbogin of the terms which he will pay for his homage *Westm.* R 1. 814 O ii 665 H 1 p iii 140.
Nov. 12	Commission to receive the oath of Sifrid abp. of Cologne to serve the K. with 1,000 horsemen. *Westm* R. 1 815 O ii 665. H. 1. p. iii 140
[Nov 12]	Credence from the K for Stephen de Baumes to A count of Savoy and bp of Lausanne. R 1 815 O ii 666 H 1 p ii 141
Nov 12	The K to the bp of Bâle, a letter of compliment. *Westm.* R. 1 815. O ii. 666. H. 1. p. iii 141
Nov. 12	The K places in the care of Florence count of Holland the money which he is about to pay to the K of the Romans *Westm.* R 1. 815 O ii 666 H 1 p iii 141
Nov 23.	The K. asks the prayers of the General Chapter of the Franciscans at Assisi. *Worcester* R. 1 815. O ii 667 H 1 p iii 141
Nov 23.	The K thanks the citizens of London for their subsidy *Worcester* R. 1 815
Dec 30	Dionysius K of Portugal sends messengers to the K on the disputes between the subjects of the Kings of England and Castile *Coimbra.* R. 1 815 O ii 667 H 1 p iii 141
1295. Jan 24	Pope Boniface [VIII] informs the K. of the voluntary resignation of pope Celestine [V.] and of his own election *Lateran* R 1 816 O ii 667. H 1 p iii 141
Feb 10	The K asks the bp of Bath and Wells to cause inquiries to be made as to those who have 40 librates of land and rent per annum, and ought to serve the K *Aberconway* R. 1. 816.
Feb 19	Pope Boniface [VIII] sends two cardinals to make peace between the K of England and the K of France. *Lateran* R 1 817 O ii 669 H 1 p iii 142
Feb. 25.	Pope Boniface [VIII] recommends to the K Peter de Hocham prior and the Knights Hospitalers of S John of Jerusalem in England *Lateran* R. 1 817. O. ii. 670 H. 1. p iii 142
March 30	Pope Boniface [VIII] exhorts the K of England to make peace with France. *Lateran.* R 1 817 O. ii 671 H 1 p iii. 142
April 6.	The K in answer to three cardinals, he is desirous of an honourable peace with France, and craves their aid therein *Aberconway* R 1. 818. O ii 672 H. 1. p. iii 143.
April 6.	The K. asks Isabella countess of Flanders to mediate with her husband in favour of Reginald count of Guelders *Aberconway* R 1 818 O ii. 673. H. 1. p. iii 143.
April 6.	The K asks G. count of Flanders to come to a settlement with the count of Guelders *Aberconway.* R. 1 818 O ii 673 H 1 p iii 143.
April 6.	Convention by which Reginald count of Guelders undertakes to serve the K. of England with 1,000 horsemen for six months *Aberconway.* R. 1. 819 O ii. 674. H. 1. p. iii. 144.

DATE	SUBJECT
1295 April 6	Outline of the above-mentioned convention, with an additional clause *Aberconway* R 1 819 O 11 675 H 1. p 111 144
April 18	The K thanks S abp of Cologne for having fixed the day of meeting with the K. of Almain. *Lammays in Anglesea* R 1. 819. O 11 676. H. 1. p 111 144.
April 23	Convention by which John duke of Lorraine and Brabant undertakes to serve the K. with 2,000 horse-soldiers against the K of France *Lammays in Anglesea* R. 1 820. O 11 676. H 1 p 111 144
April 24.	Waleran lord of Montjoy and Faukemont notifies that he has agreed to serve the K. of England for life *Lammays in Anglesea* R. 1. 820. O. 11 677. H. 1. p 111 145
April 26	John lord of Cuck notifies that he has done homage and fealty to the K of England. *Lammays in Anglesea*. R 1 120 O 11 677 H 1 p. 111 145
April 28	The K asks A King of the Romans to permit John duke of Brabant to serve under him in the war with France. *Lammays, in Anglesea* R 1 820 O. 11. 677 H 1 p 111 145.
April 28.	The K asks credence to be given by G count of Flanders to John lord de Cuck *Lammays in Anglesea* R 1 820 O 11 578 H 1. p 111 145
April 28	Similar credence addressed by the K. to F. count of Holland. *Lammays in Anglesea*. R 1 820 O 11 678 H 1 p 111 145
April 28	The K. asks Wyckebold dean of Cologne to give credence to Gerlach de Gardinis, canon of Auch *Lammays in Anglesea*. R 1 820 O 11 678. H 1. p. 111 145.
April 28.	The K of England assents to the prorogation of the day of meeting with the K. of the Romans *Lammays in Anglesea* R 1 821 O 11 678 H 1 p 111 145.
April 28.	The K. is glad to hear that Beraldus bp of Albano is coming into England to effect a reconciliation between the Kings of France and England *Lammays in Anglesea*. R. 1. 821. O 11 679 H 1 p 111 145.
June 3	The K of England explains to A King of the Romans the causes of the arrests of certain merchandise of the citizens of Lubec *Cardigan* R 1 821. O 11 678 H. 1 p 111. 145.
June 7	Letters of safe conduct for two cardinals. *Thleghython.* R. 1. 821. O. 11. 679. H. 1. p. 111. 146
June 7.	The K. asks the cardinals to let him know the form of the letter of safe conduct granted to them by the K of France *Thleghython* R 1 821 O 11 680 H. 1 p 111 146.
June 24	Summons to the clergy, barons, and others to attend the parliament at Westm. on 1 Aug. *Whitchurch.* R 1 822.
July 5.	John K of Scotland appoints commissioners to arrange a treaty with the K of France. *Stirling* R. 1 822 O 11 680 H 1 p 111 146
[July 5]	The commission referred to above, in French. *Stirling.* R. 1. 822 O 11 680. H. 1. p. 111. 146.
July 5	John K of Scotland appoints commissioners to conclude a treaty of marriage between his son Edward and a princess of France *Stirling* R 1 823 O. 11 681 H. 1 p 111 146
July 5	The above-mentioned commission in French. *Stirling* R. 1 823. O. 11. 681. H. 1. p 111 146
July 8	Pope Boniface [VIII.] asks the K. to protect certain Italian merchants going into England *Anagni* R 1 823 O 11 681 H 1 p 111 146.
July 21	Pope Boniface [VIII] asks the K. to protect the Knights Templars at Cypres *Anagni*. R. 1 823 O 11 682 H 1 p 111 147
July 31.	Pope Boniface [VIII] asks the K. to grant licence to John bp of Winchester to go to Rome. *Anagni* R 1 823 O 11 684. H 1 p 111 147.
Aug. 12	The K. of England to Margaret Q of France, inquires as to her health. *Westm.* R 1 824 O 11 684 H 1 p 111 147
Aug 12	The K of England to Mary Q of France, does not mean that recent quarrels should alter his regard for her *Westm* R. 1 824 O 11 684 H 1. p 111 147
Aug 12	The K of England to Johanna Q of France, to the same effect as the last entry. *Westm* R. 1 824 O 11 684 H. 1. p. 111 148
Aug 14	The K of England notifies to A King of the Romans that he has sent to him Wm de Ormesby and master Gerlach, canon of Aux *Westm* R. 1 824 O 11 684. H 1. p 111 148
Aug. 14.	The K to the pope, is willing to enter into a truce with France. *Westm* R. 1 824 O 11 685 H 1 p 111 148

DATE	SUBJECT
1295. Aug. 14.	The K. notifies that, in compliance with the wishes of cardinals, he is ready to make a truce with France *Westm* R 1 824 O ii 685 H 1 p iii. 148
Aug 14.	The K orders his captain and seneschal in Brittany to suspend hostilities with France. *Westm.* R 1. 825 O ii. 686 H 1 p iii 148
Aug 14.	The K. requests Amadeus count of Savoy to attend to the directions of the two cardinals, who will wait upon him. *Westm.* R. 1. 825. O. ii. 687. O 1 p iii. 149
Aug. 14.	The K. to Otho de Grandison , to the same effect as the preceding. *Westm* R. 1. 825 O ii 687 H 1 p iii 149
Aug 16	The K. asks the two cardinals to take care that the English and Gascon prisoners and hostages be surrendered up by the K. of France *Westm* R 1 825. O. ii. 687. H. 1. p iii. 149.
Aug 22	The K thanks H of Castile, his brother-in-law, for his offer of 500, 1,000, or 2,000 soldiers if needed in Gascony *Westm* R 1 825 O ii 687. H 1. p iii 149
Aug 23,	The K. of England to John K. of Scotland, credence for the bearer, Henry de Abirden. *Westm.* R. 1 826. O ii 688 H 1 p iii 149.
Aug. 28.	Mandates for the defence of the seacoasts of Essex, Norfolk, and Suffolk *Westm.* R. 1 826
Sept. 28	Proclamation to be made that the men of Holland, Zeland, and Frisland may fish in the sea near Yarmouth. *Wengeham.* R 1 826 O. ii. 688. H 1 p. iii. 149
Sept 28	Writs for the removal from the seacoast of all Norman and other foreign monks dwelling near the same *Wengeham* R 1 826
Sept 28	The K of England to the K of the Romans , the K of France hesitates to accept the truce *Wengham* R 1 826 O ii. 689 H 1 p iii. 149
Sept. 30	The K asks the clergy to meet at Westm to deliberate what ought to be done in the present state of affairs with France relative to Gascony. *Wengham* R 1 827. O. ii 689. H 1 p iii 150
Oct. 1.	The K. of England complains to the K. of the Romans that Henry count of Luceberg has seized 12,000*l.* (Turon') sent by the K. of England for the French war. *Canterbury* R 1. 827 O. ii. 690. H. 1 p iii 150.
Oct 1	Memorandum, that this day the custody of the Rolls of Chancery was committed to Adam de Osgoteby by the K's chancellor R 1 827
Oct. 2	The K. enters into an agreement with the count of Flanders and Guelders as to a debt of 100,000*l* (Turon') *Canterbury* R. 1 827. O ii 690 H 1 p iii 150
Oct 3	Writs of military summons to 19 persons to serve in Gascony with Edmund, the K's brother, at the K.'s cost *Canterbury* R 1 828. O ii 688 H 1 p iii 149.
Oct. 3.	Inspeximus and confirmation by the K. of letters of marque granted by John de Britannia to certain merchants of Bayonne against the men of Lisbon *Canterbury.* R 1. 828 O. ii. 691 H. 1 p iii 150
Oct. 3.	The sheriffs of England are to cause the election of two knights of each shire to meet the K at Westm *Canterbury.* R. 1 828
Oct. 8	Letters of credence for Luke de Tuderco going to the K. of the Romans. *Westm.* R. 1. 829 O. ii 692 H 1 p iii 151
Oct 16	The K. of England undertakes to restore to John K of Scotland the castles and towns of Berwick-upon Tweed, Rokesburgh, and Gedeworth on the ending of the war with France *Westm* R 1 829 O ii 629 H 1 p iii 151.
Oct 18.	Commission (with credence) for John Wogan, (justiciary of Ireland, and 29 others,) to raise 10,000 foot soldiers, in addition to horsemen, in Ireland. *Westm* R 1 829
Oct. 19.	The K. sends a subsidy to the men of Bourg *Westm* R. 1 829 O ii 693. H. 1 p. iii. 151.
Oct 19.	The K. informs the nobles of Aquitain that he has despatched his brother, Edmund earl of Lancaster, to aid them in Aquitain. *Westm.* R 1 829 O ii 693 H 1 p iii 151
Oct. 19.	Letters to a similar effect addressed to various other nobles of Gascony *Westm.* R. 1 830 O ii 694. H. 1 p iii 151
Oct. 23	Confederation and alliance between the Kings of France and Scotland against England. *Paris* R 1. 630. O. ii. 695. H. 1 p iii 152
Oct 23	Confirmation (by Charles count de Valois) of a treaty of marriage between the son of the K of Scotland and a daughter of the said Charles *Paris* R. 1. 831 O ii 697. H. 1. p. iii. 152.

DATE	SUBJECT
1295. Nov. 2	The K prorogues the Parliament till 27 Nov *Odymere* R 1 831.
[Nov]	Ratification by the Kings of Scotland and France of the treaty of marriage and friendship between those realms R 1 832 O ii 698 H 1 p iii 153
Nov. 17.	The K to the cardinals , will speedily send messengers to them respecting his intentions. *S. Edmund's* R 1 832 O ii 698 H. 1. p iii 153.
Nov 17.	Safe conduct for Blanche Q of Navarre coming from Gascony into England *S Edmund's* R 1 832 O ii 699 H 1 p iii 153
Nov 21	Credence for messengers going from the K. of England to the K of the Romans. *S Edmund's* R 1 832. O ii 699 H 1 p iii 153
Dec 1	The K informs the barons of England and Gascony of the illness of Edmund earl of Lancaster, by which his expedition to Gascony has been retarded. *Westm* R 1 833. O ii 699 H 1 p iii 157
Dec 4	Commission for the collection of the subsidies granted to the K for his war *Westm.* R. 1 833
Dec 13.	Pope Boniface [VIII] revokes certain acts and grants imprudently and ignorantly made by pope Celestine V. *Rome* R 1 833. O. ii. 700. H. 1 p. iii. 154.
[Dec]	The K of England to the K of the Romans , has sent messengers to Cambray to negotiate a peace with the K of France R 1 834 O ii 701 H 1 p. iii 154
1296. Jan 1	The K asks the bps. of England to pray for his success in his war with France for the recovery and defence of Gascony *S Alban's* R. 1 834 O ii 701 H 1 p iii 154.
Jan 1	The K gives the cardinals at Cambray power to conclude a truce with the K. of France *S Alban's* R 1 834 O ii 702 H 1 p iii 155
Jan 1	Commission to certain persons to treat along with the cardinals, on the terms of a truce with France *S Alban's* R. 1. 834 O. ii. 703 H 1 p iii 155
Jan 1	Commission to make a treaty of special amity with Reginald count of Guelders. *S Albans* R 1 835 O ii 703 H 1 p iii 155
Jan 1	Commission to make a similar treaty with Florence count of Holland. *S. Alban's.* R 1 835 O ii. 704. H 1 p iii, 155.
Jan. 15.	The K asks A King of the Romans to transfer the land of the late count of Holland to his son count John of Holland, who is engaged to marry Elizabeth, the K of England's daughter *Harwich* R 1 835 O ii 704 H 1 p iii 155
Jan 16	Commission from the K for a treaty of friendship with the count of Clyve *S Alban's.* R 1 835 O ii 704. H 1 p. iii 155
Jan 17.	Credence for the bearers, Reginald Ferrer and Richard de Havering, going to the K. of the Romans. *Harwich.* R 1 835. O. ii 705 H 1 p iii 155
Jan 18.	Pope Boniface [VIII] to the K in favour of certain merchants of Lucca *Rome.* R 1 835 O ii 705 H. 1 p. iii 155
Jan 22.	The K asks his bps to pray for the repose of the soul of his aunt Margaret, late Q. of France *Thetford* R 1 836. O. ii 705 H. 1 p. iii. 156.
Jan. 30.	The K asks A King of the Romans to make satisfaction for the robbery of certain of his messengers near Bâle on their way to Rome *Massingham* R 1 836 O ii 706 H 1. p iii 156
Feb. 24.	Pope Boniface [VIII] forbids the clergy to pay taxes, except by his special licence, to any secular prince *Rome.* R 1 836 O ii 706 H 1 p iii. 156
April 5.	John K of Scotland renounces his homage to Edward K of England. *Berwick-on-Tweed.* R 1. 836 O ii 707 H 1 p iii 156
April 24.	Commission from the K of England to the cardinals to negotiate peace with the K. of France. *Berwick-on-Tweed* R 1. 837. O ii 707 H 1 p iii 157
April 24.	Truce with France granted by the K of England at the request of the cardinals *Berwick-on-Tweed.* R. 1 837 O ii 709 H 1 p iii 157.
May 12	Commissioners are appointed by the K of England to treat of a truce with the K. of France. *Roxburgh* R. 1 837 O ii 709 H 1 p iii 156
May 12	The K orders his clergy and others to obey the cardinal bp of Albano, employed in negotiating the truce with France *Roxburgh* R 1 838 O ii 710 H 1 p iii 157
May 12.	The K. to his clergy (as above), nearly in the same words, but including the K of the Romans *Roxburgh* R 1 838 O ii 711 H 1 p iii 158

DATE.	SUBJECT
1296. May 12.	The K requests the duke of Brabant and the count of Bar to be present at the negociation for the truce with France *Roxburgh.* R. 1. 838. O. ii. 711 H 1 p m 158
May 12.	The K appoints commissioners to swear that he will observe the above-mentioned truce *Roxburgh* R. 1 838 O ii 711. H 1. p. iii 158
May 14.	Instructions to the earl of Lancaster, lieutenant of Aquitain, relative to the above truce *Roxburgh* R 1 838 O ii 712 H 1 p iii 158
May 14.	The K. assents to the prayer of the citizens of Bayonne for exemption from certain tolls and taxes *Roxburgh* R. 1. 839 O ii 713 H 1. p. iii 158
May 14	Robert de Brus earl of Carrick and Robert his son have power to receive into the K.'s peace the men of Annandale and the parts adjacent *Roxburgh* R 1 839 O ii 174 H 1 p iii. 159
May 14.	The custody of the castle, town, and county of Roxburgh committed to Walter Touk *Roxburgh.* R. 1 832 O ii 714 H 1 p iii 159
May 15	John the Steward, brother of James the Steward of Scotland, undertakes to serve the K. of England *Roxburgh* R 1. 839. O ii 714 H 1 p iii 159
May 16	The K of England notifies, in French, to the K of the Romans, that he has entered into a truce with France *Roxburgh* R 1 840 O ii 715. H 1 p iii 159
May 16.	Copy of the above-mentioned notification, in Latin *Roxburgh.* R. 1. 840. O. ii 715 H 1 p iii. 159
May 16	The K appoints commissioners to negociate the above-mentioned truce *Roxburgh* R 1 840 O ii 716 H. 1. p iii 160
May 16.	The castle, town, and county of Berwick-upon-Tweed committed to the custody of Osbert de Spaldington *Roxburgh* R. 1. 840 O ii 716 H 1 p iii 160.
May 16.	The castle of Jedborough and forest of Selkirk committed to the custody of Thomas de Burnham *Roxburgh.* R 1 840 O ii 717 H 1 p iii 140
May 16.	Three writs for arrangements to be made for the the conveyance into England of Scotchmen taken in the castle of Dunbar *Roxburgh* R 1 841.
June 6.	The K of England to the K of the Romans, relative to the ingratitude of Florence count of Holland. *Cluny* R 1 841 O ii. 717 H 1 p iii 160
[July 1]	The men of Holland inform the K of England of the murder of Florence count of Holland, and ask him to send over John his son R. 1 841 O ii 717. H. 1. p iii 160
July 2.	John K of Scotland resigns his realm to K Edward *Kincardin.* R 1 842 O ii 718 H 1 p tii 160
July 2.	The same resignation, in Latin. *Kincardin.* R 1 843. O. ii 718 H. 1. p. iii. 160
July 15.	The K asks the clergy and abbots to say masses for the soul of his brother Edmund. *Aberdeen* R. 1 842. O ii 719 H 1 p iii. 161
July 15.	Wm. Comyn, provost of the church of S Andrew's, and several others, renounce their alliance with France, and do homage to K. Edward *Aberdeen* R. 1 842 O ii 720. H. 1 p iii. 161.
July 26.	Robert bp of Glasgow renounces his alliance with France, and does homage to K Edward *Elgin, in Murray* R 1 843. O. ii 721 H 1 p iii 162
Aug. 18.	Pope Boniface [VIII] asks Philip K. of France to send messengers to him to treat for peace with England. *Anagni.* R. 1 843.
Aug 25	Credence for Otho de Grandison sent from the K of England to the K of the Romans *Berwick-upon-Tweed* R 1 843 O ii 722 H 1 p iii 162
Aug. 28.	The bps. of Glasgow, Aberdeen, and Candida Casa [Whithern] do fealty to the K *Berwick-upon-Tweed* R. 1 844 O ii 722. H. 1. p. iii 162.
Aug 28	Submission and fealty of Wm de Lambreton, chancellor of Glasgow *Berwick-upon-Tweed.* R 1 844 O ii. 723 H 1 p iii. 162.
Sept 2.	Credence for John de Selvesdon going from the K of England to the cardinals *Berwick-upon-Tweed* R 1. 844. O ii 723. H. 1 p. iii. 162.
Sept 2	Writs for the restoration of their lands to various Scottish ecclesiastics, who have done fealty to K Edward *Berwick-upon-Tweed.* R 1 844. O ii 723 H 1 p iii 162
Sept 3.	The K of England gives the custody of the realm of Scotland to John de Warren earl of Surrey. *Berwick-on-Tweed* R 1 845 O ii 726 H 1 p iii 164
Sept. 3	Writs for the restoration of their lands to certain widows of Scotchmen, who have taken the oath of fealty to the K of England *Berwick upon-Tweed* R. 1 845 O ii 726 H. 1. p iii 164

DATE	SUBJECT
1296 Sept. 3	Writs to allow annuities to certain Scottish married women (who have taken the oath of fealty to the K of England), whose husbands are in prison in England *Berwick-upon-Tweed* R. 1 846 O ii 728 H 1 p iii 164
Sept 8	Writ to restore his lands to Patrick de Berkeley, who has taken the oath of fealty to the K of England *Berwick-upon-Tweed* R. 1 846 O ii 728 H 1 p. iii 165
Sept 14	The K. requests the barons of Holland and Seland to arrange with him for the marriage of his daughter Elizabeth with John count of Holland *Berwick-upon-Tweed* R 1. 846. O. ii 729. H 1. p iii 165.
Sept 16	Safe conduct for certain nobles of Holland coming to the K of England *Berwick-upon-Tweed* R 1. 847. O ii 729 H 1 p iii 165
Sept 16.	The K. of England requests certain nobles and towns in Holland to give credence to the bearers of his letters *Berwick upon-Tweed* R 1 847 O ii 730 H 1 p. iii. 165.
Sept 16	Loef de Cleve count of Kyrkerode and the lord of Toeneborch have a request to the same effect *Berwick-upon-Tweed* R 1 847 O ii 730 H. 1 p iii 165
Sept. 16	Grant of 40l. per annum to the convent of Durham to do certain things in memory of S. Cuthbert, who is buried in their church *Berwick-upon-Tweed.* R 1 847. O ii. 730. H 1 p iii 165
Sept 29	The K notifies the appointment of John de Warren as guardian of Scotland and Henry de Percy as guardian of Galloway and Ayr *Morpeth* R 1 847 O ii. 731. H 1 p. iii 166
Sept 29	The K. grants the custody of the castle and county of Edinburgh, Linlisou, and Hadington, to Walter de Huntercumbe *Durham* R 1 848 O ii 731 H 1 p iii 166.
Oct 5	The K permits the bps of Scotland to make their wills *Durham* R 1 848 O ii. 732 H. 1 p iii 166
Oct. 13	Grant to Gilbert de Grimesby, clerk, who carried the banner of S John of Beverly in the Scottish war, of an annuity of 20 marks *Kirkham.* R. 1 848 O ii 732. H 1 p iii 166
Nov 21	Credence for the K's messengers going to the two cardinals on the subject of the peace with France. *S Edmund's* R. 1. 848 O ii 732. H. 1. p iii 166
Nov 21	Credence for the same messengers going from the K. of England to the K of the Romans *S Edmund's* R. 1 848 O ii 733 H 1. p iii 166
Nov 21	Commission for the same messengers to settle a treaty between the K of England and the nobles of Burgundy *S Edmund's.* R 1 848 O ii 733 H. 1. p iii 166
Nov 21	Commission to the same messengers to settle a treaty with any nobles whomsoever. *S. Edmund's* R 1 849 O 11 733. H. 1 p iii 166
Nov 21	Commission to the same messengers to treat for a peace or truce with the K of the Romans, the K of France, and others *S Edmund's* R. 1 849 O ii. 733 H 1 p iii 167
Nov 21	Commission to the same messengers to swear to the observance of the above treaties. *S. Edmund's* R 1 849 O ii 735 H 1 p iii 167.
Nov 21.	The K enjoins obedience to the same messengers in the execution of their commission. *S Edmund's* R. 1 849 O ii 735 H. 1 p iii 167
Dec 30	The K invites the bp. of London and 16 others to be present at the marriage of his daughter Elizabeth with John count of Holland *Ipswich* R. 1. 850 O ii 736 H 1 p iii 168.
1297. Jan 7	Treaty of Guy count of Flanders and K Edward against Philip K of France *Winendale.* R. 1 850 O ii 737 H 1 p iii. 168
Jan 7	Guy count of Flanders promises that his two sons, William and Philipe, and his nobles of Flanders, will put their seals to the above treaty *Winendale* R. 1. 851. O ii 739 H 1 p. iii 169
Jan 7	Guy count of Flanders notifies that he will be guided by the K of England in regard to the treaty between the K and the count of Holland *Winendale* R 1 851 O ii 740. H. 1 p iii. 169
Jan. 7	The K grants certain privileges to the merchants of Flanders trading in his dominions *Ipswich* R 1 852 O ii 740 H 1 p. iii 169
Jan 7.	The K. promises to make satisfaction for all injuries done by the English to the merchants of Flanders *Ipswich* R. 1. 852 O. ii. 741 H 1 p iii 169
Jan 7	The King notifies that he will pay 6,000l. to the count of Flanders to carry on the war with France and contract a treaty of marriage between Edward, his son and heir, and Philippa or Isabella, daughters of the said count *Ipswich.* R. 1 852 O ii. 741. H. 1 p. iii. 169.

DATE	SUBJECT
1297 Jan 7	The King notifies his intention to form a marriage between his son Edward and Isabella daughter of Guy count of Flanders *Ipswich* R. 1 852 O ii 742 H. l p iii 170.
Jan. 8	The settlement of the disputes between John count of Holland and John duke of Brabant is left to the arbitration of the K *Ipswich.* R 1 853. O. 11. 743 H. l p iii 170
Jan 9	Commissioners appointed by Guy count of Flanders to make alliance with the K of England. R 1 853 O ii 744 H l p iii l70
Jan 14	The K. appoints commissioners to inquire into the dower of his daughter Margaret duchess of Brabant *Harwich* R. 1 854 O ii 744. H l p iii 171
[Jan]	The K of England asks the K. of the Romans to assign to John count of Holland the lands due to him R 1 854 O ii 745 H l p iii 171
Jan 15	The K thanks Theodric count de Kilkerade for his care and cost incurred by him in Holland after the death of the late count *Harwich* R 1 854 O ii 745 H l p iii 171.
Jan. 17	Credence from the K of England for his messengers going to the K of the Romans *Harwich* R. 1. 854 O ii 745 H l p iii 171
Jan 17	John count of Holland swears that he will appoint Renand Ferre and Richard de Havering to his council who are nominated by the K of England *Harwich.* R. 1 854. O. 1. 745. H 1 p. iii 171
Jan 17,	Credence for the same two persons going from the K. to Wolfard de Barsle. *Harwich.* R. 1 854. O ii 746 H l p iii 171
Jan 17	Credence for the same going to Florence de Barsle. *Harwich* R. 1. 855. O. ii. 746. H. l. p iii 171.
Jan. 17	Relative to the arrest and liberation of the son of Wolfard de Barsle *Harwich.* R 1 855 O ii 746 H l p iii 171
Jan. 18	Credence for two messengers going from the K of England to the K. of the Romans to the marriage of K Edward's daughter Elizabeth. *Harwich.* R. 1 855. O ii 747 H. l. p iii. 171.
Jan 18	Receipt for 5,640*l* (Tournais) from John count of Holland as the dower of his wife the princess Elizabeth. *Harwich* R 1 855 O ii 747 H l p iii. 172
Jan 20	Commission by the K to two persons to act for the princess Elizabeth in regard to her dower *Harwich* R 1. 855 O ii 747. H l p iii 172
Jan 20,	Assignment of dower to Elizabeth, wife of John count of Holland R 1 855. O ii. 747. H. l p iii 172
Jan 20	Memorandum of the assignment in dower to the K.'s daughter Elizabeth of the manor of La Haye and the other manors between the Meuese and the Zype R. 1. 855 O. ii 748. H 1 p. iii 172.
[Feb 2]	Attestation by Henry de Beaumont and John de Kuc, envoys of the count of Flanders, that the count will keep faith with K. Edward *Walsingham* R. 1 856. O. ii. 749. H l p iii 172
Feb. 2	The K appoints Hugh de Despenser and Walter de Beanchamp to make the corresponding oath to the count of Flanders *Walsingham* R 1 856 O ii 749 H l p iii. 172.
Feb 5	Attestation by the envoys of the K of England upon the marriage of prince Edw. with one of the daughters of the count of Flanders *Walsingham* R. 1 856 O. ii. 749 H. l p iii 173
Feb 5	Attestation on the part of the K. of England by his envoys for the observance of the above-mentioned treaties *Walsingham* R 1 856 O ii 750. H l p iii 173.
Feb 6	Credence for two messengers from the K of England to the counts of Savoy and Bar *Walsingham* R 1 857. O ii 750 H. l. p. iii. 173.
Feb 6	Credence for the same messengers going from K Edward to John count of Holland. *Walsingham* R 1 857 O ii 751 H l p iii. 173
Feb 6.	Credence for the same messengers to Guy count of Flanders *Walsingham* R. 1. 857. O. ii 751. H l. p iii 173
Feb 6	Credence for the same persons to John count of Hainault *Walsingham* R 1 857 O. ii. 751. H l. p iii 173
Feb 6	Credence for the same persons to Hugh bp. of Liege, William bp. of Utrecht, and the duke of Lorraine *Walsingham.* R. 1 857 O ii 751 H p iii 173
Feb. 6	Credence for the same persons to the abp. of Cologne and the count of Guelders *Walsingham.* R. 1. 857. O. ii. 751. H. l. p iii. 173

DATE.	SUBJECT.
1297 Feb 6	Credence for the same persons to John duke of Brabant. R 1 857 O ii. 752 H. 1. p iii 178
Feb 6	Commission to renew the treaty with Guy count of Flanders *Walsingham.* R. 1. 857. O. ii 752 H 1 p iii 173
Feb 6	Commission (with various modifications) to renew the treaty with the duke of Lorraine and various other persons. *Walsingham.* R. 1. 858 O ii 753 H 1 p iii 174
Feb 6	General commission, to treat in the K of England's name, given to bp of Coventry and others *Walsingham* R 1 858 O ii 753 H 1 p iii 174
Feb 6	Commission to the same persons to treat for truce or peace between the K. of England and the K of France *Walsingham* R 1 858 O ii 754 H 1 p. iii 174
Feb 6	Commission to the same persons to swear to the above truce or peace *Walsingham.* R. 1. 859. O. ii. 754 H 1 p iii 174
Feb 7	The K informs the abp of Cologne that he has given orders for the payment of the money due to him *Walsingham* R 1 859 O ii 755 H 1 p iii 175
Feb 7.	The K. informs Wychold dean of Cologne that he hopes shortly to provide him with a prebend in the church of Dublin *Walsingham.* R 1. 859. O ii 755 H. 1 p iii 175.
Feb 12	General commission to the bp of Coventry and others to allay all disputes between the K of England's confederates *Ely* R 1 859 O ii. 756. H 1 p iii 175
Feb 12	Special commission to the same persons to allay all disputes between the dukes of Holland and Lorraine and others *Ely* R 1 860 O ii 756. H. 1 p iii. 175
Feb 12.	The K to certain cardinals, he has appointed persons to carry out the treaty of peace begun by them *Ely* R. 1 860 O ii 757 H 1 p iii 176
Feb 12	The K directs inquiry to be made respecting the losses sustained by the citizens of Bayonne plundered by the French *Ely* R. 1 860 O ii. 758 H 1 p iii 176
Feb 17	Guy count of Flanders having requested a safe conduct for the merchants of Spain and Portugal coming to Flanders, the K of England consults the lieutenant and seneschal of Gascony thereon *S Albans* R 1 680 O ii 758 H 1 p iii 176
Feb 26	Philip K of France sends envoys to the K of England to request that Scotland may be included in the truce *S Germain-en-Laye* R 1. 861.
March 8	Regulations respecting the shipping and commerce between England, Bayonne, and Flanders *Bruges* R 1 861. O ii 759 H 1 p iii 176
March 16.	Commission to treat of a marriage between A count of Savoy and Johanna countess of Gloucester, the K's daughter *Shoppesle* R 1 861 O ii 759 H 1 p iii 176
March 28	The K recommends to the pope Theobald of Bar, elected to the see of Metz *Shirburn.* R 1 863 O. ii 763 H 1 p iii 178
April 1	The K asks Guy count of Flanders to cause redress to be made to Pieres de Arthelinge, citizen of Bayonne, plundered at sea *Ford* R 1 863. O ii 754 H 1 iii 178.
April 6	Guy count of Flanders notifies that as a peer of France he has renewed his homage to the K. of France, and entered into an alliance with the K of England. *Lille* R. 1. 862 O ii 761. H. 1. p iii 177
April 6	Guy count of Flanders promises that his son Philip shall enter into the above-mentioned alliance *Lille* R 1 863 O. ii 763 H 1 p iii 178.
April 6	Guy count of Flanders promises to induce his nobility to agree to his treaty with the K. *Lille* R 1 862 O. 1 760. H 1 p iii 177
April 7	The K asks Guy count of Flanders to redress the losses sustained by Nicholas de Murtynges citizen, of Bayonne, plundered at sea *Elstington* R 1 863 O n. 765. H 1. p iii 178
May 3	The K. notifies to the men of Gascony that he has sent a subsidy for their relief *Plympton.* R. 1 864 O ii 765. H. 1 p iii 179
May 5	Writs of summons to persons holding 20 librates of land to go with the K for the defence of the realm *Plympton* R 1 864
May 6	The K orders assistance to be given to Raymund de Campania and Bernand de Pamsars, plundered in Gascony during the war *Plympton* R 1 864 O ii 765 H 1 p iii 179
May 14	The K. to the count of Flanders; has sent an answer to his letter by the count's own messengers. *Lynne* R 1 864 O ii. 766 H 1 p iii 179
May 14	The K to the countess of Flanders, will do all he can for her husband *Lynne.* R. 1. 864 O ii 766 H 1. p iii 179

DATE	SUBJECT.
1297 May 15.	Writs for the performance of military service by all persons from whom it is due, who are to meet the K. at London on 7 July *Loders* R 1 865 O ii 766 H 1 p iii 179.
May 15	Writs of military service to the bps to meet the K as above mentioned *Loders* R 1 865 O ii 767 H 1 p iii 179
May 15	Writs of military summons for the nobility to meet the K. as above mentioned. *Loders* R 1 865 O ii. 767. H. 1. p. iii 179
May 17.	The K of England asks the K of the Romans to aid the count of Flanders against the K. of France *Warham* R. 1 865 O ii 768. H 1 p iii 180
May 24	The K asks the barons of Scotland to give credence to what will be told them by the bearers of his letter as to the expedition beyond the seas. *Portsmouth* R 1 866. O ii 769. II 1 p iii 180.
May 24	Commission to Hugh de Cressingham and others to make arrangements with such Scotchmen as are willing to go with the K of England beyond the seas. *Portsmouth* R 1 866. O ii 769. H 1 p. iii 180
May 28	Bond of Simon and Richard Fraser to serve the K of England against the K. of France. *Brembre.* R 1 866 O ii. 769 H 1. p iii 180
June 4	The K urges the K of the Romans to lose no time in helping the count of Flanders against the K of France. *Canterbury* R 1 866 O ii 770 H 1 p iii 180
June 4	The K urges the K of the Romans to send immediate help to the count of Bar *Canterbury* R 1. 867 O ii 771 H 1. p iii 181
June 4	The K asks the count of Flanders to give credence to John count of Bar *Canterbury* R 1 867 O ii 771 H 1 p iii 181
June 5	The K. asks the count of Flanders to see that food be ready for the English troops on their arrival in Flanders *Canterbury.* R. 1 867 O 1 772 H 1 p iii 181
June 6	Alex Comyn of Buchan and David de Breghyn swear to serve the K of England against France. R 1. 867. O ii 772. H. 1 p iii 181
June 6	John Comyn earl of Buchan, constable of Scotland, swears to serve the K. of England against the K of France *London* R 1 867. O ii 772 H 1 p iii 181
June 10	Wm Byset, and Richard Lovel, son and heir of Hugh Lovel, swear to serve the K of England against the K of France *Canterbury* R 1 868 O ii 773 H. 1 p iii 181
June 25	Acquittance for 76,000*l* (Tournois) paid by the K of England to Guy count of Flanders for the war against France R 1. 868 O. 1. 773 H 1 p iii 181.
July 3.	The K hopes speedily to cross the sea to assist the count of Flanders against the K of France *Westm.* R 1 868 O ii 774 H 1 p iii 182
July 9	Robert Bruce earl of Carrick and others of the Scottish nobility submit to the K. of England *Irving* R. 1. 868 O ii 774. H. 1 p iii 182
July 9.	The bp of Glasgow and others of the Scottish nobility become mainpernors for Robert de Bruce earl of Carrick. *Irving* R 1 868 O ii 775 H 1 p iii 182
July 30	Memorandum as to the service of certain of the Scottish nobility (released from prison) against the K of France R. 1. 869 O ii 775 H 1 p iii 182
July 31.	Writ to restore his lands in Scotland to John earl of Athol *S Paul's, London* R 1 869 O ii 776 H 1 p. iii 183
Aug 2.	The K explains to the count of Flanders the causes of his detention in England. *Eltham* R. 1. 869 O. 1. 777. H 1 p. iii 183
Aug 2.	Similar explanation to Isabella countess of Flanders *Eltham* R 1 870 O ii 777 H 1 p iii 183.
Aug 2	Convention between the K. of England and the nobles of Burgundy against the K of France *Eltham.* R. 1. 870 O. ii. 778. H 1. p. iii 183.
Aug 2.	The K. asks the count of Savoy to march to the aid of Guy count of Flanders attacked by the K of France. *Eltham.* R 1 870 O ii. 779 H 1 p iii 184
Aug. 2	The K sends similar letters to the count of Bar and the barons of Burgundy R. 1. 871 O ii. 779 H 1 p iii 184.
Aug. 2.	The K sends similar letters to John duke of Brabant *Eltham* R 1 871 O ii 780 H 1. p. iii 784
Aug. 2	The K sends similar letters to nine nobles of Flanders *Eltham.* R 1 871 O ii 780 H 1 p iii 184
Aug 2.	The K sends similar letters to Douay, Ghent, and eight other towns R. 1. 871. O. ii 781 H 1 p iii 184

DATE	SUBJECT.
1297 Aug 2	The K orders Otho de Grandison to join him in Flanders *Eltham* R. 1. 871. O ii 781 H 1 p iii 185
Aug 2	The K asks Clay de Cachche to join him in Flanders *Eltham* R.1 871. O ii 781 H. 1. p iii 185
Aug 5	The K grants power to John le Breton, custos of the city of London, to amerce such aldermen and others as neglect their duty and take bribes. *Tunbridge* R 1 872
Aug 7	The K requests the prayers of the clergy for his success against the K of France *Cumbwell.* R. 1 872 O ii 781 H. 1. p iii 185.
Aug 12	Proclamation by the K explanatory of his dealings with the constable and marshal of England, and regretting the expenses rendered necessary by the war *Odymere.* R 1 872 O. ii 783 H. 1 p iii 185
Aug. 13.	The K excuses his delay to the K of the Romans in coming to help the count of Flanders. *Winchelsea* R 1 873 O ii. 785 H 1 p iii 186.
Aug 13	The K. informs the count of Flanders that he is now nearly ready to embark. *Winchelsea* R I 874 O ii 786 H 1 p iii 186.
Aug. 13.	Similar letter to Isabella countess of Flanders. R. 1. 874. O ii 786 H 1 p. iii 187
Aug 13	Similar letters to Bruges and eight other towns, and to various nobles of Flanders R 1 874 O ii 786 H 1 p iii 187
Aug 14.	Brian FitzAlan appointed guardian of Scotland *Odymere.* R 1 874. O. ii 786 H 1. p. iii. 187.
Aug 17.	John Comyn of Kilbride, John de Mentethe, and John de Inchemartyn, having been delivered from prison, swear to serve the K of England against the K of France R 1 872 O ii 782. H 1 p iii 185
[Aug. 17]	John de Dromman of Scotland, liberated from prison in Wisbeach castle, will serve the K of England against the K of France *Odymere* R 1. 872 O ii 782. H 1 p iii 185
Aug 19	John de Warren earl of Surrey is ordered to surrender the custody of Scotland to Brian FitzAlan *Winchelsea* R 1 874 O. ii 787 H 1 p iii 187
Aug 19	The K directs the bps of England not to excommunicate his officers for seizing corn for his use *Winchelsea.* R 1 875 O ii 787 H 1 p iii 187
[Aug]	Commission to imprison such persons as excommunicate the K 's officers acting in the discharge of their duty R 1 875 O ii 788. H 1.p.ii.187.
Aug. 21.	The K excuses himself to the barons of Gascony for having been duped by the K. of France *Winchelsea* R 1 875 O ii 789 H 1 p iii 188
Aug 21	The K requests the English barons in Gascony not to leave their posts there without the licence of the earl of Lincoln *Winchelsea.* R 1 876 O ii 790 H 1 p iii 188
[Aug 22]	John earl of Athol and others notify that they have mainprised Sir Lawrence de Strobolgy and 23 other Scotchmen about to serve the K. of England against the K of France *Winchelsea* R 1 876 O ii 790 H 1. p iii 188
Aug 22	Memorandum that this day the K. sailed for Flanders, having delivered the Great Seal into the custody of J de Benstede R 1. 876. O ii. 791. H 1. p. iii 189.
Aug 25	Pope Boniface [VIII] asks the K of England to come to terms of peace with the K of France. *Orvieto* R. 1 877 O ii 791 H 1 p iii 189.
Aug 27	Memorandum of the delivery of the seal to John de Langton at Tunbridge by prince Edward, guardian of the realm during the K.'s absence R. 1. 876. O ii. 791 H. 1 p iii 189
Aug 28	John de Hodleston is appointed keeper of the castles of Ayr, Wyggeton, Cruggelton, and Botel, and of the land of Galloway *Tunbridge* R. 1. 877. O. ii 793. H 1. p iii 189
Aug. 28.	Licence to Brian FitzAlan, guardian of the realm of Scotland, to present Englishmen to benefices in Scotland *Tunbridge* R 1 177 O ii 793 H 1 p iii. 189
Aug 28	The K decrees that the grant of au eighth for the defence of the realm, and for the confirmation of the Great Charter, shall not be construed into a precedent. *Tunbridge.* R 1 877
Sept. 7	The K forbids the holding of meetings of the people at Northampton and elsewhere. *S Paul's, London* R. 1 878
Sept. 15.	The K confirms the Great Charter of Liberties and the Forest Charter *S Paul's, London* R. 1 878 O. ii. 793. H. 1. p. iii. 189.

DATE.	SUBJECT
1297 Sept 26.	The K. orders certain of his nobility to assist Brian FitzAlan with horses and arms against the Scots *S. Paul's, London* R 1. 878 O ii. 794 H 1 p iii 190
Oct. 9.	The details by the K of England of the first truce between the Kings of France and England. *S. Bavon-sur-le-Lys* R. 1. 878. O ii. 795. H 1 p iii 190.
Oct. 9	Counterpart of the above-mentioned truce on the part of the K of France. *S. Bavon-sur-Lys* R. 1 879 O ii 795 H. 1 p iii 190
Oct 12	The K enjoins the observance of the Great Charter and the Charter of Forests. *Westm.* R. 1. 879.
Oct. 15.	The K. publishes the treaty with France, and desires that it may be observed *Ghent* R. 1 879 O ii 797 H 1 p iii 191
Oct 16	Adolph K of the Romans informs the K of England that he will send messengers to him *Andernach* R 1. 880 O ii 797 H 1 p. iii 191
Oct. 20	The K orders proclamation to be made of the truce with France *Westm.* R 1 880 O ii 797. H 1 p iii 191
Nov 5	The K confirms Magna Carta and the Charter of Forests, and adds four new clauses *Ghent.* R 1 880.
Nov. 14.	Commission to the bp of Carlisle to receive Rob de Brus earl of Carrick into the K's peace *Westm* R. 1 881 O ii 799 H 1 p iii 192
Nov 17	The K. orders proclamation to be made for the observance of Magna Carta and the Charter of Forests *Eltham.* R 1 881.
Nov 23	The commissioners of the K of France extend the duration of the truce between France and England *Groslin Abbey, near Courtray* R 1 881 O ii 799 H 1. p iii 192
Nov 23	Counterpart of the above-mentioned truce, by the commissioners of K Edward *Groslin Abbey* R 1 881. O ii 800 H 1. p iii 192
Dec. 14.	The K of England notifies the above extension of the truce *Westm.* R. 1 882 O ii. 802 H 1 p iii 193
Dec 14	The K desires various persons to come to him into Flanders with horses and arms *Tower of London* R 1 883
Dec. 14	Writ to various sheriffs to proclaim that bread and beer be ready for the Welsh soldiers as they pass on their journey into Scotland *Tower of London* R 1 883
1298 Jan 8	Writs to provide horses and arms to go with the K into Scotland as soon as he returns home *Langley* R. 1 883
Jan. 15.	Pope Boniface [VIII] to K Edward on his marriage with the sister of the K of France, and on his unjust claim to Scotland. *Lateran* R. 1 883 O ii 803 H 1 p iii 193
Jan 15	Answer by Philip K of France to certain proposals made by K Edward *Paris* R. 1 884
Jan. 22.	The K orders John de Warren earl of Surrey to march at once into Scotland without waiting for the Welsh troops *Westm* R 1 884
[Jan 29]	The English ambassadors promise that the K of England shall send an embassy to the pope respecting peace with France *Tournay* R 1 885
Jan 31.	Extension of the truce between the Kings of France and England. *Tournay,* R. 1. 885. O. ii 804. H 1 p iii 194
Feb 4.	Proclamation for the observance of the above-mentioned truce. *Langley* R. 1 886 O. ii. 807 H 1 p iii 195.
Feb 12.	Philip K of France explains a clause in the above-mentioned treaty. *Paris.* R 1. 886. O ii 808. H. 1. p iii 195
Feb 14.	The K orders shipping to be provided at Sluys for his return into England from Flanders *Langley* R 1 886
Feb. 14.	The K. orders 100 vessels to be provided at Sluys for his return from Flanders. *Langley.* R. 1. 886.
Feb 18	The K of England sends messengers to the pope to treat of the terms of peace with France *Ghent.* R. 1 887 O ii 808 H 1. p iii 195
Feb. 18.	The K of England to the cardinals on the same subject *Ghent.* R 1 887 O. ii. 808. H. 1 p iii 195
Feb. 18.	The K of England promises to abide by the decision of the pope in regard to the disputes with the K of France *Ghent* R 1 887 O ii 809 H 1 p iii 196
Feb 20	The K of England authorizes two of his messengers to appoint with the pope substitutes in the event of their absence. *Ghent.* R. 1. 887. O. ii. 810. H. 1. p. iii. 196.

DATE	SUBJECT
1298 Feb 20	The K authorizes Amadeus count of Savoy and Otho de Grandison to appoint deputies in their absence *Ghent* R 1 888 O ii 810 H 1 p iii 196
Feb. 27.	The K of England binds himself to pay to certain nobles of Burgundy 80,000*l* (Tournois) to continue the war in Burgundy. *Erdenburgh, in Flanders* R 1 888 O. ii 811 H 1 p iii 196
[March 4]	Philip K of France binds himself to adhere to the engagements made by his ambassadors at the papal court touching a peace with England *Paris* R 1 888 O ii 812 H. 1 p iii 197
March 14	Memorandum of the K's return from Flanders, and of the delivery of the great seal to the chancellor R 1 889 O ii 813 H 1 p iii 197.
March 15	Summons of certain persons to attend the K's council at Westminster on Palm Sunday *Sandwich* R 1 889
March 17	The K thanks John de Warren for his good services in Scotland *Canterbury* R 1 889
March 30	The K asks the earl of Ulster to hold himself in readiness to go into Scotland *Westm* R 1 889
March 30	Writs of military summons to 154 persons to attend at York on Whitsunday to march against the Scotch *Westm* R 1. 890
April 3	Replies by the K of England to certain questions proposed to him by the K of France respecting the liberation of John K of Scotland. *London*, R 1. 890.
April 4	Commission to inquire into the abuses imposed upon the people *Westm* R 1. 891. O ii 813 H 1 p iii 197
April 8	Commission to raise footsoldiers in Wales for the Scottish war *Westm* R 1 891
April 10	The K requires John de Warren and others to confer with him at York. *Westm.* R 1 891
April 10	The K requires the sheriffs to send knights of the shire and burgesses to confer with him at York *Westm.* R 1. 892
April 11	The K restores the city of London and the mayoralty to the citizens *Westm* R 1 892
April 20	The nobles of Burgundy appoint proctors to treat with the K of France before the pope *Besançon* R 1 892 O ii 814 H 1 p iii 197
April 25	Commission to receive 10,000 marks lent by the K. of England to Charles K of Jerusalem. *S Alban's* R 1 893 O ii 815 H 1 p iii 198
June 17	Pope Boniface [VIII] to the K of Scotland in favor of Wm de Lamberton, elected bp of S Andrews *S Peter's, Rome.* R 1 893 O ii 816 H 1 p iii 198
June 27	Pope Boniface [VIII] notifies that the Kings of the Romans and of France are severally satisfied with their rights and boundaries *S. Peter's, Rome* R. 1 893 O ii 817 H 1 p iii 199.
June 30.	Pope Boniface [VIII] grants letters to the King's procurators vouching the accomplishment of their missions to him *S Peter's, Rome* R 1. 893. O ii 817. H 1 p. iii 199
June 30	Pope Boniface [VIII] annuls the contract of marriage between prince Edward and Philippa of Flanders *S Peter's, Rome* R 1 894 O ii 818 H 1 p iii. 199
June 30.	Pope Boniface [VIII] adjudicates in the disputes between the Kings of France and England *S Peter's, Rome* R 1 894 O ii 819 H 1. p iii 200,
June 30	Notarial instrument of the compromise of the English envoys on the disputes of K. Edward with the K. of France. R 1. 896 O ii 823 H 1 p iii 201.
July 1	Dispensation by pope Boniface [VIII] for the marriage of the K. of England with Margaret sister of the K. of France. *S Peter's, Rome* R. 1. 897. O ii 826. H 1 p iii 202
July 10	Pope Boniface [VIII] solicits the K of England to cease from disturbing the peace of Scotland *S Peter's, Rome* R 1. 897 O ii 827 H 1 p iii 203
Aug. 19	Notarial instrument containing the requests of the K of France as to the infraction of the truce, and the K of England's answers *In the K's tent near Edinburgh Castle* R 1. 898
Sept 26	Writs of military summons to Roger earl of Norfolk and 117 others to meet at Carlisle, Sept. 26, to punish the rebellious Scots *Stanwick* R 1 899 O ii 828 H 1. p iii 203
Oct 8.	Pope Boniface [VIII] requests the K of England to assist the K of Armenia, who has sent messengers to the pope and the K *Rieti* R 1 900 O ii. 830 H 1 p iii 209

DATE.	SUBJECT
1298 Nov. 9.	Commission to settle the violations of the truce with France *Durham* R 1. 900. O n 830 H 1 p m 204.
Nov 16	Commission to send 40 miners from Yorkshire to the K at Berwick *York* R 1 901
Nov. 25.	Commission to draw horse and foot soldiers in the counties of Nottingham and Derby. *Newcastle-upon-Tyne* R. 1. 901.
Nov 25	Commission to Rob de Clifford to be the K's commander-in-chief in Cumberland, Westmoreland, Lancashire, and Annandale *Newcastle-on-Tyne* R 1 901
Dec 3	Summons to the barons of the Cinque Ports to perform their service at Skynburnesse on Whitsun-eve. *Tynemouth.* R. 1 901.
[Dec]	The K of England to pope Boniface [VIII] , he has sent answers to the K of Armenia and the patriarch of Jerusalem. R 1. 902 O n 831 H 1 p m 204
1299 March 12	The K. desires his lieutenants of Aquitain to send to Montreuil persons well instructed as to the aggressions of the K. of France upon Gascony *Dalton.* R 1 902. O. ii. 832 H 1 p. m. 204
March 23	Pope Boniface [VIII] exhorts the K of England to make peace with the K. of France *Lateran* R 1 902 O n. 832 H 1 p m 205
April 22	The K orders the men of Gascony to obey the papal nuncio until the end of the dispute with France *Westm.* R 1 902 O n. 833 H. 1. p. m 205.
April 22	The K notifies the appointment of the bp of Vycenza as papal nuncio *Westm* R. 1. 903. O. n. 834 H 1 p m 205
April 22.	Assurance to the citizens of London that the expedition made by them into Kent and Sussex to resist the invasion of the French shall not become a precedent *Westm* R 1 903
April 25	Pope Boniface [VIII] asks the K. to put Raynald bp of Vycenza papal nuncio in possession of Gascony *Lateran* R 1. 904. O. n. 835. H. 1. p m. 206
May 12.	Commission to Amadeus count of Savoy to complete the arrangements for the marriage of the K. of England with the princess Margaret, and of prince Edward with the princess Isabella of France *Stebenhethe* R 1 904 O n 836 H 1 p m 206
May 12	The K delegates to certain commissioners the entire business of the peace with France *Stebenheth.* R. 1 904 O n. 837. H 1. p m 206
May 15	Prince Edward appoints Henry de Lacy earl of Lincoln to settle his marriage with the princess Isabella *Stebenheth* R 1 905 O n 838 H 1 p m 209
May 23	The K requests that the bp of Vicenza may be courteously treated in Gascony and England. *Canterbury.* R 1 905 O n. 838 H 1 p m. 207
May 23	The K directs that all the lands, &c which he holds in Gascony shall be delivered to the bp of Vicenza *Canterbury* R 1. 905 O n 839 O 1 p m 207
June 3	The K orders that Gerard de Vyspeins and Amaneu de la Brette shall be added to those appointed to execute the above-mentioned business in Gascony. *Dover* R 1. 905. O u 839 H. 1 p m 207.
June 12	Pope Boniface [VIII.] apologises for the inability of the society "de Spinis " at Florence to undertake a certain loan *Anagni* R 1 905 O n 839 H 1 p m 207
June 14	The K orders that the constable of Dover deliver John de Balliol to the bp. of Vicenza at Wissant *Canterbury* R 1 906 O n 840 H 1 p m. 208
June 19	Peace between the Kings of England and France concluded by the mediation of the bp of Vicenza *Montreuil-sur-Mer.* R 1 906 O n. 840 H 1 p m 208.
June 27	Pope Boniface [VIII] asserts that the realm of Scotland belongs to the see of Rome *Anagni* R 1 907 O n 844 H 1 p. m 209
July 14	The K of England ratifies the treaty of Montreuil in the presence of the bp of Vicenza *Canterbury.* R 1 908 O n 846 H 1 p iu 210
July 16	The K notifies that he has prorogued the day of meeting at Carlisle to march against the Scotch until Aug 2 R 1 908
July 18.	The bp of Vicenza notifies that he has received John de Balliol from the constable of Dover *Wissant* R 1 909 O n 846 H 1 p m 210
July 18	Duplicate of the above-mentioned notification, in French *Wissant.* R. 1 909 O n 848 H 1 p m 211
July 21	Pope Boniface [VIII.] ordains the extension of the duration of the truce between the Kings of France and England *Anagni* R 1 910 O n 849 H 1 p. m 211

I

DATE.	SUBJECT
1299. July 29.	Pope Boniface [VIII] decrees that the Kings of France and England shall each continue to hold in Gascony what he holds at the present time *Anagni.* R. 1. 910 O. ii 850. H. 1 p iii 212
[Aug. 3]	Philip K. of France ratifies, in the presence of the bp of Vicenza, the treaty of Montreuil R 1 911. O ii 851 H 1 p iii. 212
[Aug. 3.]	Notarial copy of the treaty of Montreuil, certified by the bp. of Vicenza. R. 1 911 O ii 852 H 1 p iii 212
Aug 3.	The bp of Vicenza notifies that the assumption of the title of "Duke of Aquitain" by K. Edward shall not prejudice the rights of the K of France R 1 911
Sept. 10.	Assignment of dower to the princess Margaret of France on her marriage with K. Edward *Canterbury* R 1 912 O. ii. 854 H 1. p. iii. 213.
Sept 11	Pope Boniface [VIII] to the K of England on the prorogation of the truce with France R 1 913 O ii 857 H 1 p iii 214
Sept. 17.	Writs of military summons to proceed against the Scots, to meet at York on Nov 12 *Canterbury* R 1 913
Sept. 18	The K orders the mayor of Newcastle-upon-Tyne to arrest all French vessels in that port which were taken before the French war *Canterbury* R 1 913
Oct. 18.	Inspeximus and exemplification of a charter granted by Hen. III to John de Britannia earl of Richmond *Westm* R 1 914. O ii 857 H 1 p iii 214.
Oct 30	The K inhibits the clergy about to meet in convocation at the New Temple from meddling with matters which concern the crown *Langley* R. 1. 914.
Oct. 31.	The K asks the prayers of the Friars Preachers and Minors on his expedition into Scotland *Langley* R 1 914
Nov 3.	Amadeus count of Savoy surrenders to the K. all his right in the honor of Aquila and the manor of Coteseia *S Alban's.* R 1 914 O ii 858 H. l. p in 215
Nov. 3.	The Regents of Scotland inform the K of England that (at the requisition of the K of France) they wish to cease from hostilities with England. *Forest of Torre* R. 1 915 O. ii. 859 H 1 p iii 215
Nov 14.	Pope Boniface [VIII.] to the K of England , regrets that he cannot go to Lyons, as the K. proposes, to settle the affairs between England and France *Lateran.* R 1 915. O ii 859 H 1 p iii 215
Nov. 21.	Commission to raise foot soldiers to serve the K in Scotland by the inducement of extra pay *Wigton* R 1 915
Nov. 22.	Mandate to the see of York to send to Berwick the troops which they are bound to provide for the defence of the realm *Burton-Bishop* R 1 916
Nov 30	The K of England approves the prorogation of the truce with France recommended by the pope *Northallerton* R. 1. 916 O ii 860 H 1 p iii 216
Dec. 30.	The K prohibits tilts and tournaments in the county of York during the war *Berwick-upon-Tweed* R 1 916
Dec 30.	Writs of military summons to meet the K. at Carlisle on 24 June, to proceed against the Scotch. *Berwick-upon-Tweed.* R. 1. 916.
1300. Jan. 17.	The K. (about to march against the Scotch) asks credence for John Wogan, justiciary of Ireland, whom he sends to confer with the clergy and people of Ireland on this matter *Blythe.* R. 1. 917.
Jan. 17.	The K. (about to march against the Scotch) wishes to have the advice of Richard de Burgh earl of Ulster. *Blythe.* R 1 917.
Jan. 17.	Writs to the sheriffs of various counties to supply victuals (by June 24) for the army about to meet at Carlisle. *Blythe.* R 1. 917.
March 17.	The K. sends messengers to his daughter Elizabeth countess of Holland respecting her dower. *Westm.* R. 1. 918 O. ii 861. H. l. p. iv 1.
March 17.	The K. sends a verbal answer to the letters of Guy count of Flanders *Westm* R. 1. 918. O. ii. 861. H. l. p. iv. 1.
March 20	The K orders that the knights and burgesses sent to the parliament of Westminster shall have their accustomed reasonable expenses allowed them by their county *Westm.* R. 1. 918
March 26.	Writ to the sheriffs of England, the warden of the Cinq Ports, and justiciary of Ireland, to notify that the coins called pollards and crockards are no longer to be current R 1. 919

DATE	SUBJECT
1300. March 27.	Writs for the election of knights of the shires to meet at York for the observance of Magna Carta and the Charter of Forests *Westm.* R. 1. 919.
March 28	Writs for the proclamation, by the sheriffs, of Magna Carta and the Charter of Forests, four times each year *Westm* R. 1 919
April 7.	Pope Boniface [VIII.] informs the K. of the successes of the K. of Tartary over the Soldan of Babylon. *Lateran.* R. 1 919. O ii. 862 H. 1. p iv 1
April 11	Writ to the sheriff of Gloucester to cause those who owe military service to be ready to go with the K. against the Scotch Indorsed with the sheriffs return *S Alban's* R. 1 920.
April 15.	Writs to the sheriffs of England to cause proclamation to be made of the K's desire to alleviate the burdens occasioned by the late wars *S Alban's* R 1 920 O. ii 863. H. 1. p iv 2.
April 15.	The K. sends commissioners to pope [Boniface VIII] with powers to do whatever is required in order to complete the peace with France *S Alban's.* R 1 920 O ii 864. H 1. p iv 2
June 13.	Inspeximus and confirmation by the K. of a charter granted by him when earl of Chester (4 Nov , 43 Hen. III) to religious men and barons, &c. of the county of Chester. *York* R. 1 921.
July 15.	Commission for the punishment of persons who, having received pay to serve in the Scotch war, had deserted from the K.'s service *Dumfries* R 1 921.
July 26.	The K. appoints agents to collect 5,900 men from Yorkshire to serve in the war against Scotland. *Kircudbright.* R 1 921
Aug 24.	Pope Boniface [VIII] to the K ; has sent back one of his messengers with a reply to his letters *Sculcula* R 1 922 O ii. 865 H 1 p iv 2
Sept. 25.	The K asks the abps., bps., and certain abbots to cause masses to be sung for the soul of Edmund earl of Cornwall. *La Rose* R 1. 922 O. ii. 865. H. 1 p iv 2
Sept 26.	The K to the pope; sends commissioners to join the procurators already appointed to act for the completion of the peace with France *La Rose.* R 1 922 O ii 866 H 1 p iv. 3
Sept. 26.	The K , being about to hold a parliament at Lincoln, desires the sheriff of Cumberland to send thither two knights of the county, two citizens from each city, and two burgesses from each borough, and also such as claim forest rights *La Rose* R. 1 923
Sept 26	Writs to various abbots, priors, chapters, &c , ordering them to search their chronicles and archives for matters relative to Scotland, and to send whatever they find to the K at the parliament at Lincoln. *La Rose* R. 1. 923.
Sept 26	Writs to the chancellors and universities of Oxford and Cambridge to send to the parliament at Lincoln discreet and learned men to discuss the K 's claim to Scotland *La Rose* R. 1. 924.
Oct 7	Oath of fealty to the K. of England made by Robert bp. of Glasgow *Abbey of Holmcultram.* R. 1 924 O ii 867 H 1 p iv. 3
Oct 21	Pope Boniface [VIII] extends the duration of the truce between England and France. *Lateran* R. 1 924 O ii 868 H. 1 p iv 3
Oct. 30	The K of England grants a truce to the people of Scotland, at the intervention of Philip K of France. *Dumfres* R. 1 924 O ii 868 H 1 p iv 4.
Oct 30	The K notifies to Patrick de Dumbar earl of March that he has granted the above-mentioned truce *Dumfres* R. 1 925. O ii. 869 H 1 p iv 4
Nov. 2.	The French commissioners notify that K Edw has granted the above-mentioned truce. *York* R 1 925 O ii 870 H 1 p iv 4
Nov. 21.	The K. appoints commissioners to prove that certain citizens of Bayonne did fealty to him *Ripon* R 1 925 O ii 870 H 1 p iv 4
Nov 26.	Credence for Richard de Havering sent by the K. of England to John duke and Margaret duchess of Lorraine, *Wetherby* R. 1. 926. O ii 871 H 1 p iv 5
Nov. 27.	Commission to Richard de Havering to treat with the duke and duchess of Lorraine *Aberford.* R 1 926. O. ii. 871. H 1. p. iv. 5
Dec. 15.	Pope Boniface [VIII] exhorts the K to release from arrest the tenths collected in Ireland for the use of the Holy Land *Lateran* R. 1 926. O ii 872 H 1 p iv 5
1301 Feb, 12	One hundred and four barons, assembled in the parliament at Lincoln, write to the pope, in answer to the papal claim of sovereignty over the realm of Scotland. *Lincoln* R. 1 926 O. ii. 873 H. 1 p iv. 5.

DATE.	SUBJECT.
1301. Feb. 14.	The K confirms Great Charter and the Charter of Forests. *Lincoln* R 1. 927
Feb. 14	Writ of military summons to Roger le Bygod earl of Norfolk to proceed against the Scotch, and to be at Berwick on June 24 *Lincoln.* R. 1. 927.
Feb 14.	The K orders the bailiffs of Yarmouth and 41 other ports in England and Wales and 6 in Ireland to supply him with shipping for the expedition against Scotland. *Lincoln.* R 1 928
Feb. 14.	The K orders that search be made so as to prevent the exportation of silver of every kind from the realm *Lincoln* R. 1 928
Feb 22	Pope Boniface [VIII] to the K. he sends a verbal answer to his letters by the bearers *Lateran* R 1 928 O ii. 875 H 1 p iv 6.
Feb. 26	Pope Boniface [VIII] forgives the K. the repayment of the tenths collected for the Holy Land, and applied by the K. to other purposes. *Lateran* R 1 928 O ii 876 H 1 p iv 6
Feb 26	Pope Boniface [VIII] entreats the K not to allow himself to be diverted from the crusade by his claim to some insignificant portions of the realm of France. *Lateran.* R 1. 929 O ii 876 H. 1 p iv 6
Feb 28	The K to the citizens of Bayonne , hopes soon to be able to satisfy their demands *Lincoln* R 1 930 O ii. 879. H 1 p iv 8
[Feb]	The body of Edmund earl of Cornwall being about to be interred in the monastery of Hailes, the K. asks the presence of certain bps and abbots on the occasion R 1. 930 O. ii 879 II 1 p iv 8
March 1	Pope Boniface [VIII] permits the K to choose a confessor. *Lateran* R 1 930 O ii. 880 H. 1 p iv 8
March 1.	Pope Boniface [VIII] permits the K 's attendants to confess to the K 's chaplain in the absence of their own priest *Lateran* R 1 930 O ii 880 H ii. p. iv 8
March 1	Pope Boniface [VIII] grants the same privilege to the servants of prince Edward *Lateran.* R. 1 931 O ii. 881. H 1 p iv 8
March 1.	The K of England appoints commissioners to treat with the envoys of the French K respecting peace with Scotland *Lincoln.* R. 1 931 O ii 881 H 1 p iv 9.
March 12.	Pope Boniface [VIII.] remits to the K all the tenths which, though collected for the Holy Land, he had appropriated to his own use *Lateran* R 1 931. O. ii. 882. H 1. p. iv 9
March 18	Pope Boniface [VIII.] asks payment of the annual tribute of 1,000 marks, now 11 years in arrear *Lateran* R 1 931 O ii 882 H 1 p iv 9
April 4	The K. asks Humphry de Bohun earl of Hereford to give attendance on Edward prince of Wales at Carlisle instead of the K. at Berwick *Feckenham* R. 1 931
May 1	The K appoints commissioners to treat with the messengers of the K of France about peace with Scotland. *Lincoln* R 1 932 O ii 883 H 1 p. iv 9
May 7.	The K of England to pope Boniface [VIII.], vindicating the claim of England to superiority over Scotland *Kemesey* R 1 932 O ii 883, H. 1 p iv. 9.
May 13	The K grants to John de Kyngeston, constable of Edinburgh castle, authority to receive certain classes of Scotchmen into "the K 's peace" *Kemesey* R. 1 934 O ii 888 H 1 p iv 11
May 21.	The K commands the personal attendance of John de Wogan, justiciar of Ireland, in Scotland, together with those persons who are to accompany him *Kenilworth* R 1 934
May 27.	Philip [IV] K of France to the K of England in favor of the bp. of Avranches *S. Germain-en-Laye* R 1 934. O. ii 888 H. 1. p iv 11.
June 1.	The K of England orders the arrest of certain inhabitants of Bayonne who have attempted to deprive him of that town *Kenilworth* R. 1 934. O ii 888 H 1. p. iv. 11
June 2	The K. orders that none of his officers in Aquitain shall at this present time be arrested for debt *Kenilworth* R. 1 934 O ii 889 H 1. p. iv 11
Aug. 24.	The K of England appoints commissioners to settle peace with France in the court of Rome *Glasgow* R. 1 935 O ii 889. H. 1 p iv 12
Aug. 24.	The K asks of the pope credence for the said commissioners *Glasgow.* R 1. 395. O ii 890 H 1 p iv 11
Sept 24	Pope Boniface [VIII] asks the K to release certain merchants of Florence and their goods, arrested for homicide. *Anagni* R 1 935 O ii 891 H. 1. p iv 12

DATE.	SUBJECT.
1301. Oct 4.	Proclamation to be made cautioning masters of ships and other sailors to be on their guard in their voyage towards Gascony and other ports of France *Donypas* R 1 936.
Oct 14	The K of England appoints commissioners to settle all disputes with the K of France *Donypas* R. 1. 936 O ii 891. H. 1. p iv 14
Oct. 14	The K. appoints the same commissioners to grant a truce to the Scotch. *Donypas*. R. 1 936 O. ii 892 H 1. p iv. 12
Dec 18	The K. asks the prayers of the general chapter of the Friars Minors about to assemble at Genoa *Linlithgow* R 1 936 O ii 894 H 1 p iv 13
[Dec]	Truce granted to the Scotch by the K of England at the intervention of Philip [IV.] K. of France. R. 1. 937 O u 892 H 1 p iv 13
Dec 23	Pope Boniface [VIII] directs the further extension of the truce between England and France. *Lateran* R 1 936 O ii 895 H 1 p iv. 14
Dec. 25.	Confirmation by K Philip [IV] of the truce granted to the Scotch by his intervention. *S. Benoit Sur Loire*. R. 1. 937. O. ii. 895. H. 1 p iv 14.
1302 Jan 26	Confirmation by the K. of England of the truce granted by him to the Scotch at the intervention of K Philip of France *Linlithgow* R. 1 938 O ii 996 H 1 p iv 14
Feb. 12.	Safe conduct for Gerard de Frenay going from the K. of England to Elizabeth countess of Holland, his daughter. *Roxburgh*. R. 1. 938. O ii 896 H 1. p iv. 14.
Feb 23	Geoffrey de Geynvill and John Wogan, justiciar of Ireland, are commanded to treat with 183 magnates of Ireland on the expedition into Scotland *Morpeth* R 1 938 O ii 896. H 1 p iv 15
Feb. 23.	Geoffrey de Geynvill is to associate himself with John Wogan, justiciar of Ireland, and to treat with the magnates of Ireland. *Morpeth* R 1. 939 O ii 896 H 1 p. iv 14
March 5	The K of England notifies to the pope that he will ratify the proceedings of those commissioners at Rome who shall act in his behalf *Darlington*. R. 1. 939 O. ii. 899. H. 1 p iv 15
March 5	The K to the pope on the same subject *Darlington* R. 1. 939 O ii 899 H. 1. p iv 15.
April 6	Pope Boniface [VIII] hopes that the K will not be prejudiced against Sir John de Lovetot, who has proceeded against the bp of Coventry and Lichfield. *Lateran*. R. 1. 939 O ii 900 H 1 p iv 15
April 12	Roger le Bigod resigns to the K. the earldom of Norfolk and marshalsey of England. *Colchester* R. 1 940
April 25.	The K. appoints commissioners to conclude peace with France *Devises* R. 1. 940. O ii 901. H. 1 p. iv 16
June 12.	Agreement between the Ks of England and France as to the satisfactions to be made for the infractions of the truce *Chatham* R 1 940 O ii 901 H 1 p iv 16.
July 12	The K. restores to Roger le Bigod the earldom of Norfolk and marshalsey of England *Westm* R 1 940
July 24.	The K appoints commissioners to settle the satisfactions to be made for the infringement of the truce in Aquitain *Westm* R. 1. 941 O ii 902 H 1 p. iv. 16
Aug 10	Grant by the K of 40 oaks annually for firewood to his daughter Mary, a nun at Amesbury. *Westm* R 1 941 O ii 903. H 1. p iv. 16.
Aug. 10	The manors of Cosham, Sherston, Porstoke, Herdecote, Freshwater, and Whytefeld, together with the boroughs of Wilton and Bereford, granted for the use of the K's daughter Mary, a nun at Amesbury. *Westm* R 1 941 O ii 903 H 1. p iv 16
Aug. 10	Pope Boniface [VIII] grants a dispensation for the marriage of Humphrey earl of Hereford and Elizabeth, the K's daughter, widow of John count of Holland *Anagni* R 1 941 O ii 903 H 1. p iv 17
Aug 13	Pope Boniface [VIII] reproves the bp of Glasgow for being the originator of strife between Scotland and England *Anagni* R 1 942 O ii. 904 H 1 p iv. 17
Aug. 13.	Pope Boniface [VIII] exhorts the bps of Scotland to be at peace with the K of England *Anagni* R 1 942 O ii. 905 H 1 p iv 17
Aug. 15	The K. of England appoints commissioners to treat for peace with France *Westm* R. 1 942 O ii 905. H 1 p iv 17
Aug 15	The K. of England grants a safe conduct for two envoys from the French K coming to him upon the affairs of Scotland. *Westm*. R 1 942. O ii 906 H 1 p iv 17

DATE	SUBJECT
1302 Aug 24	The K to pope Boniface [VIII], in defence of the bp of Lichfield and Coventry, against the false charges of John de Lovetot. *Coveham* R. 1 943 O ii 907 H 1 p. iv 18
Aug 24	The K to certain cardinals , he laments to see the suspension of the bp of Lichfield from the administration of his functions, spiritual and temporal *Coveham* R. 1 943 O ii 907. H. 1. p. iv. 18.
Sept. 9	The K asks credence for certain commissioners sent by him to Rome in the matter of peace with France *Arundel* R 1 943 O ii 908 H. I p iv 18
Sept 9	The commission appointing the above envoys to Rome *Arundel.* R. 1. 943. O ii. 908 H. 1. p iv 18
Oct 8	Humphrey de Bohun surrenders to the K all his castles, manors, vills, lands, and tenements in England and Wales, as also the office of constable of England *London* R 1. 944.
Oct 13	The K of England asks the people of the comté of Bar to obey the persons whom he appoints to act in favour of the children of Henry late count of Bar *Westm* R. 1. 944. O ii 909 H I p iv 19
Oct 29	The K of England appoints commissioners to make a truce with the K of France. *Westm* R. 1 944 O ii 909 H 1 p iv 19
Oct. 29.	The K. of England appoints commissioners to make a peace with the K of France *Westm* R 1. 945 O ii. 910 H 1 p iv. 19
Nov. 7	The K informs the warden of the Cinque Ports that instead of 57 ships (which the barons of those ports are bound to furnish) he will be satisfied with 25 for the Scottish war *Westm* R. 1. 945. O. ii. 911 H. 1 p iv. 19.
Nov 7.	The K to the barons of the Cinque Ports , to the same effect as the previous entry *Westm* R 1. 945. O. ii 911. H 1 p iv 20.
Nov 7.	General order respecting the levying of the aid granted for the marriage of his eldest daughter. *Westm* R 1 945 O ii. 912 H. 1. p iv. 20.
Nov 13	In answer to the request of the K of Bohemia, the K of England sends to him certain relics of the body of S Thomas of Canterbury *Westm* R 1 946
Nov 23.	" Jehan de Bailleul," K. of Scotland, asks Philip [IV] K. of France to proceed with the business which he, the writer, has in hand against the K. of England. *Bailleul* R. 1. 946
Nov 25	The English commissioners extend the duration of the truce between the Kings of England and France *Amiens* R. 1 946 O ii 913 H 1. p iv 20
Dec. 2.	The K orders this extension of the truce to be proclaimed throughout England, Gascony, Scotland, and elsewhere *Hamstead* R 1 947 O ii 913 H 1. p iv 20
1303. Jan 10	The K of England ratifies the above mentioned truce *Odiham* R 1 947 O ii 914 H 1 p iv 21
Jan 10.	The K appoints commissioners to treat of peace with France. *Odiham.* R. 1. 947. O ii 914 H 1 p iv 21
Jan 20	The K. requests Ralph FitzWilliam and 26 others to aid John de Segrave in suppressing the attacks of the Scotch *Guilford* R 1 947
Feb. 3	The K. orders the arrest of Alexander de Balliol. *Windsor.* R. 1. 948.
Feb 11	The K gives an indemnity to the collectors of the tenths who permitted him to appropriate 10,000*l* to the affairs of Gascony *Langley* R 1 948 O ii 915 H 1 p iv 21.
Feb 17	Credence for two envoys sent from the K of England to the pope and the cardinals. *S Albans* R 1 948 O ii 916. H 1. p. iv. 21.
Feb 20	Assignment of certain castles, manors, and lands in dower to Q Margaret on her marriage with the K *Hertford* R 1 949 O ii 917 H. 1. p iv 22
March 5.	Robert bp of Glasgow declares that he holds the temporalities of his see from K. Edw as lord of Scotland *Cambuskenneth* R. 1. 949. O ii. 918 H. 1. p iv. 22.
March 12	The K of England informs Casan the emperor of the Tartars that he cannot carry out his wishes in regard to the Holy Land *Westm.* R 1 949 O ii. 918 H 1. p. iv 22
March 12.	The K. to the patriarch of the Christians in the east ; to the same effect as the preceding *Westm* R 1 949 O ii 918 H 1 p iv 22.
March 22.	Credence for the K.'s messengers going to Gascony. *Huntingdon* R. 1. 950 O. ii 919. H 1 p iv 22
March 22	The K of England orders proclamation to be made as to the extension of the truce with France *Huntingdon* R 1 950 O ii 919 H. 1. p iv. 23
March 22.	The K of England appoints commissioners to treat of a special confederation with France. *Huntingdon* R. 1. 950. O. ii. 920. H. 1. p iv. 23.

DATE	SUBJECT
1303. March 22.	The K. of England ratifies the extension of the truce with France *Huntingdon* [*cancelled*]. R 1 950 O. ii 920 H. 1 p iv 23
March 22.	The K orders the warden of the Cinque Ports to provide for the passage of the K's messengers going into France R. 1 951
April 8	The K. refers the count of Namur to the bearer for the reply to his letter *Lenton.* R. 1. 951 O. ii 922 H. 1. p. iv 24
April 9.	The K refers the councillors of Bruges and other communes of Flanders to the bearers for his answer to their letters *Lenton* R 1 951 O. ii 922 H 1 p. iv 24
April 10.	The K. of England to Henry of Spain on the marriage of prince Edw with Isabella Infanta of Spain *Lenton* R. 1 951.
April 17	The K. notifies that he will commute for a money payment the services of the clergy and others who cannot bear arms *Launton.* R. 1 952 O. ii. 923 H 1 p iv. 24
May 16	Prince Edward appoints commissioners to ratify (in his name) all treaties made between the Kings of France and England "*Rotzerbourg*" R 1 952
May 20.	Treaty of perpetual peace and friendship between the Kings of England and France. *Paris* R 1 952 O ii 923 H. 1 p iv 24
May 20.	Additional articles agreed upon by the Kings of France and England *Paris* R 1 954 O ii. 923 H 1 p iv 25
May 20	The French commissioners ratify the treaty of marriage between prince Edward and Madame Isabel, daughter of the K. of France. *Paris.* R. 1 954 O ii 928. H. 1. p iv 26
May 20.	Henry de Lacy earl of Lincoln notifies that he has received from Philip K. of France restitution of the duchy of Aquitain *Paris* R 1 955
May 20	The French commissioners certify that the K of England shall recover the debts in Aquitain due before the war *Paris* R 1 955 O ii. 928 H 1 p iv. 26
[May 21]	The French commissioners decree that 900*l* still remain to be assigned to K Edw out of 3,000*l* awarded to him by the late treaty of peace. *Paris.* R 1 955 O ii 929. H. 1. p. iv. 26.
May 25	The Scottish envoys in the French court explain to the people of Scotland the reasons why they are not expressly mentioned in the treaty of peace just concluded between England and France *Paris* R 1 955 O ii 929 H. 1 p iv. 26.
June 6	The K orders inquiry to be made respecting the robbery of the royal treasury in Westminster Abbey. *Linlithgow* R 1 956 O ii 930. H 1. p iv 27.
[June]	The K to pope [Boniface VIII.] in vindication of the conduct of the bp of Lichfield and Coventry. R. 1 956 O ii 931. H 1 p iv 27.
June 8	Pope Boniface [VIII.] to the K on the charges brought by Sir John de Lovetot against the bp. of Lichfield and Coventry. *Anagni.* R. 1. 956. O. ii. 932. H. 1 p. iv 27
June 10	Ratification by the K of England of the treaty of perpetual peace between England and France *Perth* R 1 957 O ii 934 H 1 p iv 28.
June 14.	The K asks the bp of Durham to repel the Scotch who have invaded Annandale and Liddesdale *Clacmanan.* R. 1. 957
July 10	The K orders proclamation to be made of the recent treaty of friendship and peace between England and France *Perth* R 1 958 O. ii 934. H 1 p. iv. 28
July 10	The K asks for the prayers of the Carthusians of Hampton and Selwood for his success over the Scotch. *Perth* R 1. 958 O. ii 936 H 1 p iv 29
[Aug 24]	Philip [IV] K of France admits his obligation to aid K Edward against the K of the Romans *Longchamp* R. 1 958 O ii 936 H 1 p iv 29
[Aug 27]	K Philip [IV] annuls all letters of bail between him and K. Edward in the duchy of Aquitain *Paris.* R 1 959 O ii 937 H 1 p iv 29
Sept. 30	The K of England asks the K of France to cause restitution to be made to a merchant of Lenne who had been plundered by the men of Calais. *Kynlos* R 1 959 O. ii. 937 H 1 p iv 29.
Oct. 10.	The K orders inquiry to be made into the charge against the monks of Westm of breaking into the K's treasury and stealing 100,000*l* ; John of London and Robert de Redyng are among the monks here named *Kynlos* R 1 959 O ii 938. H 1. p iv 30.
Oct. 30	Pope Benedict [XI] announces his election to K. Edward *Lateran* R 1 960. O y 939 H 1 p. iv 30.

DATE	SUBJECT
1303 Nov 10.	Commission to inquire into the robbery of the K.'s treasury at Westm *Kynlos* R 1 960 O ii 940 H 1. p iv 31.
Dec 11	The K. asks the prayers for himself, family, and realm of the general chapter of the Friars Minors about to meet at Assisi *Dunfermline* R 1 960. O ii 941 H 1 p iv 31.
1304 Jan. 21.	The K of England asks the K. of France to fix a meeting at Montreuil to settle the disputes arising out of the infraction of the truce *Dunfermline* R 1 961 O ii 941 O iv 31
Jan 28	The K of England asks the K of France to arrange for the settlement of disputes arising out of the infraction of the peace *Dunfermline* R 1 961. O ii 942 O iv 31
Jan 30.	The K. orders that the issues of the bprick. of Bath and Wells during its vacancy be assigned to Amadeus count of Savoy *Dunfermline* R 1 965
Feb 10	The K orders that the custody of the lands which belonged to Richard FitzAlan earl of Arundel, deceased, be assigned to Amadeus count of Savoy *Dunfermline*. R. 1. 961. O. ii. 650 H 1 p iv 31
April 9	The K of England orders preparations to be made for supplying the K of France with 20 ships to act against Flanders *Sandford* R 1. 961 O ii 943. H 1 p iv 31
April 10.	The K of England requires the nobility of Gascony to swear that they will renounce their allegiance to him if the marriage of prince Edward and the princess Isabella does not take place *Donary* R 1 962 O ii 944 H 1 p iv 32
April 10	The K orders his subjects and merchants to retire from Flanders, and that the Flemish merchant be expelled from England *Donery* R 1 962. O ii 944 H 1 p iv 32
April 10	The K. orders arrangements to be made for providing 20 ships for the use of the K. of France *Sandford*. R 1 962 O ii 945 H 1 p iv. 32
May 1	The K orders that John duke of Brittany be restored to his lands in England. *Stirling* R. 1 963 O ii 945 H 1 p iv 32.
May 1.	The K recommends the bp of Winchester and his affairs to the pope *Stirling*. R 1 963 O ii 946 O 1 p iv 33
May 20	The K orders certain sheriffs to send to him all crossbows and arrows in their custody to be used in the siege of Stirling castle *Stirling* R 1 963
June 8	The K informs Philip son of the count of Flanders that he cannot suffer the Flemish merchants to trade in his realm beyond 24 June *Stirling* R 1 963 O ii 946 H 1 p iv 33
June 9.	The K. notifies that the taking of the oath by the countess of Foix at Toulouse shall not be prejudicial to her rights. *Stirling* R 1 963 O ii 947 H 1 p iv 33
June 10.	The K forbids the holding of tournaments or jousts, except by his permission. *Stirling* R 1 964.
June 28	The K asks of the pope a favourable hearing for the bearers of these letters *Jedworth* R 1 964 O ii 947 H 1 p iv 33
[June 28]	The K explains the absence from the papal court of Walter de Winterburn, an English cardinal R 1 964 O ii 947 H 1 p iv 33
[June 28.]	The K recommends friar John de Wrotham to the Pope R 1. 964 O ii 947 H 1 p iv 33
[June 28]	The K recommends the same friar to Charles K of Sicily *Jeddewith.* H 1 964 O ii 948 H 1 p iv 33
[June 28]	The K recommends the same to the cardinals H. 1. 965 O ii. 948. H 1 p 4 34.
[June 28.]	The K recommends Adam de Hodelston, knight, to the pope. R 1 964. O ii 948 H 1 p iv 33
July 1	The K thanks the citizens of Bayonne for their fidelity to him *Stirling* R. 1 965 O ii 949 H 1 p iv 34
[July.]	Eric K of the Danes professes his good feeling towards K. Edward, and his willingness to forward the claim of John of Great Yarmouth. R 1 965 O. ii 949 H 1. p. iv 34
July 24	The terms and particulars of the surrender of Stirling castle to K Edward *Stirling* R 1 965 O ii 950 H 1 p iv 34
Sept. 2	Credence for Gerard Selwyn, knight, and Roger de Aselerton, clerk, sent from the K of of England to the K of France *Horton* R 1 960. O ii 952. H. 1 p iv 35
Sept 27	The K appoints the prince of Wales to act as his proctor in the approaching meeting with the K of France at Amiens *Akle* R 1 966 O ii 953 H 1. p iv 35

DATE	SUBJECT
1304. Oct 1	The K orders that 2,000 marks be allowed to prince Edward for his expenses in going into France *Northallerton* R. 1 967 O II 953 H 1 p IV 35
Oct 4	The K orders the payment of 1,000*l* sterling as a present to Mary Q of France *Thirsk.* R. 1. 967 O. II. 953. H 1 p IV. 36
Oct 4	The K orders the bp of London and other ecclesiastics of the diocese of London to say masses for the soul of the late John earl of Warren *Thirsk* R 1 967.
Oct. 14.	The K orders John de Brittania and others to superintend the expenses of prince Edward in his expedition into France *Fymmer* R 1 967 O II 954 H 1 p IV 36
Oct. 14	The K. authorizes certain others to act in the same matter *Fymmer* R 1. 967 O. II 954 H 1 p IV 36
[Dec 29]	Memorandum of the delivery of the seal by the K to Wm de Hamelton dean of York at Lincoln, to keep during the absence of the chancellor R 1 968 O II 954 H 1 p IV ,36.
Dec. 31	The K recommends to the pope William de Grenefeld chancellor of England, abp elect of York, going to Rome *Lincoln* R 1 968. O II 955 H 1 p IV 36
Dec 31	The K recommends the same person to the cardinals collectively *Lincoln* R 1 968. O II 955 H 1 p IV 36.
Dec. 31.	The K. recommends the same person to the cardinals severally. *Lincoln.* R 1 968. O II 955 H 1 p IV 36
Dec. 31	The K begs the pope to settle the disputes between the abps. of Canterbury and York respecting the carrying of the cross *Lincoln* R 1 969 O II 956 H 1 p IV 37
1305. Feb. 1	The K. orders the mayor and bailiffs of Winchester to answer before parliament for the escape of certain hostages of Bayonne *Walsingham* R 1. 969 O II 957 H 1 p IV 37
March 12.	The K orders inquiry to be made respecting certain malefactors who had attacked the masters and scholars of the university of Cambridge. *Westm* R. 1. 969. O II. 957. H 1 p IV. 37.
April 5.	The K announces that he is unable to comply with the request of the pope in favour of Hugh bp of Byblis R 1 969 O. II 958 H 1 p IV 37
April 6.	Appointment of justices of "Trailbaston" throughout the realm *Westm.* R. 1. 970 O. II 960 H 1 p IV 38
April 6	Commission to settle the exchange between the K of England and the abp of Bordeaux of certain castles in Gascony R 1 971 O II 961 H 1 p IV. 38
April 13	K Edward asks various bps. and abbots in England, Ireland, Gascony, and Scotland to pray for the soul of Johanna Q of France *Westm.* R 1 971 O II. 961. H. 1. p IV 39.
April 16	Robert count of Flanders asks the K of England to allow his men to trade with the Scotch as well as with others *Ghent* R 1 972 O II 963 H 1 p IV 39
May 26	The K asks certain bps and abbots to pray for the soul of Blanche duchess of Austria, sister of Margaret Q of England *Kenyngton* R 1 972 O II 964 H 1. p. IV. 40
May 27.	The K augments the dower of Q Margaret *Banstede* R. 1. 972 O II. 965 H 1. p IV 40
July 6.	The K orders that the tithes of the foals reared in the park of Risborough shall be paid to the abbot of Nutley. *Canterbury.* R 1 973 O II 964. H. 1. p IV 40.
Sept 4	The K appoints certain persons to be receivers of petitions presented to the parliament about to be held at Westm *Lanfare* R 1. 973 O II 965 H 1 p IV 40
Oct 4.	The K. to the pope [Clement V], regrets that neither he nor his son prince Edward can be present at the coronation of his holiness. *Westm* R 1 973 O II 966. H 1. p IV. 41.
Oct. 14	The K orders certain sheriffs to see that the Scotch are not molested in coming to or going from the K *Westm.* R 1. 973 O II 967 H 1 p IV 41
Oct 15	The K of England appoints commissioners to treat with the K. of France on the affairs of the Holy Land *Westm* R. 1 974. O. II. 969 H. 1 p IV 41
Oct. 15.	The K. grants an indemnity under certain conditions to the Scots who had opposed him *Westm* R 1. 974 O. II. 968. H 1 p IV 41.
Oct. 16	Notarial instrument reciting the bull by which pope Clement IV [A.D 1265] annuls the provisions of Oxford *London* R. 1 975. O. II. 971 H 1 p IV. 42.
Oct 26	The K appoints John de Britannia the younger to be guardian of Scotland. *Westm* R 1 975. O. II. 970. H. 1 p I– 42

DATE	SUBJECT
1305 Oct 27	The K asks credence for certain persons sent by him to the pope [Clement V.] *Westm* R 1 975 O ii 971 H. 1 p iv 42
Oct. 28	Wm. archdeacon of Lothian [*Laudoniæ*] submits to K. Edward, and asks to be admitted to his peace *Paris.* O. ii 975 O ii 971 H 1 p iv 43
Nov 2	The K. asks the pope [Clement V] to permit the canonization of Thomas de Cantilupe bp of Hereford *Westm* R 1. 976 O ii 972 H 1 p iv 43
Nov 4	The K to the cardinals, to the same effect as the preceding. *Westm* R 1 976 O. ii. 972 H 1. p. iv 43
Nov 5	The K orders a messuage and nine shops bequeathed by William Burnel to be delivered to the master and scholars of Balliol College, Oxford. *Westm* R. 1. 976. O ii. 973. H 1. p. iv 43
Nov. 7.	The K , pursuant to his father's charter, forbids jousts or tournaments to be held within five miles of Cambridge *Westm.*R 1 976 O ii 974 H 1 p. iv 44.
Nov 7	The K. orders the arrest of certain persons who had tilted near Cambridge *Westm.* R 1 977 O ii 974 H 1 p iv 44
Nov. 12.	The K. forbids jousts or tournaments being held near Oxford. *Chertsey.* R 1 977 O ii. 975. H 1 p. iv 44
Nov 16	Pope Clement [V] notifies his election to Edward prince of Wales. *Lyons* R 1 977 O ii 975 H 1 p iv 44
Dec. 18	Pope Clement [V] asks the K of England to give a patient hearing to the bearer, who will inform him of the condition of the Holy Land *Avignon* R 1 977 O ii 976 H 1 p. iv 44
Dec 19	The K , hearing that the pope has met with an accident, sends a messenger to ascertain the truth. *Ringwood.* R 1 978 O ii. 977. H 1 p iv 45
Dec 27	Pope Clement [V] asks the K to sanction the collation to his nephew cardinal Raymond of certain benefices in England *Lyons* R 1 978 O ii 977 H 1 p iv 45
Dec 29.	Pope Clement [V.] absolves the K from the obligation of observing the forced concessions made by him to his nobles while he was in Flanders *Lyons* R 1 978 O ii 978 H 1 p iv 45
1306 Jan 1	Pope Clement [V] exempts the K from excommunication, suspension, or interdict *Lyons* R. 1 979 O ii 979 H 1 p iv 45
Jan 1	Pope Clement [V] grants the same privilege to Edward prince of Wales R. 1 979. O ii 979 H 1 p iv 46
Jan 1	Pope Clement [V] announces to the bp of Worcester that he has absolved the K from observing the forced concessions made by him while he was in Flanders *Lyons* R. 1 979 O ii 975 H 1 p iv 46
Jan 20	The K forbids tournaments being held within the town and 12 miles of Oxford. *Bindon.* R 1 979 O ii 980 H 1 p iv 46.
Jan 23	Pope Clement [V] informs the K that he escaped unhurt from the accident which occurred at his coronation, but that the duke of Britanny was killed. R. 1. 980. O ii 981 H 1 p iv 46
Feb 1	Pope Clement [V] to the K in praise of Ralph bp. of London. *Lyons.* R 1. 980. O ii 981 H 1 p iv. 46.
Feb 7	Pope Clement [V] permits the K to nominate six of his clerks to ecclesiastical benefices *Lyons* R 1 980 O. ii 982. H 1 p iv 47
March 4	Pope Clement [V] apologises to the K for having detained his messengers at the papal court *S. Ciracum near Lyons* R 1 981 O ii 983 H 1 p iv 47
March 6	Pope Clement [V.] asks the K to grant the castle of Mylhano to Amanenus de Lebret *S Sirié.* R. 1 981 O ii. 984. H. 1 p iv 47
March 9	Licence to Raymund Guillelmi of Budos, knight, the pope's nephew, to embattle his house of Budos in Gascony *Winchester* R 1 981 O ii 985 H 1 p iv. 48.
March 14	Pope Clement [V] asks the K of England to conclude a peace with the K. of France *Villeneuve.* R. 1 981. O. ii 985. H 1 p iv. 48
[March 15]	Names of Scottish prisoners, with the places of their imprisonment in England R. 1. 994 O. ii. 1012. H. 1 p iv. 58
[March 15]	Names of Scottish knights and others who did homage to the K. R. 1 995. O ii. 1015. H. 1 p. iv 59.

DATE	SUBJECT
1306 April 5.	Writs to the bps., abbots, and abbesses to grant the usual aid on knighting the K.'s eldest son. *Winchester.* R. 1 982 O n 986 H 1. p. iv. 48
April 5	Similar writs to 70 earls and barons *Winchester.* R 1. 982. O n 986 H 1 p iv. 48.
April 5	Writs for the election of knights, citizens, and burgesses to meet at Westminster, to deliberate on the same subject. *Winchester.* R. 1. 982. O. n. 987. H. 1 p. iv 49.
April 5	Robert de Bruce, late earl of Carrick, having murdered John Comyn of Badenagh in the church of the Friars Minors of Dumfries, the K has appointed Aymer de Valence as his lieutenant and commander in chief in the north *Winchester* R 1 982 O n 987 H 1. p iv 49
April 6.	The K. complains to the pope of the factious behaviour of the abp of Canterbury. *Winchester* R 1 983 O. n 989. H 1. p. iv 49
April 6.	The K. orders all persons who intend to be knighted to apply to the Royal Wardrobe in London for the usual necessaries *Wolvesey.* R 1. 983 O n. 990 H 1. p iv 49
April 7.	The K. grants to prince Edward the whole duchy of Aquitain. *Winchester.* R. 1. 983. O. n. 990. H. 1. p iv. 49
April 7	The K. grants to prince Edward the Isle of Oleron *Winchester.* R. 1 983 O. n 990 H. 1 p iv 50
April 7	The K. grants to prince Edward the land of Agen. *Winchester* R. 1. 984. O. n. 990 H. 1. p. iv. 50
April 8	The K asks the prayers of the Friars Preachers about to meet in the General Chapter at Paris *Wolvesey* R. 1 984 O n 991 H 1 p iv 50
April 8.	The K. informs the pope (in answer to his letter in favour of Amanenus de Le Bret) of the recent misconduct of that person *Winchester* R. 1 984 O n 991 H 1 p iv 50
April 12.	The K recommends to the pope the petition of master Simon de Faversham *Wolvesey* R 1 984. O n 992 H 1 p iv 50
April 23.	The K. asks the pope to give credence to master Thomas de Cobham and Roger Sauvage, knight *Winchester.* R 1 984 O n 992 H 1. p iv 50
April 23	The K asks the bp of Portua to expedite the canonization of Tho de Cantilupe, late bp of Hereford *Winchester.* R 1. 985. C. n 993 H 1. p iv 51.
April 27.	The K recommends to the pope the case of the priory of Pontons in Gascony *Wolvesey* R 1 985 O n 993 H 1. p iv 51
April 30	Pope Clement [V] exhorts the K to liberate the property of certain French merchants lately arrested *Perigord* R. 1. 985 O ii 993 R 1 p iv 51
May 3	The K asks the pope and one of the cardinals to favour the ecclesiastical promotion of Baldwin, brother of the count of Luxemburg *Winchester* R 1 985. O n 993 H 1 p. iv 51.
May 6	Pope Clement [V] informs the K. that he will send a special messenger relative to the affairs of the abp. of Canterbury and the bp of Glasgow *Château-Châtillon* R 1 986. O. n 995 H 1 p iv 51
May 8.	Commission to settle the marriage of Robert, son of Otho late duke of Burgundy, and the K.'s daughter Eleanor *Winchester.* R. 1. 986 O n 995. H 1 p. iv. 52
May 8	The K. recommends to the counts of Dreux and S. Pol the affairs of his grand-nephew, Edward count of Bar *Winchester* R. 1. 986. O n 996. H 1 p iv. 52
May 8.	The K. assures the count of Dreux that he did not speak of him in the unkind terms he is reported to have done. *Winchester.* R. 1. 986. O. n. 996 H 1 p. iv. 52
May 8	The K. recommends Edward, son of the count of Bar, to Mary Q of France *Winchester.* R 1 986 O. n. 996. H. 1 p ix. 52
May 8.	The K. recommends the same person to Mary countess of S Pol *Winchester* R. 1 987. O ii 996. H 1 p iv 52.
May 8	The K recommends Agnes duchess of Burgundy to give her daughter in marriage to his grand-nephew Edward of Bar. *Winchester.* R 1. 987. O ii. 997. H 1 p iv 52.
May 8.	The K. asks Theobald bp. of Liege to promote the above marriage. *Winchester* R 1 987 O ii 997. H. 1. p iv. 52.
May 18	Pope Clement [V] excommunicates Rob. earl of Carrick and his adherents for the murder committed in the church of the Friars Minors of Dumfries *Bordeaux* R. 1 987 O. n 997 H 1. p. iv. 52

DATE	SUBJECT
1306. May 25	The K asks the pope to grant to John de Leek, the K.'s almoner, the favour which he requests *Westm.* R 1 987 O n 998 H 1 p iv 53
June 4	The K to the pope; the bearer will give a verbal answer to the letters lately sent by his holiness *Westm* R 1 988 O n. 998 H 1. p iv. 53 .
June 5.	The K. narrates to the pope the details of the double dealing of the K of France *Westm* R 1 988 O n 999 H. 1 p iv 53
June 17	Pope Clement [V] orders inquiry to be made respecting the relics deposited within the abbey of Scone *Bordeaux.* R 1 988 O n 1000. H 1 p iv 53.
June 25	Pope Clement [V] exhorts the K of England to come to peace with the K of France. *Avignon* R 1 988 O n 1000 H 1 p iv 53
June 30	Pope Clement [V] to the prior of S Neot's relative to a suit for tithes between him and the prior of Snapes. *Bordeaux* R 1 988. O n 1000 H. 1 p. iv 54
July 2	The K to the pope, further complaints of the misconduct of the abp of Canterbury. *Preston* R 1 989 O. n 1003 H 1 p iv 54
July 2	The K appoints the abp of York and the bp. of Lichfield guardians of the realm during his absence in Scotland *Preston* R 1 989 O n 1003 H 1 p iv. 54.
July 2	The K commands the admirals of the fleet of the Cinque Ports and of the coasts from the Thames to Berwick to come to him without delay in his expedition against Scotland *Preston* R 1 990.
July 7	Pope Clement [V] has already answered the K's letter about the bps. of S Andrew's and Glasgow and the abbey of Scone *Bordeaux* R. 1 990 O n 1003 H 1 p iv 54
July 11.	The K asks pope [Clement V] to cause inquiry to be made into the affairs of the priory of Durham *Tykyngtote* R. 1 990 O n 1004 H 1 p iv 55
July 12	The K asks for the prayers of the provincial chapter of the Friars Preachers about to meet at York *East Stratton* R 1 990 O n 1004 H. 1 p iv 55
July 23	The K permits Henry de Lacy earl of Lincoln to give the advowsons of the churches of Wadynton, Winelingham, Thoresby, Halton-upon-Trent, and Buckeby to a college which he is building in Oxford *Beverley* R 1 990 O n 1004 H 1 p. iv 55
July 28	The K assents to the truce between the men of Bayonne and the subjects of the K of Castile *Thirsk* R 1 991 O n. 1005 H 1 p iv 55
July 28	The K. asks the cardinal of S Prisca to interest himself in a matter concerning the burgesses of Bayonne *Thirsk* R 1 991 O n 1005 H 1 p iv 55
Aug 1.	Pope Clement [V] requires the clergy of England, Scotland, Ireland, and Wales to pay their tenths for two years for the relief of the Holy Land. *Bordeaux.* R 1. 991 O n 1,006 H 1 p iv 56
Aug. 2	Pope Clement [V] orders payment to be made to the K and prince Edward of certain tenths collected for the Holy Land *Bordeaux* R 1 992 O n 1,007 H 1 p iv. 56
Aug 2	Pope Clement [V] orders payment to be made to the K and Q. Margaret of certain tenths collected for the Holy Land *Bordeaux* R 1 992 O n 1008 H 1. p. iv 56
Aug 2.	Pope Clement [V] orders payment to be made to Q Margaret of 4,000*l* collected for the Holy Land *Bordeaux.* R 1 992 O n. 1008 H 1 p. iv 56
Aug 2	Pope Clement [V] orders payment to be made to the K of certain tenths collected for the Holy Land. *Bordeaux* R 1 993 O n 1009 H 1 p iv 57
Aug 2	Pope Clement [V] orders 2,000*l* to be paid to Q Margaret out of the tenths collected for the Holy Land *Bordeaux.* R 1. 993 O. n 1009. H. 1 p iv 57.
Aug 5.	Pope Clement [V] grants to prince Edward the whole of one year's tenths collected for the Holy Land *Bordeaux.* R 1. 993 O n 1010 H 1. p. iv 57
Aug 5	Pope Clement [V.] appoints additional collectors for collecting the tenths for the Holy Land *Bordeaux.* R 1 993 O n. 1010 H 1. p. iii
Aug 5	Pope Clement [V] permits Q. Margaret to receive 10,000*l* within five years from the tenths for the Holy Land. *Bordeaux* R 1 993 O n 1011. H. 1. p iv 57
Aug 5	Pope Clement [V] adds the bp of Lichfield to the collectors of the tenths for the Holy Land *Bordeaux* R. 1 994 O n 1011 H 1. p. iv 58
Aug 5.	Pope Clement [V] absolves the K from all sentences incurred by him for having violated holy places during the war. *Bordeaux.* R. 1 994. O n 1012 H 1 p. iv. 58.

DATE	SUBJECT.
1306. [Aug.]	Names of noble Scottish prisoners who did homage to the K. of England. R. 1. 994 O. ii 1012 H. 1 p. iv 58. *See* [March 15,] 1306.
[Aug.]	Names of Scottish landholders who did homage to the K of England R 1 995 O ii. 1015 H 1 p iv. 59 *See* [March 15,] 1307
[Aug.]	Ordinance for securing the peace of Scotland R 1 995 *See* [Feb.,] 1307.
[Aug.]	Ordinance for the transmission of the bps of S Andrew's and Glasgow and the abbot of Scone, Scottish prisoners, to their respective places of confinement in England, R. 1 996 O ii 1015 H 1 p iv 59
Aug. 7.	Writ to the sheriff of Hampshire to keep the bps of S. Andrew's and Glasgow in chains, the first-named in Winchester Castle and the other in Porchester Castle *Durham* R. 1 996 O ii. 1016 H. 1 p iv 59
Aug 7	Writ to the sheriff of Wiltshire to keep the abbot of Scone in chains in the castle of Mere *Durham* R 1 996 O ii 1017 H 1 p. iv 60
[Aug.]	The K settles the expenses which shall be allowed for the bp of S. Andrew's during his imprisonment in Winchester Castle. R. 1. 997
[Aug.]	Similar regulation as to the expenses of the bp of Glasgow in Porchester Castle R. 1. 997
Aug 14	The K. to the pope, grants his castle of Milhano to Amanenus de Lebret. *Corbridge* R. 1 997 O. ii 1017 H 1 p. iv 60
Aug 27.	Pope Clement [V] requests that his nuncios may be treated with more respect than heretofore when they come into England *Bordeaux* R. 1 997 O ii 1017 H 1 p iv 60
Aug 28	The K to the cardinal of St. Prisca , regrets that he has been compelled to refuse his requests for Wm. de Soe *Neuboro', in Tynedale* R. 1 997 O. ii. 1018. H. 1 p iv 60.
Aug. 31	The K assigns certain lands and rents to Thomas and Edmund his sons by Q Margaret *Neuboro', in Tynedale* R 1. 998. O. ii. 1018 H. 1 p iv 60
Aug 31.	The K. binds himself to pay 15,000 marks within seven years to his daughter Eleanor *Neuboro', in Tynedale* R 1. 998 O ii 1019 H 1. p. iv. 61.
Sept 6	The K. asks Tho [Jorz], cardinal of S Sabina, to let him know what passes in the court of Rome *Bradley, in the march of Scotland* R. 1. 998. O. ii. 1024 H 1 p iv 62
Sept. 6.	The K thanks R cardinal of S. Maria Nova for the interest he has taken in the K's affairs *Bradley, in the march of Scotland* R 1 998. O. ii. 1020. H. 1. p iv 62
Sept. 7.	The K. informs the pope why he has suspended the administration of the spiritualities and temporalities of the see of Canterbury and taken the latter into his own hands. *Bradley, in the march of Scotland* R 1 999 O ii 1020. H. 1 p. iv. 61
Sept. 11.	The K , relative to the suspension of the abp of Canterbury , and he asks the pope to permit his physician, Nicholas de Tyngewyk, to hold the church of Reculver along with that of Coleshill in the diocese of Sarum *Haltwhistle* R. 1 999. O. ii 1021 H. 1 p iv 61
Sept 20.	The K asks the pope to give credence to certain messengers who will inform him of the misconduct of the bps. of S Andrew's and Glasgow *Thirlwall* R 1 999. O. ii. 1025. H 1 p iv 62
Sept. 20	The K. to the cardinals, upon the same subject *Thirlwall* R. 1. 999. O ii. 1025. H 1 p. iv 63
Sept. 20. or Oct 4	The K informs the pope that William de Lamberton, bp of S Andrew, and Robert Wychard, bp of Glasgow, traitors and rebels, being in confinement, that he has granted the custody of the see of S Andrew's to master William Comyn, brother of the earl of Buchan and the custody of the bpric of Glasgow to master Geoffrey de Moubray He prays the pope's confirmation of these appointments He also informs the pope of the intended marriage between his daughter Eleanor and the son of the duke of Burgundy R 1 528 and 999 O. ii. 105. H. 1. p iv. 63.
Sept. 20.	The K. sends thank-offerings for his recovered health to S. James [of Compostella] *Thirlwall.* R 1. 997.
Oct 4.	The K. to the pope, in vindication of his right to collate John Bussh of London, his clerk, to a prebend in the cathedral of York, held *de facto* by Francis, son of Peter Gaitani *Lanercost.* R. 1. 1000. O. ii. 1026. H. 1. p iv. 63.

DATE	SUBJECT
1306. Oct. 4	The K recommends John de Drokenesford, clerk of the K.'s wardrobe, and his affairs, to the pope *Lanercost* R. 1. 1000. O. ii. 1027. H 1. p. iv. 63
Oct 7.	The K asks the pope to expedite the affairs of Nicholas de Tynchewyk, his physician, whom he had presented to the church of Reculver *Lanercost.* R. 1 1000 O ii 1027 H. 1 p iv 64
Oct. 7	The K. to the cardinal of St. Maria Nova on the same subject. *Lanercost* R. 1 1001 O ii. 1028. H 1 p iv 64.
Oct 12	The K. orders his chancellor to apply to the pope for a dispensation for the marriage of Duncan earl of Fife with Maria de Monthermer *Lanercost.* R 1 1001. O. ii 1022 H 1 p iv. 61
Oct. 23.	Notarial act, embodying the homage of James the Steward of Scotland to the K of England *Lanercost.* R 1 1001 O ii 1022 H. 1. p iv 62
Oct 28	The K solicits from the pope a dispensation for the marriage of Duncan earl of Fife with Maria de Monthermer *Lanercost* R. 1 1002 O. ii 1024 H. 1. p iv 62
Oct 28	The K asks P., a Roman cardinal, to assist in the same matter *Lanercost* R 1 1002 O ii 1024 H 1 p iv 62
Nov 4	The K commands that the monastery of Cluni shall have the assistance of all his subjects *Lanercost* R. 1. 1002. O ii. 1028. H. 1 p. iv 64
Nov. 6	The K sends as a gift to the pope 100 English does *Lanercost.* R. 1. 1002 O ii 1029 H. 1 p iv 64.
Nov 10	The K grants to John de Britannia the manors of Bywell, Wodeborne, Driffeld, Torkeseye, Kempgeston, the castle of Fodryngeheye with Nassington and Yarewell, and various other lands and rents here mentioned, in the counties of York, Lincoln, Derby, Northampton, Huntingdon, Rutland, and Middlesex, which had belonged to John de Balliol *Lanercost* R. 1 1002 O ii 1029 H 1 p iv 64
Nov 10	The K asks the pope to permit the translation of the Abbey of Scone to a safer place *Lanercost* R 1 1003. O ii 1030 H 1 p. iv. 65
Nov 10	The K to three of the cardinals to the same effect *Lanercost* R 1 1003 O ii 1031 H 1 p iv 65
Nov 15.	The K recommends Elias Gindonis, abbot of Nobiliac, to the pope *Lanercost* R. 1 1003. O ii. 1031 H 1 p iv 65
Nov. 16	The K orders that Malise earl of Strathern shall be confined in Rochester castle, but not in chains *Lanercost* R 1 1003
[Nov]	The names of the Roman cardinals. R. 1 1004 O ii 1031 H 1 p iv. 65
Nov 23	The K. orders that all persons who ought to receive knighthood shall come to him at Carlisle for that purpose. *Lanercost* R. 1 1004
Nov 24	Pope Clement [V] provides John Topham with a canonry in the church of S Asaph. *Avignon.* R 1. 1004 O ii 1031 H. 1. p. iv. 65.
Nov 28	Pope Clement [V.] urges the K to take into consideration the miserable state of the Holy Land *Vallandraut* R. 1 1005 O ii 1033 H 1 p iv. 66.
Nov. 29.	Pope Clement [V] asks the K. to give a speedy answer to the subject which will be mentioned to him by the bearers, and to dispatch them to him without delay *Bordeaux* R 1 1005 O. ii 1034 H 1 p iv 66
Dec 1	The K asks the prayers of the general chapter of the Friars Preachers in Germany *Lanercost* R. 1 1005. O ii 1034 H 1 p iv 66
Dec. 10.	The K. orders that due respect be paid to the cardinal de S. Sabina, who is coming into England, and that carriages, &c be provided for him. *Lanercost* R 1. 1005. O. ii 1035 H 1 p iv 67
Dec 10	Similar writs to the mayor, &c of Dover, Canterbury, Rochester, London, &c. *Lanercost.* R 1. 1006
Dec. 17.	Pope Clement [V] tells the K that he will forward the interests of Nicholas Tyngewyk, the K's physician. *Villandraut* R 1 1006 O ii 1035. H. 1. p. iv 67.
Dec. 22.	Pope Clement [V] informs Q Margaret that he is now recovering from his illness, but is still weak. *Villandraut* R 1 1006 O ii 1036. H 1 p. iv. 67.
Dec. 22.	Pope Clement informs the K that he is better, though weak, to recover his strength he has gone to Villandraut, where he was born, exhorts the K to undertake the crusade *Villandraut* R. 1 1006. O. ii. 1036. H. 1. p. iv 67.

DATE	SUBJECT
1307. Jan. 3.	The K. sends to Wm. de Hamelton, his chancellor, a letter in French, which is to be translated into Latin, and sent to the Pope *Lanercost.* R 1. 1006. O. ii 1037 H. 1 p. iv. 67
Jan. 3.	The K's letter to the pope, in French , he will be happy to receive the pope's messengers *Lanercost* R. 1 1007. O ii 1038 H 1 p iv 67
Jan. 3.	Translation of the above letter into Latin *Lanercost.* R. 1. 1007. O. ii. 1037 H. 1 p. iv 67
Jan 5	The K forbids the exportation of corn, cattle, horses, arms, &c., all being required for the Scottish war *Lanercost* R 1 1007
Jan. 9.	Pope Clement [V.] recommends to the King Sir John de Havering, seneschal of Gascony *Villandraut* R. 1. 1007. O. ii. 1038 H 1 p 38. 68.
Jan 16	Pope Clement [V] instructs the collectors of the tenths how the same are to be divided and applied. *Villandraut* R 1 1007 O ii 1038 H 1 p iv 68
Jan. 16.	Pope Clement [V.] to the K. relative to the fourth part of the tenths to be reserved to his holiness, according to the preceding bull. *Villandraut.* R. 1. 1008. O. ii. 1039. H 1 p iv 68
Jan 19.	The bp of Chester and the earl of Lincoln are commanded to open the parliament summoned to meet at Carlisle *Lanercost* R 1 1008
Jan. 25.	The K. to pope [Clement V.] for the prior and brethren of the order of Mount Carmel at Kingston-upon-Hull *Lanercost* R 1. 1008 O ii 1040 H 1 p iv 68
Jan 25.	The K to the cardinals, in favour of the business of Wm archbp. of York. *Lanercost* R 1 1008 O. ii 1040 H 1 p iv 68
[Jan. 26.]	The oath to be taken by the K's council in the parliament at Carlisle. R. 1. 1009. O. ii 1040 H 1 p iv 68
Feb	Regulations for securing the peace of Scotland R. 1 995
Feb. 4.	The K asks the prayers of the general chapter of the Friars Minors assembled at Toulouse *Lanercost.* R. 1 1009. O. ii. 1041. H. 1. p. iv. 69.
Feb 22.	Writ announcing the prorogation until the Sunday next after Mid Lent of the parliament to meet at Carlisle *Lanercost.* R 1 1009 O. ii 1042. H 1 p iv 69
Feb 24	Pope Clement [V.] asks the K. to give credence to the bearer on the matter of the translation of the abbey of Scone *Pessat.* R. 1 1009 O ii. 1042. H. 1. p iv. 69.
Feb 26	Notification that Piers Gaveston has sworn that he would leave England for Gascony, and would never return, and that Prince Edward also swore that he would never recall him. *Lanercost* R 1. 1010. O. ii 1043 H 1 p iv 70
Feb. 28.	The K. of England asks Ferrand K. of Castile to cause restitution to be made to certain merchants of Bayonne who have been injured. *Lanercost* R 1 1010. O. ii, 1044 H 1. p. iv. 70
March 6.	The K. of England asks the K of Norway to cause the bp of Moray, a rebel, to be arrested in the Orkney Islands and sent to the K *Linstock* R 1 1010 O ii 1044. H. 1. p. iv 70.
March 10	The K orders Tho. de Grelle to do homage to Tho earl of Lancaster for lands, &c held by him in Lancashire *Carlisle* R 1. 1011 O ii 1044 H. 1. p iv. 70
March 10.	The K. orders that Walter de Bedewynd shall have possession of the treasurership of the church of S Peter's, York *Carlisle* R 1 1011 O ii 1046 H 1 p. iv 71
March 16.	The K. orders that due respect be paid to the cardinal of S Sabina, coming to him at Carlisle *Carlisle.* R. 1. 1011 O ii 1046 H 1 p iv. 71
March 16.	Writ to the same effect for the cardinal during his stay and on his return home *Carlisle.* R. 1. 1011. O. ii. 1047 H 1 p iv. 71.
March 17	The K. to the pope, in favour of the priory of Lanercost. *Carlisle.* R 1 1012. O. H. 1047 H. 1. p iv. 71.
March 20.	Pardon for Geoffrey de Coigners, who had concealed the golden "coronella" with which Robert de Brus was crowned. *Carlisle* R 1 1012 O ii 1048 H. 1 p iv 71.
March 22	The K requests the bp. of Worcester and 13 others to accompany prince Edward on his journey into France. *Carlisle.* R. 1. 1012
March 25.	The K. intercedes with the pope for the cardinals and the house of Colonna *Carlisle* R 1. 1013. O. ii. 1048. H. 1. p. iv. 71.

DATE	SUBJECT
1307. March 26	The K orders the delivery of the abprick of Canterbury into the hands of the papal administrators of the see *Carlisle* R 1 1012 O 11
March 28	The K orders an inquisition to be made as to the distribution of the profits of the bridge between Berwick and Tweedmouth *Carlisle* R 1 1013 O. 11 1049 H 1 p 1v. 72
April 1	The K orders that the bps and clergy, &c be requested to pray for the soul of his daughter Joanna countess of Gloucester *Carlisle* R 1 1013 O 11 1049 H. 1. p 1v 72
April 1.	The K. extends the period within which B. abp of Rouen shall do homage for the lands, &c. which he holds in England *Carlisle* R 1 1013 O. 11. 1050. H. 1. p 1v 72.
April 4.	The K to the pope; he will take care to attend to the recommendation of his holiness in favour of John de Havering, seneschal of Gascony. *Carlisle* R. 1 1013 O. 11 1050 H 1 p v1 72
April 4.	The K to the cardinal of S Maria Nova, certain matters in the papal rescript connected with the priory of Okeburn, being prejudicial to the rights of the crown, cannot pass in their present form, but require amendment *Carlisle* R 1 1014 O 11 1050 H 1 p 1v 72
April 4.	The K permits the papal nuncios freely to exercise their office in England. *Carlisle* R. 1 1014. O. 11. 1051 H 1 p 1v 72
April 4	The K refuses the above-mentioned nuncios permission to carry out of England any minted English money or silver in the mass *Carlisle* R. 1 1014 O. 11 1042 H 1 p 1v. 69
April 4	The K permits the above-mentioned nuncios to hold for the pope certain sums collected for the Holy Land *Carlisle* R 1 1014 O. 11. 1051. H 1 p 1v 72
April 4	The K to Emeric de Friscobald of Florence in favour of his society *Carlisle*. R 1.1014 O. 11 1051 H 1 p 1v 73
April 16	The K orders the restitution of certain lands belonging to the abp of Rouen. *Carlisle* R 1 1015 O 11. 1052 H 1 p 1v 73
April 18	The count of Flanders to the K of England, requesting that compensation be made for injuries inflicted on one of his subjects *Ghent*. R 1 1015 O 11 1052 H 1 p 1v 73.
April 26	The K asks the pope to grant a dispensation for the marriage of Pontius de Castellione with Joanna de Peregort. *Carlisle* R 1 1015 O 11 1053 H 1 p 1v 73
May 4	The K orders that his procurations be paid to the cardinal of S Sabina, papal nuncio in England *Carlisle* R 1. 1015 O 11 1053 H 1 p 1v 73
May 6	The K orders his chancellor to urge on the pope the canonization of Robert Grosseteste, bp of Lincoln *Carlisle* R 1 1015 O 11 1054 H 1 p 1v 73
May 6	The K. urges the pope to proceed with the canonization above mentioned *Carlisle*. R 1 1016 O 11 1054 H 1 p 1v 74
May 6.	The K requests all the bps. and certain abbots to cause masses to be sung for the soul of his daughter Joanna countess of Gloucester. *Carlisle* R 1 1016 O 11. 1055 H 1. p 1v. 74
May 20.	The K. asks the prayers of the general chapter of the Augustinian Friars assembled at Lincoln *Carlisle* R 1 1016 O. 11. 1054 H. 1. p 1v 74.
May 28.	The K. requests the pope to confer on the Q.'s physician, master John de Fontibus, the first prebend which shall be vacant in the church of Rouen *Carlisle*. R. 1 1016. O. 11. 1056 H 1 p 1v 74
May 28.	The K to the abp of Rouen to the same effect. *Carlisle* R 1. 1017 O 11 1056 H. 1. p. 1v 74
June 4	Pope Clement [V] asks K. Edward to order the restitution of the castle of Mauleon to the K of France *Poitiers*. R. 1 1017 O 11 1057. H 1 p. 1v 75.
June 28.	The K grants an annual pension of 50 marks to P. cardinal of S Sabina. *Carlisle* R 1 1017 O 11 1057 H 1. p 1v 75
June 28	The K orders that no furnaces [*rogos*] be made near the Tower of London while the Q. is resident therein *Carlisle* R 1 1017 O 11 1057 H 1 p. 1v 75.
June 28.	The K orders the bp of Durham to show cause why he should not surrender the Isle of Man to the K *Caldecotes*. R. 1 1017 O 11 1058 H 1 p 1v. 75.
July 5.	The K sends messengers to the pope on his affairs with the K. of France. *Carlisle* R. 1. 1017 O 11 1058 H 1 p 1v. 75

DATE	SUBJECT
1307 July 5	The K of England to two cardinals on the same business. *Carlisle.* R 1 1018. O ii. 1058. H 1 p iv. 75.
July 7.	Memorandum respecting the death of the K at Burgh-on-the-Sands on this day. R 1 1018 O ii 1059 H 1 p iv 75

EDWARD II.

7th July 1307—20th January 1327

[July 7]	Proclamation of the K's peace R n 1 O. m 1. H 1 p iv 88
Aug 6.	Grant to Peter de Gaveston of the county of Cornwall and of the other possessions in England late belonging to Edmund earl of Cornwall *Dumfries.* R n 2. O. m 1. H 1 p iv. 88
Aug. 6.	The K orders the abbot of Hayles to pay to Peter de Gaveston 51l due annually from the town of Lechlade *Dumfries* R. ii 3 O iii 4 H 1 p iv 89
Aug 6.	Pope Clement [V] asks the K to restore to Abp Walter the temporalities of the see of Armagh *Poitiers* R ii 3 O iii 4 H 1 p iv. 89
Aug 7	Pope Clement [V] asks the K of France to grant safe conduct to the messengers of the K. of England *Villa Nova* (dioc Avignon) R ii 1 O iii 1060 H 1 p iv 76
Aug 7	Pope Clement [V] to the chancellor of France, to the same effect as the former. *Villa Nova* (dioc Avignon). R. ii 1 O. ii 1060 H. 1 p iv. 88
Aug. 21.	The K, to the pope Thanks for condolence on his father's death *Comenok* R ii 3 O iii 5 H 1 p iv 89
Aug 21	The K to the pope Will obey his advice as to making peace with France *Comenok* R. ii 1 O. iii 5 H 1 p iv 90
Aug. 21	The K to the K of France Has ordered his seneschal of Gascony to receive from him the castle of Mauleon, &c, in accordance with the treaty *Comenok* R ii 4 O iii 6 H 1 p iv. 90.
Aug 26	The K to the sheriffs of England, forbidding tournaments. *Comenok* R. ii. 4. O iii 6 H 1 p iv 90
Aug 28.	The K requests the bps, abbots, &c, to meet him at Northampton, during Michaelmas, to consult on his father's burial, and his own marriage and coronation *Comenok* R ii 4 O iii 7 H 1 p iv 90
Aug 28	The K has commissioned Aymar de Valence, guardian of Scotland, to receive into his peace all Scotchmen, excepting the murderers of Sir John Comyn. *Comenok.* R ii 4. O iii 7 H 1 p iv 90
Aug 30	The K appoints Aymar de Valence guardian and lieutenant of Scotland during pleasure *Tynewald* R ii 4 O iii 7. H. 1 p. iv. 91.
Aug 30	The K orders the payment to Ralph de Monthermer of 5,000 marks, &c by virtue of an arrangement with K Edw I *Dalgernock* R ii 5 O iii. 7 H 1 p iv 90.
Aug. 30	The K to the Barons of the Exchequer of Dublin, &c, to restore to Ralph de Monthermer all lands, &c seized in consequence of his debts to Edw I *Dalgernock.* R. ii. 5. O iii 8 H 1 p iv 91
Sept 3	The office of Marshal of England committed by the K during pleasure to Robert de Clifford. *Carlisle* R ii 5 O iii 9 H 1 p iv 91
Sept 4.	The K restores to A bp of Durham the liberties of his church, which were forfeited to Edw I *Carlisle* R. ii. 5 O iii 8 H. 1. p iv 91.
Sept 6	The K solicits of the Pope a dispensation for the marriage of Duncan earl of Fife with Maria de Monthermer, the K's niece *Bowes* R ii 5 O iii 9 H 1 p iv 91.
Sept. 6	The K to the cardinals, to the same effect *Bowes* R ii 6. O iii. 10 H 1 p iv 91.
Sept 10.	The K. appoints Eustace de Coteshache his chamberlain and receiver of Scotland during pleasure, to act with Robert Heyron, the K's comptroler *Knaresborough* R. ii. 6 O iii 11. H 1 p iv 92
Sept. 13	The K appoints John de Britannia earl of Richmond to be guardian and lieutenant of Scotland during pleasure *York* R. ii 6 O iii 10 H 1. p iv. 91.

K

DATE	SUBJECT
1307 Sept. 13	The K to the chamberlain of Scotland, to pay the earl of Richmond 10 marks per diem for his retinue of 60 men at arms *York* R II 6. O. III. 11 H 1 p IV 92
Sept. 20	The K to the sheriffs of England, to seize into the K's hands all the lands and tenements, goods and chattels, of Walter de Langton bp of Lichfield, late treasurer of K Edw 1 *Clipston* R. II 7 O III 11 H 1 p IV 92
Sept 25	The K asks the sheriff of Gascony and constable of Bordeaux to ship 1,000 tons of good wine for his coronation, to be paid for by the Friscobaldi, of Florence *Clipston* R. II 7 O III 11 H 1 p IV. 92
Sept 26	The K to Dionysius K of Portugal, respecting the restitution of an English ship recovered by the Portuguese from some pirates *Clipston* R II 7. O III 12 H 1 p IV. 92
Sept 28	The K asks the Treasurer of the Exchequer to pay the arrears of the pension of 50 marks due to Cardinal Neapoleon. *Lincoln* R II 7 O III 12 H 1 p IV 92
Sept. 29	Renunciation, by Walter de Jorz abp of Armagh, of all claims in the bulls of his appointment which are prejudicial to the K's power *Lenton.* R II 7 O III 13 H 1 p IV 92
Sept. 30	The K requests John de Britannia earl of Richmond, his lieutenant in Scotland, to proceed to Galloway to suppress the rebellion of Robert de Brus *Lenton* R II 8 O III 14 H 1 p IV 93
Oct 6	The K to pope [Clement V], has received his letters respecting peace with France, and will consider their import at Northampton with his council *Nottingham* R II 8 O. III. 14 H. 1 p IV 93
Oct 16	The K to Dolgetus K. of the Tartars, has received the letters and messengers sent by him to Edw I, is happy to hear of the success of his measures for peace. *Northampton.* R II 8 O III 15 H 1 p IV 93
Oct 18	The K. notifies that he has made new arrangements for receiving the castle of Mouléon &c from the K of France *Northampton* R II 8 O III 15 H 1 p IV 93
Oct. 18	Commission to Fortunatus de Baaz to receive the castle of Mauléon for the K from the K of France *Northampton* R II 9 O III 15 H. 1. p. IV. 94.
Oct. 18	The K directs Humphrey de Bohun earl of Essex (and 15 others) to proceed to Scotland, as soon as possible after the funeral of Edw. I to suppress the rebellion of the Scots *Northampton* R II 9
Oct. 27.	The K. orders the sheriffs of London to send to Berwick certain military stores, here specified, for the use of his army against Robert de Bruce *Westm* R II 9 O III 16 H 1 p IV 94
Oct 28	The K to the abp of York, 12 bps and other ecclesiastics, asking their prayers for the peace and prosperity of the realm *Westm* R II 9 O III 16 H. 1 p IV 94.
Oct. 28.	The K orders the sheriffs of 24 counties to permit Robert de Monthermer to have scutage from the knights' fees within their bailliwick at the rate of 40s for the array of 28 Edw I. and 40s for that of 31 Edw I *Westm* R II 10 O III 17 H 1 p IV 94
Oct. 30.	The K informs pope [Clement V] that he will reply more fully to the request of his holiness respecting the levying of the first fruits of ecclesiastical benefices *Westm* R II 10 O III 17 H 1 p IV 94
Oct. 30	The K of England to the K of France, has communicated to his prelates and others the information as to the abominable heresy [of the Templars] contained in the letters of the K of France *Westm* R II 10 O. III. 18 H 1 p IV 94
Oct. 30.	The K asks the bps, abbots, &c of England to offer masses and other ecclesiastical suffrages for the soul of K Edw I *Westm* R II. 10 O III 18 H. 1 p IV 95
Oct 31	The K recommends to the pope [Clement V] John de Leek, about to proceed to the papal court *London* R II 13 O III 18 H. 1 p IV. 95
Nov 1	The K appoints Richard de Rokesley to be seneschal of Ponthieu and Montreuil *Berkhamstead.* R. II. 11. O III 19 H. 1 p IV 95
Nov 3	Safe-conduct for the messengers of William count of Holland and Zelaud, coming to the K to arrange disputes between his merchants and the English *Berkhamstead* R II. 11 O. III. 19 H 1 p IV 95.
Nov 4	The K to William count of Holland; the commercial intercourse between the realms will be increased if the count will restore the dower of the K's sister Elizabeth, late the wife of John the count's predecessor *Westm* R. II. 11. O III 20 H 1 p IV 95
Nov. 6	Proxy by the K to the bps of Durham and Norwich and six others, to contract a marriage between himself and Isabella, daughter of the K. of France, according to the terms formerly made by pope Boniface VIII *London.* R II 11 O III. 20. H. 1. p IV 95.

DATE	SUBJECT
1307 Nov 6	Proxy to the same parties for the same purpose, but with certain alterations *London.* R ɪɪ 12 O ɪɪɪ 21 H 1 p ɪv 96
Nov. 6.	Proxy to the same parties to arrange with the K of France respecting the dower of the lady Isabella *London.* R ɪɪ 12 O m. 21 H 1 p ɪv 96
Nov 6	Proxy to the same parties to arrange a meeting between the Kings of England and France. *London* R. ɪɪ 12 O ɪɪɪ 21 H. 1 p ɪv 96
Nov 6	Commission to the earls of Lincoln and Pembroke to contract a marriage, *per verba de præsenti,* between the K of England and the lady Isabella *London* R. ɪɪ 12 O ɪɪɪ 22.
Nov 6	Letters of credence from the K. of England to the K of France in favour of the bps. of Durham and York and four others, sent to treat on special matters. *London.* R. ɪɪ 12. O ɪɪɪ 22 H 1 p ɪv 96
Nov 7	The K grants to Adam de Osgoteby the custody of the converts and their house in London *Westm* R ɪɪ 13
Nov. 8	Credence for the bp. of Norwich and another going from the K to the pope on matters between the Kings of England and France *London* R. ɪɪ. 13, O. ɪɪɪ 24 H 1. p. iv. 97.
Nov 8	The K grants for life to Amanenus de Lebret 2,000*l* of Bordeaux money arising from the pedage of St Macaire *Westm* R ɪɪ 13 O ɪɪɪ 23 H 1 p ɪv 97
Nov 8	The K. requests Robert de Kendale, constable of Dover and warden of the Cinque Ports, to take care that no bulls prejudicial to the liberties of the crown be admitted into the realm. *Westm.* R ɪɪ 13
Nov 10	The K orders the sheriff of Hampshire to pay the expenses of William bp of St Andrews (in the castle of Winchester), and of Rob Wychard bp of Glasgow (in the castle of Porchester), according to the indentures made by Edw I. *Westm* R ɪɪ 13 O ɪɪɪ 24 H 1 p ɪv. 97
Nov 10	The K orders the Treasurer of the Exchequer to pay to Humphrey de Bohun earl of Hereford and Essex, and Elizabeth his wife, the K's sister, certain sums arising from the office of constable of England. *Westm* R ɪɪ 14 O ɪɪɪ 24. H. 1 p ɪv 97
Nov 10	The K to the bp. of Bazas, will take care that the misdoings of the lords De Stagno and de Monte Olivo (of which the bp has informed him) shall be speedily punished. *Westm* R. ɪɪ 14 O ɪɪɪ 25 H. 1 p ɪv 97
Nov 10	The K requests aid for his baker, Wm Hathewy, going to France, to provide for the arrival of himself and his retinue *Westm.* R ɪɪ 14. O ɪɪɪ 25 H 1 p ɪv 98
Nov 12	The K to pope [Clement V] in favour of the affairs of "his dearest friend" Anthony bp of Durham in the papal court. *Westm* R ɪɪ 14 O ɪɪɪ 25 H. 1 p ɪv 98
Nov 14	The K asks Rob de Kendale, constable of Dover castle and warden of the Cinque Ports, to aid the departure of Peter cardinal bp of Sabina, with his plate, &c and 1,000 marks of money *Langley* R ɪɪ. 15 O. ɪɪɪ. 26 H 1 p ɪv 98
Nov 14	The K to the same, to provide all things necessary for the K's passage by Dec 19. *Langley* R. ɪɪ 14 O ɪɪɪ 26 H 1 p ɪv 98
Nov. 14	The K to the same, to permit Reginald Berardi (one of the Friscobaldi of Florence) to export with him 500 marks to make provision for the K.'s coming *Langley* R ɪɪ 14 O ɪɪɪ 26. H 1. p. ɪv 98
Nov 14.	The K to the same, to permit certain persons named (15 in number) to pass the sea with their luggage unsearched, they being employed in providing for the K *Langley.* R ɪɪ 15 O ɪɪɪ 26 H 1 p ɪv 98
Nov. 21.	The K. recommends his treasurer W Reynolds to the pope as a fitting bp for the vacant see of Worcester *Langley* R. ɪɪ 15 O ɪɪɪ 27 H 1. p. iv 98
Nov 21	The K to the cardinals, in favour of the same Walter Reynolds R ɪɪ 15 O ɪɪɪ 28 H 1 p ɪv 98.
Nov. 21.	The K grants to Peter de Gaveston, earl of Cornwall, the custody of the lands and tenements of Tho de Audeley, a minor, deceased, son and heir of Nicolas de Audeley, deceased *Langley* R. ɪɪ 16
Nov. 21	The K grants to his sister Mary, now at Amesbury, (in exchange for the manor of Cosham and the burgh of Wilton and Bereford,) the manor of Swaynston, for her life or as long as she lives in England. *Langley.* R ɪɪ. 16 O ɪɪɪ. 29. H. 1 p ɪv. 99
Nov. 21	Pope Clement [V] requests the K to give letters of safe-conduct for two of his nuncios about to proceed into England *Avignon.* R. ɪɪ. 16. O. ɪɪɪ 30 H. 1. p ɪv. 99.
Nov. 21	Letters of credence from the pope to the K. for the two nuncios. *Avignon.* R ɪɪ 16 O ɪɪɪ 30. H 1 p ɪv 99

DATE	SUBJECT
1307. Nov 22.	Pope Clement [V] requests the K to arrest (on the same day) all the Knights Templars within his realm *Poitiers.* R. ii 16. O iii 30. H 1 p iv 99.
Nov 25	The K orders the mayor and sheriffs of London to provide a ship for the conveyance of his tents [into France] *Langley* R. ii 17 O iii 32 H 1 p iv 100
Nov. 25.	The K orders the sheriff of Kent to provide, at Dover, sufficient bridges and "clays" for his passage [into France] *Langley* R ii 17 O iii 32. H 1 p iv 100
Nov 26	The K orders the seneschal of L'Agennois to meet him at Boulogne at Christmas, to give him information respecting the Templars and the condition of that country *Langley.* R ii 17 O iii 32 H 1 p iv 100
Nov 30	The K of England to the K of Armenia, in favour of Wm bp. of Lidda and various friars preachers, and others, proceeding to the Holy Land for the conversion of the heathen *Langley.* R ii 17 O iii 33 H 1 p iv 100
Nov 30	The K to the pope [Clement V] in favour of the persons mentioned above *Langley* R ii 18 O iii 33 H 1 p iv 100.
Nov 30	The K. to the emperor of the Tartars, as it is a favourable opportunity to extirpate the sect of the Mahometans, he recommends the bp of Lidda and his company *Langley* R ii 18 O iii 34 H 1 p iv 100.
[Dec. 1]	Ordinances by the K and his council for the simultaneous seizure of the Knights Templars by the several sheriffs throughout England and Ireland R. ii 18. O iii. 34. H. 1. p iv. 101.
[Dec. 4]	The K of England to the Kings of Portugal, Castille and Leon, Sicily and Aragon, cautioning them against giving credence to reports against the Knights Templars, circulated by their enemies *Reading* R. ii 19 O iii 35 H 1 p iv 101
Dec 4–10	The K to the sheriffs of Norfolk and others, to pay the expenses of certain Scottish and Welsh prisoners in the castles of Norwich, Winchester, Exeter, and Launceston *Reading and Westm* R. ii. 20 O iii 39 H 1 p iv 102
Dec 6	The K to pope [Clement V] in favour of Walter de Stapeldon, bp elect of Exeter, against whose election an appeal has been raised *Langley* R ii 19 O iii. 36. H. 1. p iv 101
Dec 6	The K to two of the cardinals, to favour the election of Walter de Stapeldon to the see of Exeter *Langley* R ii 19. O iii 37 H 1 p iv 102
Dec 10	The K to pope [Clement V], is unable to credit the horrible charges brought against the Knights Templars, who everywhere bear a good name in England *Westm.* R. ii 24. O iii 37 H 1 p iv 102
Dec 10	The K requests pope [Clement V] to make no process in the matter of the disputed treasurership of York nor in the prebend of Stynelyngton Were the writer to connive at such proceedings, his nobles would not endure it. *Westm* R. ii 20 O iii 38 H 1 p iv 102
Dec 12	The K solicits pope [Clement V] to proceed with the canonization of Tho de Cantilupe late bp of Hereford, and for this purpose sends to him Adam de Orleton *Westm.* R. ii 20 O iii 39 H 1 p iv 103
Dec 12	The K to three cardinals , thanks them for their good offices in the matter referred to above, and asks their further co operation *Westm* R ii 21 O iii 40 H 1 p. iv. 103
Dec 12.	The K. to 22 cardinals , asks their assistance in obtaining the canonization of Tho de Cantilupe *Westm* R ii 21 O iii 40 H 1 p iv 103
Dec 12	The K asks Cardinal Franciscus Gaytani to stay the proceedings instituted by his nephew for collation to the prebend of Stillington, in the church of York *Westm.* R ii 22 O iii 41 H 1 p iv 103
Dec 13	Pope Clement [V] asks the K to permit the abbots of the Cistercian order in England personally to attend their general chapter at Citeaux *Poitiers* R ii 22 O iii 42 H 1 p iv 104
Dec 13–14	The K (about to cross to Boulogne) asks the clergy and nobility of Scotland to preserve peace in that realm *Westm* R ii 22
Dec 14	The K asks that Elias de Accumbe may be assisted in erecting the K 's tents at Boulogne. *Westm* R ii 22 O iii 43 H 1 p iv 104
Dec 15.	The K orders various sheriffs to arrest the Knights Templars on the morrow of the Epiphany *Westm* R ii 23 O. iii 43 H 1 p iv 104
Dec 16	The K asks the pope to restore the abp of Canterbury to his see, for it pertains to the abp to crown the Kings of England *Westm* R ii 23 O iii 44 H. 1. p iv 105.

DATE	SUBJECT
1307 Dec 20	The K orders the simultaneous arrest of the Knights Templars throughout Ireland, Scotland, and Wales. *Byfleet* R n. 23. O iii. 45. H 1 p iv. 104.
Dec 20	The K orders all persons in West and North Wales to assist in the above arrest. *Byfleet.* R ii 24 O ii' 45 H 1 p iv 105.
Dec. 24	The K asks the cardinals to help him in preserving his rights against certain papal bulls *Westm* R ii 24 O iii. 45 H. 1. p iv 105
Dec. 26.	The K tells the pope that he will carry out his wishes in the matter of the Templars. *Westm* R. ii 24 O iii 46 H 1 p. iv 106
Dec 26	The K (going abroad) appoints Peter de Gavaston earl of Cornwall to be guardian of England during his absence *Westm* R ii 24 O iii 47 H 1 p iv 106
Dec. 26.	The K requests the pope to cause the papal legates to suspend their proceedings until he has consulted his nobility *Westm* R ii 25 O iii 47 H 1 p iv 106
Dec 30	The K of England notifies to the K of France the day of his intended arrival at Boulogne for his marriage *Canterbury* R ii 25 O iii 48 H 1 p iv 106
1308 Jan 1	The K. of England asks the K. of France to give credence to certain messengers *Canterbury* R ii 25. O iii 49 H 1 p. iv 106
Jan 3	The K orders the constable of Bordeaux to pay what is due of the dowry of Constance of Byern *Canterbury* R ii 25 O iii 49 H 1 p iv 106
Jan 6	The K. orders the sheriffs of Worcester and Warwick to levy the twentieths and fifteenths due in those counties *Wye* R ii 26
Jan. 10	The K orders the sheriff of Wiltshire to provide certain oxen, hogs, &c for his coronation *Westm* R. ii 26
Jan 15	The K assigns to John de Brittannia, guardian of Scotland, 10 marks per diem for himself and his retinue *Dover* R ii 26. O. iii 50. H. 1 p iv 107
Jan 16-20	Protections for various persons about to go abroad with the K *Dover* R. ii. 27. O iii 51 H 1 p iv. 107
Jan 18	The K. orders various ecclesiastics, nobles, and others, to be present at his coronation *Dover* R ii 27. O iii 51 H 1 p iv 108
Jan 18	The K orders the sheriffs throughout England to proclaim the day of his coronation *Dover* R ii 28 O iii 53. H 1 p iv 108
Jan 18	The K. allows Peter de Gaveston earl of Cornwall to confer benefices and to settle wards and marriages during his absence from England *Dover* R ii 28 O iii 53 H 1 p iv 108
Jan 20.	The K complains to A cardinal of S. Maria in Porticu of the conduct of the pope in regard to Walter Reynolds bp of Worcester. *Dover* R ii 28. O. iii 54 H. 1. p iv. 108
Jan. 20.	The K complains to the pope of his conduct in the same matter *Dover* R ii 28. O iii 55 H 1 p iv 108
Jan 20	The K. to cardinal Th Jorz and five other cardinals upon the same subject. *Dover* R ii 29 O iii 56. H. 1. p iv 109.
Jan 21.	Memorandum of the delivery of the great seal to Wm de Melton, who took the same with him when he went abroad with the K, and of the new seal to the chancellor, to be used in the K.'s absense R ii 29 O iii 56 H 1. p iv 109.
Jan 22	Peter de Gavaston (custos of England in the K's absence) requests Alice, widow of Roger le Bygod, and others, to meet the K and his consort at Dover coming from abroad. *Dover* R. ii. 30 O iii 57 H 1 p iv 110
Jan 26	Letters of protection for certain persons who are abroad with the K. or Q. Margaret. *Ledes* and *Dover* R ii 30. O iii. 57. H. 1. p. iv 110
Jan. 31	Philip K. of France ratifies the truce with England, and accepts the homage of the K of England *Boulogne* R. ii 30 O iii. 57 H 1 p iv 110
Feb 5	The K intercedes with the pope for Garcio count of Foix, who has been excommunicated *Whitsand* R ii 30 O iii 58 H. 1 p. iv. 110.
Feb. 5.	The K to Reymond [del Gout,] the pope's nephew, for the same Garcio de Foix *Whitsand.* R ii. 30 O. iii 58 H 1 p iv 110
Feb 7	Memorandum of the arrival of K. Edward and Q Isabella at Dover. R ii 31. O. iii 59 H 1 p iv 110.
Feb. 8	The K. invites certain persons here named, to be present at the coronation of himself and the Q. *Dover.* R. ii. 31. O. iii 59. H. 1 p iv 111.

DATE	SUBJECT
1308 Feb 9	Philip K of France sends his brother Charles count of Valois and two others to be present at the coronation *Neuf Marche* R ıı 31 O ııı 61 H. 1. p ıv 111
Feb. 9.	The K. forbids the holding of tournaments at Croydon or elsewhere before his coronation *Dover* R ıı 31 O ııı 61. H. l p. ıv. 111
Feb 9.	The K invites the abp of Cant to the coronation, and states that, if he cannot be present, he will appoint one of his suffragans as a deputy R ıı 32 O ııı 61 H. 1. p ıv 111
Feb. 12	The K of England asks Philip K of France to forgive Geoffrey Rudelli lord of Blania. *Osprynge* R ıı 32. O ııı 62. H. l. p ıv 111
Feb 15	The K orders the usual payments to be made for the support of certain Scottish prisoners in the castle of Searbro' *Eltham* R ıı 33 O ııı. 62 H 1 p ıv 112
Feb 19	The K orders the adjournment until after his coronation of the hearing of the complaints against Walter bp of Lichfield *Eltham* R ıı 33. O ııı. 62. H. l. p. ıv. 112.
Feb 20	The K orders Michael de Meldon to do homage to Peter de Gaveston for certain lands and tenements in co Oxon, lately held by Edmund earl of Cornwall *Eltham.* R ıı 33.
[Feb 24]	Account of the ceremonies at the coronation of the K. and Q. R ıı 34–36
Feb 24	An abridged account of the same ceremony, with the K's oath R ıı 36 O ııı. 63 H 1 p ıv 112
Feb 25.	The K forbids the holding of a tournament at Stebenheth *Westm* R ıı. 36 O ııı. 63 H 1 p ıv 112
Feb 27	The K orders certain sums of money to be paid towards the liquidation of the debts of Amadeus count of Savoy *Westm* R ıı 37 O ııı 64 H 1 p ıv 112
March 1	The K of England asks Philip K of France to restore to John le Latimer certain property which he has in Champagne *Westm* R ıı 37 O ııı 64 H. 1 p ıv 112
March 3	The K. promises Leo K of Armenia and John his brother, of the order of the Minorites, that at a more convenient season he will attend to their requests. *Westm* R. ıı. 37 O ııı 65 H 1 p ıv 113
March 6	The K orders that the issues of the lands lately held by Edmund earl of Cornwall be paid to Peter de Gaveston earl of Cornwall *Westm* R ıı 37 O ııı. 65 H 1. p ıv. 113
March 12	The K confirms to B count of Armignac the grant of the castle of Laree *Westm.* R ıı 37 O ııı 65 H 1 p ıv 113
March 12	The K. grants to Guy Ferre the office of the seneschalcy of the duchy of Aquitain *Westm* R. ıı. 37 O ııı 66 H. l. p ıv 113
March 12	The K grants to Hugh le Despencer the custody of the castles of Devizes and Marlbro'. *Westm* R ıı 38 O ııı 66 H 1 p ıv 113
March 21	The K. grants to Nicholas de Segrave the office of the marshalcy of England. *Westm.* R. ıı 38 O. ııı 67. H 1 p ıv 113
March 12	The K grants to Pontus lord of Castellion the office of the seneschalcy of Saintes. *Westm* R ıı 38 O ııı 67 H 1 p ıv 114
March 14.	The K directs that the messengers about to be sent into England for the furtherance of trade with Holland be courteously treated *Westm* R. ıı. 38 O ııı 67 H. 1 p ıv 114
March 14	The K of England sends to Philip K of France three commissioners to settle the affairs of Ponthieu. *Westm.* R. ıı. 38 O ııı 68 H 1 p ıv 114
March 14	The K orders Rob. de Kendale, constable of Dover Castle, to permit the messengers of the K of Armenia to embark at Dover *Westm* R. ıı 39 O. ııı 68. H 1 p ıv. 114.
March 15	The K orders the constable of Bordeaux to pay the arrears of the yearly alms due to the abbess of Fontevrault. *Westm.* R ıı 39 O ııı 68 H 1 p ıv 114.
March 15	The K remits the payment of certain sums of money due to him by Gaston count of Foix *Westm* R. ıı 39 O ııı 69 H 1 p ıv. 114
March 18.	The K orders that the judgments given against Walter bp. of Lichfield shall be levied from the temporalities of his see *Westm* R ıı 39 O ııı 69 H. 1. p ıv 114
March 18	The K appoints Richard de Rokesle to be his seneschal of Ponthieu R ıı 39 O ııı 69 H. 1 p ıv 114
March 20	The K orders Rob de Kendale, warden of the Cinque Ports, to take care that the merchants of France have liberty to trade in England. *Westm.* R ıı 39 O ııı 70. H 1 p ıv 115

DATE.	SUBJECT
1308 March 20.	The K. orders the sheriffs of Devon, Lincoln, Norfolk, and Suffolk to see that Margaret, widow of Edmund earl of Cornwall, has the liberties belonging to her dower. *Westm.* R ii. 40 O iii. 70. H 1 p iv 115
March 20	The K. of England complains to Philip K of France of an act of piracy committed on an English ship by the inhabitants of Lere in Normandy *Westm.* R ii 40 O iii 70. H 1 p iv 115
March 22.	The K orders his bailiffs and others to help the merchants of John duke of Brabant to collect their debts in England *Westm* R ii 40 O iii 71 H 1 p iv 115
March 26	The K orders the justices to proceed with the suits pending against the bp. of Lichfield *Windsor* R ii 40 O iii 71 H 1 p iv 115
March 26.	The K confirms the grant of certain houses in Paris or elsewhere in France made to Amadeus count of Savoy by Hugh le Despenser *Windsor.* R ii 40 O. iii. 72. H 1. p iv 115
April 1	The K. asks the pope to take steps for the reformation of the monastery of Bardeney, dioc Lincoln *Windsor* R ii 41 O iii 72 H 1 p iv 116
April 8.	The K asks the pope to assent to the election of Ric de Sudbury as abbot of Westm. *Windsor* R ii 41 O iii 73 H 1. p iv 116
April 9	Pope Clement [V.] asks the K to liberate from prison the bps of Lichfield, S Andrew's, and Glasgow, and to refrain from interfering in ecclesiastical matters *Poitiers.* R. ii 41. O iii 73. H 1 p iv 116
April 9.	Pope Clement [V] asks Walter bp of Worcester to urge the K to give effect to the recommendations contained in the above-mentioned bull *Poitiers* R ii. 42. O iii 76 H 1 p iv 117
April 14.	The K forbids the holding of a tournament at Stafford. *Windsor.* R. ii. 43. O. iii. 76. H 1 p iv 117
April 15	The K requests the pope to proceed with the canonization of Tho de Cantilupe formerly bp of Hereford *Windsor* R ii 43 O iii 77 H 1 p iv 117
April 16	The K requests Tho cardinal of S Sabina and two others to hasten the above canonization *Windsor.* R ii 43. O iii. 77. H 1 p iv. 117.
May 2.	The K commits the custody of the town of Oxford to Warin de Insula and Gilbert de Ellefeld *Westm* R ii 43 O iii 78 H 1 p iv 118
May 2	The K orders the restitution of the lands, &c in England belonging to Bernard abp. of Rouen, who has performed his homage to the K *Westm* R ii 43 O iii 78 H 1. p iv 118
May 8	The K orders the payment of the sums allowed for the custody of certain prisoners of Scotland and Wales *Westm* R ii 43 O iii 78 H 1 p iv. 118
May 9	The K grants to Tho earl of Lancaster and his heirs for ever the earldom of Leicester, with the office of seneschal of England thereunto pertaining *Westm* R n 43 O iii 78 H. 1 p iv 118.
May 14	The K requests Ferrand K of Castile to protect and indemnify certain citizens of Bayonne who have been plundered by his subjects. *Westm.* R ii 44. O. iii. 79 H 1 p iv 118
May 14.	The K grants all the issues of Ponthieu and Monstroil to Q Isabella for the expenses of her chamber *Westm* R ii 44 O iii 80 H 1 p iv 118
May 18	The K announces that he will not hinder the banishment which has been decreed against Peter de Gaveston. *Westm.* R. ii 44. O. iii. 80 H 1 p iv, 119.
May 20	The K thanks David earl of Athol and 12 other Scotchmen for their faithful service to his father and himself *Westm.* R ii 45 O iii 81 H 1 p iv 119.
May 21	The K orders that 100l per ann be paid to the bp of S Andrew's from the issues of his see *Westm.* R ii 44. O. iii. 80. H 1. p iv 119.
May 22.	The K. orders Everic de Friscombald to cease from hindering the abp. of Canterbury from using his own mints at Canterbury *Westm* R ii 45 O iii. 81. H 1 p. iv 119.
May 23.	The K orders the sheriff of Southampton to liberate Wm. bp of S Andrew's, a prisoner, from the castle of Winchester, and to allow him to stay in the county of Northampton. *Westm* R ii 45. O iii. 82. H. 1 p iv 119
May 24	The K orders the barons of the Exchequer not to distrain John de Britannia earl of Richmond for the debts due by his late father. *Westm* R. ii. 45. O iii. 82. H. 1. p iv 119
May 24.	The K orders that Wm Olyfart, a Scotchman, be set free from prison in the Tower of London *Westm* R ii 45. O iii. 82. H 1. p iv 119.

DATE	SUBJECT
1308 May 24	The K grants to John de Britannia earl of Richmond all the goods and chattels in England which belonged to his late father, John duke of Brittany and earl of Richmond. *Westm* R. ii 46 Ö ib. 83 H. 1 p iv 119
May 24	The K orders that Wm de la More, master of the Knights Templars in England, be delivered to A patriarch of Jerusalem and bp of Durham *Westm* R ii 46 Ö iii 83 H 1 p iv 120
May 24.	The K. to W count of Hainault relative to extending the period for treating of the complaints of the merchants of Holland. *Westm.* R. ii 46 O iii. 83. H. 1 p iv 120
May 25	The K recommends his almoner, John de Leek, to the pope *Westm.* R ii 46 O iii. 85 H 1 p iv 120
May 27	The K. restores the liberty of the see of Durham to Anthony, patriarch of Jerusalem and bp of Durham, and his successors bps of Durham *Windsor.* R ii 47. O iii. 85 H 1 p iv 120
May 27	The K grants the manor of Werk in Tynedale to Anthony, patriarch of Jerusalem and bp of Durham *Westm* R ii 47 O iii 85 H 1 p iv 121
June 1	The K and Q appoint general proctors for Ponthieu and Monstroill *Langley* R. ii 47 O iii 86 H 1 p iv. 121
June 5	The K orders his justiciary of Ireland to permit Walter abp of Armagh to carry his cross as heretofore. *Langley* R ii. 47 O iii 86 H 1 p iv 121
June 5	The K asks Arthur duke of Britanny to send Maurice de Credomio to him into England to treat of matters which concern the duke and his brother John de Britannia *Langley* R. ii 47 O iii 87 H 1 p iv 121
June 7	The K. grants various manors, castles, and honors here specified in England to Peter de Gaveston and his wife Margaret, the K's niece. *Langley* R. ii. 48. O iii. 87 H. 1 p iv 121
June 7	The K grants various lands and castles here specified in Aquitain and Gascony to Peter de Gaveston. *Langley* R. ii. 48. O iii. 89. H 1 p iv 121.
June 8.	The K grants certain jurisdictions in the diocese of Bordeaux to John Russel, knt *Langley* R ii 49 O iii 89 H 1 p iv 122.
June 16	The K authorizes the payment of 1,600 marks made by his father's orders to Amadeus count of Savoy *Reading.* R ii 49 O iii 89 H 1 p iv 122
June 16	The K of England asks Philip K of France to send mediators to appease the disputes which have arisen between his nobility and Peter de Gaveston earl of Cornwall *Windsor* R. ii 49. O iii 89 H 1 p iv. 122
June 16	The K. to the pope, with the same request *Windsor.* R. ii. 49. O iii 90. H. 1. p iv 122
June 16	The K asks the pope to revoke the excommunication pronounced by the English bps upon Peter de Gaveston earl of Cornwall. *Windsor* R ii 50 Ö iii 91 H 1 p iv 123
June 16	The K to the cardinals, to the same effect *Windsor* R ii 50 O iii. 92. H. 1. p iv 123
June 16	The K asks Otto de Grandison to intercede with the pope for the same purpose *Windsor* R ii 50. O. iii. 92. H. 1. p. iv 123.
June 16	The K appoints Peter de Gaveston earl of Cornwall to be his lieutenant in Ireland. *Reading* R ii 51 O iii 92 H 1 p iv 123
June 16	The K. grants the castle and town of Blankeford in Aquitain to Bertrand del Gout, the pope's nephew. *Reading* R ii 51 O iii. 93 H. 1. p iv 123.
June 16	The K. appoints Rob de Unfranville earl of Angus and Wm de Ros of Hanelak, conjointly, his lieutenants in Scotland *Stanlegh* R ii 51. O iii 94 H 1. p iv 124.
June 19.	The K orders Eustace de Cotesbashe, chamberlain of Scotland, to provide 3,000 salmon for the K's use in his expedition into Scotland *Marlbro'.* R. ii 51 O. iii 94 H 1 p iv. 124
June 21	The K asks John Comyn earl of Boghan and 13 others to assist in quelling the rebellion of Rob de Brus *Stanlegh* R ii. 51. O iii. 94 H 1. p iv 124
June 22	The K orders the removal from Brustwick of Elizabeth the wife of Rob de Brus, late earl of Carrick, to another place of residence. *Marlbro'.* R ii 52 O iii 94 H 1 p iv. 124.
July 14	The K orders the payment of 330*l* 16*d.* to the abbess of Fontevrauld *Windsor.* R ii. 52. O iii 95 H. 1. p iv. 124.

DATE.	SUBJECT.
1308 July 15	The K (on payment of a fine of 300l. by the cathedral of Enachdun in Ireland, for having elected a bp without his licence) permits the dean and chapter to proceed with the election *Windsor* R ii. 52 O iii 95 H l p iv. 124.
July 17.	The K intercedes with the pope for Frederic son of Manfred late K of Sicily. *Windsor* R ii. 52 O iii 96 H. I. p. iv 125.
July 23	The K to the pope, refusing to grant the liberation of the bps of S Andrew's, Lichfield, and Glasgow. *Windsor* R ii 53 O iii 96 H. l p iv. 125
Aug 6.	The K of England asks Philip K of France to grant a safeconduct to Frederic, son of K. of Sicily, going to the pope R. ii. 53. O. iii. 98. H. l p iv 125.
Aug 6	The K asks certain cardinals to obtain a hearing by the pope of the claims of the said Frederic *Northampton* R ii 53 O iii. 98. H. I. p. iv 125
Aug. 11.	W bp of S Andrew's notifies that he has taken the oath of fealty to the K. of England *Northampton*. R. ii. 54. O iii 98. H l p iv 126
Aug. 11.	Pope Clement [V] sends Arnald bp of Poitiers to promote concord between the K. and his barons *Poitiers* R ii 54 O iii 98 H l p iv 126
Aug. 11	The K permits Ralph de Monthermer to hunt in the royal parks *Northampton*. R. ii. 54 O. iii 100 H l p iv 126
Aug 12	Pope Clement [V.] instructs the K. how to act in the suppression of the Knights Templars, and narrates his own proceedings in the matter *Poitiers* R ii 55 O. iii 101. H. l. p. iv. 126
Aug 12	The K grants to John de Britannia earl of Richmond the lands here specified lately held by John de Balliol, and the lands which were of Agnes de Valencia, widow of Hugh de Balliol, and of Alianor de Geneure, widow of Alex de Balliol *Northampton*. R. ii. 56. O iii 103 H. l p. iv. 127
Aug 15	The K notifies that he has granted the above lands to the earl of Richmond. *Northampton* R ii 56 O iii 105 H l p iv 128
Aug. 16.	The K. and Q. appoint John de Alueto their general proctor in the land of Ponthieu. *Langley* R ii 57 O iii 106 H l p iv 128
Aug. 16	The K orders Alice countess of Norfolk to pay to certain merchants of Lucca 275l due by her to Walter bp of Lichfield R ii 57 O. iii 106 H l p iv 129.
Aug 16.	The K orders all persons resident between Berwick-upon-Tweed and the river Forth and in Annandale, Carrick, and Galloway, and elsewhere in Scotland to aid in suppressing the rebellion of Rob. de Brus *Langley* R ii. 57.
Aug. 18	Pope Clement [V] thanks the K for having bestowed the castle of Blancafort upon Bertrand Deugod R ii 57 O iii. 107 H l p iv 129
Aug 20	The K appoints Rob de Clifford to be captain of the whole of Scotland *Windsor* R ii 58
Oct. 3.	The K grants permission to the merchants of D. King of Portugal to trade with England. *Waltham* R. ii 58 O iii 107 H. l p. iv. 129
Oct. 3	The K. orders the restitution of the temporalities of his see to Walter bp. of Lichfield. *Westm* R. ii, 58 O iii 108 H l. p iv. 129.
Oct 4	The K. orders Rob. de Kendale, warden of the Cinque Ports, to prevent the departure of all knights and esquires from the realm. *Westm.* R ii 58.
Oct 4.	The K forbids tournaments, and orders that no one come to the parliament at Westm. with arms and horses *Westm.* R. ii. 59. O iii. 108 H. l. p iv 129
Oct. 4	Bull of pope Clement [V] to the K. relative to the liberation of the bps. of Glasgow, S Andrew's, and Lichfield from prison, and as to the application of the goods of the Knights Templars R. ii. 59 O. iii. 109 H l p. iv 129
Oct. 4	Bull of pope Clement [V.] to the bp. elect of Worcester, to the same effect. R ii. 60. O iii 111 H l p iv. 130.
Oct 13	The K forbids the holding of a tournament at Leicester. *Canterbury* R ii. 60 O iii. 111 H. l. p. iv. 130.
Nov. 12.	The K. advises the count of Foix and Amanenus Lebret to be at peace with each other. *Westm* R. ii 60 O. iii. 111. H. l. p. iv. 130
Nov. 12	The K asks Ferdinand K. of Castile to continue the old alliance with England. *Westm.* R. ii. 60 O iii. 112 H l p iv. 131.

DATE	SUBJECT
1308 Nov 14	The K orders the constable of Bordeaux to pay the arrears of the allowance due to various nobles of Gascony whose lands had been seized by the French *Westm.* R. ii. 60. O iii 113 H 1. p iv 131.
Nov 14	The K to the same constable, to the same effect, for payment of the arrears of the wages due to various other persons. *Westm* R ii 61 O iii 114 H 1 p iv 132
Nov 18	Mainprise of Mahse earl of Strathmore by Patrick de Dunbar earl of March and others. *London* R ii 62 O iii. 116 H 1 p iv 132
Nov 21	The K orders the sheriffs of Hampshire and Wilts to permit his sister Mary, now at Ambresbury, to have her usual allowance of fuel *Byflet* R ii 62 O iii 116 H 1 p iv 132
Nov 24	Inquisition upon certain articles of enquiry touching the 'converts' of London *Byfleet.* R ii 62.
Nov. 27	The K orders the constable of Bordeaux to permit certain persons (herein named) to enjoy certain lands, tenements, &c in Gascony *Westm.* R ii 63 O iii 117 H 1 p iv 133
Nov. 27.	The K. to the same constable, ordering that the same persons enjoy the premises, any assignment to the contrary notwithstanding R. ii. 63. O iii. 116. H 1 p iv, 133
Nov 29	The K of England, at the instance of the K of France, grants a truce to the Scots *Westm* R ii 63
Nov 29	The K appoints guardians for the furtherance of the said truce *Westm.* R. ii 63.
Dec. 1	The K orders the constable of Bordeaux to permit Peter de Gavaston to enjoy the grants in Gascony made to him by the K *Westm* R ii 64
Dec. 1.	The K orders that R bp. of Glasgow be delivered to Arnald bp of Poitiers to be by him conveyed to the pope *Westm* R ii 64. O iii 118 H 1 p iv 133
Dec 1	The K of England requests the K of France to consent to the prorogation of the meeting of their commissioners at Montreuil-sur-Mer R ii 64 O iii 119 H 1 p iv 133
Dec 1	The K of England thanks Philip K of France for the letters sent by his brother Louis count of Evreux *Westm* R ii 64. O iii 119 H 1 p iv 133
Dec 3	The K appoints Gilbert de Clare earl of Gloucester and Hereford to be captain of the expedition into Scotland. *Westm.* R ii 64.
Dec. 4.	The K recommends John le Breton to the pope on account of his services to his sister Mary R. ii 64 O iii 119 H 1 p iv 133
Dec. 4.	The K of England appoints proctors to treat of the affairs of Ponthieu before Philip K of France. *Westm* R ii. 64 O iii 120 H. 1 p iv 134.
Dec 4	The K to certain sheriffs and others, respecting the temporalities of the see of Lichfield. *Westm* R, ii 64 O iii 120 H 1 p iv 134
Dec. 4.	The K to the pope, respecting the atrocities of the bp of Glasgow, the liberation of the bps of St Andrew's and Lichfield, and the goods of the Templars. *Westm* R ii. 64. O iii 121 H 1 p iv 134.
1309 Jan 5	The K grants safe conduct to his mariner Percot Barde, master of the K's ship the Isabella of Westminster *Windsor* R ii 65
Jan. 8,	The K complains to Fernand K of Castile of the misconduct of his sailors towards the ships of Bayonne *Langley* R. ii 65. O iii 122 H. 1 p iv. 134
Jan 10	The K requests that the pope would nominate Stephen de Segrave dean of Glasgow to the see of Glasgow. *Langley.* R ii. 66 O. iii. 122 H 1 p iv 135
Jan 10	The K to the cardinals, to the same effect. *Langley.* R ii 66. O iii 122 H 1 p iv 135.
Feb 2	The K forbids the holding of a tournament at Stannford and elsewhere during the present Lent *Guilford* R ii 66 O iii 124 H 1 p iv. 135
Feb 15	The K. orders 20 war horses and 12 packhorses to be purchased for him in Lombardy. *Langley* R ii 67 O iii 124 H. 1 p iv 135.
Feb 26	The K orders the payment to Amadeus count of Savoy of 592*l* 4*s* 11*d* due to him out of 10,000 marks *Westm* R ii 67 O iii 125 H 1 p iv 136.
Feb 26.	The K orders the payment of 700 marks due to the same count as the arrears of his annual fee of 200 marks. *Westm.* R ii 67 O. iii 125 H. 1 p iv 136
Feb. 26.	The K appoints commissioners to punish those who had destroyed the property of Peter de Gavaston in the Isle of Wight *Westm.* R. ii. 67. O. iii. 125. H. i. p iv. 136.

DATE	SUBJECT
1309 March 1.	The K. grants certain privileges to the keepers of the royal mints at London and Canterbury. R ɪɪ 67
March 2.	The K of England asks Bernard Piletti to superintend the interests of Philip K of France in March, Angoulême, &c. Westm. R ɪɪ 67 O. ɪɪɪ 126 H 1 p ɪv 136.
March 2	The K to Philip K of France, concerning the claim of the count of Armignac to the land of Gaverdan Westm R ɪɪ 67 O ɪɪɪ 126 H 1 p. ɪv. 136.
March 3	The K grants certain liberties and privileges to John Vanne and other citizens of London Westm. R, ɪɪ 68
March 4.	The K grants letters of attorney to cardinal Francis Gaytam archdeacon of Richmond. Westm R ɪɪ 68 O ɪɪɪ 126 H 1 p ɪv. 136
March 4	Safe conduct for Oliver de Roches, messenger of Philip K of France, going into Scotland to the bp of St Andrew and Robert de Brus R ɪɪ 68 O. ɪɪɪ. 127 H. 1. p ɪv 136.
March 4.	Credence for the K of England's messengers going to Philip K of France on their way to the pope Westm R. ɪɪ 68. O ɪɪɪ 127 H 1 p. ɪv 136
March 4	The K asks Otto de Grandison and Amanenus de Lebret to give credence to his messengers going to the pope. Westm. R. ɪɪ 68 O ɪɪɪ. 127. H 1. p ɪv 137.
March 4	The K asks the pope to give credence to the above messengers Westm R ɪɪ. 69 O. ɪɪɪ. 128 H 1 p ɪv 137
March 4	The K asks the pope to give credence to certain private matters to be told him by W. bp Worcester and John de Britannia earl of Richmond Westm. R ɪɪ 69 O. ɪɪɪ. 128. H 1 p ɪv 137
March 4	The K asks the cardinals to forward the interests of his messengers sent to the pope Westm R. ɪɪ 69 O ɪɪɪ 128 H 1 p ɪv 137.
March 4	The K grants annual pensions to six cardinals. Westm. R ɪɪ 69. O. ɪɪɪ. 129. H 1 p ɪv 137
March 4	The K orders the Queen's gold to be levied. Westm R ɪɪ 69 O ɪɪɪ 130 H 1 p ɪv 137
March 4	The K orders that the lands of the Templars in England be valued. Westm R. ɪɪ 70. O. ɪɪɪ 130 H 1. p ɪv 138
March 4	The K grants letters of recommendation for John earl of Richmond going to the parts beyond the sea Westm R ɪɪ 70 O ɪɪɪ. 130 H 1 p ɪv 138.
March 10	The K appoints John de Segrave to be keeper of Scotland, with 60 men at arms Langley. R. ɪɪ. 70
March 16	The K appoints W bp of Worcester and others to settle the disputes between the citizens of Bayonne and the men of Castille Langley. R ɪɪ 70 O ɪɪɪ 131 H 1 p ɪv 138
March 29	The K sends Giles de la Mote to J count of Namur relative to the aggressions by the Esterlings upon the English traders Langley R. ɪɪ 70 O ɪɪɪ 131 H 1 p ɪv. 138
March 29	The K to R count of Flanders in favour of the same Giles sent for the same purpose Langley R ɪɪ 70 O ɪɪɪ. 131. H 1 p. ɪv 138
April 3	The K grants certain privileges to the men of Jersey, Guernsey, Sark, and Alderney Langley R. ɪɪ 70.
April 13	The K of England asks Philip K of France to suspend his anger against Peter de Gavaston La Grave R ɪɪ 70 O ɪɪɪ 132 H 1 p ɪv 138
April 15	Fernand K of Castile asks credence for his messengers sent to the K of England to settle the disputes between their subjects Toledo R ɪɪ 71 O ɪɪɪ 132 H 1 p ɪv 138.
April 16.	The K. orders Robert FitzRoger to perform homage and the other services due to John de Britannia earl of Richmond Langley R. ɪɪ 71 O ɪɪɪ 132 H 1 p ɪv 138.
April 18.	The K forbids the holding of a tournament at Newmarket Langley R. ɪɪ. 71. O ɪɪɪ. 133. H 1 p ɪv 139
April 28	The K of England asks Philip K of France to give credence to the bearers Langley R. ɪɪ 71. O ɪɪɪ 133. H. 1. p ɪv 139
May 6	The K appoints commissioners to survey the manors, &c. of the Templars in co Hertford. Westm. R. ɪɪ 71 O. ɪɪɪ. 134. H 1. p ɪv 139.
May 6	The K. orders that John de Britannia earl of Richmond have possession of the lands, tenements, &c , in England lately held by John de Balliol K. of Scotland. Westm. R. ɪɪ 72. O ɪɪɪ. 134. H. 1. p. ɪv 139
May 12.	The K complains to Rob. count of Flanders that an English ship had been plundered off Portsmouth by Flemish pirates Westm. R. ɪɪ. 75. O. ɪɪɪ. 141. H. 1. p. ɪv. 142.

DATE	SUBJECT
1309 May 12	The K endeavours to induce A cardinal of S Marcellus to renounce the deanery of S Paul's, with which he had been provided by the pope *Westm.* R. ii. 72. O. iii. 134 H. 1 p. iv. 139.
May 12.	The K informs the sheriffs throughout England that tournaments are to be forbidden for a time *Westm* R. ii. 72 O iii 135 H 1 p iv. 139
May 15	Inspeximus by the K of a grant made by Walter bp of Worcester and others of certain privileges in the dioc of Bordeaux to Raymond Guillelmi de Budos the pope's nephew *Avignon*. R. ii. 72 O iii 135 H. 1. p iv 140
May 15.	The K grants the custody of certain lands, castles, and tenements here specified in Yorkshire to Peter de Gavaston *Westm* R ii 73 O iii. 136 H 1 p iv 140
May 15	Safe conduct for the messengers of W count of Holland coming to the K of England. *Westm* R ii 73 O iii 137 H 1 p iv. 140
May 15	The K permits the warden and scholars of Peterhouse, Camb , to acquire certain messuages in Cambridge *Westm* R. ii. 73 O iii 137 H 1 p iv 140
May 15.	The K orders that the men of the islands of Guernsey, Jersey, Sark, and Alderney shall not appear in the court of the bp of Coutance *Westm.* R. ii 73
May 18	The K authorizes the correction of an error in the charter granted to Humfrey de Bohun earl of Hereford and Essex by K Edw I *Westm* R ii 74 O iii 138 H i p iv 141
May 21	Pope Clement [V] absolves the K from homicides, &c committed by him in time of war *Avignon* R ii 74 O. iii 138 H 1 p iv. 141
May 21	Pope Clement [V] permits the K to choose his own confessor *Avignon* R ii 74 O iii 139 H 1 p iv 141
May 21	Pope Clement [V] exempts the person of the K from excommunication and his chapels from interdict *Avignon* R ii 74 O iii 139 H 1. p iv. 141
May 24	The K authorizes Gilbert de Clare earl of Gloucester, and others, to assure the safety of Tho earl of Lancaster and others coming to the K at Kennington R ii 75 O iii 140. H 1 p iv 141
May 25	The K licences the brethren of St John of Jerusalem to export horses, gold, silver, &c , from England for the service of the Holy Land *Kenyngton* R ii 75. O iii 140. H 1 p iv 141
May 26	Pope Clement [V] will speedily send special messsengers to the K on matters which concern them both *Avignon* R ii 75 O iii 141 H 1 p iv 142.
May 27.	The K grants to Albertus Medici the office of judge of the Jews within the seneschalcy of Agen *Kenyngton* R ii 75 O iii 141 H 1 p iv. 142
June 5	The K. enforces the regulations which forbid tournaments, &c , being held within five miles of Cambridge *Westm.* R. ii. 76 O iii 142 H 1. p. iv 142.
June 11	The K orders the payment of 200l to certain merchants of Florence *Westm* R. ii 76. O iii 142 H 1 p iv 142.
June 14	The K forbids the holding of tournaments, &c., throughout England *Langley* R ii 76 O. iii 143 H. 1 p iv 143.
June 19	The K of England asks Philip K of France to make arrangements for a personal interview in France *Langley* R ii 76 O iii 143 H 1 p iv 143
June 29	The K recommends to the pope John de Elsefeld who is going to the Holy Land *Chester.* R ii 76. O. iii. 144 H 1 p iv. 143
July 4	The K. complains to R count of Flanders of the plunder of a ship of Bayonne by the Flemings *Heywode* R ii 77 O iii 144 H 1 p iv 143
July 15.	The K orders the payment of their allowances to Walter Olyfart, Wm bp of S Andrew's, Rob bp of Glasgow, and Mary the K.'s sister now at Ambresbury *Langley* R. ii 77. O iii 144 H 1 p iv 143
July 15	The K insists upon the preservation of his rights in presenting John de Sandale to the archdeaconry of Richmond *Langley* R ii 77 O iii 145 H 1 p iv 143.
July 16	The K orders that certain malefactors who had broken open the houses of Anthony bp. of Durham, in the parish of S. Martin's, London, should be punished *Langley* R. ii. 77 O. iii. 146. H 1 p iv. 144.
July 16	Similar order for the punishment of those who had cut down the trees of the said bp in the wood of Colynweston, co. Northamp. *Langley.* R ii 78 O. iii 146 H. 1. p iv. 144.
July 29.	Licence to 18 abbots to attend the general chapter of the Cistercians about to be held at Citeaux. *Staunford.* R. ii 78 O. iii. 147. H. 1. p. iv. 144.

DATE	SUBJECT.
1309. July 30.	Writs of military summons to the nobility and clergy to meet the K at Newcastle-upon-Tyne to march against the Scots *Staunford* R n 78 O m 147. H 1 p iv 144
July 30	The K of England to Philip K of France , regrets that their meeting must be interrupted by the state of affairs in Scotland *Staunford* R. n 79 O m 149 H. 1 p iv 145
Aug. 3	The K. of England complains to the K of France that his messenger has addressed letters to Rob. de Brus in which he is styled King of Scotland, while in those produced to the writer he is designated as earl of Carrick *Staunford* R n 79 O m 150 H 1 p iv 145
Aug 3	The K forwards to Wm count of Holland certain ordinances respecting commerce between their subjects, which he begs may be henceforth observed *Staunford*. R n. 79 O m. 150. H 1 p iv. 145
[Aug 3]	Memorandum as to the settlement of various disputes between the merchants of England and Holland R n 80. O m 151. H 1 p iv 145
Aug 5	The K appoints commissioners to settle the claims of the men of Holland against the English *Staunford.* R n 80 O iii 152 H. 1. p. iv. 146
Aug 5	The K. of England requests Fernand K of Castile to cause certain injuries done to his English subjects by the men of Bayonne to be compensated *Staunford* R n 80 O m 153 H 1 p iv 146
Aug. 5	The K informs Haco K of Norway that he will be glad to renew the ancient treaties of friendship between their realms. *Staunford.* R n 81. O m 153 H 1 p iv. 147.
Aug 5	The K. appoints general proctors for the management of his affairs in Ponthieu *Staunford.* R n 81. O m 154 H 1 p iv. 147.
Aug 5	The K ratifies the agreement made by his seneschal of Ponthieu with the mayor of Abbeville *Staunford* R n. 81. O m 155 H 1 p iv 147
Aug. 5.	The K remits to the town of Abbeville for ten years the payment of the assise of wine due to him *Staunford* R n 82 O m 155 H 1 p iv 147
Aug 5	The K confirms his previous grant made to Raymund Guilhelmi de Budos *Staunford* R. n 82 O m 155 H 1. p iv 147
Aug 5	The K orders his seneschal of Gascony to give effect to the before-mentioned grant *Staunford* R n 82 O m 156 H 1 p iv 147
Aug 5	The K orders the leying of foot soldiers in Wales to serve against the Scots. *Staunford.* R ii 82 O m 156 H. 1 p n. 148
Aug 5	The K orders the levying of foot soldiers in various counties in England to serve against the Scots *Staunford* R n 83 O m 158 H 1 p iv 148
Aug 5	The K orders that the coin in circulation at the time of his father's death shall continue to be a lawful tender *Staunford* R n. 84.
Aug. 5	The K orders that the bp of Durham and abp of York shall levy troops in their respective jurisdictions to serve against the Scotch *Staunford* R n 84 O m 159 H 1 p iv 149
Aug 6	The K. orders his earls and barons to affix their seals to a letter framed in the Parliament of Stamford against the oppressions of the pope *Staunford* R n 84. O m 159 H 1. p. iv 149.
Aug 15	The K. recommends to the pope John de Drokensford bp elect of Bath and Wells. *Langley.* R n. 84. O m 160 H 1 p iv 149
Aug 19	The K thanks the pope for kindnesses received *Langley* R n 85 O. iii. 161. H 1 p. iv 149.
Aug. 20.	The K orders that ecclesiastics and women, who cannot serve in person against the Scotch, shall pay their fines at the Exchequer *Langley* R. n 85
Aug 21	Commission to Ric de Burgo earl of Ulster to treat in the K's name with Rob. de Brus respecting peace. *Langley* R n 85 O m 163. H 1. p iv 150
Aug 21	Safe-conduct for the envoys of Rob de Brus coming to treat with R. de Burgo earl of Ulster. *Langley.* R n 85 O m. 163 H 1. p iv 150.
Aug. 21.	The K orders that the merchants of Hainault, Holland, and Zeland be civilly treated by the English *Langley.* R. n 85 O m 163 H 1 p iv 150
Aug 26	The K orders that certain vagabond Friars Preachers in Ireland be arrested. *Westm.* R. ii 86
Aug 26	The K permits Wm. Broun of Drogheda and his children. to use the English laws in Ireland. *Westm.* R n 86

DATE	SUBJECT
1309 Aug 28	The K makes a grant of additional lands and tenements to Peter de Gaveston and Margaret his wife *Westm* R ii 86 O iii 164 H 1 p iv. 150
Aug 28	The K recommends to the pope John de Leek bp elect of Dunkeld *Westm.* R ii 86 O iii 164 H 1 p iv 151.
Aug 28	The K recommends the same John de Leek to the cardinals *Westm* R ii 86. O. iii 165 H 1 p iv 151
Aug 28	The K recommends the same John de Leek to G auditor of the Roman court, and Grimerius advocate of the Roman court. *Westm.* R ii 87 O iii 166 H 1 p iv 151
Aug 28	The K orders the seneschal of Gascony to take under his protection Margaret vicomtesse of Bearn, and to see to the execution of her father's testament *Westm* R. ii 87 O iii 166 H 1 p iv 151
Aug 29	The K notifies that pope Clement [V] has reserved for himself the fourth part of the tenth given by the clergy of England, Scotland, Ireland, and Wales *Westm* R ii. 87 O iii 166 H 1 p iv 152.
Sept. 3	The K regrets that he cannot consent to the appointment of cardinal Neapoleon to a prebend in the church of York *Langley* R. ii 87 O iii 167 H 1 p iv 152.
Sept 4	The K. asks the pope to absolve the earl of Cornwall from an additional clause in an oath which he had taken. *Langley.* R ii 88 O iii. 167. H 1 p iv 152
[Sept]	Ordinance respecting the examination of the Templars at London, Lincoln, and York R ii. 88 O iii 168 H 1 p iv 152
Sept 13.	The K. orders that the emissaries sent by the pope for the examination of the Templars be treated with due respect *Westm* R. ii 88 O iii. 168 H 1 p. iv 152
Sept. 13	The K orders the abp of York and the bps of Lincoln and London to examine the Templars at Lincoln *Westm* R ii 88 O iii. 168 H 1 p iv 152
Sept 14	The K appoints commissioners to treat of concord between the men of Castile and the men of Bayonne *Westm.* R ii 88 O iii 169 H. 1. p iv. 152
Sept. 14	The K to the seneschal of Gascony relative to the same treaty of concord. *Westm* R ii 89 O iii 169 H. 1 p iv 153
Sept. 14	Details of the treaty of concord between the proctors of Castile and those of Bayonne *Westm* R ii 89 O iii 170 H 1 p iv 153
Sept 14	The K orders that such Templars as are yet at large shall be arrested and sent to London, York, and Lincoln, there to be examined. *Westm* R ii 90 O iii 173 H 1 p iv 154
Sept. 14	The K orders that the Templars are to be imprisoned in the castles of York and Lincoln and the Tower of London *Westm* R ii 90 O iii 174 H 1 p iv 155
Sept 14	The K appoints his nephew, Gilbert de Clare earl of Gloucester, captain of his army in Scotland *Westm.* R. ii. 91. O. iii. 175. H. 1. p iv 155
Sept 14	The K orders that due assistance be given to Gilbert de Clare in the discharge of the above-mentioned office *Westm* R ii 91 O iii 175 H 1 p iv 155
Sept. 16.	The K grants certain lands and tenements here specified to Ralph de Monthermer and his sons Thomas and Edward, the K's nephews R ii 92 O iii 176. H 1 p iv. 155.
Sept. 18	The K informs F King of Castile of the conclusion of a treaty of concord between his subjects and the men of Bayonne *Langley* R ii 92 O. iii. 178 H 1. p iv 156
Sept 22	Commission to enquire respecting certain concealed lands of the Templars in Essex and Hertford *Langley* R ii 92 O iii 178 H 1 p iv 156
Sept. 23.	The K orders the seneschal of Gascony to take care that the royal jurisdiction within the city of Bordeaux is not impaired *Langley* R ii 93 O iii 179 H 1. p iv 156
Sept. 23.	The K orders that the agreement made with the men of Castile be strictly observed. *Langley* R ii 93 O iii 179 H 1 p iv 157
Sept. 29	The K orders that the inquisitors going into Ireland to examine the Templars be protected *Windsor* R ii 93 O iii 179 H 1 p iv 157.
Sept 29	The K orders that the Irish and Scotch Templars be sent for examination to Dublin. *Windsor* R ii 93. O iii 180 H 1 p iv 157.
Sept. 29	The K orders the bp elect of Dublin to conduct the examinations of the Templars in Ireland. *Windsor* R ii 93 O iii 180 H 1 p iv 157
Oct 1.	The K orders the payment of 50 marks to cardinal Thomas Jorsce, being his allowance for six months *Windsor* R ii 94 O iii 181 H 1 p. iv. 157.

DATE.	SUBJECT
1309. Oct 1.	The K orders that witnesses be examined according to the treaty with the men of Castile. *Windsor* R ıı 94 O ııı, 181 H l p ıv, 157.
Oct. 3	The K requests that the inquisitor sent into Scotland for the examination of the Templars be respectfully treated *Langley* R ıı 94 O ııı 182 H l. p ıv 158
Oct. 6.	The K orders that the Templars who are yet at large in Scotland shall be arrested and kept in safe custody. *La Grove.* R ıı 94 O. iii. 182. H ı p. ıv 158
Oct. 6	The K orders his seneschal of Gascony to protect the liberties of Gasto count of Foix and his mother Margaret viscountess of Bearn *La Grove.* R. ıı 94 O ııı 182 H l p ıv 158
Oct. 6.	The K of England to Philip K. of France on the settlement of the disputes between the counts of Foix and Armignac *La Grove* R ıı 95. O ııı 182 H l p ıv 158,
Oct 7	The K respites for two years the debts due to him by Constance de Biern *La Grove* R ıı 95 O ııı 183 H l p ıv 158
Oct. 8	The K. inhibits his nobility from leaving the realm during the war with Scotland *La Grove* R ıı 95
Oct 21	The K promises that the hospitality of the abp of York to Gilbert de Clare earl of Gloucester, at Thorp, near York, shall not be quoted as a precedent. *York* R ıı 95 O ııı 184 H ı p. ıv. 158
Oct 24	The K appoints John de Hastings his lieutenant in Aquitain *York* R ıı 95 O. iii. 184 H l p ıv 159
Oct. 26	The K. promises that he will sanction the covenant between A bp of Durham and Henry de Percy concerning the castle and manor of Alnwick. *York* R ıı 96 O. ııı 185 H l p ıv, 159
Oct. 26	The K. asks the pope to help him in preserving the rights of the crown of England *York* R. ıı 96 O ııı 185 H l p ıv. 159
Oct. 26	The K to the cardinals, to the same effect. *York* R ıı 96. O ııı 186 H. l p. ıv. 159.
Oct 27	The K sends messengers to the pope to vindicate the royal prerogatives *York* R ıı 96 O ııı 186 H l p ıv 159
Oct. 28.	Pope Clement [V] exhorts the bp. of Worcester to admonish the K and his ministers to cease from oppressing the church, and to pay the yearly tribute due to the see of Rome *Priory of Grunselle* R ıı 97. O ııı. 187 H. l. p ıv 160.
Nov 15	The K. grants to Peter de Gavaston and his wife Margaret the ancient prisage of wines in the port of Dartmouth *Burton Episcopi* R ıı 98 O ııı 191 H l. p ıv 161
Nov 19	Anthony bp of Durham grants to Henry de Percy the barony of Alnwick with its appurtenances. *Kenynton.* R ıı 99 O ııı, 183 H l p ıv 158
Dec. 10	The K permits Anthony bp of Durham to hear a suit formerly reserved for himself *Westm* R ıı 99 O ııı 193 H l p ıv 162
Dec 10	The K orders that the Templars imprisoned in the castle of Marlbro' be removed to the Tower of London *Westm* R ıı 99 O ııı 193 H l p ıv 162
Dec 14	The K. appoints John de Leek to receive in the K's name the books, vestments, &c belonging to the late Matthew bp of Dunkeld *Westm.* R ıı 99 O ııı 194 H l. p ıv 163
Dec. 14	The K to the pope and cardinals in favour of Wm le Latimer *Westm* R ıı 99 O ııı 194 H l p ıv 163
Dec 14	The K orders the arrest of certain Templars who go about in the dress of seculars *Westm* R ıı 100. O ııı 194 H l p ıv 163.
Dec 15	The K. orders the keepers of the Templars to obey the directions of the inquisitors appointed for their examination *Westm* R ıı 100 O ııı 195 H l p ıv 163
Dec. 15	Rob de Clifford is appointed guardian of Scotland *Westm* R. ıı. 100. O ııı 195 H. l p ıv 163
Dec 16	The K asks R count of Flanders to remedy the injuries inflicted by his subjects upon certain English merchants at Bruges *Westm* R ıı. 100. O ııı. 196 H l p ıv 163.
Dec 18	The K apologises to the pope for the absence from his council of Wm bp of Worcester, who is prevented from attending by old age. *Westm* R ıı. 101 O. ııı 196. H l p ıv 163.
Dec. 18.	The K orders the apprehension and imprisonment, according to the form of the statute, of such persons as circulate false reports *Westm.* R. ıı. 101

DATE	SUBJECT
Dec 19	The K orders that John de Britannia earl of Richmond be acquitted of certain debts due to the K *Westm* R ɪɪ 101 O ɪɪɪ 197 H 1 p ɪv. 163
1310 Jan 1.	The K authorises the execution, by the seneschal of Gascony, of letters appointing proxies in the French court. *S. Alban's* R ɪɪ 101. O ɪɪɪ 197 H 1. p ɪv 164.
Jan 1	The K. forwards to his commissioners the proxy referred to in the previous letter *S Alban's* R. ɪɪ 102 O ɪɪɪ 198 H 1 p ɪv. 164
Jan. 14.	The K asks Wm count of Holland to see that justice is done to certain Englishmen who have been plundered by the count's subjects. *La Grove.* R. ɪɪ 102 O ɪɪɪ 198 H 1 p ɪv 164
Jan 19	The K forbids the holding of a tournament at Newmarket *Shene* R ɪɪ 102 O ɪɪɪ. 199 H 1 p ɪv 164
Jan. 23.	The K confirms the charter by which Anthony bp of Durham grants the barony of Alnwick to Hen de Percy *Shene* R ɪɪ 102 O ɪɪɪ 199 H 1 p ɪv 164
Feb 4	The K orders the arrest of all persons who form themselves into confederacies to disturb the peace *Westm* R ɪɪ 102
Feb. 7.	Philip K of France asks the K of England to favour Matthew de Caraczoli of Naples in obtaining a prebend in the church of Salisbury R ɪɪ 103 O ɪɪɪ 199 H 1 p. ɪv 164
Feb 7	The K forbids all persons from coming to the parliament at Westm. with horses and arms *Westm* R ɪɪ 103 O ɪɪɪ 20 H. 1 p ɪv 165.
Feb. 7.	The K forbids the earls of Lancaster, Hereford, Pembroke, and Warwick from coming to the parliament with horses and arms *Westm* R ɪɪ 103 O ɪɪɪ 200. H. 1 p. ɪv 165
Feb 12	The K orders Margaret, widow of Edmund earl of Cornwall, to pay to Peter de Gavaston earl of Cornwall, and Margaret his wife, 46*l*. 14*s* 11*d* according to the K 's grant. *Westm* R ɪɪ 103 O ɪɪɪ. 201. H 1 p ɪv 165
Feb 16	Commission to Wm bp of S Andrew's and others to treat with the Scotch for a truce *Westm* R ɪɪ 104 O ɪɪɪ 201 H 1 p ɪv 165
March 1	The K repeats his orders to the constable of the Tower of London for steps to be taken in proceeding with the process against the Templars *Westm.* R ɪɪ 104 O ɪɪɪ 202 H 1 p. ɪv. 165
March 3	The K sends similar orders to the sheriffs of York and Lincoln *Westm* R. ɪɪ. 104 O ɪɪɪ 202 H 1 p ɪv 165
March 3.	The K forbids the holding of a tournament at Bungay *Westm* R ɪɪ 104 O ɪɪɪ 202. H 1 p ɪv 166
March 5	The K recommends himself, his queen and kingdom, to the prayers of the approaching general chapter of the Friars Preachers *Westm* R ɪɪ 104
March 8.	The K orders the keepers of the Templars to obey the inquisitors appointed by the pope. *Westm* R ɪɪ 104 O ɪɪɪ 203 H 1 p ɪv 166
March 12	The K orders the arrest of certain Templars who have been permitted to go at large by the sheriff of York *Westm* R ɪɪ 105 O ɪɪɪ 203 H 1 p ɪv 166
March 16	The K authorises the appointment of certain persons to settle the management of the realm and the royal household *Westm* R ɪɪ 105 O ɪɪɪ 204 H 1 p ɪv 166
March 30	The K. sanctions the exchange of Maria de Brus, a Scotch prisoner in Roxburgh Castle, for Walter de Comyn *Westm* R ɪɪ 105 O ɪɪɪ 204 H 1 p ɪv 166
April 1	The K exculpates himself to the pope, and promises to obey him as far as is consistent with the liberties of the crown *Westm* R ɪɪ 105 O ɪɪɪ 204 H 1 p ɪv 166
April 1	The K orders the restitution of his temporalities in England to Rob. Putot appointed abbot of Fécamp *Westm* R ɪɪ 106 O ɪɪɪ 205 H 1 p ɪv. 167
April 1	The K orders that the petitions of various persons who had served him in Scotland shall be admitted *Westm* R ɪɪ 106 O ɪɪɪ 206 H 1 p ɪv. 167.
April 10	The K appoints John de Segrave to be guardian of Scotland *Windsor.* R. ɪɪ 106. O ɪɪɪ 206. H 1 p ɪv 167
April 16	The K orders that John Wychard, formerly archdeacon of Glasgow, shall be sent from the prison of Conway Castle to Chester, and thence to the Tower of London *Windsor* R ɪɪ 106 O ɪɪɪ 207 H 1 p ɪv 167
April 20	Protection for commissioners appointed to settle disputes between the English and the Hollanders *Windsor* R. ɪɪ 106 O ɪɪɪ 207 H 1 p ɪv 167.
April 20.	The K. recommends his clerk, Wm de Melton, to the favour of the pope. *Windsor.* R. ɪɪ 107 O ɪɪɪ 208 H 1 p ɪv 168.

DATE.	SUBJECT.
1310 May 3.	Protection for the pope's nuncios coming into England, provided they do nothing to the prejudice of the crown. *Woodstock.* R. ii 107 O iii 208. H 1 p iv. 163
May 6	Philip K. of France complains to the K of England of the injuries done by the men of Bayonne to the men of S. Malo *S Lô* R ii 107 O iii 209 H 1 p iv 168
June 1.	The K. declares his determination to punish such as interfere with the rights of the crown. *Reygate.* R. ii. 107 O. iii 209 H 1 p iv 168
June 12	The K orders the delivery to John de Britannia earl of Richmond of the lands and tenements lately held in dower by Agnes de Valence, deceased, wife of Hugh de Balliol *Westm.* R ii 108. O iii 209 H. 1 p iv 168
June 15.	The K. orders the payment of their allowances to certain Scottish prisoners in the castles of Corfe and Sherburn and in the Tower of London. *Westm.* R ii. 108. O iii. 210. H 1, p iv. 169.
June 15	The K appoints John de Caunton to be captain of the fleet about to sail for St John, Perth, to serve against the Scots *Westm* R ii 108 O iii 211. H 1. p. iv. 169
June 15	The K appoints Alex de Abernethy to be keeper of that part of Scotland which is between the Forth and the mountains. *Westm* R ii 108. O iii. 211 H 1 p iv 169.
June 18	The K orders the bailiffs of Shoreham and 35 other ports to supply him with ships to act against the Scots. *Westm* R. ii 109 O. iii 212 H 1 p iv 169
June 18.	The K grants to John de Britannia the privilege of holding fairs and markets in his manors of Newebiggyn, Boghes, Burghersh, and Bulewarhithe *Westm* R. ii 109. O iii 213. H 1. p. iv. 170
June 18.	The K appoints Ric de Burgo earl of Ulster to be captain of the Irish troops about to proceed into Scotland in the K's service. *Westm* R ii. 109 O iii 213 H 1. p iv 170
June 21	Pope Clement [V] grants dispensation for a marriage between John, eldest son of Arthur duke of Brittany, and Isabella, daughter of Sancho K of Castille *Avignon.* R ii. 109. O. iii. 214 H 1 p iv. 170
July 4.	Pope Clement [V] confirms the possessions of the monastery of S Fredeswyde, Oxford *Avignon.* R ii 110 O iii 215 H 1 p iv 170
July 5.	Philip K of France regrets that the Scots have broken the truce with England, and thus prevented his interview with K Edward *Chingiac* R ii 110 C iii 215 H 1 p iv 170
July 6.	Memorandum of the delivery of the great seal to Walter bp. of Worcester R. ii. 110
July 9	The K complains to Haco K of Norway that his subjects have plundered the ship of Wm de Tollere, burgess of Grimsby. *Westm.* R ii 110 O iii 215 H 1 p iv 171
July 12.	The K requests that the pope will not irritate the English nobles by issuing personal citations against his subjects. *Westm.* R. ii. 111 O iii. 216. H. 1. p iv. 171.
July 14.	Safe-conduct for the inquisitors sent by the pope to try the Templars in Ireland *Westm.* R ii 111 O. iii 216. H 1 p iv 171
July 17	The K. orders that the castle of Struguyll be delivered to Robert Darcy for the sustentation of his (the K's) brothers. *Westm* R. ii. 111. O. iii. 216 H 1 p iv 171.
July 18	The K grants to his brothers Thomas and Edmund the castles and manors formerly held by Roger le Bygod, late earl of Norfolk *Westm* R. ii. 111 O iii 217 H. 1 p iv 171.
July 18	The K of England to the K of France; the Scots having again broken the truce, the writer is proceeding against them in person, and on his return will visit the K. of France *Westm.* R ii 111. O iii 217. H. 1. p. iv. 171.
Aug 1.	The K confirms the agreement respecting the limits of Ponthieu and S Valery, made by his seneschal of Ponthieu and Robert count of Dreux *Northamp.* R. ii 112 O iii. 218. H 1. p iv 172.
Aug 1.	The K. confirms the agreement made by his seneschal of Ponthieu and the convent of Lonevilers *Northamp* R ii 112 O. iii. 218. H. 1. p. iv. 172.
Aug 1.	The K. confirms the agreement made by his seneschal of Ponthieu and the convent of the Cistercians of Valoiles. *Northamp* R. ii. 112. O. iii 219 H. 1. p. iv. 172.
Aug 1.	The K. requests the pope to confer a prebend in Agen or Paris upon Bernardus Pileti. *Westm.* R ii 112. O iii 219 H 1 p iv 172
Aug 2.	The K of England appoints commissioners to arrange the transfer of lands mutually occupied wrongfully by the Kings of England and France. *Northamp.* R. ii. 113 O. iii. 220. H. 1. p. iv, 172.

L

DATE	SUBJECT
1310 Aug 2	The K orders the publication throughout England of the ordinances made of late respecting the realm and the royal household. *Northamp* R ii 113 O. iii 221. H 1 p. iv. 173.
Aug. 2.	The K authorizes John de Britannia earl of Richmond to transfer the earldom of Richmond, and all his lands, &c in England, to his brother Arthur duke of Brittany. *Northamp* R ii 113 O iii 221. H i p iv. 173
Aug 2	The K. summons his nobles to join him at Berwick to proceed against Robert de Brus *Northamp* R. ii 114. O iii 222 H 1. p iv 173
Aug. 2	The K orders the mayor of Dover and of 41 other ports to provide him with ships to proceed against the Scots *Northamp* R ii 114. O iii 222 H. 1 p iv. 173
Aug 2	The K orders that foreign coins shall not circulate in the realm *Northamp* R ii 114
Aug 3	The K summons Humfry de Bohun, constable of England, to accompany him in his expedition against the Scots *Sulby* R ii 114
Aug 6	The K appoints Simon de Montacute to be captain and governor of his fleet against the Scots *Northamp* R ii. 115. O iii 223. H. 1. p. iv 174
Aug 6	The K. remits the sentence of banishment pronounced upon a burgess of Abbeville by the seneschal of Ponthieu *Rughford* R. ii 115 O. iii. 224. H 1 p iv 174.
Aug 18	The K orders certain ecclesiastical persons to provide victuals for the expedition against the Scots *Wyghton* R. ii 115
Aug. 26.	The K orders John de Crumbewelle, constable of the Tower of London, to deliver the Templars in his custody to the sheriffs of London *Beverley* R ii 115 O iii 224. H. 1 p. iv. 174
Aug 26.	The K orders the sheriffs of London to receive the Templars mentioned above *Beverley* R ii 115 O iii 224 H 1 p iv 174
Sept. 1.	The K. appoints Henry de Lacy earl of Lincoln to be guardian of England during his absence in Scotland *Newcastle upon-Tyne* R ii 116. O iii. 225. H 1 p iv 174.
Sept. 6	The K orders Humfry de Bohun to accompany him into Scotland, as he is bound to do, by virtue of his office of constable of the army *Newcastle-upon-Tyne* R. ii 116
Sept. 20	John Earl of Surrrey is exonerated from the custody of Edward de Balliol who is to reside with Thomas and Edward, the K's brothers *Roxburgh* R ii 116, O iii.225. H. 1 p. iv 175.
Oct 1	The K grants the custody of the castle of Nottingham to Peter de Gavaston earl of Cornwell *Byger.* R ii 116 O iii 225 H 1 p iv 175
Oct. 1.	The K. grants to Peter de Gavaston earl of Cornwall the office of justiciary of the royal forests on this side of the Trent. *Byger* R ii 116 O iii 226 H 1 p iv 175
Oct 6.	The K takes into his protection Henry de Lacy earl of Lincoln (the K's lieutenant in England during his absence in Scotland), and all his possessions in Cheshire *Byger* R ii 117 O iii 227 H 1. p iv. 175.
Oct 6	The K orders that the Templars in London shall be imprisoned in the four gates of the city and elsewhere *Byger* R ii 117 O. iii 227 H 1 p. iv. 175
Oct 6.	The K orders the sheriffs of London to receive the said Templars from the const of the Tower, and to deal with them as above directed *Byger* R. ii 117 O iii 227 H 1 p iv 176
Oct. 13	Protection for the papal nuncios coming into England to examine the Templars. *Linlithgow, in Scotland* R ii 117. O iii 228 H 1 p iv 176
Oct 23.	The K arranges as to the details of the reception of the said nuncios and the examination of the Templars. *Linlithgow.* R ii 118 O iii 228 H 1 p iv. 176
Oct. 23	Further regulations as to the custody, support, &c of the said Templars *Linlithgow.* R. ii 118 O. iii 229 H 1 p iv 176
Oct 25	The K orders the keeper and sub-keeper of the lands of the Templars to pay to the sheriffs of London the sums allowed for their support *Linlithgow* R ii 118 O iii 230. H 1 p iv. 176
Nov 9	The K requests R count of Flanders to give no shelter to various pretended exiles from Scotland, and who harass the English fleet. *Berwick-upon-Tweed* R. ii. 118. O ii.230 H 1 p iv. 177.
Nov 22	The K orders the mayor and sheriffs of London to deliver up the four gates of the city and certain other houses for the custody of the Templars. *Berwick-upon-Tweed* R ii 119 O iii 231 H 1 p iv 177.
Nov 22.	The K gives further orders respecting the delivering up of the said gates. *Berwick-upon-Tweed* R ii 119 O iii. 231 H 1 p iv 177.
Nov. 22	The K gives additional orders to the mayor and sheriffs of London relative to the custody of the Templars *Berwick-upon-Tweed* R ii 119. O iii 232 H 1. p. iv. 177.

DATE	SUBJECT
1310 Nov 22	The K orders the correction of all offences committed against the truce with France. *Berwick-upon-Tweed* R ɪɪ 120 O ɪɪɪ 233 H 1. p ɪv. 178
Dec 9	The K orders it to be proclaimed that he strictly forbids victuals, arms, &c being sent to the Scots *Berwick-upon-Tweed* R ɪɪ 120 O ɪɪɪ 233 H 1 p ɪv 178
Dec. 12.	The K orders that all the Templars within the province of Canterbury shall be sent to London, where a provincial council is to be held for their acquittal or condemnation. *Berwick-upon-Tweed* R. ɪɪ 120 O. ɪɪɪ 234. H 1 p ɪv. 178
Dec. 12	The K orders that allowance be made for the expenses of the Templars and their keepers journeying from Lincoln to London *Berwick-upon-Tweed* R ɪɪ 120 O ɪɪ 235 H 1 p. ɪv 178
Dec. 12.	The K appoints commissioners to settle claims for damages committed in Aquitain during the truce. *Berwick-upon-Tweed* R ɪɪ 121 O ɪɪɪ 235 H 1 p ɪv 178
Dec 12.	The K grants additional powers to the said commissioners *Berwick-upon-Tweed* R ɪɪ. 121
Dec 12	The K still further extends the powers of the said commissioners. *Berwick upon-Tweed* R ɪɪ 121. O. ɪɪɪ. 236 H 1 p ɪv. 179.
Dec. 12.	The K confers additional powers upon the said commissioners *Berwick-upon-Tweed* R. ɪɪ 121 O ɪɪɪ 236 H 1 p ɪv 179
Dec. 12.	The K of England proposes to the K of France that the settlement of disputes should be deferred until this meeting *Berwick-upon-Tweed.* R ɪɪ 122 O ɪɪɪ. 237. H 1. p ɪv 179.
Dec 15	The K. orders aid to be given towards the expulsion of the fleet which Robert de Brus is about to send to the Isle of Man *Berwick upon-Tweed* R ɪɪ 122 O ɪɪɪ 238 H 1 p ɪv 180
Dec. 16.	The K orders the arrest of the adherents of Robert de Brus as they are coming from the Isle of Man *Berwick-upon-Tweed.* R ɪɪ 122 O ɪɪɪ 239 H 1 p ɪv 180
Dec. 16	Credence for Elias de Joneston and Roger de Waldenho, employed by the K. on the affairs of Aquitain *Berwick-upon-Tweed* R ɪɪ 122 O ɪɪ 239 H 1 p ɪv 180
Dec. 16.	The K asks the pope to consider favourably the affairs of John de Sandale, the K's treasurer *Berwick-upon-Tweed.* R ɪɪ 123 O ɪɪɪ 239. H 1 p ɪv 180
Dec 16	The K to Cardinal P de Colonna and 13 other cardinals in favour of the said John de Sandale *Berwick-upon-Tweed* R ɪɪ 123 O ɪɪ 240 H 1 p ɪɪ 180
Dec. 19	Inspeximus and confirmation by the K. of the charter by which Anthony bp. of Durham grants to Henry de Percy the manor of Langeleye. *Berwick-upon-Tweed* R. ɪɪ. 123. O. ɪɪɪ 241 H 1. p. ɪv 181
Dec 20.	The K recommends to the pope the affairs of John and Philip de Friscobaldis *Berwick-upon-Tweed* R. ɪɪ 123 O. ɪɪɪ 241 H 1 p ɪv 181
Dec 20	The K to the pope in favour of the above-named John and Philip *Berwick-upon-Tweed* R ɪɪ 124 O ɪɪɪ 242 H. ɪ p ɪv 181.
Dec 20	The K to Cardinal P de Colonna in favour of the above-mentioned John and Philip *Berwick-upon-Tweed* R ɪɪ. 124 O ɪɪɪ 242 H 1 p ɪv 181.
Dec 20	The K to Bernard de Gote marquis of Aucon in favour of the above-mentioned John and Philip *Berwick-upon-Tweed* R ɪɪ 124. O ɪɪɪ 242 H. 1 p ɪv. 181
Dec 29	The K grants to Ralph de Monthermer and his sons Tho and Edw, the K's nephews, the manor of Warblyngton *Berwick-upon-Tweed* R ɪɪ 124. O ɪɪɪ 243 H 1 p ɪv 182
Dec 30	The K exhorts the mayor and sheriffs of London to remedy and correct the robberies and murders so rife in that city *Berwick-upon-Tweed.* R ɪɪ. 124
1311 Jan. 1.	The K orders his treasurer, John de Sandale, to forward certain letters which he sends into Gascony, transcripts of which he sends for his information. *Berwick-upon-Tweed.* R. ɪɪɪ 125 O ɪɪɪ 243 H 1 p ɪv 182
Jan 4.	The K orders the sheriff of York to put into safe custody such vagabond Templars as he may happen to find. *Berwick-upon-Tweed* R. ɪɪ 125 O. ɪɪɪ 243 H 1 p ɪv. 182.
Jan. 6	The K orders John Wogan, justiciary of Ireland, to seize the temporalities of the see of Dublin, vacant by the resignation of Richard de Haveryng *Berwick-upon-Tweed* R ɪɪ 125 O ɪɪɪ. 244 H 1 p ɪv 182.
Jan. 15.	The K grants to Ralph de Monthermer and his sons Thomas and Edward, the K's nephews, the manor of Westenderle in recompense for the manor of Warblynton. *Berwick-upon-Tweed.* R. ɪɪ. 125. O ɪɪɪ. 244. H. 1 p. ɪv 182

DATE	SUBJECT
1311 Jan 15	The K forbids the holding of a tournament at Northampton *Berwick-upon-Tweed* R ıı 125 O ııı 245 H. 1 p ıv 182
Feb 1.	The K asks the pope to arrange that Robert bp of Glasgow shall never return into Scotland *Berwick-upon-Tweed.* R ıı 126 O. ııı 245 H 1 p. ıv 182
Feb 1	The K asks B. cardinal of SS John and Paul, and 15 other cardinals, to request the pope as above prayed *Berwick-upon-Tweed* R ıı 126 O ııı 246 H 1 p ıv 183
Feb 6.	The K asks the pope to favour the affairs of John de Sandale, the K's treasurer. *Berwick-upon-Tweed* R. ıı 126 O ııı 247. H 1 p ıv 183
Feb 6.	The K writes to two of the cardinals to the same purpose *Berwick-upon-Tweed* R. ıı 127. O. ııı 247. H 1 p ıv 183
Feb 6.	The K requests J bp of Norwich and two others to visit Abbeville on their return from Gascony, and settle the disputes in that town *Berwick-upon-Tweed* R ıı 127 O. ıı 248 H. 1 p ıv 183
Feb 10	The K orders the arrest of certain persons who pretend that they are appointed by the chapter of St John of Beverley to collect contributions for the repair of their church *Berwick-upon-Tweed.* R ıı 127 O ııı 248 H 1 p ıv 184
Feb. 15.	The K (having heard of the death of cardinal Thomas Jorz) asks the pope to appoint John de Lenham, the K's confessor, to the vacant dignity *Berwick-upon-Tweed.* R ıı 127, O ıı 249 H 1 p. ıv. 184
Feb. 16	The K asks certain cardinals to give credence to Henry Spigurnel and John de (?) Benstede, going to the papal court *Berwick-upon-Tweed* R ıı 128. O ııı 249 H 1 p ıv 184.
Feb. 17	The K gives his certificate that the bearer, Peter Auger, wears a long beard in compliance with a vow, and is not a Templar *Berwick-upon-Tweed* R. ıı 128 O ııı 250 H 1 p ıv 184
Feb 17	The K recommends the said Peter Auger to the pope. *Berwick-upon-Tweed* R ıı 128 O. ıiı 250 H 1 p ıv 184
Feb. 18.	The K asks the pope to give credence to Henry Spigurnel and Nicholas (?) de Benstede *Berwick-upon-Tweed* R ıı 128 O ııı 250 H 1 p ıv 184
Feb. 18.	The K asks 10 cardinals and Otto de Grandison to give credence to John de Wrotham, going to them upon a special matter which the K has much at heart. *Berwick-upon-Tweed.* R. ıı 128. O. ııı. 250 H. 1 p ıv 184.
Feb. 28.	The K asks the loan of 4,000 marks from the executors of the will of Henry de Lacy earl of Lincoln for his expedition into Scotland *Berwick upon-Tweed* R ıı 128
March 3	The K. orders the seizure of the goods and chattels of Anthony bp of Durham, lately deceased *Berwick-upon Tweed* R. ıı. 129 O ııı 251. H. 1 p. ıv. 185
March 4	The K orders the seizure of the lands and tenements, goods and chattels, of the said bp *Berwick-upon-Tweed* R ıı 129 O ııı 251, H 1 p ıv 185
March 4.	The K commits the custody of the see of Durham to Rob Baygnard and Rob. de Barton *Berwick-upon-Tweed* R ıı 129 O ıı 252 H 1 p ıv 185.
March 4	The K. commits the custody of his realm, during his absence in Scotland, to his nephew, Gilbert de Clare earl of Gloucester *Berwick-upon-Tweed* R. ıı. 129 O ııı 253 H 1 p ıv. 185.
March 9	The K reminds the pope that he is bound to preserve the rights of the crown, and cannot give effect to certain papal mandates. *Berwick-upon-Tweed* R ıı 130. O. ııı. 253. H 1 p ıv 185
March 9.	The K reproaches F cardinal of S Maria in Cosmedyn for having procured the issue of letters of citation in a suit in the papal court. *Berwick-upon-Tweed.* R. ıı. 130 O. ıı. 254 H 1 p ıv 186
March 10	The K asks the pope to support the interests of Guy de la Val, the K's cousin, nominated to the church of Maidenston, dioc Canterbury *Berwick-upon-Tweed.* R ıı 130. O ııı 254 H 1 p ıv. 186.
March 14.	The K to the pope's chamberlains in support of the suit of the said Guy de la Val *Berwick-upon-Tweed* R. ıı 131 O ııı 255 H 1 p. ıv. 187
March 14,	The K to his two proctors in the papal court to the same effect. *Berwick-upon-Tweed.* R ıı 131 O ııı 256 H 1 p ıv 187.
March 18	The K of England asks credence for two of his messengers going to Philip K. of France. *Berwick-upon-Tweed.* R. ıı 131 O. ııı 256 H 1 p ıv. 187.
March 20.	The K forbids the holding of a tournament at Leicester. *Berwick-upon-Tweed* R ıı. 131. O. ııı. 256 H 1 p ıv 187

DATE	SUBJECT
1311. March 26	The K. appoints Henry de Percy to be keeper of the vacant see of Durham *Berwick-upon-Tweed.* R. ii 131. O iii 257 H 1 p iv 187
March 26	The K. appoints Rob. de Barton to be receiver of the issues of the vacant see of Durham. *Berwick-upon-Tweed* R. ii. 132. O. iii 257. H 1 p. iv. 187.
April 5.	The K thanks the pope for having promoted John de Lek to the abprick of Dublin *Berwick-upon-Tweed* R ii 132. O iii 258 H 1 p. iv. 187.
April 14.	The K asks the abp. of Canterbury to induce the clergy of his province to grant him a subsidy of 12d. in the mark for the Scottish war. *Berwick-upon-Tweed.* R. ii. 132. O. iii. 258. H 1. p. iv 188.
April 20.	The K of England complains to Philip K of France that certain English merchants have been plundered by the French at the port of Whitsand. *Berwick-upon-Tweed* R ii 132 O iii 259 H 1 p iv 188
April 28.	The K. orders the mayor, aldermen, and commonalty of London to aid the inquisitors in proceeding with the examination of the Templars *Berwick-upon-Tweed* R ii 133. O iii 260. H 1. p. iv 188
April 30.	Proclamation to be made throughout England that those who have complaints against the Flemings are to report the same to the deputies at London appointed to hear the same. *Berwick-upon-Tweed* R ii 133 O iii. 260 H 1 p iv 188
May 1.	The K. orders that the issues of the see of Canterbury, which are in his hands, shall be delivered to the pope *Berwick-upon-Tweed.* R. ii. 133 O. iii. 260 H 1. p. iv 188
May 1.	The K orders that the portion of the mint at Canterbury belonging to the abp shall be delivered to the pope *Berwick-upon-Tweed* R ii 133 O iii 261 H 1 p iv 188.
May 5.	The K requests that Haco K. of Norway will make compensation for injuries committed by his subjects upon the sailors of an English ship which had been wrecked upon the coast of Norway *Berwick-upon-Tweed.* R ii. 133 O iii 261 H. 1. p. iv 189.
May 7.	The K directs his commissioners in Guienne and Gascony to settle disputes with France, and to send deputies to the general council at Avignon. *Berwick-upon-Tweed.* R. ii. 134 O. iii. 262. H 1. p. iv 189
May 20.	The K grants certain favours to the heirs, executors, and successors of Anthony bp of Durham *Berwick-upon-Tweed* R ii 134 O iii 263 H 1 p ii. 189
May 20.	The K. orders that Henry de Percy be not molested in holding the castle and honor of Alnwick *Berwick-upon-Tweed.* R ii 135. O iii 264 H 1 p iv 190
May 20.	The K orders that proclamation be made forbidding tournaments during his absence in Scotland *Berwick-upon-Tweed.* R ii 135 O iii 265 H 1 p iv 190
May 20.	The K orders three messengers to prepare for their departure with a message from him to Philip K. of France. *Berwick-upon-Tweed* R. ii 135
June 1.	The K appoints John de Ergadia to be admiral of his fleet on the coast of Ergaille, Inchegall, &c *Berwick-upon-Tweed* R. ii 135 O iii. 265 H. 1 p iv 190
June 1.	The K. orders W abp of York and others to come to London and arrange for their departure as nuncios to the approaching general council *Berwick-upon-Tweed.* R ii 135 O iii 265 H 1 p iv 190
June 1.	The K orders that certain allowances in Gascony be made in lieu of dower to Constantia de Bearn, widow of Henry de Alemannia *Berwick-upon-Tweed.* R. ii. 136 O. iii. 266. H. 1. p iv 190
June 1.	The K orders the constable of Bordeaux to pay to Constance de Bearn the arrears of her dower *Berwick-upon-Tweed.* R ii 136 O. iii 266 H. 1 p iv 191
June 5.	The K orders John de Britannia earl of Richmond, his seneschal of Gascony, and the constable of Burgundy, to carry out his orders in favour of Constantia de Bearn. *Berwick-upon-Tweed.* R ii. 136. O iii. 267 H 1. p. iv. 191.
June 7.	The K asks Philip K of France to grant letters of protection to his messengers going to the general council *Berwick-upon-Tweed.* R. ii. 136 O iii. 267. H 1. p iv 191
June 7.	The K. appoints Otto de Grandison to go as one of his nuncios to the general council. *Berwick-upon-Tweed.* R. ii. 136 O iii 267. H. 1 p iv 191.
June 7.	The K confirms the privileges granted by his father, K Edw I, to the merchants of the Teutonic Guildhall in London *Berwick-upon-Tweed.* R. ii. 137. O. iii 268. H 1 p iv. 191.
June 15.	The K. cautions Stephen de Segrave and seven others not to break the peace at Norwich. *Berwick-upon-Tweed.* R. ii 137.

DATE.	SUBJECT
1311 June 15	The K. of England appoints commissioners to settle the preliminaries for a conference with the deputies of Philip K of France *Berwick-upon-Tweed* R. ii. 137. O iii 268 H l. p iv 191
June 16.	The K of England asks Philip K. of France to permit the silver of Constance de Bierne to be conveyed through his realm. *Berwick-upon-Tweed* R. ii 137 O iii. 269 H l p iv. 192
June 20	The K of England asks Philip K of France to give credence to certain messengers sent to him from the K of England to treat on the affairs of Gascony *Berwick-upon-Tweed* R ii 137 O iii. 269 H l p iv. 192
June 20	The K of England informs Philip K of France that he cannot consent, without the sanction of the common council of the realm, to relax certain duties in favour of the merchants of Amiens *Berwick-upon-Tweed* R ii 138 O iii 269 H l p iv 192
July 1	Wm abp of York authorizes Tho. bp of Whithern to receive Walter bp. of Lichfield, prisoner in the K.'s prison at York, and to transfer him into the prison of the abp. *Thorpe near York* R ii. 138. O. iii 270. H. l p iv 192.
July 1	The K asks the pope to grant a dispensation for the marriage of Roger de Moubray with Margaret the daughter of Alexander de Abernethy. *Berwick-upon-Tweed* R ii 138. O iii. 270 H. l p iv 192
July 6.	The K asks the pope to provide quarters for his nuncios going to the council at Vienne. *Berwick-upon-Tweed* R ii 138 O iii 270 H. i p iv 192
July 6	The K. makes the same request to B cardinal of SS John and Paul, the pope's chamberlain. *Berwick-upon-Tweed* R. ii 138 O iii 271 H l p iv 192
July 6	The K invites Bertrand de Saubiat count of Champagne, the pope's nephew, to come into England *Berwick-upon-Tweed* R ii 139
July 6.	The K asks the pope to permit his nephew Bertrand de Saubiat to come into England *Berwick-upon-Tweed* R ii 139
July 6.	The K. asks three cardinals to intercede with the pope to the same effect *Berwick-upon-Tweed* R ii 139
July 14.	The K summons Rob de Umframvill earl of Angus, and 37 others, to meet him at Roxburgh, to proceed against the Scots *Berwick-upon-Tweed* R. ii 139 O. iii. 271 H l p iv 192
July 20	The K asks the pope to appoint John de Lenham, or some other Englishman, to the dignity of a cardinal *Berwick-upon-Tweed* R. ii. 139 O. iii. 272 H l p iv 193.
July 20.	The K applies to seven cardinals on the same subject. *Berwick-upon-Tweed* R. ii 140 O. iii 272 H l p iv 193
July 20.	John de Lek, abp elect of Dublin, having renounced certain clauses in the papal bulls prejudicial to the rights of the crown, the K orders the restitution of the temporalities of his see *Berwick-upon-Tweed* R ii 140. O iii 273 H l p iv 193.
July 20.	The K. forbids Nicholas de Segrave and Wm le Mareschal to come to the parliament at London with arms *Berwick-upon-Tweed* R ii 140
July 22.	The K orders that certain Templars who have been freed by the provincial council shall be conveyed into the diocese of Worcester *Berwick-upon-Tweed* R ii. 140
July 24	The K informs the pope that W. bp of S Andrew's is unable to attend the general council to which he has been summoned *Berwick-upon-Tweed* R. ii 141. O. iii 274 H. l p iv 193.
July 26.	The K orders W. abp of York to attend the next parliament at London instead of going to the general council *Berwick-upon-Tweed.* R. ii 141.
Aug 16	Letters of safe conduct for R. bp of London and H. bp of Winchester going to the general council. *Westm.* R ii 141 O iii 274. H. l. p iv. 194
Aug 18.	The K orders that all the Templars in the custody of the sheriff at York shall be delivered to Rob. de Pykeryng, vicar-general of the abp *London.* R ii. 141. O iii. 274 H l p iv 194
Aug. 20.	The K requests the pope to excuse W. bp of Worcester, the K's chancellor, from attending the general council *London.* R ii. 141. O iii. 275. H. l. p iv 194
Aug. 20	The K. makes the same request to B cardinal of SS John and Paul, the pope's chamberlain *London.* R ii 142 O iii 275 H l p iv. 194.
Aug. 24.	The K. requests the pope to be favourable to the order of the Carmelites. *London.* R. ii. 142 O iii. 276. H l p. iv. 194.

DATE.	SUBJECT
1311. Aug. 25.	The K. orders that a safe and free passage be provided from Dover for his chancellor the bp. of Worcester, going to the general council. *London.* R ii 142 O iii 276 H. 1 p iv 194
Aug 27.	Memorandum concerning the delivery of the Great Seal to the K. by Walter bp. of Worcester, his chancellor, on his going to the general council. R. ii. 142. O iii. 276. H. 1. p. iv. 194.
Aug. 27.	The K orders that his relative, Ric de Cornubia, shall not be molested by papal citations in respect to his possession of the prebend of Northnenbald, in the church of York. *London* R. ii. 142. O iii. 277 H. 1 p iv 195
Aug. 27.	The K orders that such persons as serve the papal citations shall be arrested. *London.* R. ii 143 O. iii 277. H. 1. p. iv. 195.
Aug 28	The K acknowledges that he is indebted in 1,386*l* 13*s* 4*d*. for gold plate, &c bought from the executors of Anthony late bp. of Durham *London* R. ii. 143 O iii 277 H 1. p. iv 195
Sept. 12.	The K. forbids Rob. de Retford and 16 others of his Council from departing from the parliament at London *Haddeleys* R ii 143
Oct. 8.	The K grants to Gilbert de Bohun, constable of the castle of Loghmaban, and Rob de Applynden, power to receive the Scotch who came to the K's peace. *London* R ii. 143 O iii 279 H 1 p iv 195
Oct 8.	Protection for Peter de Gavaston earl of Cornwall coming to the K. by his command. *London.* R. ii. 143. O. iii. 278. H. 1. p. iv 195.
Oct. 9.	The K. regrets that he cannot lend to the K of Castile the sum of money which had been asked. *London* R ii 144. O. iii. 278 H 1 p iv 195
Oct. 9	The K grants his commission to certain persons to take charge of the lands and tenements of the Templars and of Walter de Langeton, bp of Lichfield. *London.* R. ii. 144. O iii 279 H 1 p iv 195.
Oct 9	The K earnestly requests J duke of Brabant and M duchess of Brabant his sister favourably to receive his especial friend, Peter de Gavaston earl of Cornwall, who shortly intends to visit their dominions R. ii 144. O. iii. 279. H. 1. p. iv. 196.
Oct 9	The K asks Edw le Butiller and four others to promote good will among his subjects in Ireland *London* R ii 144 O. iii 280 H 1 p iv 196
Oct 9	The K orders his seneschal of Gascony to revoke all donations in Gascony made by virtue of writs dated after 16 March, 3 Edw. II. *London.* R. ii. 145. O iii 280. H. 1. p. iv. 196.
Oct 10.	The K. of England asks Philip K of France to give credence to two messengers sent to him *London.* R ii 145 O iii 281. H 1 p iv 196
Oct. 10	The K of England tells Philip K of France that he is anxious to have a personal interview with him. *London* R. ii 145 O. iii. 281. H. 1. p. iv 196.
Oct 10.	The K asks credence for certain messengers sent by him to the pope *London.* R ii. 145. O iii 281 H 1 p iv. 196.
Oct. 10	Instructions by the K to the messengers going to the pope. *London.* R. ii 145. O iii 282. H. 1. p iv. 197.
Oct 10	The K orders that certain ordinances for the government of his household and realm shall be proclaimed by the sheriffs, and copies thereof preserved in monasteries *London* R ii 146
Oct 12.	The K orders the seneschal of Gascony to take care that certain of the society of the Friscobaldi be arrested and kept in prison until they render their accounts of all issues. *London.* R ii. 146. O iii 282. H ii. p. iv. 196.
Oct. 15	Philip K of France complains to the K of England of various injuries inflicted upon his merchants by the English *Abbey of Longpont* R. ii 146 O iii 283. H 1 p iv 197
Oct. 17	The K. requests the pope to excuse the absence of the bp of Durham from the general council on account of the Scotch war. *Windsor.* R. ii. 146. O. iii. 283. H. 1. p iv. 197
Oct 23	Pope Clement [V.] complains to the K that Aymer cardinal of S Anastasia has been prevented from obtaining possession of certain ecclesiastical benefices in England. *Avignon.* R. ii. 147 O. iii. 284. H 1 p iv 197
Oct 26	The K asks the pope to grant a dispensation to John de Hothum in regard to a petition which will be read to his holiness *Eltham.* R. ii. 147 O iii. 285. H 1. p iv 198.
[Oct.]	Pope Clement [V] urges the K. to restore to liberty Walter bp of Lichfield, a prisoner in York castle *In the priory of Granselle, in the dioc of Bazas* R. ii 147 O iii 286. H 1 p iv. 198.

DATE	SUBJECT
1311 Nov 4	The K commits to John de Ferrars the custody of the lands in Gloucestershire belonging to Waller bp of Lichfield *Windsor* R ii 148 O iii. 287. H 1. p. iv. 199.
Nov. 4	The K commits to various persons the custody of the lands belonging to the Templars and to the bp of Lichfield in various counties *Windsor* R. ii. 148. O iii 287 H 1 p iv 199
Nov 8	The K asks the cardinal of S Nicholas in Carcere Tulliano to protect the interests of the master and brethren of the House of Asherugge. *Westm.* R. ii. 148. O. iii. 288. H 1. p iv 199.
Nov 13	Pope Clement [V] appoints Roland Jorz to the archbishoprick of Armagh, vacant by the cession of Walter Jorz *Vienne* R ii 149 O iii 289 H 1 p iv. 199
Nov 14	The K. appoints Wm de Hillum to collect the fruits and obventions belonging to the church of the Templars at Whitechirche, co York. *Westm.* R. ii 149. O. iii 290. H 1 p iv 200.
Nov 16	The K forbids the holding of a tournament at Northampton *Westm* R. ii 149 O. iii 290 H 1 p iv 200
Nov. 24.	The K. of England informs Philip K of France that he has caused restitution to be made for a robbery committed upon a merchant of Rochelle, but that he cannot send his subjects out of his own realm to be punished abroad *Westm* R. ii 149 O iii 290. H 1 p iv 200
Nov 25	The K makes arrangements for receiving the issues of the lands and tenements of the Templars and of Walter bp. of Lichfield. *Westm.* R ii. 150 O. iii. 291. H. 1. p iv 200
Nov 25	The K orders that pensions out of the manors here specified formerly belonging to the Templars be paid to various persons who have been in the service of the said Templars. *Westm* R ii 150 O iii 292 H 1 p iv 200
Nov 28.	The K. forbids Gilbert de Clare earl of Gloucester, and five other nobles, to come to the parliament at Westm with horses and arms *Westm.* R. ii 151
Nov 30	The K orders that search be made for Peter de Gavaston, who is wandering from place to place in Cornwall, Devon, Somerset, and Dorset *Westm* R ii 151 O. iii 294 H 1 p iv 201
Dec. 9.	The K asks the chancellors and masters of the university of Oxford to protect the rights of the Friars Preachers studying in their university *Westm.* R. ii 152
Dec 15	The K orders that the sums allowed for the support of certain Templars in Somerset and Dorset be paid to their keepers *Westm* R ii 152 O iii 295. H. 1. p. iv 202
Dec 16.	The K of England regrets that the rebellion of Robert de Brus prevents him from having an interview with Philip K of France, as he had intended *Westm* R. ii 152 O. iii 295 H 1 p iv 200
Dec. 16.	The K informs the pope that he is unable to comply with the request conveyed by the messengers returning from his Holiness, nor, indeed, could he do so, without the consent of the prelates and nobles of the realm *Westm* R ii 152 O iii 296 H 1 p iv 202.
Dec 19	The K orders the sheriffs of London to seize all the lands and tenements of the Templars within the city and suburbs *Westm* R ii 153 O iii 296 H 1 p iv 202
Dec 26	The K asks credence for certain messengers sent by him to the K of France *Westm.* R. ii. 153 O iii. 298. H. 1. p iv 203.
Dec 26	The K orders the keepers of the lands of the Templars and of Walter bp. of Lichfield to pay over to the Exchequer all the issues of the same *Westm.* R ii 153. O. iii 297. H 1 p iv 202
1312 Jan 18.	The K. orders it to be proclaimed throughout the realm that Peter de Gavaston earl of Cornwall had been illegally banished, and that he has returned by the K's commandment *York* R ii 153. O iii 298. H. 1. p. iv 203
Jan. 20.	The K orders it to be proclaimed that Peter de Gavaston is prepared to stand to the law, and directs that his castles, vills, lands, &c shall be restored to him *York*. R. ii. 154. O iii 298 H 1 p iv 203
Jan. 21.	The K orders that the castle of Knaresboro' shall be victualled from the issues of the manor of Ribbestayn, lately belonging to the Templars *York* R. ii. 154. O. iii. 299. H 1 p iv 203
Jan. 23	The K (having restored his manors, lands, and tenements to Walter de Langeton bp. of Lichfield) orders that the arrears of the issues of the same be paid to the said bp. *York*. R ii 154 O. iii 299 H 1 p iv. 203.

DATE.	SUBJECT
1312. Jan 24	The K informs the pope that he has liberated the bp of Lichfield, whom he commends to the favour of his Holiness *York.* R ıı 154. O ııı. 300 H 1 p ıv 204
Jan. 26.	The K. orders it to be proclaimed that the peace, laws, and ordinances of late enacted are to be firmly observed R ıı 154. O. ııı 300 H. 1 p ıv 204
Jan. 26.	Commission to David earl of Athol and five others to treat with the Scots for a truce *York.* R ıı 155 O ııı 300. H 1. p ıv 204
Feb 6	The K. orders that Elizabeth, wife of Robert de Brus, and her family, be imprisoned in Windsor Castle *York* R ıı 155 O ııı 302 H 1 p ıv 205.
Feb 8.	The K grants to David earl of Athol (along with the custody of the manors of Etton and Cave, late belonging to the Templars) the gift of the corn, &c within the said manors. R ıı 155 O. ııı 303 H 1 p ıv 205
Feb. 8.	The K recommends the pope to favour the promotion of Wm de Saint Clare to the see of Dunkeld *York.* R ıı 155. O ııı 303 H 1 p. ıv. 205.
Feb 8	The K orders the mayor and citizens of London to take care that the city is not endangered by assemblages of bps, earls, and barons *York* R ıı 156 O ııı 304. H 1 p ıv 205
Feb. 10.	The K restores to Peter de Gavaston the castle and honors of Wallingford and S. Waleric. *York.* R ıı 156. O. ııı. 304. H. 1. p. ıv 205
Feb. 10	The K asks the pope to give credence to his nephew Bertrand count of Champagne *York* R ıı 156 O ııı 305 H 1. p ıv 205
Feb 10.	The K to 32 cardinals and other prelates to the same effect. *York.* R. ıı. 156. O ııı 305 H 1 p ıv 206
Feb 14.	Protection for the said count Bertrand de Salviaco count of Champagne coming into England from the pope. *York* R. ıı. 157 O ııı 306 H 1 p ıv 206
Feb. 16	The K of England recommends John de Feraniis, his seneschal of Gascony, to Philip K of France *York* R ıı. 157 O ııı 307 H 1 p ıv 206
Feb 18.	Protection for Reymund cardinal of S Maria Nova, archdeacon of Leicester and dean of Sarum, and two others, going abroad. *York* R ıı 157 O ııı 307 H 1 p ıv 206
Feb 23.	The K. asks the pope to give to Oliver of Bordeaux the place of the Templars at Bordres near Tarbes. *York.* R. ıı. 157. O. ııı. 307. H 1 p ıv 206.
Feb 24.	The K grants the manors of Cosham, Newport, and Watlyngton, and houses in London, to Peter de Gavaston earl of Cornwall *York.* R ıı 158 O ııı 308. H 1. p ıv 207
Feb 24	The K orders proclamation to be made, week by week, in various counties, for the preservation of the rights of the crown and the safety of the realm *York* R ıı 158
Feb. 24	The K. orders that no heavier duty than heretofore shall be levied upon the merchants who bring silver in mass for coinage at the K's mint. *York.* R ıı. 158.
March 2	The K grants to Peter de Gavaston earl of Cornwall the marriage of Tho. son of John Wak, deceased. *York.* R ıı 158 O ııı 308 H 1 p ıv 207
March 7.	The K. asks the pope to excuse the absence of W bp of S. Andrew's from the general council *York* R ıı 158 O ııı 308. H 1 p. ıv 207
March 7	The K. to three cardinals, to the same effect *York.* R. ıı. 159 O. ıu. 309. H. 1. p. ıv 207.
March 8.	The K. of England asks the K. of France to protect certain merchants of Genoa *York* R. ıı 159 O ııı 309 H 1 p ıv 207.
March 8	Commission to J. bp of Norwich and others to treat respecting the amendment of certain ordinances prejudicial to the K *York* R. ıı 159 O ııı 310 H 1 p ıv 207
March 8	The K. to the bps. of the province of Canterbury and certain nobles on the same subject *York.* R. ıı. 159.
March 14	The K. appoints W. bp of Lichfield to the office of treasurer of the Exchequer *York.* R. ıı. 159. O ııı 310. H 1 p ıv 208
March 21	The K. orders the sheriffs to take measures for ending disputes between the English and Flemings. *York.* R ıı. 160.
March 21.	The K. orders the observance of certain rules in keeping the accounts of the Exchequer. *York.* R. ıı 160.
March 22.	The K. orders the customs on wools and hides in the port of Berwick to be assigned to Peter de Gavaston. *York.* R ıı. 160. O. ııı. 310. H. 1. p. ıv. 208

DATE.	SUBJECT
1312. March 24.	The K orders that the lands and tenements late of John de Balhol shall not be charged with the debts due to the K. on being transferred to John de Britannia earl of Richmond. *York.* R. u. 160. O. m. 311. H 1. p iv 208.
March 28	Credence for Bertrand de Salviaco count of Champagne and others going from the K to the pope *York* R u 161 O m 311. H 1 p iv 208
March 28.	Credence for Walter de Maydenestan and Stephen le Bygot, the K.'s clerks, going on his business to certain cardinals and others. *York.* R. n. 161. O. m 311 H 1 p. iv. 208.
March 28	The K asks Bertrand de Salviaco count of Champagne to give credence to the clerks mentioned in the previous article *York* R u 161. O. m. 312 H 1 p iv 208
March 28	The K orders the sheriffs of England to make a return of the names of such persons as pretend that they have commissions from others than himself for keeping the peace. *York* R u 161
March 28	The K requests the chancellor and regents of the university of Oxford to favour Roger de Baketon, of the order of the Friars Preachers *York* R u 161
March 29	The K. asks the chancellor and regents of the University of Oxford to permit the Friars Preachers of Oxford to enjoy their privileges until the next parliament *York* R u 162
March 30	The K forbids the breaking of the public peace by assemblages of armed persons going about by night. *York.* R. u. 162
April 1	The K asks B bp of Frascati and several cardinals to promote the K's interests at the papal court *York* R u 162 O m. 312 H. u p i 1.
April 1.	The K. of England asks Philip K. of France to give credence to Thomas of Cobham and Henry of Canterbury, his messengers. *York* R. u. 162. O. m. 313. H u p. i. 1.
April 1	The K of England informs Philip K of France that Rob de Brus being about to besiege Berwick, he, the writer, must hasten thither *York* R. u. 162. O m 313 H. u p i. 1.
April 3	The K appoints Peter de Gavaston earl of Cornwall to be custodian of the office of justiciar of forests on this side of the Trent. *York.* R. ii. 163. O. m. 313 H. u p. i. 1.
April 5	The K urges Amenenus de Lebret to come to him without delay *York* R u 163. O m 314 H u p i 2.
April 5.	Writs of military summons to Gaston de Berne count of Foix and 121 others, barons, &c. of Gascony, to attend the K with horses and arms *York.* R u 163 O m. 315. H u. p i 2
April 6	The K asks F King of Castile to show favour to Maria, widow of Rotheric de Ispania, and her children *Northallerton.* R. u. 164. O. m 316 H. u. p. i. 2.
April 8	Credence for Thomas of Cobham, Walter of Thorpe, and Henry of Canterbury, the K's clerks going to the K of France *Allerton* R u 164. O m 316 H u p i 2
April 8.	The K, unable to attend personally at the court of French peers at Paris, has expressed his wishes respecting the count of Flanders through his messengers. R. u 164 O u 317. H. ii p i. 2.
April 13.	The K. advises W bp of Lichfield not to be deterred by threats from discharging the office of the treasurer *Newcastle-upon-Tyne* R u 164
April 14.	Credence to the K of France for certain messengers sent to urge the preservation of the K of England s rights in Aquitain *Newcastle-upon-Tyne* R u. 164. O. m 317. H u. p i 3.
April 14	The K asks Amanenus de Lebret to aid in preserving his rights in Aquitain. *Newcastle-upon-Tyne* R u 165. O m 318 H u p i 3.
April 14	The K. asks Jordan Moraunt, constable of Bordeaux, to aid him as above mentioned *Newcastle-upon-Tyne* R u 165 O m 318 H u p i 3
April 14	The K asks his councillors in Aquitain to deliberate and act for the preservation of his rights in that duchy *Newcastle-upon-Tyne* R ii 165 O m. 318. H. u. p i. 3.
April 14	The K makes the same request to Bernard Peleti, prior "de Manso." *Newcastle-upon-Tyne.* R u 165 O m 319. H u p. i 3
April 14	The K. asks John de Ferarius, seneschal of Gascony, and others, to settle the disputes respecting the liberties of Bordeaux *Newcastle-upon-Tyne* R u 165 O m 319. H H p i. 3.
April 15.	Commission to Alex de Abernithy and others to settle a meeting between the K of England and Philip K of France at Boulogne-sur-Mer *Newcastle-upon-Tyne.* R. u. 166. O m 320 H u p i 4
April 15	Credence for the above-mentioned commissioners sent to the K of France *Newcastle-upon-Tyne.* R. u. 166. O. m. 320. H. u. p i. 4

DATE	SUBJECT.
1312. April 16.	The K asks A cardinal of S Maria in Porticu and two others to assist in the arrangement of a marriage between Roger de Moubray and Margaret, daughter of Alexander de Abernythy *Newcastle-upon-Tyne* R n 166 O m 320 H n p 1 4
April 20.	Commission to Wm de Bevercote to collect the fruits of the church of the Templars at Marnham, co Notts, for the K.'s use. *Neweastle-upon-Tyne* R n 166. O m 321 H n p 1. 4.
May 1.	Safe conduct for W. bp of Lichfield going abroad on the K's affairs *Newcastle-upon-Tyne* R n 166 O m. 321 H n p 1 4
May 1	The K requests the pope to revoke the sentence of excommunication pronounced upon W bp of Lichfield *Newcastle-upon-Tyne.* R ii 167 O m 322 H. n. p 1 4
May 1.	The K requests R abp of Cant to take care that his men do not interfere with the men of W abp of York, going through Kent to the general council *Newcastle-upon-Tyne* R n 167 O. m 322 H n p 1 5
May 2.	Pope Clement [V] grants the entire goods of the order of the Templars to the Hospital of S John of Jerusalem *Vienne.* R. n 167 O m. 323 H n p 1 5.
[May 4.]	Memorandum respecting the delivery to the K of the great seal at Newcastle on this day, the K's departure on May 5 from Tynemouth to Scarboro', and of the delivery of the great seal to Adam de Osgodeby and others at York on Wednesday in Whitsun week R n 169 O m 329 H n p 1 7
May 16	Pope Clement [V.] informs the K. of the grant to the Hospitalers made with the sanction of the general council at Vienne *Liberon, dioc Valence* R n 168 O m 326. H n p 1 6
May 16	Pope Clement [V] asks the aid of the abps and ops of England in carrying out the above-mentioned grant *Liberon* R. n 168 O m 326 H n p 1 6.
May 16.	Pope Clement [V] to the nobility of England, to the same effect. *Liberon.* R. n 169. O m 327. H n p 1 7.
May 17.	The K desires that the usual payments be made for the charges of such Templars as have been sent to do penance within monasteries *York.* R. n 169 O m 327 H n p 1 7
May 17	The K commands that the siege of Scarbro' Castle shall be raised. *York* R n 169. O m 327 H. n. p 1 7
May 17	The K orders John de'Warren earl of Surrey, Aymer de Valence earl of Pembroke, Henry de Percy, and Rob de Clifford to desist from the same siege *York* R. n 169 O ni 328. H. n p 1 7.
May 26.	The K orders Griffin de la Pole to cease from besieging Pole Castle belonging to John de Cherleton *York* R n 170 O. m 328 H n p 1 7
May 26	The K orders the mayor of London to guard the city on the K's behalf *York* R n. 170
June 11	The K of England informs Philip K of France that, although grievously annoyed by his subjects, he will follow the advice contained in the letters of K Philip *Hoveden* R n 170. O n 329 H. n p 1 7
June 31	Henry emperor of the Romans informs the K of his coronation at Rome, and of the events which preceded it *Rome.* R. n 170
July 3.	The K recommends to the pope W. bp of Lichfield then at the papal court *Stril.* R n 171. O m 329 H n p i 7.
July 5	The K. orders payment of their wages to be made to various persons formerly in the service of the Templars *Kirkstede.* R n. 171 O m 331 H n p. 1 8
[July]	The form of the oath to be taken by the sheriffs R n 171
July 11	The K begs the pope to excuse the absence of the bp of S Andrew's from the general council *Mildenhale* R. n. 172. O in 332. H n, p. 1 8
July 11	The K. to three cardinals, on the same subject as the preceding *Mildenhall* R n 172 O. m. 332 H n. p 1 8
July 20.	The K forbids unlawful assemblies, and threatens to punish those who disturb the peace *Westm* R ii 172 O. iii. 333 H. n p. 1. 9
July 23	Protection for John de Bonkhil, of the order of the Carmelites, going to Jerusalem on the K.'s behalf. *Westm.* R n. 172 O m 333 H n p 1 9
July 24.	Proclamations to be made throughout England against unlawful assemblies and persons who disturb the peace *London* R n. 172 O m 334. H n. p. 1 9
July 24.	The K. to the constables of 27 castles and the mayors of 16 towns, ordering them to guard the same. *London.* R n. 173.

DATE	SUBJECT
1312 July 28.	The K orders payment to the bp of Ely of the usual allowances for the support of the Templars. *London* R. u. 173 O. iii 334 H u p i 9
July 28	The K orders the keepers of the passage of the port of Dover to permit the abbots of 17 houses of the Cistercian order to cross on their way to Citeaux *London* R ii 173
July 30	The K orders John de Moubray to seize the lands, tenements, &c. of Henry de Percy. *London.* R ii 173 O iii 334 H ii p i. 9
July 31	The K orders John de Moubray to arrest Henry de Percy, who, contrary to his mainprise, had permitted the death of Peter de Gavaston earl of Cornwall *London.* R. ii 173. O iii 334. H ii p i 9
July 31.	Proclamation to be made that all persons who have lands to the annual value of 40l, or one knight's fee, be knighted *London* R ii 174 O. iii. 335 H. ii p. i 9
July 31	The K grants various lands, &c in S Macaire and elsewhere in Gascony to Bertrand de Salviaco count of Champagne. *London* R. ii 174 O iii 335 H ii p. i. 10
Aug 1.	The K charges the prior of the hospital of S John of Jerusalem in England not to meddle with the goods of the Templars by virtue of any bull from the pope. *London.* R. ii. 174. O iii 337 H ii p i 10.
Aug 4	The K directs that certain ordinances prejudicial to the crown shall be corrected, and that no one shall come to parliament with horses and arms *Canterbury* R ii 175. O iii 337 H ii p i 10.
Aug. 5.	The K. arranges for the settlement of disputes which had arisen between John de Ferrariis, his seneschal of Gascony, and Amanenus de Lebret R. ii. 175. O iii 338 H. ii. p i 10
Aug 6	Credence for Aymer de Valence earl of Pembroke and Henry de Beaumont, going from the K. of England to Philip K of France *Dover* R ii. 175. O. iii. 339 H. ii. p i. 11.
Aug. 6.	Credence for Bertrand de Salviaco count of Champagne and others, going from the K to the pope *Dover* R. ii 175 O iii 339 H ii p. i 11.
Aug. 6	Credence for Aymer de Valence earl of Pembroke and Henry de Beaumont, going from the K to A cardinal of S Prisca and the bp of Poitiers. *Dover.* R ii 176. O. iii. 339. H ii p i 11
Aug. 8.	Credence for Bertrand de Salviaco count of Champagne, and others, going from the K to the cardinals *Dover* R ii 176 O iii. 340 H ii p i 11.
Aug. 8.	Special credence for Bertrand de Salviaco count of Champagne, going from the K. to the pope on important business. *Dover.* R. ii 176. O. iii. 340. H. ii. p i 12.
Aug 10	Pope Clement [V] to John de Ferrariis, seneschal of Gascony, on the disputes between him and Amanenus de Lebret *Priory of Granselle.* R ii 176. O. iii 340. H ii p i 12
Aug 13.	The K. orders Roger de Mortimer, justiciary of Wales, and the sheriff of Shropshire, to arrest Griffin de la Pole, who has besieged the castle of Pole. *Chartham.* R ii. 177.
Aug 16	The K orders Amanenus de Lebret to appear before him in England for the settlement of the disputes between him and John de Ferrariis, seneschal of Gascony *Canterb.* R. ii. 177. O iii. 342 H ii p i 12
Aug 19	Writ from the K to John de Ferrariis, to the same effect as the preceding. *Eltham.* R ii. 177 O iii 343 H ii p i 13
Aug. 23.	The K orders the sheriff of Bedfordshire to arrest such persons as hold illegal meetings. *Westm.* R. ii. 177. O iii 343. H ii p i. 13
Aug 24.	The K. to the pope in favour of Malachi bp of Elphin, elected to the abprick of Tuam. *Westm.* R. ii 178 O. iii. 344. H ii p i 13
Sept. 3.	The K forbids Thomas earl of Lancaster and his followers from coming to him with horses and arms. *Westm.* R ii. 178. O iii 344 H ii p i 13.
Sept. 6.	The K intercedes with the pope in favour of the suit of the Friars Preachers of Oxford against the chancellor and masters of the university *Westm* R. ii 178 O iii 345. H. ii p. i 13
Sept. 14	The K to the pope, in favour of W. bp of Lichfield, his treasurer. *Westm* R ii. 178. O. iii. 345. H ii. p i. 13
Sept 14	The K to the cardinal of S Angelo, in favour of the same. *Westm* R. ii 178 O. iii. 345 H ii. p i. 13.
Sept. 14.	The K to 20 other cardinals, in favour of the same *Westm* R. ii 179. O. iii. 346. H. ii p. i. 14.

DATE.	SUBJECT.
1312. Sept. 15.	The K asks the pope to expedite the canonization of Thomas de Cantilupe, late bp of Hereford. *Westm.* R n 179 O m. 346 H n p i. 14.
Sept. 15	The K to two cardinals, upon the same subject. *Westm* R n 179 O m. 347. H i. p i 14.
Sept. 15.	The K. of England asks Philip K. of France to aid the above petition to the pope *Westm.* R n. 179 O. m 347 H n. p i 14
Sept 16.	The K. asks the pope to excuse Ingelard de Warle on account of his proceedings in the matter of W bp of Lichfield. *Westm* R n. 180 O m 348 H n p i 14.
Sept. 16.	The K. orders the payment of their usual allowance to certain Templars in the custody of the bp of Worcester. *Westm.* R. n. 180 O. m. 349 H n p i 15.
Sept. 28	The K undertakes to discuss his disputes with his nobles in the presence of A cardinal of S Prisca and the other papal delegates. *Windsor* R. n 180 O m 349 H n p i. 15
Sept. 30.	The K forbids the holding of tournaments at Sudbury, Exeter, and Lewes. *Windsor.* R n. 180 O m 349 H n p i. 15
Oct. 3.	The pope recommends Thomas de Colewelle, abbot of S Augustine's, Canterbury, to the K. *Avignon* R. n. 181 O m 350 H. n p i 15
Oct. 5.	The K appoints John Lenfant as his seneschal of Ponthieu. *Windsor* R. ii 181. O m 351 H. n p i 15
Oct. 5	The K orders the mayor and sheriffs of London to take care that the earl of Hereford and others be not admitted within the city of London *Windsor* R n 181. O m. 351 H n p i 16
Oct. 5	The K orders W bp of Worcester to receive the great seal into his custody *Windsor* R. n. 181
Oct 8	The K again undertakes to discuss his disputes with his nobles (the address to whom is modified in the duplicate and triplicate of these letters), in the presence of the papal delegates. *Windsor.* R ii. 182. O m 351. H n p. i 16
Oct 12.	The K forbids the holding of meetings and tournaments *Windsor* R. n. 182 O m. 352. H n p. i 16
Oct. 12.	The K forbids Edmund earl of Arundel from sheltering the people who, with Griffin de la Pole, had disturbed the K's peace in the marches of Wales *Windsor* R n 182.
Oct. 13.	The K orders the removal to Shafton of Elizabeth, wife of Robert de Brus earl of Carrick *Windsor* R n. 182. O m 352 H n. p i 16
Oct 17.	General proxy given by the master and convent of the house of the hospital of S John of Jerusalem to Albret de Castro Nigro, as visitor general of the order. *Rhodes.* R n. 182 O. m. 459. H n p i 57
Oct. 20.	The K authorizes his wife, Q. Isabella, to dispose by will of her goods and jewels *Windsor* R. n 184
Oct 22	Pope Clement [V.] informs the K that he has appointed John de Valle to the see of Ardfert *Avignon* R n. 184. O. m 352. H n p. i 16
Oct 28.	The K recommends John de Sandale to the pope *Westm.* R. n. 185 O m 353 H n. p i 16
Oct. 28	The K. asks the pope to give a favourable hearing to the petition of John de Sandale. *Westm* R n. 185. O. m 354 H n p i 17
Oct. 28	The K of England recommends Arnold Guilhelmi de Marsano to the K. of France *Westm* R. n 185. O m 354 H n p i 17
Oct. 28.	The K appoints Stephen Ferioli as his seneschal of Gascony. *Westm* R. n. 185. O. m. 354. H n p i. 17.
Oct. 28.	The K assigns his wages to Stephen Ferioli as seneschal of Gascony *Westm* R ii. 185 O m. 355. H n. p i 17
Nov 1.	The K forbids tournaments throughout England. *Windsor.* R. n. 185 O iii 355 H n p i. 17.
Nov 2	Safe conduct for Thomas earl of Lancaster and five others coming to discuss their disputes with the K *Shene* R n 186 O m 355 H n p i 17
Nov 4	The K asks the pope to exonerate Ingelard de Warle from blame in his dealings with the goods of the W. bp. of Lichfield. *Windsor* R n 186 O m. 356 H. n p i. 17
Nov. 6.	The K. gives directions to the bps. of Exeter and Norwich how to act in regard to the processes about to be brought against him in the parliament at Paris *Windsor.* R n. 186 O. m. 356. H. n. p. i. 18.

DATE.	SUBJECT
1312 Nov 12	The K. recommends Wm de Melton to the pope *Windsor* R ii 187 O iii 357 H n p i 18
Nov 12	The K recommends Wm de Melton to R cardinal S Mariæ Novæ and the pope's nephew, Bertrand del Gout *Windsor* R ii 187, O. iii 358 H. ii p i 18.
[Nov. 13]	Memorandum of the birth and baptism of the K's eldest son at Windsor R ii 187. O iii 358 H ii p i 18
Nov 19	The K forbids the holding of a tournament at Dunstable *Windsor* R ii. 187. O iii 358 H ii p i 18
Nov 20	The K grants certain manors here specified to John Comyn *Windsor* R ii 188 O. iii 359 H ii, p i, 19
Nov 20	The K orders the constable of Bordeaux to pay the arrears of the annuity of the count of Audoigne *Windsor* R ii 188 O iii 359 H ii p i 19
Nov. 20.	The K recommends Arnold Guillelmi de Marsano to the pope *Windsor* R ii 188. O. iii. 360. H. ii p. i. 19.
Nov 26	The K appoints two commissioners to settle the claims of the Flemings against the English *Windsor* R. ii 188 O iii 360 H ii p i 19
Nov. 26.	Credence for two messengers going from the K to R count of Flanders *Windsor*. R ii 188 O iii 360 H ii p i 19
Nov 27	The K orders the mayor and bailiffs of Winchester to permit their fellow citizen Peter de Nottelegh, falsely accused of being a leper, to dwell among them peaceably. *Windsor* R ii 189
Nov. 30	The K asks the pope to give a favourable hearing to the petitions of W bp of Lichfield *Windsor* R ii 189 O iii 361 H ii p i 19
Nov 30	The K asks the pope to expedite the business of W. bp of Lichfield *Windsor* R. ii. 189 O iii. 361 H. ii p i 19
Nov 30.	The K notifies that he has received the homage of Giles abp of Rouen *Windsor* R ii 189 O. iii 362 H ii p i 20
Dec 3	The K repeats his request to the pope in favour of Ingelard de Warle. *Windsor* R ii 189 O iii 362 H ii p. i. 20
Dec 3	The K asks the pope to suffer the goods of Emericus de Friscobaldis and his brother Bettinus to be arrested within the papal court. *Windsor* R ii. 190 O iii 362 H. ii p i 20
Dec 4.	The K begs the pope not to trouble W bp of S Andrew's on account of his absence from the general council at Vienne. *Windsor* R ii 190 O iii 363 H. ii p. i 20
Dec 4	The K orders the customary payments to be made for the support of Robert Wychard bp of Glasgow, prisoner at Porchester castle, and for the annuity to the K's sister Mary. R. ii 190 O iii 363 H ii p i 20
Dec 15.	The K orders the bp of Norwich and 20 others to meet him to deliberate upon the conferences lately held at Perigort *Westm* R ii 190 O ii. 364 H ii p i 20
Dec 15	The K orders John Guytard, controuller of Bordeaux, to send the processes referred to in the above-mentioned meeting *Westm* R ii 191 O. iii. 364 H ii. p i 21
Dec 16	Safe conduct for Rob de Clifford, Tho earl of Lancaster, and 4 others, coming to discuss certain matters of importance *Westm* R ii 191.
Dec 19	The K orders his seneschal of Gascony and constable of Bordeaux to pay certain sums to Bertrand de Salviaco count of Champagne *Windsor*. R ii 191. O. iii. 365 H ii p i 21.
Dec 20	Settlement, before the papal legates and others, of the disputes between the K and his nobles relative to the death of Peter de Gavaston *London* R ii 191 O iii 366 H. p i 21
Dec 22	The K. orders the proclamation of his peace throughout England, and forbids new prisage to be taken *Windsor* R ii 192 O iii 368 H ii p i 22
Dec 30	The K orders the mayor, aldermen, and sheriffs of London to desist from shutting the gates of the city, and stretching chains across the streets *Windsor* R ii 193 O iii 368 H ii p i 22
1313. Jan 1	The K orders the payment of the expenses of the residence of his sister Mary, nun of Amesbury, at Windsor, in Dec last, and of her journey to Amesbury *Windsor*. R. ii. 193 O iii 369 H ii p i 22
Jan 1	The K orders that such charters as are to be confirmed shall be left at the Exchequer. *Windsor*. R. ii. 193.

DATE.	SUBJECT.
1313 [Jan.]	The K. orders certain regulations to be observed respecting the chaplains of the chapel of S Edward in Windsor Castle. R. ii 193 O iii 369 H ii. p i 22.
Jan 1.	The K. informs Margaret countess of Foix of the steps which he had taken for the redress of injuries done to her by the K of France *Windsor* R ii 193 O iii 369 H ii p. i 23.
Jan. 1.	The K. instructs Stephen Ferioli, his seneschal of Gascony, as to the form of the oath to be made by the mayor, &c. of Bordeaux. *Windsor.* R ii 194 O iii 370 H ii. p i. 23.
Jan 1.	The K. orders that the citizens of Dax be no longer injured by the commissioners of the K of France. *Windsor.* R ii 194 O. iii 70 H ii. p i 23
Jan 7.	The K. asks the pope to be favourable to the affairs of John de Sandale *Windsor* R. ii. 194. O. iii 370 H ii p i 23.
Jan 7.	The K. appoints two commissioners to receive the jewels and horses taken from Peter de Gavaston at Newcastle-upon-Tyne *Windsor* R ii 194 O iii 371 H ii p i 23.
Jan 8.	The K orders his seneschal of Gascony to protect Margaret countess of Foix from the commissioners of the K of France *Windsor.* R. ii. 194. O ii. 371 H ii p i 23
Jan 8.	The K asks the pope to give credence to John de Crombwell and Walter de Maidenstan *Windsor* R ii 194 O iii 371 H ii p i 23
Jan 12	The K asks Ardinald cardinal of S Marcellus to protect the rector and brethren of the house of Asherugge *Windsor.* R. ii. 194 O. iii 289 H. l p iv 199.
Jan. 13.	The K commits the custody of the castles, lands, and tenements in Cornwall and Devonshire which formerly belonged to Peter de Gavaston to Thomas de Ercedekne *Windsor* R ii 195 O iii 372 H ii p i 24.
Jan. 16.	The K grants the castle and vill of Blancafort to Bertrand de Guto. *Windsor* R ii 195. O. iii. 372. H ii p i 24.
Jan. 16.	The K confirms certain grants formerly made by him to the same Bertrand *Windsor* R ii 196 O iii 374 H ii p i 25
Jan 17.	The K forbids the holding of a tournament at Newmarket *Windsor.* R ii 196 O iii 375 H. ii p i 25.
Jan. 17	The K warns his nobles generally, and seven of them by name, not to attend the tournament at Newmarket. *Windsor* R ii 196 O iii 376 H ii p i 25
Jan. 20	The K. hopes that the pope will be able to let him have the loan of the sum already solicited *Windsor.* R ii. 196. O iii 376 H ii p i 25
Jan 21	Pope Clement [V] asks the K. to accept the nomination of Lawrence bp. elect of Elphin *Avignon* R ii 197 O iii 377 H ii p i 25
Jan. 23.	The K. asks 17 cardinals and several other ecclesiastics to favour his application to the pope (for a loan) *Windsor* R ii 197 O iii. 377 H ii p i. 26
Jan 31.	The K forbids the holding of a tournament at Bedford *Westm* R ii 198 O iii 379 H ii p i 26
Feb 1.	The K informs the pope that the charges brought against him in the pope's presence, by the proctor of the university of Oxford, are false *Westm.* R. ii 198. O. iii. 379 H ii. p. i. 27
Feb 1	The K informs the pope of the true import of the letter which he had written to the University of Oxford in favour of the Friars Preachers *Westm.* R ii 198. O iii. 379 H ii p i 27
Feb. 1.	The K asks four cardinals to favour the suit of the Friars Preachers of Oxford against the chancellor and masters of the university. *Westm.* R ii 198 O iii. 380 H ii. p i. 27
Feb 2.	The K orders certain payments to be made to the executors of Wm de la More, late master of the Temple in England, in liquidation of his debts *Westm.* R ii 198 O iii. 380 H ii p i 27.
Feb. 3	Commission to Aymer de Valence earl of Pembroke to revoke the appointment of Stephen Ferioli, seneschal of Gascony. R iii 198 O iii. 381 H ii p i 27.
Feb 4	Commission to Walter bp of Exeter and others to act as the K's proctors in the court of France. R. ii 199 O iii 382 H. ii. p i 27
Feb. 4.	Credence for the above-mentioned commissioners going from the K. of England to the K. of France. *Westm.* R ii 199 O iii 382 H ii p i 27
Feb. 4.	Credence for the above-mentioned commissioners from the K. of England to Charles count of Valois and five others. *Westm.* R. ii. 199. O. iii. 382. H. ii. p i 28.

DATE	SUBJECT
1313. Feb 4	The K recommends Reymund de Byern canon of Pavia to the pope *Westm.* R ii 199. O. iii. 382. H. ii. p. i 28.
Feb 4	The K asks the pope to expedite the affairs of Walter bp of Lichfield. *Westm.* R ii. 199. O iii 383 H ii p i 28
Feb 4	The K to N bp of Ostia and 18 cardinals to the same effect. *Westm.* R. ii. 200. O. iii 383 H. ii. p i 28
Feb 4	The K to A cardinal of S Maria de Pelagru (to whom the examination of the affairs of the bp of Lichfield had been intrusted), in favour of the said bp *Westm* R. ii 200 O iii 384 H ii p i 28
Feb 4	The K orders inquiry to be made respecting the request made by Bertrand de Gout for the extension of his jurisdiction in Gascony *Westm.* R ii. 200. O. iii 384 H ii. p i 28
Feb 8.	Record of the process respecting the forging of the K.'s privy seal by John de Redinges. *Windsor* R ii 200
Feb 8.	The K orders that a passage be provided from Dover for Walter bp. of Exeter going abroad on the K's affairs. *Windsor* R ii 201
Feb 10	The K of England complains to Philip K. of France of an attack made by Wm. Reymundi de Gensaco upon Arnaldus Calkuli of Bordeaux. *Windsor* R ii 201. O iii 384. H ii. p i 28.
Feb 12	The K. orders the usual allowance to be made for the support of Elizabeth de Brus, dwelling at Shafton *Windsor.* R ii 201 O iii 385 H. ii p. i 29
Feb 13.	The K informs Pandulf de Sabelli that he will not permit the liberties of the crown to be interfered with in the collation of benefices. *Windsor.* R. ii. 202. O iii 385. H. ii. p i 29.
Feb 14	The K instructs the bp of Exeter and Aymer de Valence earl of Pembroke, his proctors in France, how to act *Windsor* R ii 202 O iii 386 H ii p i. 29
Feb 15	The K informs R count of Flanders that he accepts the proposed settlement of the disputes with the Flemings *Windsor* R ii 202 O iii 386 H ii. p i 29
Feb 15	The K asks R count of Flanders to prevent the export of victuals, arms, &c from Flanders into Scotland *Windsor* R. ii. 202 O. iii. 386 H. ii p i 29.
Feb. 16	Safe conduct for the transmission to London of the horses, jewels, &c given at New- castle to Thomas earl of Lancaster *Windsor* R ii 202. O iii. 387 H ii. p i 29
Feb. 20	The K (fearing the inroads of the Scots) requests the bps of Durham and Carlisle and 10 nobles not to leave the parts in which they are at present. *Westm* R ii 203.
Feb. 22	Commission to W bp of Worcester and John de Sandale to receive the horses and jewels taken at Newcastle *Windsor* R ii 203 O iii 387. H ii p i 30.
Feb 27	Acquittance by the K for jewels received by him from Tho earl of Lancaster and others, lately the property of Peter de Gavaston R ii 203. O iii 387 H ii p i. 30.
March 4.	The K recommends to the pope Ric de Draghton, abbot elect of St Edmund's. *Windsor.* R. ii 205 O iii 393 H ii p i 32.
March 4	The K thanks the pope for having granted him a loan. *Windsor* R ii. 205. O. iii 394 H ii p i. 32
March 5.	Credence for Hen de Beaumont and Alex de Abernythy going from the K of England to the K of France *Windsor* R ii 205 O iii 394 H ii p i 32
March 15	The K recommends Wm of Toulouse to the Kings of Castile and Navarre, he going into Spain to buy 30 war horses for the K of England. *Windsor.* R. ii 206
March 15.	General recommendation of the same person going into Spain for the purpose named above. *Windsor* R, ii 206 O iii 394 H ii p i 32.
March 19	The K forbids the holding of a tournament at Reading. *Langley Marcis.* R. ii. 206 O iii. 395. H ii p i 32
March 21.	Inspeximus by the K of a grant made to K. Edw I by John duke of Lorraine of the city of Antwerp, &c , in fee *Langley* R. ii 206
March 28.	The K of England complains to Haco K of Norway of the imprisonment of certain English sailors in Norway *Westm* R ii 206 O iii 395 H ii p i. 33
April 1	The K recommends John and Thomas, sons of Adam Gurdoun, to the pope. *Westm.* R ii. 207 O iii 396. H ii p i. 33.
April 1.	The K orders the arrest of the lands and tenements of certain persons who had tilted at Reading and Sudbury. *Westm.* R. ii. 207. O. iii. 396. H. ii. p. i. 33.

DATE.	SUBJECT.
1313. April 1.	The K recommends to the pope the suit of Guy de la Vale, the K's relative, nominated by the Q to the church of Maydenstan *Windsor.* R ii 207 O iii 397 H. ii p i 33
April 3	The K complains to Haco K of Norway of the imprisonment in Norway of certain merchants of Lynn. *Westm.* R. ii 207. O iii 397 H ii p i 33.
April 7.	Pope Clement [V] asks the K. to favour the appointment of Richard de Draughton as abbot of the monastery of S Edmund's, dioc. Norwich. *Avignon.* R ii 208 ·O iii 398 H ii. p i 34
April 15.	The K orders the payment of 150*l* sterling to Bertrand de Salviaco, the pope's nephew, for his expenses in the papal court. *Windsor* R ii 208 O iii 399 H ii p i 34
April 16.	The K. of England complains to Haco K of Norway of the treatment experienced by the English merchants in Norway *Windsor* R. ii 209 O iii. 400 H ii p i. 34
April 16.	The K. of England asks Haco K. of Norway to listen to the petition of the said merchants of England *Windsor* R ii 209 O iii 401 H ii p i 35
April 28.	The K orders that Isabella, widow of John earl of Buchan, be freed from her imprisonment at Berwick-upon-Tweed *Westm.* R. ii. 209. O iii 401 H ii p i 35
April 30	Protection for Walter bp of Lichfield, staying in the court of Rome *Windsor.* R ii 209. O iii 401 H ii p i 35
April 30	The K. commits to John de Kyngeston the custody of the manor of Thornton and of the other lands of the Templars in Northumberland *Westm* R ii 209 O iii 402 H ii p i 35
April 30.	The K congratulates the emperor of the Romans upon his coronation and conquest of Brescia *Westm* R. ii 210 O iii 402 H ii p i. 35,
May 1.	The K. asks R count of Flanders to join with him in settling the disputes which have arisen between their subjects, and complains of aid being given by the Flemings to the Scots *Westm.* R ii 210 O iii 402 H ii p i 35
May 1.	The K orders W abp of York to come to him without delay. *Westm.* R. ii. 210.
May 2.	The K orders the sheriff of Gloucester to seize the liberties of the town of Bristol into the K's hands *Westm* R ii 210
May 3	The K. orders that the manors of South Cave and Etton, granted by him to David earl of Athol (who now has joined the Scots), shall be seized *Westm* R ii 211 O. iii 404 H. ii p i 36
May 3.	The K. grants the custody of the manor of Wylnghton to Alexander de Abyrnythy *Westm.* R. ii 211 O iii 404 H ii p i. 36.
May 3.	Safe conduct for Thomas earl of Lancaster and five others, with their retainers, coming to treat with the K. in the presence of the papal legates and others *Westm* R. ii 211. O. iii. 404. H ii p. i. 36
May 3.	The K of England (being about to attend the knighting of the eldest son of Philip K of France at Paris) requests Otto de Grandison to meet him before he reaches Paris *Westm* R ii 211. O ii. 393 H ii p i 32
May 3.	The K orders that ships be got ready for his departure in order to be present at the solemnity of the assumption of arms by the K of Navarre *Westm* R ii 211 O iii 405 H. ii p. i. 36.
May 3.	The K. orders that a passage from Dover be permitted to his messengers going abroad *Westm* R. ii. 211.
May 3.	The K. orders that bridges and cleyes be provided at Dover for his embarkation at that port. *Westm.* R ii 212 O iii 405 H ii p. i 36
May 3	Letters of protection for 220 persons about to accompany the K beyond the sea *Westm* R. ii 212. O iii 405. H ii p i 37
May 3.	The K grants to Wm. de Casis certain land in Agenois which had been forfeited on account of the heresy of Hugo de Castro Maurone *Westm* R ii 213 O iii 407. H ii p i 47.
May 3.	The K. asks the canons of S. Severin of Bordeaux to grant a canonry to Gailard de Margeis. *Westm.* R ii 213. O iii 408 H ii p i 37
May 4	Credence for certain persons sent by the K. of England to ask letters of protection for him from Philip K. of France. *Windsor* R ii 213 O iii 408. H ii p i 38
May 4	The K asks the pope to favour the cause of Richard de Cornubia, the K.'s relative. *Westm.* R ii. 213. O. iii 408. H. ii. p. i. 38.
May 5.	Anthony de Pessaigne of Genoa pledges himself to restore to the K. the authority which he has received to borrow 20,000*l.* for the K. if the loan is not effected. *London.* R. ii. 214,

M

DATE.	SUBJECT
1313 May 5	The K. orders that the custody of the manors of Dynesle, Langenok, Chelse, Crissing, and Wyam, lately belonging to the Templars, be given to Anthony de Pessaigne and Francis Bascheme　*Windsor*　R ii 214　O iii 409　H ii p i 38
May 10.	Safe conduct for John Roberti and another going from Philip K of France into Scotland. *Windsor*　R. ii 214.　O. iii 410　H. ii p i 38.
May 12.	The K orders the constable of Bordeaux to pay to Margaret countess of Foix the arrears of dower due to Constance late viscountess of Bearne　R. ii 214　O iii. 410　H ii p i. 38.
May 13.	The K. orders a return to be made to him of the mode in which the election of the mayor of Bayonne is made　*Windsor.*　R. ii 215.　O. iii. 411.　H ii p i. 39.
May 16	The K asks the pope to dispense with the attendance of Robert de Cisterne, the K's physician, at his prebend of Wengeham　*Westm*　R ii 215　O iii 411　H ii p. i 39
May 17.	Commission, granted to Robert de Umframvill and others at the request of Philip K of France, to treat of a truce with the Scots. *Westm.*　R. ii. 215.　O. iii. 411.　H. ii. p i 39.
May 17.	Philip K of France having sent Lowys de Cleremund and others with the request as above mentioned, the commission is issued. *Westm.*　R ii 215.　O iii 412　H ii p i 39
May 20	The K. asks the pope to favour the business of John de Sandale. *Canterbury.*　R ii. 215. O iii 412　H. ii. p. i. 39
May 20.	The K to Arnald cardinal of S Maria in Porticu, to the same effect. *Canterbury*　R ii 216　O iii 413　H ii p i. 39
May 20.	The K., being about to go abroad, directs that his peace be strictly kept during his absence *Canterbury*　R. ii. 216.　O iii. 413.　H. ii. p i. 39.
May 20	Safe conduct for cardinal Wm de Testa, returning from England to the Roman court. *Canterbury*　R. ii 216　O iii 414　H ii. p. i 40
May 21.	The K. requests J bp. of Norwich to suspend until his return from France the publication of certain sentences against John de Warren earl of Surrey, who has been entrusted with the keeping of the peace. *Canterbury*　R. ii 216.　O iii 414　H i p ii. 40
May 22.	The K of England asks David K of the Jurgiani, the emperor of the Trabizond, and others, to aid Guillerinus de Villanova, a Minorite bp going to preach to the infidels. *Dover.* R. ii 216.　O iii 415　H ii p i 40.
May 22.	The K. asks the pope to send to him certain Florentine merchants, arrested at his suit in the papal court for having defrauded the English revenue　*Dover.*　R. ii. 217.　O iii 415　H. ii. p i 41.
May 23.	The K requests the keepers of the vacant see of Canterbury to send him 200*l* for the expenses of his passage into France　*Dover.*　R. ii. 217.　O. iii 416.　H ii p. i. 41.
May 23.	The K. orders the barons and others of Cumberland carefully to guard those parts against the Scots　*Dover.*　R. ii 217　O. iii 416　H ii p i 41
[May 23]	Memorandum of the passage of the K. and Q. from Dover into France, and of the delivery of the Great Seal. *Dover*　R ii 217　O iii 416　H. ii 4 p i. 41
June 14.	The K. asks the pope to favour the business of Boniface de Salucis, the K.'s relative. *Puntose.*　R ii 218.　O ii 417　H. ii p. i. 41
June 15.	Safe conduct for Isabella countess of Warren, the K's niece, going to join him abroad. *London*　R. ii 218　O iii 417　H ii. p i. 41
June 16.	The K orders provisions to be laid in for his use during the approaching parliament at Westminster　R ii 218　O iii 417　H ii. p i. 41
June 19.	The K. recommends to the pope Berenger de Mar, a friar preacher　*Puntese*　R ii. 218　O. iii 418.　H ii. p. i. 42
June 19.	The K. asks the pope to permit Anthony de Pessaigne and Lanfrankin, although minors, to hold certain ecclesiastical benefices　*Puntese.*　R. ii 218　O iii 418　H ii. p i 42
June 19.	The K. orders the mayor and sheriffs of London to arrest all the Flemish ships within their bailiwick. *Pountese*　R ii 219　O iii. 419.　H ii p i 42
June 29.	Inspeximus and confirmation by the K of an agreement between Gaston count of Foix and his mother Margaret countess of Foix. *Pontisara.*　R ii 220　O. iii. 419.　H ii p i 42.
July 1.	The K appoints commissioners to open the parliament summoned to Westminster during his absence. *Pontisara*　R ii 220.　O. iii. 422.　H. ii. p i 43.

DATE.	SUBJECT.
1313. July 2.	Philip K. of France grants an indemnity to all the officers and subjects of the K of England in Aquitain and the district of Bordeaux for offences committed against France *Poissy* R ii 220 O m 423. H ii. p i. 43
July 3.	The K of England (by the advice of Philip K of France) grants 20,000*l* (Tourn.) to Amanenus de Lebret. *Poissy*. R ii 221 O m. 424 H ii p i. 44.
July 4.	The K. orders his seneschal of Gascony and constable of Burgundy to take care that the above payment is regularly made. *Poissy*. R ii. 221 O m. 424 H ii p i. 44.
July 5.	The K orders that the expenses incurred by Almaric de Croun in attending the parliament of Paris shall be allowed him *Poissy* R ii. 221. O. iii. 424. H. ii. p. i. 44.
July 6.	The K. renews and confirms to Bertrand de Salviaco certain grants already made to him in Gascony *Pontissara*. R ii 221 O m 425 H ii p i. 44.
July 8.	The K. commits to Gaston count of Foix the custody of the "bastida" of Florentia. *Ybovillere* R. ii 222 O m 427. H ii p i. 45.
[July 16]	Memorandum of the arrival of the K. at Sandwich. R. ii. 222. O. iii. 427. H. l. p i. 45
July 17	Safe conduct for Thomas earl of Lancaster and five others throughout the realm, provided they travel unarmed *Sandwich* R ii 222 O. iii. 427 H ii p i 45
July 25	The K. of England informs Philip K of France of his arrival at London, and of the troubled state of the realm. *London*. R. ii 222. O m 427 H ii p i 45
July 26	The K. forbids the holding of a tournament at S Edmund's. *Westm* R. ii. 223. O m. 428 H ii. p. i 45
July 26.	The K. permits Margaret countess of Foix to appear by proxy in the court of S. Severe. *Westm*. R. ii. 223 O m 428 H ii p i 45
July 26	The K. asks loans of various sums of money from ten bishops and others for resisting the attacks of Robert de Brus *Westm* R ii 223 O m 428 H ii p i 45
July 26	The K. orders that various ships and mariners be provided for the use of the realm. *Westm* R. ii. 223. O iii 429. H. ii p i. 46.
Aug 3	The K. asks the pope to interpose in the disputes between the K of the Romans and the K of Sicily. *Bistlesham*. R. ii 224 O m 430 H. ii p. i 46
Aug 3	The K. to A bp of S. Sabina and 17 cardinals to the same effect. *Bistlesham*. R ii 224 O m 431. H ii p i 46
Aug 9.	The K orders that seven abbots here named of the Cistercian order be permitted to attend the general chapter at Citeaux. *Windsor* R ii 224
Aug 12	The K. orders it to be proclaimed throughout England that tournaments are forbidden. *Windsor*. R. ii. 224. O. iii. 432 H ii. p. i 47.
Aug 13	The K requests a loan from the abbot and convent of Whitby and 57 other ecclesiastics to defend the realm against the Scots. *Windsor* R ii 225 O m 432 H ii p i 47
Aug 16	The K forbids John Giffard of Brymsefeld and four others from holding tournaments. *Windsor*. R ii 225 O iii. 434. H. ii. p i. 48
Aug 18	The K. forbids Gilbert de Clare earl of Gloucester and Bartholomew de Badlesmere to besiege the town of Bristol. *Windsor* R ii 225. O iii 434 H. l p ii 48
Aug 28	The K of England asks Philip K of France to send his brother L. count of Evreux and Ingelram de Maregny to attend the parliament at London. *Windsor* R. ii. 226. O. iii. 434 H ii. p. i. 48
Aug 28.	The K. of England asks the K of Navarre to help the attendance of the above-named persons at the parliament at London *Windsor* R ii 226. O iii 435 H l p ii 48
Aug 28	Credence for certain messengers from the K. of England to Philip count of Burgundy, Charles count of Nevers, and Charles count of Valois. *Windsor* R ii 226. O iii. 435. H ii p. i 48.
Aug. 28.	Credence for Edward de Mauley going from the K of England to L count of Evreux and Ingelram de Maregny *Windsor* R ii 226 O m 435 H ii p i. 48
Aug. 28.	Credence for certain messengers sent from the K. to the pope. *Windsor*. R ii 226. O iii. 436 H ii p i 48
Aug 28.	The K. asks the help of A. bp. of S Sabina and six others in the furtherance of the above-mentioned messengers *Windsor* R. ii 227 O m 436 H. l p i 48
Aug. 30.	The K asks the K of France to sanction the gift made by him to Ingelram de Maregny of 1,000*l*. (Tourn) per ann. *Windsor*. R ii 227 O iii 436 H ii p i 49.

DATE	SUBJECT
1313 Sept 8	The K forbids the holding of a tournament at Brackley. *Windsor.* R. ii. 227. O iii 437. H ii p i 49
Sept. 10.	The K. forbids his barons and others to hold a tournament at Brackley. *Windsor.* R ii 227 O iii 437 H ii p i 49
Sept 10	The K forbids Edmund earl of Arundel and four others to attend the tournament at Brackley *Windsor.* R. ii 227. O. iii 438. H. ii p i 49
Sept. 16.	The K. empowers his serjeants at arms to arrest all persons who meet at Brackley for the tournament *Windsor* R. ii. 228 O iii 438. H. ii p i 49
Sept 16	The K censures Thomas earl of Lancaster and five others for intending to attend at Brackley instead of at the parliament *Windsor* R ii 228 O iii 438. H ii p. i. 49.
Sept. 24.	Safe conduct for Thomas earl of Lancaster and six others to come to the parliament, provided they come without arms *Westm* R ii 228 O iii 439. H ii p i 49
Oct 1.	Pope Clement [V] announces to the K that he has cancelled the election of Thomas de Cobham, and appointed Walter bp of Worcester to the see of Canterbury R. ii. 228. O iii 439 H ii p i 50
Oct. 12.	The K asks Andronicus emperor of Constantinople to liberate Giles de Argenteym taken prisoner near Rhodes *Westm* R ii 229 O iii 440 H ii p i 50
Oct 12.	The K to Michael emperor of Constantinople to the same effect *Westm.* R ii 229, O iii 441 H ii p i 50
Oct 12	The K to the empress of Constantinople, to the same effect *Westm* R ii 229 O iii 441 H ii p i 50
Oct 12.	The K. to the marquis of Montferand and six others, to the same effect. *Westm* R. ii. 229 O. ii 441 H ii p i 50.
Oct 13	The K to Wm cardinal of S Ciriac upon the payment of the loan of 2,000 marks sterling made by the cardinal to the K while in France *Westm* R ii. 229 O iii 442 H ii p i 51
Oct. 16.	The K. desires proclamation to be made throughout England that no one shall be molested for the death of Peter de Gavaston *Westm* R ii 230 O. iii 442 H ii p. i 51.
Oct 16	The K pardons Thomas earl of Lancaster and about 359 others (here named) for their part in the death of Peter de Gavaston *Westm.* R ii. 230. O. iii 443. H. ii. p. i. 51.
Oct 28	The K pledges the issues of Aquitain and Gascony for the loan of 160,000 florins made to him by pope Clement *Westm* R ii 231 O iii 446 H ii p i 52
Oct. 28.	The K of England asks Philip K. of France to confirm the document above mentioned. *Westm* R ii 232 O iii 447 H ii p i 53
Oct 29	The K orders the seizure of the goods and chattels of John late abp of Dublin for debts due to the K *Westm* R ii 232 O iii 447 H ii p i 53
Oct 30.	Proclamation that it is within the K's prerogative to forbid the carrying of arms *Westm.* R ii 232. O iii 447 H ii. p i 53.
Nov 5	Acquittance from the K to Thomas earl of Lancaster and others for the goods and horses received by them at Newcastle-upon-Tyne. *Westm* R ii. 232. O iii 448. H ii p. i. 43
Nov. 6.	The K confirms the ordinances made in the recent parliament that no one shall be troubled on account of the death of Peter de Gavaston *Westm* R ii. 233. O iii 448 H ii. p i. 53
Nov 7	Notification of exemption from trouble on account of the return of Peter de Gavaston. *Westm* R ii 233 O. iii. 449. H. ii. p i 54.
Nov. 14	The K of England asks the K of Norway to restore the goods of certain English merchants detained in Norway *Westm* R ii 233 O iii 449 H ii p i 54.
Nov. 16.	The K informs R. count of Flanders that full justice shall be done to his subjects in respect to their goods if they will sue for the same in the courts of law. *Westm* R ii 233
Nov 18	The K forbids the imposition of taxes upon houses of the Premonstratensian order in England *Westm* R ii 234
Nov 18	The K exempts the chancellor and scholars of Cambridge from the payment of tallages due to the K *Westm* R. ii. 234.
Nov 20	The K directs that Robert bp of Glasgow shall be imprisoned in at his own expense in the convent of Ely. *Westm* R ii 234. O iii 450. H. ii p. i 54

DATE.	SUBJECT
1313. Nov. 21.	Safe conduct for A. cardinal of Albano returning from England to the papal court *Westm* R. u 234 O. m. 450 H u p i 54
Nov. 25.	Protestation by the K. that he did not prejudice the rights of the crown in transferring the goods of the Templars to the Hospitalers of S John of Jerusalem, at the request of the pope *Westm* R u. 235 O m. 451 H u p i 54
Nov. 28	The K. grants fees, &c in Aquitain to the annual value of 500*l* (Tourn) to cardinal Arnald de Pelagru *Westm* R u 235 O m 453 H u p i 55
Nov 28.	The K solicits the cardinals, collectively and singly, to hasten the despatch of the pall to W abp. of Canterbury *London* R u 236 O m 453 H u p i 55,
Nov 28.	The K orders the delivery to the order of the Hospitalers of Jerusalem of various manors, lands, and tenements formerly belonging to the Templars *Westm* R u 236 O m 454 H. u p i. 55.
Nov 28	The K orders the sheriffs of 37 counties to protect the Hospitalers in obtaining possession of the lands, churches, and tenements lately belonging to the Templars *Westm* R u. 237 O m. 457. H u p i 57
Nov. 28.	The K exhorts such of the people of Scotland as have come to his peace to continue steadfast in the same *Westm* R u 237 O m 458 H u p i 57
Nov 28	The K desires that the immunities of the free royal chapel of S Martin the Great in London be preserved intact *Westm* R. u 238
Dec 3.	The K grants certain privileges to the citizens of Dort to continue during the life of his sister Elizabeth countess of Holland *Westm* R u 238 O m 358 H u p i 57
Dec 15.	Commission for collecting the twentieth and fifteenth granted to the K. *Dover.* R u. 238
[Dec 20]	Memorandum of the voyage into France made by the K, who left Dover for Boulogne on Dec 12, and returned to Sandwich on Dec 20 R u 238 O u 463 H u p i. 59.
Dec 23	Writs of military summons to Thomas earl of Lancaster and 93 others to meet the K at Berwick-upon-Tweed to proceed against the Scots *Westm* R u 238 O m 463 H u. p i 59
Dec. 23.	The K. orders all ecclesiastics and women to send their service for the same expedition. *Westm* R. u 239. O m 464. H u p i. 59
1314 Jan 1.	The K. forbids the holding of a tournament at Blythe. *Windsor* R u 239 O m 465. H u p i 60
Jan. 3.	Attestation that the abp of Cant. had renounced certain clauses in the bull of his nomination which were prejudicial to the rights of the crown *Windsor* R u 239. O m. 465. H. u. p. i. 60.
Jan. 6	The K orders the arrest of such persons as impugn the rights of the crown *Windsor* R u 240 O m. 466. H. u. p i. 60
Jan. 14.	The K. of England asks the K. of France to send one of his subjects to the pope in conjunction with the messenger sent by the writer *Westm.* R u 240. O m. 466. H u p. i 60.
Jan 14.	The K of England asks the K. of France to remedy the inconveniences arising from a regulation made by him respecting the currency of Aquitain *Westm.* R. u 240. O. m. 467. H u p i 60.
Jan 27	The K asks the pope to interfere in his favour in a dispute which he has with the bp of Saintes. *Windsor* R. u. 240. O m 467 H u p i 60
Jan 27	The K thanks the pope for having assented to his requests. *Windsor.* R u 240. O m 467 H u p i 61.
Jan. 27	The K orders that the cardinal bp. of Albano, whom he has appointed to be of his council, shall have an annual pension of 50 marks. *Westm.* R. u 241. O. m. 468. H. u p. i. 61.
Jan 29	The K recommends to the pope Alexander Bykenore abp. elect of Dublin. *Windsor.* R u. 241. O m 468 H u p i 61.
Jan 30	Settlement of the disputes which had arisen between the K. and Wm count of Holland by reason of the injuries done to English merchants. *Westm.* R. u. 241. O ui 469. H. u p i 61.
Feb 6.	The K. orders the sheriff of Kent to accept fines from persons who are in prison for having violated the K's parks and fish ponds *Eltham* R u 242
Feb. 7.	The K asks the pope to favor John Sandale, dean elect of S. Paul's, London *Eltham.* R. u. 242. O. m 471 H u. p. i. 62

DATE.	SUBJECT.
1314. Feb 7.	The K. to four cardinals and others for the said John Sandale *Eltham* R ıı 242. O ııı 471 H. ıı. p ı 62.
Feb 7	The K asks Almeric de Credonio, his seneschal of Gascony, to protect the mayor and citizens of Bayonne from the French. *Eltham* R. ıı 242 O ııı 472. H ıı p ı 62.
Feb. 8	The K. orders that the allowances heretofore made for the support of certain Templars shall be continued. *Eltham*. R ıı 243 O ııı 472 H ıı p ı. 62.
Feb 21	The K asks two cardinals to expedite the affairs of John de Sandale, dean of S Paul's, with the pope *Canterbury* R ıı. 243. O ııı 473. H ıı p ı 63
Feb. 22.	The K. asks the pope to expedite the affairs of John de Sandale *Canterbury*. R. ıı. 243. O. ııı. 473 H. ıı. p. ı. 63.
Feb. 22.	The K asks the pope to protect Bernard Peleti, prior of Manso, from the persecution of Amanenus de Lebret *Canterbury*. R ıı 243 O. ııı 473. H. ıı. p. ı. 63
Feb. 26	The K orders Almeric de Credonio, his seneschal of Gascony, to assist in the matters relative to Gascony before the parliament of Paris *Hadley*. R. ıı 243 O. ııı 474 H. ıı. p ı 63
Feb 26.	Credence for Gilbert de Clare, earl of Gloucester, and others, going from the K. of England to the K of France. *Hadley* R. ıı. 244. O. ııı. 474. H. ıı. p. ı. 63.
March 1	The K. orders that the lands of such persons as go abroad to tourney shall be seized. *Hadley* R. ıı 244 O ııı 475. H ıı p ı 63.
March 12.	The K. appoints John Sturmy and Peter [Bard to be admirals of his fleet going to Scotland *Westm.* R. ıı. 244. O. ııı. 475. H. ıı. p ı. 63.
March 12	The K orders that Elizabeth, wife of Robert de Brus, shall be removed from the nunnery of Barking to Rochester Castle, with an allowance for her support therein *Westm.* R. ıı 244. O ııı. 475 H ıı. p ı 64.
March 14.	The K. forbids the purchase by any goldsmiths of uncoined silver. *Westm.* R ıı. 245.
March 21.	The K excuses the service due at Berwick from his brother Thomas de Brotherton, earl of Norfolk *Westm* R ıı 245 O ııı 476 H ıı p ı 64
March 22.	The K. asks the assistance of Eth' Okonhar and 25 others, Irish chieftains, against the Scots *Westm.* R. ıı. 245 O. ııı. 476. H. ıl. p. ı. 64.
March 24	The K asks the pope to favor the matters respecting the hospital of S Leonard, York, which are before him on the part of Walter bp. of Lichfield, keeper of the said hospital *Westm* R ıı 245 O ııı 477 H ı p ııı 64
March 24.	The K appoints Aymar de Valence earl of Pembroke to be guardian and lieutenant of Scotland. *Westm* R. ıı 245 O. ııı. 477 H ıı. p ı 64
March 26	The K appoints Richard de Burgh earl of Ulster to be captain of the Irish serving the K. of England in the Scottish war *Westm.* R. ıı 246. O ııı 478 H ıı p ı 65.
March 27.	The K orders the clergy of the two provinces to meet and contribute an aid against the Scots *Westm* R ıı 246
April 1.	The K orders the barons of the Cinque Ports to send to him for the Scottish war the service of ships which they are bound to provide *S. Albans* R ıı 246 O ııı. 478 H. ıı. p ı 65
April 1.	The K grants to the house of the converts of London (for the completion of their chapel) the alms called deodands *S. Albans* R ıı. 247
April 23.	The K orders Henry de Cobham, constable of Rochester Castle, to permit certain persons (here named) to reside with Isabella de Brus in that castle *Torksey* R. ıı 247. O ııı. 479. H. ıı p. ı. 65.
May 10	The K asks for the prayers of the general chapter of the Friars Preachers for himself, his queen, and his son *Osyngwold.* R ıı 247 O ııı 479. H ıı. p ı 65
May 26.	The K orders that certain measures be adopted in regard to the issues of the duchy of Aquitain pledged by him to the pope. *Durham.* R. ıı 247. O ııı. 480. H. ıı. p ı 65
May 27.	Credence for certain persons going from the K. to the cardinals and others upon the affairs of Aquitain *Durham* R ıı 247. O ıı 480 H ıı p.ı. 66.
May 27.	The K orders various sheriffs and nobles in England and Wales to levy foot soldiers, and send them with all speed to the siege of the castle of Stirling *Newminster*. R. ıı 248 O ıı 481 H. ıı. p. ı. 66,

DATE.	SUBJECT.
1314 May 28	Philip K. of France asks the K of England to compel his merchants to bring their wools to the staple at S. Omer, and to abandon the fair at Lille. *Lorris.* R. u. 248. O. m. 481. H. u p 1 66.
June 12.	Credence for certain persons going from the K. to the convocation of the clergy assembled at York *Newminster* R. u 249. O iii. 483 H u. p. 1 66
June 27.	The K., having mislaid his privy seal, requests that no attention be for the present paid to writs sealed with it. *Berwick-upon-Tweed* R u 249. O. m. 483. H u. p. 1. 66.
June 28	Credence for two persons sent from the K of England to Philip K. of France. *Berwick-upon-Tweed* R ii 249. O m 284 H. u. p 1 66.
June 29.	The K., having heard of the death of pope Clement V., asks the cardinals collectively to proceed with the election of a successor. *Newcastle-upon-Tyne.* R. u. 249. O. iii. 484. H. u. p. 1. 66.
June 29.	The K to several of the cardinals and others singly to the same effect. *Newcastle-upon-Tyne.* R u 250 O. m 485. H. u p 1. 65
July 2.	The K of England asks the K of France to revoke a prohibition which he had made respecting the K.'s coinage in Aquitain. *Berwick-upon-Tweed.* R. u. 250. O m. 486. H. u. p. i. 68.
July 2.	The K of England asks the K. of France to grant indemnities to certain citizens of Dax. *Berwick-upon-Tweed* R u 250 O. iii. 486 H. u p 1. 68
July 2	Philip K. of France notifies that Amanenus de Lebret has renounced all the appeals which he had made against K. Edw. *Poissy.* R. ii. 250. O. m 487. H. u p 1. 68.
July 6.	The K. of England to James K of Aragon, intimating that he is in good health. *Berwick-upon-Tweed* R u. 250. O m 487 H u. p 1 68
July 8.	Philip K. of France asks the K of England to permit certain burgesses of Ypres to trade with England. *Arras* R. u. 251. O. m 488. H. ii. p. 1. 68.
July 16.	The K of England informs the K of France that he will deliberate with his council relative to the staple of wool at S Omer R u 251 O. m 488 H u. p 1. 69
July 18.	The K orders that Robert bp of Glasgow, Elizabeth wife of Robert de Brus, and others be brought to him at York *York.* R u 251. O m 489. H. u. p. 1. 69
July 18	The K. orders that Christina, sister of Robert de Brus, widow of Christopher de Seton, be brought to him at York *York.* R u 251 O m 489 H i p u. 69.
July 18.	The K. asks certain cardinals and others to permit certain payments to be made on his account from the issues of Aquitain assigned to the late pope Clement V. *Saltwood.* R. ii. 251. O m. 490 H u p. 1. 69.
July 25.	Philip K of France asks the K of England to permit the inhabitants of Ypres to trade with England. *Compiègne* R ii 252 O. m 490 H u p 1 69.
July 26.	Robert count of Flanders asks the K to permit his subjects to trade with Flanders, and to consent to the establishment of a staple at Bruges. *Bruges.* R. u. 252. O. m. 490. H. ii. p. 1. 69.
Aug. 10.	The K appoints Aymar de Valence earl of Pembroke to be captain of the troops about to repel the invasion of the Scots. *York* R. u. 252 O. m. 491. H u. p. 1. 70.
Aug 12.	Credence for John de Hothum going from the K to confer with Richard de Burgh earl of Ulster and 28 others in Ireland. *York.* R. u. 252. O. ii. 492. H. u. p 1 70.
Aug. 12.	The K. directs that the nobles of Ireland shall be summoned to confer with John de Hothum. *York* R u 252. O m 492 H u p 1 70
Aug. 18.	The K certifies that the hospitality shown to John de Warren earl of Surrey by Ralph de Monthermer at Clyfton near York shall not prejudice his rights in the same vill. *York.* R u. 253 O m. 492. H. u. p. i. 70.
Sept. 3.	The K. forbids W abp. of York from interfering with the right of the abp. of Canterbury to carry his cross within the province of York *York.* R. u. 253. O m 493 H. l. p. 1. 70.
Sept. 3.	The K. to the dean and chapter of York upon the same subject *York.* R. u. 253. O m 494 H u p. 1. 71
Sept. 3.	The K. forbids John de Warren earl of Surrey from interfering with the abp of Canterbury in the above matter. *York.* R. u. 253 O m 494 H u p 1. 71.
Sept. 7.	The K , being unable to be present, authorizes W. bp of Exeter and other persons to open the parliament at York *Wolston.* R u 253.
Sept. 10.	The Italian cardinals inform the K of the riot which occurred when they were assembled at Carpentras to elect a pope, and of their escape. *Valence.* R. u. 254. O. iii. 494. H. u. p 1 71.

DATE	SUBJECT
1314. Sept 18.	The K. intimates, that at the request of Robert de Brus he has given a safe-conduct to certain Scotchmen to meet him at Durham *York.* R. ii. 254. O. iii. 495. H. ii. p. i 71.
Sept 25	Safe-conduct for W. bp. of S Andrew's going abroad *York* R ii 254. O iii. 496. H ii p i 72
Oct 2.	The K sends to the castle of Carlisle Robert bp. of Glasgow, together with the wife, sister, and daughter of Robert de Brus. *York.* R. ii 256. O iii 496. H ii. p i. 72.
[Oct. 3]	Memorandum of the delivery by the K of the great seal to his chancellor John de Sandale at York R. ii 255
Oct 6.	Commission to Robert de Pikeryng, dean of York, and others, to treat with the ambassadors of Robert de Brus respecting a truce *York* R ii 255 O iii 497 H. ii. p. i. 72.
Oct 6	Commission to the same effect as the preceding, but with the provision that the terms shall be submitted to the King *York* R ii 255 O iii 497. H ii p i 72
Oct 6.	Commission to the same effect, said to be granted at the request of the K of France, but not as an ally of the Scotch *York* R. ii 255. O iii. 497. H ii. p. i. 72.
Oct 6	Commission to the same effect as above, with authority to conclude a peace with the Scots *York* R ii 255 O iii 498 H ii p. i 72
Oct 9	Commission to levy men-at-arms in co Lancaster to repel the inroads of the Scots. *York* R ii 256. O iii 498 H ii. p. i 73
Oct 10	Safe-conduct for six persons coming from Scotland to treat of peace *York* R ii. 256 O iii 499 H ii p i 73
Oct 10	Richard de Burgh earl of Ulster and Theobald le Botiller, guardian of Ireland, are to attend the parliament at Westminster. *York* R ii 256 O iii 499. H ii p i 73
Oct 16.	The K. asks the dukes of Lorraine and Brabant to arrest Anthony Fazeul, who had carried off 500l stg which he had been employed to collect for the K. *Lincoln* R. ii. 256 O iii 500 H ii p i. 73
Oct 24.	Commission to assess and levy the tallage due in the city and suburbs of London. *Spalding* R ii 257.
Nov 3	The K informs his clergy that no heed is to be given by them to any commission or mandate which will interfere with his ecclesiastical rights *Ely* R ii 257 O. iii 500 H. ii. p. i. 73.
Nov 19.	The K to certain cardinals and others to withdraw the heavy demand made upon the abp of Canterbury upon his translation from the see of Worcester. *Northampton.* R ii 257 O iii 500 H ii. p i 73
Nov 20	The K orders the delivery of certain Scottish prisoners in the Tower of London to be exchanged for John de Segrave the elder, a prisoner in Scotland *Northampton.* R ii 257 O iii 501. H ii p i 74
Nov 22	The K of England asks Philip K of France to restore to Maurice de Rocheford the manors of Cenerech and Trenyuz in Poitou R ii. 258 O iii 502 H. ii. p i 74.
Dec 5	The K asks the cardinals to lose no time in electing a pope *Berkhamstead* R ii. 258. O iii 502 H ii p i 74
Dec 15	The K asks the abps and bps of England and 29 abbots to celebrate the exequies of Philip K of France, deceased *Langley* R ii 258 O iii 503 H ii. p i 74
Dec 16.	The K asks the bp of Norwich to advance him 1,000 marks from the tenths. *Langley.* R. ii 258
Dec 17	The K asks Bertrand de Guito to lend him 60,000 florins of gold. *Northampton.* R ii. 259 O iii 504 H ii p i 74.
Dec 20	The K recommends Ingelram de Maregny to L King of France. *Bustlesham* R. ii 259. O iii 504 H ii. p. i. 75
Dec. 22.	Safe-conduct (at the request of Ralph de Monthermer) for Duncan de Fife and his family going abroad *Windsor* R ii 259 O iii 505. H ii p i 75
Dec 26	The K orders his seneschal of Gascony to remedy the wrongs done to Margaret countess of Foix *Windsor* R ii 259 O iii 505 H ii p i. 75
Dec 27	The K orders the payment of 20l to the chancellor and scholars of Oxford for the soul of Peter de Gavaston. *Windsor.* R ii 259. O iii 506 H ii p i. 75
1315 Jan 4	The K of England asks L King of France to restore to Edward de Baliol the fees belonging to his late father John de Baliol. *Langley.* R. ii. 260 O iii 506. H ii. p. i 75.

DATE.	SUBJECT.
1315. Jan. 4.	The K. excuses the absence of W abp of York and the bp of Durham from the parliament, summoned to Westm in the octaves of Hilary, on account of the inroads of the Scots *Langley* R ii 260 O iii 506 H. ii p i 75
Jan. 4.	The K. excuses the absence of Marmaduke de Twenge and 8 others from the same parliament for the like cause. *Langley*. R. ii 260. O iii 507. H ii p i. 76
Jan. 4.	The K appoints Edmund le Botiller to be justiciary of Ireland *Langley* R. ii 260
Jan 12.	The K orders the payment of the arrears of the grant of 20,000l [Turon] made by him to Amanenus de Lebret *Langley*. R. ii 261 O iii 507 H ii. p. i. 76
Jan. 24.	The K orders the payment to Bernard de Spinasia of 80l stg by the seneschal and treasurer of l'Agenois *Westm* R ii 261 O iii 507 H ii p i 76
March 4.	Proxy by Yolendis de Solerio, viscountess of Fronsac, to treat with the proctors of K Edw *Boys Gyrart, near Paris*. R. ii. 261. O. iii. 508 H ii p i 76.
March 4.	The mayor and citizens of Bayonne complain to the K of the losses sustained by them off the coast of England *Bayonne* R ii 262 O iii 509. H ii p i 77.
March 10.	Proclamation that no convicted conspirator shall come to the K's court *Westm* R ii 262
March 14.	The K. requests 84 ecclesiastics, nobles, and communities of Ireland to give credence to Edmund le Boteller and two others. *Westm* R ii 262 O iii 510 H ii p i 77
March 14.	The K. regulates the prices at which various articles of food shall be sold *Westm* R ii 263
March 15.	The K. asks the prior and convent of Winchester and 89 other religious houses to lend him money to repulse the invasions of the Scots *Westm* R. ii 263 O iii. 511 H ii p i 77.
March 15	The K orders the usual allowances to be made to certain Welsh hostages. *Westm*. R ii 264
March 15	The K directs that the tenth granted by the clergy in the province of Canterbury shall be collected *Westm* R ii 264.
March 15	The K orders that certain grants made by the lords ordainers shall be revoked. *Westm* R ii 265
March 27.	The K. orders John de Butetour, with the help of the men of Yarmouth, to arrest 13 great Scottish coggs lying in the port of Sluys in Flanders *Westm* R ii. 265.
March 27	Composition between the K and Yolendis de Solerio in regard to their respective rights in Aquitain and Gascony R ii 265 O iii. 514. H. ii. p. i 78.
April 10.	The K. repeats and enforces the ordinance as to the prices of various articles of food. *Windsor* R ii. 266
April 13.	B count of Flanders complains to the K of the pillage of a Flemish ship in the port of Orwell *Ghent* R ii 266 O iii 516 H ii p i 79
April 18	The K. appoints Maurice de Berkley to be keeper of the castle and town of Berwick-upon-Tweed. *Westm*. R ii. 267 O iii 516 H ii p i 79
April 20	The K commissions Almaric de Credonio, his seneschal in Gascony, to settle some disputes in Gascony *Westm* R. ii. 267 O iii 517 H ii p i 79
April 20.	Articles of the peace and concord between the K and Reymund viscount of Fronsac. *Westm* R. ii. 267 O iii 517. H ii p i 80
April 20	Ratification of the treaty between the K. and Yolendis de Solerio *Westm* R ii 267. O iii 519 H ii p i 80
April 21.	The K is requested to send further instructions to the seneschal and treasurer of l'Agenois in the matter of Bernard de Spinasia. *Agen*. R. ii. 268. O iii 519. H. ii p i 80
May 4.	The K orders that the tin produced in Cornwall shall be stamped before being exported *Westm* R. ii 268.
May 28	The K of England announces to A. King of Castile that he will do his best to preserve amity between the citizens of Bayonne and the people of Castile *Westm.* R. ii 268. O iii 520 H ii. p i 80
May 30.	The K settles the retail price of wine within the city and suburbs of London. *Westm.* R. ii 268.
June 1.	The K appoints Stephen le Blund to be his chamberlain and receiver of Scotland R. ii 268. O iii 520. H. ii p i 81.
June 2.	The K orders that all the money due to him in Ireland shall be levied for the use of the fleet in Ireland. *Westm*. R. ii, 269,

DATE.	SUBJECT.
1315 June 4	The K. orders that the ships arrested in Surrey, Cornwall, Devon, Hants, and Dorset for the Scottish war shall be freed from arrest *Westm* R 11 269.
June 11.	Proclamation against clipped or false money *Canterbury.* R. 11. 269.
June 15	Louis K. of France informs his subjects in Aquitain that he desires to be on friendly terms with the K of England *Paris* R 11. 269. O 111 521. H. 11 p 1. 81.
June 15.	Vidimus of a letter of Louis K of France containing regulations for the preservation of peace with the K. of England *Paris* R. 11 269. O 111 521. H 11. p. i. 81.
June 15.	Vidimus of another letter of the same King, confirming letters of his late father to the same effect. *Paris* R. 11 270 O 111 522 H 11 p 1 81.
June 18.	Louis K. of France asks the K of England to arrest all the Flemings (and their goods) whom he shall find in England. *Crecy* R 11 270. O. 111. 478. H 11 p 1 69
June 26.	Commission by Louis K of France for the completion of the peace between France and England *Paris.* R. 11. 270. O 111 522. H. 11. p 1 82
June 30.	The K. orders Henry de Lancaster and 8 others to be ready at Newcastle to help the K. to repel the Scots *Berwick-upon-Tweed* R 11. 271. O. 111 523 H. 11. p. i. 82.
July 4	The K. issues regulations as to the form for the election of the mayor and sheriffs of London *Westm* R 11 271
July 5.	The K appoints Aymar de Valence earl of Pembroke to be his captain and lieutenant between the Trent and Roxburgh. *Westm* R 11 271. O. 111. 524. H 11 p. i. 84.
July 10	The K. urges W. count of Holland to pay the arrears of the dower of Elizabeth countess of Holland, wife of Humfrey de Bohun earl of Hereford *Westm* R. 11 271. O 111 625. H 11 p 1 82
July 14.	Louis K. of France states his complaints against the Flemings, and what he has done in retaliation. *Paris.* R 11 272. O 111 525 H 11 p 1 82.
July 17.	Credence for Almaric de Credonio, seneschal of Gascony, and others, going from the K. to Aquitain *Langley* R 11 273 O 111 528. H 11. p. 1 82
July 17.	Credence for John de Benstead and Tho de Cantabr' going from the K to the mayors and inhabitants of 60 towns and districts in Gascony and to 130 nobles and others there. *Langley* R 11 273 O. 111 528 H 11 p 1 84
Aug 6	The K retains Carolus de Flisco to be of his council *Langley* R 11. 274. O 111 531. H. 11. p. 11 85
Aug 6	The K of England to Louis K of France, he will refer his letter about the Flemings to the English council *Langley* R 11. 274. O 111 531 H 11. p. 1 85
Aug 6	The K regulates the number of courses which shall be served at the tables of his nobles and churchmen *Langley.* R 11 274
Aug. 8	The K. orders that the statute of Winchester shall be observed as to the armour which is to be kept by occupants of lands *Langley.* R 11 275
Aug 30	The K orders the attendance of Edward earl of Arundel and 65 others to repel the incursions of the Scots. *Lincoln* R 11 275 O 111 531 H 11 p 1. 85.
Sept. 1.	Commission to John de Hothum to make arrangements for the expulsion of the Scots who have invaded Ireland *Lincoln.* R 11 276 O 111 532 H 11. p. 1 85
Sept. 1	The K. thanks those persons who assist in expelling the Scots from Ireland. *Lincoln* R 11. 276. O. 111. 532. H 11. p 1 86.
Sept. 1.	The K orders that no corn or victuals shall be conveyed to the Scots, or to his enemies elsewhere. *Lincoln* R 11 276.
Sept 1.	Commission to John de Hothum and Edward le Botiller to remove insufficient officers from their offices in Ireland, and to appoint others *Lincoln* R 11. 276. O. 111. 533 H. 11. p. 1. 86.
Sept. 1	Proclamation that no aid is to be afforded to the Flemings, enemies of Louis K. of France *Lincoln* R 11 277 O 111 533 H 11 p 1. 86
Sept 16	The K urges 24 cardinals to elect a new pope *Ramsey.* R. 11. 277. O 111. 534. H. 11. p. 1. 86.
Sept. 18.	The K of England excuses himself to the K of France that he cannot help him with a fleet against the Flemings *Dytton* R. 11 227. O 111 535 H 11. p 1. 87.
Sept. 18.	The K. orders the captains of his fleet to do all possible injury to the Flemish shipping. *Dytton* R. 11 278 O 111 535 H 11 p 1 87.
Sept. 18.	The K forwards to his seneschals of Ponthieu and Gascony the above requisition of the K of France against the Flemings. *Dytton.* R. 11. 278. O. 111 536. H. 11. p. 1. 87.

DATE.	SUBJECT.
1315 Sept. 18.	The K grants to Andrew de Harcla the custody of the city of Carlisle and the parts adjacent. *Dytton.* R. ii 278 O. iii. 536. H. ii p. i 87.
[Sept 21.]	Memorandum that Edward de Balliol appeared this day before the K.'s chancellor in his house near Algate R ii 278 O iii. 537 H ii p i 87.
Oct. 5.	The K. urges the cardinals collectively to proceed with the election of the pope. *York* R ii. 278. O. iii. 537. H ii p i. 87.
Oct. 5.	The K. urges the cardinals severally to the same effect. *York* R. ii 278. O iii. 538. H ii p i 88
Oct. 14.	Safe conduct for the servants of Alice countess of Norfolk (dwelling in Holland) buying corn in Norfolk for her use *Ditton* R ii 279. O. iii. 539 H. ii. p i. 88.
Nov. 2.	The K of England complains to the K of France of the conduct of certain pirates of Calais *King's Clipston* R ii. 279 O iii. 539 H ii. p i 88
Nov. 2	Complaint to the same effect on the part of certain merchants of the Germanic Hanse in England *King's Clipston*. R. ii. 280 O iii. 540 H. ii. p. i. 88.
Nov. 4.	The K forbids the men of the bprick of Durham to make private truces with the Scots. *Clipston* R ii 280. O. iii 540 H ii p i 88
Nov. 9.	The K orders the arrest of all Flemings within the realm, the period for their departure having expired *Clipston* R. ii 280 O iii 541. H ii p. i 89
Nov. 23.	The K indemnifies the bp of Durham for having lent him the castle of Norham. *Clipston* R. ii 280 O iii. 541 H ii p i 89
Nov 25.	The citizens of Agen ask the K to be favourable to Bernardus Laispinassa, who has protected his rights in that city. *Agen* R ii. 281. O. iii 542 H ii. p i. 89.
Dec. 5	The K of England complains to the K of France, on the arrest of certain Spanish ships at Dover, on their way to Flanders *Clipston* R ii 281 O iii 542 H. ii p i 89
Dec 16	The K. of England complains to Louis K of France that certain English merchants have been plundered by the French. *Doncaster.* R ii 281 O iii. 543 H ii p i 89
Dec. 16.	The K orders that deliberation shall be entered into respecting the establishment of a staple between Calais and the Seine *Doncaster* R ii 281 O iii 543 H ii p i 90.
Dec 18	The K. thanks the men of Newcastle-upon-Tyne for having repelled the Scots *Doncaster* R. ii 282. O. iii. 544 H. ii p. i 90
Dec. 18	The K. of England asks L King of France and J Duke of Brittany to permit the men of Newcastle-upon-Tyne to export corn from their ports. R ii 282 O iii. 544 H ii p i. 90.
Dec. 19.	Commission to Anthony de Lucy to receive the Scots into the K's peace *Doncaster.* R ii 282. O iii. 545. H. ii. p. i. 90
Dec. 20	The K promises that the grants made to him by various towns in Gascony for the Scottish war shall not be considered as a precedent *Doncaster.* R ii 282 O iii 545. H ii p i 90
Dec. 30.	The K permits Ralph de Monthermer (going in pilgrimage to S James) to appoint deputy-keepers of the forests beyond the Trent. *Clipston.* R. ii. 282. O iii. 546. H ii p i. 91.
1316 Feb. 4.	John FitzThomas and 9 other Irish nobles pledge themselves to defend Ireland for the K against the invasion of the Scots *Dublin.* R ii. 283 O iii. 546 H ii p i 91.
Feb 6	The K. orders the men of the forest of Dene to obey Wm. de Monthermer, his captain against the insurgent Welsh. *Lincoln.* R. ii 283. O iii. 547 H. ii. p. i 91
Feb 7	The K. orders the levying of troops in Wales to proceed against the insurgent Welsh. *Lincoln.* R. ii 283. O iii 548. H ii p. i 91.
Feb 7.	The K appoints Humfrey de Bohun earl of Hereford and others to be his captains to act against the insurgent Welsh. *Lincoln* R ii 283. O. iii. 548. H ii p. i. 91
Feb 7	The K. decrees that certain ancient customs shall be observed and certain abuses removed in North Wales. *Lincoln.* R. ii. 284 O iii 548. H. ii p. i 92
Feb. 7.	Similar decree as to the customs of West Wales and South Wales. *Lincoln.* R. ii 284. O. iii. 549. H ii p. i 92
Feb 7	The K. confirms the liberties enjoyed by Amanus bp. of Bangor and his predecessors. R. ii. 284. O iii. 550. H. ii. p i 92.
Feb. 8.	Safe conduct for Wm de Melton abp elect of York going to the pope *Lincoln.* R. ii 285 O iii. 551. H ii p i 93
Feb. 11.	The K appoints Humfrey de Bohun earl of Hereford to be his captain against the insurgent Welsh. *Lincoln.* R ii 285. O. iii. 551. H ii p i 93.

DATE	SUBJECT
1316 Feb 13	Commission to Humphrey de Bohun to receive the Welsh into the K.'s peace *Lincoln.* R ii 285 O. iii 551 H ii p i 93
Feb 16	Permission for the men of Elanus bp of Nidros to trade with England for one year. *Lincoln.* R ii 285. O iii. 551. H. ii p. i 93.
Feb 16	The K summons a meeting of the convocations of Canterbury and York to grant him a subsidy against the Scots *Lincoln* R ii 285.
Feb. 20	The K. of England asks the K of Norway to make compensation for injuries inflicted by his subjects upon certain burgesses of Berwick. *Lincoln* R ii 286. O. iii 552. H ii p. i. 93.
Feb 20	Commission to Roger de Mortimer of Chirk to receive the Welsh into the K.'s peace *Lincoln* R. ii 286 O iii 552 H ii. p i 93.
Feb 20.	Summons to the earl of Lancaster, and Tho. de Brotherton earl of Norfolk to march against the Scots *Lincoln* R. ii. 286. O. ii. 553. H ii. p i 93.
Feb 20	The K orders that victuals shall be sold at the same reasonable prices, as before the recent proclamation *Lincoln* R. ii 286
Feb 22.	Commission to Robert de Umframville earl of Angus and others to treat with the Scotch for a truce *Lincoln* R ii 286 O iii 553 H ii p i 93
Feb 26	Writs to the justiciary of Chester and sheriff of Shropshire to march against the rebellious Welsh. *Lincoln* R. ii. 287. O. iii 553 H ii p i 93
Feb. 28.	Proclamation ordering all persons to be knighted who are duly qualified. *Lincoln.* R ii 287 O iii 554 H ii p. i. 94
March 5	Inquiry to be made, for the K.'s information, as to who are the lords of hundreds, cities, vills, &c. throughout England *Clypston.* R. ii 287.
March 6.	The K orders that the ordinances lately made by the prelates and nobles of the realm be carefully observed. *Clypston* R ii. 287. O iii. 554. H ii p i 94
March 14	The K requests Amanenus de Lebret to attend the parliament at London. *Clypston* R ii 287 O iii. 555. H. ii. p. i 94.
March 16.	Commission to Wm de Montacute to receive the Welsh into the K.'s peace. *Oneston* R. ii 288 O. iii 555 H ii p i 94.
March 19	The K assures G. de Castelione, constable of France, that no victuals have been conveyed into Flanders from England. *Leghtone Busarde.* R ii. 288. O. iii. 555. H. ii. p i. 94.
April 12.	Commission to treat for the redress of grievances and increased commerce between the men of England and Norway *Windsor.* R ii 288 O iii 556 H ii p i 94.
April 12	The K. of England to the K. of Norway, on the same subject. *Windsor.* R ii. 288 O iii 556. H ii p i 94
April 17	Safe conduct for certain merchants going to Norway upon the same business. *Westm.* R ii 288 O iii 556 H. ii. p i. 94.
April 24	The K asks the prayers of the general chapter of the Friars Preachers about to meet at Toulouse *Westm.* R ii. 288 O. iii 556 H ii. p. i 95
April 28.	The K. authorises John Walewyn and others to give safe conducts to Robert de Brus and other Scots coming into England to treat of a truce *Westm.* R ii 289 O iii 557 H. ii. p. i 95
April 28	Commission to John de Walewyn and others to treat with Robert de Brus and other Scots as to a peace or truce *Westm.* R ii. 289 O iii. 557. H. ii. p. i 95
[April]	Schedule of instructions for the framing of letters on the affairs of France and Gascony. R ii 289 O iii 558 H ii p i 95
May 15.	The K asks Charles count of Valois to continue his good offices in the court of France. *Westm* R ii. 289. O iii 259 H. ii. p i 96
May 15	The K thanks A. bp of Agen for his good offices. *Westm.* R. ii 290. O. iii. 559. H ii p i. 96
May 16	The K permits Richard son of John Makeshiteruk and Rob Osheth, Irishmen, to use the English laws in Ireland. *Westm* R. ii. 290
May 17	The K of England asks the K of France to continue on kindly terms with him. *Westm.* R ii 290 O iii. 560 H ii p i 96
May 17.	The K. of England to Elizabeth queen of France, to the same effect. *Westm.* R ii 290. O iii 560. H. ii. p i 96
May 18.	The K annexes the city of Bordeaux to the crown of England and the royal chamber in perpetuity. *Westm.* R. ii 290 O iii. 560. H ii p i 96.

DATE.	SUBJECT
1316. May 18	The K orders the arrest of the goods within Gascony of the men of Castile to the value of 165 marks and 20d *Westm* R ii 290 O iii 561 H ii p i 96
May 20	The K orders the levying of the fifteenth, granted in the parliament of Lincoln, within the city of London *Waltham*. R ii. 290 O iii 561. H ii. p i 97
May 27.	The K prorogues the day of the summons to Newcastle to serve against the Scots *Westm*. R. ii. 291
May 30	The K encourages the men of Northumberland to continue to resist the incursions of the Scots *Westm* R ii 292. O iii 563 H ii p i 97.
June 1.	The K orders that the town and university of S. Foy and certain other towns in Aquitain be annexed to the English crown *Westm* R ii 292 O iii 563 H ii p i 97
June 16	The K of England to the council of France, collectively and singly, complaining of the capture of an English ship by the French *Westm* R ii 292 O iii 564 H ii p i 97.
June 18	The K. complains to the city of Genoa that the Genoese furnish the Scotch with ships and arms *Westm* R ii. 292. O iii 567. H ii p i 98
July 28	Haco K of Norway informs the K of England that he will meet any complaint brought against his subjects respecting the arrest of a ship in the port of Selay *Bergen* R ii 293. O iii 571 H ii p i. 100
Aug 4	The K confirms the grant of 500l. sterling made to Theophania de S Petro in Campis, the nurse of Q Isabella. *Lincoln* R ii 293 O iii 566 H ii p i 98
Aug 6	The K orders that no monk be permitted to export coin from the realm pursuant to the statute made at Carlisle *Lincoln* R. ii. 293
Aug 8	The K. orders that a parliament of the clergy, nobility, and commons of Ireland be summoned. *Lincoln*. R ii. 294
Aug 9	Haco K. of Norway narrates to the K of England the facts of the complaint of the merchants of Berwick *Bergen* R ii 294. O iii. 566. H ii p i 98
Aug. 20.	The K recommends to the cardinals, Geoffrey de Ailham, a friar minor, as worthy to occupy the vacant see of Cashel *York*. R ii 294. O. iii 567 H ii p i 98
Aug 20	The K. requests Andrew Sapiti to forward the election of the said Geoffrey de Aylsham *York* R. ii 295 O iii 567. H ii p i 99.
Aug 20	The K. requests the general of the friars minors in Ireland to correct the misconduct of the friars in Ireland *York* R ii. 295 O iii 568 H ii p i 99.
Aug. 20.	Military summons to Thomas earl of Lancaster and 169 others to meet the K at Newcastle to proceed against the Scots. *York*. R ii 295 O. iii 569 H. ii. p. i. 99.
Aug. 20.	Proclamation requiring all persons having 50 librates of land to serve against the Scots. *York* R ii 295. O iii 569 H ii p i. 99
Aug 20.	The K. orders the levy of a subsidy in Gascony and the Bordelais to assist him in the war with Scotland *York* R. ii 296. O iii 569. H ii p i 99.
Aug 24	The K. asks the prayers of the provincial chapter of the friars preachers, about to meet at Sudbury, for himself, his queen, his children, and especially for John of Eltham. *York* R. ii 296. O iii 570 H ii p i. 100.
Sept 9.	The K recommends to Wm de Melton, Robert Abbot of Bardney, he having business in the court of Rome *Beverley*. R. ii 296. O iii 571 H ii p i. 100.
Sept 16.	The K asks the cardinal of S Mary in Portieu, and six other cardinals, to interest themselves in the matter of the issues of Aquitain, assigned to pope Clement V *York* R. ii. 297. O. iii 571 H ii p i 100
Sept. 26.	The K thanks the cardinals of S Maria in Portieu and of S Agatha for having informed him of the election of a pope. *York*. R ii. 297 O iii. 572 H ii. p i 100.
Oct 1.	The K informs the cardinal of S Prisca that he cannot permit his rights in regard to his royal chapels to be interfered with. *York* R. ii 297 O iii 573 H ii p i 101
Oct. 1.	The K asks the clergy of the two provinces of Canterbury and York to aid him with a subsidy to be employed against the Scots. *York*. R. ii. 297.
Oct. 1	The K to 15 cardinals, urging the completion of the business of William de Melton, elect of York *York* R. ii 298 O iii 573 H ii p i. 101
Oct. 1.	The K. recommends the cause of Wm de Melton to Reymund de Baucio count "Anelmi" *York* R ii 298 O iii 574 H ii p i. 101
Oct 4	The K. orders the payment of the wages of certain Welsh soldiers *York* R ii 299
Oct. 9	The K. grants to Johanna, daughter of Peter de Gavaston, the fine arising from the marriage of Thomas son and heir of John Wake *York* R ii. 299. O. iii 575. H ii. p. i. 101.

DATE	SUBJECT.
1316 Oct 12	The K of England recommends to Louis of France and four others the affairs of Anthony Pessaigne of Genoa. *York.* R 11 299 O in 575 H. 11 p 1 102.
Oct. 12.	The K requests Leonard de Tibercus, visitor-general of the order of S John of Jerusalem, not to molest the said Anthony de Pessaigne. *York* R 11 299 O. 111 576 H 11 p 1 102.
Oct 20	The K informs the lieutenants of the regent of France that he will promote concord between the men of Bayonne and the Normans *Crayk* R 11. 299 O 111. 576. H 11 p 1 102.
Oct 30	The K of England informs the K of Norway that he cannot at present answer his letters. *Newburgh* R. 11 300 O 111 577 H 11 p 1 102.
Nov 5	The K to certain cardinals, urging expedition in the affairs of W de Melton abp elect of York *Newburgh* R 11. 300 O 111. 577. H. 11. p 1 102
Nov. 6	The K to the pope to the same effect as the preceding *Newburgh* R. 11 300 O 111 577 H 11 p 1 102.
Nov 12	Commission to John Giffard of Brymmesfeld and others to receive the insurgent Welsh into the K's peace. *York* R 11 300 O 111 578 H 11 p 1 103
Nov. 15	The K orders the liberation of the Welsh imprisoned for the late insurrection *York.* R 11. 301. O 111 579 H. 11 p 1 103.
Nov 20	The K. orders that the lands of various Welshmen, forfeited for their insurrection, shall be restored to them *York* R 11 301. O 111. 579 H. 11 p 1 103.
Nov 23	The K appoints Roger de Mortimer of Wygemore guardian and lieutenant of Ireland. *York* R 11 301. O 111. 580 H 11 p 1 103.
Nov 23	The K grants various additional powers to the said Roger de Mortimer *York* R. 11 301. O 111 580 H 11. p 1 103
Nov 23.	The K grants to the said Roger de Mortimer power to remove officers in Ireland and substitute others *York* R 11. 302. O 111 580 H 11. p 1 103.
Nov. 23.	Additional powers granted by the K. to the said Roger de Mortimer *York* R 11. 302 O 111 586 H 11 p 1 104
Nov 23	The K asks the pope to appoint Lewis de Beaumont to the bprick of Durham *York* R 11 302 O 111 581 H 11. p. 1. 104.
Nov 23	Safe conduct for Thomas Randolf and Sir John de Menteth coming from Scotland to the King *York* R 11 302 O 111 582 H 11. p 1 104
Nov 23	Commission to Robert de Hastang and others to treat for a truce with Robert de Brus. *York.* R. 11. 302 O. 111 582 H 11 p 1. 104.
Dec. 6.	Credence for the bps. of Norwich and Ely and others, going from the King to Amadeus count of Savoy, who is requested to assist them in going to the pope. *Scroby* R. 11 302 O 111 582 H 11 p 1 104
Dec 6.	The K to Otto de Grandisson, to the same effect as the preceding *Scroby.* R 11 303 O 111 583 H 11. p 11 104
Dec 7	Peace being concluded between Flanders and France, the Flemings may now trade with England *Scroby* R 11. 303 O 111. 583. H 11. p 1 105.
Dec 15	Credence for the bps of Norwich and Ely and others, specially recommended by the K. to the pope. *Clipston* R 11 303 O 111. 584 H 11 p 1. 105.
Dec 15	The K to 22 cardinals, to the same effect as the preceding *Clipston* R 11 303 O 111 584 H 11 p. 1 105
Dec 15	Safe conduct for the same persons going to the pope. *Clipston.* R. 11. 304 O in 584 H 11 p. 1 105
Dec. 15	Credence for the above persons going to the pope *Clipston* R. 11 304 O 11. 584. H 11 p 1. 105.
Dec 16.	Commission to the above persons to treat respecting the issues of Aquitain assigned by the K. to the late pope Clement V *Clipston.* R 11 304. O 111. 585 H. 11. p 1. 106.
Dec. 20	The K of England regrets that he cannot be present at the coronation of Philip K of France *Clipston.* R 11 304. O. 111 585 O 11 p 1. 105
Dec 20	The K permits David earl of Athol to take all the plunder he can win from the Scots *Clipston* R. 11. 304 O 111 587. H. 11 p 1. 106.
Dec. 20.	The K orders a free passage to be provided for Roger de Mortimer and the troops going from S Wales into Ireland *Clipston* R 11 305 O 111. 587 H 11. p 1 106.
Dec. 25.	Credence for the bps of Norwich and Ely and others going from the K to the court of Rome *Nottingham.* R 11 305. O 111. 588 H. 11 p 1. 106

DATE.	SUBJECT
1316 Dec. 26.	The K. asks the pope to interfere for the settlement of the disputes between the university of Oxford and the friars preachers *Nottingham* R. ii 305 O iii 589. H. iii. p. i. 106.
Dec. 26.	The K to the cardinals, to the same effect. *Nottingham* R ii 305. O iii. 589. H. ii. p i. 107.
Dec 26.	The K expostulates with the pope upon the injuries done to the church and the realm by the delay in the matter of Wm. de Melton, abp elect of York. *Nottingham* R ii. 305 O. iii 589. H. ii p i 107
Dec 26	The K. to the cardinal of Albano, in vindication of the character of Wm de Melton *Nottingham*. R ii 306 O iii 590. H ii p i 107
Dec 26.	The K to the cardinal of S. Prisca, in favour of Wm. de Melton. *Nottingham*. R. ii. 306. O iii 591 H. ii p. i 107
Dec 26	The K to the cardinal of S Maria in Porticu, to the same effect *Nottingham*. R ii 307 O. iii 592 H ii p. i 108
Dec. 26	The K to the cardinal of S. Ciriac in Thermis, to the same effect. *Nottingham* R ii. 307. O iii 593. H ii p. i 108
Dec. 26.	The K. to the cardinal of S Adrian, to the same effect. *Nottingham* R ii 307. O. iii 593 H. ii p. i 108
Dec. 26.	The K. to the cardinal of S Agatha, to the same effect. *Nottingham*. R. ii. 307. O iii 594. H ii p. i. 108.
1317. Jan 1.	Pope John confirms the truce for two years between the King of England and Robert de Brus, who carries himself for K of Scotland . "gerentem se pro rege Scotiæ " R ii. 308. O iii. 594. H ii. p i 108
Jan 4.	The K gives authority to the bps of Norwich and Ely and others to grant pensions to the cardinals in the K's name *Clipston* R ii 308 O. iii 595 H ii p i 109
Jan 4.	The K asks the pope to appoint Geoffrey de Aylsham to the abprick. of Cashel *Northampton* R ii 308 O iii 595 H ii p i 109
Jan 4	The K requires 15 of his nobles to go to Ireland to repulse the invasion of Edward de Brus *Clipston* R ii 309 O iii 596 H ii p i 109
Jan 4	The K authorizes the bps of Norwich and Ely and others to prorogue the period of his journey to Jerusalem *Clipston*. R ii 309 O iii 597 H. ii p. i 109
Jan 4.	The K forbids the holding of a tournament at Thetford. *Clipston*, R. ii. 309. O. iii. 597 H ii p i 110
Jan 4.	The K. orders the arrest of those who tourney at Thetford *Clipston* R ii 309 O. iii. 597. H ii p i 110
Jan. 6	The K. recommends to the pope, Alexander de Bykenore to be abp. of Dublin. *Clipston*. R. ii. 309 O iii 598. H ii p i 110
Jan. 7	The K to 8 cardinals in favour of the same person *Clipston*. R. ii 310 O iii 597 H ii. p i 110
Jan. 7.	The K to the pope, in favour of William de Melton abp. elect of York. *Clipston*. R ii. 310. O. iii. 599. H. ii. p i 110
Jan. 8.	The K to cardinal G. the pope's vice-chancellor, in favour of the same. *Clipston* R. ii. 310 O iii 600 H. ii p i. 111
Jan. 8	The K to the pope, in favour of Thomas de Cherleton. *Clipston*. R. ii. 310. O iii. 600. H ii. p. i 111.
Jan. 10.	The K to the pope and cardinals, in favour of John bp of Winchester, his chancellor. *Clipston* R ii. 311 O. iii. 600. H. ii p i 111.
Jan 10.	Proclamation against the introduction into the realm of clipped or false coin. *Clipston*. R. ii 311
Jan. 12	The K. asks the cardinals in the papal court to forward the petitions presented by his ambassadors to the pope. *Clipston*. R. ii. 311. O. iii. 601. H. ii p i. 111.
Jan. 12	Philip K. of France tells the K. of England that he hopes to receive his homage at Amiens. *Paris*. R ii. 311 O iii. 602. H. ii. p. i. 111.
Jan 16	The K orders the arrest of all persons who tourney anywhere in England. *Clipston*. R ii 312 O iii 602 H ii. p. i. 112.
Jan. 11.	The K asks the pope to give credence to the private matter to be told to him by the K's ambassadors. *Lichtburgh* R. ii 312 O iii 603. H. ii. p i. 112.

DATE.	SUBJECT
1317 Jan 19	The K asks the pope to favour the promotion of Louis de Beaumont, bp elect of Durham. *Leicester.* R ii 312 O iii 603. H ii p i 112
Jan 20	The K asks the pope to favour the promotion of Wm de Melton, abp elect of York. *Daventry.* R ii. 312 O iii 603. H ii p i. 112
Jan. 20.	Credence from the K. for the ambassadors going to the pope in favour of the abp. elect of York *Daventry* R ii. 312. O iii. 603 H ii p i. 112.
Jan 20	The K to three cardinals, in favour of the same R ii. 313 O iii. 604. H ii p i. 112.
Jan 31.	The K asks the citizens of Genoa to furnish him with five galleys, armed and manned, for the war with Scotland *Andover.* R. ii. 313. O. iii 604 H. ii. p. i 112.
Feb 9.	Pope John to the K, in favour of Louis bp elect of Durham *Avignon* R ii 313. O iii 605 H ii p i 112.
Feb 12.	The K. to the pope, in favour of the convent of Sempringham, in which Wenciliana daughter of Llewelin prince of Wales, and many noble women of England, are nuns R. ii. 313 O iii 606 H ii p i 113
Feb 13	The K again appeals to the pope in favour of Wm de Melton, abp. elect of York. *Lincoln* R ii 314 O. iii 606 H ii p i 113
Feb 13	The K to 22 cardinals on the same subject. R. ii. 314. O. iii. 607 H. ii. p. i. 113.
Feb 17	The K congratulates the pope upon his election *Clarendon* R. ii. 315 O iii 608 H ii p i 114
Feb. 20	The K grants certain privileges to the university of Cambridge *Clarendon* R. ii. 315. O iii 609 H ii p. i. 114.
Feb 20	The K intercedes with the pope in favour of William de Melton, abp elect of York *Clarendon* R ii 315
Feb 20	The K asks for a return of such persons as resist and disobey his officers. *Clarendon.* R. ii. 315.
Feb 20	The K asks for a return of such persons as interfere with his rights in the matter of hundreds, &c. *Clarendon* R ii 315
Feb 20	Proclamation that (according to Magna Charta) one measure for wheat (viz the London quarter) shall be used throughout England *Clarendon* R ii 316
Feb 23	The K. asks the pope to sanction the consecration of Louis de Beaumont as bp of Durham *Clarendon* R ii 316 O iii 610 H ii p i 114
Feb 23	The K to the cardinal of S Maria in Porticu to the same effect *Clarendon* R ii 316 O iii 610 H ii p i 114
March 12	The K. asks the pope to favour the order of the Carmelites in England *Clarendon* R ii 316. O iii 610. H ii p i 114
March 12	The K to two cardinals in favour of the same order *Clarendon* R ii 317. O iii 611. H ii p i 115
March 17	Pope John exhorts the K to make peace with Robert Brus, " who at this time governs the realm of Scotland" *Avignon* R ii. 317. O iii 611 H ii p i 115
March 17	Pope John authorizes two cardinals to go into England, Scotland, Ireland, and Wales, to promote the said peace *Avignon.* R. ii 317. O. iii. 612 H ii p i 115
March 17	The pope authorizes the same cardinals to proceed against Robert de Brus, " qui regnum Scotiæ gubernat ad præsens" *Avignon* R ii 318 O iii 613 H ii p i 215
March 25	The K to the pope, in favour of Geoffrey de Aylsham, abp elect of Cashel *Clarendon.* R ii 318. O iii 615. H ii p i. 116.
March 25	The K. to cardinal James, to the same effect. *Clarendon.* R ii 319. O. iii. 616. H. ii. p i 117.
March 27	The K to the pope, in favour of Wm. de Melton, abp elect of York. *Clarendon.* R. ii. 319 O. iii. 616. H ii. p i. 117.
March 28.	The K to five cardinals, in favour of Wm. de Melton, abp. elect of York. *Clarendon.* R. ii. 319. O iii 615 H. ii. p. i 116.
March 28	The K asks the pope to promote Tho de Cheilleton to the see of Hereford. *London.* R ii. 319. O. iii 617. H. ii. p. i. 117.
March 28.	Pope John grants to the K. the tenths which have been collected for one year. *Avignon.* R ii. 319. O. iii. 617. H. ii p. i. 117.

DATE	SUBJECT
1317 March 28	Pope John orders the collectors of the tenths to pay the same to the K *Avignon* R ıı 320 O. ııı 618. H ıı p ı 117
March 28	Pope John postpones the period at which the K ıs required to pay certain debts due to him *Avignon.* R ıı. 320 O. ıı. 619 H ıı p. ı. 118.
March 28	Pope John excommunicates all who are hostile to the K or who ınvade his realm. *Avignon* R ıı 320 O ııı 619 H ıı p. ı 118
March 28	Pope John excommunicates Robert de Brus, late earl of Carrıck, and his brother Edward. *Avignon.* R ıı 321. O ııı 620 H. ıı. p. ı 118
March 30	The K. to W cardınal of S Cırıac ın Thermıs ın favour of the appointment of Thomas de Cherleton to the see of Hereford *London* R. ıı 321 O ııı 622 H ıı p ı 119
Aprıl 1.	Pope John translates Wm bp of Ossery to the abprıck of Cassel *Avignon* R. ıı 322 O. ıiı. 622. H. ıı p ı 119.
Aprıl 1.	Pope John's dıspensatıon for the K's chıldren to marry wıthın the prohibıted degrees *Avignon* R ıı 322 O ııı 623 H ıı p ı 119
Aprıl 1	Pope John orders that nothıng be done agaınst the exemptıons enjoyed by the K.'s free chapels *Avignon.* R ıı 322 O ııı 623 H ıı p ı 119
Aprıl 1	Notarıal ınstrument upon the terms agreed to between the Englısh ambassadors and the executors of the wıll of pope Clement V upon the ıssues of Aquıtaın *Avignon.* R. ıı. 322 O ııı 624 H ıı p ı 120
Aprıl 4	The K. asks the prayers of the General Chapter of the Frıaıs Preachers about to meet at Pampeluna, ın Arragou *Clarendon.* R ıı 324 O ııı 630 H ıı p ı 122
Aprıl 7	The K thanks the pope for havıng presented Louıs de Beaumont to the bprıck. of Durham *Clarendon* R. ıı. 325 O ııı 630 B ıı p ı 122
Aprıl 10	Pope John orders that such mendıcant frıars and others as excıte the Irısh to rebellıon shall be punıshed. *Avignon.* R ıı 325. O. ııı. 631 H ıı. p. ı. 122
[Aprıl 12]	The ınhabıtants of Bermeıo ask the K to free them from the exactıons of the seneschal of Gascony, who has no jurısdıctıon over them R ıı 325 O ıı 632 H. ıı p ı 122
Aprıl 12	Alfonso K of Castıle to the K of England, to the same effect as the precedıng *Carrıon* R ıı 325. O. ııı. 632 H ıı p ı 123
Aprıl 13.	Acquıttance by pope John for the annual trıbute of 1,000 marks for England and Ireland, paıd by the K *Avignon* R ıı 326 O ııı 632 H ıı p ı 123
Aprıl 16	Order of Councıl that no sherıff or coroner henceforth be a justıce of assıze, gaol delıvery, or to hear and determıne trespasses R ıı 326
Aprıl 20.	Pope John assures the K that he wıll act justly ın the case of Wm de Melton, elect of York *Avignon* R ıı 326 O ııı 633 H ıı p ı 123
Aprıl 20	The ınhabıtants of Bayonne ask the Kıng of England to provıde a remedy for them agaınst the crafty dealıngs of the K of France *Bayonne.* R ıı 326. O ııı 633 H ıı p ı 123
Aprıl 23.	The K asks Roger de Mortımer of Wyggemore, guardıan of Ireland, to ınform hım of the reasons for the arrest and ımprısonment of Rıchard de Burgo earl of Ulster. *Westm* R ıı 326 O. ııı 634 H ıı p ı 123
Aprıl 27.	The K. ınforms Roger de Mortımer, guardıan of Ireland, that he reserves to hımself the hearıng of the charge agaınst the earl of Ulster *Wındsor.* R ıı 327 O. ııı. 634 H. ıı. p. i. 123.
Aprıl 28	The K asks Robert K of Jerusalem to ıntercede wıth the pope for Wm de Melton, elect of York. *Wındsor* R. iı 327. O ııı. 635. H. ıı p ı 124
Aprıl 28.	The K. thanks Rıchard de Clare and 50 other nobles, mayors of towns, &c of Ireland, for theır good servıces agaınst the Scots *Wındsoı.* R ıı 327.
May 1.	Pope John authorızes two cardınals, hıs nuncıos, to arrange a truce between the K and Robert de Brus *Avignon* R ıı 327. O ııı 635 H ıı p ı 124
May 4.	Renuncıatıon by Louıs de Beaumont bp. of Durham of everythıng prejudıcıal to the K's. rıghts ın hıs bull of nomınatıon. *Wındsor* R. ıı 328. O ııı 636. H ıı p ı 124.
May 6.	The K asks the pope to appoint Thomas de Cherleton (and not Adam de Orleton) to the see of Hereford. *Wındsor* R ıı 328. O. ııı 637. H. ıı p ı 124
May 6	The K. enjoıns Adam de Oreleton to refuse the see of Hereford ıf ıt be offered to hım hy the pope *Wındsor* R iı 328. O ııı. 637. H ıı p ı 125.
May 6	The K ınforms the pope why he urges the claıms of Thomas de Cherleton to the see of Hereford. *Wındsor* R. ıı. 329 O ııı 638 H ıı p ı 125
May 6.	The Kıng to the cardınals, severally, on the same subject as the precedıng *Wındsor* R. ıı. 329. O. ııı 639 H. ıı. p ı 125

DATE	SUBJECT
1317. May 8	Safeconduct for two of the pope's nuncios coming into England with Bulls. *Windsor.* R ıı 329. O. ııı 639. H. ıı p. 1. 125.
May 10	The K of England complains to Philip K of France, Charles Count of Valois, and 21 others, that Aymer de Valence earl of Pembroke has been seized near Etampes by certain malefactors, and carried into Germany *Windsor* R ıı. 329. O ııı. 640. H. ıı p 125.
May 10	Credence for Ebulo de Montibus going from the K of England to Edward count of Bares and 17 others *Windsor* R ıı. 330 O ııı 641 H ıı p ı 126.
May 20	The K of England annexes the town and castle "Senhorn" (dioc. Agen) to the crown of England. *Windsor* R ıı 330 O ııı 641 H ıı p ı 126.
May 24	The K of England complains to Philip K. of France that the liberties of the men of Bayonne have been invaded by his officers *Westm.* R ıı. 330 O ııı 642 H ıı p ı 126
May 24.	The King orders Gilbert Pecche, his seneschal of Gascony, to see that justice be done to Wm Arnaldi de Campana, who was plundered in Gascony by the men of the K. of Castile. *Westm* R ıı 331 O ııı 642 H. ıı p ı 126
May 26.	Terms agreed upon for a marriage between John son and heir of Thomas de Multon lord of Egremond, and Johanna daughter of Piers de Gavaston late earl of Cornwall *Westm* R ıı. 331 O ııı 644 H ıı p ı 127
May 28	The K forbids the assemblage of men at arms and other unlawful conventicles. *Westm.* R. ıı 332.
June 6	The inhabitants of Bayonne complain to the K of the conduct of the seneschal of Gascony *Bayonne.* R. ıı 332 O ııı 635 H ıı p ı 127
June 8	The K intercedes with the pope in favour of Wm de Melton abp. elect of York. *Westm.* R. ıı. 332. O. ııı. 645. H ıı p. ı 128.
June 8	The K to the cardinals and others, to the same effect *Westm* R ıı 333 O ııı 646 H ıı p ı 128
June 8	The K thanks Pandulf de Sabelli and two others for having ceased from annoying the abp elect of York in the papal court *Westm* R. ıı 333. O ııı 646. H. ıı p ı. 128
June 11	The K authorizes David de Strabolgy earl of Athol to receive the rebellious Scots into the K's peace *Westm* R ıı 332 O. ııı 644 H ıı p ı 127
June 12	The K gives orders as to the conveyance into England of 1,400 barrels of wine given to him by the inhabitants of Bordeaux and S Macaire for his use in the Scottish war *Westm.* R. ıı 333 O ııı 647. H ıı p ı 128.
June 13	The K. of England asks Philip K of France to postpone the homage of Henry of Lancaster for the lands of John de Lancaster, his ancestor *Westm.* R. ıı 334 O. ııı 648 H ıı p ı 129
June 13.	The K directs Roger le Sauvage and seven others to accompany from Dover to London two cardinals coming from the pope. *Westm* R ıı 334 O ııı 648 H. ıı. p ı. 129
June 15	The inhabitants of Bordeaux complain to the K of England of the encroachments upon their liberties by the K of France *Bordeaux* R ıı 334 O ııı 648 H ıı p ı 129
June 17	The K. orders the payment of the allowances made to certain Welsh prisoners in the Tower of London *Westm* R ıı 334 O ııı 649 H ıı p ı 129
June 17.	The K orders the constable of Dover and the sheriff of Kent to pay all respect to the two cardinals coming to the King *Westm* R ıı 334 O ııı 649 H ıı p ı. 129.
June 20	The K orders that the merchants of Brabant trading with England shall be kindly treated *Westm* R. ıı 333 O ııı 647 H ıı p ı 128
July 1.	The K desires to have a conference with certain of his clergy, nobility, and others, before the arrival of the cardinals *Woodstock* R. ıı 335. O ııı 650 H. ıı p ı. 129.
July 3.	Agreement upon the settlement of various disputes between the English and the subjects of William count of Holland. *Northampton* R. ıı 335. O. ııı. 650 H ıı p. ı. 130
July 6	The King directs the bailiffs of Yarmouth and Lynn how to proceed upon the settlement of certain disputes with Holland *Northampton* R ıı 336. O ııı. 352. H. ıı. p. ı. 130.
July 6	Pope John absolves Isabella duchess of Britanny from her vow to visit the shrine of S James the Apostle *Avignon* R ıı 336 O ııı. 653 H ıı p ı 131
July 6.	Pope John grants an indulgence of 10 days to all who pray for the said duchess. *Avignon.* R. ıı. 336 O ııı 653 H ıı p ı 131
July 7.	Pope John permits the said duchess to choose her own confessor. *Avignon.* R. ii. 336. O ııı. 654. H. ıı. p. ı. 131.

DATE	SUBJECT
1317 July 13.	The K thanks the pope for having refused to accept Stephen de Donydor, a Scot, as bp of Glasgow, and urges the claims of Wm. de Melton, abp. elect of York *Leicester.* R ii 337. O iii 654. H. ii p i 131.
July 16	Safeconduct for two precursors of the cardinals, going into Scotland *Nottingham* R ii. 337. O iii 655 H ii p i 131.
July 19.	The citizens of Agen complain to the K. of England of the conduct of the seneschal of Gascony and treasurer of Agen. *Agen* R ii. 337 O iii 655 H. ii. p. i. 131.
July 25	The citizens of Agen ask the K of England to grant them the favour which will be told to him by the bearer *Agen* R ii 337 O iii. 656 H ii p i 132
July 26	The K. asks John duke of Brittany to promote a commercial intercourse between their subjects *Nottingham.* R. ii. 338. O iii. 656 H ii p i. 132.
July 27	Safe conduct for the cardinals going into Scotland on the affairs of the church *Nottingham.* R ii 338 O iii 657 H ii p i 132
July 27	Safe conduct for the messengers of the said cardinals, going into Scotland. *Nottingham* R. ii 338 O iii 657. H ii p i. 132
July 28	The K. informs the duke of Brabant that the dispute mentioned in the duke's letters has been settled *Nottingham.* R ii 338. O ii. 658 H ii. p. i 132
July 28	R count of Flanders complains that his subjects have been plundered by the English at Crasdun and la Rye R ii 338 O iii 658 H ii p i 132
Aug 4	The K asks the pope to complete the translation of Wm bp. of Ossory to the abprick of Cashel *Nottingham.* R ii 339 O iii. 658. H ii p i 133.
Aug 6	The K. asks the pope to settle the disputes between the abps of Canterbury and York as to the right of carrying the cross. *Nottingham* R ii 339 O iii. 659 H ii p i 133.
Aug .6	The K. orders the bp of Ferns to be tried for having, as it is said, given aid in Ireland to Edward and Robert de Brus *Nottingham* R ii 339 O iii 660 H ii p i 133
Aug 7	Power granted by the K to Andrew de Harcla to receive the Scots into the K 's peace *Nottingham* R ii 339 O iii. 660 H ii p. i 133
Aug 12	Robert count of Flanders exonerates the burgesses of Ypres from having injured the English R ii 340 O iii 660. H. ii p i 133
Aug 21.	The K of England asks Philip K. of France to liberate an English ship which had been arrested by the duke of Brittany. *Lincoln* R ii 340 O iii. 661 H ii. p i 133.
Sept 7.	[The papal nuncios in England] to the pope, giving him an account of their interview with Robert de Brus *Durham* R ii 340. O iii 661. H ii p i 134
Sept. 10	The K. informs the pope of the particulars of the robbery perpetrated upon the papal legates near Derlington *York* R ii 341 O iii 663 H ii p i 134
Sept. 10.	The K intercedes with the pope in favour of Wm de Melton, abp elect of York. *York* R. ii 341 O. iii. 664 H ii p i 134
Sept 10	The K informs the pope that the contending parties leave the question of the election of Wm de Melton to the archbishopriek of York to the decision of his holiness *York.* R. ii. 341 O iii 665. H ii p i 135
Sept 10.	The K. asks the abp of Mayence to give credence to the letter of Walter abp of Canterbury *York.* R ii. 342 O iii 665. H. ii p i. 135
Sept 13.	The K asks R count of Flanders to promote concord between his subjects and the men of the Cinque Ports *York* R ii 342. O iii 665 H ii p i 135
Sept. 16	The K. orders that the same customs shall be paid at Bordeaux by the married clerks who trade in wine equally with others *York* R ii 342. O iii 666 H ii p i 135.
Sept. 20.	Proclamation that the K will punish the sons of iniquity who lately plundered the cardinals at Ache *York.* R. ii 342 O iii 666 H. ii. p i 135.
Sept 24.	Commission to the earls of Pembroke and Hereford to free such adherents of Thomas earl of Lancaster as have been arrested. *York.* R ii 343 O iii 667 H ii p i 136
Sept. 24	Protection for Rigald de Asserio coming into England as special nuncio from the pope. *York.* R. ii. 343. O. iii. 667. H. ii. p i 136
Sept 26	The K. certifies that the earl of Lancaster and his adherents may safely come to the parliament at Lincoln *York.* R ii 343 O. iii 668. H. ii. p. i. 136.
Oct. 6.	The K forbids tournaments throughout England. *Sutton-upon-Trent.* R. ii. 343. O. iii 668. H. iii. p i. 136.

DATE.	SUBJECT
1317 Oct 8	The K restores the temporalities of the see of York to Wm. de Melton archbp. elect of York *Corby* R ıı 344 O ııı 669 H ıı p. ı. 136
Oct. 15.	The K asks the cardinals who are in England to inquire into the conduct of Walter bp of Exeter, falsely accused by his enemies *Waltham* R ıı 344 O ııı 670 H ıı p. ı. 137
Oct 18	Proclamation that the Flemish merchants are to be well used in England. *Westm* R. ıı. 344
Oct 18	The K asks the pope to permit the consecration of Louis de Beaumont elect of Durham (who had been carried off prisoner by robbers) to take place within the diocese of York. *Westm* R. ıı. 344 O ııı 670 H. i p ıı 137
Oct 29.	Commission from pope John to Rigaud de Asserio, canon of Orleans, to receive the annual tribute to be paid by England. *Avignon.* R ıı 345 O. ııı 671. H. ıı p ı. 137
Nov 2	The K grants to Wm de Montacute the ransom of three Welsh prisoners. *Westm.* R ıı 345 O. ııı 671 H ıı p ı 137
Nov 3	The K grants to Anthony Pessaigne of Genoa the seneschalcy of Aquitain *Westm* R. ıı 345. O in 671. H ıı. p i. 137.
Nov 3.	The K orders Thomas earl of Lancaster to desist from besieging several castles in Yorkshire belonging to John de Warren earl of Surrey *Westm* R. ıı 345 O. ııı 672. H. ıı. p ıı 137
Nov 3	The K orders Thomas earl of Lancaster to restore to the sheriff of York the castles of Knaresbro' and Alveton, of which the earl's men had taken forcible possession *Westm.* R. ıı 345 O ııı 672 H ıı p ı 138
Nov 3.	The K orders Nicholas de Grey, sheriff of Yorkshire, to take possession of the castle of Knaresbro' *Westm* R ıı 346 O ııı 672. H. ıı. p ı. 138.
Nov 4	The K. asks the pope to give no credence to the charges brought against Bertrand de Gutto and Amanenus de Lebret. *Westm* R ıı 346. O ııı. 673 H ıı. p i 138
Nov 4.	The K asks four persons to intercede with the pope in favour of Bertrand de Gutto and Amanenus de Lebret *Westm* R. ıı 346 O ııı 674 H. ıı p ı 138
Nov. 4	The K authorizes Anthony Pessaigne of Genoa, his seneschal of Gascony, to borrow 20,000 marks sterling on the security of the duchy of Aquitain. *Westm* R ıı 346. O ııı 675 H ıı p. ı 139
Nov. 4.	The K of England asks Philip K of France to favour the university of Floren', in the duchy of Aquitain *London* R ıı 347. O ııı 675 H ıı p ı 139
Nov. 4	The K asks J bp of Ely to provide for the security of the Isle of Ely, and directs the sheriff of Cambridgeshire to assist the bp *Westm* R ıı. 347.
Nov 5.	The K orders the Cinque Ports to be so guarded that no one can go abroad without the K's special licence *Westm* R ıı. 347
Nov 8	Credence for Anthony Pessaigne of Genoa, seneschal of Gascony, going from the K. to the pope *Windsor* R ıı 347. O ııı 676 H ıı p ı. 139.
Nov. 8.	The K to 22 cardinals, to the same effect. *Windsor* R ıı 347 O ııı 676. H ıı. p ı 139
Nov. 11	The K appoints Peter Doze, the pope's brother, and Peter de Vie and Arnald de Tyran, his nephews, to be of his council abroad. R ıı. 348 O ııı 676. H ıı. p. ı. 189
Nov. 11.	The K. grants annuities to the persons mentioned above *Windsor.* R. ıı. 348. O ııı. 677 H. ıı p ı 139
Nov. 15	Writ for the payment of his pension of 50 marks to Gaucelin, cardinal of SS. Marcellinus and Petrus. *Windsor* R ıı 348 O ııı 677 H ıı p ı. 139
Nov. 15.	The K authorizes his envoys at Rome to grant pensions to certain cardinals and lawyers in the papal court *Windsor* R. ıı 348 O ııı 677. H ıı p ı 140
Nov 20	The K orders his officers in Gascony and Ponthieu to respect the liberties of the men of Biscay *Westm* R ıı 348 O ııı 678 H ıı p ııı 140
Nov. 22.	Commission to four persons to examine the petitions of the cardinals in England in regard to presentations to benefices *Westm* R. ıı. 349 O ııı 679 H. ıı p ı 140
Nov. 22	The K asks the cardinal of S Ciriac in Thermis to aid the settlement of an oppressive claim made by the Papal Court against the abbot of Westminster. *Westm.* R ıı. 349. O ııı. 679 H. ıı p ı 140
Nov 22.	The K asks the pope to help Wm abbot of Westminster in the said matter *Westm.* R ıı 349 O ııı 680. H. ıı p ı 140

DATE.	SUBJECT
1317. Nov 28.	The K of England asks Philip K of France, Charles of Valois, and two others, to favour certain merchants of Florence resident in France *Windsor.* R. ii 349 O. iii 680 H. ii. p. i. 141.
Dec. 1	The K. complains to Philip K of France of the capture of a ship called Dromond and of other injuries committed by the French *Windsor* R ii 350. O iii 681 H. ii, p i 141.
Dec. 6	The K of England recommends to Philip K of France Wm Daniel, marques de Careto, and his brothers, going into France *Windsor* R ii 350 O iii 681 H ii p i. 141.
Dec. 6.	The K to the pope and 7 cardinals, in favour of the same persons *Windsor.* R. ii. 350. O iii 681 H ii p i 141
Dec 6.	The K appoints the said marquis to be of his council and livery for the parts beyond the sea *Windsor* R ii 350 O iii 682 H ii p i 141
Dec 10	Indemnity to the citizens of Dublin for having burnt the suburbs of Dublin during the late inroads of the Scots. *Windsor* R ii 350 O iii 682 H ii p i 141.
Dec. 20.	Adam de Neuton, guardian of the minorites of Berwick, to the cardinals in England, recounting his interview with Robert de Brus near Holdecambehus *Berwick* R ii 351 O. iii 683 H. ii. p i 141.
Dec 22	Articles of complaint delivered to the K against Arnaldus Calculi, seneschal of Xantoigne, with the K.'s judgment upon the same. *Windsor.* R ii. 351. O iii. 684 H ii p. i. 142.
Dec 27.	The K. confirms the grant made to the children of Theophania de Sancto Petro, the Q's nurse *Westm* R ii 352 O iii 687 H ii p i 143
Dec 27.	The K. forbids the holding of tournaments in England. *Windsor.* R. ii. 352 O iii. 687 H. ii. p. i. 143
Dec 29	Pope John excommunicates those who invade the realm of England, or disturb its peace *Avignon* R ii 353 O iii. 688. H ii p. i 143
1318. Jan. 1.	The K. orders the arrest of such persons as neglect his proclamation against tilting. *Windsor.* R ii 353 O iii 689 H ii p i 144.
Jan. 2.	The K orders that certain towns, &c in Aquitain be annexed to the crown of England. *Windsor* R ii 353 O iii 689 H ii p i 144
Jan. 8.	The K. complains to the pope of the injuries inflicted on his subjects by the subjects of the K of France. *Westm.* R. ii 354 O iii 690 H ii p i 144
Jan. 8.	The K. of England complains to Philip K of France of the said injuries *Westm.* R. ii 354. O iii. 690. H ii. p. i 144
Jan. 10.	The K. and council complain to the pope of his late constitution, whereby he reserves to himself the disposal of certain pluralities *Windsor* R ii 354 O iii 691. H. ii. p. i. 144.
Jan. 10	The K. to 14 cardinals against the said constitution R ii. 354 O iii. 691. H ii. p i 145.
Jan. 21.	The K. urges the pope to proceed with the canonization of Thomas de Cantilupe bp. of Hereford. *Windsor.* R. ii 355 O iii. 692 H ii p i 145
Jan. 28	Philip K of France complains to the K of England of the illegal detention in London of the goods of some French merchants *Paris* R ii. 355 O iii 693 H ii. p i 145
Jan. 28.	The K notifies the completion of a truce between the citizens of Bayonne and the Normans. *Westm* R ii 355 O. iii 693. H ii p i. 145.
Feb 4.	The K. of England asks Philip K of France to proclaim the above-mentioned truce in Normandy *Windsor.* R. ii. 355 O iii. 694 H ii. p i 146
Feb 6.	The K. prohibits Rigaud de Asserio from doing anything prejudicial to the rights of the crown *Windsor* R ii 356 O iii. 694 H. ii p. i 146.
Feb. 8.	The K of England asks the K. of France to prevent his officers from injuring the people of Aquitain *Windsor* R ii. 356. O iii 695. H ii p i 146
Feb 16.	The K forbids the clergy, about to meet in convocation at London, from doing anything prejudicial to his crown. *Shene* R ii 356. O iii 695. H ii p i 146
March 1.	The K orders that his subjects shall not be unduly oppressed in the collecting of the Peter's pence. *Westm* R ii 357 O iii 696 H ii p i 146
March 4	Protection and safeconduct for Thomas earl of Lancaster and his adherents to go anywhere in England *Westm.* R. ii 357. O iii 696. H ii p i. 147.
March 6.	Writ for the payment of 150*l* to the cardinal of Albano. *Westm* R. ii. 357. O. iii. 697. H. ii. p. i. 147.

DATE	SUBJECT.
1318 March 18.	The K asks the pope to extend and perpetuate the privileges of the university of Cambridge. *Westm.* R ii 357 O iii. 698 H ii p i 147.
March 18.	Commission to W ahp. of York and others to make a truce with Robert de Brus and his adherents *Westm* R ii 358. O iii 698 H ii p i. 147
March 18.	The K annexes to the crown of England the castle and vill de Podio Lorman (in Aquitain) R ii 358 O iii 699 H ii p i. 147
March 20.	The K recommends his relative James de Berkele to the pope. *Westm.* R. ii. 358. O iii. 699 H ii p i 148
March 20.	The K licences the collection in Ireland of the procurations for the cardinals who had come into England from the pope *Westm* R ii 358 O iii 699 H ii p i 148
March 20	The K pardons Wm. Melksop for having killed Wm. de Ponton in a tournament at Luton *Westm* R ii 358. O. iii 700 H ii. p i 148
March 30	The K of England complains to Philip K of France of the misconduct of his officers in Aquitain. *Haddele* R ii 359 O iii. 700 H ii p i 148
April 7.	The K forbids the holding of tournaments throughout England. *Mortlake* R. ii. 359. O iii. 701 H i p ii. 148
April 8	Commission for the settlement of a truce between the men of Bayonne and the Normans. *Mortlake.* R ii 359. O iii 701 H ii p i 148
[April 8]	The K. (intending to found a house for sisters of the order of the Friars Preachers at Langley) asks the pope to give credence to Richard de Birton and Andrew Aslakeby, the bearers of this letter R ii 359 O iii 702. H. n p i 149
April 9	The K orders the payment of his pension of 2,000l of Bordeaux money to Amanenus lord of Lebret *Mortlake.* R ii 359 O iii 702 H ii p i 149
April 13.	The K. orders the arrest of such of the goods of the commonalty of Berwick-upon-Tweed as are at Kingston-upon-Hull *Mortlake* R. ii. 360
April 15.	Philip K of France requires the K. of England to do homage to him for the duchy of Aquitain *Paris* R ii 360 O. iii 703 H ii. p i 149
April 18.	The K grants certain privileges to his brothers, the executors of the will of Margaret late Q of England *Windsor* R. ii 360 O iii 703 H ii p i 149.
April 27.	The K to three cardinals, in favour of his intended foundation for sisters of the order of the Friars Preachers at Langley. *Wallingford* R ii 360 O iii 704 H ii. p. i. 149
April 27.	The K asks the master of the order of the Friars Preachers to have seven sisters ready to be despatched when required *Wallingford* R ii 361. O iii 704. H ii p i 149
April 28.	The K annexes 41 towns, &c in Aquitain to the crown of England. *Windsor.* R ii 361. O. iii 704 H. ii p i 150
May 20.	The K asks R count of Flanders to send commissioners to treat with the English about peace *Westm* R ii 361
May 27.	Pope John complains to the K of the treatment which his nuncio had lately received at Valence *Avignon.* R ii 361 O iii 705 H ii p i. 150.
May 28.	The K. orders the payment of the arrears due to Margaret countess of Foix. *Westm.* R ii 362. O iii 707 H ii p i 150.
May 30.	The K tells the pope of his joy on hearing of the renewal of the process for the canonization of Thomas de Cantilupe *Westm* R. ii. 363 O iii 709. H. ii p. ii. 151.
May 30.	The K to the cardinal of S Ciriac in Thermis to the same effect *Westm* R. iii 363. O iii 710 H ii p i 152
June 1.	The K asks the pope to depose Wm de Lamberton and substitute Tho de Riverus in the bprick of S Andrew's. *Westm* R ii 363 O iii 710 H ii. p i 152.
June 5.	Pardon to John Manduyt for having killed Roger de Chedele in jousting at Cirencester *Westm* R ii 364 O iii 711 H ii. p i 152
June 6	Pope John informs the K that he has ordered the cardinals to excommunicate Robert de Brus for his various offences. *Avignon.* R ii 364 O iii 712 H. ii. p i 152.
June 7.	The K asks the pope to grant certain privileges to the clerks of the Chancery *Westm.* R ii 364 O iii 712 H. ii p i. 152.
June 8.	The K announces to the nobility and clergy that he will not hold the parliament summoned to meet at Lincoln *Westm* R ii 365 O iii 712 H ii p i 153
June 8.	The K. orders a general proclamation to be made to the same effect. *Westm.* R. ii. 365. O. iii, 713 H ii p, i. 153.

DATE.	SUBJECT.
1318. June 10.	Thomas earl of Lancaster is ordered to proceed with his retinue against the Scotch, who have taken the town of Berwick *Westm.* R ii. 365 O iii 713. H ii p. i. 153.
June 16.	Philip K. of France is requested to postpone the period for the reception of K Edward's homage for Aquitain *Westm.* R. ii 365 O. iii 714. H ii p i 153
June 16.	The K. authorises the bp of Hereford and another to take the oath of fealty in his name to the K of France for the duchy of Aquitain *Westm* R. ii. 365. O. iii. 714. H ii. p. i. 153.
June 16.	The K. orders that the servants of the cardinals in England shall be assisted in procuring provisions *Fulmere* R ii 366 O iii 714. H ii p. i. 153
June 22.	Safeconduct for the cardinals going to Northampton *Woodstock* R ii 366 O. iii. 715. H. ii p i 153
June 24.	The K orders that the arrears of his annual fee be paid to Amadeus count of Savoy. *Woodstock.* R ii. 366. O iii. 715. H. ii p i 154
June 28	Pope John excommunicates Robert de Brus for his various acts of rebellion, the particulars of which are recorded *Avignon* R ii. 362. O iii 707 H ii p i 151
[July.]	Pope John complains to the K of the misconduct of the seneschal of Gascony *Avignon.* R ii 366 O iii. 716 H ii p i. 154
July 4	The K orders that aid be given to the servants of the cardinals in England in procuring victuals. *Northampton* R ii. 367. O. iii 717 H ii p i 154
July 11.	Proclamation by the K. throughout England against the assemblage of armed men. *Northampton* R. ii. 367. O iii 717 H ii p i. 154.
July 13	The K settles with R count of Flanders the particulars of a meeting of their commissioners for the establishment of peace *Northampton.* R ii 367 O iii, 718. H. ii. p i 155
July 13.	The K orders that the men of Flanders trading to England shall not be molested *Northampton.* R ii. 368 O iii 718 H ii p i 155
Nov 13	Safeconduct for the commissioners coming from Flanders to treat with the English. *Northampton.* R ii 368 O iii 719 H ii p i 155.
July 15.	Recommendation from the K for Reymund Subirani going to the pope. *Northampton.* R. ii. 368 O iii. 719 H ii. p. i 155.
July 15	The K to certain nephews of the pope and others, to the same effect. *Northampton* R. ii 368 O iii 720 H ii p i 155
July 16.	Protection for the Flemish commissioners coming to treat with the English. *Northampton* R. ii. 368 O. iii 720 H ii p i 155
July 20.	The K asks J duke of Brittany to help him in promoting concord between their subjects *Northampton.* R ii 369. O iii 720 H ii p i 156
July 29.	The K again asks the pope to favour his relative James de Berkele. *Northampton.* R. ii 369 O iii. 721 H. ii p i 156
July 29	The K to Robert K of Sicily for the same James *Northampton.* R ii. 369. O iii 721. H ii p i. 156
July 29.	The K again asks the pope to cease from urging the extravagant demand of the court of Rome upon Wm. abbot of Westminster. *Northampton.* R. ii. 369. O iii 721. H ii p. i. 156.
July 29.	The K asks the pope to show favour to the abbey of Westminster in the above demand. *Northampton.* R ii 369. O iii 722 H. ii p. i. 156.
[Aug.]	Settlement in parliament of the disputes between the K. and Thomas earl of Lancaster. R ii. 370. O. iii. 722 H. ii p i 156.
Aug. 12.	Safeconduct for the abbot of Menrose, in Scotland, going to the house of Holmcultram. *Nottingham* R ii 370 O iii 724 H ii. p i 157
Aug 12	The K. of England asks Philip K of France to excuse his delay in doing homage to him in France *Nottingham.* R ii. 371 O. iii. 725. H ii. p i 157
Aug 12	The K. orders the arrest of Castellus de Janua, who had obtained money by false pretences *Nottingham.* R ii 371. O iii 725 H. ii p i 157
Aug 18	Safeconduct for the messengers of the cardinals going into Ireland *Clipston.* R ii 371. O iii. 726. H. ii p i 158.
Aug 24.	The K asks the pope to punish those who raise false accusations in the papal court *Nottingham* R. ii. 371. O iii. 726. H. ii. p. i 158

DATE	SUBJECT.
1318 Aug. 24.	The K informs the pope of the good service done in England by Aymerieus Quirardi, a servant of the cardinals in England, and commends him to His Holiness *Nottingham* R ii. 371. O iii. 726 H. ii p i 158
Aug.	The K , on the return of the cardinals to Rome, gives the pope a statement of what they have effected in England *Nottingham*. R ii 372. O iii. 727. H. ii p i. 158
Aug. 25.	Safeconduct for the said cardinals returning from England to Rome. *Nottingham* R. ii. 372 O iii 728 H ii p i 159
Aug 25	The K of England asks the bp of Hereford to state to the K of France the injuries done by his officers to K Edward's subjects in Aquitain. *Nottingham* R ii. 372 O iii. 729 H ii p i 159
Aug 26	The K of England complains to Philip K of France of the same injuries. *Nottingham*. R ii 373. O iii 728 H ii p i 159
Sept 10	The K of England complains in detail to Philip K of France of the injuries done by his subjects to the English *Clipston* R. ii 373 O iii. 729. H. ii. p i 159.
Sept. 18.	Pope John informs the K that he cannot depose Wm bp of S Andrew's in favour of Thomas de Riverus *Avignon* R ii 374 O iii 733 H ii p i 160
Oct 5	The K recommends his clerk, Roger de Northburgh, to the pope *York* R ii 374 O iii 733 H ii p i 160
Oct 5	The K to certain cardinals and others in commendation of the said Roger. *York*. R ii 374 O iii 733 H ii p i 160
Oct 22.	General pardon granted up to 7 Aug last for Thomas earl of Lancaster *York* R ii 374 O iii 733 H ii p i 160
Oct 22.	Similar pardon for David de Strabolgy earl of Athol and 42 others *York*. R ii 374. O iii 734 H ii p i 161
Oct 26.	The K. asks the pope to appropriate the church of Kingsclere to the sisters of the order of the Friars Preachers at Guilford. *York* R ii 375 O. iii. 734. H ii p i. 161.
Oct. 26.	The K to Peter Fabry, the pope's notary, on the same subject. *York* R ii. 375 O iii. 735 H ii p i 161
Nov 2	The K orders that the liberties of Thomas earl and Alice countess of Lancaster be preserved intact *York* R ii 375. O iii 735 H ii p i 161.
Nov. 11.	The K protests to the cardinals that the pardon granted by him to Thomas earl of Lancaster and his adherents does not cover the robbery committed upon the said cardinals *York* R ii 375 O iii 735 H ii p i 161
Nov. 11.	The K pardons John earl of Richmond the payment of arrears due to the crown for the wapentakes of Gillynghang and Halikeld *York* R ii 376. O iii 736 H. ii p i. 162
Nov 12	Grant by the K to the said earl to hold for life the wapentakes of Gillynghang and Halikeld on the payment of 36*l* *York* R ii 736 O iii 736 H ii p i 162
Nov 15	The K orders that his clerk Wm de Aremynne shall honorably hold his prebend in S. Paul's, London *York* R ii 376 O iii 736 H ii p i 162
Nov 20	The K explains how he will act in regard to the truce between the men of Bayonne and the Normans *York* R ii 736 O iii 737 H ii p i 162
Nov 20	The K grants certain privileges to the citizens of Bayonne *York* R. ii 376. O iii 737 H. ii p i 162
Nov. 20.	The K. exempts certain persons who served his father in the war in Gascony from paying certain taxes *York* R. ii 376 O iii 738 H. ii p i 162
Nov. 20.	The K appoints Wm de Montecute to be seneschal of the duchy of Aquitain. *York* R. ii 377 O iii 738 H ii p i 162
Nov 20	The K. defines the powers of the said seneschal. *York* R. ii. 377. O ii 738. H. ii p. i. 162.
Nov 20	The K states the wages and allowances to be paid to the said seneschal. *York* R ii 377 O. iii 739 H ii p i. 163.
Nov 20	The K in addition to the above gives a present of 5,000*l* Turon to the said seneschal *York*. R ii 377 O iii 739 H i p i 163
Nov 20	The K grants certain powers in Gascony to the said seneschal *York*. R. ii 377. O iii 740. H. ii p i. 163
Nov. 20.	The K grants the custody of the isle of Oleron to the said seneschal *York* R ii 378. O. iii. 740. H ii p. i. 163.

DATE.	SUBJECT.
1318. Nov. 22.	General summons to citizens and merchants to a conference to discuss the establishment of a staple in Flanders *York.* R ii 378 O iii 740 H. ii. p i 163
Nov 23.	The K. orders the sheriffs of 15 counties to see that no injuries be inflicted upon the Flemings. *York* R ii 378 O iii 741. H. ii p i. 163.
Nov. 24.	The K asks the pope to permit the annexation of the church of Horncaster (dioc Lincoln) to the see of Carlisle, and that the bp and clergy may free this dioc from the Scots *York* R ii 378 O. iii 741 H ii p i 164
Nov 24.	The K orders the distribution of 40 barrels of wine among the inhabitants of Northumberland, endamaged by the Scots. *York* R ii. 378 O. iii 742 H. ii p i. 164.
Nov. 25.	The K. orders a convocation of the clergy for the purpose of granting him a subsidy for the Scottish war *York* R ii 379.
Nov 28.	The K promises that the aid given him by the city of London shall not become a precedent. *York.* R. ii 379 O iii. 742 H ii p i. 164
Nov 28	The K. orders the abp of York to cease from troubling the people by vexatious citations *York.* R. ii 379.
Nov 28	The K asks three cardinals to intercede with the pope for the promotion of Simon de Montacute, a student at Oxford. *York* R ii 379. O iii 743 H. ii p i. 164.
Nov. 28.	The K asks for a dispensation from the papal court for the said Simon *York* R ii 379. O. iii 743 H ii p i 164
Nov. 29	The K asks the pope to grant a dispensation to the said Simon. *York* R ii 380. O iii 743 H ii p i 164.
Dec. 4.	Credence for Wm de Montacute, seneschal of the duchy of Aquitain, going to Philip K. of France *York* R. ii 380. O iii 744 H ii p i 164
Dec. 4	The K directs that tenths shall no longer be levied according to the ancient taxation of benefices *York* R ii. 380
Dec. 7.	The K sends to Robert count of Flanders certain delegates to settle peace between Flanders and Holland *York* R ii. 380 O iii 744 H ii. p i 165.
Dec. 7.	The K asks certain nobles to aid the delegates mentioned above in the said settlement *York* R ii. 381. O iii 745 H ii. p i 165
Dec. 7.	Commission to the said delegates to execute the said treaty of peace *York* R ii 381 O iii 745 H ii p i 165
Dec 7.	The K orders the arrest of all persons that tourney anywhere in England. *York* R ii. 381 O iii 745. H. ii p i. 165.
Dec 10.	The K asks of the pope a dispensation for the marriage of Edward son of the K of England and Margaret daughter of William count of Holland *York* R ii 381 O iii 746. H ii p i 165
Dec 10	The K to 28 cardinals and others, on the same subject. *York* R ii. 382 O iii 747. H ii p i 165
Dec. 16.	The K asks various nobles, clergy, &c , to levy men to resist the incursions of the Scots *York* R ii 382 O iii. 748 H ii. p i 166
Dec 20	The K asks the pope to excuse the absence of the abps of Dublin and Cashel from the Roman Court *York* R ii. 382 O iii. 749 H ii p i 166
Dec. 20.	The K. to the cardinals, to the same effect *York* R ii 383 O iii. 750 H ii. p. i. 167.
1319 Jan 1.	The K orders the arrest of those who attend tournaments. *Bursley* R ii. 383 O iii 750 H ii p i 167.
Jan 1.	The K orders the arrest of those who go to the tournament at Dunstable. *Bursley* R. ii 383 O iii 751. H ii. p i 167
Jan 1	Credence for Robert de Wyrsop, John de Benstede, and John de Nevill, going from the K. to the pope. *Bursley* R ii 383 O iii 751 H ii p i 167
Jan 1	Credence for the same persons to the cardinals. *Bursley* R. ii, 383 O iii 752. H ii. p i 167.
Jan. 1	Credence for Hugh le Despenser the elder, going on a special matter from the K to the pope *Bursley* R ii 384 O iii 751 H ii. p. i 167
Jan 9	The K requests five cardinals to take heed that the sentence against the Scots is neither removed nor mitigated *York.* R. ii. 384 O iii 752. H ii p i. 167.
Jan 12.	The K returns to the pope certain letters which he had intercepted on their route from the papal court to Scotland. *York.* R. ii. 384. O. iii 752. H. ii p i. 168

DATE	SUBJECT.
1319. Jan. 12	The K asks three cardinals to see that the writers of the said letters be punished. *York.* R II 384. O. iii. 753. H. n. p i 168
Jan 12.	The K asks the pope to further his wish for the foundation of a sisterhood of the order of the Friars Preachers at Langley *York* R II 384 , O III 753 H II p. i. 168
Jan. 17.	The K asks the pope to proceed with the canonization of Thomas de Cantilupe, bp of Hereford *York.* R. II. 385. O III 753 H II p i 168
Jan 17	The K to 10 cardinals, on the same subject. *York.* R II 385. O III 754. H II. p i 168
Jan 25.	The K excuses the payment of various sums due from the tenants of the castle of Knaresburgh, they being impoverished by the inroads of the Scotch *York* R II 385.
Jan 27	The K asks the prayers of the general chapter of the Friars Minors, about to meet at Marseilles *York* R II 385 O III 754. H II p i 168
Feb 1	Protection for Hugh le Despenser the elder, employed abroad in the K's service *York* R II 385 O. III 754 H ii p i. 168.
Feb. 2.	The K. forbids the introduction of clipped or false money into the realm. *York.* R II 386
Feb. 2.	The K issues certain new regulations for the management of the Exchequer accounts. *York* R II 386
Feb 3.	The K informs the pope (for the quieting of his conscience) of certain facts connected with the priory of Fruterwell, dioc. London *York.* R. II 386 O. III 755 H ii. p i 169
Feb 6	Credence from the K for certain persons sent to the pope upon private matters of importance *York* R II 387 O III 755. H II p i 169
Feb. 6	Credence for two clerks sent from the K. to the bp of Sabina *York.* R. ii. 387. O III 756 H II p i 169
Feb 6	The K. asks the bp of Hereford to obtain, before his return, a final answer from the pope. *York.* R II 387. O. III. 756. H II p i 169
Feb 7.	The K asks the pope to grant a dispensation for a marriage between Thomas son of Guy de Beauchamp earl of Warwick, and one of the daughters of Roger de Mortimer lord of Wygemor *York.* R. II 387 O. III. 757 H II p i 169.
Feb 9.	The K. directs that the military summons in Ireland, issued by the justiciary without the assent of the nobles, shall be revoked. *York.* R II. 387 O III 757. H. II p. i. 169
Feb 15	The K orders that no tournament be held within the bprick. of Durham *York* R II 388 O III 758 H II p i 169
Feb 28	The K orders Richard de Maundeville to cease from besieging the castle of Crakfergus. *York* R II. 388.
March 1	The bp of Hereford is directed to obtain the pope's permission to effect exchanges with the bps and convents in Aquitain *York* R. II 388 O III 738 H II p i 170
March 8	The K. asks the pope to permit him to treat of peace with the Scots, who have been excommunicated *York.* R. II 388 O III 758 H II p i 170.
March 14	The K forbids the abp of Canterbury from proceeding with certain pleas in his ecclesiastical court *York* R II 388
March 19	The K grants to his son, John of Eltham, all lands which have been forfeited by the Scotch, on this side of the Trent *York.* R II 389
March 20	Bond by the K to pay to the pope 36s of borrowed money. *York.* R. II. 389. O III 759 H II p i 170.
March 20	Bond by the K. to pay to the pope 37l 19s. 9d. of borrowed money. R. ii 389 O III. 759 H. II p i 170
March 25	The K requests Robert count of Flanders, the duke of Brabant, and various towns in Flanders, to cease from trading with the Scots *York.* R II 389 O III. 759. H. II. p i 170.
March 26	The K asks the pope to proceed still further with the punishment of the Scots found in the papal court, who had sent rebellious letters into Scotland *York* R II. 390 O III 761. H II p i. 171.
March 28	The K of England informs Philip K of France that he will consult the parliament at York upon the contents of his (Philip's) letter *York* R. II. 390 O. III 761 H II p i 171.
April 1.	The K asks the pope to expedite the affairs of Roger de Northburgh. *York.* R II. 390. O. III. 762. H. II p. i. 171.

DATE	SUBJECT
1319 April 4.	The K. asks the pope to proceed with severity against the Scots *York* R. ii 390 O iii 762. H. ii. p. i. 171.
April 4.	The K to the cardinal of S. Ciriac in Thermis to the same effect. *York* R. ii 390 O iii 762. H ii p. i 131
April 9	The K. appoints Andrew de Hartcla as sheriff of Cumberland and Westmorland. *Kirkham.* R ii 390. O iii 762 H. ii p i 171.
April 15.	The K complains that his rights have been violated by the pope. *York* R. ii. 391 O iii 763 H ii p i 171
April 18.	The K complains to the pope of the misconduct of Wm de Somerton, a monk of St Alban's, made prior of Bynham, a cell of S Alban's *York* R ii 391 O iii 764 H ii p i. 172
April 24.	Pope John permits the K to treat with excommunicated persons. *Avignon* R. ii 391 O. iii 764. H. ii. p. i 172
April 24	The K. asks the pope to be favourable to Louis bp. of Durham. *York.* R ii. 391. O iii. 765 H ii p i 172.
April 24.	The K. asks the cardinals to excuse the delay of Louis bp of Durham in paying certain sums due by him to them. *York.* R. ii. 391. O. iii. 765. H ii p i. 172.
April 24.	The K of England asks the King of Jerusalem to intercede with the pope for the bp. of Durham *York* R. ii. 392 O iii 765. H ii p i 172
April 26	The inhabitants of Mechlin assure the K. that they will not assist the Scotch R. ii. 392 O iii. 766. H ii p i 172
May 1.	John duke of Brabant assures the K. that the Scotch shall have no aid from his territories. *Tonamag'* R. ii 392 O iii 766 H. ii. p i 173.
May 10.	The K asks the pope to appoint Henry de Burgherghs to the archdeaconry of Canterbury *York.* R. ii. 392 O. iii 767. H ii p i. 173
May 12.	Creation of John de Birmyngeham to be earl of Loueth in Ireland, for his good service against Edward de Brus. *York* R ii. 393. O iii 767. H. ii p i 173
May 14.	The K complains to the pope of an injury done to his rights by a papal provision respecting the church of Rutherfeld. *York.* R. ii 393. O. iii. 768. H ii p i 173
May 14	The K asks the bp of Sabina to suspend the proceedings before him in the case of the provision referred to above *York* R. ii 393. O iii. 769 H ii p i. 174
May 14.	The K trusts that the cardinal S. Martin in Montibus will so act in the above matter that other remedies shall be unnecessary. *York.* R. ii 394. O. iii 770 H ii p i 174
May 17.	Robert count of Flanders informs the K. (in answer to his letters), that Flanders is open to all comers, and that he cannot deny an entrance into it to the subjects of "the K of Scotland" *Bruges* R ii 394 O iii 770 H ii p i 174
May 17	The burgesses of Bruges to the K to the same effect as the preceding *Bruges* R ii 394. O iii. 771. H. ii p. i 174.
May 22	The burgesses of Ypres inform the K that they will give no aid to his enemies, nor will they trade with Scotland. R ii 394 O iii. 771. H. ii p i 174
May 24.	Commission to the bps of Exeter and Hereford, &c , to perform the homage due by the K. of England to the K. of France *York.* R. ii 395. O. iii 772. H ii p i. 775
May 24.	The K of England acknowledges that he is bound to do homage to Philip K. of France for the duchy of Aquitain. *York* R ii 395 O iii. 772 H ii p i 175
May 24	The K of England authorizes his commissioners to apologize to Philip K of France for his delay in doing homage *York.* R. ii. 395.
May 24	The K. of England acknowledges that he is bound to do homage to Philip K. of France for the comté of Ponthieu and Montreuil. *York.* R. ii 395 O iii 773. H. ii. p i. 175
May 24	Credence for the above-mentioned commissioners going from the K of England to Philip K of France *York* R. ii 395 O iii 773 H. ii. p i 175
May 24	The K authorizes the above-mentioned commissioners to fix the day and place for the rendering of the homage *York* R. ii 395 O iii 773 H. ii p i. 175.
May 30	The K. directs that enquiry be made as to the adherents of Edward de Brus in Ireland. *York.* R. ii. 396. O iii. 774. H. ii p i. 175.
June 4	The K. orders that footsoldiers shall be levied in Wales for the war in Scotland *York* R ii 396 O. iii. 774. H. ii. p i. 176
June 5	The K. confirms to Thomas earl of Lancaster and his brother Henry all rights devolving upon them in the comté of Provence. *York.* R. ii 396. O. iii. 775. H. ii. p. i. 176.

DATE.	SUBJECT.
1319 June 5	The K (for the quieting of his conscience) informs the pope that during the vacancy of the see of York he had presented Roger de Northburgh to the prebend of Wistowe, void by the death of Peter of Savoy　*York*　R ii 396　O iii 776　H. ii p i 176
June 6	The K thanks the pope for having punished the Scotch, and tells him that England is tranquil　*York*　R ii 397　O. iii. 777.　H. ii p i. 177.
June 7	The K grants 20 librates of land to Edmund de Bermengeham for his good service against Edward le Brus in Ireland　*York*　R ii 397　O iii 777　H ii p i. 177.
June 7	The K. grants certain liberties to John de Bermyngeham earl of Loueth, for his good service against Edward de Brus in Ireland.　*York.*　R. ii 397.
June 7	The K complains to the pope of the proceedings of cardinal Reymund de Fargis respecting the prebend of Ketene in the church of Lincoln　*York*　R. ii 398.　O iii 778　H ii. p i 177
June 8	The K instructs the treasurer and barons of the Exchequer how to proceed in the settlement of the debts of Anthony late bp. of Durham, and the claims of Rigaud de Asserio.　*York*　R ii 398　O iii 779.　H ii p i 177
June 8	Attorneys appointed for the above-mentioned settlement of debts.　*York.*　R. ii. 398.　O iii 780　H ii p i 178
June 8.	The K asks the pope to permit him to delay the payment of the yearly tribute of 1000 marks　*York*　R ii 399　O iii 780　H ii. p. i 178
June 8	The K to the cardinals, with the same request　*York*　R ii 399　O iii. 781.　H ii. p i 178
June 8	The K of England asks the K of Sicily to assist his proctors in the Roman court　*York*　R ii 399　O iii 781　H ii p i 178.
June 8.	The K directs that the fines due for absence from personal service against the Scots shall be forthwith paid into the Exchequer　*York*　R ii. 399　O iii. 781　H. ii. p. i. 178.
June 8	The K asks the pope to appoint John de Wrotham to the office of papal penitentiary, in the place of Nicholas de Wysebech　*York.*　R ii 399　O iii 781　H ii p i. 178.
June 9	The K informs the pope of the particulars connected with the nomination of Wm de Ayremynne to a prebend in Lincoln cathedral.　*York.*　R ii. 400　O iii 782　H ii. p. i. 179
June 9	The K authorises the granting of a pension of 25 marks to some resident agent in the papal court　R. ii 400
June 12.	The K asks Haco K. of Norway to cause Botulph Bix of Northherg' to pay debts due to certain merchants of Lynn　*York*　R ii 400　O ii 783　H ii p i 179
June 26	The K thanks the pope for permitting the translation of the body of Thomas de Cantilupe formerly bp of Hereford　*York*　R ii 400　O ii 784.　H ii p. i. 179
July 1.	The K orders Thomas earl of Lancaster to levy 2000 foot soldiers to serve against the Scotch　*York*　R ii 400　O iii 784　H ii p i 179
July 12	The K orders that no one shall be put into possession of the prebend of Grimston and Yateminster, in the church of Salisbury, without his knowledge, as he had conferred it on Tho de Stanton　*York.*　R ii. 401.　O iii 784.　H ii p i. 180.
July 19	The K grants various prebends, churches, &c in Scotland to various persons specified in the letters patent　*York*　R ii 401　O iii 785　H ii p i. 180
July 20.	The K (going into Scotland) asks the prayers of the abps and bps of England　*York.*　R ii 402　O iii. 786.　H ii. p i 180.
July 20.	All persons worth 50l. per ann in lands are to be knighted　*York.*　R ii 402.
July 20	The K orders that all fines due for non-attendance in the expedition to Scotland be paid to the Exchequer　*York*　R. ii 402
July 20	The K asks a loan from the clergy, cities and towns in England, the same to be employed against the Scots　*York*　R ii 402　O iii 787.　H ii. p i 181
July 20	The K grants an annual pension of 50 marks sterling to Nicholas bp. of Ostia　*York.*　R. ii. 403　O iii 788　H ii p. i. 181.
Aug 12	The K. pardons Ralph de Monthermer for having married Isabella, widow of John de Hastynges, without the K's permission　*Goseford,*　R ii. 403　O. iii 789　H ii p i. 181
Aug 18	The K recommends Anthony de Pessaigne of Genoa to the pope　*Auebel'.*　R. ii. 403.
Aug 18	The K recommends the same Anthony to Peter de Via, the pope's nephew, and the cardinal of S Aquino　*Auebel'*　R ii 403　O iii 789　H. ii. p i 181.
Aug 18.	The K informs L cardinal of S Maria in Via Lata that the said Anthony is innocent of certain charges brought against him.　*Auebel'.*　R ii. 403　O iii 789　H ii p. i. 181.

DATE.	SUBJECT
1319 Oct. 16.	Proclamation that arms are not to be worn within the city of London, except by the retinue of the King, Queen, and nobility *York* R ii 404 O iii 790 H ii p i 182
Oct. 20.	The K forbids the holding of a tournament at Eggefeld. *York.* R ii 404. O. iii 790. H. ii. p i. 182.
Oct. 20.	The K. informs his nobility and others of the above prohibition. *York* R ii 404. O. iii. 791. H ii. p. ii 182
Oct. 24.	Safeconduct for 12 persons coming from Scotland to Newcastle-upon-Tyne there to treat of peace *York* R ii 404 O iii 791 H ii p i 182
Oct 25.	The K orders that payment of his expenses in Gascony be made to Wm de Montacute, seneschal of Gascony *York.* R. ii 404 O iii 791 H. ii. p i 182
Oct. 26.	Memorandum of orders given by the K to John de Hotham bp. of Ely, his chancellor, respecting the sealing of the K.'s mandates *York* R ii 405 O iii 792 H ii. p. i. 182
Nov. 2	The K asks the pope for a dispensation for the marriage of the K's son Edw with Sibilla, daughter of Rob count of Hainault. *York.* R ii 405 O iii 792 H ii p i 182
Nov. 2.	The K. asks three cardinals to promote the above dispensation. *York.* R ii 405 O. iii 793 H ii. p i 183
Nov. 2	The K of England to R King of Sicily, to the same effect R ii 405 O iii. 793. H ii p i 183.
Nov. 2	The K asks the pope to promote Hen de Burghash, nephew of Barth de Badelesmere, to the vacant see of Winchester *York* R ii 405 O iii 793 H ii p i. 183
Nov. 5.	The K asks the pope to promote Thomas de Rivarus to the see of S Andrew's in Scotland. *York* R ii 406. O iii 794 H. ii p i 183
Nov. 6	The K orders that no one shall be required to plead out of the realm *York.* R ii 406. O iii 795 H ii p i 183
Nov. 6.	The K, gives the custody of the duchy of Gascony (vacant by the death of Wm. de Montacute, seneschal of the same) to Amaneus de Fossato. *York.* R ii. 406. O iii 795 H. ii p i. 184.
Nov. 9.	The K again asks the pope to promote Henry de Burghasshe to the see of Winchester *Gaynesburgh* R ii. 406 O iii 796 H. ii p i. 184
Nov. 9.	The K to various cardinals, &c, in favor of the said Henry *Gaynesburgh* R ii 407 O iii 796 H ii. p i 184.
Nov. 9.	The K to A bp. of Hereford and Andrew Sapiti, to the same effect *Gaynesburgh* R. ii. 407. O iii 797. H ii p i. 184.
Nov. 17	Pope John authorises his legates to excommunicate Robert de Brus and others *Avignon* R ii 407 O iii 797 H ii p i. 184
Nov 23	The K asks the citizens of Bayonne to continue in their fidelity to him *York.* R. ii. 409 O iii 801. H ii p i 186
Nov 25.	The K. exempts various vills in Yorkshire here specified (burnt by the Scots), from the payment of the tax of the eighteenth *York.* R ii. 409. O. iii. 801. H ii p i 186
Nov 27.	Philip K of France complains to the K of England of injuries done to Toco Guidi of Amiens, by the English merchants *Vincennes.* R ii 409. O iii 802 H ii p i 186
Dec. 1.	Commission to J bp of Ely, the K's chancellor, and others, to treat with the Scots for a truce *York* R ii 409 O. iii. 803. H ii. p i. 187
Dec. 1.	Commission to the above to swear to the observance of the said truce *York.* R. ii 410 O iii 803 H ii p i 187
Dec 1.	Commission to the above to treat for a peace with the Scots. *York* R. ii 410 O iii 804 H. ii p i 187
Dec. 1.	Commission to the above to swear to the observance of the said peace. *York.* R. ii 410. O iii 804. H ii p i. 187.
Dec 1.	Commission to the above to swear the observance of the said truce *York* R ii 410 O. iii 804 H ii p. i 187
Dec. 1.	Commission to the above to grant safeconducts to the Scots coming to Newcastle to treat of peace or truce. *York.* R ii 410 O iii 805 H ii p i 187.
Dec. 1.	Commission to the above to assure the above peace or truce *York* R ii 411 O. iii 806 H ii p i 187
Dec. 4.	The K informs the pope of what he has done as to the above treaty with the Scots. *York* R ii 411. O. iii 806 H. ii. p i 188
Dec. 4.	The K orders his seneschal of Gascony to attend the parliaments of France. *York.* R. ii. 411 O iii 806 H ii. p i. 188

DATE	SUBJECT
1319. Dec 5.	The K renews his application to the pope in favour of Henry de Burgherssh. *York* R. ii 411 O iii 807 H ii p i 188
Dec 5	The K. to the cardinals for the same. *York* R ii 412. O. iii 808 H 1 p i. 188
1320 Jan 6	The K forbids the holding of a tournament at Dunstable *York* R ii 412. O. iii 808 H. ii p i 189
Jan 6	The K orders the arrest of persons going to the said tournament *York.* R. ii. 412 O iii, 809. H. ii. p i 189
Jan 7	Safeconduct for 12 persons coming to the K from Scotland to treat of a truce. *York* R ii 412 O iii 809 H ii p i 189
Jan. 8	Pope John orders the republication of the bull of excommunication of Robert de Brus for the murder of John Connyn. *Avignon* R ii. 412. O iii. 810 H ii p. i. 189.
Jan 8	Pope John excommunicates the Scottish nobles and others who invaded Ireland *Avignon.* R ii 413 O iii 810 H. ii p i 189
Jan. 9	The K. grants certain privileges to Thomas Norman, barber in Suthwerk. *York* R. ii 413.
Jan 9	The K to the pope in favor of Roger de Stanegrave, a knight hospitaler, who had been a prisoner with the Saracens for more than 30 years *York.* R ii 413. O iii 812 H ii. p i 190
Jan. 9	The K to the cardinals for the said Roger. *York.* R ii 414 O iii. 812. H. ii. p i 190
Jan 10	The K asks the master of the hospital of S John of Jerusalem to renew the privileges formerly held by the said Roger *York* R ii 414 O iii 812 H ii p i 190.
Jan. 11	The K of England informs Philip K of France respecting the true state of the case of Totto Guidi *York* R ii 414 O iii. 813 H ii p i 190
Jan 12	The K asks the pope not to press the payment of the sums due by Wm abp of Cashel in the papal court *York* R ii 414 O iii 813 H ii p i 190
Jan 15	The K asks the pope to appoint Henry de Burgherssh to the see of Lincoln *Knaresburgh* R ii 414. O. iii 814. H. ii p i 190
Jan. 15.	The K. to the cardinals, to the same effect *Knaresburgh* R ii 415. O iii 815 H ii p i 191
Jan. 15	The K. to his four agents in the papal court, to the same effect. *York* R. ii. 415. O iii 815 H ii p i 191.
Jan. 24.	The K appoints persons within Cumberland and Northumberland to keep the truce with Scotland *York* R ii 416 O iii 816 H ii p i 191
Jan. 24	The K. authorizes (under certain circumstances) the destruction of the castle of Herbottle, according to the terms of the truce with Robert de Bruys. *York* R ii 416 O iii 817. H ii p i 192
Jan. 26.	The K forbids the abbot of S Alban's from going abroad under the pretext of a citation *York* R. ii. 416.
Jan. 26	Memorandum as to the delivery of the great seal by the K at York to J bp of Norwich R ii 415
Jan 28.	Safeconduct for the K's niece, the countess of Fife, going into Scotland for the deliverance of Ellen, the widow of Robert de Nevill *York* R ii 416 O ii. 817. H. ii p i 192
Jan. 29	The K informs R count of Flanders, and others in Flanders, that he is ready to do justice for any injury inflicted by his subjects upon the Flemings *York* R ii 417
Jan 29	The K commands the sheriffs of London and other persons not to arrest the goods of the Flemings. *York* R. ii. 417.
Feb. 3.	Commission to Thomas earl of Kildare, and three others, to inquire who rendered help to Edward de Brus in Ireland *Clipston* R ii 417
Feb 19.	The K of England informs Philip K of France that he will meet him at Amiens to do homage. *Westm.* R. ii 417. O iii 818 H. ii p i. 192
Feb 20.	Commissions to provide for the K's lodgings on his visit abroad *Westm* R. ii 417 O iii 818 H. ii p i 192
Feb 25	The K of England asks Philip K of France to permit the said commissioners to provide lodgings for him at Amiens *Westm* R ii 418 O iii 818 H. ii p. i. 192
Feb 28.	The K commits to Maurice de Berkeleye the office of seneschal of the duchy of Gascony *Westm* R iii 418 O iii 819 H. ii p i 192
Feb 28.	The K orders the adjustment of all disputes in Gascony *Westm* R. ii. 418. O iii. 819. H. ii p i. 192

DATE	SUBJECT
1320 Feb 28	The K. forbids the holding of tournaments throughout England *Westm.* R. ii. 418 O. iii. 820. H. ii p i. 193.
March 6.	The K again urges the pope to appoint Henry de Burghersh to the see of Lincoln *Canterbury* R ii. 418 O iii 820 H ii p i 193
March 6	The K to 11 cardinals, to the same effect *Canterbury* R. ii. 419. O ii. 821 H ii p i. 193.
March 13.	The K asks the cardinal of S. Maria Nova to cease from annoying Robert de Wodehouse in his prebend of Ketene, in the cathedral of Lincoln. *Sturreye* R ii 419. O. iii. 821. H ii. p i. 193
March 14	Pardon for Wm Baud for having jousted in England *Stureye* R. ii. 419. O iii 822 H ii p i. 193.
March 15	Commission to A. bp of Hereford and others to settle the interview of the K of England with Philip K. of France *Sturreye* R ii 419 O iii. 822 H ii p i 194
March 15	Credence for the above-mentioned messengers going from the K of England to the K. of France. *Stureye* R. ii 419 O iii 822. H ii. p i 194
March 15.	Credence for A bp of Hereford and others going from the K to the pope. *Westm* R ii 420. O. iii 823 H ii p. i 194
March 15.	The K to 28 cardinals, to the same purport. *Westm* R ii 420. O iii. 823 H ii p i 194
March 19	The K. of England recommends Anthony Pessaigne, of Genoa, to Philip K of France *Sturrey* R. ii 420 O. iii 924 H ii p i 194
March 19	The K. recommends the same Anthony to the pope. *Sturrey* R ii 420. O iii. 924. H. ii. p. i 194.
March 19	The K. recommends the same Anthony to the cardinals *Sturrey* R. ii 420. O iii 924 H ii p i 194
March 19	The K recommends the same Anthony to R King of Jerusalem and Cicily. *Sturrey*. R. ii 421 O iii 825 H ii p i 195
March 24.	Safeconduct for the K of England going to meet Philip K. of France. *Paris* R ii 421 O iii 825 H ii p. i 195
March 25	The K. grants an annual pension of 50 marks sterling to Bertrand cardinal of S. Maria, in Aquiro. *Stureye.* R iii 421 O. iii 826 H ii p i 195
April 7.	The K asks the prayers of the general chapter of the Friars Preachers about to meet at Rouen for himself and his family *Westm* R ii 421 O iii 826 H ii. p i 195
April 10	The K forbids Edmund earl of Arundel and John de Hastings coming to an assize at Southwark with a retinue of armed men *Westm.* R ii 422
April 11.	Pardon for John de Flete for having jousted. *Westm* R ii. 422 O iii 826 H. ii. p i 195
April 16.	Protestation by the K on the admission of Rigaud de Asserio to the bprick of Win- chester, and the renunciation by the same Rigaud on the reception of the temporalities of the said see. *Lambeth.* R ii 422 O iii 827. H ii p i 195
April 17.	Writ for the restitution of the said temporalities *Lambeth* R. ii. 422 O iii 828 H ii p i 196
April 17	The K suspends the payment of the tenths due by three cardinals beneficed in England *Lambeth* R ii 423 O iii 829 H. ii p i 196
April 23.	Protection for Reymund cardinal of S Maria Nova, dean of Sarum and archdeacon of Leicester *Westm* R ii. 423 O iii 832 H ii p i 197
April 25.	Safeconduct for James de Conyngham and Reginald de More, two Scotchmen passing through England *Westm* R ii 423 O. iii. 829. H iii p i 196
April 26.	The K. directs the abp of Canterbury to admit no imperial notary public to appear in any cause before him *Westm* R. ii 423 O iii 829 H ii p i 196
April 26.	General proclamation against such notaries and their instruments *Westm.* R ii 423. O. iii. 830 H. ii p i. 196
April 28	The K of England replies to Philip K. of France respecting the claim made by Totto Gudi *Westm.* R. ii. 424. O. iii. 830. H ii p i. 196
April 28.	Commission to Robert de Kendale and Andrew de Bruges to settle the details of the meeting between the K of England and the K of France. *Westm* R ii 424 O iii 830 H ii p i 197.
April 28	Credence for the persons named in the above commission going upon private matters to Philip K. of France *Westm.* R. ii. 424. O. iii. 830. H. ii. p. i. 197.

DATE.	SUBJECT
1320 April 28	The K. asks the pope to appoint John de Wrotham, a friar preacher, as penitentiary in the Roman court *Westm* R ii 424 O iii 831 H. ii, p i. 197
April 28.	The K. recommends the same person to the cardinal of S. Maria in Via Lata. *Westm.* R ii. 424. O iii 832 H. ii p i. 197
May 8	The K of England asks the K of France to interfere in his behalf in the disputes between the mayor and commonalty of Abbeville *Fulmere* R ii. 425. O. iii. 832. H ii p i 197
May 8	The K to Robt de Funes, seneschal of Ponthieu, respecting the said disputes *Fulmere.* R ii 425 O iii 833 H ii p i 197
May 23.	The K appoints his butler, Stephen de Abindon, to provide wine for him on his journey abroad *Odiham* R ii 425 O iii 833 H ii p i 198
May 27.	Bull of pope John appointing Henry de Burghersh to the bprick. of Lincoln *Avignon* R ii 425 O. iii 833 H ii p i 198
June 3	The K appoints John de Weston to provide lodgings for him on his journey abroad *Westm* R ii 426 O iii 835 H ii p i. 198.
June 4	The K. appoints Aymer de Valence earl of Pembroke to be guardian of the realm during his absence *Westm* R ii 426 O iii 835 H ii p i 198
June 5.	Writs for the provision of wines for the K's use during his absence abroad. *Westm* 426 O iii 835 H ii p i 198
June 7.	The K forbids the holding of a tournament at Leicester. *Westm* R ii 426 O. iii 835 H ii p i 198
June 8	Writ to the treasurer and barons of the Exchequer to inquire respecting the lands and liberties belonging to the K *Havering-atte-Boure* R ii 426.
June 11.	Renewal of safeconduct for the K of England going to visit Philip K. of France *Pontoise* R ii 426 O iii 836 H ii p i 198
June 18	The K orders the arrest of all persons who attend tournaments *Dover* R. ii. 427. O iii 836 H ii p i 199
June 18.	Proclamation that no one shall come armed before the K's justices *Dover.* R ii 427 O iii 837 H ii p i 199
June 18	The K orders that no heed is to be given to citations, commissions, &c, derogatory to his royal rights. *Dover* R ii 427 O iii 838 H. ii. p. ii. 3.
June 18.	Writ to the treasurer and barons of the Exchequer against clipped and false money. *Dover* R ii 428
June 19	Memorandum as to various transactions connected with the delivery of the royal seals, and of the departure of the K from Dover R ii 428 O iii. 838. H ii p ii 3
June 25	The K asks the pope to appoint Richard de Ponteftracto, a friar preacher, to the vacant bprick of Dumblane *Westm* R ii 428 O iii 838 H ii p ii 3.
July 22.	The K. notifies his safe arrival at Dover. *Dover* R ii 428. O. iii 839 H. ii. p. ii 4.
July 22.	The K asks the pope to appoint Guy de Valle, canon of Agen and rector of Maidstone, to the bprick of Dol *Dover* R ii 429 O iii 840 H ii p ii 4
July 26.	The K. permits Peter son of John de Greille to sell to Amaneus count of Savoy certain lands in Savoy *Haddele* R ii 429. O iii 840 H. ii. p. ii. 4
Aug. 6.	The K fixes a day for a conference between the English and the Flemings *Westm.* R ii. 429 O iii 841. H ii p ii 4.
Aug 6	Safeconduct for the messengers of R. count of Flanders coming to the said conference *Westm* R. ii 429 O iii 841 H ii p ii 4
Aug. 6.	Writ for the restitution of the lands and tenements on this side and beyond the Trent, belonging to the abp of Rouen *Westm* R. ii 429 O iii 842 H ii p ii 4
Aug 6	Terms upon which the K consents to the creation of a new district ["nova bastida"] at Apantanha, in Aquitain. *Westm* R ii 429 O iii 842. H ii, p ii. 4
Aug. 7.	Ordinances for the custody of certain castles belonging to the K of England in Gascony. *Westm* R. iii 430 O iii 844 H ii p. ii 5
Aug 7	The K of England (at the request of Philip K. of France) grants certain privileges to the men of Amiens. *Westm* R ii 430 O iii 844 H. ii p. ii. 5
Aug. 7.	The K recommends to the pope Wm bp "Munaten," (? Mande "*Minatensis Episcopus,*") sent into England to inquire into the life and miracles of Thomas de Cantilupe, formerly bp. of Hereford *Westm* R ii 431 O iii 845 H ii p ii. 6

DATE.	SUBJECT.
1320. Aug. 7.	The K asks the pope not to press the payment of the debts due by Roland abp. of Armagh, impoverished by the Scotch *Westm.* R ıı 431. O. ııı 844. H. ıı p ıı 6
Aug 8.	The K. orders the payment of the arrears of the pension of A cardinal of Albano. *Westm* R. ıı 431. O. ııı 845 H ıı p ıı. 6
Aug. 9.	The K. recommends Roger de Northburgh, archdeacon of Richmond, to the pope *Stratford-atte-Bogh.* R. ıı. 431. O. ııı 846. H. ıı. p. ıı. 6.
Aug 9.	The K to the cardinal of S Maria ın Aquıro ın favour of the same Roger. *Stratford-atte-Bogh* R ıı 431. O ııı 846 H ıı p ıı 6
Aug. 10.	Pope John recommends the K. to make peace with the Scots. *Avignon.* R. ıı. 432. O ııı. 846 H. ıı. p. ıi. 6.
Aug. 14	The K asks W. count of Holland to do justice to certain English merchants *Langeley.* R ıı 432 O. ııı 847. H ıı p ıı 6
Aug. 18.	Pope John informs the K of the proceedings which have taken place between the envoys of Robert de Brus and himself. *Avignon.* R ıı. 432 O ııı. 848. H. ıı p. ıı. 7.
Aug. 27.	The K asks the pope to appoint Roger de Northburgh to be a cardinal *Odyham* R. ıı. 433 O ııı 849 H ıı p ıı 7
Aug 27.	The K to 27 cardinals on the same subject. *Odyham* R ıı 433. O ııı 850 H ıi p ıi 7.
Aug. 27.	The K of England asks the K. of Cyprus to protect three Friars Preachers going to preach to the Saracens. *Odyham* R ıı 433 O ııı 851. H ıı p ıı 8
Aug 23	The K asks the prayers of the provincial chapter of the Friars Preachers at Staunford *Polhampton* R ıı 433. O ııı 851 H ıı p ıı 8
Sept. 15	Commissioners appointed to treat with the Scotch for a final peace *Clarendon* R. ıı. 434. O ııı. 851. H ıı p ıı 8.
Sept 15.	Mandate to the above-mentioned commissioners to proceed forthwith to Carlisle. *Clarendon.* R ıı 434
Oct. 5.	The K of England informs Philip K of France of his proceedings towards obtaining a final peace with Robert de Brus *Shene* R ıı 435 O ııı 853. H ıı p ıı 9
[Oct 5]	Credence for the bp of Hereford and others who will inform Philip K of France what the K. is doing ın regard to a peace with Scotland R ıı. 435. O ııı 853 H. ıı p ıı. 9.
Oct. 7.	The K complains to the pope of the invasion of his Royal rights ın regard to his free chapel at Boseham *Westm* R ıı 435 O ııı. 154 H ıı p ıı 9.
Oct 7.	The K to the cardinal of S Maria ın Aquıro, on the same subject. *Westm.* R. ıı 435. O. ııı. 855 H. ıı. p ıı 9.
Oct. 7.	The K. to the cardinal of S Cırıac ın Thermıs, to the same effect. *Westm.* R. ıı 436 O ııı. 855. H ıı p ıi 10
Oct. 7.	The K to the cardinal of SS Marcellınus and Petrus, to the same effect *Westm.* R ıı. 436 O ııı. 856 H. ıi. p ıı. 10.
Oct 7.	The K. to the cardinal of S. Maria ın Vıa Lata, to the same effect R. ıı. 436. O. ııı 856. H ıı p ıı 10.
Oct. 8.	Proclamation to be made at various places that a truce is concluded between the English and the Bretons *Westm.* R ıı 436 O. ııı 856. H. ıı p ıı 10.
Oct. 11.	The K. to Philp K of France upon the claims of Anthony [Pessaigne] of Genoa and Totto Guidı *Westm* R ıı 436 O ııı 857 H ıı p ıı 10.
Oct. 13.	Settlement of all disputes between the K of England's council and the nuncıos of Robert earl of Flanders R ıı 434. O. ııı 852 H ıı p ıı 8.
Oct. 14.	The K to Philp K of France on the claims of Anthony Pessaıgne of Genoa and Totto Guidı. *Westm.* R. ıı. 436 O ııı 857 H ıı p. ıı. 10
Oct. 24.	Safe conduct for Johanna, widow of Alexander Comyn, going to Scotland *Westm* R ıı 437. O. ııı 857 H. ıí p. ıí 10.
Nov. 1	The K authorizes the levy of the money yet due to the Scotch, who would have burnt the town of Rıpon had not ıt been redeemed by the payment of 1,000 marks. *Westm.* R. ıí. 437. O. ııı. 858. H. ıí. p. ıı. 11.
Nov. 9.	The K asks the pope for a dispensation for the marriage of the K's son Edward with Margaret, daughter of the count of Holland. *Westm* R ıı 437 O ııı. 859. H ıı. p ıı 11.
Nov. 10.	The K. informs the two cardinals who had been plundered that he cannot punish the robbers because he does not know their names, nor recover the plunder, because he does not know where ıt ıs to be found *Westm.* R ıı. 437 O. ııı 859 H ıı. p. ıı. 11.

O

DATE	SUBJECT.
1320 Nov. 11	The K to the pope upon the intended treaty of peace with Robert de Brus. *Westm.* R ii 438. O iii 860. H. ii. p ii 11.
Nov. 16.	The K orders the payment of the arrears of the pensions to Peter d'Oze, the brother, and the nephews of the pope *Westm* R ii 438. O iii 860 H. ii p ii 16
Nov 16.	The K. to Peter de Osa the pope's brother, Peter de Via and Arnald de Trian, his nephews, respecting the above pensions. *Westm* R ii 438. O ii 861. H. ii. p ii 12
Nov 17.	Safe conduct for certain persons coming from Scotland to treat about peace. *Westm* R ii 438 O iii 861. H ii p ii 12
Nov. 17.	The K authorizes certain persons to receive the Scots to the K's peace. *Westm.* R. ii. 438. O. iii 862 H. ii p ii 12
Nov 18.	The K to the cardinal of S Maria in Via Lata, upon a question respecting a prebend in Salisbury cathedral *Westm.* . R ii 439 O iii 863. H. ii p ii 12
Nov. 20.	The K authorizes the collection of alms for the shrine and church of S Thomas of Hereford. *Westm* R ii 439 O. iii. 863 H ii p. ii. 13.
Nov. 24.	The K asks the duke of Brittany to forward a treaty of concord between their subjects. *Westm* R. ii 440 O iii 864 H ii p ii 13
Dec 11.	The K appoints commissioners to pardon forfeitures incurred by the Scotch *Windsor.* R ii 440 O. iii. 864. H. ii. p ii 13.
Dec 12	The K asks the pope to help the society of the Bardi of Florence against the knights of the Hospital of Jerusalem *Windsor* R ii 440 O iii 865 H ii p ii 13.
Dec. 13.	The K summons all persons who hold processes against the Flemings to come with the same to Westminster *Windsor.* R. ii 440.
1321 Jan 12	Safe conduct for John de Pilmor, monk of Coupre, coming from Robert de Brus to the K *Yeshampstede* R ii 440 O iii 865. H. ii p ii 13.
Jan. 13.	Protection of Robert de Compton going to Berwick on the affairs of the countess of Fife *Yeshampstede* R ii 441. O iii 866 H ii p ii 14.
Jan 14.	The K orders that no associations or meetings shall be held within the city of London. *Windsor.* R ii 441 O iii 866 H. ii. p. ii, 14.
Jan. 19.	Commission to W abp of York and others to treat for a peace with Robert de Brus. *Westm* R ii 441 O. ii 866 H ii p ii. 14
Jan 24	Safe conduct for a messenger coming from Philip K of France into Scotland. *Westm.* R ii 441 O iii. 867. H ii. p. ii 44
Jan. 25.	The K orders that victuals shall be sold for a reasonable price within the city of London notwithstanding the proclamation of the King's justices *Westm* R ii 442
Jan 30	The K forbids Humfry de Bohun earl of Hereford, and 28 others of the nobility, to collect assemblies of men *Westm* R ii 442. O iii. 867. H ii p ii. 14
Feb. 11	Safe-conduct for the messengers of Philip K of France going to the north. *Haveryngatte-Boure* R ii 442 O iii 868 H ii p ii. 14
Feb. 16.	Safe-conduct for a messenger from the pope going to the north *Westm* R. ii. 442 O iii 869. H. ii. p ii 15
Feb. 20.	Proclamation respecting the settlement of disputes between the English and the Bretons *Westm* R ii. 443 O iii 869 H ii p ii. 15
Feb. 24.	The K asks the pope to sanction the translation of Thomas formerly bp of Hereford. *Westm* R ii 443 O iii 870 H ii. p ii. 15.
March 1.	The K asks the pope to permit Robert Hereward archdeacon of Taunton to study the civil law *Westm.* R ii 443 O iii 870 H ii p ii 15.
March 2.	The K orders that the measures throughout the realm shall be of one uniform capacity according to "Magna Carta *Shene.* R ii 443
March 4	The K. asks the pope to deal yet more severely with Robert de Brus. *Westm.* R. ii. 443. O. iii 870. H ii p ii. 15.
March 4.	The K to Andrew Sapeti, to the same effect. *Westm.* R. ii 443. O. iii. 871 H. ii. p ii 16
March 7.	The K. asks the prayers of the general chapter of the Friars Preachers at Florence. *Fulmere.* R ii 444. O. iii. 872 H ii p ii. 16
March 10.	The K asks the pope to excuse the delay of Louis de Beaumont bp of Durham in paying his debts on account of the scottish incursions. *Windsor* R. ii 444 O. iii 872 H. ii p ii 16
March 12	The K. to three cardinals on the same subject. *Henle.* R. ii 445. O. iii 873. H. ii p ii 16.

DATE	SUBJECT
1321 March 12	The K of England to the K of Jerusalem, to the same effect *Henle* R. ıı 445 O ııı 873 H ıı p ıı 17.
March 27	The K forbids the holding of meetings at Usk and Tregruok and elsewhere in Wales, whereby the peace is endangered *Gloucester*. R. ıı 445
March 28	The K summons John de Hastynges and seven others to meet at Gloucester to suppress the said meetings *Gloucester* R ıı 445
March 28	Credence for a messenger going from the K. of England to Peter K of Aragon *Gloucester*. R ıı. 446 O ııı 874. H. ıı p ıı 17
March 28.	The K asks the pope for a dispensation for a marriage between Aymer de Valence earl of Pembroke and Mary daughter of the countess of S Paul *Gloucester* R ıı. 446 O. ııı 874 H ıı p ıı 17
March 28.	The K. to the cardinal of S Prisca, to the same effect. *Gloucester*. R, ıı. 446. O ııı 875. H ıı. p. ıı 17.
March 30.	The K asks W count of Holland whether he has obtained the dispensation for which he applied to the pope *Gloucester* R. ıı 446 O ııı. 875 H ıı p ıı 17
March 30.	The K asks Clementina Q of France to interfere for the liberation of Matilla princess of Achaia, carried off by John, brother of the K. of Sicily. *Gloucester*. R ıı 446 O ııı 876. H ıı. p. ıı 17.
March 30.	The K of England to R King of Sicily, to the same purport *Gloucester* R. ıı. 447. O ııı. 876. H ıı p ıı 17
March 30	The K. to the pope, to the same purport. *Gloucester*. R, ıı 447 O ııı 876 H ıı p ıı 17
March 30	The K renews his complaints to the pope respecting the collegiate church of Boseham *Gloucester* R. ıı 447. O ııı 877 H ıı p ıı 18
March 30.	The K complains to the pope of the misconduct of Reimund bp of Condom *Gloucester* R ıı 447. O. ıı 877. H ıı. p ıı 18.
April 21.	The K directs Thomas de Berkeleye and 70 others to arrest those who disturb the peace and spread false reports *Bristol* R. ıı 447 O ııı 878 H ıı p ıı 18
April 21	The K. asks the bps. to punish the said persons by ecclesiastical censures *Bristol* R ıı 447 O ııı. 879 H ıı p ıı 18.
April 26.	Proclamation that no knight or man-at-arms leave the realm *Devises* R ıı 447
May 3	The K orders the bailiffs of Ravenesrodde to liberate a certain Scottish ship which they had arrested *Wallingford* R. ıı 448. O. ıı. 879. H ıı. p. ıı 18
May 4	The K. of England to Philip K of France respecting the arrest of certain French ships by the English during the truce with Scotland. *Wallingford* R ıı 448 O. ııı 880 H ıı p ıı. 19
May 12	The K sanctions the sale of a house called the Earl's Hall at Condom', which had become a place of resort for improper women *Westm* R ıı 449 O ııı 880 H ıı p ıı 19
May 12	The K., to satisfy the pope's conscience, informs him of certain particulars affecting the church of Ufford, dioc Lincoln. *Westm* R ıı 449 O ııı 882. H ıı p. ıı 20
May 12	The K to Raymund, cardinal of S Maria, in Cosmedyn, respecting the said church of Ufford *Westm.* R. ıı. 449 O. ııı. 882. H. ıı p. ıı. 20
May 14	The K recommends Bertrand Bonifacii to the pope for the services rendered by him in the treaty with Scotland *Westm* R. ıı. 450. O. ıı 883. H ıı p ıı 20
May 14	The K to four cardinals, to the same effect. *Westm.* R ıı 450 O. ııı 883. H. ıı. p ıı. 20.
May 14	The K recommends bishop "G Munaten," [? Mimaten' *Mande*] to the pope for his services in same treaty. *Westm* R ıı. 450. O ııı. 883 H ıı p. ıı. 20.
May 14.	The K to certain cardinals and others, commending the services of the said bp in the inquiry respecting the life and miracles of Thomas bp. of Hereford. *Westm.* R ıı. 450. O. ııı 883 H. ıı p. h 20.
May 14.	The K explains to the pope why certain papal letters had not been presented to Robert de Brus *Westm.* R ıı. 450 O ııı 884 H. ıı. p. ıı 20.
May 21.	The K orders that the custody and mayoralty of the city of London be redelivered to Hamo de Chiggewelle, citizen of London *Westm.* R. ıı 451. O ııı. 885 H ıı p ıı 21
May 24.	Protection for the servants of Maria countess of Fife coming from Scotland to London. *Westm* R. ıı. 451 O. ııı 885. H. ıı. p. ıı. 21.

DATE	SUBJECT
1321 May 24	The K orders his seneschal of Gascony to endeavour to procure the extension of the truce between the English and the Bretons *Westm*. R ii 451. O. iii. 885. H. ii. p. ii 21.
May 29	The K orders that the town and castle of Bristol be safely watched. *Westm* R ii. 451
June 27	The K asks the pope to confirm the appropriation of the church of Stampford Magna with the chapel of Hampstede to Battle Abbey. *Westm* R. ii. 451.
July 4	The K notifies that he will maintain his rights in the prebend of Aylesbury in the cathedral of Lincoln *Westm* R ii 452. O iii 886 H ii p ii 21
July 4	The K orders that the city of Canterbury be carefully guarded. *Westm* R ii. 452
July 5	The K sanctions the foundation of various houses for teaching theology and logic in the university of Cambridge *Westm* R ii 452 O iii 817 H ii p ii 21
July 24	The K asks the pope to appoint Roger de Northburgh archdeacon of Richmond to the cardinalate *Westm.* R. ii. 452 O iii 887. H ii p. ii. 22
July 26	The K asks the prayers of the provincial chapter of the Friars Preachers at Pomfret for himself, his Queen, and his children *Westm* R ii 453
Aug 9	The K. asks 28 cardinals to aid the promotion of Roger de Northburgh to the cardinalate *Westm* R ii 453 O. iii. 887. H. ii p ii. 22.
Aug 9	The K of England to the K of Sicily, to the same effect *Westm* R ii 453 O iii 889 H ii p ii 22
Aug 12	The K orders that the manor of Kilham, co York, be delivered to the abp and dean and chapter of Rouen *Westm* R ii 453. O. iii. 889. H ii p. ii. 22.
Aug 20.	The K confirms the ancient privileges enjoyed by the inhabitants of S Omer in trading with England *Westm* R ii 454 O iii 890 H ii p ii 22
Aug 20.	The K. pardons Bartholomew de Badelsmere certain pains and forfeitures which he had incurred. *Westm* R. ii. 454. O. iii 890. H ii p ii 23
Aug. 20.	The K undertakes that no one shall be called in question for what may have been done in prosecuting Hugh le Despenser, the father and the son *Westm* R ii. 454 O iii 891. H ii p ii 23
Aug 25	The K. explains to the pope how he has been prevented from treating with the Scotch. *Westm* R. ii. 454. O iii 891 H ii p ii 23.
Aug. 25.	The K asks the cardinals and others to induce the pope to punish the Scotch *Westm*. R ii 455. O. iii 892 H ii p ii 23.
Aug. 25.	The K orders the destruction of the castle of Herbotel according to the treaty with the Scots *Westm* R ii 455 O iii 893 H ii p ii 24
Aug 25	The K. orders various persons to assist in the destruction of the said castle. *Westm* R ii 455 O iii. 893 H ii p ii 24
Aug. 25.	The K of England complains to Philip K of France of the capture, by his subjects, of a ship called Dromond from Genoa to England, freighted for the English market *Westm*. R ii 455 O iii. 894 H ii p ii. 24
*Aug 29	Commission for the settlement of disputes between the men of the Cinque Ports and those of Pool, Weymouth, Melcombe, Lynn, and Southampton. *Westm*. R. ii. 456
Aug 31.	Agreement for the settlement of disputes between the mariners and men of England and Brittany R ii 456.
Sept 8	The K. orders that the manors of Leyham, Wykes, Kereseye, Lammersh, and Dachet which had belonged to Hugh le Despenser the younger, shall be delivered to Gilbert de Eborum *Sandwich*. R ii 456
Sept 26.	The K asks the pope to protect the cathedral of Enachdun from the aggressions of Malachias abp of Tuam *Westm* R. ii. 457. O iii 895 H. ii p ii 25
Oct. 1.	The orders that those who circulate false reports shall be punished *London*. R. ii. 457' O iii 896 H ii p ii 25
Oct 8	The K. asks the pope to permit Robert de Duffield, the K's confessor, to converse while at table, although forbidden to do so by his rule, he being a Friar Preacher. *Porchester*. R. ii 457. O. iii 896 H ii p ii 25.
Oct. 16.	Summons to the men of Essex, Hampshire, Surrey, and Sussex to assemble before Ledes Castle, in co Kent, to which entrance had been refused to Q Isabella *Tower of London*. R ii 457. O iii. 897. H ii p ii 25.
Oct 16.	Proclamation as to the causes which induce the K. to lay siege to Ledes Castle in co. Kent *Tower of London*. R ii. 458. O. iii. 898 H. ii. p. ii. 26.

DATE	SUBJECT.
1321 Oct 16.	The K orders the men of Kent to assist in the seige of Ledes Castle　*Tower of London.* R ii. 458　O. iii 898　H ii. p ii 26.
Oct 18	The K orders that the fortifications of Shrewsbury be strengthened　*Tower of London* R. ii 458.
Oct 25	The K. permits the citizens of London to elect one of their number to govern the city. *Tower of London*　R. ii 458
Nov 11	The K orders that Warwick Castle, held against him, be beseiged　*Westm*　R ii 459 O iii. 899　H ii p ii 26
Nov. 12.	The K forbids Thomas earl of Lancaster to hold the meeting which he had summoned at Doncaster　*Westm.*　R. ii. 459　O. iii 899　H. ii p. ii 26
Nov 12	The K forbids Humfrey de Bohun and 106 others to attend the said meeting　*Westm* R. ii 459　O iii 900　H ii p ii 26
Nov 15	The K. commands the sheriffs of London and all others throughout England to see that the peace is kept.　*Westm.*　R. ii. 460.　O iii. 901.　H ii. p ii 27
Nov 18	The K orders the sheriffs to arrest those who spread false reports　*Rumford*　R. ii 460 O iii 902　H ii p ii. 26
Nov 25.	Safe conduct for the servants of Mary countess of Fife coming to London and returning into Scotland.　R ii 460.　O iii 902.　H ii p 27.
Nov. 26.	The K asks the pope not to interfere with his liberties in the matter of the prebend of Aylesbury.　*Ilford.*　R. ii. 460　O iii 902　H ii p ii 27
Nov 26	The K to three cardinals, to the same effect　*Ilford*　R. ii. 461.　O. iii. 903.　H ii. p ii. 28
Nov. 28.	The K orders the personal attendance at Cirencester of Roger de Mortimer of Chirk, justiciary of Wales.　*Pountefreit-on-Thames.*　R ii 461　O iii 904　H ii p ii 28
Nov 30	Credence for certain messengers going from the K to the bps. of the province of Canter- bury assembled in a provincial council at London.　*Pountfreyt on-Thames*　R. ii. 461
Nov 30.	The K. orders that no suspected persons shall enter London while the provincial council is sitting there　*Pountfreyt-on-Thames*　R. ii. 461.　O iii 904　H ii p ii 28
Nov 30.	Proclamation throughout England for keeping the peace　*Pountfreyt-on-Thames* R ii. 461.　O iii 904　H. ii p. ii. 28.
Nov 30.	Summons for all knights, esquires with horses and arms to meet the K at Cirencester· *Pountfreyt-on-Thames*　R. ii 462
Nov 30.	The K makes arrangements for the suppression of an apprehended insurrection　*Pount- freyt-on Thames*　R ii 462　O. iii 904　H. ii. p. ii. 28
Nov 30.	The K. asks the pope to appoint Robert de Baldok to the bprick of Lichfield.　*Pountfreyt- on-Thames*　R. ii. 462　O iii 905　H ii p ii 29
Dec 3.	The K. authorizes his justiciary of Ireland to remove inefficient officers and substitute others in their stead　*Istelworth*　R ii 462.
Dec. 6.	Proclamation that the truce with Brittany is prolonged　*Westm*　R ii 463.　O iii 907 H. ii p. ii. 19
Dec 6	Safe conduct granted by James lord of Douglas to Richard de Topclif to come to Jedburgh. *Etlebredehelys.*　R ii 463　O iii. 907.　H ii p ii 29
Dec. 8.	The K. orders that Hugh le Despenser the younger and Hugh le Despenser the elder be not injured nor molested　*Westm.*　R ii 463.　O iii 907　H ii. p ii. 29
Dec. 8	Credence for various persons going from the K to the pope.　*Westm.*　R. ii 463 O. iii 908.　H ii p ii. 30
Dec. 8.	Credence for the same persons, who will explain to the pope the troubles to which the K is subjected.　*Westm.*　R. ii 464.　O iii 909　H ii p ii 30.
Dec. 8.	Credence for the same persons, who will explain to the pope the disqualifications of Henry de Burghersh lately appointed bp of Lincoln　*Westm.*　R ii 464　O iii 909　H ii p ii. 30.
Dec. 11.	The K. to the bp of Sabina and 32 cardinals and others in favour of the above messengers. *Reading.*　R. ii. 464.　O iii 910　H ii p ii 30
Dec. 12	The K of England asks Philip K of France to protect his rights in the city of Condom from the aggressions of the bp　*Reading*　R ii 465　O. iii 911　H ii p ii. 31
Dec. 12.	The K to the count of Boulogne and three others to the same effect　*Reading.* R. ii. 465.　O. iii. 912.　H ii p. ii 31.

DATE	SUBJECT
1321. Dec 12	The K. to the pope, against the said bp *Reading*. R. ii. 465 O iii. 912 H ii. p ii 31
Dec 12	The K to the cardinal of S Maria in Porticu, to the same effect *Reading* R. ii 465. O iii 913 H ii p ii. 32.
Dec. 12	The K recommends the above messengers to the special consideration of the pope. *Reading* R. ii 466. O. iii. 913 H ii. p. ii. 32.
Dec 12	The K begs the pope to respect the liberties of the crown in the matter of the prebend of Leighton Buzzard *Reading* R ii 466 O iii 914 H ii p ii. 32.
Dec 12.	The K. to three cardinals, to the same effect. *Reading.* R ii 466. O iii 915. H. ii. p ii. 32.
Dec 12	The K orders that every man shall have arms in his house, for the preservation of the peace, according to the statute of Winton *Shrewsbury.* R ii 466
Dec 13	The K insists upon the preservation of his rights in the matter of the church of Crunda, dioc. Winton. *Newbury.* R. ii. 467. O. iii. 915. H. ii. p ii. 32.
Dec. 17.	The K asks a subsidy from the citizens of Aquitain and others, to be employed in the Scottish war *Okebourn* R ii 467. O iii 916 H ii p ii 33
Dec 20	The K asks Andrew Sapiti to proceed in the matter of the bp. of Condom *Cyrencester.* R. ii 468. O iii 917 H ii p ii 33
Dec 22.	The K asks the pope to promote Robert de Baldok archdeacon of Middlesex to the bprick of Lichfield *Cirencester* R ii 468 O iii 918. H ii p ii 33
Dec 24	The K. to the pope, in vindication of his rights in the prebend of Aylesbury. *Cirencester* R ii 468 O iii 918 H ii p. ii 33
Dec 24.	The K to 6 cardinals in favor of Robert de Baldok *Cirencester* R ii 469 O. iii 919 H ii p ii 34.
Dec 26.	The K. orders all sheriffs throughout England to arrest Bartholomew de Badelesmere. *Cirencester.* R ii 469
1322 Jan. 4	The K thanks the pope for having appointed Roger de Northburgh archdeacon to the see of Lichfield, and complains of the cardinal of S Lucia in Silice. *Worcester* R ii 469. O iii. 920. H ii p ii 34
Jan 4.	The K to the cardinals, in favour of Roger de Northburgh *Worcester* R ii, 469 O iii 921 H ii p ii 35
Jan 4.	The K. of England assures the K. of Sicily that Vannus Fortigair is not of the party of the Ghibellines. *Worcester* R ii 470 O iii. 921. H ii p. ii. 35.
Jan 4	The K to the pope in favour of Vannus Fortigair *Worcester*. R ii. 470. O. iii 922 H ii p ii 35
Jan. 4	The K to the cardinal of S. Prisca and Andrew Sapiti, on the same subject. *Worcester* R. ii 470 O iii. 922. H ii p ii 35
Jan 4	The K. asks to be informed by the bps whether they consent to the decision of the abp. and bps in the provincial council at London respecting Hugh le Despencer, the father and the son *Worcester* R ii 470.
Jan. 4.	The K recommends R. bp of Worcester to the pope. *Worcester.* R. ii. 471. O. in 922. H ii p ii 35
Jan 4.	The K of England to Philip K of France, to the same purport. *Worcester.* R ii. 471. O iii 923 H ii p. ii 35.
Jan 4	The K. to Charles count of Valois, to the same purport. *Worcester.* R ii. 471. O iii 923 H. ii p ii. 35
Jan. 9	Safe conduct for Hugh le Despenser the younger. *Doderhulle.* R. ii. 471.
Jan. 15.	The K orders the arrest of the persons who had burnt the town of Bridgenorth. *Shrews-bury* R ii 471. O. iii 923 H ii p ii. 35
Jan 15.	Proclamation for the keeping of the peace and for praying for the K. *Shrewsbury.* R ii 471.
Jan 15.	Safe conduct granted by Thomas Randolf earl of Murray to Richard chaplain of Topclif, to come to the said earl *Corbridge* R ii 472 O iii 924 H ii. p. ii. 36
Jan. 17	Safe conduct for Roger de Mortimer of Wigmore coming to confer with the earls of Richmond, Pembroke, Arundel, and Warren *Shrewsbury* R. ii. 472.
Jan. 20.	The K. forbids suspected persons from entering the town of Oxford. *Shrewsbury.* R ii 472.

DATE	SUBJECT.
1322. Feb. 8.	The K orders that no one shall associate himself with Edmund earl of Kent and his adherents. *Gloucester.* R ii 472 O. iii 924. H ii p ii 36
Feb. 8.	The K regrants to the citizens of London the office of the mayoralty of their city *Gloucester* R ii. 472 O iii. 925 H. ii. p ii 36
Feb. 9.	Authority from the K. to Andrew de Hartela to treat with the Scots for peace or truce. *Gloucester,* R. ii 473. O. iii. 925. H. ii p ii 36
Feb. 11.	The K orders the arrest and imprisonment of all persons who oppose him. *Gloucester.* R ii 473.
Feb. 16.	Safe conduct granted by Thomas Randolf, lieutenant of Scotland, to John de Monbray and Thomas de Cifford, to treat with him in Scotland, with copies of two letters by James de Douglas *Caveris* R ii 474. O iii. 926. H ii. p ii. 36.
Feb. 16	The K going to raise the seige of the castle of Tykhulle, asks a subsidy from 128 clergy *Gloucester.* R. ii. 474 O iii 927. H. ii p ii 37.
Feb. 16.	The K of England asks the K. of France and certain of his nobles to aid him against Thomas earl of Lancaster and his adherents. *Gloucester* R ii. 475. O iii 929. H. ii p. ii 38.
Feb. 17.	Charles K. of France complains to the K. of England of injuries inflicted at Southampton upon merchants of Amiens *Paris* R. ii 475.
Feb. 18.	The K. asks the people of Aquitan to forward with all speed the aid which they have granted him for his Scottish war. *Gloucester.* R. ii. 475. O iii. 930. H. ii p. ii. 38.
Feb. 19.	The K of England asks the K. of France to permit the men-at-arms coming to him from Aquitan to pass through France. *Chiltenham* R ii 475. O iii 930. H ii p ii 38.
Feb. 25.	The K informs the pope of the rebellion of his nobles, of the invasion of England by the Scotch, &c. *Weston-under-Edge.* R ii 476. O. iii. 930. H. ii. p. ii. 38.
Feb 25.	The K. to 12 cardinals and others, on the same subject *Weston-under-Edge.* R ii 476 O iii 932 H ii p ii. 39.
Feb. 28.	The K. thanks the pope for having promoted Roger de Northburgh to the see of Lichfield. *Coventry* R. ii. 476 O iii. 933. H. ii p ii. 39.
March 3.	The K asks the prayers for himself and his family of the General Chapter of the Friars Preachers about to meet at Vienna *The Abbey of Miraval* R ii. 477 O iii 933 H ii p ii 39
March 11.	The K. orders the arrest of Thomas earl of Lancaster and 10 other nobles for rebellion. *Tuttebury.* R. ii. 477. O iii. 933 H. ii. p ii 39.
March 18.	The K informs the pope of the defeat of the above-mentioned rebels *Doncaster* R. ii 477. O. iii 934 H ii p ii 40
March 18	Credence for Robert de Wirksop going from the K. to 6 cardinals. *Doncaster.* R ii. 477. O iii 935 H. ii. p. ii. 40.
March 19.	Credence for the same Robert going to the pope on the matter of the prebend of Aylesbury. *Pomfret.* R ii 478 O iii. 935 H ii. p ii 40.
March 20	Credence for the same, going to the pope on the matter of the prebend of Leighton Buzzard *Pomfret.* R ii. 478. O. iii 935. H. ii. p ii 40.
March 20.	Credence for the same, going to three cardinals. *Pomfret* R. ii. 478. O. iii. 936 H. ii p ii 40
March 22.	The K orders the ports to be guarded, to prevent the escape of rebels. *Pomfret.* R. ii 478 O iii 936 H ii. p ii. 40.
March 23.	The K grants to Aymer de Valence earl of Pembroke the New Temple of London, late the property of Thomas earl of Lancaster. R. ii 480 O iii 940 H ii. p ii 42
March 23.	The K grants to John de Britannia earl of Richmond certain vills and tenements late the property of Roger de Clifford and others. R. ii. 480. O iii. 940 H ii. p. ii 42.
March 24.	The K. grants to various persons the custody of various castles, lands, and tenements, late the property of Thomas earl of Lancaster and others *Pomfret.* R. ii 480. O iii 941 H. ii. p. ii. 42
March 25	The K. creates Andrew de Hartela earl of Carlisle for his good service against Thomas earl of Lancaster. *Pomfret* R ii 481. O. iii. 943. H ii p ii. 43.
March 25.	The K informs the pope of his success over the rebels, and asks him to proceed with increased severity against the Scotch who have invaded England *Pomfret.* R. ii 481. O iii 944 H ii p ii 43.
March 26.	The K. orders the men of Cornwall (who had neglected to send their contingent to serve against Thomas earl of Lancaster) to supply the requisite number to march against the Scotch. *Pomfret.* R. ii. 482. O. iii. 945. H ii. p. ii 44.

DATE	SUBJECT
1322. March 29.	Process before the K. against Thomas earl of Lancaster and his adherents at Pomfret *York* R ii. 478. O iii. 936. H. ii. p. ii 40.
April 2.	The K asks aid against the Scots from the people of Aquitain. *Altoftes.* R. ii 482. O iii. 945 H. ii. p ii 44
April 2.	The K. asks the people of Aquitain to supply him with troops to serve against the Scots. *Pomfret.* R ii 482. O. iii. 946. H. ii. p. ii. 45.
April 6	The K appoints Reymond de Mille Sanctis to be captain of the above-mentioned troops from Aquitain. *Altoftes* R ii. 482 O iii. 946. H ii p. ii. 44.
April 12.	The K informs R count of Flanders that he is willing to renew the treaty of commercial intercourse between their subjects. *Pomfret* R ii 483 O iii 947 H ii. p ii 45
April 13	The K asks the pope to facilitate the consecration of Roger de Northburgh as bp. of Lichfield *Pomfret.* R ii 483 O iii 948 H. ii p ii 45.
April 13.	The K to 7 cardinals on the same subject. *Pomfret* R ii 483 O. iii. 948. H. ii. p ii 45.
April 14.	The K of England informs the K of Aragon that he will gladly enter into a treaty with him *Pomfret.* R ii 483 O. iii 948 R. ii p. ii. 45.
April 14	The K asks the K. of France to correct the injuries inflicted upon the English in Aquitain. *Pomfret* R ii 483. O iii. 949. H ii p ii 45
April 14	The K to the count of Valois on the same subject. *Pomfret.* R. ii 484 O iii 949. H ii p. ii 45.
April 18.	The K orders that 24 men from N Wales and as many from S. Wales shall be present at the parliament at York *Rothewelle.* R ii 484
April 20	The K directs the men of Great Yarmouth and of the Cinque Ports to be ready to check the insolence of the Flemings and other enemies. *Rothewelle* R ii. 484. O iii 949. H ii p. ii 45.
May 5.	Pope John orders the excommunication of those persons who disturb the K's peace. *Avignon* R ii. 484. O. iii 950 H ii p i 46.
May 5.	Pope John absolves from their oaths those persons who have conspired against Hugh le Despenser the father and Hugh le Despenser the son. *Avignon.* R. ii. 484. O. iii. 950. H. ii. p. ii. 46.
May 6.	The K informs the count of Flanders that he is ready to renew a treaty of peace between their subjects *York* R ii 485 O iii 251 H ii p ii 46
May 7.	The K tells the men of the Cinque Ports that he is waiting for an answer from the count of Flanders, of the import of which he will inform them. *York.* R ii 485. O iii. 951. H. ii. p ii 46
May 11.	The K informs the abp of Canterbury and 16 bps that he has postponed the summons for military service at Newcastle-upon-Tyne *York.* R ii. 485 O iii 952 H ii. p ii 46
May 11.	Similar intimation to Edward earl of Chester and 84 other nobles. *York* R ii. 485. O iii 952 H ii p ii 47
May 11.	The K orders the proclamation of the same notice to be made throughout England. *York.* R. ii 486 O iii 954. H. ii. p. ii. 47.
May 15.	The K to the nobles of Gascony on the said prorogation, and on the supply of provisions for the said expedition against Scotland *York.* R ii 486 O iii 954 H ii p ii 47
May 18.	Commission to inquire into an assault by the mayor and bailiffs of Cambridge upon the masters and scholars of the university *York.* R ii 487
May 20	The K appoints Robert de Leyburn to be admiral of the fleet on the west coast of Scotland, with power to receive the Scots to the K.'s peace *York* R ii. 487. O iii. 955. H ii p ii 48
May 23	Pope John grants to the brethren of the hospital of S John of Jerusalem the lands and possessions lately belonging to the Templars in England *Avignon* R. ii 487. O iii. 956. H. ii. p ii 48
June 4.	The K of England complains to the K. of France of the attacks made upon his subjects in Aquitain *Rothewell* R ii. 488. O. iii. 959. H. ii. p. ii. 49.
June 6.	The K orders that the goods and merchandize of the subjects of John duke of Brabant shall not be arrested *Rothewell* R ii 489.
June 13	The K appoints wardens of the Eastern and Western Borders towards Scotland, and orders them to repulse the Scotch who have invaded the realm. *Hathelsaye.* R. ii. 489. O. iii 959. H ii p ii. 49.

DATE.	SUBJECT.
1322 June 20.	The K. of England complains to the K of France of the conduct of his officers who have introduced new usages into the isle of Oleron *York* R ii 489. O iii 960. H. ii. p. ii 50.
July 2.	The K orders Andrew de Harcla to levy soldiers from Cumberland, Westmorland, and Lancashire for the repulsion of the Scots. *York* R ii 489 O iii 960 H ii p ii 50
July 2	The K. appoints Henry de Beaumont to protect the ports of England, which have been invaded by the Scotch. *York* R ii 489 O iii 961 H ii p ii 50
July 3.	The K. orders that the cattle of the northern counties of England shall be driven into Yorkshire for fear of the Scotch *York* R ii 489 O iii 962 H ii p ii 50
July 4	The K grants to farm to various persons the lands and tenements in 33 counties which had belonged to his enemies and rebels *York.* R ii 490 O iii 962 H ii p ii 50.
July 9.	The K. grants to his niece Eleanor, wife of Hugh le Despenser the younger, the lands which had belonged to John de Moubray and Bartholomew de Badelesmere, rebels R ii 491 O iii 964 H ii p ii 51
July 13.	The K orders that the clergy and others who do not personally serve in the army against Scotland shall pay fines for the same. *York* R ii 491
July 22.	Certificate that the contingent of troops sent by the bp of Durham to serve against Scotland shall not prejudice the liberties of the see *York.* R ii 491 O iii 964. H. ii p ii 51.
Aug. 3.	The K. informs the pope that he has suppressed the rebellion, and complains of the way in which he has been treated in regard to the prebends of Aylesbury and Leighton Buzzard *Newcastle-upon-Tyne.* R. ii 491 O iii. 965. H. ii. p. ii. 51
Aug 4.	The K to 9 cardinals, with the same complaints *Newcastle-upon-Tyne* R ii 492 O iii 966 H ii p ii 52
Aug. 4.	The K. asks the pope to increase the severity of the sentences against the Scotch *Newcastle-upon-Tyne.* R ii 492. O iii 967 H ii p ii 52.
Aug. 7	The K. to the seneschal of Gascony relative to the gift of 1,000 marks sterling made by the K to cardinal Gaucelin Johannis *Gosford* R ii 492 O iii 967 H ii p ii 52
Aug. 8.	The K notifies that Thomas earl of Lancaster was beheaded at Pomfret on Monday 22 March for high treason, and that the advowson of the church of Bradeford has come into the K.'s hands by forfeiture *Felton.* R. ii 493. O iii 968 H ii p ii. 53.
Aug 8	The K asks the cardinal of S Lucia in Silice to abandon his claim upon the prebend of Aylesbury. *Gosford* R ii 493 O. iii 968 H ii p ii 53.
Aug 8.	The K. to 26 cardinals, upon the unjust claims made to the prebends of Aylesbury and Leighton Buzzard *Gosford* R ii 493 O iii 969 H ii p ii 53
Aug 8.	The K asks the cardinals to excuse his delay in the payment of the yearly tribute of 1,000 marks, and to desist from claims prejudicial to his rights *Newcastle-upon-Tyne* R ii 494. O iii 971 H. ii p ii 54.
Aug. 8.	The K. grants annual pensions to the brother and two nephews of the pope, and asks them to procure the cessation of the annoyances to which he has been subjected in the papal court *Gosford* R ii 494 O iii 971 H ii p ii 54
Aug 12	The K cites John Luterel, late chancellor of the University of Oxford, and the master and scholars of the same, to inform him respecting the discords which have arisen between them. *Felton.* R. ii. 494
Aug 16	Pope John informs the K that he has conferred the archdeaconry of Richmond upon Helias Talairandi. *Avignon* R. ii 495 O iii 972. H ii p ii 54
Sept. 2.	The K. thanks the pope for having promoted Rog de Northburgh to the see of Lichfield. *Newcastle-on-Tyne.* R. ii. 495. O iii 972 H ii p ii 54
Sept. 15.	The K appoints Andrew de Hartcla Earl of Carlisle and several others to the custody of various counties and castles on the borders towards Scotland *Newcastle-upon-Tyne* R. iii. 495. O. ii 973 H ii p ii 55
Sept. 18	The K notifies the extension of the truce with the duke of Brittany *Newcastle-upon-Tyne.* R ii. 496. O iii 974. H ii p ii 55
Sept. 18.	The K. summons W. abp. of York to attend a conference at Ripon with the other prelates and magnates of the realm. *Newcastle-upon-Tyne* R ii 496 O iii 974 H ii p ii 55.
Sept. 20	The K summons 42 nobles to meet him at Newcastle to march against the Scots. *Newcastle-upon-Tyne.* R. ii. 496. O. iii 975 H ii p ii 55
Sept 27	Proclamation that no one shall molest the men who are driving their cattle northwards to escape from the Scots. *Durham.* R. ii. 496.

DATE	SUBJECT
1322 Sept 28	Writ to John de Bermingham, justiciary of Ireland, to aid David earl of Athol against the Scotch. *Durham.* R. ii 495 O. iii. 974 H ii p ii 55.
Sept 28	The K directs Fulco Lestraunge how to proceed in allaying disputes which have broken out in Gascony *Durham.* R ii 497 O iii 975. H ii p ii 55
Oct 2.	Summons to Simon Warde and 10 others to meet the K. on Blakhoumor to repulse the Scotch *Barnard Castle* R ii 497
Oct 6	The K orders the bps. of London and Lincoln to send to the Exchequer a copy of the taxation of benefices made by their predecessor, the bp of Lincoln. *Yarum.* R. ii 497
Oct 15.	The K having lost his privy seal, directs that no heed is to be given to letters sealed with the same *Bridlington* R ii 498 O iii 976 H ii p ii 56
Oct 21	John duke of Brittany announces the extension of the truce between his sailors and the English *Gaunte.* R ii 497 O iii 977. H ii p ii. 56
Oct 27	The K. having recovered his privy seal, authorises the validity of documents sealed with it. *York* R ii. 498. O. iii. 977. H. ii p. ii. 57.
Oct. 27.	The K. permits 7 persons to reside with John de Brittannia earl of Richmond, prisoner in Scotland *York* R ii 498 O iii 978 H ii p ii 56
Oct 28	Grant to Wm de Morle, called Roi de North, the K.'s minstrel, of the houses in Pomfret lately belonging to John le Botiler, called Roi Brunaund R ii 498. O iii. 978 H ii. p ii 56
Oct 30	Proclamation that the parliament summoned to meet at Ripon shall be held at York *York* R ii 499 O iii 978 H ii p ii 56
Oct. 31.	The K complains to the pope of the annoyances occasioned him in regard to the prebends of Aylesbury and Leighton Buzzard *York* R. ii 499 O iii. 979. H. ii. p ii 57.
Nov 4	The K orders that the abp of Canterbury shall be permitted to carry his cross within the province of York *York* R. ii 499 O. iii 979 H ii p ii 57
Nov. 4	Louis count of Flanders proposes a truce between the Flemings and the English. *Ypres.* R ii 499.
Nov 27	The K orders the clergy of the two provinces to meet and grant him a subsidy. *York* R ii 500
Dec 3	The K asks the pope not to interfere with his rights in the prebend of Stoke in the church of Lincoln *York* R ii 500 O iii 980 H. ii p ii 57
Dec 4	The K asks the pope not to disturb the cardinal of S. Lucia in Silice in regard to his benefices in England *York.* R ii. 500. O iii. 980 H. ii. p ii 57
Dec. 4	The K orders that no one shall disturb the said cardinal as above. *York.* R. ii. 500. O iii 980 H i p iii 57
Dec 4	The K asks the said cardinal to expedite his affairs in the papal court *York* R ii 500. O iii. 981 H. ii. p. ii. 57.
Dec. 4	The K informs Louis count of Flanders that he will be glad to treat with him about a truce, provided he will not aid the Scots *York.* R ii 500 O ii. 981 H. ii p ii 57
Dec 8	The K. asks Richard de Burgo earl of Ulster and 11 other noblemen of Ireland to help him against the Scots *Hathelsey* R ii. 501.
Dec 10	The K of England to the K of France relative to a decree obtained against him by the prior of S. Eustropius *Hathelsey* R. ii. 501. O iii 981. H. ii. p ii. 58
Dec 23.	The K orders that Q Isabella be aided with carriages and other necessaries while going in pilgrimage to various places in England *York.* R. ii 501 O iii 982 H. ii. p ii 58.
Dec. 28.	Safe conduct for the men of Henry Lord de Sully, taken prisoner by the Scotch *York.* R ii 501 O iii 982 H ii p ii 58.
Dec. 30	The K orders the arrest of those who tourney at Newport, co Stafford *York.* R ii 501 O iii 982 H ii p ii 58
1323. Jan 8	The K orders that no truce shall be made with the Scotch unless with his knowledge. *Couwyk* R ii 502 O. iii 983 H ii p ii 58
Jan 8.	The K orders Andrew de Hartcla Earl of Carlisle to inform him personally respecting the said truce with the Scots *Couwyk.* R ii 502 O. iii 984. H ii p. ii 58
Jan. 18.	The K asks the pope to grant a dispensation to Wm de Culpho to hold a plurality of benefices. *Parcus de Stowe.* R ii. 502. O iii 984. H. ii. p ii 59.
Jan. 20.	The K of England to Charles K of France, complaining of the capture of the ship called Dromund of Genoa by the men of Calais. *York.* R. ii 502 O iii. 985 H. ii. p ii. 59.

DATE	SUBJECT
1323 Jan 30	Credence for John bp. of Ely and Almaric de Credonio sent to settle the affairs of Gascony. *Newerk.* R ıı 503 O ııı 986. H ıı p ıı 59
Jan 30	The K. orders that assistance be given to the said persons employed as above-mentioned *Newerk.* R ıı 503 O ııı. 987 H ıı p ıı. 60
Jan. 30.	The K asks the prelates, &c of Gascony (52 ın number) to give him a subsidy for his Scottish war *Newerk.* R. ıı 503 O ııı 987. H. ıı. p ıı 60
Feb. 1.	The K. orders Henry FitzHugh to arrest Andrew de Hartcla earl of Carlisle, who has joined the Scotch *Newerk* R ıı 504 O ııı 988 H. ıı p ıı 60.
Feb. 2.	The K complains to the pope that the bps of Lıncoln and Bath and Wells have joined the rebellıous barons *Newerk* R ıı 504 O ııı 989 H ıı p ıı 61
Feb. 2.	The K. to 21 cardinals against the said bps *Newerk.* R. ıı. 504. O ıu. 989. H. ıi. p ıı. 61.
Feb 2	K Edward complains to the K of France of the misconduct of his officers ın Gascony. *Newerk* R ıı 505. O ııı 990 H ıı p ıı 61
Feb 8	The K. asks the pope to permit him to select his own confessor. *Pomfret* R. ıı. 505. O. ııı. 991. H. ıı p ıı 61.
Feb. 8.	Regulations by the K and council at York for the *government* of Gascony *Pomfret* R ıı 506 O ııı 991 H. ıı p ıı. 61.
Feb. 8.	The K. forwards the above-mentioned regulations to J bp. of Ely and Almaric de Credonıo. *Pomfret* R ıı. 506 O ııı 993 H ıı p ıı 62.
Feb 9.	The K appoints Edmund earl of Kent to be lieutenant ın the Marches of Scotland. *Pomfret.* R ıı 506 O ııı. 993 H ıı p ıı 62
Feb 10	The K sharply rebukes the ınertness of L. bp. of Durham, by reason of whıch the north of England has been destroyed by the Scots. *Pomfret.* R. ıı 506 O. ııı 994. H. ıı p. ıı. 62
Feb 12.	The K cancels all powers given to Andrew de Hartcla, and transfers the same to Edmund earl of Kent *Pomfret* R ıı 507 O ııı 994. H ıı p ıı 62
Feb. 12.	The K. ınforms the pope as to the nature of his title to certaın portions of Provence and Forcalquıer. *Pomfret.* R. ıı. 507. O ıı 995 H. ıı. p ıı 63
Feb. 15.	Pope John asks the K to procure the liberation of John de Brıtannıa earl of Richmond and Henry lord of Sully, taken prisoners by the Scots *Avignon.* R ıı. 507 O ııı 995. H ıı. p ıı 63
Feb. 16.	The K. asks the cardınal of S. Lucıa ın Sılıce whether he is willing to accept the prebend of Stoke ın the church of Lıncoln *Pomfret* R ıı 507 O. ııı 996 H. ıı p ıı. 63
Feb. 18.	The K. of England asks Robert K of Sıcıly to restore to him his rights ın Provence and Forcalquıer *Pomfret* R ıı. 507 O ııı. 996. H. ıi. p. ıi. 63.
Feb. 26	The K. asks the commissioners of Louis count of Flanders to settle the particulars of a truce which the count wishes to make with England. *Knaresbro'* R ıı 508 O. ıu 997 H. ıı. p ıı. 63.
Feb 26	The K orders the publication of the above-mentioned truce, if drawn up ın the terms which he requıres. *Knaresbro'.* R. ıı 508. O ııı 998 H ıı p ıı 64.
Feb. 26	The K asks the prayers of the general chapter of the Frıars Preachers about to assemble at Barcelona *Knaresbro'* R ıı. 508. O ııı 998 H ıı p ıı 64
Feb 27	Commissıon to Edmund earl of Kent and 5 others for the degradation and execution of Andrew de Hartcla earl of Carlisle *Knaresbro'.* R ıı 509. O. ııı. 999 H ıı p ıı 64
Feb. 27.	Instructıons for the execution of the above-mentioned sentence *Knaresbro'.* R ıı 509. O. ııı 999 H ıı p. ıı 64
March 4.	The K. grants to Henry le Scrop the lands and tenements of the late Andrew and Mıchael de Hartcla, traıtors, ın Caldeswell and Occurby and ın Horneby. R ıı 509. O. ııı. 1000 H ıı p ıı 65
March 4.	Credence for Robert de Cantuarıa going to the pope from the K. *Knaresbro'.* R ıı 509 O ııı 1001. H ıı p ıı 65.
March 4	Credence for the saıd Robert going to John de Stratford archdeacon of Lıncoln, resident ın the papal court. *Knaresbro'.* R. ıı 509 O ııı 1001. H. ıı p ıı. 65
March 9.	The K. asks Hervey master of the Frıars Preachers to send ınto England four sisters of the Domınıcan order. *Knaresbro'.* R. ıı. 510.

DATE.	SUBJECT.
1323 March 14	The K notifies that he has entered into a truce with the Scots *Knaresbro'*. R. n. 510 O m 1001 H. n. p n. 65
March 14	The K orders that the said truce shall be observed. *Knaresbro'*. R n 510 O m. 1002 H n p n 65
March 14	Authority to Wm de Herle to swear to the observance of the above truce on the part of the English *Knaresbro'*. R. n. 510. O. m. 1002 H n p. n. 65
March 15.	Credence for the bp of Ely going from the K of England to the K of France. *Knaresbro'* R n 510 O m 1002 H n. p n 66.
March 15,	K Edward asks the K of France to join with him in denouncing Henry bp. of Lincoln to the pope. *Knaresbro* R n 510. O. m. 1002. H. n. p. n. 66.
March 21.	Robert K of Scotland informs Henry de Sully that he will not accept the truce proposed by K Edw because in it the writer is not recognized as K of Scotland *Berwick* R n 511. O m. 1003. H n p n 66
March 24	Pope John complains to the K that his subjects have plundered Bernard Brachifort, merchant of Placenza *Avignon* R n 511 O m 1004. H n p n 66
April 1	Safe conduct for Thomas Randolf earl of Murray coming to Newcastle to treat for a final peace with Robert de Brus. *Westm* R. n 511 O m. 1004 H n p n 66.
April 1.	Safe conduct for Alex de Seton, Will de Mounttichet, and Walter de Twynham coming to Newcastle to treat upon the above-mentioned peace *Westm* R n 512 O. m 1005 H n p n 66
April 3	Military summons to Thomas earl of Norfolk and 78 others to proceed with the K against the Scotch. *Westm* R. n. 512.
April 4	The K of England complains to the K' of France of the conduct of the seneschal of Toulouse towards certain of the K.'s subjects in Gascony *Westm* R. n. 512 O m. 1005 H n p n 67
April 4	The K. to Fulco Lestraunge, seneschal of Gascony, on the same subject. *Westm* R n. 513 O. m 1006 H n p n 67.
April 5	The K orders that the truce between the English and the Flemings be proclaimed. *Westm* R n 513 O m 1006. H n p n 67
'April 5.	The K. notifies that he has appointed Nicolas de Farnedone to be mayor of London. *Westm* R n 513
April 6	The K forbids his subjects to molest the Flemings returning home from Scotland. *Westm* R n 513 O m 1007 H. n p n. 67.
April 6.	The K authorizes Henry lord of Sully to prorogue the truce with Scotland. *Tower of London* R n 513 O m 1007. H n p n 67
April 7.	The K asks the prayers of the general chapter of the Cistercians about to meet at Citeaux *Westm*. R n. 514 O m. 1008. H n p n. 68
April 7	Commission to inquire as to the persons who had planned the seizure of the castle of Wallingford, the Tower of London, and the castle of Windsor *Westm* R. h. 514.
April 10	Notification of the settlement of all disputes between the captains of 5 galles of Venice and the town of Southampton. *London.* R n 514 O. m. 1008. H. n. p n 68
April 11	Pope John to the K in favor of Peter abbot of Cluny *Avignon* R n 514 O m. 1009 H n p. n 68
April 12	The K. of England complains to the K. of France of the unjust claims made by his ministers in Gascony. *Tower of London* R n 515 O m 1010 H n p n 68
April 13	The K asks the pope to proceed with vigour against the bps of Lincoln and Bath and Wells *Tower of London* R n 515 O. m 1010. H n p n 69
April 13.	The K. complains to the pope of an attempt made by the abbess of Saintes to transfer the tenure of her temporalities to the K. of France. *Tower of London* R n. 515 O. m. 1011. H. n p n 69.
April 16	The K having pardoned the misconduct of the five Venetian galles at Southampton, the Venetians may therefore trade with England in safety *Tower of London*. R h. 516. O m 1011 H. n p n 69.
April 17.	The K orders the barons of the Cinque Ports to provide 57 ships to aid him against the Scotch *Westm* R n 516 O m 1012 H n p n 69
April 18.	The K orders that the Flemish merchants coming into England be not molested *Westm.* R h 516. O. m 1012. H n p n 69
April 18	The K orders Edward earl of Chester and 78 others to provide saddles for the sumpter horses during the expedition into Scotland. *Westm.* R. n. 516.

DATE	SUBJECT
1323. April 19	The K of England informs the K. of France that he cannot consent to a further delay in the payment of certain sums due by him to the writer. *Westm.* R. ii. 517. O iii 1013. H. ii. p. ii. 70
April 20	The K of England cautions the K of France against giving credence to certain statements made to him by the merchants of Amiens *Westm* R. ii 517 O iii 1014 H ii p ii 70
April 26	The K asks the pope to promote Robert de Baldok to the bprick. of Winchester. *Thynden.* R ii 517. O. iii. 1015. H. ii p ii 70.
April 27-28.	The K to five cardinals, to the same purpose *Thynden and Bishopsthorpe* R. ii 518 O. iii 1015 H. ii p ii 70.
April 29.	The K notifies the extension of the truce with the Scotch *Newerk.* R ii 518. O iii 1016 H. ii p ii 71.
April 29.	The K appoints three commissioners to take care that the said truce be observed *Newerk* R ii 518 O iii. 1017 H. ii p ii 70
April 29.	The K appoints Wm de Herle to swear to the observance of the said truce. *Newerk.* R ii 519. O iii 1017 H. ii p ii 71
April 29.	The K. appoints the said William de Herle to swear that he will observe certain covenants for the security of Thomas Randolf earl of Murray coming into England to treat for peace. *Newerk* R ii 519. O iii. 1017 H ii p ii 71
May 20	The K sends to J bp of Ely and Almaric de Credenio certain articles respecting the K.'s castles in Gascony, with instructions concerning the same. *Cowyk.* R. ii. 519. O iii 1018. H. ii. p ii. 71
May 28.	The K. to the pope in favor of Robert de Baldok archdeacon of Middlesex *Bishopsthorp* R ii 519. O iii 1019 H ii p ii 72
May 28.	The K to four cardinals, to the same effect. *Bishopsthorp* R ii. 520. O iii 1020. H ii. p. ii. 72.
May 28.	The K to the cardinal S Lucia in Silice on the disputes respecting the prebends of Aylesbury and Stoke, for the promotion of Robert de Baldok to the see of Winchester. *Bishopsthorp* R ii 520 O. iii 1021 H ii p ii 72
May 30.	Statement as to the disrespectful conduct of Henry de Beaumont towards the K. in the council at Bishopsthorp, and on the proceedings thereupon. R. ii. 520. O iii 121. H ii. p. ii. 73.
May 30.	Truce with Robert de Brus for 13 years. *Thorp, near York* R. ii 521 O iii 122. H. ii p ii 73
May 30.	The K. orders the publication of the said truce. *Thorp, near York.* R ii 521. O. iii. 124 H ii p ii. 74.
June 1.	Safe conduct for the messengers of Robert de Brus returning into Scotland. *Bishopsthorp* R. ii 522. O iii 125 H. ii p ii 74
June 1.	The K. appoints commissioners to receive the oath of Robert de Brus and others for the observance of the said truce *Bishopsthorp* R ii 522. O. iii. 125 H. ii. p ii 74
June 1.	The K appoints commissioners to attend to the observance of the said truce *Bishopsthorp.* R ii. 522. O iii 1026 H ii p ii 74
June 1.	The K informs the nobles of Ireland that their services against Scotland are no longer required. *Bishopsthorp.* R. ii. 523 O. ii 1027 H. ii. p. ii. 75.
June 2.	The K to the nobles of Gascony, to the same effect. *Bishopsthorp* R ii 523 O iii 1027 H ii. p ii 75
June 4.	Protection for the messengers of Sancius K of Majorca returning home. *Bishopsthorp* R. ii 523. O. ii 1028 H. ii. p. ii. 75.
June 4.	The K. of England to Sancius K of Majorca ; he has appointed a special commission on the grievances complained of *Thorp, near York.* R ii 523 O. iii 128 H. ii. p ii 75
June 5.	Letters of attorney for John de Britannia earl of Richmond, prisoner in Scotland. *Bishopsthorp* R ii 524. O. iii 1029. H. ii p ii. 75.
June 5.	The K asks the pope to stay proceedings against Aymer de Valence earl of Pembroke respecting the advowson of the church of Holtham. *York* R ii 524 O iii 1029 H ii p ii 76
June 6.	The K informs Charles count of Valois that he will lay before the parliament the count's proposal for a marriage of his daughter with Edward the K's son *Thorp, near York* R ii. 524 O. iii. 129, H ii. p. ii. 76.
June 6.	The K of England to Charles K of France, to the same effect *Thorp, near York* R. ii 524 O iii. 1030. H. ii p ii 76

SYLLABUS OF RYMER'S FŒDERA

DATE	SUBJECT.
1323 June 7	Robert K of Scotland confirms the truce with England dated 30 May last *Berwick-upon-Tweed* R ıı 524 O ııı. 1030. H ıı p ıı 76.
June 7	The K. asks the cardinal of S Adrian to induce the pope to promote Robert de Baldok the see of Winchester *Bishopsthorp.* R. ıı. 524 O. ııı 1031 H. ıı. p. ıı. 76.
June 9	The K grants to Matthew de Trye, marshal of France, certain possessions ın Areynes ın Ponthıeu *Cowyk.* R ıı 525. O ııı 1032 H ıı p ıı 77
June 20.	Pope John ınforms the K that he has appoınted John de Stratford to the see of Wınchester. *Avıgnon.* R. ıı 525 O ııı. 1032. H ıı p ıı 77.
June 28	The K censures Stephen bp of London and the dean and chapter of London for havıng permıtted the people to belıeve that mıracles are wrought at a pıcture of Thomas late earl of Lancaster ın the church of S Paul s. *York* R ıı 525 O ııı 1033 H ıı p ıı 77
July 4.	The K ınforms the count of Savoy and others that he cannot support theır applıcatıon that the count's nephew should succeed to the see of Wınchester , he havıng already recommended Robert de Baldok to the pope *York* R. ıı 526 O ııı. 1034. H. ıı. p. ıı 77.
July 8	The K asks the pope to wıthdraw hıs provısıon of John de Stratford to the bprıck of Wınchester, and to leave the electıon to the chapter *Faxflete.* R. ıı 526 O ııı 1035 H ıı p ıı. 78
July 8	The K. to 32 cardınals and others agaınst the provısıon of the saıd John de Stratford *Faxflete* R ıı 526 O ııı 1035. H. ıı. p ıı. 78.
July 8	The K orders that search be made at the Cınque Ports and other ports for papal letters concernıng the see of Wınchester. *Faxflete* R. ıı. 527. O. ıv. 1. H. ıı. p. ıı 78.
July 15.	Pope John permıts the K to chose hıs own confessor *Avıgnon.* R ıı 527. O. ıv 1. H ıı p ıı. 79
July 15.	The K orders that the tenth and sıxth granted to hım at York he collected. *Brustwıck.* R. ıı. 527
July 18	The K ınforms three cardınals that he cannot grant the petıtıon of Raymond de Bussolers, as ıt ıs supported by John de Stratford, agaınst whom the K. ıs exceedıngly ıncensed. *Brustwıck* R ıı. 527 O ıv 2 H ıı p ıı 79
July 18.	Credence for two messengers sent by the K of England to the K. of France on the affaırs of Aquıtaın *Brustwıck* R ıı 527 O ıv 2 H ıı p ıı 79
July 19	The K to Charles count of Valoıs and fıve others, on the same subject *Brustwıck.* R ıı 528 O ıv. 2. H ıı p. ıı. 79.
July 22	The K notıfıes the extensıon of the truce wıth the subjects of Louıs count of Flanders. *Brustwıck* R ıı 528 O ıv 3 H ıı p ıı 79
July 26	The K grants to Anthony de Lucy the manors of Meuburn Regıs and Grendon lately forfeıted by Andrew de Hartela. R ıı 528 O. ıv 4 H. ıı. p ıı 79.
July 28	The K asks the pope to revoke any gıft whıch he may have made of the see of Wınchester to John de Stratford *Cowyk* R ıı 528 O ıv 4 H ıı p ıı 80
July 28	The K to the cardınal of S Adrıan agaınst the saıd John de Stratford *Cowyk* R. ıı 529. O ıv. 5. H ıı. p ıı 80.
July 28.	The K to Bernard Jordanı and two others agaınst the saıd John. *Cowyk* R. ıı. 529. O. ıv 6 H ıı p ıı 80
July 31.	Wrıt to the justıcıary of Ireland for the restıtutıon of hıs temporalıtıes to Stephen elect of Armagh *Cowyk.* R. ıı. 529 O ıv. 7. H. ıı. p ıı. 81.
Aug 6	The K forbıds the holdıng of tournaments ın England *Kırkham* R. ıı. 530
Aug 6	The K orders the aprehensıon of Roger de Mortımer of Wıgmore, who has escaped from the Tower of London *Kırkham.* R ıı 530, O. ıv. 7 H. ıı. p ıı. 81.
Aug. 6.	The K orders that ıncreased precautıons be taken for the arrest of the saıd Roger de Mortımer. *Kırkham* R ıı. 530. O ıv 7 H. ıı p ıı 81
Aug 10	The K appoınts Hugh le Despenser earl of Wınchester to attend to the saıd arrest. *Pıckerıng.* R ıı 530. O ıv. 9. H ıı p ıı 81.
Aug 15.	The K. orders that Thomas Henry, merchant of Florence, be delıvered to Charles K. of France *Pıckerıng* R ıı 531
Aug 15	K Edward sends some "runnıng dogs" to Charles K. of France *Pıckerıng* R ıı 531
Aug 16	The K. authorızes J bp of Ely to appoınt a keeper of the Isle of Oleron *Pıckerıng.* R ıı. 531 O ıv 9 H ıı p ıı 81.
Aug. 17,	The K. of England asks the K. of Sıcıly to let hım have peaceable possessıon of hıs rıghts ın Provence and Forcalquıer. *Pıckerıng.* R. ıı. 531. O. ıv. 9 H. ıı. p. ıı. 82.

DATE.	SUBJECT.
1323 Aug. 17	Credence for Adam Myrymouth going from the K. to the pope against J de Stratford, bp elect of Winchester, and on other matters *Pickering.* R. II 531. O. IV. 10. H II. p. II 82.
Aug 17.	The K. to 30 cardinals and others, on the same subject as the preceding. *Pickering* R. II 532. O IV. 11. H II p II, 82
Aug. 17.	The K. orders J. de Stratford to deliver up to Adam Mirimouth all bulls, &c. connected with the bprick. of Winchester. *Pickering* R. II 532. O IV 12 H II p II 82
Aug. 19.	The K informs the abp. of Canterbury that he will support the rights of John de Bruxton in the archdeaconry of Canterbury *Pickering.* R II 532
Aug 20.	Pope John to the K., on having appointed John de Stratford to the bprick of Winchester *Avignon* R II. 533. O. IV 12. H II p II. 83
Aug 22.	Safe conduct for the messengers of Robert de Bruys coming to the K *Pickering.* R. II. 533. O IV 14 H II p II 83
Aug 29	Credence for Hugh de Engolisma coming from the pope to the K *Avignon* R. II 533 O IV 14. H II p II 83.
Aug. 30	The K of England to James K of Aragon on a claim for compensation for his losses made by Berenger Lecionis *Grenhou* R. II 534 O iv. 15. H II. p. II. 84.
Aug 31.	The K. grants to John de Britannia earl of Richmond (a prisoner with the Scots) the custody of the lands which belonged to John de Northwode, deceased *Grenhou* R II 534 O IV 15 H. II. p. II. 84
Sept. 1.	The K asks the tenants of John de Britannia earl of Richmond to grant a subsidy for his ransom from prison in Scotland *Grenhou* R II 534 O IV. 16. H. II. p II 84
Sept 13.	Pope John asks the K to excuse the long residence of John bp of Winchester in the papal court *Avignon* R II 534. O. IV 16 H II p II. 84.
Sept. 13.	Pope John informs the K that he will gladly assist him in recovering his rights in Provence *Avignon* R II. 534 O IV 17 H II p II 84
Sept. 16.	The K. asks the pope to postpone the personal attendance of the abp of Canterbury at the papal court. *Jeroval.* R. II. 535. O IV 17 H II p. II. 84
Sept. 16.	The K to four cardinals, on the same subject. *Jeroval* R. II. 535. O IV. 17. H II p II 84.
Sept. 16.	The K to the pope, exonerating the abp of Canterbury from having arrested the clerks of the cardinal of S. Maria in Cosmedyn at Dover. *Jeroval* R II 535. O IV. 18. H II. p II 85
Sept 16	The K to the cardinal of S. Maria in Cosmedyn and three other cardinals on the same subject as the preceding. *Jeroval* R II 535. O IV 19 H II p II 85
Sept. 17	Pope John informs the K that he cannot consent to depose the bps of Bath and Lincoln, of whom the K has complained without hearing them *Avignon* R II 356 O IV 19 H. II p II 85.
Sept 17.	Pope John asks the K to pay the quarter of the yearly tenth due to the papal camera. *Avignon.* R II. 536 O IV 19 H II p II 85
Oct. 1.	The K orders John and Robert de Fienles to arrest Roger de Mortimer of Wiggemer if he should venture within their jurisdiction *Skipton in Craven* R II 536 O. IV. 20. H. II. p. II. 85
Oct. 2.	Commission of inquiry as to miracles stated to have been performed at Bristol over the bodies of certain felons executed for treason. *Skipton in Craven* R II 536. O IV 20. H II p II 86
Oct 2.	The K orders the arrest of such Scotchmen as reside in England. *Skipton in Craven.* R. II 536.
Oct. 10.	The K asks the pope to depose John bp of Bath and substitute the abbot of Langedon in his stead *Hightenhill* R II 537. O IV 21 H II. p II 86
Oct. 12.	Pope John asks the K to protect Bernard Jordani lord of Insula *Avignon.* R. II 537 O IV 21. H. II p II. 86.
Oct. 24.	Commission to inquire into the truth of the miracles said to have been performed at Bristol *Liverpool* R II 537 O IV 22. H. II p II 86.
Nov. 14.	Writ to the sheriffs throughout England and 15 noblemen to deal with Roger de Mortimer as a rebel. *Nottingham* R. II. 537 O IV 22 H. II p. II 86
Nov. 20.	The K. summons a convocation of the clergy to deliberate on the state of the church and realm *Nottingham* R. II. 538

DATE	SUBJECT
1323 Nov. 24.	Ordinances for the government of Ireland. *Nottingham* R. ii. 538. O. iv. 23. H. ii. p ii. 87
Nov 24.	The K orders the chancellor of Ireland to publish the said ordinances *Nottingham.* R ii 539 O iv 24 H. ii p ii 87.
Nov 28.	Safe conduct for Guy of Flanders coming into England. *Ravensdale* R. ii 539
Nov 29	The K appoints Hamo da Chygwelle to be mayor of London. *Ravensdale* R. ii 539
Dec 28	Protection for the papal nuncio and sub-collectors in England *Kenilworth.* R ii 539. O. iv. 25 H ii p ii 87.
1324 Jan 1	The K asks the pope to put an end to various annoyances to which he and the bp of Ely have been subjected *Kenilworth* R ii 539 O iv 25 H ii p ii. 88
Jan 3.	The K to the cardinal of S Ciriac in Thermis, asking him to desist from the above-mentioned annoyances. *Kenilworth.* R. ii 540 O. iv 26 H ii. p. ii. 88
Jan 3.	The K asks John Lescapon, canon of Dublin, (employed by the above cardinal,) to abandon his proceedings *Kenilworth* R. ii 540 O iv 27 H ii. p ii 88
Jan 5	Pope John to the K , in answer to his requests respecting the bps of Winchester, Lincoln, and Bath, and Robert de Baldok *Avignon* R. ii 540. O iv 27. H. ii p ii 88.
Jan 8	The K orders the arrest of the prior of Bermondsey and others, adherents to the K 's rebels *Henley.* R ii 540
Jan 13.	Pope John to the K in favour of Henry de Sully, butler [buticularius] of France. *Avignon.* R. ii. 541. O. iv 28. H. ii. p. ii. 88
Jan 13.	Pope John explains to the K the reasons why he has addressed Robert de Brus as "king of Scotland" *Avignon* R ii 541 O iv 28 H ii p ii 89
Jan 15	Process in the K 's Bench against John de Stratford, bp of Winchester, relative to his proceedings in the papal court. *Worcester* R ii 541 O iv. 28. H. ii. p. ii. 89.
Jan. 26.	Proclamation against the introduction into England of clipped or false money. *Bristol* R ii 544
Jan 28	The K orders that all ships belonging to the subjects of the count of Zealand be arrested. *Berkley* R ii 544
Feb 23	The K. permits the abp of York to carry his cross in the province of Canterbury when coming to the parliament at Westminster *Fulham* R ii 544.
Feb 25	Credence from the K for J bp of Ely and others to John count of Armignac and to 76 other bps and towns in Gascony *Fulham* R. ii. 545. O. iv. 36 H ii p. ii. 92.
March 6	Credence for Wm. de Weston, canon of Lincoln, going to Charles K of France on matters connected with Aquitain. *Westm.* R ii 545. O iv 37. H. ii p ii. 92
March 6.	Credence for the same person, going to the parliament of France *Westm.* R. ii. 546. O iv 38 H ii p ii 92
March 6	Proxy for the same, to prosecute the K. of England's affairs in the court of France *Westm* R ii 546 O. iv. 38 H ii p ii 92.
March 6	Proxy for the same, to excuse the K of England's absence from the court of France R ii 546 O iv 38 H. ii p ii 92
March 10	The K pardons the crew of the 5 gallies of Venice who had misbehaved at Southampton and the Isle of Wight *Westm* R. ii 546. O iv 39 H ii. p. ii. 93.
March 11	The K orders the burial of the bodies of all rebels which are still hanging on the gallows *Westm* R ii 546.
March 11.	The K. authorizes certain persons to fix a day and place for a meeting between the King's of France and England *Fulmere* R. ii. 547. O. iv 40 H ii p ii. 93.
[March 11]	Pope John exhorts the K of England to do homage for Aquitain to Charles K. of France R ii 547. O iv. 41. H. ii. p ii. 94
March 15	The K appoints Robert de Shirland to be seneschal of Aquitain *Westm.* R ii 547 O iv 41. H ii p ii. 94.
March 16	The K. orders inquiry to be made respecting the miracles said to have been performed at Bristol. *Westm.* R. ii 547 O iv 42. H. ii p ii 94.
March 30	The K orders inquiry to be made respecting the excesses said to have been done at S Sacerdos in Agenois *Westm* R ii 547 O. iv. 42 H. ii p ii 94
March 30	The K appoints commissioners to settle the cases of appeal in Gascony from him to the court of France *Westm.* R. ii. 548. O. iv. 43. H. ii. p. ii. 94.

DATE.	SUBJECT
1324. March 30.	The K. requires all prelates, nobles, and communities in the duchy of Aquitain to be obedient to the said commissioners. *Westm.* R. ii 548 O iv. 43. H. ii. p. ii. 94.
March 30	The K requests John count of Armignac to be obedient to the said commissioners. *Westm* R ii 548. O iv. 44 H ii p ii 94
March 30	The K. of England to James K of Aragon upon a marriage between Edward the K.'s eldest son and a daughter of the K of Aragon *Westm.* R ii. 548. O iv. 44. H. ii. p ii 95.
March 30.	Credence for two messengers going from the K of England to James K of Aragon on the above marriage. *Westm* R ii 548 O iv 44 H ii p. ii 95.
March 30.	Commission to Alexander abp of Dublin and others to treat with James K of Aragon on the above marriage *Westm* R. ii 549 O iv. 45 H ii. p. ii 95.
March 30	Commission to the same persons to treat of general and special peace and concord with the K. of Aragon *Westm* R ii. 549. O iv 45 H. ii p ii 95
April 1.	Credence for three persons to treat with Philip infant of Spain and 11 of the nobility of Spain *Westm* R. ii 549 O iv. 46 H ii p ii 95.
April 1.	The K. to the pope on withholding the title of king from Robert de Brus, on the treason of Adam bp of Hereford, and on the lands of the Templars in England. *Westm* R ii 549. O iv 46. H. ii p ii 95
April 1	Proclamation of the extension of the truce with the Flemings *Westm* R ii 550. O iv. 47 H. ii p ii 96.
April 18	The K orders inquiry to be made respecting the attempt of the French to capture the castle of Montpezat *Langley.* R. ii 550 O iv 48 H. ii p. ii 96.
May 1.	Pope John asks the K. to permit cardinal Raimund of S Mary in Cosmedin to enjoy the archdeaconry of Canterbury *Avignon.* R ii 550. O iv 48. H ii p ii 96
May 4	Protection for Gerard de Orum going to John de Britannia, earl of Richmond, prisoner in Scotland. *Westm* R ii 551 O. iv 49 H ii p ii 96
May 8	The K informs the pope that, notwithstanding the aggressions of Charles K of France, he is willing to be at peace with him. *Westm* R ii 551 O iv. 49 H ii p ii 97.
May 10	Louis count of Flanders to the K. upon the complaints of Wm de Querle, warden of the Friars Minors of London. *Males, near Bruges* R. ii 551 O iv 50 H ii p. ii 97.
May 10.	The K orders all persons who possess 40 librates of land to be knighted *Westm* R. ii 552 O iv 51 H. ii p ii 97.
May 10.	Proclamation that all who are to be knighted shall apply for necessaries at the K's wardrobe *Westm.* R. ii. 552. O. iv. 52 H ii p ii 97
May 10.	The K, being about to vindicate his rights in Aquitain, orders the mayor of Southampton and 12 other ports to provide him with shipping *Westm* R ii 552
May 10.	The K. orders that the said ships shall be ready upon three days' notice. *Westm.* R. ii 552.
May 12.	The K annexes the town "de Forcessio" [Fources ?] in the Agenois to the crown of England *Westm.* R ii 553 O iv. 52 H ii p ii. 98.
May 21	The K asks the pope to remove Raymund, bp. of Condom, to another diocese *Westm.* R ii 553 O. iv. 52. H ii. p. ii. 98.
May 21	The K to 12 cardinals, to the same purport. *Westm.* R ii. 553. O. iii 1019 H ii p ii. 72
May 21.	The K asks 3 cardinals to procure the correction of some errors in the papal letters which he sends by the bp of Cork. *Westm.* R ii. 553. O iv 53. H. ii. p. ii. 98.
May 21.	The K asks John de Lescapon to aid the bp. of Cork in the matters on which he applies to the pope. *Westm.* R ii 554. O iv 53 H ii p ii 98
May 21	Louis count of Flanders informs the K. that he will send messengers with an answer to the K's letters *Males, near Bruges.* R. ii. 554 O iv 54. H. ii. p ii 98.
May 28.	The K. asks the pope to unite the poor bpricks of Ireland to more wealthy cities and localities *Westm.* R ii. 554 O. iv 54. H. ii p ii 98.
May 28.	The K complains to the pope of the conduct of the French at S. Sacerdos and Montpezat *Westm.* R ii 554 O. iv. 55. H. ii. p. ii. 98.
June 4.	The K orders that foot soldiers shall be levied to proceed into Aquitam. *Westm.* R ii 555 O iv. 57. H. ii p ii. 99
June 6.	The K informs 6 cardinals that he cannot grant their request as to the presentation to the prebend of Leighton upon Brouneswold in the ch of Lincoln. *Westm* R ii. 555. O iv 57. H ii p ii 100.

P

DATE	SUBJECT
1324 June 6.	The K. to 5 other cardinals about the said prebend of Leighton-upon-Brouneswold. *Westm* R ii 556 O. iv. 58 H ii p ii 100
June 6.	Letters of attorney for John de Britannia, earl of Richmond, prisoner in Scotland. *Westm*. R ii 556 O iv 58 H ii. p ii. 100.
June 12	The K orders the sheriff of Cumberland to deliver certain prisoners to the wardens appointed for the preservation of the truce, to be tried by them *Westm* R. ii 556. O iv 59 H ii p ii. 100
June 12.	Commission to receive into the K's peace those persons who had joined the Scotch. *Westm* R ii 556. O iv 59 H ii p ii 100.
June 15.	The K asks the pope to grant the accompanying petition of the monks of Burton-upon-Trent. *Westm* R ii 557. O. iv. 60. H. ii p ii. 101
June 18.	The K orders the restitution of the temporalities of the see of Winchester to John de Stratford *Tonbridge* R ii 557 O iv 61. H ii. p ii 101.
June 30	Protestations made by the K and the bp upon the above restitution *Westm* R ii 557. O iv 61 H. ii p ii 101.
July 2.	Safe conduct for Edward de Balliol coming to the K. into England *Rotherfield* R ii 558. O iv 61 H ii p ii 101
July 2.	Pope John exhorts the K. of England to do homage to Charles K of France, and to continue at peace with him. *Avignon.* R. ii. 558. O. iv. 63. H ii. p ii. 102.
July 8	The K. authorizes John bp of Norwich, and others, to arrange the time and place for an interview with Charles K. of France *Porchester.* R ii 558. O iv. 64 H ii p ii 102.
July 8	Commission to John bp of Norwich and others to settle all disputes respecting the attempt made by the K. of France to seize the castle of Montpezat *Porchester.* R. ii. 558. O. iv 64 H. ii p ii 102.
July 8	Commission to swear that the K of England will observe the treaty of peace with Charles K of France *Porchester* R ii 559 O iv 65. H. ii p ii 103.
July 8.	The K commits the custody of the castle of Montpezat to John de Stonore *Porchester.* R. ii 559. O iv. 66 H ii. p. ii. 103.
July 8.	Commission to John de Stonore to deliver the said castle to the K. of France *Porchester.* R ii 559 O iv 66 H ii p ii 103
July 8	Writ to John de Stonore, to the same effect. *Porchester.* R ii. 559. O iv 67. H. ii. p. ii 103.
July 8.	Richard de Grey, seneschal of Gascony, ordered to demand and receive the said castle from the K of France *Porchester.* R. ii. 560. O. iv 67 H ii. p ii. 103.
July 10.	The K. grants to the said seneschal and others authority to appoint a new keeper for the said castle. *Porchester* R. ii 560.
July 10.	The K thanks the pope for various kindnesses, and asks him to patronise Robert de Baldok, his chancellor *Porchester.* R. ii 560 O iv. 68 H ii p ii. 104
July 15.	The K informs Edward earl of Kent of the arrangements which he has made for the government of Aquitain *Porchester.* R ii 560. O iv 69 H. ii p ii. 104
July 15.	Safe conduct for Wm bp of S Andrews and Tho Randolf, earl of Murray, coming to treat of a final peace with Robert de Brus. *Porchester* R ii 561 O. iv 70 H ii p ii 104.
July 16.	Letters of special protection for Henry lord of Sully going into and returning from France on the K.'s business *Porchester.* R ii 561 O iv 70 H. ii p ii. 104.
July 16.	The K appoints John Segrave and Fulco FitzWarin to be captains of the troops going into Gascony *Porchester* R ii 561. O iv. 71 H ii p ii. 105
July 16	The K. appoints John de Cromwell admiral of the fleet sailing for Gascony. *Porchester.* R ii 562 O iv 71 H ii p ii 105.
July 20.	The K appoints his brother Edmund earl of Kent to be his lieutenant in Aquitain, the Agenois, and Gascony *Porchester* R ii. 562 O iv. 72 H ii p ii. 105
July 21.	The K orders the arrest of all the subjects of the K. of France, with their ships, &c., throughout England. *Porchester* R ii 562. O iv 72 H ii. p. ii 102
July 22.	The K. orders that ships of war to serve against France shall be ready at Sandwich, Dover, &c *Porchester* R. ii. 562. O iv 73. H ii. p ii 105
July 26	Letters of special protection for Henry lord of Sully going into and returning from France on the K.'s business *Porchester.* R. ii. 563 O iv. 73. H ii p ii 106.

DATE	SUBJECT
1324. July 28.	The K informs the pope of the aggressions of the K of France, in Oleron, notwithstanding which he has endeavoured to keep peace *Dartford.* R. ii 563 O. iv 74 H. ii p. ii 106.
July 29	Protection for the messengers of Louis count of Flanders returning home from England *Wittele* R. ii 564 O iv 75 H ii p ii 107
July 31	Safe conduct for the merchants of Flanders coming to trade in England *Guilford* R ii 564 O iv 77. H ii p ii 107.
Aug 3.	The K orders that Hugh de Engolisma, the pope's messenger, be not annoyed in the discharge of his duties *Guilford* R ii 564
Aug. 4.	Commission to various bps to receive the oaths of persons appointed by the K to guard the ports of the realm. *Guilford.* R. ii 564 O. iv. 77. H ii p ii 107
Aug. 4.	Writs to the bailiffs of Sandwich and others not to annoy the French shipping unless first annoyed by them *Guilford* R. ii 565 O iv 78 H ii p ii 107.
Aug 6.	The K appoints commissioners to array horse and foot soldiers to be ready to embark for the defence of Gascony. *Guilford.* R ii. 565 O iv 78. H ii p ii 107
Aug. 6.	The K extends the period within which qualified persons must receive knighthood. *Guilford* R ii 566 O. iv 80 H ii p ii 109
Aug. 10	The K asks the prayers of the General Chapter of the Friars Preachers at Cambridge *Windsor* R ii 566
Aug 14.	The K. asks the count of Flanders to extend the duration of the truce with England *Windsor* R. ii 566.
Aug 18	The K asks 52 nobles, bps, &c of Ireland to continue to assist in the defence of Ireland *Westm* R ii 567
Aug. 20.	Safe conduct for Edward de Balliol coming into England to the K. *Westm* R ii 567 O. iv 81 H. ii. p ii 109
Aug 20	The K orders possession to be taken of the manors of Temple Neusem, Strode, and Daneye, lately belonging to the Templars, granted to him by the prior of the hospital of S. John of Jerusalem *Westm.* R ii 567 O iv 81. H ii p. ii 109
Aug. 24.	Safe conduct for the merchants, mariners, and others of Spain coming into England *Tunbridge.* R ii. 567.
Aug 30.	Pope John advises the K of England to be at peace with Charles K. of France *Avignon.* R ii 567 O. iv 81 H ii p ii 109
Sept 17.	The K. permits cardinal Gaillard de Mota to retain for life the portion of Milton in the prebend of Aylesbury *Tower of London* R. ii 568 O iv 82 H ii p ii. 109
Sept. 18	The K of England assures Sanctius K of Majorca that he is ready to do justice in the matter of his ships which are said to have been plundered by English pirates *Porchester* R ii 568 O iv 82. H. ii p ii 109.
Sept. 18.	The K. of England to James K of Aragon on the same subject *Porchester* R ii 568 O iv 83. H ii p ii 110
Sept. 18	The K takes into his own hands the county of Cornwall, the castles, lands, &c belonging to Q Isabella, being apprehensive of the invasion of the French *Porchester* R ii. 569. O. iv 84. H ii p. ii. 110.
Sept. 18	Notification to various persons in several counties to the same effect *Porchester* R ii 569 O. iv 85 H ii. p ii. 110
Sept 22.	Commission to Thomas de Sandwich and Henry de Goshale to provide for the safety of the coasts threatened by the French. *Porchester.* R. ii 569
Sept. 23.	Letters of protection for the messengers coming to treat of a final peace with Robert de Brus. *Porchester* R ii. 570. O iv 85. H ii. p. ii. 110
Sept 23	Letters of safe conduct for the same persons coming for the same purpose. *Porchester* R. ii 561 O iv 70. H ii p. ii. 105.
Sept. 24.	Summons to John de Brittania, earl of Richmond, to attend with the other magnates the conference at London *Porchester* R ii. 570 O iv. 86 H ii p ii 111
Sept 28.	The K. orders the arrest of all the French in England *Porchester.* R. ii 570. O. iv 87 H ii. p. ii. 111.
Sept 30.	The K. exhorts the nobles, prelates, mayors, &c of Aquitain (144 in number) to continue faithful to him against the French *Porchester.* R. ii. 570 O. iv 86 H ii p ii. 111.
[Sept]	Narrative of the unjust dealings of the K of France towards the K of England in regard to the duchy of Aquitain. R ii 572. O. iv. 90. H. ii p ii 112

DATE	SUBJECT.
1324 Sept 30	The K of England asks the Kings of Aragon and Castile to aid him with troops against Charles K of France *Porchester* R ii 572 O iv 91 H ii p ii 113.
Sept 30	The K asks John infant of Biscay and others to favour his agents in providing victuals for his troops in Aquitain. *Porchester* R ii 572 O iv. 92. H. ii p ii 113.
Oct 1	The K appoints commissioners to form treaties of confederacy with all who will join England. *Porchester.* R ii 573 O iv. 92 H ii p ii 113
Oct 1	Commission for the same persons to treat of a marriage between Edward the K's eldest son and a daughter of James K of Aragon *Porchester.* R ii. 573. O. iv 93. H. ii p ii 113
Oct 1	The K asks the men of Lynn and Norwich to be ready to repel any descent of the French on the coast of Norfolk. *Porchester* R ii 573 O iv 93 H ii p ii. 114
Oct 6	The K complains to the duke of Britanny of the conduct of the K of France, who has violated the rights of the peers of France. *Porchester.* R ii 573 O iv. 94. H ii. p ii 114
Oct 8	The K. requires the abp of Canterbury to refrain from molesting the abp. of York in carrying his cross in the province of Canterbury, while coming to the K. at London. *Guilford* R ii 574 O iv 95 H ii p ii 114
Oct 12	The K orders that aid be given to the bps in removing foreign monks, &c from their houses near the coast (the Flemings excepted), a descent of the French being apprehended. *Byfleet* R ii 574 O iv 96 H ii p ii 114
Oct 12.	The K. requires the bps. of England to take charge of the benefices and goods of the foreign religious persons. *Byfleet* R ii 575 O iv 97. H ii p ii. 115
Oct 18	The K informs several of the cardinals of the manner in which he has been treated by the K of France *London* R ii 575 O iv 98 H. ii p ii 115
[Oct]	Statement of facts for the information of the pope and cardinals on the same subject. R ii 576 O iv 100 H. ii p ii. 116.
Oct. 20	The K asks the lords of Hainault to take prisoners those of his enemies whom they may find in their marches. *Tower of London* R ii 577
Oct. 22	The K orders that no annoyance be offered to Neapolion, cardinal of S Adrian, in regard to his prebend of Kynges Sutton in the church of Lincoln. *Tower of London* R. ii 577. O iv 102 H ii. p ii 117
Nov 3	Protection for the messengers of Robert de Brus coming to treat for final peace *Mortlake.* R ii 577 O iv. 102 H ii p ii. 117
Nov 8	The K. appoints commissioners to treat with the messengers of Robert de Brus. *Westm* R ii 578 O iv 104 H ii p ii 118
Nov 10	The K orders that cardinal Gaucelm shall not be molested in his benefices in England R ii 578 O iv 104 H ii p ii 118
Nov. 12	The K. orders that a cessation of hostilities with France be proclaimed in anticipation of peace *Westm* R ii 578 O iv 105 H ii p ii 118
Nov 12.	Protection for the messengers of the K of France coming to treat of peace *Westm* R ii 579. O. iv. 106. H. ii. p. ii 119.
Nov 15	Commission to treat with the said messengers respecting peace with France *Westm* R. ii. 579. O. iv 106 H ii p ii 119
Nov. 15	Commission to treat with the said messengers for a truce with France *Westm* R ii 579. O iv. 106 H. ii p ii 119.
Nov 15	Commission, with additional powers, for the same purpose *Westm* R ii 579. O iv. 107 H ii p ii 119
Nov 17	Instructions to various persons for the array of soldiers to proceed into Gascony for its defence against the French *Westm.* R ii. 580. O. iv. 107. H. ii. p. ii 119
Nov. 18.	Protection for cardinal Raymund, archdeacon of Canterbury. *Westm* R ii. 580. O iv 109. H. ii p. ii. 120
Nov 19	The K informs the pope of the misconduct of the K. of France, in consequence of which he cannot pay the annual tribute to Rome. *Westm* R. ii. 581. O iv. 109. H ii p ii 120
Nov. 19	Renewal of protection for Hugh de Engolisma, papal nuncio. *Westm.* R ii 581 O. iv. 110 H ii p ii. 120.
Nov. 22.	The K. exonerates John de Britannia, earl of Richmond, from various manucaptions for Frenchmen in his service. *Tower of London* R ii. 581. O iv. 110. H ii p. ii. 120.

DATE.	SUBJECT
1324 Nov. 24.	The K orders the arrest of all the men of such parts of Gascony who may be found in England as have rebelled against him *Pokeriche* R ii. 581. O iv 111 H ii p ii. 120.
Nov. 25.	The K asks the pope to dispense with the obstacles which prevent marriages between various families in England who are now at hostility with each other *Bassingburn*. R. ii 582. O. iv 112. H ii p. ii, 121.
Nov. 25.	The K. to 11 cardinals for the same dispensations. *Bassingburn*. R ii 582 O ii 113. H ii p ii 121.
Dec. 18	The K. orders that search be made at various ports for letters from abroad prejudicial to the Crown. *Nottingham* R ii. 582
Dec 21.	Summons to Thomas earl of Norfolk (and 53 other nobles) to accompany the K into Gascony to resist the inroads of the K of France. *Nottingham* R ii 583. O iv 113. H ii p ii 121
Dec 23	The bp. of Durham is commanded to provide soldiers to accompany the K into Gascony. *Nottingham*. R ii 583. O. iv. 114 H ii. p ii. 122
Dec 23	Commission to receive to the K's peace the persons who have rebelled against him in Aquitain. *Nottingham* R ii 583. O iv 115. H ii p ii 122
Dec. 28	The K receives back into his fealty Bernard de Durford, lord of "Flamareus," who had rebelled against him by joining the French. *Nottingham*. R. ii 583. O ii 115 H ii p ii 122.
Dec. 28.	The K receives to his peace the same Bernard and 31 other nobles of Gascony who had joined the French *Nottingham*. R ii 584 O. iv 116 H ii p ii 122
Dec. 30.	The K. summons Thomas earl of Norfolk and 97 other nobles and prelates to confer with him on the state of Aquitain *Nottingham* R. ii. 584 O iv. 116 H ii p ii 123
1325 Jan 5	The K grants various privileges to the men of Castile *Ravensdale* R ii. 585 O iv 118 H ii p ii. 124.
Jan 8	Protection for Aymo de Sabaudia, prebendary of Strenshall, and Thomas de Sabaudia, prebendary of Novewyk, and various other persons *Ravensdale*. R ii 585. O iv 119 H. ii. p. ii. 124.
Jan. 18	The K to Alfonso K of Castile, on the proposed marriage of Edward, the eldest son of the K. of England, with Eleanor, sister of the K of Castile *Langley* R ii 585 O iv 119 H ii p. ii 124
Jan. 18.	The K of England to John, guardian of the K of Castile, on the said marriage and on the aggressions of the K of France. *Langley* R ii. 586 O iv 120 H ii p ii 124
Jan 18	The K complains to the bp of Burgos [in Spain] of the misconduct of the K of France. *Langley* R ii 586 O iv 121. H ii p ii 124
Jan. 18.	The K. asks Martinus Ferrandi, guardian of the K. of Castile, to aid him against the French. *Langley*. R. ii 586 O. iv. 121 H ii p ii 125
Feb 6	Proxy by the K of England for treating of a marriage between Alfonso K of Spain and Eleanor, daughter of the K of England *Westm*. R ii. 586. O iv 122. H. ii. p ii 125.
Feb. 6	Proxy by the K of England for treating of a marriage between his son Edward and Eleanor, sister of the K of Spain. *Westm* R ii. 587 O iv 123. H ii p ii 125
Feb. 6.	Another proxy respecting the said marriage *Westm* R ii 587. O iv 123 H ii. p ii. 125.
Feb. 6	Another proxy respecting the marriage of Alfonso K. of Spain and Eleanor, daughter of the K of England. *Westm* R ii. 587. O v. 124 H ii p ii 125
Feb. 6.	Commission for the same proctors to treat of a confederacy between K Alfonso and the K of England and the nobles of Spain. *Westm*. R ii 587 O iv 124 H. ii. p ii 126
Feb 6.	Credence for the same proctors going to John, guardian of the K. of Castile, and to Mary lady of Biscay. *Westm*. R. ii 587. O. iv. 124. H. ii. p. ii 126
Feb. 8.	The K. orders the liberation of the French lately arrested in England *Westm* R ii 588. O. iv. 126 H. ii. p ii 126
Feb 10.	Credence for messengers sent from the K. to the guardians of the K. of Castile. *Westm*. R. ii 588 O. iv. 126 H ii p ii. 126
Feb. 12.	The K grants a commission to make a truce with John duke of Brittany *Westm*. R. ii 588. O. iv 126 H ii p ii 126.
Feb 15	The K asks the pope to extend the period for the personal appearance of W abp of Canterbury at Rome *Westm* R ii 588 O. iv. 127. H. ii p ii 127.
Feb 15	The K. to four cardinals, on the same subject. *Westm* R ii. 589. O iii 127 H. ii. p. ii. 127.

DATE	SUBJECT
1325 Feb 16	The K thanks several of the nobles of Gascony for having repelled the K of France *Tower of London* R ii 589 O iv. 128. H ii. p. ii 127
Feb 16	The K of England to James K of Aragon on the treaty of marriage between their children *Westm* R ii 589 O iv 128 H ii p ii 127
Feb 16	The K to Alfonso infant of Aragon upon the said treaty of marriage. *Westm* R. ii 589 O iv 129 H ii p ii. 127.
Feb 16	Will de Dene and Steph de Abyndon appointed to settle terms of peace between the English and the Flemings *Westm* R ii. 589 O iv 129 H ii p ii 127
Feb 17.	The K of England informs the councillors of the K of Norway that he desires to have peace with their realm. *Westm.* R. ii 590 O iv. 130 H ii p ii 127
Feb 18	The K of England to James K of Aragon respecting the seizure of the galleys of the K of Majorca *Tower of London* R ii 590 O iv 130 H ii p ii 128.
Feb 19	Commission to settle a marriage between Alfonso, heir of Aragon, and Johanna, daughter of K Edward *Tower of London.* R ii 590 O iv 131. H ii p. ii 128
Feb 19	Letters patent respecting the said contract of marriage *Tower of London.* R. ii 591 O iv 132 H ii p ii 128
Feb 19	Commission to treat of a special confederation with James K. of Aragon. *Tower of London.* R. ii 591 O. iv. 133. H ii p ii 129
Feb 19	Similar commission to treat with Alfonso K of Aragon *Tower of London* R. ii 591 O iv 132 H ii p ii 129
Feb. 20	The K. informs the nobles and prelates whom he had previously summoned, that he has postponed his expedition into Aquitain *Westm* R ii 591 O iv 133. H ii p. ii 129.
Feb 20	The K orders Wm de Bradeshawe and 149 others to be ready at Portsmouth to proceed to Gascony, notwithstanding the above prorogation *Westm* R ii 591 O. iv 133. H ii p ii 129
Feb 26	The K orders certain payments to be made to John de Warren, earl of Surrey, going into Aquitain *Tower of London* R ii 592 O iv 135 H ii p ii 130
Feb 26	Similar order for Peter de Montfort. *Tower of London* R ii 593 O iv 135 H ii p ii 130
Feb. 26	Similar order for Rob FitzPaine *Tower of London* R ii 593 O iv 136 H ii. p ii 130.
Feb 26	Similar order for David Strabolgi, earl of Athol *Tower of London.* R. ii. 593. O. iv. 136 H. ii p ii. 130
Feb 26	Ordinances for the levying of troops in North and South Wales for the service of the K in Aquitain *Westm* R. ii 593 O iv 136. H ii p ii 130
Feb 26	Safe conduct for merchants and mariners coming into England from Venice. *Westm* R ii 593 O. iv. 138 H ii p ii 131
March 2	The K warrants John de Warren, earl of Surrey, that an arrangement which he had made about 100 men at arms shall not be drawn into a precedent. *Tower of London* R ii 594 O iv 138 H ii. p ii 131
March 3	The K pardons all the cardinals in England from the payment of tenths, &c due to the Exchequer *Tower of London* R ii 594.
March 5	Writ for the payment of 5 marks to Wm Herle going to York to treat with the Scotch. *Tower of London.* R ii 594 O iv 139. H. ii. p. ii. 131
March 6	Writ for the payment of 100s to Wm. de Beauchamp [going into Aquitain] *Tower of London.* R ii 594 O iv 139 H ii p ii 131
March 6	The K asks the prayers of the General Chapter of the Friars Preachers about to meet at Venice *Tower of London* R ii 594 O. iv 139. H. ii. p. ii, 132.
March 7	The K orders 5,000*l* to be paid to Wm de Oterhampton for the expenses of the expedition into Aquitain *Tower of London* R ii 595. O iv 139 H ii p ii 132
March 8	The K informs the pope that he has sent Q Isabella into France to procure peace, that the Scotch refuse to come to terms, and that he has exempted the cardinals beneficed in England from the payment of tenths *Tower of London* R ii 595 O iv 140. H ii p ii.132.
March 8	The K. informs the said cardinals of the exemption mentioned above *Tower of London* R ii 595 O iv 141 H. ii p ii 132
• March 18	The K. orders that springalds and other engines of war be provided for the castles and towns of Aquitain *Westm* R ii. 596 O iv 142 H ii p ii. 133

DATE	SUBJECT.
1325. March 18	The K thanks 14 nobles of Gascony for their good service against the French *Westm.* R ıı 596. O. ıv. 142 H. ıı. p. ıı 143
April 1	The K appoints John de Warren, earl of Surrey, captain of the men at arms going to Aquitain. *Merewell* R. ıı 596. O ıv. 143. H ıı. p ıı 133.
April 2.	The K orders that messengers coming from abroad shall be prevented from publishing news. *Merewell.* R. ıı. 596
April 8	Protection for the bp of Orange and Henry lord of Sully coming from France as messengers to the K *King's Beaulieu* R ıı 596 O ıv. 143 H ıı p ıı 133
April 11	The K authorizes Edmund earl of Kent and others to receive into his peace the people of Gascony who had joined the French. *King's Beaulieu* R ıı. 597. O ıv 143 H. ıı p. ıı. 133.
April 14.	The K appoints commissioners to see that the truce with the Scotch is observed in Northumberland *King's Beaulieu* R. ıı. 597. O ıv. 144 H. ıı p ıı 133
April 18	Proclamation that the truce with France is prolonged *King's Beaulieu.* R ıı 597. O. ıv. 144 H ıı. p ıı 134.
. April 20	The K. orders that wheat be sold at a reasonable price in London *King's Beaulieu* R. ıı 597
May 6	Commissioners appointed to treat with the K of France for the extension of the truce *Winchester* R. ıı 597 O ıv. 145. H ıı p. ıı. 134.
May 6	Additional powers to the said commissioners for the settlement of the disputes with the K. of France *Winchester.* R. ıı. 598. O ıv 145 H ıı p ıı 134
May 7	The K of England asks Alfonso K of Portugal and his mother Isabella to permit provisions to be conveyed into Gascony *Winchester* R ıı 598 O ıv 146 H ıı p ıı 134
May 8	The K. appoints commissioners to secure the observance of the truce with the Scotch in Cumberland and Westmorland *Winchester* R. ıı 598 O ıv 146 H. ıı. p ıı. 134.
May 8	Grant of additional powers to the commissioners appointed by the K to treat for peace with France *Winchester* R ıı. 598. O ıv 147 H ıı p ıı 134
May 10.	The town of Bruges appoints proctors to treat with the K. respecting commercial intercourse between Flanders and England. R ıı. 598 O ıv 147 H. ıı p ıı. 135
May 12	The K orders Richard de Sobbury to see that the letters sent by the K. to the pope be presented without delay *Forchester* R ıı 599. O ıv. 148 H ıı p ıı. 135
May 14.	The K. informs the pope of the position of affairs respecting the Queen Isabella and the Scotch. *Porchester* R. ıı 599. O ıv 148 H ıı p ıı 135
May 25	Charles K. of France appoints commissioners to treat of peace with England *Font Briand.* R ıı. 600 O ıv 150 H. ıı p ıı 136
May 28	The K extends the duration of the truce between England and Flanders *Chertsey* R ıı. 600. O ıv 151. H. ıı p ıı 136.
May 28	The K asks the pope to depose the abp of Dublin from his see, he having betrayed Reole to the K of France *Chertsey* R. ıı 600. O ıv 152. H ıı p ıı. 137.
May 28	The K. asks the pope to depose the bp of Hereford from his see, he having joined the K's rebels *Chertsey.* R. ıı 600. O ıv. 153 H ıı p ıı 137.
June 13.	Agreement between the commissioners of England and France respecting Guienne and Gascony *Westm* R ıı 601 O ıv. 153. H ıı p ıı 137
[June 13.]	Agreement respecting the interchange of lands in Guienne and Gascony according to the previous document. *Westm* R ıı 602. O ıv 156. H ıı p ıı 138
[June 13.]	The commissioners of the K of France announce that they have extended the period for the homage to be made by the K of England *Paris* R. ıı 602 O ıv. 156 H ıı. p ıı 138.
June 13	The K confirms the agreements mentioned above *Westm* R. ıı 603. O. ıv. 157. H ıı p. ıı. 138.
June 13	The K orders the proclamation of the extension of the truce with France *Kennington.* R ıı 603. O ıv 157 H ıı p ıı 138
July 19	The K. informs Alfonso K of Portugal that he cannot treat of a marriage unless accredited messengers be sent. *Tower of London* R ıı 603 O ıv. 158. H. ıı. p. ıı 138.
July 20.	The K (about to go into France) appoints conservators of the truce with Scotland during his absence *Tower of London* R ıı 603 O ıv 158 H ıı p. ıı 139
July 20.	The K. appoints commissioners to watch the ports and sea-coasts in Northumberland during his absence in France. *Tower of London.* R. ıı. 603 O ıv 158 H ıı p ıı 139

DATE.	SUBJECT
1325 July 29	The K orders the constable of Dover and warden of the Cinque Ports to provide shipping for his voyage into France *Writle* R ii 604
Aug 8.	The K orders the abp of Canterbury, the mayor of London, and others, not to molest the abp of York in carrying his cross *Havring atte Bower* R ii 604
Aug 15	The K orders the warden of the Cinque Ports to see that no abbots or other religious person leave the realm. *Pomfret* R. ii 604
Aug. 21.	Letters of protection and attorney for various persons about to accompany the K to the parts beyond the sea *Sturrey* R ii 604 O iv 159 H ii p ii 139.
Aug. 24	The K, being detained by illness, appoints commissioners to settle another meeting with the K of France *Langedon, near Dover* R ii 604. O iv 163 H ii p ii 141
Aug 27	The K orders that the truce with Flanders be strictly observed. *Langdon* R. ii 605
Sept 2	The K grants to his son Edward the comté of Ponthieu and Montreuil *Abbey of Langdon, near Dover* R ii 605 O iv. 163 H ii p ii 141
Sept. 4.	Charles K of France notifies that he has received the homage of Edward son of the K of England *Château-Neuf-sur-Loire* R ii 607. O iv. 164. H ii p ii. 141.
Sept. 10.	The K grants to his son Edward the entire duchy of Aquitain. *Dover* R ii 607 O iv. 165 H ii p ii. 142
Sept 10	The K requires all archbps, &c in Aquitain, Ponthieu, and Montreuil to obey his son Edward. *Dover* R. ii 608 O iv 166 H ii. p ii 142.
Sept. 10	The K of England to James K of Aragon on the complaint made by his subjects of having been plundered by English pirates *Dover.* R ii 608 O iv. 166. H ii p ii 142.
Sept 10.	The K thanks John Eximinius de Urrea for the offer of aid *Dover.* R ii. 608 O. iv 167 H ii p ii 143.
Sept 10	Proclamation by the K that he has remitted all ill will which he had against the K. of France. *Dover* R ii 608
Sept. 12	Safe conduct for the messengers of Wm count of Holland coming to treat with the K. *Dover* R. ii 609
Sept 12	Memorandum that Edward, the K's eldest son, embarked at Dover for France, to do homage to the K of France R ii 609 O iv. 168 H ii p ii 143
Sept. 23	The K advises Edmund earl of Kent how to proceed on the reported death of Regina countess of Armignac. *Marsfield.* R ii. 609. O. iv. 168. H ii p ii 148
Sept. 24	The K asks the pope not to revoke the censures which he had issued against the Scotch. *Marsfield.* H ii 609 O iv 168. H ii p. ii 143
Sept 25	The K to various cardinals on the same subject *Marsfield* R. ii 609. O iv. 169. H ii. p ii 143
Sept 30	The K appoints various persons to arrest all suspected persons at the ports, and to search for the same *Marsfield* R ii 610
Oct. 2.	The K orders Edmund earl of Kent to take care that the interests of the K's son Edward be not prejudiced by the death of the countess of Armignac. *Marsfield.* R. ii. 610. O iv. 170. H ii p ii. 144.
Oct. 15.	The K asks 25 of the nobles, bishops, and others of Gascony to continue their good services to his son Edward *Shene* R ii 610 O. iv. 171. H ii p ii 144.
Oct 15.	The K. informs the papal nuncios that he has made every effort for the preservation of peace with France, but with what success he does not know. *Shene.* R. ii 611. O iv. 172. H ii p ii 144.
Oct. 15.	The K. to Alfonso K of Aragon, will be glad to proceed with the treaty for a marriage. *Shene.* R. ii 611). O iv 172 H ii p ii 144.
Oct 15	Credence for two messengers going from the K of England to K Alfonso for the same purpose. *Shene* R ii. 611 O iv 173 H. ii p ii 145.
Oct 15	The K to the bp of Burgos [in Spain] and 5 others, on the same subject. *Shene.* R. ii. 611. O. iv. 173 H. ii p ii 145
Oct 15	The K. thanks 26 noblemen of Spain for their offer of help, and asks credence for the said messengers *Shene* R ii 611. O iv 173 H ii p ii. 175
Oct 15	Credence for the same messengers going from the K. to the abp of Saragossa *Shene.* R. ii 612. O iv. 174 H ii p. ii. 145
Oct. 16.	The K asks his son Edward to remit a certain fine due by Mata, wife of Bernard de Lebret. *Shene.* R. ii. 612. O. iv 174 H ii p ii 145.

DATE.	SUBJECT.
1325 Oct. 16	The K asks 13 cardinals to grant dispensations for two marriages between his children and Alfonso K. of Spain and his sister *Shene.* R ii 612. O. iv. 175. H. ii. p. ii 145
Oct. 18.	Credence for Petrus Galiciani going from the K of England to Alfonso, eldest son of the K. of Aragon. *Shene.* R. ii. 613. O iv 176. H. ii. p ii 146.
Oct 18.	The K thanks the pope for having rejected the petition of the Scotch, and informs him of the state of his own affairs with France. *Shene.* R. ii. 613 O. iv. 176. H. ii p ii 146.
Oct. 18.	The K to two cardinals, on the same subject. *Shene* R ii 613 O. iv. 177 H ii. p ii 146
Oct. 18	The K asks John de Warren, earl of Surrey, and three others to continue to hold their offices in Gascony *Shene* R ii. 613 O. iv 178 H ii p ii 146
Oct. 20.	The K orders the extension of the truce with John duke of Brittany *Chippenham.* R ii 614 O iv 178 H ii p. ii 147
Oct. 20.	The K. asks Arnald Guilhelmi, lord of Lescun, to co-operate along with Petro de Galiciano in promoting the Spanish matches *Chippenham* R ii 614 O iv 179 H ii p ii 147.
Oct. 29	The K. orders that the forfeited manors and lands of certain of his enemies and rebels be let to farm. *Chippenham.* R ii 614
Nov 8	The K orders the discharge of the ships which had been arrested for his service. *Chippenham.* R ii 614.
Nov. 27.	The K proposes the interchange of letters of safe conduct between the English and the subjects of Wm. count of Holland *Westm* R ii 614 O iv 179 H. ii p ii 147
Dec 1.	The K of England informs the K of France, and 16 bishops and nobles of France, of his disquietude in consequence of the unexpected and lengthened absence of Q Isabella and his son Edward, and cautions them against English traitors in the French court *Westm.* R. ii. 615 O. iv. 180 H. ii. p. ii. 147.
Dec. 1.	The K. urges Q Isabella to return home with prince Edward, and to avoid the company of certain English traitors in the French court *Westm.* R ii 615 O iv 181. H. ii. p ii. 148.
Dec 2.	The K orders his son to return home with his mother, if possible, or if not, without her. *Westm* R ii 616. O. iv. 182 H ii p ii 148.
Dec 5	The K informs the pope by a special messenger of the state of affairs between him and France *Westm* R ii 616 O iv. 182 H ii p ii 148.
Dec 5	The K to 18 cardinals and others on the same subject as the preceding *Westm.* R. ii 616. O. iv. 183. H ii. p. ii. 148.
Dec 10.	The K orders the arrest of all persons introducing into England letters from abroad. *Tower of London.* R ii 616 O iv. 183 H ii p ii 148.
Dec 12	The K orders that all persons be knighted who are duly qualified. *Tower of London.* R. ii. 616. O iv 184 H. ii. p. ii. 149
Dec 26.	The K orders certain abps , bps , and abbots to see that nothing be done to prejudice the rights of the crown *S Edmund's* R ii 617 O iv. 184. H ii p ii. 149.
1326. Jan. 1.	The K informs the lady Majora Garcia that his son Edward is not married, and is not about to be married, in France *S Edmund's* R ii 617 O iv 185 H ii p ii 149.
Jan 3.	The K appoints inspectors at ports and elsewhere throughout the realm to prevent the introduction of letters from abroad. *Haule.* R. ii. 617 O iv 186 H ii p. ii 149
Jan 3	The K. asks the pope not to grant a dispensation for any treaty of marriage between the royal families of France and England without the express approval of the writer *Haule.* R ii 618 O. iv 186 H ii p ii 150
Jan. 13.	The K. orders that no persons (merchants only excepted) be allowed to cross from England *South Elmham* R ii. 618
Jan 22.	The K. assures Wm count of Holland that he is ready to satisfy all the reasonable demands of his merchants *Norwich* R ii 618. O iv. 187. H ii p ii 150
Jan. 23.	The K. informs the burgomasters, &c of Bruges of the extension of the truce with England. *Norwich.* R. ii 618. O. iv 188. H. ii p. ii. 150.
Jan 26.	The K. commands the prior and brethen of the hospital of S, John of Jerusalem not to export money from England. *Norwich* R ii. 618.
Feb. 4.	The K. orders proclamation to be made against the exportation of horses, arms, gold and silver from England. *Walsingham* R. ii 619

DATE	SUBJECT
1326 Feb 8	The K., fearing a descent of his enemies upon the seacoasts, orders all sheriffs, the admirals of his fleet and others, to be prepared to repel the invaders *Gaywood* R ii 619. O iv. 188 H. ii p i 150
Feb. 18	The K orders inquiry to be made respecting a whale cast ashore upon the manor of Walton, belonging to the church of St Paul's, London. *Barnwell* R. ii 619
Feb 20	The K intercedes with the pope in favour of the university of Oxford against cardinal Gaillard, archdeacon of Oxford *Barnwell* R. ii 620 O iv 189 H ii p ii 151.
Feb 20.	The K asks cardinal Gaillard to permit the said dispute to be heard and determined in England. *Barnwell.* R ii. 620 O iv 190 H ii. p ii 151.
April [?] 20 Feb ?	The K asks the cardinal of S Maria in Aquiro to intercede with the pope in favor of the university of Oxford in the above dispute *Kenilworth* R. ii 620 O iv 190. H ii. p ii. 151
Feb. 25.	Credence for Arnold Calculi [? Caillau] going to Bernard Jordani, lord " de Insula " *Langeton.* R. ii. 620. O. iv. 191. H ii p. ii. 151.
Feb 25	Credence for Arnold de Duro Forti [? Durfort] going to the same, and for Peter de Greylin *Langeton* R ii 621 O iv 191 H. ii p ii 151
Feb. 25	Credence for Arnald Calculi [? Caillau] going to various persons on the K's service *Langeton* R ii. 621. O iv. 191. H. ii p. ii 151.
Feb. 25	Credence for the same going to James K of Aragon. *Langeton* R ii. 621 O iv-192. H ii p ii 152
Feb 25	Credence for the same going to Alfonso, son of the K of Aragon, and various other noble personages in Spain *Langeton* R ii. 621. O iv. 192. H ii p ii 152
Feb 25	Credence for the same and Wm de Weston going to the pope *Langeton* R. ii 621. O iv. 192. H ii p ii. 152
March 6	The K orders Wm de Aremynne (said to be bp. of Norwich) to appear before the K. and council to give an account of his proceedings in France *Leicester.* R ii 622 O iv 193 H. ii p. ii. 152
March 10	The K orders that proclamation be made of a statement of recent transactions between himself and the K of France *Mireval* R ii 622
March 13	The K orders the arrest of John de Britannia, earl of Richmond *Tamworth.* R ii 622 O iv 193 H ii p ii 152
March 18	The K of England informs the K of France of the causes of his dissatisfaction with the conduct of Q Isabella *Lichfield* R. ii. 622 O iv 194 H ii p ii. 153.
March 18	The K orders his son Edward to enter into no contract of marriage, and to return without delay into England. *Lichfield* R ii 623 O iv. 195 H ii p. ii 153.
March 18	The K orders that his previous proclamation be enforced as to strict search being made for suspicious persons coming into England *Lichfield.* R. ii. 623 O. iv. 196. H. ii. p ii 153
March 24	The K (as guardian of his son Edward) orders compensation for the loss of certain of his lands in Aquitain, seized by the French, to be made to Reymund Duran *Kenilworth* R ii 623 O iv 197. H ii p. ii 154
March 24.	The K (in the same capacity) grants to the same Reymund the office of seneschal of Les Landes in the duchy of Aquitain *Kenilworth.* R ii. 624 O iv 197 H ii p ii 154.
March 24.	The K (in the same capacity) asks to be certified as to the services of Pontius Amaneri de Madalhano in the war in Gascony. *Kenilworth* R ii 624 O iv. 198 H. ii. p ii 154.
March 25	The K cautions Henry de Percy and Anthony de Luscy to be more careful in granting safe conducts to the Scotch to come into England *Kenilworth* R ii. 624 O iv 198. H ii p ii. 154
April 1.	The K asks the pope to grant another pall to Wm. abp. of York, the previous one having been stolen out of his chapel. *Kenilworth.* R. ii 624. O iv 199 H. ii p ii 154
April 1.	The K. orders proclamation to be made that " truce has been entered into with the Flemings. *Kenilworth* R ii 624. O iv 199 H ii p ii. 154
April 2	The K notifies to the burgomasters of Bruges the publication of the above mentioned truce *Kenilworth* R ii 625 O. iv 199 H ii p ii. 155.
April 15	The K asks the pope to give no heed to various false reports respecting his conduct towards his wife and his son Edward. *Kenilworth* R ii. 625 O iv 200 H. ii. p ii 155.
April 15	The K of England informs Alfonso K. of Portugal that he is not at present at liberty to treat with Alfonso relative to the marriage of his son Edward *Kenilworth* R ii. 625. O. iv. 201 H ii p ii 155

DATE	SUBJECT
1326. April 15.	The K to Beatrice Q of Portugal, on the same subject as the preceding *Kenilworth* R. ii. 626. O. iv 201. H ii p ii 155
April 18.	The K orders the arrest of such persons as circulate false reports. *Kenilworth.* R. ii. 626. O iv. 202. H. ii p. ii. 155.
April 25	Safe conduct for the messengers of the K. of Portugal coming into England. *Kenilworth* R ii 625 O. iv. 200 H ii p ii 155
April 28	The K orders the arrest of certain armed persons who wander about the realm *Kenilworth.* R ii 626. O iv 202 H ii p ii. 156.
April 28.	The K orders that a free passage into England be granted to Hugh de Ingoliama, coming from the pope *Kenilworth* R ii 626 O iv 203 H ii p ii. 156.
April 29.	The K orders L bp of Durham and others to fortify and victual the castles of Norham, Alnwick, Dunstanburgh, Werk, and Toteneys, against the Scotch. *Kenilworth* R ii 626-7
May 12	The K orders the 2 abps and 17 bps to prepare for the defence of the church and realm of England *Gloucester* R. ii 627 O iv 203 H ii p. ii 156
May 12.	The K orders increased vigilance to be exercised in Kent and Essex against the introduction of treasonable letters into England *Gloucester.* R ii 627 O iv. 204. H. ii p ii. 156
May 18.	Safe conduct for Wm abp of Vienne and Hugh bp of Orange, nuncios coming from the pope to the K. *Marlbro'* R ii 627 O iv 205. H ii. p ii 157.
May 19	Instructions to Ralph Basset, constable of Dover, as to the mode in which he shall receive the nuncios above-mentioned *Marlbro'.* R. ii. 628. O iv 205 H ii p. ii 157
May 19.	The K orders the sheriff of Kent to assist the constable of Dover in receiving the said nuncios. *Marlbro'* R ii 628 O iv 206 H ii p ii. 157.
May 19	The K orders Nicholas Kyriel, admiral of the fleet to the west of the Thames, to assist in the above reception *Okebourne.* R ii. 628 O. iv. 207. H ii p ii 157
May 20.	The K. orders the constables of 16 castles carefully to guard the prisoners confined therein. *Crokeham* R ii 629
June 3	The K notifies the extension of the truce with the merchants of Flanders. *Saltwood* R ii 629 O iv 207 H ii p. ii. 158
June 10	The K. to the pope relative to the arrival of his nuncios, to the delay in the payment of the annual tribute, and to other matters *Sturreye* R ii 629 O iv 208 H ii. p. ii. 158.
[June 10]	The answer made by the K to the said nuncios on their presentation to him on their arrival R ii 629 O iv 209 H ii p ii 168
June 18.	The K to the pope upon the ingratitude and disobedience of John de Britannia earl of Richmond. *Tower of London* R ii 630 O iv 209 H ii. p. ii 158
June 19.	The K complains to the bp of Beauvais of the misconduct of Q Isabella, and of the long absence of his son Edw in France *Westm* R. ii 630. O iv 210 H ii p ii 159
[June 19.]	The K rebukes his son Edward for his disobedience, and orders him to return to England forthwith. R. ii. 630 O. iv 211. H ii p ii 159.
[June 19.]	The K of England to the K. of France, complaining of the disobedience of his wife and son R ii 631 O iv 212 H. ii p ii 159
[June 20]	Regulations for the preservation of peace and order within the city of London R ii 631
June 23.	Credence for three messengers sent from the K. to treat of a truce with Robert de Brus *Tower of London.* R ii 631 O iv. 212 H ii p ii 159
June 24.	Commission to Oliver de Ingham and others to receive into the K.'s fealty certain of his subjects in Gascony who had joined the French. *Tower of London* R. ii. 632 O iv 213. H. ii p ii 160
June 24.	The K receives into his favour Amanemus lord of Lebret, who had joined the French *Tower of London.* R ii 632. O iv 213 H ii p. ii 160
June 27.	The K. (as guardian of his son Edward) informs various cities, &c. in Gascony of the reforms to be introduced into the administration of the duchy. *Westm* R. ii. 632. O iv 214 H ii p ii. 160
June 30	The K (in the same capacity) issues orders for the security of the castles in Gascony belonging to Berard de la Brette. *Westm.* R ii 633. O. iv. 215. H. ii p ii. 161.
July 1	The K asks the pope to substitute the bp of Orange for some one of the English bps. whose deposition he had previously solicited *Westm* R ii 633 O. iv 216. H. ii. p ii 161

DATE	SUBJECT
1326. July 6.	The K. of England asks the citizens of Bayonne to annoy and injure all the subjects of the K. of France excepting the Flemings *Heule* R ii 633 O. iv. 216. H. ii. p. ii. 161
July 10.	Proclamation of the postponement of the military service about to proceed into Gascony until the K shall be informed of the issue of a treaty now pending with France *Westm.* R ii. 633. O iv 217 H ii p. ii 161
July 10.	The K informs Thomas earl of Norfolk and 42 other nobles of the prorogation of the said expedition *Westm.* R. ii 634 O. iv. 217. H ii p ii. 161.
July 16	Safe conduct for two messengers returning to France with the answer to the letters which they had brought from the K of France to the K of England *Westm.* R. ii. 634.
July 18.	The K. notifies that he has explained his pleasure to Ralph Basset of Drayton and Ralph de Camoys as to the war with France. *Westm* R. ii. 634 O iv 218 H ii. p ii. 162
July 18	The K encourages the men of Shoreham to annoy the shipping of the subjects of the K of France (the Flemings and Bretons excepted) *Westm* R iv. 634 O iv 218. H ii p ii 162.
July 20	The K grants facilities for increased intercourse with foreign merchants, the French excepted. *Westm.* R. ii. 635. O. iv. 219 H. ii. p. ii. 162.
July 90	Commission to collect the gold found in the tin mines in Devon and Cornwall. *Westm.* R ii 635
July 21.	The K appoints John atte Gotere of Boston to be his steward of the lands lately belonging to John de Britannia, earl of Richmond *Westm* R. ii 635. O iv 220. H ii p. ii 162
July 23	The K orders that two standards of the new coin lately issued for Aquitain be preserved at the Exchequer *Westm* R ii 636
Aug 4.	The K orders it to be proclaimed that no one is to introduce into the realm from abroad letters prejudicial to the K *Porchester* R ii 636. O iv 220 H ii p ii 163.
Aug 4	The K to the persons appointed to search along the sea-coasts, to the same effect as the preceding *Porchester* R. ii. 636 O iv 221 H ii p ii 163
Aug 4	The K orders the persons appointed to array men-at-arms in various counties to proceed with the execution of the same according to the statute of Winchester *Porchester.* R ii 636
Aug 10	The K. orders the above commissioners to provide for the erection and firing of beacons along the coast, wherever necessary *Clarendon* R. ii. 636.
Aug 11.	The K directs the abps of Canterbury and York to see that the people are informed of the state of the realm, and of the K's desire for peace with France *Clarendon* R ii. 637. O iv. 221 H ii p ii 163.
Aug 12	The K. summons his navy to assemble at Portsmouth to repel the descent of the French. *Clarendon* R ii. 637.
Aug 15	The K orders that watch be kept from the mouth of the Thames northward against the apprehended invasion of the realm *Clarendon* R ii 638
Aug 26.	The K orders the arrest of all subjects of the K of France (the Flemings and Bretons only excepted) who are found in England *Clarendon.* R ii 638 O iv 222. H. ii p. ii 163.
Aug 26.	Similar order applicable to the islands of Jersey, Guernsey, Alderney, and Sark. *Clarendon* R ii 638. O. iv. 223 H ii p ii 164
Aug 29	Commission to Peter de Geyton to arrest all Frenchmen found in England *Fontelie* R ii. 638 O iv 224. H. ii. p. ii. 164.
Aug 29.	Credence for Robert de Welle, going from the K. to explain to Robert de Brus certain matters connected with the truce with Scotland. *Fonteleye* R ii 639. O. iv. 224 H ii. p ii 164.
Sept 3	Commission to inspect the ships required for the K's service against the French. *Porchester* R. ii 639. O iv 225. H. ii. p. ii 164.
Sept. 3	The K. orders that such alien monks, natives of France, as reside near the sea, in England, shall be removed to other houses further from the coast *Porchester* R. ii 640.
Sept 4	The K orders the men of Bayonne to attack all subjects of the K of France, the Flemings excepted, and to aid him with shipping for this purpose. *Porchester.* R. ii. 640. O. iv 226. H. ii p ii 165
Sept. 4.	The K. orders seven citizens of Bayonne to expedite the dispatch of the above shipping. *Porchester.* R. ii. 640. O. iv. 227. H. ii. p. ii 165.

DATE	SUBJECT
1326 Sept. 6.	The K asks the prayers of the universities of Oxford and Cambridge for himself and his realm, suffering from the malice of the K of France *Porchester.* R II 640–1. O IV 227. H. II. p II 165
Sept. 6.	The K. asks the prayers of the general chapter of the Friars Preachers about to meet at Oxford. *Porchester.* R. II. 641.
Sept 8.	The K orders the bailiffs of Bristol to arrest all the men of Marmand found within their jurisdiction, that town having treasonably surrendered to the French. *Porchester.* R. II 641 O II. 228. H II p II. 166
Sept. 10.	The K. orders the arrest of all French found within the realm. *Porchester* R. II. 641. O. IV. 228. H. II p. II 166.
Sept 12.	Proclamation to be made that the men, &c of Wm. de Ayremynne, bp. of Norwich, shall be protected *Porchester* R II 641
Sept 14.	The K. requests W abp. of Canterbury to postpone for a time the meeting of the provincial council of his province. *Porchester* R. II. 642.
Sept 24.	The K. directs the constable of Dover and the mayor and bailiffs of 71 other places to search for letters coming from abroad, and to arrest all suspected persons *Marsfield* R II. 642 O IV 229 H II p. II 166
Sept 25.	The K. to the mayors of Antwerp, Brussels, &c, asking them to procure the liberation of Wm. de Weston, his clerk, taken prisoner while returning from the pope *Tower of London.* R II 643.
Sept 25	The K to John duke of Brabant and Margaret duchess of Brabant, to the same effect as the preceding. *Tower of London* R II 643.
Sept. 27.	The K orders all persons to assist Robt de Watevylle to suppress the rising occasioned by the arrival in England of the Queen, prince Edward, and Roger de Mortimer. *Tower of London* R. II. 643 O IV. 231 H II p II 167.
Sept 28.	The K promises to pardon those persons who abandon Roger de Mortimer, and sets a price upon him, alive or dead *Tower of London* R. II 644 O. IV 232 H II. p II 167
Sept 28.	The K orders that no heed is to be given to any writs issued by his wife, his son, or the earl of Kent, his brother, and that no aid is to be afforded them. *Tower of London.* R. II. 644. O IV 233 H II p II 167
Sept. 28.	The K. orders aid to be given to Daniel de Burgham in raising men against Roger de Mortimer *Tower of London* R II 645 O IV 234 H II p. II 168
Sept. 28.	Similar aid to be given to Simon de Redding and John de Bray. *Tower of London* R. II. 645 O IV. 234. H. II p. II 168
Sept 28.	Similar aid to be given to Ralph de Wedon. *Tower of London* R II 645 O IV 235. H II. p. II 168
Sept 30 *	The K orders Ralph de Cammoys and Rob. de Kendale, constable of Dover Castle and warden of the Cinque Ports, to be diligent in arresting suspected persons and in searching for letters. *Marsfield* O IV 235 H. II. p. II. 169.
Oct. 11.	The K orders the deliverance of certain prisoners, provided they serve him against his enemies *Gloucester.* R II 645
Oct. 15	Queen Isabella, her son Edward, and Edmund earl of Kent, notify the causes which have induced them to rise against the K and invade the realm. *Wallingford* R II 645. O. IV. 236. H II. p. II. 169
Oct. 26	Narrative of the circumstances connected with the resignation of the K and the surrender of the great seal to the Queen and the prince. R II 646 O. IV 237. H II p II. 169
Oct. 29.	The K. orders the levying of horse and foot-soldiers in Wales for his defence against the rebels *Kerfilly.* R. II. 646 O IV 238. H. II p. II. 170.
Nov 10.	Protection for certain messengers going from the K. to the Queen and prince Edward *Neeth* R II 647 O. IV 239. H II p II 170
Nov 30.†	Safe conduct for two nuncios coming from the pope into England. *Ledbury* R. II 647. O. IV 239. H. II p II. 170
Dec. 3.	Writ for the payment of 10*l* to certain sailors of Bayonne who had aided Queen Isabella in coming into England from abroad *Ledbury.* R. II. 647 O IV 239. H. II p II 170.
Dec 5.	The K. restores to the aldermen, sheriffs, and commonalty of London the free election of a mayor for the city of London. *Kenilworth.* R II 647

---

* This document has been accidentally omitted in the Record edition of the Foedera
† From this point to the end of his reign the King was in prison

DATE	SUBJECT
1326 Dec. 6	The K orders the warden of the Cinque Ports to provide a free passage for the men-at-arms of Hainault, returning from Dover into Flanders. *Kenilworth.* R ii. 647.
Dec 12.	The K forbids the holding of tournaments in England *Kenilworth* R, ii 648.
Dec 14	The K orders the barons of the Exchequer to provide a free passage for the men-at-arms from Germany and Hainault, returning from Dover to the Swyn in Flanders. *Kenilworth* R. ii. 648.
Dec. 14	The K orders that 60 does from the park of Braburn be salted for the use of the approaching parliament at Westminster *Kenilworth.* R. ii 648 O iv 240 H ii. p ii. 170
Dec 18	The K recommends to the pope John Bercleye, as well qualified to fill the vacant see of Exeter. *Kenilworth* R ii. 648. O iv 270 H ii p. ii 170.
Dec 18	The K to certain cardinals, to the same effect *Kenilworth.* R ii 648 O. iv 240 H. ii. p ii 170
Dec 25	The K orders his castles and manors to be restored to John de Britannia earl of Richmond *Kenilworth* R. ii. 648. O iv 241. H ii. p. ii. 171.
- Dec 26	Commission to treat with Robert de Brus for a final peace *Kenilworth* R ii 649
1327. Jan 4	The K pardons John de Felton for having held the castle of Kerfilly against the Queen and prince Edw *Kenilworth* R ii 649
Jan. 4.	The K pardons the garrison of Kerfilly (excepting Hugh de Despenser the younger) for having held the castle of Kerfilly against the Queen and prince Edw *Kenilworth* R. ii 649
Jan 11	The K summons 24 men, English and Welsh, from N Wales, to attend the parliament at Westminster. *Kenilworth.* R. ii 649. O iv. 242 H ii p ii, 171.
Jan 12	The K orders Wm de Synythwayt to surrender the custody of the chase of Wenslaydale to John de Scargill, appointed keeper of the same by John de Britannia, earl of Richmond *Kenilworth* R ii 649 O iv 242 H ii p ii 171.
[Jan]	Deposition of K. Edward II in the parliament held at Westminster, and the election of his son K. Edward III. R ii 650

EDWARD III.

(25 *Jan* 1327–21 *June* 1377)

Jan, 24.	Proclamation of the K's peace at London. R ii p ii 683. O iv 243. H ii p ii. 171.
Jan 28	Delivery of the great seal to John bp of Ely. *Westm* R. ii p ii 683. O iv 243 H. ii p ii 171
Jan 29	The K signifies the voluntary abdication of his father, and orders his peace to be proclaimed by the sheriff of York, the warden of the Cinque Ports, and nine others *Westm.* R ii p ii 683 O iv 243 H ii p ii 171
Feb 1	Coronation of the K. at Westminster Present nine bishops, five earls, and others R ii. p. ii 684 O. iv 244. H. ii. p ii. 172.
Feb 3.	Petitions in parliament by the adherents of Thomas earl of Lancaster for the restitution of their lands, with the answers. *Westm* R. ii p ii. 684 O. iv. 245 H. ii p ii 172
Feb 4 *	John de Britannia, earl of Richmond, appointed to confer with the French nuncios *Westm* O. iv. 246
Feb 4	The K restores to the prior of Newport Paynel and 64 other alien priories their lands in England, seized on account of the war in Aquitain. *Westm.* R ii p ii 684 O iv. 246. H ii p. ii 173
Feb 4	The K. forbids tournaments. *Westm.* R. ii. p. ii. 685.
Feb 6.	The K. restores the temporalties to William bp of Norwich *Westm* R. ii p ii 685. O. iv. 248. H ii. p ii. 173.
Feb 7.	The K grants a pension of 1,000 marks yearly to John de Hainault out of the customs in the port of London, until the K. provides him with land to that amount in England *Westm* R ii. p. ii. 686 O. iv 249. H ii p ii 173
Feb. 8.	The K. repays to Dinus Forcetti, of the company of the Bardi of Florence, 2,000*l* lent to Q Isabella when abroad, for the expenses of the late K. *Westm* R. ii. p ii 686 O iv 249. H. ii p ii. 174

* This document has been omitted in the Record Edition, and also in the Hague Edition, but it occurs in another form on the 23rd of February. See p. 240.

DATE	SUBJECT.
1327 Feb 8	Warrant for 360*l* 6*s* 8*d* to be paid to Thomas de London, late keeper of the Queen's wardrobe, for Dinus Forcetti, as above *Westm* R n p n 686 O iv 249 H n p. n 174
Feb 8	Letters of credence addressed to 101 persons and communities for Berard de la Bret, John de Weston, constable of Bordeaux, Arnald Edmundi, Bernard de Semyux, and Peter Descorte. *Westm.* R. n. p ń 686. O. iv. 249. H. ii. p n. 174.
Feb 9	The K cancels a recognizance of the bp of Winchester to the late K for 2,460*l*. 5*s* 10*d* *Westm.* R n. p n 687 O iv 251 H n p n 174
Feb 10	The K orders the sheriff of Leicester to deliver to Henry de Beaumont and Alicia his wife, one of the co-heirs of John Comyn, late earl of Bogban, the manor of Whitewyk, of which Hugh le Despenser had possession by virtue of a recognizance. *Westm* R. n p n 687 O iv. 251 H. n p n. 175.
Feb 12.	The K directs the treasurer and barons of the Exchequer to restore to the abp of Rouen the lands, &c taken from him by the K.'s father on account of the war in Aquitain *Westm* R n. p n 687 O. iv 252 H n p n. 175
[Feb. 12.]	Similar letters for the dean and chapter of Rouen R. n. p n 688. O. iv. 252 H n. p. ii. 175.
Feb 13.	Warrant to Thos de Eynill, keeper of Pontefract Castle, to pay to Ralph de Bulmere, a knight banneret, 60*l* , as wages for keeping the said castle. *Westm* R n p n 688 O iv 253. H n p n 175
Feb. 13	Warrant for the payment to Henry de Percy, warden of the Marches, 1,000 marks for his expenses *Westm* R n p n 688 O iv. 254. H n. p n 176
Feb. 13	The K informs Maurice FitzThomas and 18 others in Ireland of his accession, and appoints Thomas FitzJohn earl of Kildare his justiciary *Westm* R. n p. n 688 O iv 254 H n p ii. 176
[Feb 13]	Similar letters to the bp of Ossory and eight other bishops R n p n 688 O iv 255 H n. p n 176
Feb 14.	The K , pursuant to an act of parliament, cancels the fines imposed upon Edmund de Nevill and nine others of the party of the earl of Lancaster. *Westm* R. n p. n 689 O. iv. 256 H n p n. 176.
Feb. 15	The K orders Henry de Percy, Ralph de Nevyll, Roger Heron, Willm Rydell, and Gilbert de Boroughdon, to maintain the truce with Robert de Bruys *Westm* R n p. n 689 O iv 256 H n p n. 176
Feb. 16	The K appoints Thomas FitzJohn, earl of Kildare, justiciary of Ireland *Westm.* R. n. p. n 689. O. iv. 255 H. n. p n. 176.
Feb. 16	The K restores the temporalties to the bp of Hereford, who had taken part with Thomas earl of Lancaster *Westm.* R. n. p n 689 O. iv 257 H n p n 177
Feb. 17.	The K orders the sheriff of each county to make restitution to William de Kaerdiff and 203 other adherents of the earl of Lancaster. *Westm* R n p n 690 O. iv. 258 H ii. p n 177.
Feb. 19	Order to pay 20,000*l* to John de Oxindon, keeper of the wardrobe of Queen Isabella, for the payment of her debts *Westm.* R n p n 691 O iv 262 H n p n 179.
Feb. 19	The dean and chapter of St Patrick's, Dublin, are not to exact the tenth from benefices of less value than six marks *Westm.* R n p. n. 692.
Feb. 22	Letters of restitution to several sheriffs, for Willm. FitzWaryn and 16 others, adherents of the earl of Lancaster *Westm.* R. n p. n. 692. O. iv. 262. H n p n 179.
Feb 22	Similar letters for Margaret, wife of Bartholomew Badelesmere, and 11 others, to the several keepers of their lands *Westm.* R n p n 692 O. iv 262 H. n. p. n. 179.
	The K annuls the fines imposed on Howel ap Howel and six others, adherents of the Earl of Lancaster. *Westm.* R ii. p ii 693 O iv. 264 H n p n 179
Feb. 22	Commission to John bp. of Winchester, Wm bp. of Norwich, John earl of Richmond, John de Hainault, and Hugo de Audeleye, for making a truce with Charles K of France *Westm* R n p ii. 693 O. iv 264 H. n p n 180
Feb 22	Power for them to treat of all matters in dispute R. n. p. n. 693. O. iv 265. H. ii. p. n 180.
Feb 22.	Power for them to pardon offences in Aquitain during the war. *Westm.* R. ii p. n. 693 O iv 266 H n p n. 180.
Feb. 22.	Power for them to treat of making submission to the K. of France. *Westm* R. ii. p. n. 694 O iv 266 H n p ii. 180.

DATE	SUBJECT.
1327 Feb 22.	The K orders the seneschals, constables, &c of his lands beyond sea, and the seneschal of Gascony, to obey them R ıı p ıı 694 O ıv 266 H. ıi p ıı. 181.
Feb 22	Power for them to treat for friendship and alliance with the K of France *Westm* R. ii. p ii. 694 O. ıv 267 H ıı p ıı 181
Feb 23	The K pardons the debts of the cardinals for their benefices in England *Westm* R ıı p ıı 694 O ıv 267 H. ıı p ıı 181
Feb. 23	John of Brittany, earl of Richmond, ordered to join the K's ambassadors in France. *Westm* R ii p ıı 694 O ıv 268. H ıı p ıı 181
Feb 23	The K confirms the grant of 10 casks of wine yearly to his aunt Mary, a nun at Amesbury *Westm.* R ıı p ıı 694 O ıv 268 H ıı p ıı 181.
Feb 28	The K requests of the pope the canonization of Thomas late earl of Lancaster, and sends to him Walter de Burle, Sir Wm Trussel, and John Thoresby, clerk. *London.* R. ıı p ıı 695 O. iv. 268. H. ıı. p. ıı. 181.
March 1	The K desires his justiciary in Ireland to allow to James le Botiller, son and heir of Edmund le Botiller, the prisage of wines in Ireland *Westm* R ıı p ıı 695 O ıv 269 H ıı p ıı 182
March 3.	Reymund de Farges, a Romish cardinal, dean of Salisbury, archdeacon of Leicester and parson of Leek, appoints John de Pinibus, archdeacon of Bazas, and John de Tarenta, canon of Leghtredebury, his attorneys in England. *Wesim* R. ıı p ıı 695 O. ıv. 270 H ıı p ıı 182
March 4.	Power to the abbot of Ryvall and Ivo de Aldeburgh, to treat for peace with Robert de Brus *Westm* R ıı p ıı 695 O ıv 270 H. ıı p ıı 182
	Power to the above to swear to a truce R ıı p. ıı 696. O. ıv 271. H. ıı p. ıı. 182.
March 5.	The K pays to Adam de Bridlelyngton 20*l.* for the keep of the horses of the men of Hainault in the Queen's retinue *Westm* R ıı p ıı 696 O ıv. 271. H ıı p ıı 182.
March 6.	The K confirms the truce granted by his father to the Scots, 30 May 1323. *Westm* R. ıı. p ii 696. O. ıv 271 H. ıı p ıı. 182.
March 8	The K pardons Robert de Malverthorp for having given judgment on Thomas earl of Lancaster *Westm* R ıı p ıı 696 O ıv 271 H p ıı. 182
March 8	The K requests the pope to canonize Robert de Winchelsey, late archbp. of Canterbury. *Westm* R ıı p. ıı. 696. O. ıv 272 H ıı. p. ıı. 183
March 8.	The K releases the clergy of the diocese of Carlisle from their debts, except those for the victuals of the late K *Westm.* R ıı p ıı 696
March 10.	The K. orders Benedict de Fulsham, his butler, to restore to W. archbp of York, the prisage of wines at Hull, pursuant to the Royal charters to the archbps of York. *Westm.* R. ıı. p ıı. 697 O ıv 272 H ıı p ıı 183.
March 10	The K releases H bp. of Lincoln from the fines imposed on him by the late K, through the influence of Hugh le Despenser the younger. *Westm.* R. ıı. p ıı 697. O ıv 274. H ıı. p ıı. 183.
March 10	The K. grants to Pontius de Controne, his physician, 100*l* yearly for services to the late K and Queen Isabella *Westm* R ıı p. ıı 697 O ıv 274 H ıı p ıı 183
March 11	The K requests the pope to canonize John de Daldenby, late bp of Lincoln. *Westm.* R. ii p. ıı 698 O. ıv 275 H. ıı p. ii. 184.
March 13	Release to the K by Maria de St Paul, wife of Adomar de Valentia, late Earl of Pembroke, of the castles of Hertford and Haverford, and manors of Hegham Ferers, Monemuth and Hodenak *Westm.* R. ıı p ıı 698 O ıv 275. H ıı p ıı 184
March 17	The K. orders Richard de Kenebrok, his clerk, to sell certain ships. *Westm.* R ii. p ii 698.
March 24	The K orders the seneschal of Gascony to inquire into the seizure by Oliver de Ingham, late seneschal, of a whale taken in the territory of the viscount de Benanger. *Westm* R. ıı p ıı 698 O. ıv 276 H. ii p ıı 184
March 24.	Letter of credence to the pope for A bp of Hereford, Bartholomew de Burghassh, and Thomas de Astleye, canon of Hereford. *Westm.* R. ii. p. ıı 698. H ıı. p ıı 184
March 24.	Letter of credence for the same to 18 cardinals and nine others R. ıı. p. ii 699. O. ıv. 276. H ıı. p. ıı 184
March 25	The K of England will endeavour to procure from the K. of France the restitution of the lands of Peter de Greyle, viscount de Benanger *Westm* R ıı p ıı. 699 O ıv 277 H ıı p. ıı 185.

DATE.	SUBJECT.
1327. March 26	The K grants to Gaucelinus, a Roman cardinal, the power of obtaining the debts due from his benefices in England, notwithstanding previous prohibitions *Westm.* R. ii. p. ii 699 O. iv 277. H ii p ii 185
March 27	The K. writes to the pope in favour of Roger de Mortimer, clerk *Westm* R ii. p. ii 699
March 29.	The K orders the sheriffs to proclaim the prorogation of the truce with Flanders for two years from next Easter *Westm* R ii p ii 700 O iv 278. H ii p ii. 185
[March 29]	The K writes to the burgomasters of the towns of Bruges and Ypres on the same subject. R ii p ii 700 O iv 278 H ii p ii 185
March 30.	Proclamation to be made at all the ports that no injury is to be done to French merchants *Westm.* R ii p ii 700
March 31	Treaty between England and France *Paris* R. ii. p ii. 700. O. iv. 279. H. ii. p. ii. 185.
April 3.	The K. forbids all religious persons leaving the kingdom without licence. *Huntingdon.* R. ii. p. ii 701
	The K. appoints as councillors Bernard Lebret and Gycard de Lebret, viscount of Tartas. R. ii p ii 701. O iv 281 H ii p. ii 186
April 5	The K summons Thomas earl of Norfolk, marshal of England, and 85 others, to meet him at Newcastle-on-Tyne on the Monday before Ascension Day, to serve against the Scots *Ramsey.* R. ii p ii. 702. O iv. 281 H. ii p ii 186
[April 5]	Similar letters to W. abp of Canterbury and 44 other bishops, abbots, and priors. R ii p ii 702 O iv 283. H. ii. p. ii. 187.
[April 5.]	Writs to all the sheriffs to proclaim the above-mentioned summons R ii. p ii 702 O iv 283. H. ii. p. ii. 187
April 5	The K orders the mayors of Dover and eight other towns to send their service of ships to Skymburnesse by the same day. *Ramsey* R ii. p. ii 703. O. iv. 284. H. ii p. ii. 187
April 11.	Ratification by the K of England of the treaty with France. *Peterborough.* R. ii. p. ii. 703. O iv 284 H. ii p. ii. 187.
April 15.	The K orders the sheriffs of Northampton, Lincoln, and Rutland to aid the abp. of York on his journey to Staunford. *Peterborough.* R ii p ii. 703 O iv 285 H ii p. ii 187
April 15.	The K. requests Barnabas, master of the order of Friars Preachers, to pray for him and his mother *Peterborough.* R ii. p ii. 703.
April 15.	The K orders his treasurer and barons of the exchequer to inquire into the counterfeiting and clipping of money *Peterborough.* R ii. p. ii 703.
April 22.	The K. orders the arrears of the revenues of the lands of Henry earl of Lancaster to be restored to him, viz., the issues of the castles and honours of Lancaster, Tutbury, and Pykeryng, and of the manors of Melburne and Staynford, Belteford, Donynton, Hertyndon, Croudecote and Wirkesworth, Esingwold, Hoby, Berleye, Passenham, Rydelinton, Bagworth, and Lindrich. *Staunford* R ii p ii 704 O iv 285 H ii p ii 188
April 23.	The K. orders Ivo de Aldeburgh to arrange with Robert de Brus for the safe passage of the abp of York, and the other ambassadors whom he is about to send, and for the time and place of meeting *Staunford.* R ii p ii 704 O iv. 287. H. ii p ii 188
April 24.	The K. orders Matthew de Cranthorn, receiver of Glamorgan, to pay 100s a day to Thos. de Berkele and John Maltravers for the expenses of the late K. *Staunford.* R. ii p ii. 704. O iv 287. H ii p ii 188
April 29.	The K. orders the mayors and commonalties of London and of 42 other towns to make preparations against the intended invasion by the Scots. *Nottingham* R. ii. p. ii. 703. O. iv. 287 H ii p ii. 188
April 30.	The K to the burgomasters of Bruges, offering to make reparation for the capture near Boulogne of a ship of Newport by men of Sandwich and Winchelsea. *Nottingham* R. ii p ii 705 O iv. 288. H. ii p. ii 189
April 30.	The K forbids English merchants to leave the kingdom until they belong to a staple. *Nottingham* R. ii p. ii 705.
May 1.	Proclamation of the above to be made at London and eight other towns. *Nottingham* R. ii p ii 705.

Q

DATE	SUBJECT.
1327 May 16	The K writes to the pope on behalf of Geoffrey, prior of Lenton, concerning the church of Radeclive on Sore in the diocese of York *Nottingham* R ii p ii 706 O iv 289 H 1 p ii 189
[May 16]	Similar letter to the cardinal of St Susanna R ii p ii 706. O. iv 290. H. ii p ii. 189.
May 18	The K orders 500 marks to be paid to John de Hainault *Nottingham.* R ii p ii 706. O iv 290 H ii p ii 189
May 29	The K commissions Alexander de Northampton, John de Melford, and John of York, to provide for the pantry, butlery, and kitchen of John de Hainault *York.* R ii p ii 706. O. iv. 290 H ii p. ii 190
June 1	The K orders the seneschal of Gascony to observe the treaty of peace with France *York* R ii p ii 707 O iv 290 H ii p ii 190
June 1	Similar letters to the seneschals, sheriffs, &c. of Aquitain *York* R. ii. p. ii 707. O. iv 291 H. ii p ii. 190.
June 3	The K informs Otto de Grandison, custos of Guernsey, Jersey, Sark, and Alderney, that he has received the fealty of Nichola, abbess of the Holy Trinity, Caen *York* R. ii. p ii 707. O iv 291 H ii p ii 190
June 8.	The K authorizes Robert de Weryngton, clerk, to collect alms for building a chapel on the hill where Thomas Earl of Lancaster was beheaded *York* R. ii. p ii 707. O. iv. 291 H ii p ii 190
June 14	The K. orders Henry le Scrope, Walter de Beauchamp, John de Heslarton, Nicholas de Langton, and Simon Croyser to inquire into a fray at York between English foot soldiers of the counties of Lincoln and Northampton and those of Hainault *York* R ii. p ii 707 O iv 292. H. ii. p ii 190
June 17	The K orders the arrayers of the east and west ridings of York and of Lancashire, to meet him at York with the men of their districts *York* R. ii p. ii 708. O. iv. 292 H ii p ii 190
June 28.	Warrant for payment of 700*l* to John de Hainault, for the wages of himself and company *York* R. ii p ii 708 O iv 293 H ii p ii 191
July 4	Commission to William de Irland to provide carriages for John de Hainault *York* R ii p ii 708 O iv 294 H ii p ii 191
July 5	Warrant for the payment of 200*l* to Thomas de Berkeley and John Mautravers, for the expenses of the late King *Aldewerk* R ii. p. ii. 708. O iv 294 H. ii. p. ii. 191.
July 6	The K forbids the mayor of Oxford to encroach upon his and Queen Isabella's rights in the honour of St Waleric *York* R ii p ii 708 O iv 294 H ii p ii 191
July 12	The K. orders Thomas FitzJohn, justiciary of Ireland, to warn the nobles of Ireland to fortify their castles against the Irish rebels. *Topcliff.* R. ii. p ii. 709. O. iv. 295. H ii p ii 191
July 12	The K orders his treasurer at Dublin to provide money for resisting the Irish rebels *Topcliff* R. ii. p ii 709 O iv 295. H. ii p. ii. 191
July 12.	Safe conduct until Christmas for Edward de Bahol, coming to England from over sea. *Topcliff* R ii p ii 709 O iv 295 H. ii p ii 192
July 13	The K orders Thomas de Mounceaux and John de Sourdeval, arrayers in the wapentake of Holdernesse, and the bailiffs of Beverley, to conduct the men under their charge to Carlisle to resist the Scots. *Northallerton.* R. ii. p ii. 709. O. iv. 296. H. ii p ii 192
July 5. Sic Qu 15	The K orders the mayor of York to fortify the city, as the King's mother, brother, and sisters are there *Durham* R ii p ii 709 O iv 296 H ii p ii. 192
July 15	The K informs Roger Mortimer, custos of Castle Barnard, and of the lands of Guy Beauchamp late, earl of Warwick, that the royal liberties of the bp of Durham have been restored to him R. ii. p. ii 710 O iv 297 H. ii p ii 102.
[July 15]	Similar letter to Robert de Clifford, keeper of the manors of Hert and Herternes, which belonged to the late Roger de Clifford. R ii p ii 710 O iv. 298 H ii p. ii. 192
July 16	The K directs Maurice FitzThomas and four others to obey Thomas FitzJohn, earl of Kildare, his justiciary. *Durham.* R. ii p ii. 710. O. iv. 298. H ii. p ii. 193
July 17.	The K orders Richard de le Pole, his butler, to allow the abp of York his prisage of wine at Hull *Durham* R ii p ii 710. O iv. 299. H. ii p ii 193
July 26.	The K. orders the mayor of London to search for certain malefactors in the city of London *Tudham.* R ii p ii 711
Aug 5.	The abp and the mayor of York make arrangements for the defence of the Old Bailey [Vetus Ballium] there. *York* R ii p ii. 711.

DATE	SUBJECT.
1327. Aug 2.	Obligation of the K. to Jacobo Nicholas, Giovanni Francisci, and Petro Reyneri of Florence, for 1,000 marks lent for the war against Scotland, and 148*l* 13*s* 8*d* paid by them at the desire of the late K ; which sums the K orders to be paid out of the customs of Southampton and Sandwich *Stanhope.* R II p II 712. O IV 300 H. II. p. II 193
Aug. 7.	Summons to W. abp. of Canterbury to a parliament to be held at Lincoln, Sept. 15, for defence of the realm *Stanhope.* R. II p II 712 O IV 301 H II. p II '194
Aug 8	The K. orders Bartholomew de Burghersh, constable of Dover Castle and warden of the Cinque Ports, to make proclamation that no injuries shall be done to Frenchmen. *Stanhope.* R II p II 712 O IV. 302 H. II p II 194
Aug 15	The K. hopes the pope will not delay the dispensation for his marriage on account of the reports about Wm. de Hainault *York* R. II. p II 712. O IV 302 H II p, II 194
Aug. 15.	Restitution of the temporalties to John archbp of Cashel, if there be nothing in his appointment by the Pope prejudicial to the crown *York.* R. II p II 713. O IV. 303 H II p II 194
Aug. 18.	The K orders the removal of his Exchequer to York. *York* R II p II 713
Aug 20.	The K. orders the payment of 4,000*l* as wages to John de Hainault, for which, if needful, jewels in the Tower are to be pledged. *York.* R. II. p. II. 713. O. IV. 303 H II p. II 194
Aug. 20.	Warrant to John de Insula, for carriages and other necessaries, for the conduct of John de Hainault to Dover *York* R. II. p II 713 O IV 304 H. II p II 195
Aug. 20.	The K. orders the sheriff of Oxford to take bail for Wm de Aylemere, accused of an attempt on Berkeley Castle for the purpose of seizing the late King. *York.* R. II. p II. 714 O IV 304 H. II p II 295
Aug. 20.	The K. writes to the pope in behalf of Henry Clif, clerk, in a suit with Thomas de Cherleton R II p II 714. O IV 305 H. II p. II 195.
Aug 20.	The K writes to the cardinal of SS. Marcellinus and Peter on the same subject. *York.* R. II p II. 714. O. IV. 305. H II. p, II. 195
[Aug 20]	Also to the cardinal bp de Sabino, the cardinal of St Adrian, and the bp. of Palestrina (Penestrinus), vice-chancellor R II p II 714
Aug 30	Papal dispensation for the marriage of the K with Philippa, daughter of William de Hainault. *Avignon.* R. II, p II 714 O IV. 306. H II p. II. 196.
Aug. 30.	The K asks William de Hainault to make restitution to Henry le Palmere, of Lincoln, and Nicholas de Castre, of Great Yarmouth, whose ship was taken by his subjects *Nottingham* R II p II 715 O IV. 307 H II p II 196
Sept. 5.	The K. appoints Henry Percy warden of the Marches towards Scotland. *Nottingham.* R II. p II. 715
Sept 6	The K writes to the pope in favour of Wolstan, prior of Worcester, elected to the bishopric *Nottingham* R II p II 715 O IV 308 H II p II 196.
[Sept. 6.]	Similar letters to the cardinal of SS Marcellinus and Peter and 10 others. R II p II. 716. O. IV. 308. H. II. p II 196
[Sept. 6]	Similar letters to Andrew Sapiti and the other agents of the K R II p II. 716. O IV 308. H II p II. 197
Sept. 10.	The K forbids W. archbp. of Canterbury to object to the cross being carried before the archbp. of York on his way to meet the K. at Lincoln. The K. writes also to the mayor and sheriff of Lincoln to assist the said archbp. of York *Nottingham.* R. II. p II. 716. O IV. 310. H II p II. 197
Sept 18	The K grants to William de Clynton, for services to Q. Isabella, the castle, hundred, and manor of Halton, in Cheshire and Lancashire Similar letters to Richard Damory, justiciary of Cheshire, and to the knights and others of the said manor *Lincoln* R II p II. 716 O. IV. 311 H II p II, 197.
Sept. 23.	The K. bids the mayor of London assist in the movement of the Exchequer and King's Bench to York. *Lincoln* R. II. p II 717
Sept. 25.	The K orders Richard Damori, justiciary of Chester, to deliver the boys whom he holds as hostages to the citizens of Chester *Lincoln* R. II p II 717 O IV 311. H II p II 179
Sept. 28.	The King grants to Thomas de Rokesby 100*l.* a year for bringing him within sight of his enemies *Lincoln.* R. II p II 717. O. IV 312. H. II p. II. 198
Oct 1.	The K complains to Richard Damory, justiciary of Cheshire, of the neglect of the sergeants of the peace *Nottingham.* R. II p II. 717
Oct. 3.	The K. orders proclamation to be made for the making of a new great seal. *Nottingham.* R II. p. I. 718.

DATE.	SUBJECT.
1327. Oct 6	The K orders an alteration to be made in his great seal for Ireland *Nottingham.* R n p. n 718
Oct 6	Agreement of the abbot of Crokesden to hold an anniversary for the late king on St. Matthew's day *Crokesden* R n p n 718 O iv 312 H i i p n 198
Oct 6	Safe conduct for William de Hainault, count of Holland *Nottingham.* R ii p. n. 718 O iv 313. H. n p il 198
Oct 8.	Power for R bp of Coventry and Lichfield to treat for a marriage between the K and Philippa, daughter of William de Hainault *Nottingham* R n p n 718 O iv 313. H n p n 198
[Oct. 8.]	Similar power for contracting marriage *per verba de præsenti* R n p ii 719 O. iv. 313. H n p n 198
Oct 9.	Power for Henry de Percy and William de Denum to treat with the Scots. *Nottingham.* R n p n 719 O iv 314 H n p n 198
Oct. 10.	Order for the payment of 10*l* to Wenthliana, daughter of Lewelin, late prince of Wales, being her pension for six months. *Nottingham.* R n p. n. 719. O. iv. 314. H. n. p n 199.
Oct. 16	Protection to Augustin le Walys, clerk, while providing for the consecration of the bp of Worcester. *Nottingham* R. n p n 719. O iv 314 H n p n 199.
Oct 20.	Relative to hay, corn, and other provender for the use of the horses belonging to the K and to the prelates and magnates summoned to the parliament to be holden at New Sarum *New Sarum* O iv 315 H n p n 199 *See* 20 Oct 1328
Oct 23.	Bull of Pope John against certain Bavarian heretics who deny the papal supremacy. *Avignon.* R n p n 719. O iv 315 H. n p n 199
Nov. 8.	The K. forbids arms to be carried in the city of London *Nottingham.* R. ii. p. ii. 723.
Nov. 17.	The K forbids the prior and convent of Christ Church, Canterbury, to hinder the consecration of Wolstan bp elect of Worcester Similar letter to the sub-prior of Worcester *Pontefract* R n p n. 723 O iv 325 H n p n 203
Nov. 20.	Safe conduct for 100 Scots coming to treat for peace. *Pontefract.* R. n. p. ii 723 O iv 325 H n p n 203
Nov. 23	Power to William archbp of York, H bp of Lincoln, John de Warenne, earl of Surrey and 10 others, to treat with the Scotch *Pontefract* R n p n 723. O iv. 325. H n. p. n. 203.
[Nov 23]	Power for the same to treat for a truce R. ii. p. n 724 O iv 326. H n p n 203
[Nov 23]	Power for the same to grant safe conduct to the Scotch ambassadors. R. n p n 724 O iv 326 H ii p n. 203
[Nov. 23]	Power to Henry de Percy, one of the above, to swear to the peace for the K. R n p n 724 O iv 327 H n p n. 203
Nov 28.	The K of England requests Charles K. of France to do justice to William de Rydale, an English merchant, whose woad was arrested at Amiens *Clipstone.* R n p n 724 O iv 327 H n p n 203
Nov 28	Safe conduct for Bartholomew de Burghersh, constable of Dover Castle, and William de Clynton, who are to accompany William count de Hainault and his daughter Philippa into England *Clipstone.* R n p n 724 O iv 327 H n p n. 203.
Nov. 29.	The K asks the pope to confirm the decision of the dispute between the archbp of York and the dean and chapter about the right of visitation *Clipstone.* R n p. n. 725 O iv 327 H n p n 204
Dec. 7.	The K forbids an intended tournament at Dunstable He appoints John de Gynes to assist the sheriff in the said matter *Leicester* R n p n 725
Dec 10.	Summons to the archbps of York and Canterbury to a parliament to be held at York on Feb 7 for reforming the peace with Scotland *Coventry* R. n p. n 725. O. iv. 328. H n p n 3
Dec. 12	The K. orders the sheriffs of Norfolk and Suffolk to release the goods of certain merchants of Bruges now under arrest. *Coventry.* R n p n 725 O. iv 328 H. n p n 3.
Dec 12	The K orders search to be made at London, the Cinque Ports, and Canterbury, for papal letters prejudicial to his rights *Coventry* R. n p n 726 O iv 329 H n p. ii. 3
Dec. 12.	The K writes to Adam de Orleton, late bp of Hereford, to the same effect as to the prior of Christchurch, Canterbury, on Nov. 17. *Coventry* R n. p. n. 726. O. iv. 330. H. n. p iii 4

DATE.	SUBJECT.
1327. Dec. 15.	The K. orders the arrest of certain persons who are collecting alms for the pretended purpose of building a chapel on the hill where Thomas late earl of Lancaster was beheaded *Chipping Cambden* R. ii p. ii 726. O. iv. 330. H. ii p. iii. 4.
Dec. 16.	The K orders Peter de Galiciano and Robert de Wyvill to restore to the archbp. and the dean and chapter of Rouen their lands in England seized by the late King *Winchcombe* R ii p ii 726 O iv 331. H. ii p. iii 4
Dec. 26	Summons to Adam de Orleton, late bp of Hereford, to appear at the parliament at York on Feb. 7, to answer for his attempts to procure his translation to the see of Worcester, and for obtaining papal letters prejudicial to the King *Worcester* R. ii. p. ii. 726 O. iv. 321 H ii p iii 4
1328. Jan. 5.	The K. of England writes to Alfonso K of Castile on behalf of Richard Baret, merchant of Exeter, whose ship was taken by subjects of Alfonso *Nottingham.* R. ii p ii 727. O iv. 332. H ii p. iii. 4.
Jan 6.	Safe conduct for Simon de Mepham, archbp elect of Canterbury, who is going to Rome about his election *Nottingham* R ii p ii 727 O iv 332 H ii p ii 4
Jan 6.	The K writes to the pope about the troubles during the reign of his father, and commends Simon de Mepham, archbp elect of Canterbury *Nottingham.* R ii p ii. 727. O iv. 332. H ii p. iii 4
[Jan 6]	Similar letters to 16 cardinals and others at Rome R ii p ii 727 O iv 333 H. ii. p iii 5
Jan 22.	The K writes to L bp of Durham, the sheriffs of Yorkshire and Northumberland, and the mayor of Newcastle, for the honorable reception of 100 persons coming from Scotland to treat with the King at York *York* R ii p ii 728. O iv 334 H ii p iii. 5
Jan 22	Safe conduct for the said 100 persons *York* R ii p ii 728 O iv 334 H ii. p iii 5
Jan 22	Safe conduct for 12 Scots sent beforehand to make provision for them. *York.* R ii. p. ii 728. O iv 334 H ii p iii 5
Jan. 30.	The K. orders Henry de Percy, Ralph de Nevill, and seven others to observe the truce with Scotland. *York* R. ii p ii. 728 O iv 335 H ii p iii 5
Feb. 12.	The K orders the bailiffs of Lyme to observe his grant of that town to Q. Isabella, dated 1 Feb, 1 Edw III *York* R. ii p ii 728.
Feb. 13.	The K. orders Otto de Grandison, custos of Guernsey, Jersey, Sark, and Alderney, to restore the lands of religious persons and others, French subjects, seized by the late King *York* R ii p ii 729 O iv 335 H ii p iii 6
Feb. 15.	Safe conduct for John le Long, John de Kirkintolach, and three others, sent by the Scotch ambassadors into Scotland *York.* R ii. p. ii. 729 O iv 336 H ii p iii. 6.
Feb. 20.	The K. requests the pope to canonize John de Dalderby, late bp of Lincoln *York* R ii p ii 729 O iv 336. H ii p iii 5
Feb. 26.	The K orders Simon de Grymesby, his escheator, to abstain from molesting John of Brittany, earl of Richmond, whose lands were restored by the late king. *York* R. ii. p. ii 729 O iv 336 H ii. p iii 6
Feb. 26.	Safe conduct for Eleanor, late wife of Hugh le Despenser the younger, coming from London to York *York* R ii. p. ii 729 O iv 337 H. ii p iii 6
Feb 29.	Licence to the abbot of St Peter's, Gloucester, to appropriate the churches of Wyrardisbury and Chipping Norton, Linc dioc , and of Camine, Worc dioc., for the purpose of saying masses for the late king *York* R. ii. p. ii. 729 O. iv 337 H. ii p iii 6
March 1.	The K of England renounces all his pretensions to dominion in Scotland *York* R ii p. ii. 730. O. iv 337 H ii p iii 6.
March 1.	Power for Henry de Percy and William la Zouche de Assheby to swear to the said renunciation *York.* R. ii. p ii 730
[March 1.]	The K renounces all his rights by virtue of certain sentences in the court of Rome against Robert K. of Scotland *York.* R. ii. p ii 730
March 1.	Power to H bp. of Lincoln, William bp. of Norwich, Henry de Percy, and two others, to treat for a marriage between the king's sister Joan, and David, son and heir of Robert de Bruce *York* R ii. p ii. 730.
March 2.	Warrant to all sheriffs to provide carriages, &c. for Queen Isabella during her intended journey through England *York* R ii p ii 731
March 3.	Memorandum that John bp of Ely, at that time the K's chancellor, delivered up the great seal to the King at York, who delivered it to Henry de Clyf, keeper of the rolls, and William de Herlaston, clerk of the chancery *York.* R. ii. p. ii. 731.

DATE	SUBJECT.
1328 March 3.	The K annuls the sentence on Thomas late earl of Lancaster, at the petition of Henry, his brother and heir *York* R n p ii 731.
March 4	The K writes to the pope in favour of Henry de Clyf, his clerk, engaged in a suit with Thomas de Cherleton, bp. of Hereford, about the prebend of Blebury in the church of Salisbury. *York* R ii p ii 732. O iv. 338. H. ii. p iii 7.
March 4	Similar letters to the cardinals of SS Marcellinus and Peter and of St Adrian. *York* R ii. p ii 732 O iv 339 H ii p iii 7
March 5.	The K writes to Alfonso K of Castile on behalf of Gerard de Boyle or Byole, merchant of Southampton, whose ship and goods have been taken by the subjects of Alfonso. *York* R ii. p ii. 732 O iv 340 H. ii p iii 7
March 5	The K forbids tournaments in Northamptonshire. *York* R ii p ii 732.
March 5	Restitution of the temporalties to Adam bp of Worcester, late bp of Hereford *York* R ii p ii 788
March 6.	The K promises to pay to John de Hainault for his wages and expenses in coming twice to his assistance, 14,406*l* 6*s* 9*d*., in two instalments *York* R. ii. p ii 733
March 7	Proclamation that no person, at the ensuing parliament at Northampton, shall take lodgings without the assent of the K's marshals and harbingers of his household *York*. R ii p ii 733
March 8	The seneschal of Gascony and the constable of Bordeaux are to inquire into the claim of Gerard de Tastys, lord of Sainte Croix des Mont, to receive certain fines for blows struck within his lordship. *York* R ii. p. ii 733 O iv 340 H. ii p iii 7.
March 9.	Similar letters to the commonalties of Bordeaux, Bayonne, and 10 other towns. *York*. R ii p ii 734. O. iv. 342. H ii. p iii. 8.
March 10.	Credence for Peter de Galleiano, canon of Agen, addressed to Berard de la Bret [d'Albret], lord de Vairs [Varies], and 60 others *York* R ii p ii 733 O iv 341 H ii p iii 8
March 10.	Exemplification of the patent granted to Cardinal Gancelin, 26 March, 1 Edw III. *Pontefract*. R. ii. p ii. 734. O iv. 342. H. ii p iii. 8.
March 17	Treaty between Robert K of Scotland and the commissioners of the K. of England. Perpetual peace; marriage between David, son of the K of Scotland, and Joan, sister of the K of England , restitution by the K of England of all deeds touching the subjection of Scotland to him , payment by the K of Scotland of 20,000*l* st to the K. of England, in three years , and other articles. *Edinburgh*. R. ii. p. ii 734.
March 25	The K. requests the pope to expedite the matter of Simon de Mepham, elected to the see of Canterbury. *Barlings* R ii p ii 735 O. iv 342 H ii p. iii 8.
[March 25]	Similar letters to nine Roman cardinals. R. ii. p ii. 735. O iv 343 H. ii p iii 9.
March 28.	The K asks the consent of Alfonso K. of Castile to a marriage between John de Eltham, his brother, and the daughter of John late lord of Biscay. *Lincoln* R. ii p ii. 736 O iv 344. H ii p iii 9.
March 28	The K.'s letter to Mary lady of Biscay on the same subject. *Lincoln*. R ii. p ii. 736. O. iv 344. H. ii. p. iii. 9
March 28.	The K informs John de Haustede, seneschal of Gascony, and John de Weston, constable of Bordeaux, that he has received their letters sent by Bertram de Codene, and that he intends to recover his rights and inheritance, and wishes them to treat of it secretly with the nobles and commons. *Lincoln*. R ii. p ii 736 O iv 344 H. ii. p iii. 9
[March 28]	Similar letters to Bernard de la Brette and Arnald de Montpesat R ii. p ii. 736. O. iv. 345 H. ii. p iii 9
March 28.	The K. asks Rauffre lord of Montpesat to continue faithful to him, and the K will make restitution for his losses *Lincoln* R. ii. p. ii. 737. O iv 345. H. ii. p. iii 10
[March 28.]	Letter to Reymond Durant about his intention to recover his inheritance R. ii. p ii 737. O. iv 346. H. ii. p iii. 10.
[March 28.]	Letter on the same subject to Bertram de Codene R. ii. p. ii. 737. O iv 346 H ii. p iii 10
March 28.	The K writes to Arnard Guilliam, lord of Eygremond, and to the several nobles and commonalties of Navarre and Languedoc, on the same subject, and desiring credence for Reymond Durant *Lincoln*. R ii p ii. 737. O iv 347. H ii p iii 10
March 28.	Letter of credence to the pope for William de Weston, canon of Lichfield, and Benedict de Paxton, canon of Exeter [?Oxon] *Barlings* R ii p ii 738 O iv. 348. H ii p iii. 10.
[March 28.]	Similar letters to 19 cardinals R. ii. p ii. 738 O iv. 348. H. ii. p iii 10.

DATE.	SUBJECT.
1328 April 4.	Order of the sheriff of Lincoln to pay to Wenthliana, daughter of Lewellin late prince of Wales, a nun at Sempringham, 10*l.*, being her pension for half a year. *Sempringham.* R ii p. ii. 738 O iv 348. H ii p iii 11
April 6.	The K has received from Nicholas de Leek the letters of the burgomasters of Bruges, and requests them to send nuncios to treat with him by the 24th of next June *Sempringham* R. ii p ii 738. O iv. 349. H ii. p. iii. 11.
April 12.	The K. desires the abbot of Ramsey to maintain Janet le Sautreour, Q Isabella's minstrel. *Staunford* R ii. p ii 738.
April 20	The K. to the pope; he hears that there has been some defect in the election of Simon de Mepham to the see of Canterbury, and if it be so he requests the pope to promote Henry bp of Lincoln. *Oundle* R ii p ii. 739 O iv 349. H. ii p. iii. 11.
[April 20.]	Similar letters to 10 cardinals R. ii. p. ii 739 O iv. 350 H ii. p. iii 11.
April 25	Sheriff of Northampton ordered to provide safe conduct for the abp of York during his journey to the parliament at Northampton. *Northampton.* R. ii p. ii. 739.
April 30.	The K forbids tournaments. *Northampton* R. ii. p. ii 739.
May 3.	The K requests the pope to revoke all processes in the court of Rome against Robert K. of Scotland or his subjects Similar letters to 17 cardinals. R ii. p ii *Northampton.* 739 O iv 350–351 H. ii p iii. 11
May 4	Ratification by the K of England of the treaty with Scotland concluded at Edinburgh, 17 March. *Northampton.* R ii p. ii. 740
May 4.	Ratification by the K of England of the obligation of the K of Scotland to pay 100,000*l.* for the K's renunciation of his rights in Scotland, and for the marriage between prince David and the K.'s sister. *Northampton* R ii. p ii 741
May 10.	The K releases the Roman cardinals beneficed in England from the payment of the tenth granted by the clergy. *Northampton* R ii. p. ii. 742 O. iv. 351 H ii p iii 12
May 14.	The K. to the pope, repeating his request relative to the elect of Canterbury. *Northampton.* R. ii. p ii 742. O. iv 352 H ii p iii 12.
May 11	The K requests the burgomasters of Bruges to send commissioners to treat of peace. *Northampton* R ii. p ii 742 O iv 352. H ii p iii 12.
May 12.	The K. asks the pope to confirm the appropriation of the churches of Wyzardisbury, Chipping Norton, and Camme, for the support of three priests performing religious services for the late K. in the abbey of S. Peter's, Gloucester. *Northampton.* R. ii p. ii 742. O iv. 353 H ii p iii 12
May 12.	Memorandum of the delivery of the great seal by the King to H bp. of Lincoln. *Northampton* R ii p. ii 743.
May 15.	The K. promises to assign lands to the value of 15,000 livres Tournois for the dowry of Q. Philippa within a year *Northampton* R ii p ii 743 O iv. 353 H ii p iii 12.
May 16	Power to Adam bp of Worcester and Roger bp. of Chester to demand and receive for the K. his rights as heir to the crown of France *Northampton* R ii. p ii 743. O. iv. 354 H ii p iii 13
May 18	The chancellor of the University of Oxford and the mayor of Oxford are commanded to appear before the K and council at York for the settlement of their respective liberties. *Northampton* R ii p ii. 743.
May 21	The K., with the assent of Isabella queen mother, appoints Sir Roger Manduyt and Robert de Tughale to receive, for his sister Joan, the lands to the value of 2,000*l.* a year assigned for her dowry by Robert K. of Scotland. *Northampton.* R ii. p ii 743 O iv. 354 H ii p iii. 13
May 21.	Warrants for the payment of 50 marks to Roger Manduyt and 20 marks to Robert de Toghal for their expenses *Northampton* R. ii p ii 742 O iv. 355. H. ii. p. iii 13
June 9.	Sir Reginald de Cobeham and Sir John de Chidiok empowered to treat with John duke of Brabant and the cities of Brabant and Flanders. *Woodstock.* R ii. p. ii. 744 O iv. 355. H ii p. iii 13.
June 15.	Relative to the remuneration to be made to Peter de Greilly, vicomte de Benauges, for the detention of rents and rights in the vills of Langoun and Bazas. *Worcester* R. ii p ii. 744 O iv. 355 H. ii. p. iii 13.
June 24.	The K. prohibits John de Bermyngeham earl of Louth, and five other nobles in Ireland, from making war on each other. *Evesham* R ii p ii 744. O iv 356. H ii p iii 13.
June 28.	The K. revokes his permission to Cardinal Gaucelin to summon his debtors for the tithes and the fruits of benefices before the ecclesiastical courts, such being contrary to the common law of the realm *Evesham.* R ii. p. ii. 744. O iv. 356 H ii p iii 14

DATE	SUBJECT
1328. June 28	Order to the K.'s treasurer to pay to John de Hainault 7,000*l.*, part payment of 14,000*l.* due to him for wages, &c. *Evesham.* R ii p ii 745. O. iv. 357 H. ii. p. iii, 14.
June 28	The sheriffs of Southampton and London are to arrest the goods of Frenchmen, in consequence of the plunder of English ships in Poictou and Normandy *Evesham.* R ii. p ii 745. O iv 357. H ii p iii 14
July 1.	Memorandum that H bp of Lincoln, chancellor, who is about to go to Berwick with Q. Isabella, delivers the great seal to Henry de Clyf, keeper of the rolls of Chancery. *York.* R ii p ii 745. O. iv. 358 H ii p iii 14
July 7	The sheriff of Lancashire ordered to make proclamation against the wearing of arms, pursuant to a statute of Northampton *Bridgenorth* R ii p ii 745 O iv. 358. H ii p. iii 14
July 8.	Protection and safe conduct for the merchants of Aragon, Majorca, Catalonia, and Spain for three years *Bridgenorth* R. ii p ii 746.
July 12.	Proclamation throughout England that all who have claims to make for damage done by the Flemings must appear at York on August 1. *Bridgenorth* R. ii p ii 746 O iv. 359 H ii p iii 15
July 23.	The K. commends to the pope Stephen de Segrave, abp of Armagh, who is going to Rome *Nottingham* R ii p ii 746 O iv 359 H ii p iii 15.
Aug 3	Proclamation that no persons are to leave the realm without licence *York.* R ii p ii. 746 O iv 360 H ii p iii 15
	The K recommends to the pope Henry de Gower, bp elect of S David's, and asks him to desire the bps. of Worcester and Hereford to assist the said bp elect in preventing rebellion among the Welsh R ii p ii 747 O iv 360 H. ii p iii. 15.
Aug 7	Credence for John de Chidiok, sent by the K to the town of Bruges. *York.* R. ii. p ii. 747 O. iv. 361. H. ii. p. iii. 15.
Aug. 8	Inspeximus and confirmation of the charter granted to foreign merchants, 1 Feb. 31 Edw I *York* R ii. p ii 747 O iv 361 H ii p iii 15.
Aug. 10.	The K orders Antony de Lucy, warden of Carlisle Castle, to deliver the quarter of the body of Andrew de Harcla, which was hung over the wall by the order of the late K , to Sara widow of Robert de Leyburn, sister of the said Andrew. Similar letters to the mayors of London, Newcastle, and Bristol, and the bailiffs of Shrewsbury, for the delivery¹ of the head and remaining quarters *York* R ii p ii 748 O iv. 364 H. ii p. iii. 17
Aug. 16.	The K. to the pope, in favor of Henry bp of S. David's, whose request to go to Rome he is unable to grant on account of the Welsh disturbances *York.* R ii. p ii 748 O iv. 365 H ii p iii 17.
[Aug. 16.]	Similar letter to three cardinals. R ii p ii 749 O iv 365. H ii p iii 17
Aug. 22.	Power for Sir Reginald de Cobham and John de Hildcale, canon of Chichester, to treat for the K with John duke of Brabant *Pontefract.* R ii p ii 749. O. iv 366. H ii. p. iii 17.
[Aug. 22]	Power for the same to treat with the count of Los and others R ii p. ii. 749 O iv. 366 H ii p iii. 17
Aug 22.]	The K. to John Darcy le Neveu, justiciary of Ireland, granting licence to the bps of Ireland to acquire waste lands on the marches, for the purpose of fortifying them against the incursion of the Irish *Pontefract.* R. ii. p. ii. 749.
Aug. 30.	The sheriffs of London are to provide 120 targets, painted with the K's arms, and 120 crossbows, to be sent to John de Roches, custos of Guernsey, Jersey, Alderney, and Sark, for the defence of the said islands *Clipstone* R ii p ii 749 O iv. 367 H. ii p iii. 18
Aug. 30.	The K orders John de Roches above-mentioned to compel all bishops and others of Normandy who hold land in Guernsey, &c to perform their homage and service. *Clipstone.* R ii p ii 750 O iv 367 H ii p iii 18
Aug. 30.	The K. orders the same John de Roches to complete the castle at Girburgh in Guernsey. *Clipstone.* R ii p ii. 750
[Aug. 30.]	The K orders the same John de Roches to fortify the castles in the islands above-mentioned R. ii p. ii. 750
Sept. 15	John de Haustede, seneschal of Gascony, John de Weston, constable of Bordeaux, and John Travers empowered to treat with John count d'Armagnac and Bernard Ezii, lord de Lebret *Wisbeach* R ii p ii 750 O iv 367 H ii p iii 18
Sept. 16.	The K. promises to indemnify John count d'Armagnac and three others for any losses they may sustain in his service. *Wisbeach.* R. ii p ii 750. O. iv. 368. H ii. p iii. 18.

DATE.	SUBJECT
1328 Sept. 16.	The K forbids assemblies of armed men *Wisbeach* R ii p ii 751
Sept. 19.	The sheriff of Southampton commanded to arrest French merchandize, by way of satisfaction for damages inflicted on English ships *Walsingham.* R ii p ii. 751. O iv 369 H ii p iii 18
Sept 22.	The K asks the pope to revoke the collation of the bp of Auxerre to the prebend of Blebury, which is to the prejudice of Henry de Clyff. *Norwich.* R ii p ii 751. O. iv. 369 H ii p iii 19
Sept. 22.	The K on the same subject to the bp of Auxerre, a Roman cardinal. *Norwich.* R ii p ii. 752 O iv. 370 H ii p iii 19
[Sept. 22]	The K. on the same subject to Bernard Stepham, notary and chaplain to the pope. R ii p ii 752 O iv 371 H ii p iii 19
Sept. 27	The K orders John de Flete, keeper of his wardrobe in the Tower of London, to deliver to John de Montgomery the armours of the late Bartholomew de Badelesmore, for the use of his son Giles *Cambridge* R. ii p ii 752 O iv. 371. H. ii p iii 19
Oct 15.	The K deputes his chancellor, H bp of Lincoln, and Walter Hervey, archdeacon of Salisbury, to open the parliament at Salisbury. *Marlborough* R ii p ii 752 O iv 372 H ii p iii 20.
Oct. 20.	Order for the provision of fodder for the horses of persons attending the parliament. *New Sarum* R. ii. p ii 752 O iv. 315 H ii p ii 199
Oct. 28	The K releases from arrest the goods of John de Mes and 14 other French merchants *New Sarum* R ii p ii 753 O iv 372. H ii p iii 20.
Oct 28.	The K orders the pensions of the abbots of Jedworth, Melrose, and Kelso, also to Dundreynam, to be paid to them as before the war with Scotland. *New Sarum.* R. ii. p. ii. 753 O iv. 373. H. ii. p iii 20.
Nov 10.	Proclamation throughout England to forbid the wearing of arms, pursuant to the statute of Northampton *Wallingford* R ii p ii 753
Nov. 11.	John bp of Winchester summoned to answer before the K. for leaving the parliament without his licence *Wallingford* R. ii p ii 753.
Nov. 15	The K orders the several sheriffs to arrest persons who take corn, carriages, &c , on pretence of being the K's purveyors. *Windsor* R ii p ii 754
Nov 28.	Exemplification of letters patent to Thomas de Savoy of a prebend at Ripon, dated 13 June, 28 Edw I *Westm* R ii p ii 754 O iv 373. H ii p iii 20.
1329 Jan. 15.	Memorandum of the delivery of the great seal to the K , and of the sealing of writs with the same, and of their delivery to William de Herlaston, clerk of the Chancery, to be deposited in the K's wardrobe, and of the re-delivery of the seal to the bp of Lincoln. *Northampton* R ii p ii 754. O iv 374 H ii p iii. 20.
Jan 30	Bartholomew de Burghassh, John de Cobham, and John de Feld, appointed keepers of the peace in Kent. *Windsor.* Seven other counties have similar commissions. R. ii. p ii 755.
Feb. 2.	John de Grantham, mayor of London, and four others, commanded to make inquisition concerning certain malefactors in the city of London. *Windsor* R. ii p ii 755
Feb 5	Roger de Mortimer, earl of March, justiciary of Wales, commanded to protect the castle of Kaerfilly, besieged by William la Zousche de Mortimer *Windsor.* R ii. p. ii. 755. O. iv 374 H. ii p iii 21.
Feb 5	John de Gynes commanded to attach the said William de la Zousche. *Windsor* R. ii p ii 756 O iv. 375. H ii p iii 21
Feb 8	Proclamation for the adjournment of parliament to Feb. 9 at Westminster. *Tower of London.* R ii p ii 756.
Feb. 9	The K. deputes Thomas bp of Hereford his treasurer, Henry de Clif, and Adam de Herwynton, to open the parliament at Westminster *Tower of London* R. ii p. ii 756
Feb. 15.	The K requests Cardinal G[ailard] to desist from suits at Rome prejudicial to the rights of the university of Oxford *Westm* R ii p ii 756 O iv 375 H ii p iii 21
Feb 19	John Darcy le Cosyn, appointed justiciary of Ireland, with a fee of 500l a year. Letters to Roger Utlagh, prior of St John's, and others, informing them of the fact. *Westm.* R ii p. ii 756.
Feb. 20.	The K. requests the pope to canonize William de Marchia, formerly bp of Bath and Wells. Similar letters are sent to the cardinals. *Westm.* R ii p. ii. 757. O iv 376 H. ii p. iii. 21.

DATE.	SUBJECT.
1329 Feb 20	The K orders the sheriff of Lincoln to allow merchants, both foreign and English, either to come to or to leave the kingdom *Westm* R ıı p ıı 757.
Feb. 23	The K to the pope, in favor of Peter de Joceux, nommated to the priory of Lewes by John de Warenne, earl of Surrey, and against the appointment of Adam, monk of Winchester, nommated to the same priory by papal provision. Similar letters to the cardinals. *Eltham*. R ıı. p. ıı. 757. O ıv 376. H. ıi. p. ııı, 21.
Feb 27.	A letter to the pope in favour of Hugh de Camera, archdeacon of Lincoln, against the interference of the court of Rome *Eltham* R ıı p. ıı. 757. O ıv 377 H ıı p. ııı 22.
March 2	The K. confirms the grant of his father to Arnald de Tryan, nephew of the pope, of 300 *livres Tournois* a year, and orders the constable of Bordeaux to pay the said pension R ıı. p ıi. 757. O ıv. 377. H ıı. p ııı 22
[March 2]	Confirmation of a similar grant to Peter de Via, nephew of the pope. R. ıı. p ıı. 758 O ıv 377 H. ıı. p ıı. 22
March 2	Power to John Darcy le Cosyn, justiciary of Ireland, to let crown lands in Ireland on the marches, except the lands " de Saltu Salmonis, Lymeryk, and Tassehagard." *Eltham* R ıı p ıı 758.
March 2	Power to John Darcy le Cosyn to pardon felons and outlaws in Ireland, and to allow Irishmen to use and enjoy the laws of England *Eltham* R. ıı p ıı 758.
March 3	The K. requests the pope to appoint Leonard de Tibercis, prior of Venice, to the priory of St. John of Jerusalem in England, vice Thomas Larcher, incapacitated by age. *Eltham* R ıı p ıı 758 O ıv 378 H ıı p ıı 22
[March 3]	Letter on the same subject to Elion de Villa Nova, master of the hospital of St John of Jerusalem R ıı. p ıı 758. O ıv 378 H. ıı. p ııı. 22
March 4	The K. requests the pope to promote Simou de Montacute, his clerk, to some benefice in the diocese of Wells *Eltham* R ıı p ıı 759 O ıv 379 H ıı p ııı. 22
March 4	The K grants to Peter [de Mortuomari], cardinal of S. Peter *in Cœlo Monte*, a pension of 40 marks *Eltham*. R ıı p ıı 759 O ıv. 379. H ıı p ııı 23
March 8	The K. repeats his order to Roger de Mortimer earl of March, justiciary of Wales, to raise the siege of the castle of Kaerfily *Guildford*. R. ıı p ıı. 759
March 12	The K has received the petition of Bernard de le Bret, and will answer it when his council meets after Easter *Chertsey* R ıı p ıı 759 O ıv 379 H ıı p ıı 23
March 15	The K informs Bernard de la Bret, lord de Varus [Vayres], and 18 others, that he will send envoys to them after Easter *Wycombe* R ıı p ıı 759. O. ıv. 380 H ıı p. ııı. 23.
March 15.	Order to pay to William count of Juliers 300*l* due at Mich , part of his pension of 600*l*. *Wycombe* R ıı p ıı 759 O. ıv 380 H ıı p ııı 23
April 1	Restitution of the temporalities to Ralph de Kilmessan, bp. of Down. *Wallingford*. R. ıı. p. ıı. 760 O ıv 381. H ıı p. ııı 23
April 14	K Edward informs Philip K of France that he intends to do homage to him, but has been prevented by his affairs; desires credence for Thomas bp of Hereford and Bartholomew de Burghersh. *Wallingford*. R. ıi p. ıi. 760 O ıv 381 H ıı p ıı 23
April 14	Pardon for John Mautravers Similar letters for Bartholomew de Burghersh *Wallingford* R. ıı p. ıı 760.
April 14	Protection until St John's day for Thomas bp of Hereford, who is going with the K.; for four persons going with the said bp , and for 73 persons going with the K. *Wallingford*. R. ıı. p ıı. 764. O. ıv. 387. H ıı p ııı 26.
April 17	Safe conduct for Thomas Randolf, earl 'of Murref, in Scotland, on his way through the kingdom to foreign parts *Wallingford*. R. ıı. p. ıı. 760. O. ıv. 381. H. ıı p ııı 23
April 22	The K orders his treasurer and chamberlains to receive from the keeper of the privy seal all documents relating to his disputes with France. Warrant to Adam de Lymberwe, keeper of the privy seal, to deliver tehm. *Wallingford*. R. ıi. p. ıı 761.
April 24	Proclamation that no persons are to leave the realm without licence. *Wallingford* R ıı. p. ıı. 761. O ıv 382. H ıı p ııı 24.
April 26.	Letters to Bartholomew de Burghersh, constable of Dover and warden of the Cinque Ports , to the mayor of London, and to the mayors and bailiffs of 25 other towns on the same subject. *Wallingford* R. ıı. p. ıı. 761. O ıv 382. H ıı p ııı 24.
April 28.	The K writes to Gerard count of Holstein, desiring him to make restitution to Robert de Musgrave of Newcastle-on-Tyne for the capture of his ship. *Windsor* R ıı p ıı 761. O ıv. 383 H. ıı p ııı. 24

DATE.	SUBJECT
1329 [April 28]	Similar letter to Kanute duke of Halland in Dacia, and three others, who took the said ship R ii p. ii. 762 O iv 383 H. ii p. iii 24
May 8.	The K orders Bartholomew de Burghersh, constable of Dover, and the other officers of the Cinque Ports, to assist Stephen le Blount in providing ships at Dover for the K's passage to France *Eltham* R. ii. p ii 762 O. iv 383. H. ii. p. iii 24
May 8	Safe conducts for William la Zousche, the K's clerk, and five others, to make provision for the K. across the sea. *Eltham.* R. ii. p ii. 762. O. iv. 383. H ii. p iii 24
May 9.	Commission to Thomas Cary to bring before the K. John le Rous and William de Dalby, who can make silver by alchemy. *Eltham.* R ii p ii 762 O. iv 384 H ii p. iii 24
May 12.	Restitution to Sir James Douglas of the manor of Faudon in co Northumberland, which was forfeited by his father William Douglas *Eltham* R. ii. p ii 762. O iv 384. H. ii. p. iii. 25.
May 13.	The K. consents to receive from Robert K of Scotland 5,000, marks on account, due on S. John's day, in part payment of 10,000 marks ; the remainder to be paid at Martinmas. *Eltham.* R ii p ii 763 O. iv. 385. H ii p iii 25
May 13.	The K. informs the treasurer and barons of the Exchequer of the above arrangement. *Eltham.* R. ii. p. ii 763. O. iv 385 H ii p iii 25.
May 13.	The K. writes to four cardinals in favour of the university of Oxford, touching the dispute between them and Gaillard de Mota, cardinal of S Lucia in *Cilice*, archdeacon of Oxford. *Eltham* R ii p ii 763. O iv, 385 H. ii p iii 25
May 22	The K forbids tournaments during his absence abroad. *Canterbury* R ii p ii 763 O iv 386 H. ii p iii 25
May 25.	The K. appoints his brother, John de Eltham, earl of Cornwall, regent of the realm during his absence *Dover* R ii p ii. 763 O iv 386 H ii p iii. 25.
May 25	Power for John de Eltham to grant *congés d'elire* *Dover.* R. ii. p ii. 763 O iv 386 H ii. p. iii. 26
May 25.	Warrant for payment of 2,000*l* to Dinus Forcetti and other merchants of Florence, who have lent the K. 5,000*l.* for his passage to France, and 7,000*l* for the payment of John de Hainault *Dover.* R ii p ii 764 O iv. 387 H ii p iii 26.
May 26.	The K set sail from Dover in a ship of Winchelsea at noon, accompanied by H. bp of Lincoln, his chancellor, and other nobles R. ii. p. ii. 764. O. iv. 387. H ii. p iii. 26.
May 29.	The K forbids all interference with his presentation of Robert de Tanton to the prebend of Thlanarthuen, in the collegiate church of Abirgwylly in S David's dioc. *Wingham.* R ii. p. ii. 764 O. iv. 388 H ii. p iii 26
May 31.	Memorandum of the delivery of the great seal by Bartholomew de Burghersh to Henry de Clyf at Canterbury, with a letter from the K. R ii p ii. 764 O. iv 389 H ii. p. iii. 27.
June 2.	The K forbids tournaments in Leicestershire R ii p ii. 765
June 6.	K. Edward performed homage to Philip K. of France for the duchy of Guienne, under protestation that the act should not prejudice his rights. *Amiens.* R ii. p ii. 765. O. iv. 389 H ii p iii. 27.
June 11	The K , accompanied by his chancellor H bp of Lincoln, Henry de Percy, and others, arrived at Dover , and on the 14th of June Henry de Clyf delivered the great seal to the said bp at Canterbury R. ii p ii 765. O. iv, 391 H. ii p iii 27.
June 12	The K. requests the pope to promote Robert de Wyvill, canon of Lincoln and Lichfield, to the bishopric of Bath and Wells , and desires credence for Roger de Huntyngfeld. *Dover.* R ii p. ii. 765. O. iv. 391. H. ii p iii. 27.
[June 12]	Similar letters to 24 cardinals and others R ii p ii 766. O iv. 391. H. l. p iii. 27.
June 14.	The K orders the abp of York to be present at Windsor, July 23, with the other prelates and magnates of the realm, notwithstanding his dispute with the abp. of Canterbury about bearing the cross in his province. *Canterbury.* R. ii. p. ii. 766. O. iv. 391. H. ii. p iii. 27.
[June 14]	Similar command to the abp. of Canterbury. R. ii. p. ii 766. O iv. 391 H. ii p iii 27.
June 16.	Power for Henry bp of Lincoln, the K's chancellor, Ralph de Nevill, and three others, to treat with Philip K of France for a marriage between his eldest son and Eleanor, sister of the K. of England. *Canterbury* R. ii. p. ii 766 O iv 392. H ii p iii 28
[June 16.]	Power for them to treat for a marriage between John de Eltham, earl of Cornwall, and one of the daughters of the K. of France. R. ii. p ii. 766 O. iv. 392. H. ii. p iii 28.

DATE.	SUBJECT.
1329 June 18	Acquittance of Guillaume Amaneni de Chastillon for his losses in the war in Gascony. *Canterbury* R ii p ii 767 O. iv 392 H ii p iii. 28.
June 18.	The K warns the pope against believing Richard bp of Ossory, who secretly left the kingdom when summoned to answer for fostering disturbances in Ireland. *Canterbury.* R ii p. ii. 767. O iv 392. H ii. p. iii. 28
[June 18]	The K writes to Peter, cardinal of S Stephen *in Cœlio Monte*, on the same subject. R ii p ii 767 O iv 393 H ii p iii. 28.
June 18.	The K again requests the pope to revoke the promotion of John de Courtenay, monk of Tavistock, to the priory of Lewes *Canterbury.* R. ii. p ii. 767. O. iv 394. H. ii. p. iii. 28.
[June 18]	Similar letters to 13 cardinals. R ii p ii 768. O iv. 394. H. ii p iii 29
June 19	Commission to Bartholomew de Burghersh, warden of the Cinque Ports, and to John de Ifeld, to inquire into damage done to English subjects in France, in fulfilment of the recent treaty at Amiens. Similar commissions to W. bp of Norwich and Thomas Bardolf. *Canterbury* R. ii p ii. 768. O. iv. 395. H ii, p, iii. 29
June 19	Proclamation of the said inquiry to be made by the sheriffs of London and by 20 others. *Canterbury* R ii p ii 768 O iv. 396 H ii p iii. 29
June 20.	Pardon for Lewelin ap Kenewrik for offences committed while assisting the K. against the Despensers *Canterbury.* R ii. p. ii. 768 O. iv. 396. H ii, p iii. 29
June 24 ? B	The K sends Thomas de Garton, comptroller of his household, to receive from David K of Scotland the 5,000 marks due on S John's day. *Rochester.* R ii p. ii 769. O. iv. 397. H ii p iii 30
June 28	John de Hainault appoints Dyne Forset and the company of the Bardi in London to receive his pension of 1,000 marks. R ii p ii. 769. O iv 397 H ii. p. iii 30
June 30	The K orders William de Weston, clerk, to consult with the cardinal of S. Stephen *in Cœlio Monte* for the prevention of the designs of Richard bp. of Ossory. *Eltham* R ii. p ii 769 O iv 398. H. ii. p. iii. 30.
July 2.	The K. orders Roger de Mortimer, earl of March, justiciary of Wales, to assist Nicholas de Acton, chamberlain of North Wales, in repairing the castles in North Wales *Dover.* R ii p ii 769
July 29.	The K requests the duke of Brittany to prevent his subjects from injuring English merchants *Windsor.* R ii. p. ii 769. O. iv 398. H ii. p. iii. 30.
July 29.	Letters of credence to the K of Aragon for Reymund Cornelin, who is returning to the K of Arragon *Windsor.* R ii p. ii. 770. O iv 399 H ii p iii. 30
July 30	Similar letters to Leonora Q of Aragon and [John Pratal of Alexandria, for the same Reymund Cornelii *Reading.* R ii p. ii. 770. O. iv. 399. H. ii. p. iii. 30.
Aug 2	Letters to the pope and cardinals in favour of Robert de Wyvill, late bp of Bath and Wells *Wallingford* O iv 399 H ii p iii 31 This entry is omitted in the Record Edition
Aug. 27.	Grant to Maurice Fitz-Thomas, created earl of Desmond, of the advowson of the church of Dungarvan. *Gloucester* R ii p ii 770 O iv. 400. H ii p. iii. 31.
Aug 27	Release to Maurice Fitz-Thomas of the rent of Dungarvan, amounting to 200 marks a year *Gloucester* R ii. p ii 770. O. iv 400. H ii. p iii. 31.
Sept 1.	Protection for James lord of Douglas going to the Holy Land with the heart of Robert late K. of Scotland *Gloucester* R. ii p ii 770. O iv 400. H ii. p. iii 31.
Sept 1	The K commends James lord of Douglas to Alfonso K. of Castile. *Gloucester.* R ii. p ii 771
Sept. 1.	The K. commends Walter de Twynham, clerk of the K. of Scotland, to the pope. *Gloucester.* R ii. p ii 771 O iv. 400. H. ii p. iii. 31
Sept. 1	Similar letters to three Roman cardinals. *Gloucester* R ii. p ii 771. O. iv 401. H. ii p iii 31
Sept. 1.	The K grants the county of Ponthieu, which Q Isabella holds for life, to her executors for three years for the performance of her will *Gloucester.* R ii p. ii 771.
Sept 1.	Similar grant of the county of Cornwall *Gloucester* R ii. p ii 771.
Sept. 3.	The K orders the pension of William count of Juliers, 600*l* a year, to be paid by the customer of S. Botolph's. *Gloucester.* R ii p ii. 771 O iv 401. H. ii. p iii 31
Sept. 12	Protection for Henry earl of Lancaster, William de Montacute, Bartholomew de Burghersh, and 30 others, who are going across the sea. *Hereford.* R. ii. p. ii. 772. O. iv. 401. H. ii. p. iii. 31.

DATE.	SUBJECT
1329. Sept. 15.	The K. asks the pope to confirm the dispensation of pope Clement V. for defect of birth to John de Chedewynd, abbot elect of Lilleshull *Gloucester.* R ɪɪ p ɪɪ. 772 O ɪv 402. H. ɪɪ p ɪɪɪ. 32
Sept. 20.	Pardon to the Roman cardinals beneficed in England of the tenths of their benefices. *Gloucester* R ɪɪ. p. ɪi. 772. O ɪv 403 H ɪi p ɪɪɪ 32.
Sept. 20.	Power to W. bp. of Norwich, Sir John de Insula, and three others, to treat with Philip K. of France R ɪɪ p ɪɪ 772 O ɪv 403 H ɪɪ p ɪɪɪ 32
Sept. 24.	Power to Sir John de Hausted and Peter de Galicien, canon of Agen, to treat for a marriage between John of Eltham, earl of Cornwall and Mary, daughter of John late lord of Biscay. *Gloucester* R ɪɪ p ɪɪ 773. O ɪv 403 H ɪɪ p ɪɪɪ. 32
Sept. 24.	Credence for John de Haustede and Peter de Galicien to the commonalty of Durance, and 13 other commonalties and persons. *Gloucester* R. ɪɪ p ɪɪ. 773 O ɪv. 404 H ɪɪ p ɪii. 32
[Sept. 24]	Credence for the same to Mary lady of Biscay and John Manuel R ɪɪ p ɪɪ 773. O ɪv 404 H ɪɪ p. ɪɪɪ 33.
Sept. 24.	Power to Bartholomew de Burghersh and William de Montacute to treat with the lord de Cuk about coming to England to join the K.'s council. *Gloucester.* R. ɪɪ. p. ɪɪ. 773. O ɪv 404 H. ɪɪ p. ɪɪɪ 33
Oct. 24.	Safe conduct for merchants of Brabant for five years. *Northampton.* R ɪɪ p ɪɪ. 773.
Oct. 28.	The K. summons W abp. of York and L. bp of Durham to appear before the council at Northampton on the morrow of S. Nicholas, for the settlement of their dispute. *Northampton* R ɪɪ p. ɪɪ 774 O ɪv 405 H ɪɪ p. ɪɪ. 33
Oct. 29.	The K. orders the sheriff of York to put down the disturbances in the diocese of York. *Northampton* R ɪi p ɪɪ. 774 O ɪv. 405 H ɪɪ p ɪɪɪ 33
Oct. 30.	The K. sends William de Kestevene, his clerk, to David K of Scotland, to receive the 5,000 marks due at Martinmas. *Kenilworth.* R. ɪɪ p ɪɪ 774 O. ɪv. 406. H p ɪɪi 33.
Nov. 2	The K. forbids the mayor of London to close the gate of the New Temple leading to the river *Kenilworth* R ɪɪ p ɪi 774 O ɪv 406. H ɪɪ p ɪɪ 33
Nov. 4.	The K. forbids the officers of the Mint to leave London without licence. *Kenilworth* R. ɪɪ p ɪɪ 774.
Nov. 12.	Receipt by the K of 5,000 marks from David K. of Scotland. *Kenilworth.* R ɪi. p. ɪɪ 775
Nov. 14.	Protection for L. bp. of Durham coming to the council relative to his dispute with the abp of York. *Kenilworth.* R ɪɪ p ɪɪ 775 O ɪv 407. H ɪɪ p ɪɪɪ. 33.
Dec. 3.	The K. orders W. bp of Norwich and Henry earl of Lancaster to go to the French King, and will send them instructions. *Kenilworth.* R ɪɪ p. ɪɪ 775 O. ɪv 407. H. ɪɪ p. ɪɪɪ. 34.
Dec. 7.	The K. orders Geoffrey le Scrope and the other justices in eyre in Northampton to arrest those who are spreading reports of the coming of foreigners into the kingdom Similar letters to the justices in eyre of Nottingham and the sheriffs of 4 other counties. *Kenilworth.* R. ɪɪ. p. ɪɪ. 775.
Dec. 12.	Grant of privileges by the K. of England to the burgesses of Deest in Brabant at the request of Q Isabella. *Gloucester.* R ɪɪ. p. ɪi 776. O ɪv. 408 H ɪɪ p. ɪɪ 34
Dec. 26.	Safe conduct for Archibald count de Peregore, Gaston earl of Foix, and 5 others, who are coming into England *Kenilworth* R ɪi p ɪɪ 776. O ɪv. 409 H ɪɪ p. ɪɪɪ. 34
1330 Jan. 6.	Reymund [de Farges], cardinal of S Maria Nova, dean of Sarum, archdeacon of Leicester and parson of Leek, appoints John de Pinibus, archdeacon of Bazas, and John de Tarent, parson of Berwick, his attorneys in England. *Worcester.* R. ɪɪ p ɪɪ. 776. O. ɪv 409 H. ɪɪ p ɪɪɪ 35
Jan. 7.	The K requests the pope to confirm the promotion of Hugh de Camera to the archdeaconry of Lincoln, notwithstanding the claim of Archambaldus de Petragons. *Leicester.* R ɪi. p ɪɪ 776 O ɪv. 409. H ɪi. p. ɪɪɪ. 35
Jan. 17.	The K gives to Q. Isabella the 10,000 marks due to him from the K of Scotland on S John's day next *Oseney* R. ɪi. p. ɪɪ 777 O ɪv. 410 H. ɪi. p ɪɪɪ. 35.
Jan 27	Power for A. bp. of Worcester, W bp of Norwich, Henry earl of Lancaster, and two others to treat with the K of France *Eltham* R. ɪɪ p. ɪɪ. 777. O. ɪv 410. H. ɪɪ. p ɪɪɪ. 35
Jan. 27.	Power for them to treat of a marriage between John, the eldest son of the K of France, and Eleanor, sister of the K. of England. *Eltham* R ɪɪ. p ɪɪ 777. O ɪv. 411 H ɪɪ. p. ɪɪɪ. 35

DATE	SUBJECT
1330 [Jan 27]	Power for them to treat of a marriage between John of Eltham, earl of Cornwall, and Mary, daughter of the K of France R. ii p ii 777. O. iv. 411. H ii p iii. 35
Feb. 2.	The K. commends to the pope the petitions of the masters of the university of Oxford. *Eltham.* R. ii. p ii 777 O. iv. 411 H. ii. p iii 35.
Feb 2	The K to the pope, asking him to support the university against the encroachments of cardinal Gayllard de Mota, archdeacon of Oxford *Eltham* R ii p ii 777. O iv 411. H ii p iii 35
Feb 2	Letters to the said cardinal on the same subject. *Eltham.* R. ii p. ii. 778 O. iv 412 H ii p iii. 36
Feb 2	Similar letters to 7 other cardinals *Eltham* R ii p ii 778 O iv 412 H ii p iii 36
Feb 5	The K instructs the bps of Worcester and Norwich and his other ambassadors relative to the homage done by him at Amiens *Eltham.* R. ii p ii. 778. O. iv. 413. H ii. p iii 36.
Feb 5	Power to the same persons to resume the negotiations for peace between France and England, begun at Montreuil in the time of Edward I *Eltham* R ii p. ii 778 O. iv 414. H ii p iii 36.
Feb 5.	Power for the same to resume the negotiations commenced at Perigord in the reign of Edward II *Eltham* R ii p ii 778 O. iv 415 H. ii p iii 37
Feb 10.	The K. requests the cardinal bp of Palestrina (Penestrinensis) and Bernard Stephani to obtain from the pope the confirmation of the grant by Geoffrey le Scrope of the advowson of the church of Sadbergh to the abbey of Coverham. *Tower of London.* R ii p ii 780 O iv. 417. H. ii p iii. 37
Feb. 11.	The K writes to the pope on the same subject *Tower of London* R. ii p n 780. O iv 417 H ii p iii 38
Feb 11	The K writes to the pope, objecting to the union of the see of Enachdoen to that of Tuam, and desiring credence for Thomas bp. of Enachdoen. *Tower of London.* R. ii. p ii. 780. O iv 418 H. ii. p iii 38
Feb 15	The K asks the pope to ratify a bull of Honorius IV touching certain benefices granted to the Chapel Royal at Westminster *Tower of London* R. ii p ii. 781. O iv 419. H ii p iii 38
Feb 22	The K warns the pope against believing Richard bp of Ossory. *Windsor.* R. ii. p ii. 781 O iv 419 H ii p iii 38
*Feb 28	The K orders Bartholomew de Burghersh, constable of Dover Castle, to summon the barons of the Cinque Ports to the coronation of his consort Philippa at Westminster on the *Sunday** before the feast of S. Peter *in Cathedra.* *Eltham* R ii p ii. 781. O iv 420. H. ii p iii 39
Feb 28.	The K desires William abp of Tolouse to deliver to Henry of Canterbury, his clerk, the French K's letters of pardon for Oliver Dinguehen and seven others, banished for the rebellion in Guyenne *Guildford* R ii p ii 781 O iv 420 H ii p iii 39
March 7	The K. requests the pope to canonize Thomas late earl of Lancaster. *Winchester* R. ii p ii 782. O. iv. 421 H ii p iii 39
March 7	Similar letters to 5 cardinals *Winchester* R. ii p ii 782 O iv 422 H ii. p iii 39
March 14	Warrant to Nicholas de Langford and John Payne to take the countess of Kent and her children, and deliver them to the sheriff of Wiltshire, and her goods to William de Holyns and Roger atte Asbe *Winchester* R ii p ii 782
March 15.	The K orders the several sheriffs to make search for the personal property of the two Despensers, Edmund, late earl of Arundel, Edmund late earl of Kent, and Rob. de Baldok, and to deliver the same into the K.'s wardrobe. *Winchester.* R. ii p ii 782.
March 18.	The K orders the abps of Canterbury and York to assemble the clergy for the purpose of obtaining a subsidy from them to carry on the war with France *Winchester* R. ii. p ii 783 O. iv 422 H ii p iii 40
March 20.	The K to the doge of Venice, in favour of the company of the Bardi of Florence in their dispute with him *Winchester* R ii p ii 783 O. iv. 423 H. ii p iii. 40.
March 24.	The K informs the pope of the trial and execution of Edmund late earl of Kent. *Reading.* R ii p ii 783 O iv 424 H ii p iii 40

---

* This would be the 18th. The date of the document must be wrong

DATE	SUBJECT.
1330 March 24	Letters of credence for John Walewayn, canon of Hereford *Reading* R. ii p ii 784 O iv 425 H ii p iii 41
March 27.	Commission to John le Small, the K's clerk, to provide 40 ships for the passage of John of Eltham earl of Cornwall to Aquitain. *Wallingford.* R. ii. p. ii. 784. O iv 425 H ii p iii. 41.
March 28	The K requests Alfonso K of Castile to make restitution to Gerard de Byole of Southampton, whose ship was taken by subjects of Alfonso. *Woodstock.* R ii p ii 784 O iv. 426 H ii p. iii 41
April 2	Warrant for the payment to Robert de Veer earl of Oxford, hereditary chamberlain of the Queen, of 100 marks, in lieu of her bed, and her shoes, and 3 silver basins, his fee for attending at her coronation *Woodstock* R. ii p ii 784. O iv 428. H ii. p iii 41
April 3	The K orders the sheriffs of Surrey and Sussex and of 15 other counties to forbid all persons from going about armed *Woodstock* R ii p ii. 784. O. iv 427. H ii p iii 41.
April 3.	The K orders Thomas de Garton, his clerk, to pay to Q Isabella the 5,000 marks received from David K of Scotland *Woodstock.* R. ii. p. ii. 785
April 10	Power to A bp of Worcester, W bp of Norwich, John Walewayn, and John de Shordich to continue the negotiations begun at Amiens *Woodstock* R ii p ii 785 O iv 437 H ii. p iii 42.
April 10	Power to the same to treat for a marriage between John, son of Philip K of France, and Eleanor, the K's sister *Woodstock* R ii p ii 785. O iv 428 H ii p iii 42
April 10	The K. deputes John de Sordiche, John de Fenton, and William de Culpho to excuse his absence at the parliament of the K. of France, and to act for him *Woodstock* R. ii p ii 785
April 10	Power for the same to object to the jurisdiction of the K of France *Woodstock* R. ii p ii 786
April 12	The K will pay to the pope the half of the tenth granted by the clergy, and also the arrears of the annual census of 1,000 marks due to the holy see. *Woodstock* R ii p ii 786 O iv 428. H ii p iii 42
April 12.	The K. orders the sheriff of Devon to provide fittings for 20 ships for the conveyance of certain nobles to Aquitain *Woodstock* R. ii p ii 786
April 13	The K orders the several sheriffs and the justiciary of Wales to proclaim the death of Edmund late earl of Kent, and to arrest those who say he was unjustly put to death, or that the late king is still alive *Woodstock* R ii p ii 787 O iv. 430 H. ii p. iii 43.
April 13.	The K orders John de Londham. Thomas de Hindringham, and Robert Houel to make inquisition in the counties of Norfolk and Suffolk for adherents of the late earl of Kent *Woodstock.* R. ii p ii. 787
April 15	Credence for Robert de Wodehous, archdeacon of Richmond, the K's treasurer, John de Gray John de Stonore, and Simon de Swanlond, mayor of London, going to the convocation of the province of Canterbury at Lambeth *Woodstock* R. ii p. ii 787. O. iv 431. H ii p ii 43
April 18.	The K orders the sheriff of Southampton to provide fittings for 20 ships for the passage of certain nobles to Aquitain *Woodstock* R. ii. p ii. 787.
April 24.	The K. orders the officers of the Cinque Ports to assist John le Smale in providing 40 ships to cross to Aquitain *Woodstock.* R ii p ii 788
April 25.	The K orders the arrest of all those who endeavour to disturb the presentation of Simon de Montacute to the archdeaconry of Wells. *Woodstock* R ii. p ii 788. O iv. 431. H ii p iii 43.
April 27.	Power to John Darcy le Cosyn and William de Seintz, lord de Pomeris, to treat with the nobles and commonalties of Aquitain *Woodstock* R ii p ii 788 O iv. 432 H. ii p iii 43.
April 27.	Power to the same persons to treat for alliance, and for the coming of the nobles to the K *Woodstock* R ii p ii 788. O. iv. 432. H ii. p iii. 43
April 27.	Credence for the same and 115 other nobles and commonalties. *Woodstock* R ii. p. ii 788 O. iv 432. H ii. p iii. 44
[April 27.]	The K. commissions his brother John of Eltham, earl of Cornwall, to reform abuses in Aquitain. R ii. p ii 789. O iv 434 H ii. p iii. 44

DATE	SUBJECT.
1330 April 28	Obligation of the K to the Bardi for 1,318*l* 16*s* 8*d*, advanced by them to William de Montacute and Bartholomew de Burghersh, for the payment of 1,000 marks annual tribute to the pope, and for their expenses Warrant to the treasurer and barons of the Exchequer for the payment of the above sum *Woodstock* R. ii p ii. 789. O. iv. 484–5. H ii p iii 44
April 28	The K grants an annuity of 500*l* to Berard de la Brette Warrant to the constable of Bordeaux to pay the same *Woodstock.* R ii p ii 790 O iv 436 H ii. p. iii 45
May 1	The K appoints Berard de la Brette custos of the castle of Puy Normand [de Podio Normanni] and of the bastide of Villefranche *Woodstock* R ii p ii 790 O. iv 435. H ii p iii 45.
May 5.	The K informs the lord de Caumont and 7 others that the French K's letters of pardon will be shortly put into effect. *Woodstock* R. ii p ii 790 O iv 436 H ii p iii 45
May 5.	Credence for William Trussel and Reymund Cornill to the Ks of Aragon, Portugal, Majorca, and Castile. *Woodstock* R ii p ii 790 O iv 436. H. ii. p iii. 45.
[May 5]	Credence for William Trussel to Reymund Cornill R ii p ii 791 O iv 437 H. ii. p iii 45
May 6	The K grants to David de Strabolgi, earl of Athol, son and heir of David de Strabolgi, livery of the lands inherited by his late mother Johanna, daughter of Aymer de Valence, late earl of Pembroke. *Woodstock* R ii p ii. 791 O ii 437. H. ii p iii 45.
May 8	Treaty between England and France Restitution of places taken, the duchy of Guyenne to retain its liberties, Edward III. to pay 50,000 marks and 6,000 livres de Paris; confirmation of the two treaties made by Edward II and Edward III, &c. *Bois de Vincennes* R ii p ii 791 O iv 437–41 H ii p iii. 46
May 10.	Obligation to Dinus Forsetti for 25 marks paid by him for the K. as a reward to Colard Maloysel, valet of the countess of Juliers, the K's sister, for bringing news of her delivery to Q Philippa, and 20 marks to Henry of Canterbury, for his expenses in going abroad Warrant to the treasurer to pay the above sums *Woodstock* R ii p ii 792. O iv 441 H ii p iii 47
May 11.	The K requests the pope to admit the bearer as proctor for Thomas de Lavenham, parson of Great Okle, who desires to go to his holiness on a matter of conscience, but is prevented by his age *Woodstock.* R ii p ii 792 O iv 441 H. ii p iii 47
May 19.	Credence for William Trussel and Reymund Cornelius to the K of Aragon, concerning the defence of the Holy Church against the Saracens *Woodstock* R. ii p ii. 793. O iv. 442 H ii p iii 47
May 31.	The K appoints Walter de Shobdon, overseer of the ships for the passage of John of Eltham, earl of Cornwall, to Gascony *Woodstock.* R. ii p ii 793 O iv. 442. H. ii. p iii 47
June 6	The K orders his treasurer to pay to the count of Juliers his annuity of 600*l* *Woodstock.* R ii p. ii 793 O iv 442 H ii p iii 48
June 19.	The K orders Maurice FitzThomas earl of Desmond to desist from his dissensions with William de Burgh earl of Ulster *Woodstock* R. ii p. ii 793
July 8	Ratification by Edward III of the recent treaty with France. *Woodstock* R ii p ii. 793 O iv 443 H. ii p iii 48
July 8	Power for Roger bp of Coventry and Lichfield, William bp of Norwich, John Walwayn, canon of Hereford, John de Shordich, and Thomas Sampson to treat with France about certain matters not yet settled *Woodstock* R ii p ii 794 O iv 443 H ii p iii 48.
July 8	Power for the same commissioners to estimate the debts of the K of England to the K of France *Woodstock* R ii p ii 794. O iv 444. H ii p iii 48
July 8	Power for the same commissioners to treat of marriage (*See* April 10) *Oseney.* R ii. p ii. 794. O iv 444 H ii p iii. 48
July 12	The K orders the several sheriffs to proclaim that all knights and others shall be ready to defend him against his rebels. *Oseney.* R. ii. p ii 794
July 12	The K forbids tournaments. *Oseney.* R. ii. p ii. 794.
July 25 ? 15	The K informs Simon de Bereford and John de Bolyngbrok, his escheators, that he has granted to John of Brittany, earl of Richmond, a respite for performing his homage *Woodstock* R ii p ii 795 O iv 444 H ii p. iii 48
July 25 ? 15	Receipt by the K for 10,000 marks from David K. of Scotland *Woodstock* R. ii. p ii 795 O .v 445 H. ii. p. iii 48.

DATE	SUBJECT
1330. July 20	Safe conduct and protection for Edward de Balliol coming to the K. *Woodstock* R. ii. p ii 795 O. iv 445 H. ii p iii 49
July 25	The K commends Thomas de Abtot, his clerk, going to the pope to consult his holiness on matters of conscience *Woodstock* R ii. p ii 795 O iv 445 H ii p. iii 49
July 25	The K appoints John le White of Limerick, constable of the castle there *Woodstock.* R. ii p ii 795.
Aug 2	The K. allows Thomas de Mont Hermer to pay the 200 marks by instalments for his pardon as an adherent of Henry late earl of Lancaster *Northampton* R ii. p ii 796 O iv 445. H. ii p iii 49
Aug 3.	The K to the pope, requesting him to promote his clerk, Peter de Galiciano, constable of Bordeaux, to the pontifical dignity in Gascony. *Northampton* R. ii p ii 796 O iv. 446 H. ii p iii 49.
[Aug. 3]	The K writes on the same subject to 13 cardinals R. ii p ii 796 O iv. 446 H ii p. iii 49
Aug 8	The K orders Roger de Mortimer, earl of March, justiciary of Wales, to arrest Rees ap Griffyn and the other adherents of Edmund de Wodestok, late earl of Kent. *Clyve* R. ii p ii 796 O iv 447 H ii p iii. 49.
Aug 10.	The K orders L bp of Durham to appoint Ralph de Nevill arrayer for his bishopric. *Stamford* R ii p ii 797 O iv 448 H ii p iii 50
Aug. 26.	The K forbids A abp of Dublin, to exact tithes from benefices of less value than six marks *Lincoln.* R ii p. ii. 797
Sept. 1	Philip VI of France summons Edward III to appear at Paris a fortnight after St. Andrew's day, as he was not present at the late parliament *Retoisel* R. ii p. ii 797.
Sept 9	The K. informs the seneschal of Gascony and the constable of Bordeaux that the K of France has not yet accepted the K. of England's confirmation of the treaty of May 8, and desires him to observe the treaty, saving the rights of the duchy. *Nottingham.* R. ii. p ii 798 O iv 449 H ii p iii. 50
Sept. 16	The K orders Oliver de Ingham, justiciary of Chester, to pay 500 marks annually towards the expenses of the household of his eldest son Edward *Nottingham* R ii p ii 798
Sept. 20	The K requests the pope to persuade the K of France to maintain peace *Nottingham* R ii p ii. 798 O iv 449 H ii p. iii 50
Sept 20	The K informs John Darcy and John de Haustede, seneschal of Gascony, that the K of France will not come to terms, and that he intends to maintain his rights by force *Nottingham* R ii p ii 798 O. iv 450 H ii p iii. 50
[Sept. 20.]	Power for the same persons to make grants to the commonalties of the duchy, and to treat with the people of Agennois, the counts of Foix and Comenge, and others R ii p ii 799 O iv 451 H ii. p iii 51
Oct 1	Power for Sir William FitzWaryn, Hugh Elys, dean of Wolverhampton, and John de Hildesle, canon of Chichester, to treat with John duke of Brabant and the count of Flanders. *Pontefract* Also to treat with the counts of Geldres, Los, and Chyny *Nottingham* 11 *Oct* R. ii p ii. 799. O iv. 451. H ii p. iii 51.
Oct. 16	Safe conduct and protection for one year for Edward de Balliol *Nottingham* R. ii. p ii 799 O. iv 452 H ii p. iii. 51.
Oct 20	The K orders proclamation to be made by the sheriff of Yorkshire of the arrest of the earl of March, Oliver de Ingham, and Simon de Bereford, and of his intention to govern the kingdom himself Similar letters to the several sheriffs *Nottingham* R ii p ii 799. O iv. 452 H. ii p. iii. 51
Nov. 3	The K orders the several sheriffs to proclaim that grievances shall be redressed at the approaching parliament at Westminster, complains of the character of the members of the late parliament, and orders a new election. *Woodstock.* R ii. p ii 800 O iv. 453 H ii. p. iii 52
Nov 4.	The K orders the customers of St. Botolph's to pay the annuity of 900 marks granted to the count of Juliers. *Woodstock* R. ii p ii. 800 O iv 454 H ii p iii 52
Nov. 6.	The K orders the customers of London to pay the annuity of 1,000 marks granted to John de Hainault. *Woodstock.* R. ii. p ii. 800. O. iv. 454. H ii p. iii 52
Nov. 28	Memorandum of the resignation of the great seal by Henry bp of Lincoln, the K's chancellor, and of its transfer by the King to John bp. of Winchester, who takes the oath as chancellor *Westm* R ii. p. ii 800. O. iv. 454 H ii p iii 52

DATE	SUBJECT.
1330. Dec 3	Warrant to the sheriffs of Northampton, Cornwall, Southampton, and Wilts, for the restitution of his lands to Edward de Mont Hermer, suspected of complicity with the earl of Kent. *Westm* R. u p u. 800 O iv 454 H u p ui 52
Dec 3	Warrants to the several sheriffs for the arrest of John Mautravers, Thomas de Gurneye, John Wyard, William de Exon, late constable of Wallingford Castle, John Deveroill, and William de Ocle. *Westm* R u. p u 801.
Dec 3	Similar warrants to the mayors and bailiffs of Faversham, Dover, and six other ports *Westm* R u p u. 801
Dec 4	The K requests the pope to confirm to St Mary's College, Oxford, the grants of the churches of St Mary, Oxford, of Aberford (in York dioc.), and of Coleby (in Linc. dioc.), and to delegate to the abbots of Oseney and Rewley [de Regali loco] near Oxford the power of reconciliation for the church of St Mary's and the cemetery polluted by the effusion of blood *Westm* R u p u 801 O iv 454 H u p ui. 52.
Dec. 10	The K requests the pope to forbid cardinal Ambaldo molesting Manser Marmyon, presented by the K to the church of Hoghton in Durham dioc. *Westm*. R u p u 801 O iv 455 H u p ui 53
[Dec. 10]	The K writes to the said cardinal on the same subject R u p u 801 O iv 456 H u p ui 53
Dec. 11.	The K recommends Merton College, Oxford, to the pope *Westm* R u p u 802 O iv 456 H u p ui 53
Dec. 11.	Similar letters to two cardinals *Westm* R u p u 802 O iv. 456. H u p ui 53
Dec. 12	The K pardons and cancels the recognizances of Henry earl of Lancaster and his adherents for taking arms against Roger de Mortimer. *Westm.* R u p u 802. O iv 457. H u p ui 53
Dec. 13.	The K requests the pope to allow John de Godelee, dean of Wells, to reside away from Wells, for the sake of his health *Westm* R u p u 802 O iv 457. H u p ui 53
Dec. 13.	Similar letter to the cardinal bp of Albano. *Westm* R u p u 802 O iv. 458 H u p ui 53
Dec 14.	The K requests the pope to revoke the promotion of the cardinal of St. Stephen *in Cœlio Monte* to the treasurership of York *Westm*. R. u p u 803 O iv. 458. H u p ui 54
Dec. 14.	The K writes to the cardinal of St Stephen *in Cœlio Monte* on the same subject *Westm* R u p ii 803 O iv 459 H u p ui 54
Dec. 14.	The K writes to the pope for the confirmation of the bull of Honorius IV to Westminster Abbey, relative to Sabrichesworth, Kellevedene, and Langedon *Westm* R. n. p u 803 O iv. 460 H u p. ui 54
[Dec 14]	Similar letters to the vice-chancellor of the pope and another cardinal. R. u p. u 803 O iv 460. H u p ui 54
Dec. 14	The K orders the sheriffs of London to proclaim a pardon for those who rose against the K at Winchester and Bedford *Westm* R. u p u 804
Dec 15	The K informs the mayors of London and of three other towns and the bailiffs of Dover that he has allowed the friends of Hugh le Despenser the younger to collect and bury his bones *Westm* R u p u 804. O iv. 461 H u p ui 55.
Dec. 20	The K requests David K. of Scotland to make restitution to Thomas Wake, lord of Ledel, and Henry de Beaumont, earl of Boghan, according to the treaty with Robert late K of Scotland *Westm* R u p u 804 O iv 461. H u p ui 55
Dec 26.	The K requests the pope to confer upon his secretary Richard de Bury the prebends in the cathedrals of Hereford, London, and Chichester, vacant by the death of Gilbert de Middleton, archdeacon of Northampton. *Guildford* R. ii. p. u. 804. O iv. 462 H. u. p ui. 55.
1331. Jan 10	Receipt by the K for 10,000 marks due on next St. John's day from David K. of Scotland *Westm* R u p u 804 O iv 462 H u p ui 55
[Jan 10]	Three other receipts for 5,000 marks, 3,000 marks, and 2,000 marks, due from David K of Scotland *Westm.* R u p u 805. O iv. 463. H u p ui 55
Jan. 12	The K requests David K. of Scotland to pay 10,000 marks to the company of the Bardi of Florence. *Westm* R. u. p u 805. O iv. 463. H. u. p. ui. 56
Jan 14	The K ratifies the appointment by the pope of cardinal Arnaldo to the treasurership of Salisbury and the prebend of Calne. *Westm.* R. u p u. 805. O. iv 463 H. u p. ui 56

DATE	SUBJECT
1331 Jan. 15.	The K orders John de Pulteneye, mayor of London, to repair the gate of the New Temple and the bridge leading to the Thames. *Westm.* R. ii p ii 805. O iv 464 H ii p iii 56
Jan. 16.	Power to Adam bp of Worcester, William de Norwich, Henry de Percy, Hugh de Audeleye, and John de Shordich to treat with the K. of France. *Westm.* R ii p ii 805 O iv. 464 H. ii p. iii. 56.
Jan 16	Power for the same to treat of the mutual debts of the two Kings. *Westm* R. ii p ii 806 O iv.-465. H ii p. iii. 56.
Jan 16.	Power for the same to treat of all matters in debate. *Westm* R. ii p ii 805 O iv. 456 H ii p iii. 56
Jan 22.	The K. revokes his presentation of John de Charnebrok to the church of Otery St. Mary, which church was granted to the dean and chapter of Rouen by Edward the Confessor *Westm* R ii p ii. 806. O iv. 466 H ii p iii. 57
Jan. 22.	Warrant for the payment of 1,000 marks to William de Grandisson, executor of Blanche late Queen of Navarre *Westm.* R ii p ii 806 O iv. 466 H ii p iii 57
Feb 3	The K requests David K. of Scotland to order Patrick earl of Dunbar to restore the town of Upsethngton to the bp of Durham, in accordance with the late treaty with Robert late K of Scotland. *Langley.* R. ii. p ii. 806. O iv. 467 H. ii. p. iii 57
[Feb 3]	The K writes on the same subject to Thomas earl of Murref, guardian of the land of Scotland R ii. p. ii. 807 O. iv 468 H ii p iii. 57
[Feb 3]	Similar letter to Patrick de Dunbar, earl of March. R ii. p. ii. 807. O. iv. 468. H. ii, p iii. 57.
Feb. 5.	The K orders the sheriffs of Gloucester and Somerset to allow William de Clyvedon and two others to export 600 quarters of corn to Ireland, where there is great scarcity, *Langley.* R. ii p ii 807.
Feb, 6, ? 5	The K orders the seneschal of Gascony and the mayor of Bayonne to forbid alienations in mortmain. *Langley* R. ii p ii 807. O iv 468 H ii p iii. 57.
Feb 8	The K writes to the pope in favour of Guichard de Jou, prior of Montacute, whose title is disputed by the cardinal of St Stephen. *Langley* R ii. p iii. 807 O iv 469. H ii p. iii 58.
[Feb. 8.]	The K writes to the cardinal of St Stephen on the same subject. R. ii. p. ii. 808 O iv 469. H ii p iii 58
Feb. 10.	The K orders the seneschals of Gascony and the Landes to inquire into the acquisition, by William Arnaldi de Brokars de St Sever of ignoble birth, of the fee-noble of St Sarnan and the whole land of Guauzon, Seint Barba, and Sauboet, which are of the barony of Gualhart, from Reymund Gulhelmi, lord of Marsan. *Langley.* R ii p ii 808 O iv 470 H ii p iii 58
Feb. 12.	The K requests the chapter general of the Friars Preachers to pray for him, his Q, and his son Edward *Langley* Similar letters to the Friars Minors, also to the Carmelite Friars *Eltham.* 12 *April* R ii. p. ii 808
Feb. 13.	Respite of the homage of John de Britannia, earl of Richmond, who is beyond the seas in the K.'s service. *York.* O iv. 470. H. ii. p. iii 58 Omitted in the Record Edition
Feb. 14.	The K. forbids tournaments throughout England *Windsor.* R ii. p ii 808
Feb 16	The K appoints William abp of York, William prior of Durham, Henry de Percy, and six others, his justiciaries for enforcing the observance of the treaty with Scotland Similar letters for John de Haryngton, Ralph de Dacre, and Richard de Denton *Windsor* R ii p ii 802. O iv 470-1. H ii p. iii 58
Feb. 20.	The K grants to Otho lord of Lauret, at the request of Reymund Durand, the bailiwicks of Miremont, Genoa, Serrafronte, Pymbol, and "de Castro Novo," and other places *Windsor* R ii. p ii 809 O iv 471 H ii p iii 59
Feb. 24.	The K requests David K of Scotland to make restitution of their lands and possessions to Thomas Wake and Henry de Beaumont, according to the treaty. *Croydon* R. ii p. ii. 809. O iv. 471 H. ii p iii. 59.
[Feb. 24.]	Letter to Thomas Rondulf, earl of Morref, on the same subject. R ii. p ii 809 O. iv. 472. H. ii. p. iii. 59
[Feb 24.]	Letters to J. bp of St. Andrew's, J. bp. of Dunkeld, and five others, on the same subject. R. ii p ii 809. O. iv. 472. H ii. p. iii 59
Feb. 24.	Pardon for Thomas West, John de Nevill, and William de Clynton, for the death of Hugh de Turphton and Richard de Monemuth, at the arrest of Roger de Mortimer. *Croydon* R. ii. p. ii. 810. O iv. 473. H ii. p. iii 59.

R 2

DATE	SUBJECT
1331. Feb. 24.	The K orders the several sheriffs, and William de Clynton, constable of Dover Castle and warden of the Cinque Ports, to proclaim that neither men at arms nor horses nor armour shall leave the kingdom *Croydon* R ii p ii 810.
Feb 25	The K writes to the pope in favour of A bp of Dublin against the bp of Ossory *Croydon* R ii p ii 810 O iv 473 H ii p iii. 59.
[Feb. 25]	Similar letters to the bp of Albano and five others R ii p. ii 811. O. iv. 474 H ii p iii. 60.
Feb 25	The K directs the seneschals of Gascony and the Landes to inquire into the complaints of the nobles of the barony of Miremont *Croydon* R. ii p ii. 811 O iv 474 H. ii p iii 60
Feb 25	The K grants to Q. Philippa the revenues of the duchy of Chester, for the maintenance of his son Edward and his sister Eleanor. *Croydon.* R ii p ii 811.
Feb 27	The K orders William de Burgh, earl of Ulster, James le Boteler, earl of Ormond, and 34 others, to assist Antony de Lucy, justiciary of Ireland. *Croydon.* R.ii p. ii 811
March 3	The K appoints William de Burgh, earl of Ulster, his lieutenant in Ireland *Croydon* R ii p ii 811 O iv 475 H ii p iii 60.
March 3	The K sends to the justiciary, chancellor, and treasurer of Ireland certain articles decreed in the late parliament at Windsor for the reformation of Ireland. *Croydon.* R. ii p ii 812 O iv 475 H. ii p iii 60
March 5	Resumption of all grants whatsoever in Ireland since the K assumed the government *Croydon.* R. ii. p ii. 812. O iv. 476 H ii. p. iii 61.
March 6	The K grants to Q Philippa the power of disposing of the lands assigned for her dowry. *Croydon* R. ii p ii 812
March 21.	Safe conduct for the merchants of Louvain, at the request of John duke of Brabant. *Westm* R ii p ii. 812.
March 24	The K annexes for ever to his crown Chirk in Wales, which escheated to him by the forfeiture of Roger de Mortimer *Westm* R ii p ii 813
March 28.	The K. orders the seneschal of Gascony and the constable of Bordeaux to send information of the value of his lands there for the assignment of pensions to Arnold Dosa, viscount of Caraman, to Peter de Via and to Arnold de Tryn *Eltham* R. ii p ii 813. O iv. 477 H ii p iii 61
March 30.	Letters patent declaring that the homage performed by the K of England to the K of France should be considered liege homage, and giving the form which the K. and his successors shall use *Eltham* R ii p ii 813 O. iv 477 H. ii p iii 61.
April 3	The K urges on the pope the canonization of Thomas late Earl of Lancaster *Eltham,* R ii p ii 814 O iv 478 H ii p iii 61
April 3	Letters on the same subject to the cardinal of St. Angelo and 13 others *Eltham* R. ii p ii 814 O. iv 479 H ii p iii 62
April 8	The K orders proclamation to be made throughout England that no person shall import false money *Eltham* R ii p ii 814
April 4	John de Eltham, earl of Cornwall, appointed regent of the realm during the K's intended absence in France *Dover* R ii p ii 814 O iv 480 H. ii p iii 62
April 4	Memorandum that the K sailed from Dover for France, to fulfil a vow, and for other purposes, accompanied by J bp of Winchester, his chancellor, William de Montacute, and others The chancellor left the great seal in the custody of his brother, Master Robert de Stratford R ii p ii. 815. O iv 480. H ii p iii 62
April 11	The sheriffs of Norfolk, Suffolk, and London are ordered to forbid tournaments *Eltham.* R ii p ii 815.
April 12	The sheriff of Lincoln, notwithstanding the prohibition, is ordered to allow 400 quarters of corn to be bought for the K of Scotland. *Eltham.* R. ii p. ii. 815 O iv 481. H ii p. iii 62
April 13	Philip K of France accepts the homage of the K. of England according to the form in his letter of March 30. *S Christopher en Halate* R. ii p. ii 815 O. iv. 481 H ii. p iii 63
April 13	Philip K of France releases the K of England from any penalties in consequence of the imperfect homage paid by him at Amiens *S. Christopher en Halate* R ii. p. ii. 815 O iv 482 H. ii p iii. 63

DATE	SUBJECT
1331 April 13.	Philip K. of France promises to pay to the K of England 30,000 *livres Tournois* as reparation for the damage done to the town and castle of Saintes by the count of Alençon. S. *Christopher en Halate.* R. ii. p ii 816 O iv 483 H ii p. iii. 63
April 18	Philip K of France pardons his exiles in Guyenne *S Christopher en Halate* R ii p. ii. 817. O iv 485 H ii p iii. 64
April 18	Philip K. of France annuls the penalties for receiving the exiles *S Christopher en Halate* R ii p ii 817. O iv. 485. H. ii. p. iii. 64.
April 18	Philip K of France consents that the castles of Sainte Croix, Madillan, Pui Pymes, and Don Bardill, in Gascony, shall not be demolished, as stipulated in the late treaty *S Christopher en Halate* R ii p ii 817 O iv 486 H ii p iii 65
April 20.	Memorandum that the K arrived at Dover on his return from France, and spent the night at Wengham R ii p. ii. 818 O iv 487 H ii p iii 65.
May 4.	The K orders the sheriffs of Lancashire and Cheshire to provide ships for the passage into Ireland of Antony de Lucy, justiciary of Ireland, and Thomas de Burgh, treasurer of Dublin *Havering atte Bower* R ii p ii 818
May 10.	The K grants to John de Nevill, of Horneby, the manors of Lodres, Phelipston, Up Wymburn, Chelrete, and Wynterburn Houton, as a reward for his assistance in the arrest of Roger de Mortimer, earl of March *Havering atte Bower.* R. ii p ii 818 O iv 487. H. ii p. iii 65.
May 10	Restitution of the temporalties to the bp of Ossory *Havering atte Bower* R ii p ii 818 O iv 488. H ii p iii 65
May 20	The K requests Alfonso K. of Castile to deliver up Thomas de Gourney, in custody at Burgos, to John de Haustede, seneschal of Gascony *Havering atte Bower* R ii. p. ii 819. O iv 488 H ii p iii. 65.
[May 20]	Similar letter to the mayor and commonalty of Burgos R. ii p ii 819 O iv 489 H ii p iii 66
May 20	The K acknowledges that the treaty between St Louis K of France and Henry late K of England has been fulfilled. *Havering atte Bower* R ii p ii 819 O iv 489 H ii p. iii. 66.
May 20.	The K of England will send ambassadors to K Philip for the settlement of his debts before next Christmas *Havering atte Bower* R ii p ii 819. O iv 489 H ii p iii 66
May 20	The K. directs John de Pulteneye, mayor of London to attend to the maintenance of the chantries in the city *Havering atte Bower.* R ii p iii 819
May 28	The K requests Alfonso K of Castile to cause Thomas de Gourney to be examined, and his confession transmitted to him. *S Edmund's* R ii p ii 820 O iv 490 H ii p. iii 66
[May 28]	Similar letters to the mayor and commonalty of Burgos R ii p ii 820 O. iv 491 H ii. p iii 66
May 28	K Edward desires John de Leynham, chamberlain of the K of Spain, to deliver Thomas de Gournay to the mayor of Bayonne Letters on the same subject to the mayor of Bayonne *S Edmund's* R ii p ii 820 O iv 491 H ii p iii 66
May 30	Warrant to Giles de Ispannia to bring Thomas de Gurney to England *S Edmund's* R ii p ii 820 O iv 491. H ii p iii 67
June 8	The K requests the K of Navarre to allow safe conduct to those who conduct Thomas de Gournay to Bayonne *Norwich* R ii p ii 820 O iv 492 H ii p iii 67
June 23.	Warrant to the constable of Bordeaux to pay 300*l* to John Martyn de Leyna, of Spain, for the arrest of Thomas de Gurney *Norwich* R ii p ii 820 O. iv 492. H ii p. iii 67
June 23.	The treasurer ordered to pay 50*l* to Ferando Ivaynes de Greynoun, who came from Spain with the news of the capture of Thomas de Gurney. *Norwich* R ii p ii 821. O iv. 492 H. ii p iii 67
June 29	Warrant for the payment of 20*l* to Giles de Ispannia, for his expenses in bringing over Thomas de Gourney from Spain *Gaywood* R ii p ii 821. O iv. 492 H ii. p iii. 67.
July 4.	Acquittance by the K of England of all claims on the K of France or the count of Alençon, for the damage done to Saintes. *Lincoln.* R. ii. p. ii. 821. O iv. 492. H ii p iii 67
July 5.	Credence for John Darcy and William Trussell to the Kings of Castile, Portugal, France, Navarre, Arragon, and Majorca. *Lincoln.* R. ii. p. ii 821. O. iv. 494 H. ii. p. iii. 68.

SYLLABUS OF RYMER'S FŒDERA.

DATE	SUBJECT
1331 July 5	The K orders the seneschal of Gascony and constable of Bourdeaux to proclaim the accord lately made with the K of France *Lincoln* R ii p ii. 822. O. iv. 494. H ii. p iii 68
July 15	Power to John Darcy and William Trussel to treat for a marriage between prince Edward and the daughter of the K of France *Lincoln* R ii. p ii 822 O. iv 494 H. ii p iii 68
July 16	The K writes to the pope in favour of Simon abp of Canterbury, who is accused of outrages on the servants of Icherius de Concoreto, the papal nuncio *Lincoln.* R ii. p. ii. 822 O iv. 495 H ii. p. iii 68.
July 18	The K desires the seneschal of Gascony and the constable of Bordeaux to inform him of the losses suffered from the French by Peter de Moncan and three others. *Lincoln* R ii p. ii. 822 O iv 495 H ii p iii 68
July 22.	Warrant for the payment of the annuity to William count of Juliers. *Lincoln* R ii. p. ii 822.
July 28	Licence to John Kempe of Flanders, weaver, to practise and teach his trade in England, and promise of similar licence to others *Lincoln* R ii p. ii 823 O iv 496 H ii p iii 68.
Aug 10.	The K. writes to four cardinals on behalf of Simon abp. of Canterbury *Clapstone* R ii p. ii 823 O iv 496 H ii p iii 69
Sept 4.	The K orders William de Clynton, constable of Dover Castle and warden of the Cinque Ports, to send ships to Whitsand for the passage into England of the countess of Holland *Ashbourn in the Peak* R ii. p ii 822 O iv 497 H ii p iii 69
Oct. 1.	Order to pay 20 marks, part of the annuity of 40 marks granted by the K. to Thomas Priour, for bringing him word of the birth of his son Edward *Westm* R ii p ii. 823. O iv 497. H ii p iii 69
Oct. 2.	The K writes to the pope in favour of John bp elect of Cashel, and asks him to remit the papal dues *Westm* R ii p ii 823 O iv 497. H ii p iii 69
Oct. 4.	The K writes to the pope in favour of the abbey of Glastonbury. *Westm.* R ii. p ii 824. O iv. 498. H ii p iii. 69
Oct 8	The K. forbids tournaments throughout England *Westm* R ii. p. ii 824
Oct 8	Payment of 200l for the expenses of the countess of Hainault ordered to William de Coleby, treasurer of the household of Q Philippa *Westm*. R. ii. p. ii. 824 O iv. 498 H. ii. p. iii. 69.
Oct 8	Warrant for the payment of the annuity of 40 marks granted by the K. to Nicholas de Aubricicourt, on whom knighthood has been conferred *Westm* R ii p ii 824 O iv 498 H ii p iii 69
Oct. 10.	The K. requests David K of Scotland to desist from molesting Lewis bp. of Durham and his tenants at West Upsetlyngton *Westm* R ii p ii 824 O. iv 499 H ii p iii 70.
Oct. 14.	Warrant for the payment of the annuity to the count of Juliers *Westm* R. ii. p ii. 825 O. iv 500 H ii p. iii 70
Oct 14.	William de Clynton, constable of Dover Castle and warden of the Cinque Ports, is commanded to allow fishermen to be paid for their goods in English money, notwithstanding the act against taking money out of the realm *Westm* R ii p ii 825 O iv. 500 H ii p iii 70
Oct. 15	The K. has received from William de Remmesbury, his chaplain, relics of The Innocents, S Silvester, S Laurence, and S John the Baptist, a picture given by the K. of France, and certain jewels *Westm* R ii p. ii 825.
Oct 15	The K orders Thomas earl of Norfolk, marshal of England, and 24 others, to provide for the defence of their lands in Ireland *Westm* R ii p ii 825
Oct. 16.	The K allows the cardinal of S Stephen *in Cœlio Monte* to enjoy his right to the treasurership of York *Westm* R ii p ii 826 O. iv 500 H ii p iii. 70.
Oct 16	Inspeximus of a patent of Edward II, dated Feb 7, 9 Edw II, annulling the customs in West and South Wales, called Amobragium, Blodwyte, and Westrua. *Westm*. R ii p ii. 826
Oct. 20	Power to J bp of Winchester, the K's chancellor, W bp. of Norwich, Geoffrey le Scrop, and William de Herle, to treat for a marriage between the count of Gueldres and Eleanor the K's sister *Windsor*. R ii p ii. 826. O iv 501 H ii p iii 70.
Oct. 20.	The K informs W count of Hainault of the intended marriage above mentioned. Similar letter to the count of Guelders *Windsor*. R ii p. ii. 826 O iv 501 H ii p iii 71

DATE	SUBJECT
1331 Oct 22	The K. requests J. duke of Brabant to send persons to London on the morrow of the Ascension, for the settlement of mercantile disputes *Windsor* R ii p ii 827
Oct. 25.	Protection for Hugh de Preissak, deputy of Peter de Mortimer, cardinal of S. Stephen *in Cœlio Monte* *Odiham.* R ii p. ii 827 O iv 502 H. ii p iii 71
Oct 25	The K of England requests the pope to write to the K of France in favour of peace *Windsor* R ii p ii. 827. O iv 502 H ii p iii 71
Nov. 3	The K orders his treasurer to make allowance to the customers of S Botolph's for the pension paid by them to the count of Juliers *Odiham.* R ii p. ii 827 O iv 503. H ii p. iii 71
Nov. 5	The K orders William de Burgh, earl of Ulster, James le Botiller, earl of Ormond, Sir William de Bermyngham, and Walter de Burgh to come to him to arrange for his intended visit to Ireland *Hungerford* R. ii p ii 828. O iv 503 H ii p. iii. 71
Nov 7	The K orders the Friars Minors of Coventry to deliver the body of Roger de Mortimer to Joan his widow and Edmund his son. *Wherewell* R ii p. ii. 828
Nov 14	The K. desires the bp. of Agen to appoint a perpetual vicar in the church of S Saurin Grand Cast * *alias* Puch Mirol *Windsor* R ii p ii 828 O iv 503 H ii p iii 71
Nov 18	The K. orders the several sheriffs to make proclamation of the act of the late parliament as to the sale of wines *Guildford.* R ii p ii 828.
Nov 19	Warrant for the payment of the annuity to the count of Juliers *Guildford* R ii p ii 829 O iv 504 H ii p iii 71.
Nov 20	Inquisition ordered to be made as to the damages committed by Richard de Kynebelle and others on the property of the cardinal of Naples, prebendary of Sutton, at Bukyngham, Ganecote, Leythyngburgh, and Bourton. *Guildford.* R ii p. ii 829 O. iv 504. H ii. p. iii 71
Nov 25.	The K desires his chancellor in Ireland to order all persons to provide for the defence of their lands against the Irish *Alton.* R ii p ii 829
Nov. 30.	The K orders the sheriff of Wiltshire to repair the manor house at Clarendon, for the residence of Q Philippa during her pregnancy *Clarendon.* R. ii p ii 829
Dec 5	Warrant for the payment of 10 marks to the messengers of John Alfonso de Carriello, baron of Spain, for their expenses in coming to the K *Wymborne* R ii p ii 830 O iv 504. H. ii. p iii. 72
Dec 6	Warrant for the payment of 20*l* 2*s* 10*d* to Thomas de Walepole, goldsmith, for certain silver cups bought of him, and given to certain knights in the company of the count of Eu *Clarendon.* R. ii. p ii 830 O iv 505 H ii p iii 72
Dec. 29	The K informs Alfonso K of Castile that he sends Arnald Garsy to recover money sent by the late K to Spain for the purchase of war horses, and to buy therewith 50 war horses Similar letter to the commonalty of Burgos, and to the merchants to whom the money was sent *Wells* R ii. p ii 830 O. iv 505. H. ii p iii 72
1332 Jan 6	The K writes to the pope in favour of Simon abp of Canterbury *Wells* R ii p ii 830 O iv 505 H. ii. p. iii 72.
Jan. 10	Pardon for William de Montacute, for the death of Sir Hugh de Turphton and Richard de Monemuth, at the arrest of Roger de Mortimer *Westm* R ii p ii. 830 O. iv 506 H ii p iii 72
Jan 28	The K orders Thomas earl of Norfolk, marshal of England, Ralph count of Eu, and 21 others, having lands in Ireland, to be ready to go thither with him on Aug 1 *Westm.* R. ii p ii. 831. O. iv 507
	The K. orders Johanna, late wife of Roger de Mortimer, countess of Pembroke, and two others, to send men-at-arms for the same purpose H. ii. p iii 73.
Feb 2	The K orders Ralph de Nevill, steward of his household, Richard de Bury, Walter de London, and John de Langetoft, to examine the condition of his scholars in the university of Cambridge. *Hertford* R ii p ii 831
Feb 3	The K. orders the arrest of those Friars Minors who, having left their religion, are wandering about the country. *Waltham* R ii p ii 831 O iv. 507 H ii p iii 73.
Feb 6	The K. orders Anthony de Lucy, justiciary of Ireland, to send information relative to the supply of victuals there *Waltham.* R ii p ii. 832
Feb 7	The K orders the constable of Bourdeaux to repair the castle of Saintes *Waltham* R ii p. ii 832 O iv 508 H ii p iii 73

* Ecclesia S Saurini Grandis Castri

DATE	SUBJECT
1332. Feb 8	Power to John Travers, canon of Lichfield, and John de Hildesle, canon of Chichester, to meet the French deputies for the redress of injuries. *Waltham.* R. ii. p. ii. 832 O. iv 508 H. ii p iii 73
Feb 12	Power to J bp of Winchester and his colleagues to treat with Otto lord of Kuye and two others, for a marriage between Reynald count of Gueldres and Eleanor the K's sister *Waltham* R ii p ii 832 O iv 538 H ii p iii 73
Feb 13	The K desires the mayor and commonalty of Bayonne to assist Peter Bernardi de Pynsole, whom he sends to bring Thomas de Gournaye into England. *Waltham* R ii p ii 832 O iv 509 H ii p iii 74
Feb 16	The constable of Bordeaux to pay to John cardinal bp of Albano his pension then due *Pontefract* (¹) O iv 509 H ii p iii 74
Feb. 16.	Warrant to the same constable to pay the said cardinal 400*l* granted to him by Edw I *Pontefract* (¹) O iv 510 H ii p iii 74
Feb. 22	Warrant for the payment of 20*l* to Sii James Parobam, ambassador of Louis of Savoy, for his expenses in returning to his home *Langley* R ii p ii 833 O iv 510 H ii p iii. 74
Feb. 25	The K orders the constable of Bourdeaux to make the necessary repairs in the offices of the artillery in several of his castles in Aquitain *Langley* II ii p ii 833 O iv 510 H ii p iii 74.
Feb 26.	The several sheriffs are to proclaim that commissioners will meet at Westminster on the morrow of the Ascension, for the redress of mercantile disputes with Brabant. *Langley.* R ii p il 833 O iv, 511 H. ii p. iii 74
March 21	Order to pay 1,000 marks to the Bardi, for the payment of the ambassadors about to go to France and Rome, and for the expenses of the voyage of the K's sister Eleanor *Westm* R ii p ii 833 O iv 511 H ii p iii 74
March 24	The sheriffs of Northumberland, Yorkshire, Lancashire, Cumberland, and Westmoreland are commanded to prevent breaches of the peace with Scotland *Westm* R ii. p ii 833 O iv 511 H ii p iii 75
March 25.	Ratification by the K of the treaty of marriage between Reynald count of Gueldres and Eleanor the King's sister *Westm* R. ii p ii 834 O iv. 512 H. ii p iii. 75
March 29	The K grants to Q Isabella, his mother, for life, the manors of Roffer Dolpenmayn and Pennehan, and the commote of Meney, in North Wales, the castle and town of Haverford in South Wales, the hundred of Gertre in Leicestershire, and certain rents to the value of 1,000*l* a year, in compensation for the 3,000*l* granted to her by the late parliament at Westminster *The Tower of London.* R ii p ii 835
March 30	Warrant for the payment of 40 marks to the ambassador of the King of Armenia. *The Tower of London* R ii p ii 835 O iv 515 H ii p iii 76
March 30	The K orders William de Clynton, constable of Dover Castle and warden of the Cinque Ports, to prepare ships at Dover by the close of Easter for the passage of the King's sister Eleanor *The Tower of London* R. ii. p. ii 835. O. iv 615. H. ii. p ii 76
March 30	Order to repay Robert de Tong for his expenses in going with the K's sister Eleanor, and returning to England *The Tower of London* R ii p ii 835 O iv 515 H ii p iii. 76
March 30.	The K. orders William de Clynton to prepare ships at Dover by the Wednesday in Easter week, for the passage of John bp of Winchester and Adam bp. of Worcester to France *The Tower of London* R ii p ii 836
March 31.	The K requests from the K of Navarre safe conduct for Arnald Garsy going to Spain *The Tower of London* R ii p ii 836 O iv 516 H ii p iii 76
March 31.	Similar letter to the Q of Navarre. *The Tower of London.* R. ii. p ii. 836 O iv 516. H ii p iii 76
April 13	The K orders the sheriffs of Norfolk and Suffolk to proclaim that foreign merchants are at liberty to visit the realm according to the charters of Edward I *Staunford* R ii p ii 836 O iv 517 H ii p iii 76
April 18	The K orders the bailiffs of Sandwich to provide ships for the passage of Eleanor the King's sister, at Sandwich, on May 1 *Staunford* R ii p ii. 836. H ii p. iii 77.
April 21.	Pope John exhorts the K. to preserve peace with France *Avignon* R ii p ii. 837 O. iv 5187 H ii p iii 77
April 22.	The K reminds Thomas earl of Murref that restitution has not yet been made to Thomas Wake, lord of Lydel *Staunford* R. ii p ii 837 O iv. 518 H ii p. iii 77

(¹) The two instruments relating to Cardinal Albano are omitted in the Record Edition, but are placed under 16 Feb. 1333

DATE	SUBJECT
1332 April 24	Warrants for the payment of 100*l* to the bp of Winchester, the K.'s chancellor, 100 marks to Adam bp of Worcester, 40*l* to William de Clynton, and 20*l* to John de Shordich, for their expenses *Staunford.* R II p ii. 837. O IV. 518 H II p III 77
April 26	Power to the bp. of Winchester, the K.'s chancellor, and his colleagues, to treat with Philip K of France about an expedition to the Holy Land. *Nottingham* R II p II 837 O. IV. 518 H II p. III 77
[April 26.]	Power for the same to treat for an interview between the Kings of England and France. R II p II 837 O. IV 519 H II p III 77
[April 26.]	Power for the same to treat for a marriage between Edward earl of Chester, the K.'s eldest son, and Joanna, daughter of the K. of France. R. II. p. II 838 O IV 519 H II p. III 78
May 1.	Warrant for the payment of the pension to the count of Juliers *Nottingham.* R II p II 838. O. IV. 519 H II p III 78
May 2.	The K. having been informed by the petition of John Mounfichet, his clerk, that certain English merchants are imprisoned in Saintes and Brittany, and that a toll is exacted at Langon, contrary to the treaty, he desires the sheriffs of London to call a common hall, and obtain from the citizens any letters giving information thereof *Woodstock* R II. p. II 838 O IV 519. H II p III 78
May 16.	Recognisance of Ralph de Yarewell, parson of Cotum, Simon de Staunton, parson of Staunton, Thomas de Outheby, parson of East Bridgeford, and William de Gonalston, parson of Knyveton, to cardinal Ambaldo, archdeacon of Nottingham, for 280*l*. *Woodstock* R II p II 838 O IV 520 H. II. p. III 78
May 20.	The K requests the pope to give credence to Robert de Luffenham, archdeacon of Salisbury, on behalf of Margaret, widow of Edmund earl of Kent *Woodstock* R. II p II 838 O IV 320 H II p III. 78
May 28.	The several sheriffs throughout England are ordered to proclaim that, at the request of the Duke of Brabant, the proposed conference is postponed until Michaelmas. *Woodstock.* R. II. p II. 839. O. IV. 521 H II p. III 78
June 18	The K orders proclamation to be made throughout England that charters will be confirmed and fines levied for the wardship of archbishoprics, bishoprics, &c., at Martinmas. *Woodstock* R II p II 839
June 20.	The K. informs the duke of Brabant that he has publicly notified the postponement of the conference, and asks him not to fail to keep the day now fixed *Woodstock* R II. p II 839 O IV 521 H II p III 79
June 23	Memorandum of the delivery of the great seal by Henry de Clyf, Henry de Ednestowe, and Thomas de Baumburgh, keepers thereof, to master Robert de Stretford, the chancellor's brother, at the desire of John bp. of Winchester, chancellor. R II p II. 839 O IV 522 H. ii. p. III. 79
June 25	The K. requests the K of Navarre to desire Henry lord de Suilly to deliver Robert Lynel de Spain to Giles de Ispania, who had arrested him, and placed him in the custody of the said lord de Soilly *Woodstock* R II p II 839 O IV 522 H. II. p. III 79
June 25.	The K appoints William de Denum, Thomas de Baumburgh, and Robert de Tughale, assessors of the tallage in Northumberland, Cumberland, Westmoreland, and Lancashire. Similar appointments for 31 other counties *Woodstock* R II. p II. 840
June 26.	The K. sends Thomas de Brayton, his clerk, to ask a subsidy of the archbp of York, for the expenses of the marriage of his sister Eleanor, which he promises shall not be taken as a precedent *Woodstock* Similar letters to the bishops, abbots, and priors R II p II 840 O IV 528. H. II p III 79
July 1	The K commissions Giles de Ispannia to attach certain persons in foreign parts accused of conspiring for the death of the late King *Woodstock* R. II p II 840
July 12.	The K informs Thomas earl of Norfolk, marshal of England, and others, that his visit to Ireland will be postponed until Michaelmas *Woodstock* R. II p II. 840. O. IV. 523 H II. p. III. 79
July 13	Cardinal Reymund de Fargis, dean of Salisbury, archdeacon of Leicester, appoints Bernard Vivens, canon of Bazas, and John Vivens, clerk, his attorneys in England *Woodstock* R. II p. II 841 O. IV 523 H II p III 79
July 24	The K thanks Alfonso K of Portugal for having appointed as his admiral Manuel de Pessaigne, brother of Antony de Pessaigne, the K.'s councillor *Woodstock* R II p. II 841. O IV 524. H. II. p. III. 97.
[July 24.]	The K writes in favour of Manuel de Pessaigne to Lupus de Ferariis, councillor of K. Alfonso R. II. p II 841 O IV 524. H. ii p III 79

DATE	SUBJECT
1333 July 25.	The K orders Antony de Lucy, justiciary of Ireland, to arrest all ships in the ports of Ireland, and send them to Holyhead by Sept 9 for his passage *Woodstock*. R ii p ii 841. O iv 524 H ii p iii 80.
July 26	The K requests the pope to allow the appropriation of the church of St Lawrence, Candlewick Street, London, in the patronage of Westminster Abbey, to a chantry founded near the church by John de Pulteney, mayor of London, and also of other benefices in the province of Canterbury, to the value of 20*l.* *Woodstock* R ii. p ii. 841. O iv 525 II ii p iii. 80
July 29	The K orders Roger de Chaundos, John Giffard, and Nicholas de Acton to provide 400 foot soldiers in South Wales for his visit to Ireland *Woodstock* Similar letters for John de Leybourn and two others for North Wales. R. ii. p ii 842 O. iv 525. H. ii p iii. 80
Aug 4	Power for Roger Outlawe, prior of St John of Jerusalem in Ireland, to treat with the Irish rebels, and receive them into the K.'s peace. *Hanley* R ii p ii. 842
Aug 4	The K desires the archbp of Cashel, William de Burgh, earl of Ulster, and 14 others, to assist Roger de Outlawe in his treaty of peace *Hanley* R ii. p ii. 842. O iv. 526 H ii p iii. 80.
Aug 4	The K orders the sheriffs and seneschals of Ireland to make proclamation concerning the treaty above mentioned. *Hanley* R. ii. p ii 842 O iv 526 H ii p. iii 81.
[ ]	Ordinances to be observed in the chapel of St Edward in Windsor Castle. O. iv. 527 H ii p. iii. 81 Omitted in the Record Edition
Aug 7	The K desires Henry lord de Scilly to deliver Robert Lynel to Giles de Ispannia Similar letter to Simon de Mounbreton *Hanley* R. ii. p ii 843 O iv 528. H. ii p iii 81.
[Aug 7]	The K orders Reymund de Monceuz, castellan of Mailloune, to deliver John Tilli, whom he arrested in Spain, to Giles de Ispannia R ii. p ii 843. O iv 528. H. ii. p iii 81
[Aug 7]	The K orders the Seneschal of Gascony and the constable of Bordeaux to provide Giles de Ispannia with a ship and necessaries for bringing Robert Lynel and John Tylly to England R. ii p ii. 843 O iv 528 H ii. p. iii 81.
Aug 9.	The K having been informed that Henry de Beaumont and others are preparing to invade Scotland, appoints Henry de Percy, warden of the Marches, with full power to prevent breaches of the peace in the counties of Northumberland, York, Lancaster, Cumberland, and Westmorland *Wigmore* R ii p 843 O iv 529 H ii p iii 81
Aug 9	The K orders the sheriffs of five northern counties to proclaim the above facts *Wigmore* R ii p ii 844 O iv 530 H ii p iii 82
Aug 18	The K desires S archbp of Canterbury to allow the cross to be carried before the archbp. of York in the province of Canterbury while he is on his way to the approaching parliament at Westminster *Kidderminster*. R ii p ii 844 O iv. 531 H. ii. p iii. 82.
Aug 18	Safe conduct for William archbp. of York until the feast of All Saints. *Kidderminster*. R ii p ii. 844. O iv 531 H ii p. iii 82
	The K forbids the archbp of Canterbury and the clergy in convocation to treat of anything prejudicial to him, and desires credence for John Peeche and John de Pulteneye, mayor of London *Northampton*. R ii p. ii 845
Sept 13	The K orders W. archbp of York to desist from demanding tithes from cardinal Gauselin, John, parson of Hemingburgh and prebendary of Driffield, and from cardinal Bertrand de Monte Faventio, parson of Brantingham. *Westm* R ii p ii 845 O iv 531. H ii p iii 82
Sept 16	The K. appoints John Daundelyn and Eustace de Brunneby, with a clerk, to assess in Northamptonshire the tenth and fifteenth granted by the present parliament. Similar letters for the other counties *Westm* R ii p. ii 845
Sept 20	Inspeximus of a patent dated at York, 7 Dec 13 Edw. II, concerning a covenant between Alicia, daughter and heir of Geoffrey Rudell, lord of Blania, and William de Montacute, late seneschal of Aquitain. *Westm*. R. ii p. ii 845 O iv 532 H ii p iii 82
Oct 7.	William de Clinton, justice of Chester, is commanded to cause to be chosen 300 bowmen of his country for defence against the Scots, and to send their names to the K. *Nottingham* R. ii p ii 846 O iv 534 H ii p iii 83

DATE.	SUBJECT
1332. Oct. 7.	The K. orders John de Denum, Edmund Nevill, and Robert de Shreburn to provide 400 archers and 100 hobillers in the county of Lancaster for defence against the Scots Similar commissions to Ralph de Bulmere and Nicholas de Wurcelay in Yorkshire, and Nicholas de Langeford and Ralph de Brayleford in Derbyshire. *Nottingham* R n p n 846. O iv 534. H. ii. p. iii. 83
Oct. 26.	The K empowers John Darcy and William de Denum to go to Newcastle to treat with Sir Robert de Loweder and Ralph de More, who have been sent to the K by the guardian of the land of Scotland, and are detained by the illness of Loweder *York.* R. n p n 847 O iv 535 H u p. iii. 84
Oct 26	The K requests the pope to promote Robert de Ayleston, archdeacon of Berkshire, his treasurer, to the bishopric of St. Andrew's *York* R. n p. n. 847. O. iv. 535. H. n p iii 84.
[Oct. 26.]	Letters on the same subject to the cardinal of St Eustace and 10 others R n p n 847. O iv 536 H n p iii 84
Nov. 23.	Edward [Balliol] K. of Scotland, states that he has performed homage to Edward III for the kingdom of Scotland, and he grants to him the town and county of Berwick, and promises to marry his sister Joan, if she do not marry David de Brus *Roxburgh.* R. n. p n 847 O iv. 536. H. n p. iii. 84.
Nov 23.	Edward K of Scotland promises to come with his whole force to the assistance of the K of England when required. *Roxburgh* R n p n 847 O iv 539 H n p m 28
Dec 1.	Power to W archbp of York, Robert de Stratford, and Geoffrey le Scrop to open the parliament at York. *Knaresborough.* R. n. p. n 848 O. iv. 532. H. n p m 85
Dec. 12.	Safe conduct for six Scotchmen to come to the K. in England *York* R n p n 849 O iv 539 H n p m 85
Dec. 14.	Power to Ralph Basset de Drayton and William de Denum to treat with the guardian and nobles of Scotland *York* R n p n 849 O iv 540 H n p m 85.
Dec 15.	The K informs the pope that Edward Balliol having caused himself to be crowned K of Scotland, he has gone to the North, to defend the kingdom, if necessary, instead of going to Ireland *York* R. n p n 849. O iv. 540. H n p m 86
1333. Jan. 30	Protection for weavers and other manufacturers of cloth of whatever country Proclamation thereof to be made by the several sheriffs. *York.* R. n p n. 849
Feb. 3	The K requests the pope to remove the interdict imposed on the church of S Peter at York by the abp of Dax, in consequence of the suit between the cardinal of S Stephen and William de la Mare, about the treasurership *York* R n p n. 849. O iv 541 H n p m 86
Feb. 3.	The K orders the justices of the bench to decide the right of the abp. of York to prisage of wine at Hull *York* R n p n 850 O iv. 541 H n p m 86
Feb. 3	The K forbids the exportation of corn *York* R. n p n 850
Feb 4.	The K of England requests Philip K of Navarre to desire Henry lord de Soilly to deliver Robert Lynel de Ispannia to Giles de Ispannia. *York* R n p n 850 O iv 542 H. n p m 86
[Feb 4]	The K orders the seneschal of Gascony and the constable of Bordeaux to supply Giles de Ispannia with a ship and other necessaries for the purpose of bringing over to England Robert Lynel and John Tyth R. n p n 850 O n. 542 H n p m 86
Feb 11.	The K of England requests Philip K of France to release two ships of Dover, arrested in consequence of a dispute about the salvage of a ship of Rouen, wrecked at Dover *Pontefract* R n p n 850 O iv 542 H n p m 86.
Feb 12.	The K orders his treasurer and barons of the Exchequer to levy the sums promised by certain of the prelates and religious persons for the marriage of his sister Eleanor The bp of Ely had promised 100*l.*, the bp of Chichester 20*l*, and 42 others, the smallest sum being five marks *Pontefract* R n p n. 851 O. iv 543 H n p m 87.
[Feb. 12]	The K desires the above-mentioned persons to pay the sums granted by them R n p n 851 O iv 544 H n p m 87.
Feb. 12	The K having received no answer to his request for the money above mentioned from the bp. of Lincoln, the abbot of Croyland, and 103 others, repeats it *Pontefract* R n p n 851 O iv. 544 H n p m. 87.
Feb. 12.	The K refuses to accept the excuses made in this behalf for the money in question by the abbot of Bardenaye, the prior of Sixhill, and 140 others *Pontefract.* R n p. n 852 O iv. 546. H n. p m. 88

DATE.	SUBJECT
1333. Feb 12	The K requests a subsidy for the purpose mentioned above from the priors of Buttele and Marton and nine others who have not yet been asked. *Pontefract.* R. ii. p. ii. 853 O iv 547 H. ii. p iii. 89
Feb 12	Edward K of Scotland empowers Alexander de Moubray and John de Felton to swear to his conventions with the K of England "*Burgh*" R ii p ii 853 O iv 548 H ii p ii 89
Feb 16.	The K orders the constable of Bordeaux to pay to cardinal John bp of Albano the arrears of his pension of 50 marks. *Pontefract.* R. ii p ii. 854
Feb 16	The K. orders the constable of Bordeaux to pay to the said cardinal the 400l. granted to him when nuncio in England by the late K *Pontefract.* R ii p ii 854
Feb 18	The K desires Arnaldo do Unsa and three others to assist Richard de Byry and Sir John de Sordiche in their mission to the pope *Pontefract* R. ii. p ii 854 O. iv 548 H ii p iii 89.
Feb 24	Power for Adam bp of Worcester, Sir Bartholomew de Burghersh, Sir William Trussel, and William de Cusantin, to treat with Ralph count of Eu for a marriage between his daughter Joan and John earl of Cornwall, the K's brother *Pontefract* R ii p ii 854 O iv 549 H ii p iii 89
March 4	The K. orders his treasurer to pay 200 marks to Pontius lord of Castelhone in recompense for his losses in the late war in Aquitain *Pontefract* R ii p ii 854 O iv 549 H ii p iii 90
March 9	The K again requests the pope to promote Robert de Ayleston, archdeacon of Berkshire, to the bishopric of St Andrews. *York* R ii p ii 854 O iv 549 H ii p iii 90.
March 11.	The K informs John duke of Brabant that he cannot comply with his request to appoint Francis Rauland customer of Southampton, as he has not the property required by the statute *Pontefract* R ii p ii 855 O iv 550 H ii p iii 90
March 20	Proclamation to be made throughout England that all persons with lands or rents worth 40l a year shall take the order of knighthood at the feast of the Holy Trinity *Pontefract.* R. ii. p ii. 855. O. iv. 550 H ii p iii 90
March 20	The K orders proclamation to be made by the sheriffs of Lincoln and 15 other counties for the carriage of corn to the north of England. *Pontefract* R ii p ii 855
March 21	Writs of military summons to Thomas earl of Norfolk, marshal of England, Henry earl of Lancaster, and 143 others, to meet at Newcastle-on-Tyne at the feast of the Holy Trinity *Pontefract.* R ii. p ii 855
March 23	The K orders the sheriffs of Northumberland, Cumberland, and Westmoreland to proclaim that those persons, who are obliged to move southwards in consequence of the invasion of the Scots, may pass through and remain in the royal forests and pastures. *Pontefract.* R ii p ii 856 O. iv. 551. H. ii p iii 90
March 25	Licence to Peter de Luk, abp of Bourdeaux, to fortify his *manile* of Luc, in the eastlery of Blancheforte *Pontefract* R ii p ii 856 O iv 551 H ii p ii 90
March 26.	The K orders the abbot of St Mary's, York, receiver of the tenth and fifteenth, to provide Richard le Goldsmyth with homes for the making of certain engines *Cowyk* R ii p ii 856
March 28	The K. orders Ralph de Dacre, constable of Carlisle castle, to keep in irons William Douglas de Polerte and William Bard, prisoners of war *Pontefract* R ii p ii 856 O iv 552 H ii p iii 91
March 28	The K orders the sheriff of Cumberland to proclaim that all persons who have Scotch prisoners are to keep them safely *Pontefract* R ii p ii 857.
March 30	The K orders John de Warenne, earl of Surrey, to send 300 men from his lands at Bromfield and Yal to Newcastle, by next Easter, in consequence of the invasion of the Scots *Aberford* R ii p ii. 857. O. iv 552
	Letters to the same effect to Richard earl of Arundel, the justiciaries of North Wales South and West Wales, and Chester, and to nine others. R ii. p ii 857 O iv 552 H ii p iii 91
April 1.	Proclamation to be made throughout England that the conference with the deputies of Brabant will be held within a fortnight after Michaelmas. The K. requests the duke of Brabant to send his deputies by that day *Cowyk* R ii p ii 857.
April 2.	Ralph bp of Bath and Wells informs the K that he is impoverished by suits at Rome, and will grant a subsidy of 40l. for the marriage of the K's sister Eleanor. *Wiveliscombe* R. ii p ii 858

DATE	SUBJECT
1333 April 5	The K will not alienate from the crown provostry [prepositura] Entre-deux-Mers and Croén *Knaresborough* R ıı p ıı 858 O ıv 552 H ıı p ııı 91
April 8	The K. requests Alfonso K of Castile to excuse the absence of Guitard viscount de Tartoys, who ıs occupied ın servıng K Edward. *Durham* R ıı p ıı 858 O ıv 552 H ıı p ııı 91
April 11	The abbot and canons of Nuttele ask the K to be content with six marks as their subsidy towards the marrıage of the K's sister Eleanor *Nuttele* R ıı p ıı 858
April 22	The K orders the baıliffs of Tadcaster to assıst Thomas de Pabenham ın buyıng stones for the K's engınes *Newcastle* R ıı p ıı 858
April 23	The K requests the abps of Canterbury and York to exhort their clergy to pray for his success *Newcastle* R ıı p ıı 858 O ıv. 553 H ıı p ııı 91
April 23	The K assures the dean and chapter of Lichfield, the abbot of St Albans, and 38 others, that their grants towards the expenses of his sister's marrıage shall not be taken as a precedent. *Newcastle* R ıı p ıı 859 O ıv 553. H. ıı, p ııı. 91
April 24	The K requests Alfonso K of Castile to make restitutıon to Thomas Symon of Sandwich, whose ship was attacked off the Needles [apud Nedleu] by subjects of Alfonso *Newcastle* R ıı p ıı 859 O ıv 555 H ıı p ııı 92
April 24	Inspexımus and confirmatıon of a grant of Edward II of certain prıvileges to the burgesses of St. Omer's, dated 8 June, 16 Edw II. *Newcastle*. R ıı p ıı 859 O ıv. 555 H ıı p ııı 92
April 27	The K requests L count of Flanders to prevent his subjects from assisting the Scotch. *Newcastle* R ıı p ıı 860 O ıv. 556 H ıı p ııı 92
April 29.	Safe conduct till Michaelmas for Ferrarıus de Pınkeny and Peter Gawayn dean of St. Omer's, ambassadors of Phılıp K of France *Newcastle* R ıı p ıı 860 O ıv 557 H ıı, p ııı 93
May 7.	The K of England ınforms the K of France that the guardıan of Scotland and others have several tımes ınvaded the realm of England *Belford.* R ıı p ıı. 860 O ıv. 557 H ıı p ııı. 93
May 16.	The K. desıres excommunıcatıon to be pronounced against all felons, breakers of the peace, and other malefactors *Doncaster* R ıı p ıı 860
May 20	Licence to John of Brıttany, earl of Richmond, to remaın ın foreign parts. *Tweedmouth.* R ıı p ıı 861
May 27.	The K requests the abbot of Vale Royal to send to the Exchequer at York the 100*s* promised by hım as a subsıdy for the marrıage of the K's sister Sımilar letters to the abbot of Chester and to four others *Tweedmouth* R ıı p. ıı. 861 O ıv 558 H ıı p ııı 93
May 30.	Phılıp K of France orders his Exchequer [les gıens de nos comptes] at Paris to delıberate on certaın complaınts of English merchants *Chauntecot* R ıı p ıı 861 O ıv 558 H ıı p ııı 93
May 30.	The K orders Wıllıam le Taıllour of Carlisle, Haver Macoter, and Gılbert Makstephan to take possessıon of the Isle of Man for hım *Tweedmouth* R ıı p ıı 861 O. ıv 559 H ıı p ııı. 93
June 2	The K orders the constable of Bourdeaux to make ınquisıtion as to a sum of 3,000*l* receıved by Olıver de Ingham, seneschal of the duchy, from the property of Garsıa Arnaud de Conpenne, late bp of Dax, which the pope claıms, the bp. havıng dıed ıntestate. *Tweedmouth* R ıı p ıı 861 O ıv 559 H ıı. p. ııı. 93
June 4	The K assıgns the annuıty of 100*l* granted by hım to Pantıus de Coutrone, his physıcıan, to be paıd by the baıliffs of Norwich *Tweedmouth* R ıı. p ıı. 862 O. ıv. 560. H. ıı p ııı. 94
June 5	The K requests L count of Flanders to remove the recent ımposıtions on Englısh subjects untıl the arrıval of his ambassadors Sımılar letters to the commonalties of Ghent, Bruges, and Ypres. ' *Tweedmouth.* R ıı. p. ıı. 862 O ıv 560, H ıı p ııı 94
June 6.	K Edward asks Phılıp K of France to grant a safe conduct to Asnarot Burgensıs de Pampelyon and John de Gernache, who have bought certaın war horses ın Spaın for the K. *Tweedmouth* R ıı p ıı 862 O. ıv. 561 H. ıı p. ııı. 94.
June 7.	The K desıres credence for John de Hıldesle, canon of Chester, baron of the Exchequer, Wıllıam de la Pole, and Robert de Kelleseye, whom he ıs sendıng to L. count of Flanders, and the towns of Bruges, Ghent, and Ypres, to treat about the aıd gıven by the Flemıngs to the Scotch *Tweedmouth.* R ıı p. ıı 862. O ıv 561. H. ıı. p ııı 94

DATE	SUBJECT
1333 June 8	The K commits to William de Montacute the custody of the Isle of Man until Michaelmas *Tweedmouth* R ii p ii 863 O iv 562 H ii p iii. 94
June 11	The K. orders John de Warenne, earl of Surrey and Sussex, lord of Broomfield and Yale, in Wales, to make proclamation forbidding all assemblies tending to the disturbance of the K's peace Similar letters to Richard earl of Arundel, lord of Clon and Osewaldestre, Edward de Bohun, justiciary of North Wales, Gilbert Talbot, justiciary of South Wales, and 10 others. *Tweedmouth.* R. ii p ii 863
June 26	The K orders his treasurer and barons of the Exchequer to arrange for the anniversary of K Edward (I), his grandfather, which will be held on the feast of the translation of S. Thomas of Canterbury *Tweedmouth* R ii p ii 863 O iv 562 H. ii p iii 95.
July 2	Warrant for the payment of 17*l* 0*s* 10*d*. to Nero Peryn of the company of Peruth, for silver plate given to the count of Eu and the other ambassadors of the K of France *Tweedmouth* R ii p ii 863 O iv 562 H ii p iii 95
July 5.	The pope acknowledges the receipt of 1,500 marks from Richard de Bury, dean of Wells, being the pension from England and Ireland for 1½ year *Avignon.* R ii p ii 864 O iv 563 H ii p iii 95
July 6	The K requests R bp of Bath and Wells to pay to the abbot of S Mary's, York, the K's receiver, his contribution of 40*l* to the subsidy for the marriage of the K's sister Similar letters to the abbot of Keynesham and 100 others *Tweedmouth* R ii p. ii 864 O iv 563 H ii p iii. 95
July 15	Capitulation of Patrick Dunbar, earl of March, for the surrender of Berwick to the K on July 20. *Berwick.* R ii p. ii 864 O iv 564 H ii p. iii 96
July 16	Similar capitulation of William de Keth, warden of Berwick. R. ii p ii 865 O iv 566 H ii p iii 96.
July 22.	The K informs the apbs of Canterbury, York, and Bordeaux, and the bps of England, Wales, and Aquitaine, of his victory near Berwick over the Scots on July 19, and desires thanksgiving to be offered *Berwick* R ii p ii 866 O iv. 568. H. ii. p. iii 97
July 24	The K requests the pope to promote Robert de Tanton, the K's secretary and treasurer of his wardrobe, to the bishopric of S Andrews The K writes on the same subject to the card of S Stephen. *Berwick.* R. ii p. ii. 866 O iv 569 H ii p iii 97
July 26.	Protection for Patrick de Dunbar, earl of March, Adam de Bodyngton of Berwick, and 17 others *Berwick* R ii p ii 867 O iv 570 H ii. p. iii 98
June 28	Release of the debts to the crown of John de Warenne, earl of Surrey, in consideration of his great expenses at the siege of Berwick *Berwick* R ii p ii 867 O iv 571 H ii p. iii. 98.
June 28	The K , to commemorate his victory near Berwick, orders a nunnery in the neighbourhood to be repaired at his cost, and grants to it 20*l* a year from the revenues of Berwick, for the performance of mass on the anniversary of the battle Warrant to the sheriff of Berwick to attend to the repairs of the nunnery. *Berwick* R ii p ii 867 O iv. 571. O iv 572-3 H ii p iii 98.
July 30	The K requests Alfonso K. of Castile to make restitution to Bartholomew de Berys, son and heir of John de Berys, of 800 marks taken from his late father, John de Berys, by subjects of Sancho, late K of Castile *Berwick.* R ii p ii 867. O iv. 573. H ii p iii 98
Aug 4	The K. orders the several sheriffs to take sufficient bail of those who have received his pardon in consequence of their services in the Scotch campaign *Newcastle-upon-Tyne* R ii. p ii 868 O iv 573 H ii p iii 99
Aug. 9.	Release of the K's claim to the Isle of Man, in favour of Richard de Montacute *Topcliffe* R ii p ii 868 O. iv 574 H ii p iii 99.
Aug 16	Protection and safe conduct for merchants of all nations. *Knaresborough.* R ii p ii 868. O iv. 574. H. ii p iii 99
Aug. 26.	The K orders Thomas Bacoun and John Claver to inquire into the charge against Henry Tristrem de Rokelound, bailiff of Louthyglond, and Reginald Reynald, constable of Lowestoft, of having allowed certain Scots and others to take silver out of the realm. *Great Yarmouth* R ii p ii 869 O. iv 575 H ii p iii 99
Aug. 28	The K appoints the abbot of S Mary's, York, to receive the subsidy for the marriage of his sister from the persons whose names are enclosed. *St Edmund's* R ii p. ii. 869 O. iv 576 H ii p iii 100.
Sept. 8.	The K. desires the several sheriffs, in accordance with the late treaty with the count of Flanders, to release from arrest all Flemish persons and goods, and to proclaim a safe conduct for them. *Eltham* R ii. p. ii. 869. O. iv. 576. H. ii. p. iii. 100.

DATE.	SUBJECT
1333. Sept. 27.	The K orders his treasurer to deliver to John de Nevill de Horneby, to hold until the next parliament, the hundred of Bradford, Shropshire, the grant of which has been resumed *Norwich* R. ii p. ii 869
Sept 30.	The K appoints W bp of Norwich, Sir Geoffrey le Scrope, and Thomas Sampson, canon of York, to reform the state of Ponthieu *Waltham*. The K. informs Bartholomew de Burghersh, seneschal of Ponthieu, of the above. R. ii p ii 870
Oct 1	The K. orders Henry de Percy, Ralph de Nevill, steward of the household, William de Shareshill, and Thomas de Baumburgh, to attend the approaching parliament in Scotland, for the confirmation of the treaty between Edward de Balliol and himself. *Waltham* R ii. p ii 870 O iv 576 H ii p. iii 100
Oct. 3	The K orders the several sheriffs to arrest those Friars Preachers who have deserted their religion *Waltham*. R. ii. p. ii. 870.
Oct. 6 ? 5.	The K requests Alfonso K. of Aragon to withdraw the letters of marque granted to Berenger de la Tone *Waltham* R ii p ii 870. O iv 577 H ii p iii 100
Oct 6.	The K orders the several sheriffs to proclaim that the conference with the ambassadors from Brabant will be prorogued till a month after Easter, at the request of the duke of Brabant *Waltham* R. ii. p ii 871 O iv 578 H ii p. iii. 101
[Oct. 6.]	The K. informs John duke of Brabant that he consents to the prorogation, and asks him to keep the day fixed R ii p ii 871. O iv 578 H ii p iii 101.
Oct 6	The K. orders the sheriffs of York and seven other counties to proclaim that all who have claims for damage against the Flemings must appear at York on the morrow of All Souls The men of Kent and the other counties to appear at York on the morrow of Martinmas *Waltham* R ii p ii 871 O. iv 579 H ii p iii 101
Oct. 6.	The K desires S abp of Canterbury to summon a convocation of the clergy of his province at London on Nov 22, to grant an aid to the K Similar letter to the abp of York to summon a convocation at York for 28 Nov *Havering atte Bower*. R. ii p ii 871 O iv 579–80 H ii p iii 101
Oct. 8	The K releases the cardinal of Naples from the tenth due to the K from his prebends of Southcave and King's Sutton *Waltham*. R. ii p ii 872 O iv. 580 H ii p iii 102
Oct 15.	The K orders his treasurer to inflict fines on those who have not obeyed his proclamation of March 20 concerning knighthood *Havering atte Bower* R. ii p ii 872 O. iv 580 H ii p iii. 102
Oct. 29.	The K. orders the sheriffs of York to receive the four remaining hostages given by the town of Berwick, and to send two to the abbey of Peterborough and two to the abbey of Ramsey. *Shene*. R ii p. ii 872. O. iv. 581. H. ii p. iii. 102
Nov 8	The K appoints Thomas de Brayton and Simon de Stanes to execute the settlement of the disputes with Flanders. *Marlborough* R ii p ii. 872 O. iv 582 H. ii p iii 102
Nov 18.	The K informs the pope that he has assented to the unanimous election of John bp of Winchester, the K's chancellor, to the see of Canterbury, vacant by the death of abp Simon *Clarendon* R ii p ii 873. O. iv 582 H. ii p iii 102.
Nov. 18	The K. requests the pope to confirm the election above mentioned *Clarendon* R ii p ii 873 O. iv 583 H ii p iii. 103
[Nov. 18.]	The K. requests the pope to send a pall to John bp of Winchester. R ii. p ii. 873. O iv 583. H ii. p. iii 103
[Nov 18.]	The K. writes on the same subject to 9 cardinals. R. ii p ii 873. O iv. 584. H ii p. iii 103
Nov 22.	Inspeximus of a grant by John de Brittany, earl of Richmond, of the castles, towns, and manors of Richmond and Bowes, and his other lands in England, to his niece, Mary de S Paul, countess of Pembroke, at a yearly rent of 1,800*l*. *Shireborne* R. ii p ii 873 O iv. 584 H ii. p iii 103
Dec 21.	Philip K of France orders his seneschal of Toulouse, Saintonge, Perigord, and Agennois, and his bailiff of Amiens, to treat English subjects honourably in their courts. R ii p. 874 O iv 586 H ii. p iii 104.
1334. Jan. 5	Inspeximus of an acquittance by Mary de S Paul, countess of Pembroke, to John de Brittany, earl of Richmond. *Wallingford* R ii p ii 874 O iv 586 H ii p iii 104.
Jan. 7.	The K. sends Sir Robert de Scorburg to the count of Flanders, to take the place of Thomas de Brayton *Wallingford* R ii p ii. 874 O iv 586 H ii p iii. 104

DATE	SUBJECT
1334 Feb. 1	The K appoints Edward de Bohun, William de Montacute, Henry de Percy, Ralph Nevill, steward of the household, and Geoffrey le Scrop, chief justice, to attend the parliament of the K. of Scotland as his deputies, and to confirm the treaties with him. *Woodsto* R ii p ii. 875 O iv 588 H ii p. iii. 104.
Feb. 3	The K orders his treasurer to pay a sufficient sum for their expenses to David de Wollo. his clerk, and William de Sireston, notary public, whom he sends to Scotland. *Woc stock* R ii p ii 875 O. iv 588 H. ii. p iii 105
Feb 5	The K. informs Louis count of Flanders that he sends certain persons to treat with hi *Woodstock* R ii p ii 875 O iv 589. H ii. p iii. 105
Feb 5	The K appoints Simon de Stanes, Robert de Kelleseye, Reginald de Conductu, and Jo de Causton, to act as his deputies in Flanders, and orders Simon de Stanes to be at Brug four days before Lent *Woodstock* R. ii p ii 875 O iv 589 H ii p iii 105.
[Feb 5]	The K. orders John de Pulteneye, mayor of London, to choose one of the three abo named to accompany Simon de Stanes R ii p ii. 876 O iv. 590 H ii p. iii 105
Feb 12	Acts of the parliament held at Edinburgh confirming the homage done by Edward Balhol to the K. of England, and the surrender of Berwick R ii p ii 876 O iv 59 H ii p iii. 105.
Feb 13	The K forbids tournaments throughout England. *Woodstock* R ii p ii 878
Feb 14	The K orders his treasurer of Ireland to cancel the fine of 100 marks imposed upon th bp of Down for absence from the late parliament, as he is informed that he was presen *Dublin.* R. ii. p ii 878 O iv 595 H. ii. p iii 107
March 2	The K directs Henry de Beaumont, earl of Boghan, not to allow any process to made before him respecting the earldom of Strathern forfeited for treason by Malisius e of Stathern *York* R ii p ii 878 O. iv 595 H ii p iii 108.
[March 2]	The K of England informs Edward K. of Scotland that he hears that Malisius, la earl of Strathern, claims the county of Strathern, which the K of Scotland had granted John de Warenne, earl of Surrey , and he requests the K. of Scotland to act with deliber tion R ii p ii 879 O iv 596 H ii p iii 108
March 3	The K. orders it to be proclaimed throughout England that staples of wool shall cease, accordance with a petition presented to the present parliament. *York* R ii p ii 879.
March 3	The K. forbids customs to be levied on the goods of the citizens of Bayonne, when the ships are driven on to the coast of England on their way to other countries. *York* R p ii 879
March 6	The K grants to Q Philippa the rents of Cheshire, Beston, Rhuddlan, Flint, and Ingle field, with wardships, marriages, &c , for the maintenance of his son Edward, and h daughters Isabella and Joan The K. informs the justiciary of Chester of the abov *York* R ii p. ii 880
March 16.	The K. desires the abps of Canterbury and York, and all other bps. in England an Wales, to pronounce the sentence of excommunication every Sunday against all breakers his peace and other malefactors *Towcester* R. ii p ii. 880 O iv. 596 H. p iii. 108
March 26	The K empowers W bp of Norwich, H. bp of S David's, Sir William Trussel, & John de Shordiche, and others, to renew the negotiations with France commenced Perigueux, Agen, and elsewhere *Rockingham.* R ii. p. ii 880 O iv. 597. H p iii 108.
March 26.	The K orders John de Peres, his clerk, to deliver to the ambassadors all documents r lating to the previous negotiations. *Rockingham* R ii p ii. 881 O iv. 599 H. p iii. 109.
March 26.	Power to Sir William de Clynton, Sir Bartholomew de Burghersh, Sir William Trusse Sir John de Shordich, and others, to resume the negotiations commenced at Montreu Agen, and elsewhere *Rockingham* R. ii p ii 881 O. iv 600 H ii p iii. 109.
March 26	The K orders the presidents of his courts and all others to assist both embassies *Roc ingham* R ii p ii 882 O iv, 601 H ii p iii 110
March 30.	William abp of York, pardoned for confirming the election of Robert de Graystan, mo of Durham, to the bpric of Durham, without the K.'s assent. *Rockingham.* R. ii. p. ii. 88 O iv. 602 H ii p iii 110
March 30.	The K. appoints John abp. of Canterbury and Sir Geoffrey le Scrop to treat with th duke of Brittany concerning certain lands, late the property of John de Brittany, earl Richmond *Rockingham* R ii. p. ii 882. O. iv. 602 H. ii. p. iii 110

DATE	SUBJECT
1334 March 30.	Power to the abp of Canterbury, William de Clynton, and Geoffrey le Scrop, to receive the homage of the duke of Brittany. *Rockingham* R. ii p ii 883 O iv 603 H ii p iii 110
March 30.	Power to the abp of Canterbury and others to treat of all matters in debate with the K of France touching Aquitan. *Rockingham* R ii. p. ii. 883 O iv 603 H ii p iii 111
[March 30]	Power for the same to treat for an interview with the K of France, to arrange for an expedition to the Holy Land. R ii p ii 883 O iv p ii 604. H ii p iii 111
March 30.	Power for the abp of Canterbury and others to treat for a marriage between John, son and heir of Edmund, late earl of Kent, and the daughter of some French noble *Rockingham* R. ii p ii. 883 O iv 605 H ii p iii 111
March 31.	Power to the same to reform the state of the county of Ponthieu. *Rockingham* R ii p. ii 884. O. iv 605 H ii p iii 111.
[March 31].	The K orders Bartholomew de Burghersh, seneschal of Ponthieu, and the inhabitants of the county, to assist them R ii p ii 884 O iv 606 H. ii p iii 111
April 1	Pope John orders the abbot of S Mary's, Salbury, to procure the restoration of property alienated by the abbots of the greater monastery at Tours *Avignon* R ii p ii 884 O iv 606 H ii p iii 112.
April 1.	Warrant to the treasurer and barons of the Exchequer to pay to Simon de Stanes, sent by the K to Flanders on Feb 8, 50 marks for his expenses for 50 days, in addition to his expenses for his passage and the wages of his clerks Also for 20*l* to Wilham Fox, of York, sent with Simon de Stanes *Rockingham* R. ii p ii 884 O iv 606–7 H ii. p iii 112.
April 5	The sheriffs throughout England are to proclaim that a treaty was concluded on the 23rd March, with the count of Flanders, for free mercantile intercourse until the Feast of the Assumption *Rockingham*. R ii p ii 884 O iv p ii 112
April 9.	Power for John abp. of Canterbury and William de Cusance, canon of Ripon, to treat for a marriage between John earl of Cornwall, the K's brother, and Mary, daughter of the count of Blois *Huntingdon* R ii p ii 885 O iv 628 R ii. p iii 112
April 9	Power for them to treat with any French nobles for a marriage with the earl of Cornwall *Huntingdon.* R ii p ii 885 O iv 608 H ii p. iii. 112
April 10.	Inspeximus and confirmation of an indenture, dated Bourdeaux, 15 March 1333, relative to the claim of the abp of Bourdeaux to the third part of all the money coined by the K in Aquitain. *Huntingdon.* R. ii p. ii. 885. O. iv. 608. H ii p. iii. 112.
April 16	Pardon of a fine of 100s imposed on John bp of Lismore for neglecting to appear at the court of Exchequer of Dublin respecting the manor of Bergrarold. *Dublin.* R. ii p ii 886 O iv 611 H iii. p. iii. 113
April 31	Power for J abp of Canterbury, Sir William de Clynton, Sir Geoffrey le Scrop, and Sir John de Shordich, to treat with any person on matters concerning the county of Ponthieu. *Rockingham* R. ii p. ii 886.
May 24	William de Clapham, escheator of Yorkshire, Northumberland, Cumberland, and West-moreland, is ordered to deliver to John duke of Brittany (born and baptized abroad), cousin and heir of John de Brittany, late earl of Richmond, the lands lately belonging to the said earl, the said duke John having done his fealty for the same, and paid his relief Similar writs to five other escheators *Beverley* R ii p. ii 886. O iv 611 H. ii p iii 113
May 31	The K desires J abp. of Canterbury to summon a convocation of the clergy to grant him an aid for the Scotch war *Helmesley.* R ii p ii 887. O iv 612 H ii p iii 114
June 2.	The K orders John Travers, constable of Bourdeaux, and Arnald Pagani, canon of Bourdeaux, to proceed to the restitution of lands in the duchy, according to the late treaty with France. *Northallerton* R ii p ii 887 O iv 612 H ii p iii 114.
June 11	Philip K of France orders Bertrand Boniface, canon of Paris, and Pierre Remond de Rabastang, seneschal of Agennois, to carry out the recent treaty with the K of England *Maubusson.* R ii p ii 887 O iv 613 H ii. p iii 114
June 12.	The K. desires W abp of York to summon a convocation for granting him an aid for the Scotch war *Newcastle.* R ii p ii 888 O iv 614 H ii p iii 114
June 12.	The K desires W abp. of York to allow the cross to be carried before the abp of Canterbury while passing through the province of York on his way to the K Letters of safe-conduct to the sheriffs of Nottingham and York for the abp of Canterbury *Newcastle.* R. ii. p. ii. 881. O iv. 614. H. ii p iii. 114.

DATE	SUBJECT
1334 June 12.	Edward K of Scotland, in the 2nd year of his reign, grants to Edward K of England two thousand librates of land in the Marches of Scotland, and in part payment of the same he concedes the castles, towns, and counties of Berewyk-upon-Tweed and Rokesburgh, the town, castle, and forest of Jedworth, the town and county of Selkirk, the forests of Selkirk and Etryk, the town, castle, and county of Edenburgh, with the constabularies of Hadyngton and Lynhseu, and the towns, castles, and county of Pebles, Dumfres. *Newcastle-upon-Tyne.* R II p II 888 O IV 614 H II p III 115
June 15	The K appoints Geoffrey de Moubray, John de Kyngeston, Gilbert de Bourghdon, Peter Tilhol, Robert de Maners, and William de Pressen, to take possession of the above-mentioned places *Newcastle.* R II. p II 889 O IV 616 H II p III 116
June 15.	The K appoints the same persons sheriffs of the respective counties and wardens of the castles *Newcastle* R u p II 889 O IV 617 H. II p III 116.
June 15	The K appoints Robert de Lowedre his justiciary in Lothian, according to the law of Scotland *Newcastle* R II p II 889 O IV 617 H II p III 116
June 18	The K restores to Edward K of Scotland his hereditary lands of Botel, Kenmore, and Kirkandres, in the county of Dumfries *Newcastle* R II. p II 889. O IV 618 H II p III 116
June 21.	The K appoints John de Bourdon, his clerk, chamberlain of all his lands in Scotland, in Berwick, Edenburgh, Hadyngton, Lynhscu, Rokesburgh, Dumfries, Pebles, Selkirk, Jedworth, and Etryk *Chester* R II p II 890 O IV 618 H II p III 116
June 23.	Warrant for the payment of the pension of the count of Juliers *Raby.* R. II. p. II. 890. O IV. 619 H II p III 116
July 4	The K orders Gilbert de Ledred, his escheator in Lincoln, Northampton, and Rutland, to deliver to John duke of Brittany and earl of Richmond the revenues of his lands from May 8 Similar writs to five other escheators *York* R II p II 890 O IV 610–20 H II. p. III 117
July 16	Power for William de Cusance, canon of Ripon, and James de Lukes to treat for a marriage between John earl of Cornwall and Mary, daughter of William de Gynes, lord of Coucy *Nottingham* R II p II 890 O IV 620 H II p III. 117
July 16.	The K orders Robert de Bousser, whom he has appointed chief justice in Ireland, to be at Dublin by Michaelmas Similar letters to Adam de Lymbergh, chancellor, Robert de Stoiburgh, and Hugh de Colewyk, barons of the Exchequer, and Thomas de Louth, Thomas de Dent, and John de Kirkebythore, justices *Nottingham.* R II p II 890
July 23	The K writes again to J abp of Canterbury, desiring him to summon a convocation *Northampton* R II. p II 891 O IV 619 H II p III 116
Aug. 2	Power to William Trussel and Richard de Bynteworth, professor of civil law, to receive the homage of the count of Savoy. *Windsor* R. II p II 891 O. IV. 620. H II p III 117
Aug 2	The K of England requests the seneschal of the K of Jerusalem and Sicily, in Provence, to arrest Richard de Thurmarton, a rebel, and deliver him to William de Trussel. *Windsor.* R II p II. 891. O IV 621 H II p III 117
Aug 2	The K orders Richard de Thurmarton to come at once to England *Windsor* R. II p II 891 O IV. 621 H. II p III 117
Aug. 2.	The K orders the sheriffs of Lincoln and Oxford to prevent the masters and scholars, who have seceded from the university of Oxford, from studying at Staunford. *Windsor.* R II p II 891 O. IV 621 H II p III 117
Aug. 20	The K orders proclamation to be made throughout England, that those who have received pardons in consequence of their services at Berwick shall repair to Newcastle at Michaelmas to resist the attempts of the Scotch. *Clarendon* R II p II 892.
Sept. 2.	The K summons the chancellor of the university of Oxford, and the mayor of Oxford, to appear at Westminster on Sept 22 *Guildford* R II p II 892
Sept. 15.	The K orders Ralph de Nevill and Anthony de Lucy to inquire into the claim of Geoffrey de Moubray to be sheriff of Roxburgh and warden of Selkirk forest, in right of his wife, Isabella countess of Mar *Westm* R II p II 892 O IV 622 H II p. III 117
Sept 20.	The K appoints Richard bp of Durham, Roger bp of Coventry and Lichfield, and William bp of Norwich, to settle the dissensions in the university of Oxford *Westm.* R II p II 892 O IV 622 H I p III. 118
Sept. 22	Power to Oliver de Ingham, seneschal of Gascony and John Travers, constable of Bourdeaux, to treat with Guitard de la Bret [d Albret] about coming to reside with the K. *Westm* R II p II 893 O IV 623 H II. p. III 118

DATE	SUBJECT
1334 Sept 24	Grant to Q Isabella for life of the county of Ponthieu and Montreuil *Westm* R ii p ii 893 O iv 628 H ii p iii 118
Sept 27	Proclamation to be made by the several sheriffs of safe conduct for Flemish merchants until Whitsuntide. *Westm* R ii p ii 893
Sept. 28	Memorandum that J abp of Canterbury delivered the great seal to the K at Westminster, and that the K transferred it to R. bp of Durham, whom he appointed chancellor R ii p ii 893
Sept. 30.	Inspeximus and confirmation of the marriage settlement between John earl of Cornwall and Mary de Hispania, daughter of Ferdinand de Hispania, lord of Lara, dated London, Sept 28, 1334. *Westm.* R ii p ii 893 O iv 624 H ii p iii 118
Sept. 30.	The K appoints cardinal A bp of Frascati as one of his councillors with an annuity of 50 marks *Westm* R ii p. ii. 894. O iv 626 H ii p iii 119
Sept 30.	Power to J. abp. of Canterbury, the abbot of Dore, and Sir William de Clynton, to treat with Philip K of France about certain causes in his courts *Westm* R ii. p ii 894 O. iv. 626. H ii p. iii. 119
Sept 30.]	Power for the same to treat for an interview between the Kings of England and France, to arrange for an expedition to the Holy Land R ii p ii 895 O iv 627. H ii p iii 119
Sept. 30.	The K informs the chamberlain of Kaernarvan that he has appointed Stephen le Blount and Ambrose de Newburgh, his clerks, to fortify his castles in North Wales, Similar letter to the chamberlain of Kaermarthen for South Wales. *Westm* R ii p ii 895
Oct 1	Power for Nicholas de la Beche to appoint an agent for the K at Rome in place of Andrew Sapiti *Westm* R ii p ii 895
Oct. 3.	Warrant to the customers of London to pay to Otho lord of Kuyk the last half year's portion of his pension of 250*l* *S. Alban's* R. ii p ii 895 O iv. 627. H ii p iii 120
Oct 4.	The K appoints the abbot of Cerne and John Mauger to collect, in the county of Dorset, the tenth and fifteenth granted in the recent parliament, in consequence of the extortions of the collectors of the last subsidy The K informs the nobles and commonalties, and the sheriff of Dorset, of the above Similar appointments are made in the other counties *York* R ii p ii 895.
Oct 23.	The K requests his abps and bps to pray for him during his expedition against the Scots. *York* R ii p ii 896 O iv 628 H ii p iii 120.
Oct. 24.	Warrant for the payment of 24s to David de Wolloure, for his expenses at the parliament at Edenburgh at 3s a day, in addition to what he has before received. *York* R ii p. ii 897. O iv. 628. H ii. p. iii. 120
Oct. 24.	The K orders the abps of Canterbury and York to appoint collectors of the tenth granted by the clergy *York* R ii p ii 897
Oct. 24	Warrant to the treasurer and barons of the Exchequer to repay William de Montacute for the repairs done by him at the manor and park of Woodstock, and in Rosamound's chamber there. *York* R. ii. p ii 897 O iv 629 H. ii p iii 120
Nov 1	The K repeats his order of Aug 2 to the sheriffs of Lincoln [relative to the scholars of Oxford at Staunford] *Newcastle* R ii p ii 898
Nov 5	The K orders Sir William de Clynton and eight others to suspend all agreements and processes commenced with the K of France until a fortnight after Michaelmas. *Newcastle.* R ii p ii 898 O iv 629. H ii p iii 120
Nov 6.	The K orders the sheriff of Yorkshire to provide waggons from other parts of the county for carrying the K's stuff, &c, and not to take those which bring victuals to York *Newcastle* R ii. p ii 898
Dec 1.	Safe conduct until Easter for Andrew bp of Tournay and Hugh lord de Bovill, ambassadors of the K of France. *Roxburgh* R ii. p. ii 899. O iv 631. H ii. p iii. 121
Dec. 10.	The K, hearing of the death of pope John [XXII], orders the companies of Bardi and Peruch, dwelling in England, to retain the tenths and other papal dues now in their hands The K orders the mayor and sheriffs of London to seize all such sums of money found in their bailiwick *Roxburgh.* R ii. p. ii. 899 O iv 631. H. ii. p iii 121
Dec 16	The K appoints Nicholas Usomare warden of Bourdeaux Castle and constable of Bourdeaux. The K intimates this to the seneschals of Saintonges and Gascony, and others in Aquitain. *Roxburgh.* R ii. p. ii 899 O. iv. 632 H ii p iii. 121.
Dec. 20.	All persons having property to the amount of 40*l*. a year are to take the order of knighthood. *Roxburgh.* R. ii. p. ii. 899.
Dec 30	Proclamation that all persons are to arm themselves in accordance with the statute of Winchester. *Roxburgh.* R. ii. p. ii. 900,

DATE.	SUBJECT
1335. Jan 7	The K. orders William de Clynton, constable of Dover Castle and warden of the Cinque Ports, to send some person to Whitsand to inform the chancellor of the coming of the French ambassadors *Roxburgh* R. ii. p. ii 900 O iv 632. H ii p. iii. 122
Jan 9.	Benedict [XII] informs the K of England, as the first of all Christian princes, of the death of Pope John XXII, and of his own election to the papacy *Avignon* R. ii. p ii 900 O iv 633 H ii p iii 122
Jan. 26.	An order to pay 40*l* to Thomas Powis, the K's clerk, and master of the boys whom the K supports at the university of Cambridge *Roxburgh.* R ii p ii 900 O iv 634 H ii p iii. 122
Jan 26.	The K appoints Roger de Somerville and Robert le Conestable de Fleynburgh, to see that the men of the East Riding of Yorkshire are armed according to the statute of Winchester 40 similar commissions *Roxburgh.* R. ii p ii 901
Feb. 16.	The K. respites the debts of John duke of Brittany, earl of Richmond, till a fortnight after Michaelmas *Newcastle* R. ii p ii 902 O iv 634 H ii p iii 122.
Feb. 22.	The K grants to Isabella countess of Marr the goods and chattels which her husband Geoffrey de Moubray, forfeited for his adhesion to the Scots. *Newcastle.* R. ii. p iii 902 O. iv 635 H. ii p iii 122
[Feb 22]	The K orders Robert Darreys and Stephen de Thoresby to deliver to the countess of Marr the said goods and chattels above referred to, in the county of Northumberland R ii p ii 902. O iv 635 H ii p iii 122.
Feb. 22.	The K desires Hugh de Courtenay, senior, to assume the name of earl of Devon, as heir of Isabella de Fortibus, late countess of Devon *Newcastle* R ii p. ii 902 O. iv 636 H. ii. p iii 123
[Feb. 22]	The K. orders the sheriff of Devonshire to proclaim the above-mentioned notification R ii p ii. 902. O iv 636 H ii p iii 123.
Feb 23.	The K orders his treasurer to pay to Hugh de Courtenay the fee of 18*l*. 6*s* 8*d* from the county of Devon, which his predecessors received. R ii p ii. 903
March 6.	The K. permits Edward K of Scotland to have a constable and marshal of his army with the power to punish offences in his army. *Coventry.* R. ii p. ii 903 O iv 636 H. ii. p. iii 123
March 22	Safe conduct for 30 Scots to come to Newark to treat with the bp. of Evreux and Peter de Tierslen, ambassadors of Philip K of France *Cattywade* The safe conduct extended as far as Gedelyng *Nottingham,* 1 *April* R ii p ii 903 O iv 637–8 H ii. p iii 123
March 28	The K appoints William Trussel to carry out his orders relative to the members of the university of Oxford retiring for study to Stamford *Nottingham.* R. ii. p ii. 903 O iv 638 H ii p iii 124.
April 1	The K orders the several sheriffs to put in force the statute of Westminster the first passed in the reign of Edw I, against circulators of false reports. *Nottingham* Similar writs to the bailiffs of Kingston-on-Hull, Norwich, Lynn, Yarmouth, and Ipswich *Cowick* 15 *May.* R n p ii. 904 O iv. 639 H. ii. p iii. 124.
April 2	Safe conduct for Sir William de Keth and Sir Godfrey de Ros, with 60 men-at-arms bringing Richard de Talbot, a prisoner in Scotland, to the English marches. *Nottingham* R ii p ii. 904 O. iv 639. H ii p iii 124
April 4.	The K informs the bp. of Evreux and Peter de Tyerzleu, the French ambassadors, that at their request, he has promised to grant an armistice with Scotland until S. John's day on condition of a proclamation being made in Scotland forbidding hostilities. *Nottingham* R ii p ii. 904. O iv 640. H ii p iii 124
April 9	W abp. of York is directed to permit the cross to be carried in the province of York before the abp of Canterbury on his way to the parliament at York *Clipston.* R. ii p ii 904 O iv 640 H ii p iii 124
April 22	Safe conduct for John de Floto and Thomas of Bologna, nuncios from the pope Benedict [XII], coming to England and Ireland. *Clipstone* R. ii p. ii 905. O. iv 640 H ii p iii 125.
April 24	The K orders the sheriffs of Nottinghamshire and Yorkshire to protect the abp of Canterbury made his cross) on his journey to the parliament summoned to York, on the morrow of Ascension day *Clipston.* R ii p ii 905 O iv. 641 H ii. p iii. 125.
May 8.	The K requests an aid from the clergy and laity of Ireland, for the war against the Scots, and promises that it shall not be taken for a precedent, *Cowick* R. ii p ii 905 O. iv 641 H. ii p iii. 125.
May 8	The K desires the abps and bps. of Ireland to provide armed men, to be brought to him on S John's day, by John Darcy, the justiciary. *Cowick.* R. ii. p. ii 905. O iv 642 H ii. p. iii. 125.

DATE	SUBJECT.
1335 [May 8]	The K. orders James le Botiller, earl of Ormond, Maurice FitzThomas, earl of Desmond, 54 knights, 14 Irish chiefs, and 111 esquires to come to him with John Darcy. R II p II. 906 O IV. 643 H II p III 125
[May 8.]	The K requests the city of Dublin to grant him a subsidy, and desires credence for John Darcy, justiciary, and John de Ellerker junior, treasurer of Ireland R II p II. 907. O IV 645 H. II p III 126.
[May 8.]	Letter to the justiciary, chancellor, and treasurer of Ireland, on the same subject R II p II 907 O IV 645 H II p III 127
May 11	The K desires the mayor and commonalty of London to give instructions to their deputies at the approaching parliament, if they wish to pay a fine in lieu of the fifteenth granted at the late parliament *Cowick* R II p II 907
May 16.	Power to William de la Pole, and others, to treat with Louis count of Flanders, and the commonalties of Bruges, Ghent, and Ypres about the piracies, &c committed on both sides. *Cowick.* R. II p. II 907 O. IV 645 H II p. III 127
May 16	The K recommends William de la Pole, and his other ambassadors, to Louis count of Flanders *Cowick* R II p II 908 O IV 646 H II p III 127
[May 16.]	Similar letters to the commonalties of Bruges, Ghent, and Ypres. R II p II 908 O. IV 546. H. II. p. III. 127
May 26.	The K. requests John duke of Brittany, earl of Richmond, to make redress for four anchors taken by his subjects from the ship of John Perbroun, of Great Yarmouth, wrecked on the coast of Garound in Brittany *York* R II. p II 908 O IV 647. H. II. p. III 127
May 26.	The K. requests the Friars Preachers, at their approaching chapter general at London, to pray for him, his queen and children, and recommends to them Friar Nicholas de Herle. *York.* R II p II 908.
May 27.	Warrant for the payment of the annuity of the count of Juliers *York* R II p II. 908 O IV 647 H II p III 127
May 29.	Protection till Michaelmas for Ralph de Campionis and Henry de Monte Felici, of Normandy, in the suite of the French ambassadors *York* R II. p II 908 O IV. 647 H. II p III 127
June 5.	The K grants permission to William de Montacute during his lifetime to hunt for one day in all the royal forests, chaces, and parks *York* R II p II 909.
June 6.	Memorandum that the bp of Durham delivered the great seal to the K , in the chamber of the Friars Minors at York, where the K was residing ; and he then delivered it to J abp of Canterbury, whom he appointed chancellor R II p. II 909
June 8	The K orders Paul de Monte Florum, his clerk, to return to the chamberlains two gold crowns pledged to him for 8,000 marks, which sum has been repaid *York* R. II p II. 909. O. IV 647 H II p III 127.
June 8,	Pardon to the Roman cardinals for the dues of their benefices in England. *York.* R II p II 909
June 10.	The K orders Oliver de Ingham, seneschal of Gascony, and Nicholas Usomare, constable of Bourdeaux, to obtain from the abp and chapter of Bourdeaux letters declaring that they only claim the third part of the profit of the coinage there *York* R II p II 909 O IV 648 H II p III 128
June 14.	The K desires Alfonso K. of Castile to give credence to Berard de la Bret, William Fitz-Waryn, and Gerard de Puteo, judge of the duchy of Aquitain *York* R II p II 909. O IV. 648. H II. p. III. 128.
June 14.	Power for the above-named persons to treat for a marriage between the eldest son of K Alfonso, and Isabel, the K.'s eldest daughter *York.* R II p II 910 O. IV 648 H. II p. III 128
June 15.	Safe conduct till Michaelmas for Sir Theodoric Schinman, marshal of the count of Juliers *York* R II p II. 910 O IV 649 H II p II 128
June 16	Inspeximus and confirmation of a grant by Eleanor Q of Henry III of her inheritance in Provence to Thomas and Henry, sons of Edmund earl of Leicester, dated May 1286 , and of the confirmation thereof by Edward I , dated May 1286, 14 Edw I *Newburgh* R. II. p. II 910. O IV 649 H II p III 128
June 18	The K desires the prayers of the abps and bps of England and Wales for his success in the Scotch war *Newcastle* R II p II 910. O IV 650 II II p III 129.

DATE.	SUBJECT.
1335 June 24	Adam de Lymbergh, Geoffrey de Edenham, and Thomas de Sibthorp, appointed to levy the 500*l* granted by the county of Lincoln, exclusive of Lincoln, Grantham, and Stamford, in lieu of 300 hobilers and 1,000 archers Twenty-six similar appointments *Newcastle* R. ii p ii 911
June 28	William de Clynton, constable of Dover Castle and warden of the Cinque Ports, ordered to ascertain if the Scots have prepared any ships at Calais or elsewhere to serve against the English. Similar letters to the bailiffs of Great Yarmouth. *Newcastle.* R ii p ii 911 O iv 651 H ii p ii 129.
June 28	The K sends Edmund de Grymesby, his clerk, to ask John de la Gotere for the loan of 100*l* promised by him Similar requests are sent to John de Tumby, Hugh de Edelyngton, junior, and Richard and Thomas de Kele. R ii. p. ii 912 *Newcastle*
July 1.	Safe conduct until All Saints for the ship called La Nicholas, of Hull, (William de Fenby, master,) laden with victuals for the count of Juliers and his retinue, who are coming to the K *Newcastle* R ii. p ii 912. O iv 652 H ii. p. iii 129
July 2.	The treasurer and barons of the K's Exchequer ordered to impose fines on those who are qualified for knighthood, but have neglected to assume the order. *Newcastle* R. ii p ii 912
July 2.	The K requests John duke of Normandy to make redress for a ship belonging to Robert Atte-Grene, Nicholas le Coifster, and John de Weston, which was taken by the Normans and Scots at the mouth of the Seyn in Normandy. *Newcastle.* R. ii. p ii. 912 O iv 652 H. ii p iii 129.
July 3,	Permission to William de Herle, justice of the King's Bench, to resign his office, in consequence of old age. *Newcastle* R ii. p ii 913
July 6	The K of England writes to Philip K. of France in favour of Robert Atte Grene and the other merchants mentioned above. *Carlisle* R. ii p ii 913 O. iv. 653 H ii p iii 130.
July 8	Thomas bp. of Hereford commanded to maintain the peace in his diocese in the marches of Wales *Carlisle* R. ii p ii 913 O iv 654 H ii p iii 130
July 8.	Warrant for the payment of the annuity of Otho lord of Kuyk *Carlisle* R. ii. p ii 914. O. iv. 654. H. ii. p. iii. 130.
July 10	Thomas Bacon, William Scot, and Richard de Kelleshill ordered to inquire about the finding of a certain treasure under a pear tree in the garden of Thomas earl of Lancaster, in the parish of St Clement Danes. *Carlisle* R ii p ii 914
July 12.	Safe conduct until Michaelmas for the count of Namur, who is coming with men-at-arms to the K's assistance against the Scots *Carlisle* R. ii p ii 914 O iv 654. H. ii p iii 130.
July 12.	Proclamation to be made throughout England that no one shall deceive the people by alleging that the K. exacts more than the ancient custom for wool *Carlisle* R ii p ii 914
July 18.	Power for William bp of Norwich, Thomas Wake, lord of Lidel, the abbot of Dore, and Richard de Bynteworth, to treat with Philip K. of France about certain questions in his court *Carlisle* R ii p. ii 914 O. iv 655 H. ii. p iii 130
[July 18]	Power for the above-mentioned commissioners to treat for an expedition to the Holy Land R ii p ii 915 O iv. 655 H ii p iii 130.
[July 18]	Power for William Trussel and John de Shordich to treat of a marriage between the eldest son of the duke of Austria and Joan the K's daughter R ii p. ii 915 O iv. 655 H ii p iii. 131
July 25.	Oliver de Ingham, seneschal of Gascony, ordered to send out ships from Bayonne to resist the fleet which is being prepared to assist the Scotch rebels against Edward Balliol, K of Scotland, the K of England's vassal *Carlisle.* R ii p ii. 915. O. iv 656 H ii p iii 131
July 26	The K. writes on the same subject to the commonalties of Bayonne and Bourdeaux *Carlisle* R ii p. ii 915 O iv 656 H. ii p. iii 131
July 28.	Order to repay Bartholomew de Bard and other merchants of Florence the money advanced to the abp of Canterbury, William de Clynton, John Peres, William Trussel, and James Fakk. *Carlisle* R ii p ii 915 O iv 657 H ii. p. iii 131
Aug. 1	The several sheriffs commanded to proclaim that all persons between the ages of 16 and 60 are to arm themselves according to the statute of Winchester. *Erthe.* R. ii. p ii 916.

DATE.	SUBJECT.
1335. Aug 3	The K orders his treasurer to deliver to Philip, brother of the count of Namur, a silver gilt cup and ewer, as a reward, and a similar cup to a knight in his company. *Erthe* R ii p ii 916 O iv 657 H ii. p iii 131
Aug. 7.	Summons to W bp of Norwich, five other bishops, five abbots, the prior of S Swithins, the earl of Norfolk, and 18 others to a council to be holden at London on Aug 25 Margaret, widow of the earl of Kent, Mary, widow of the earl of Pembroke, and Joan, widow of Thomas de Botetourt, are desired to send discreet members of their household thither *Perth* R. ii p. ii. 916.
Aug. 11.	Safe conduct until Michaelmas for the count of Namur, who is returning home *Perth* R ii p ii 917 O iv 58. H ii p iii 131
Aug. 12.	The K commends to Robert K of Jerusalem and Sicily, Andrew de Portivaris, whom the K. sends to buy six war horses. *Perth.* R ii p ii 917 O. iv 658. H ii p. iii. 132.
Aug. 12	S bp of London, A. bp of Winchester, and Laurence Fastolf are appointed as the K's deputies at the council to be held at London on Aug 25 *Perth.* R. ii p ii 917 O iv 658 H ii p iii 132
Aug. 12.	John de Pulteneye and Reginald de Conductu, citizens of London, appointed to array and lead the men of London, should the realm be invaded *Perth.* R. ii. p ii 917. O iv. 659. H. ii p. iii 132
Aug. 13	Nicolas de Langford and John de Feriby, appointed to bring the earl of Murref [Murray], prisoner of war, from York to Nottingham Castle. Letters on the same subject to the sheriff of York and to William de Eland, constable of Nottingham Castle. *Perth* R ii p ii 918 O iv. 660 H ii p iii 132
[Aug. 13]	Warrant to the sheriff of Nottinghamshire to pay to the constable of Nottingham Castle 20s a week for the expenses of the earl of Murref R u. p ii 918. O iv 660 H ii p iii 132
Aug 16.	The several sheriffs and the warden of the Cinque Ports are commanded to proclaim the truce lately concluded with the count of Flanders, until Christmas *Perth.* R. ii p ii. 918 O. iv. 661 H. ii. p iii 133
Aug 16	The count of Flanders, and the commonalties of Bruges, Ghent, and Ypres, are informed that the K has ordered the truce to be proclaimed *Perth* R ii p ii 918 O iv 662 H ii. p iii 133
Aug. 17.	Warrant for the payment of 32l to John de Denton, of Newcastle-upon-Tyne, his expenses in conveying the earl of Murref from Bamborough Castle to York *Perth.* R ii p.. ii 919 O iv. 662. H ii. p iii 133
Aug 18.	William de S Omer, steward of Edward earl of Chester, the K's son, and J de Burnham, his treasurer, are commanded to convey the Prince and his household to Nottingham Castle *Perth* R ii p ii 919
Aug. 20.	Warrant for the payment of 32s. to Peter de Middleton, sheriff of York, for his expenses in keeping the earl of Murref for eight days *Perth.* R. ii p ii 919. O iv 663. H. ii. p. iii 133
Aug. 20	Warrant for the payment of sums from 40s to 40 marks as rewards to the lord de Karendon, the lord of Walecourt, the lord of Licheroles, and John de Bovyne, clerk, companions of the earl of Namur, also to deliver to lord Theodoric de Walecourt a cup and ewer gilt *Perth* R ii p ii 919 O iv. 663. H ii p iii 133
Aug. 20.	The K. orders John de Langeford, constable of Carisbrook Castle, to garrison the castle, as he hears that a fleet has been prepared by Scots and others to attack the realm *Perth* R ii p ii 919
Aug 20	The K orders William de Montacute and Henry de Ferrers, wardens of Guernsey, Jersey, Sark, and Alderney, to provide for the defence of the islands *Perth* R ii p ii 919
Aug 24.	Safe conduct for the fleet which is about to convey Blanche, sister of the count of Namur, to Norway, the King of which country she is going to marry Similar letters to the bailiffs of Great Yarmouth and the Cinque Ports, and to the admirals of the fleets North and South of the Thames *Perth* R ii p ii 920 O iv 663 H ii p iii 134
Aug. 24.	The sheriffs of Hertfordshire, Lincolnshire, Kent, Northumberland, and Norfolk, and the bailiffs of Wark, are ordered to restore to David de Strabolgi, earl of Athol, the lands he forfeited for his adherence to the K's enemies, for which he has excused himself *Perth* R ii. p ii 920 O. iv 664 H ii p iii 134
Aug. 26.	The mayor and sheriffs of London are commanded to send to the K the ships arrested in the port of London, and to pay 60 marks of the 500 marks granted by them in lieu of men *Perth* R ii p ii. 920 O. iv. 664 H. ii p iii 134

DATE.	SUBJECT
1335. Aug 26	The K grants an annuity of 400 marks to Guy count of Namur for his services. *Perth.* R ii p ii 920. O. iv. 665. H. ii. p iii. 134.
Aug 26	Indenture by which the count of Namur agrees to serve the K *Perth.* R ii. p ii 921 O iv 666 H. ii p iii 134
Aug 27.	Warrant to the treasurer for the payment of the pension of the count of Namur *Perth.* R ii p. ii 921 O iv 666 H ii p iii 135
Aug 30	Warrant for the payment of 12*l.* 7*s* 9*d* to the count of Namur for his expenses in returning from Scotland *Perth* R. ii p ii 921 O iv 666. H ii. p iii 135
Aug. 30.	Safe conduct for Henry count of Mont Bellegarde, lord of Montfaucon in Burgundy, who is coming to assist the K. against the Scots *Perth* R. ii. p. ii. 921 O iv 666. H. ii p iii 135
Sept 16	Safe conduct for R bp of Morinensis [Terouenne] and John de Chastellor, who are coming on an embassy from Philip K. of France *Edinburgh.* R. ii p ii 921 O iv 667. H ii p iii 135.
Sept 16	Safe conduct for Giles de Coucy, ambassador of the K of France, who is returning thither *Edinburgh* R ii p ii 921 O iv 667. H. ii. p. iii. 135
Sept 19.	Warrant for the payment of 500*l* to the count of Juliers, for his expenses in serving with the K. against the Scots Another warrant for 200 marks *Edinburgh* R ii p ii. 922. O iv. 667 H ii p iii 135
Sept 20.	The K orders William de Clynton, warden of the Cinque Ports, to provide ships for the return home of certain knights in the company of the count of Juliers *Edinburgh.* R ii p ii 922
Sept 21	The bailiffs of Great Yarmouth and 18 other ports are ordered to proclaim that no person leaving the country is to exchange money except at the appointed tables of exchange. *Edinburgh* R ii p ii 922 O iv. 668. H ii p iii 135.
Sept. 23.	Safe conduct for certain men and horses whom the count of Juliers is sending home. *Cole Brantespeth* R ii p ii 922 O iv 668 H ii p iii 135.
Sept. 24.	Warrant for the payment of 10 marks to Alice countess of Meneteth, who is residing in England. *Edinburgh.* R ii. p. ii. 922. O. iv 669 H ii. p. iii. 136
Sept 28	Safe conduct for Hugh bp of S Paul de Trois Chateaux ["Tricastrinensis Episcopus"] and Roland de Ast, canon of "Landunensis," chaplain and auditor of the pope, who are coming as nuncios from him *Edinburgh.* R n. p ii 923. O iv. 669. H ii p iii 135
Oct 6.	The K requests Guy count of Namur to release Jordan de Staunford, servant of William Tonnok, mariner of Newcastle-upan-Tyne, who is imprisoned at Lescluses [Sluys]. *Berwick* R ii p ii 923 O iv 669 H ii p iii 136
[Oct. 6]	Similar letter to Louis count of Flanders R ii. p ii 923 O iv. 670. H. ii. p iii 136.
Oct. 10	The K. grants to William de Presfen (who took John Earl of Murref prisoner) of the town of Ederynton, the fishery of Edermuth, and mills at Berwick and Ederyngton, at a yearly rent of 110 marks *Berwick* R ii p ii 923 O iv. 670. H ii. p iii. 136.
Oct. 10.	Licence to Duncan earl of Fife to grant the manor of Caldore, in the county of Edinburgh, to Thomas de Fereres *Berwick* R ii p ii 923 O iv 671 H ii. p iii 736
Oct 10	The K. grants to William de Montacute the forest of Selkirk and Etryk, and the town and sheriffalty of Selkirk, for a yearly rent of 30*l* The K also grants to him the town and county of Peebles *Berwick* R ii p ii 924. O iv. 671 H iii p iii 136.
Oct 10	Proclamation to be made throughout England that merchants are at liberty to come into the realm until a year from next Christmas. *Berwick* R ii p ii 924 O. iv. 672 H ii p iii 137
Oct. 11	Bull of Benedict [XII] confirming the election of William de Bernham as abbot of the monastery of S Edmunds Bury, vacant by the death of Richard late abbot. *Avignon.* R ii p ii 924 O iv 672 H ii p iii 137
Oct 14	The K grants to John duke of Brittany, earl of Richmond, a respite of his debts until a fortnight after Easter *Berwick* R ii p ii 925. O iv 674 H ii p iii 138
Oct 16	The K orders his treasurer to pay to Thomas de Ughtred the remaining 200*l.* of the 300*l.* which the K promised to lend to Edward K. of Scotland *Berwick* R. ii. p ii 925. O. iv 674 H ii p iii. 138
Nov 1.	Power for William de Montacute, Robert de Ufford, and Ralph de Nevill to treat with Andrew de Murref of Scotland *Dodyngton* R ii p ii. 925. O. iv. 674. H ii p iii 138

DATE.	SUBJECT
1335 Nov 8	The K. grants a truce until Nov 25 to Andrew de Murref of Scotland and his adherents *Alnwick.* R u p u 925 O iv 675 H u p iii 138.
Nov. 16.	The truce above mentioned prorogued until Dec 10 Similar letters for the prorogation of the truce until Dec. 3. *Newcastle upon-Tyne* R. ii. p u 925. O. iv. 675. H ii p iii 238
Nov 16.	Power for Geoffrey le Scrop, Nicholas de la Beche, and Richard de Byntewarth, professor of civil law, to treat with Andrew de Murref *Newcastle-upon-Tyne* R u p u. 926 O iv 675 H u. p iii 138
Nov. 16.	Warrant for the payment of 10 marks a day to the count of Juliers, from Sept. 25. *Newcastle-upon-Tyne* R u p. u 926 O. iv. 675. H u p iii 138.
Nov 20	The K. requests W abp of Cologne, and the counts of Hainault and Gueldres, to give safe conduct for 30 casks of Rhenish wine, bought by John de Cologne *Newcastle-upon-Tyne* R u p u 926 O iv 676 H u p iii 138.
Nov. 23.	The K , at the request of the pope and Philip K of France, prorogues the truce with Scotland until Christmas The K. orders Anthony de Lucy, justiciary of Lothian, to proclaim the prorogation *Newcastle-upon-Tyne.* R. u. p u 926 O iv 676. H u. p. m. 138.
Nov 23	Safe conduct for six Scots with a retinue of 40 horsemen to come to Newcastle to treat with the K. *Newcastle-upon-Tyne* R u p u 926 O iv 677. H u p iii 139
	Safe conduct for Andrew de Murreff, William de Keth, Robert de Lowethre, and William Douglas of Scotland to come into England. R u p. u. 926 O iv. 677. H u. p iii 139.
Nov. 26.	Safe conduct until March 25 for John de Calseto [? Chasteller], courier of R. "Epis Morinensis" [bp Terouenne,] the French ambassador *Newcastle-upon-Tyne* R u p u 927 O iv 677. H u p u 139
Nov 27.	Benedict [XII] commends, to the King, Arnald de Durfort and his son Arnald. *Avignon.* R. u p. u 927. O iv 678 H. u. p. iii. 139.
Dec 12.	The K orders Paul de Monte Florum, his clerk, to pay 40l to the ambassadors of Ermonye [? Armenia] *Auckland.* R u p u 927 O iv 678 H u p iii 139
Dec. 12.	The above-mentioned Paul is also to pay 205l 13s. 4d. to the count of Juliers, 100 marks to the provost of Dax, and 20l to Sir Matthew Stumble and his companion *Auckland.* R u p u 927 O iv. 678. H u p iii 139.
Dec 13.	The K orders William de Clynton, constable of Dover Castle and warden of the Cinque Ports, to find ships for the return home of the count of Juliers. *Auckland* R u p u 927
Dec 13.	The K. has received the letters of Leo K of Armenia, by his ambassador, George Sighke, and will, if possible, assist him against the infidels. *York* R u. p. u. 927. O. iv. 679 H u p iii 129.
Dec. 14	Warrant for the payment of 200l. to the count of Juliers *Auckland.* R. u p u 928 O iv 679 H u p iii 140
Dec. 14.	The K orders his treasurer to deliver certain silver plate and two palfreys to the count of Juliers, for himself and his countess , and certain plate to the dean of Ase, [Dax?] and Matthew Stumble and his companion *Auckland* R u. p u 928 O. iv 679 H u p. iii. 140.
Dec. 18.	Power to Sir William Trussel and Sir John de Shordich to treat with the abp of Cologne, John duke of Brabant, and the counts of Hainault and Gueldres , the K also empowers them to treat with the count of Juliers *Auckland.* R u p u 928.
Dec. 18.	Protection and safe conduct for three years for Bernard Sistre, canon of S Hilary, Poitou, the pope's nuncio *Auckland.* R. u p u. 928. O iv 680 H u p u 140
Dec. 21	The K , at the request of the pope and the K of France, will prorogue the truce with Scotland until Jan 25 The K desires proclamation thereof to be made by Anthony de Lucy, justiciary of Lothian *Auckland.* R u p u 928. O iv. 681. H. u p iii 140
Dec 26	The K orders Thomas de Burgh, chamberlain of Berwick, to restore to Edward K of Scotland his hereditary lands in Lowederdale and elsewhere in the counties of Berwick, Roxburgh, Edinburgh, Peebles, and Dumfries *Newcastle-upon-Tyne* R u p u 929 O iv 681 H. u p iii 140
Dec 28	Power for William Fitzwaryn and John de Shordich to treat for a marriage between Joan, the K 's daughter, and Frederic, eldest son of Otho duke of Austria. *Newcastle-upon-Tyne.* R u p u 929 O iv 682 H u p iii 141
Dec. 29.	The K. orders William de Eland, warden of Nottingham Castle, to send John earl of Murref to Thomas de Foxele, constable of Windsor Castle *Newcastle-upon-Tyne* R u p u 929 O iv 682. H u p. iii 141
[Dec. 29.]	The K orders the sheriff of Nottingham to pay 10 marks to William de Eland, warden of Nottingham Castle, for his expenses in taking John earl of Murref to Windsor R u p. u. 929. O. iv. 682 H u p iii. 141.

DATE	SUBJECT
1335. Dec 30	The K orders Robert Tonge, receiver of the K.'s victuals at Berwick, to deliver 10 casks of flour and six casks of wine to Edward K of Scotland. *Newcastle-upon-Tyne.* R. ii. p ii. 929 O iv 683 H ii p iii 141.
Dec. 31	Power for Sir William d'Aubeneye and John Coupegorge to treat with John duke of Brittany about a marriage between John earl of Cornwall and the daughter of Guy of Brittany, the duke's niece *Newcastle-upon-Tyne* R ii p ii 929. O iv 683 H ii p iii 141.
1336. Jan 17.	The K reduces to 20*l* the fines, amounting to 106*l.* 13*s* 4*d.*, imposed on Maurice Fitz Nicholas, for his absence from the parliament held at Dublin in the 6th and 7th years of the K's reign *Teste Johanne Darcy, apud Dublin* R ii p ii 930 O. iv 683 H ii. p iii 141
Jan 22	The K prorogues the truce with Scotland until Jan 31 *Berwick-upon-Tweed.* R ii. p. ii 930 O iv 684 H ii. p iii 141
Jan 22	Safe conduct until Feb 2 for Alexander bp of Aberdeen, John abbot of Coupre, Thomas de Fyngask, John de Monypeny, and John de Orak, who are sent into Scotland by the ambassadors of the pope and the K of France at Berwick *Berwick-upon-Tweed* R. ii p ii. 930. O iv 684 H ii p iii. 141
Jan 26	Safe conduct for the envoys of David de Brus, now in France, to come to London. The K notifies this to William de Clynton, warden of the Cinque Ports *Berwick upon-Tweed* R ii p ii 930 O iv 685 H ii p iii 142-143
Jan 26	The K prorogues the truce with the Scots until April 14, but stipulating that they shall raise the siege of the castles of Coupre and Loghenndorn *Berwick-upon-Tweed* R ii. p ii 930 O iv 683 H ii p iii 142
Jan 27.	Warrant for the payment of five marks a day to Edward K of Scotland for his expenses. *Berwick upon-Tweed* R. ii p ii 931 O iv 686 H ii p iii 142
Jan 27.	The K orders Robert de Tong, receiver of his victuals at Berwick, to deliver victuals to the value of 10 marks a day to Alice countess of Meneteth, who cannot receive her rents in consequence of her adherence to the K *Berwick upon-Tweed* R. ii. p. ii 931. O iv 686 H ii p. iii 142
Feb 6	Warrant for the payment of 200*l* as a reward to Paul de Monte Florum, the King's clerk. *Knaresborough* R ii p ii 931 O iv 687 H ii p iii 142.
Feb 16	All people between the ages of 16 and 60 are commanded to arm themselves, according to the statute of Winchester *Walsingham* R ii p ii 931. O iv 687 H. ii. p iii 142
March 3	The K thanks Alfonso K. of Castile for his reception of the K's ambassadors, and requests him to send persons to K Edward to complete the treaty. *Westm* R. ii p ii 932 O. iv. 687 H ii p iii 143.
March 3,	The K thanks Fernando Sancu de Valle Leti for the assistance he has given to his ambassadors, and wishes that K Alfonso would send him to England. *Westm.* R. ii p. ii 932. O iv 688 H ii p. iii 143
[March 3]	The K thanks Guitard de Lebret, viscount of Tartas, for the favour he has shown to his ambassadors R ii p ii 932 O iv. 688 H ii p iii 143
March 3	Proclamation is to be made in London against unlawful assemblies during the session of Parliament which will be held on March 11 *Westm* R ii p ii 932.
March 12	Licence to Elizabeth de Burgh to grant the advowson of the church of Lythington in Cambridgeshire to university hall, Cambridge *Westm* R. ii p ii 932 O iv 688 H ii p iii 143.
March 15	The K orders the mayor and bailiffs of Bristol to take sureties from all masters of ships of the Cinque Ports which come to Bristol that they will return to their proper ports, to be equipped for the defence of the realm *Westm* R ii p. ii 933
March 17.	Warrant for the payment of 40*s* a week to Mary countess of Fife while she remains in England *The Tower of London.* R ii p ii. 933. O iv 690. H ii p iii 143
March 18	The K prorogues the truce with Scotland until May 12, at the request of the pope and the K of France Proclamation to be made by Anthony de Lucy, justiciary of Lothian *Westm* R ii p ii 933 O iv. 690 H ii p iii 144
March 20	The K commands the mayor and bailiffs of Cambridge not to liberate any malefactors given into their custody by the chancellor of the university *Westm.* R. ii p ii 933. O iv 693 H. ii p iii 144
March 20.	The K grants the petition of the chancellor and scholars of the university of Cambridge, that the mayor, bailiffs, aldermen, and burgesses of the town shall take an oath to maintain the peace of the university and town *Westm* R ii p ii 934 O. iv 692. H ii. p iii 144

DATE	SUBJECT
1336 March 20	The mayor and bailiffs of Cambridge are commanded to make an assay of bread and ale, when required by the chancellor of the university, according to the grants of the K's predecessors *Westm* R. п p ii 934 O iv 693 H п p iii 144
March 20.	The K. permits Gilbert de Umframville, earl of Anegos, to keep the prisoners of Redesdale in his castle of Prudhou, as that of Harbodill is out of repair *Westm* R il p ii 934.
March 20	The K will send an envoy to complete the treaty with the count of Flanders at St John's day, and desires the count to prorogue the abstinence of war until Easter *London* R ii p п 935 O iv 693 H п. p iii 145.
[March 20]	Similar letters to the communalties of Bruges, Ypres, and Ghent R п p п 935 O iv 694. H п p iii 145
March 24	Warrant for the payment of 100*l* to Edward K of Scotland, and other sums, amounting to 986*l* 13*s* 4*d*, to Henry de Lancaster, Thomas de Beauchamp, earl of Warwick, Gilbert de Umfrevill, earl of Anegos, John de Veer, earl of Oxford, William de Bohun, John Tibetot, Eustace de Makeswell, Henry de Beaumont, earl of Boghan, Henry de Percy, Ralph de Nevill, and John de Segrave, as wages for their services in Scotland *Westm* R. п. p п 935 O. iv 694. H. п p iii 145
March 24.	Warrant for the payment of 55*l* to Edward K of Scotland, being the residue of 200*l* granted to him for the payment of his debts in the north. *Westm* R п p п 935 O. iv 694. H. п p iii 145
March 24.	Warrant for the payment of 66*l*. 13*s* 4*d* to William Bullok, the K's clerk, for coming with other messengers from Scotland to the parliament at London, and for certain works at Coupre Castle, also for the payment of 40*l* to sir Michael de Wymes, 20*l* to William de Mohaut, and 10*l* to Henry de Rameseye *Westm*. R п p п 935 O iv 694 H п p iii 145.
March 26.	The K desires the archbp of York to summon a convocation before Whitsunday for the purpose of granting an aid. *Westm* R п p п 935 O iv 689 H п p iii 143
April 7.	Henry de Lancaster appointed captain of the K's army against the Scots, and Antony de Lucy, justiciary of Lothian, to lead the men of Northumberland, and William de Bohun those of Cumberland and Westmoreland *Waltham* R п p п 936 O iv 695 H п. p iii 146
April 10	Power for Henry de Lancaster to receive the fealty of the enemies of the K in Scotland. *Waltham Holy Cross* R. п p. п 936. O iv 696 H п. p. iii 146
April 11.	The K. requests the K of France to defer taking any steps about the lands of Blanquefort, "de Virmis," and "de Lurano," the restitution of which to the count of Armunac was refused by his commissioners, until the arrival of the K.'s ambassadors *Waltham Holy Cross.* R п p п 936 O iv 696 H. п p iii 146
April 11	John earl of Cornwall has a grant of the coinage of 4,000 cwt of tin in Cornwall *Waltham Holy Cross* R. п. p п 937.
April 15	The K retains Nicolin de Flisco, cardinal of Genoa, as his councillor, with an annuity of 20*l* and a knight's robes *The Tower of London* R п p п 937. O iv 697 H п. p iii 146
April 17.	The K grants an annuity of 10 marks to Matilda de Plumton, nurse of Edward earl of Chester *The Tower of London.* R п p п 937.
April 18.	The mayor and sheriffs of London commanded to proclaim that halfpence and sterlings will be coined, in accordance with an act of the late parliament at York. *Guildford* R п p п 937 O iv 697 H п p iii 146
April 20.	Hildebrand de London, John de Temyse, and William de Tydelsyde are commanded to make inquiry concerning a certain treasure belonging to the K's father found at Glamorgan and Morgannok in Wales *Guildford* R п p п 937 O iv 697. H. п p iii 147
May 2	John de Elleker, treasurer of Ireland, is commanded to make provision for certain miners, refiners, and comers, whom the K. sends to discover a silver mine in Ireland *Westm* R п p п 938
May 3.	The exportation of timber or boards fit for shipbuilding forbidden *Westm.* R ii p n. 938
May 4	The K forbids tournaments throughout England, as the truce with Scotland has expired *Westm* R п p п 938 O iv 698 H. п. p п 147
May 4	Power for Henry de Lancaster, Thomas de Beauchamp, earl of Warwick, Henry de Beaumont, earl of Boghan, and William de Bohun, to treat with Sir Andrew de Murref, or other Scots, for a truce until St John's day. *Westm* R п p п 938 O iv 699 H п p iii. 147
May 4	Safe conduct until Aug. 1 for Perot de Nevill, the French ambassador, who is going to Scotland *Westm* R п p ii. 938 O. iv. 699. H. п. p. iii 147.

DATE	SUBJECT
1336 May 6	The K orders John de Cobbam, John de Segrave, and John de Wyndesore to pay 100 marks to Alexander Hurtyn of Dover, deputy of William de Clynton, warden of the Cinque Ports, as part payment of the 87*l* 10*s* which he has spent on the passage of the count of Juheis　*Windsor*　R u p ii 939　O iv 700. H ii p iii 147
May 25	The K orders Thomas de Foxle, constable of Windsor Castle, to conduct John earl of Murref, to Winchester Castle　The K orders John de Sturcs, sheriff of Southampton, to receive and take charge of the said earl, and to allow him 20*s* a week.　*Woodstock.*　R u. p ii 939　O iv 700　H ii p iii 148
June 2	The K having been informed that the justiciary, chancellor and treasurer of Ireland, administer justice partially, orders them in future to treat all persons equally.　*Woodstock.* R ii p ii 939
[June 2]	The K thanks the people of Ireland for their grant of a subsidy, and desires credence for the justiciary, chancellor, and treasurer　R ii p ii 939
[June 2]	The K desires the commonalties of Ireland to consult with the justiciary, &c. as to the coinage of small money　R ii. p ii 939.
June 4	The K requests the duke of Austria to give credence to his proctors as to the marriage between the duke's eldest son Frederick and the K's daughter, Joan.　*Woodstock.*　R ii. 940　O iv 701　H ii p iii 148
June 4	The K orders that the castles of Corfe, Tintagel, Launceston, Restormel, Bristol, Carisbrook, Porchester, Pevensey, Hastings, Dover, Rochester, and Tower of London, be put in a state of defence　Similar letters to the earls of Arundel and Surrey as to their castles of Arundel and Lewes　*Woodstock*　R. ii p ii 940
June 10	Safe conduct for John de Pratis, dean of Beauvais, John de Castell, and William de Sanguinac, the French ambassadors, who are about to return home　*Northampton*　R. ii. p. ii 940　O iv 701　H ii p iii 148.
June 10	The K orders William de Clynton, constable of Dover Castle and warden of the Cinque Ports, to prevent any religious person from leaving the kingdom.　*Northampton*　R ii. p ii 940
June 20.	The K. appoints J archbp. of Canterbury, his chancellor, H bp of Lincoln, his treasurer, and John earl of Cornwall, to preside at the council to be holden at Northampton on June 25　*Newcastle-upon-Tyne*　R ii p ii 940　O iv. 701　H ii. p iii. 148
June 26	Pardon for Ralph count of Eu for having acquired without the K's licence the moiety of the manor of Wyghton and the moiety of the hundred of Northgrenehou, in co Norfolk, from Margaret, daughter of Drogo de Merlawe　*Berwick-upon-Tweed*　R. ii. p ii. 941　O iv 702　H. ii. p iii 148
June 28	The K having heard that the crews of the ships arrested in North Wales refuse to serve without being prepaid their wages, orders Richard earl of Arundel, justiciary of North Wales, to survey the ships, and give the crews a reward　Similar letter to the justiciary of South Wales　*Perth*　R ii p ii 941
July 4.	The K. releases the commonalty of Genoa from the payment of customs to the amount of 8,000 marks, in recompense for a ship of Yvan Lucian, taken by Hugh le Despenser.　*Perth.*　R. ii p ii 941　O iv 702　H ii p iii 148
July 6	Power for Richard bp of Durham, Adam bp of Winchester, Sir William Trussel, and Richard de Byntesworth, to treat with Philip K of France for a joint expedition to the Holy Land, and to arrange an interview between the two Kings in France　*Perth*　R ii. p ii 941.　O iv 703　H. ii. p iii 149.
July 6	Power for the same commissioners to treat about certain processes depending in the French courts　*Perth*　R ii p ii 942.　O iv 704　H ii p iii. 149
July 6	Power for the same to treat with David de Brus　*Perth*　R ii p ii. 942　O iv. 704. H ii p iii 149
July 12	The K empowers Paul de Monte Florum, canon of London, and Laurence Fastolf, canon of London, to contract a loan in his name for 60,000*l*　Similar letters for 50,000*l*, 40,000*l*, 30,000*l*, and 20,000*l*　*Perth*　R ii p ii. 942.
July 12	Simon Croyser and Hugh del Croft, collectors of the tenth and fifteenth in Bedfordshire, are ordered to give the inhabitants of Luton a respite until Michaelmas, in consequence of the damage caused by the late fire there.　*Perth*　R ii p ii 942
July 14	Warrant for the payment of 200*l* to the ambassadors going to France　*Perth.*　R. ii p ii 943　O iv 705　H. ii. p iii 149.
July 18.	Safe conduct for Lambert le Ulynt de St Omer, who brings letters from the K of France　*Perth.*　R ii p. ii. 943.　O. iv. 705.　H. ii p. iii. 149.

DATE.	SUBJECT
1336 Aug 5.	The K orders John de Norwich, admiral of the fleet from the Thames northwards, who is searching for hostile galleys with a fleet consisting of ships of Great Yarmouth, to hold no communication with the men of the Cinque Ports, in consequence of the dissensions between them and the men of Yarmouth Similar letter to Geoffrey de Say, admiral of the fleet south of the Thames *Perth.* R. n. p n 943.
Aug 5.	The K orders the bailiffs of Great Yarmouth to send three or four burgesses to treat with the chancellor, John archbp of Canterbury, and certain persons from the Cinque Ports, concerning the dissensions above mentioned *Perth* R n p n 943.
Aug. 12.	The K orders the customers of London to place the seal called "Coket" in a safe place under the seals of the mayor and others, and to allow no wool or leather to be exported. Similar letters to the mayors and bailiffs of Newcastle and 14 other ports. *Perth* R n p n 943.
Aug 20.	The K orders Oliver de Ingham, seneschal of Gascony, to proclaim that no man-at-arms is to leave the duchy without licence. *Perth* R n p n 944.
Aug. 24.	The K. summons the archbps and bishops, 27 abbots, 4 priors, the earls of Norfolk, Surrey, Lancaster, Arundel, Devon, and Hereford, and 35 others, to a council to be held at Nottingham on Sept 23, to deliberate about defending the country from the threatened invasion by France on behalf of the Scots *Perth* R n p n. 944. O iv 705–6 H n p in 150
Sept. 1.	Safe conduct till All Saints day for 30 persons coming from David de Bruys into England with the French ambassadors *Perth* R n p n 945 O iv 707 H n p in 150.
Sept 3	Safe conduct for the bishop of Beauvais, Ferric de Pynguiac, and Guido Peytevin, ambassadors from France *Perth.* R n p n 945 O iv 707 H n p in 150
Sept 3	Safe conduct till Nov 30 for Adam bp of Brechin, Walter de Moffete, and Gartenet Byset, coming as ambassadors from David de Brus These letters of safe conduct were afterwards extended until Easter, but John Heumere, lord of Wasnes, was put in place of of Ferric de Pigniac R u p n 945 O iv 707–8 H n p in 150
Sept 3	The K informs the commonalty of Bayonne that a fleet is at sea off the coast of Normandy for the purpose of assisting the Scots, and requests them to send their ship of war to join those of England. *Perth* R n. p n 946 O iv 708 H n p. in. 150
Sept. 3	The collectors of the tenth and fifteenth in Northampton are ordered to grant a respite to the inhabitants of Hoghton Parva until Feb 2 for 67s 3d at which they are assessed, as their corn and goods have been destroyed by fire *Perth* R n p n 946
Sept 28.	The constable of the Tower of London is commanded to receive John earl of Murryf, from the sheriff of Southampton, and to keep him safely in irons at the Tower *Nottingham.* R. n. p. n. 946 O iv. 708 H n p in 151.
Sept. 29.	Warrant for the payment of the arrears of the pension of 40s. a week granted to Mary countess of Fife. *Nottingham.* R. n p n 946 O. iv 709 H n p in 151
Oct 2	The K thanks Robert K. of Jerusalem and Sicily for having stopped the equipment of ships which, under colour of assisting the Holy Land, were intended to be used against England , and desires credence for Nicolin Flisco, of Genoa. *Leicester.* R n. p n 946. O. iv. 709 H n. p in. 151.
Oct. 2,	The K thanks the Genoese for having burnt certain galleys which were being prepared against him , and desires credence for Nicolin de Flisco. *Leicester.* R n p. n 946. O. iv 709 H n p in. 151.
Oct 2	Power to Nicolin de Flasco, called "cardinal of Genoa," to hire galley for the K's service *Leicester* R n p n 947 O iv 710 H n p in 151
Oct. 3	Warrant for the payment of 100l. as a gift to Edward K of Scotland for his household expenses *Leicester.* R n p n 947 O iv 710. H n p ni 151
Oct 3	The K orders Robert de Tong, receiver of his victuals at Berwick, to deliver to Edward K of Scotland wine and other victuals to the value of 100l *Nottingham.* R. n. p n. 947. O. iv. 710 H n p in 151.
Oct 4	The K orders Thomas Sampson and John Piers to consult with Henry of Canterbury and Roger de Staunford as to the questions pending in the French courts, and to report to him *Nottingham.* R n. p. n. 947.
Oct 5.	Inspeximus and confirmation of an indenture dated Perth, 12 Sept 1335, by which Edward K of Scotland grants to John de Insula the islands of Ysle, Githe, Golwouche, Mull, Skye, and Lewethy, and the moiety of the island of Dure, the lands of Kentyre, Knappedoll, Kenalhadon, and Ardinton, and the wardship of Loghaler, until the son and heir of David de Strabolgy, last earl of Athol be ot full age , in return for which he takes the oath of allegiance to the K of Scotland *Auckland.* R n, p n. 947 O iv 711. H n p in 152

DATE	SUBJECT
1336 Oct 5	The K orders the sheriff of Norfolk and Suffolk to arrest all Flemish merchants and merchandise, as English merchants have been arrested in Flanders Similar writs to the sheriffs of London and 15 counties, to the bailiffs of Great Yarmouth, Ravenserod, and the Cinque Ports, and the admirals of the fleets *Auckland* R ɪɪ p ɪɪ 948 O ɪv 711 H ɪɪ p ɪɪɪ 152
Oct 16	Nicolin de Flisco, called the "cardinal of Genoa," agrees to the sum of 8,000 marks, assigned by the K as redress for the losses of Yvan Luccan The said Nicolin on the 30th of October following came into the K 's chancery at York, and acknowledged his act and deed *Lenton* R ɪɪ p ɪɪ 948 O ɪv 712-13 H ɪɪ p ɪɪɪ 152
Oct. 18	The K requests Louis count of Flanders and Nevers to release the English merchants arrested in Flanders Similar letters to the commonalties of Bruges, Ghent, and Ypres *Auckland* R ɪɪ p ɪɪ 948 O ɪv 713-14 H ɪɪ p ɪɪɪ 152-3
Oct 20.	The K desires the seneschal of Gascony and the constable and mayor of Bourdeaux to do their utmost to preserve the rights of the duchy *Auckland* R ɪɪ p ɪɪ 949
Oct 28	The K appoints Andrew Sapiti as his proctor to assert his rights against the bishop elect of Norwich, who has gone to the apostolic see for confirmation without having obtained the royal assent *Newcastle-upon-Tyne* R ɪɪ p ɪɪ 949 O ɪv. 714 H ɪɪ p ɪɪɪ 153
Oct 28	Commission to Nicholas de Atton, the K 's chamberlain, to exhibit, copy, and make known all records necessary for the assertion of the K 's rights in the court of Rome *Newcastle-upon-Tyne* R ɪɪ p ɪɪ 949 O ɪv 714 H ɪɪ p ɪɪɪ 153
Nov 3.	K Edward requests the K of Norway to forbid his subjects letting ships to his enemies. *Newcastle* R ɪɪ. p. ɪɪ 949. O ɪv 715 H ɪɪ p ɪɪɪ 153
Nov 3	Similar letter to the count of Hainault *Newcastle-upon-Tyne*. R ɪɪ p. ɪɪ. 249. O ɪv 715 H ɪɪ p ɪɪɪ 153
[Nov 3]	Similar letter to the count of Gueldres R ɪɪ p ɪɪ 950 O ɪv 715 H ɪɪ p ɪɪɪ 153
Nov 4	Warrant for the payment to R bp of Durham of five marks a day from 12 July to 29 Sept., during which time he was on an embassy in France *Stirling* R ɪɪ p ɪɪ 950 O ɪv. 716 H ɪɪ p ɪɪɪ 153
[Nov 4]	Warrant for the payment of the money spent by him on couriers R. ɪɪ. p ɪɪ 950 O. ɪv 716. H ɪɪ. p. ɪɪɪ 154
Nov 6.	The K orders all the ships from the Thames westward to meet at Portsmouth on Dec 7 to protect the merchantmen going into Gascony. Letters to this effect are sent to Bristol and 37 other ports *Stirling* R ɪɪ p ɪɪ. 950. O ɪv 716 H. ɪɪ. p. ɪɪɪ. 154
[Nov 6]	The K orders the bailiffs of Great Yarmouth and 24 other ports to send their ships to Orwell by Dec 1 R. ɪɪ p ɪɪ 951 O. ɪv 718. H ɪɪ p ɪɪɪ 154
Nov 20	The K orders the treasurer and barons of the Exchequer in Ireland to pay 10*l* to O'Dymsy for his expenses in fighting against Lessagh O'Moyche and his accomplices *Teste Johanne Darcy, Dublin* R ɪɪ p ɪɪ 951 O ɪv 718 H ɪɪ p ɪɪɪ. 155.
Nov. 27.	Hugh de Courtenay, earl of Devon, and Philip de Columbar, wardens of the sea-coast of Devon, are directed to provide for the defence of Dartmouth and other places. *Bothwell.* R ɪɪ p ɪɪ 951
Nov 27.	The commonalty of Bayonne are ordered to send into the English sea all their ships which are fit for war, and with them the English merchant ships now at Bayonne *Bothwell.* R ɪɪ p ɪɪ 951
Nov 28	The K grants 1,000 marks to Richard earl of Arundel in recompense for the office of seneschal of Scotland, which belongs to him by hereditary right Warrant to Robert de Hambury, chamberlain of North Wales, to pay the said sum *Bothvill.* R ɪɪ. p. ɪɪ 952 O ɪv 719 H ɪɪ p ɪɪɪ 155
Dec 3	Oliver de Ingham, seneschal of Gascony, is commanded to detain all English merchant ships until the fleet is ready to start from Bayonne, and to arrest all Flemish ships *Bothwell.* R ɪɪ p ɪɪ. 952 O. ɪv. 719 H ɪɪ p ɪɪɪ 155.
Dec 3	The K cannot grant the request of J duke of Brabant to establish staples of wool in his duchy until there is safe and free access there for English merchants *Stirling* R. ɪɪ p. ɪɪ. 952 O. ɪv 720. H. ɪɪ p ɪɪɪ 155.
Dec. 4	Letters of credence to the count of Juliers for John de Frandeston, the K 's valet. *Bothwell* R. ɪɪ p ɪɪ 952. O. ɪv. 720. H. ɪɪ. p. ɪɪɪ. 155.
[Dec 4]	Credence for the same to the bishop of Liege. R. ɪɪ. p. ɪɪ 952. O. ɪv. 720. H ɪɪ. p. ɪɪɪ. 155.

DATE	SUBJECT
Dec 11.	The K deputes John archbp of Canterbury, S bp of London, John de Warenne, earl of Surrey and Sussex, Henry de Lancaster, and William de Clynton, to expound his intentions at the approaching council at London. *Bothwell* R. ii p. ii. 953 O iv 721 H ii p iii. 156
Dec. 11	The K appoints his chancellor, John archbp of Canterbury, and the four others mentioned above, to consult with the nobles and commonalties of the sea-ports from the Thames westwards, for the defence of the country against David de Bruys and his adherents, who have taken some ships near the isle of Wight, and have attacked Guernsey and Jersey. *Bothwell* R. ii p ii 953 O iv. 721. H ii p. iii 156
Dec 12	Protection for one year for William and Hanekin, weavers of Brabant, coming into England to exercise their trade at York. *Bothwell.* R ii p ii 954 O iv 723 H ii p iii 156
Dec. 13	The K desires the commonalty of Bourdeaux to prepare for the defence of the duchy, and to compose any dissensions with their fellow subjects Similar letters to Bayonne and nine other towns. The K also writes to exhort them to maintain their old fidelity. R ii p ii 954.
[Dec. 13]	The K thanks lord de la Spar for his fidelity in defending the K's rights Similar letters to the seneschal of the Landes, Arnald Edmundi, and five others R ii p ii 954
Dec 15.	The K orders the several sheriffs to proclaim that no persons are to leave the realm with ships, merchandise, or victuals, without special licence, except those bringing necessaries to him in Scotland *Bothwell* R ii p ii. 954. O iv 723 H ii p iii 156
Dec. 15.	Credence for sir John de Montgomery and John Waweyn, canon of Darlington, to the archbp of Cologne and the bp of Liege *Bothwell* R ii p ii 955 O iv 724 H ii. p iii 157
[Dec. 15.]	Credence for the same to the duke of Austria and the counts of Juliers, Hainault, and Gueldres. R ii p ii. 955 O iv 724 H ii p iii 157.
Dec 16	Power to William earl of Hainault to treat with certain nobles and other persons about entering into the K's service *Bothwell* R ii p ii 955 O iv 724. H ii p iii 157
[Dec 16]	Similar power to William count of Juliers, sir John de Montgomery, and John Waweyn R ii p. ii 955 O iv 725 H ii p iii 157.
[Dee 16]	Similar power for John de Montgomery and master John Waweyn, canon of Darlington. R ii p ii 955 O iv 725 H ii p iii 157
Dec. 22	Power to Richard de Bynteworth, professor of civil law, Paul de Monte Florum, canon of Lincoln, and John de Ragenhill, to treat with any persons for protecting ships passing between England and France. *Doncaster* R u p. ii. 956 O iv 726 H ii. p iii 157.
[Dec 22]	Power for the persons above mentioned to treat with Philip K. of France on the same subject R ii p ii 956. O iv 726 H ii p iii 157
1337 Jan. 14.	William de Montacute appointed admiral of the fleet from the Thames westward The K orders the masters and mariners of the fleet to obey him, and orders him to use all possible diligence in executing his office. *The Tower of London.* R. ii p. ii. 956. O. iv 726. R ii p iii 157
[Jan. 14]	Robert de Ufford and John de Ros, appointed admirals of the fleet north of the Thames R. ii. p ii 956 O. iv 727 H ii. p iii 158
[Jan 14]	William de Montacute is empowered to impress as many men as are required for his fleet. Similar power for Ufford and Ros R ii p ii 956. O iv 727 H ii p iii 158
Jan. 15	The K orders the prior of Ware, a foreigner, to detain the tribute due to his superior monastery, and forbids him to leave the realm Similar letters to the priors of Goldeclyve and Chepstow, and 51 other monasteries. *The Tower of London* R ii p ii 957
Jan 16	Nicholas Uso Mare appointed vice admiral of the fleet of galleys and other ships of Aquitain The K exhorts him to act with diligence, and orders the masters and mariners of the fleet to obey him *The Tower of London* R ii p ii 957. O iv 728 H ii p iii 158
Jan. 18	Power to Oberto Uso Mare, of Genoa, and Richard de Gadenton, to hire galleys and transport ships with their masters and crews for the K's service *The Tower* R ii. p. ii. 957. O iv 728. R ii p iii 158
Jan. 18.	Antonio Usomare, lieutenant of Nicholas Usomare, constable of Bourdeaux, appointed as vice-admiral of the fleet while he is absent The K orders his subjects in the duchy to obey him *The Tower of London.* R. ii. p. ii 957. O iv. 728. H ii. p. iii. 158
Jan. 24.	Warrant to the sheriff of Essex to pay to Nicholas de la Beche, constable of the Tower of London, 20s a week from Oct. 10, for the expenses of the earl of Murref, a prisoner there. *The Tower of London.* R. ii. p. ii. 958. O. iv. 958. H. ii. p iii. 159.

DATE	SUBJECT
1337 Jan 26	The mayor and bailiffs of Dover ordered to prevent all persons from leaving the country, and to arrest and send to the archbp of Canterbury all letters intended for foreign parts *The Tower of London.* R ii p ii 958 O iv. 729 H ii p iii 159
Jan 27	The prior of Blith [Blida] is ordered to deliver to William de Kelm, the K's carpenter, 40 oaks which he has provided at Kingston-on-Hull for building a galley. *Langley.* R ii p ii 958 O iv 730 H ii p iii 159
Jan 28	The sheriffs of London are ordered to deliver to Thomas de Sapleford, overseer of the works in the Tower, 5,000 of iron, 200 Eastland boards, and 100 qrs of sea-coal, for making anchors for the *Cristoffre* and the *Cogge Edward*, and for other works. *The Tower of London.* R ii p. ii. 958. O. iv. 730 H ii p iii. 159.
Jan 28	Safe conduct until Ascension Day for the ambassadors about to be sent by the K of France The keepers of the K's passage at Dover are commanded to receive them Similar letters for the ambassadors about to be sent by David de Brus from Scotland. *Langley* R ii p ii 958 O iv 730 H ii p iii 159
Feb 10	Credence to the earl of March for John de Thraudeston, the K.'s valet *London.* R ii p ii 959 O iv 731 H. ii p iii 159.
Feb 10	Credence for John de Thraudeston to the commonalty of Brussels for the purpose of establishing a staple of wool in Brabant Similar letters to the commonalties of Louvaine and Malines. *London* R ii p ii 959. O iv 731 H ii p iii. 159
March 10.	Credence to the pope for Master Bernard de Sistre *Westm* R. ii. p. ii 959. O. iv 731. H. ii p iii 159
March 14.	Benedict [XII] informs the K that he has promoted Antony [de Beck], dean of Lincoln, to the bishopric of Norwich *Avignon.* R ii p ii 959 O iv 732 H ii p iii 160
March 14	Benedict [XII] promotes Thomas de Hemenhale, monk, of Norwich, to the bishopric of Worcester, void by the translation of Simon, late bishop, to the see of Ely. *Avignon.* R ii p. ii 959 O iv 733 H ii p iii 160
March 16.	Ralph de Dacre, Peter de Tilliol, and Clement de Skelton, are commanded to ascertain the names of those persons in Eskedale, Lidelesdale, Ewithesdale, Walughopdale, and Bretellaugh, who assist his enemies. *Westm* R ii p. ii 960. O iv 734 H ii p iii 160
March 16	The K, at the parliament held at Westminster on March 1, acquits Thomas de Berkeleye of all blame for the death of the late K, his father *Westm* R. ii p ii. 960. O iv. 734. H ii p iii 161
March 16	The K. increases the allowance for the earl of Murref, a prisoner in the Tower of London, from 20s to 26s 8d a week *Westm* R ii p ii 960 O iv. 735. H ii p. iii. 161
March 17	The sheriff of Cornwall is informed that the K has granted the stannary to his eldest son, Edward duke of Cornwall, with the reservation of 1,000 marks granted to William de Montacute, earl of Salisbury *Westm* R ii p ii 961 O iv 735 H ii p iii 161
March 18.	Alfonso K of Castile is requested to forbid his subjects to trade with Flanders. *Westm* R ii p ii 961 O iv 736 H ii p ii 161
[March 18]	The K of England is glad to hear that K Alfonso intends to send ambassadors to complete the treaties between them R. ii p ii 961 O iv 736 H. ii p iii 161
[March 18]	The K of England writes on the same subjects to Ferando Rodryes, chamberlain to the K of Spain, Sancio Sanches de Royas, chief sergeant, and 5 others. R ii p. ii. 961. O iv. 737 H ii p iii 162
March 18	The treasurer and barons of the Exchequer are commanded to stay their writs to the bp. of Durham, demanding a return of those who have neglected to assume knighthood, until they have investigated the privileges which he claims. *Westm.* R ii p. ii 961 H. iv. 737. H ii p iii 162
March 20	The sheriff of Sussex is commanded to send to Nicholas de la Beche, constable of the Tower, two large oaks given by the earl of Surrey from his forest of Werch for the making of a great engine in the Tower *Westm* R. ii. p ii 962. O. iv. 738. H ii. p iii 162
March 20	The K asks the pope to grant to sir Bartholomew de Burghersh, brother of the bp of Lincoln, a dispensation from his vow to visit the Holy Sepulchre. *Westm.* R. ii p. ii. 962. O iv 738 H ii p iii 162
March 20	The K requests the pope to send letters to the clergy of the province of York, ordering the renewal of the ancient taxation, which had been suspended in consequence of the damage done by the Scots *Westm* R ii p ii 962 O iv. 739 H. ii p iii 162
March 20	The commonalty of Bayonne are requested to send 20 ships of war, their customary contribution *Westm.* R. ii p ii 963 O iv 740. H ii p iii 163.

DATE.	SUBJECT
1337 March 20.	The K appoints Berard de la Bret to reside in the castle of Blania for the purpose of defending the neighbourhood. *Westm.* R. ii p. il. 963. O iv. 740 H ii p. iii. 163.
March 20	The K declares that he will make no truce or peace without including the city of Bayonne. *Westm* R. ii p ii 963 O iv 740. H ii p iii 163.
March 20.	The K commends the fidelity of the commonalty of S. Macaire, and will attend to their petition presented by John de Navi. *Westm* R ii p ii 963 O. iv 741. H. ii p. iii. 163.
March 24.	R bp of Durham, Thomas de Beauchamp, earl of Warwick, John Darcy, steward of the household, and Geoffrey le Scrop are appointed to consult with the council to be held at York on April 6, about marching towards Scotland against the K's enemies *Westm* R ii p ii. 963 O iv 741. H ii p iii 163
March 24.	The K orders that Irishmen who are living among the English, and are faithful subjects to him, may be admitted into religious houses among the English in Ireland. *Westm* R. ii p ii. 964.
March 24.	Memorandum that John abp of Canterbury delivered the great seal to the K in the palace at Westminster, and the K transferred it to Robert de Stretford, archdeacon of Canterbury, whom he appointed chancellor R ii p. ii. 964
March 29.	Inspeximus of the confirmation by Philip K of France, dated at S Christopher en Halace 13 *April* 1337, of the article in the treaty concluded at Paris 9 March 1330, relating to the sums claimed by K Edward from the K of France. *Westm.* R ii. p. ii. 964.
March 30.	The K informs the commonalty of Bayonne that the Scotch and French are preparing a fleet against him in Normandy, though he has made offers of peace to K Philip, and he desires them to send out all their ships of war to search for the enemy's ships *Windsor.* R. ii p ii 965. O iv 742 H ii p iii 163
April 1.	The K promises indemnity to the commonalty of Bayonne for all the damages inflicted on them by French subjects *Westm* R ii p ii 965 H ii. p iii. 164
April 6.	The K orders Anthony de Lucy, justiciary of Lothian, and Thomas de Burgh, chancellor and chamberlain of Berwick-upon-Tweed, to make restitution to Geoffrey de Moubray, of Scotland, according to the conditions agreed to at Perth for the restoration of the earl of Athol. *Westm* R ii p ii. 965. O iv 743. H ii. p iii 164
April 8.	Safe conduct till the feast of S. John Baptist for lord de Rotenay, Henry de Cairs, William de Cairs, Peter de Biores, and Ivo de la Chevoie, ambassadors of John duke of Brittany and earl of Richmond *Windsor* R ii p ii 965 O iv 743 H ii p iii 164.
April 10	The K requests the pope to expedite the bulls for the translation of Simon de Montacute (brother of William de Montacute, earl of Salisbury,) from the bishopric of Worcester to that of Ely. *The Tower* R. ii p ii 966 O iv 743 H ii p iii 164
April 15	Power for H bp of Lincoln, William de Montacute, earl of Salisbury, and William de Clynton, earl of Huntingdon, to treat with the count of Flanders, and the cities of Bruges, Ghent, and Ypres Similar power to Reginald de Cobham, William Trussel, and Nicholas de la Beche. *Windsor.* R ii p. ii. 966. O iv. 744 H ii. p. iii. 164.
April 15	Power for the bp of Lincoln and his colleagues above mentioned to treat with the K's allies for establishing staples of wool Similar power to Cobham and the others. *Windsor.* R. ii p ii 966. O. iv. 745. H ii. p. iii. 165
April 18	Power for the above-named ambassadors to treat with Philip K of France about disputes relating to the duchy of Aquitain. *Windsor.* R. ii. p. ii 966 O. iv. 745. H. ii. p. iii. 165.
April 19.	Power for the same ambassadors to treat with any persons about entering into alliance with the K. *Windsor* R. ii. p ii 967. O. iv 746 H. ii. p. iii. 165.
April 19.	Power for the same to treat for a marriage between the eldest son of Louis count of Flanders and the K.'s daughter, Johanna *Windsor.* R ii p ii 967. O iv. 746 H ii. p. iii 165.
April 23.	Licence to Robert de Artoys to stay at the K's castles of Guildford, Wallingford, and Somerton, and to hunt in the K's park of Guildford. *Westm* R ii p ii. 967 O iv. 747. H. ii. p iii 195.
April 24	Protection until Aug 1 for Henry bp. of Lincoln and 30 persons going abroad in his company. *Windsor* R ii. p. ii 967. O iv. 747. H ii p. iii 166
April 24.	The collectors of the stannary in Cornwall are informed that the K. has granted to William de Montacute, earl of Salisbury, 1,000 marks a year from the revenues of the coinage. *Windsor.* R. ii. p. ii. 967. O iv. 748. H ii p. ii. 166.

T

DATE	SUBJECT.
1337. April 29	The K. grants to William de Montacute, earl of Salisbury, 5,000 marks from the issues of the coinage, by half-yearly instalments of 1,000 marks, in payment of the same sum which he has spent on the K's business *Windsor* R. ii p. ii 968 O. iv 749 H. ii p. iii 166
May 2.	The K. requests the pope not to allow A. bp of Winchester to appeal to the court of Rome for the decision of his cause against William Inge, archdeacon of Canterbury *Westm.* R. ii p. ii 968 O. iv. 749. H. ii p. iii 166
May 2.	The K. writes on the same subject to cardinal B. bp of Ostia and Veletri and 15 other cardinals *Westm* R. ii p. ii 968 O. iv. 750 H. ii p. iii 167
May 3	Protection for Leffyn de Holand, John de Hilford, and 13 other clothworkers of Zealand, coming to England *Westm.* R. ii p. ii. 969 O. iv 751 H. ii p. iii 167.
May 5	The K. grants to Robert de Artoys a pension of 1,200 marks *Dunstable* R. ii. p. ii 969 O. iv 752 H. ii p. iii 167
May 11	The K. appoints Thomas de Ferrers to array the inhabitants of Guernsey, Jersey, Sark, and Alderney which have been invaded by the adherents of the K's Scotch enemies. *York.* R. ii p. ii 969 O. iv 752 H. ii p. iii 167
May 12.	The bp of Lincoln and his colleagues retain Henry de Geldonia, canon of Cambray, for the K's service, with a pension of 100 gold florins of Florence *Valenciennes* R. ii p. ii. 969 O. iv 752 H. ii p. iii 167
May 15	The K. takes Adolph count of Monte into his service, with a pension of 1,200 gold florins of Florence *York.* R. ii p. ii 970 O. iv 753 H. ii p. iii 168
May 15	The K. grants to the count of Monte 12,000 gold florins, and 1,500 gold florins a month, for the wages of 100 men-at-arms *York* R. ii p. ii 970 O. iv. 753 H. ii p. iii. 168
May 15	Henry bp of Lincoln and his colleagues engage for the K's service lord Henry de Grauschaf and lord Arnold de Baghem, promising to each of them 400 florins *Valenciennes* R. ii p. ii 970 O. iv 754 H. ii. p. iii 168
May 24.	The ambassadors above-mentioned give licence to the counts of Hainault and Gueldres and the marquis of Juliers to levy, at the K's expense, 1,000 men-at-arms, or 2,000 if needful, for the defence of their countries against the French, at the wages of 15 florins a month R. ii p. ii 970 O. iv 755 H. ii p. iii 168
May 24	The same ambassadors also promise William de Hainault, count of Zealand, that if his father dies he may have the above-mentioned men-at-arms *Valenciennes* R. ii. p. ii. 971 O. iv. 755. H. ii p. iii 168
May 24	They also promise the same William de Hainault that all the treaties with his father shall still remain in force with him *Valenciennes* R. ii p. ii 971 O. iv 755 H. ii p. iii 168
May 24	The K. grants to Adolph count of Marha 3,000 small florins of Florence, and promises him the same wages as other lords while in his service *York* R. ii p. ii 971 O. iv 756 H. ii. p. iii 169
May 24	The K. grants to Henry de Gemenith, knt, 300 small gold florins of Florence, and promises him similar wages Similar grants to Ernest de Mulenarkin of 300 florins and to Winand de Dunzenchoyven of 400 florins *York* R. ii p. ii 971 O. iv 756 H. ii p. iii 169
May 24	Licence to the citizens of Louvain, Brussels, Antwerp, and 15 other towns subject to John duke of Lorraine, Brabant, and Lembourgh, to buy wool in England. *Everwyk* R. ii. p. ii 971. O.. iv 757. H. ii p. iii. 169
May 24.	The bp of Lincoln and his colleagues promise to the counts of Hainault and Zealand that if the K takes the towns of Crèvecuer, Allues, or S. Surpleth, he will deliver them up to the said counts. *Valenciennes.* R. ii p. ii 972 O. iv 757. H. ii p. iii. 169
May 26	The K confirms the covenant made by his ambassadors with Everhard, eldest son of Thideric count of Limburg, as to his becoming the King's vassal *Westm* R. ii. p. ii. 972. O. iv 758 H. ii p. iii 169
May 27	Henry bp. of Lincoln and his colleagues grant to William marquis of Juliers 5,000l. st., *Mons in Hainault* R. ii p. ii 972 O. iv. 759 H. ii p. iii 170
May 28	The same ambassadors grant 100 marks st. to Herman de Blankart, dean of Ays and provost of Werde. *Bintz* R. ii p. ii 973. O. iv 759 H. ii p. iii 170
June 1	The same ambassadors promise to recompense the marquis of Juliers to the amount of 1,400l. st. if the K of France confiscates his heritage or that of his mother Isabel, countess of Juliers. *Valenciennes.* R. ii p. ii. 972. O. iv 760. H. ii. p. iii 170.

DATE	SUBJECT.
1337 June 3	The K. orders Nicholas de la Beche, constable of the Tower of London, to allow Adam de Cailly (who was imprisoned in Dunbar Castle) to deliver to John Randolf, earl of Murref, a letter from his sister the countess of March, and to examine it *Staunford.* R ii p ii 973 O iv 761. H ii p iii 171
June 7.	The ambassadors of the K. of England grant to William de Dunenvorde, lord of Costerhout, 500*l* st *Brussels.* R ii p ii. 973 O iv 761. H. ii. p. iii 171.
June 8	The K. confirms the grant of 10,000*l* st made to John duke of Lorraine and Brabant by his ambassadors *Staunford* R ii p. ii 974. O iv 762 H ii p iii 171.
June 12.	The K. orders Gawan Corder, marshal of the household, to make provision of victuals at Portsmouth, where he intends to embark with his nobles for Aquitain. *Berwick.* R ii. p. ii. 974. O iv. 762 H. ii p iii. 171.
June 12	The K thanks Gerard de Spinula, marshal of the K. of Sicily, for his diligence in executing some special business Similar letters to Nicholas de Spinula and four others *Berwick* R ii. p ii 974 O iv. 763 H ii p iii 171
June 20	The K orders John de Ros, admiral of the fleet north of the Thames, to go with 40 ships to Durdraght, to convoy home the bp of Lincoln and his colleagues, the K's ambassadors. *Staunford.* R ii p ii 974 O. iv 763. H ii p. iii. 171.
June 25	Power to Oliver de Ingham, seneschal of Gascony, and John Dyens, to retain the nobles and others for the K's service Power for them to treat with lord Louis de Sanneye and Antony de Fossibus, baron of Aragon *Staunford.* R ii p ii. 975. O iv, 764. H. ii p. iii 172
June 25.	Confirmation of the engagement by Oliver de Ingham of Hugh de Geneve, lord of Vareia and Anchou, with an annual pension of 500 marks st. *Staunford* R ii p ii 975. O. iv. 765. H. ii. p. iii. 172.
June 25.	Confirmation of the engagement of John Eynard, lord of Chalanco, with an annuity of 100 marks st. *Staunford* R ii p ii 975. O iv. 765 H ii. p. iii 172
[June 25]	Confirmation of the engagement of lord Amadeus de Peyteyz, with an annuity of 100 marks st. R. ii. p ii 975 O iv. 765 H.. ii. p. iii 172.
June 25	The K thanks the viscount of Tartas, Berard de la Bret, and 66 others, for their fidelity, and desires their assistance in defending his rights Similar letters to the mayors and jurats of Bourdeaux and 20 other towns. *Staunford* R ii p ii 976 O iv 766 H ii p iii 172.
June 25.	The K writes similar letters to John de Colom and the citizens of Bourdeaux and other towns. *Staunford.* R ii p. ii. 976. O iv 767 H ii p iii 173
June 26	Grant of an annuity of 20*l.* to Joan and Eleanor, daughters of Hugh le Despenser, nuns of Sempryngham *Staunford.* R ii p. ii. 976
June 27	The K. is expecting the ambassadors of Alfonso K. of Castile, and is sorry to hear that he is engaged in war, as he desired his assistance *Staunford* R ii p ii 977. O iv. 767. H. ii p. iii. 173
June 27	The K. desires the commonalty of Bayonne to send all their ships to join his fleet under the command of Nicholas Usomare. *Staunford.* R. ii p ii. 977 O iv. 768 H. ii p. iii 173
June 27	The K. commends the conduct of the commonalty of Bourdeaux and the commonalties of Aquitain, and desires them to assist him in defending his rights against the K. of France *Staunford.* R ii p ii. 977 O iv 768 H ii p iii 173
June 27	The K orders Nicholas Usomare, vice-admiral of the fleet of Aquitain, to put to sea and destroy all hostile ships in the ports of Normandy and elsewhere *Staunford.* R. ii. p. ii. 977. O iv. 769 H ii. p ii. 173.
June 27.	The K commends the viscount of Tartas, and desires the continuance of his fidelity *Staunford.* R ii p ii 978. O. iv 769. H. ii. p. iii 174
[June 27]	Similar letters to John Colom and seven other citizens of Bourdeaux, 12 citizens of Bayonne, six of S Sever, eight of Solers, and five of Dax R ii p ii 978 O. iv. 770 H ii p. iii. 174
June 27.	Similar letter to John Dyet, knt. *Staunford* R ii p ii 978. O iv 770. H ii p. iii. 174.
June 27.	Also to Hugh de Gavadon, knt , William Amaneni, knt , Gerald de Puteo, clerk, and four others. *Staunford* R ii. p. ii 978. O iv 770 H ii p iii 174
[June 27.]	Credence for the seneschal of Gascony to Guitard de Lebret, viscount of Tartas R ii p ii 979. O. iv 771 H ii. p iii 174

DATE.	SUBJECT.
1337 June 27	The K thanks Bertrand Ferandi for his diligence in executing the K's business in Spain, and desires his assistance in maintaining his rights in Aquitain *Staunford* R II p II 979. O IV 772 H II p III 174
[June 27]	The K. desires the assistance of Fortinarius de Lescun in maintaining his rights in Aquitain R. II p II 979. O IV 772 H II p III 175.
June 27	The K retains Rodulph lord of Haut Ville as an officer of his wardrobe. *Staunford.* R. II p II 979 O IV 772 H II p III 175
June 28	Richard bp of Durham, William la Zousche, dean of York, the K's treasurer, Thomas de Beauchamp, earl of Warwick, Henry de Percy, Ralph de Nevill, and Geoffrey le Scrof, are deputed by the K to inform the parliament about to be held at York of what has been determined by the council for the defence of the kingdom against the Scots, and to make any further arrangements *Stamford* R II p II 979 O IV 772. H. II p III 175
June 30	Henry bp of Lincoln and his colleagues engage Rupert count palatine of the Rhine and duke of Bavaria to serve the K with 150 men-at-arms, promising him 15,000 florins, and 15 florins a month for each man *Frankfort* R. II. p II 979 O IV. 773. H. II p III 175
June 30.	The same ambassadors also promise to Rupert count palatine 16,000 gold florins, beside his wages, to be paid at Michaelmas *Frankfort* R II p II. 980 O IV 774. H II p III 175
June 30.	The same ambassadors retain Marqua de Randegg as one of the K's councillors with an annuity of 150 florins *Frankfort.* R. II. p II 980. O IV 774. H. II p. III. 175.
July 1.	The K desires the count of Geneve and 19 others to enter into alliance with him. *Staunford.* R II p II. 980 O IV 775 H II p III 176
[July 1.]	The K makes a similar request to Louis de Savoy R II. p II 981 O. IV. 775. H II p III 176
[July 1.]	The K thanks Berard de Lebret for his services R. II p II. 981 O IV 776 H. II. p III 175.
[July 1]	The K is glad to hear that Hugh de Geneva, lord of Varrays, has entered into an alliance with Oliver de Ingham, on his behalf Similar letters to Amadeus de Peytters and John Eynard, lord of Chalanco R II p II 981 O IV 776 H II p II 176
[July 1.]	Similar letter to Antony de Fossibus, of Aragon R II p. II 981. O IV 776 H II. p. III 176
July 1.	Obligation for 60,000*l* to the duke of Brabant. *Staunford.* R. II. p II. 981 ¦O IV 777. H II p III 176
July 1	The K orders John de Molyns, and two others, to seize all priories, benefices, and other property in Holderness, in co York, belonging to subjects of the K. of France, (Bretons only excepted,) leaving them sufficient for their sustenance Similar commission to the same in the Isle of Wight, and another commission for all priories in England, Wales, and Ireland. *Staunford* R II p II 982 O IV 779 H. II p III 177
July 3.	Henry bp of Lincoln and his colleagues retain the services of Nicholas de Dordraco, clerk of the count of Hainault, with an annuity of 100 fl *Frankfort* R II p II 982. O IV 779 H II. p. III 177
July 7.	The same ambassadors retain Robert de Tonbourgh, lord of Vernich, promising him 3,000 florins *Brussels.* R II p. II 982 O. IV. 779. H. II. p. III 177
July 7	They also receive the fealty of the said Robert de Toubourgh, and promise him an annuity of 300 "regales aureos" *Brussels* R. II. p. II. 983 O. IV. 780 H. II p II 178
July 7.	Engagement for the K's services of Walran de Steyne, Lambert Deppy, Philip de Kenteny, and Craye de Hofstat, who have sworn fealty to the K. *Brussels* R II p. II 983 O IV 780 H II p II 178
July 10.	Promise of 2,700 fl to Rupert count palatine of the Rhine, on certain conditions *Cologne* R II p II 983 O IV 781 H II p. III. 178.
July 10	Theobald Russel is appointed captain of the men of the Isle of Wight. The K orders the wardens of the coast, and the arrayers of the Isle of Wight, and the sheriff of Southampton to assist him *The Tower of London.* R II p II 983 O IV. 781. H. II. p III 178.
July 10	The castles in South and North Wales are to be put in a state of defence *Westm.* R. II. p II 984 O IV 782 H II p III 178.
July 12	Treaty with William count of Hainault, who promises to assist the K. of England against France. *Staunford.* R. ii. p. ii 984. O iv. 783 H. II. p III. 179.

DATE	SUBJECT.
1337. July 12.	The K. confirms the covenant made by his ambassadors with Renant count of Gueldres and William marquis of Juliers. *Stamford.* R. ıı p. ıı. 985. O ıv 785. H. ıı. p ıı. 179
July 13	Treaty with John duke of Lorraine, Brabant, and Lembourgh, who will serve the K , when he has crossed the sea, with 1,200 men *Stamford.* R ıı. p. ıı. 985. O. ıv. 785 H. ii. p. ııı 180
July 13.	John Quatremars ıs retained for the K's service, with 10 men-at-arms *Ruremunde.* R ıı p ıı 985 O ıv 786 H. ıı. p. ııı. 180.
July 13	Hugh le Despenser and Gilbert Talebot appointed captains of the men of South Wales *The Tower of London.* R u p ıı 985 O ıv. 787 H ıı p ııı 180
July 13	The K. orders Henry earl of Derby to arm his tenants in Kedewelly, Grosemund, Skenefrith, and Bergevenny, in S. Wales Similar letters to John de Mowbray, lord of Gower, Alice de Lascy, countess of Lıncoln, lady of Builth, and 13 others, ın S Wales R ıı p ıı 986. O. ıv 787 H u p ııı 180
July 19.	The bp. of Lincoln and his colleagues empower William marquis of Juliers to raise 400 men-at-arms at the K. ın the K's expense R u p ıı. 986. O ıv 788 H ıı p ııı, 181.
July 23.	Philip de Thame, prior of the hospital of St. John of Jerusalem, summoned to appear before the K on Nov 12. to answer for having sent money out of the kingdom. *Westm.* R ıı p ıı 986 O ıv 789 H ıı p ııı 181
July 24.	The K orders Robert de Wardecop, his clerk, to restore the lands or goods which he has seized belonging to Isabella lady of Mota, now residing with his daughter Joan and Mary de St. Paul countess of Pembroke. *Westm* R. ıı. p. ıı. 987. O ıv. 790. H. ıı p. ııı. 182.
July 25	Notarıal attestation of the renunciation by Thomas bp. of Worcester of all words prejudicial to the K. ın the papal bulls relating to the restitution of the temporalties. *The Tower of London* R ıı. p. ıı. 987. O. ıv 790 H ıı p ııı 182.
July 28.	Peter Hayward and Thomas de St. Nicholas are commanded to be more diligent in arraying the men of the hundred of Ryngeslow ın the Isle of Thanet, and also to compel religious persons, as well as others, to find men. *Westm.* R, ıı. p. ıı. 987. O ıv. 791. H ıı p. ııı 182.
Aug. 1.	The K orders William Fraunk and Reginald de Donyngton to deliver a ship to William de la Pole of Kingston-on-Hull and Reginald de Conductu, for the purpose of exporting 30,000 sacks of wool. Similar letter to the mayor and sheriffs of London *Clarendon.* R. ıı p ıı 988
Aug 3	Warrant to the treasurer of Dublın to pay the wages of 200 Welsh foot-soldiers who are goıng to Ireland under the command of John de Cherleton, senıor, justıcıary *Clarendon.* R. ıı p. ıı. 988.
Aug 11	Walter de Manny appoınted admıral of the fleet from the Thames northward The K. orders the masters and marıners of the fleet to obey hım, and orders hım to execute his office with dilıgence. *The Tower of London* R ıı p. ıı 988 O. ıv 792. H ıı. p ııı 182
[Aug 11]	Bartholomew de Burghersh ıs appointed admiral of the fleet from the Thames westward R. ıı p ıı 988 O ıv 792. H. ıı. p nı 182.
Aug 12	Protection for John Junensan, baılıff of the duke of Brıttany, at hıs manors of Bassingbourne and Munden *The Tower of London.* R. ıı. p ıı. 989. O. ıv. 792. H ıı. p ııı 182
Aug. 16.	Letters of ındemnıty for the merchants who have bought 30,000 sacks of wool for the K , for whıch they have gıven obligations to the amount of 200,000*l. Westm.* R. ıı. p. ıı 989.
Aug 20	The K promises not to deliver to the emperor the treaties between himself and the duke of Lorraine, and to make neither truce nor peace without the consent of the said duke of Lorraine. *Westm.* R ıı p ıı. 989. O ıv. 793. H ıı. p. iii. 183.
Aug 21.	In consequence of the invasion of the Channel Islands and duchy of Aquitan by the French, the K. orders all ecclesiastical and lay persons throughout the realm to meet at certain places on Sept. 15, for the purpose of being ınformed of his intentions. *Westm.* R ıı p ıı. 989. O. ıv. 793. H ıı. p. ııı 183
Aug 21	The K desıres the archbps. and bishops of England to summon convocations of the clergy of their respective dioceses for the purpose of granting hım a subsidy. *Westm.* R. ıı, p. ıı, 990. O. ıv, 794. H. ıı, p, ııı. 183.

DATE	SUBJECT
1337. Aug 21	The K deputes J archbp of Canterbury and William de Clynton, earl of Huntingdon, to explain the decision of the council at Westminster to the inhabitants of Kent assembled at Rochester on Sept 14. *Westm.* R. ii. p ii 990. O iv. 795. H ii p. iii. 184
Aug 26	The K forbids any appeals or processes to be made against the collation of William de Kildesly to the prebend of Castre in the see of Lincoln *Westm* R. ii p ii 990 O iv 796. H ii p iii 184.
Aug. 26.	The K. orders William de Shareshull and the other justices of assize in the counties of Gloucester, Hereford, Worcester, Shropshire, and Stafford to postpone all assizes of novel disseisin against John de Cherleton, senior, whom the K. has appointed justiciary of Ireland. *Westm.* R. ii p ii 991 O iv 797 H. ii p iii 184
Aug. 26.	The K offers alliance to the Emperor Louis *Westm* R ii. p. ii 991. O iv. 798. H ii p iii 184.
[Aug. 26.]	The K engages to pay 300,000 gold florins to the emperor, who has promised to assist him with 2,000 men R ii p ii 991 O iv 799 H ii p iii. 185
Aug 26	The K grants 30,000 gold florins to Theodoric count of Los and Hensebergh and lord Blankenbergh, who has engaged to serve him with 200 men at 15 florins each a month. *Westm.* R. ii p ii 992. O. iv. 799. H. ii p iii 185.
Aug. 26.	Engagement of Theodoric lord of Montyoie and Valkenborgh, with 100 men at arms *Westm* R ii p ii. 992 O iv 800 H ii p iii 185
Aug 26.	Ratification of the covenants made by Henry bp. of Lincoln and his colleagues *Westm.* R ii p ii 992 O iv. 801 H. ii p iii 186
Aug. 26	Similar ratification of other covenants made by them *Westm.* R ii p ii 993 O iv 801 H. ii p iii 186
Aug 27	The K. having received the homage of Corrard de Ash, Corrard de Lyseny, John de Bosenham, Winmer de Gomeny, and William de Urley, grants to each of them 500 florins, and admits Geoffrey de Bergh as his special knight *Westm* R ii p ii 993 O. iv 802. H ii p iii 186
Aug 28	The K desires the alliance of Peter K. of Aragon *Westm* R ii p ii 993. O iv 802. H ii p iii 186.
Aug 28	Protection until Easter for Peter Burgundion, chaplain and nuncio of the pope. *Westm* R. ii p. ii 993 O iv 803 H. ii. p iii 186
Aug 28	The K desires Robert de Hambury, chamberlain of North Wales, and Richard de Welles, chamberlain of South Wales, to array the 1,000 Welshmen whom he has ordered to be sent to Canterbury by Michaelmas in tunics and mantles of similar cloth *Westm* R. ii. p. ii. 993 O. iv 803 H ii. p iii 186.
Aug 28	The archbp of Canterbury and William de Clynton, earl of Huntingdon, are commanded to inform the men of Kent of the offers made by the K. of England to the K of France for the purpose of avoiding war, viz, the marriage of his eldest son, his sister, or his brother, a reasonable sum of money, and his assistance in a crusade, but the K. of France has not accepted them, has assisted the Scots, and invaded Aquitain Similar commissions are issued for 34 other counties R. ii p. ii 994 O iv. 804 H. ii p. iii 187
Sept 1.	The K informs the pope that Paul de Monte Florum has resigned, by the K's permission, the prebend of Bannebury, to which the K had collated him, as the pope had presented another person, and that he never had the money for the pope which he is supposed to have received *Westm* R. ii p. ii 995. O iv 807 H. ii p iii 188
Sept 2	Letters patent by which the K promises to fulfil all the obligations entered into by Henry bp of Lincoln and his colleagues. *The Tower of London.* R ii p ii 995 O. iv. 807. H. ii. p. iii 188.
[Sept. 2]	Similar letter of indemnity for William de Montacute, earl of Salisbury R ii. p ii 995. O iv. 807. H. ii p. iii. 188.
Sept 2	Confirmation of the engagement of Lambert and Everard de Heynesbergh for the King's service *Westm.* R. ii. p. ii. 995. O. iv. 808. H ii. p. iii. 188
[Sept 2.]	Confirmation of the agreement with Louis marquis of Brandenburg, count palatine of the Rhine, duke of Bavaria, and chief chamberlain of the empire. R. ii p ii 996. O iv. 808. H ii p iii 189.
Sept 2	The K desires Otto and Albert, dukes of Austria, to excuse the delay of their ambassador, Henry Gaseler, knt, and the king's daughter, Isabella, as the sea is infested with pirates. *The Tower of London* R. ii. p. ii. 996. O. iv. 809. H. ii. p. iii. 189

DATE.	SUBJECT.
1337. Sept. 4	The K. orders Bartholomew de Insula and the other wardens of the coast of Southampton to prepare beacons to be lighted on the approach of an enemy. Similar letters to Hugh Courtenay, earl of Devon, and John de Beauchamp of Somerset *Woodstock.* R. ii p. ii 996.
Sept. 18.	The mayors and bailiffs of Sandwich and four other ports are commanded to receive Reginald count of Gueldres, and inform the K of his arrival *Woodstock.* R. ii. p. ii 996. O. iv. 809. H. ii. p. iii, 189
Sept 20	Warrant for the payment of 100*l* to Eustace Piscair, knt of Flanders. *The Tower of London* R. ii p ii 997 O iv 810 H ii. p iii 189
Sept 24.	Sir John de Langeton and others, arrayers in South Wales, are informed that the K has postponed his expedition, and that their compliment of 500 men must be ready to come to Canterbury at 12 days' notice. Similar letter to the arrayers of North Wales. *The Tower of London.* R. ii p ii. 997 O iv 810 H. ii. p. iii 189.
Oct. 3	Protection for William de Bohun, earl of Northampton, and for John FitzWauter, and 63 others, who are going in the earl of Northampton's company across the sea in the K's service. *Westm.* R ii p ii 997 O iv 811. H. ii p iii 189
Oct. 3.	Power to Henry bp. of Lincoln, William de Bohun, earl of Northampton, Robert de Ufford, earl of Suffolk, and John Darcy, steward of the household, to treat of perpetual peace with the K of France. Another commission adding a clause for treating for a truce R. ii p ii 998. O. iv 812 H. ii p iii 190
Oct 3.	Power for the same persons, and Richard de Wynkele, provincial of the Friars Preachers, John de Ufford, canon of London, Paul de Monte Florum, sir John de Montgomery, and John Wauwayn, canon of Darlington, to treat with the French king. They are also empowered to treat with David de Bruys. *Westm* R ii p ii. 998. O. iv. 812. H ii p iii 190
[Oct. 3.]	Power for the same persons to treat with the King's allies about establishing a staple of wool. R. ii p. ii 998. O iv 813 H ii p iii. 190.
Oct 3	Power to the same to treat with Louis count of Flanders about a marriage between his eldest son and the K.'s daughter Joan. *Westm.* R. ii. p. ii. 998. O. iv 813. H ii p iii. 190.
Oct. 3	Power for the same to treat with the count of Flanders and the commonalties of Bruges, Ghent, and Ypres *Westm* R. ii. p ii 999 O iv 814 H ii p iii. 191.
[Oct 3]	Power for the same to make alliance with any persons whomsoever. R. ii. p ii. 999 O iv 815 H ii p iii. 191.
[Oct. 3.]	Power for the same to treat with the emperor Louis. R. ii. p. ii 999 O. iv. 815 H ii p iii 191.
[Oct 3]	Power to the same to grant lands belonging to the K in reality or in expectation to such persons as they think fit R ii p ii 999 O iv. 815. H. ii. p iii 191
[Oct 3]	Power for the same to grant money R ii p ii. 1000. O iv 816 H ii p iii 191
Oct 4	The K grants to Theoderic Pytan, chamberlain of the archbp of Cologne, an annuity of 300 florins of Florence; also an annuity of 400 florins to Robert de Foresta. R. ii p. iii 1,000 O iv 816–17. H ii. p iii. 192.
Oct. 4	The K grants annuities of 600 florins to John Moyllard, provost of Arnheim [Arnham], Herman Blackard, dean of Dax and provost of Werde, and Renard de Ghore, canon of Liege. *Westm.* R. ii p ii. 1000 O iv. 817. H ii p iii 192.
Oct 6	Power for Richard bp of Durham and others to explain the K's intentions to his subjects in the north, and to treat with them about occupying the K.'s dominions in Scotland. *Westm* R ii p ii 1000 O iv. 817 H ii p. iii 192
Oct 7	Commission to John duke of Brabant and Lorraine to take possession of the kingdom of France in the K.'s name. Similar commissions to William marquis of Juliers, the count of Hainault, and William de Bohun, earl of Northampton *Westm* R ii p ii 1000. O iv 818. H. ii p iii 192
Oct. 6.	The K. appoints the duke of Brabant his lieutenant and vicar-general in France Similar commissions to the marquis of Juliers, the count of Hainault, and the earl of Northampton R ii p ii 1001 O iv 818 H ii p iii 192. These commissions are in duplicate, one set styling K. Edward "Rex Angliæ et Franciæ," and the other "Rex Franciæ et Angliæ"
Oct 7.	The K desires all Frenchmen to obey the duke of Brabant as himself Similar letters for the others named above R ii p ii. 1001. O iv. 819. H ii p iii 193
Oct 7.	Power to the bp of Lincoln and his colleagues to treat with David de Bruys for a truce or peace *The Tower of London.* R ii p ii 1001 O iv 820 H. ii. p. iii 193.

DATE	SUBJECT
1337 Oct 7	The K again excuses his delay in sending his daughter Joan to Otho and Albert, dukes of Austria *Westm.* R. ii. p. ii. 1001 O iv 820. H. ii p. iii 193.
Oct 7	Credence for Henry bp. of Lincoln, the earls of Northampton and Suffolk, and John Darcy, to P cardinal of S Praxedis and P cardinal of S Mary *in Aquiro* *Westm* R. ii p ii 1002 O iv 821 H ii p iii 193.
[Oct 7]	Credence for the same to Guido de S Germain, chaplain of the pope, Peter Burgundionis, and Nicholas de Capucio R ii p ii. 1002 O. iv. 821. H ii p iii 193.
Oct 7	The K appoints Thomas Powys warden of his hall at Cambridge, and grants to the hall the advowson of the church of S Peter, Northampton, and of the chapels thereto annexed *The Tower of London* R ii p ii 1002. O iv 821. H ii p iii. 193.
Oct 15	Safe conduct for Peter cardinal of S Praxedis and Bertrand cardinal of S Mary *in Aquiro* *Westm* R ii p ii. 1002 O iv 822. H. ii. p iii 194
Oct. 15.	Safe conduct until Feb 2 for Alexander de Seton and Lawrence de Preston, who are coming to London *Westm.* R ii p ii. 1003 O iv 823. H ii p iii. 194.
Oct 15	Power to Richard earl of Arundel and William de Montacute, earl of Salisbury, to treat for a truce with the Scots. *Westm* R ii p ii 1003 O iv 823 H ii p iii 194.
Oct. 15	Power for the same commissioners to treat for a final peace *Westm.* R ii p ii 1003 O iv 824 H ii p iii 194
Oct. 15.	Power for the same commissioners to receive into the K's peace those Scotch who have not adhered to his enemies *Westm* R ii p ii 1003 O iv 824. H ii p iii. 195
Oct. 16	The K requests the pope to confirm his grant to his hall in Cambridge university. *Westm.* R ii p ii 1003 O iv 825 H ii p iii. 195
Oct. 16	The K writes on the same subject to the bps of Palestrina and Albano and the cardinal of S Adrian *Westm* R ii p ii 1004 O iv 825 H. ii p iii 195.
Oct. 17.	The K explains to the pope why he has declared war on the K of France, and entered into alliance with the emperor *Westm.* R ii. p ii. 1004 O iv. 826. H. ii. p iii 195.
Oct. 17	The K has received the letters of the cardinals of S Praxedis and S. Mary *in Aquiro*, and sends them letters of safe conduct *Westm* R ii p ii 1004 O. iv 827. H. ii. p iii 196.
Nov 1	Geoffrey le Scrop and five others are appointed to treat with the convocation of the clergy at York on Nov. 12 about granting a subsidy. *Thame.* R ii p ii 1005 O iv. 827. H ii p ii 196.
Nov. 2.	The K congratulates the commonalty of Bayonne on their victory at sea, and informs them that six ships of their fellow citizens have been arrested for dealing with the enemy, but he has caused them to be liberated *Thame* R. ii. p ii. 1005. O iv 828, H ii p iii 196.
Nov. 14.	The sheriff of Essex is ordered to pay the arrears due to Nicholas de la Beche, constable of the Tower, for the expenses of the earl of Murref. *Querendon.* R. ii. p ii 1005. O. iv. 828. H. ii p iii 196
Nov 24.	The K orders Walter de Manny, admiral of the northern fleet, to put to sea and attack his enemies, if he thinks it advisable, but to return to Orewell or Sandwich in three weeks. *Querendon* R ii p ii 1005. O iv. 829 H ii p iii 196.
[Nov 24.]	The sheriff of Norfolk and Suffolk is commanded to supply Walter de Manny with victuals for three weeks, and if he cannot provide a sufficient quantity, the sheriff of Essex is to procure the remainder. R. ii p ii 1006 O iv 830 H. ii. p. iii. 197.
Nov. 27.	The collectors of the tenth and fifteenth in Cambridgeshire are ordered to pay 40l. to Thomas Powys, master of the K's scholars in Cambridge university. *Querendon.* R. ii. p ii 1006. O iv 830 H. ii p iii. 197.
Nov. 29.	The K orders William de Clynton, earl of Huntingdon, constable of Dover castle and warden of the Cinque Ports, to receive the papal nuncios *Reading.* R ii. p ii 1006. O iv 831 H ii p iii 197
Dec 3.	Safe conduct till Whitsuntide for John de Insulis, who is coming to England. *Aldermarston* R ii p ii 1006 O. iv 831 H ii p iii 197.
Dec. 4.	Power to William de Montacute, earl of Salisbury, to treat with John de Insulis. *Reading.* R ii p ii 1006 O iv 831 H ii p iii 197.
Dec 20	General summons to the clergy of England to the parliament to be held at Westminster, on Feb. 3. *Westm* R. ii p. ii 1007. O. iv. 832. H ii. p iii. 197.

DATE	SUBJECT
1337. Dec 24.	In consequence of the mediation of the papal nuncios, the K. promises not to invade France before March 1, and has forbidden any attack to be made upon the French by sea or land from Jan. 6 until that date. *Guildford.* R II. p. II. 1007 O IV 833. H II p III. 198.
1338. Jan 2.	The abp of Dublin is ordered to allow the cross to be carried before the abp of Armagh, when he attends the parliament at Dublin on Jan 14 *Bukeden* R II. p II 1007 O. IV. 833 H. II p III 198
Jan 3.	The K writes on the same subject to the sheriffs and his other bailiffs in Ireland. *Bukeden.* R II. p II 1007 O IV. 834 H. II p III. 198
Jan. 3.	Warrant for the payment of 20l. to Edward K. of Scotland, or his clerk, Ralph de Malton *The Tower of London* R II p II 1008 O. IV 834 H II. p III 198
Jan. 3	Protection for the galleys of John de Aurea and Nicholas Blancus, which the K. sends to scour the sea towards Scotland. *The Tower of London* R II. p II. 1008. O IV 835. H II. p III 199
Jan. 4.	Protection for certain servants of the cardinal of S. Mary in *Aquiro* whom he sends to Aquitain to buy wine *The Tower of London* R II. p II. 1008 O IV 835. H II p III. 199.
Jan. 4	Roger Norman and Collard Mundenard, of Southampton, are ordered to restore the goods of John Gomyz, who was sent by the K of Spain with letters for the K of England. *The Tower of London.* R II p II 1008 O IV. 835 H II p. III 199.
[Jan. 4]	The K. writes on the same subject to the mayor and bailiffs of Southampton. R. II p. II. 1008. O. IV 835. H. II. p. III 199.
Jan. 4.	The K orders the seneschal of Gascony to compensate the viscount of Tartas for his losses out of the goods of the K's enemies confiscated in the duchy *The Tower of London* R II p. II 1009. O IV 836 H II p III. 199
Jan. 5	Power to Oliver de Ingham, seneschal of Gascony, to treat with John Eximini de Urrea. *The Tower of London* R II p II 1009. O IV 837 H II p III. 199
Jan. 5.	The K orders proclamation to be made at the Cinque Ports, Great Yarmouth, and S Botulph's, that no attempts are to be made against the French until March 1. *The Tower of London* R II p. II 1009. O. IV. 837. H II p III 200
Jan. 6.	The K thanks Raimund Corneln, lord of Arbertha and " Castrum Asinorum," (?) for his offer to assist the K. in a war to maintain his rights. *The Tower of London.* R II p II. 1009. O IV 838. H II p III 200
Jan. 7.	The K desires Mary Q of Castile to urge her husband to send ambassadors to complete the negotiations already commenced. *The Tower of London.* R. II p II 1010 O. IV. 839. H II p III. 201.
Jan. 8.	The K. writes on the same subject to Alfonso K of Castile. *The Tower of London.* R. II. p. II 1010. O. IV. 839. H. II p II 200.
Jan. 8.	The K of England states that he does not wish the subjects of K Alfonso, who trade with Flanders, to be injured by the English, but he warns Alfonso that it is dangerous for his subjects to trade with the Flemings *The Tower of London.* R II. p. II. 1010. O. IV. 839 H II p III 200.
Jan. 8.	The K desires Ferrando Rodriges, chamberlain of the K. of Spain, and five others, to persuade him to complete the negotiations. *The Tower of London* R II p II 1010. O IV 840 H. II p II 201
Jan 8	Credence for Arnald de Duro Forti, knt., going to Robert K. of Jerusalem and Sicily, and to Alfonso K. of Castile. *The Tower of London* R II p II 1011 O IV 841. H. II. p III 201.
[Jan. 8]	Credence for Arnald de Duro Forti going to the Q of Sicily. R. II. p. III. 1011. O IV. 841. H. II p III 201.
[Jan 8]	Credence for him going to the duchess of Durache R. II p II. 1011. O IV 841. H II. p III 201.
[Jan 8]	Credence for him going to Charles duke of Durache. R. II p II 1011. O IV 841. H II p III. 201
Jan 8	Credence for Nicholas Usomare, constable of Bourdeaux, going to Guirard, Nicholas, and Frederick Spinula, of Luculo, and seven others. *The Tower of London.* R II p. II. 1011. O IV 842 H II p. III 201
Jan 8	The K desires the commonalty of Genoa to stop the sailing of certain galleys, which have been equipped for his enemies. *The Tower of London.* R. II. p. II. 1011 O. IV. 842. H II. p. III 201.

DATE	SUBJECT
1338 Jan 8	Power to Nicholas Usomare, constable of Bourdeaux, to treat with Yvano Luciani concerning the redress he seeks for his ship, plundered by Hugh le Despenser in the reign of Edw II *The Tower of London.* R ii p ii 1011. O iv 842. H ii p. iii 201
Jan 8	The K desires lord de la Brette to treat with his brother, the viscount of Tartas, and the seneschal of Gascony, about confirming their alliance with the K *The Tower of London.* R ii p ii 1012 O iv 843 H ii p iii 202.
Jan 8	Credence for Arnald de Duro Forti, knt, going to Oliver de Ingham, seneschal of Gascony, John de Norwich, John de Insula, mayor of Bourdeaux, Fortunarius de Lescun, seneschal of the Landes [Laudarum], Bernard de Bearne, called "Lespoya," and the mayor and commonalty of Bayonne *The Tower of London.* R ii p ii 1012 O. iv. 843. H ii p iii 202
Jan. 10	The K desires the viscount of Benanges, and lords de Rosan and de Laudinas, to maintain their fidelity to him *The Tower of London* R ii. p ii 1012 O iv. 844 H ii p iii. 202.
Jan 10	The K desires William de Clynton, earl of Huntingdon, constable of Dover and warden of the Cinque Ports, to allow the messengers of the papal nuncios to leave the kingdom. *Hertford.* R ii p ii 1012 O iv 844 H ii p iii 202
Feb 12	Warrant to the constable of Bourdeaux to pay to the Friars Minors of S. Macaire 20s " Chipotenses " [viginti solidos Chipotenses] for one repast every week, granted to them by Edward I and Elianor his queen *Westm.* R ii. p. ii 1012 O v 1 H ii p. iv. 3
Feb 16	The K orders the collectors of the scutage, granted 1 Edw III, to defer levying it until they have further orders *Westm.* R ii p ii 1013
Feb 17	The K requests the pope to grant a dispensation to Edward de Leteham, of Scotland, and Joan de Clifford, of England, who, being of the third and fourth degree of affinity, have clandestinely contracted marriage. *Westm.* R ii. p ii 1014 O v 2 H ii p iv. 3
Feb 22	The K appoints Henry Darcy, mayor of London, and certain knights and others in 34 counties, to keep the peace during his absence, and orders them to attend at the council at Westminster at the close of Easter *Westm.* R ii p. ii. 1013
Feb 24	Prorogation of the truce with France until the Feast of S John the Baptist *Westm.* R ii p ii 1014 O v 3 H. ii. p iv 4
Feb 24	Bartholomew de Burghersh, admiral of the fleet from the Thames westward, is commanded to provide ships at Orwell by a fortnight after Easter, for the passage of the K to the continent. Similar commission to Walter de Manny, admiral of the northern fleet, to provide ships at Great Yarmouth, and writs to the sheriffs of the maritime counties to assist them. R ii p ii. 1015 O v. 4 & 5 H ii p iv 4
Feb 24	Similar writs to the mayor and bailiffs of Southampton and the bailiffs of Caermarthen and other ports *Westm* R. ii. p ii 1015. O. v 5 H ii p iv 4
[Feb 24]	Similar writs to Edward duke of Cornwall, John de Moubray, lord of Gower, and Hugh le Despenser, lord of Glamorgan and Morgannowe , also writs to the bailiffs of Yarmouth, &c , to assist Walter de Manny R ii. p. ii. 1015. O. 5. H ii p. iv. 4.
Feb 25	The K orders the sheriffs of Kent, Surrey, Sussex, and Southampton to furnish the admirals above-mentioned with the necessary fittings for the transport of horses. *Westm.* R ii p ii 1015 O v 6 H ii p iv 7
Feb 25.	The K orders John de Warenne, earl of Surrey, lord of Broomfield and Yale, to send 50 archers and 50 spearmen by a month after Easter Similar letters to Richard earl of Arundel, lord of Osewaldestre, Chirke, and Clonne, John de Cherleton, senior lord of Powys, William earl of Salisbury, lord of Dynebegh, Roger de Grey, lord of Deffrencloyd, and Hugh Tyrrel, warden of Radenore, Kery, and Werth Eynon, for 400 men R ii p ii 1016 O v 7 H. ii p iv 5
Feb 26	Similar writs to Henry de Lancaster, earl of Derby, lord of Kedwelly and Carnwathlan, and 11 other lords in South Wales, for 950 men *Westm.* R. ii. p ii. 1016
Feb 26	John de Langeton, William Broun, John de Avene, Howel ap Howell, Griffin Dun, and John Norreys, are commanded to muster and bring to Ipswich the men furnished by the lords of South Wales The justiciary of South Wales is commanded to assist them. R ii p. ii 1017.
Feb 28	The K orders Fulco FitzWaryn, John de Cherleton, junior, sir Robert de Harleye, and Griffin Cragh, to array and conduct the men from North Wales mentioned in document dated 25 Feb *Westm* R ii p ii 1017 O. v 8. H ii p iv 5
Feb 28	Warrant to Robert de Hambury, chamberlain of North Wales, to pay the wages of the 700 men (500) from North Wales Similar warrant for 200 men from the county of Chester R. ii p ii 1017. O v 9. H. ii. p iv 6

DATE.	SUBJECT
1338 March 1.	Richard de Taleworth and others are ordered to send 40 archers to Portsmouth by a fortnight after Easter, in addition to the 80 he has already ordered to be sent to Norwich. Similar writs sent to 14 other counties for 300 archers, in addition to the 755 previously ordered. R. u. p ii 1018
March 3.	The K orders Edmund de Bereford, his clerk, to pay 50*l* to Isabella Seneschal [? Stewart], countess of Mar, the arrears of her pension *Westm* R ii p ii 1019 O v 9. H ii p iv 6.
March 3.	The K., at the petition of Matilda countess of Ulster, whose husband has been killed by felons in Ireland, and who dares not return thither, takes into his possession her lands, and he will assign her lands of equal value in England, and grants her an annuity of 200 marks. Warrant to the treasurer for the payment of 100 marks for Easter next R ii p ii 1019. O v. 9 H ii p iv. 6.
March 3	The K orders those Englishmen who have castles and fortresses in Ireland to reside there, for their safe keeping *Westm* R ii p ii. 1019
March 3.	The K. informs the justiciary of Ireland that the justices of the common pleas in Ireland are in future to be Englishmen, and orders him to send word who are fit to fill the office. *Westm* R. ii p ii 1019
March 3.	The K desires the emperor Lous to grant the title of king to Imbert, dauphin of Vienna *Westm* R ii. p ii. 1019 O. v 10 H ii p iv. 6
March 4.	Credence for Radulph, joint lord of Haute Ville, and Friar Geoffrey de Maldon, going to Imbert, dauphin of Vienna *Westm* R. ii p 1020 O v 10 H ii p iv 6
March 4	Power to Hugh de Jabennis [Geneva], lord of Varre and Autone, and Geoffrey de Maldon, to treat with the above-mentioned dauphin. *Westm.* R. ii p ii 1020. O v 11. H ii p iv 7
March 4.	Credence for Radulph, joint lord of Haute Ville, and Geoffrey de Maldon, to Hugh de Jabennis [Geneva] *Westm.* R ii p ii 1020 O v 11 H ii p iv 7
March 4	The K. grants to John duke of Brittany, earl of Richmond, respite for his debts due at the Exchequer until a fortnight after Easter. *Westm* R. ii p ii 1020 O. v. 11 H ii p iv 7
March 6	Bartholomew de Burghersh, admiral of the fleet from the Thames westward, is commanded to provide 70 ships at Portsmouth by a week after Easter, for the passage of some of the K.'s nobles to Aquitain. *Westm.* R ii p ii 1020 O v 12 H ii p iv 17.
March 8.	William de Dunstaple is commanded to provide wheat, beans, peas, beer, salt, bacon, beef, mutton, herrings, and cheese, at Yarmouth and Orwell Writs to the sheriffs of York, Nottingham, and Derby to arrange for payment for the above. *The Tower of London* R. ii. p ii 1021. O v 12 H ii p iv 7
March 8.	The K orders Stephen le Blount, his clerk, to furnish the like provisions, as well as stock fish and horse shoes *The Tower of London* R ii. p. ii. 1021 O. v. 12 H ii p iv 8
March 8	The K desires H. bp. of Lincoln to order Paul de Monte Florum to provide for the reception in Germany of Q Philippa. *The Tower of London.* R ii p ii 1021. O v 14 H ii. p. iv 8.
March 10	The K orders William de Clynton, earl of Huntingdon, constable of Dover castle and warden of the Cinque Ports, and the bailiffs of Yarmouth and S Botulph's, to observe the truce with France until the Nativity of S. John Baptist *Westm.* R ii. p ii 1022. O v. 14 H ii p iv 8
March 10	The K. orders Oliver de Ingham, seneschal of Gascony, to observe the same truce *Westm.* R ii p ii 1022 O v 1⁵ H ii p iv 8
March 10.	The K thanks his subjects in the castellany of Burgos for their defence of his rights, and desires credence for Hugh de Guanadon and Roger de Norwich. Similar letters to the lord of Mont Ferrand, Thaleran de Graynoles, and seven others. *The Tower of London* R ii. p ii. 1022. O. v. 16. H ii. p iv 9
March 10	The sheriff of Yorkshire is ordered to proclaim that no wool is to be bought or exported until the quantity granted by parliament is collected *Westm* R ii. p ii 1022.
March 13	The K. commends the commonalties of Gascony for their fidelity, and desires credence for Oliver de Ingham *The Tower of London* R ii p ii 1023 O v 16 H ii p iv 9
March 15	The K appoints John de Norwich, lieutenant of Oliver de Ingham, seneschal of Gascony *The Tower of London.* R. ii p. ii. 1023.
March 15	Credence for Oliver de Ingham going to the prelates and nobles of the duchy of Aquitain *The Tower of London.* R ii p ii 1023 O. v 17. H ii p iv 9
March 15.	The K desires Oliver de Ingham to thank the prelates and nobles, and the commonalties of Aquitain, for their fidelity, and to encourage them to resist his enemies *The Tower of London.* R ii. p. ii. 1023 O. v 17. H. ii. p. iv. 9.

DATE.	SUBJECT
133? March 15	Power for Rodulph, joint lord of Hauteville, and Friar Geoffrey de Maldon, to treat wit Amadeus count of Gehenna [Geneva] , also to treat with Eimon count of Savoy. *Th Tower of London* R u p ii. 1023. O. v 17 H ii p iv 9
March 15	The K admits John Coupgorge, clerk, Peter de Richmond, sir William de Daubigne Luke de Cheveigne, parson of Swaffham Market, and Roger de Meres, as attorneys fo John duke of Brittany and earl of Richmond *The Tower of London.* R. ii. p. ii. 1024 O v 18 H ii p iv 9
March 16	Confirmation of the grant by Oliver de Ingham, seneschal of Gascony, of an annuity c 500 marks to Hugh de Geneva, lord of Vareys and Authton. *The Tower of London.* R. i p ii 1024 O v 18 H ii p iv 9
March 16	The K. confirms the presentation of cardinal John de Columpna to the benefice c Dounton *The Tower* R. ii. p ii 1024 O. v 19 H. ii p iv 10.
March 25	Warrant for the payment of 564l 3s 4d for horses, plate, jewels, &c required by Quee Philippa for her journey abroad. *Newcastle* R ii p ii 1024 O v 19. H. ii p iv 1C
March 26	The K grants to Robert de Artoys an annuity of 800l. payable by the priors of Sel Prittlewell, and nine others. Writs to the priors to pay the half-yearly portion at Easte *Darlington.* R. ii p ii. 1024 O. v. 19. H ii p. iv. 10.
March 28	The K. requests J archbp of Canterbury to order the clergy of his province to pra for him, and to explain to the people that he is compelled to impose tallages and other bur dens upon them *Berwick-upon-Tweed* R ii p ii 1025. O v 20 H ii p iv. 10
April 1	Henry Husee, Thomas de Ponynges, and Edward de St John, warden of the sea coast o Surrey and Sussex, are commanded to attach those who refuse to contribute to the defenc of the country *Newcastle* R ii p ii 1025.
April 6.	The K directs Stephen Blount, purveyor of victuals for the K 's passage, not to take an victuals except wine within 12 leagues of the sea, as the enemies' fleet is near at hand *Langley* Similar writ to William de Dunstaple, purveyor in Essex, Norfolk, and Suffolk *Havering atte Bower* April 30 Similar writ to the sheriff of Kent *Langley.* 6 Apri R ii p ii 1025
April 6	The K orders the arrayers of archers in Kent not to choose men within 12 leagues o the sea *Langley* R. ii p ii 1026
April 6	The K appoints Theobald Russell captain of the men of the Isle of Wight. *Langley* R ii p ii 1026 O v 22 H ii p iv. 11.
April 10.	William archbp. of York sends to J bp of Carlisle a copy of the K 's letter [28 March] and desires him to order his clergy to pray for his success *Cawood.* R. ii p ii. 1026 O v 21 H ii p iv 10–11 ♦
April 10.	Protection until Michaelmas for Henry bp of Lincoln and 57 persons in his compan going over the sea *Havering atte Bower* R. ii p ii 1027 O v. 22 H ii. p iv. 11.
April 15	The K is surprised that Walter de Manny, admiral of the fleet north of the Thames, ha not provided sufficient ships for his passage, and orders him to assemble all ships capabl of crossing the sea at Yarmouth by a month after Easter Similar letter to Bartholomew d Burghersh, admiral of the fleet west of the Thames, to provide ships at Orwell *Haverin atte Bourc* R ii p ii 1027 O v 23–24 H ii p iv 11
April 15.	John de Langeford, warden of Carisbrook Castle, Bartholomew de Isle, and Theobal Russel are commanded to compel all persons in the Isle of Wight to furnish men for th defence of the island The K orders the sheriff of Southampton to assist them. *Haverin atte Bower* R ii p ii 1027 O v. 24 H ii p iv 12.
April 16.	The sheriffs of London are commanded to pay to William de Bohun, earl of Northampto his pension of 200l Similar warrants to the customers of London for 200l , the sheriff c Essex for 50l , and the sheriff of Northampton and Wm de la Pole for other sums. *Towe of London* R ii p ii 1028
April 18.	The sheriff of Gloucestershire and the bailiffs of Gloucester are commanded to put stop to the riot caused by the arrest of William de Hassefeld, a preaching friar, who ha deserted his religion *Westm* R. ii. p. ii. 1029
April 21	The K. orders the sheriff of Cumberland to arrest those who send arms or victuals int Scotland *Westm.* R. ii. p ii 1029. O v 26 H ii p iv 12
April 23	The K desires the bailiffs of Great Yarmouth to provide a ship for Reginald de Cobham whom he sends to Henry bp. of Lincoln. *Westm* R. ii p ii 1029 O. v. 26. H i p iv 13.

DATE.	SUBJECT
1338 April 25	Richard earl of Arundel is appointed captain of the army against the Scots. The K orders the sheriffs of Yorkshire and six other northern counties, Richard Talbot, warden of Berwick castle, and the wardens of the castles at Edinburgh, Roxburgh, Stirling, and the town of St John [Perth], to obey the earl of Arundel. *Westm.* R ii p. ii 1029. O. v 27–29. H ii p iv. 13
[April 25.]	The K. orders Gilbert de Umframvill, earl of Anegos, and the sheriff of Northumberland, to furnish men for the earl of Arundel R ii p ii 1030 O. v 29 H ii p iv 14.
[April 25.]	Similar letter to Antony de Lucy and Ralph de Dacre to supply men from Cumberland and Westmoreland, and to the sheriffs of those counties to assist them R ii p ii 1030 O v. 30. H ii p iv 14
April 25	Power for Richard earl of Arundel to conclude a truce with the Scots *Westm* R ii p ii 1031 O v 30 H. ii. p iv 14
[April 25]	Also to conclude peace R ii p ii 1031. O v. 30. H ii. p iv 14
April 25	Also to receive the fealty of those Scots who have been his enemies *Westm.* R ii p ii 1031 O. v. 30 H ii p iv 14
April 25	The K orders proclamation to be made by the several sheriffs that a new privy seal has been made *Westm.* R ii p ii. 1031. O v 31. H ii p iv 14
April 28	The K grants the manor of Strode in Kent to Mary de St. Paul, countess of Pembroke, guardian of his daughter Joan of Woodstock *Westm* R ii p ii 1031 O v. 31 H ii. p iv 14
April 28	The K. orders Walter de Manny, admiral of the northern fleet, to conduct from Ipswich certain merchants of Brabant whom he has licensed to export 2,200 sacks of wool. *Westm.* R ii p. ii. 1031. O v 32 H ii p iv 15
April 28	The K orders the sheriff of Suffolk to pay the annuity of 20*l* which he has granted to Robert de Ufford, earl of Suffolk *Westm* R ii p ii 1032
April 30.	Power to Henry bp of Lincoln, William de Bohun, earl of Northampton, and Robert de Ufford, earl of Suffolk, to retain Radulph, joint lord of Haute Ville, for the King's service *Westm* R ii p ii 1032 O. iv 32 H ii p iv 15
April 30	Power to Radulph, joint lord of Haute Ville, and Geoffrey de Maldonan, Augustin friar, to retain for the K's service Hugh de Joyvill, lord of Gaye, Walter de Vienna, lord of Mirabelle, and four others. *Westm.* R ii p ii 1032. O v 32 H ii. p iv 15.
April 30.	Confirmation of the covenant made by Oliver de Ingham, seneschal of Gascony, with Matha de la Brette, lady of Montynak and Genssac *Westm.* R ii p ii. 1032 O v 33. H ii p iv 15
April 30.	Bernardet lord de la Brette is desired to refrain from assisting Philip K of France, and to surrender the lands he holds of him. *Westm.* R. ii. p. ii 1033. O v. 34. H ii p iv 16.
April 30.	The K promises to indemnify William Raymund, lord of Camount, for any losses he may incur in assisting him *Westm* R ii p ii 1033 O v 34 H ii p iv 16.
May 1.	The K orders William de Clynton, earl of Huntingdon, constable of Dover Castle, to convey the messengers of the papal nuncios across the sea. *Westm.* R ii p. ii. 1033 O. v. 35. H. ii. p iv 16.
May 2.	Protection for the German merchants at the guildhall of the Teutons in London. *Westm* R. ii p. ii 1033.
May 6.	The K informs William de Clynton, earl of Huntingdon, that the cessation of hostilities with France is to be revoked, as the French king refuses to observe it. *The Tower of London.* R. ii p ii. 1034. O. v. 35. H. ii. p iv 16.
May 7.	The K. orders the bailiffs of St Botulph's to prevent the exportation of live rams for the purpose of improving foreign wool, which would deteriorate the value of wool in the kingdom *The Tower of London.* R ii p ii 1034. O v 36 H ii p iv 17
May 8.	The K repeats his order to Richard earl of Arundel, William de Montacute, earl of Salisbury, and John de Cherleton, senior, to send archers and spear men from their lands in Wales *The Tower of London.* R. ii. p. ii 1034. O. v 37 H ii. p iv 17.
May 8.	The K thanks the commonalty of Ghent for their friendship *The Tower of London* R ii. p ii. 1035 O v 38. H ii p iv 17
May 8	Similar letters to the commonalties of Bruges and Ypres. *The Tower of London* R ii. p ii 1035. O v 38 H ii p iv 17
May 8.	Credence for the lord of Craydonk and Reginald de Shanow going to J duke of Brabant, G count of Hainault, Reginald count of Gueldres, William marquis of Juliers, and three others. *The Tower of London* R ii p ii 1035. O v 38 H ii p iv. 17.

DATE	SUBJECT.
1337 May 8	The K promises indemnity to the lord of Contresyn for any losses he may have sustained *The Tower of London* R II p II 1034. O v. 99 H. II p IV 17.
May 10.	The K orders Richard de Suthorp and John Moneroun to take all the tin in Cornwall and Devonshire to assist in defraying the expenses of the war, giving security for it to the owners The K orders the sheriffs to assist them, and provide conveyance for the tin to Southampton *The Tower of London* R II p II. 1035 O v. 39. H n. p. IV. 19.
May 12	Power to Antony de Lucy, sir Thomas de Rokeby, and sir John de Lilleburne, to grant pardons to the Scots who have sided with his enemies *The Tower of London* . R II p II 1036 O v II 1036 H II p IV 18
May 12	Safe conduct for Rodolph, joint lord of Haute Ville, and Geoffrey de Maldonan, Augustin friar, whom the K sends on a mission to the emperor *The Tower of London* R. II p II. 1036 O v 41 H II p IV 18
May 12	Power to Henry bp of Lincoln, and William de Bohun, earl of Northampton, to treat for a marriage between the K's eldest son Edward and one of the daughters of the duke of Brabant *The Tower of London* R II p II 1036 O v 41. H II p IV. 19
May 12.	Memorandum that the mayor, sheriffs, and aldermen of London have promised the K to keep the city safely, and maintain peace during his absence. *The Tower of London.* R II p II 1036 O v 42 H II p IV 19
May 13	Safe conduct until June 24 for William lord of Cravendouk, John Bernage de Flemyng, John de Thraudeston, and their servants, going abroad on the K's business. *The Tower of London* R II p II 1037 O v 42 H. II p IV 19
May 15	The K releases the cardinal Gaucelin, prebendary of Driffield and parson of Hemming-burgh, Peter, archdeacon of York and prebendary of Wistow, and Bertrand, parson of Brantingham, from the payment of the triennial tenth *The Tower of London* R II p II 1037 O v 43 H II p IV 19
May 15	The K orders the widow of John de Glanton, late constable of Carlisle Castle, to deliver Henry de Douglas, prisoner of war, to Antony de Lucy, sheriff of Cumberland. *The Tower of London*. R. II p. II. 1037. O. v. 43. H II. p IV 19
May 15	The K. appoints Thomas bp of Hereford guardian of Ireland, with an annuity of 500*l* The K orders John de Cherleton, late justiciary, to resign his office, and the K's castles, &c , to the said bp , and orders the clergy and nobles and his other subjects to obey him. *The Tower of London* R II p II 1037 O v 43 H II p IV 19.
May 16	Manumission of John Simondson, William Godwyn of Esyngton, and Alan Mason of Esyngton, natives of the K's manor of Brustwyk *The Tower of London* . R II p II 1038 O v 45 H II p. IV 20
May 18	Safe conduct until Aug 1 for the attorneys of certain cardinals carrying 80 sacks of wool which the K has licensed to be exported to Brabant for the pope and the said cardinals *Windsor* R II p II 1038 O v 44 H II p IV 20
May 8	Indenture between the K and Bernardet de la Brette, viscount of Tartas, by which he becomes the K's vassal, and the K grants him the castellanies of S Macaire, Dax, and S Severin, and other lands, in recompense for the lands he will lose in consequence. *The Tower of London* R II p II 1038 O v 45. H II p. IV 20
May 20	The K has been petitioned by Peter de Puyane, admiral of the fleet at Bayonne, to grant him the rent of 6*l* on every whale caught at Biarritz, and other rents and dues in Bedured in the bailiwick of Goes, and desires the seneschal of Gascony and the constable of Bordeaux to report as to their value *The Tower of London.* R II p II. 1039. O v. 46 H II p IV 21.
May 23	Sir John Engayne and Robert de Teye are appointed attorneys for William de Bohun, earl of Northampton. *The Tower of London* R II p II 1039 O. v. 47. H. II. p IV. 21
[May 23.]	Protection till All Saints day for the earl of Northampton, and for 74 persons going abroad in his company R II p II 1039 O v 47. H. II p IV 21
May 26.	Receipt for a chalice and paten worth 32*l* 14*s* from the abbot of Oseney, as a loan to the K. *The Tower of London* R II p II 1039 O. v 48 H II p IV. 21.
June 3	Receipt for a loan of 50 marks from the abbot of S Augustine's, Canterbury *Bury S Edmunds* R II p II 1040 O v 48 H II p IV 21.
June 3.	Receipt for silver cups, chalices, &c worth 11*l* 5*s* 4*d* from the abbot of Thorneye. *Bury S Edmunds* R II p II 1040 O v 48. H II p IV. 21
June 3.	Receipt for a gold chalice and paten from the abbot of Thornton *Bury S. Edmunds.* R II p II 1040 O v 49 H II p. IV 21

DATE	SUBJECT.
1338 June 3	Receipt for a silver cross, gilt cups, chalices, and other plate worth 22*l* 4*s* 8*d* from the abbot of Peterborough *Bury S. Edmunds* R n p n 1040 O v 49 H n. p iv 22
June 4	Receipt for gold and silver plate worth 100*l* 15*s* 6*d* from the abbot of Ramsey. *Bury S. Edmunds* R u. p. n. 1040 O v. 49 H u p iv 22.
June 4	Receipt for gold and silver plate and jewels worth 276*l* 3*s* from the abbot of Reading *Bury S. Edmunds* R n p. n 1041 O v 50 H n p iv 22
June 8.	Receipt for plate worth 7*l* 14*s* 10*d* from the abbot of Bardney *Lopham.* R. n. p n. 1041. O. v. 50. H. n p. iv. 22
June 8	Receipt for a chalice and a cope worth 9*l* 7*s* 1*d* from the abbot of Croyland *Lopham* R n p n 1041 O v 50. H n p iv 22
June 8.	The K orders the warden, chancellor, and treasurer of Ireland to compel the constables of his castles to put them in a state of defence *Lopham* R. n p n. 1041.
June 9.	The K orders Walter de Manny, admiral of the northern fleet, to send ships to Orwell to protect and convey home certain merchants of Brabant *Lopham* R n p n 1041 O v 51. H n p iv 22.
June 9	The K. remits the triennial tenth due from the town of Portsmouth, which has been burnt by the enemy Letter to the collectors on the same subject *Lopham* R n. p n. 1042.
June 12	Protection until Christmas for William de Northwell, John Chaucer, and 43 others going across the sea in the K's company *Walton* R n p n 1042 O v 51 H n p iv 23
June 12	The K. permits Humphrey de Bohun, earl of Hereford and Essex, to grant, on account of his infirmities, the office of constable of England and the manor of Fulmodeston, in co. Norfolk, to William de Bohun, earl of Northampton, his brother *Lopham* R n p n. 1042. O v. 52. H n p iv 23.
June 10	Treaty between Henry bp of Lincoln and his colleagues, for the K of England and the commonalties of Flanders, granting to the Flemings free mercantile intercourse, on condition of their not assisting Scotland or France *Antwerp* R n p n 1042 O v 53. H n p iv. 23
June 21.	Power for J abp of Canterbury, and others, to treat with our "cousin of France" A similar power to treat with "Philip K of France" *Walton* R n p n 1043 O v 55 H. n p iv. 24
June 21	Similar powers to the same persons and John duke of Brabant, William count of Hainault, Reginald count of Gueldres, William marquis of Juliers, and William de Dunort, lord of Oustrehout *Walton* R n p n 1044. O. v 56 H n p iv. 24
June 22.	Protection for John de Bury, and 75 others, going abroad in the company of Q Philippa *Walton* R n p n 1044 O v 57 H n p iv 25
June 23	The K orders William de Clynton, earl of Huntingdon, constable of Dover Castle and warden of the Cinque Ports, to provide ships for the passage of the abp of Canterbury and the bp of Durham, going abroad on the K's service. *Walton.* R n. p. n. 1045 O v 58 H n p iv. 25
June 23	Protection for the abp of Canterbury and the bp of Durham *Walton* R. n p n 1045. O. v. 58 H n p iv 25
June 23.	Receipt for a golden cross jewelled and two chalices worth 32*l* 15*s* as a loan to the K. from the abbot of Hide *Walton* R n p n 1045 O v 59. H n p iv 26
June 23	The K orders William de Stury to pacify the mutiny among the soldiers assembled at Norwich. *Walton* R n p n 1045
June 26	Confirmation of the treaty with Flanders of June 17 *Walton* R. n p n 1045 O v 59 H n p iv 26
June 26.	The K orders proclamation of the treaty to be made throughout England *Walton* R n p. n 1046.
June 28.	The K informs the Emperor Louis that he will set sail with the first favourable wind, and desires credence for William de Bohun, earl of Northampton, and sir Geoffrey le Scrope. *Walton* R n p n 1046. O v 59 H n p. iv. 26
June 28.	Receipt for gold and silver plate and jewels worth 157*l* 1*s*. 8*d* from the prior of Christchurch, Canterbury, as a loan to the K *Walton* R n p n. 1046 O. v 60 H n. p. iv 26.
June 29	The K directs John Roos, treasurer of Ireland, to pay the wages of certain miners, refiners, and coiners, whom he sends into Ireland *Walton* R n p n 1047.

DATE	SUBJECT.
June 29.	The K. orders John Roos to receive from John de Flete, keeper of the exchange at London, dies for pence, halfpence, and farthings *Walton.* R. ɪɪ p. ii. 1047.
July 1.	The K appoints Bernardet lord de la Bret, viscount of Tartas, and Oliver de Ingham, seneschal of Gascony, his lieutenants in the duchy *Walton.* R. ɪɪ p. ɪɪ 1047. O. v 61. H ɪɪ. p. ɪv 26
July 6.	Memorandum that Robert bp of Chichester resigned the great seal to the K , who delivered it to Richard de Bynteworth, bp elect of London, as chancellor. *Walton.* R. ɪɪ. p ɪɪ 1047 O v. 61. H. ɪɪ. p. ɪv. 27
July 7	The K promises that the grant by the city of London of 40 men-at-arms and 60 archers to serve with him shall not be prejudicial to their privilege of not serving or sending men to serve beyond the city *Walton* R ɪɪ p ɪɪ 1048.
July 8.	Warrant for the repayment of money supplied to Edward K of Scotland by Robert de Darreys, sheriff of Northumberland, at the K 's order *Walton.* R ɪɪ p ɪɪ 1048 O v 62 H ɪɪ p ɪv 27
July 8.	Protection until Christmas for William de Brun and two others going abroad in the company of Edward de Mont Hermer *Walton* R. ii. p ii 1048. O v 63. H. ɪɪ p. ɪv. 27
July 10	Protection for Robert de Burton and 25 others going abroad in the company of William de Montacute, earl of Salisbury *Walton* R ɪɪ p ɪɪ 1048 O v 63. H ɪɪ. p ɪv 27.
July 10.	The K orders publication to be made throughout England, Ireland, Wales, and Aquitain, of the impression of his new great seal. *Walton.* R. ɪɪ. p. ɪɪ. 1048. O. v. 63. H. ɪɪ. p ɪv 27.
July 11.	Memorandum of the sending of the impressions with the preceding letters. *Walton* R ɪɪ. p. ɪɪ. 1049 O v 64. H ɪɪ p ɪv 28
July 11.	The K. appoints Edward duke of Cornwall, his eldest son, regent of the kingdom during his absence. *Walton* R. ɪɪ. p ɪɪ. 1049 O v. 65. H. ɪɪ. p. ɪv 28.
July 12.	The K sends to R. bp of London, his chancellor, certain ordinances for the regulation of the exchequer, which he desires to be read before the council *Walton* The K orders the treasurer and barons of the exchequer to observe the regulations. *Windsor.* 6 *Sept* R. ɪɪ p ɪɪ 1049
July 14	Memorandum that John de S Paul, keeper of the rolls, and Thomas Baumburgh, delivered the great seal to the K ɪɪ the *Cristope* at Orwell, and he gave it to William de Kyldesby R ɪɪ p ɪɪ 1050 O v 65. H ɪɪ p ɪv 28
July 16.	Memorandum that on July 12 the K went from Walton to Orwell, from which port he set sail between six and seven o'clock on July 16, and was joined by the fleet from Yarmouth under the command of the earl of Derby. R. ɪɪ. p. ɪɪ 1050 O. v 65. H. ɪɪ. p. ɪv 28.
July 16	The several sheriffs are ordered to send four merchants from each county to consult with the regent and council at Northampton on Aug 3 *Ipswich* R ɪɪ p ɪɪ 1051
July 19.	Memorandum that John de S Paul and Thomas de Baumburgh, on coming from Orwell, delivered the great seal to Richard bp. of London, chancellor, at Fulham R. ɪɪ. p. ɪɪ. 1051. O v. 65 H ɪɪ p. ɪv. 28.
July 22.	Revocation of all powers to treat with Philip de Valois, as K. of France *Antwerp.* R. ɪɪ. p ɪɪ 1051 O. v. 66 H. ɪɪ p ɪv 28
July 27.	The K. appoints Robert Howel and Robert de Watford to superintend the exportation of the wool granted for the expenses of his expedition. *Northampton.* R. ɪɪ. p ɪɪ. 1051. O v 66 H ɪɪ p ɪv. 29
July 30	Commission to Ralph de Hastyng, sheriff of York, John de Percebrigg, clerk, and John de Barton of Hull, to send wheat, barley, oats, and wine to Berwick, for the K.'s castles in Scotland *Northampton* R ɪɪ p ɪɪ 1052 O. v 67. H ɪɪ p. ɪv 29
Aug 1.	Warrant for the payment of the annuity of Robert de Artoys *Northampton.* R. ɪɪ. p ɪɪ 1052 O. v. 69. H ɪɪ p ɪv 30
Aug 2	Warrant to the treasurer to pay the portions of the annuity assigned on the priories of S Neots and Thetford, the rents of which have been already paid. *Northampton.* R ɪɪ. p ɪɪ 1052 O v 69. H ɪɪ p ɪv 30
Aug 4	The K desires Edward K of Scotland to deliver the town of S John of Perth to Thomas Ughtred, for the better defence of the neighbourhood. *Northampton.* R. ɪɪ p. ɪɪ. 1053. O v 70 H ɪɪ p ɪv 30.
[Aug. 4.]	The K desires Henry de Beaumont, earl of Boghan, justiciary of Scotland, to appoint Thomas Ughtred as his lieutenant. R ɪɪ p ɪɪ 1053. O. v 70. H ii. p. ɪv. 30

DATE.	SUBJECT.
1338 Aug 4	Licence to the prelates, nobles, and others in Devon to dig for gold, silver, or hidden treasure, of which, when refined, the K will claim one third *Northampton.* R n p n. 1053 O v 71 H n p iv 30
Aug. 5.	The abps of Canterbury and York are desired to summon convocations of the clergy *Northampton.* R. ii p. n 1053. O v. 72. H n p. iv. 31
Aug. 7.	John Waweyn, William de Kyngeston, and Thomas de Baddeby are ordered to collect and send to Antwerp the wool granted to the K. by Parliament. *Antwerp.* R. ii. p. n. 1054. O v 73 H n p iv 31
Aug 9.	The K takes into his service Conrad de Marea, lord of Hurde, with 50 men. [*Antwerp*] R n p n 1054 O v 74 H n p iv. 32
Aug. 15	The several sheriffs are ordered to prepare beacon fires to warn the country in case of an invasion *Kennington* R n p n 1055
Aug 16	The K releases the commonalty of Ghent from the payment of ulnage on cloth. *Antwerp.* R. n p n 1055 O iv. 74 H n p iv 32
Aug 18	The K retains Robin de Forest as one of his councillors, with an annuity of 100 marks *Antwerp* R n p n 1055 O. v 75 H n p iv 32
Aug. 18.	The K. orders Roger Norman, Nicholas Pyk, and Thomas de Snetesham to make inquisition concerning the capture of ships of Gueldres by Englishmen, between Blaunkebergh and Heste near the coast of Flanders Similar letters to Thomas de Drayton, admiral of the fleet from the Thames northwards, Peter de Barde, admiral of the fleet from the Thames westward, and two others Aug 28 *Kennington.* R n p n 1055 O. v 76 H n p iv 32
Aug 18	Inspeximus and confirmation of a charter to the merchants and burgesses of Louvain, dated Havering atte Bower 23 May, 5 Edw III *Antwerp* R n p n 1056. O. v 77 H n p iv 33
Aug. 18.	Licence to the merchants and burgesses of Louvain to buy wool and sell cloth in England *Antwerp.* R n p n 1057 O. v 78 H n p iv 34
Aug 18	Power for Thomas bp of Hereford, guardian of Ireland, to retain horsemen and footmen for the defence of the country. *Kennington* R. n p n 1057.
Aug. 18.	Power for the bp of Hereford to pardon rebels in Ireland and receive their fealty *Kennington* R n p. n 1057
Aug 18	Power for the bp of Hereford to remove sheriffs, constables, and other officers in Ireland, and appoint others in their place *Kennington.* R. n. p n 1057.
Aug. 20.	The K orders Robert de Chikewell, his clerk, to assist John Waweyn, William de Kyngeston, and Thomas de Baddeby, in sending the wool granted by Parliament *Herrenthals* R n. p n. 1057 O v 80 H n p. iv 34
Aug 26.	The K orders the treasurer and barons of the Exchequer to send dies for halfpence, farthings, and sterlings to the abbot of Reading, whom he has licensed to establish a mint at Reading *Windsor* R n p n 1058
Aug 28.	The K grants free mercantile intercourse to the merchants of Diest and Brussels. Similar grants to the towns of Thenen' [Theux ?], Mechlin, and Leuwen, [? Louvain], dated Sept 19th and 24th and Oct 26th *Antwerp.* R n. p. n. 1058. O. v. 80. H n. p. iv 34
Sept. 6.	The K., in consideration of the services of Nicolas Blank de Flisco, master of a galley, releases him from his engagements with Nicolin de Flisco, called the cardinal of Genoa, the K's proctor *Coblenz* R ii p n 1058 O v 81 H n p iv 35.
Sept. 6	Respite until June 24 for the wool to be contributed by the town of Arundel, the greater part of which has been accidentally burnt *Windsor* R n p n 1059.
Sept 8.	Warrant to the customers of London to pay 564*l* 3*s* 4*d*. for the use of the Queen *Windsor* R n p n 1059 O v 82 H n p iv. 35
Sept 16.	The K. grants to the inhabitants of Westminster a respite for the payment of the tenth and fifteenth, and for their contribution of wool, as the town is not a borough nor mercantile, and is impoverished by the absence of the K and the courts of law *Windsor.* R. ii. p n 1059.
Sept 18.	Confirmation of the privileges granted by the K's predecessors to the inhabitants of Cologne. *Mechlin* R n p n 1059 O v 82 H n p iv 35
Sept 20.	Grant to William de Montacute, earl of Salisbury, of the office of marshal of England for life, the same being in the K.'s hands by death of Thomas late earl of Norfolk, the K.'s uncle. *Antwerp.* R. n. p. ii. 1060. O. v. 83. H. n. p. iv. 35.

U

DATE	SUBJECT
1338. Sept. 25	Power to John de Roos and Reginald de Donyngton to contract a loan of 100,000 guld florins of Florence *Antwerp.* R. ii p. ii 1060 O v 83 H. ii. p. iv 35
Sept 27	The K orders Peter Barde, admiral to the west of the Thames, and Thomas de Drayton, admiral of the north of the Thames, to prepare to resist the French galleys which have taken divers English ships. *Windsor.* R. ii p. ii 1060 O v 83.' H ii p iv 36
Oct 4	The K forbids the exaction of the tenth due from the deanery of Lincoln and the churches of Cestrefeld, Ashebourn, Wyrk', Maunnesfeld, and Leverton, thereto annexed, and the prebend of Kelleseye and the church of Wyrkesworth, now in the hands of the pope by reason of the promotion of Anthony to the see of Norwich *Kennington.* R. ii. p ii 1060. O v 84 H ii p iv. 36.
Oct 4	The K orders R. bp of Chichester to remove those monks in the priory of Lewes who are French subjects to houses farther from the sea Similar letter to J bp of Exeter, as to the priory of Mount S Michael Oct 12 *Westm* R ii p ii 1061
Oct 12.	Warrant to Michael Mynot, the K's butler, to deliver six casks of wine to Edward K of Scotland *Kennington* R ii p ii 1061 O v 85 H ii p iv 36
Oct. 14	The K orders H bp of Rochester, Roger de Northwode, the prior of Rochester, and seven others to fortify the Isle of Sheppey, which is threatened by the enemy's fleet *Kennington* R ii p ii 1061 O v 85 H ii p iv 36
Oct 15	The K orders the admirals Peter Bard and Thomas de Drayton to unite their fleets and attack the enemy *Kennington* R ii p ii 1061
Oct. 20	The K. informs the constable of Wallingford Castle that he has appointed it as the residence of Robert de Artoys *Kennington* R ii p ii 1062 O v 86 H ii p iv 36
Oct 20	The abbots of Sherborne, Cerne, Bindon, Abbotsbury, and Milton, the priors of Warham, Cranborne, Frompton, Lodres, and Horton, and 30 other persons, are ordered to remove to manors nearer the sea for the defence of the coast *Kennington.* R ii p ii 1062
Oct 23	The K orders the mayor and sheriffs of London to fortify the city on the waterside *Kennington* R ii p ii 1062 O v 86 H ii p iv 37
Nov 7	James Coterel and 43 others are ordered to join the K in arms at Ipswich. Similar writs to 10 persons in Wales *Kennington.* R ii. p ii 1062
Nov 10	The K permits William Trussel and his tenants, of the manor of Shoteshroke, in Windsor Forest, to keep dogs not expeditated *Antwerp.* R. ii. p ii. 1063 O v 86 H ii p iv 37
Nov 12	Power to Reynold count of Gueldres to treat for a marriage between the eldest son of Louis count of Flanders and the K's daughter Isabella *Antwerp* R ii p ii 1063 O v 87 H ii p iv 37.
Nov 12	Power to the count of Gueldres to treat with the count of Flanders and the commonalties of Bruges, Ghent, and Ypres, about establishing a staple of wool and hides in Flanders Also to treat for a perpetual peace *Antwerp* R ii p ii. 1063. O v 87 H ii p iv 37.
Nov. 13.	Pope Benedict [XII] remonstrates with the K for entering into an alliance with the emperor, who is excommunicated, and states that he did not grant the tenths to the K. of France with the intention of assisting him against the K of England. *Avignon* R ii p ii 1063 O v 88. H ii p iv 37
Nov. 14.	Receipt for 11,000l as a loan from William de la Pole, merchant, for the expenses of the K's household abroad *Antwerp* R ii p ii 1065 O v 91 H ii p. iv 39
Nov 14	The K promises indemnity to William de la Pole for 7,500l., lent by him to the count of Gueldres *Antwerp.* R ii p ii 1065 O v 92 H. ii p iv 39
Nov 15	The K., at the pope's request, empowers J abp of Canterbury, R. bp. of Durham, H. bp. of Lincoln, William de Montacute, earl of Salisbury, Sir Bartholomew de Burghersh, Sir Geoffrey le Scrop, and John de Offord, archdeacon of Ely, to treat with Philip de Valois, "our cousin" Similar power to treat with Philip de Valois, who styles himself K of France. *Antwerp* R ii p ii 1065 O v 92 H ii p iv 39
[Nov. 15.]	Power to the same to treat with the cardinals of S. Praxedis and S. Mary *in Aquiro* about the differences between the K. and any catholic person R. ii p. ii. 1065. O. v 93. H. ii. p. iv 39
Nov. 16.	The K. forbids his commissioners to treat with Philip de Valois as K. of France. *Antwerp.* R ii. p ii. 1066. O. v. 93. H. ii. p. iv. 39.

DATE	SUBJECT.
1338 Nov 20	The K. orders that in Kent and in 15 other maritime counties only one bell shall be rung in the churches within seven leagues of the sea, so that in case of an attack the people may be warned by the ringing of all the bells *Kennington* R ii p ii 1066
Nov 24	William de Clynton, earl of Huntingdon, is ordered to victual Dover castle *Kennington.* R ii. p. ii. 1066.
Nov. 25	Proclamation is to be made at the ports that no letters prejudicial to the K are to be brought into the realm. *Kennington* R. ii. p ii 1066.
Nov 30	The K orders Nicolin de Flisco and John Petri to receive the account of Jacobin de Sarzana, for the money delivered to him for providing galleys *Antwerp* R. ii. p ii 1066 O. v. 94 H ii p iv 40
Dec 3	John Bardolf and Robert de Morleye are ordered to provide for the defence of Great Yarmouth *Byfleet* R ii p ii 1067
Dec 8.	Warrant for the payment of 700*l* for the expenses of Edward earl of Cornwall, regent of England *Byfleet* R ii p ii. 1067 O v. 94. H ii p iv 40
Dec 8.	The towns of Portsmouth, Fodyngton, Portsea, and Estene, which have been burnt by the enemy, have a respite for the wool which they ought to contribute *Windsor* R. ii. p ii. 1067
Dec 12	The K. grants 100*l* to John de Bures, for bringing him word that Q Philippa has been delivered of a son *Antwerp* R. ii. p. ii 1067 O v. 95. H ii. p iv 40
Dec 15	The K grants to the abbess and nuns of Barking licence to take wood from their woods within the metes of the forest. *Antwerp* R ii p ii. 1067 O v 95 H ii p iv 40
	The K. renews, at the request of the pope, the powers to his commissioners to treat with Philip de Valois Similar renewal of the power to treat with Philip K of France R ii p ii 1068. O v 95 H ii p iv 40
[Dec 15]	Power for the said commissioners to treat with the papal nuncios for peace with any catholic person R ii. p. ii 1068 O v 96 H ii p iv. 40
1339 Jan 6.	The K grants to Nicolin de Flisco, called the cardinal of Genoa, an additional annuity of 20 marks, and annuities of 20*l* to his sons Gabriel and Anthony, after his death *Antwerp* R ii p ii 1096 O v 96. H ii p iv 41
Jan. 7	Warrant to Thomas de Baddeby to deliver one cask of flour and one of wine to Robert de Artoys for his maintenance *Windsor.* R ii p ii. 1068 O v. 97. H ii p iv. 41
Jan 12	The K explains to Elion de Villeneuve, grand master of the hospital of S. John of Jerusalem, that the money taken from his house at Clerkenwell was for a loan to the K. *Berkhamstead* R ii. p. ii. 1068. O. v 97 H ii p iv 41
Jan 14	The K promises indemnity to Reinold count of Gueldres for an obligation of 600 marks to Simon de Hale. *Antwerp.* R. ii p ii 1069. O. v. 98 H. ii. p iv 41.
Feb 3	Warrant for the payment of the arrears of the annuity of Nicolin de Flisco, called the cardinal of Genoa *Berkhamsted* R ii p ii 1069. O v 98 H ii p iv. 41.
Feb 4	The K grants 800 florins of Florence to the commonalty of Middelburgh in recompense of all the injuries done to them by the English *Antwerp* R ii. p. ii. 1069. O v 98. H ii p iv 41
Feb. 8	The abp of York is ordered to convoke his clergy, and exhort them to grant the K. an aid, which they refused at the last convocation *Byfleet.* R. ii. p. ii. 1069.
Feb 15.	The treasurer and barons of the Exchequer are ordered to send new balances for weighing goods to the customers at Southampton, the former balances having been carried away by the enemy. *Westm* R ii p ii 1070. O v 99. H. ii. p. iv 41.
Feb 16.	William abp. of York, Henry de Percy, Thomas Wake de Lidel, William de Ros de Hamelak, and Ralph de Nevill, are commanded to muster 200 men-at-arms, 500 armed men, and 500 archers from the county of York Similar writs for 36 other counties *Westm* R ii p ii 1070
Feb 16	The K orders W. abp. of York to convoke the clergy of his province at York on the Wednesday after Palm Sunday, that they may furnish men for the defence of the country Similar letters to the abp of Canterbury and 15 bishops. *Westm* R. ii. p ii 1072
Feb. 16	Albert and Otto, dukes of Austria, have promised the K. to invade Burgundy, and the K engages not to make peace without them. *Antwerp.* R. ii. p ii 1072. O. v. 99 H. ii. p. iv. 42.

DATE	SUBJECT.
1339 Feb 20	Proclamation is to be made throughout England against molesting Flemish merchants *Kennington* R ii p ii 1073 O iv 100 H ii p iv 42
Feb 27	Covenant between Henry bp of Lincoln and his colleagues, and Baldwin abp of Treves, who agrees to assist the K of England with troops, and receives the hereditary crown of England as a pledge. R ii. p ii. 1073 O v 101. H ii p. iv 42
March 1.	John de Flete, keeper of the K's exchange at London, is ordered to send to Dublin dies of pence, halfpence, and farthings *Kennington.* R. ii. p ii. 1074. O. v. 104 H. ii. p. iv. 43.
March 1.	The circulation of black money called "Turneys" is prohibited in Ireland. *Kennington.* R ii p ii 1074.
March 3.	Thomas bp of Hereford, guardian of Ireland, is ordered to survey the K's castles there *Kennington* R. ii p ii 1075.
March 4	Robert de Inghale, chamberlain of Berwick-upon-Tweed, is ordered to pay 20 marks yearly to the Friars Minors there, which sum they were wont to receive as alms from the Kings of Scotland *Byfleet.* R ii p ii 1075. O v 104 H ii p iv 44
March 5	The bp of Hereford, guardian of Ireland, is ordered to send information concerning lands in Ireland granted by the K *Kennington* R ii p ii 1075
March 6	Warrant to the sheriffs of London to pay 50 marks to Henry Darcy, mayor of London, for the expenses of his office *Kennington.* R ii p ii. 1075. O v 105. H. ii p iv. 44.
March 6.	The abbot of Glastonbury is ordered to arm his servants Similar letters to 30 abbots and 14 priors *Byfleet* R ii p ii 1076 O v. 105–6. H ii p. iv 44
March 6.	The treasurer and barons of the Exchequer are ordered to allow letters sealed with the K's secret seal called "Griffoun" *Kennington* R ii p ii 1076 O. v. 106. H ii p iv. 44.
March 11.	The K grants an annuity of 3,000 florins of Florence to Otes, lord of Cuyc, and his lady Joan, in recompense for the lands they have lost in France. *Antwerp* R. ii. p. ii. 1076. O v 107 H ii p iv 44
March 15.	Simon, bp of Ely is relieved from contributing to the defence of Norfolk and Suffolk, as he is defending Cambridgeshire and the Isle of Ely. *Winchester* R. ii p ii. 1076
March 15	The sheriffs of Hampshire and Wiltshire are ordered to provide workmen and materials for fortifying Southampton with a wall. *Winchester.* R. ii p ii 1077.
March 16	The inhabitants of Southampton are ordered to remain in the town and defend it. *Winchester.* R ii p ii 1077
March 16	Nicholas Devenyshe, mayor of Winchester, Robert Inkepenne, John de Nuttele, and Nicholas de Exon, are ordered to repair the walls of Winchester *Winchester.* R ii. p ii 1077
March 18.	Confirmation of the covenant with the abp. of Treves. R. ii. p ii 1077. O. v. 107. H ii p iv 45
March 25	Protection for the citizens of Chichester who have been ordered to fortify the city. *Berkhamsted.* R ii p. ii 1078.
March 31	The K desires John de Veer, earl of Oxford, and the wardens of the coast of Essex, not to exact men from the abbot of S Albans, as he has armed his household, by the K's order *Berkhamsted.* R ii. p. ii. 1078
April 1	The K desires the mayors and bailiffs of London and 11 other ports to advise the merchantmen going to Antwerp to arm themselves, as the enemy intends to intercept them *Berkhamsted* R. ii p. ii. 1078.
April 7.	Warrant for the payment of 100 marks for the expenses of Edward K of Scotland. *Berkhamsted.* R ii p ii. 1078 O v 108 H ii p iv 45
	Warrant for the payment of 40*l* of the annuity to Robert de Artoys.' R. ii. p. ii 1078. O v 108 H ii p iv. 45
April 12.	The prior of S John of Jerusalem in England is ordered to send 30 men-at-arms to Southampton. *Berkhamsted.* R ii. p. ii. 1079.

DATE	SUBJECT.
1339 April 15.	The sheriff of Somerset is ordered to examine the neighbourhood of Wells for a reported silver mine *Berkhamsted.* R ii p ii 1079
April 20	Thomas FitzWilliam de la Rynde and Henry FitzThomas de Eton, the Scotch hostages for the town of Berwick, are sent from the abbey of Glastonbury to that of Abbotsbury *Berkhamsted.* R ii. p. ii 1079.
April 23	Warrant to the sheriff of Cambridgeshire to provide carriage for materials for the repairs of Kings hall at Cambridge. *Berkhamsted.* R ii p ii 1079.
April 27.	Confirmation of the grant by the K's commissioners to Roupert count palatine of the Rhine, dated Frankfort, 30 June 1337 *Antwerp* R ii p ii 1079 O v. 116 H ii p. iv, 48.
April 27.	Power to Oliver de Ingham, seneschal of Gascony, to treat with Bernardet lord de la Brette *Antwerp.* R. ii p. ii 1080. O. v 108 H ii p iv 45
April 28	Power for Oliver de Ingham to treat with William Reymond, lord of Caumont *Antwerp* R ii p ii 1080 O v 108 H ii p iv 45
May 1.	Warrant to John de Flete, keeper of the armoury at the Tower of London, to send springalds, crossbows, &c to Southampton Arnald Dexcestre and Robert de Colyngbourne are ordered to receive them *Berkhamsted.* R. ii p ii. 1080
May 3.	Warrant for the payment to Edward K of Scotland of 30s a day in time of peace and 50s in time of war *Berkhamsted* R. ii. p ii 1080. O v. 109. H ii p iv. 45.
May 6.	The K forbids any sums of money to be paid out of the Exchequer until his return, except for the defence of his towns in Scotland and to the companies of the Bardi and Peruch. *Antwerp.* R ii p ii 1080 O v 109 H ii p iv. 45
May 10.	The sheriffs and Cambridgeshire and Huntingdonshire are ordered to deliver to Thomas Powys, master of the K's scholars at Cambridge, for the repair and building of their house, the oaktrees granted by Q Philippa and by Elizabeth de Burgh, from the forests of Sappele and Hundone *Berkhamsted* R ii p. ii. 1081. O. v 110. H. ii, p. iv 46.
May 12.	The K. promises that the armed men raised by the city of London shall not be taken as a precedent prejudicial to their privileges. *Berkhamsted* R ii. p ii. 1081.
May 10	Letters obligatory for the payment of 140,000 florins of Florence lent to the K. by Nicholas Bartholomew of Lucca. *Antwerp.* R. ii, p ii. 1081. O v 110. H ii p. iv 46
May 25	Thomas Ughtred, warden of the town of S John of Perth and master of the K.'s galley of Hull, is ordered to restore a ship of Gueldres which he has taken *Berkhamsted* R. ii. p ii 1082 O v. 112 H ii p iv 46,
May 25.	Licence to the University of Oxford to erect a stone cross in the High Street near the "Bocheria" in the parish of S Mary Magdalene opposite the north gate *Berkhamsted* R. ii. p. ii 1082
June 3.	The K orders the guardian and chancellor of Ireland to revoke all writs issued against Richard bp. of Ossory concerning the charge of heresy made by Alexander abp of Dublin, as the said bp has appealed to Rome *Berkhamsted* R. ii p ii 1082 O v 112 H ii p iv 47.
June 12.	Revocation of the order against the use of black money ["nigra moneta"] called Turneys in Ireland. *Berkhamsted* R.ii p ii 1082 O v 113 H ii p iv 47
June 15.	Hugh de Haudele, earl of Gloucester, is ordered to go with the men he has mustered to Orwell, which the enemy intend to attack *Berkhamsted.* R ii p ii 1083
June 22	Treaty of marriage between Edward, eldest son of the K , and Margaret, daughter of John duke of Brabant *Brussels* R ii. p ii. 1083 O v 113 H ii p iv. 47.
July 1.	Power to the abp of Canterbury, the bishops of Durham and Lincoln, the earls of Derby, Salisbury, and Suffolk, and three others, to treat with Philip de Valois, who is acting as K. of France *Antwerp.* R. ii. p. ii 1084 O v. 117. H ii p. iv 49.
July 6.	The treasurer and chamberlains are ordered to renew the wax which covers the body of Edward I. in Westminster Abbey *Berkhamsted* R ii p ii. 1084 O v 118. H. ii p iv 49
July 6.	Letters obligatory for 54,000 gold florins of Florence, lent to the K by John Richier, William Kerman, and Walter Campsor, of Mechlin. *Antwerp.* R. ii. p ii 1085. O v 118 H. ii. p. iv. 49.

DATE	SUBJECT
1339 July 8	The English standards of weights and measures are to be used in North Wales *Berkhamsted.* R II p. II 1085
July 16.	Proclamation to be made at Southampton that all persons having tenements in the town are to return thither *Kennington.* R II p II 1085.
July 16	The K explains his title to the crown of France, to the pope and college of cardinals. *Antwerp* R. II p II 1086
July 16	Warrant for the payment of the arrears of his fee to Thomas bp of Hereford, guardian of Ireland *Kennington.* R II p II 1087 O v 119 H II p IV 49
July 20.	The K. orders Thomas bp, of Hereford, guardian of Ireland, to report those constables of castles who have neglected the defences of their castles *Kennington* R II p II 1087
July 20.	The abp of Dublin is ordered to repair his castles at Castelkenyn and other places in Leinster *Kennington* R II p II 1088
July 20.	Also to cultivate and colonise his waste lands *Kennington* R. II p II. 1088
July 20.	Summons to the abp of Dublin to attend the K's council in England at Martinmas *Kennington* R II p II 1088
Aug 2	Declaration by the K and the imperial ambassadors that the treaties between the two sovereigns have been observed. *Filford [Vilvorde]* R II p II 1088 O. v. 120. H II p IV 53.
Aug. 12	Receipt by the K for 9,600 fl of Florence from the company of the Bardi, who have received jewels in pledge Receipt for 6,400 fl from the company of Peruch *Filford [Vilvorde]* R II p II 1088 O. v 120 H II p IV 50
Aug 13	The K, as vicar of the Holy Empire of Rome, promises that he will not do any damage to the count of Hainault *Brussels* R II p II 1088 O. v. 120. H II p. IV. 50
Aug 15	The K desires the abps and bps. of England to pray for his success in France *Windsor* R II p II. 1089 O v 121. H II p IV 50
Aug 20	The K, as vicar of the Holy Empire, declares that the aid given to him by the count of Hainault shall not be used as a precedent to oblige him to give further assistance. *Brussels* R II p II 1089 O. v 122 H II p IV 50
Sept 6	The cardinal of Naples, prebendary of Sutton, is released from the payment of tenths or aids. *Windsor* R. II p II 1089 O. v 122 H II. p IV 50
Sept. 19	Protection for two Roman cardinals who are coming to the K. *Valenciennes.* R II p II 1090 O v 123 H II p IV. 51
Sept 16	Grant of the advowson of the priory of Montacute to William de Montacute, earl of Salisbury, marshal of England. *Quevrain* R II. p II. 1090 O v 123. H II p IV 51
Sept. 21.	The K. grants an annuity of 1,000*l.* to Reinald duke of Gueldres and count of Zutphen, who has done homage to him. *Brussels.* R II p II 1690 O v 123 H II p IV. 51
Sept 22.	Writs for the election of sheriffs in Somerset, Dorset, Essex, Sussex, Surrey, and Cambridge. *Windsor* R II p. II 1090.
Sept 26.	Power to Edward duke of Cornwall, John abp of Canterbury, the bps of Durham and London, and five others, to pardon debts to the crown not exceeding 10*l* *Markoyn infra marcham Franciæ [? Marchiennes]* R II p II 1091. O v 124. H II. p IV 51
Sept 26	Power to the same to grant releases and pardons *Markoyn infra marchiam Franciæ [? Marchiennes].* R. II. p. II 1091. O v 125. H II. p IV 52
Sept 27	Indenture specifying the powers granted *en chaump de la ville de Markoyn deins la marche de Franciæ [? Marchiennes]* R II p II. 1001 O v 125 H II p IV 52
Oct 4	At the request of John duke of Brabant, the K grants a safe conduct to persons coming to treat of peace with Philip de Valois *Markoyne [? Marchiennes]* R II. p II 1092 O. v. 126 H II p IV. 52.
Oct 10.	The K desires the abp of York to convoke his clergy, and exhort them to grant an aid *Windsor* R. II p II 1092 O v 127. H II. p IV. 53
Oct 12	Pope Benedict XII. remonstrates with the K for his proceedings against William bp. of Cambray, and for assuming the title of vicar of the empire *Avignon.* R II p II 1092 O. v 128 H II p IV 53
Oct 13	The K grants the title of earl of Pembroke to Laurence de Hastynges, nephew of Aymer de Valence, late earl of Pembroke *Mont Martin* R II p II. 1093. O v 130 H II p IV. 54
Oct 15.	Warrant for the payment of the wages of 64 men-at-arms and 1,200 hobillers, going to Scotland with Edward Balliol. *Westm.* R II. p II 1093 O. v. 131. H. II. p. IV 54

DATE.	SUBJECT
1339. Oct 17	Letter informing the K of England that the K of France will give him battle on the following Thursday or Friday. *S Quentins* Hugh de Geneve writes in answer that the K. will remain in France till the time mentioned. *Ormy de S. Benedict.* 18 Oct R ii p ii 1093.
Oct. 26.	Edward K of Scotland is appointed captain of the army against the Scots. *Windsor* R ii p ii 1094 O v 126. H ii p iv 52
Oct. 29.	Pardon to Thomas Ughtred for having surrendered the town of S John of Perth. *Kennington.* R. ii. p. ii. 1094 O. v. 131. H ii p iv. 54.
Nov 1	The K sends an account of his campaign to Edward duke of Cornwall and the council. *Brussels* R. ii p ii 1094
Nov. 2	Ratification of an indenture between Oliver de Ingham, seneschal of Gascony, and Gaston de Insula, who does homage to the K.; dated Bordeaux, 31 March 1339. *Ghent.* R. ii. p. ii. 1095. O. v. 132. H. ii. p. iv. 54
Nov 8.	William Trussel, admiral of the fleet west of the Thames, is ordered to deliver a ship to Robert de Artoys *Langley* . R ii p ii 1095 O v 127 H ii p iv 52
Nov. 8.	Warrant to William Trussel to deliver the *Seint Jak* of Bayonne, or another ship, to Robert de Artoys. R. ii. p. ii. 1095 O. v. 133. H. ii. p iv 55
Nov 8.	Warrant to the treasurer of the Exchequer to allow the sheriffs of London for 100 marks paid to Henry Darcy, late mayor of London *Langley* R. ii p ii 1096
Nov. 13.	Benedict [XII] blames the K for acting as vicar to the emperor, who is excommunicated , denies that he has aided the K. of France against the K of England, and reminds him that he has sent nuncios to negotiate a peace *Avignon.* R ii p ii 1096
Nov 13	Power for William de Montacute, earl of Salisbury, marshal of England, Henry de Ferrers, the K.'s chamberlain, Geoffrey le Scrop, and Maurice de Berkele, the K.'s secretaries, to treat for a marriage between the eldest son of Louis count of Flanders and the K's daughter Isabella *Antwerp* R ii p ii 1097 O v 134. H ii. p iv 55
Nov. 15.	Power to John duke of Brabant, the earls of Northampton, Salisbury, and Suffolk, and three others, to enter into a treaty of alliance with Flanders, and for the redress of injuries in the island of Cagent. *Antwerp.* R. ii p ii. 1097. O. v. 135 H. ii. p iv. 55
Nov 15	William Trussel, admiral of the fleet west of the Thames, is ordered to supply Hugh le Despenser with two ships, one called " La Seinte Marie Cogg," and the other " La Cogg de Clyve." *Langley* R ii p ii. 1098 O v 135 H ii p iv 56
Nov. 16.	Summons to the abps. and bps to attend a parliament at Westminster in the octave of S Hilary. *Langley* R. ii p ii 1098 O v. 136. H. ii p iv. 56.
Nov 17.	The K grants 1,500 florins of Florence to Robert count of Varnebergh for his homage and service *Antwerp.* R ii p ii 1098 O v. 136. H ii. p. iv 56
Nov 25	Licence to Thomas Blanket and other burgesses of Bristol to construct machines and to make woollen cloth. *Langley.* R. ii. p. ii. 1098. O v. 137. H ii. p. iv. 56.
Nov 28.	The abp of Canterbury is ordered to summon a convocation at London on Jan 27 The abp of York is ordered to summon a convocation at York on Feb 9. *Langley* R ii. p ii 1099 O v 137 H ii. p iv 56–7.
Nov. 28.	The K grants to the marquis of Juliers, whilst he is in the K.'s service, 8l. a day and the expenses of his retinue. *Antwerp* R ii p ii 1099. O. v 138. H ii p iv. 57.
Nov 28.	The K promises to make William marquis of Juliers an earl in England *Antwerp* R ii p ii 1099. O. v. 139. H ii p iv. 57.
Dec. 3	The marshal of the household of Edward duke of Cornwall, Robert de Bilkemore, James de Wodestok, and Hugh de Berewyk are empowered to try felonies committed within the verge of the duke's court during the K.'s absence abroad. *Langley* R. ii. p ii 1100 O v. 140. H ii p. iv. 57
Dec 4	The K , who is on his way back to England, promises the duke of Brabant to return by the end of June, and leaves the earls of Derby and Salisbury as hostages. *Antwerp* R ii p ii 1100 O v 140 H ii p iv. 57–8.
[Dec 4]	The duke of Brabant is allowed to retain 1,000 men at the K.'s expense during his absence. R. ii. p ii 1100 O. v 141. H ii. p iv 58
Dec 8	The K acknowledges that he owes 20,000 small gold florins of Florence to the marquis of Juliers for the loss of horses and other damages suffered in his service. *Antwerp* R ii. p. ii. 1101. O v 142. H ii p iv 58
Dec 8	The K also acknowledges that he owes the said marquis 7,000 gold florins *à l'Escu* for his wages R. ii. p. ii 1101 O. v. 142. H ii p. iv. 58.

DATE	SUBJECT
1339 Dec 8	Memorandum that on the death [at the house of the bp of Winchester in Southwerk] of Richard bp of London, the K's chancellor, the great seal was taken to the abp. of Canterbury at Lambeth, who sent it to the house of the Carmehte Friars in Fleet Street, where the K's council was then sitting, and the council delivered it to John de S Paul, keeper of the rolls of Chanery, Michael de Wach and Thomas de Baumburgh. R. ii p ii i1101. O v 143. H ii p. iv 58.
Dec 9	The masters of the ships of Bayonne at Sandwich and elsewhere in those parts are ordered to have their ships ready to sail with the admiral about S Hilary's day *Langley.* R ii p ii. 1191 O v. 143. H. ii p. iv 59
Dec 10	The K grants an annuity of 100*l* to Peter Moryn, lord of Caumpaignes. *Antwerp* R. ii. p ii. 1101. O v 144 H ii p iv. 59
Dec 10	The K grants the advowson of Thingden, in the diocese of Lincoln, to the convent of S Michael at Antwerp, where a son was born to him, and where the Q. is now staying, expecting her confinement *Antwerp* R ii p ii 1102 O v 144 H. ii. p. iv 59
Dec. 20.	Safe conduct for two Roman cardinals who are coming to Valenciennes to treat of peace *Antwerp* R ii p ii 1102 O v 145 H ii p iv 59
Dec 20	Warrant to the treasurer of the Exchequer to pay Nicholas de la Beche, constable of the Tower of London, for the wages of 20 men-at-arms and 50 archers. *Langley.* R ii. p ii 1102
Dec 22.	The K. promises to Otes lord of Cuyc compensation for the lordships he has lost in 14 French towns *Antwerp.* R. ii p ii 1102 O v 145 H ii p. iv 59
Dec 23	Richard de Potenhale, the K.'s valet, is ordered to provide herrings and other fish at Yarmouth, Blakenheth, and S Botolph's. *Langley* R. ii p ii. 1103. O v. 146. H. ii. p iv 60
Dec 23	Pope Benedict [XII] offers to mediate in person between the Kings of England and France *Avignon.* R ii p ii. 1103 O v 146 H ii p iv 60
Dec. 28	The K. grants a pension 1,500*l.* to John duke of Lorraine and Brabant *Antwerp.* R. ii p ii. 1103 O v. 147 H. ii p iv 60
Dec. 28.	Obligation for 5,000*l*, the residue of the fee of the duke of Brabant, which amount was settled by the arbitration of the earl of Salisbury and the lord of Cuyc. *Antwerp.* R ii p ii. 1103 O v 148 H ii p iv 60.
Dec 28	Grant of a pension of 24*l* to Henry Bertaldi, lord of Duffle and Geyle. *Antwerp* R ii. p ii. 1104 O v 148 H ii p iv 61.
Dec. 29	The K writes to the seneschal of the K of Sicily, in Provence, for restitution of a sum of money for the purchase of galleys at Monaco within the district of Genoa, which was sequestrated by him *Antwerp.* R. ii p. ii 1104. O v 148 H ii p iv 61
1040. Jan 1	The K. assigns the sums promised to Oto lord of Cuyk to be paid out of the customs at London *Antwerp* R ii p ii 1104 O v 149 H ii p iv 61
Jan 2.	Power to H bp of Lincoln, the earls of Derby and Salisbury, William de Exon, and Alexander de Oneby, to treat with Philip de Valois *Antwerp* R ii p ii. 1104 O v 149 H. ii p iv. 61
[Jan 2]	Power for the said commissioners to treat with the papal nuncios. R ii. p ii 1104. O v 150 H ii p iv 61
Jan 2	The K promises to make neither peace nor truce with Philip de Valois without comprehending Bernardet lord de la Bret *Antwerp.* R ii. p ii. 1105 O. v 150. H ii. p iv 61.
Jan. 3.	Bernardet lord de la Bret and Hugh de Gebennis [? Geneva], lord de Vorray and Athon, are appointed the K's lieutenants and captains in Aquitain *Antwerp.* R ii p ii. 1105 O v 151 H ii p iv 61
Jan 3	The K orders his subjects in Aquitain to obey and assist the above-mentioned Bernardet and Hugh *Antwerp* R ii p ii 1105 O. v. 151 H. ii. p iv 62
Jan. 4.	Indemnity to the duke of Gueldres for 5,000 florins promised by him to certain citizens of Cologne *Antwerp* R ii p ii. 1105 O v. 151 H. ii p iv 62
Jan 4.	The K. promises to repay the duke of Gueldres for his expenses in his service *Antwerp* R. ii. p ii 1105 O v 152 H ii p iv 62.
Jan 4.	Power to the earl of Salisbury, Henry de Ferrers, the K.'s chamberlain, and Sir Geoffrey le Scrop to treat for a marriage between Louis, eldest son of the count of Flanders, and the K's daughter Isabella *Antwerp* R ii p ii 1106 O v 152 H ii. p. iv. 62
Jan 4	Power for the same to treat with the count and the commonalties of Flanders about assisting the K. against France *Antwerp* R. ii p. ii 1106 O v 153. H ii p iv 62

DATE.	SUBJECT.
1340 Jan. 19.	John archbp of Canterbury, William la Zousche, dean of York, Richard de Wylughby, John de Stonore, and John de St Paul are deputed to open the parliament at Westminster on Jan 20 *Langley* R II p II. 1106 O v 153 H II p iv 63.
Jan. 21.	Letters obligatory for 10,000*l.* lent by John de Ponte, Leo de Mirabella, Louis Pellet, and Antony Abolon The bp of Lincoln and four others are also bound for the same sum. *Antwerp.* R. II p. II 1106. O v 154 H II p IV. 63.
Jan. 26.	The K releases Guy de Flanders, taken prisoner by Walter de Manny, admiral of the fleet. *Ghent* R. II. p II 1107. O v. 155 H II p IV 63
Jan. 26.	The K. will not make peace with Philip de Valois without comprehending Hugh de Gebennis, lord of Athon and Vorray. *Ghent.* R II p II 1107. O. v. 155. H II. p IV. 63
Jan 28.	The K deputes Reinold duke of Gueldres to swear for him to the covenants with Ghent, Bruges, and Ypres *Ghent* R II p II 1107 O v 155 H II p IV 63
Jan 30.	Nicholin de Flisco is allowed 13*s* 4*d* a day while travelling on the K.'s service. *Ghent* R II p II 1107 O v 156. H II p IV 63.
	The K. writes to the pope that no offers have been made to him by Philip de Valois through the cardinals or otherwise, and though he would have been contented with a moderate offer to avoid war, he does not see what more he can do for peace *Ghent* R II. p. II. 1107. O v 156 H II p IV 64
Feb 2	Obligation for 65,982 florins of Florence to Gabriel de Monte Magno and Matthew de Canachoen, merchants *Ghent* R II. p. II 1108 O v. 157 H. II. p. IV. 64.
Feb 6.	Obligation for 64,066 florins to Reynand, duke of Gueldres *Ghent.* R II p II 1108 O v 158 H II p IV 64.
Feb 8.	The K of England declares that the Flemings have recognized him as K. of France, and invites the French to do the same, promising to observe the laws of St Louis *Ghent* R II p II 1108. O. v. 158 H II p IV 64
Feb. 8	The K orders his letters patent declaring his title to the crown of France, and the refusal of his offers by Philip, to he affixed to certain church doors R. II p II 1109
[Feb. 8]	K Edward's declaration setting forth all the overtures and advances he had made to Philip from time to time, and the refusal of his offers by Philip, and the many injuries he had received from him *Ghent* R II p II 1109 O v 160. H II p IV 65
Feb. 8.	Power to Nicolin de Flisco to hire galleys for the K.'s service. *Ghent.* R II p II 1111. O v. 163 H II p IV 66
Feb. 8.	Declaration to the people of France as to the K of England's title to the French crown, and his intentions. *Ghent* R II. p. II 1111 O. v 163 H II p. IV 66
[Feb. 8]	Similar declaration to the towns of Lille, Douay, Bethune, Aire, Arras, St Omer, and Tournay. R II p II 1111 O v 164 H II p IV 67
Feb. 13.	John de St Pool is appointed keeper of the great seal *Kennington* R II p. II. 1111 O v 165. H. II. p IV 67.
Feb. 14.	The K orders the sheriff of Berwick to restore to the prior of Durham the barony of Coldingham, notwithstanding the privy seal obtained by the late prior of Coldingham, who had been deprived for his crimes. *Kennington* R II p II 1112 O v 165. H II p. IV 67.
Feb. 16.	The K orders J bp of Exeter to assist Hugh de Courtenay, earl of Devon, and the other wardens of the coast, as he hears that the French are preparing for an invasion *Kennington.* R II p II 1112.
Feb. 18.	Thomas Wake de Lydel, William de Ros de Hamelak, Thomas Ughtred, and two others, are deputed to arrange with the prelates and nobles at York for sending men to Scotland with Edward Bahol Similar commissions to Nicolas de Cantilupe and two others, for Nottinghamshire and Derbyshire, and to Gilbert de Clyderowe and Robert de Radeclyf, for Lancashire *Kennington.* R II p II 1113 O v 168. H II p IV 68
Feb. 18.	The K. offers to send a safe-conduct to John duke of Brittany and earl of Richmond for persons to seek redress for injuries done to Bretons by English *Kennington* R II p IV 1113
Feb. 20.	Warrant for the payment of 26*s.* 8*d.* a week to Alice countess of Mynteth *Kennington.* R II p II 1113. O v 168. H II p IV 68.
Feb. 20	The mayor and bailiffs of Ipswich are ordered to inquire into the claim made by the merchants of Ghent on the executors of John de Whatfeld. *Kennington* R II p II 1113 O. v. 169. II II p IV 68.

DATE	SUBJECT
1340 Feb. 20	The K orders Reginald de Conductu and 136 merchants and others to attend on the council at Westminster on the Monday in Mid-Lent. *Kennington.* R ii p ii 1114
Feb. 21.	Impressions of the new seals with the title of K of France are to be published throughout the K's dominions *Herewicz* R. ii p. ii. 1115. O. v 169 H. ii. p iv 69.
Feb 21	Memorandum that the K landed at Orwell on his return to England, the bishop of Lincoln, the earls of Derby and Northampton, and others, being in his company. R ii p ii. 1115 O v 170 H ii p iv 69
Feb 21	The K. summons a parliament at Westminster on the Monday in Mid-Lent, and will explain the reasons for his change of style *Harwich* R. ii p ii. 1115 O v 170. H. ii. p. iv 69
March 1.	The K delivers a new great seal to John de St Paul, keeper of the rolls of Chancery, in the cage-chaumbre at Westminster R. ii p ii 1115 O v 170 H ii. p. iv 69
[March 1.]	John de St Paul delivers to the K the great seal which he had kept during his absence R. ii p ii 1115 O v 171. H ii p iv 69
March 1.	Commission to Henry bp of Lincoln, Robert de Sadyngton, John de Thoresby, and nine others, to contract a loan for the K *Westm* R ii p ii 111b O v 171 H. ii p iv. 69
March 1	The K orders Henry Trenchard and the lord of Glamorgan to return with their men to the Isle of Wight *Westm.* R ii p ii 1116
March 2.	Licence to Hugh de Gebennis, banneret of Burgundy, to export 100 sacks of wool to Bruges without paying the customs. *Westm* R ii p ii. 1116 O v. 712. H. ii. p iv 70
March 2	Licence to Adam de Thorpe, the K's barber, to perform by deputy his office of keeper of the K's seal for the recognizance of debts at Lincoln *Westm.* R ii p. ii 1117
March 5.	Pope Benedict [XII] exhorts the K to lay aside the title of K of France *Avignon* R. ii p ii 1117. O v. 173. H. ii. p iv 70.
March 6.	Grant to William de Montacute, earl of Salisbury, of the manor of Merton, in co Somerset, forfeited by John de Fienles *Westm* R ii p ii 1117 O v 174. H ii. p. iv. 70
March 6	The K. forbids an intended tournament at Canterbury. *Westm.* R. ii. p ii 1118.
March 14.	The K informs the pope that the French ambassadors were not ready to meet his ambassadors at Tournay, but he has written to express his willingness to resume the treaty; he desires credence for William de Kyldesby, archbp elect of York, John Wawayn, and Fnar Thomas de Insula, concerning William la Zouche, who claims to be the archbishop elect. *Langley* R ii p ii 1118 O. v. 175. H. ii. p iv. 71.
	Credence for John Wawayn and Thomas de Insula to six cardinals R. ii p ii 1118 O v 176. H ii p iv 71
March 15	Proclamation to be made in the maritime counties against injuring Spanish merchants trading with Flanders *Westm.* R. ii. p ii 1118.
March 16	The K. asks the pope to confirm the foundation of a priory at Bustlesham in the diocese of Sarum by the earl of Salisbury *Westm* R. ii p ii 1119. O v 176 H ii p iv 71
March 16	The K requests the pope to grant a dispensation for the marriage of Hugh le Despenser and Elizabeth, daughter of the earl of Salesbury *Westm* R ii p ii 1119 O v 176. H ii p iv 71.
April 4	Power to Oliver de Ingham, seneschal of Gascony, and Antony Usumaris, lieutenant of the constable of Bordeaux, to treat for a marriage between Amanenus, eldest son of Bernardet lord de la Bret, and Margaret, daughter of the late earl of Kent *London* R ii p ii. 1119 O v 177. H. ii. p. iv. 71.
April 8	Confirmation of the grant by Edward K of Scotland to Sir Thomas Ughtreth of the manor of Bonkhill and other lands forfeited by John Stiward, dated Roxburgh. 20 Oct. 1 Edw. III *Westm* R ii p ii. 1119. O. v 178. H ii p iv 72
April 10	The K orders Richard Talebot, warden of Berwick-upon-Tweed, to deliver William Mason of Berwick, who was arrested within the liberties of the bp of Durham, to the constable of Norham castle *Westm* R. ii p ii. 1120. O. v. 178 H ii. p iv 72
April 10	The mayor and sheriffs of London are ordered to prevent butchers selling meat unfit for food, by sewing it to good meat *Westm.* R ii p. ii 1120.
April 12.	The K forbids the exportation of wool for fear of its being taken by the enemy. *Westm.* R ii p ii. 1120
April 12.	Protection for the merchants of Spain, Catalonia, and Majorca, going to Flanders *Westm.* R ii p ii. 1120 O. v. 179. H. ii. p. iv 72

DATE.	SUBJECT
1340 April 18	Warrant for the payment of the annuity of the count of Juliers *Windsor* R ii p ii 1120 O. v 179 H ii p iv 72.
April 16	The K grants certain privileges to the clergy of England, with the assent of parliament. *Westm* R. ii. p. ii. 1121.
April 20	The K allows Edward of Brussels, a converted Jew, to reside in the house of converts in the suburbs of London, with a pension of twopence a day *Westm.* R ii p ii 1121
April 25	Credence for Dr Richard de Wyncle to the pope. *Westm* R. ii p ii 1121. O v 179 H ii. p. iv 72.
April 28	Memorandum of the delivery of the great seal by the K to John abp. of Canterbury, as Chancellor *Westm* R. ii p ii 1122 O v 180 H ii p iv 72
April 18	Power for Gilbert de Umfravill, earl of Anegos, Henry de Percy, and Ralph de Nevill, to treat with the K's Scotch enemies Similar power for Robert de Clifford and Anthony de Lucy *Westm.* R ii. p ii 1122. O v. 180 H ii p iv 76
[April 28.]	Power for Richard bp of Durham, Gilbert de Umfravill, Henry de Percy, Ralph de Nevill, and Geoffrey le Scrop, to treat for a truce or final peace with the Scotch R ii p ii 1122 O v 181 H ii p iv 73
April 28	Power for Robert de Clifford and Anthony de Lucy to grant pardons and receive fealty Similar power to Umfravill, Percy, and Nevill, above-mentioned *Westm* R ii p ii. 1122. O. v. 181 H ii p iv. 73
May 3	If the K. fails to obtain a papal dispensation for the marriage of the duke of Cornwall, his eldest son, with Margaret, daughter of the duke of Brabant, he will repay double the dowry already received *Westm* R ii p ii 1122 O v. 181 H ii p iv 73
May 3	The K grants an annuity of 200 marks to Geoffrey le Scrop *Westm* R. ii. p ii 1123
May 3	The K grants to Mary countess of Fyff 40s. a week, two robes a year, and the manor of Colde Kenyngton Warrants for the performance of the grant to the K's treasurer, to Thomas Crosse, clerk of the great wardrobe, Thomas de Foxle, constable of Windsor Castle, and to the sheriff of Middlesex *Westm.* R ii p ii 1123 O v 182-3 H ii p iv 74
May 7	The K grants to Walter de Manny 8,000*l* for the ransom of Guy de Flanders and other prisoners whom he detains *Westm* R ii p. ii 1123 O v 183 H ii p iv 74
May 9	The K grants an annuity of 20*l* and the robes of a valet to John Stykerape, councillor of Ypres Similar grants to John Hoost, Baldewin Vandenwalbe, and Nicholas Scotelare, of Ghent and Bruges *Westm* R ii p ii 1124 O v 183 H ii p iv. 74
May 12.	Similar grant to William de Bomere, prebendary of Northmusk *Westm* R ii p ii. 1124 O v. 184 H ii p iv 74
May 12	William marquis of Juliers is created earl of Cambridge, with a pension of 1,000*l* a year. *Westm* R ii p ii 1124 O v 184 H ii p iv. 74
May 17.	The K assigns certain dues in Berkshire, Buckinghamshire, and Rutland for the payment of 11,720*l* 2s , lent by Anthony Bache on the security of two crowns belonging to the K and one to the Queen Writs to the receivers and others in the above counties. *Westm* R ii. p ii 1124 O v 185 H ii. p. iv 74.
May 20.	Credence for Thomas de Cerfe, clerk, to the bailiffs and jurats of Jersey *Westm* R ii p ii. 1125 O iv. 186 H ii. p iv 75.
May 26.	The K grants 40s. a day during peace and 60s during war to Edward K of Scotland, for the expenses of his household Warrant for the payment thereof *Westm* R. ii p ii 1125 O v 186 H. ii p iv 75
May 27.	The K appoints his eldest son Edward duke of Cornwall regent during his intended absence abroad *Westm* William de Clinton, earl of Huntingdon, and J. archbp of Canterbury are appointed his councillors. *Westm* , 28 *May* Also Henry de Percy, Thomas Wake de Lydel, and Ralph de Nevill *Shotley,* 21 *June* R ii p ii 1125 O iv 187 H ii p iv 75
May 29.	Power for Edward duke of Cornwall to grant letters of *congé d'elire*, appoint justices and other officers, sell wardships, &c *Westm.* R ii p. ii 1125 O v 188 H ii p iv. 76
June 1.	The K demands justice from the pope for the seizure of his ambassador Nicholin de Flisco at Avignon and his abduction into France, and cannot send other ambassadors unless he is assured of their safety *Clare* R ii p ii. 1126. O v. 188 H ii. p iv. 76
June 18.	The K orders the archbishops and bishops to repay the money lent to him by the papal nuncios, out of the biennial tenth *Shotley.* R. ii. p. ii 1126 O v 189 H ii p iv 76

DATE	SUBJECT.
1340. June 21	The K grants 3,333*l* 6*s* 8*d*, from the subsidy of sheaves, lambs, and fleeces in Kent, for the payment of the wages of the archbp of Canterbury during his embassy. *Shotley.* R 11 p 11 1126. O v 193 H 11 p 1v 77
June 21	The K excuses Wolstan bishop of Worcester from attendance in parliament in consequence of his infirmity *Shotley* R 11 p 11 1127. O. v 191 H 11 p 1v 77
June 21.	Bartholomew de Fayete is appointed remembrancer and registrar of the castle of Bordeaux, with the fee of 12*d* a day *Shotley* Letter informing the seneschal of Gascony thereof R 11 p 1v. 1127
June 21	The K. promises that his assumption of the crown of France shall not affect the privileges of his subjects in Gascony *Shotley* R. 11 p 11. 1127. O.v. 191 H. 11. p 1v 77
June 21	The K of England explains his title to the crown of France to the nobles and commonalties of Gascony, and desires their assistance *Shotley* R 11 p 11 1127 O v 191. H. 11 p 1v 77
June 21.	The K desires the assistance of the commonalty of Montfort and 81 other commonalties and lords in Aquitain *Shotley* R 11 p 11 1128 O v 192 H 11 p 1v. 77
June 21.	The K orders the seneschal of Gascony and the constable of Bordeaux to fortify the town of Bonnegarde with a wall and bridge. *Shotley.* R 11 p 11 1128.
June 22.	The archbp of Canterbury returned the great seal to the K at Orwell on June 20, and resigned the chancellorship on account of his infirmity, the K thereupon ordered the seal to be broken, and a new seal to be made, which he sent on June 22 to John de St. Paul, keeper of the rolls, for the purpose of being delivered to Robert bp of Chichester, who was appointed chancellor R 11 p 11 1129 O v 194 H 11 p 1v 78
June 22	John de St Paul delivered the seal to the bp. of Chichester in the palace at Westminster. R. 11 p 11 1129 O v 195. H 11 p 1v. 79.
June 22	The K. sailed from Orwell about 6 a.m R. 11 p 11 1129
June 28	The K. informs the archbishops and bishops of England and Wales of his victory over the French fleet at Swine, on June 24th, and desires their prayers *Waltham Holy Cross* * R 11 p 11 1129 O v 195 H 11 p 1v 79
July 2	The treasurer and chamberlains are ordered to renew the wax about the corpse of Edward I in Westminster Abbey. *Waltham* R 11 p 11 1130. O. v 196 H 11 p 1v 79
July 5.	The pope has received the K's letters by Dr Richard de Wyncle, a friar preacher, and is ready to interpose for the preservation of peace *Avignon* R 11 p 11 1130 O v. 196. H 11 p 1v 79
July 9	The K informs the parliament of his victory at Zwyne, and that he is marching towards Tournay with 100,000 men, and Robert de Artoys with 50,000 towards S. Omers. *Bruges* R 11 p 11 1130 O v 197 H. 11. p. 1v. 79.
July 18	Warrant to the sheriff of Yorkshire to deliver John earl of Murref to the bp of Durham, Gilbert Umframville, earl of Anegos, Henry de Percy, and Ralph de Nevill *Kennington.* R 11 p 11 1130 O 1v 197 H 11 p 1v 79
July 22	Warrant to John de Ellerker, receiver of the subsidy in the northern counties, to pay 60*l*. for the repair of the walls of Carlisle. *Westm* R 11 p 11 1131.
July 24	The K. promises that the contribution of men by the city of London shall not be prejudicial to their privileges *Kennington* R 11 p 11 1131
July 27	Robert de Hanbury, chamberlain of North Wales, is ordered to repair and victual the K's castles in those parts *Kennington* R. 11 p 11. 1131
July 26	The K challenges Philip de Valois to decide their quarrel either by a single combat, by a combat of 100 a side, or by a general engagement before Tournay in 10 days *Chyn.* R 11 p 11. 1131. O. v 198 H 11 p 1v 80
July 30	The K of France refuses to acknowledge the challenge as directed to him, considers K Edward's invasion of France as contrary to his duty to him as his liege lord, and intends to drive him out of the kingdom *Near the priory of St Andrew's* R 11 p 11 1131
Aug 1	Indenture for the liberation of John Randolf, earl of Murref, to arrange about his ransom, the earl of March and four others being hostages for him *Bilibrig* R 11 p 11 1132. O v. 200 H 11 p. 1v. 80
Aug 20	Confirmation of the above-mentioned indenture *London* R 11 p 11 1132 O v 200 H 11 p 1v. 81

* The documents dated in England during the King's absence are attested by the duke of Cornwall.

DATE.	SUBJECT
1340. Aug 20.	The mayor, sheriffs, and aldermen of London are ordered to preserve the peace and repress crime in the city and suburbs *Berkhamstead.* R. ii p. ii 1132.
Aug 20	Peter cardinal of St Praxedis is licensed to export 60 sacks of wool to Bruges without paying the duty *Berkhamsted* R. ii p. ii. 1133
Aug. 24.	The admirals of the fleets of the north and of the Cinque Ports are ordered to unite for the defence of the kingdom *Windsor.* R. ii. p. ii 1133. O. v 201-2. H. ii p. iv 81
Aug 24.	The town of Spondon, in Derbyshire, is released from payment of the subsidy until Feb 2, in consequence of its destruction by fire *Berkhamsted.* R. ii p. ii 1133
Aug 25	Power to R. bp of Durham and three others to receive William de Douglas and other Scots in place of the earl of March as hostage for the earl of Murref, if he wishes to defer his return. *Berkhamsted* R. ii p. ii. 1134. O. v. 202. H. ii p. iv 81
Sept 1.	Proclamation is to be made by the sheriffs of Norfolk and Suffolk and 17 other counties that no injury is to be done to Spanish merchants trading with Flanders. *Windsor* R. ii p. ii 1134 O. v 203 H. ii p. iv 81
Sept. 6	Transfer of the annuity of 100 marks granted to Robin de Forester to Godekin de Revele, merchant. *In the field near Tournay.* R. ii. p. ii. 1134 O. v 203 H. ii p. iv 82
Sept 13	Protection till All Saints' day for Peter Cenu and Bernard Dini of Florence, agents of the cardinal of S. Praxedis *Windsor* R. ii p. ii 1135 O. v 204 H. ii p. iv. 82
Sept 20.	The bishops of England and Wales are ordered to send the collectors of the cardinals to the council at Westminster at Michaelmas *Andover.* R. ii. p. ii. 1135 O. v. 204. H. ii. p. iv 82.
Sept. 25	The sheriff of York is ordered to receive the earl of Murref, unless his surrender is prorogued *Andover* R. ii p. ii 1135 O. v 205 H. ii p. iv 82
Sept. 25.	Truce between England and France and between England and Scotland. *Espechin.* R. ii. p. ii. 1135. O. v 205-6. H. ii p. iv 83
Oct 6.	Proclamation of the truce to be made throughout England, Ireland, and Wales *London* R. ii. p. ii 1137 O. v 209 H. ii p. iv. 84
Oct. 7.	The K. orders the assessors not to levy the tax on sheaves, lambs, or fleeces in the Cinque Ports until their claim of exemption is settled *Andover* R. ii p. ii 1138.
	The K. asks the pope to confirm the grants of forfeited lands to sir John de Gatesdene by the city of Spoleto in recompense for his services against the Ghibellines R. ii. p. ii 1138 O. v 210 H. ii p. iv 84.
Oct 10	Tournaments are prohibited throughout England *Andover* R. ii p. ii 1138.
Oct. 11.	The sheriffs of the maritime counties are ordered to prevent ships being sold or given to foreigners *Andover* R. ii p. ii 1138. O. v 210 H. ii p. iv 85
Oct. 18	Credence for sir Reginald de Cobham to the pope. *Westm* R. ii p. ii 1139. O. v. 211. H. ii p. iv. 85
Oct. 18	The K. requests the pope to grant a dispensation to Robert, son of sir Robert de Burghcher, for holding a benefice, notwithstanding his illegitimate birth. *Westm* R. ii. p. ii 1139 O. v. 211. H. ii p. iv 85.
Oct 18	The K. assures the pope that William de Kildesby was not concerned in the arrest of the messenger whom Oliver de Cerzeto, papal chaplain, sent with a summons to the bp of Coventry and Lichfield and Robert de Kildesby. *Westm* R. ii p. ii 1139 O. v. 212. H. ii p. iv 85.
Oct. 18	John de Pulteneye is licensed to export 160 sacks of wool to Bruges for the ransom of William de Montacute, earl of Salisbury. *Andover* R. ii p. ii 1139
Oct 25	Henry de Percy and Ralph de Nevill are ordered to deliver John earl of Murref to the constable of Windsor *Wallingford* R. ii p. ii 1140 O. v 213 H. ii p. iv. 86.
Oct. 25.	The constable of Windsor Castle is ordered to receive the earl of Murref *Wallingford* R. ii. p. ii 1140 O. v 214. H. ii p. iv 86.
Oct 26	The K. grants the earl of Murref to the earl of Salisbury *Wallingford.* R. ii p. ii 1140 O. v. 214 H. ii. p. iv 86.
Oct 30.	The K. asks the pope for a dispensation for the marriage of his eldest son Edward duke of Cornwall with the daughter of the duke of Brabant *Westm* R. ii p. ii 1140. O. v. 214 H. ii p. iv 86.
Nov 6	The archbp of Canterbury, the bps. of London and Ely, the earls of Arundel, Salisbury, and Gloucester, and Ralph Basset of Drayton, are summoned to a council at Westm. Nov. 14 *Reading.* R. ii. p. ii 1141.

DATE	SUBJECT
1340 Nov 15	Licence to Peter cardinal of S Praxedis, to export 60 sacks of wool yearly, without payment of customs *Ghent* R. ii p ii 1141 O v. 215 H. ii p iv. 86.
Nov. 24.	Thomas de Drayton of Great Yarmouth is ordered to send to London the bishop of Man in Scotland who was arrested in a ship at Kirkele. *Wallingford* R. ii p ii 1141 O v 215 H ii p iv 86
Nov 30	Memorandum that the K arrived at the Tower of London on Thursday about midnight. Robert bp of Chichester, then chancellor, the next morning delivered to him the great seal which had been used in England during the K's absence, which he gave into the keeping of William de Kildesby, and the seal brought by the K from abroad is ordered to be henceforth used R. ii p ii 1141 O iv 216. H ii p iv. 87
Jan 1,	Thomas de Evesham, clerk, delivered the great seal to Robert de Burghcher, chancellor, at the house of the bp of Worcester without the bar of the New Temple R ii p 1142.
Dec 2	The rolls, bundles, and memoranda of the chancery in the keeping of John de S. Paul were sent to the Tower of London, delivered on Dec 2 to William de Kyldesby, keeper of the privy seal, and on Jan 3 were delivered to Thomas de Evesham, who took the oath as keeper of the rolls R ii p ii 1142 O v 216 H ii p iv 87
Dec 12	Letters of indemnity for Thomas Wake de Lidell, Henry de Lancaster, earl of Derby, and 9 others, who are appointed to examine into the extortions of the king's officers *The Tower of London* R ii p ii 1142.
Dec. 14	The K appointed Robert de Burghcher chancellor, and delivered the great seal to him at the Tower R ii p ii 1142
Dec 17	Protection until Whitsuntide for the bp of Man in Scotland, who is going to Rome. *The Tower of London* R ii p ii 1143. O v.
1341. Jan. 1	The archbp of Canterbury warns the K that the conduct of some of his advisers and officers will alienate the hearts of the people from him, and begs him to inquire into the manner in which the subsidies have been levied and spent *Canterbury* R ii p ii 1143
Jan 10	Licence for the exportation of 1000 sacks of wool at a duty of 40s a sack, to Matthew Canaceon and the company of Leopardi, who have released Henry de Lancaster, earl of Derby, arrested in foreign parts, for the king's debts *Westm* R ii p. ii 1143 O v 217. H ii p iv 87
Jan 18	Commission to Hugh de Courteneye earl of Devon, William Trussel, senior, and John l'Ercedekne, to inquire into the infractions by English subjects of the truce with France. *The Tower of London* R ii p ii 1144 O v 218 H ii p iv 87
Jan. 18	Licence to Robert de Eglesteld to found a hall in the parish of S Peter's, Oxford, under the name of the Queen's Hall *The Tower.* R ii p ii 1144
Jan 20	The K desires Bernard Ezii, lord de Lebret, and Hugh de Geneva, lord of Varry and Hanton, his lieutenants, and Oliver de Ingham, his seneschal in Aquitain, to observe the truce with France *Westm.* R ii p ii 1144 O v. 218 H. ii p iv 88
Jan 20	The K orders Hugh de Geneva, lieutenant of Aquitain, to resist the intended attack of the count of Foix on the lord de Lebret *Westm* R ii p ii 1144 O v 219 H ii p iv 88
Jan 20.	The K desires Oliver de Ingham, seneschal of Gascony, to come to him in England *Westm* R ii p ii 1145 O v 219 H ii p iv. 88
Jan 20	The K commends the fidelity of the commonalties of Bourdeaux, S Macaire, and S Emilion, and desires credence for sir John Dyieus, Gerald de Puy chief justice of Aquitain, and William de Radnore *Westm.* R ii p ii 1144 O v 220 H ii p iv. 86.
Jan 20	Credence for the same to the lords of Lebret and Varry and Oliver de Ingham *Westm* R ii p ii 1145 O v 220 H ii p iv 88
Jan 20	The K desires the lords of Lebret and Varray and Oliver de Ingham to appease the dissensions between the nobles and others in the duchy of Aquitain *Westm* R. ii p ii. 1145 O v 221 H ii. p. iv. 89.
Jan 20.	The K will not alienate from the crown of England the manors of Gerald and Reymund de Puy, in Entre-deux-mers *Westm* R ii p ii. 1145. O. v. 221. H. ii p iv. 89
Jan 20	Similar concession to the commonalty of S Emilion *Westm* R. ii p ii 1146. O. v. 222 H ii p. iv 89
Jan 26.	Exemplification of the grant of the castle of Puy Normand to Berard de la Brette, dated Antwerp, 13 May, 13 Edw. III *Westm.* R. ii. p. ii 1146. O. v 222 H ii. p iv. 89

DATE	SUBJECT
1341. .Jan 26.	Protection for the archbp of Canterbury, who fears to come to the K in consequence of his enemies. *Westm.* R ii. p 1146 O v. 223 H n p iv. 89
Feb 1	Indemnity for John bp of Exeter, for the detention of Margaret, daughter and heir of Thomas de Monthermer, and for delivering her to the earl of Salisbury *Westm.* R ii p ii 1146 O v 223. H n p iv 89
Feb. 5.	The K forbids tournaments throughout England, with the exception of one lately proclaimed at Norwich *Langley* R. ii. p. ii. 1146 O. v 223 H n p iv 90.
Feb 8	The K informs the customers of Hull that he has licenced the exportation of 240 sacks of wool, as an aid for the ransom of the earl of Salisbury *Westm* R ii p. ii 1147 O v 224 H n p iv 90.
Feb. 8.	Protection until June 24 for John earl of Murref, who is going abroad *Westm* R ii p. ii. 1147. O. v. 224 H. ii. p. iv 90
Feb 26	The treasurer and barons of the Exchequer are to receive all revenues and pay all issues *Westm* R ii p ii 1147 O v 224 H ii p iv 90
Feb 10.	The K orders the abp of Canterbury, and the bps of his province, to desist from fulminating ecclesiastical censures against the collectors of the ninth of sheaves, fleeces, and lambs *Westm.* R ii p ii. 1147 O v 225 H ii p iv. 90
Feb 10	The K orders the bps and deans and chapters of England, the abbot of S Augustine's, and the prior of Christ Church, Canterbury, to publish an account of the neglect of the abp of Canterbury in collecting the taxes for the support of the K while abroad, his refusal to appear before the K except in full parliament, and his complaints of the K's oppression *Langley* R ii p ii 1147 O v. 225. H n p iv 90
Feb. 11.	The K. requests John duke of Brittany and earl of Richmond to protect the merchants of Bayonne when trading in his dominions *The Tower of London* R ii. p. ii. 1149. O v 228 H ii p iv 92
Feb 11	Similar letters to the burgomasters of Bruges, Ghent, Ypres, and Sluys *The Tower of London* R ii p ii 1149 O v 229. H ii. p iv 92.
Feb. 11.	The K desires Bernard Ezu, lord of Lebret, to redress the injuries done by his bastard brother Peter to the citizens of Bayonne *The Tower of London* R. ii p ii 1149. O. v 229 H ii p iv 92
Feb 11.	The K orders Hugh de Geneva, lord of Vareys and Hauton, his lieutenant of Aquitain, and Oliver de Ingham, his seneschal in Gascony, to maintain the rights of the citizens of Bayonne, which have been violated by the lords of Lebret and Laspaie and John de Gerly, captain of Buch *The Tower of London* R ii p ii 1149 O. v. 230. H ii p. iv. 92.
Feb, 11	The K orders the warden of the Cinque Ports to enter into a treaty with the commonalty of Bayonne *The Tower of London* R ii p ii 1150 O v 231 H ii p iv 92
Feb. 12	The K orders that all ships of 60 tons and upwards, belonging to Sandwich, Great Yarmouth, and 26 other ports, be ready for service by a week after Easter, and orders deputies to be sent from each port to Westminster in the middle of Lent *Westm* R ii p ii 1150 O. v 231. H ii p iv. 93.
Feb 12	Power to Bernardet lord of Lebret to resume the treaty with Alfonso K of Castile. *The Tower of London.* R ii p ii 1150 O v 232 H ii p iv 93.
Feb 12	Power to Reymund Cornehi to treat with the Kings of Aragon and Majorca, and the count Urgium, for a perpetual alliance against Philip de Valois *The Tower of London.* R. ii. p. ii. 1151. O. v 233. H ii p iv 93
Feb 14	Memorandum that Robert de Burghcher, the K's chancellor, went from London to the K. at Norwich, having left the great seal at the house of the bp of Norwich beyond Temple Bar, where he the said chancellor was then residing, and he returned on March 3 to London. R ii p ii 1151 O v 233. H ii p iv 93
Feb 21.	The K appoints master John de Thoresby keeper of the rolls of chancery in the room of Thomas de Evesham *Woodstock* R ii p ii 1151 O v 233 H. ii p iv. 93.
March 6	The K orders John bp of Exeter to revoke his censures against Hugh de Courteneye, earl of Devon, and the other commissioners, for inquiring into the misconduct of his officers. *Westm* R ii p ii 1151 O v 234 H ii p iv. 94
March 6.	The K. orders the sheriff of Kent to proclaim that all the statutes relating to subsidies are to be observed *Westm* R ii p ii 1152. O v 235 H ii p iv 94
March 11.	Warrant to John de Ellirker, receiver of the biennial tenth in the province of York, to repay the loan of 586l. from the papal nuncios *Langley.* R ii. p ii 1152. O. v 236. H. ii, p. iv. 94

DATE	SUBJECT
1341. March 13	The K, informs the treasurer and barons of the Exchequer that letters sealed with the privy seal called "Griffoun" are sufficient warrants. *Westm* R ɪɪ p ɪɪ 1152 O v 236. H ɪɪ p ɪv 94
March 14.	The K desires credence from the pope for John Wawayn, Friar Thomas de Insula, and William de Norwich, dean of Lincoln, as to the conduct of the abp of Canterbury *Langley* R ɪɪ, p ɪɪ. 1152. O v 236 H ɪɪ p ɪv 95
March 15	The K desires Margaret, widow of Thomas de Monthermer, to pay 100 marks a year to the earl of Salisbury, for the support of her daughter Margaret, whose wardship the K. has granted to him *Langley* R ɪɪ p ɪɪ 1153. O v 239 H ɪɪ p ɪv 95
March 15.	Warrant to Bartholomew de Burghersh, keeper of the forest on this side of the Trent, to deliver timber to John Crabbe and William Hurel, the K.'s chief carpenter, for making military engines *Langley.* R ɪɪ p ɪɪ 1153.
March 20	The K. orders the bps and collectors of the biennial tenth in London and 11 other dioceses to pay to Michael Petri de Cuellario agent of the bp of Sabina, the sum due to him *Langley* R ɪɪ p ɪɪ 1154 O v 239 H ɪɪ p ɪv 96
March 23	The K appoints Thomas de Hampton to survey the defences of Guernsey, Jersey, Alderney, and Sark *Langley* R ɪɪ p ɪɪ 1154
March 26	Warrant to William de Edynton, receiver of the subsidies lately granted by parliament, to pay 1,500*l* to Terric ord of Manny, and Claus de Dordrech, provost of Oelderburgh, agents of the earl of Hainault, as compensation for horses lost in the K.'s service *Shene* R ɪɪ p ɪɪ 1154 O v 240 H ɪɪ p ɪv 96
March 31	The K orders the bp of London to publish his letters, justifying his conduct towards the abp of Canterbury, notwithstanding any mandate he may have received from the abp. *The Tower of London* R ɪɪ p ɪɪ 1154 O v 240 H ɪɪ p ɪv. 96
March 31	Warrant for the payment of the arrears of the daily allowance to Edward de Balliol, K of Scotland. *The Tower of London.* R ɪɪ p ɪɪ 1155 O. v 242 H ɪɪ p. ɪv. 97.
April 1	Writ to the treasurer and barons of the Exchequer to examine Philip de Thame, prior of S John of Jerusalem, who is accused of sending tribute out of the kingdom. *Westm* R ɪɪ p ɪɪ 1155 O v 242 H ɪɪ p ɪv 97
April 1.	The K orders proclamation to be made throughout England that he has licensed certain merchants to export wool, at an increase of 40s on the usual customs. *Langley.* R. ɪɪ. p ɪɪ 1155
April 10.	Power to R bp of Durham, Hugh d'Audele, earl of Gloucester, William FitzWaryn, Nicholin de Fusco, and William Trussel to treat for peace with Philip de Valois *Langley* R ɪɪ p ɪɪ 1156. O v. 242 H ɪɪ p ɪv 97.
[April 10]	The K desires them to send speedily reports of the negotiations R ɪɪ p ɪɪ 1156 O v 243 H ɪɪ p ɪv 97
April 10. 243⟩	The K orders Robert de Morle, admiral of the fleet west of the Thames, to provide 100 ships, called "pessoners and creyers," for his passage to France. *Langley.* R. ɪɪ. p ɪɪ 1156. O v 243. H ɪɪ p ɪv 97 !
April 12	The K informs Simon Buccanigra, duke of Genoa, that he has offered to his ambassadors, in compensation for injuries done by English men, 10,000*l* on the security of Flemish merchants, which they refused, desiring jewels as pledges; he asks if he will accept the offer, and is willing to enter into a treaty with him *The Tower of London* R ɪɪ p ɪɪ 1156 O v. 244 H ɪɪ p ɪv 97.
April 18	The K orders the sheriff of York and of 20 counties, the duke of Cornwall, and the mayor of Bristol, to provide bows and arrows by Whitsuntide *Westm.* R ɪɪ p ɪɪ 1157 O v 245 H ɪɪ p ɪv 98
April 20.	Proclamation to be made throughout England, enjoining the assumption of knighthood by persons possessing 40*l* a year *Westm* R ɪɪ p. ɪɪ 1157 O v 245. H ɪɪ. p ɪv 98
April 22	The K writes to the communalties of Ghent, Bruges, and Ypres, explaining the increase of the customs on wool *Westm* R ɪɪ p ɪɪ 1157
May 1.	Licence to the goldsmiths of London to found almshouses for men of their trade who have been blinded by fire and the fumes of quicksilver *Westm.* R. ɪɪ p ɪɪ 1157 O v 246 H ɪɪ p ɪv 98
May 2	The abbot of S Augustine's, Bristol, is released from attending parliament, as he is not a tenant by barony or in chief, and his house not of royal foundation *Westm* R. ɪɪ p ɪɪ 1158 O v 246 H ɪɪ p ɪv 98
May 3	The K cannot now pay his debt to Gerlae count of Nassau, who has sent to demand it, but will do so at S John the Baptist's day, or release him from his homage. *Westm* R ɪɪ. p ɪɪ 1158. O v 247 H ɪɪ. p ɪv 99

DATE.	SUBJECT
1341 May 3	The sheriffs of Kent and four other counties are ordered to forbid the exportation of timber *Westm* R ii p. ii 1158
May 4.	The K. orders the customers of Ipswich and 13 other ports to allow the exportation of wool on payment of 50s a sack *Westm.* R. ii. p. ii. 1158.
May 5.	The K promises to marry his son Lionel to Elizabeth, daughter of William de Burgh, late earl of Ulster. *Westm* R ii. p ii 1159. O v. 247 H ii p iv 99
May 8.	The abbot of Thornton is released from attending parliament as he is not a tenant by barony nor in chief of the K. *Westm.* R ii p ii. 1159 O v 248. H. ii p iii 99.
[May 8]	Similar letter for the prior of Sempringham. R. ii p ii 1159. O. v 248 H. ii. p iv 99
May 12	The K orders the collectors of wool in Northampton and eight other counties to deliver certain quantities of wool to the several sheriffs for the ransom of Henry de Lancaster, earl of Derby. *Westm.* R ii p ii. 1159 O v 248 H ii p iv. 99
May 16.	Thomas de Fencotes and Peter de Richemund are appointed custodes of the landed possessions in England belonging to the late duke of Brittany and earl of Richmond *Westm* R. ii p. ii. 1159 O. v 249 H ii p iv 99.
May 19	The rents of the lands of the late duke of Brittany are assigned for the maintenance of Lionel, John, Isabel, and Joan, the K.'s children. *Westm.* R. ii p. ii. 1160. O. v. 249. H. ii p iv 100.
May 20.	Protection until June 24 for Charles and Matthew Mountmorensy, who are coming from France into England. *Westm* R ii p ii 1160 O v 250. H ii p iv 100
[May 20]	Protection for John Randolf, earl of Murref, who is coming from France into England R. ii. p. ii. 1160. O v 250 H ii. p iv 100.
May 24	Warrant for the payment of the arrears of the allowance to Mary countess of Fife. *Westm* R ii p ii. 1160 O v 250 H ii p iv 100
May 24.	Warrant to Thomas de Crosse, keeper of the great wardrobe, to deliver the robes granted to Mary countess of Fife. *Westm.* R ii p ii. 1160. O v 250 H. ii p iv 100.
May 24.	Power to John duke of Brabant, Reynold duke of Gueldres, William marquis of Juliers, William earl of Hainault, and John de Hainault, lord of Beaumont, to treat for a truce with Philip de Valois *The Tower of London* R ii p ii. 1160. O v. 251. H. ii p iv. 100.
May 26.	The K. forbids tournaments in Essex *Westm* R ii p. ii. 1161.
May 28	The K. orders the constable of Bourdeaux to pay the wages due to Garsias Arnaudi, Vitalis lord of Castellar, and 50 others *Westm* R ii p ii 1161. O v 251-2 H ii p iv. 100.
May 30.	The K. promises not to alienate the city of Dax from the crown of England. *Westm.* R. ii. p. ii. 1161. O v 252 H. ii p iv 101
June 3	Licence to the mayor and aldermen of London to reform the customs of the city of London *The Tower of London* R ii p ii 1162. O v 253 H ii p iv 101.
June 3.	Pardon for the offences of the commonalty of the city of London against the K and his predecessors. *The Tower of London* R ii p ii 1162 O v 253 H ii p iv 101.
[June 3]	Grant to the city of London, that justices in eyre shall not sit in the Tower of London for seven years *The Tower of London* R ii p ii 1162. O. v. 253 H. ii p iv 101
June 4.	The K approves of the execution of those persons who assaulted Andrew Aubrey, mayor of London, and rescued malefactors whom he had arrested. *The Tower of London* R. ii p ii 1162 O v 254 H ii. p iv 101
June 4	The K thanks Arnald de Villa, Arnald de Bourdeaux, and 10 other citizens of Bayonne, for their promise to furnish him with 8 or 10 ships, and desires them to appoint an admiral for them. *The Tower of London.* R ii p ii 1163. O v. 255 H ii p iv 102
June 4	Warrant to William de Edyngton, receiver of the subsidy lately granted to the K , to pay 1,000 marks to the agents of the count of Hainault, in compensation for horses lost in the K 's service *The Tower of London.* R. ii. p ii 1163 O v. 255. H. ii. p iv 102
June 8.	Warrant for the payment of the wages of Guillerme Reymund, lord of Caumont, William Sanns, lord of Pomers, and 16 others *The Tower of London* R ii p ii 1163 O v 255 H ii p iv 102
June 12	The K congratulates Alfonso K of Castile on his victory over the Moors, and informs him of the negotiations for peace with France. *The Tower of London.* R. ii. p ii 1164 O v 257 H. ii. p. iv. 102

DATE	SUBJECT
1341 June 12	The K informs Albert duke of Austria, that in consequence of the reported defection of the emperor from him, he thinks it best to postpone the marriage of his daughter Joan with the duke's cousin Frederick *The Tower of London* R ii. p ii 1164 O v 258. H ii. p. iv. 103
June 15	Notarial certificate of the money left by the late duke of Brittany in the church of Nantes R ii p ii 1164 O v 258 H. ii p iv 103
June 26	The K promises that he will not alienate the town of S Severin from the crown *The Tower of London*. R ii p. ii. 1165 O v 260 H ii p iv 104.
June 18	The K asks for the assent of the commonalties of Bruges, Ghent, and Ypres, to the prorogation of the truce with France until the Decollation of S John the Baptist. *The Tower of London* R. ii p ii 1165 O v 260. H ii p iv 104
June 21	As no news has yet come of the confirmation of the prorogation of the truce by Philip de Valois, and as the K hears that he is preparing a fleet, he orders the fleets to be prepared, and the men of Kent and other counties to be arrayed *The Tower of London*. R ii p ii 1165 O v 261 H ii p iv 104
June 25	The emperor Louis informs K. Edward that the K of France has empowered him to act as mediator, blames him for making a truce without his consent, and revokes the appointment of the K as vicar of the empire. *Frankfort* R. ii. p. ii. 1166. O v 262 H. ii p iv 104
July 1	Safe conduct for John Randolf, earl of Murref, going to Scotland *Langley* R ii p ii. 1166 O v 262 H ii p iv 105
July 1.	The K promises indemnity to Peter de Ronynham, lord of Caumont, who has done homage to the K's lieutenants *Langley* R ii p ii 1166 O r v. 263 H. ii. p. iv. 105.
July 1.	The K. informs the treasurer and barons of the Exchequer that he has ordered the loan of the papal nuncios to be repaid from the biennial tenth in the diocese of Norwich *Langley*. R ii. p. ii. 1167
July 3	Grant to the commonalty of Bourdeaux, for six years, of the fines for acts of violence committed in the city *Langley* R ii p ii 1167 O v 263 H. ii p iv. 105
July 5	The K promises not to alienate the town of Bourg in the duchy of Aquitain from the English crown. *Langley*. R. ii. p. ii 1167. O v 263 H ii p. iv. 105
July 10.	The K confirms all the privileges of the inhabitants of Jersey, Guernsey, Sark, and Alderney *The Tower of London* R ii p ii 1167
July 14	The K declines the emperor's mediation, is surprised that he has allied himself with Philip, justifies his having made a truce, and reminds him that he was appointed vicar until he obtained the kingdom of France, or the greater part of it. *Westm* R ii p ii. 1167. O. v. 264. H. ii. p. iv. 105.
July 14	The K confirms the agreement with Bernard Ezii, lord of Lebret, and Matha de Lebret, lady of Montinhac and Gensac *The Tower of London* R ii p ii. 1168. O v 265. H ii p iv 106
July 14	Power for William de Clynton, earl of Huntingdon, Bernard lord de le Bret, Bartholomew de Burghersh, John de Offord, archdeacon of Ely, and Nicolin de Flisco, to treat with Philip de Valois about the crown of France and other matters *The Tower of London* R ii p. ii 1168 O v 266 H ii p iv 106
[July 14]	Similar powers for the dukes of Brabant and Gueldres, the marquis of Juliers, the earl of Hainault, and John de Hainault lord of Beaumont. R ii p ii 1169. O v 267 H. ii p iv. 106.
[July 14]	Power for the same commissioners to send reports of their negotiations to the K. R ii p ii 1169 O v 267 H ii p iv 107
July 15	The K. licenses the hastide of Hastyngs, on the frontier of Navarre, to be a port for ships of Bayonne and other places *The Tower of London*. R. ii. p ii 1169 O v 267 H ii p iv 107
July 20	Safe conduct for the earl of Murref, who is returning to prison in England, and for sir William de Lemyngston, with 10 horsemen, coming with the said earl *The Tower of London* R ii p ii 1169 O v 268 H ii p iv. 107.
July 20.	The K orders Bartholomew de Burghersh, John de Offord, and Nicholas de Flisco, to cross to Auntoyne as speedily as possible to commence the treaty. *The Tower of London*. R ii. p ii 1169
July 23.	Warrant to the sheriff of Gloucestershire to send 1,000 bows and 800 sheaves of arrows to the Tower of London. *The Tower of London*. R ii p ii. 1169. O. v. 268. H. ii. p iv 107.

DATE	SUBJECT
1341. July 24.	The K orders Hugh de Gebennis [Geneva], lord of Vaire and Hauton, and Oliver de Ingham, seneschal of Gascony, to seize the property of all ecclesiastics who adhere to the French party, and to recompense Bertrand Ferandi for the benefice he has lost in France *The Tower of London* R ii p ii 1170 O v 268 H ii p iv 107
July 25	Warrant for the payment of 500*l* towards the ransom of Robert de Ufford, earl of Suffolk. *Havering atte Bower* R ii p ii 1170 O. v 269 H ii p iv 107
July 26	Warrant to the abbot of S Mary's, York, collector of the biennial tenth, to pay 1,000*l* for the same object *The Tower of London* R ii p ii. 1170. O v 269 H. ii p iv. 107
July 26.	The K. asks Alfonso K. of Castile for redress for William Jue, Stephen Yok, and William atte Welle, of Sandwich, whose ship was taken by Spaniards. *The Tower of London.* R ii p ii 1170 O v 270 H. ii p. iv 108.
July 27	The K. orders John Darcy, justiciary of Ireland, to remove those officers who are Irish, or are English with wives and property in Ireland, and substitute for them persons with property in England *The Tower of London* R ii p ii 1171
July 27	Power to R. bp. of Durham. Henry earl of Derby, Henry de Percy, Ralph de Nevill, and Robert de Dalton, to treat with the K 's subjects in the north for the defence of the country against the Scots *Havering atte Bower* R ii p ii. 1171 ,
July 28	Warrant for the payment of 100*l* to the K of Scotland *Havering atte Bower*. R ii p ii 1171 O v. 270 H ii. p iv 108
July 31	Warrant to the abbot of S Mary's, York, to pay 300*l* to the K of Scotland, for the defence of the marches. *Havering atte Bower* R ii p ii 1171 O v. 271 H. ii p iv 108
Aug 1	The K appoints Edward K of Scotland captain of the army against the Scots *Havering atte Bower* R ii p ii 1171. O v 271 H ii p iv 108
Aug 1	The K orders the sheriffs of Northumberland and Yorkshire, the bp of Durham, the warden of Berwick, and his other subjects beyond the Trent and in Scotland, to assist him *Havering atte Bower* R ii p ii 1172 O v. 272 H ii p iv 108
Aug 7	Memorandum that Robert de Burghcher, chancellor, (then residing at the house of the bp of Worcester, near the Stone Cross, in the parish of S Mary atte Stronde, beyond Temple Bar,) sent the great seal to the K at the Tower, and received it there again on the next day. R ii p ii. 1172 O v 272. H ii. p iv. 109
Aug 8	The K orders a staple of wool to be established at Bruges in Flanders *The Tower of London* R ii p ii 1172 O v. 273 H. ii p iv 109.
Aug. 8.	Hugh de Ulseby is appointed mayor of the staple at Bruges. *The Tower of London* R. ii p. ii 1173. O v 275 H. ii p. iv. 109
Aug 10.	The K assigns 12 sacks of wool, at 10 marks, for the wages of Edward de Montacute and 44 men *The Tower of London* R. ii p ii. 1173
Aug. 12.	The K. desires the commonalty of Bayonne to send 20 ships and 10 galleys for his passage to France. *The Tower* R ii p ii 1173 O v 275 H ii. p iv. 110
Aug. 13.	The election of Peter de Puyan as mayor of Bourdeaux, at the K 's request, shall not be prejudicial to the privileges of the city *The Tower* R ii p ii 1173 O v 276 H ii p iv 110
Aug 14.	Power to Bernard Ezii, lord of Lebret, to receive persons in the dominions of Philip de Valois into the K 's service. *Westm.* R ii p ii. 1174 O v 276. H ii p iv 110
Aug. 14.	The K assigns 400 sacks of wool for the payment of the wages of Robert d'Artoys and his company Warrant to Hugh de Ulseby, Henry Goldbeter, and Thomas Colle, to pay the above *The Tower of London* R ii p ii 1174 O v 276 H ii. p. iv 110
Aug 20	The K. repeats his order to the abbot of S Mary's, York, to pay 300*l*. to the K of Scotland. *The Tower of London* R ii. p ii. 1174 O v 277. H ii. p iv 110
Aug. 24.	Warrant to the sheriffs of Lincolnshire and six other counties to sell wool for the ransom of the earl of Derby *The Tower.* R ii p ii 1174 O v 277 H. ii. p iv. 110
Sept. 1	The K orders John de Moubray, Ralph de Bulmere, and John de Fancomberge, to furnish the K of Scotland with men from Yorkshire Similar letter to Ralph de Nevill for Northumberland. *Westm.* R ii. p ii 1175 O v 278. H ii. p iv 111
[Sept. 1]	Similar warrant to the bp. of Durham R ii. p ii 1175 O v 279 H ii p. iv. 111.
Sept 2	The K informs the commonalty of Bayonne that he will not require their ships, as the truce with France is prorogued. *Westm* R ii p. ii. 1175 O v 279. H ii p iv. 111.
Sept. 10	Warrant to the sheriff of Cambridge to pay 20*l* a year to William marquis of Juliers, earl of Cambridge. *The Tower of London.* R ii p ii. 1175. O. v. 279. H ii p. iv 111

x 2

DATE	SUBJECT
1341 Sept 10	Warrant to the customers of London, S Botolph's, and Hull, to pay the annuity of the duke of Gueldres *The Tower of London* R ɪɪ p ɪɪ 1176 O v. 280 H ɪɪ p ɪᴠ 111
Sept. 10	Warrant to Walter Prest, of Melton Mowbray, and Geoffrey de Astwyk, to pay 2,100*l.* for the redemption of jewels pledged by the earl of Derby for the K *The Tower* R. ɪɪ p. ɪɪ 1176
Sept 18	Power to John Darcy, Reginald de Cobham, and Walter de Manny, to treat with Amadeus lord of Aula Nova *Westm* R ɪɪ p ɪɪ 1176
Sept 24	The K grants the earldom of Richmond to John duke of Brittany and earl of Montfort, in compensation for the county of Montfort, confiscated by the K. of France. *Westm* R ɪɪ. p ɪɪ. 1176. O. v 280 H ɪɪ p ɪᴠ 112
Sept 25	Warrant to John de Thyngden, receiver of money for the Scotch war, to pay 200*l* to John bp of Carlisle for the wages of himself and men defending the marches *Westm.* R ɪɪ p ɪɪ 1176 O v 281 H ɪɪ p ɪᴠ 112
Sept 27	Proclamation to be made in Kent and 10 other counties of the prorogation of the truce with France until June 24 *Westm* R ɪɪ p ɪɪ 1177 O v. 281. H ɪɪ. p. ɪᴠ 112
Oct 1	Repeal of a statute passed in the late parliament, which is contrary to the laws of England, and to which the K assented, fearing that the parliament would be dissolved without finishing the public business *Westm* R ɪɪ p ɪɪ 1177 O v 281 H ɪɪ. p. ɪᴠ. 112.
Oct 3	Commission to Robert Chamberleyn, John de Mounceaux, and three others, to arrest ships for the passage of certain nobles to Brittany *Westm* R ɪɪ p ɪɪ 1177. O v 282 H ɪɪ p. ɪᴠ 112
Oct 6.	The K orders the collectors of wool in Norfolk to send to the chancery the names of those who have refused to contribute *Westm.* R. ɪɪ p. ɪɪ 1178
Oct 6	The K orders William de Kelleseye, his receiver at Bruges, to pay the arrears of the annuity of Oto, lord of Cuyk *Westm* R ɪɪ p ɪɪ 1178
Oct 7.	The K accepts the homage of Bernard Ezii, lord of Lebret, performed on Oct. 7, for the castle of Lebret, the viscounty of Tartas, the castles of Gensac, Mauron, and other places *Westm.* R ɪɪ p ɪɪ 1178 O v 284 H ɪɪ. p ɪᴠ 113
Oct. 7.	Also his homage for the castle of Dartions, the lordship of Vaires, the parishes of Marean, Prinhae, &c *Westm* R ɪɪ p ɪɪ 1178 O v 285 H ɪɪ p ɪᴠ 113.
Oct 10	Henry de Lancaster, earl of Derby, is appointed captain of the army against the Scots, and is empowered to negotiate a peace *Westm* R. ɪɪ. p. ɪɪ 1179 O v 285 H ɪɪ. p ɪᴠ 114
Oct 12.	Protection for the subjects of the K of Majorca *Westm.* R ɪɪ p ɪɪ 1179. O v. 286. H ɪɪ p ɪᴠ 114.
Oct 18	Grant to the lord of Lebret of the pedage of S. Macaire and the land of Blancheforte *Westm* R ɪɪ p ɪɪ 1179 O v 286. H. ɪɪ. p. ɪᴠ 114
Oct. 20	The K orders the seneschal of Gascony to receive the fealty of Elias de Sancto Chesterio, and to deliver to him his castle de Monte Regali *Westm* R ɪɪ p ɪɪ. 1180 O v. 287. H. ɪɪ. p ɪᴠ 114.
Oct 20	Letters testimonial of the payment of the ransom of 400 florins by Peter Arnaud de Fytor, lord de Unissa, who was taken prisoner by John de Brocas at S Arnaud *Westm* R ɪɪ p ɪɪ 1180 O v 288 H ɪɪ p ɪᴠ 114
Oct. 22.	The K revokes his grant of the land of Bort to Arnald de Duro Forti Writ to the seneschal of Gascony to occupy it. *Westm.* R. ɪɪ p ɪɪ 1180 O v 288 H ɪɪ. p ɪᴠ. 115
Oct. 23	Warrant for the payment of the sums assigned to Robert d'Artoys *Westm.* R ɪɪ p ɪɪ 1180 O v 289. H ɪɪ p ɪᴠ. 115
Oct. 27.	Memorandum that the great seal was resigned by Robert de Burgheher, and Sir Robert Parnyng appointed chancellor. R ɪɪ p ɪɪ. 1180 O v 289 H ɪɪ p ɪᴠ. 115
Oct 28.	The K. states that if the abbot of S Mary's cannot pay the sum assigned to the K of Scotland, he must request the prior of Durham to do so. *Westm* R. ɪɪ p ɪɪ. 1181 O v 289. H. ɪɪ p ɪᴠ 115
Nov 4	Summons to William de Bohun, earl of Northampton, to be at Newcastle on Jan 24 with 120 men at arms and archers. Similar writs to Richard earl of Arundel and 23 others with companies of from 10 to 100 men *Newcastle.* R. ɪɪ. p ɪɪ. 1181 O. v 290 H. ɪɪ p ɪᴠ. 115
Nov 10	Warrant for the payment of 860*l* to Robert de Artoys, Robert de Morle, Walter de Manny, Henry de Ferrers, John Tibetot, and John Bardolf, going to Brittany in the K.'s service *Staunford* R ɪɪ p ɪɪ 1181. O v 291 H ɪɪ p ɪᴠ 116.

DATE	SUBJECT
1341 Nov. 15.	Warrant to William de Kelleseye, receiver of wool in Flanders, to pay 1,200*l* to the lord of Falquemont. *Staunford* R. ii p ii 1181 O v. 291. H ii p iv 116
Nov 20.	The K orders William de Bohun, Richard de Kelleshull, and the other justices of Oxfordshire to show favour to the officers of cardinal Guillard de Mota, archdeacon of Oxford *Staunford.* R ii p ii. 1182 O v 292 H ii p iv 116.
Nov 20	John Darcy, justiciary, Robert de Askeby, chancellor, and Hugh de Burgh, treasurer of Ireland, are ordered to prevent the transporting of arms and victuals to Scotland. *Stamford.* R ii p. ii 1182. O v 292 H ii p ii 116
Nov. 30.	Pardon for Arnald R viscount of Anorta for disturbances at Gouossa and Senhans, on payment of 2,000 livres de Bourdeaux *Bourdeaux* R ii p ii 1182 O v 293 H ii p iv 116
Dec. 3.	Receipt by Antony Ususmaris, lieutenant of Nicholas Ususmaris, constable of Bourdeaux, of the above-mentioned fine *Bourdeaux* R ii p ii 1183 O. v. 294 H. ii p iv 117
Dec. 3	Warrant for the payment of 840*l* to the bp of Lascale, Bernard de Bearn, and 5 others, who came to the K concerning the affairs of Aquitain *Newcastle* R ii p ii 1183 O. v 295 H. ii p iv. 117.
Dec. 4.	The K promises that the grant of 20 men at arms and as many archers by the bp of Durham shall not be prejudicial to his privileges *Newcastle* R ii p ii 1183 O v. 295. H. ii. p. iv. 117.
Dec 4.	Summons for the earls of Northampton, Arundel, and Huntingdon, and 22 others to be at Newcastle with their men on Jan 24 *Newcastle* R ii p ii 1183
Dec. 5.	The K orders Hugh de Jebennis [? Geneva], lord of Varroi, and Anton, his lieutenant in Aquitain, to execute justice on certain persons of Bayonne who took a Spanish ship. *Newcastle.* R ii p ii 1184
[Dec 5]	Similar letter to the mayor, jurats, and 100 others of Bayonne R ii p ii 1184
Dec. 5.	The K informs the alcaldes and councillors of Castro and Vern that he has ordered the outrage above-mentioned to be punished, and asks that it may not be considered a violation of the truce. *Newcastle* R. ii p ii 1184
Dec 27	The K grants the revenues of the prebend of Thame to William de Kyldesby, as the cardinal of Peregoitz, who holds it, adheres to the K's enemies in France Letter informing the sheriff of Oxfordshire thereof *Menrose* R. ii p ii 1184 O v 206 H ii p iv 118
1342 Jan 4	The K desires the bp of S Davids, John de Offord, Simon de Islip, and William Trussel, to go to Auntoyn to treat with ambassadors from France *Menrose* R ii p ii 1185.
Jan 10.	The K. orders John de Ellerker, chamberlain of North Wales, to defer the payment of wages to his officers there in consequence of his great expenses *Menrose* R ii p ii 1185
Jan. 10.	The K. orders all writs, &c for North Wales to be sealed with his seal, and not that of the justiciary *Menrose* R ii. p ii 1185
Jan. 22.	The K wonders that he has not received an answer from Simon Buccanigra, duke of Genoa, to his offer of compensation for the ships taken by his subjects, and desires his friendship. *Morpeth.* R ii p ii 1185 O v 296 H ii p iv 118
Feb. 1.	The K. forbids trading by religious persons of the order of S. Gilbert, the Cistercian, and other orders in Lincolnshire. *The Tower of London.* R ii. p. ii. 1186.
Feb 10	The K appoints John de Mansergh, clerk, Roger de Sprotle, Nicholas de Appleby, and John de Harum, to inquire into the use of weights and measures in Yorkshire which differ from the standards *Dunstable* R ii p ii 1186
Feb 14	The K requests the judges and commonalty of Cologne to desire their fellow citizens who hold his pledges for loans to desist from their complaints, as he has given orders for payment. *Westm* R ii p ii 1186 O. v 298 H. ii p iv. 118
Feb 14	The K has received the letters of James K. of Majorca about a marriage and an alliance, and will send ambassadors to him *Westm* R. ii p. ii 1187 O v. 298 H ii p iv 118.
Feb. 14.	The K. of England desires the friendship of Philip de Castris, baron of Aragon, and asks him to dissuade the K of Aragon from favouring his enemies *Westm* R ii. p. ii. 1187. O. v. 299 H ii p iv 119
Feb. 14.	The K thanks Glasons d'Alegon, lord of Pina, for his kindness to William de Pulcro Monte and his companions imprisoned for homicide at Pina. *Westm* R ii p. ii 1187. O iv. 299 H. ii. p. iv. 119.
Feb 20	Grant of the earldom of Richmond to John duke of Brittany, earl of Montfort. *Westm.* R. ii. p ii 1187. O. iv. 299. H. ii. p. iv. 119.

DATE	SUBJECT
· 1342 Feb 20	Commission to Walter de Derleston, Roger Power, and Thomas Ursewyk to provide 40 ships for the passage of certain persons to Brittany, at Orwell on March 27 Similar commission to Walter de Betell and Thomas de Ursewyk for 60 ships *Westm.* R ii p ii 1187. O v 300 H ii p iv 119.
Feb 20	Proclamation to be made throughout England forbidding earls, barons, knights, and men at arms to leave the kingdom *Westm* R ii p ii. 1188
Feb 22	Protection until June 24 for John earl of Murref going to France *Westm* R ii p ii 1188 O v 300 H ii p iv 119
Feb 24	The K will not alienate from the crown of England the city of Bazas and the town of Sauveterre. *Westm* R ii p ii 1188
Feb 28	The K grants to the citizens of Bazas freedom from the customs on wine at Bourdeaux Castle *Westm* R. ii p ii 1188. O v 301 H ii p iv 120
March 10	The K. orders the justiciary of Ireland and John Larcher, prior of S John of Jerusalem in Ireland, to prepare 1,000 men for his expedition *The Tower of London.* R. ii p. ii 1188
March 10	The K appoints Walter de Manny to receive and keep the towns and castles in Brittany belonging to the duke of Brittany *Westm* R ii. p. ii. 1189. O v 301. H ii, p iv. 120
March 10	Receipt for a loan of 1,000*l* from Joan duchess of Brittany, countess of Montfort, and Almaric de Cluzon, guardian of the duke *Westm* R ii. p ii 1189. O. v 302 H ii. p iv 120
March 10	The K sends persons to Brittany to coin money for his subjects there, and promises that it shall not be to the prejudice of the duke or duchess of Brittany. *Westm.* R. ii, p. ii. 1189. O v 302 H ii. p iv. 120
March 15	The K will not allow money to be coined in Brittany without the consent of the duke *Westm.* R. ii p ii 1189 O v. 302 H ii. p iv 120
March 20.	The K recommends Malcolm de Incheffery, bp. elect of Dunkeld, and Martin de Ergaill, bp elect of Argyle, to cardinal —— *Westm* R. ii p. ii 1189. O. v. 303 H. ii. p iv 120
March 20	Safe conduct for Adam bp of Brechin, Patrick earl of March, sir William de Douglas, sir Thomas de Carnoto, and William Bullok, ambassadors of David de Brus *Westm* R ii. p ii 1189. O v 303 H ii p iv. 120
March 20.	The K orders the mayor and sheriffs to search in the port of London for letters from spies *Westm* R ii p ii 1190 O v. 304. H ii. p iv 121
March 20	The K orders the justiciary of Ireland and the prior of S John of Jerusalem in Ireland to have 600 hobillers ready for service. *The Tower of London.* R ii p. ii. 1190.
March 27	Warrants to John de Watenhull and Richard de Cortenhale to provide ships at Portsmouth for the passage of William de Bohun, earl of Northampton, to Brittany. *Eltham.* R ii p ii 1190 O v 304 H ii p iv 121
March 28	Protection until June 24 for Benedict Fernandi, ambassador of the K. of Spain *Eltham* R ii p. ii 1190 O v 304. H. ii p. iv. 121.
March 28	The K informs Alfonso K of Castile that he intends to send ambassadors to France , and that he has ordered the constable of Mauleon to restore the goods of his subjects which he has seized *Eltham* R ii p ii 1190 O v 305 H. ii p iv 121
April 3	Power for R. bp of Durham, Henry de Lancaster, earl of Derby, Ralph de Nevill, John de Stryvelyn, William de Careswell, warden of Berwick-upon-Tweed, Walter de Creyk, and Robert de Manero to treat for peace with David de Brus. *Eltham.* R ii p. ii. 1191. O v 305 H ii p iv 121.
April 3	Commission to them to inform the K of their negotiations *Eltham.* R. ii. p ii. 1191 O v 306 H ii p iv 121
[April 3.]	Power for them to treat for a truce R. ii. p ii 1191 O v. 306 H ii p iv 122
April 5	Commission to Bernard Ezii, lord of Lebret, John de Offord, archdeacon of Ely, William FitzWaryn, and Nicolin de Flisco to treat with Philip de Valois *Westm.* R ii p ii 1191 O v 306 H ii p iv 122.
[April 5]	Power for them to treat with Philip de Valois, with the advice of John duke of Brabant, Reynald duke of Gueldres, William marquis of Juliers, William earl of Hainault, and John de Hainault, lord of Beaumont R ii p ii 1191. O. v. 307. H ii. p. iv. 122.
[April 5]	The K commissions them to refer the negotiations to him R ii. p ii 1192 O. v. 307 H ii p iv 122.
April 10	The K orders Philip ap Rees and Milo Pichard to muster 60 archers in Blenleveny by Ascension day *Dittm* R ii p ii 1192. O v 307. H ii p iv 122

DATE	SUBJECT
1342. [April 10]	The K. orders Humfrey de Bohun, earl of Hereford and Essex, and lord of Breighennok, to muster 140 men in the lands of Penkethly and Brunles R. ii. p ii 1192. O. v. 308 H. ii. p. iv. 122.
April 13.	Protection for the agents of cardinal Reymund de Farges, dean of Salisbury, archdeacon of Leicester. *Westm* R. ii. p. ii. 1192. O v 309 H ii p iv. 122
April 14.	The K. grants the petitions of his subjects in Ireland, desires them to fulfil his orders for men, and informs them of the annulling of a statute passed in the late parliament at Westminster. *Westm.* R. ii p. ii. 1193 O. v. 309. H ii p. iv 123.
April 15	The K. orders the mayors and bailiffs of Winchelsea and 24 other ports to send two mariners from each port to the council at Westminster on April 29. *Westm* R ii p ii 1193
May 3	The K releases Wolstan bp of Worcester from attendance at parliament, in consequence. of his age. *Westm* R. ii. p. ii 1193. O. v. 310. H. ii. p. iv. 123.
	The K. requests the college of cardinals to proceed speedily to the election of a pope R u p 1193 O v 310 H. ii p. iv 123
May 7.	Cardinal Ambaldus, bp. of Fiascati, and Reymund cardinal of S Maria Nova, inform the K of the election of Clement VI. on the 7th of May. *Avignon.* R. ii p. ii 1194 O v. 312. H. ii. p iv. 123.
May 12	The K. orders the sheriff of Hampshire, and Bartholomew de Insula, John de Kyngeston, and Henry Romyn, in the Isle of Wight, to proclaim that the men of the island must be ready for its defence by a week after Trinity Sunday *Westm*. Similar order to the sheriff for Sept 14 *The Tower of London, 28 Aug* R ii p ii 1194
May 16	Memorandum that sir Robert Parnyng, chancellor, delivered the great seal to the K., who gave it to the earls of Derby and Northampton, to seal pardons. It was then returned by the K to the aforesaid chancellor *Westm* R u p ii 1194. O. v 312 H. ii p. iv 124.
May 18.	Inspeximus and confirmation of pardons granted by sir Oliver de Ingham, seneschal of Aquitain, and Nicholas Usomare, constable of Bordeaux, dated 30 Nov. and 3 Dec *Westm* R. ii. p ii 1194 O. v. 312 H ii p. iv 124
May 20.	Proclamation to be made throughout England, except in Yorkshire, Northumberland, Cumberland, and Westmoreland, that those men who desire to serve the K abroad must be ready by June 24 *Westm* R. u p ii 1195 O v 312 H ii p iv. 124
May 20	Licence to William de Montacute, earl of Salisbury, prisoner in France, to swear that he will not bear arms against Philip de Valois in France *Westm.* R. u p ii. 1195. O v 313 H. ii. p iv 124.
May. 22.	The K congratulates pope Clement [VI] on his election *Westm* R ii p ii 1195 O. v. 313 H. ii. p. iv. 124.
[May 22]	The K thanks the cardinals for their intimation of the election of a pope R. ii p ii 1195 O. v. 314 H. ii p iv 124.
May 23	The K. informs the commonalty of Bayonne that he did not believe the reports of their intended surrender of their city to Philip de Valois R. ii p. ii. 1195. O v 314. H. ii. p. iv. 124.
May 24.	Power for R. bp. of London, Thomas de Beauchamp, earl of Warwick, Nicholas de Cantilupe, Bartholomew de Burghersh, and John de Offord, archdeacon of Ely, to treat with the K.'s allies about the war with France, and also to treat with Philip de Valois *Westm.* R ii. p ii 1196 O v. 314 H ii p iv 125.
May 24.	Warrant to Hugh de Ulseby to pay 2,000l. in money called " l'english " to Reynold duke of Gueldres. *Westm.* R. ii. p ii 1196. O. v. 315. H. ii p. iv. 125.
May 25	Receipt by Bernard Ezii, lord of Lebret, of 600l. from the K's treasuries *London* R. ii. p ii. 1196. O. v. 315. H ii p iv. 125.
May 28.	Credence for Francis Drizacorne to Simon Buccanigra, duke of Genoa. *Wsetm* R ii p. ii 1196. O. v 316. H ii p iv. 125.
June 1	Grant of 4,382l. 15s. to the commonalty "de Medicino " [? Mezin] in compensation for 600 houses pulled down by order of the K.'s officers. *Westm* R. ii p. ii 1196 O v 317 H. ii p. iv. 125.
June 1	Licence for the men of same community to carry arms in the duchy of Aquitain. *Westm* R. ii p ii. 1197. O v. 317. H. ii. p. iv. 126.
June 1.	The K. annuls all grants made by Philip de Valois of property in the above-mentioned town *Westm.* R. ii. p. ii. 1197. O. iv. 317. H. ii p iv 126.

DATE	SUBJECT.
1342 June 1	The K confirms his father's promise that he will not alienate the town of S. Macaire from the English crown. *Westm* R. ii. p ii 1197. O. v. 318. H. ii. p. iv. 126.
June 1	Similar confirmation to the town of "Castrum Comitatus" *alias* Damazan. *Westm* R. ii p ii 1197 O v 318 H. ii. p iv 126
June 1.	Similar grant to the town of Bourg in Aquitain. *Westm.* R. ii. p. ii. 1198 O. v. 318. H ii p iv 126
June 1	The K accepts the fealty of Reymund viscount of Fronzac, and will include him in any truce with Philip de Valois *Westm* R ii p ii. 1198 O v. 319. H ii p. iv 126
June 1.	Warrants to the constable of Bordeaux for the payment of the wages of Arnald Reymundi, viscount d'Ortiæ, Arnald lord d'Assac, and 31 others. *Westm* R ii. p ii 1198. O. v 319 H. ii p iv 127.
June 2	The K grants to cardinal Peter, bp of Sabina, 60 sacks of wool a year for the clothing of his household *Westm* R ii p ii 1199 O. v. 321. H ii p iv 127
June 3.	Warrant for the payment of 10*l* to A bp of Frascati and R. cardinal of S *Maria Nova*, bringing letters of the pope's election, and 5*l* to Amenen, valet of the lord of Pounte and Brigerak. *Westm* R ii p. ii 1199. O v 321. H. ii. p. iv. 127.
June 4.	In consequence of letters from the pope, the K. sends John de Offord, archdeacon of Ely, to treat for a prorogation of the truce with France *Westm* R ii p ii 1199 O v 322 H. ii p iv 128
June 8	The K orders the treasurer and barons of the Exchequer to make allowance to Thomas de Hampton, warden of Guernsey, Jersey, Sark, and Alderney, as these islands are occupied and devastated by the French *Westm* R ii p ii 1199
June 12.	Inspeximus and confirmation of two indentures between the seneschal of Gascony and the lieutenant of the constable of Bordeaux, and Gausbert de Mayrac, lord of Tenbon, who promises to aid the K, dated Hyson, 29 March 1240 (?1340), and Bourdeaux, 29 May 1341. *Westm.* R ii p ii 1200 O v 323 H ii p. iv. 128
June 20	The K orders the wax covering the body of Edward his grandfather in Westminster Abbey to be renewed *Woodstock* R. ii p ii 1201 O. v 325 H ii p iv 129
June 20	Warrant to the mayors and bailiffs of Sandwich, London, and 37 other ports to provide ships at Portsmouth by July 12 for the passage of the earl of Northampton and other lords going to Brittany *Woodstock* R ii p ii 1201
June 25	Warrant to the collectors of wool to deliver 57 sacks to Ralph de Stafford, who is going to Brittany in the K.'s service with 100 men-at-arms, soldiers and archers *Woodstock* R. ii. p ii 1201 O v 325. H ii p. iv. 129
July 3	The collectors are also to deliver 158 sacks of wool for the wages of Robert de Artoys and his company of 240 men *The Tower of London* R ii. p ii. 1201 O v 326 H. ii. p iv. 129
July 3,	Grant of 85½ sacks of wool for the wages of William de Kildesby and 150 men *The Tower of London* R ii p ii 1202 O v 326 H ii p iv 129
July 3.	The K informs the seneschal of Gascony and the constable of Bourdeaux that he has granted compensation to the Bastide of Credon in Entre-deux-Mers for their losses in consequence of the war. *Westm.* R. ii p ii. 1202.
July 5	Protection till Michaelmas for John de Portevare to whom the K. has granted 334½ sacks and four cloves * of wool (quatuor clavos lanæ) in part payment of 2,500*l*. for the redemption of the two crowns of Philippa the Queen *The Tower of London.* R. ii p. ii. 1202. O. v 326 H ii p iv 129
July 10	The K orders the mayors and bailiffs of London, Southampton, and five other ports, to arrest French merchants and merchandise, in retaliation for the capture of the ship of Walter Bernard of London by the French *Westm* R ii p ii 1202
July 13	The K assigns various quantities o f wool for the payment of the wages of Robert de Ufford, earl of Suffolk, Reginald de Cobham, and nine others, with their companies *The Tower of London* R ii. p. ii 1203 O v 327 H ii p iv 129.
July 15	Power to Edward de Balliol, K of Scotland, to pardon all men called " grithmen," in Beverley, Ripon, Tynemouth, Hextildesham, Wordehale, and elsewhere in the ecclesiastical liberty who are willing to serve the K in Scotland *Westm* R ii p ii. 1203 O. v. 328 H ii. p. iv. 130
July 16	The K desires the earl of Kildare, Maurice FitzThomas, earl of Desmond, and seven other Irish lords to come to him with men-at-arms and hobillers R ii p 1203.

* A clove of wool is 7 lbs. weight

DATE.	SUBJECT
1342. July 20.	Power for Oliver de Ingham, seneschal of Aquitain, and Walter de Weston, treasurer of the army, to treat with Reginald de Pons, archdeacon Gaillard de Duro Forti, and Gaston count of Foiz, about giving aid to the K *Windsor* R ii p ii 1204 O v 329 H ii. p iv 130
[July 20]	Power for the same commissioners to receive any persons or commonalties in France into the K's obedience R ii p ii 1204 O v 329 H ii p iv 130
[July 20]	Power for them to grant lands and privileges to those whose fealty they receive. R ii. p ii 1204 O v 329 H ii p iv 130
July 20.	The K orders them [Oliver de Ingham and Walter de Weston] to muster the army once a month, to value the horses, and to send information of excessive grants which have been extorted from him *Windsor* R ii p ii 1204 O. v. 330. H ii. p. iv 130
July 20.	The K appoints William de Bohun, earl of Northampton, his lieutenant and captain in France Notification to the prelates, nobles, and people of France, enjoining obedience to him *Windsor* R ii p ii. 1204 O v 330 H ii p iv 131
July 20.	William de Bohun, earl of Northampton, is also appointed the K's lieutenant and captain in Brittany Mandate enjoining obedience to him *Windsor*. R ii p ii. 1205. O v 331. H ii p iv 131
July 20.	William de Kildesby, the K's clerk, is ordered to go with the earl as his councillor *Windsor* R ii p ii 1205
July 20.	Warrants to 15 sheriffs, the mayor of Bristol, and the duke of Cornwall, to send bows and arrows to Sandwich by Aug 10 *The Tower of London* R ii p ii 1205.
July 21.	The K forbids Walter de Weston to pay old debts out of the money for the war. *Westm.* R ii. p ii 1205
July 22.	Power to the earl of Northampton to grant honours and possessions in France. *Windsor.* R ii p. ii. 1206. O v 332 H ii p iv 131
[July 22]	Power for the same earl to enter into alliances against Philip de Valois R. ii p ii 1206 O v 333 H ii p iv 132
July 20.	Power for him to contract a loan in the K's name to the amount of 40,000*l.* *Windsor.* R. ii p ii. 1206.
July 23	The K appoints the lieutenant of the justiciary of Ireland, the chancellor, the treasurer, and Simon FitzRichard to treat with the nobles of Ireland for sending assistance to Brittany *The Tower of London.* R ii. p. ii. 1207. O v 333. H. ii p iv 132
July 23	Power for Bernard Ezii, lord of Lebret, William Amynion de Castillon, lord of Blevyades, and two others, to treat with Alfonso K of Spain for a marriage between his eldest son and one of the K's daughters, and for mutual assistance *Windsor* R ii p ii 1207 O v 334 H. ii. p iv. 132
July 23	Credence for the above-mentioned lord of Lebret to the K of Spain *Windsor* R. ii. p. ii 1207. O v. 334. H. ii. p. iv. 132
July 23.	Warrant for the payment of the wages of Laurence de Hastynges, earl of Pembroke, and his company of 60 men-at-arms and 100 archers *The Tower of London* R ii p ii 1207 O. v 335. H ii p iv 132
July 26.	Grant of an annuity of 20*l.* and the robes of a valet to Peter de S. Marcello, sent by Pope Clement VI with letters announcing his election and coronation. *The Tower of London* R ii p. ii 1207 O v 335 H ii p iv 132.
July 28.	The K informs the papal chaplains and auditors of the royal prerogatives in ecclesiastical matters in detail *The Tower of London* R ii p ii 1208 O v 335 H ii p iv 133
July 30.	Power for Edward Balliol, K of Scotland, to array the inhabitants of the counties north of the Trent *The Tower of London* R. ii p ii 1208 O v 336 H ii p iv 133
Aug 1.	The K assigns 42 sacks of wool for the wages of Robert de Ferrers and his company of 80 men *The Tower of London.* R ii p ii 1208 O v 337 H ii p iv 133
Aug 5.	The K grants to Cardinal Gaillard de Mota respite until All Saints' day for the subsidy of the ninth *The Tower of London* R ii p ii 1208 O. v 337. H ii p iv. 133
Aug. 8.	The K informs [the papal nuncio] that his sending ambassadors to France has been useless, and that his adversary has violated the truce, and asks him to send word to what his adversary will agree. *The Tower of London.* R ii p ii. 1208 O v 337. H ii p iv 133
Aug 15	The K informs the archbp. of Canterbury of his intended expedition to France, and desires him to summon a convocation at St Paul's on Oct 5 Similar letter to the archbp. of York *The Tower of London.* R. ii. p ii. 1209. O v 339. H ii p iv 134

DATE.	SUBJECT.
1342 Aug 20	The K desires the archbp of Canterbury and 18 bishops to offer prayers and masses, &c., for his success *The Tower of London* R ii p ii 1209 O v 339. H ii p iv 134
Aug. 29	Safe conduct for Peter de Marcello on his return to pope Clement VI. *Ledes.* R ii p ii. 1210 O. v 340. H ii p iv 134.
Sept 8.	The sheriffs of London are ordered to forbid all persons to molest, while on his way to the K, William la Zouche, who is said to be consecrated archbp of York Similar letters to the sheriff of Kent, &c *Eastry.* R ii p ii 1210 O v 340. H ii p iv. 134
Sept 10.	Proclamation is to be made at Southampton for the defence of the town, which is threatened by the same galleys which have burnt Portsmouth *Eastry* R. ii. p. ii. 1210
Sept 15	Hugh de Ulseby, mayor of the staple at Bruges in Flanders, is ordered to pay 800*l.* to Francisco Drisactorn for the redemption of Queen Philippa's crown. *Eastry.* R. ii p ii. 1210 O v 341 H ii p iv 135
Sept. 19.	Restitution of the temporalities to William la Zouch, archbp. of York. *Eastry.* R. ii p ii. 1210
Sept 24	Licence to the inhabitants of the Isle of Man to enter into a truce with Scotland *Eastry* R ii p ii 1211 O v 241 H ii p iv 135
Oct 1	The K sends Francisco Dirzacorne to treat with Simon Buccanigri, duke of Genoa. *Eastry* R. ii p ii 1211 O v 341 H ii p iv 135
Oct. 1.	The K informs [the papal nuncios] that his adversary has continually put him off with negotiations, and that he intends to go in person to France, where he will be ready to treat for peace. *Eastry* R ii. p ii 1211 O v 342 H. ii p iv 135
Oct. 4.	Memorandum that Robert Parnyng, chancellor, delivered the great seal to the K. in the ship called *La George* at Sandwich, and the K gave him another seal to be used during his absence abroad. R ii p ii 1212 O v 342 H ii p iv 135
Oct 5	Edward duke of Cornwall and earl of Chester is appointed regent during the K.'s absence abroad. *Sandwich.* R. ii p ii 1212 O v 343 H. ii. p iv. 135.
Oct 5	The duke of Cornwall is empowered to grant letters of *congé d'elire*, to restore temporalities, and to receive fealty during the K.'s absence. *Sandwich* R ii p ii. 1212 O v. 343 H ii p iv. 135
Oct. 6.	Grant to Robert de Artoys, who has gone abroad in the K.'s service, of 400*l* of his annuity due next Easter *Eastry.** R. ii p ii 1212 O. v. 344 H ii. p. iv. 136
Oct 8	The sheriffs of London are ordered to arrest foreigners adherents of Philip de Valois. *Westm* R ii p ii 1213 O v 344 H ii p iv 136
Oct. 12	Acquittance to Bartholomew de Burghersh for jewels and money of the K's, which he had in his possession for the K's business Mandate to the treasurer and barons of the Exchequer on the subject *Kennington.* R, ii. p. ii. 1213 O v. 345 H. ii. p. iv. 136
Oct. 25	The K desires Berengarius Deuerose, prior of Barlet, and Gerard de Montacute, marshal of the convent of Rhodes, visitors general of the hospitallers, to send back prior Philip Thame *Kennington* R ii p ii 1213 O. v 345 H ii p. iv, 136.
Nov. 10	The sheriff of Kent is ordered to send a certain military engine from Sandwich to the Tower of London *Kennington* R. ii p ii 1213
Nov. 12.	The K. orders Thomas de Wake, lord of Lydel, to come to him with his men Similar summons to the earls of Warren and Anegos and 17 others *La Rosere.* R ii. p. ii. 1213 O v 346 H ii p iv. 136
Nov. 16	John Cory is sent to Λ bp of Winchester to ask for a loan of 200*l* Similar requests for various sums to the abbots of Ramsey and Peterborough, and 58 other bishops, priors, abbots, and deans. *Kennington.* R ii p ii 1214 O v 346-7 H. ii p. iv 137.
Nov 20	Grant of the earldom of Richmond to the K's son, John of Ghent ; the custody of the earldom being granted to the Q *Kennington.* R ii p ii 1214 O v. 348. H. ii p iv. 137.
Nov 20	Licence to Henry Galeys, attorney of Robert de Artoys, who is reported to be dead, to export 11¼ sacks of wool, at a duty of ½ mark. *Kennington* R. ii p. ii 1215. O. v. 349 H. ii p iv. 139.
Nov. 27.	Commission to John de Wynewyk, lieutenant of the constable of the Tower of London, and William de Hurle, chief carpenter, to convey a certain engine from Sandwich to the Tower. *Kennington* R ii p ii 1215. O. v. 350. H. ii p iv. 138

* Documents dated in England during the King's absence are attested by the Duke of Cornwall.

DATE	SUBJECT.
1342 Nov 29	The commonalties of Ghent, Bruges, and Ypres promise to fulfil their engagements with the K. *Ghent* R ii p. ii 1215. O v. 350 H ii p iv 138.
Dec 5	William de Northwell, late keeper of the wardrobe, is ordered to receive the accounts of Bartholomew de Burghersh *Kennington.* R. ii. p. ii. 1216. O. v. 351. H ii p iv. 138.
Dec. 12.	Pope Clement [VI] exhorts the K to consent to a truce with France. *Avignon,* R ii p. ii. 1216 O v 251. H. ii p iv 139.
Dec. 20	The K. desires John de Warren, earl of Surrey, to be ready to come to France on March 1 with 40 men-at-arms and 100 archers Similar letters to Humphrey de Bohun, earl of Hereford, John de Moubray, and 20 others *Westm* R. ii. p. ii 1216. O v 352. H ii. p. iv. 139.
1343. Jan 3	Richard earl of Arundel, justiciary of North Wales, John de Warren, earl of Surrey, John de Cherleton, and 17 others, are ordered to send lancemen from their several lands in Wales to the K. in Brittany Similar letters to Gilbert Talebot, justiciary of South Wales, and 11 others *Winchester* R ii p ii 1216 O v 353 H ii p iv 139, 140
Jan. 26.	The earl of Arundel is ordered to preserve peace in North Wales. *Westm.* R ii. p. ii. 1218.
Jan 26	Summons to Robert de Morle, Nichol Frаunceys, and five others, to come to Brittany with their men in March. *Westm* R ii p ii 1218
Jan. 26	Warrants to Robert Beaupel and William Trussel, admirals of the fleet west and north of the Thames, and John de Watenhull and the sheriffs of seven counties, to prepare ships at Portsmouth for the passage of the earls of Arundel and Huntingdon on the 1st of March *Westm* R ii p ii 1218
Jan 27	The sheriff of Leicester is forbidden to exact tenths or aids from cardinal J bp of Porto, prebendary of Leicester *Kennington.* R. ii p ii 1218. O v 356. H ii p iv 140
Jan. 28.	Peter de Greece and John de Charyngworth are ordered to inquire concerning the discovery of treasure at Caumpden *Kennington* R ii p. ii 1219
Jan 30	Warrant for the payment of the arrears of the wages of Nicholin de Flisco *Kennington* R. ii p. ii 1219 O v 356 H ii p iv 141
Feb 1.	Proclamation to be made by the several sheriffs south of the Trent that all persons who are willing to serve the K. in Brittany must be ready to accompany the earls of Arundel and Huntingdon *Kennington* R ii p ii 1219.
Feb 6	The K orders the admirals and the sheriffs of Devon, &c to stay the arrest of ships until further orders *Kennington* R ii. p ii. 1219.
Feb. 20.	The several sheriffs, the bp of Durham, the justiciaries of Ireland, Chester, and Wales, and the warden of the Cinque Ports, are ordered to proclaim a truce with France until Michaelmas 1346 *London* R ii p ii. 1219 O v 357 H ii p. iv. 141
Feb 27	The K.'s mother Isabella is released from payment of the subsidy. *Kennington* R ii. p ii. 1220.
March 2	Memorandum that the K. arrived at Weymouth on Sunday March 2, and on the following Tuesday arrived at Westminster Robert Parvyng, the chancellor, delivered to him the seal he had used during his absence, and the K gave him that which he had carried into Brittany R ii p. ii 1220. O v 377 H ii. p iv 141.
March 8	Guido, K. of Armenia, desires credence for his ambassadors *Adhene* R ii p. ii. 1220 O v 358 H. ii. p iv 141.
March 14.	Protection for William de Kildesby, the K.'s secretary, who is going to the Holy Land *Westm.* R. ii p ii 1220. O v. 358 H. ii p. iv 141
March 14	The K requests the pope to grant letters of protection to William de Kildesby *Westm.* R. ii p ii 1220. O v. 358. H ii p. iv 141.
[March 14]	The K. writes to the Roman cardinals, recommending William de Kildesby *Westm.* R ii p ii 1220 O v 359. H ii. p iv 141
March 17.	The K. requests the Kings of Cyprus, Sicily, Castile, and Armenia, the doges of Venice and Genoa, and the grand master of St. John's, to give W de Kildesby safe conduct. *London* R ii p. ii 1221 O v 359. H. ii p iv 142.
March 17.	The K. recommends W de Kildesby to Martin Zacharias de Castro, whom he thanks for his treatment of Englishmen in the East. *Westm* R ii p ii 1221 O v. 359. H. ii p iv 142
March 20.	The K. asks cardinal . . . to favour his request in the enclosed letter to Berengarius de Aurosio, prior of Barlet [Baroli], commissary of the Grand Master of the Order of S. John of Jerusalem *Westm* R. ii. p. ii. 1221. O. v 360 H. ii p. iv. 142.

DATE.	SUBJECT
1343 [March 20]	Request to the above-mentioned prior of Barlet [Baroh] to admit William de Northwode, the Q's page, cousin of the earl of Salisbury, as a knight of the order R. ii p ii 1221 O v 360 H ii p iv. 142
[March 20]	The K desires Peter de S Marcello to speak to the pope in favour of the above mentioned William de Northwode. R ii p ii. 1221 O. v 361 H ii p iv 142.
April 6	The K desires Oliver de Ingham, seneschal of Gascony, to come to him in England. *The Tower of London* R ii p ii 1222
April 18	The K forbids John de Wolde and Tideman de Lymbergh to demand the custom on the wool granted to the cardinal bp. of Sabina. Similar letter to Francis Bandini and his company of Lucca, merchants *Westm* R ii p ii 1222 O v 361 H ii p iv 142.
May 1	The K appoints John de Thoresby to settle with the creditors of Robert de Artoys, who is now dead *Westm* R ii p ii 1222 O v iv 143
May 1	Protection for William de Kyldesby, for his prebend of Wetewang with its members Fynmere, Frydaythorp, Holme, Kirkeby, and Elghton, the prebends of S Andrews in Beverley, Cank, Saltemersh, Kynges Sutton, with its members of Horlege and Bukyngham; the prebend in the church of Deon, chapel of Tykhull with its members ; the hospital of S Katherine, the prebend of Drlyngtonham, and the church of Lampadervaur *Westm* R ii p ii 1222 O v 363 H ii p iv 143
May 12.	The K requests the pope to revoke his commission for hearing at Rome a cause relating to the patronage of certain churches against R bp of Chichester, such commission being contrary to the K's prerogative *Westm* R u p ii 1223 O v 363 H. ii p iv 143.
[May 12]	Similar letters to three Roman cardinals R ii p ii. 1223. O. v 364. H ii p. iv. 143
May 14.	The K exempts cardinal Gaucelm, bp of Albano, from payment of the subsidy for his prebends of Driffield, Lude, and Sallowe, and for the churches at Hackney, Stepney, Pageham, Hollyngbourn, Lemyng, and Hemmyngburgh, of which he is parson Similar exemption for Peter cardinal of Palestrina, archdeacon of York and prebendary of Wistowe. *Westm* R ii p ii 1223 O v 364 H ii p iv 143
May 17.	The K. forbids the exportation of timber or ships. *Westm*. R ii p ii. 1223.
May 19	Pope Clement [VI] desires the K to send ambassadors to Avignon, to meet those of the K of France, and informs him that the K of France will liberate the earl of Montfort, when he can find securities *Avignon* R ii p ii 1224 O v 365 H ii p iv 144
May 20	Power to Hugh le Despenser, lord of Glamorgan, Ralph baron of Stafford, William de Norwich, dean of Lincoln, Sir William Trussell, and Master Andrew de Offord, to treat with the French ambassadors before the pope, not as a judge, but as a private person and common mediator *Westm* R ii p ii 1224 O v 366 H ii. p iv. 144.
[May 20]	William de Norwich and William Trussell are sent on to inform the pope that the K. cannot send a solemn embassy until he has received satisfaction from Philip for breaches of the truce R. ii p ii 1224 O v 367 H ii p iv 144
May 20	The K orders Gilbert de Umframvill, earl of Anegos, Henry de Percy, and six others, in Northumberland, to observe the truce concluded with the Scots until Michaelmas 1346 Similar letter to the bp of Carlisle and seven others in Cumberland and Westmoreland *Westm* R ii p ii 1225
May 20	The K orders Richard de Aldeburgh and four others to make inquisition concerning the carrying away of two whales and two sturgeons worth 3,000*l* from the manor of Hoveden , the bp of Durham having wrecks of the sea and the right to royal fish there *Westm*. R u p ii 1225 O v 368 H ii p iv 145
May 20	Proclamation to be made by the several sheriffs that no person is to buy wool under certain fixed prices, in accordance with a statute of the present parliament. *Westm*. R ii. p ii 1225 O v 369 H ii p iv 145
June 4	The K desires Alfonso K of Castile to give redress to Robert Annels, master of the ship called *La James* of Harwich, which was taken by his subjects *Westm* R ii p ii 1226 O v 370 H. ii. p iv 146
June 8	Warrant to the mayor and sheriffs of London to arrest two ships which deserted the fleet at Brest Similar warrant to the bailiffs of Strode, Margate, Dover, Sandwich, and Hythe *Westm* R ii p ii 1226. O. v 370 H ii p iv 146
June 15.	Commission to Thomas de Rokeby, Roger de Blakeston, and Hamon de Sesseye of York to arrest persons having papal bulls for benefices in the K's gift *Westm* R ii p ii. 1226. O v. 371. H ii p iv 146
June 20	The K orders the wax which covers the body of K. Edward his grandfather in Westminster Abbey to be renewed *Windsor* R ii p ii 1227. O v. 372. H. ii. p iv 146.

DATE	SUBJECT.
1343. June 24	The K. informs Alfonso Ř of Portugal that he has ordered restitution to be made for the plunder of a Portuguese ship at Dartmouth *Westm.* R n. p n 1227 O. v 372 H n. p. iv 146
July 1	Power to Ralph de Stafford, steward of the household, Sir William Trussel, Philip de Weston, canon of York, and master John Wawayn to treat with Flanders. *Windsor.* R n p n. 1227 O v. 370 H n p iv 147
[July 1.]	Power for the same persons to treat with the nobles and people of Germany R n. p. n. 1227 O v 373 H n p iv. 147
[July 1]	Power for them to report their negotiations to the K R n. p n 1227 O. v 373. H n p iv. 147
July 2.	The K. orders his treasurer to pay 200*l* to the customers of London for 100 sacks of wool which he has licensed the cardinal bp of Frascati to export *Windsor* R n p n. 1227 O v 373 H n p iv 147
July 6.	The K sends the earls of Derby, Arundel, Warwick, Suffolk, and Huntingdon, and others, to the pope, relative to the charges against Nicolin de Flisco, and to treat concerning his adversary of France, he desires letters of safe conduct from his holiness. *Clarendon.* R. ii. p. ii. 1228. O. v. 374. H n p n. 147.
July 6.	The K desires the nobles and commonalties to seal certain letters against provisors, which are to be sent to the pope *Windsor* R. p n 1228.
July 9.	Clement [VI] writes to the K in favour of John bp of Exeter *Avignon* R n p ii. 1228 O v 375 H n p iv. 148
July 9	Also in favour of Friar Antony de Valentia and Gregory de Sogio, knight, ambassadors of Guido K of Armenia. *Avignon* R n p n 1228 O v 375 H n p iv. 148
July 9.	Philip de Weston and Hugh de Ulseby are appointed to redeem the great crown and other jewels pledged in foreign parts. *Westm.* R n p n. 1229 O v 375 H. ii. p iv 148
July 19.	The K. requests Peter K of Aragon to revoke the letters of marque granted for the capture of two vessels by men of Aquitain, he has ordered the mayor of Bayonne to make redress *Clarendon* R n p n 1229 O v 376 H n p iv 148
July 20.	The K orders the sheriff of Southamptonshire to provide three ships for Nicholas de la Beche *Clarendon* R n. p n 1229
July 20.	Nicholas de la Beche is appointed seneschal of Gascony The K orders Oliver de Ingham to resign the office to him *Lyndhurst* R n p n 1229
July 23.	Proclamation to be made throughout England, at the request of Parliament, forbidding the execution of the pope's grants of benefices to strangers *Clarendon.* R n p n 1230 O v 377 H n p iv. 149
July 26.	Grant of 100 marks to Edward Balliol, K of Scotland *Clarendon* R n p. n 1230 O v 378 H n p iv. 149.
July 30	The mayors and bailiffs of London and the other ports of England are ordered to arrest all persons bringing papal bulls into the kingdom *Clarendon* R n p n 1230 O v. 378 H n p n 149
Aug. 18.	Power for Henry de Percy, Maurice de Berkeley, and Thomas de Lucy to treat with William de Douglas. *Westm* R n. p n 1230 O v 379. H n p iv 149
Aug. 18.	Power to the bps of Durham and Carlisle, Gilbert de Umframvill, earl of Anegos, Henry de Percy, and six others, to treat with the Scots for the preservation of the truce. *Westm* R. n p n 1230 O v 379 H n p iv 149
Aug 22.	The K orders Saier Lorymer to pay 20*l* to John de Thoresby for the debts of Robert de Artoys *Westm* R. n p. n. 1231. O. v. 380. H. n p. iv 150
Aug 26.	Robert Parnyng, the K's chancellor, being dead, John de Thoresby, John de S Paul, and Thomas de Brayton are appointed keepers of the great seal. *Westm.* R n p ii 1231. O. v 380. H. n p iv 150.
Aug 26.	Memorandum that Robert Parnyng, the K's chancellor, died on the 26th of August at Worcester House beyond Temple Bar ; and of the delivery of the great seal to John de Thoresby, keeper of the rolls of chancery, Thomas de Brayton, a clerk of the chancery, and John de St Paul. R. n. p n 1231 O v. 381 H n. p. iv 150
Aug 29	Power to Henry de Lancaster, earl of Derby, and 11 others, to treat with the ambassadors of Philip de Valois before the pope, as a private mediator, not as a judge. *Westm.* R n p n 1231 O. v. 381. H. n. p. iv. 150

DATE	SUBJECT.
1343 Aug 30	The K informs the pope that the nobles and commonalty assembled in parliament will no longer endure the injuries occasioned by the immense number of provisors who have invaded the kingdom *Westm* R ii p ii 1231 O v 381 H ii. p iv 151
Aug 30	Credence for Henry earl of Derby and William de Montacute, earl of Salisbury, to Alfonso K. of Castile *Westm* R. ii p ii. 1232. O. v 383 H ii. p iv 151
Sept 2	The K requests Alfonso K of Castile to grant redress to Garsio Hernaut de Verger, of Ort, whose ship has been taken by his subjects *Westm* R. ii p ii 1232. O v 383. H ii p iv 151
Sept 2.	Power for Henry de Lancaster, earl of Derby, and William de Montacute, earl of Salisbury, to treat with Alfonso K of Castile *Westm* R. ii p ii 1233 O v 384 H ii p. iv. 151.
Sept 4	The K sends Philip de Weston, canon of York, John Costre, archdeacon of the East Riding, and Thomas de Melchebarn, mayor of the staple, to treat with the commonalties of Flanders about certain complaints made by English merchants *Nottingham* R ii p ii 1233
Sept 10	The K complains to the pope of the presentation to benefices of foreigners not residing in England *Westm* R ii p ii. 1233 O v 385 H ii p iv 152
Sept 18	The K empowers Nicholas de la Beche, seneschal of Gascony, to treat with the nobles and others, and to grant pardons to rebels *Westm*. R ii. p. ii 1234 O v 386. H ii. p iv. 152
Sept. 20	Also to remove unfit officers, and to do what is necessary for the government of the duchy *Westm* R ii p ii 1234
Sept 20	Grant of 400*l* to the cardinals of Palestrina and Frascati, in lieu of a former grant of 200 sacks of wool *Westm* R ii p ii 1234 O. v. 387. H ii p. iv 152.
Sept 20	The K is glad to hear of the resistance made by Leo K of Armenia to the infidels, and would assist him but for the wars in which he is engaged *London* R. ii. p ii 1234 O v 387 H ii p iv 152
Sept 21	Pope Clement [VI] complains to the K. of the violations of the truce by him in Brittany, and sends Stephen de Mulceone to compel the observance of the truce, on pain of ecclesiastical censure. *Villeneuve* R ii p ii 1235 O iv 387 H ii p iv. 153
Sept 23	The K desires Nicholas de la Beche, seneschal of Gascony, to treat with the inhabitants of the duchy for a subsidy of 12*d* in the pound on merchandise *Westm*. R. ii. p ii 1235 O. v. 388. H. ii p iv 153
[Sept 23]	Letters on the subject to the commonalties of Bourdeaux and seven other towns R ii p ii 1235
Sept 23	The K desires the above-mentioned Nicholas to send information about the value of the grants he has made in Gascony *Westm* R. ii p ii. 1235
Sept 23	The K orders him to examine the men at arms before he pays them their wages *Westm* R ii p ii 1235
Sept. 26	K Edward, as K of France, empowers John de Sordich to hear all complaints and appeals relating to the duchy of Aquitain. *Westm* R ii p. ii. 1236. O v 388. H. ii. p. iv. 153
Sept 29	Memorandum of the appointment of Robert de Sadyngton to the office of chancellor, and the delivery to him of the great seal *Westm* R ii p ii 1236 O v 389 H ii p iv 153
Oct 4	The K.'s grant to Peter de Greyly, viscount of Bénanges, and John de Greyly, capital de Buche, of 12*d* in the pound on merchandise for the repair of their fortresses, but which shall not be to the prejudice of the rights of the town of Libourne *Westm*. R ii p ii. 1236 O v 389 H ii p iv 153
Oct 8	The K forbids the priors of Lewes, Prittlewell, and 19 other priors, to send money to their superiors abroad, or to pay it to their agents *Westm* R. ii p ii 1236
Oct 9	Clement [VI] desires the K to procure the liberation of Ralph de Montfort and others who were captured by Hugh de Wrocelesse and others of the retinue of the court of Narantone during the truce *Avignon* R ii p ii 1237 O v 390 H. ii. p iv. 153
Oct 18	The K grants an annuity of 20 marks to Druet Godyn, for his services to Robert de Artoys *Westm*. R ii p ii 1237 O v 390 H ii p iv 154
Oct. 20 ?	The sheriffs of the maritime counties and the earl of Huntingdon, warden of the Cinque Ports, are ordered to prevent the importation of bulls or letters prejudicial to the crown or the people *Westm* R. ii p ii 1237

DATE.	SUBJECT
1343. Oct. 24.	Clement [VI] licenses Richard bp of Durham to institute a perpetual vicarage and five prebends from the revenues of the church of Houghton *Avignon* R ii p. ii. 1237. O. v. 391 H. ii. p iv. 154
Nov 4	Tournaments are forbidden throughout England *Langley* R ii p ii. 1238
Nov. 20.	Pope Clement desires the dean of Lichfield, Matthew de Trevaur, canon of Bangor, and Emyon Vap Jerweth, canons of S Asaph's, to bestow the canonry of Bangor and the next vacant prebend on John de Trevaur R. ii. p. ii 1238 O v 392. H ii. p iv 154
Nov. 29.	The K. consents to the prolongation of the negotiations before the pope until Christmas 1344, and will send the earls of Derby and Warwick and other ambassadors, informs the pope that he has observed the truce, but his adversary has violated it, and that he has done nothing new relating to provisions *Westm* R ii p ii 1289 O v 394 H ii p. iv 155
Nov 29	William de Bohun, earl of Northampton, and Bartholomew de Burghersh, are ordered to protect John archbp. of Canterbury in his visitation of the diocese of Norwich *Westm* R ii p ii 1239 O v 395 H ii p iv 155
Dec. 1.	Gilbert de Umframvill, earl of Anegos, Henry de Percy, Ralph de Nevill, and fourteen others, are ordered to punish the transgressors of the truce with Scotland *Westm* R ii p ii 1229 O v 396 H ii p iv 156.
Dec 2	John de Gatesden is appointed warden of the castle and town of Brest and the viscounty of Lyoun *Westm* R ii p ii 1240 O v 397 H ii p iv 156
Dec. 6	Proclamation to be made throughout England that all persons who capture falcons and hawks must bring them to the sheriffs *Thetford* R. ii. p. ii. 1240.
Dec. 7.	Proclamation to be made in London, Hull, Southampton, Yarmouth, and Bristol, that no wine is to be sold or sent away without being gauged by Thomas de Colleye or his deputies. *Westm* R ii p ii 1240
Dec 8.	The K. desires the seneschal of Gascony and the constable of Bourdeaux to inform him of the condition and value of Bearys [Biarritz], which the commonalty of Bayonne have petitioned to be granted to them, that they may fortify it. *Westm* R. ii p ii 1240
Dec. 10.	The K. orders the commonalty of Bourdeaux to pay to his receiver the customs due to the duke of Brittany *Westm* R ii p ii 1241 O v 397 H ii p iv 156 ·
Dec. 10.	The K orders the constable of Bourdeaux to repay the loans of the citizens of Bourdeaux *Ditton* R ii p ii 1241
Dec. 10.	Power to the bp of Bayonne, Nicholas de la Beche, seneschal of Gascony, John de Shordich, Bernard de Bearne, provost of Bayonne, Dominic de S John, and John de Gistede to treat with Alfonso K of Castile *Ditton* R ii p ii 1241 O v 398 H ii p iv. 156
Dec. 18	The K desires the bp of Bayonne to undertake this commission *Westm* R. ii p ii. 1241. O v. 398 H ii p iv 157
[Dec 18]	Similar letter to Bernard le Berne, called l'Espes R ii p. ii 1241 O v 399 H ii p iv 157
Dec. 23.	The K commends the fidelity of the bp. of Corneivaille (Quimper), and desires credence for Almeric de Chezon Similar letters to the captains and commonalties of Quimper, Quimperlé, and four other towns, and to five lords *Westm* R ii. p ii 1242 O. v. 399 H ii p iv 157
Dec 23.	The K. desires the bp. of Quimper to allow certain impositions on merchandise for the defence of Brittany Similar letters to ten other persons and commonalties. *Westm* R ii. p ii 1242 O v 399 H. ii. p iv. 157
Dec. 24	The K orders John de Montgomery, admiral of the fleet west of the Thames, to provide 24 ships at Dartmouth and Southampton by Jan 2, for the passage of men at-arms and archers to Brittany *Westm* R ii p ii. 1242
1344. Jan 1.	Protection for all persons coming to the tournament at Windsor on Jan. 18. *Ditton*. R. ii p. ii. 1242. O v. 400 H ii p iv 157
Jan 3	The K desires the pope not to allow certain processes commenced at Rome against Robert bp of Chichester, as they are contrary to the rights of the crown. *Woodstock* R ii. p ii 1242. O. v 400 H ii. p. iv 157.
[Jan. 3]	Similar letters to three Roman cardinals. R. ii p ii 1243. O. v. 401. H. ii. p. iv. 158

DATE.	SUBJECT
1344 Jan 8	K Edward has received the letter of Alfonso K of Portugal, stating that he has ordered his subjects to treat the English in a friendly manner, and he has ordered proclamations to be made in England in favour of the subjects of the K of Portugal. *Woodstock* R. II p II 1243 O. v 402 H II. p iv. 158
[Jan. 8]	Proclamations to the effect above-mentioned to be made in London, Sandwich, and four other ports R II p II 1243 O v 402 H II p. iv 158
Jan 15	Warrant for the payment of the arrears of the annuity of 1,500*l* to John duke of Brabant *Westm* R II p II 1244 O v 403 H II p iv 158
Jan 27.	The K orders proclamation to be made in London for the circulation of three new gold coins, one worth 6*s*, another worth 3*s*, and the other 1s 8*d* *Westm* R III p I. 1 O v 403. H II p iv 158
Jan. 28	The seneschal of Gascony and the constable of Bourdeaux are ordered to appoint a captain and garrison for the defence of Bourg *Westm* R III p. I. 1.
Jan 29	Tournaments are forbidden throughout England *Westm* R III. p. I 1.
Jan 29	Clement [VI] writes to the abbot of Valle Crucis [Stratmarkell ?] and the deans of Lichfield and Chichester for the promotion of John de Trevaur, canon of S. Asaph. *Avignon.* R III. p I. 1. O. v 403. H. II p. iv. 158.
Jan 30	The K orders proclamations to be made throughout England against provisors *Westm* R III p I 2
Jan 31.	John de Houton and Nicholas de Rook are ordered to ascertain the manner in which the late earl of Norfolk held the office of marshal of England *Westm* R III p I 3. O. v. 405 H II. p. iv 159.
Feb 2	Protection for one year for William Wariner, of Southampton, who is providing victuals in England for the K 's forces in Brittany *Westm.* R III p I. 3 O. v. 405. H II. p iv. 159
Feb. 3.	The K orders the justiciary of Ireland to forbid his officers to leave the country. *Westm.* R III p I 3
Feb 3.	The several sheriffs are ordered to send the names of those who propose to hold tournaments, with the values of their horses and arms *Westm* R. III p I 4
Feb. 3.	The coiners at Canterbury and Bury S Edmund's are ordered to come to the Tower of to London coin money *Westm* R III p I 4
Feb. 6.	The bailiffs of Great Yarmouth, Newcastle, and 43 other ports are ordered to send persons to London, to inform the council of the state of the navy *Westm.* R III p I 4. O. v. 405. H II p iv. 161
Feb. 9.	Proclamation is to be made by the several sheriffs and the mayors and bailiffs of 13 ports that no earl, baron, man-at-arms, religious person, or foreigner is to leave the kingdom without the K 's licence *Westm* R II p I 4
Feb. 10.	Thomas de Beauchamp, earl of Warwick, is appointed marshal of England. *Westm.* R. III. p I. 5 O. v. 406 H II p iv 160.
Feb 10	Ralph de Ufford is appointed justiciary of Ireland Mandate to the people of Ireland, ordering them to obey him, and to John Darcy, to resign his office *Westm.* R III p I 5
Feb 10	Licence for an annual tournament to be held at Lincoln on the Monday after S. John the Baptist's day, of which the earl of Derby is to be captain *Westm* R. III p I 5 O. v. 407 H. II p iv. 160
Feb 12	The sheriffs of London and the mayors and bailiffs of Newcastle and 12 other ports are ordered to prevent the exportation of money and plate *Westm.* R. III p I 5
Feb 13	Memorandum that Robert de Sadyngton, the K 's chancellor, sent the great seal to the K, who received it in his chamber at Westminster called La Oriole, and directed to be sealed therewith four pardons for Geoffrey State of Ipswich and three others, and then sent back the seal to the chancellor *Westm* R III p I 6 O v 407 H. II. p iv 160
Feb 25	Memorandum that the chancellor sent the great seal to the K, and of the sealing of pardons for John Swerd of Hull and four others by the earl of Warwick by the K.'s command, and of the return of the seal to the chancellor. *Westm.* R III p I 6. O v 408. H II p. iv 160
Feb 26	William de Horle, the K 's carpenter, is authorized to select carpenters for the works at Windsor Castle Similar commission to William de Rameseye, the K 's mason, to select masons *Westm* R. III. p. I. 6
Feb 28.	William de Langele and Stephen de Harpham commissioned to provide carriage for stone and timber from Oxfordshire, Berkshire, and Middlesex for the same works *Westm.* R. III. p. I 6

DATE	SUBJECT
1344. [Feb. 28.]	Commission to John Knyght to provide conveyance for the K's estovers between London and Windsor R. iii p. i. 6
March 1.	The K. informs Frederic duke of Austria that he has received his letter by Henry Corzeleyn, his butler, but cannot decide about the marriage with his daughter Joan until she is of age to consent *Westm* R. iii p. i 7 O v 408 H ii p iv 160.
March 2	Proclamation to be made by the several sheriffs for the circulation of the three new gold coins. *Westm.* R. iii. p. i. 7.
March 9.	Clement [VI] desires the archdeacon of London to induce the prior and convent of Dunmow-Parva to admit John de Dunmowe-Magna to a canonry. *Avignon* R. ii. p. i 7. O. v 408 H ii. p iv 160.
March 10	Thomas de Melcheburn and William his brother are commissioned to receive the great crown from Conrad Clypping and the other German merchants to whom it is pledged. *Westm* R iii p i 7 O v 409 H ii p iv 160
March 10	The K. orders Nicholas de la Beche, seneschal of Gascony, and John Wawayn, constable of Bourdeaux, to coin such gold pieces as the council think advisable *Westm* R iii p i 7.
March 12	The K orders the constable of Bourdeaux to pay the wages of an additional company of 20 men for Nicholas de la Beche, senachal of Gascony *Westm* R. iii. p. i 8.
March 24.	Power for Henry de Lancaster, earl of Derby, and Richard earl of Arundel, to make alliances with any persons whomsoever. *The Tower of London* R iii p i. 8 O v 409. H. ii p iv 161.
[March 24]	Power for the same commissioners to retain persons for the K's service R iii. p i. 8. O v 410 H. ii. p. iv. 161.
March 24.	Power for the same persons to treat with Alfonso K of Castile, Alfonso K of Portugal, and Peter K of Arragon *The Tower of London* R iii p i 8 O v 410 H ii p. iv 161
March 24.	Power for the same commissioners to treat with the K of Castile for redress of injuries. *The Tower of London.* R. iii p i. 9. O v 410 H ii p. iv 161
March 24.	Power for the same commissioners to reform the state of Aquitain *The Tower of London.* R iii. p i 9. O. v. 411 H ii. p. iv 161
[March 24]	The K. orders his subjects in Aquitain to assist the above-named commissioners. R iii p i 9 O v. 412. H. ii p iv, 162.
March 24	Power for the same commissioners to revoke excessive grants *The Tower of London.* R iii p. i 9 O v 412 H. ii. p iv 162
March 24	Power for the same commissioners to enforce the observance of the truce with France. *The Tower of London* R. iii. p. i 10. O. v 413. H. ii p iv 162
March 24.	Protection for one year for William de Percy and 28 others going abroad in the company of the earl of Arundel *Westm* R iii p i 10
March 25	The K. orders Bartholomew de Burghersh, constable of Dover Castle and warden of the Cinque Ports, to compel the barons of the Cinque Ports to provide eight ships fit for war, and to detain all the ships of 30 tons and over *The Tower of London* R iii p. i 10
March 25.	The K. orders Bartholomew de Burghersh to prevent any persons leaving the kingdom, except merchants *The Tower of London* R iii p i 10
March 25	The men of Bayonne, who are occupying the castles in Brittany, are ordered to remain there for their defence. Letter to the same effect to the mayor and commonalty of Bayonne. *The Tower of London* R. iii p i 10
March 25.	Warrants to the sheriffs of London and the bailiffs of all the ports of England to arrest ships of 30 tons and upwards *The Tower of London.* R. iii p i 11
March 26	Protection for one year for Sir William Marmyon, Sir Hugh de Menill, and 30 others going abroad in the retinue of the earl of Derby *Westm* R iii, p i, 11.
April 5.	The mayor and bailiffs of Sandwich are ordered to release two Carmelite friars, lately consecrated as bishops by the pope, whom they had arrested with Papal Bulls and other letters prejudicial to the K. *Marlborough* R iii p i 11 O. v 413 H. ii p iv 162
April 8	The K orders John de Flete, keeper of the exchange at the Tower of London, to coin the new gold pieces and sterlings ordered by parliament. *Marlborough.* R. iii p. i. 11.
April 24	The K. orders Thomas and William de Melchebourn to deliver the great crown to the treasurer and chamberlains Warrant to the latter to receive it. *Westm.* R iii p i 12 K of Castile. O. iv. 414. H. ii p. iv 162.
April 26	The K. informs the provost of Fontis Rabidi [Fuentarabia] of the truce with the K. of Castile. *Westm.* R. iii. p. i. 12.

Y

DATE.	SUBJECT.
1344 April 28.	Power for Peter de S John, bp of Bayonne, and five others, to treat with the K. of Castile for the redress of injuries and for peace. Two similar powers for the above, with others ; and one power for Nicholas de Beche, seneschal of Gascony, Sir John de Shordich, and John Wawayn, constable of Bourdeaux, dated 26 April R. iii p. i 12 O. v 414–15 H ii p iv 163
May 8	Reginald de Cobham is appointed admiral of the fleet from the Thames westward. The masters and mariners are ordered to obey him Robert de Ufford, earl of Suffolk, is appointed admiral north of the Thames *Rising* R iii p i 13
May 8	The K forbids the sheriffs of London to implead the clerks of the Chancery, except in that court. *Westm* R iii p i 13
May 30.	The K. congratulates the K. of Castile on the conquest of the town of Algiers. *Westm.* R iii. p. i. 13 O. v. 415 H ii p iv. 163.
June 4.	The K does not wish Ralph de Ufford, justiciary of Ireland, to remove justices, barons of the Exchequer, or others who hold offices by the K's letters patent *Westm.* R iii p i 13.
June 8	The K. orders the mayor and bailiffs of Dover to allow Robert de Eye and Robert Archer to pass to France to ransom Adam de Everingham *Westm* R iii p. i 13
June 10	R. bp of Chichester, William de Clynton, earl of Huntingdon, Hugh de Courtney, earl of Devon, Thomas Wake de Lydel, and Thomas de Berkele, are appointed to hear complaints of delay of justice. *Westm.* R iii. p i 13
June 14	The K orders Ralph de Ufford, justiciary of Ireland, to make inquisition as to lands granted by his predecessors for the defence of the Marches. *Westm.* R iii p i. 14.
June 14	Proclamation to be made in Ireland that the money used in England shall be current in Ireland. *Westm* R iii p i. 14
June 16	The K sends the letters of Peter K of Arragon, about certain injuries to his subjects, to the seneschal of Gascony, who, he has ordered, is to do justice *London* R. iii p i. 14
June 20	Power to William Trussel, John de Wodehous, canon of York, chancellor of the Exchequer, and Thomas de Rokeby, to explain the K's affairs to the convocation of the province of York *Westm* R iii p. i. 15.
June 20	The K. orders the seneschal of Gascony to deliver to his mother Isabella the land formerly belonging to the viscount of Castellion, the pedage of Peyrafrice, &c *Westm.* R iii. p i. 15.
June 28	The admirals Robert de Ufford, earl of Suffolk, and Reginald de Cobham, are ordered to provide ships at Portsmouth and Southampton by Sept 8 for the K.'s passage to France. *Westm.* R. iii p i 15
June 29	Pardon for Peter de Reppes, of Great Yarmouth, for breaches of the K's peace. Similar letters for 400 other men of Yarmouth *Westm* R iii p i. 15
June 30	The K orders the wax around Edward his grandfather's body in Westminster Abbey to be renewed. *Westm.* R iii. p i 16. O v. 416. H ii. p. iv 163
June 30.	Proclamation to be made for the assumption of knighthood by persons with 40l. a year or upwards. *Westm* R iii p i 16
July 1.	The sheriffs of Norfolk and Suffolk and eight other counties are ordered to provide fittings for shipping horses *Westm* R iii p i 16.
July 7.	The sheriff of Yorkshire is ordered to make proclamation that no person shall be compelled to receive gold coin for a less amount than 20s *Westm* R. iii. p i 16.
July 9	Proclamation to be made in London for the circulation and exchange of the new coinage. *Westm.* R iii. p i. 16 O v 416 H ii. p iv. 163.
July 10.	Summons to Maurice FitzThomas, earl of Desmond, to join the K. with 20 men at arms and 50 hobillers, at Portsmouth, on Sept 8 Similar summons to Maurice FitzThomas, earl of Kildare, and 10 others. *Westm* R iii p i 17. O v 417 H ii p iv. 164.
July 10	Grant to William Fraunk, constable of Tykill Castle, of five marks a week for the expenses of the duchess of Brittany *Westm.* R iii p i 17. O. v 418. H ii p iv 164.
July 28	The K. repeats his prohibition of tournaments. *Merewell.* R. iii p i. 17
July 30.	The K orders the mayor and bailiffs of Dover to give free passage to Benedict " Episcopus Cardicensis," who is going on a pilgrimage in the name of Q. Philippa *Merewell.* R iii p i 18 O v 418. H ii p. iv 164
Aug 3	The K asks the pope to send letters of protection and safe conduct for his ambassadors, John de Offord, dean of Lincoln, Hugh de Nevill, and Nicholin de Fhsco. *Rising.* R. iii. p i 18 O. v 419. H ii p iv 164

DATE.	SUBJECT.
1344. Aug 3	The K. informs the pope that he sends John de Offord and others to treat for a final peace with France. *Rising.* R. m. p i 18. O v 419 H. n p iv 164
[Aug. 3.]	The K. desires W. bp of Norwich to present the above-mentioned letters to the pope. R. iii. p. i. 18 O v 420 H ii. p. iv. 165.
[Aug 3]	Similar letter to Andrew de Offord. R iii p i. 19 O. v. 420. H ii p iv 165.
Aug 4	Power for William bp of Norwich, John de Offord, Thomas Fastolf, archdeacon of Norwich, Sir Hugh de Nevill, Nicholin de Flisco, and Andrew de Offord, to treat with the ambassadors of Philip de Valois before the pope *Rising.* R. iii p. i. 19. O v. 420. H ii. p iv. 165
Aug. 4	Credence for Nicholin de Flisco to John abp of Milan, and Luchino viscount of Milan. *Rising* R. iii p i. 19 O v 421 H ii. p iv 165.
Aug. 6.	Credence for Nicholin de Flisco to Andrew K. of Jerusalem and Sicily. *Westm* R. iii p i 19 O v. 421 H.iii. p iv 165.
Aug 12	The K. informs Alfonso K of Castile that he had intended to visit him when he heard of the surrender of Algiers, and that he will send ambassadors to resume the treaty of marriage. *Rising.* R iii p i. 19. O v 422 H. ii p iv. 165.
[Aug. 12]	The K thanks Alfonso for the two jennets he has sent by John de Brocas and the lord de Pomerus R. iii p i 20 O v 422. H ii p iv 166.
Aug 12	The K forbids appeals to Rome against judicial sentences of the chancellor of Oxford university *Westm.* R ii p. i.20.
Aug 16	The K requests Ferando Zancu de Vailhedolit [Valladolid] to favour the treaty of marriage with the K of Castile Similar letters to John Alfonso de Broket and three others *Windsor* R. iii p i. 20 O v 423 H ii p iv. 166
Aug. 18.	The K desires Peter del Serayn and two others to remain in the castles of Brittany for their defence *Westm* R iii. p i 20 O v 423 H. ii p iv. 166.
Aug 20	Proclamation to be made throughout England for the circulation of the new coinage. *Westm* R. iii p i 21 O v. 424. H ii p iv 166
Aug. 25.	Edward de Balhol, K. of Scotland, is appointed captain of the army against the Scots The abp of York, the sheriffs of the northern counties, and seven others, are ordered to assist him. *Westm.* R iii. p. i 21 O. v 424 H ii p iv. 166.
Sept. 1	The K of England informs Alfonso K of Castile that he will send Sir William Trussell and Sir William Stury to treat of a marriage between his daughter Joan and Alfonso's eldest son. *Westm* R iii. p. i 21. O v 425 H. ii. p iv 167
[Sept 1]	The K. desires the assistance of Alfonso K. of Castile in composing the differences between his subjects and the city of Bayonne R. iii p. i 21. O. v 426 H ii p iv 167.
Sept. 1.	The K recommends William Trussel and William Stury to Ferando Zanchi of Valladolid and four others. *Westm.* R. iii p i 22. O v 426 H. ii p. iv. 167
Sept. 1.	Safe conduct for Nicholin de Flisco going to the pope *Westm* R iii. p. i 22 O v 426 H ii. p iv 167
Sept. 1	Crédence for Nicholin de Flisco to Simon Buccanigra, duke of Genoa *Westm.* R. iii p. i 22 O v 427 H ii p iv. 167.
Sept 1.	The K. thanks Giles Buccanigra, brother of the duke of Genoa, admiral of the K of Castile, for his reception of the earl of Derby, and for his offers of service, and desires credence for Nicholin de Flisco. *Westm* R. iii p i 22 O v. 427 H. ii p iv. 167
Sept 2	The K assigns 200l, payable at Easter, for the arrears due to Nicholin de Flisco. *Westm* R iii p. i 22 O v 427 H ii p. iv. 167
Sept 10.	Instructions for Sir William Trussel and Sir William Sturey to treat with the K of Castile. *London.* R. iii. p i 22 O v 428. H. ii p. iv 168
Sept. 18.	The K desires Nicholas de la Beche, seneschal of Gascony, to settle the dissensions between the people of Bayonne and of Labourde. *Waltham.* R iii. p i. 23. O v 429 H ii p iv 168.
Oct. 5.	Warrant for the payment of the annuity of Druet Godyn for his services to Robert d'Artoys *Waltham.* R. iii p i 23 O v 429. H. ii p. iv. 168
Oct. 12	Protection for all foreign cloth workers coming to England. *Westm.* R. iii. p i. 23. O v. 429. H i p. iv. 168.
Oct. 13.	The K desires the abbot of S. Peter's, Gloucester, to provide a house for Thomas de la Mare de Ryndecombe and John de Weston, collectors of the tenth and fifteenth in Gloucestershire Similar letters to 30 other abbots, priors, and deans. *Westm.* R. iii. p. i. 24 O. v. 430. H ii p. iv. 168.

DATE	SUBJECT
1344	
Oct. 15.	The K. forbids men-at-arms leaving the country *Westm.* R. iii p. i 24.
Oct. 21	The K. informs the consuls and échevins of Cologne that Thomas de Melcheburn, mayor of the staple at Bruges, will redeem the jewels in pawn on Nov 28　*London.* R. iii. p i. 24. O. v 432 H ii p iv 169.
Oct. 26.	The K asks the pope for a dispensation for marriages between his eldest son and the daughter of the duke of Brabant, and between his daughter Isabel and the duke's eldest son *Westm* R. iii p i. 25　O v 432　H ii p iv. 169.
Nov 4	Memorandum of the delivery by Robert de Sadyngton, the K's chancellor, to John de Houton and John de Etton, chamberlains of the receipt of Exchequer, of nine papal bulls and other letters arrested at Sandwich　R. iii p i 25　O v 433　H ii. p iv 169
Dec 6	Clement [VI] desires the K to send the promised embassy, including one member of the royal family. *Avignon*　R iii p i 25　O v 433　H. ii p. iv 169.
Dec. 27.	The K. informs the K. of Castile that, in consequence of a report that one of his ambassadors had been wrecked, he has renewed the commissions, and intends to send them to his ambassadors at Bayonne. *Norwich.* R iii p i 25　O v 434　H ii p. iv. 170
1345	
Jan 2.	Power to Peter bp. of Bayonne and others to treat with Alfonso K. of Castile. *Westm.* R iii p i 26. O v 434　H ii p. iv 170.
Jan. 2.	Letters of recommendation for the ambassadors to John Stephani, chancellor of the K. of Castile, and two others *Westm* R. iii. p i 26. O v 435　H ii p iv. 170.
Jan 5.	The K desires the assistance of John Stephani and the others in the negotiations. *Norwich* R. iii p i 26. O v 435. H. ii p. iv 170.
Jan. 14.	The K. grants to Senebrun lord del Sparre the castellany of Lanerdale, to be held during the war with France for the use of Cardinal Taillerand, who claims it as his inheritance The seneschal of Gascony is ordered to deliver it to the lord del Sparre *Westm. Jan. 17.* R. iii p i 26　O v 436　H ii p iv. 171.
Jan 18	The K. orders the seneschal of Gascony to inquire into the cardinal's claim to the above. *Westm.* R iii. p i 27. O v. 437. H ii p. iv. 171.
Jan. 18	Credence for John prior of Rochester and sir William Trussell to the Q. of Castile. *Westm* R iii. p i 27　O v. 437　H ii p iv 171
Jan 20	Credence for the same persons to the K of Castile　*Westm.* R. iii. p. i 27. O. v 438. H ii. p iv 171.
Jan. 20.	The K. informs the pope that the charges of John Bodemon and Thomas Dunclent against Wolstan bp of Worcester are false, and asks that the said bp may be allowed to answer them by proxy in consequence of his age *Westm* R iii p i 27. O. v 438. H. ii. p iv. 171.
Jan. 20.	The K writes on the same subject to W bp of Norwich, John de Offord, dean of Lincoln, and Friar Thomas del Isle *Westm.* R. iii p i 27. O v. 438 H ii p iv. 172.
Jan 21	Protection for a year for the agents of cardinal Reymund de Farges *Westm.* R. iii. p i 27 O v 439 H ii. p iv. 172.
Jan 26.	The K. orders the collectors of the tenth and fifteenth in Cornwall to desist from taxing the tin-workers, who are exempt *Westm.* R iii p i 28.
Jan. 27.	The K informs the cardinals whom the pope sends to treat for peace that he can make no peace without the consent of his allies *Westm.* R. iii p i 28. O. v. 439. H. ii. p iv. 172
Feb. 1.	Clement [VI.] sends John Bonde to tell the K of the capture of Smyrna by the Christians, and exhorts him to consent to a peace *Avignon.* R iii. p. i 28. O. v. 439. H ii p iv 172
Feb 8.	Safe conduct for Nicholas abp. of Ravenna and Peter abp. of Astorga, who are coming from the pope to England. *Westm.* R. iii. p. i 29 O. v. 441. H. ii. p. iv. 172.
Feb 10.	Proclamation is to be made throughout England that wool is to be exported only from certain ports. *Westm* R. iii p i. 29
Feb. 20.	The K forbids the exaction of the triennial tenth on the English benefices of cardinals Gancelin, parson of the churches of Hemmyngburgh, Stepney, Hackney, Lymyng, Holyngbourn, Pageham, and prebendary of Driffield, Louth, and Sallowe, John the bp. of Palestrina (Penestrinensis), archdeacon of York, and prebendary of Wistowe, Taillerand dean of York, parson of Whitchurch, and prebendary of Thame, and four others. *Tenham.* R iii p i. 29. O. v. 442. H. ii. p. iv. 173.
Feb. 20.	The K. desires the commonalties of Ghent, Bruges, and Ypres not to treat with the count of Flanders without the K.'s consent. *Tenham.* R. iii. p. i. 30.

DATE.	SUBJECT
1345. Feb 20	The K informs the same commonalties that his letters desiring them to receive honorably the count of Flanders, were authentic *Tenham.* R. iii p. i 30
Feb. 20.	Bartholomew de Burgherssh, constable of Dover Castle and warden of the Cinque Ports, is ordered to forbid the exportation of horses exceeding 60s. in value. *Tenham.* R iii. p i 30
Feb 20.	Also to prevent men-at-arms leaving the kingdom *Tenham* R iii p i 30
Feb. 22.	The K asks the pope to confirm the dissolution of the marriage of Richard earl of Arundel with Isabel, daughter of the late Hugh le Despenser, and to grant a dispensation for his marriage with Eleanor, daughter of the earl of Lancaster. *Tenham* R. iii p. i 30. O. v. 443. H ii p iv. 173
Feb. 22.	Bartholomew de Burgherssh is to allow the papal nuncios to pass on their return to the pope, and all other persons except men-at-arms. *Tenham* R. iii. p i 31.
Feb. 23.	Richard earl of Arundel is appointed admiral of the fleet west of the Thames *Tenham* R. iii p. i 31.
Feb 23.	The K tells the pope that he has been falsely informed that certain statutes have been passed in England to the prejudice of the church of Rome, and a council will be held to answer the nuncios *Tenham.* R iii. p i 31 O v. 443 H ii p iv. 173
Feb. 23.	The K desires the pope to give credence to Michael de Northburgh, canon of Lichfield and Hereford, and sir Nigel de Loryng, touching the dispensation for the marriage of the prince of Wales with the daughter of the duke of Brabant *Tenham.* R iii. p. i. 32 O. v. 444. H. ii, p. iv. 174.
Feb. 23.	Power for Otto lord of Cuyk and Philip de Weston, canon of York, to treat with Louis K of the Romans *Tenham* R iii p i. 32. O v 445 H ii p iv 174
Feb. 25.	Ralph baron of Stafford is appointed seneschal of Aquitain. Edmund de la Beche, lieutenant of the seneschal, is ordered to resign the office to him *Tenham* R iii. p. i 32.
March 1.	Richard earl of Arundel, admiral of the fleet from the Thames westward, is ordered to provide 13 ships at Bristol for the passage of the baron of Stafford *Westm* R iii p i 32
March 10	The K forbids any persons leaving the kingdom, except merchants, from any port except Dover *Westm.* R iii. p i. 32.
March 10.	The sheriffs of the maritime counties and the mayors and bailiffs for the sea ports are ordered to proclaim that no injury is to be done to the merchants of the K. of Spain or the K's other allies *Westm* R iii p i 33
March 12.	The K forbids the exaction of the triennial tenth from the benefices of cardinal Reymund de Farges, archdeacon of Leicester and parson of Leek. *Westm* R iii p i 33. O. v. 445. H. ii p iv 174.
March 14	The mayors and bailiffs of Dover, Hastings, and seven other ports are ordered to send their ships to Sandwich on May 9. *Westm* R iii p i. 33.
March 16.	Ralph baron of Stafford, seneschal of Gascony, is ordered to make inquisition as to excessive grants extorted from the K. *Westm* R. iii p i 33. O v 446. H ii. p iv 174
March 18.	Pope Clement [VI.] exhorts the K to make peace with France *Avignon* R iii. p i. 34 O. v 446 H ii p iv. 174
March 30.	The K orders Ralph baron of Stafford, seneschal of Gascony, to send information concerning the custom of exposing the bodies of murdered persons, and the exaction by the bailiffs of a ransom for their burial. *Sheen* R iii p i 34.
April 10.	Warrant to the customers of S. Botolph's for the payment of an annuity of 20l to William de Melchebourn in compensation for his trouble in redeeming the K's great crown. *Westm.* R iii. p i 34 O v 447 H ii p iv. 175
April 10.	Henry de Lancaster, earl of Derby, is appointed the K.'s lieutenant in Aquitain *Westm.* R. iii. p. i. 34
April 10.	Power for John lord Disyke and A. Ingram des Champs to treat with the K.'s allies for serving him Similar commission to John de Say. *Westm.* R iii p. i. 35.
April 12.	The K repeats his request to the pope for a dispensation for the marriage of the prince of Wales with the daughter of the duke of Brabant, and desires credence for friar John de Reppes, the pope's chaplain, in a matter concerning Thomas de Hatfield, his secretary *Westm.* R iii p i. 35. O. v. 448. H. ii p. iv. 175
April 16.	Richard earl of Arundel is ordered to provide ships for the passage of men sent by the earl of Devon in the company of the earl of Northampton *Westm* R iii. p i 35.
April 20.	Protection for Ralph baron of Stafford and 34 persons in his company. *Westm.* R. iii. i.36.

DATE	SUBJECT.
1345. April 23.	The K. confirms the election of Peter de Puteo as mayor of Bayonne. *Westm.* R. III. p. 1. 36
April 24.	Power to William de Bohun, earl of Northampton, to defy Philip de Valois for his violations of the truce *Westm.* R. III p. 1 36. O v 449. H. II p IV 175.
April 24.	William Stury is appointed mayor of Bourdeaux. The seneschal of Gascony and the constable of Bourdeaux are ordered to deliver the office to him, and the jurats and commonalty are ordered to obey him *Westm* R III p 1 36
April 24.	William de Bohun, earl of Northampton, is appointed the K.'s lieutenant and captain in France and in Brittany Two similar commissions, omitting the clause *prout pro commodo nostro videritis faciendum.* *Westm.* R. III p 1 37. O v. 449-50. H. II p IV 175-6.
April 27,	Indenture between the K. and the earl of Northampton, containing his instructions. *Westm.* R, III p 1 37 O. v. 450 H. II. p. IV 176
May 10	Henry de Lancaster, earl of Derby, is appointed the K.'s lieutenant and captain in Aquitain *Westm.* R III p. 1 37
May 10.	Power for him to enter into alliances and to retain persons for the K.'s service. *Westm* R III p. 1. 38
May 10	The K orders Robert de Mildenhale, keeper of the wardrobe at the Tower of London, to receive 1,200 bows, 1,000 sheaves of arrows, and 4,000 bow-strings from the mayor and sheriffs of London. *Westm* R III. p 1. 38
May 13	Power for John prior of Lewes, Otto de Grandison, knt, and Thomas de Baddeby, clerk, to treat with the K of Jerusalem and Sicily and the K of Hungary. *Westm.* R. III p 1. 38 O v 451 H. II p IV. 176.
May 17.	Protection for William de Bohun, earl of Northampton, and 68 persons in his company, going to Brittany *Westm.* R. III p 1 38
May 18	Protection for John Darcy, the cousin, going abroad on the K.'s service, also for John Darcy, the father, and 34 persons in his company. *Westm* R. III p 1 39
May 20.	Memorandum that John de Montfort, duke of Brittany, did homage to the K. of England as K. of France, in the abp's palace at Lambeth. R. III p 1 39 O v 452 H. II. p IV 177.
May 20	Protection for Henry de Lancaster, earl of Derby, for John de Norwich, and 49 others in his retinue, going abroad *Westm* R III p. 1 39.
May 23.	Protection for John de Veer, earl of Oxford, who is going to Brittany, and for 51 persons in his retinue *Westm* H. III p 1 40
May 24	Power for the abbot of S. Mary's, York, and Henry de Ingelby, to receive the fealty of Thomas de Hatfeld, bishop elect of Durham *Westm* R III. p. 1. 40. O v. 452 H. II p IV 177
May 24.	Safe conduct for Mary de Monthermer, countess of Fife, who is about to return to Scotland *Westm.* R III p 1 41 O v. 452. H II p IV 177
May 26	The K informs the pope of the violation of the truce by Philip de Valois, who has arrested in Brittany, and put to death at Paris, certain noblemen, the K.'s adherents, and has committed great outrages in Brittany and Aquitain, complains of the conduct of the nuncio in Brittany, who has rather excited contention than promoted peace, and informs him that he has defied Philip. *Westm* R III p 1 41 O v 453 H. II p IV 177
[May 26]	Letters on the same subject to the cardinal bishops of Palestrina (Penestrinensis) and Frascati and to two others R. III p 1. 41 O v. 454. H. II. p IV. 178
[May 26]	The K desires friar John de Reppes to present the above-mentioned letters to the pope and cardinals R III p 1 42 O v 455. H. II p IV 178
May 28	Protection for Roger, son of Roger Beler, and 10 others, going abroad in the company of John de Grey, of Codnore *Westm* R. III p 1 42
May 28	Protection for Lawrence de Hastings, earl of Pembroke, and 35 persons in his retinue *Westm* R III p. 1. 42.
June 3	The K orders William de Bohun, earl of Northampton, to assist John duke of Brittany in recovering his rights *Westm* R III p. 1 42
June 4	The K orders proclamation to be made in London that the men at arms and archers going to Brittany with the earl of Northampton must be at Portsmouth on the next Monday or Tuesday. *Westm.* R III p 1. 42 O v. 455 H. II p. IV 178.
June 6,	The K. has received the letters of Louis marquis of Brandenburg and duke of Bavaria, by Simon Brenner de Vynstynge, and is willing to confirm the league made with his father. *Westm.* R. III p. 1. 43. O. v. 455. H. II. p IV. 178.

DATE.	SUBJECT.
1345 June 6	Power for Philip de Weston, canon of York, and sir William Stury to treat with the marquis of Brandenburg *Westm.* R. iii p. i. 43 · O v 456. H ii. p iv. 178.
June 6	Safe conduct for Robert lord of Eienles, castellan of Bourbourgh, who is going to Flanders. *Westm.* R iii. p ii 43.
June 7.	The K. orders the treasurer and barons of the Exchequer not to exact from the abbey of Oseney [which was founded by Robert de Olleio, and not by any of the K.'s progenitors,] the amount of wool granted by the parliament, as the abbot was not summoned to parliament, and has paid the amount granted by the convocation of the diocese of Canterbury. *Westm.* R iii p. i. 43. O. v. 456. H ii p iv 178.
June 8	Power for Philip de Weston, canon of York, Peter de Gildesburgh, canon of Lincoln, and sir William Stury to demand from John duke of Brabant, William Dunort, and the K.'s other allies, the fulfilment of their obligations *Westm.* R iii p. i 44 O. v 458. H ii. p. iv 179.
June 10.	Licence to John Blome of London to search for the body of Joseph of Arimathea in the abbey of Glastonbury, about which he has received a divine revelation *Westm.* R. ii. p ii 44. O v 458 H ii p. iv 179
June 11	Proclamation to be made in London, ordering the men of the earl of Derby going to Gascony to hasten to Southampton *Westm* R iii. p. i. 44 O v 458 H ii p iv 179
June 13.	The K. promises compensation for the lands lost by Godefrey de Harecourt, who has done homage to him as K. of France. *Westm.* R. iii. p. i. 44. O. v 459. H ii p iv 179
June 14.	Declaration of the K.'s rights to France, and the injuries he has received from Philip de Valois, *Westm.* R. iii. p. i 44. O v 459 H. ii p iv 179
June 14.	Commission to sir Thomas Spigurnel and sir William de Cusance to treat with persons willing to enter the K.'s service in France and elsewhere. *The Tower of London.* R iii. p i. 45. O. v. 460 H. ii p iv. 180.
June 14.	The K intends to maintain and defend those persons in France who voluntarily come into his obedience, and will observe the laws of S Louis *The Tower of London.* R. iii. p. i 45 O. v. 460. H ii p iv. 180.
June 15	The K. desires the clergy of England to pray for his success against Philip de Valois. *Westm.* R iii p i 45. O. v. 460. H. ii p iv. 180
June 15.	The K. orders the earl of Derby, lieutenant in Aquitain, to restore to Bernard Ezii, lord of Lebret, the castle of Gensak, which he had granted to the lord of Moissidan, to induce him to take the K.'s part, and to recompense the latter, if he deserve it. *Westm.* R i p. i 45
June 18.	The K has received the message of the K of Castile by John prior of Rochester and sir William Trussel, consents to the dowry of 400,000 florins, and will send Peter bp of Bayonne and Gerard de Puy to him. *Sandwich* R iii p. i 46. O v 461. H ii p iv. 180
June 18.	The K requests the Q of Castile to obtain a diminution of the dowry, and he would be willing to treat for a marriage between his son John and her sister, the daughter of the K of Portugal *Sandwich* R iii p. i. 46. O. v. 462. H. ii p iv. 181
June 18.	The K. writes on the same subject to John Stephani, chancellor of the K of Castile *Sandwich* R iii p i. 46. O v 463. H ii. p. iv 181
June 18	The K. thanks John Alfonsi de Bona Vita for his offers of assistance *Sandwich.* R iii p i 46. O v 463 H ii p iv 181.
June 20.	Power for Peter bp of Bayonne and Gerard de Puy, justice of Bourdeaux, to treat with Alfonso K of Castile *Sandwich.* R iii p i. 47. O v 463 H ii p iv 181
June 20.	Instructions for the bp. of Bayonne and Gerard de Puy *Sandwich* R iii p i 47 O. v 464 H ii p iv. 181.
June 20.	The K. thanks John Martyn de Lene for his offers of assistance. *Sandwich.* R iii p i 47. O. v 465. H ii p iv. 182.
June 20.	Protection for Walter de Wodelond, sir John de Ferrers, and 11 others, going abroad in the retinue of Edward prince of Wales. *Sandwich* R iii p i 47.
June 20.	Protection for William de Clynton, earl of Huntingdon, and for Walter de Hopton and 17 others, going abroad in his retinue *Sandwich* R iii p. i 48
June 20.	Protection for Richard earl of Arundel, Roger Wodelok, and 47 others in his company. *Sandwich* R. iii p. i. 48.
June 20.	Protection for Guy de Bryan, John de Wynwyk, clerk, and 61 others going abroad with the K. *Sandwich.* R. iii. p. i. 48.

DATE.	SUBJECT.
1345. June 20.	Protection for Robert de Ufford, earl of Suffolk, for sir Thomas Visdelu, and 13 others in his company *Sandwich.* R III p I 49.
June 20.	Protection for Thomas de Beauchamp, earl of Warwick, and for John de Foleville, and 14 others in his retinue. *Sandwich.* R. III. p. I. 49.
June 20	Protection for Simon Flemmyng and nine others in the retinue of Maurice, son of Maurice de Berkeley *Sandwich.* R. III p I 49.
June 26.	Warrant for the payment of the wages and expenses of William Trussel going into Spain *Sandwich.* R III p. I. 49. O v 471 H II p IV. 184.
July 1.	The K. appoints his son Lionel regent of England during his absence. *Sandwich.* R III p I 50. O v. 471. H II p IV 184.
July 1.	The K appoints as the councillors of his son Lionel, J. abp of Canterbury, R. bp. of London, R bp of Chichester, Thomas bp. elect of Durham, Henry earl of Lancaster, John de Warenne, earl of Surrey, Robert de Sadyngton, the K.'s chancellor, William de Edyngton, the K's treasurer, the prior of Rochester, Simon de Islep, William Trussel, and Andrew de Ufford. *Sandwich.* R. III p I 50.
July 1	Power for the abp of Canterbury and seven others to treat with merchants for loans and advances *Sandwich* R III p I 50
July 3	Memorandum that Robert de Sadyngton, the K.'s chancellor, delivered the great seal to the K at Sandwich, who gave him another for use during his absence The K left Sandwich in the *Swaleue* immediately after noon R III p I 50 O. v. 472. H II p IV 184.
July 4.	Summons to Hugh de Courteneye, earl of Devon, to be ready with his retinue by Aug. 10 to cross the sea to the K.* Similar summons to lords James de Audele and John de Segrave and 22 bannerets , also to John de Heyling and 322 other knights and squires. *Westm.* R III p I 50. O. v 472–3 H II p IV 184–5.
July 10	Peter Heyward, Thomas de S Nicholas, and William de Manston are appointed to put the ports in the Isle of Thanet in a state of defence. The people of Thanet and of Kent are ordered to assist them *Southwick.* R III p I 53.
July 21.	Clement [VI.] rebukes the K for not sending as an ambassador a person of the blood royal, which he had promised to do ; excuses the alleged infractions of the truce by the K of France , complains of the occupation by Vennes and the expulsion of the papal troops, and exhorts him to resume negotiations for peace. *Avignon.* R III p. I 53 O v 465. H II p IV 182
July 26	Memorandum that the K arrived at Sandwich from Flanders on July 26, and on the 30th sent the great seal by John de Thoresby, keeper of the privy seal, to Robert de Sadyngton, who delivered the seal he had used during the K's absence to John de Etton and John de Houton, chamberlains of the Exchequer R III p. I 53 O v 474 H II. p IV 185
July 31	The pope desires John de Thoresby, canon of Lincoln, to give credence to Thomas [Lisle], whom he has lately consecrated bp of Ely *Avignon.* R III p I 55 O v 474 H II p IV. 185
Aug 3	The K informs the sheriffs of Lancaster, London, and 21 others that he has been driven back to England by the wind, but intends soon to go again to France, and he orders all men at-arms between the ages of 16 and 60 to be ready to accompany him. *Westm* R III. p I 55. O v 474 H II p IV 185
Aug 5.	Protection for Peter Bernardi of Toulouse and four other masters of ships who assisted the K against his enemies Similar letters for four others *Westm.* R III p I 56
Aug 5.	Protection for sir John Mautravers, senior, who complains that he was condemned unheard, until his sentence is annulled or confirmed by parliament. *Westm.* R III p. I 56
Aug 28	The K orders the earls of Arundel and Suffolk, his admirals, and Philip de Whitton, and Reginald de Donyngton, their lieutenants, to assemble the ships of 30 tons and upwards at Portsmouth by a week after Michaelmas. Similar order to Robert Flambard to arrest ships in the port of London *Westm* R III p I 57
Aug 28	The K orders Peter Bernardi of Toulouse, Peter de Farges, and the other captains of the galleys of Bayonne to deliver to Thomas de Ferrers, warden of the Channel Islands, the castle of Cornet in Jersey which they have taken and now occupy *Westm* R III p I 57.
Aug 28	The K orders a new assessment of the tenth and fifteenth to be made in Tamworth, which town has suffered from fire *Westm* R III p I 57.
Aug 28	The sheriffs of Lancashire and Staffordshire are ordered to proclaim that all persons who have received pardons on condition of serving the K. must be at Portsmouth by a week after Michaelmas. *Westm.* R. III p, I. 57.

---

* Documents dated in England during the King's absence are attested by the Regent.

DATE.	SUBJECT.
1345. Aug. 30.	Power for Peter bp. of Bayonne and others to treat for the marriage of the K.'s daughter Joan and the eldest son of Alfonso K. of Castile. Similar power to Andrew de Offord. *Westm.* R. iii. p. i 58. O. v. 475. H. ii. p. iv. 186.
Aug. 30.	Andrew de Offord is appointed proxy of Johanna the K.'s daughter to contract marriage *per verba de præsenti* with Peter, eldest son of the K. of Castile. *Westm.* R. iii. p. i. 58. O. v. 476. H. ii. p. iv. 186.
Aug. 30.	The K. informs K. Alfonso of the mission of the above-mentioned ambassadors. *Westm.* R. iii p. i 58. O. v. 476. H. ii. p iv. 186
Aug. 30.	The K. writes to the Q. of Castile on the same subject, and desires credence for Andrew de Offord concerning the proposed marriage with her sister. *Westm.* R. iii. p. i 58 O. v. 477. H. ii p iv 186.
Aug. 30.	The K. writes on the same subject to [Eleanor de Gusman, the mistress of the K of Castile], and offers to receive one of her sons as companion to the prince of Wales. *Westm.* R. iii. p. i. 59. O. v 478. H. ii. p iv 187.
Aug. 30.	Letters on the same subject to John Stephani, chancellor of Castile, and two others. *Westm.* R. iii. p. i. 59. O. v. 478. H. ii. p. iv. 187.
Sept. 7.	Clement [VI.] desires the K. to send letters of safe conduct for Nicholas abp. of Revenna. *Avignon* R. iii. p. i 59 O. v 478 H. ii p. iv. 187.
Sept. 8.	William Stury and Thomas de Melchebourne are appointed to treat with the commonalties of Flanders about the circulation and coinage of nobles in Flanders. *Westm.* R. iii. p. i. 59.
Sept 10.	The K. desires Thomas bp. of Ely to grant a pension to Robert de Burton, the K.'s clerk. *The Tower of London* R. iii. p. i 59. O. v 479 H. ii p iv. 187.
Sept 15.	Summons to the priors of Totness and 31 other alien priories to appear before the council at the octave of Michaelmas, as they neglected the last summons, when an annual tenth was granted. Similar summons to 58 abbots, priors, &c. to appear on the day after Michaelmas. *Westm.* R. iii. p. i 60.
Sept 29	The Prince of Wales is ordered to have 2000 men ready to be sent to Portsmouth. *Westm.* R. iii p. i 60.
Sept. 30.	The K. informs the abbess of Shafton that, being newly elected, she is bound to provide a pension for one of his clerks. *Wolmer.* R. iii. p. i. 61. O. v 479. H. ii. p. iv 187
Oct 6.	Protection for the agents of cardinal Reymund de Farges, dean of Salisbury, archdeacon of Leicester, and parson of Leek and Hornsey. *Westm.* R. iii p. i. 61. O. v 479 H. ii. p iv 187.
Oct. 10.	Power to William de Stury, Thomas de Melcheburn, and Gilbert de Wendlynburgh, to receive Flemings into the K.'s obedience, as K. of France. *Westm.* R. iii. p. i. 61. O. v 480 H. ii p iv 187.
Oct. 10.	Warrant for the payment of 6d a day to Coursus de Gangeland, apothecary of London, for his attendance on the K when ill in Scotland. *Westm.* R. iii p. i. 61 O. v. 486. H. ii p iv 180
Oct. 20.	Power for John de Hainault, lord of Beaumont, and others, to take possession of the inheritance of Q Philippa by the death of her brother, William count of Hainault. Letter informing the people of Zealand thereof. Similar commission and letter, omitting John de Hainault. *Westm.* R. iii p i 61.
Oct 24	The inhabitants of the northern counties are ordered to bring their cattle to the forests of Galtres and Knaresborough, as the Scots are preparing for an invasion. *Westm.* R. iii. p i. 62.
Oct. 26.	Memorandum of the appointment of John de Offord to the office of chancellor, in place of Robert de Sadyngton. *Westm.* R. iii p. i 62.
Nov. 8.	Power for the prince of Wales, John abp. of Canterbury, Ralph bp of London, William bp. of Norwich, the earls of Arundel and Huntingdon, John de Offord, and William de Edyngton, to treat with the abp. of Ravenna, the papal nuncio. *Westm.* R. iii p 62 O v 481. H. ii. p iv. 188.
Nov. 8.	Credence for Andrew de Offord, Richard de Saham, and Philip de Barton, sent to Alfonso K of Portugal. *Westm.* R. iii p. i 62 O. v 482 H. ii. p. iv. 188.
Nov. 8.	Power for the same commissioners to treat for a marriage between one of the K.'s sons and one of the daughters of the K. of Portugal. *Westm.* R. iii p. i. 63.
Nov. 8.	Credence for the same commissioners to the Q. of Castile. *Westm.* R. iii. p. i. 63. O. v. 482. H. ii. p. iv. 188.

DATE	SUBJECT.
1345 Nov 11	The K has received the pope's letters blaming him for having broken the truce, and will send him an answer on the arrival of the abp of Ravenna. *Westm.* R. iii., p. i 63. O v 483. H. ii p iv 188
Nov 15	The K., as guardian of John son and heir of the late duke of Brittany, appoints John de Charveles, his clerk, receiver of the duke's revenues in the duchy of Aquitain. *Westm* R iii p i 63 O v 483 H. ii p. iv 189
Nov 15	Power for Nicholas de Flisco and Anthony, Usomare to treat with the Genbese, *Westm.* R iii p i 63 O v 484 H ii p iv 189.
Nov 25	Pope Clement [VI] desires John de Thoresby to assist his nuncios, cardinal Anibaldus, bp of Frascati, and Stephen cardinal of SS John and Paul *Avignon.* R. iii p i 64. O v. 484. H ii p iv 189
Dec. 9	Pope Clement [VI] informs the K that he has appointed William de Edyngton, canon of Salisbury, to the bishopric of Winchester. *Avignon.* R. iii. p i 64. O. v. 484. H. ii. p. iv. 189.
Dec 9.	The K orders John de Charvels, his receiver in Brittany, to obey the earl of Northampton. *Rockingham* R iii p i. 64. O v 485. H ii p iv. 189
Dec. 10	The K orders his treasurer to deliver 51,000 florins to Peter Gretheved for rewards to the earls of Lancaster and Pembroke and to Walter de Manny *Clipstone.* R. iii. p. i. 64 O v. 485 H. ii p iv 189
[Dec 10]	The treasurer and chamberlains of the Exchequer are to deliver to Peter Gretheved 270 casks of flour, 188 qrs 4 b of wheat, and 1500 qrs of oats, to be sent to Gascony R. iii p i. 64 O. v. 486. H ii p iv 190
Dec 19.	The K orders the constable of Bourdeaux to take security from the masters of English ships for their appearance at Portsmouth within a fortnight after Candlemas. *Westm* R iii p i 65
Dec 20	The K desires the pope to grant a dispensation for the marriage of the earl of Arundel with Eleanor de Lancaster *Westm* R iii p i 65 O. v 486. H ii p iv 190
[Dec 20.]	Letter on the same subject to cardinal [.] R iii. p. i. 65. O. v. 487 H. ii. p iv 190
Dec 27	Power for Otto lord of Cuyk, sir Roger de Beauchamp, sir John de Levedale, sir William Stury, sir Wulfard de Gistell, and Ivo de Clynton, to recover the inheritance of Q Philippa *Woodstock* R iii. p i 65 O v 487 H ii p iv. 190.
Dec 27	Power for the same to treat with the Emperor Lows *Woodstock.* R. iii. p. i. 65 O v 488 H. ii. p iv 190.
[Dec 27]	Also to treat with Louis marquis of Brandenburg R iii p. i 66
1346. Jan 1	The K appoints Gawain Corder and William Bisshop, serjeant-at-arms, to send the ships of Kent and Sussex to Portsmouth, by a fortnight after Candlemas *Langley.* R. iii p i 66
Jan 3.	The sheriff of Lancashire is ordered to proclaim that all persons who have letters of pardon must be at Portsmouth by March 1. *Woodstock* R iii p. i 66
Jan 8	The K desires the pope to give credence to Richard Vaghan, canon of London, concerning the dissolution of the truce with France *Woodstock.* R iii p i 66 O v. 489 H ii p iv 191
Jan. 9	The K informs the sheriff of Yorkshire that Edward de Balliol has been paid his wages in gold nobles, and that the people are to receive them *The Tower of London.* R iii p i 66 O v 489 H ii p iv 191
Jan. 20.	The sheriffs of the counties south of the Trent are to order the men-at-arms of their several counties to be at Portsmouth by the middle of Lent. *Leicester.* R iii p i. 67 O. v 489 H. ii p iv 191
Jan. 27	The K orders all persons who have captured falcons and hawks to bring them to the sheriffs of their respective counties to be claimed *Westm.* R iii p. i. 67.
Jan 28	Protection for William de Bohun, earl of Northampton *Westm.* R iii. p i. 67.
Feb 3	The stewards of the earl of Northampton in Melenyth are ordered to send 150 Welsh men to Portsmouth by the middle of Lent. Similar letters to 22 others. *Westm.* R iii p i. 67.
Feb. 4	Peter Donynyan, admiral of the fleet of Bayonne, now in England, and Robert Mounseux, serjeant-at-arms, are empowered to arrest ships of Bayonne. *Langley.* R. iii p i. 68.
Feb. 4.	The masters and mariners of the ships of Bayonne in England are ordered to obey him. *Langley.* R iii p i. 68.

DATE.	SUBJECT
1346. Feb. 12.	The K to Clement [VI], excusing the caption into the K's hands of the revenues of benefices held by foreigners, for the necessary expenses of the war *Westm* R. iii p. i 68 O v 490 H ii p iv 191
Feb. 12.	The K. requests the loan of 1,000 marks from Ralph bp. of Bath and Wells Similar request to 89 others of the clergy for various sums. *Westm.* R. iii p. i. 68 O v 491 H. ii. p iv. 192.
Feb. 15	Restitution of the temporalities to William de Edyngton, bp of Winchester *Westm* R iii p. i 69
Feb 17.	Sir Roger la Zousch, sir William Moton, and five others, are exempted from military service, being of the retinue of the abp of York Similar exemptions for John de Bruyz and John de S Andrew *Westm.* R iii. p i 69
Feb. 18.	Power for William marquis of Juliers to engage Theodoric lord of Falquemont for the K.'s service. *Westm.* R iii p ii 70
Feb. 20.	Robert Flambard and Richard atte Wode are appointed to send the ships of London to Portsmouth. *Westm* R iii p i. 70.
Feb 22	Grant of an annuity of 10l to Isolda Neweman, nurse of John of Ghent. *Westm.* R iii p i 70
Feb. 23.	The earls of Suffolk and Arundel, the admirals, are ordered to search for letters prejudicial to the K. and to the realm. *Westm* R iii p i 70
Feb. 27	The K requests the abp. of Canterbury to pray for his success *Westm* R iii p i. 70 O v 492 H ii p iv. 192
March 5.	The K informs the mayor and bailiffs of Norwich, that the fleet has been dispersed by a storm, and he will therefore postpone his departure till a fortnight after Easter, at which time they are to send their contribution of 150 men to Portsmouth Similar letters to the mayors and bailiffs of 130 other towns *Westm.* R iii. p. i. 71. O. v. 493. H ii. p. iv 192.
March 6.	The K orders the sheriffs of London to enforce the statute against the circulation of false reports *Westm* R iii. p i 72
March 15.	The several sheriffs are ordered to prepare beacon fires, to give warning of attacks by the French. *Westm.* R iii. p. i 72. O. v. 496. H. ii. p. iv 193.
March 15	The K orders the provincial of the Friars Preachers to explain to the people the K's title to the French crown, and his reasons for war Similar letter to the prior of S Augustine's, London. *Westm.* R iii p i 72. O v 496 H ii p iv 193
March 15	The K empowers Henry earl of Lancaster, his lieutenant in Aquitain, to appoint a seneschal in place of Ralph de Stafford, who desires to be released from the office. *Westm.* R. iii p i 73
March 17.	Power for Peter bp of Bayonne, Gerald de Puy, and three others to ratify the treaty of marriage between the K's daughter Joan and the eldest son of the K. of Castile *Westm.* R iii p i 73 O v 498 H ii. p iv. 194.
March 17	The K thanks [Eleanor de Gusman] for her advocacy of the marriage above-mentioned. *Westm.* R. iii. p i 74. O. v 499 H ii. p iv 195
[March 17]	The K. recommends the bp of Bayonne and his colleagues to John Stephani and John Alfonsi. R iii p i 74 O v 500 H ii p iv. 195.
[March 17.]	The K. desires Gerald de Puy, justice of Gascony, to undertake this embassy R iii p i 74. O. v. 500 H ii. p iv. 195
March 17.	Credence for the bp of Bayonne and his colleagues to Alfonso K of Castile *Westm* R. iii. p i. 74 O. v 501 H. ii p iv. 195
[March 17]	Credence for William de Lindeford, one of the ambassadors to the Q of Castile, about the marriage of her sister. R. iii p i 75 O v 502. H ii p iv. 196
[March 17.]	The K. writes concerning the embassy to Fernando Sanchu de Valle Oleti [Valladolid?], the abp. of Toledo, and John Furcado de Mendoce , also a letter of thanks to the abbot S Croix, Bourdeaux R. iii p i 75. O v 503 H ii p iv. 196
March 18.	The K. condoles with Louis K of Hungary for the death of Andrew K of Sicily, his brother. *Westm.* R iii p i 75 O. v. 503. H. ii p. iv. 196
[March 18.]	Credence for friar Walter de Mora to the K. of Hungary. R iii p i 75. O. v 504 H. ii. p. iv. 196.
[March 18.]	Letter of condolence to the mother of the K. of Sicily. R. iii. p. i. 76. O. v. 504. H. ii. p. iv. 196.

DATE.	SUBJECT.
1846. March 18	The K. orders the sheriff of Kent to make proclamation that all the men-at-arms and archers who have been summoned must be at Portsmouth by a fortnight after Easter *Westm* R III p 1 76
March 23	The people of Normandy agree to furnish the duke with 44,000 men for the invasion of England. *Bois de Vincennes* l'an 38 * R III p 1 76. O. v 504. H II. p IV. 196–7.
March 24	William Stury and Gilbert de Wendelyngburgh are appointed to treat with the commonalties of Flanders for the circulation and coinage of gold nobles *Westm.* R III. p 1 77 O. v. 506 H II p IV 197
March 26	Grant of an annuity of 1,000 marks to Theodoric lord of Faukemont. *Westm.* R. III. p. 1 77 O v 506. H. II. p. IV 197.
March 27.	The archers who are going to Gascony are ordered to assemble at Totehill near Westminster on the next day *Westm* R III p 1. 77
March 30	The K orders Reginald Grey, warden of the coast of Essex, to remain near the coast. *Westm.* R. III p 1 77 O v. 507. H II. p IV. 197.
March 30	The K. grants an annuity of 100*l* to John de Falkemont, lord of Bendekynbagh and Berghen super le Soem [Bergen op Zoom] *Westm* R. III p 1 77 O. v 507 H II p. IV 198.
March 31	Richard Talbot, steward of the household, and John de Codyngton, clerk, are authorized to levy fines in lieu of service from men-at-arms, hobillers, and archers, in the counties of Worcester, Hereford, Oxford, and Berks 13 similar letters for other counties. *Westm* R. III p. 1 77
April 1	Commission to Guy de Brian to send 40 miners from the forest of Dean to accompany he K *Westm* R III. p 1 78.
April 6.	The K appoints Philip de Whitton, lieutenant of the earl of Arundel, to provide shipping at Portsmouth for his passage *Westm* R III p 1 78
April 8.	The inhabitants of Southampton are ordered to remain in the town and defend it from the expected attack *Westm.* R III p 1 78.
April 12.	Licence to William de Flisco, son of Nicholin de Flisco, to receive the revenues of his prebend of Stransale Similar licences for John de Flisco, prebendary of Teyngton and Yalmpton, and parson of Terring. *The Tower of London.* R III p 1 79 O v. 507 H II p IV 198
April 20	The men furnished by the earl of Northampton and 22 other lords in Wales are ordered to be at Portsmouth in a month after Easter. *Westm.* R. III. p 1. 79. O v. 508 H. II. p. IV 198.
[April 20]	Similar letter to Edward prince of Wales R III p 1 79 O v. 509 H II p. IV 198
April 20	The men of the several counties south of the Trent are to be at Portsmouth by a month after Easter. *Westm.* R. III. p 1. 79.
April 20.	Power to Ivo de Clynton and Sir Adam de Shareshull to recover the inheritance of Q. Philippa come to her by the death of the count of Holland *Westm.* R III p 1. 80. O. v 509 H II p IV 199.
April 20.	Power for the same persons to treat with the bp of Utrecht and other persons in Hainault, Holland, Zealand, and Friesland *Westm.* R. III p 1 80. O. v. 510. H. II. p IV 199
April 20.	Andrew de Offord and William de Bomere, canon of Southwell, are deputed to receive the message of the cardinals, the bp of Frascati and S. de Claremont, whom the pope sends as mediators between the K. of England and Philip de Valois. *Westm.* R. III. p 1 80. O. v 511 H II p IV 199
April 20.	Credence for Andrew de Offord to the cardinals *Westm.* R. III. p.; 80, O. v. 511. H. II p IV 199
April 22.	The K informs the commonalties of Ghent, Bruges, and Ypres that he intends to send Andrew de Offord and William de Bomere to meet the nuncios, and asks their advice. *Westm.* R. III. p. 1 80 O v. 511 H. II p IV 199.
April 30	The K informs the arrayers in Somerset and six other maritime counties that persons living within six leagues of the sea are exempt from military service. *Westm.* R. III p 1 81.
May 4.	The K orders the sheriff of Wiltshire to deliver 12 oaks a year from the forest of Chut to Isabell de Lancaster, nun of Ambresbury. *Westm.* R III p. 1 81.

* Apparently out of date.

DATE.	SUBJECT.
1346 May 6.	The K. orders the priors of the Friars Preachers, the Carmelite and the Augustine Friars, the warden of the Friars Minors, and the bp. of London, to offer thanksgivings and prayers for the successes of the earl of Lancaster in Gascony. *Westm.* R. iii. p. i. 81. O. v 512. H. ii. p iv. 199–200
May 12	Ralph Turville, farmer of the deanery of York, is ordered to pay the 500*l* due to the agents of the cardinal who holds the deanery, to be kept for the K.'s use Similar writs to the agents of other foreigners beneficed in England *Westm.* R ii p. i. 81
June 3	Protection for Thomas Ughtred, Gilbert Chastellein, and 30 others, going abroad in the retinue of Thomas de Beauchamp, earl of Warwick. *Porchester* R. iii. p. i 82.
June 6.	Bull of pope Clement [VI] of provision of the canonry of Lichfield for Richard d'Aston. *Villeneuve.* R. iii. p i 82 O v 512 H ii p. iv 200
June 20.	Hugh de Hastynges is appointed the K.'s lieutenant and captain in Flanders. The K informs the people of Flanders thereof. *Porchester.* R iii. p. i. 83. O. v. 514. H. ii p iv 200
June 20.	Another commission and letter to the same effect *Porchester.* R iii. p i. 83. O. v 514 H. ii p iv 200.
June 25.	The K. appoints Theodoric, lord of Montjoye and Falkynburgh, arbiter of the claims of Q. Philippa. *Porchester* R iii. p i 83 O v 515 H ii. p. iv. 201.
June 25.	The K.'s son Lionel is appointed regent of England during the K.'s absence abroad. *Porchester* R iii p. i 84 O v. 516. H ii. p iv 201.
June 26.	Licence for Edward prince of Wales to make a will arranging for the payment of his debts. *Porchester* R iii. p i 84 O v i 516 H ii p iv 201.
June 28.	Power for Hugh de Hastynges to redress the reciprocal injuries of Englishmen and Flemings. *Porchester* R iii p i 84 O v. 516. H ii p iv 201
July 1.	Power for J abp of Canterbury, W bp of Winchester, the K.'s treasurer, and John de Offord, dean of Lincoln, the K.'s chancellor, to treat with merchants and others for loans to the K *Porchester* R. iii. p i 84. O. v. 517. H ii. p. iv. 201.
July 2.	The K informs the papal nuncios that he has no leisure to speak with them, and that he cannot treat without the consent of his allies. *Porchester.* R iii p i. 84 O v. 517 H ii p iv 202
July 2.	Memorandum that John de Offord, chancellor, by order of the K. when in the Isle of Wight, delivered the great seal, used during the K.'s presence in the realm to John de Thoresby, in Fareham church near Porchester, and received from him the seal to be used during the K.'s absence. R. iii. p i. 85 O. v 518. H ii p iv 202
July 6.	Warrant for the payment of 40*l* as reward to Raso Maskerel, Adam Adereyn, and Gerard de Wendenthorp, German knights, also for the same sum to Silvanus de Rodynburg and to Otto de Illyngburgh. *Porchester* * R iii p. i 85. O. v. 518 H ii p iv 202
July 10.	The mayors and sheriffs of London are forbidden to allow any person (except the company of Hugh de Hastynges) to leave the kingdom for eight days. Similar letters to the mayors and bailiffs of Dover, Winchelsea, and Sandwich. *Windsor.* R. iii. p i. 85. O v. 518. H ii. p. iv. 202.
July 10.	The treasurer and chamberlains are ordered to renew the wax covering the body of Edward I in Westminster Abbey. *Windsor.* R. iii. p. i. 85. O. v 519. H. ii. p. iv. 202
July 10.	The K. desires the commonalties of Bruges, Ghent, and Ypres, to maintain their fidelity to him. *At sea, near the Isle of Wight* R iii. p. i. 85.
July 11.	Power for John abp of Canterbury, William bp of Winchester, Ralph bp of London, John de Offord, and Simon de Islep, to open letters and treat with ambassadors during the K.'s absence. *St Helen's, in the Isle of Wight.* R. iii. p i 85. O. v. 519. H ii. p. iv. 202
July 12.	Pardon for Roger Normaund, in the retinue of John de Montgomery, who had omitted to assume the order of knighthood *Windsor.* R. iii p i 86. O. v. 519 H iii. p iv 202
July 20	Warrant for the payment of 500*l*. for the expenses of the purification of Q Philippa. *Windsor* R iii. p i. 86. O iv. 520. H ii. p. iv. 202.
July 20.	The abbot of Hide, John Lenglish, and John de Bokeland, are appointed wardens of the town of Southampton and of the coast adjacent to the New Forest. *Windsor.* R. iii p. i 86

DATE	SUBJECT.
1346 July 20	The K desires the earls of Desmond and Kildare to come to England. *Windsor.* R. ш. p 1 86
July 24	The master of the hospital of S Giles-in-the-Fields, without London, and John de Holbourn, are ordered to collect certain tolls for two years for the repair of the highway from the said hospital to the New Temple, and another road called "Pourtepol" *Windsor.* R. ш p 1 86 　O v 520 　H п p iv. 202.
July 25	Credence for Richard de Saham to W abp of York, J bp. of Carlisle, and others in the north 　*Windsor* 　R ш p 1 87 　O v. 521. 　H. п p. iv 203.
July 25.	The mayors and bailiffs of the several seaports are ordered to make ready all the ships in the ports for their defence 　Letters on the same subject to the earls of Suffolk and Arundel, the admirals 　*Windsor* 　R. ш p 1. 87
[July 25]	The wardens of the sea-coast are also ordered to prepare to resist an invasion. R. ш. p 1 87.
Aug. 1.	Writs to 14 sheriffs to send bows and arrows to the Tower of London for the war with France 　*Windsor* 　R. ш p 1 87
Aug 3	The K informs the abp of Canterbury of the landing of his army at La Hogue, in Normandy, and desires him to celebrate masses and solemn processions for his success. Similar letter to the abp of York and the bps of England 　*Windsor* 　R ш p 1. 88. O v 522. 　H п p iv 203
Aug 3	The several sheriffs are ordered to make proclamation of the successes in Normandy, and that all who are willing to serve the K must be ready to come when summoned. *Windsor.* R ш p 1 88. 　O v 522 　H п p iv 203
Aug. 3	Safe conduct for the papal nuncios who are coming to the K to negotiate for peace. *Lisieux* 　R ш p. 1 88 　O v 523 　H п p iv 204
Aug 12	Thomas de Haukeston, Robert Houel, William de Catesby, and Augustine Waleys, are appointed to exercise the office of marshal within the verge of the court. Letters on the subject to the marshals of the regent's household and to the sheriffs and other officers of the K 　*Windsor* 　R ш p 1 88 　O v 523 　H. п p iv 204
Aug 20	Nicholas de Cantilupe is ordered to be ready with 40 men at arms and a number of archers to serve against the Scots 　*Westm* 　R ш p 1 89. 　O. v 524. 　H п p iv 204
Aug 20	The mayor and bailiffs of York are ordered to furnish 200 men at arms 　*Westm.* R. ш p 1 89. 　O. v 524 　H. п p iv. 204
Aug 21	William Fraunk and Thomas de Haukeston are appointed constable and marshal of the army about to sail to the K 　*Westm.* R. ш p 1 89 　O v 525 　H п p. iv 204
Sept. 6	The K writes to the several sheriffs, the bp of Durham, and the mayors and bailiffs of seaport towns, informing them of the victory at Cressy; and desires victuals, bows, and other necessaries to be sent to his camp before Calais 　*Windsor.* R iii p 1 89. 　O v 525. H п p iv 205
Sept. 8.	The K deputes Bartholomew de Burghersh, John Darcy, chamberlain, John de Thoresby, keeper of the privy seal, and John de Carleton, to expound his intentions to the parliament about to meet on Sept 11 　*Before Calais* 　R. ш p 1. 90 　O v. 526 　H ii p iv. 205
Sept. 8.	The bp of Durham, the earls of Northampton, Arundel, Warwick, Oxford, and Suffolk, Hugh le Despenser, and the other lords with the K , inform the parliament that the K has knighted the prince of Wales, and ought therefore to receive an aid from his kingdom. *Before Calais* 　R ш p 1 90 　O. v 527 　H п p iv 205
Sept 10	Protection for Gilbert de Imworth and three others going abroad with the Q. Philippa *Westm.* R. ш p 1 90
Sept. 17.	The bps are ordered to send the names of foreigners who hold benefices in their respective dioceses 　*Westm* 　R. ш p 1 90.
Sept. 18	Hugh de Audele, earl of Gloucester, and the prior of S John of Jerusalem, are ordered to send men to man a fleet to protect the victuallers going to Calais 　*Westm* 　R. iii. p 1 91
Sept. 18	Similar letters to John de Molyns and eight others 　*Westm* 　R ш. p 1. 91.
Oct 3	The K desires Margaret countess of Kent to send her son John earl of Kent to join him with as many men as possible, as Philip de Valois has assembled his whole force at Compeigne 　*Windsor* 　R ш. p. 1 91 　O. v. 527. 　H п. p iv 205
Oct 14.	The sheriffs of London are to summon the aldermen and citizens for the election of a mayor 　*Westm* 　R. iii p. i. 91.
Oct 20	Letters of thanks to the abp of York, Gilbert de Umframvill, earl of Anegos, Henry de Percy, and nine others in the north, for their service against the Scots. *The Tower of London.* R ш. p 1 92 　O v. 528. 　H п p. iv 205.

DATE	SUBJECT
1346 Oct. 22	The K, at the request of the cardinals of Naples and of Cleremont, empowers William marquis of Juliers, William de Bohun, earl of Northampton, and six others, to treat with Philip de Valois *Before Calais* R iii p. i 92 O. v. 959 H. ii p. iv 206
Oct 25,	Corn is forbidden to be exported except for the K's use at Calais *Westm.* R iii. p. i 92
Oct. 28.	Power for Sir William FitzWaryn, Sir Wolford de Gystelles, Michael de Northburgh, canon of Lichfield, and Sir Robert de Forest, to make alliances with any princes or nobles. *Before Calais* R. iii p i 92. O v 529. H ii p. iv 206
Oct. 30	Power to Gilbert de Umframville, Henry de Percy, and Ralph de Nevill, to grant pardons to the K's Scotch enemies *Westm* R. ii p i 92 O v. 530 H ii p iv 206.
Nov. 4.	The K. informs Walter de Bermyngeham, justiciary of Ireland, of the victory over the Scots near Durham, and desires him to treat with John de Insulis, or if he refuse to attack him. *Westm.* R. iii p i 93 O. v 530 H ii p iv 206
Nov. 4.	Indenture between the K and Percival de Porche, of Lucca, master of the Mint *Westm* R iii p. i 93
Nov. 8.	Safe conduct until Christmas for William Mauvesyn, prisoner of Robert Darcy, to obtain his ransom *The Tower of London* R. iii. p. i 93. O. v 531 H ii p iv 207
Nov 12	Obligation for 253l 6s 8d received from Bernard Viventis, agent of cardinal Reymund de Farges *Westm* R iii p i 93 O v 531 H. ii p iv 207
Nov. 12	The earl of Huntingdon and the prior of S John are ordered to go with their men to Sandwich on Nov. 27 The mayor of London is ordered to send 100 men *The Tower of London* R iii. p. i. 93.
Nov 15.	The abbot of Colchester is ordered to deliver to the sheriff of Essex a prisoner, calling himself the archdeacon of Paris, whom he has bought from certain deserters *The Tower of London* R iii. p i 94 O v 531 H ii p iv 207
[Nov. 15]	The sheriff of Essex is ordered to arrest the deserters, and to send the prisoner above-mentioned to Westminster R iii p i. 94. O. v. 532 H. ii p iv 207
Nov. 20	Persons who have taken Scotch prisoners are ordered to bring them to London to arrange with the council for their ransom *The Tower of London.* R. iii. p i 94 O v 532 H. ii p iv 207
Nov. 24.	Thomas de Drayton, William de Redenhale, and John de Wolmere, are commissioned to provide 20 fishing smacks and 10 boats for the siege of Calais Similar commission for 30 vessels to Thomas Spigurnel and Philip de Whitton *The Tower of London* R iii p i 94
Nov. 26.	The sheriffs of Kent, Surrey, Sussex, and Norfolk and Suffolk, are ordered to provide ladders for the siege of Calais *The Tower of London* R iii. p i 95.
Nov 30.	Reginald de Grey and four others are requested to go to the K with their men *The Tower of London* R iii p. i. 95. O. v 533 H ii p iv 208
Dec. 8.	The K. orders Robert de Ogel to send his prisoners taken at the battle of Durham, viz, the earl of Fife, Henry de Rameseye, and Thomas Boyde, to the Tower of London Forty-three similar writs *The Tower of London* R iii p i 95 O v 533 H ii p iv 208
Dec. 8.	Reginald de Grey, Ralph de Wylyngton, and six others are desired to be at Sandwich with their men by Jan 1. at the latest *The Tower of London* R iii p. i. 96.
[Dec. 8.]	John Bardolf de Wirmegaye, Hugh de Audele, earl of Gloucester, and nine others are ordered to send men-at-arms and archers at the same time Similar summons to Philip de Nevill, Henry Hillary, and Saier de Rocheford R iii. p. i 96.
[Dec. 8]	The mayor of Norwich is ordered to send 40 men. Writs to the bailiffs and mayors of 13 other towns R iii p i. 96.
[Dec. 8.]	Writs to the sheriffs of Somerset and Dorset, and 18 others to send archers. R iii p i 97
Dec 10.	Summons to Gilbert de Umframvill, earl of Anegos, and 15 other lords of the north to come to Westminster to consult about the war with the Scots *The Tower of London,* R iii. p. i. 97 O. v 535. H. ii p. iv 208
[Dec 10.]	Similar summons to the abp of York and the bishops of Durham and Carlisle. R iii p i. 97. O v. 535. H. ii. p. iv. 208
Dec. 12.	Warrant for the payment of 20l to John Darcy, the father, and 20 marks to John de Carleton for going to the north to bring the prisoners taken at the battle of Durham to London. *Eltham* R iii p i. 97. O. v. 535. H ii. p iv 208

DATE.	SUBJECT.
1346. Dec. 12.	Warrant for the payment of 10*l.* as a reward to William Hugate, valet of Wilham abp. of York, who brought the news of the victory at Durham. *Eltham.* R. m. p. l. 98. O. v 536 H. u. p. iv. 208.
Dec. 12	Nicholas de Stanweye and John Ballard are ordered to deliver the prisoner, who is said to be the archdeacon of Paris, to the court of Chancery. *The Tower of London.* R m p i 98
Dec 12.	John de Watenhull is appointed to survey and arrest ships at Sandwich for the passage of certain nobles. *The Tower of London* R m. p i 98.
Dec. 13	Commission to Thomas de Lathum, John de Haveryngton le Filz, and Nicholas le Botiller to make inquisition in Lancashire concerning those who have released their prisoners taken at the battle of Durham, or allowed them to escape. Four similar commissions for the northern counties *Eltham.* R. m. p l. 98 O v 536 H m p i l.
Dec. 15	John Darcy "le Pyere" is ordered to receive David de Brus and Malcolm Flemyng, Scotch prisoners, and forward them to the Tower of London *Eltham* R m p. l. 98. O v 537 H. m p i l.
Dec 16.	Thomas de Rokeby is ordered to receive Malcolm Flemyng from Robert Bertram, who took him prisoner at the battle of Durham, and bring him to the Tower of London. *Eltham.* R. m p i 99 O. v. 587. H m. p i l.
Dec 16.	Warrant for the payment of 50*l* to John Darcy, constable of the Tower of London, for the expenses of David de Bruys and the Scotch prisoners *Eltham* R m p i. 99.
Dec. 17.	The commissioners for inquiring into the release of Scotch prisoners taken at the battle of Durham are ordered to imprison those who have released them. *Eltham.* R m. p l. 99. O v 537 H m p i l.
1347 Jan 1.	Letters and writs concerning the county of Ulster will be made in the name of the K.'s son Lionel. *Eltham* R m. p i 99 O. v. 538. H m. p. i. 2
Jan. 1.	Receipt by John Darcy "la Piere," constable of the Tower of London, of David de Bruys, calling himself K of Scotland, from Thomas de Rokeby, sheriff of York. *The Tower of London.* R. m p i 99 O v 539 H m p i 2
Jan 8	Summons to Henry Buk, of London, to appear before the K.'s council with Beringarius de Monte Alto, a French prisoner calling himself archdeacon of Paris. The sheriffs of London are ordered to see that he appears. *Eltham.* R. m. p. i. 100. O v 539 H. m. p i 2
Jan. 10	Thomas de Daggeworth is appointed the K.'s lieutenant and captain in Brittany during the war *Redyng* R m. p i 847 O v. 540. H m p. i 2
Jan. 15	Clement [VI.] desires the K. to disclose his mind concerning peace to the cardinals. *Avignon.* R. m p i 100.
	The K informs the pope that he has always made reasonable offers to the nuncios and others who wished to treat of peace, and desires him to compel his adversary to acknowledge and redress his injuries. R. m. p i. 100
Jan 16.	Richard de Kelleshull and four others are appointed to examine the justification of the abbot of Colchester for his conduct to the French prisoner called the archdeacon of Paris. *Eltham* R m p i 101 O v 540. H m p i 2.
Jan 17	Ralph de Cahours is appointed the K.'s lieutenant and captain in Poicton and Rays *Eltham* R m p l. 101. O. v. 542. H. m p i 3.
Jan 17.	Power for him to receive fealty and grant pardons *Eltham.* R. m p i 101.
Jan 17	Power for him to treat with the commonalty of Nantes *Eltham* R m p l. 102.
Jan. 18.	Loan of 20,000 marks to the K by Henry Pycard and his company. *Westm.* R. m. p l. 102
Jan 19.	The bailiffs of Portsmouth are ordered to protect certain Bretons who have gone thither by desire of Thomas de Dagworth *Eltham* R m p i 102
Jan. 20.	Warrant for the payment of 10 marks to Thomas de Clyfford for the expenses of sending his prisoner, Walter de Halyburton of Scotland, to the Tower of London *Eltham* R. iii. p i 102. O v 542 H m. p. i 3
Jan. 20	Warrant for the payment of 10 marks to Bertin Beneyt, for the expenses of sending to the Tower of London William de Rameseye, a Scotch prisoner. *Eltham* R m p i 102 O. v. 542 H. m. p. i. 3.
Jan. 20	John de Coupeland, who took David de Brus prisoner at the battle of Durham, is made a knight banneret, with an annuity of 500*l* Warrants to the customers at Berwick, London, and Newcastle for payments to him. *Eltham.* R. m. p. l. 102. O. v. 543. H m. p. i. 3

DATE.	SUBJECT.
1347. Jan 20	Pardon to John de Coupeland, for his services in Scotland, especially at the battle of Durham, for homicides and felonies, also for Sir Robert Bertram and William Silvertop, senior *Before Calais* R iii p i 103 O v 548 H iii p i 4
Jan 21.	Clement [VI] sends Constantus, secretary of Constantius K of Armenia, to tell the K of England of the outrages of the Turks, and exhorts him to make peace with France. *Avignon* R. iii. p i. 103 O. v 544 H iii p. i 4
Jan 26.	The earl of Kildare and seven other Irish lords are summoned to join the K. with men-at-arms and hobillers *Eltham.* R iii p i 103. O v 544 H iii p i. 4.
Jan 26.	Henry de Percy and Ralph de Nevill engage to serve under Edward de Balliol, K. of Scotland, with 180 men-at-arms and 180 archers *London.* R. iii p i 104 O v 545. H iii p. i. 4.
Jan 30	Henry Romyn, constable of Carisbrook Castle, is ordered to compel persons residing in the Isle of Wight to remain there, for its defence *Eltham* R iii p i 104
Feb 1	The K. releases Henry earl of Lancaster from his office of captain in Aquitain *Before Calais* R. iii p i 104 O v 546 H iii p i 5
Feb 5	Protection for John de Craven, proctor of the cardinal of Spain, archdeacon of Chester. *Eltham* R iii p i 105 O v 546 H iii p i 5
Feb 6	Warrant for the payment of a quarter's wages to Edward de Balliol and his company *Eltham* R iii p i 105 O v 547 H iii. p i 5
Feb 7.	Protection for Robert de Redynges, proctor of cardinal Bertrand de Embrun, archdeacon of Dorset, and Robert de Shirwode and two others, his farmers *Eltham.* R. iii p i 105. O v 547 H. iii p i 5.
Feb 10	Hugh earl of Devon is licensed to appear in parliament by proxy in consequence of his infirmities *Calais* R iii p i 105.
Feb. 14.	W abp of York is ordered to keep safely William de Lyvynston, William Moubray, and David FitzWalter FitzGilbert, Scotch prisoners taken at the battle of Durham *Reading* R iii p i. 105. O v 447. H iii p i 5
Feb. 15.	The mayors and bailiffs of Great Yarmouth and 31 other ports are ordered to send persons to Westminster to give information of the state of the navy *Reading.* R. iii p i 105. O v 548 H. iii. p i. 5
Feb. 15.	The sheriffs of Kent and other maritime counties are ordered to send persons to Westminster to consult about the defence of the coast. *Windsor* R iii p i 106.
Feb 15	The exportation of victuals from the Isle of Wight is forbidden *Reading* R iii. p i 106
Feb. 15.	The K.'s admirals are ordered to arrest ships to convey certain lords and others to the K *Reading* R. iii p i 106
[Feb. 15.]	Letters on the same subject to the mayors and bailiffs of Yarmouth and 43 other ports R iii p i 107
Feb. 18.	William Chaumbernoun, John Louterel, Roger de Whitele, and the sheriff of Devon are commissioned to provide 60 archers by next Easter 28 other similar commissions *Reading.* R. iii p i. 107..
Feb. 22	Robert de Sadyngton, William de Thorp, William Trussel, and Geoffrey de Wychyngham, mayor of London, are ordered to try John de Graham, earl of Monteith, and Duncan de Fife, earl of Fife, who were taken in the battle near Durham, for rebellion The sentence of the council at Calais is enclosed. *Windsor* R iii p i. 108 O v. 549. H iii. p. i 6
Feb. 22	Sentence of death as traitors against the earls of Monteith and Fife, the latter being reprieved on account of his relationship to the K *Westm* R iii p i. 108 O v 550. H iii p i 6.
Feb. 23.	Power for Bernard Ezii, lord de Lebret, lieutenant of the seneschal of Gascony, and also for the constable of Bourdeaux, to receive the fealty of the K.'s subjects, and to promise that the K will not grant their lands to any one except to his heir. *Reading* R iii. p i 109. O. v. 550 H. iii. p. i 6.
Feb 23.	John de Montgomery is appointed admiral of the fleet west of the Thames. *Reading.* R iii p i 109
Feb. 27.	Power for John de Stryvelyn to pardon Scotch rebels *Reading.* R. iii p. i 109. O v 551 H iii p i 6.
March 1.	The treasurer and barons of the Exchequer are ordered to pay to John Darcy "le.Piere," 20s. a day, for his expenses in bringing the Scotch prisoners taken at the battle of Durham to the Tower of London. *Reading* R. iii. p i 109. O. v. 551. H iii. p i. 7

Z

DATE.	SUBJECT
1347 March 3	Power for the seneschal of Gascony, the lord of Lebret, Gerard de Puy, the mayor and constable of Bourdeaux, and William de Fenton to redress violations of the truce with Castile *Calais* R ɪɪɪ p ɪ. 109 O v 552 H. ɪɪɪ p ɪ 7
March 5.	The bailiffs of Weymouth are ordered to deliver to John le Noir, armourer of Edward prince of Wales, the jewels and other goods of Godfrey de Harecourt, confiscated for his adhesion to Philip de Valois *Reading* R ɪɪɪ p ɪ. 110 O v 552 H ɪɪɪ p ɪ 7
March 6	William de Morlee and Robert de Kenton, sergeants-at-arms, are appointed to convey the quarters of John de Graham late earl of Menteith to York *Reading* R ɪɪɪ p ɪ 110.
March 7.	Warrant to Robert de Mildenhale, keeper of the jewels at the Tower of London, to deliver two chests of ornaments for the chapel to William de Lamehithe, to be conveyed to the K *Reading* R ɪɪɪ p ɪ 110 O v 553 H ɪɪɪ p ɪ 7
March 7	Summons to the earl of Kildare, Richard Tuyt, and six others, to repair to the K. with men-at-arms and hobillers *Reading* R. ɪɪɪ p ɪ. 110
March 12.	Warrant for the payment of the annuity of 100s granted to Thomas de Brynchesle, for bringing news of the defeat of the Scots at Durham *Reading.* R. ɪɪɪ p ɪ 111 O v 553 H ɪɪɪ p ɪ 7
March 12	John Darcy, constable of the Tower of London, is ordered to deliver William Douglas to Thomas de Aspale, sheriff of Southampton, and Duncan, son of Duncan MacDowel, to John de Cobham, constable of Rochester Castle Letter to Cobham to receive MacDowel. *Reading.* R. ɪɪɪ p ɪ 111 O v. 554. H ɪɪɪ p ɪ 8
March 12	Thomas de Foxle, constable of Windsor Castle, is ordered to receive William de Ramesey and Walter de Haliburton, Scotch prisoners, at the Tower of London. *Reading* R ɪɪɪ p ɪ 111 O v 554 H ɪɪɪ p ɪ 8
March 8	John Howard is appointed admiral from the Thames to Berwick. *Reading.* R. ɪɪɪ. p ɪ 111
March 13.	Promise of Louis count of Flanders to marry the K's daughter Isabel within a fortnight after Easter *Dunkirk* R ɪɪɪ p ɪ 111 O v 554 H ɪɪɪ p ɪ 8
	The K promises to give 25,000 *livres* a year as Isabel's dowry till she can enjoy peaceably Ponthieu, Monstreuil, and Provoste Chastel, and also the sum of 400,000 *deniers d'or* R ɪɪ p ɪɪ 112
March 13	John Darcy, constable of the Tower of London, is ordered to take charge of Sir Walter de Maundevill of Ireland, taken prisoner at Calais *Reading* R ɪɪɪ p ɪ 112
March 14	Proclamation to be made throughout England that complainants against the subjects of the K of Castile must attend at Bayonne at the Nativity of S John the Baptist. *Reading* R ɪɪɪ p ɪ 112 O v 556 H ɪɪɪ p ɪ 8
March 16	Warrants to the warden of the Cinque Ports and the sheriffs of the maritime counties to provide ships prepared and manned for war at Sandwich by the day after Easter *Reading* R. ɪɪɪ p ɪ 112
March 20	John de Wodehous, receiver of the lay and clerical subsidies in the north, is ordered to pay the wages of the K of Scotland, the earl of Anegos, and 12 others, with their men, 480 men-at-arms, and 480 mounted archers, amounting to 3,222*l* 3s 4d. *Reading* R. ɪɪɪ p ɪ 113 O v 556 H ɪɪɪ p. ɪ 8–9
March 22	Agreement of Henry Husee to guard the Isle of Wight with 40 men-at-arms and 60 archers *Westm* R ɪɪɪ. p ɪ. 114
[March 22]	Agreement of Henry Romyn to guard Carisbrooke Castle with 20 men-at-arms and 20 archers. R ɪɪɪ p ɪ 114
March 30	William de Allerton, valet of the scullery, is ordered to purvey pewter and wooden vessels, firewood, salt, &c, for the K's household beyond sea *Reading* R. ɪɪɪ p. ɪ. 114.
March 31	Robert de Morle is summoned to come with his retinue to the K at Calais. *Reading* R ɪɪɪ p ɪ 114
[March 31]	Summons to the prior of St John of Jerusalem and Friar John de Pavely R ɪɪɪ p ɪ 114
March 31	Sir John de Dalton is ordered to appear before the council with Margery de la Beche, wife of Gerard del Isle, whom he and others had carried away by force from the manor of Beaumes, near Redynges. Similar summons to Sir Matthew Haydok, sir William Trussel, son of John Trussel, and Sir Edmund de Mancestre *Reading* R ɪɪɪ p ɪ 114
April 3	William de Clopton and John Herlyng, customers of London, ordered to pay 297*l*. 2s. 11d to Q. Philippa. *Reading* R. ɪɪɪ. p ɪ 115
April 5.	John de Montgomery and John Howard, the admirals, are not to exact ships from towns distant from the sea, or which are too poor to furnish any *Reading.* R. ɪɪɪ. p. ɪ. 115

DATE.	SUBJECT
1347 April 5	Bartholomew de Burgherssh, constable of Dover Castle and warden of the Cinque Ports, is ordered to provide ships for the passage of the earl of Huntingdon with men-at-arms to Calais. *Reading* R. iii. p i 115.
April 8	Nicholas de Staunford, clerk, is sent to request the abp of York and 43 abbots, priors, and others in Yorkshire to grant a loan of wool to the K Similar appointments in the other counties of England *Reading* R iii p i 116
April 8.	Warrant to the collectors of the subsidy to buy flags for four ships. *Reading.* R. iii. p i 116
April 10	John abp. of Canterbury, William, bp of Winchester, Richard de Stafford, and Peter de Gildesburgh are to prevent lord de Tankervill, who is in their custody, from having communication with any person Similar letter to Thomas de Holand respecting the count of Eu, constable of France *Reading* R. iii. p i 116 O v 558. H iii p i 9
April 10.	Protection for one year for Venetian merchants *Before Calais.* R. iii. p i 116. O v. 558 H. iii. p i 9
April 12	The K forbids any money to be collected by virtue of the letters sent to England by the papal nuncios *Reading* R. iii p i 117 O v 558 H iii p i 9
April 12	Ralph de Baggleye, constable of Corfe Castle, is ordered to provide for the defence of the maritime places within the forest of Purbeck *Reading* R. iii. p i 117.
April 13	Antonio Usomare, William de Flisco, canon of York, and Antony de Flisco are commissioned to hire 12 galleys to go to Flanders, and to treat with the duke and council of Genoa *Before Calais* R iii p i 117 O v 560. H. iii p i 10
April 13	Summons to the prior of S John of Jerusalem in England to come with friar John Pavely and his retinue to the K at Calais *Reading* R iii p i 117
April 26	The K informs G. cardinal of S Mary in Cosmodyn that he has seized the temporalities of the see of Norwich in consequence of the misconduct of the bp, and not at the instigation of the abbot of S Edmund's *Before Calais* R. iii p i 118 O v 560 H iii. p iv 10
April 28.	The sheriffs of London are ordered to provide ships for the passage of the K.'s daughter Joan to Calais *Reading* R iii p i 118.
May 1	Pardon for Ralph de Shelton, on account of his services at the battle of Cressy, for neglecting to assume knighthood *Reading.* R. iii p i. 118 O v 561 H. iii p i 10
May 1.	Warrants to the several sheriffs for the arrest of John de Dalton and his accomplices. *Reading* R iii p i 118
May 1	Warrant to John Darcy, constable of the Tower of London, to receive Sir John de Dalton and 17 others *Reading* R. iii p i 119
May 6.	The K and William marquis of Juliers promise to indemnify Ronald duke of Gueldres if he become subject to any fine for not marrying the daughter of John duke of Brabant *Before Calais.* R iii. p i 119. O v 561 H iii p i 10
May 8.	Safe conduct for William de Tours, of Scotland, going thither to obtain money for the expenses of David de Bruys and the other prisoners *Reading* R iii p i 119. O v 562 H iii p i 10
May 10	Commission to John Wawayn, constable of Bourdeaux, and Walter de Weston, his lieutenant, to survey the castles and towns in Aquitain, the coinage, and to do other matters there. *Before Calais* R iii p i 119
May 12	William Trussel of Cublesdon, constable of Odiham Castle, is ordered to receive sir William de Rameseye and sir Walter de Haliburton, Scotch prisoners, from Thomas de Foxle, constable of Windsor Thomas de Foxle, constable of Windsor Castle, is ordered to deliver them up *Reading* R. iii. p. i 120 O v. 562 H iii. p i 11.
May 14	Summons to Henry earl of Lancaster, John de Veer, earl of Oxford, and 31 others, to join the K as soon as possible, as the French K is preparing to give battle before Whitsuntide. *Reading* R. iii p i 120. O. v 562 H. iii. p. i. 11.
[May 14.]	Hugh de Audele, earl of Gloucester, Humfrey de Bohun, earl of Hereford and Essex, and six others, are ordered to send men to the K. R. iii. p i. 120 O v. 563. H iii p i 11.
May 16	The mayors and bailiffs of London and other ports are ordered to prepare their ships by June 1 *Reading.* R. iii p. i 120
May 19.	John de Montgomery, admiral west of the Thames, is ordered to provide ships for the conveyance of the earl of Lancaster to Calais. *Reading.* R. iii. p. i 121. O. v. 563. H. iii p i 11

DATE	SUBJECT
1347 May 19.	Letter to the mayor and bailiffs of Sandwich on the same subject *Reading* R iii. p i 121 O v 564 H iii p i 11
May 28.	Engagement of Wynand Dynscheu, Ernold Dalselowe, and the Burghgrave of Ouderkryke, for the K's service *Before Calais* R iii p. i 121. O v 564 H iii p i 11
May 28	The K desires William de Acum of York, and 26 other merchants, to send the loans they have promised by June 20 *Reading* R iii p i 121
May 28	Summons to Richard de Leyham of Ipswich, and 70 others in various counties, to appear before the council on June 20 *Reading* R. iii p i 122
May 28.	Warrant to the sheriff of Norfolk to attach Edward Cosyn and Geoffrey Botiller, merchants, who did not answer the summons to grant a loan. Similar warrants for attaching 25 other merchants R iii p i 122
June 1.	Grant of the town and castellany of Bragerac to Henry earl of Lancaster, who has lately taken it by assault The seneschal of Gascony and the constable of Bourdeaux are ordered to deliver it to him *Before Calais* R iii p i 123. O v 565 H iii p i 12
June 2	Letters commendatory to the lord de Labret, the archdeacon of Durford, the lord of Lasparre, and 11 others *Before Calais* R iii. p i 123 O v 565 H iii p i 12
[June 2.]	Similar letters to the commonalties of Bourdeaux, Bayonne, and nine other towns. R iii p i 123 O v 567 H iii p i 12
June 2	Restoration of the temporalities to John Gynwell, bp. of Lincoln. *Reading* R iii p. i. 124
June 2.	William de Gategang, Henry de Baa, and Walter de Harewell, lieutenant of the admiral John de Montgomery, are appointed surveyors of the receipt of the subsidy for providing 60 ships between London and Mousehole in Cornwall The collectors at the several ports are informed therof *Reading* R iii p i 124
June 3.	The K. promises not to alienate the town of la Reole from the crown. *Reading.* R iii. p i 125 O v 568 H iii p i 13
June 3	Grant of 2,000 florins to the said town of la Reole in compensation for the damage done by the army of the earl of Lancaster *Reading* R iii p i 125
June 3	Confirmation of a grant to the said town of la Reole by K. John, dated at la Rochelle, 2 Nov, 8 John *Reading* R iii p i 125
June 3	The K orders the seneschal of Gascony and the constable of Bourdeaux to compel the observance of the compact between the commonalties of Bourdeaux and la Reole *Reading.* R iii p i 125
June 10.	The treasurer and chamberlains are ordered to renew the wax covering the body of Edward I in Westminster Abbey. *Reading.* R. iii p i 126 O. v 568 H iii p i 13
June 16.	Obligations for the payment of 80,000 florins to Thomas de Holand, who has delivered the count of Eu, his prisoner, to the K *Before Calais.* R. iii. p. i 126. O. v 568. H iii p i 13
June 18.	Thomas de Berkele, William de Shareshull, Roger Hillary, and four others, are com- missioned to make inquisition concerning certain rebels at Bristol who have assumed the royal authority *Reading* R iii p. i 126
June 23	The several sheriffs are ordered to explain that the late proclamation about the exporta- tion of wool does not forbid the sale of wool in the kingdom *Reading* R. iii p i 126
July 5.	Treaty concluded by Antony Usomare and Antony de Flisco, the K's ambassadors, with John de Murta, duke of Genoa *Genoa* R iii p i 126 O v 569 H iii p i 13
July 7	Power for Robert de Stratton, canon of Chichester, and Richard de Saham, to treat for a marriage between Edward prince of Wales and Leonora, daughter of Alfonso K of Por- tugal. *Before Calais.* R. iii. p. i. 128. O. v. 573. H iii p i 15.
[July 7]	Power for them to arrange for the coming of the said Leonora to England. R. iii. p i. 128. O v 574 H iii p i 15
July 7.	The K. writes to Guncelm Ispannii, chancellor of the K. of Portugal, about the proposed marriage. *Before Calais.* R iii. p. i. 129 O. v 574 H iii. p i. 15
July 23.	The mayors of Sandwich and London are ordered to send merchants with victuals to Calais, as the French army is within three leagues of the K. *Reading.* R. iii. p i. 129. O. v 575 H iii p i. 15
	The K to the archbishop of Canterbury, informs him of the negotiations between the earls of Lancaster and Northampton and others on his part, and the duke of Bourbon and others on the French part, and of the retreat of the French army. R iii. p. i 129.

DATE.	SUBJECT.
1347 Aug 2	The K promises not to alienate from the crown the town of Lanardac Release of the crown revenues for four years, in compensation for the damage done the enemy *Aug.* 1 Letter on the subject to the seneschal of Gascony and the constable of Bourdeaux *Before Calais.* R. iii p 1 129
Aug. 12.	Proclamation to be made throughout England that houses will be assigned to English persons willing to reside at Calais. *Reading* R. iii p. 1. 130 O v. 575. H. iii p. 1 16
Aug 20	Proclamation to be made by the sheriff of Kent that all persons who have returned to England from the army, the archers of the county, and others willing to serve, must be at Calais on Sept 2 Similar writs to the several sheriffs south of the Trent *Reading* R iii p 1 130
Aug. 20.	Request to the dean and chapter of York and 24 other religious foundations, for a loan either in wool or money *Gloucester* R iii p 1 130 O. v. 576–7. H iii p. 1 16.
Aug 20	Request to the abbot of Melsa for a loan of two sacks of wool, in addition to that already granted Requests to 265 others of the clergy, for wool and money *Gloucester* R iii p 1 131 O v 578–583 H iii p 1. 17–19
Aug. 20.	Warrant to John Darcy, constable of the Tower of London, to deliver David de Anand and William de Douglas, senior, to John de Verdon, constable of Rockingham Castle ; also to deliver William de Vaus and Andrew de Cambel to Stephen Romyl, constable of Nottingham Castle , also to deliver Walter de Maundevill, to John Crabbe, constable of Somerton Castle , also warrants for their reception *Gloucester* R iii p 1 133. O v 583–4 H iii p 1 19
Aug. 30.	Grant of an annuity of 10l to John de Merle, for bringing news of the capture of Charles de Bloys. *Calais.* R. iii p 1 134
Sept. 1	Commission to John de Chalon, lord of Arlay, and the prior of Lewes, to treat for a marriage between the eldest son of the duke of Austria with one of the K 's daughters *Calais* R iii p 1. 134 O v 585 H iii p 1 19
Sept 3	Summons to Walter Turk, John de Bedeford, and 13 others, to attend the meeting of the citizens of London at the Guildhall, on public business. *Gloucester* R iii p 1 134
Sept. 4	The mayors and bailiffs of Bristol and four other ports are ordered to provide ships for the conveyance of forces to Gascony Power to John de Montgomery, admiral of the fleet west of the Thames, to arrest ships *Evesham* R iii p 1 134.
Sept. 7.	Warrant to John de Cobham, constable of Rochester Castle, to deliver Duncan Magdowell and his son, Scottish prisoners, to John de la Dale, serjeant at-arms, to be taken to York The sheriff of Yorkshire is ordered to receive them, and deliver them to Henry de Percy and Ralph de Nevill *Worcester* R iii p 1 135 O v 585 H iii p. 1 19
Sept. 8.	Repetition of the proclamation (Aug 20) summoning men-at-arms and archers to Calais *Worcester* R iii p 1 135 O v 586 H iii p 1 20
Sept. 13.	The sheriff of Essex is ordered to send 100 quarters of wheat to Calais Similar writs to eight other sheriffs to send corn *Worcester* R. m. p. 1 135 O v 587 H iii p 1 20
Sept. 25	Pope Clement [VI] desires credence for Friar Nicholas Herle, in answer to the K.'s letters *Avignon* R iii p. 1 136 O v 587 H iii. p 1 20
Sept 25	Power for Ralph lord Stafford, Reginald de Cobham, John Darcy, and Robert de Burgcher, to treat for peace or truce with Philip de Valois Similar power for the earls of Lancaster and Huntingdon *Calais* R. iii p 1. 136 O v 588 H iii. p 1 20.
Sept 28.	Truce until July 8 between the K s of England and France, including their allies, through the mediation of the papal nuncios *Calais.* R. iii p. 1 136 O iii 588–592 H iii. p 1 20–22
Oct. 3.	The K grants to Henry earl of Lancaster the lands and goods of his prisoners taken at the capture of S. Jean d'Angely, who have refused to pay their ransoms and have joined the enemy Letters on the same subject to the constable of Bourdeaux, the seneschal of Gascony, and the castellan of S Jean d'Angely. *Calais* R iii p 1 138. O v 592 H iii p 1 22
Oct. 5.	Protection for the agents of the cardinals of Naples and Clermont *Calais.* R. iii. p 1 138 O. v. 593. H. iii. p 1. 22.
Oct. 8.	An annuity of 40 marks to Eustace de S. Pierre for the custody of Calais *Calais.* R. iii. p 1 138
Oct. 8.	John de Montgomery is appointed captain of Calais, and Sir John de Gatesden marshal of the same place *Calais* R iii p 1. 138 O v 593. H iii p 1. 22 Articles to be observed for the government of Calais. R. iii p 1. 139

DATE.	SUBJECT
1347. Oct 8	Robert bp of Chichester is released from the subsidy of wool for the lands which have escheated to the see　*Eltham*　R iii p i 139.　O v 593　H iii p i 23
Oct 12	Memorandum that the K landed at Sandwich on Oct. 12th, and came to London on the 14th ; on the 15th John de Offord, the chancellor, delivered the great seal which had been used during the K 's absence to the bp of Winchester, and on the following day the K sent to the said chancellor the seal which had been used while the K. was abroad　R iii. p i 139　O. v 594　H iii p i 23.
Oct 16.	The exportation of corn, except to Calais, is strictly forbidden　*Westm*　R. iii p. i 139
Oct. 18	The K orders the sheriffs of Northumberland and Cumberland not to arrest Gerard de Wydryngdon, who permitted the escape of Scotch prisoners, as the earl of Northampton has given surety for his appearance　*Westm.*　R iii p i 140　O v 594　H iii. p. i. 23.
Oct 18	Grant to the burgesses of Dunkirk of freedom from arrest in England for debts, except as principals or pledges　*Westm.*　R iii p i. 140　*See* Oct 28.
[Oct 18]	Proclamation to be made in London, forbidding knights and esquires to leave the kingdom　R iii p. i 140
Oct 20	The K. desires Alfonso K. of Castile to send fresh commissioners to redress injuries and arrange a truce　*London*　R. iii p i 140　O v 595　H. iii p i 23
Oct 20	William de Salop is appointed keeper of the mint at Calais　*Westm.*　R iii. p i 140
Oct 20	The K intending to go hawking, orders the sheriff of Essex and Hertford to repair the bridges from Stratford to Ware and thence to Staines, and to forbid hawking　Similar writs to the sheriffs of Middlesex, Bucks, Hants, Wilts, and Berks.　*Westm*　R iii. p. i 141　O. v. 596.　H iii. p i 23.
Oct. 28.	The K hearing that many knights and squires are about to go to Sprucea and other foreign parts, orders the mayors of Sandwich, Dover, and Winchelsea, and the warden of the Cinque Ports, to prevent their departure　Letter to the captain of Calais to arrest any who arrive there　*Newmarket*　R ii p i 141
Oct. 28	The K thanks the burgesses and inhabitants of Dunkirk for their good services, and permits them to bring their goods into the realm without distraint, after they have paid the accustomed duties for the same　*Westm*　O v 594　H iii. p. i 23　*See* Oct 18
Nov 12	Tournaments are forbidden throughout England　*Westm*　R iii p i 141
Nov 26.	Thomas de Foxle, constable of Windsor Castle, is ordered to allow 2s. a day for the expenses of William de Rameseye and Walter de Halyburton, Scottish prisoners.　*Westm*　R iii p i 141.　O. v. 596　H iii p i. 24.
Nov 26	The K. allows the exportation of wool to the staple in Flanders　*Westm.*　R iii p i 141
Nov. 28.	The K orders ships to go to Calais, and not at Whitsand or Boulogne.　Letter on the same subject to the captain of Calais　*Westm.*　R iii p. i. 142.
Dec. 1.	John de Chivereston is appointed captain of Calais.　Intimation thereof to the bailiff and inhabitants of Calais　*Calais*　R iii p i. 142　O v 584　H iii. p. i. 19
Dec. 3	The K confirms the laws of Calais.　*Westm*　R iii p i 142
Dec 3.	The K has received the letter of Corard de Kyrkel, provisor of the see of Mayence, by Corad, provost of S Maurice in Mayence, and Heylmann de Prymheyn , and desires credence for them　*Westm*　R iii p i 144　O v 597　H iii p i 24
Dec. 4.	Credence for Henry the bearer to [Louis duke of Bavaria, marquis of Brandenburg]　*Westm*　R iii p i. 144　O v 597　H iii p. i 24
Dec 4.	William Stury is appointed seneschal of Calais　*Westm*　R iii p i 145
Dec 7.	Safe conduct for William de Levingeston, banneret, Friar Walter Blanntyr, and Walter le Clerc, coming from Scotland at the request of David de Bruys, a prisoner in the Tower of London　*Evere*　R iii p i 145　O v. 597.　H iii p i. 24
Dec. 12	Credence to the pope for Sir Hugh de Nevill, John de Carleton, canon of Wells, and John Reppes, papal penitentiary.　*Westm.*　R iii p i 145.　O. v. 598　H iii p i 24
[Dec. 12]	Letters of commendation for the same persons to seven cardinals.　R. iii p i 145.　O. v 598.　H iii p i 24
Dec 12	Warrant to the bailiffs and jurates of Jersey to arrest William le Conte, prisoner of William de Wynchelese, who has broken his parole　*Westm*　R. iii p i 145.　O v. 598.　H iii p i 24
Dec 12	The sheriff of Nottingham is ordered to allow 2s a day for the expenses of William Douglas, senior, and William Vaux, Scots taken prisoners at the battle of Durham　*Westm.*　R. iii p i. 146.　O v. 599.　H. iii p i. 24.

DATE.	SUBJECT
1347 Dec 13.	Warrant to the sheriff of Gloucester to allow 12d. a day for the expenses at Bristol Castle, of William Anand, who was taken prisoner at the battle of Durham. *Rising.* R iii p ı. 146 O. v 599 H iii. p ı 24
Dec 27	Henry de Baa is ordered to provide 40 ships at Plymouth for the conveyance of the K's daughter Joan to Gascony Richard de Holmesle, Nicholas Lovy, and eight others are ordered to assist him. *Guildford* R iii p ı 146 O v 599 H iii p ı 25
Dec. 28.	Renewal of the protection for sir John Mautravers, senior. *Guildford* R. iii p ı. 146 O v 600 H iii. p ı 25
1348 Jan. 1.	The K informs Alfonso K of Castile that he is about to send his daughter Joan to Gascony, accompanied by Robert Burghcher, a baron, Andrew de Offord, canon of York, and Gerald de Puy, sacristan of Bourdeaux. *Westm* R iii p ı 147 O v 601 H iii p. ı 25
[Jan 1]	Similar letter to the Q of Castile. R. iii p. ı. 147. O. v. 601. H. iii p ı 26.
[Jan 1]	Similar letters to [Aleanora Gusman.] R iii p ı 147. O v 602 H iii p ı 26
[Jan. 1]	Letters on the same subject to John lord of Lare and Biscay, John Emanuelis, and two others. R. iii p ı 147. O. v 602 H iii p ı 26
[Jan. 1]	Letters on the same subject to the bp of Palencia, Fernando Sancii de Vallesleti [Valladolid], and John Stepham, the chancellor R iii. p ı 148 O v 603 H iii p ı 26.
[Jan 1.]	Also to Peter, infante of Castile. R iii p. ı 148 O. v 603 H iii p ı 26
Jan 2	Clement [VI] commends to the K Arnold, son of Arnold de Duroforti, viscount of Laburde. *Avignon* R iii p ı 148 O v 603 H iii p ı 26
Jan 8	The sheriff of Devon is ordered to assist Thomas de Weryngton, Thomas Poleyn, and Alexander le Bakere, whom the K. has commissioned to provide victuals, &c for his daughter Joan *Mortlake.* R. iii p. ı. 148. O. v. 604. H. iii. p. ı 26.
Jan. 15.	Grant to William de Careswell, of the custody of the lands of Isabella, late countess of Mar Intimation thereof to William de Kelleseye, chamberlain of Berwick *Westm.* R iii. p ı 148 O v. 604 H iii p ı 27.
Jan 28.	The several sheriffs are ordered to send wheat, barley, &c to Calais *Westm* R iii. p ı. 149
Jan. 29.	Warrant to the sheriffs of Somerset and Dorset, Devon and Cornwall, to assist Thomas de Weryngton and his colleagues *Westm* R iii p ı 149
Feb. 1.	The K. desires the seneschal of Gascony and the constable of Bourdeaux to observe the truce till Easter 1350, concluded with the count of Perigord *Westm.* R iii p ı 149. O. v. 605 H iii p ı 27.
Feb 1	Commission to Robert baron Burghcher, Andrew de Offord, and Gerald de Puy, to obtain security that if the infante Peter and the K's daughter have a son, he shall be K of Castile, after his father's death ; and to treat of other matters concerning the marriage *Westm.* R iii p ı 150 O v 606 H iii. p ı 27
Feb. 6.	William de Salop is appointed keeper of the mint at Calais. *Westm* R iii p. ı. 150.
Feb. 10.	Commission to William de Salop to pay the soldiers and workmen in Calais, Oye Marke, etc. *Westm.* R. iii p. ı 150.
Feb. 12	The K.'s admirals, seneschals, and other officers in England and abroad are ordered to assist John bp. of Carlisle and sir Robert Burgher, who are going to Gascony with the K.'s daughter Joan *Westm* R iii. p. ı. 151 O v 607. H iii p ı 28.
Feb 18.	Proclamation to be made throughout England for the destruction of "lussheburghs" and other false coins, and the importation of silver plate. *Westm* R iii. p ı 151.
Feb 14	Summons to J abp. of Canterbury to a parliament to be held at Westminster in mid-Lent, to arrange for sending ambassadors to ascertain the pope's wishes about the preliminaries of a treaty with France. *Westm.* R iii p ı 151 O v. 608 H iii p. ı 28.
Feb 14	The K appoints John de Vilario and others arbiters between his subjects and those of the K of Castile. Similar commissions for the bp of Bayonne and 26 others, and for the bp. and 11 others. *Westm.* R iii p ı 152 O v 609. H. iii. p. ı. 28.
Feb 14	The K desires the commonalties of Ghent, Bruges, and Ypres, to allow Lombard merchants to buy the wool imported by the English. *Westm.* R. iii p. ı. 153. O. v. 611. H iii. p. ı. 29.
Feb. 14.	Summons to Edward K. of Scotland to come to a parliament at Westminster. *Westm.* R. iii p. ı. 153. O. v 611. H. iii. p. ı. 29.

DATE	SUBJECT
1348 Feb 15	Instructions for Robert Burghcher and Andrew Offord concerning the marriage of the K.'s daughter Joan　*Westm.*　R ɪɪɪ p ɪ 153　O ᴠ 612–14　H ɪɪɪ p ɪ 30.
Feb. 16	Protection for sir Stephen de Colyngton and three others in her company.　*Westm*　R ɪɪɪ p ɪ 154
Feb 16	Protection for Friar Barnabas Maffey of Florence, James Ramanany, parson of Sevenoaks, James Francisci, parson of Ivinghoe, and John de Bonaura, canon of Chichester, agents of Ambaldo, cardinal of Naples　*Westm*　R ɪɪɪ p ɪ 154.　O. ᴠ. 614　H. ɪɪ p ɪ 30
Feb 18.	The K orders William Trussel of Cublesdon to release Maurice FitzThomas, earl of Desmond, as Ralph baron of Stafford, Thomas de Berkele, Richard Talbot, and Reginald de Cobham are sureties for him　*Westm*　R ɪɪɪ p ɪ 154
Feb 18	The K writes to three cardinals against the claims of the abp. of Armagh, which are prejudicial to the privileges of the see of Dublin.　*Westm*　R. ɪɪɪ p. ɪ, 154.
Feb. 18.	The K orders R abp. of Armagh to return to his diocese, and provide for its defence against the rebels　*Westm*　R ɪɪɪ p ɪ 155
Feb. 20.	Writs to the sheriffs of Somerset and Dorset and Devon to provide 180 archers to accompany the K.'s daughter Joan　*Westm.*　R. ɪɪɪ. p. ɪ 155
Feb 20	The K. orders the chancellor of Ireland to disregard prohibitions in ecclesiastical causes fraudulently obtained from the English chancery　*Westm*　R ɪɪɪ p ɪ 155
Feb. 26.	The K requests the K of Castile to make redress to William Turk of London, whose ship has been plundered by his subjects　*Westm.*　R. ɪɪɪ p ɪ 156　O ᴠ 614　H ɪɪ. p ɪ. 31
March 2.	Commission to sir Thomas de Uvedale and others to arrest ships for the passage of the K.'s daughter Joan　*Westm.*　R ɪɪɪ. p ɪ 156　O ᴠ 615　H ɪɪɪ p ɪ 31
March 8	John de Dale, serjeant-at-arms, is appointed to arrest Thomas de Toltham and his son, agents of Eleanor duchess of Gueldres, who have embezzled money collected for her.　*Westm*　R ɪɪɪ p ɪ 156　O. ᴠ. 616　H. ɪɪɪ p ɪ 31
March 14	Walter de Manny is appointed admiral from the Thames to Berwick.　*Westm.*　R. ɪɪɪ. p ɪ 156
[March 14.]	Reginald de Cobham is appointed admiral from the Thames westward　R ɪɪɪ p ɪ 157.
March 16	Safe conduct until Whitsuntide for Garsias de Gyvill, minstrel of the infante of Castile.　*Westm*　R ɪɪɪ p ɪ 157　O ᴠ 616　H ɪɪɪ p ɪ. 31.
March 20	Truce with Johanna Q of Navarre till Christmas 1849.　*Westm.*　R ɪɪɪ. p. ɪ. 157.　O ᴠ 617　H ɪɪɪ p ɪ 31
March 20	Protection for one year for Johanna Q of Navarre in Aquitain　*Westm*　R. ɪɪɪ p ɪ 157.　O ᴠ 617　H ɪɪɪ p ɪ. 32
March 20	Warrant to the treasurer and chamberlains to deliver standard weights and measures to John de Thyngden, keeper of the victuals at Calais　*Westm*　R ɪɪɪ p ɪ 157
April 4	The burgesses and inhabitants of Calais are released from pontage and other tolls for three years　*Westm.*　R ɪɪɪ p. ɪ 158
April 4.	The captain of Calais is not to take into the K.'s service any of the inhabitants.　*Westm.*　R ɪɪɪ p ɪ. 158
April 4	The K orders the captain of Calais to take security from all persons going to England that they will land at Dover　*Westm*　R ɪɪɪ p. ɪ 158
April 5	The K appoints a staple at Calais for tin, lead, feathers, and cloth, for seven years.　*Westm*　R ɪɪɪ p ɪ 158　O. ᴠ 618　H ɪɪɪ p ɪ 32.
April 16	Safe conduct during their return to Scotland for John bp of Murray, Adam bp of Brechin, Robert de Herskyn, lord of Herskyn, and William de Melidram, and lord of Bachynnanebe, who came to England to treat for liberation of David de Bruys　*Westm*　R ɪɪɪ. p. ɪ 158　O ᴠ 618　H ɪɪɪ. p ɪ. 32.
April 24.	Amerigho de Pavia is appointed captain of the K.'s galhes.　*Westm.*　R. ɪɪɪ. p ɪ 159.　O. ᴠ. 619　H ɪɪɪ p ɪ. 32.
April 26.	The K directs the sheriffs of Dumfries not to interfere with the lands of Botillkenmore and Kirkandres, which are part of the inheritance of Edward de Balliol.　*Windsor.*　R ɪɪɪ. p ɪ 159　O ᴠ 620　H ɪɪɪ p ɪ 33.
April 28.	John de Stretle is appointed warden of Bourdeaux castle.　*Westm.*　R. ɪɪɪ. p ɪ. 159.
May 1.	Grant to Reymund Gullielmi, lord de Cava Penna, of the royal revenues in Toulonsote St. Edward's and other places　*Westm.*　R ɪɪɪ. p. ɪ. 159.　O ᴠ. 620.　H. ɪɪɪ. p. ɪ. 33

DATE	SUBJECT.
1348 May 1.	Confirmation of the privileges formerly enjoyed by the town of Alewe, the charters of which have been destroyed by the enemy *Westm* R iii p i 160
May 3.	Tournaments are forbidden throughout England *Westm* R. iii. p. i. 160
May 4.	Commission to Sir Hugh de Nevill, and Ivo de Glynton, clerk, to treat with the duke of Brabant for redress of injuries Similar commission, with the addition of William marquis of Juliers *Westm* R iii p i 160 O v 621 H iii p i 33.
[May 4.]	Similar commissions to treat with the duchess of Gueldres R. iii. p. i. 160 O v 622 H iii. p i. 33
May 4.	Also to make a league with the bp of Liege and the count of Loos *Westm* R iii. p i. 160 O v 622 H iii p. i 33.
May 10.	Credence for Hugh de Nevill and Ivo de Glynton to Henry bp of Mayence, Rudolf and Rupert, counts palatine of the Rhine, and Louis marquis of Brandenburg, who have proposed the K.'s election to the empire *Westm* R. iii. p i. 161 O. v 622. H. iii. p. i. 34.
May 15	Power for Thomas Fastolf, archdeacon of Wells, John de Carleton, canon of Wells, and friar John de Reppes to prorogue the truce with France *Westm* R. iii p i 161. O v. 623 H ii p i 34
May 17.	Safe conduct for William le Keu and other servants of Charles de Bloys coming to him in the Tower of London *Westm.* R. iii. p i 161.
June 1	The K confers knighthood on John de Guillo, burgess of Linde in Aquitain *Westm.* R. iii p. i 151 O. v. 623. H iii p i 34
June 4.	The K forbids men-at-arms leaving the country *Westm.* R. iii p i. 161.
June 5.	Credence for John Mantravers and Gilbert de Wendlynburgh sent by the K to the commonalties of Ghent, Bruges, and Ypres *Westm* R iii •p i 162. O v 624. H iii. p i 34
June 6.	Robert de Morle is appointed admiral from the Thames to Berwick-upon-Tweed. *Westm.* R iii. p i 162
June 11	The K orders the seneschal of Gascony and the constable of Bourdeaux to settle the variances between the lords of Rosano and Penolns and the lord of Muchdane, and between the lord de Sparre and the lord of Castellion *Westm* R iii p i. 162.
June 11.	Warrant to the constable of Bourdeaux to seize the goods of rebels. *Westm.* R. iii. p i 162
June 24.	Order for the renewal of the wax about the corpse of Edward I in Westminster Abbey *Westm* R. iii p i 162 O v 624 H iii p i 34
July 1.	The K orders the restitution of the fruits of the prebend of Wetewang to John de Melbourn, which had been seized for the K as belonging to the cardinal bp of Frascati. Letters to the sheriff of York, the farmers of the prebend, and the agents of the cardinal *Westm* R iii p i 162 O v 624 H iii. p i 34
July 3	Safe conduct until Michaelmas for Adam bp. of Murray and the other Scotch ambassadors. *Westm.* R. iii p i 163 O v 625. H iii p i 35
July 3.	Oliver le Fur is appointed macebearer in Brittany with 12d. a day. *Westm* R iii. p. i. 163.
July 3.	Safe conduct for the servants of Charles de Bloıs, who are about to return to Brittany *Westm* R iii p i 163
July 4.	Grant of 1,000l. a year to Ralph de Caours. *Westm.* R. iii. p. i. 164. O. v 626. H. iii. p i 35.
July 6.	Licence to Reymund Bernardi de Duro Forti to restore the castle of Belaic to the bp of Cahors *Westm* R iii p i 164.
July 12.	The K. orders the constable of Bourdeaux to pay the the arrears of the weekly alms granted by Edward I to the friars minors of S Macaire *Westm* R. iii p i 164. O v. 626. H. iii p i 35.
July 20.	Permission to John son of Stephen Leynath of Breksys and six other Irish persons to use English law *Westm* R iii p i 164
July 24	Grant of 20s a week to the friars minors of La Reol *Westm.* R iii. p. i 164. O. v. 627 H. iii p i 35
July 24.	The K promises not to alienate the town of Thouny Charante *Westm.* R. iii p i 165.
July 28.	The K. requests the pope to send a safe-conduct for W bp of Norwich, Henry earl of Lancaster, Richard earl of Arundel, and Bartholomew de Burghersh, whom he intends to send as ambassadors to his holiness. *Westm.* R iii. p i 165.

DATE.	SUBJECT.
1348 July 29	John de Wolmere, serjeant-at-arms, is appointed to furnish men for four ships captured from the French, and to send them to John de Beauchamp, captain of Calais. *Westm.* R iii p i 165
July 30	Safe conduct until Christmas for John lord of Ryeux, Bonables de Rouge, lord of Dernal, and seven others, coming to treat for the ransom of Charles de Bloys, a prisoner in the Tower of London. *Westm.* R. iii p i 165 O v 627 H. iii p i 35
Aug 1	The captain of Vennes is ordered to observe the truce concluded with Charles de Bloys *Westm.* R iii p i 166 O v. 628 H iii p i 36
Aug 3	John de Dale is commanded to arrest the agents of the duchess of Gueldres *Westm* R. iii p i 166 O v 628 H iii p i 36
Aug. 4.	Renewal of the appointment of Bernard de Bernes, called Aspeys, Peter bp. of Bayonne, and others, as arbiters between the K.'s subjects and the Castilians. *Westm.* R. iii p. i. 166 O v 628–9. H iii p i 36
Aug 6.	Prorogation of the truce with France for one year *Westm* R iii p i 166. O. v 629. H iii p i 36
Aug. 6	Thomas de Daggeworth, the K.'s captain in Brittany, is ordered to enforce the truce with Charles de Bloys *Westm* R iii p i 166 O v 629. H iii p. i 36
Aug 6	Licence to the agents of the cardinals of Naples and Cleremont to collect their dues. *Westm* R iii p i 167 O v 630 H iii p i 37
Aug 6	Grant to the dean and canons of S Stephen's, Westminster, of a house in Lombard Street, with the advowsons of the churches of Dewsbury and Wakefield *Westm.* R iii. p i 167. O v 631 H iii p i 37
Aug. 8	Safe conduct until Martinmas for William bp of S. Andrews, Thomas bp of Caithness, and five others, coming to England to the K and David de Brus. *Odiham* R iii. p i 167. O v. 632 H iii p i 37
Aug. 8.	The K orders William de Kelleseye, chancellor of Berwick-upon-Tweed, to allow Edward de Balhol, K of Scotland, to enjoy his rights in Lowederdale. *Westm* R iii p i 168. O v 632 H iii p i 37
Aug. 9.	Grant to Ralph de de Caourz of 1,000 librates of land in Rayes in Brittany, and other parts in Poiton gained by him. Intimation thereof to the K.'s officers in those parts *Westm.* R iii p i 168 O v 633 H iii p i 38
Aug 9	An indenture which by Ralph de Caourz engages to the serve the K. *Westm.* R iii p i 168 O v 633 H iii p i 38
Aug 10	The K orders John de S Paul, archdeacon of Cornwall, to urge the people to defend the coast *Westm* R iii. p i 168
Aug 10	Grant to Thomas de Daggeworth, captain of Brittany, of the revenues of the duchy. *Westm* R iii p i 169
Aug 10	Reginald de Cobham, admiral of the western fleet, is ordered to provide shipping to convey Thomas de Daggeworth to Brittany *Westm* R iii p i 169
Aug 12	Safe conduct for Alexander de Seton, master of S John of Jerusalem in Scotland, coming to David de Bruys in the Tower of London *Westm.* R. iii. p i 169. O. v. 634 H iii p i 38.
Aug 12	Also for Patrick de Dunbar, earl of March, coming to treat for the liberation of David de Bruys *Odiham* R iii p i 169 O v 634 H iii. p i 38
Aug 12	Power for R. abp of Armagh to consult with the sheriffs of Ireland for the preservation of peace *Westm* R iii. p i 169 O v 634 H iii p i 38
Sept 4	Grant of 25,000 florins to Thomas de Daggeworth for the capture of Charles de Bloys. calling himself duke of Brittany *Westm* R iii p i 170.
Sept 4	The seneschal of Gascony and the constable of Bourdeaux are ordered to publish the truce concluded by Henry earl of Lancaster and the count of Eu, constable of France. *Westm* R. iii p i 170
Sept 5.	The several bishops of England are informed of the licence granted to the agents of the papal nuncios in the collecting of procurations. Similar letter to the abbot of Faversham. *Clarendon.* R iii p i 170 O v 635 H iii p i 38
Sept. 5	Truce for six weeks concluded between Henry earl of Lancaster and Ralph count of Eu, to allow Q Johanne of France and Q Isabel of England to meet and treat for peace. *London.* R. iii. p i 170 O v. 635. H iii p i 39.
Sept. 11.	The K. orders the publication of the truce above-mentioned in England, Wales, and Flanders. *Westm.* R. iii p i 171. O v. 641. H. iii. p. i. 39.

DATE	SUBJECT
1348. Sept 15	The K. informs Alfono K of Castile of the death at Bourdeaux of his daughter Joan, who was betrothed to Peter, infante of Spain *Westm* R III p 1 171. O v 642 H III p 1 40
[Sept 15]	Letter on the same subject to the infante of Castile. R. III p 1 172. O. v 642 H III. p 1 40
Oct. 12	Letter to the Q of Castile on the subject. *Westm* R III p 1 172. O v. 643 H III p 1 40
Sept 21.	Commission of Philip K of France to the abp of Rouen, the bp of Laon, the dukes of Burgundy and Bourbon, and nine others, to treat for peace with England *Bois de Vincennes* R III p 1. 172 O v 644 H III p 1 40
Sept. 24.	Clement [VI.] recommends John [de Offord] dean of Lincoln to the vacant see of Canterbury *Avignon* R III p 1 173 O v. 644. H III p 1 41
Sept 25	Commission to William bp of Norwich, the earl of Lancaster, Robert de Ufford, earl of Suffolk, sir Walter de Manny, and John de Charleton, to treat for peace with France Commission to them to swear for the K of England *Westm.* R III p 1 173 O v 643 H III p 1 42
Sept 25	Henry earl of Lancaster is appointed the K's lieutenant in Flanders and Calais *Westm* R III p 1 174 O v 644 H III p 1 42
Oct. 1	Writs to the sheriffs of London and the mayors and bailiffs of 17 seaports to unload merchant ships, and send them to join the fleet *Westm* R III p 1 174
Oct. 8	Men at arms, hobillers, and archers willing to serve the K abroad are to muster at Sandwich on Oct 26 *Westm* R. III p 1. 174 O v 644 H. in p 1 42
Oct 10	Safe conduct until June 24 for Joan, wife of David de Bruys, who is coming to remain with her husband in the Tower of London *Westm* R III p 1 174 O. v. 645 H. III p 1 42
Oct 11	Commission to William bp of Norwich, Henry earl of Lancaster, and seven others, to treat with the count and people of Flanders *Westm* R. III p 1. 175 O. v. 645. H III. p. 1 42
Oct 18	Safe conduct until Dec. 7 for Thomas bp of Caithness and his colleagues coming to England to treat for the liberation of David de Bruys from the Tower of London *Westm* R. III p 1 175 O v 646 H III p 1 43
Oct 22.	Truce with the Scots until June 24. Letters enjoining the observance thereof by Henry de Percy and Ralph de Nevill, wardens of the marches, and five other officers of the K *The Tower of London.* R III. p 1 175. O v 646 H III p 1 43
Oct 22	Proclamation to be made in various counties of the K's intended voyage from Sandwich on Oct 30 *The Tower of London* R III p 1 175
Oct. 23.	Safe conduct for Ralph de Haneford and Richard de Crosedale to buy wine and other necessaries for the household of Joan the Scottish Q, and to convey them to Scotland. *Westm* R III p 1 176 O v 647 H III p 1 43
Oct 25.	Warrant for the payment of five marks a day for the expenses of John bp of Carlisle conveying Johanna, the K's daughter, now deceased, to Gascony *Westm.* R. III. p 1 176. O v. 648. H III p 1. 43.
Oct 25.	The bps of England are desired to pray for the K's success. *Westm.* R. III. p 1 176
Oct 29.	Memorandum of the sending of the great seal by John de Offord, chancellor, to the K at Sandwich, and of the chancellor's receipt of the seal for use during the K's absence from William de Edyngton, bp of Winchester, the K's treasurer. R III p 1 176 O v 648 H III p i 43
Nov 4.	The sheriff of Kent is ordered to repair the barriers and benches for the assize of the justices in eyre in Kent. *Sandwich* R III p 1 177
Nov 13	Truce concluded between the English commissioners until Sept 1, with comprehension of allies *Between Gusnes and Calais* R III. p. 1 177. O v 649 H III p 1 44
Dec. 1.	The K desires those persons of Calais who obtained from him the establishment of a staple of wool to appear before the council at London, as there are complaints that it is injurious *Westm* R III p. 1 178
Dec. 10.	Treaty between the K and the count of Flanders *The Tower of London.* R. III. p. 1 178. O v 652 H. III p 1 45
Dec. 10.	Confirmation by the K. of the above treaty. *The Tower of London.* R III. p. 1. 179. O. v 654 H III p. 1. 46.

DATE.	SUBJECT
1348 Dec 14	Notarial attestation of the taking of the oath of fealty by John de Offord, abp. of Canterbury *The Tower of London* R iii. p. i 179.
Dec. 14.	Restitution of temporalties to John de Offord abp of Canterbury *The Tower of London* R iii p i 180
Dec. 19.	The K orders the bailiffs of Scarborough to release from arrest a ship of Middilsburgh, in Sealand, laden with Scotch goods, which was driven into their harbour. *Westm.* R iii p i 180 O v 654 H iii p i 46.
1349 Jan 1.	The K informs W bp of Winchester that the parliament is prorogued until a fortnight after Easter, in consequence of a sudden pestilence at Westminster *Westm* R iii p i 180. O v 655 H iii p i 46
Jan. 1.	John de Beauchamp is appointed captain of Calais *Westm.* R iii p i. 181. O. v. 655. H iii p i 46
Jan 23.	The K orders proclamation to be made by the sheriffs of London that matters relating to the common law which concern the K are to be referred to the chancellor *Langley.* R iii p i 181
Feb 1	Power for William marquis of Juliers to treat for the marriage of Charles K of the Romans and the K's daughter Isabella *Westm.* R iii p i 181 O v 655 H iii. p i 46
Feb 5.	Commission to Richard Talbot, the K's seneschal, John de Carleton, and sir Stephen de Cosington, to receive renewed oaths of fealty from the burgesses, &c of Flanders *Westm.* R iii p i 181 O v 656 H iii p i 47
[Feb 5]	Commission for the same to receive the oaths of Flemish exiles R iii p i. 181. O. v. 656. H iii p i 47.
Feb 25.	Safe conducts until Aug 1 and Nov 1 for William abp of S Andrews and five other ambassadors coming from Scotland for the liberation of David de Brus from the Tower of London *Langley* R iii p i 181 O v 657 H iii p i 47
March 8	Commission by Philip K of France, to the abp of Rouen, the bp of Laon, the duke of Athens, and four others, to treat for peace or truce with England *Apud Fontem Blundi* [*Fontainebleau*] R iii p i 182 O v 657 H iii p i 47
March 10.	Prorogation of the parliament until further notice, in consequence of the plague. *Westm.* R iii p i 182. O v 658 H iii. p i. 47.
March 10.	Commission to William bp of Norwich, William de Bohun, earl of Northampton, Wilham de Clynton, earl of Huntingdon, the prior of Rochester, and three others, to treat for peace or truce with France *Westm* R iii p i 182. O. v. 658. H iii p i. 47.
March 12	Protection for the bp of Norwich and eight persons in his company. *Westm* R iii. p i 183
March 14	Licence to Henry earl of Lancaster to establish a mint at Bergerac Intimation thereof to the seneschal of Gascony *Westm* R iii p i 183 O v. 659 H iii. p i. 48.
April 2	The K rebukes John Wylyot, Philip de Codeford, and three others, for the riots at the late election of a chancellor by the university of Oxford, and for the expulsion of Robert Ingram, the proctor; and forbids them to hold assemblies in Oxford *Westm.* R iii. p i 183
April 2	The K orders them to restore the contents of the university chest, which they had carried away *Westm* R iii p i 183
April 13	Power for William bp of Norwich and his colleagues to prologue the truce with France. *Langley* R iii p i 184. O v 660 H iii. p i 48
April 15	The K orders the mayor and commonalty of Bayonne to remove the prisoners in the new prison to the castle where they ought to be kept *Westm* R iii p i 184
May 2	Prorogation of the truce between England and France until Whitsuntide, 1350. *Between Calais and Guisnes* R iii p i 184 O v 660 H iii p i. 48
May 9	The K orders the treasurer and barons of the Exchequer to levy the marshal's fees due to him since the death of Thomas earl of Norfolk *Woodstock.* R iii p i 185
May 28	William de Shrouesbury, treasurer of Calais, is ordered to buy draught horses for the works there. *Woodstock* R iii p i 185
May 28	The K orders the captain and council of Calais to coin what money they think advisable there. *Woodstock* R. iii. p i 185

DATE.	SUBJECT
1349. May 28.	Memorandum that John de Offord, abp. elect and confirmed of Canterbury, the K.'s chancellor, died at Totenhall, near London, on May 20 , that Andrew de Offord, his brother, took the seal to the K at Woodstock, and on the 28th Bartholomew de Burghersh, by the K's command, gave it into the custody of David de Wolloure, John de S Paul, Thomas de Brayton, and Thomas de Cotyngham R iii. p 1 185 O v 662 H iii p 1 49
June 16.	Memorandum that the K delivered the great seal to John bp of S David's as chancellor *Westm.* R iii p 1 186
July 8.	Clement [VI] confirms the election of Thomas abbot of Tynemouth to the abbacy of S Alban's *Avignon* R iii p 1. 186.
July 12	John de Beauchamp is appointed captain of Calais *Clarendon* R. iii p 1 186.
July 16.	Safe conduct for Duncan Cambell and Gilbert de Levenax, coming to sir Andrew Cambell, prisoner in the Tower of London. *Clarendon.* R. iii p. 1 187 O v. 663 H. iii. p 1 49.
July 25	Protection for the castellany of Belac and the other possessions of Mary de S Paul, countess of Pembroke, in Aquitain *Clarendon* R iii p 1 187
July 30.	Warrant to Richard Molineux, collector of the tenth and fifteenth in Lancaster, for the payment of 18 li to Edward de Balliol, K of Scotland Warrant to Robert de Mulcastre for 16l. *Clarendon* R. iii p 1 187 O v 664. H iii p 1 50
Aug. 4.	Power for John de Beauchamp, captain, and the bailiffs of Calais, to let and grant lands and tenements in Calais *Westm* R iii p. 1 187
Aug. 17.	John de Beauchamp is appointed admiral of a fleet for protecting the passage to Calais. *Westm* R iii p 1 188
Aug. 19.	Commission to Gilbert de Aclom, master mason of Calais, to take 20 masons and 12 carpenters from Kent *Westm* R iii p 1 188
Aug. 23.	The K forbids the exportation of arms or other merchandise to Scotland. *Westm.* R. iii. p. 1. 188.
Aug. 28.	Commission to Henry earl of Lancaster to send information of the grants made by the K in Aquitain *Westm* R iii p 1. 188 O v 664 H iii p 1 50.
Aug 28.	Power for Michael de Northburgh, archdeacon of Suffolk, Andrew de Offord, archdeacon of Middlesex, Richard de Wymondwold, and Robert de Askeby, canon of Salisbury, to reform and prorogue the truce with France *Westm.* R iii p 1 188 O v 664 H. iii. p 1 50
Aug 28	Henry earl of Lancaster is appointed the K 's lieutenant and captain in Aquitain *Westm* R iii p 1 189.
Aug 28	Commission to the earl, conferring on him full powers of jurisdiction there. *Westm.* R. iii p 1 189
Aug 28	Power for him to make alliances with persons and commonalties of any nation. *Westm.* R iii p 1 189
[Aug 28]	Power for him to retain persons for the K.'s service R iii p 1 189
Sept. 26	Power for Sir Robert de Herle, lieutenant of Calais, and Sir Richard Totesham, to treat with Louis count of Flanders for the confirmation of the articles concluded at Dunkirk *Westm.* R iii. p 1 189, O v 665 H iii p 1 50
Oct. 15.	Similar power for sir William de Burton and Ivo de Glynton, canon of S Paul's *Westm.* R iii p 1. 190 O v. 665. H. iii. p 1 50.
Oct. 18.	Henry earl of Lancaster is appointed the K.'s lieutenant and captain in Poictou Intimation thereof to Moniquot de France and eight others. R. iii. p 1. 190. O. v 665 H iii. p. 1 50
Oct. 28.	Memorandum that James de Bononia, agent of the cardinal bp. of Frascati, protested in the presence of the bp of S David's, the K's chancellor, and others, that he would do nothing prejudicial to the K 's rights concerning a bull of provision for the cardinal of the treasurership of York *Westm* R. iii p 1 190. O v 666 H iii p 1 50
Nov 6.	Proclamation to be made by the sheriffs of London that no merchants are to buy salt at le Bay or elsewhere in Poictou from any one except the earl of Lancaster *Westm* R. iii p 1 190.
Nov. 20.	The K. revokes his licence to the abp of Armagh to have his cross borne before him in any part of Ireland *Westm* R iii p 1. 190 O. v 666 H iii p. 1 51.
Dec. 1.	The K forbids any persons leaving England in consequence of the plague. *Westm.* R. iii. p i. 191. O v 668. H. iii. p. 1 51

DATE.	SUBJECT.
1350 Jan 15	Safe conduct for John Estnie and seven other servants of the count of Eu going to France for his ransom *Westm* R iii. p. i 191.
Feb. 12.	Warrants to nine sheriffs to send arrows to the Tower of London *Westm* R. iii p i 192
Feb 18	The K. writes to Andomar, cardinal of S. Anastasia, against the pretensions of the abp of Armagh to carry the cross, also to the cardinal of Palestrina, the papal vice-chancellor. *Westm* R iii p i 192. O. v. 668. H iii p i. 51.
Feb. 18	The abp. of Armagh is ordered to repair to his see and provide for its defence. *Westm.* R iii p i 192 O v 669. H iii p i 52
Feb 24	Thomas de Rokeby, justiciary of Ireland, is ordered to send Robert de Emeldon, late treasurer, to the K *Rotherhithe* R. iii p i 192
March 9	Robert de Herle is appointed captain of Calais *Westm.* R iii p i 193
March 18	Warrant to Hugh de S Albans, master of the painters in the chapel at Westminster, to take painters and other workmen in the counties of Kent, Middlesex, Essex, Surrey, and Sussex Similar warrants for other counties to John Athelard and Benedict Nightegale. *Westm* R iii p i 193 O v 670 H iii p i 52.
March 20.	The mayor and sheriffs of London are ordered to provide 100 armed men by June 6 Similar writs to the mayors and bailiffs of 109 other towns *Westm* R iii p i 193
March 20	Proclamation to be made by the several sheriffs that men willing to serve the K. must be at Sandwich on June 6 *Westm.* R iii p i. 194
March 20.	Philip de Whitton is appointed lieutenant of John de Beauchamp, admiral of the fleet west of the Thames *Westm* H iii p i 194
March 20	Foundation of the Cistercian house of S Mary of Grace, London certain messuages at "La Tourhulle" granted *Westm* R iii p i 194
April 1	Grant of an annuity of 200 marks to Guy de Bryan for his bravery in a battle at Calais *Westm* H iii p i 195 O v 670 H iii p i 52
April 20	Release to the tenants of the abp of Canterbury from the exaction of a palfrey at the death of John de Offord. *Westm* R iii p i 195 O v 670 H iii p i 52
April 30	Safe conduct until Christmas for Duncan earl of Fife, a prisoner in the Tower of London, going to Scotland to obtain his ransom *Westm* R iii p i 195 O v 671 H. iii p i 52
May 1	Commission to William Passelewe and Robert Shipman, constable of the ship called *la Cog Thomas*, to procure 100 sailors in Kent and Sussex Nine similar commissions. *Westm.* R. iii p i. 195
May 12	Richard de Thoresby, keeper of the hanaper, is ordered to pay 7*l.* 1*s* 8*d* to the bp. of Worcester, the K's chancellor, being the excess over the usual expense of the robes for the clerks of the chancery *Westm* R iii. p i 196
May 15.	Power for William bp of Norwich, Robert de Ufford, earl of Suffolk, Thomas Cok, and Robert de Herle, captain of Calais, to treat for peace or truce with France *Westm.* R iii p i. 196. O v 671 H iii p i 52
[May 15]	Power for them to take an oath for the K R iii. p. i 196 O v. 672 H iii p i 53
May 20	Commission to Thomas de Swetesham to purchase rigging, &c for the K's ships *Westm.* R iii p i 196
May 24	Safe conduct until June 24 for Peter Warineys and four other servants of the count of Eu going to France *Westm* R iii p. i. 196.
May 30.	Safe conduct for one year for Joan de Bar, countess of Surrey and Sussex, going on a pilgrimage abroad *Westm* R iii p i. 196
June 8	Order for the renewal of the wax covering the corpse of Edward I. in Westminster Abbey *Westm.* R iii p i 197. O v 672 H iii p i. 53
June 13	Prorogation of the truce with France until Aug 1. *Near Calais* R. iii. p. i. 197. O v 672 H iii p i 53
June 18.	Proclamation to be made by the several sheriffs that, in consequence of the death of great numbers of workmen and servants from the plague, all men and women without estates or trades are to enter into service at the wages which have been ordinarily paid in their localities for the last five or six years, and tradesmen are forbidden to enhance their prices. *Westm* R iii p. i 198
June 23	The K forbids all persons leaving the country *Westm.* R. iii p. i. 199
June 23	The K forbids the exportation of corn *Westm* R iii p i. 199

DATE	SUBJECT
1350. June 24.	Safe conduct for Thomas le Bastard de France, knt., to come to England to fight a duel with sir John Viscontes *Westm.* R in p l. 199. O v 676. H ii. p. 1. 54
July 1	The K. orders the truce with France to be published throughout England. *Westm.* R iii p l. 200 O v. 676 H iii p 1 54
July 2	Protection till Easter for James Ramananii, parson of Sevenoaks, agent of Anibald, cardinal of Naples *Westm* R iii p l 200 O v 677 H iii p l. 55
July 18.	Licence to Adam Brabazoun, citizen of London, to go to Rome to obtain absolution *Westm.* R iii p l. 200 O v 677 H. iii p l. 55
July 22	Robert de Morlee is appointed admiral of the fleet north of the Thames. *Westm.* R iii p l 200.
June 22.	The K appoints William de Clynton, earl of Huntingdon, and Bartholomew de Burghersh, senior, wardens of the sea-coast. *Westm.* R iii p. l. 200
July 28	The K requests the pope to send a safe conduct for W bp of Norwich, the earls of Lancaster and Arundel, and Bartholomew de Burghersh, his chamberlain, whom he intends to send to his holiness about Michaelmas *Westm* R iii. p l 201. O v 678. H iii. p. l 55.
Aug 6	Power for Robert de Herle, captain of Calais, to hear causes and appeals there. *Rotherhithe.* R. iii. p l 201 O v 678. H. iii. p l 55.
Aug 10	The K informs S abp of Canterbury of the intended invasion of England by the Spaniards, and desires his prayers. Similar letter to the abp of York *Rotherhithe* R iii p l 201 O v 679 H iii. p l 55
Aug. 28.	Proclamation to be made by the sheriffs of London and Norfolk, and the bailiffs of Hull and three other ports, that the commissioners for the redress of injuries by the Flemings will meet at Calais on Sept 9 *Winchelsea.* R iii p l 202
Sept 3	Clement [VI.] exhorts the K to make peace with John K of France, successor of Philip de Valois, and desires credence for Raymund Pelegrini, canon of London. *Avignon* R iii p l 202 O v 680 H iii. p l 56
Sept. 3	Power for Michael de Northburgh, the K's secretary, John de Carleton, dean of Wells, and sir Robert de Herle, captain of Calais, to confirm the articles treated of at Dunkirk *Winchelsea* R iii p l 202 O v 680 H iii p l 56
Sept. 8	The K desires the mayor and commonalty of Bayonne to prepare their fleet to resist the Spaniards *Westm.* R. iii. p l. 202. O v. 681. H. iii p. l. 56.
Sept 8	The K orders Bartholomew de Burghersh, constable of Dover Castle and warden of the Cinque Ports, to allow William Fitzwaryn to pass on his pilgrimage to Rome Similar letter for Henry de Ingelby, Ida lady Nevill, and 153 others. *Rotherhithe* R iii p l 203 O v 681-2. H iii p l 56
Sept. 8.	Walter de Bentele is appointed the K's lieutenant and captain in Brittany and Poictou *Sandwich.* R. iii p l 204. O. v. 683 H iii p l 57
Sept. 12	Grant to Walter de Bentele of all the revenues of Brittany as well those pertaining to the K. as to John son and heir of John de Montfort, late duke of Brittany *Hertford.* R iii p l 204 O v. 684. H iii p l 57
Sept. 13	The K. licences the agents of the cardinals of Naples and Clermont to collect their dues. *Hertford* R iii. p l 204 O v 684. H iii. p l 57
Sept. 24.	Safe conduct till Feb. 2 for Ivo Gautier, Peter Burchon, and the servants of Charles de Bloys, prisoner in the Tower, to go to France Similar letters for John Raymond and Poulet de la Viccigne. *Hertford* R iii p l 204 O v 685 H iii. p l 58.
Oct. 12.	Declaration of the judicial combat between Thomas de la Marche, bastard of France, and John Viscount, at Westminster, Oct. 4 *Westm* R iii p l 205 O v. 685 H iii. p. l 58
Oct 14	Power for Thomas bp of Durham, Ralph baron of Stafford, Henry de Percy, and Ralph de Nevill to treat for peace with Scotland. *Westm* R. iii p l. 205 O v 686. H iii. p l 58
Oct 16.	Power for Robert de Herle, captain of Calais, and Andrew de Offord, archdeacon of Middlesex, to treat with Louis count of Flanders for redress of injuries. *Westm* R. iii. p l. 205 O. v 687. H. iii p. l 58.
Oct. 18.	Inspeximus and ratification of the treaty with Genoa, dated 5 July, 21 Edw III *Westm* R iii p l 205 O v 687. H iii p l 58
Oct. 20.	The K appoints Roger Larcher, sergeant at arms, and Peter de Maners, collectors of the subsidy of 40d. a cask on Gascon wine Intimation thereof to the seneschal of Gascony and the constable of Bourdeaux *Westm.* R. iii p l 206. O v. 688. H. iii p l 59.

DATE	SUBJECT
1350. Oct 20.	Safe conduct till Whitsuntide for 15 persons sent abroad by the count of En. to procure money for his ransom *Westm.* R. iii p. i. 206 O v. 688. H iii p. i. 59.
Oct 21	Power for sir Walter lord of Manny, sir William de Burton, sir William Stury, and Ivo de Clynton, clerk, to treat with the empress Margaret concerning the government of the Low Countries Similar power for the said Stury and Clynton *Westm* R. iii. p i 206 O v 689 H iii p i 59
Oct. 21	Power for the same persons to enter into alliance with the empress and her son William duke of Bavaria. *Westm* R iii p i 206 O v 689 H iii p i 59
Oct. 26	Commission to sir William de Stury to receive the custody of the Low Countries, committed to the K of England by the empress Margaret *Westm.* R. iii p i. 207 O v 690 H iii p i 60
Oct. 27.	The exportation of corn is forbidden except for the use of the town of Calais *Westm* R iii p i 207
Nov 2	Commission to Robert de Herle, captain of Calais, and Andrew de Offord, archdeacon of Middlesex, to confirm, with K John of France, the truce of Calais Four similar commissions, dated 4th, 7th, 12th, and 16th Nov *Westm* R. iii p i 207 O. v 690–1 H iii p i. 60
Nov 2	Thomas Bannstre, on account of his good service in a sea fight with the Spaniards, is pardoned for the homicide of Ralph de Blakeburn. *Westm* R iii p i 207 O v 691 H iii p i. 60
Nov. 3	Trial, before Richard earl ofArundel, Thomas de Beauchamp, earl of Warwick, and three others, of sir William de Thorpe, chief justice, for receiving bribes Sentence of death was passed, but remitted by the K *Westm* Nov 19 R iii p i 208
Nov 11	Power for Robert de Herle, captain of Calais, Andrew de Offord, Henry Pycard, and John de Wesenham, to treat with the Spanish seamen at the ports of Flanders *Westm* R iii p i 210 O v 691 H iii p i. 60.
Nov 11.	Commission to Henry Pycard and John de Wesenham to treat with and grant a safe conduct to the crew of a Genoese vessel now at Swyne in Flanders *Westm.* R iii. p i 210 O v 692 H iii p i 60
Nov 18	Pardon for William la Zouche, abp of York, for homicides, during the reigns of Edward II. and Edward III, especially at the battle of Durham *Westm.* R iii p. i. 210. O v. 692. H iii p i 61
Nov 18	Andrew de Bures, and five others, are appointed to carry out in Suffolk the proclamation of June 18, relating to the moderation of wages and prices Similar commission to William de Skipwith and three others in Lindsey *Westm.* 12 *Nov* R iii p i.211 O v. 693–6 H. iii p i. 61–2.
Nov 19.	Memorandum that John bp of Worcester, chancellor, delivered the great seal to the K, who gave it to John de Grey of Retherfeld, his seneschal, to seal a commission and a writ, after which it was returned to the chancellor *Westm.* R iii p i 211
Dec 8	The K orders the justiciary, chancellor, and treasurer of Ireland to prevent assemblies of armed men for the purpose of maintaining the privileges of the abp of Armagh about carrying the cross *Westm* R iii p i 211 O v 695 H. iii p i 62
Dec 16	Power for sir Nigel de Loryng, sir William de Stury, Ivo de Clynton, and Stephen Rumilowe to treat concerning the payments to be made to the K of England for the government of the Low Countries, Similar power, omitting Stury *Westm* R. iii. p i. 212. O v 696 H iii p i. 62.
Dec. 20	Safe conduct until Easter for William Buynet, servant of sir Geoffrey de Charny, the K's prisoner *Westm.* R iii p i 212
1351 Feb 4	The K desires the abbot of Beaulieu to send some of his brethren to the new house of S. Mary of Grace, near the Tower of London *Westm* The K desires Friar Walter de S Croix, president of S Mary of Grace, to receive them *Westm.* 6 *Feb.* R iii p i. 212
Feb. 20	The K orders the seneschal of Gascony and the constable of Bourdeaux to coin money at Bayonne. *Westm* R. iii. p i. 213
Feb. 23.	Commission to the abbot of Aachos, the prior of the hospital of S Sepulchre, and Dominic de Vico of Dax, to hear the appeal of Galhard lord of S Paul against a sentence of sir Thomas Cok, seneschal of Gascony. *Westm* R iii p i 213 O v 696 H. iii. p i 62
March 1	Grant of an annuity of 1,000*l.* to Bernard Ezii, lord of Lebret *Westm.* R iii. p i 213. O v. 697 H iii p. i 63
March 1.	The K desires the abp of Canterbury to summon convocations for the purpose of granting an aid *Westm* R. iii. p i 214

DATE	SUBJECT.
1351. March 1.	Similar request to the abp. of York *Westm* R iii p i 214. O v 698 H iii p. i 63.
March 4.	Protection for Eleanor countess of Ormond (widow of sir Thomas de Daggeworth) and her men and tenants in Brittany *Westm* R. iii p. i 214. O v. 699. H iii. p. i. 63.
March 4.	K Edward accepts the protestation of Edward de Balliol, K of Scotland, that his negotiations with the Scots shall not prejudice his treaty with the K of England *Westm* R. iii. p i 214 O v 699 H iii p i 63
March 5.	Safe conduct for Edward de Balliol to come to Hextildesham [Hexham] *Westm.* R. iii. p i. 215. O v. 700 H. iii. p i. 63
March 8	Power for William de Bohun, earl of Northampton, Henry de Percy, Ralph de Nevill, Henry le Scrop, and William Legat to treat at Hextildesham [Hexham] with the Scots for the ransom of David de Bruys *Westm* R iii p i 215. O v 700 H iii. p. i 64
March 8.	Henry duke of Lancaster is appointed admiral of the fleet west of the Thames, and William de Bohun, earl of Northampton, of the fleet north of the Thames *Westm* R. iii. p. i. 215
March 10	Commission to Andrew de Guldeford and Walter Warde, sergeants at arms, to arrest ships in Ireland for the K's passage to France. *Westm* R iii p i 215
March 20.	Commission to Henry duke of Lancaster, John de Carleton, dean of Wells, and Andrew de Offord, archdeacon of Middlesex, to treat with Louis count of Flanders for redress of injuries *Westm* R iii p i 216 O v. 700 H. iii p i 64
March 20	The same commissioners may make a league with the empress Margaret *Westm* R iii p i 216. O v 701 H iii p i 64
March 20	Similar power to the same commissioners to treat with the empress and her son, William duke of Bavaria *Eltham* R iii p i 216. O v. 702 H. iii p i 64
March 20	The K forbids common pleas in Ireland to be tried in the court of Exchequer there *Eltham.* R iii p i 216
March 20	The K orders the dismissal of Thomas de Dente and John Gernon, justices of the K's Bench in Ireland, and the appointment of Richard Brown, third justice of the King's Bench, as the second justice. *Eltham* R iii p. i. 216.
March 20	The K forbids the sealing of judicial writs in Ireland with the seal of the exchequer of Dublin. *Eltham* R iii. p i. 217.
March 20.	Pardons for felonies in Ireland are not to be granted without the assent of the chancellor and treasurer there *Eltham* R iii p i 217
March 22.	The K orders the mayor and sheriff of London to enforce the statute of the last parliament against ingrossers and regraters *Eltham* R. iii p i 217
May 1.	William de Bodrygan and John Dabernon are appointed wardens of the sea coast of Cornwall Ten similar commissions *Westm* R iii p i. 217
May 1	The K. promises his eldest daughter Isabel in marriage to Bernard Ezii, heir of the lord of Lebret, and grants them an annuity of 1,000 marks *Westm.* R. iii p. i 218. O. v 702. H iii p i. 64.
May 1.	Commission to Antonius and Pascasius Ususmaris to procure the observance of the treaty with Genoa. *Westm* R iii p i 218 O v 703 H iii p i 65
May 4	The K. grants 4,000 marks as the dowry of his daughter Isabel. *Westm* R iii p i. 218. O. v. 704 H. iii. p i 65
May 8.	Declaration that the lord of Anghen has purged himself before the K. and his council of the accusation of having attempted to poison the count and countess of Flanders and Monsieur Louis de Namur. *Westm* R. iii p i. 219 O v 704 H iii p i 65
May 12	Protection until Aug 1 for Gerard count of Mountz and Ravensberg and his brother William, sons of the marquis of Juliers *Westm* R iii p i 219 O v. 706. H iii. p. i. 66
May 12.	Power for Bernard de Caulason, archdeacon of Ely, Richard de Wymondeswolde, advocate of the Roman court, and Robert de Askeby, canon of Salisbury, to treat for an alliance with the K. of Arragon *Westm* R iii p. i 219 O v 706 H iii p i 66
May 14	The abbot of Quarre, Thomas Haket, and Robert Chaumberleyn are ordered to put the Isle of Wight in a state of defence. *Westm.* R. iii. p. i. 220
May 20.	Pardon for the inhabitants of Ghent. *Westm.* R. iii. p i. 220. O v 707. H. iii. p. i. 66.

DATE	SUBJECT.
1351. May 22.	The K. sends Walter lord of Manny to act as mediator between the empress Margaret and her elder son, Louis duke of Bavaria, on one part, and her younger son, William duke of Bavaria, on other part *Westm.* R iii p i 220 O. v. 707 H iii p ii. 66.
June 10	Proclamation to be made in London that a commission for the redress of injuries will sit at Bruges in the octave of Trinity Sunday *Westm.* R iii p i 220.
June 15.	Henry duke of Lancaster is ordered to provide 80 spearmen for his lands of Monmouth and other places in Wales Similar writs to 17 others in Wales. *Westm.* R. iii. p i 221.
June 15	Commission to Roger de Beauchamp, Thomas de Seymore, John Bluet, sergeant-at-arms, John de la Roche, and Thomas de la Ryvere, sheriff of Wilts, to provide 150 archers in Wilts Twenty-nine similar commissions *Westm.* R iii p i. 221
June 20.	Indenture with Robert de Herle for his office of captain of Calais *Westm.* R iii p. i. 222 O. v 707 H. iii p. i. 66
June 20	Indenture relative to the appointment of Henry de Brisele and John de Cicestre as masters of the mint in the Tower of London *The Tower of London.* R iii p. i 222 O v 708 H iii p i 67
June 21.	Proclamation to be made by the sheriffs of London, Norfolk, and Suffolk, and Lincoln, for the circulation of groats and half-groats, and forbidding the exchange of money except by the authorised exchangers *The Tower of London* R iii p i. 220.
June 21	Proclamation to be made by the sheriffs of London forbidding the exchange of money as above. *The Tower of London* R iii p i 224
June 22	Power for Franco de Hale and Stephen de Cosyngton to treat with the count and commonalties of Flanders *Westm.* R iii p i 224 O v 710 H iii p. i 67.
June 27	Instructions for the duke of Lancaster to treat of a marriage between the earl of Richmond and the daughter of the count of Flanders, and other matters *The Tower of London.* R. iii p. i 224 O v 710. H iii p i 67
June 27	Power for William bp of Norwich, William earl of Huntingdon, Bartholomew de Burghersh, and Robert de Herle to treat for a final peace or truce with France *Westm.* R iii p i 225. O v. 711 H iii p i 68
June 28	Safe conduct for the bps of S Andrew's, Brechin, Caithness, and Dumblane to come as ambassadors to Newcastle-upon-Tyne , also for the earls of March, Mar, Angus, and Sutherland, and five others *The Tower of London.* R iii p i 225 O v 711 H iii p i 68
June 28	Power for Thomas bp of Durham, Richard earl of Arundel, Henry lord Percy, Ralph lord Nevill, sir Hugh de Nevill, and John de Wynewyk, treasurer of York, to treat with the Scotch ambassadors at Newcastle, for the ransom of David de Bruys and for a final peace *The Tower of London* R iii p i 225. O. v 712 H iii p i 68.
June 28	The K writes to the chapter general of the Cistercian order on the subject of the house of S Mary of Grace *The Tower of London* R iii p i 225
June 30	Robert de Herle is appointed captain of Calais. *Westm.* R iii p. i 226 O v 712. H iii p i 68
July 1	Order for the renewal of the wax around the body of Edward I in Westminster Abbey *Westm.* R iii p i. 226 O v 713 H iii. p i 68
July 1.	Power for William Dyryan, seneschal of Brittany, to hear at Vannes causes relating to the town of Rennes, now occupied by the enemy *Westm.* R iii p i 226. O v 713. H iii p i 68
July 6	The K. forbids all persons leaving the kingdom *The Tower of London.* R iii p i 226
July 10	Warrant to the farmers of the customs and subsidies to pay the annuity of 200 marks granted to Robert Bertram, the captor of William de Douglas at the battle of Durham. *Westm* R iii p i 226. O v 713 H. iii p i 69.
July 12	Exemplification of the grant dated May 1 to Isabel the K 's daughter and the son of the lord of Lebret *Westm* R iii. p i 227 O v 714 H iii p i 69
July 18.	Safe conduct for William duke of Bavaria coming to England. *Westm* R. iii. p i. 227. O v 714 H iii p i 69
July 26	Power for William bp of Norwich, William earl of Huntingdon, Bartholomew de Burghersh, and sir Robert de Herle to treat for peace with France *The Tower of London* R iii. p i 227. O. v. 714 H. iii. p. i. 69
July 27.	Power for the said commissioners to prorogue the truce. *The Tower of London.* R iii. p i. 227 O v 715. H iii p i. 69.
July 27.	Licence to sir Richard de Totesham to pursue his right as to the lord of Garenseres, whom he took prisoner according to the law of arms *The Tower of London.* R iii. p. i. 228 O. v 716. H. iii. p. i. 70.

DATE	SUBJECT.
1351 Aug 1	Treaty between the Kings of England and Navarre R ɪɪɪ. p ɪ 228 O. v. 716. H. ɪɪɪ. p ɪ 70
Aug 1	Truce for 20 years with the towns on the coast of Castile and the county of Biscay. London. R ɪɪɪ p ɪ 228 O v 717 H ɪɪɪ p ɪ 70
Aug. 2.	The K. orders William Basset, John Mynyot, Peter de Richemond, and Nicholas Gower to examine the complaint of Hugh abp of Damascus that John abbot of " Bella Landa " and others stole a horse and deer from his park at Newstead, near Boghland Westm. R. ɪɪɪ. p. ɪ 229 O v 719 H ɪɪɪ p ɪ. 71
Aug 10	The K orders his admirals, Henry duke of Lancaster and the earl of Northampton, to publish the truce with Spain in the ports under their jurisdiction. Westm. R. ɪɪɪ. p ɪ. 229. O v 720 H. ɪɪɪ p i. 71.
Sept. 1	Richard earl of Arundel, William de Clynton, earl of Huntingdon, William de Shareshull, and John de Stonore are appointed to examine the petitions presented to Parliament by the abp. of Canterbury and the clergy of his province. The Tower of London. R. ɪɪɪ p ɪ 230. O v 721. H ɪɪɪ p ɪ 71
Sept. 4	Safe conduct for Joan wife of Charles de Bloys, the K's prisoner, to come to Calais to her husband The Tower of London. R. ɪɪɪ p ɪ. 230 O. v. 721. H. ɪɪɪ. p. ɪ. 72.
Sept. 4.	Power for Michael de Northburgh, archdeacon of Suffolk, the K.'s secretary, to receive security from Charles de Bloys for the conditions of his release. The Tower of London. R ɪɪɪ p ɪ 230 O v 721 H ɪɪɪ p ɪv 72
Sept 4	Power for Michael de Northburgh to confirm the truce lately concluded at Calais. The Tower of London R ɪɪɪ p ɪ 230. O v 722 H ɪɪɪ p. ɪ. 72.
Sept. 4	Power for Thomas bp of Durham, Henry de Percy, and Ralph de Nevill to receive an oath from David de Bruys for his going into and return from Scotland. The Tower of London R ɪɪɪ p ɪ 230 O. v 722. H ɪɪɪ p ɪ. 72
Sept. 4	Power for Henry de Percy, Ralph and Hugh de Nevill, and Ivo de Clynton to receive the oaths of the Scots. The Tower of London. R. ɪɪɪ. p. ɪ 231. O. v. 723. H. ɪɪɪ. p ɪ. 72
Sept 4.	Safe conduct for the bp of S Andrews, Patrick earl of March, William earl of Sutherland, Thomas earl of Angus, and William lord of Douglas, going to David de Bruys, the K's prisoner The Tower of London R. ɪɪɪ p. i. 231 O v 723 H ɪɪɪ. p ɪ 72
Sept. 5.	Safe conduct for John son and heir of the seneschal of Scotland, John de Dunbar, son and heir of the earl of March, and five others coming to England as hostages for David de Bruys The Tower of London R. ɪɪɪ p ɪ 231 O. v 724. H ɪɪɪ p ɪ 73
Sept 6	Writs to the constable of Nottingham Castle and the sheriff of Yorkshire to receive the hostages The Tower of London R. ɪɪɪ. p ɪ 231. O. v 725 H. ɪɪɪ p ɪ. 73
Sept. 11	Prorogation of the truce with France till 12 Sept 1352 R ɪɪɪ. p. ɪ. 232. O. v. 725. H. ɪɪɪ. p ɪ. 73
Sept 25	Protection for persons banished from Flanders for adherence to the K. Westm. R. ɪɪɪ. p ɪ 232 O v 727 H. ɪɪɪ p ɪ 74
Sept 28	Protection for the Hanse merchants in England whose goods have been arrested for their supposed complicity in the death of Richard Curteys of Bristol, at Lecluse [Sluys]. Westm. R ɪɪɪ p ɪ. 232
Oct. 1.	Order for the publication of the truce with France Westm R. ɪɪɪ p ɪ 233. O. v 727. H. ɪɪɪ p ɪ 74.
Oct 12	The K orders the mayor and commonalty of London to stay the action against John de Weston and Richard de Wycombe, who are charged with having granted the loan to the K. without the consent of their fellow citizens Westm. R ɪɪɪ p. i. 233.
Oct 20	The K. orders the mayor and sheriffs of London to publish certain articles Westm. R. ɪɪɪ p. i. 233
	Articles for the regulation of the sale of victuals in London R ɪɪɪ. p. ɪ 233.
Nov 3.	The K orders John de Coupeland, sheriff of Northumberland, to keep David de Brus, the K's prisoner, at Newcastle, if his surrender is not effected Letter bidding the inhabitants of Northumberland and the marches assist Henry de Percy and Ralph de Nevill in their charge concerning David de Brus. Westm R ɪɪɪ. p ɪ 234 O vɪ. 724-5 H. ɪɪɪ p ɪ 74.
Nov 3.	The K. orders the sheriff of Yorkshire and the constable of Nottingham Castle to keep the Scotch hostages. Westm R. ɪɪɪ p ɪ 234 O. v 728. H. ɪɪɪ. p ɪ 74
Nov. 6	The K deputes Sir William Stury and Sir William de Burton to receive the castles and fortresses in the Low Countries. Westm R. ɪɪɪ. p. ɪ 234.

A A 2

DATE.	SUBJECT
1351. Nov. 12.	Safe conduct for William duke of Bavaria, coming to England　*Westm.*　R. iii p 1 235　O v 728　H iii p 1 74
Nov 12	The K promises Matilda eldest daughter of the duke of Lancaster in marriage to the duke of Bavaria　*Westm.*　R. iii p 1 235　O v 729　H iii. p 1 74
Nov. 15.	Walter de Harewell, sergeant-at-arms, is ordered to provide five ships for the passage of the K.'s daughter Isabella to Gascony　*Westm.*　R iii p 1 235　O v 729. H iii. p 1 75
Nov 16	The K orders J bp of Lincoln to appoint another collecter of the tenth in place of the abbot of Croxton, whose house and church have been damaged by fire and who has lost several brethren by pestilence　*Westm*　R. iii p 1 235.　O v 729.　H iii p 1 75
Dec 1.	Power to Bernard Ezii, lord of Lebret, John de Cheversdon, seneschal of Gascony, and John Charnels, constable of Bordeaux, to engage Cenoille, count d'Astarac, for the K's service　*Westm*　R iii p 1 235.　O v 730　H iii. p 1 75
Dec 4.	The K promises that John de Beauchamp, prisoner in France, about to be released to obtain his ransom, shall not be prevented from returning to prison.　*Westm.*　R iii p i. 236.　O. v. 730　H iii. p 1 75.
Dec. 14 (?).	The K's ordinance relative to the dissensions between Margaret empress of the Romans and William duke of Bavaria concerning castles and fortresses in the parts of Holland and Seland, and he intimates that it is not his intention that the dukes of Brabant and Gueldres and the count of Flanders or their subjects shall be injured by his decision.　*Westm.*　R iii p. i 236　O v 731　H. iii. p. i. 75.
1352 Jan. 6.	The K forbids men-at-arms leaving the duchy of Aquitain　*Westm.*　R iii. p 1 236
Jan 20.	Thomas Dautry and Robert de Baildon, sergeants-at-arms, are appointed to provide ships for the passage of Bernard lord of la Bret to Gascony.　R iii p 1 236
Jan 27	The K orders Henry de Percy and Ralph de Nevill to allow certain Scots who are under the K's dominion, to enjoy the laws and customs of the time of Alexander formerly K. of Scotland　*Westm*　R iii p 1 237　O v 732　O v 732　H iii p 1 76
[Jan. 27]	Letter on the same subject to the chancellor and chamberlain of Berwick-upon-Tweed.　R iii p 1 237.　O v 732.　H iii p. 1 76.
Feb 1	Power for Thomas bp of Durham, Henry de Percy, and Ralph de Nevill to treat with the Scots for the ransom of David de Bruys and for a final peace.　*Westm*　R iii p 1 237.　O. v 733　H iii p 1 76
Feb 1	Safe conduct for Edward de Balliol, K. of Scotland, to come to England　*Westm.*　R iii. p 1 237　O v 733　H iii p 1 76
Feb. 3.	Safe conduct for one year for the ambassadors of the town of Pyse.　*Westm*　R. iii. p 1. 238.　O v 734.　H. iii. p 1 76
Feb. 6	The K orders William de Fifhide, John de Ingepenne, and Walter Chamberleyn, mayor of Winchester, to compel the return of those citizens of Winchester who have left the town to escape taxation　*Westm.*　R. iii p 1 238
Feb. 24.	Thomas Dautre and Walter de Harewell, sergeants-at-arms, are ordered to send ships of 40 tons and upwards to Southampton by Mid-Lent　*Westm*　R. iii p 1. 238.
March 6.	The K. releases the abbot of Gloucester from personal attendance at parliament　*Westm.*　R. iii p 1. 238.
March 6.	The K. forbids the exportation of victuals from the Isle of Wight　*Westm.*　R. iii. p. 1. 238
March 6.	The K. orders the men in the isle to be arrayed and beacons to be made on the hills.　*Westm.*　R. iii p 1 239.
March 6.	William de Dale, constable of Carisbrook Castle, is to order all persons to return to the island by March 25　*Westm*　R iii p. 1 239
March 6.	The K appoints Ralph earl of Stafford his lieutenant and captain in Aquitain.　*Westm.*　R. iii p 1 239
March 8.	Powers conferred on the earl of Stafford.　*Westm.*　R. iii p 1 239.
March 8.	Power for the earl of Stafford to make leagues and retain persons for the K.'s service　*Westm.*　R iii. p. 1 240.
March 9.	The K. of England to Alfonso K. of Portugal.　William le Palmere, of Rouen, arrested for piracy, says that he is a Lisbon merchant and was there when the act was committed, about which the K. requests information.　*Westm.*　R iii p 1. 240.

DATE	SUBJECT
1352. March 10	The K. orders Ralph earl of Stafford, captain of Aquitain, to assign lands to the lord of Lebret in compensation for Gensac, which he granted to the lord of Mochidan. *Westm.* R iii p. i. 240 O v. 734. H iii p. i. 77
March 16.	Safe conduct for the empress returning home from England *Westm* R iii p i 241 O v 735 H iii p i 77.
March 18.	Safe conduct for William, bp. of S Andrews, Patrick de Dumbarre, earl of March, Sir William de Lymyngeston, Robert de Irskin, and two others coming to Berwick to treat for the [liberation of David de Bruys. *Westm.* R. iii. p. i 241 O v. 736. H. iii. p i 77
March 26.	Commission to Michael de Northburgh, archdeacon of Suffolk, keeper of the privy seal, and Robert de Herle, captain of Calais, to receive the ransom of Charles de Blois *Westm.* R. iii p i 241. O v 736. H. iii p. i. 77.
March 28	The sheriff of York is ordered to send the Scotch hostages to Berwick to be released on the return of David de Bruys *Windsor.* R iii p i 241 O v 736. H iii p. i. 77.
March 28	John de Coupeland, sheriff of Northumberland, is ordered to receive David de Bruys, the K.'s prisoner, from the bp of Durham and the other commissioners, and to deliver up the hostages in his custody. *Windsor* R iii p i. 241. O. v 737 H iii p i 78.
	Secret instructions to Roger de Beauchamp relative to the imprisonment of David de Bruys He is to remain at large if it seem advisable. R iii p. i. 242. O. v. 737. H. iii. p i. 78
April 3.	Power for Ralph earl of Stafford, lieutenant of Aquitain, to appoint a seneschal and a constable of Bordeaux *Westm* R iii p i 242
April 20.	The K. orders the mayors and bailiffs of Dover and six other ports to prevent all persons leaving the kingdom, and to search persons entering the kingdom for anything prejudicial to the kingdom *Westm* R iii p i 242
April 20	Commission to Walter de Bentele, captain of Brittany, to survey the fortresses and provide for the security of the duchy *Windsor* R iii. p. i 242
May 6.	The K. desires the duke and commonalty of Genoa not to assist the K of France. *Westm.* R. iii p. i. 243 O v 738 H iii p i 78.
May 24	Commission to Arnald Sauvage, Walter Colpepir, Henry de Apulderfeld, and the sheriff of Kent to provide 120 archers 32 similar commissions *Westm* R. iii p i. 243
May 24	Henry duke of Lancaster and 16 others are ordered to array spearmen from their lands in Wales by June 17. *Westm* R iii p i 244
[May 24]	Writ to the prince of Wales to provide 700 spearmen R iii p. i. 244
June 14	William earl of Huntingdon and Bartholomew de Burghersh, constable of Dover Castle and warden of the Cinque Ports, are appointed to defend the coast of Kent from the expected attack by the French fleet 10 similar appointments. *Westm.* R. iii. p. i. 245.
June 18	Warrant to William Passelewe, master of the ship called *la Jerosalem*, to impress 80 sailors Similar warrants to 14 other masters of ships *Westm* R iii p i 245
June 20	Order for the renewal of the wax covering the body of Edward I. in Westminster Abbey. *Westm* R. iii. p. i 246. O. v 738 H iii. p. i 78.
June 20.	Safe conduct for Pontius de Morteyn, viscount of Danneye, the K.'s prisoner, coming to England *Westm* R iii. p. i 246
July 17.	Indenture for the liberation of William Douglas, the K.'s prisoner, who engages to serve the K *London* R iii p. i. 246 O v. 738. H. iii. p. i. 78.
July 24.	Ralph de Nevyll is ordered to deliver the castle and manor of the Hermitage in Scotland to William Douglas, late the K.'s prisoner. *Westm.* R. iii. p i. 247. O. v. 740. H iii. p i 79
July 25.	Protection for one year for Portuguese merchants to come to England, also for seven Portuguese masters of ships. *Westm.* R. iii. p. i. 247. O v. 740. H. iii. p i 79
July 28.	John Maynard is appointed warden of Brest Castle in Brittany. *Westm* R. iii. p i. 247. O v 741 H iii. p i. 79.
Aug 1	The K informs Alfonso K of Portugal that he has granted protection to his subjects. *Westm.* R iii p i 247 O v. 741 H. iii. p. i. 79.
Aug. 23.	Licence for Henry duke of Lancaster to leave the country to clear himself from the accusations of the duke of Brunswick. *Westm.* R. iii. p. i. 248. O. v. 742. H. iii. p. i 80.

DATE	SUBJECT.
1352 Aug 30.	Warrant to the collectors of the tenth and fifteenth in the East Riding of York to pay 200*l.* to Edward de Balliol, K. of Scotland. *Westm* R. III. p 1 248. O v 742. H. III. p 1 80
Sept 6.	Safe conduct for one year for Edward de Balliol, K of Scotland, coming to England by the K's order *Westm.* R III p 1 248 O v 742 H III p 1 80.
Sept. 6.	The K will grant a safe conduct to the ambassadors of the town of Pyse coming to obtain redress for a ship plundered at Sandwich. *Westm.* R. III p 1. 248. O. v. 743. H III p 1 80
Sept. 12.	The K. excuses J abp of Armagh from personal attendance at the parliament at Dublin, as he cannot go thither in safety with his cross borne before him. *Westm* R. III p. 1. 248 O. v 743. H III p 1 80
Oct 15.	Warrant for the payment of the annuity of 400 florins granted to Engelbert count of Mark. *Westm* R III p 1 249 O v 744 H III p 1. 80.
Oct 17	Bull of Clement [VI] appointing John bp. of Worcester to the abprick of York when vacant *Avignon* R. III p 1 249 O v 744 H III p 1 80
Oct 22	Bull of Clement [VI] appointing Reginald bp of S David's to the see of Worcester *Avignon* R III p 1 249 O v 745 H III p i 81
Nov 2.	Proclamation to be made in London against the mixing of old and new wine. *Westm.* R. III p 1. 249.
Dec 6.	Safe conduct for Hector Leche, valet of David de Bruys, prisoner in the Tower of London, to go to Scotland and return *Westm* R III p 1 250. O v. 746. H III p. 1. 81.
Dec. 10	Power for Andrew de Offord, archdeacon of Middlesex, and Sir John Avenel to treat with William duke of Bavaria *Westm* R. III p 1 250 O v. 746. H III p. 1. 81.
Dec 30	Safe conduct for the bp. of Vannes, the lord of Beaumanoir, and three others, who have come to treat for the ransom of Charles de Bloys, the K.'s prisoner. *Westm.* R III p 1 250. O v 746 H III p i. 81.
1353. Jan 20	The K forbids the exaction of first fruits by Hugh Pelegrim, papal nuncio. *Hertford.* R III p 1 250 O. v 747 H III p 1 81.
Jan. 28.	The K. forbids the exportation of corn, boards, iron, or victuals. *Westm.* R. III. p. 1. 250
Feb. 5.	Safe conduct for the servants of John de Clermont, of France, coming to prepare for his arrival *Westm.* R. III. p. 1 251
Feb 5	Safe conduct for John de Clermont coming to obtain justice for wrong done to him by John de Charnels. *Westm* R III p 1. 251.
Feb 8	Restitution of the temporalities to John de Thoresby, bp of Worcester, translated to York *Westm.* R III p 1 252
Feb 16	Protection for one year for Dominic and Sanchio Piers and two other Spanish merchants *Westm* R III p. 1. 252.
Feb. 17.	Treaty between the K and William duke of Bavaria, count of Holland and Zealand. *Westm* R III p 1 252.
Feb. 19	Commission to Simon abp of Canterbury, William bp of Norwich, Henry duke of Lancaster, Richard earl of Arundel, Guy de Bryan, lord of Lagherne, and Michael de Northburgh, archdeacon of Suffolk, keeper of the privy seal, to reform the peace with France. *Westm* R III p 1 253. O. v. 747. H. III. p 1 82
Feb. 24	The K forbids men-at-arms leaving Ireland *Westm* R. III. p. 1 253 O. v. 748. H III p. 1 82.
March 8	The K. promises that the treaty with the Scots shall not prejudice the rights of Edward de Balliol *Westm* R. III p. 1. 253 O v 748 H III. p 1. 82.
March 10	Safe conduct for Walter bp. of Vannes and seven others coming to England to treat for the ransom of Charles de Bloys *Westm* R III p 1 254. O v 749 H III p. 1 82.
March 10	Truce with France until Aug. 1. R III p 1 254 O. v. 749. H. III. p 1 82.
March 20	The K orders the publication of the truce by the warden of the Cinque Ports, the admirals, and the sheriffs of London *Westm* R III p 1. 255 O v 752 H III p 1 83
· March 20 *	The K has received letters of the pope [Innocent VI.] announcing his election, and he congratulates him. *Westm.* R. III p 1 259 O v 754 H III p. 1. 84
March 20.	The K will attend to the pope's request relative to the liberation of Charles [de Bloys], duke of Brittany *Westm* R. III p. i 255. O. v 753. H III p i 84.

* Misdated 20th June

DATE.	SUBJECT.
1353 March 26	Declaration that Nicholas de Hethe, clerk, who accused Henry de Ingelby and others of imprisoning him to make him resign his benefices, was arrested for fraudulently obtaining money on the promise of procuring a general indulgence *Westm.* R iii p i 255.
March 28.	Indenture between the K. and Henry de Brisele, master of the mint in the Tower of London, for the coinage of nobles, groats, &c. *Westm* R iii p i 256
March 30.	In accordance with a petition presented by the clergy in the late parliament, the K. promises that he and his heirs will not present to benefices falling vacant while the temporalities of bishoprics are in the K.'s hand. *Westm.* R iii p i. 256.
April 1.	The K orders the sheriffs of London and Middlesex to prevent any molestation in the city or suburbs to the abp of York, the K.'s chancellor, for carrying his cross while engaged in the duties of his office of chancellor. *Westm.* R iii p i 257. O v 753. H iii p. i 84
April 4	John Avenel is appointed lieutenant and captain in Brittany and Poictou. *Westm.* R iii p i 257. O. v. 754. H iii p. i. 84.
April 17	Robert de Gersyngdon, parson of Rickinghale, Godfrey Folejaumbe, and two others are appointed collectors in Ireland of the fees due to Thomas de Beauchamp, earl of Warwick, marshal of Ireland *Westm* R iii p i. 257. O v 754 H iii p i 84.
April 20.	James d'Audele, of Helegh, released for life from attending parliament and from military service. *Westm* R iii p. i. 257 O iv. 74. H iii p i 84.
April 23.	The K orders Thomas de Rokeby, justiciary of Ireland, to allow R. abp of Armagh to come to England. *Windsor.* R iii p i 257.
May 1	The K orders his officers in Aquitain to observe his grant to the commonalty of Bazas. *Westm* R iii p i. 258.
May 2,	The K orders his treasurer to deliver two dies to the abp. of York for his coinage at York *Westm.* R iii p i 258 O v. 755. H iii p i 84.
May 3.	The K orders Reginald de Cobbeham and Robert de Herle, captain of Calais, to allow wager of battle to John de Spaigne, who is accused of treason by a woman of Calais. *Westm* R iii p i 258 O. v. 755. H iii p i 85.
May 16.	Protection for Anselm de la Viscoigne, servant of Charles de Bloys, going abroad *Westm.* R iii p i 258
May 20	The K. orders the sheriffs of London to forbid tournaments Similar order to 16 other sheriffs *Westm.* R iii p i 258.
June 18	Protection for Norman le Viscounte and Hugh de Redynges, servants of Charles de Bloys, duke of Brittany, to buy victuals for his sons, who are in the K.'s custody *Westm.* R iii p i 259. O v 756 H iii. p i 84
June 20 *	The K congratulates Innocent VI on his creation. *Westm.* R. iii p i. 259. O. v 752. H iii p i. 84 *See March 20*
June 29.	Reginald de Cobham is appointed captain of Calais, Guisnes, Mark, Colne, Oye, and Sandgate *Westm* R iii p i 259.
July 1.	Thomas Ferre, sergeant-at-arms, and John Ramme are appointed to select 100 mariners in Kent. Three similar commissions *Westm* R iii p. i 260
July 5	Safe conduct until Michaelmas for the merchants of Portugal and Algarve. *Westm* R iii p i. 260 O v. 756. H iii p i 85
July 6.	The sheriff of Northumberland is ordered to forbid the conveyance of wool, fleeces, and hides to Berwick or Scotland. *Westm* R iii p i 260.
July 7	Peter de Nuttle is ordered to convey David de Bruys from London to Newcastle-upon-Tyne Letters to John de Coupeland, sheriff of Northumberland, to receive him, and to the constable of the Tower of London to deliver him up *Westm* R iii p i 260 O v 756. H iii. p. i 85
July 10	Power for Simon, abp of Canterbury and five others to prorogue the truce with France till Martinmas *Windsor.* R iii p i 260. O. v. 757 H iii p i. 85
July 13	The K sends Richard Lenglish to those captains who refuse to obey John Avenel, captain of Brittany *Westm* R iii. p i 261
July 18	The K. orders the sheriff of Yorkshire to deliver to Henry de Brisele and William Hunt, keeper of the exchange at York, houses fit for a mint *Westm.* R iii p i. 261.
July 25.	William de Rothewell, keeper of the exchange at the Tower of London, is ordered to deliver standards and trestles for coining to Henry de Brisele. *Westm* R iii p i 261.

* Evidently a mistake for 20 March

DATE	SUBJECT
1353. July 26	Prorogation of the treaty with France concluded at Guisnes till a fortnight after Michaelmas, and of the truce until Martinmas *Paris* R iii p. i 262 O v. 757. H iii p i 86
July 30.	Safe conduct until Christmas for Joan wife of David de Bruys, to come to England *Westm* R iii. p i 262 O v 758 H iii p i 86
Aug 6.	Safe conduct for Edward K of Scotland for one year, coming to England by the K's command *Westm* R iii p i 262 O v. 759. H iii. p i. 86
Aug. 6.	Warrant to the abbot of S. Mary's, York, collector of the biennial tenth to pay 100l. to Edward de Balhol, K. of Scotland. *Westm.* R iii p i 262 O v 759. H iii. p i 86
Aug 18	The K orders John de Boulton, chancellor and chamberlain of Berwick, and John de Coupeland, sheriff of Roxburgh, to seize the lands of Duncan Magdowaill, who has joined the K.'s enemies contrary to his oath. *Woodstock.* R iii p. i. 262. O v. 759 H iii. p i 86
Sept 24.	The K to Reginald de Cobham, captain of Calais, refuses a safe conduct to French ambassadors to go to Scotland, and orders him to let no foreigners pass without the K's knowledge *Westm* R iii p. i 262
Oct. 14	Power for Henry duke of Lancaster to treat with William duke of Bavaria. *Westm.* R iii p i 263 O v 760 H iii p i 86
Oct 14	Power for him to mediate between the duke and the empress Margaret *Westm* R iii p i 263 O. v. 760 H. iii p i 86
Oct. 14	Power for Henry de Percy and Ralph de Nevill to treat with Elizabeth, widow of William Douglas, for the surrender of Hermitage castle. *Westm.* R iii. p i.263. O. v 760 H iii p i 87
Oct. 14	The K forbids men-at-arms leaving the realm *Westm* R iii p i 263
Oct 15	Power for Thomas bp of Durham, Gilbert bp of Carlisle, William de Bohun, earl of Northampton, and five others to treat with David de Brus and others, for his liberation and for a final peace *Westm.* R iii p i 264 O v 761 H iii p. i 87.
Oct. 15.	Safe conduct for Catalonian merchants coming to England. *Westm.* R iii p i. 264 O v 762 H iii p i 87.
Oct 26	Power to Reginald de Cobham, captain of Calais, to prorogue the truce with France for 15 days *Westm.* R iii p i 264 O v 762 H iii p i 87
Oct 20	Treaty with the merchants of Portugal for intercourse with England for 50 years *London* R iii p. i. 264 O v 763 H iii p i 88
Oct 20	Letters of acquittance of William, marquis of Juliers and earl of Cambridge, for the K's grants and debts to him, and promise of the K that the alliances between them shall remain in force *Westm.* R iii p i. 265 O v 764 H iii. p i 88
Oct 25	Notarial attestation of the declaration by the marquis of Juliers that he signed the above-mentioned letters of his own free will *London* R iii p i. 266. O v 766 H iii p i 89
Oct. 26.	Power to Reginald de Cobham to prorogue the truce with France till a fortnight after Martinmas. *Westm.* R. iii. p. i. 266.
Oct 29	Treaty of peace between the commonalty of Bayonne and the inhabitants of the coast of Castile Ratification dated *Westm*, 9 *July.* R iii p i. 266 O v. 767. H iii. p i 89.
Oct. 30.	The marquis of Juliers promises to return to the K before June 24 the letters patent granting him wages while on the K's service *Westm.* R. iii. p. i. 268. O. v. 772. H iii p. i. 91
Oct. 30	Licence to' John de Crespy to go to France, and a release from his fealty if he is unable to return. *Westm* R iii p i 268.
Nov 6	Power for Simon abp of Canterbury, William bp of Norwich, and five others to treat with France *Westm* R. iii p i 268 O. v 772 H iii p i. 91
Nov 8	The K informs the pope that he is about to send ambassadors to treat for peace. *Westm.* R iii. p i 269. O v 772 H iii p i 91
Nov 20	John Avenel, captain of Brittany, is ordered to publish the truce till Feb. 2, concluded with Charles de Bloys Credence for John de Ellerton to the K.'s officers in Brittany. *Westm.* R. iii. p. i 269 O v 773 H iii p. i 92.

DATE	SUBJECT
1353. Nov 20.	The K. appoints John de Bedeford to collect certain tolls for the repair of the road leading from Temple Bar to Westminster Abbey. *Westm* R iii p i 269 O v 774 H iii p i 92
Nov 20	Safe conduct for Hector de Balliol, a French knight, to come to England to clear himself from the accusations of Thomas de Rippesford *Westm.* R iii. p. i. 270. O. v 775 H. iii. p i 92
Dec. 21.	Treaty between the men of Bayonne and of Biscay. R iii p i 270 O. v 776 H. iii p. i 93
1354 Jan 14	Protection for Nicholas Conte, who is about to fight a duel. *The Tower of London.* R iii p i 270 O v 776 H iii p i 93
Jan 26.	Power for Henry duke of Lancaster to treat with the K. of Navarre. *The Tower of London* R iii. p. i 271 O v 777 H iii p i 93
Jan 30	Safe conduct for John Meyngre, *alias* Bussigand, the K.'s prisoner, to go to the Holy Land *Westm* R iii p i 271 O iv 776 H iii p i 93
[Jan 30]	Licence to John Meyngre, *alias* Bussigand, the K.'s prisoner, to import 600 casks of Gascon wine. R iii p i 271 O. v. 778. H iii p i 93
Jan 30	Safe conduct till a fortnight after Easter for Charles de Bloys to go to Brittanny *Westm* R. iii p i 271.
[Jan. 30]	The K orders Thomas Durannt, sergeant-at-arms, to provide ships for Charles de Bloys. R. iii p. i 271
Feb. 1.	The K orders the seneschal of Gascony and the constable of Bordeaux to publish and enforce the statute against engrossing and forestalling Gascon wine *Westm.* R iii p i 272
[Feb 1]	The K orders the pound, and not the florin, to be used in mercantile transactions in Gascony R iii p. i. 272.
[Feb 1.]	The K orders the constable of Bourdeaux to reduce the expenses of the mint there R iii p i 272
Feb. 10	Writ to the sheriffs of London, forbidding pilgrims to leave the kingdom. *Westm.* R. iii p i 272
Feb. 20	The K forbids all men and pilgrims leaving the kingdom *Westm* R. iii p i 272
March 4.	The K. orders the sheriff of Carlisle to arrest Scotch spies. *Westm.* R iii p i 273
March 6.	John Gybon is appointed admiral of the fleet going to Normandy under Henry duke of Lancaster *Westm* R iii p. i. 273.
March 10.	The K orders John Pavely, prior of S John of Jerusalem in England, to repair the bridge of the New Temple. *Westm* R iii p i 273 O. v. 778 H. iii p i 94
March 14.	Protection for the lady Hazagana, Roland de Redebourne, Bernard de Kenalro of Alexandria, lord Nicholas de Checole of Cairo, and the masters and crews of three "taritæ" now anchored at the Channel Islands *Westm.* R iii p i 274.
March 18	The K. summons to England William de Bromle, treasurer of Dublin, John de Carru, escheator of Ireland, and John de Rednesse, one of his justices· *Westm.* R iii p i 274
March 18.	Thomas de Holand is appointed the K.'s lieutenant and captain of Brittany and Poictou. *Westm.* R iii p. i. 274.
March 18.	Grant to Thomas de Holand of the revenues of the duchy. *Westm.* R. iii p i. 274
March 18	The K orders William de Hameldon and William Walkelate, serjeants-at-arms, to convey ships from London and the Medway to join the fleet at Plymouth. *Westm.* R iii p. i 274.
March 18.	The admiral of the North, or John de Haddon, is ordered to provide three ships for carrying to London from Newcastle or Hertipole the victuals of the bp of Durham, who is coming to parliament *Westm* R iii p i 275 O v 778 H iii p i 94.
March 19.	Thomas de Roos, of Dounesby, is appointed mayor of Bourdeaux Intimation thereof to the seneschal of Gascony, and the constable and commonalty of Bourdeaux *Westm.* R. iii p. i. 275.
March 20	Sir William Stury is appointed warden of Guernsey, Jersey, Sark, and Alderney. *Westm.* R. iii. p. i. 275.
March 23.	The sheriffs of London are ordered to forbid the sale of cloths before they are examined by the alnager. *Westm* R. iii. p. i. 275.

DATE.	SUBJECT.
1354 March 30	Power to William bp of Norwich, William de Clynton, earl of Huntingdon, Michael de Northburgh, canon of York, keeper of the privy seal, and Reginald de Cobeham, captain of Calais, to treat for a final peace or truce with France, and for the renunciation of the K.'s claims　*Westm.*　R. iii p. i 275.　O. v. 779　H. iii p. i. 94.
April 1	The K releases Roger David and Joan de Rosterven, viscountess of Rohan, from subsidies and aids on their lands　*Westm*　R. iii p. i 276　O v. 780　H iii p i. 94
April 1	The K grants to Roger David, the castle, castellany, and town of Kemenetguengant, and the castle of Pestyngen.　*Westm*　R. iii p. i 276　O v. 780–1.　H iii. p. i. 94–5
April 6	Truce with France until April 1　Thomas de Holand, captain of Brittany, and the seneschal of Gascony are ordered to publish it　*Before Guisnes.*　R iii p. i 276.　O v. 781–784　H iii p i 96
May 18.	Arnald de Duroforti, lord of Fespuch, and Pontius de Belleville, lord of Roquetorn, are appointed conservators of the truce in Aquitan　Six similar commission for the Landes, the Bordelais, Saintouge, Perigord, and Agen.　*Westm*　R iii p. i. 277.　O. v. 784.　H iii p i 96
May 20	The K orders the seneschal of Gascony and the constable of Bourdeaux to pay the annuity of 100l. granted by the duke of Lancaster and the earl of Stafford to Blanche de Foix, "Capitalesse" de Buch, as recompense for her services in victualling S. Jean d'Angely　*Westm*　R iii p. i 278　O v 785　H iii p i 96
June 6.	Protection for John de Aldenardo, Cistercian monk, agent of cardinal William bp of Frascati　*Westm.*　R iii. p i 278　O v 786　H iii p i 96
June 10	The custody of the castellany of Kymperelle is committed to Roger David.　Intimation thereof to Thomas de Holand, captain of Brittany　*Wetm*　R iii p i. 278　O v. 786　H iii p i 96
June 12	The K orders the renewal of the wax covering the corpse of Edward I in Westminster Abbey　*Westm.*　R. iii p. i 278　O v 786　H iii p i 97
June 16	The K. orders the sheriff of Norfolk to assist William de Stretford in selecting eight carpenters and eight masons for the works at Guisnes, near Calais.　*Westm.*　R iii p i 279.
June 18	Safe conducts for William bp of S Andrews, the bp of Brechin, the earl of Sutherland, Patrick de Dunbarre, earl of March, and four others to come to Newcastle to treat for the liberation of David de Bruys, the K.'s prisoner　*Westm.*　R. iii. p. i. 279.　O. v 787.　H. iii. p i 97
June 18.	Power for Thomas bp of Durham, Gilbert bp. of Carlisle, William de Bohun, earl of Northampton, and six others, to treat with the above-named persons　*Westm*　R. iii p. i 279　O v 787　H iii p i. 97.
June 30.	The K promises to Edward K of Scotland that the present negotiations shall not be to his prejudice if the treaty be not concluded　*Westm*　R iii p i. 279.　O v. 788.　H iii p i 97
July 1	Grant to Gilbert de Pelagrua, lord of Aymet, of five years respite for doing homage, as his castle of Somensac is on the enemy's frontier.　*Westm.*　R. iii p i 280.　O v 789.　H iii p i 98
July 5	Protection for one year for Edward K of Scotland　*Westm*　R. iii. p i. 280　O v. 789.　H iii p i 98
July 8	The K informs the captain and council of Genoa that he has assigned the duty on 1,000 sacks of wool for the redress of injuries to Genoese ships　*Westm*　R iii p i 280　O v 789　H iii. p i 98
July 9.	Inspeximus and confirmation of the treaty between the men of Bayonne and of Castille.　*Westm.*　R iii p i 280　O v 790　H iii p i 98
July 9	Inspeximus and confirmation of the treaty between Bayonne and the county of Biscay.　*Westm.*　R. iii. p i 280.　O v. 790.　H iii p i. 98
July 10	Commission to Ralph de Bokkyngg, William le Heir of Dersham, and four others, to inquire into the use of measures which differ from the standards at Bury S Edmunds and elsewhere in Suffolk　*Westm*　R iii p i 281.
July 13.	Agreement for the ransom of David de Brus for 90,000 marks, payable in nine years, during which time there is to be a truce, including Edward Balliol ; 20 hostages to be given.　*Newcastle-upon-Tyne.*　R. iii p i 281　O v. 791　H iii. p i 98
July 18.	Proclamations forbidding tournaments to be held in London, Yorkshire, Herefordshire, and Huntingdonshire.　*Westm.*　R iii p. i. 282

DATE	SUBJECT.
1354 July 20	The K. orders Thomas de Holand, captain of Brittany, to allow Walter de Bentele and his wife Johanna de Belleville, lady of Chuzon and Blengi, to hold the castellany of Pount Calet, and the parishes of Beaubri and Questeynt. *Westm.* R. iii p. i 282
July 26	Obligation to Bernard Ezil, lord of Lebret, for 1,672*l* 5*s* 2½*d* to be paid a fortnight after Easter *Westm.* R. iii p. i 283 O. v. 793. H. iii. p. i. 99.
Aug. 28	Power for William bp of Norwich, Michael bp of London, Henry duke of Lancaster, Richard earl of Arundel, Bartholomew de Burghersh, and Guy de Bryan, lord of Lagherne, to treat with the French ambassadors before the pope *Rockingham* R. iii p. i 283 O. v. 794 H. iii p. i 100
Aug. 28.	Power for the same persons to treat for a final peace and for the renunciation of the K.'s claims, and for the submission of the K.'s dominions in France to the jurisdiction of the pope. *Westm.* R. iii. p. i. 283 O. v 794 H. iii p. i 100.
[Aug. 28.]	Power for them to submit to the pope's decision R. iii p. i. 284 O. v. 795 H. iii. p. i 100.
Aug. 28	Power given by the abps and bps of England to Richard de Wymondeswold, Richard de Drax, William de Loughteburgh, Edmund de Grymesby, and John de Wellewyk, to consent to the treaty in their names. *Westm.* R. iii. p. i. 284 O. v 795. H. iii p. i 100
Aug. 28.	Similar power given by the K.'s sons, Edward duke of Cornwall, Lionel earl of Ulster, and John earl of Richmond, and 85 noblemen to William de Wymondeswold and others *Westm.* R. iii p. i 284. O. v. 797. H. iii p. i 101.
Oct. 5.	Confirmation of the treaty for the ransom of David de Bruys. *Westm.* R. iii p. i 285. O. v. 799 H. iii. p. i 101.
Oct 5	Confirmation of the same treaty by Edward prince of Wales *Westm.* R. iii p. i 285 O. v 800 H. iii. p. i 102
Oct. 5.	Power for William de Bohun, earl of Northampton, constable of England, to swear to the said treaty for the K. *Westm.* R. iii. p. i 286 O. v 800 H. iii p. i 102
Oct. 5.	Power also given to the above-named earl to swear for the prince of Wales. Similar powers for the duke of Lancaster and earl of Arundel *Westm.* R. iii p. i 286 O. v 801 H. iii. p. i 102
Oct 15	Indemnity for the bps. of Durham and Carlisle and the other commissioners for the liberation of David de Bruys from prison *Westm.* R. iii. p. i 286 O. v. 801. H iii p. i 102
Oct. 5.	Power for them to receive David de Bruys from John de Coupeland, sheriff of Northumberland, and to deliver him from prison *Westm.* R. iii p. i. 286 O. v 802. H iii p. i. 103
Oct. 5.	The K orders Ralph de Nevill to liberate the son and heir of the earl of March, and receive the son of the seneschal of Scotland, on the payment of the first 10,000 marks for the ransom of Bruys *Westm.* R. iii p. i 286 O. v 802 H iii p. i. 103
Oct. 5.	Power for the bps of Durham and Carlisle and nine others to perform and complete the treaty with Scotland *Westm.* R. iii p. i 287. O. v. 803 H iii p. i 103.
Oct 8.	The K orders the sheriffs of Yorkshire, Lincolnshire, and Nottinghamshire to receive the Scotch hostages *Westm.* R. iii p. i 287 O. v 804 H iii p. i. 104
Oct. 8.	Restitution of Hermitage Castle and the vail of Liddell to Elizabeth widow of William de Douglas. *London.* R iii p. i 287 O. v. 804 H iii p. i. 104
Oct. 8.	Power to Ralph de Nevill to restore the hostages for the late William de Douglas The K. orders the abbot of S Mary's, York, and the prior of Whatton to deliver them to Nevill *Westm.* R. iii p. i 288 O. v 805 H. iii. p. i 104
Oct. 8.	The K appoints Henry de Percy, Ralph de Nevill, William baron of Graystok, and John de Coupeland, conservators of the truce with Scotland in the east marches Similar appointment of Thomas de Lucy, William de Dacre, and Thomas de Musgrave for the west marches. *Westm.* R. iii p. i 288 O. v 805. H iii p. i 104.
Oct. 10.	Writ to John de Coupeland, sheriff of Northumberland, to deliver David de Bruys up to the commissioners for his liberation *Westm.* R. iii p. i 288. O. v. 806 H iii p. i 104
Oct. 15.	Power for Richard Tempest, constable of Berwick Castle, and John de Boulton, chamberlain of Berwick, to receive the oaths of the Scotch ambassadors *Westm.* R. iii p. i 288 O. v. 807. H. iii. p. i. 105.

DATE	SUBJECT
1354. Oct 15	The K orders John de Coupeland, sheriff of Northumberland, to warn the barons and knights of the county to be present at Newcastle at the liberation of David de Bruys. *Westm.* R. iii p i 289 O v 807 H iii p i 105
Oct 17	Safe conduct for the Scotch hostages at the liberation of David de Bruys *Westm.* R iii p. i 289 O v 807 H iii p i 105
Oct. 28.	Licence to William Heroun to go to Scotland for wager of battle against John Walayse and William Prudhomme *Westm* R iii p i 289. O v. 808 H. iii p i 105.
Oct 30	Power for William bp of Norwich, Michael bp elect of London, Bernard Ezii, lord of Lebret, Guy de Brian, lord of Laghern, William de Pomeris, Bertrand lord of Montferrand, and Gerard de Puy to treat before the pope concerning the K's castles and lands in France. *Westm* R iii p i. 289. O v 808 H iii p i 105
Nov 1	The K orders the dean and chapter of S Andrew's, Bourdeaux, to fine those who bring persons before the ecclesiastical courts on false charges *Westm* R iii p i 290 O. v 809. H iii. p i 106
Nov 6	The K orders Bartholomew de Burgherssh, constable of Dover Castle and warden of the Cinque Ports, to prevent persons leaving England from Mergate and other private places *Westm* R. iii p i 290.
Nov 10.	Safe conduct till June 24 for Charles de Bloys the K's prisoner to go to Brittany and return *Westm* R iii p i 290 O v. 809 H iii p i 106
Nov 10.	Safe conducts for John viscount of Rohan, Theobald lord of Rochefort, and 14 others to go to Brittany, and to return as hostages if Charles de Bloys is unable to return *Westm.* R iii p i 290 O v 810 H iii p i 106
Nov. 11.	Truce with Charles de Bloys, the K's prisoner, until June 24 *Westm* R iii p i 291. O v 811 H iii p i. 106
Nov. 12.	The K appoints Roger David and William Smale to provide ships for the passage of Roger David to Brittany *Westm* R. iii p i 291 O v 811. H iii. p. i. 107
Nov 22.	Treaty for the ransom of David de Bruys *Berwick* R. iii. p i 291. O v 812. H. iii p i 107
Nov 30	The sheriff of Southamptonshire is ordered to publish the statute for the regulation of measures *Westm* R iii. p. i 291
Dec 4	Proclamation to be made throughout England for the regulation of the price of wine. *Westm* R iii p i 292
Dec 5.	Confirmations of the treaty of Berwick for the liberation of David de Bruys by the K. and the prince of Wales *Westm* R iii p i 293 O v 812. H iii p i 105.
1355 Jan 4	The K orders Reginald de Cobham, captain of Calais, to observe the truce with France, and to demand its observance from the French admiral and the captains of the frontiers. *Hampstead* R iii p i 293
Jan 20	The K forbids the exportation of horses *Westm* R. iii p i 293
Jan 21	The K. appoints Gilbert Mason to purchase 1,000 qrs of lime in Kent for the works at Calais. *Westm* R iii p i 293
Jan 22	Protection for Roger de Beauchamp and for 10 persons in his retinue. *Westm.* R. iii. p i 294
Jan 23	Roger de Beauchamp is appointed captain of Calais, Guisnes, Mark, Colne, Oye, and Sandgate *Westm* R iii p. i. 294
Jan 30	The K orders the mayor and sheriffs of London to compel vintners and taverners to expose their wines for sale at the regulated prices *Westm* R. iii p. i. 294
Feb 4	The K orders John de Stretele, constable of Bourdeaux, to deliver the customs due to the duchy of Brittany to Thomas de Holand, captain of Brittany *Westm.* R iii. p. i 295. O v 813. H iii p i 107
Feb 6	The K. forbids pilgrims leaving the kingdom. *Westm.* R iii p. i 295.
Feb 8	Thomas de Holand is appointed lieutenant of the K and the duke of Brittany, and captain in Brittany and Poictou *Westm* R. iii p i. 295.
Feb. 14	The K. orders the mayor and jurats of Bourdeaux to allow those persons employed in the K's mint to enjoy their privileges as burgesses *Westm* R iii. p i. 295.
Feb. 16	The K orders the seneschal of Gascony to maintain the right of William Bernard, lord of Dornon, to the barony of Camparian *Westm* R iii. p i 296.
March 5	John de Beauchamp of Warwick is appointed admiral of the fleet from the Thames westward, and Robert de Morley of the fleet northward. *Westm,* R. iii. p. i. 296.

DATE	SUBJECT
1355 March 8	The K orders Adam Purfde and Peter de Grymmesby to deliver the priory of Burstall to his eldest daughter Isabel *Westm.* R III p 1. 296
[March 8.]	Warrants to Thomas Ughtred and John de Botherhy to pay annuities of 20 marks and 100s. to the K's daughter Isabel R III. p. i. 296.
March 10.	The K orders Robert de Ledred, Walter de Harewell, and Richard de Bosevill, sergeants-at-arms, to arrest ships for the passage of Thomas de Beauchamp, earl of Warwick, and others to Gascony *Westm* R III p 1 297
March 12.	The sheriff of Northumberland is ordered to forbid all persons taking the new Scotch money, which is of less value than the English. *Westm.* R III p 1 207 O v 813. H III p 1. 107
March 15.	John de Chyveryston is appointed seneschal of Gascony *Westm* R III p 1 297
March 15.	The K. orders Richard de Stafford, Henry Grene, and his other justices at Oxford to remove Richard de Williamescote from the office of sheriff of Oxford and Berks. *Westm* R III. p 1 297
April 2	Safe conduct for John bp of Elne [Eluensis Elnensio ?] and Andruynus, abbot of Clugny, papal nuncios *Woodstock.* R. III p 1 297. O. v 814 H III p i 108
April 14.	The exportation of corn, except to Calais, is forbidden. *Westm.* R. III. p i. 298.
April 18.	Bartholomew de Burgherssh, constable of Dover Castle and warden of the Cinque Ports, Roger de Northwode, Arnald Sauvage, and Stephen de Valoignes are appointed wardens of the coast of Kent *Westm* R III p 1 298
April 27	Richard de Cortenhale and Robert de Baildon are appointed to arrest ships of 20 tons and upwards from the Thames to Lynn, and bring them to Southampton by June 11 for the conveyance of Edward Prince of Wales to Gascony. Three similar commissions *Westm.* R III p 1 298
April 28	The K sends William Walkelate to bring a great ship from Sluys to England. *Westm* R III p 1 299
May 4.	The K. orders the sheriff of Lincolnshire to issue a proclamation forbidding the false rumours spread by merchants, that foreigners are not allowed to make cloth *Westm* R III. p 1 299.
May 6.	The K orders the sheriff of Cornwall to provide clayes and bridges for the transport of horses for the passage of the prince of Wales Similar warrants to the sheriffs of Devon and Southampton *Westm* R III p 1 299 O v. 814 H III. p. 1. 108.
May 13.	The K. orders his officers in Ireland to protect Maurice FitzThomas, earl of Desmond, and his possessions *Westm* R. III p 1 300 O v 815 H. III p 1 108
May 15.	Submission of the university of Oxford to the decision of the K in their disputes with the town. *Oxford.* R. III p 1 300
May 18	Licence to the inhabitants of Libourne to sell wine to English merchants at their town. *Westm.* R III. p 1 300
May 18.	The K informs the seneschal of Gascony and the constable of Bourdeaux of the above licence *Westm.* R III p 1 301
May 19.	Safe conduct for one year for Edward K of Scotland coming to England by the K's command *Westm.* R III p 1 301 O v 815 H III p 1 108.
May 19.	Submission of the mayor and commonalty of Oxford to the K's decision *Oxford* R III p. 1 301.
[May 19]	The K , at the request of the chancellor and others of the university of Oxford, orders the sheriff of Oxford to receive certain prisoners named by them, and liberate them on bail R. III p 1 301
May 25.	Confirmation of the inspeximus by sir John de Chiverston, seneschal of Aquitain, dated Reule, 10 Dec 1354, of a grant by the duke of Lancaster of certain tolls to the commonalty of Libourne, for the repairs of their fortifications, dated Bergerac, 14 Aug. 1346 *Westm.* R III. p 1 302.
May 27.	The K appoints Thomas de Hoggeshawe, lieutenant of John de Beauchamp, to accompany the fleet of the prince of Wales. *Westm.* R III p. 1 302.
May 28	Warrant to William Baret, master of the ship called *la Juliane*, to arrest 36 mariners Seven similar warrants *Westm* R. III. p 1 302 O v 816 H III p 1 108.
May 30	Safe conducts for Raynfrid le Veir, precentor of Dol, and Robert de S. Pierre, knight, coming to England in the company of Charles de Bloys, the K.'s prisoner *Westm.* R III p. 1 303. O. v 816. H III. p 1 108

DATE.	SUBJECT.
1355 June 1	The K. informs the abps and bps. of England that as the French ambassadors have refused to confirm what had been agreed on, he determines to renew the war, and desires them to pray for his success *Westm.* R m p ı 303. O v 816 H m p ı 109
June 6.	The K orders the mayor and sheriffs of London to appraise the armour at the armourers' shops, as they are asking exorbitant prices *Westm* R. ni. p ı. 303. O. v. 817. H. ın p ı 109
June 6.	Similar order to the mayor and sheriffs and Henry Picard, the K.'s butler, touching vintners *Westm.* R m p ı. 303.
June 11	The K has restored the privileges of the university of Oxford, and granted a general pardon, and orders the masters to resume their lectures *Westm* R m p. i 304.
June 12.	The K congratulates the emperor Charles [IV.] on his coronation at Rome last Easter. *The Tower of London* R. m p ı 304. O v 818 H m p ı 109
June 28	Order for the renewal of the wax around the body of Edward I. in Westminster Abbey. *Westm* R m p ı 304 O v 818 H. m p ı 109
July 1	The K receives the homage of Hugh de Dacre (who has married Elizabeth de Douglas), for Hermitage castle and Liddesdale. *Westm.* R. m. p ı 304 O v 818. H. m. p ı 109
July 1	The K appoints, as regents during his absence, his son Thomas, Simon abp. of Canterbury, John abp of York, the chancellor, William bp of Winchester, treasurer, Richard earl of Arundel, and Bartholomew de Burgherssh *Northfleet* R m p ı. 305
July 6	Grant to John de Greyly, captal de Bogio [Buch], of the K's rights in the towns of Bénauges, Ilas, and other places Intimation thereof to the seneschal of Gascony and the constable of Bourdeaux *Westm* R m p ı 305 O v 819 H m. p ı '110.
July 8	Grant to William de Montacute, earl of Salisbury, of respite for his debts in Gascony. *Westm* R m. p i 305 O v. 820 H. m p ı 110
July 8	Power for Michael bp of London, Franco de Hale, Roger de Beauchamp, captain of Calais, and Andrew de Offord, archdeacon of Middlesex, to treat with Peter abp of Rouen, and Peter duke of Bourbon. *Westm* R m p ı 305 O v 820 H. m. p ı 110
July 8	Maurice FitzThomas, earl of Desmond, is appointed justiciary of Ireland, with an annuity of 500*l*. Intimation thereof to the people of Ireland, the K's officers, and Thomas de Rokeby, late justiciary *Westm.* R m p ı 306.
July 10	Release to William earl of Ulster, James earl of Ormond, and the other sureties for the earl of Desmond *Westm.* R m. p ı 306
July 10.	The K informs Alfonso K of Castile that he has retained Martin de la Gytarye, master of the ship called *La S. Antoyne de Gyteria* *Westm.* R m p ı. 306. O v 821 H. m p ı 110
July 10	Resumption of the grant of the castellany of Kemenetguengant Castle of Pestynyen and the vill of Kymperelle to Roger David. *Westm.* R m p ı. 306. O. v 821. H m. p ı. 110
June 10	Grant of the revenues of Britany to Thomas de Holand, captain of Brittany. *Westm.* R m p. ı. 307 O v 822 H m p ı. 111.
July 10.	Edward prince of Wales is appointed the K's lieutenant in Gascony. *Westm.* R m. p ı 307
July 10	Power for him to make alliances and to retain persons for the K.'s service. *Westm.* R m p. ı 307 O v 822 H. m p ı 110
July 10	Proclamation to be made in Ireland ordering the annual election of sheriffs and escheators by each county, and for the election of customers in the towns where there is a staple, and permission for the importation of iron there. *Westm* R. m p. i. 308.
July 11.	Power for Michael bp of London and his colleagues to treat concerning violations of the truce with France *Westm* R m p. ı. 308
July 15	Roger de Beauchamp, captain of Calais, is ordered to arrest John Danseye, captain of Guisnes, for having burnt a bastide near Guisnes, in violation of the truce. *Northfleet* R m p ı. 308 O. v 822. H m p. ı 111
July 16	The K authorizes William Stury, warden of Guernsey, Jersey, Sark, and Alderney, John de Bokelond, and three others, to arrest the ships of Bayonne for the conveyance of the prince of Wales. *Northfleet* R. m p ı 308 O v 823 H m p ı 111.
July 16	The K. orders the constable of Bourdeaux to appraise and mark horses for the purchase of the prince of Wales and his company *Northfleet* R. m p ı. 309. O v. 823 H. m. p. ı 111.

DATE	SUBJECT.
1355. July 16	The K orders the mayor and bailiffs of Oxford to levy 250*l* for the payment of the damages suffered by the scholars of the university *Westm.* R m p. ı. 309
[July 16.]	The K orders them to search for and restore the goods and chattels taken from scholars. R. ııı. p. ı. 309
July 17.	Agreement between Humfrey de Cherleton and John de Carleton, junior, for the university, and John de S Frideswide, mayor, John de Bedeford, and John de Norton, burgesses, on the part of the town of Oxford, for the settlement of their disputes. *Westm.* R ııı p ı. 309
July 22.	The K. orders John de Eyncourt and three others to appraise and mark the horses of the prince of Wales, the earls of Warwick, Suffolk, Oxford, and Salisbury, Reginald de Cobham, and others, going to Gascony. *Northfleet* R m p ı 310 O. v 824 H. ııı. p. ı. 111
July 25.	The K. orders that tonsured clerks who are married at Bourdeaux are to enjoy their rights as burgesses *Sandwich* R. m p ı 310 O. v. 824. H. iii. p ı 111
July 26.	Restitution of the liberties and privileges of the town of Oxford, with certain exceptions *Westm.* R ııı. p ı 311
Aug 2.	Order for the assignment of a spot near the wall of the Friars Preachers, for depositing the offal from the market of S Nicholas, London *Sandwich* R m p ı 311
Aug. 3.	The K desires the prince of Wales to hear the complaint of Amanen de la Bret, lord of Logoyran, against Thomas de Roos, mayor of Bourdeaux, who condemned and executed his squire Dominic Deunant. *Westm* R ııı p ı 311. O v 825 H. m p. ı 112
Aug 4.	Power for Edward prince of Wales to receive homages in the duchy of Aquitain *Sandwich* R ııı p ı 312 O v 826. H. ııı. p ı. 112
Aug. 30.	The K orders the justices and chancellor of Ireland to examine the complaints of persons that their lands have been seized in consequence of errors in records and processes *Westm* R. ııı. p. ı 312.
Sept 14.	Thomas de Holand is ordered to deliver to the duke of Lancaster the castles of Brittany *Portsmouth.* R ııı. p. ı 312 O. v 826 H ııı p ı 112.
[Sept. 14]	Letters to Bernard de Chastel Breton, sir Thomas de Liston, and 17 others, bidding them obey the duke of Lancaster R ııı p ı 312 O. v 827 H ııı p ı 113.
Sept. 15	The K forbids ships to leave the kingdom before Michaelmas *Southwich* R ııı p ı 313
Sept. 26.	Writs extending the prohibition for a week to the mayor and bailiffs of Lynn, the bailiffs of Yarmouth, and 12 other ports. *The Tower of London.* R ııı p ı 313
Oct. 1.	Proclamation to be made by the several sheriffs for the uniformity of measures *Westm* R ııı. p. ı. 313.
Oct 23.	The K forbids Thomas bp of Ely to leave the country, as a parliament has been summoned for Nov 23. *Westm* R. iii. p. ı 314 O. v. 827. H. ııı. p. ı. 113.
Nov 23.	Commission to John Maykyn to arrest 100 sailors in Kent and Essex for the ship called *la Plente.* *Westm* Nine similar commissions to masters of other ships, dated *Westm* , 18 *Dec.* R. ııı. p ı 314
Dec. 3.	Pardon to certain nobles for hunting in Inglewood Forest, in the company of Edward de Balhol, K of Scotland *Westm.* R ııı p ı. 314. O. v. 828 H ııı p. i 113
Dec 23.	The sheriffs of Yorkshire and eight other counties are to issue a proclamation ordering men-at-arms and archers to meet the K at Newcastle-upon-Tyne on Jan 1, to resist the invasion of the Scots *Durham* R ııı p. ı 314 O v 828 H ııı p ı 113
Dec 23.	Writs of military summons to Robert de Colvill of Bytham, Thomas de Furnivall, and eight others. *Durham* R. ııı p. i. 315. O ıv 829 H ııı p. ı. 113.
[Dec. 23]	Also to the seneschals of the prince of Wales in North Wales. R. iii. p. ı. 315. O. v. 829 H ııı p ı 113.
1356. Jan 6.	John Kiriel, Otto de Grandisson, and Arnald Savage are appointed arrayers in Kent *Newcastle-upon-Tyne.* R. iii. p. i 315
[Jan. 6]	Letters desiring the abp. of Canterbury, J bp of Rochester, the abbots of S. Augustine's, Canterbury, and of Faversham, and the prior of Christchurch, Canterbury, to assist them. R. ııı p ı 315.
Jan 9	The constable of Dover Castle and warden of the Cinque Ports is ordered to send to Calais the stones for warlike engines at Folkestone *Newcastle-upon-Tyne* R ııı p ı 315.
Jan 12.	The K. orders the constable of Bourdeaux to obey and assist the prince of Wales. *Westm.* R. ııı. p. i. 316. O. v. 829 H. ııı. p ı 114.

DATE.	SUBJECT.
1356 Jan 14	John de Beauchamp of Warwick is appointed captain of Calais, Guisnes, Marke, Colne, Oye, and Sandgate Roger de Beauchamp is ordered to resign the office to him. *Newcastle-upon-Tyne* R iii p i 316
Jan. 18.	The K. orders the prior of S John's of Jerusalem in England to go with his men-at-arms to his manor near Southampton. *Newcastle-upon-Tyne.* R. iii. p i 316. O. v. 831. H. iii p. i. 114.
Jan 17	The mayor and sheriffs of London are ordered to array the men of the city and suburbs. *Newcastle-upon-Tyne* R iii p i 317
Jan 17.	Commission of Robert seneschal of Scotland to William bp of S Andrew's, Patrick bp. of Brechin, sir William de Levingston, and sir Robert de Erskyne to treat with the K. for the liberation of David K of Scotland. *S. John of Perth* R iii. p i. 317. O. v. 831. H iii. p. i. 114.
Jan 20	Cession by Edward de Balliol of the kingdom of Scotland to the K of England. *Roxburgh* R. iii p i 317 O v 832. H iii. p i 114.
Jan 20.	Cession to the K. of England by Edward de Balliol of Galloway and the rest of his inheritance not annexed to the Scotch crown. *Roxburgh* R iii. p i 318. O v. 833. H iii p i 115
Jan 20	Another deed of cession by Edward de Balliol of the kingdom, government, and crown of Scotland to the K of England *Roxburgh* R. iii p i 318 O v. 835 H iii p i 116
Jan. 20	Indenture by which the K of England grants to Edward de Balliol an annuity of 2,000*l* in recompense for the above cession *Bamborough* R iii p i 319 O v 836 H iii. p i 116
Jan 20	Charge of the above annuity on the customs at Hull and S Botolph's. *Bamborough.* R. iii. p i 319. O v. 838. H. iii. p. i 117.
Jan 23	Power to John de Grey of Rotherfield, steward of the K 's household, John de Cherleton, the K 's chamberlain, and three others, to remove John de Coupeland from the office of sheriff of Northumberland *Newcastle-upon-Tyne* R iii p i 320
Jan. 25.	Resignation to the K. of England by Edward de Balliol of his rights in Scotland. *Roxburgh* R iii. p i 320 O v 840 H iii p. i 118
Jan 25	Release by Edward de Balliol to the K of England of all promises and contracts before the 20th inst. *Roxburgh* R iii p i 321. O v 84 H iii p i 119
Jan 27	Acquittance to the K of England by Edward de Balliol for all his rights and claims in Scotland *Roxburgh* R iii p i. 321 O v 842 H iii p i 119
Jan 28	Power for the justiciary and chancellor of Ireland to remove one of the three barons of the Exchequer *Newcastle-upon-Tyne* R. iii p i 322
Jan 30	Writs to 14 sheriffs to send bows and arrows to William de Rothewell, keeper of the wardrobe in the Tower of London *Bamborough* R iii p i 322
Feb 6	Protection for Menald de Insula, alias de Caressa, a married clerk at Dax *Bamborough.* R. iii. p i 322
Feb 7	Power for Edward prince of Wales to hear the appeal of the commonalty of Bayonne against the decision of the lord of Lebret in their cause with the inhabitants of Labourde. *Newcastle-upon-Tyne* R iii p i 322. O v 843 H iii p i 119
Feb 7.	Protection for the mayor and commonalty of Bayonne. *Newcastle-upon-Tyne* R iii p i 323.
Feb 8	Protection for sir Thomas de Felton in the retinue of the prince of Wales , also for sir Richard de Stafford and seven others *Bamborough* R iii p i. 323. O v 844 H iii. p i 119.
[ ]	Letters of protection for persons going to Brittany O. v 844–5. H. iii. p i 119
March 8	The K. orders the sheriff of Devon to send clayes for the conveyance of the prince of Wales's horses to Thomas Durant at Plymouth by Easter. *Westm.* R. iii p. i. 323. O v 845 H iii. p. i 120
Feb. 10	The K appoints Roger de Sutton to purvey timber, &c. for the repair of his ships. *Bamborough* R iii p i 323
Feb 10.	Indenture between the K and John de Beauchamp, brother of the earl of Warwick, for the custody of Calais *Westm* R iii p i 324
March 1	The K orders the sheriff of Essex to enforce the ordinance for regulating the price of wine *Hertford* R iii p i. 324
March 12.	The K releases Edward de Balliol from his homage *Westm* R. iii. p. i. 324. O. v 845 H iii p. i 120

DATE.	SUBJECT
1356 March 15	The K. orders the chancellor and chamberlains of Berwick, and the sheriffs of Berwick and Roxburgh, to proclaim that he intends to maintain in Scotland the ancient laws and customs of Scotland *Westm* R. iii p i. 325 O v 846 H iii p. i. 120.
[March 15]	Similar proclamation to be made in Scotland by William de Bohun, earl of Northampton, warden of the marches R iii p i 325 O v 846 H iii p i 120
March 25.	Power to the bps. of Durham and Carlisle, the earls of Northampton and Anegos, and three others, to treat with the Scotch for the liberation of David de Bruys, and for peace. *Westm* R iii. p. i 325 O. v 847. H. iii. p. i 120.
March 28	John de Palyngton is appointed to provide bacon for the prince of Wales *Westm.* R iii p. i 325 O v 847 H iii p i 121
	Protection for sir Edward le Despenser, sir William de Morlee, sir Edward de Courtenaye, and 119 others, going to Aquitain in the retinues of the prince of Wales, the earls of Suffolk and Salisbury, and other lords R iii p. i. 325 O v 847–8. H iii p i. 121.
March 30	Maurice FitzThomas, earl of Kildare, is appointed justiciary of Ireland, with an annuity of 500*l* Letter ordering the prelates, nobles, and people to obey him. *Westm.* R iii p i 326
March 31.	Power for sir John de Gatesden and Godfrey Foljaumbe to treat with John de Insulis [des Isles] for entering the K's service *Westm* R iii p i 326 O. v 849. H. iii. p i. 121.
March 31	Power for the earl of Kildare, sir John de Gatesden, and Godfrey Foljambe to pardon Irish rebels. *Westm* R iii. p. i 327
April 18.	Truce between William lord of Douglas and William de Bohun, earl of Northampton *Roxburgh* R iii p i. 327. O v. 849. H iii p. i. 122
April 23	Warrants to the customers of Hull and S Botolph's to pay the annuity of ·Edward de Balliol *Westm* R iii p i 327 O v 850 H iii p i 122
April 27	Restitution of the temporalities to John bp of Emly, late archdeacon of Fernes. *Westm.* R iii p i 327
April 28	The K orders the customers in England to allow Irish hides to be imported free, if the duty has been paid in Ireland Similar licence for wool and other goods *Westm* R iii p i 327.
May 1.	Guy de Bryan is appointed admiral of the fleet from the Thames westward. *Westm* K iii. p i. 328
May 2	The K has received the pope's letters by Simon de Sudebiria, and excuses himself for not sending ambassadors to treat again for peace with France, as he has been so often deceived *Westm* R iii p i 323 O v 851 H iii p i 122
May 12.	Safe conduct for John lord of Morbek, and William Carbonel, lord of Buverannce, coming to England as ambassadors of Philip de Navarre *Westm* R iii p i 328 O v 851. H iii p i 122
May 10.	Protestation of the bp of S Andrew's that what he and his colleagues may say according to the commission of Robert, seneschal of Scotland, dated 17 Jan., shall not be to their prejudice *London* R iii p i 328 O v 852 H iii p i 122
May 12.	Safe conduct until June 24 for the lords of Morbek and Buveraunce *Westm* R iii. p i 329
May 14.	The K assures the pope that Charles K of Navarre had not conspired with him against K. John of France, as the latter alleges *Westm.* R iii p i. 329 O v 852 H iii. p. i 123
[May 14.]	Similar letter to the emperor Louis R iii p i 329 O v 853 H iii p i 123
[May 14]	Letters patent to the same effect R iii p i 329 O v. 853 H iii p i. 123.
May 14.	The K forbids Alan del Strothre, the Queen's bailiff of Tyndale, to make exactions contrary to the privileges of the miners of Carlisle *Westm.* R iii p. i. 330
May 18	The K. orders the bailiffs of Sefford, great part of which has been burnt, and the inhabitants dead of pestilence, to prevent James Archer of Assheton from pulling down the remaining houses, and carrying away the material *Westm* R iii p i 330
May 29	Safe conduct for Martin de Navarre to come to England *Westm.* R iii. p. i. 330. O. v. 854. H. iii p. i 123
May 30.	The K. orders Henry duke of Lancaster to issue no more commissions for general inquisitions in Aquitain. *Reading* R. iii. p. i. 330

B B

DATE	SUBJECT
1356 June 3	The K orders the bailiffs of Rochester and the Medway to allow vessels with timber and stone for the palace at Westminster to pass under the bridge over the Medway *Westm.* R. iii p i 331.
June 6	The K orders Geoffrey de Say, constable of Rochester Castle, to remove the obstructions in the river at the bridge *Westm.* R iii p. i 331.
June 8	The K orders the chancellor and chamberlain of Berwick to allow to the men of Tevy-dale the privileges enjoyed by them in the time of Alexander, formerly K of Scotland *Westm.* R iii p i 331 O. v. 854 H iii p i 123
June 24.	Safe conduct till Aug 1 for Philip de Navarre and Godfrey de Harecourt coming to England. *Westm.* R iii p. i 331 O. v. 854 H. iii. p i 123.
June 25	Warrants to the customers of Kingston-upon-Hull and S Botolph's, for the payment of the annuity of Edward de Balliol *Westm.* R iii p i 331 O. v 855 H iii p i 123–4
July 1	The K orders Henry de Ingelby, warden of the house of converts, London, to receive John de Chastel, a converted Jew. *Westm.* R. iii. p i. 332.
July 2	Commission to John Musard, the K's valet, to select 120 archers for the K's body guard *Westm.* R iii p i 332 O v 855 H iii p i 124
July 18	Homage of Godfrey de Harecourt, viscount of S Sauveur and lord of Dangoville, in Cotentin. *S Sauveur le Visconte* R. iii p i. 332 O. v. 856. H iii p i 124.
July 26	The K appoints Roger del Wych, John Syward, John Cruys, William FitzAdam, and Thomas de Rokeby, the nephew, to arrest ships for the passage of Thomas de Rokeby, justiciary, to Ireland *Westm.* R iii p i 332.
Aug 1	Protection for Godfrey de Harecourt, viscount of S. Sauveur. *Westm.* R. iii p i 332 O. v. 857 H. iii p i 124
[Aug 1]	Protection for William de Croucy, who has done homage to the K. R iii p i. 333 O v 857. H iii p i 124
[Aug 1]	The K appoints Piers Pigache, clerk, lord of Tourtleville, judge and governor of Normandy R iii p i. 333. O v 857 H iii. p i 125
Aug 1	Proclamation to be made by the several sheriffs, enjoining the assumption of knighthood by persons possessing 40l a year *Westm.* R iii p i 333. O v 858 H iii p i 125
Aug. 1	At the pope's request, the K empowers the prince of Wales to treat with France Similar letters dated Dec 15. *Westm.* R iii p i. 333 O v. 858. H. iii p i 125.
Aug 6	The K., in consequence of his great expenses, delays the payment of 4,000 marks to Edward de Balliol, assigning him this sum on the tenth of the province of Canterbury Exemplification of the above, dated Westm., Aug 13 *Westm.* R iii p. i. 384 O v 859. H iii p i 125
Aug. 6.	Power for Thomas de Rokeby, justiciary of Ireland, to let forfeited lands. *Westm.* R iii p i 334
Aug. 6.	The K orders Thomas de Rokeby, justiciary of Ireland, to make inquisition as to the goods of felons which have not been accounted for. *Westm.* R iii p i 334
Aug 6	Power for the said justiciary to pardon rebels *Westm.* H. iii p i. 335.
Aug 7	Safe conduct for Charles de Bloys, the K's prisoner, going to Brittany. *Westm.* R. iii. p i 335 O. v 860. H iii. p i 126
Aug 7	Safe conduct for Charles de Bloys, the K.'s prisoner, Robert de S Pierre, Evanne Charruel, and others in his company, returning to England. *Westm.* R iii p i. 335. O. v 861. H. iii p i. 126.
Aug. 8	Henry duke of Lancaster is appointed lieutenant of the K. and John de Montfort, duke of Brittany, in the said duchy and the parts adjoining. *Westm.* R ii. p ii 335 O. v. 861 H. iii p i. 126.
Aug 10.	Agreement for the ransom of Charles de Bloys for 700,000 florins. *Westm.* R. iii p i. 336. O v 862–5. H iii p i. 126–128.
Aug. 10	The K. orders the men of the counties between Norfolk and Hampshire to be prepared to resist an invasion Edward de Montacute is substituted in the commission for Norfolk for John de Bardolf. *Westm.*, *Aug. 24* R iii. p i. 337.
Aug 10	The abbot of S Augustine's, Canterbury, is ordered to array his household servants. Intimation thereof to the arrayers of Kent. *Westm.* R ii. p ii 338
Aug 15	The K has received the letter of the cardinal bp of Albano, and will accept him as a mediator with France if he can show any way of attaining peace *Westm.* R. iii. p. i. 338. O v 866 H. iii p i 128.

DATE.	SUBJECT
1356 Aug 18.	Robert de Drousse, of Cork, is appointed admiral of the fleet on the coast of Ireland. *Westm* R. iii p 1. 338
Aug. 20	Safe conduct for Philip de Navarre returning to Normandy *Westm.* R. iii. p 1. 338. O v 866. H iii. p 1. 128.
Aug. 20.	Safe conduct for sir Thomas Byset, sir Walter Moigne, and Norman Lesselyn, and Walter his brother, Scotchmen, to pass through England on their way to Prussia. *Westm* R iii. p 1 339. O. v 866 H iii p 1. 128.
Oct. 20.	The K forbids the trial of common pleas in the court of the Exchequer at Dublin. *Westm.* R iii p 1 339
Aug. 24.	Safe conduct for 16 German knights in the retinue of Philip de Navarre, count of Longue-ville. *Westm.* R. iii p. 1. 339. O v. 867. H iii. p 1. 128
Aug. 24	Protection for the Norman subjects of the K of Navarre *Westm* R. iii p 1 339
Aug. 25.	The arrayers of Sussex and Kent are ordered to keep their men near the sea-coast. *Westm* R iii. p. 1 339.
Sept 4	Treaty between the K. and Philip de Navarre, who does homage to the K, of England as K of France and duke of Normandy *Clarendon* R iii p 1. 340. O v. 867 H iii p. 1 128
Sept 12	The K forbids the purveyors of his household and of the lords of Ireland to take pro-visions there without payment *Westm.* R iii. p 1 340
	Memorandum that Geoffrey Hamelyn, valet of the prince of Wales, arrived from Gascony with the tunic and bassinet of the K of France R. iii p. 1 340 O v 869 H iii p 1 129
Oct 8.	The K orders Guy de Seintiler, sheriff of Norfolk, and John Mayn, sergeant-at-arms, to prevent sir John de Caston or other persons coming armed to the inthronisation of Thomas bp of Norwich *Westm.* R iii p. 1. 341. O v. 869. H. iii p 1. 129.
Oct. 10.	The K informs the abps and bps of the victory of the prince of Wales, and the capture of John de Valois, at Poictiers, on Sept 19, and desires them to offer up thanksgivings and prayers *Westm* R iii p. 1 341 O v 869. H iii p 1 129
Oct. 19.	Pardon to Scotch nobles for hunting and fishing at Haytefield, in Yorkshire, in the company of Edward de Balliol *Westm.* R iii p 1 341 O. v. 870 H iii p 1 129
Oct 20.	Credence for William de Lynne, dean of Chichester, going to the cardinal of Perigord, and another, about the affairs of France *Westm* R. iii p 1. 341 O. v. 871. H iii. p 1 130
Oct 30.	Philip de Navarre, count of Longueville, is appointed the K's lieutenant and captain in Normandy *Westm* R iii p 1 342 O v 871 H iii p 1. 130
Oct. 30.	The K. orders his subjects going to Normandy to observe the covenant with Philip de Navarre *Westm* R iii p. 1. 342 O v. 872. H iii. p 1 130
[Oct. 30]	The K. orders Henry duke of Lancaster, captain of Brittany, to assist Philip de Navarre. R. iii. p 1 342 O v 872 H iii p 1 130
Nov 12.	Letters of credence to the pope for Philip de Codeford concerning the renewal of the privileges of the colleges in the palace of Westminster and Windsor Castle. *Westm.* R. iii p 1. 342 O v. 872 H iii p 1. 130.
Nov. 13.	The K to the emperor, would be glad if peace could be had, that it should be by means of his offered mediations, and is not disposed to favour the count of Flanders against the emperor's brother. *Westm* R iii p 1 343 O v 873 H iii. p 1 131
Nov 15	Grant by Edward prince of Wales to sir John Chaundos for his services at the battle of Poictiers, of two parts of the manor of Kirketon in Lindsey, at the rent of a red rose. *London.* R iii p 1. 343 O v 874 H iii p 1 131
Nov. 24.	The K orders Thomas de Beaumont to return to captivity in Scotland, as Walter de Haliburton and other Scotch prisoners consider that they are released from their parole by having obtained his liberation *Westm* R iii p 1. 343 O v. 874. H. iii p. 1. 131.
Nov. 25.	Licence to Thomas de Gray, prisoner in Scotland, to export 100 sacks of wool from Berwick. *Westm.* R. iii p 1 343 O. v. 874. H. iii p 1 131.
Nov. 27.	Memorandum of the transfer of the great seal from John abp of York, at his request, to the bp of Winchester, thereby appointed the K.'s chancellor. *Westm* R. iii p 1. 344 O. v. 875. H iii p. 1. 131.
Dec 12.	Licence to the merchants of Ireland to export wool to England, paying only the customs in Ireland. *Westm.* R. iii. p. 1 344

DATE	SUBJECT
1356. Dec 18	Safe conduct for William bp of S Andrew's, Patrick bp of Brechin, Thomas bp. of Caithness, sir William de Levyngston, sir Robert de Erskyne, and sir Thomas de Fauside, to come to London to treat for the release of David de Bruys, the K's prisoner. *Westm* R. III. p 1 344 O v. 875 H III p 1 132
Dec 15. 1357	Power for the duke of Lancaster to treat with the French for a truce in Brittany and Normandy *Westm.* R III p 1 344 O v. 876 H III p 1. 132.
Jan 18.	The K orders Robert de Tughale, chamberlain of Berwick, to complete the works at the Douglas Tower, near the castle of Berwick *Westm* R III p 1 344 O v 876 H III. p. 1. 132.
Jan 20.	Safe conduct for Peter Pounkellen, valet of the children of Charles de Bloys, to leave England *Westm.* H III p 1 345 O v 876 H III p 1 132.
Feb 4	The K promises to pay his debts to Edward de Balliol, late K of Scotland *Westm.* R. III p 1 345. O vi 1 H III p 1 132
Feb. 4.	Warrants to the customers of S Botolph's and Hull to pay Edward Balliol, late K of Scotland, his annuity. *Westm.* R III. p 1 345. O vi 1 H III p 1 132
Feb. 6	The K declares that Piers Pigache, lord of ,Tourtleville, governor of Cotentin and S Sauveur le Viconte, is not under the jurisdiction of any of his officers *Westm.* H III. p 1 345
[Feb 6]	The K orders Pigache to seize the lands of those who refuse to do homage R III. p 1 345
Feb. 10.	John de Beauchamp of Warwick is appointed captain of Calais, Guisnes, Mark, Colne, Oye, and Sandgate. *Westm.* R III. p 1 346.
Feb. 12.	Edward prince of Wales purchases James de Bourbon, count of Ponthieu, from John de Graylin, captal de Buch, Estienne Daex, and five others, his captors, for 25,000 crowns *Bourdeaux* R III p 1 346 O vi 2 H III p 1 132
Feb. 15.	Simon de Newenton and Richard de la Vache are appointed wardens of S. Sauveuer le Visconte and the other towns and castles of Godfrey de Harecourt *Westm.* R. III p 1 346.
Feb 15.	Piers Pygache is ordered to repair the above towns and castles *Westm* R. III p 1 346.
Feb. 16	The K orders John Gruynard and William de Neuburgh to provide ships for carrying timber to Calais *Westm* R III p 1 347.
Feb 18.	The K. orders William de Loundres to repair his castle of Wykinlowe in Ireland *Westm.* R III p 1 347
Feb 18	The K orders the earl of Ormond to put his lands in Ireland in a state of defence *Westm* R. III p. 1 347
Feb 28.	The K orders John de Ellerton and Thomas Dautre to arrest ships for the passage of persons going to Normandy and Brittany *Westm* R III p 1 347.
March 1.	Henry Pycard, the K's butler, is ordered to deliver a pipe of Gascoon wine to David de Bruys *Westm* R III. p 1 347.
March 20.	Proclamation to be made in Northumberland and Yorkshire that all persons willing to live at Berwick upon Tweed shall enjoy the right of burgesses *Westm* R III p 1. 348.
March 20	The K orders John Dabernoun, sheriff of Devon, to provide victuals and conveyance for Edward prince of Wales, who is about to arrive at Plymouth with John of France. *Westm.* R III p 1. 348. O vi 3. H III p. 1 133.
March 23	Truce until Easter 1359 between England and France, by the mediation of cardinal Talairant de Pierregort and Nicholas cardinal of S Vitalis; with comprehension of allies and appointment of conservators. *Bourdeaux* R III p 1 348 O vi. 3-10 H III. p 1. 133-6
March 23.	Safe conduct for five Venetian galleys going to Flanders. *Westm* R. III p 1 351 O vi 11 H III p 1 137
March 25.	Thomas Dautry, sergeant-at-arms, is ordered to take two vessels to Southampton for the conveyance of Philip de Navarre to Normandy *Westm.* R III. p. 1 351 O. vi 11. H III p 1. 137
March 25	The K. informs his subjects in Normandy of the appointment of Philip de Navarre as captain. *Westm* R III p 1 351. O. vi 11 H III p. 1 137.
March 25	The K orders the mayor and bailiffs of Southampton to allow Thomas de la Dyto, chancellor of Navarre, to take with him six horses free of duty *Westm* R III p 1 352
March 28	Prorogation of the safe conduct of the Scotch ambassadors (for the liberation of David de Bruys) until a fortnight after Easter. *Westm.* R. III. p i. 352 O. vi. 12. H III. p i 137
April 1	The K orders the customers and searcher of London to allow no pilgrims to leave the realm, and to search all persons entering the kingdom. Similar writ to the sheriffs of London. *Westm* R. III. p. 1 352.

DATE	SUBJECT
1357.	
April 1.	The K. forbids R abp. of Armagh leaving England. *Westm* R iii p i 352
April 4	Safe conduct for William de Leth, of Scotland, going to Scotland for Q Isabella *Westm.* R iii p i 352 O. vi 12 H iii p 1. 137
April 7	The sheriffs of London and the mayors and bailiffs of Sandwich and seven other ports are ordered to prevent all persons leaving England without licence, and friars of the order of the hermits of S Augustine even with licences of a previous date *Westm.* R. iii. p i. 353.
April 12.	Warrant to the customers of S. Botolph's to pay the annuity of Edward de Balliol, late K of Scotland *Westm* R. iii p i 353. O vi 12 H iii p i 137
April 25.	Pardon to Cecilia, widow of John Rygeway, who has been 40 days in prison without eating or drinking, which is a miracle contrary to nature She had stood mute when indicted for the murder of her husband *Westm* R iii p i. 353 O vi 13 H iii p. i.
April 28.	The K orders the duke of Lancaster to raise the siege of Rennes, in accordance with the truce concluded at Bourdeaux. *Westm* R iii p i 353 O vi. 13 H iii p 1. 137.
April 29.	The K of England to the K. of Portugal ; he refuses to restore the Portuguese merchandise which had been taken by the French, and from them by the English *Westm* R iii p i 354 O vi 14 H iii. p i 138
May 5.	General pardon for the escape of prisoners and the goods of felons. *Westm* R. iii. p i 354
May 8.	Truce with Scotland until Martinmas *Westm.* R. iii p 1. 354. O vi 14 H iii. p i 138
May 10.	Henry de Percy and Ralph de Nevill are appointed to preserve the truce with Scotland on the East March, and Thomas de Lucy on the West March *Westm* H. iii p i 355 O vi. 16 H iii p 1. 139
May 12.	Exemplification of the truce with Scotland *Westm* R. iii p i. 355. O. vi 17 H. iii p. i 139
May 20.	Declaration that sir Sagremors de Pomerus is ready to disprove the charges of Pandulphus de Malatestis against Barnabo Visconti. *Westm.* R. iii p 1. 355 O. vi 17. H. iii p i 139
May 23.	Order for the renewal of the wax covering the body of Edward I. in Westminster Abbey. *Westm* R. iii p i 355 O. vi 17. H iii p i 139
May 25.	Safe conduct for John le Grys, cup-bearer of the K. of France, going to France. *Westm* R. iii p i 355 O vi 18. H. iii p i 139.
May 25	Also for Guerryc de Montacher, comptroller of the chamber, and Peter, valet of the chamber of the French K., coming to England. *Westm* R iii p i 356. O vi 18 H iii p. i. 139
May 27.	The K desires Simon de Sudbury, chancellor of Salisbury, to assist sir Nicholas Damory and sir Thomas de Fulnetby, whom he sends to the pope *Westm* R iii. p i 356 O. vi 18. H iii p i 140.
May 29.	Innocent [VI] expresses his pleasure at the late treaty of peace, and sends Peter, cardinal of the Twelve Apostles, to France. *Villeneuve* R iii p 1. 356. O. vi. 19. H. iii. p. i 140
May 28.	The K orders Thomas de Lucy, warden of the West March, to prevent the intended combat between English and Scotch *Westm* R iii p i 356
June 1.	Protection for Henekin de Brabant, messenger of John Mayngre, called Bussiquaut, the K's prisoner *Westm.* R. iii p. i 357. O. vi 20. H iii p i 140.
June 1.	Renewal of the appointment of Simon de Newynton as castellan of S. Sauveur le Viscount *Westm.* R. iii p 1. 357.
June 1.	The K orders John de Stok to deliver the towns and castles in his charge to Simon de Newyngton. *London* R iii p i 357.
June 1.	Licence to Boniface de Casteletto to provide victuals for the cardinals of Albano and S Vitalis, who are coming to England. Similar licence to William Attewelde and another to provide poultry *Westm* R. iii p. i. 357 O. vi. 20. H iii p. i. 140
June 3.	Safe conduct for cardinal Talairand, bp of Albano, and Nicholas cardinal of S Vitalis. *Westm.* R. iii. p. i 357. O. vi. 21. H. iii. p i 140.
June 15.	Safe conduct for Peter cardinal of the Twelve Apostles. *Westm.* R. iii. p. i. 358. O. vi. 21. H. iii. p i 140.

DATE.	SUBJECT
1357 June 16	Safe conduct for Peter bp. of Lectoure, John de Muris, Peter de Caumont, and lord Delopy *Westm* R III p 1 358 O vi 21 H III p 1 141
June 26	Safe conduct for Theobald de Chaunteville and Baldwin Danequyn. *Westm.* R iii. p. 1 358. O vi 21. H. iii p. 1 141.
	Safe conduct for John Faveralus, taken prisoner at the battle of Poictiers. *Westm* R, III. p 1 358 O vi 22 H. III. p 1 141
June 30	Safe conduct for Thomas earl of Mar coming from Scotland *Westm* R III. p 1. 358. O. vi 22 H III p. 1. 141
July 3.	Safe conducts for John Malapart, messenger of the count of Dampmartin, John de Buribet, and John Philippe, messengers of the cardinal of Rouen, and 43 others *Westm* R III p 1 358 O vi 22–3 H. III. p 1 141.
July 4.	The K. repeats his order to the duke of Lancaster to raise the siege of Rennes *Westm.* R. III p 1 359
July 8.	Safe conduct for Alexander de Menteth, prisoner of Thomas Fichet, and William de Rameseye, to come to England *Westm.* R III p 1 359. O vi 23 H III p i 141
July 10	Safe conduct for Charles Jory, armour of the pope, coming to England *Westm.* R iii p i 359.
July 12.	Safe conduct for Tristan lord of Maguelers, prisoner of Thomas de Walkefare, to go to France and return *Westm* R III p 1 359 O. vi. 23 H III p 1 141
July 13.	Letters of safe conduct to the duke of Lancaster and the K 's other officers in Brittany for Charles de Bloys, the K 's prisoner, with three knights and two squires ; also for Peter Poulart, James le Moenne, John Monbouch, and others *Westm* R III p 1 360 O vi 23 H. III p 1 142
July 13	Acquittance for the letters patent and letters of renunciation received from John de Monbourcher and James lui Moigne, messengers of Charles de Bloys, the K 's prisoner *Westm* R III p 1. 360 O vi 24 H III p 1. 142
July 13	Letters of acquittance for 25,000 nobles, being the ransom of Charles de Bloys, the K 's prisoner. *Westm.* R III. p 1. 360 O vi 25 H III p. 1. 142.
July 14.	Aymer de S. Amand is appointed justiciary of Ireland Intimation thereof to John de Bolton, clerk, vicegerent of the justiciary, and to the prelates, nobles, and people of Ireland *Westm* R III p 1 361
[July 14.]	Grant of an annuity of 500l. to Aymer de S. Armand as justiciary of Ireland R iii. p. 1 361
[July 14.]	Power for him to remove inefficient officers R III p 1 361
[July 14]	Power for him to seize and let deserted lands R III p 1. 361
[July 14]	Power for him to let forfeited lands *Westm.* R III p 1. 361.
July 25.	Renewal of the commission of Henry duke of Lancaster as captain of Brittany, in the names of the K and John de Montfort, duke of Brittany. *Westm* R III p 1 361 O. vi 26 H. III p 1 143
[July 25]	The K orders the prelates, nobles, and people of Brittany to obey the duke of Lancaster R iii p 1 362 O vi 26 H. III. p 1 143
[July 25]	Commission to the duke of Lancaster as captain of Brittany, in the K 's name R III p i 362 O vi 27 H III. p 1. 143.
July 28.	Safe conducts for Guy de Rochefort, squire of the count of Auxerre, the K 's prisoner, John Tranchemontaygne, squire of the count of Juny, the K.'s prisoners, and for 24 others *Westm* R. III p 1 362. O vi 27–8. H III p 1. 143.
July 30.	The K. orders the seneschal of Gascony to attend to the complaint of Ivo de Kerembars, of Brittany, who took Aquem Guillem, son of the lord of La Sparre, prisoner at the battle of Poictiers, and who has refused to keep his oath. *Westm.* R III p 1 362 O vi 28 H III p 1 144.
Aug. 1.	Safe conduct for a valet of Joan, daughter of the count of Bourbon, who calls herself duchess of Normandy. *Westm.* R. III. p. 1. 363.
Aug. 4.	The K. authorizes John Avenel to make and demand redress for violations of the truce with France *Westm.* R III p 1. 363.
Aug. 5.	The K. declares the Spanish merchants are at liberty, under certain conditions, to trade with France *Westm.* R III p 1. 363. O. vi. 29. H III. p 1 144
Aug. 10.	Robert del Eves is appointed warden of the fortress of Seint Vache in Normandy . *Westm.* R. III. p. i. 363.

DATE.	SUBJECT.
1357. Aug 12.	Safe conduct for William duke of Bavaria who is leaving England *Westm.* R iii. p. 2 364. O. vi 30 H iii p i 144
Aug. 12.	Safe conduct for William de la Launde and James Compere, squires of the lord of Crahoun, the K.'s prisoner. *Westm.* R iii. p i 364 O vi 30. H iii. p. i. 144.
Aug. 12.	The K. orders Henry de Percy and Ralph de Nevill to release Archibald Douglas, John de Gordon, William and John de Tours, and other Scotch prisoners, taking security for their return *Westm* R iii p i 364 O vi 30 H. iii p i. 144
Aug 12	Safe conduct for Sir Thomas del Fawesside, who is returning to Scotland, having come to England on the affairs of David de Bruys, the K's prisoner *Westm* R iii p i 364 O vi 30 H iii p. i. 144
Aug 13.	Safe conduct for Sir Robert d'Erskyne, coming to England on the affairs of Robert de Bruys, the K.'s prisoner. *Westm* R iii p i 364 O vi 31 H iii p i 144.
Aug. 13.	Safe conduct for John Barber, archdeacon of Aberdeen, and three scholars coming to study at Oxford, granted at the request of David de Bruys *Westm* R iii p i. 364 O vi 31. H. iii p. i. 144.
Aug 16	Power for John abp of York, Thomas bp. of Durham, Gilbert bp of Carlisle, Henry de Percy, Ralph de Nevill, Henry le Scrop, and Thomas de Musgrave to treat for the liberation of David de Bruys, and for a truce for 10 years *Westm* R iii. p. i 365 O vi 31 H iii. p. i 145
Aug 16.	Power for Richard Tempest, Ingelram Umframvill, and William Heroun to receive security for the ransom of David de Bruys. *Westm* R. iii p i 365. O. vi 32 H iii p i 145
Aug 16	Safe conduct for the bp of S. Andrews, coming to England about the liberation of David de Bruys. *Westm* R iii p i 365 O vi 32 H iii p i 145
Aug 16	Also for the earls of Angus, Sutherland, Murray, and March, the bps of Caithness and Brechin, and John Seneschal, lord of Kyle *Westm* R iii p i 365. O vi. 33. H. iii. p i 145.
Aug 16	Power to Henry de Percy and Ralph de Nevill to take the oath to the Scotch treaty for the K *Westm.* R iii p i 366. O vi 33 H iii p i 145
Aug 16.	Safe conduct for David de Bruys after his liberation. *Westm.* R. iii. p. i. 366. O. vi 33 H iii p. i. 146
Aug 16.	Safe conduct for the 20 hostages to be given for David de Bruys. *Westm* R. iii p i 366 O vi. 34 H iii p i. 146
Aug 16.	The K. promises that the hostages shall not be detained after stipulated time, unless guilty of some crime against the laws of England. *Westm.* R. iii. p. i. 366. O. vi. 34. H. iii. p i 146.
	Names of the hostages ; John son and heir of the seneschal of Scotland, Umfred son and heir of Roger de Kirkpatrick, and 18 others. R iii p i. 366 O vi. 35. H iii. p i 146.
Aug. 16.	Safe conduct for the earls of Angus, Sutherland, and Murray coming with the hostages for the liberation of David de Bruys. *Westm.* R iii p. i 367. O. vi. 35
Aug 16	The K. states that David de Bruys will be entirely free after the fulfilment of the conditions of his ransom. *Westm.* R iii. p. i 367. O. vi. 36. H iii p i 147
Aug. 16.	The K orders Sir William Trussell, of Cublesdon, and Sir Richard de Totesham to deliver up David de Bruys to the abp of York and the other commissioners *Westm.* R. iii. p. i. 367. O. vi. 36. H. iii. p. i 147.
Aug 16.	Commission to the abp of York and his colleagues to receive David de Bruys. *Westm.* R iii p i 367. O. vi. 37. H. iii. p. i 147.
Aug. 16.	Indemnity for the above-named commissioners for delivering up David de Bruys. *Westm* R. iii. p i 368. O. vi. 37. H iii p i. 147.
Aug 16	Safe conduct for Peter bp of Lectoure to go to France and return to England. *Westm.* R iii p i 368.
Aug. 21.	Safe conduct for Stephen de Paris, John de Campellis, and Reginald de Acisco, councillors, and Matthew Guliery, secretary of the K. of France ; also for the servants of the count of Dampmartin and others *Westm* R, iii p i. 368. O. vi. 38 H iii p. i. 147
Aug 30.	Maurice FitzThomas, earl of Kildare, is appointed lieutenant of Aymer de S. Amand, justiciary of Ireland. The people of Ireland are ordered to obey him. *Westm.* R. iii. p. i. 368.

DATE.	SUBJECT
1357. Aug 31	The K orders John de Greyly, Capital de Buch, William Saucii, lord of Pomeris, Bertrand lord of Montferrand, and Elyas de Pomeris to make redress for violation of the truce in the Auvergne Similar commission to Bernard Ezii, lord de Lebret. *Westm.* R iii p i 368 O vi 38 H. iii p i 147
Sept. 9	Safe conduct for the messengers of Philip of Navarre. *Westm* R. iii p i 369.
Sept 13	Letters of Alexander bp of Aberdeen appointing P bp. of Brechin, David de Mar, canon of Aberdeen, and John archdeacon of Aberdeen, proctors for the ransom of David de Bruys Similar letters of John bp of Murray, the chapters of Murray and Ross, and six others. *Fetherin* R iii p i 369 O vi. 40. H iii p i 148
Sept 26	Power given by Robert seneschal of Scotland, lieutenant of David K of Scotland, to the bps of S Andrews, Caithness, and Brechin, and three others, to treat with the English at Berwick R. iii p i 370 O vi 41 H iii p i 148
Sept 26	Power given by the Scotch bps to the bps of S. Andrews, Caithness, and Brechin. *Edinburgh.* R. iii p i 370. O vi. 41. H iii p i. 149.
Sept 26	Power given by the magnates of Scotland to the earls of March, Angus, and Sutherland, Thomas de Murray, pantler of Scotland, Sir William de Levyngston, and Sir Robert de Griffyn *Edinburgh* R. iii p i 370 O vi 43 H iii p i 149
Sept. 26.	Power given by the burgesses of Edinburgh, Perth, Aberdeen, and 14 other towns to Alexander Gilyot, Adam Tore, and nine others. *Edinburgh* R. iii p i 371. O vi 44 H iii p i 150
Sept 30.	Safe conducts until Christmas and Easter for Peter cardinal of the Twelve Apostles, who has come to England to treat for peace with France *Westm* R. iii p i 372 O. vi 46. H iii p i 150
Oct. 3.	Treaty for the ransom of David de Bruys for 100,000 marks payable in 10 years, during which time there will be a truce. *Berwick-upon-Tweed* R iii p. i 372 O vi 46–52. H iii p i 151–3
Oct 3.	David K of Scotland appoints Alexander Bur, archdeacon of Murray, to agree to the ecclesiastical censures for enforcing the treaty. *Berwick-upon-Tweed.* R. iii. p. i. 374. O vi. 52. H. iii p i. 153.
Oct 5	Ratification of the treaty by David K of Scotland *Berwick* R iii. p i 374 O vi 52. H iii p i 153
Oct. 5	Ratification of the treaty by Patrick earl of March and the other deputies of the Scotch nobles *Berwick* R iii p i 376 O vi. 56 H. iii p. i 155
Oct 5.	Ratification by Alexander Gyllyot and the other deputies of the Scotch commons *Berwick* R. iii p i 377 O. vi 59 H iii p i 155.
Oct. 6.	Obligation of the bps of S Andrews, Caithness, and Brechin to pronounce ecclesiastical censures if the treaty be not observed. *Edinburgh.* R iii p. i 378 O vi. 61. H. iii. p vi 156
Oct 8.	The K orders his admirals and other officers to allow the subjects of the K. of Castile to come to the ports of England, France, Flanders, Guienne, and Brittany *Westm* R iii p. i 380.
Oct. 10	The K orders the sheriffs of London to examine all persons arriving from abroad for letters and instruments prejudicial to the realm *Westm* R iii p i 380 O vi 65. H iii p. i 158
Oct 12.	The K orders that after the death of William Sanxii, lord of Pomeris, the castelanny of Reule shall be committed only to Englishmen *Westm* R iii p i 380.
Oct 12.	The K forbids his officers in Aquitain to claim wrecks in the Gironde and other fresh-water streams *Westm* R iii p i 380
Oct 14	Protection for the bp of Terouenne [episcopus Morinensis], now in England. *Westm.* R iii p i 381. O vi. 66. H iii p i 158.
Oct. 16	Safe conduct for Tristan Kerety, prisoner of Matthew de Gorneye, to go to France and return , also for the count of Ventadour and others *Westm.* R iii p i 381 O vi. 66. H iii p i 158
Oct 20	The K appoints Thomas Dautre, sergeant-at-arms, to prevent men-at-arms leaving the country from Winchelsea and Dover by the coast to Weymouth Similar commission to William Walkelate from Weymouth westward *Westm* R iii p i 381
Oct 25.	Safe conduct for Duncan Walays, valet of Thomas de Murref, hostage for David de Bruys, the servants of the earls of Sutherland and Angus, and 14 others *Westm.* R. iii. p. i. 381. O. vi. 66. H. iii. p. i. 158.

DATE.	SUBJECT
1357 Oct. 28	Protection for three years for Scotch scholars to come to Oxford or Cambridge for the purpose of study. *Westm* R iii p i. 382. O. vi. 67 H iii p. i. 159
Nov 1.	Receipt for 25,000 nobles, the second payment for the ransom of Charles de Bloys, the K's prisoner. *Westm* R iii p i 382 O vi. 67. H iii p i 159
Nov. 6	Ratification by David K of Scotland of the treaty of Berwick. *Scone.* R. iii. p i 382. O. vi 68. H iii. p. i, 159.
Nov 7	Warrant for the payment to the cardinals of Albano and S Vitalis of their procurations from the bprick of Ely *Westm* R iii p i 382 O vi 68 H iii. p i 159.
Nov. 8.	The K orders, Henry de Percy and Ralph de Nevill to release on bail Archibald Douglas, John Gordoun, John and William de Tours, and other Scotch prisoners, and to ascertain whether they were taken during the truce or not *Westm* R. iii p. i 383 O. vi. 69. H. iii p i, 159.
Nov. 16.	Safe conduct for Sir Archibald de Douglas and William de Tours to come to London and Canterbury *Westm* R. iii p i. 383 O. vi 69 H iii p i 160.
Nov. 18.	Safe conduct for Ivo de Keneken, who is providing necessaries for John and Guy, sons of Charles de Bloys *Westm* R. iii p. i 383 O vi 70 H. iii. p. i. 160.
Nov 18.	Thomas de Holand is appointed warden of the fortresses at Cruyk in Normandy Donald Aselrig, Lewis Chfford, and Walter Mewe are ordered to deliver them to him. *Westm.* R iii p. i 383
Nov. 20.	Confirmation of the grant by the duke of Lancaster of the castle of Brest and the town of S. Mathieu to Matthew de Gourney. *Westm.* R. iii. p i 383. O. vi 70. H iii p i 160
Nov 27.	Innocent [VI] exhorts the K to make peace with France. *Avignon.* R iii. p i 384. O vi 70. H iii p. i 160.
Dec 3.	Power for John de Cheveresdon, seneschal of Gascony, Gerald de Puy, justice, and John Guitard to make redress to the French for violations of the truce. *Westm.* R. iii. p. i 384 O. vi. 71 H iii. p i. 160.
Dec 26.	Safe conduct for Sir John de l'Isle, of Scotland, prisoner of the prince of Wales, to go to Scotland for his ransom. *Westm* R iii p i 384 O vi 71. H iii p i 161.
Dec. 16.	The K. informs the officers of the prince of Wales that the bprick of S. David's is not in the prince's jurisdiction, but pertains to the crown *Westm* R iii p i 384
Dec 20.	Declaration that Denys de Morbeke has delivered his prisoner, the K of France, to the K of England *Westm* R iii p. i 385 O vi 72 H iii. p i 161
Dec 20	Philip de Navarre, count of Longueville, is appointed the K's lieutenant and captain in Normandy. *Westm.* R iii. p. i 385 O vi 72 H iii p i. 161.
Dec 22	Confirmation of the appointment by the prince of Wales of Peter Vernhes to the custody of the mint at Bourdeaux, dated Bourdeaux, 2 April 1357 *Westm* R iii p i. 385
Dec 25	Safe conducts for Joan, wife of David de Bruys, William bp of S. Andrews, and Patrick de Dunbarre, earl of March, coming to England *Marlborough* R iii p i 385. O. vi. 72, H iii p. i. 161.
Dec. 28.	Safe conduct for the lord of Auhigny, the K's prisoner, to go to France; also for the count of Vendosme and the lord of Derval *Westm* R iii p i 386. H iii p i 161
Dec 28	Safe conduct for William Radicis, physician of the K's adversary [John de Valois], to go to France, also for William Cove and eight others. *Westm.* R. iii. p. i. 386. O vi. 73 H iii. p. i 161
Dec 30.	Licence to the count of Ventador, the K's prisoner, to go to France on account of his ill health, leaving his eldest son Louis as his hostage. *Westm.* R iii p i. 386 O. vi 74. H iii. p i 162
Dec 30.	Henry de Percy and Ralph de Nevill are ordered to give safe conducts to Joan, wife of David de Bruys, the bp. of S Andrew, and the earl of March, if they require them. *Marlborough* R. iii p. i. 386 O vi 74 H iii. p i 162
Dec. 30.	Commission to Sir Richard de Totesham and Sir Stephen de Cusyngton to redress violations of the truce with France. *Westm.* R iii p. i. 387 O. vi. 75. H. iii. p. i. 162
1358 Jan 16.	Credence for Sir Milo de Stapelton of Bedale to the K's officers in Normandy *Westm.* R iii p i. 387.
Jan 17.	Safe conduct for Michael, bp. of Candida Casa [Whithern], to come to England. *Mortlake* R iii p. i. 387. O. vi. 76. H. iii p i 162
Jan. 23.	Licence for 40 men-at-arms and 60 archers to go to Roger David in Brittany. *Westm.* R. iii. p. i. 387.

DATE.	SUBJECT
1358 Jan 27	Safe conduct for Sir Archibald de Douglas and William de Tours to come to England *Hampstede Mareschal.* R. iii p 7 388 O. vi 76 H iii p i. 162
Jan. 30.	Safe conduct for William de Fortia, chaplain of the cardinal of Perigord, going to France , also for three servants of James de Bourbon, and for Nicholas de S. Paul. *Westm* R iii. p. i 388 O vi 76. H iii. p i 163
Feb 14	Safe conduct for John de Newers, count of Juny, and John Dartoys, count of Eu, the K's prisoners, to go to France , also for William lord of Douglas to come to England *Westm* R. iii p i 388 O vi 77 H iii p. i 163
Feb 20	The K orders the bailiffs of Sandwich and seven other ports to publish the truce with France, and to prevent men-at-arms going to Brittany or Normandy. *Westm.* R iii. p i 388
Feb 26	The K orders the customers of London to allow oil, almonds, and other provisions for Nicholas cardinal of S Vitalis to pass free of duty *Westm* R iii p i. 288 O vi 78 H iii. p i 163.
Feb 28	Safe conduct for ambassadors about to be sent by Charles de Bloys *Westm.* R. iii. p. i 389
March 1.	The K. orders Thomas de Uvedale, lieutenant of the duke of Lancaster, to publish the truce with France in Brittany *Westm* R iii p i 389 O vi 78. H. iii p i 163.
March 10	Declaration of the innocence of Thomas bp of Durham of the charge of having attacked with a body of armed men Thomas bp of Chrysopolis, near Kexeby in Yorkshire *Westm* R iii p. i 389, O vi. 79 H iii p i 163
March 16.	Ralph de Ferrers is appointed captain of Calais, Guisnes, Marlee, Colne, Oye, and Sandgate *Westm.* R. iii. p. i 389 O vi 79. H iii p i. 164
March 20	Licence to Thomas earl of Angus, hostage for David de Bruys, to go to the north until S George's Day *Westm* R. iii p i 390 O vi 80 H iii p. i 164
March 20	Protection for Peter, cardinal of the Twelve Apostles *Westm* R iii p i 390 O vi 80. H iii. p. i. 164.
April 2	The K confirms the transfer to William de Wenlok, clerk, of the annuity of 10*l* granted to John de Merle, the captor of Charles de Bloys *Westm* R. iii. p i 390. O. vi. 80. H iii p i 164.
April 8.	Warrants for the payments of the annuity of Edward de Balliol, K of Scotland. *Westm* R. iii p. i. 390 O vi. 81. H. iii p i. 164
April 16	Commission to the seneschal of Gascony, Elias de Pomerus, Peter de Mouncant, and the castellan of Bergerac to make reparation for the capture of Pontius lord of Gordoun and Elis Guilhelmi by Arnald Amanyo of Bergerac and Nicholet Danuseran, captain of Nadaillak *Westm* R iii p i 390 O vi. 81 H iii p i 164
April 24	Safe conduct for John Quaykyn, prisoner of Martin de Ferrers in Brittany *Westm.* R iii p. i 390 O vi 82 H iii p i 165
May 1.	Protection for the abbey of S Mary's de Alneto in Normandy *Westm.* R iii p. i 391
May 1.	Protection for the abbey of S Eberulfus in Normandy *Westm* R iii p i 391
May 1.	Inspeximus and confirmation of a grant by the prince of Wales of the lordship of Vilaton to Fortinus Sancii, lord of S Aralha, dated Bourdeaux, 24 March 1356 *Westm.* R. iii p i 391.
May 6	Safe conduct for Sir William de Levyngston, Eleanor de Bruys, countess of Carrick, and 21 others *Westm* R. iii p i 391 O. vi 82. H iii p i. 165
May 12	Safe conduct for Peter de Firno, servant of the cardinal of Perigord, to go to France and return , also for servants of the counts of Dampmartin, Dancere, Sacrocesare, the marshal Dodenham, and John de Valois R. iii p i 392
May 18.	Protection for Sir Matthew de Gourneye, sir Nicholas de Poyntz, and Thomas de Beauchamp going to Brittany *Westm* R iii. p. i. 392 O vi. 80. H. iii. p i 165
May 22.	Power for Richard earl of Arundel, Guy de Briane, lord of Chastel Guyon, and sir William de Thorp to treat with Wenteslau duke of Lucenburg, Lorraine, Brabant, and Lemburg, and with Joan his duchess *London.* R iii p. i 392. O. vi. 83. H iii. p i. 165
May 27.	Safe conduct for John viscount of Rohan, prisoner of Thomas de Holand, John lord of Beaumanoir [de Pulcro Manerio], Guy de Rocheford, and six others. *Westm.* R iii p i 392.
June 1.	Safe conducts for the counts of Eu, Sarebruce, Juny, Vendome, and Pontieu, the K's prisoners, and three ambassadors of Charles de Bloys. *Westm.* R. iii. p. i. 393. O vi. 84. H. iii. p. i 166

DATE.	SUBJECT.
1358 June 2.	Commission to Gilbert Chastelleyn and Stephen de Cusyngton to restore the castles and lands in Normandy taken by the English, which belong to the K. of Navarre and his brother Philip *Westm* R. iii p 1 393 O vi 84 H m p 1 166
[June 2.]	Commission to the same persons to redress the injuries suffered by Philip de Navarre. R. iii. p. 1. 393. O. vi. 85. H. iii p 1 166
June 6.	The K appoints Thomas de Musgrave, Thomas de Gray, and William de Heroun arbiters for deciding whether Hermitage Castle is to be delivered up to him or not *Westm*. R. iii p 1 393. O vi 85. H iii. p 1 166
June 6	Commission to the above-named persons to inquire as to the captivity of Archibald de Douglas, William de Tours, and other Scotch prisoners. *Westm* R iii p. 1 394 O. vi. 86. H iii. p 1 166.
[June 6]	Safe conduct for Robert seneschal of Scotland, Patrick de Dunbar, earl of March, the earl of Rosse, and William lord of Douglas, coming to take the place of the hostages for David de Bruys. R iii. p. 1 394 O vi 87 H iii p 1 167
June 7.	Commission to Henry de Percy, Ralph de Nevill, and John de Coupland, warden of Berwick, to receive 10,000 marks on June 24 for the ransom of David de Bruys. *Westm* R iii p. 1. 394 O. vi. 87. H. iii p. 1. 167
June 16.	The K allows merchants to sell their cargoes at Dublin without landing, as the harbour is dangerous *Westm* R iii p 1. 394
June 17.	Safe conduct for John de Monbourcheri and five others whom Charles de Bloys, the K's prisoner is about to send with his ransom *Westm*. R. iii. p 1. 395 O. vi 88 H iii p 1 167.
June 18	Power to Henry de Percy and Ralph de Nevill to grant a safe conduct to the Scotch nobles bringing the ransom of David de Bruys *Westm*. R iii p. 1 395 O vi 88 H iii p 1 167.
June 19 *	Safe conduct for Patrick de Dunbarre, earl of March, to come to Berwick with the ransom *Westm* R. iii p 1 395
June 20	Power for Reynaud de Schonon, lord of Schonenorst, to prorogue the time for the completion of the treaty with the duke and duchess of Brabant until Michaelmas or All Saints Day *Westm* R iii p 1 395 O vi 89 H iii p 1 167
June 21.	Innocent [VI] to David K of Scotland; will not allow the clergy of Scotland to be bound for the K *Villeneuve* R iii p 1 396 O vi 89 H iii p 1 168
June 24.	Receipt by the K. of the apostolic letters upon the treaty with Scotland *Westm*. R iii p. 1. 396. O vi 90 H iii. p 1 168
June 24.	Receipt of the apostolic letters of censure in default of paying the ransom. *Westm* R iii p 1. 396. O vi 90. H iii p 1. 168
June 24.	The K informs Robert seneschal of Scotland that on receipt of the 10,000 marks he has released his eldest son John, and received his brother as hostage in his place. *Westm*. R iii p 1. 396 O vi 91. H iii p 1 168
June 24	Receipt for 10,000 marks, the first instalment of the ransom of David de Bruys *Westm* R. iii p 1 397. O vi 91. H. iii p 1 168.
June 25.	Licence to Arnald count . . and his wife Maria to plead by proxy in Aquitain *Westm*. R iii p. 1 397
July 1.	Licence to the earl of Angus, one of the Scotch hostages, to go to Scotland. *Westm*. R. iii. p 1 397. O. vi 92. H iii. p. 1 168.
July 3.	Protection until Christmas for Venetian galleys going to Flanders. *Westm*. R. iii. p i. 397. O vi 92. H iii p 1 169
July 3	Safe conduct for John Malapert, messenger of the count of Dampnomartin, going to France on the count's affairs Letters of safe conduct for 20 going to or coming from France on various matters. *Westm* † O. vi 92 H iii p 1 169.
July 3	The K. grants to Gilbert de Pelagrua, lord of Aymet, a respite of 5 years for doing homage for his castle of Somensac *Westm* R iii p 1 397 O vi. 93. H. iii. p. 1 169.
July 4.	Grant to Reymund Guilhelm, lord of Campenna, of the castle and castellany of Tailhebort, and an annuity of 1,000 florins. Intimation thereof to the seneschal of Gascony and the constable of Bourdeaux. *Westm*. R iii p 1 397

DATE.	SUBJECT
1358. July 5	The K presents the head of S Benedict to the convent of Westminster, to be placed among the other relics belonging to the Abbey. *Westm* R III p L. 398. O. VI 98. H III p I 169.
July 5.	Safe conduct for Peter, cardinal of the Twelve Apostles, to go to France, and return *Westm* R III p I 398 O VI. 94 H III. p I 169
July 5.	Licence to merchants to unload their ships at Dublin notwithstanding the ordinance of the staple *Westm*. R. III. p I 398
July 6	Safe conduct for Alean de Plessys, whom sir Peter de Craon, the K's prisoner, sends to Brittany to procure his ransom *Westm*. R. III p I 399 O VI 94 H III p I 169
July 6	Grant of the manors of Kildroght and Kilmacridok in Kildare, Lotereles Myll, and Lynekan in Dublin, for life, to Robert de Clynton, who took the abp of Mans prisoner at the battle of Poictiers. *Westm* R III p I 169
July 6	Warrant for the payment of 20 marks to John de Montfort, duke of Brittany, for his expenses in coming to England by the K's command *Westm* R III p L. 399 O VI. 95. H III p I 170
July 6	Inspeximus and confirmation of a grant by the prince of Wales of Damasan and other places to William Reymundi, lord of Caumont, dated Bourdeaux, 16 April 1356 *Westm* R III p I 399
July 6	Inspeximus and confirmation of a grant by the prince of Wales of the castle of Blanquefort, Vernies, and other places to Galhard Durfort, dated Bourdeaux, 6 April 1356 *Westm* R. III p I 400
July 6.	Inspeximus and confirmation of a promise by the prince of Wales that the lord of Caumont shall be comprehended in any truce with France, dated Bourdeaux, 16 April 1356, also of a grant of a toll on wine *Westm* R III p I 400
July 6	Inspeximus and confirmation of a grant of the prince of Wales, releasing William de Brideport, secretary of the marshal of the army, from all exactions by the mayor of Bourdeaux, 10 April, 1357 *Westm* R. III p I 401.
July 7	Philip son of the K of France Charles count of Longueville, John count of Joigny, and seven others, become sureties for Bonabes de Rouge, lord of Derval, the K's prisoner, who is going to France on matters touching the peace between the two kingdoms *The Savoy* R III p I 401. O. VI p 95–8. H. III p. I. 170
July 14	Safe conduct for David de Bruys to come to England *Westm*. R. III p I 402 O VI 98. H III p I. 171.
July 30	The K orders the delivery of Monflanquin to John de Galhard, lord of Lymholio, in accordance with a grant to him by the prince of Wales. *Westm* R III p I. 403. O. VI. 99. H III p I 171
Aug 1	Innocent [VI] writes to the K on behalf of Thomas bp of Ely *Villeneuve*. R. III. p. I 403 O. VI 99 H III p I 171
Aug. 2	The K confirms the grant of the prince of Wales of two houses in Bourdeaux to Walter de Gales, his physician *Westm* R III p I 403
Aug 3	Safe conduct for John, eldest son of the seneschal of Scotland, coming to England *Westm* R. III. p I 403 O VI 100 H III p I 172
Aug. 5	The K orders Thomas Donnedale, lieutenant of the duke of Lancaster in Brittany, to deliver the custody of the duchy to those whom the K. shall appoint *Westm*. R. III. p I 403 O VI 100 H III p I 172
Aug. 5	Similar letter to the captains and receivers of Vannes, Roche des Anes, Pymer, and 12 other places. *Westm* R. III. p. I 404 O. VI 101 H III p I. 172
Aug 8.	The K appoints sir Robert de Herle and John de Bukyngham, clerk, lieutenants and captains in Brittany in his name and that of John de Montfort, the duke. *Westm*. R III p I. 404
Aug 8.	Commission to Robert Grenacres to survey the castles and fortresses in Brittany *Westm*. R III p I. 404.
Aug. 10.	Prorogation until Christmas of the safe conduct of James de Bourbon. *Westm*. R III p I 405 O VI 101 H III. p. I. 172
Aug 12	The K explains that his prohibition of building castles in the territory of Bourg [in Burgesio] does not apply to the restoration of old castles, and that his prohibition of markets elsewhere than at Bourg does not apply to customary markets *Westm* R. III. p. I 405.
Aug. 24.	The K orders William de Forses, captain of Brentholm (Brantôme), to deliver the abbey to the abbot if he will take the oath of fealty *Westm*. R. III. p. I. 405. O. VI. 102. H. III. p. I. 172.

DATE.	SUBJECT.
1358. Aug 24	Safe conducts for the cardinals of the Twelve Apostles and of Albano to go to Rome *Westm.* R vii p 1 405 O vi. 102. H iii p 1 173.
Aug. 24	Safe conduct for Peter Iteru, bp of Sarlat, of the household of the cardinal of Albano. *Westm.* R iii p. 1 405 O vi 103 H. iii p 1 173
Aug 30	The pope desires the K to allow the cardinals of Albano and of S Vitalis to leave England for the purpose of mediating between Charles K. of Navarre and Charles duke of Normandy. *Avignon.* R iii p 1 406 O vi 103 H. iii p 1 173
Sept 6	Henry de Tatton is appointed treasurer and receiver in Brittany *Westm.* R. iii. p 1 406.
Sept 8	The K orders the seneschals of Gascony to restore the goods of the companions of John de Gualardo, lord of Lymolio *Westm.* R. iii. p. 1. 406 O vi 104 H. iii. p. 1 173
Sept. 10	Safe conducts for the three cardinals. *Westm* R iii. p. i. 406. O vi 104 H iii p i 173
Sept. 13.	Safe conduct for Peter bp. of Sarlat. *Westm.* R iii. p 1. 407.
Sept. 18.	Safe conducts for William Vidal and John Hoquyn, officers of the K. of France, and others *Marlborough* R iii p 1 407 O vi 105 H iii p. i 174
Sept 19.	Notarial attestation of the publication of the bull of June 21 in the church of the Friars Preachers in Edinburgh. R iii p 1 407. O vi 105 H iii. p. 1. 174.
Oct 6.	Protection for sir Thomas de Holand going to Normandy on the K's service *Westm.* R iii p 1 408
Oct 8.	William Smale of Dartmouth and two others are appointed to provide ships for the conveyance of Oliver lord of Clikzon to Brittany. *Westm* R. iii. p 1. 408. O vi 106. H iii. p. 1. 174
Oct 10	Thomas de Holand is appointed warden of S Sauveur le Visconte and the other lands of Godfrey de Harecourt Sir Stephen de Cusyngton and Simon de Neuton are ordered to deliver them to him *Westm* R iii p 1 408 O vi 106 H iii p 1. 174.
Oct. 24.	Declarations that Malatesta Ungarus de Arimino, knt., and Nicholas de Beccariis of Ferrara, visited S. Patrick's purgatory in Ireland, and remained there a day and a night. *Westm* R iii. p. 1. 408. O vi 107 H iii p 1 174.
Oct 24	Safe conducts for the counts of Salebrugg and Vendôme, the K's prisoners. *Westm.* R iii p 1 408 O. vi 107 H iii p 1 175.
Oct. 24.	Safe conducts for sir Walter de Lesleye, William de Seyntoler, lord of Rosseleye, William de Kethe, marshal of Scotland, and four other Scotchmen, going abroad *Westm.* R. iii. p 1 409 O vi 108 H iii p 1 175
Oct 26	Safe conduct for William earl of Sutherland, one of the hostages of David de Bruys, to go to Scotland *Westm.* R iii p 1. 409 O vi 108 H iii p 1 175
Oct. 26	Safe conduct for the bps. of Andrew's and Brechin and the earls of March and Douglas to come to England on the affairs of David de Bruys *Westm* R iii p 1 409. O vi 108. H iii p i 175
Oct 26.	Protection for sir John la Warre, sir Otto de Holand, and seven others, in the retinue of Thomas de Holand *Westm* R iii p 1 409
Nov. 3.	The K grants the exchange of money and plate to Henry Pycard of London, for 200 marks a year. The sheriffs of London are ordered to publish the above. *Westm* R iii. p. 1. 409.
Nov 7	Warrant for the payment of the procurations from the see of Ely to the cardinals of Albano and S Vitalis. *Westm* R. iii. p. i. 410. O. vi. 109. H. iii p i. 175.
Nov. 8.	The K forbids the sheriff of Yorkshire to make his turn oftener than twice a year. *Westm.* R. iii p 1 410
Nov. 9.	Licence to R bp of Chichester to receive an annuity of 10s. from the mayor and commonalty of Chichester. *Westm* R iii p. 1 410 O. vi 109. H iii p 1. 175
Nov. 10.	The K orders Alan de Strother, late sheriff of Northumberland, to deliver Thomas Flemyng and five other Scotch hostages to Henry del Strother, the present sheriff. *Westm.* R iii. p 1 410. O vi 109. H. iii. p 1 175
[Nov. 10.]	Order to the sheriff of Northumberland to receive them. R. iii p i 411. O. vi 110. H iii. p 1. 175.
Nov. 20.	The K orders Roger de Mortimer, earl of March, constable of Dover Castle and warden of the Cinque Ports, the mayor and bailiffs of Sandwich and Margate, to prevent all persons leaving the kingdom. *Westm* R. iii. p. i 411.

DATE	SUBJECT
1358 Nov. 20	The K orders the sheriffs of London and Middlesex to clean Bishopsgate street and Algate street before the arrival of the corpse of Q Isabella, his mother. *Westm.* R iii p i, 411. O vi 110. H iii p i 176.
Dec. 1.	The K orders the treasurer and barons of the Exchequer to make allowance to the sheriffs of London and Middlesex for the costs of cleaning the above-mentioned streets, amounting to 9*l* *Westm* R iii p i 411. O. vi. 110 H. iii. p i 175
Dec 3	The K orders Henry Pycard, his butler, to take four casks of wine to Somerton Castle, for the use of his adversary of France. *Westm.* R, iii, p. i 411. O. vi. 110 H iii p i 176
Dec. 5.	The sheriffs of London are ordered to proclaim that no wine is to be sold before it has been ganged *Westm* R iii p i 411
Dec. 8	Safe conduct for Thomas de Murref, one of the hostages of David de Bruys, to go to Scotland *Westm* R iii. p i 412. O vi 111. H iii p i. 176
Dec 8.	The K appoints Thomas Durant, Thos. Dautre, and others, to provide ships at Sandwich by Palm Sunday for his passage to France *Westm.* R iii p i 412
Dec 10.	Warrant for the payment of 15*l* 14*s* to Robert de Langeton and William de Teye, for attendance on the cardinal of Perigord *Westm* R iii. p i 413 O vi. 111. H iii. p i 176
Dec. 10.	The K grants to the bailiffs and echevins of Calais the wardship of the tenements of persons dying without heirs or whose heirs are absent *Westm* R iii p i 413
Dec. 12.	Warrant for the payment of 10*l*. to sir Roger de Beauchamp and less sums to 41 others, for the custody of John of France at the Savoy *Westm.* R iii p. i. 413. O vi 111. H. iii. p. i 176
Dec. 14	Safe conduct for ambassadors from Languedoc [Lingua Occitana] coming to John of France *Westm* R iii p i 414 O vi 112 H iii p i. 176.
Dec 14	Safe conduct for Yvo Deriani, secretary to John of France, to come to England *Westm* R. iii. p. i 414 O. vi 112. H iii p i 177
Dec. 20.	Safe conduct for Peter de Vregin, squire of the lord of Craon, coming to England *Westm* R iii p i 414 O vi 112. H iii p i 177.
Dec 20	Safe conduct for Theobald de S. Albin, squire of the lord of Craon, going to France. *Westm* R iii. p i. 414. O vi 113. H iii, p. i. 177.
1359. Jan 2	The K orders the several sheriffs to assist William Deyncourt in providing for the K's adversary of France at Somerton castle in co. Lincoln. *Westm.* R. iii. p. i 414. O vi 113. H iii p i 177
Jan. 2.	The K. orders nine sheriffs to send bows and arrows to the Tower of London *Westm* R. iii p i. 414
Jan 6	Protection for sir Thomas de Courtenay, senior, John Prousz, and six others, going abroad with Thomas de Holand *Westm* R iii p i 415.
Jan 11	Safe conduct for sir Hugh de Eglynton and sir Archibald de Douglas coming from Scotland to England *Westm* R iii p i 415 O. vi 113. H iii p i 177
Jan. 12.	Safe conduct for Andrew de Murref and Alan Erskyn, Scotch merchants. *Westm.* R iii p i. 415 O vi 114. H iii. p i 177.
Jan. 12	The K. orders John de Ferres, James de Cobham, Walter de Brankescombe, and the sheriff of Devon to furnish 60 archers to accompany the K. by Sunday in mid-Lent. Twenty-seven similar commissions. *Westm* R iii. p i 415
Jan. 12.	Henry duke of Lancaster, Roger de Mortimer, earl of March, and nine other lords, are ordered to provide archers and spearmen from their lands in South Wales. *Westm.* R iii p i. 416
Jan. 17.	Power to Walter lord of Manny to receive the fealty of the French to the K. of England as K. of France at the expiration of the truce. *Westm.* R iii. p. i. 417. O. vi. 114. H iii p ii 177
Jan. 17	Power for Walter lord of Manny to grant protections *Westm.* R iii. p. i. 417. O. vi. 114 H iii p i 177
Jan. 17.	Safe conduct for the earl of Marr to come to England. *Westm.* R. iii, p. i. 417. O. vi. 116 H. iii p i 177
Jan. 28.	Safe conduct for Peter Willebert, Gerald de Habard, and four other servants of lord de Daubeny, the K.'s prisoner. *Westm* R. iii. p. i 417. O. vi. 115. H. iii. p. i. 178.

DATE.	SUBJECT
1359. Feb 1.	Commission to Guy de Bryan, keeper of the forest of Dean, John atte Hale, and three other miners, to provide four smiths and 40 miners for the K's service. *Westm.* R. iii. p. i. 417
Feb 2	Prorogation until March 3 of the surrender of the earl of Angus, one of the hostages for David de Bruys *Westm* R iii p i 418 O vi. 115 H. iii. p i 178.
Feb. 5.	Stephen de Cusyngton is appointed castellan of S Sauveur le Visconte, and custos of the other lands of Godefrey de Harecourt. *Westm.* R iii. p i. 418. O. vi. 116. H. iii. p i 178.
Feb. 7	Indenture between the K and sir Thomas de Holand for the safe keeping of S Sauveur le Visconte, Danvers, Dangouville, and S Marie de Mount *Westm* R. iii. p i 418
Feb. 8.	The K orders Henry de Percy, Ralph de Neyill, and Thomas de Lucy to attend to the complaint of sir William de Lydell of Scotland (taken prisoner at the battle of Durham by John de Standish) that he has been imprisoned by John, son of Hugh de Louthre and Thomas de Louthre, cousin of the said Hugh de Louthre, contrary to the law of arms. *Westm* R iii. p i. 418 O. vi 116 H iii p i 178.
Feb. 13.	Safe conduct for Bernard de Vineis Armand, Bernard Ruphi, knights of Toulouse, and six other ambassadors of Languedoc [Lingua Occitana], coming to the K's adversary of France [John de Valois] *Westm* R. iii p i. 419 O vi 117 H iii. p i 178
Feb. 16.	James le Botiller, earl of Ormond, is appointed justiciary of Ireland, with an annuity of 500l. Aymer de S Amand, late justiciary, is ordered to resign the office, and the people of Ireland are ordered to obey him *Westm* R iii p i 419
[Feb. 16]	Grant of the annuity of 500l to the earl of Ormond R iii p i. 419
[Feb. 16.]	Power for the earl of Ormond to remove inefficient officers R. iii. p. i. 419.
Feb. 21.	Declaration of David K. of Scotland that the respite which the K. of England has granted for the payment of his ransom shall not invalidate his rights. *London* R iii p i. 419. O vi. 117–119. H iii p i. 178
Feb 24.	Indenture between the K and Thomas earl of Mar, who does him homage, the K. granting him an annuity of 600 marks *Westm.* R iii. p i. 420. O vi 119 H. iii. p i 179
Feb 24.	Protection for six Venetian galleys going to Flanders. *Westm.* R. iii p i 420. O vi. 120 H iii p i 179.
March 1	The K orders the seneschal of Gascony to deliver the castle of Lanerdac and the rest of the inheritance of the cardinal of Perigord to Bertrand lord of Montferrand, in the cardinal's name *Westm* R iii p i 420 O vi 120 H iii p i 179
March 4.	Safe conduct for John de Fricamps, Robert Porte, Oliver de Mountmorel, and Peter Dutertre, ambassadors of the K of Navarre R iii p i 421 O vi 121 H iii p i 180.
March 6	The K appoints William de Wyndesore and Bernard Brocas to compel Robert Mareschal to restore the revenues of Dounfrount and Messy, which he has unjustly exacted ; also to compel Thomas Fogg and others to obey the duke of Lancaster. *Westm* R iii. p i 421.
March 8.	Warrant for the payment of 13l 8s 11d to John duke of Brittany for his expenses at the tournament held at Smithfield on March 4. *Westm* R iii. p i 421 O. vi. 121. H iii. p i 180
March 12.	Arnald Sauvage is appointed mayor of Bourdeaux Intimation thereof to the seneschal of Gascony and the constable and commonalty of Bourdeaux *Westm.* R. iii. p i 422.
March 12.	Protection for Tilman de Cologne and other miners at Aldeston Moor *Westm* R iii p i. 422
March 13	Safe conducts for Andrew de Ormeston and Walter de Despenser, servants of David de Bruys *Westm.* R iii p i 422. O vi. 121. H. iii. p. i. 180.
March 25.	The K orders the abp of Bourdeaux to punish Arnald Amenien de Vassoun, who was convicted of the murder of Peter de Curvyn, and delivered to the abp. as a clerk *Westm.* R iii p i 422.
March 18.	Prorogation by John K of France of the truce with England until June 24. *London* R iii. p i 422 O. vi 121 H iii. p. i 180.
March 20.	Safe conduct for the abp of Sens, prisoner of the earl of Warwick, whom the K's adversary [John de Valois] sends to France concerning the truce. *Westm* R. iii p i 423 O vi 123 H iii p i 180.
March 20.	Safe conducts for Thomas earl of Mar, sir Thomas Bisset, and four others, coming to England *Westm.* R. iii. p. i 423. O. vi. 123. H iii p. i. 181.

DATE.	SUBJECT.
1359. March 22	Safe conduct for John Bigoti of Beziers [de Biterus] and Berengarius Loc, of Narbonne ambassadors of Carcassonne, coming to the K.'s adversary of France. *Westm* R. III. p. 1 423 O vi 123 H III p 1 181
March 30.	Safe conducts for servants of the counts of Tankervill and Juny, the K.'s prisoners, going to France to purchase war horses and other articles for the said counts. *Westm* R. III. p 1. 423.
April 1	The K. appoints Gerald de Menta his councillor, with an annuity of 20 marks. *Westm.* R III p 1 424
May 1.	Warrants to the customers of S. Botolph's and Hull for the payment of the annuity of Edward de Balliol *Westm* R. III. p 1 424 O vi 124. H III p i 181
May 1.	Power for John de Stretlee and Peter Aymer to hear appeals in the duchy of Aquitain for the K. of England as K of France *Westm* R. III p 1 424. O vi. 125. H III p 1 181
May 1.	The K. forbids any person to act as notary in Aquitain, unless he be a native, and appointed by the pope, the K of England, or his officers *Westm* R III p 1 424 O. vi 125 H III. p i 181
May 1	The K orders that no ship going to Aquitain for wine shall be laden before arriving at the proper ports. *Westm.* R. III p 1 425
May 1.	The K. directs the chancellor of the university of Oxford to send the names of persons excommunicated by him to the chancellor of England, who will issue warrants for their arrest *Westm* R. III. p 1 425
May 10	The K orders the seneschal of Gascony and the constable of Bourdeaux to search for goods and profits which ought to have come to the K. *Westm* R. III p : 425
May 11	Safe conduct for the abp of Sens, the counts of Tankerville and Dampmartin, the marshal of Dodenham, the lord of Aubigny, and John Rotaru, clerk, going to France touching peace; also for John Bigoti of Beziers, Berengarius Laci of Narbonne, and Guy Forase, squire of the count of Auxerre *Westm* R III p 1 425 O vi 126 H III p 1 182
May 16.	Writs to 13 sheriffs to provide arrows for the Tower of London *Westm.* R III p. 1. 426.
May 23	Safe conduct for John de la Val, lord of Tyntyviak, John lord of Beaumanoir, and six others, ambassadors of Charles de Bloys, coming to England *Westm.* R III p 1 426
May 23.	Safe conducts for John Olivern, servant of the marshal Dodenham, the K's prisoner, William de Bolona, equerry of the K of France, and three others *Westm* R III. p 1 426.
May 25.	Indenture between the K and Patrick de Chartres, for the custody of the castle of S Grymolyn in Brittany *London* R III p. 1 427
May 25.	Pardon to Roger de Mortimer, earl of March, for having sent John de Boa to his prison at Radnor for complicity in the escape of felons at Ewyas Lacy. *Westm.* R III p 1 427.
May 30	The K orders the captains of S Sauveur, Daunfrount, and S Vedast to punish those who have injured the convent of S. Mary de Alneto *Westm* R III p 1 427.
June 1	Power for John de Cheveresdon, seneschal of Gascony, and John de Stretele, constable of Bourdeaux, to treat with the K. of Castile. *Westm* R. III. p. i. 427 O vi 126. H III p 1 182
June 5.	The K appoints Michael de Grendon, sergeant-at-arms, and others, to prepare ships at Sandwich by July 6, for his passage to France. *Westm.* R. III p i. 427.
June 6.	Safe conduct for sir Archibald de Douglas coming from Scotland to England. *Westm.* R. III p. 1. 428 O vi 127. H. III p 1 182
June 7	Warrant to Thomas Clerk, master of the ship called *La Edward*, to arrest 60 mariners Seventeen similar warrants *Westm* R III p 1 428.
June 12.	Grant of 2d, a day, 10s for a robe, and 4s. 8d for shoes to John de Dunstaple, disabled at the battle of Cressy, to be received annually *Westm.* R. III. p 1 429. O vi. 127. H. III p 1 182
June 17.	Raulyn Barry is appointed warden of Henbon in Brittany. *London* R. III p. i. 429.
June 17	The K. orders the abbot of Whalley, Thomas de Lathum, and two others, to inquire concerning Margaret, daughter and heir of sir Thomas Danyers, whose guardian, John de Radeclyf, is said to have married her against her will to an unfit person. *Westm* R. III. p. 1. 429
June 18.	The K forbids the canons of S Andrew's, Bourdeaux, to prevent the levying of the custom called Lissak on wine. *Westm.* R. III. p. 1. 429.

DATE.	SUBJECT
1359 July 6.	The K orders the justiciary of Ireland to inquire into the complaint of the citizens of Waterford that ships continue to land at Rosponte, in spite of the prohibition. *Westm.* R. iii p. 1 429.
July 8.	The K. orders the constable of Bourdeaux to seize offices which have been granted to unfit persons without the K.'s licence. *Westm.* R. iii p 1 430.
July 8.	Power for John de Cheverston, seneschal of Gascony, and John de Stretele, constable of Bourdeaux, to receive persons to the K.'s obedience. *Westm.* R. iii. p 1. 431.
July 10.	Commission to William Herlond, John Berholte, and John Haveryng to provide 50 carpenters at Sandwich by Aug. 16. Three commissions to other persons to provide masons, smiths, and farriers. *Westm.* R iii p 1 431
July 11.	Sir Robert de Herle is appointed captain of Brittany in the name of the K. and the duke of Brittany. *Westm.* R. iii. p. 1. 431.
July 11.	Sir Robert de Herle and Oliver lord of Clisson are appointed captains in Poictou. *Westm.* R iii p 1. 431
July 12.	Robert de Grenacres is appointed warden of Beaufort Castle on the Rance in Brittany. *Westm.* R. iii. p i 432.
July 14.	The K orders the constable of Bourdeaux to pay 1,000 gold crowns to Berard de Lebret *Westm.* R iii p 1. 432.
July 15	William de Wakefeld is appointed keeper of the writs concerning Brittany. *Westm.* R. iii. p. 1. 432. O. vi 127 H. iii p 1. 182.
July 16	The K orders the seneschal of Gascony and the constable of Bourdeaux to grant letters of marque to William de Wakefeld, citizen of Bourdeaux *Westm.* R iii p. 1 432 O vi. 128 H iii. p 1 182
July 18.	The K desires James Botiller, earl of Ormond, justiciary of Ireland, to make use of the counsel of John abp. of Dublin *Westm.* R iii p 1 432.
July 18	Letter to the abp , desiring him to assist the justiciary. *Westm.* R. iii. p ii 433.
July 20.	The K desires the earl of Ormond to give his eldest daughter in marriage to Gerald, younger brother of the late Maurice Fitz Maurice, earl of Desmond *Westm* R iii. p 1 433.
July 20.	Power for the justiciary of Ireland to pardon rebels. *Westm.* R iii. p 1 433
July 20	The K orders that the seal for judicial writs in Ireland shall be kept by the chief justice, and that the rolls of the pleas shall be kept in bags under his seal. *Westm.* R. iii. p 1 433
July 20.	Similar order for the rolls of the justices of the pleas *Westm* R iii. p. 1 433.
July 20.	The K orders the justiciary of Ireland to make proclamation that lords having castles on the marches must put them in a state of defence and dwell therein *Westm* R. iii p 1 434.
July 20.	The K orders the justiciary, chancellor, and treasurer of Ireland to exact an account of the money received by officers of the crown. *Westm.* R. iii. p i. 434.
July 20	Warrant for the payment of 200l to the earl of Ormond for executing the K.'s business *Westm.* R iii p 1 434
July 20.	The K forbids Irish persons being appointed to mayoralties or other offices or to ecclesiastical benefices. *Westm.* R. iii. p 1 434
[July 20.]	The K. forbids the sessions of the justices to be held in parts of Ireland exposed to war R. iii p 1. 434.
July 20.	The K orders the justiciary of Ireland to make inquisition as to lands there granted at rents below their value *Westm.* R iii p 1 435
July 20.	Commission to the justiciary of Ireland to survey castles and to remove inefficient officers R. iii. p 1 435.
July 20.	Also to remove officers who have been indicted for felonies *Westm* R iii p i 435.
July 20.	Also to revoke charters of pardons to felons for the murder of those who indicted them. *Westm.* R iii p i. 435.
July 20.	Also to seize devastated and deserted lands. *Westm* R iii p 1 435
July 21.	Safe conduct for Gassins de Lahingue, Ralph de Grandpont [de Magno ponte] and 25 others, going to France , also for the servants of the count of Salebrugg and seven other prisoners of the K. *Westm* R iii. p. 1 436 O vi 129 H iii p 1 183.
July 22.	Grant to Berard de Lebret, son and heir of Berard de Lebret, lord of Puy Normand, of respite for doing homage *Westm* R. iii p. 1 436. O. vi. 129 H. iii. p 1 183.
July 20.	Release to the tenants of the abp of York in Hextildesham [Hexham] from the payment of tenths and fifteenths during the abp.'s life *Westm* R iii p 1 436

C C

DATE.	SUBJECT.
1359 July 22	The K orders the justiciary of Ireland to enforce the statute forbidding the K.'s officers to acquire lands within their bailiwicks. *Westm* R. III p 1 436
July 24	Protection for sir Thomas Byset of Scotland, and for his lands at Upsetelyngton, Lambden, and Kymbryngham. *Westm.* R. III. p 1 437 O vi 129. H. III. p 1 183.
July 25.	Safe conduct for Guichard de Lorays and Denys Bouis, bringing wine from France for the use of the K. of France *Westm* R III p 1 437. O vi 130 H. III p i 183
July 26.	Protection for William Radicis, physician, and 19 other attendants on the K.'s adversary of France. *Westm* R III p 1 437
[July 26]	Protection for Eustace de Brolio, tailor, John de Milano, falconer, and 19 others, servants of the K.'s adversary of France R III p 1 437
July 26	The K appoints William Deyncourt to take the K.'s adversary of France from Hertford to Somerton Castle. *Westm* .R III p 1. 438 O vi 130 H. III p 1 183.
July 27.	Indenture between the K and William Deyncourt, William Colevill, John de Kirketon, John Deyncourt, and Saier de Rocheford, for the custody of the K.'s adversary of France. *London* R. III p 1 438 O vi. 131 H III p. 1 184
July 27	Warrant to the collectors of S Botolph's to pay the expenses of taking the K.'s adversary of France from the castle of Hertford to Somerton Castle. *Westm.* R III p 1. 438. O vi 131 H. III p 1 184
July 27.	Warrant to Roger de Beauchamp to deliver the K.'s adversary of France to William Deyncourt and others named above. *Westm.* R. III p 1 439. O vi 132 H III. p 1 184
July 27.	The K orders his officers to assist William Deyncourt and others in executing the above commission. *Westm.* R. III. p 1 439 O vi 132. H III p 1 184.
July 28.	Safe conducts for Margaret countess of Douglas, and for Patrick de Dunbar, earl of March, to visit the shrine of S Thomas at Canterbury. *Westm.* R. III p. 1. 439 O vi 133 H III p 1 184
July 28	Safe conducts for James Penquadyk, prisoner of sir John de Dalton, for Tristan Maniles and Hugh de Amboys *Westm* R III. p. 1 439 O vi. 133. H III p 1 184
July 30	Protection for sir John de Gros, going abroad in the retinue of Milo de Stapelton of Bedale, also for 15 others, of various dates to Aug 20 *Westm* R III p 1 439
Aug. 4.	The K orders Thomas Horsey to conduct to Sandwich the 30 archers furnished by the county of Somerset , 27 similar commissions. *Westm.* R III p. i. 440
Aug 8	Protection for Thomas earl of Anegos, returning to England from Scotland *Westm* R. III p 1 441. O vi 133 H III p i 185
[Aug. 8]	Safe conduct for four ships of Flanders, commander Copin Wolp, sent to assist the K. by Thomas earl of Anegos R III p 1. 441 O. vi 133. H III. p. 1. 185
Aug 12	The K informs the abps of Canterbury and York of the fruitlessness of the negotiations for peace with France, and his intention of resuming the war, and desires their prayers. *Westm* R III p 1 442 O. vi 134. H III p 1 185
Aug 12	The K. orders Nigel de Haukynton and three others to arrest John de Cornewaille and William de Derby, French spies *Westm* R III. p 1 442.
Aug 14	Warrant for the payment of 28*l* to William Deyncourt for his expenses in conducting the K.'s adversary of France from London to Somerton *Westm* R III. p 1. 442. O vi. 135 H III p 1 185.
Aug. 16	Protection for Henry Comyn, John de Grey of Codnore, and 26 others, going abroad in the retinue of John earl of Richmond *Westm* R III p i 442
Aug. 18	Protection for sir Thomas Fichet, Walter de Thorp, and 109 others, going abroad in the retinue of the prince of Wales *Westm* R. III p 1. 443.
Aug. 20	Safe conducts for John Reteril, secretary of John of France, the K.'s adversary, and for Charles count of Dampmartin, coming to England, and for Copin Messagier, servant of the lord de Daubeny, the K.'s prisoner, going to France *Westm* R III p. 1. 444. O. v. 135. H III p 1 185
Aug 20	Protection for Richard Foune and Lambert de Thrikyngham, clerks, and for 14 others in the retinue of John Chaundos *Westm* R. III p 1 444
Aug. 20.	Protection for Richard Longeford of Guildford, in the retinue of Thomas de Beauchamp of Warwick, and for five others in the retinues of other lords *Westm* R. III p. 1. 444.
Aug. 23.	Protection for John Bekke and Adam Delbon, in the retinue of James de Audele, and for eight others. *Westm* R III p 1. 444.

DATE.	SUBJECT.
1359. Aug. 26	Protection for ships of Sluys, Dunkirk, and Gravelines, coming to 'assist the K. in his passage. *Westm.* R. iii p i 445.
Aug. 27.	The K. grants that if Edward prince of Wales shall die during his expedition abroad, his executors shall take possession of his possessions in England, Wales, and elsewhere. *Leeds* R. iii p. i 445 O. vi 135 H. iii. p. i 185.
Aug. 28.	Grant of an annuity of 100*l* to Blanche countess of Richmond *Westm.* R. iii p i. 445. O. vi 136. H iii. p i 185
Aug. 28.	Protection for William de Botreaux and 12 others in the retinue of Guy de Brian. *Westm.* R iii p. i. 445.
Sept. 1.	Protection for sir John de Northwod and six others in the retinue of John de Cobeham, son of the countess Marshal *Westm* R iii. p i 446 O vi 136 H iii p. i 186
Sept 2.	Protection for sir Gilbert Turbervill and five others in the retinue of Edward le Despenser. *Westm* R iii. p. i. 446. O. vi 136 H. iii. p. i. 186.
Sept. 3.	Protection for sir John de Cokrington and seven others in the retinue of Thomas de Roos of Hamelak *Westm* R. iii. p i 448
Sept. 6	Protection for sir John de Lysors and 20 others in the retinue of Thomas de Beauchamp, earl of Warwick *Westm.* Also for the earl *Sandwich.* Oct. 14 R. iii. p i. 446
Sept. 8.	Protection for John Bosoun and nine others in the retinue of John de Montacute. *Westm.* R. iii p. i. 446. O vi. 136 H. iii. p. i. 186.
Sept 9.	Inspeximus and confirmation of a grant by the prince of Wales of the manors of Nevyn and Purthely in N Wales, to sir Nigel de Lohereyn, for his services at the battle of Poictiers, dated London, 8 Sept, 33 Edw III. *Sandwich* R iii p i 447
Sept. 11.	Licence to Henry le Potier and John Cornard of France, in the retinue of the prior of Frompton, to remain in England for one year. *Westm* R. iii p i, 447
Sept 12.	Protection for William, son of Roger de Esh, sir Nicholas de Poyntz, and two others in the retinue of William de Montacute, earl of Salisbury. *Sandwich* R. iii. p i 447. O vi 137 H. iii p i 186
Sept. 13.	Power for Ralph de Nevill to treat with Patrick Dunbarre, earl of March. *Sandwich.* R. iii p i, 448. O. vi. 137. H iii p i 186
Sept. 18	The K forbids markets for provisions to be held elsewhere in Kent than at Sandwich, Dover, and Canterbury *Westm* R iii p i 448
Sept 26.	Indemnity for the inhabitants of Leeds and Bromfield, in co Kent, for the burial without an inquest of William de Malmesbury, who was drowned at Leeds Castle. *Leeds* R. iii. p i 448.
Sept 30	Indenture between the K and Barthelmeu Guidonis of Castilon, and Adam · de St Ive of London, for the exchange of money *Westm* R iii p i 448
Oct. 1.	Warrants for the payment of the annuity of Edward de Balliol, late K. of Scotland. *Westm.* R. iii p. i 449 O vi. 138. H iii. p i 186
Oct. 3.	The K appoints—sir Alexander de Nevill, sir Marmaduke de Lomele, and two others arrayers in the North Riding of York, according to the statute of Winchester 33 similar commissions. *Sandwich.* R iii. p i 449
Oct. 4.	The K. orders the sheriffs of London to make proclamation that no exchange of money is to be made except by the said Guidonis and St. Ive. *Sandwich.* R iii. p. i 450
Oct. 10.	The K summons S. abp. of Canterbury, six bps., the priors of S John of Jerusalem and Christchurch, Canterbury, the abbot of Westminster, and three others, Richard earl of Arundel and 22 other lords, to a parliament at Westminster on Nov 10 *Sandwich* R iii p i 456 O vi 138. H. iii p i 186.
Oct. 12	Safe conduct for Hanekin le Chaumberlayn, and Galepin de Nyvers, servants of the marshal de Doudenham, the K/s prisoner *Westm.* R iii p i 451 O. vi. 138 H. iii. p i 187
	Safe conduct for John de Gibiac, servant of Louis, son of the count of Ventadour, the K's prisoner. R iii. p. i 451. O. vi 139 H. iii. p. i. 187.
Oct. 13.	The K. appoints his son Thomas regent of the realm during his absence abroad *Sandwich* R. iii. p i. 451. O vi. 139 H. iii. p i. 187.
Oct 13.	Power for prince Thomas to grant letters of *congé d'élire*, receive fealty, &c during his father's absence from England *Sandwich* R iii p i. 451 O vi 139 H iii p i. 187
Oct. 16.	The K. orders Richard de Ravensere, receiver of the lands belonging to the late Q. Isabella, to pay the expenses of her anniversary to John de Neubury, keeper of the wardrobe. *Sandwich.* R. iii. p i 452. O vi 140. H iii p i. 187

DATE.	SUBJECT
1359. Oct. 18.	The K. orders the mayor and sheriffs of London to proclaim protection for Flemish mariners *Sandwich* R iii p i. 452 O vii 140 II iii p i. 187
	Similar letter to Roger de Mortimer, earl of March, warden of the Cinque Ports, and the mayors and bailiffs of all the ports in England. R iii p i 452.
Oct. 20.	Warrant for the payment of five marks to John de Chichestre, goldsmith of London, for making a seal for the K's son Thomas, to use during the K's absence *Sandwich.* R. iii p i 452 O vi 141 H iii p i 187
	Memorandum of the delivery of the great seal to John de Wynewyk, keeper of the privy seal, and of the receipt by the chancellor of the seal to be used during the K.'s absence, from the treasurer and chamberlains. The K., before his embarkation, stayed at the house of Robert Goueire, at Stonore, in the isle of Thanet, near Sandwich, and he left Sandwich at sunrise on Oct. 28 in *la Philip* of Dartmouth, and arrived the same evening at Calais. R iii. p i 452 O vi. 141. H iii p i 188
Oct 28.	The K appoints Philip de Navarre, count of Longueville, and sir Thomas de Holand his lieutenants and captains in Normandy. *Sandwich.* R. iii. p i 452 O vii. 142. H. iii. p. i. 188.
Oct 30	Receipts for 5,000 marks, for the ransom of David de Bruys *Calais* Also for 2,500 marks *Viriiy* 1 *Jan.* R iii p i 453. O vi. 142 3 II iii p i. 188
Oct. 31.	Power for the treasurer of Calais and John Walewayn, governor of the merchants at Bruges, to receive the remainder of David de Bruy's ransom. *Calais* R. iii. p i. 453. O. vi 143 H iii p. i 188
Nov. 6.	Safe conduct for sir William More of Scotland, to come to Canterbury. *Woodstock* * R iii p i 453 O vi 144 H iii p i 189
Nov. 8	Twenty-one writs to sheriffs to send bows and arrows to William de Rothewell, keeper of the wardrobe at the Tower of London. *Windsor* R. iii. p. i 454.
Nov. 10.	Safe conducts of various dates for Bernard Gilebert and Sicard de Lagrissoul, squires of the count of Vendôme, and other servants of the French prisoners Protection for John Retarii and John Briton *Woodstock.* R iii p i 454. O vi 144 H iii p i. 189
Nov. 12.	Richard Tempest and John de Coupland are ordered to assist Gilbert de Umframvill, earl of Angus, and Ralph de Nevill in preserving the truce with Scotland *Woodstock.* R. iii p. i 454 O vi 145. H. iii p. i 189.
Nov. 17.	Innocent [VI] exhorts the K. to make peace with France, and desires credence for Symon, master of the order of Friars Preachers, and William de Lenne, dean of Chichester. *Avignon.* R. iii p. i 455. O vi 145. H. iii p. i. 189.
Nov 16.	John Bardolf of Wyrmegeye, William de Kerdeston, and 14 others are appointed arrayers in Norfolk. 65 similar commissions. *Westm.* R iii p i 455.
Nov. 18.	The abps of Canterbury and York are desired to summon convocations. *Woodstock.* R iii p i 458 O vi 146. H. iii p i. 190.
Nov. 20	The several sheriffs are ordered to publish the regulations for wages contained in the statute of 25 Edw III *Westm* R. iii p i 459.
Nov. 22	Proclamation of protection for the Flemings is to be made in London and Lenn. *Reading.* R iii p i 459 O vi 147 H iii p i. 190.
Nov. 22.	The mayor and bailiffs of Dover are ordered to appoint collectors of the subsidy of 6d. in the pound for providing a fleet Similar writs to the mayors and bailiffs of 58 other ports. *Woodstock.* R iii p i 459
Nov. 29.	Exemplification of a certificate of the services due to the K. from the Cinque Ports. *Reading* R iii. p. i 460.
Dec. 1.	Capitulation of sir John de Delton and Dauquin de Hatton, captains of Regennes and la Mote de Chanlay, to Robert lord of Fienes, constable of France. *Auxerre* R. iii. p i 461. O. vi. 147–150. H. iii p. i 190–1.
Dec. 1	Lease to Henry de Briselee and Richard de Colle of the gold and silver mines in Devonshire for 15 years *Westm* R iii p i 462.
Dec. 4.	John de Mouhray, Sauer de Rocheford, Thomas de Ingelby, and three others are appointed justices of the peace in Holland, in Lincolnshire 39 similar commissions for other countries *Woodstock* R. iii p i. 463.

* Documents dated in England during the King's absence are attested by his son Thomas

DATE.	SUBJECT
1359. Dec. 5.	Safe conducts for Stephen Fouque, cook of the count Daunsoire, Jaquelin de Tornay, servant of the French K., and other servants of the French prisoners. *Woodstock.* R. m. p. 1. 464. O. vi 150–1. H. iii p. 1 191.
Dec. 23	Receipt for 2,500 marks, part of the ransom of David de Bruys. *Westm.* R. m. p 1 465 O vi. 151 H. iii p 1 191.
Dec. 30.	The K accepts the election of Walter de Frompton and Geoffrey Beauflour, as collectors of the subsidy at Bristol, and of Thomas Deye and Martin Haaf, at Lostwithiel and Fowy. *Reading.* R iii p 1 465.
Dec. 30.	The K orders Robert de Herle, captain of Brittany, to restore to Oliver lord of Clizon, the lands granted to his mother Johanna and her husband Walter de Bentele, who are now dead. *Westm* R m. p i 465 O vi 151. H. iii p 1. 192.
Dec 30.	The seneschal of Gascony and the constable of Bourdeaux are ordered to restore to Oliver de Clizon his mother's right of custom at Bourdeaux. *Westm* R. iii p 1. 466. O vi. 152. H. iii. p 1 192
Dec 30.	Oliver lord of Clizon is appointed warden of Pymmere Castle in Brittany. Intimation thereof to Robert de Herle. *Westm* R m p 1. 466 O vi 153 H iii p. 1 192
1360. Jan 1.	Hugh Martyn, deputy of the earl of Lancaster, late captain of Aquitain, is ordered to deliver to John de Stretele, [constable of Bourdeaux, all writs and other profits of Brittany. *Westm* R iii p 1. 466. O vi 154 H. iii p 1 192.
Jan. 12	Thomas bp of Durham, Gilbert de Umframville, earl of Angus, and Ralph de Nevill are ordered to release persons imprisoned for resisting the arrayers, if they think their punishment has been sufficient. *Reading.* R iii p. 466.
Jan 12.	The sheriffs of London are ordered to issue a proclamation forbidding the importation of letters prejudicial to the kingdom, and summoning foreign merchants to appear before the council. *Westm.* R. iii. p. 1 467.
Jan. 13.	Declaration of Rauf Spigurnell and three other clerks in Chancery that sir Denys de Morbek is unable, from illness in a street near Barking chapel at London, to appear before the K. for the settlement of his dispute with Bernard de Troie, a Gascon squire, as to the capture of the French K at the battle of Poitiers. *Westm* R. iii. p i 467. O vi 155. H. iii p 1 193.
Jan. 18	Summons to the dean of Hereford to appear before the council, to give information concerning Henry de Shupton, archdeacon of Salop, and Andrew de Wermynstre, rector of the church of Melles, who prevent him from acting as coadjutor to the bp of Hereford. Similar summons to the bp if his health allows him to come. *Reading.* R. iii. p. i 467. O vi 155 H. iii. p 1 193.
Jan. 18.	The K. accepts the election of Thomas de Pykenham and Thomas Atte Cornerth as collectors of the subsidy in London. *Reading.* R. iii p 1. 468.
Jan. 20.	John de Neubury, keeper of the wardrobe, is ordered to deliver robes to the sister of John duke of Brittany. *Reading* R iii p 1. 468 O vi 156. H. iii p 1. 193.
Jan. 23.	The collectors of the subsidy are ordered to levy 2s on each cask of wine and sack of wool, instead of 6d. in the pound. *Reading.* R. iii p. 1. 468.
Feb 10.	Writs of parliamentary summons for March 17 at Westminster. Certain bps, abbots, and lords are commissioned to treat with the commons at Worcester, Taunton, Lincoln, and Leicester. *Westm* R iii p. 1. 468
Feb. 15.	The K forbids his captains and other officers in Normandy, Anjou, and Maine to grant safe conducts to enemies. *Westm* R iii. p. i 469
Feb. 15.	Gregory Seys, captain of Beaumont le Visconte, is ordered to hear the complaint of Richard Wiriot, that Piers Duzers has deprived him of the receivership of Plessiburet. *Westm* R iii p 1 469
Feb. 16.	Safe conduct for John de Polaynill and John Jubeat, servants of Louis, son of the count of Ventadour. *Westm* R. iii. p. 1 470.
Feb. 18.	Safe conduct for William Radicis, physician, and 20 other servants of the K's adversary of France. *Westm.* R iii p 1. 470. O vi. 157. H. iii p 1. 194
March 1.	John de Bukyngham, keeper of the privy seal of the K's son Thomas, and Ralph Spigournell are appointed to remove the K's adversary of France and the other prisoners from the castle of Somerton to the castle of Berkhampstede. *Westm* R. iii p. 1 470. O vi 158 H. iii p 1 194
March 2.	William Deyncourt and the other keepers of John of France, the K's adversary of France, are ordered to deliver him up with the other prisoners. *Westm.* R. iii. p. 1. 470. O. vi. 159. H. iii. p. 1 194.

DATE	SUBJECT.
1360 March 2	The arrayers of the several counties are ordered to prepare to resist an expected invasion by the French　*Westm.*　R. iii. p. i. 471　O. vi. 160　H. iii. p. i. 195.
March 2	Letters to the same effect to Hugh de Courteneye, earl of Devon, and the prior of S. John of Jerusalem in England.　*Westm.*　R. iii. p. i. 471.
March 2.	Similar letters to the mayors and bailiffs of Lenn and 48 other ports, the bp. of Durham, Isabella Felica, R. lady of the Isle of Wight, and the warden of the Cinque Ports, who are also ordered to have all ships drawn on shore　*Westm.*　R. iii. p. i. 471.
March 2.	Similar orders to John de Wesenham, Philip de Whitton, and William Smale of Dartmouth, lieutenants of the admirals　*Westm.*　R. iii. p. i. 472
March 4.	Innocent [VI.] desires credence for Andryn abbot of Clugny and Hugh de Gebenna, lord of Hauton, concerning peace　*Avignon.*　R. iii. p. i. 472.　O. vi. 160.　H. iii. p. i. 195.
March 8	Commission to Ralph Spigournel and Thomas de Baddely, clerk, to remove the French K. and the other prisoners from Somerton　*Westm.*　R. iii. p. i. 472　O. vi. 161　H. iii. p. i. 195
March 9	The abp. of Canterbury is ordered to array his men and send them to the coast　*Reading.*　R. iii. p. i. 472.
March 10	Truce for three years with the duke of Burgundy, who pays the K. 200,000 *deniers d'or*, or *Moutons d'or*, the K. giving up the town of Flavigny　*Guillon*　R. iii. p. i. 473.　O. vi. 161–4　H. iii. p. i. 195
March 10	Obligations of Philip duke of Burgundy and the nobles of the duchy for the payment of the above-mentioned sum.　*Guillon.*　R. iii. p. i. 474.　O. vi. 164.　H. iii. p. i. 196.
March 10	Safe conducts for John de Milano, falconer, and seven other servants of the French K., to return to France, and for Roger Chicy and seven others to remain in England.　*Westm.*　R. iii. p. i. 474　O. vi. 157　H. iii. p. iv. 194.
March 10.	Safe conduct for Nicholas Curez de Someres and three other servants of the count of Salehrigge.　*Westm.*　R. iii. p. i. 475.
March 11.	The sheriffs of London are ordered to arrest ships of 100 tons.　*Westm.*　R. iii. p. i. 475
March 12.	Safe conducts for Peter de Gyndree and Hugh le Faucouner, servants of the count of Dancerre, and 22 other servants of the prisoners.　*Westm.*　R. iii. p. i. 475.　O. vi. 158.　H. iii. p. i. 194.
March 14	William de Ayremynne, John de Buscy, and Thomas de Meaux, arrayers of Kesteven, are ordered to bring men at arms and archers to Somerton on March 20, to conduct the adversary of France to Grantham　Similar order to the sheriff of Lincoln and to the arrayers of Northamptonshire, Bedfordshire, and Buckinghamshire, to conduct him from Grantham to Stamford, and thence to London.　*Reading.*　R. iii. p. i. 175.　O. vi. 166–7.　H. iii. p. i. 197.
March 15	Robert de Causton and John de Wesenham are appointed to arrest ships fit for war from the Thames northwards, and to man and prepare them, as the French have taken Winchelsea　*Reading.*　R. iii. p. i. 476.
March 16	Writs to the mayors and bailiffs of Sandwich and 28 other ports to arrest ships and to prevent men or victuals leaving the country.　*Reading.*　R. iii. p. i. 476.　O. vi. 167.　H. iii. p. i. 198
March 16.	The arrayers of Essex and 22 other counties are ordered to send their men to London.　*Westm.*　R. iii. p. i. 477.
March 16.	The sheriffs of Wiltshire are ordered to repair the castles of Old Sarum and Marlborough.　*Westm.*　R. iii. p. i. 477.
March 16.	Summons to Thomas earl of Anegus to return to London as a hostage, the day for his return having passed　*London.*　R. iii. p. i. 477.　O. vi. 168.　H. iii. p. i. 198.
March 17.	Thomas de Brodestan, warden of Gloucester Castle, is ordered to keep safely the count of Juny, the K.'s prisoner. Similar orders for the custody of the lords of Creon, Duryvall, and Daubeneye, the K.'s prisoners, at Bristol, Pontefract, and Tykhill　*Westm.*　R. iii. p. i. 477　O. vi. 169　H. iii. p. i. 198
March 18	Safe conduct for Hanekyn de Moneyvill and three other servants of the count of Saresbruch, who is at Wallingford Castle.　*Westm.*　R. iii. p. i. 478.
March 18.	The arrayers of Essex and six other counties are ordered to send men to London by March 23　The mayor and sheriffs of London are ordered to provide 400 men at arms and 600 archers.　*Westm.*　R. iii. p. i. 478.

DATE	SUBJECT.
1360. March 19.	John Walewayn, governor of the English merchants at Bruges, is ordered to arrest English ships in the Flemish ports *Westm.* R. iii. p. i 478.
March 24.	John Bech, master of the ship called "La Cogg Johan," of Sandwich, is ordered to unload his ship and prepare it for war Similar orders to six other masters. *Bishop's Waltham* R. iii p. i 478 O vi 169. H iii p i. 198.
March 26	John Pavely, prior of S. John of Jerusalem in England, is appointed admiral of the fleet. *Westm* R iii p. i 479. O vi 170. H. iii. p. i. 199.
March 26.	The arrayers of Berkshire and five other counties are ordered to send men at arms and archers for the fleet *Westm.* R. iii p i 479
March 28	Proclamation to be made in London that all men at arms and archers going to Normandy or Brittany are to go in the said fleet. *Westm.* R. iii p i. 479.
March 31	The collectors of the tenth and fifteenth in Essex and seven other counties are ordered to pay the wages of the men at arms, &c , of their respective counties *Reading* R. iii. p. i. 480. O vi 170. H iii p i. 199.
April 1.	Safe conduct for Constance, wife of Robert de Knolles, who is going to her husband in Brittany. *Westm.* R iii. p. i. 480. O vi. 171. H iii p i 199
April 2	The sheriffs of Wiltshire and Somersetshire are ordered to exhort the collectors of the tenth and fifteenth to do their duty *Westm* R iii p i 480.
April 6	John Chandos 'is appointed warden of the castle of Fretty and the tower of S. Christopher, in Normandy. *Chantilly.* R. iii. p. i. 480.
April 8.	Protections of various dates for sir William de Overton, Thomas de Roos, and 13 others, going abroad *Westm.* R iii p i. 481
April 10.	Henry Peverell is appointed warden of Southampton. *Westm.* R. iii. p. i 481
April 14.	Protections of various dates for Richard de Sulby, of Northampton, and nine others. *Reading and Westm.* R iii p i 481
April 16.	Protection for sir William Talemache and William de Lodewyk, in the retinue of the earl of Northampton, and for Peter Albertyn, in the retinue of John de Cobham. *Westm.* R. iii. p. i. 482.
April 16	Protection for Nicholas Thomasyn, apothecary of London, sir Norman de Swyneford, and seven others in the retinue of the prince of Wales. *Westm.* R iii p i 482
April 16.	John de Saham, William Gates, and John Landesdale are ordered to garrison the castle of Q Philippa at Pevensey *Westm* R iii p i 482 O vi 171 H iii p i 199.
April 16.	James le Botiller, earl of Ormond, justiciary of Ireland, John abp of Dublin, and Thomas de Baddeby, treasurer of Ireland, are ordered to search for gold and silver mines in Ireland . *Westm* R iii p i. 482. O vi 172 H iii. p i 199.
April 20.	Protections of various dates for sir John de Nowers, sir Thomas Moygne, and 20 others. *Westm.* R iii p i 482.
April 20.	Also for Alan Cheyne, in the retinue of Edward prince of Wales, and for 30 others , various dates. *Westm.* R. iii p. i. 483.
April 20.	Also for sir William de Huntyngfeld and eight others in the retinue of Henry duke of Lancaster. *Reading.* R. iii. p i 483
April 20.	Safe conduct for Tristan de Chalon, son of the count of Dancerre [Auxerre], John de Chalon, his grandson, and three others. *Westm.* R. iii. p. i. 484.
April 21.	Protection for sir John Fitzwauter and three others in the retinue of William earl of Northampton. *Westm.* R iii. p i. 484.
April 22.	Protection for John Vathque and Hanekin Polayn, servants of James de Bourbon, the K.'s prisoner, at Hertford Castle *Westm.* R. iii. p i 484. O. vi. 172 H iii. p i 200.
April 24	Innocent [VI] desires to the K. to abstain from plundering churches and churchmen in France *Avignon.* R. iii p. i. 484 O vi. 172 H iii. p. i. 200.
April 28.	Protection for three Armenian monks to collect alms in England for their churches in Armenia. *Reading* R. iii. p i 484 O vi. 173. H. iii. p. i. 200.
April 28.	Richard de Ravenesere, keeper of the hanaper of the Chancery, is ordered to pay 60s to Jordan de Barton, a clerk in Chancery, for the expenses of removing the rolls from the Great Tower in the Tower of London, in which tower the French K. was confined. *Reading.* R iii. p. i 485. O vi. 174 H. iii p. i. 200
April 28.	The mayor and bailiffs of Dartmouth are ordered to release the ships they had arrested to serve in the fleet. *Westm.* R. iii. p. i. 485. O. vi. 174. H. iii. p. i. 200.

DATE.	SUBJECT.
1360 April 29	Protection for Walter de Verneye, in the retinue of Ralph earl of Stafford. *Westm.* R iii p i 485
April 30	Thomas Fishacre, master of the ship "*la George*," of Plymouth, and four others, are ordered to convey Constance, wife of Robert de Knolles, to Brittany. *Westm.* R. iii. p i 485 O vi 174 H. iii p. i 200
May 6.	The collectors of S Botolph's are ordered to pay 50 marks to John de Kirketon, William de Colvill, Saier de Rocheford, and John Deyncourt, the keepers of the K.'s adversary of France. *Reading* R. iii p i 485. O vi 174. H iii p. i. 200.
May 7.	Charles duke of Normandy, eldest son of the K of France, orders the proclamation of the truce concluded with the K. until Michaelmas 1361. *Chartres.* R iii p. i. 485. O vi 175 H iii p i 201.
May 7	Proclamation by Charles duke of Normandy of the above-mentioned truce *Chartres.* R. iii p i. 486 O. vi 177 H iii p i 201
May 8.	Jehan le Mangre, Gauchier de Lor, and four others are appointed conservators of the truce in France. *Chartres* R iii p i 486.
May 8	Treaty in French and Latin between England and France The K of England retains Guyenne, Gascony, Poictou, Saintonge, Agennois, Perigord, Limousin, Caoursin, Bigorre, Gaure, Angoulême, Rovergne, Montreuil, Ponthieu, Calais, Guisnes, Mark, &c, and renounces his claims to the crown of France, to Normandy, Touraine, Anjou, Maine, Brittany, and Flanders The K. of France will pay 3,000,000 gold crowns Hostages to be given by France Forty articles. *Bretigny.* R iii. p. i. 487. O. vi. 178–196. H iii p i 202–209
May 14.	Safe conduct for John Sutherland and Nicholas de Creghton, of Scotland, and two others coming to William earl of Sutherland, one of the hostages for David de Bruys. *Westm* R iii p i 494 O vi 196 H. iii p i 209
May 18.	Memorandum that the K arrived at Rye from France on May 18, and at Westminster on the day following, and delivered the great seal to the chancellor R iii p i 494. O vi 196 H iii p. i 209
May 22	Declaration of the innocence of John Taillart, accused of holding Roche des Amis against the order of the lieutenant of Brittany *Westm.* R iii p i 494.
May 22.	Warrant to John de Alveton, constable of Wallingford Castle, and John de Laundeles, sheriff of Berks, to arrest John Launeslond, and two others, suspected of an assault on the earl of Salesbrigge *Westm* R iii p i 494.
May 24	The K orders the proclamation of the truce with France throughout England. *Westm.* R iii. p. i. 495. O. vi. 197. H iii p. i. 209
May 28.	The K summons to London one arrayer and one collector of the subsidy in each county to arrange for the payment of the troops *Westm.* R iii p i 495.
May 28	Similar summons to the collectors of the subsidy of 6d in the pound. *Westm.* R iii. p i 496
May 28	The collectors of the clerical tenth are ordered to pay one half by July 1 *Westm* R iii p. i 496
June 5	The sheriff of Devon is ordered to assist Henry de Brusele and Richard de Colle in bringing wood and timber to the mines in Devonshire Similar letters to the sheriff of Nottingham and Derby, the abbot of Buckland, and 13 others *Westm.* R. iii. p. i. 497.
June 8.	The K of France desires the mayor and échevins of Rochelle to send deputies to him at Calais by July 15. *London* R. iii p. i. 497. O. vi. 197. H. iii. p. i. 210
June 13.	Power for John de Coupeland, warden of Berwick-upon-Tweed, to receive the next instalment of the ransom of David de Bruys. *Westm.* R. iii p. i. 498. O. vi 197. H. iii. p i 210.
June 13.	Henry de Percy and Ralph de Nevill are ordered to release the second son of the seneschal of Scotland on the delivery of the next instalment of the ransom and the seneschal's third son *Westm* R iii p i 498. O vi 198 H iii p i 210.
June 13	The custody of the castles of Gravelle, Fengery, and Chastelblank, in Brittany, is committed to Robert de Knolles *Westm* R iii p i. 498
June 15	Power for John Walewayn, governor of the merchants at Bruges, and Richard de Eccleshale, treasurer of Calais, to receive the money due from the duke of Burgundy. *Westm.* R iii p i 498.
June 16.	Safe conduct for John de Polaymill and two other servants of the count of Ventadour to go to France *Westm.* R. iii p. i 498. O. vi 198. H. iii. p. i. 210

DATE.	SUBJECT.
1360. June 17.	John de Beauchamp, constable of Dover Castle and warden of the Cinque Ports, is ordered to arrest ships for the passage of the K.'s cousin [the K. of France] to Calais. *Westm.* R iii p 1 499. O. vi 198 H iii p. 1 210
June 18.	Safe conduct for Charles de Blois to come to Calais for the decision of his claims to the duchy of Brittany. *Westm* R iii p 1 499. O. vi 199 H iii p 1 210.
June 18.	Safe conduct for John count of Tankarvill, the K.'s prisoner. *Westm* R. iii. p 1 499. O. vi 199 H iii. p. i. 210.
June 18.	Licence for the lord of Derval, the K.'s prisoner, to leave England. *Westm.* R. p 1 499. O. vi 200. R. iii. p. 1 211.
June 20.	Safe conducts for the marshal of Dodenham, the lord d'Aubigny, and five other French prisoners returning to France. *Westm* R iii. p 1 499. O vi 200 H. iii p 1 211
June 22.	The K orders the justices and chancellor of Ireland to restore lands fraudulently alienated from the hospital of S John of Jerusalem in Ireland. *Westm* R iii. p 1 499
June 24.	Receipt of 50,000 *deniers d'or*, called "*Moutons*," from the duke of Burgundy. *Westm* R iii. p 1. 500. O. vi. 200. H iii p 1 211
June 24.	Receipt for 10,000 marks, part of the ransom of David de Bruys. *Westm.* R. iii. p i. 500 O. vi. 201 H. iii. p. i. 211.
June 26	The K orders the cessation of the collection of the subsidy for the fleet. *Westm.* R. iii. p. 1. 500.
June 27	The K. forbids John de Couton, provincial prior of the Carmelite friars, infringing the liberties of the chancellor of Oxford university. *Westm.* R. iii. p. 1. 501.
June 27.	The sheriffs of London and Middlesex are ordered to provide 16 carts for the conveyance of the baggage of the French K to Dover *Westm.* R iii. p 1 501.
June 30.	Innocent [VI] congratulates the K on having made peace with France *Villeneuve.* R. iii. p 1 501 O vi. 201. H iii p 1. 211.
June 30	Innocent [VI] empowers the bps of London, Winchester, Rochester, Paris, Teronenne, and Arras, and Androyn abbot of Clugny, to absolve the Kings of England and France from oaths contrary to the treaty *Villeneuve* R iii p 1. 501 O. vi 202 H iii p 1 211
June 30.	Innocent [VI] empowers the bps of London, Rochester, and Bazas, and the abbot of Clugny, to absolve the subjects of the two Ks. from ecclesiastical censures. *Villeneuve* R. iii. p. i. 502 O vi 202 H. iii p 1 212
July 6.	Innocent [VI.] is rejoiced at the peace between England and France, and at the release of the K. of France, he desires credence for the abbot of Clugny and Hugh de Gebenna, lord of Auton. *Villeneuve* R. iii p 1 502. O vi 203 H iii. p 1 212
July 10	The K. desires Edmund de Northcost, William de Enefeld, and two other collectors of the tenth and fifteenth in Essex to make their payments by July 27. *Westm.* R. iii. p 1. 503.
July 10.	Safe conducts for James de Bourbon, the lord of Craon, Marshal Doudenham, and William de Plescy, to go to France. *Westm.* R iii. p. 1 503
July 13.	The K. sends Stephen de Cusyngton to conduct the lord of Fenes, constable of France, and five others going to France for redress of violations of the truce. *Westm.* R iii. p 1. 504. O. vi 205. H. iii. p i 213
[July 13]	Safe conduct for the above-mentioned persons. R. iii. p. 1 504. O. vi. 205. H iii. p. 1. 213
July 13.	Warrants to Bartholomew Stygan and eight other masters of ships to arrest sailors. *Westm.* R. iii. p. 1. 504.
July 18.	The French K, who arrived at Calais on the 8th, desires the commonalty of Rochelle to send deputies to him. *Calais.* R. iii. p 1 504 O. vi 206 H iii p 1 213.
July 18.	John de Beauchamp, earl of Warwick, is appointed admiral of the whole fleet. *Westm.* R iii p 1 505.
July 22	Protection for Robert bp of Avranches and his manors of S Philbert on Bell, Parc, and Champeaulz. *Westm.* R iii. p 1. 505 O vi 206. H. iii. p. 1. 213
July 22.	Protection for the abbey of B Maria de Voto, near Cherbourg. *Westm.* R. iii. p. 1. 505.
July 22.	Restitution of the priory of Hagh to the said abbey. *Westm* R iii. p. 1. 505.
July 26.	Safe conducts for the abbot of Clugny and Hugh de Geneve, coming to the K. from the pope. *Westm.* R. iii. p 1. 505. O. vi. 206-7. H. iii. p. 1. 213.

DATE.	SUBJECT.	
1360 July 26.	Safe conducts for Patrick bp of Brechm, Patrick de Dunbarr, earl of March, Walter de Wardlau, Robert de Erskyn, and John de Preston, coming to treat with the K. *Westm.* R iii p i 506　O vi 207　H iii, p i 213	
Aug 11.	The K forbids men at arms going to Normandy or Brittany. *Westm.* R. iii. p i 506	
Aug 13.	Commissions to Thomas de Stafford and William Walkelate, sergeants at arms, to enforce the above order　*Westm*　R iii p i 506	
Aug 13	Giles de Wyngreworth is appointed the K's treasurer and receiver in Brittany. *Westm-* R. iii. p i 506　O vi 207　H iii p i. 213.	
Aug. 20.	Power for John abp of York, Thomas bp. of Durham, Gilbert bp. of Carlisle, Henry de Percy, and four others to treat for a perpetual league with Scotland. *Westm.* R. iii. p i. 506.　O. vi 207　H iii. p i 214.	
Aug 20.	Commission to Richard de Stafford, Miles de Stapleton, and Nigel de Loryng to redress violations of the truce with France　Similar commission to Amanen de Lebret, lord of Logozan, and Amanen de Pomerus. *Westm.* R. iii. p i. 507.　O. vi. 208.　H iii p i 214	
Aug 22.	John Chaundos is appointed warden of Barfleur in Normandy. *Westm.* R iii. p i, 507.	
Aug 23	The K orders John de Pembrok, escheator of Ireland, to inquire into the admission of Irish to the privileges of citizens and burgesses　*Westm*　R iii. p i. 507	
Aug. 24.	Power for Edward prince of Wales to treat for the performance of the treaty of Bretigny. *Westm.* R. iii p i 508.　O vi 209　H iii p i 214	
Aug 29	The K orders the captain of Brittany and Giles de Wyngreworth, treasurer, to pay the expenses of Henry de Kaer and the six other deputies of John de Montfort, duke of Brittany, coming to Calais. *Westm.* R iii. p i 508.　O vi 210　H iii p i 215	
Aug. 31	Safe conduct for Charles de Bloys to come to Calais and return. *Westm.* R. iii. p. i. 508.　O v 210.　H. iii. p i 215.	
Sept. 20	Commission to Ralph earl of Stafford, sir Walter de Manny, John de Carleton, dean of Wells, and John Barnet, archdeacon of London, for the decision of the claims of Charles de Bloys and John de Montfort. *London.* R. iii. p i 508.　O vi 211　H iii p i 215	
Sept. 21.	Innocent [VI] grants a dispensation for the marriage of two of the K's children with persons within the fourth grade of consanguinity or affinity. *Avignon.* R. iii. p i 509.　O. vi 212　H iii p i. 215.	
Sept. 25.	Pope Innocent [VI.] urges the K. to preserve the peace with France　*Avignon.* R iii p i 509.　O. vi. 212.　H. iii. p i. 215.	
Sept 25	Pope Innocent [VI] desires the assistance of the K against sir Barnabo de Vicecomitibus [dei Visconti] of Milan, who has invaded the patrimony of the Church. *Avignon* R. iii p i 509.　O vi 213　H iii p i 216.	
Sept 30.	Thomas de Holand, earl of Kent, is appointed the K.'s lieutenant and captain in France and Normandy　*Westm.* R iii p i, 509　O. vi. 213　H iii. p i. 216.	
Sept 30	Commission to John Maynard and William Corby to provide 10 ships for the passage of the Earl of Kent　*Westm*　R iii p i 510	
Sept 30	Indenture between the K. and the earl of Kent. *Westm.* R. iii p i 510.	
Sept 30	Warrant for the payment by Giles de Wryngeworth, treasurer of Brittany, of the bills of William Latymer, captain of the duchy　*Westm.* R iii p i 510.	
Sept. 30	Indenture between the K and Bartholomew Guidonis, of Castilon, and Adam St. Ives, of London, for the exchange of money in England. *Westm.* R. iii p i 510.	
Oct 2.	Letters obligatory, by which Reynaud lord of Aubigny, the K's prisoner, promises to return to Calais by All Saints Day　*Calais*　R. iii p i. 511.　O. vi. 214.　H. iii. p i 216.	
Oct 16.	Licence to the duke of Orleans, hostage for the K. of France, to import victuals free of duty. *Calais,* R iii. p i 511.　O vi. 215.　H iii p i 216.	
Oct. 16.	Safe conduct for the household of the duke of Orleans. *Calais.* R. iii p. i 511. O vi 215　H iii p. i, 217.	
Oct. 18.	Licence to the count of Tankerville to import victuals. *Calais.* R iii. p. i 512. O vi 216　H. iii p i 217.	
Oct. 20.	Safe conduct for two French merchants to import wine and other goods for the dukes of Berry and Anjou, who are coming to England as hostages. *Calais.* R. iii. p. i. 512. O vi 216　H iii. p. i 217.	
Oct. 22.	Letters obligatory of Giles bp. of Noyon for the payment of his ransom. *Boulogne.* R. iii. p. i. 512.　O. vi. 216.　H. iii. p. i. 217.	

DATE.	SUBJECT.
1360. Oct 22.	Letters obligatory of John count of Tankerville and Robert de Lornz, lord Dermenoville *Calais.* R. iii p 1 512 O. vi 217. H m. p 1. 217.
Oct. 22.	Privileges granted by the K. to the commonalty of Rochelle *Calais* R iii p 1. 512. O. vi. 217. H iii., p. 1 217.
Oct. 22.	Grant to the said commonalty of Rochelle of mercantile intercourse with England, &c. *Calais.* R iii p.1 513.
Oct. 22.	Freedom from arrest for Simon de Roney, count of Brena, one of the French hostages *Calais.* R. iii. p. 1. 514.
Oct. 23.	John K of France appoints the provost of Paris, the bailiff of Chartres, and three others to preserve the truce with England. *Calais.* R. iii. p 1. 514. O. vi. 219. H. iii. p. i. 218.
Oct. 24.	Ratification by the K of France of the treaty of Bretigny, some articles having been corrected at Calais. *Calais.* R. iii. p. 1 514 O vi 219. H iii p. u 3.
Oct. 24	Ratification of the same treaty by the K. of England. *Calais.* R. iii. p. 1. 518. O. vi 229. H. iii p ii. 6.
Oct. 25.	Attestation by Androyn abbot of Clugny, papal nuncio, of the ratification by the French K. *Calais.* R. iii p 1. 518. O vi, 230. H. iii. p ii 7.
Oct 24.	Letters promissory of the K of France for the delivery of the letters of renunciation and cession at Bruges. *Calais.* R iii. p.1 519. O vi 230 H iii p ii. 7
Oct. 26	Confirmation of the treaty by Charles duke of Normandy, dauphin of Vienne, eldest son of the K. of France *Boulogne.* R iii p 1 519 O. vi 232 H iii p ii 8
Oct..24.	Letters promissory of the K of England for the delivery of the letters of renunciation. *Calais.* R. iii. p 1 519 O vi 232 H iii p ii 8
Oct. 24.	Notarial attestation of the taking of the oath to the treaty by the two Ks. *Calais.* R. iii p. 1 520. O vi. 233. H. iii. p. 1 8
Oct. 24.	Form of the oath taken by the K of France. *Calais.* R. iii. p 1 520. O vi 234. H. iii p ii 9
Oct. 24.	Form of the oath taken by the K. of England Similar of the French K.'s oath, dated Boulogne, Oct 26. Confirmation by the dauphin and attestation by the nuncio. R. iii. p 1. 520. O. v. 234. H. iii p. ii. 9.
Oct. 24.	John K of France promises to obtain the oaths of his prelates and nobles before Candlemas Similar letter, dated Boulogne Oct 26 Confirmation by the dauphin. *Calais.* R. iii p 1 521. O v. 236 H iii p ii 9.
Oct. 24.	Similar promise on the part of the K. of England. *Calais.* R iii. p. i, 521. O vi 236 H. iii. p ii. 9.
Oct. 24.	The K of England orders Thomas de Holand, earl of Kent, and his other captains in France to publish the peace. *Calais.* R iii. p 1 521. O. iv 237 H iii. p. ii 10.
Oct. 24.	Renunciation in French and Latin by John K. of France according to the treaty Attestation by the nuncio. *Calais.* R. iii. p i. 522. O. vi 237-243 H iii. p ii 10-12.
Oct. 24.	Renunciation by the K of England. *Calais.* R. iii. p. 1. 524. O. vi. 243. H iii. p ii 12
Oct. 25.	Attestation by the papal nuncio of the French K.'s renunciation. *Calais.* R. iii. p 1. 525. O vi. 247. H iii. p. ii. 13.
Oct. 26.	Confirmation of the letters of renunciation by the French K. and his son. *Boulogne.* R iii. p 1. 527. O vi. 251 H. iii. p. ii. 15
Oct. 24.	Confirmation by the K. of England of his renunciation. *Calais.* R. iii. p. i. 528. O vi 256. H iii. p ii. 17
Oct. 26.	Confirmation by Charles the dauphin of a treaty of friendship between the two Kings against all persons but the pope and emperor, dated Boulogne, Oct. 26 Attestation by the nuncio. *Boulogne* R iii. p 1. 530. O vi. 260. H. iii. p ii. 19.
Oct. 24.	Counterpart of the above treaty on the part of the K. of England. *Calais.* R iii. p. i, 531. O. vi 263. H iii p. ii. 20.
Oct. 24.	Protestation on the part of the K of England that the above treaty shall not injure his alliance with Flanders, but he will not make use of that alliance until the delivery of the renunciations. *Calais.* R. iii. p. i. 531. O. vi. 264. H. iii. p. ii 21.
Oct. 24.	Similar protest and promise by the French K. as to his alliance with Scotland. *Calais* R. iii. p. i. 531. O. vi. 264. H. iii. p. ii. 20.

DATE	SUBJECT.
1360 Oct 26	The French K promises that the alliance shall not prejudice the article in the treaty concerning Brittany *Boulogne* R. iii. p. i. 532 O vi. 265 H iii p ii 21
Oct. 24.	The French K promises that his being called the K of France in the documents concerning the treaty shall not prejudice the right of the K. of England or his successors to the crown *Calais* R iii. p i 532. O. vi 265. H. iii p. ii 21.
Oct 26	Letter of the dauphin Charles as to the use of the title of duke of Normandy by the dauphin *Boulogne* R iii p i 532 O vi. 266. H. iii p ii. 21.
Oct. 24.	The K of France acknowledges that the K of England has kept his promise of sending him to Calais, and providing for him there for one month *Calais*. R. iii. p. i 532. O vi. 266 H iii p ii 21
Oct 24	Receipt by the K of England for 10,000 "roialx" from the K of France for his expenses at Calais *Calais* R iii p i 533 O. vi 267 H iii p ii 21.
Oct. 26	Obligation of the K of France for the payment of the remainder of the 300,000 crowns Confirmation by the dauphin *Boulogne* R iii p i 533. O vi 267 H iii p. ii. 22
Oct 24	The K has received 400,000 cr of the 600,000 cr payable at Calais, and grants respite till Feb 2 for the remainder *Calais* R iii p i 533 O vi. 268. H. iii p. ii 22.§
Oct 24	The K. of France promises to deliver on his arrival at Boulogne the K's two sons, who are there as hostages *Calais* R iii p i 533. O vi 269. H iii p ii 22
Oct. 24.	Renunciation by the K of France of all wars and processes against England Renewed at Boulogne, Oct 26 Confirmation by the dauphin *Calais*. R. iii p i 534 O vi 269 H iii p ii. 22
Oct. 24	Similar renunciation by the K of England *Calais* R iii p i. 534 O vi 271. H. iii p ii 23
Oct. 24	Obligation of the K of England for the delivery of the fortresses named in the treaty to France Exemplifications by the French K, dated Calais, 24 Oct, and Boulogne, 26 Oct. Confirmation by the dauphin *Calais* R iii p. i 535. O vi 272 H iii. p ii 24.
Oct 26	Confirmation by Charles, dauphin, of the French K's obligation for the delivery of the lands mentioned in the treaty *Boulogne* R iii p i 536 O vi 275 H iii. p ii 25.
Oct 26	Confirmation by Charles the dauphin of the promise of the French K that the failure on K Edward's part to deliver one or two fortresses shall not [h]inder the execution of the treaty. *Boulogne* R iii p i 536 O vi 277 H iii. p ii. 25
Oct. 24.	The K of England will punish as traitors those who violate the peace. Similar letter by the French K, and confirmation by his son dated Boulogne, Oct 26 *Calais*. R. iii. p i 537 O vi 277 H iii p ii 25
	Obligation of Philip duke of Orleans, Louis count of Anjou, John count of Poictiers, Louis duke of Bourbon, and 47 other French lords to remain in England as hostages *Calais* R. iii. p. i 537. O. vi. 278. H. iii p ii 26
Oct 24.	The K promises to deliver the dukes of Orleans, Anjou, and Berry, John d'Estampes, and Pierre d'Alençon, on the surrender of Poitou, Agen, &c, the payment of 400,000 crowns, and the delivery of the letters of renunciation , the remainder of the hostages to be released on the performance of other articles *Calais* R iii p. i 538 O vi 280 H. iii p ii 26
Oct 24	Promise of the K of France to compel the return of the prisoners taken at Poictiers, who are included among the hostages, and who are in France on parole. Renewed at Boulogne, Oct 26 *Calais*. R iii p i. 538 O vi 281. H iii. p ii 27.
Oct 24	The K of England releases from their ransoms 16 prisoners taken at the battle of Poictiers, who will remain as hostages *Calais*. R iii. p. i 539. O. vi. 282. H. iii. p ii 27.
Oct 24	The K. releases Philip de France, James de Bourbon, John d'Artois, the earls of Tanquarville, and Joigny, and six other hostages. R iii p i. 539. O. vi 282 H. iii. p. ii 27.
Oct 24	Promise of the K to deliver the hostages on the performance of the treaty, and to treat them well while in England *Calais*. R iii p. i 539. O. vi 283 H iii p ii. 28
Oct 25.	Confirmation by the K. of the privileges and laws of the commonalty of. Rochelle. *Calais*. R. iii p i. 540
Oct 26.	Confirmation by Charles the dauphin of the obligation of the French K. to deliver Rochelle within a month after All Saints' Day, or his son Philip as a hostage. *Boulogne*. R. iii. p. i. 541. O. vi. 284. H iii. p. ii. 28.

DATE.	SUBJECT.
1360. Oct. 26.	The K. of France declares+that the release of his son Philip and the 10 other hostages shall not prejudice the K.'s right to receive them as hostages for Rochelle. *Boulogne* R iii p. i 541. O vi 284 H. iii p ii 28.
Oct. 26.	The K promises to release the French K's son Philip on the surrender of Rochelle. R. iii. p i 541. O vi 285 H. iii p ii 28
Oct. 24.	The French K promises to deliver fresh hostages in place of any who do not come to Calais or who leave without licence Renewed at Boulogne, 26 Oct. *Calais.* R iii p i. 542 O vi. 286. H, iii p ii. 29.
Oct. 24.	The K of England will allow the hostages to be changed once a year *Calais* R. iii p i 542. O vi 286 H iii p ii 29
Oct. 24.	Confirmation by the French K of the article for the delivery of burgesses of Paris and 19 other towns as hostages. Renewed at Boulogne, Oct 26. *Calais.* R iii p i. 542 O vi 287. H iii p ii 29.
Oct. 24	The French K. will deliver separate letters for the surrender of each land. Renewed at Boulogne, Oct 26, and confirmed by the dauphin *Calais* R iii p i. 542. O vi 287. H iii. p ii 29
Oct. 26.	The French K releases his subjects in Calais and the neighbouring places from their allegiance, and desires them to do homage to the K. of England. *Boulogne.* R. iii. p i 543 O. vi 288. H. iii. p. ii. 29.
Oct. 26	Ratification by the French K of the article giving the county of Montfort to John de Montfort. *Boulogne* R. iii. p i 543 O vi 289. H iii p. ii. 30
Oct. 24.	Also of the article of restitution to Philip de Navarre *Calais.* R. iii. p. i. 543. O. vi 289 H. iii p ii 30
Oct. 26.	Confirmation by Charles the dauphin of the French K's ratification of the grant by the K. of the lands of Godfrey de Harecourt to Sir John de Chandos. *Boulogne* R. iii. p i 543. O vi 290 H iii p. ii. 30.
Oct. 24.	Confirmation by the French K of the article for the restitution of exiles, excepting the viscount of Trousac ¦and John de Galard. Renewed at Boulogne, Oct 26 Similar confirmation by the K of England *Calais* R iii. p i. 544. O vi 291 H iii p ii 31.
Oct 24	Confirmation by the French K of the article for the freedom of scholars at the universities of either country. Renewed at Boulogue, Oct 26. *Calais.* R iii p i 544. O vi 292 H iii p ii 31
Oct. 24.	Confirmation by the French K of the article, that presentations to benefices during the war shall be held valid Renewed at Boulogne, Oct 26 Similar confirmation by the K of England *Calais.* R iii p i. 544 O vi. 292. H iii. p ii. 31
Oct. 26.	The two Kings promise to restore all lands taken from the church during the war, dated Boulogne, Oct 26, and Calais, Oct 24 R iii. p. i. 545. O. vi 293. H. iii. p. ii 31
Oct. 26.	Confirmation by Charles the dauphin of the French K's ratification of the article against procuring anything at Rome contrary to the treaty. *Boulogne* R iii. p i 545 O vi 293. H iii. p ii 32
Oct 26.	The K retains William de Serezio, knt, as his councillor. *Calais.* R. iii. p i 545.
Oct. 26.	The K orders Sir Nichol de Tamworth to compel Jaque Wyne, whom he holds as a prisoner for having plundered Clameci, a town of the countess of Flanders, to surrender letters of obligation and pledges for 7,000 crowns, which her subjects owe him *Calais* R iii p i 545. O vi 294 H iii p ii. 32
Oct. 28.	The K releases¦the count of Salebruche, one of the hostages of the K. of France. *Calais.* R. iii p. i.¦546 O vi. 295. H iii p ii. 32.
Oct. 28.	Safe conduct for the two burgesses of Beauvais coming as hostages. *Calais.* R iii p. i 546 O. vi 296. H iii p ii 32.
Oct. 28.	Commission to sir William Graunson and Sir Nicol de Tamworth to deliver the fortresses in Champagne, Brie, and elsewhere, to the French K Similar commissions to Thomas Fogg, the lords of Lebret and Pomers, the capital de Buch, the earl of Kent, and others. *Calais.* R. iii p i 546 O. vi. 297. H iii p. ii. 33
Oct 28	Inspeximus and confirmation of a letter of protection granted by Henry [II] to the abbey of Clugny, dated Winchester. *Calais* R iii p i 547
Oct. 30.	The K forbids William de Hatton and Roger de Wolfreton, his escheators¦in Kent and Suffolk, seizing the temporalities of the see of Rochester, now vacant, as they were granted to the abp of Canterbury by K John. *Sandwich.* R iii. p i. 547.
Oct 30.	The K. appoints Matthias de Aqua Cava his advocate in Saintonge *Calais.* R iii p. i. 548

DATE.	SUBJECT.
1360 Oct 30.	The K appoints William de Serezié, knt , his president in Rochelle and Saintonge. *Calais* R. iii p i 548
Oct 30	The K appoints Bertram lord of Monferran his governor and captain in the above places. *Calais* R iii p i 548
Oct 30	John Gemel and Peter de Sarlac are appointed keepers of the mint at Rochelle *Calais*. R iii p i 549
Oct 30	Collin Gaillard is appointed weigher at the mint at Rochelle *Calais*. R. iii. p i 549
Oct. 31.	The K releases the duke of Burgundy from the payment of 12,000 "motons" in compensation for violations of the truce *Calais*, R iii. p i 549 O. vi. 298. H iii. p. ii 33.
Oct. 31.	Commission to sir William de Grantzon and sir Nichol de Tamworth to grant fresh terms for payment to the duke of Burgundy *Calais* R. iii p i 549 O vi. 299. H iii. p ii 34
Oct 31	The K. retains as his councillor Laurence Poussard, burgess of Rochelle. *Calais*. R iii p i 549
Nov 1	Inspeximus and confirmation of a grant of nobility to Lawrence Poussart by K John of a tower France, dated Paris, March 1335 *Calais* R iii p i 550
Nov. 1.	Inspeximus and confirmation of a licence by the dauphin to Lawrence Poussart to maintain a tower which he has built near Rochelle, dated Boulogne, Sept. 1360. *Calais*, R iii. p i 550.
Nov. 1	Inspeximus and confirmation by K. Edward of a grant of nobility by Charles the dauphin to William Boulart, burgess of Rochelle, dated Boulogne-sur-Mer, Sept 1360. *Calais*. R. iii. p i 551 O vi 299 H iii p ii. 34.
Nov 1	Protection for Peter Buffet of Rochelle. *Calais*. R. iii p i, 552
Nov 1	Declaration by John K of France that the K of England has allowed him to leave Calais, and go to his own kingdom according to the treaty. *St. Omer*. R. iii p. i 552 O. vi. 301. H iii p ii 34.
Nov 2	Confirmation of the above by Charles the dauphin. *St. Omer*. R. iii p i 552. O vi 301. H iii p ii 34.
Nov 1	The French K. promises to send the counts of Vaudemont and Grantpre, the castellan of Lille, and four others as hostages by Christmas. *St Omer* R. iii p i. 552. O. vi. 301 H. iii. p ii. 35.
Nov 14.	The K forbids the exportation of corn or malt *Westm* R iii. p i 553
Nov 26	Grant of the prebend of Aldrokesburgh in the cathedral of Glasgow to Roger de Bromleye. Intimation thereof to the bishop and dean and chapter of Glasgow. *Westm* R iii. p i 553. O vi. 302. H iii p ii 35
Dec 8.	The K orders the people of Brittany to obey William lord de Latymer as his lieutenant. *Westm* R. iii p i 553 O vi 302. H iii p ii 35
Dec 10	Obligation of Philip duke of Burgundy for the payment of the sum due from him. *Dijon* R iii p i. 553. O vi. 303. H. iii p ii 35.
Dec 26	Safe conduct for Piers de Rosiers, squire of the duke of Bourbon, to go to France and return. *Woodstock* R iii. p. i 554
Dec 27.	Pope Innocent refuses the K.'s request for the promotion of Androyn abbot of Clugny, to the cardinalate *Avignon* R. iii p i 554. O. vi 303 H iii p ii 35
1361 Jan 12.	Safe conducts for William archbishop of St Andrews, Patrick bpt of Brechin, Patrick earl of March, and four other Scots to come to England; also for the servants of the duke of Bourbon *Westm*. R iii. p i. 554. O. vi. 305 H iii. p. ii. 36
Jan 20	Thomas Dautre, sergeant-at-arms, is ordered to provide ships for the passage of John Chaundos to France *Westm*. R iii. p i 554.
Jan 20	Sir John Chaundos, baron of St Sauveur in Normandy, is appointed the K.'s lieutenant and captain general in France, and conservator of the peace *Westm*. R. iii. p. i. 555. O vi 304 H iii p ii 36
Jan 20	Power for John Walewayn, governor of the English merchants in Flanders, and Richard Eccleshale, clerk, to receive the French K.'s ransom. *Westm*. R. iii p. i. 555. O vi 305. H iii p ii 36
Jan 20	Confirmation of the liberties and privileges of the inhabitants of Arde. *Westm*. R. iii. p i 555 O vi. 306 H iii p ii. 36.
Jan. 20.	Similar grant to the inhabitants of Daudrinc. *Westm*. R. iii. p. i. 555. O. vi. 306 H. iii. p. ii. 37.

DATE.	SUBJECT.
1361. Jan. 26.	Safe conduct for Simon de Roucy, count of Braynne, one of the French hostages, to go to France for three months; also for Robert de la Rochette, esquire of the duke of Berri. *Westm.* R iii p ii. 597 O vi. 307. H iii p. ii 37
Jan. 26	Robert de Herle is appointed constable of Dover Castle and warden of the Cinque Ports. *Westm.* R iii p. ii 597
Jan. 26.	Robert de Herle is appointed admiral of the whole fleet *Westm* R. iii p ii 597
Jan 28.	The K. of England's acquittance for the delivery of Rochelle *Westm.* R. iii. p. ii. 597. O. vi 307 H iii, p. ii. 37.
Jan. 30.	Guy de Bryen, steward of the K's household, William de Thorp, and three others are appointed justices of assay of the money for the ransom of the K of France *Westm* R. iii. p. ii 598 O vi 307. H iii p. ii. 37.
Jan 31.	Indemnity for the bp. of Norwich and the others who negotiated the peace *Westm* R. iii. p ii 598.
Feb 2	Safe conduct for Jaquet Dusages, squire of the duke of Anjou *Westm.* R iii. p. ii. 598. O. vi 308 H iii p ii 37
Feb 2.	Receipt for 100,000 crowns from the K. of France. *Westm.* R iii. p. ii 598.
Feb 3.	Safe conduct for Bertram du Glerguun, knt., servant of the duke of Orleans *Westm.* R. iii. p. ii 599. O vi 308 H iii p ii 37
Feb 4	Safe conducts for Louis duke of Anjou and John lord of Hangest, two hostages to go to France. *Westm* R iii p ii 599 O. vi 309. H iii p. ii. 37.
Feb. 4.	Safe conducts for John de Saintre, seneschal, and John Hanceme, secretary of the duke of Anjou. *Westm.* R iii p ii 599 O vi. 309 H iii p ii 38
Feb. 4.	Safe conducts for Piere de Vannes, Gylet de Usey, Colyn Prodhome, and Philpot de Vannes; minstrels of the duke of Orleans, and for Botecun le Taboricr, Guilmyn le Mestre, Bandet de Seint Omer, minstrels of the duke of Berry. *Westm* R. iii. p. ii. 599. O vi 309. H. iii. p. ii. 38.
Feb. 4.	Warrant for the payment of a portion of the 25,000 crowns for which the prince of Wales has bought James de Bourbon, count of Ponthieu, taken prisoner at the battle of Poitiers, from John de Grely, capital de la Buche *Westm.* R. iii p ii 599. O vi. 310. H. iii p ii 38.
Feb. 8.	Similar warrant for another portion of the said payment. *Westm.* R. iii p. ii. 599 O vi 310 H iii. p. ii 38
Feb. 8.	The K orders the collectors of customs at London and seven other ports to observe the privileges granted by his predecessors to German merchants. *Westm* R iii p ii. 600.
Feb. 9.	Inspeximus and confirmation of a confirmation by Odo duke of Burgundy of the laws and customs of Merk, dated Arras, Oct. 1330. *Westm* R iii p ii 600
Feb. 16.	Restitution to the alien priories of Montacute, in Somersetshire, Northampton, Arundel, and nine others *Westm.* R iii. p. ii 602. O. vi 311 H iii p ii. 38.
Feb 16.	Licence to the duke of Orleans to hunt and hawk anywhere within the kingdom. *Westm* R. iii p ii 603 O vi. 311. H. iii. p ii. 38.
Feb 17	The K. forbids the exportation of corn or malt except to Calais or Gascony. *Westm.* R. iii, p ii 603.
Feb. 20.	The K desires Magnus K. of Norway to make restitution to William de' Stokesby and other English merchants, whose ship was plundered at Cost in Norway. *Westm* R iii p ii 603. O vi 312. H iii. p ii 39
Feb. 20	Obligation of Louis duke of Bourbon, Peter d'Alanson, John d'Estampes, and 16 other French hostages R. iii. p. ii 604. O vi 313. H. iii p. ii 39
Feb. 25.	The butchers of London are to slaughter their beasts at Stratford or Knightsbridge, in order that the blood and offal of the beasts may not be thrown into the Thames *Westm* R iii. p. ii. 604
Feb. 26.	Safe conduct for Roland de Quoythels, servant of the children of Charles de Bloys, the K's prisoner *Westm* R iii p. ii 605. O. vi. 315. H iii p ii 40.
Feb 26.	The K promises the hostages of Paris and S Omer that he will observe the treaty as to their treatment. *Westm* R iii p ii. 605
Feb. 28.	Safe conducts for William bp of S. Andrew's, John Martyn, burgess of Edinburgh, and 10 others, going on a pilgrimage to S. James; also for two servants of David de Bruys, to come to England on his business. *Westm.* R. iii p. ii. 605. O. vi. 315 H iii. p. ii 40.

DATE.	SUBJECT.
1361. March 3	Warrant for the payment of 9*l* to John duke of Brittany, for his expenses in going to and returning from Walsingham on a pilgrimage. *Westm.* R III p. II. 605 O. VI. 315. H. III p II 40
March 3.	Warrant for the payment of 50 marks to William marquis of Juliers, in part payment of the K.'s debt to him *Westm.* R III p II 605. O VI 315 H. III. p. II. 40.
March 4	The K directs his justiciary and chancellor of Ireland not to molest beneficed Irish clerks, who are faithful subjects, in consequence of the late order against giving benefices or offices to Irishmen *Westm* R III p. II. 605.
March 4	The K. orders the proclamation of certain ordinances for the government of Ireland. *Westm* R. III p II 606
March 5.	Protection for Spanish merchants [of Castile and Lapuscoa]. *Westm* R in. p II 606. O VI 316 H III p II 40.
March 6.	Protection for the same merchants trading at Rochelle. *Westm.* R. iii. p II. 607. O. VI. 316. H III p. II 40
March 10	The K orders the sheriff of Kent to provide wheat and other provisions for John duke of Brittany, who is going abroad on the K.'s service. *Westm.* R III p. II 607. O. VI. 316. H III p II. 40
March 10.	John de Neubury, keeper of the K.'s wardrobe, is ordered to deliver robes to Petronella Talleworth and the other servants of Joan, sister of John duke of Brittany. *Westm.* R. III. p II. 607 O. VI. 317. H III p II 40.
March 10	Power for John Walewayn, governor of the merchants in Flanders, and Richard de Eccleshale, clerk, to receive the ransom of the bp. of Noyon *Westm* R III p II 607.
March 12.	Pope Innocent desires credence for Androyn abbot of Clugny, concerning the settlement of the dispute between Charles duke of Brittany and John count of Montfort. *Avignon.* R. III p II 608 O VI 317 H III p II. 41
March 12	Power for le sire de Boutressein, sir William de Burton, sir Nichol de Lovayne, and Nichol de Louthe, clerk, to receive the county of Ponthieu *Westm* R III p II 608 O VI 317 H III p. II 41
March 12	Safe conduct for merchants and burgesses of Amias [Amiens] *Westm.* R III p II 608.
March 13	Indenture between the K. and Bartholomew Guidonis de Castilon and Adam de St. Ive, for the exchange of money *Westm* R III p II. 608
March 15.	The K. writes on the subject to the warden of the mint in the Tower of London. *Westm.* R III p II 609.
March 15	Proclamation to the same effect to be made by the sheriffs of London. *Westm.* R. iii. p II 609
March 15.	The K summons a council to discuss the state of Ireland. *Westm.* R iii. p. II 609 O VI 318 H III. p. II 41.
March 15	The K orders the justiciary and chancellor of Ireland to forbid the exportation of victuals, as his son Lionel is going thither with an army. *Westm.* R III p II 610
March 15.	The K. forbids the customers to exact customs from Castilian merchants for merchandise which they bring to England for sale in other countries *Westm.* R. III. p II. 611.
March 16.	Licence to le sire de Maulevier, Mahien sire de Roye, and Gerard sire de Boubcrchie, French hostages, to go to any part of England. *Westm* R III p. II. 611. O. VI 321. H. III p II 42
March 19	The justiciary of Ireland is ordered to send all the prisoners to Dublin Castle. *Westm.* R III p II 611.
March 24.	The K informs the abps, bps, &c of Ireland, of his recent order to the justiciary about the holding of benefices by Irishmen. *Westm.* R. III p II. 611. O. VI. 320. H III p. II 42
March 24.	Power for the justiciary of Ireland to pardon rebels by advice of the abp, chancellor, and treasurer *Westm* R. III p II 612
March 24.	Commission to Henry le Scrop, warden of Guisnes and Calais, Robert de Herle, constable of Dover Castle, John de Carleton, dean of Wells, and John Barnet, archdeacon of London, to treat with the French commissioners concerning the treaty between the duke of Brittany and Charles le Bloy *Westm* R III p II 612 O VI 322 H III p ii 43.
March 24.	Commission to the count of Vendôme, sir Simond de Vendosme, and Walter de la Roke, clerk, to receive the county of Montfort from the French K. *Westm.* R III p. II. 612. O. VI 323 H. iii p. ii. 43.

DATE	SUBJECT
1361 March 27	Commission to Thomas de Brantyngham, receiver of Calais, Antoin de Vale, and Bartholomew de Malpiles, to receive the money due from the duke of Burgundy at Easter *Westm.* R III p II 612
March 28	Receipt for 40,000 "motons" of French money from the duke of Burgundy *Westm.* R III p II. 613
April 6	The justiciary of Ireland is ordered to seize the lands acquired by Robert de Hohwode while holding office in Ireland *Westm* R III p II 613
April 12	The K. appoints Gerard de la Hayth, lord of Bontrissem, to be seneschal in Ponthieu and Montreuil. *Westm.* R. III. p. II 613
April 15	The K. forbids the exportation of falcons *Westm.* R III p. II 613.
April 16	The K orders the several sheriffs to enforce the statute of wages, and forbids any person employing workmen who have deserted his service in consequence of the reduction of their wages. *Westm* R III p. II 613
April 16	Similar letter to Robert Herle and 39 other justices *Westm* R III p. II 614
April 30.	The K forbids any persons except merchants leaving the kingdom. *Westm.* R III. p II. 614.
May 1.	Privileges granted by the K to the inhabitants of Crotoy and Marhot. *Westm.* R III p II. 615.
May 6	Licence to John duke of Berry, and the vallets of the count of S Paul, French hostages, to go to France, also safe conducts for the servants of other hostages. *Westm.* R III p II. 616. O VI 323 H III p II 43
May 10.	The courts of law are prorogued until June 25, in consequence of a pestilence. *Westm* R III p II 616
May 10.	Safe conducts for William de Yeio, chaplain and secretary of the duke of Orleans, John de Puteo, his squire, and John de Mante, his chancellor *Westm.* R. III. p II 617.
May 10.	The K desires the council of Ireland to give credence to Thomas de Baddeby, concerning the coming of the earl of Ulster. *Westm* R. III. p. II. 617
May 14	Safe conduct for sir Peter de Seymur, chamberlain, Aleman de S. Venaunt, squire, and John Loen, secretary of the duke of Berry *Westm* R III p II 617
May 16	The K summons the merchants of the staples of Westminster, Lincoln, and nine other towns to appear before the council, also six burgesses of Calais *Westm.* R II p II 617.
May 21.	Licence to the duke of Anjou to visit the shrines of S Thomas of Canterbury and our Lady of Walsingham. *Hadley* R III p II 618 O VI 324 H III p II 43
May 25.	Safe conduct for servants of the dauphin of Auvergne, French hostage. *Westm* R. III. p. II 618
June 5	Licence to John and Stephen de Forges, burgesses of Tours, hostages, to go to any part of England Similar licence to 32 others *Westm* R. III p II. 618 O VI 324–5 H III p II 43
June 13	Thomas de Kyngeston is appointed warden of Calais Castle *Westm* R. III. p II. 619
June 25.	The K, at the request of the commonalty of Abbeville, orders his seneschal of Ponthieu to take an oath similar to that taken by his ancestors as counts of Ponthieu *Westm* R III p II 619 O. VI 325 H III p II 44
June 20.	Indenture between the K and Robert de Portyco, whom he appoints master of the mint in the Tower of London Similar indenture with Walter de Barde, dated *Westm*, 5 *March.* *Westm* R III p II 619 O. VI. 326 H. III. p II. 44
June 23.	Further adjournment of the courts of law until the octave of Michaelmas on account of the pestilence *Westm* R III p II 621
June 25.	The K. confirms the liberties and privileges of the commonalty of Abbeville *Westm* R III. p. II 621 O VI 325 H III p II 44
July 1	Licence to the duke of Anjou to go where he pleases in England *Westm.* R. III. p. II 621 O. VI 326 H III p II 44
July 1	The K appoints his son Lionel earl of Ulster his lieutenant in Ireland Intimation thereof to the K's officers and to the people of Ireland *Westm.* R III. p. II. 621. O VI 327 H. III. p II 45.
July 2	Proclamation to be made by the several sheriffs in England that those having lands in Ireland, occupied by the K's enemies, are to go thither at once *Westm* R III. p. II. 622. O VI 327 H. III. p II 45

D D

DATE	SUBJECT
1361 July 2	The K desires the earl of Ulster to make use of the advice of the abp of Dublin, the earl of Stafford, Rauf de Ferreres and others *Westm* R iii p ii 622
July 12.	Thomas Dautre is ordered to provide shipping for the passage of Robert de Knolles to Brittany *Westm* R. iii p. ii 622.
July 12	The custody of the castles of Fugerey and Chastelblank, in Brittany, is committed to Robert de Knolles *Westm* R iii p ii 622
July 13.	The K informs the treasurer and barons of the Exchequer that Robert de Knolles has paid the 2,000 florins for the farm of Gravele and the castles of Fugery and Chastelblank Similar letter to the sheriffs of London. *Westm* R. iii. p ii 623
July 10	Pope Innocent [VI] informs the K that he has suspended the causes touching the late bp. of Ely and the convent of Spalding, will consider the promotion of John Barnet to the bishopric of Hereford, and cannot at present reply to his request for the promotion of the abbot of Clugny to the cardinalate *Avignon* R. iii p ii 623 O vi. 328. H iii p ii 45
July 20	Licence to Guilhelma de Coroiles, widow of James de Thalemont, to marry John Buffet within a year after her husband's death *Henley* R iii p ii. 623 O. vi. 329. H iii p ii 45
July 21	Innocent [VI.] desires the K's assistance against Bernabo dei Visconti [de Vice-comitibus] *Avignon* R iii. p ii 623 O vi. 329. H iii p ii 45
July 27	Cession by John K. of France, of Poictou, Belleville, and Thouart to the K, also of Rovergne, Gaure, Angoulême, and six other territories *Bois de Vincennes* R. iii p ii. 624 O vi. 331 H iii p ii 46
Aug. 12.	John K. of France desires Le sire de Basalhac to do homage to the K. of England. *Bois de Vincennes* R iii p ii 624 O. vi. 332 H iii p ii. 47
Aug 13	Warrant for the payment of 100 crowns to Peter Burgeois for bringing to the K the news of the birth of a daughter to Joan, Q. of Navarre *Beaulieu* R. iii p ii 625. O vi 333 H iii p ii 47
Aug 17	Safe conduct for Guy Quieret, archdeacon of Glasgow, councillor of Charles K of Navarre, and others, to pass through England on the way to Scotland *Beaulieu.* R iii p ii 625
Aug 25	John de Atherstone is appointed warden of Ouderwyk Castle in the county of Guisnes Henry Lescrop, governor of the K's castles at Mark, &c, is ordered to deliver it to him. *Beaulieu.* R. iii. p ii. 625
Sept. 30	The K orders his subjects in Brittany to obey William lord de Latymer, whom John duke of Brittany has appointed his lieutenant and captain *Windsor* R iii p ii 625
Sept. 30	Giles de Wyngreworth is appointed treasurer and receiver in Brittany *Westm.* R iii. p. ii. 626
Sept 7	Pope Innocent's bull of dispensation for the marriage of Edward of Wodestok prince of Wales with Joan countess of Kent, being within the third degree of consanguinity *Avignon* p ii 626 O. vi 333 H iii. p ii 47
Oct 18	Declaration by Simon abp of Canterbury, of the solemnization of the marriage of the prince of Wales with the countess of Kent at Windsor, Oct. 10 *London.* R. iii. p ii 626. R. ni O vi 334-5. H. iii. p ii 47
Oct 25.	The K orders Richard de Stafford, seneschal of Gascony, Richard de Totesham, governor of Rochelle, and his other officers abroad, to punish infractions of the treaty with France. *Westm.* R. iii. p. ii. 628. O. vi 333 H iii p ii 49
Oct 25	The K. orders Richard de Stafford to publish the peace *Westm.* R iii. p ii. 628.
Oct 25.	Safe conduct for Charles de Bloys to come to S Omer on the subject of the above-mentioned peace. *Westm* R iii p ii 628 O vi. 358 H iii p ii. 49
Oct 29	Pope Innocent [VI] requests the K to receive by proxy the oath of Symon, bp elect of London. *Avignon* R iii p ii 628. O vi 339 H iii p ii 49.
Nov 8	Safe conduct for Henry de Maud and Stephen de Balhie, French hostages, to go to Dover. *Westm.* R iii. p ii. 629.
Nov 12	Grant of certain tolls to the commonalty of Abbeville, for the fortification of the town *Westm.* R iii. p. ii 629.
Nov 15	Commission to sir Thomas de Uvedale and Thomas de Dunclent, to make certain requests to the K of France for the performance of the treaty, and to receive his renunciations. *Westm* R. iii. p. ii. 629. O. vi. 339. H iii. p. ii. 49

DATE	SUBJECT.
1361 Nov. 15	Licence to the mayor and commonalty of Maiot, Crotoy, and Bertoncourt, in Ponthieu, to rebuild and endow a hospital burnt during the war *Westm* R iii p ii, 629.
Nov 16	Grant to the same mayor and commonalty of certain tolls for their fortifications. R iii. p. ii 630
Nov 17	John Tyrell is appointed warden of the castle of Oye. *Westm.* R iii p ii 630
[Nov 17]	Hugh de Escote is appointed warden of the castle of Sandegate R. ni p ii 630.
Nov. 18.	Safe conduct for Odo de Selande and William de Dyjoun, valets of the earl of Marre, coming from France to England with horses *Westm.* R. iii p. ii 630. O. vi 340. H iii p ii. 50.
Nov 18	Commission to John Hound and Richard de Immeworth to arrest English men at arms and archers who are living in France by plunder *The Tower of London.* R iii. p ii 630. O vi 340 H iii p ii 50
Nov 20.	Power for Thomas de Uvedale to receive the next payment from the duke of Burgundy *Windsor.* R iii p. ii. 631
Nov. 20.	John K. of France desires the count of Fois to do homage to the K. of England *The Louvre lez Par* R iii p ii 631 O vi 339 H.. iii p ii 49
Nov 25	John K of France orders the lord of Chastelbeat, castellan of Lourde, to surrender the said castle to the K of England. *The Louvre.* R. iii. p. ii. 631. O. vi 341 H iii p ii 49.
Nov. 18.	The K confirms the grant of nobility by the dauphin to Peter Buffet, burgess of Rochelle. *Westm* R iii p. ii 631 O vi 342. H iii p ii. 50
Dec 8	Power for Thomas de Brantyngham, treasurer of Calais, and Esmon Savage, to receive the money due from the duke of Burgundy *Westm* R iii. p ii. 632 O vi 342. H. iii p ii 50
Dec. 10.	Safe conduct for Wilham bp of S. Andrew's, Patrick bp. of Brechin, and three others, to come to England *Westm* R iii p ii 632 O vi 343 H iii p. ii 51
Dec 11	Receipt for 23,000 "motons" of French money from the duke of Burgundy. R. iii. p ii 632
Dec. 11.	Pope Innocent confirms the marriage between the prince of Wales and the countess of Kent. *Avignon* R iii p ii 632. O vi 343 H iii. p ii 51
Dec 20	Licence to Cossmius prior of Lewisham to go to Flanders *Westm.* R iii. p ii. 633
Dec 24	Obligation of Othes, lord of Gransson, Henry de Vienn, lord of Mirebele, and seven other hostages for the duke of Burgundy. *Calais* R iii p ii. 633. O vi. 345 H iii. p ii. 51.
Jan. 1.	The K desires John, soi-doisant duke of Brittany and count of Montfort, to come to S Omer the week after Easter, to meet the English and French commissioners, for deciding his claim to the duchy of Brittany *Westm* R iii p ii 633 O vi 346 H iii. p ii 52.
Jan 4	Safe conduct for sir Oliver de Manny, in the service of the duke of Orleans. *Westm* R. iii. p ii. 634. O. vi. 346. H iii p ii 52.
Jan. 13.	Innocent [VI.] desires the K to perform fully the recent treaty with France. *Avignon.* R iii p ii 634. O vi 347 H iii p ii 52
Jan. 14.	Innocent [VI] excuses sir Guy de Brien for having requested him to translate his brother Reginald from the see of Worcester to that of Ely. *Avignon* R iii p. ii. 634. O vi 347 H iii p. ii. 52.
Jan 18.	Receipt by the agent of the "capitan de Buche" of 23,000 florins for Jakes de Barbon, count of Ponthieu *London* R iii p ii. 635 O vi 348. H. iii p ii 53
Jan 20.	The K orders the abbot of Waltham to pay to the prince of Wales and the countess of Kent the annuity of 50l., formerly paid to Thomas de Holand. *Westm.* R iii. p ii. 635 O vi 348 H. iii p ii. 53.
Jan. 21.	Licence to Andrew de Allyncrom and John de Allyncrom of Scotland to study at Oxford or Cambridge. *Westm* R iii p ii. 635 O vi 349, H iii. p. ii. 53.
Jan 23.	Licence to William earl of Sutherland, Scotch hostage, to go to Scotland. *Westm.* R iii p ii 635. O vi 349 H. iii p. ii. 53
Jan 28	The K informs Robert de Tughale, chamberlain of Berwick, that he has appointed John de Coupeland sheriff of Roxburgh. *Westm* R iii p ii 635.
Jan. 30.	Licence to sir John de Loveyns and Assalhida de Farges to plead by deputy in Aquitain *Westm.* R. iii p. ii 635.
Feb. 3.	Henry le Scrop is appointed governor of Calais. *Westm* R iii p. ii. 636
Feb. 6.	Clement Spice is appointed attorney to the prince of Wales. *Westm.* R iii p ii. 636.

DATE.	SUBJECT.
1362 Feb 8	Commission to the bp of Worcester elect and confirmed, Robert de Ufford, earl of Suffolk, and three others, to treat for a marriage between Edmund de Langley, the K's son, and the duchess of Burgundy, daughter of the count of Flanders *Westm.* R. iii p. ii 636. O vi 349 H iii p n 53
Feb. 9.	Protection for John de Greneburn, coming from Scotland to England on the business of the earl of Sutherland. *Westm* R, iii. p ii 636.
Feb 10	Summons to Thomas de Furnyvall, Thomas earl of Oxford, and 51 others, to send men to Ireland, and to attend a council to consider the state of that country. *Westm* R iii. p ii 636 O vi 350 H iii p ii 53
Feb. 15	[The earl of Perigord] promises to serve the K of England *Montignac* R iii p ii 637. O. vi 361. H. iii p ii. 54.
Feb. 15	Grant of 200 marks a year to the prince of Wales in compensation for land held by the heir of the late earl of Salisbury *Westm* R iii p ii 638
Feb 15	The K. orders the treasurer and barons of the Exchequer to allow the earl of Salisbury to hold the castle of Trowbridge in Wiltshire and certain manors in Dorset and Somerset *Westm* R iii p ii 638
Feb. 18.	The K orders John Chaundos, viscount of S Sauveur, William de Felton, seneschal of Poictou, and 20 others, to receive the castles of Melle, Cunay, Chisek, and other places, according to a treaty between the K and the duke of Orleans and other hostages *Westm.* R. iii. p. ii. 639
Feb. 21.	Obligation of John K of France to pay to the K of England the remainder of the sum due from the late duke of Burgundy *Paris* R iii p n. 689 O vi 351. H iii p ii. 54.
Feb. 21.	John K of France acknowledges that the K. of England has fulfilled his part of the treaty with the duke of Burgundy. *Paris.* R iii p ii 640 O. vi. 354. H iii. p ii 55.
Feb 22	Commission to Hugh de Courteneye, earl of Devon, John Moubray, and Edmund de Chelreye, to inquire into the plunder of the ship called *Tarrit* and other ships wrecked at Plymouth *Windsor* R iii p ii 641
March 11	Warrant to Bartholomew Stygan, master of the ship called *Phelippe de la Toure*, to arrest 26 sailors, also to John Grene, master of the *Edward de la Tour*, for the same number R. iii p ii 641
March 14	The custody of Lochmaban Castle and Annandale is committed to John de Denton. *Westm* R iii p ii 641.
March 15.	Licence to nine French burgesses, hostages, to return to France. *Westm.* R. iii p ii 641 O vi 355 H iii p ii 55
March 19	Restitution of the temporalities to Simon bp of Ely, late abbot of Westminster *Westm.* R. iii p ii 642
March 20.	Grant to Walter Huet, captain of Colet Castle in Brittany, of the rents and revenues of Boaye, S Jean de Freyne, and other parishes *Westm.* R iii p. n. 642
March 21.	Licence for eight other French burgess to return home *Westm* R iii p ii. 642.
March 22	The K allows Archembald count of Perigord to enjoy his inheritance until the arrival of the prince of Wales *Westm* R. iii. p. ii 642 O. vi. 355. H iii p ii. 55.
March 26	Licence to the friends of sir John de Lucemburch, a French hostage, who has died in London, to take his body to France for burial. *Westm* R. iii p ii 643 O vi 356 H iii p. ii 56
	Safe conduct for Thomas de Stafford, valet of the duke of Bourbon R. iii. p. ii. 643. O vi 356 H iii p ii 56
March 29	Safe conducts for Robert Clerk, David Comyn, and Alexander Frisell, of Scotland *Westm* R iii p ii 643
March 30.	Safe conduct for the count of Vendôme and his brother Simon de Vendôme to come to England. *Westm* R. iii. p ii. 643. O vi. 356 H. iii p ii 56.
April 1	Pope Innocent thanks the K for remitting 100,000 florins of the sum due from the French K, which sum will be paid from the clerical subsidy granted to his holiness *Avignon* R iii p ii 643. O. vi. 357 H iii p ii 56
April 1.	Pope Innocent desires the abp of Canterbury and the bp. of Ely to collect the said subsidy. *Avignon.* R iii p ii 644 O vi 357 H iii p ii 56
April 1.	Acquittance by Thomas de Beauchamp, earl of Warwick, for the ransom of Gillem de Melleun abp of Sens, his prisoner, taken at the battle of Poitiers. *London* R iii p ii 644 O. vi. 359 H. iii. p ii 57

DATE	SUBJECT.
1362 April 10	The K. orders John de Chaundos, baron of S Sauveur le Visconte, to make restitution to the abbey of S Ebrulfus for injuries done by his subjects *Westm.* H. iii p. ii. 644. O vi 360. H iii. p ii. 57
April 10.	Release of Jodoin à la Gueule, burgess of Orleans, hostage in England *Westm* R iii· p ii 645
April 15	Safe conducts for William bp of S. Andrews, Patrick bp of Brechin, and three others, to come to England on the affairs of David de Bruys *Westm.* R. iii. p ii. 645. O vi. 361. H. iii. p ii 57.
April 18.	Safe conduct for David de Bruys to come to England. *Westm* R. iii p ii. 645 O. vi. 361 H. iii. p. ii 57.
April 20	Henry de Percy and Ralph de Nevill are appointed conservators of the truce with Scotland. *Westm* R iii p ii. 645
April 28	The K. orders Giles de Wyngresworth to allow John de Loco Monachorum, archdeacon and bp elect of Vennes, to receive the revenues of the bishopric *Westm.* R iii p ii 646 O. vi 361 H iii p ii. 58.
April 28	The K forbids the ships, merchandize, &c of the Scots to be molested at English ports *Westm* R iii p ii 646 O vi 362 H iii p ii 58
April 28	Renewed licence to William earl of Sutherland to return to Scotland *Westm* R iii p. ii. 646 O. vi. 362 H ii p ii 58
April 30	Commission to Marmaduke le Constable, sheriff of Yorkshire, and Henry de Ingelby, canon of York, to receive an oath from the earl of Sutherland for his return *Westm.* R iii p. ii 646 O vi 363 H iii p ii 58.
April 28.	Safe conducts for John Wyggemere and three other Scotch merchants. *Westm* R. iii p ii 646
April 28	Also for John de Petscoty and 23 other Scotch merchants *Westm* R iii p ii 647
May 1.	Receipt for 6,000 cr from William abp of Sens, taken prisoner at the battle of Poictiers. *Westm.* R iii p ii 647 O vi 363 H iii p ii 58.
May 1	Receipt for 108,800 crowns from the K of France *The Tower of London* R iii p. ii 647. O vi 363 H iii p ii. 58
May 2.	Safe conduct for John Heryng, in the service of Joan queen of Scotland *Westm* R iii p ii 647 O vi 364 H iii p ii 58
May 2	Safe conduct for Roger Hogg, burgess of Edinburgh *Westm* R. iii p. ii. 647
May 2.	Warrant to John de Cheverston and Richard Grenvill, to arrest seven ships to convey the said John de Cheverston to Gascony *Westm* R iii p ii 648.
May 3	Inspeximus of an acquittance for a recognisance of Edward le Despenser, lord of Glamorgan, and others. *Westm.* R iii. p. ii. 648
May 4	Receipt for 17,000 "moutons" French money from the K of France, for the duchy of Burgundy *Westm.* R iii p ii 649 O vi 364 H. iii p. ii 59.
May 5.	Annexation of Mountsegur in Aquitain to the English crown *Westm* R iii p ii 649
May 10.	Confirmation of the appointment by John Chaundos of William de Lyvenne to the offices of the execution of the seal and the sergeantry of Peracel. *Westm* R iii p. ii 649
May 14.	Release of John de Millevill, burgess of Douay, hostage, for exchange. *Westm.* R iii p ii 649 O vi 364 H iii p. ii 59
May 15	Restitution of the temporalities to Simon de Sudbury, bp of London *Westm* R iii. p ii 649
May 20.	The K orders Henry del Strother to deliver to Roger de Wyderyngton, sheriff of Northumberland, John Gray and Thomas del Haye, Scotch hostages. Roger de Wyderyngton is ordered to receive them *Westm* R iii p ii 650 O. vi 364. H iii p ii 59.
May 20	Walter Hewet is appointed warden of the forests of Poictiers and Poictou *Westm* R iii p ii 650.
May 26.	Protection for the abbey of S Eperche near Angoulême *Westm.* R. iii p. ii. 650
May 26.	Licence to William de Vallaquarta and Isabella his wife to plead by proxy in Aquitain *Westm* R iii p ii 650
June 28	Safe conduct for six servants of Blanche Q of France and Philip de Navarre coming to England. *Westm* R. iii p ii 650 O vi 365. H iii p. ii 59
May 28.	Grant of the first vacant prebend at Abbeville to John Bethelell de Ansere, master of arts and medicine Intimation thereof to the seneschal of Ponthieu *Westm* R iii p ii 651

DATE	SUBJECT
1362 June 2	Safe conduct for the cardinal of Clugny. *Westm* R iii p ii 651 O' vi 365 H iii p ii 59
June 2	The K orders the seneschal of Gascony and the castellan of Bourg to restore Olyvardre to Gerald de Tartas, lord of Puyane. *Westm.* R iii. p ii. 651
June 2	Safe conduct for Giles de Caumont, companion of the abp of Sens, and for four councillors of the K of France *Westm* R iii p ii 651 O vi 366 H. iii p ii 59.
June 4	Grant of certain tolls for paving the town of Crotoy *Westm* R iii. p. ii 651
June 4	The K. orders Walter Hewet to arrest ships for the passage of the prince of Wales to Gascony *Westm* R iii p ii 652.
June 6	Grant of the chapel of S. Nicholas, Cressy, to James Vintus of Paris Intimation thereof to the seneschal of Ponthieu *Westm* R iii p ii 652 O vi 366 H iii p ii 59
June 6.	Respite until Easter to the abbot of S Germain des Pres near Paris for the homage due for his lands in Saintonge *Westm.* R iii p ii 652 O vi 365 H iii p ii 59
June 7	Pardon to Peter de Fontibus and others for homicide at Abbeville *Westm.* R iii p ii 652.
June 7	The K appoints as his sergeant-at-arms Simon Raymon de Curson, servant of the cardinal of Clugny, with a fee of 12d a day Intimation thereof to the receiver and seneschal of Poictou *Westm* R iii p ii 653 O vi 367 H iii p ii 60
June 8	Richard Tempest is appointed warden of Berwick John de Coupeland, late warden, is ordered to resign the office to him *Westm* R iii p ii 653
June 8	John de Chevereston is appointed seneschal of Aquitain in place of Richard de Stafford. *Westm* R iii p ii 653
June 10.	Safe conduct for John Turpyn, in the service of the duke of Anjou, to go to Robert de Knolle in Brittany. *Westm* R iii p ii 653 O vi 367 H iii p ii 60
June 10.	The K forbids the mayor of Sandwich to exact toll from merchants of Bourdeaux. *Westm* R iii p ii 653
June 10.	The K. desires the council of Limoges to elect a conservator of the town *Westm* R iii p ii 654
June 10	The K orders William de Felton, seneschal of Poictou, Amanen lord of Poyane, and sir Amanen de Pomers, to restore Chazelles Savari in Touraine to John le Maingre *alias* Boucıquant, marshal of France Similar letter to Richard de Totesham, seneschal of Saintonge *The Tower of London* R iii p ii 654 O vi 367 H iii p ii 60
June 13	The K. orders the seneschal of Limousin to proclaim that his officers have the right of deciding appeals, and not the viscount *Westm* R iii p. ii. 654. O vi. 368. H iii p ii 60
June 13.	Thomas de Kyngeston is appointed warden of Calais Castle. *Westm* R iii p li 655
June 13	The K. orders the seneschal of Limousin and Poictou to observe the rights and privileges of the town of Limoges *Westm* R. iii p ii 655
June 14.	The K orders guards to be placed on the walls of Limoges *Westm* R. iii. p. ii. 655.
June 20	The K orders the seneschal of Limousin to punish the workmen in the mint at Limoges who refuse to work *Westm* R. iii. p. ii. 656
June 20	Protection for sir John Basset, abroad in the K's service *Westm* R iii p. ii 656.
June 21	Protection for Roger Berners, lieutenant of Giles de Wyngreworth, treasurer of Brittany *Westm* R iii. p. ii. 656.
June 22	Treaty of alliance with Peter K of Castile *London* R. iii. p ii. 656. O vi 369. H iii p ii 60
June 22	The K resigns the duchy of Brittany to John duke of Brittany and earl of Montfort, now that he is of age *Westm* R iii p ii 658 O vi 377. H. iii. p ii 62.
June 24.	William lord de Latymer is ordered to deliver to the duke of Brittany the towns and castles which he holds in Brittany. *Westm* R iii p ii. 658 O vi 374. H iii p. ii. 62.
June 24	Similar order to William lord de Latymer and the K's other officers in Brittany. *Westm* R. iii p ii 658 O vi 374 H iii p ii 63
June 24	Acquittance to the duke of Brittany for all sums received from the K. for his maintenance. *Westm* R iii p ii 659 O vi 375 H iii p ii 63.
June 25.	Power for John abp of York, Thomas bp of Durham, Gilbert bp of Carlisle, Henry de Percy, and three others, to treat with David de Bruys for a final peace *London* R iii p ii 659. O vi 375 H iii p ii 63

DATE.	SUBJECT
1362. July 1.	Confirmation of the appointment by John Chaundos, viscount of S Sauveur, of Barnard de Marceux to the office of sergeant general, dated Poietiers, 23 Sept 1361. *Westm* R m. p. n. 659.
July 3	Warrant to William de Latymer, and Robert de Latymer, captain of Vannes, to arrest Roger Berners, late receiver of Vannes *Westm* R m. p n 659.
July 6	Inspeximus of the attestation of the homage performed by the citizens of Limoges, to John Chandos, viscount of S Sauveur, the K's lieutenant *Westm* R m p n 660
July 6	The K. promises to deliver to the duke of Brittany, his letters of obligation, on payment of 64,000 nobles. *Westm.* R m p n 661
July 7	Power for the bps of Winchester and Ely, Richard earl of Arundel, Walter lord of Manny, and John duke of Brittany to prorogue the truce with Charles de Bloys for one year *Westm.* R m p n. 662 O vi 377 H m p n. 64
July 7	John duke of Brittany will submit the decision of his cause to the K. of England if Charles de Bloys will similarly submit to the K. of France *Westm* R m p n 662. O vi 378. H m. p. n. 64.
July 7	Treaty of alliance between duke of Brittany and the K of England. Ratification by the K *London* R m p n 662 O vi. 379 H m p n 64
July 7.	John duke of Brittany promises not to marry without the K's leave *Westm* R m p n 663. O vi. 381. H m p n. 65
July 8	The K desires his officers in Rochelle to allow the duke of Brittany to have the profits enjoyed by his ancestors *Westm* R m p n. 664 O vi 382 H m p n 67
July 8	The K orders the sheriff of Southampton to assist William Bridport and two others in providing victuals for the duke of Brittany and William Latymer *Westm* R m p n 664 O vi. 382 H m p n 66
July 9	The K. promises letters of acquittance to John duke of Brittany whenever he shall pay the 64,000 nobles of English money which he owes to the K *Westm* R m p n 664 O vi 376. H m p n 63
July 10	The K receives the towns of Rochelle and Trongof from the duke of Brittany as a pledge for 64,000 nobles which he owes *Westm.* R m. p n 664. O vi. 383 H m p. n 66.
July 10	The custody of Becherell and Trungo in Brittany is committed to William Latymer. *Westm* R m. p. n. 664
July 10.	Power for the prince of Wales to receive homages and to confirm privileges in the lands ceded to the K. of England by the K. of France. *Westm.* R. m. p. n. 665 O vi 383. H m p n 66
July 11.	The mayor and bailiffs of Bristol are ordered to send ships to Plymouth for the passage of the prince of Wales to Aquitain *Westm.* R m p n 665
July 12	The K exempts Gasbert de Bovis Villa (Boyville) from the jurisdiction of the communalties of Agen and Cahors *Westm.* R m p n 665.
July 15	Grant of a tax of 6d. in the pound for the defence of Limoges *Westm* R m p n 665
July 15.	The sheriffs of Devon, Cornwall, and Southampton are ordered to provide clays for the transport of the horses of the prince of Wales *Westm* R. m p. n 665.
July 15.	Commissions to Thomas Dautre, John de Ellerton, and others, to provide ships for the duke of Brittany and the prince of Wales *Westm* R. m p n 666
July 16.	Safe conduct for Ingelram de Umframvill of Scotland and his wife Katherine to come to England *Westm* R. m. p n 666.
July 16	Safe conduct for Robert bp. of Avranches. *Westm.* R. m p. n 667, O. vi. 384. H m. p n 66.
July 18	Warrant to John Ram, master of the ship called *Seynte Marie*, to arrest 100 sailors *Westm* R m p n. 667
July 19	The K creates the prince of Wales prince of Aquitain. *Westm* R m. p. n. 667 O vi 384 H m p n 66
July 19	Letter communicating the fact to the inhabitants of Poictiers and Poictou *Westm* R. m. p. n. 668. O. vi 386 H. m p n. 67.
July 19.	Similar letter to the inhabitants of Aquitain and Gascony *Westm.* R. m p n 668 O vi 387 H m p n 68
July 19	The prince of Wales does homage to his father for Aquitain, and undertakes to pay an ounce of gold annually as an acknowledgement of his sovereignty *Westm* R m p n 668 O vi 388. H m p n 68

DATE	SUBJECT
1362 July 19.	Exemplification of a patent of Henry [III] concerning the homage done by the town of Limoges, dated the Tower of London, 14 July 47. Hen [III] *Westm.* R. III p II 669.
July 19.	Exemplification of the grant to the prince of Wales, the K reserving the sovereignty. *Westm* R III p II 669
July 22.	Safe conduct for Adam Tore and Andrew de Ormiston, Scotch merchants *Westm.* R. III p. II 670
Jnly 22.	Safe conducts for Walter archdeacon of Lothian coming to England on a pilgrimage, John de Peblys, treasurer of Glasgow, and two others *Westm* R III. p II 671
July 24.	Release of Matthew le Feur, burgess of Lyons, a French hostage. *Westm.* R. III p. II 671.
July 30	Power for the prince of Wales to receive 60,000 crowns in gold due from the French K *Havering* R III p II 671 O VI 390 H III p II 69
July 30	The sheriffs of London are ordered to provide bows and arrows for the prince of Wales *Westm.* R. III. p II 671
Aug 1.	Inspeximus of a treaty between Alfonso [IV.] K of Castile and Henry [III], dated Toledo, 22 April 1292 [1254 A D], and of the treaty with Peter K. of Castile, dated London, 22 June 1362 *Westm* R III p II 671
Aug. 3	Exemplification of the patent of K John of France ceding Rochelle to the K. of England, dated Calais, 24 Oct 1360. *Westm.* R III p II 674
Aug 4	Protection for Sir William de Felton, abroad in the K's service *Westm.* R III. p II 675
Aug 5.	Robert de Herle, constable of Dover Castle and warden of the Cinque Ports, Stephen de Valeyns, and the sheriff of Kent, are ordered to send armed men and archers to Calais *Westm* R III. p II 675
Aug 6	Revocation of grants fraudulently obtained in Aquitain *Westm* R III. p II 675 O VI. 391 H III. p II 69
Aug 10	Robert Monk is ordered, after conveying the duke of Brittany, to bring his ship to Plymouth for the passage of the prince of Wales *Westm* R III p. II 675
Aug 29	Licence to the prince of Wales to make a will for the payment of his debts *Shipton near Whichwood* R. III p II 676 O VI 391 H III p II 69
Sept 3	The K orders the dean and chapter of Lincoln to defer the election of a bishop The sheriff of Lincolnshire is ordered to prevent the holding of the election on the day fixed *Beckley.* R III p II 676
Sept 13.	Thomas Dantre and Robert de Appelby are ordered to deliver ships to Thomas de Beauchamp, earl of Warwick, who will accompany the prince of Wales. " *Yeshempstede* " R III p II. 676
[Sept 13]	Confirmation of the appointment of Bernard de Martellis to the office of sergeant-general in Poictou, by John Chaundos R III p II 677.
Sept. 23.	Power for William bp. of Winchester, Simon bp of Ely, and sir Thomas de Uvedale to prorogue the truce with Charles de Bloys until Michaelmas 1363 *The new Castle, Sheppey* R III p II 677 O VI 391 H III p II 69
Sept 27	The K forbids the exportation of wool, hides, or fleeces after next Michaelmas *Westm* R III p II 677
Sept 29	Receipt for 10,000 " moutons " in gold from the K of France for Burgundy *Westm* R III p II 677 O. VI 392 H III. p. II 69
Oct 1.	Similar receipt for 500 " montons " in gold *Westm* R III p II 677. O VI 392. H III p II 70
Oct. 1	Release by John duke of Brittany for all revenues and emoluments received by the K from the duchy during his minority *Betherel* R III p II 678 O VI 393. H III. p II 70
Oct 6	Power to John Chandos, viscount of S Sauveur in Normandy, to receive 30,000 crowns in gold from the K of France *Westm* R III p II. 678. O VI 393 H III p II 70
Oct 10	The K. orders the sheriffs of London to proclaim that no cloth must be sold without the seal of the collector of the subsidy. Similar writs to the sheriffs of Southampton, Surrey, and Sussex *Westm* R III p II 678
Oct 10	Similar writs to the sheriffs of Gloucester and Wilts *Westm* R III p II 678.

DATE	SUBJECT
1362 Oct 24	The K orders the treasurer and barons of the Exchequer to release John Chaundos from the payment of the profits of the territories received by him from the French K, for the receipt of which he has appointed officers *Westm* R iii, p ii 679 O vi 394. H iii p ii 70.
Oct. 26.	Safe conduct for the bp of S Andrew's, coming on a pilgrimage to S Thomas of Canterbury *Westm* R iii p. ii. 679. O. vi 395. H. iii. p. ii. 70. Letters of safe conduct for 17 Scotch nobles with their attendants. O vi 395. H iii p ii 71 Omitted in Record Edition
Oct 26	The K. orders John de Cheverston, seneschal of Gascony, to obey the prince of Wales *Westm* R iii p ii 680
Nov. 3.	Safe conduct for Richard de Fogon, canon of Glasgow, going to Flanders *Westm.* R iii p. ii 680.
Nov 4	Safe conducts for Sir Thomas Somervyll and 17 other Scots *Westm* R iii p ii 680.
Nov 14	Safe conduct for Ingelram de Umframvill and Katherine his wife. *Westm.* R iii p.ii 680.
Nov. 20	Grant to Edmund de Langele, earl of Cambridge, of the fines at the sessions of John Moubray and other justices for the repair of his castles in Yorkshire *Westm* R iii p ii. 681. O vi 395 H iii p. ii. 71.
Nov	Treaty for the release of the dukes of Orleans, Anjou, Berry, and Bourbon , Belleville and other places being given as security *London.* R iii p ii 681 O vi 396 H iii p ii 71
Nov. 21.	Release of Dominic de Bardilly, burgess of Orleans. *Westm.* R iii p ii. 682.
Nov 22.	Protection for Robert de Grendon, clerk, in the retinue of John Chaundos *Westm.* R iii p ii 682,
Nov 24	Receipt for 9,500 "moutons" in gold from the K of France for Burgundy *Westm* R iii p ii 682 O vi 398 H iii p. ii. 72.
Nov 24.	The K orders the prince of Wales to inquire into the imprisonment of certain citizens of Bayonne by the castellan of Machecol. *Westm* R iii p ii 682.
Nov 26	The K orders the seneschals of Bigorre, Roverge, Perigord, and other districts, to summon the clergy, nobles, and commons to consult as to the best place for holding the sovereign resort of Aquitain *Westm* R. iii. p ii. 682.
Nov 26	The K. forbids the exportation of corn, lead, and cloth called Worstedes *Westm* R iii. p. ii 683.
Nov 26	Protection for Edmund Bulstrode, son of Edmund Bulstrode, in the retinue of John de Stretle going to Gascony *Westm* R iii p ii 683
Nov. 26.	Protection for John de Berkeleye and Edmund Bulstrode, son of Matilda Bulstrode, in the retinue of John de Stretle, and for John de Stretle, dean of Lincoln, in the retinue of the prince of Wales *Westm* R iii p ii 683
Dec. 4.	Safe conducts for the count of Brene, the lords of Hangest, Montmorency, and S Venaunt, to go to France *Westm* R iii p ii 684 O. vi 398. H iii p. ii. 72.
Dec 8	Pardon to Ingelram lord Desquelles of Guisnes for banishment and forfeiture in consequence of the war. *Westm* R iii p ii 684. O vi 399 H iii p ii 72
Dec. 8.	The K of England requests John K of France to pay 400 crowns in gold to William de Dormantz, chancellor of Normandy : *Windsor* R iii p ii 684 O vi 399. H iii p ii 72.
Dec. 10.	Protection for Bernard and Arnold Brocas, clerks, and Robert de Chisenhale, going to Gascony *Westm.* R iii p ii 684
Dec. 10.	John Wroth is appointed warden of Hammes Castle Intimation thereof to Henry Lescrop, governor of Guisnes and Calais *Westm* R iii p ii 684
1363. Jan 15	Release of Stephen de Foulgnes, burgess of Tours, French hostage *Westm.* R iii. p ii. 685
Jan 18.	Robert de Appelby and Richard de Imworth, sergeants-at-arms, are ordered to arrest ships for the passage of the prince of Wales to Gascony Similar commission to John de Haddon and John de Ellerton *Westm* R iii p ii 685
Jan 18	The K orders John count of Tanquarvill, John de Chaundos, viscount of S Sauveur, and William de Felton, seneschal of Poictou, to arrest James de Pipe, Hugh Calverle, and others, who have broken the peace with France *Westm.* R iii p ii 685
Jan 26	The K of France thanks the K for having released his brother and sons, desires the substitution of Pierre d'Alençon, the dauphin of Auvergne, and the lord of Coucy, for the count of Grandpre and two others, and requests him to prolong the term allowed to the count of Brenne and the lord of Hangest *Villeneuve* R iii p ii 685. O vi. 400. H iii. p ii 72

DATE	SUBJECT
1363 Jan. 26.	The K grants the prebend of S Wolfran in Abbeville to John Wycard. Intimation thereof to the seneschal of Ponthieu *Westm* R. iii. p ii 686 O. vi 400 H. iii p. ii 73.
Jan. 27.	The K. appoints John de Hatfelde, clerk, and two others, "achators" for the provision of timber for the works at Calais, in accordance with the statute of the present parliament Commission to Robert Crull, clerk, to provide workmen. *Westm* R. iii. p ii 686.
Feb 1	Confirmation of the treaty with Castile, dated June 22, 1362 *Westm* R iii p ii 686. O vi. 401 H iii p ii 73.
Feb 3	Robert de Langeton, sergeant at-arms, is appointed warden of Ouderwyk Castle, near Guisnes *Westm* R iii p ii 687
Feb 3	Henry le Scrope is appointed governor and overseer of Mark, Calais, Sandgate, Cologne, Hammes, Wale, Oye, and Guisnes. *Westm* R iii p. ii. 687.
Feb. 5.	Safe conduct for David de Berclay, of Scotland, going to Prussia, also for Thomas earl of Marr, 20 Feb *Beskwood* R iii p ii 687 H iii p ii 402
Feb. 8	The K assigns the revenues of the queen Philippa's castles and lands for six years, for the payment of her debts. *Westm* R iii p ii 687
Feb 8.	Power for the bps. of Saintes and Sarlat, Thomas de Felton, seneschal of Aquitain, and six others, to deliver the confirmation of the treaty to the K of Castile, and to receive his confirmation Similar power to the bp of Saintes, William de Loigne, and three others *Westm* R. iii p ii 638 O vi 402 H iii p ii 73
Feb 9.	The collectors of S Botolph's, Sandwich, and 10 other ports, are ordered to allow all goods, except lead, tin, and cloth, to be exported to Calais Letter on the same subject to the mayor of the staple at Norwich *Westm* , 10 *April* R iii p ii. 688.
Feb 10	The K orders Henry le Scrop, governor, Thomas de Brantyngham, treasurer, and John de Wessenham and John Wroth, mayors of Calais, to restore a house to Philip Fitzwaryn *Westm* R iii p ii 689
Feb 19	Memorandum of the transfer of the great seal from William bp. of Winchester to Simon bp of Ely. *Westm* R iii p ii 689. O. vi 403. H iii p ii. 73
Feb. 19.	John bp of Worcester is appointed treasurer of the Exchequer, *vice* Simon bp of Ely *Westm* R iii p ii 689
Feb. 20.	Thomas de Brantyngham is appointed receiver of the profits from the mint at Calais, and is ordered to pay Henry de Brisele for the tools bought by him. *Westm* R. iii. p ii 689.
Feb 20	Release of Henry de Brisele and Richard Colle from the rent of the K.'s mines in Devon *Westm* R iii p ii 690
March 1.	Confirmation of the treaty with Peter K of Castile *Westm* R. iii p ii 690. O vi 403 H iii p ii 74
March 1	Grant of an annuity of 200*l.* to Eleanor countess of Ormond *Westm* R iii p ii 690
March 1	The K grants certain privileges to the mayor, aldermen, and burgesses of Calais *Westm* R iii p ii. 690
March 1	The K orders Henry le Scrop, governor, and Thomas de Brantyngham, treasurer of Calais, to perform the above grant. *Westm.* R iii p ii 692
March 1.	John Philipot of London and William Freeman of Brackley are appointed to receive forfeitures on merchandise at Calais *Westm* R iii p ii 693
March 3	The K grants to the officers of the exchange at Calais the privileges enjoyed by the officers of the exchanges at London and Canterbury *Westm* R iii. p ii 693
March 11.	Indemnity for Peter de Bardes and Nicholas de Maryn, in case of forfeitures incurred by their partner Gautron de Bardes, master of the mint at the Tower of London. *Westm.* R iii p ii 693
March 14	Safe conducts for William bp of S Andrew's, Patrick bp of Brechin, sir Robert de Erskyn, the abbot of Dunfermline, and three others, coming to England. *Westm* R iii p. i 693 O vi. 404 H. iii. p ii 74
March 13	The K of France accepts the treaty for the release of his brother and sons, without the alterations he proposed, to which the K of England will not agree *Villeneuve.* R. iii. p ii 694 O vi 405 H. iii p ii 74
March 16	The K of France desires the dukes of Orleans, Anjou, Berry, and Bourbon to confirm the treaty *Villeneuve* R iii p ii 694 O vi 405 H iii p ii 74
March 16	The K of France writes on the same subject to the count of Brenne, the lord of Hangest, and two others *Villeneuve* R. iii p ii 694 O. vi. 406 H iii p ii 75.
April 6	The K forbids the exportation of horses, falcons, worsted, or flax *Westm* R iii p ii 694

DATE	SUBJECT
1363. April 7.	Robert de Mackeneye and 23 others are appointed achators for the K's household Walter Husy and three others are appointed to take charge of the K's hawks and hounds *Westm* 20 *April* R. iii p ii 695
April 8.	Receipt for 10,000 "moutons" in gold from John K of France, for Burgundy. *Westm.* R iii p ii 696. O vi 406 H iii p ii. 75.
April 8	Release of William de Noe, burgess of Arras, and five other French hostages *Westm*, *various dates.* R iii p ii 696. O. vi. 407 H iii p. ii 75
April 20.	Exemplification of the acquittance of the earl of Warwick to the abp. of Sens, dated April 1, 1362. *Westm.* R iii p ii 697. O vi. 407 H. iii. p. ii, 75
April 20	Safe conducts for the lord of Hangest and the count of Brene to go to France *Westm* R iii p ii 697.
April 22.	Licence to Geraud le Boucher, burgess of Compiegne, hostage, to visit our Lady of Walsingham and S. John of Beverley. Similar licence to Amand de Landa, burgess of Douay. *Westm* 7 *June.* R. iii. p. ii. 697
April 26	Safe conducts of various dates for sir Thomas de Somervill, John de Ros, and five other Scots, coming to visit the tomb of S Thomas at Canterbury *Westm.* R iii p ii 697. O vi 407 H iii p ii 75
April 28.	The wardens of the passage at Dartmouth and Weymouth are ordered to provide shipping for men-at-arms and archers going to Robert de Knolles in Brittany *Westm* R iii p. ii 697
April 28	The K orders the customers at Great Yarmouth to go to Ipswich to weigh wool which John de Wesenham has there for exportation *Westm* R iii p ii 697
April 29	Power to the prince of Wales to receive 60,000 crowns in gold from the K. of France. *Westm* R iii p ii. 698. O vi. 408. H iii, p. ii 75.
May 4.	The K grants the chapel of S Nicholas of Cressy to Peter Vetule. Intimation thereof to the seneschal of Ponthieu. *Westm.* R iii p ii 698 O vi 409 H iii p ii 76.'
May 4.	The K orders the customers of Southampton and 10 other ports to take security from merchants exporting wool that they will take it to Calais *Westm* R. iii. p. ii 698
May 8	Protection for sir Roger Davy going to Brittany *Westm* R. iii p. ii 699
May 10	The K forbids any money to be used in Calais except what is coined there. *Westm.* R iii p ii 699
May 12	Power for John Chaundos, viscount of St Sauveur, sir William de Felton, and sir William de Serys to receive Chiset and other castles as pledges for the duke of Orleans and the other hostages *Westm.* R iii p ii. 699 O vi 409 H iii p ii 76
May 12	Safe conduct for a ship laden with the property of the duke of Orleans *Westm.* R. iii. p. ii 699
May 12	Commission to John Chaundos, Wm Felton, and Wm. Serys to ascertain the value of the castles of Roche-sur-Yon, Ynay, and Dun le Roy, in Berry *Westm* R iii p ii. 699.
May 13	Obligation of John lord of Audresel, a French hostage, whom the K. has permitted to go to France *London* R. iii p ii 700 O. vi 410. H. iii. p. ii. 76.
May 15	Obligation of the dukes of Orleans, Anjou, Berry, and Bourbon R. iii p. ii 700 O vi 411 H. iii p. ii. 76.
	Renewal of the obligation of Pierre d'Alençon, Guy de Bloys, and 10 others, who remain as hostages R iii p ii 700 O vi 411 H iii p ii. 77.
May 15.	Protection for sir John de Cobeham of Kent going to Calais *Westm* R iii p ii 701
May 17	Warrant for the payment of 50l to Joan "domicella" of Brittany *Westm* R iii. p. ii 701 O. vi 412 H iii p ii 77
May 26.	Ratification of the treaty for the delivery of the French hostages. *Westm.* R. iii. p ii. 701 O. vi 412 H. iii. p ii 77.
May 26.	Promise of the K of England to deliver the hostages on receipt of the castles to be given by the French K. *Westm* R iii p ii 701 O vi 413 H iii p ii 77
May 26	Power for Gerard lord of Bontreshem to receive the castle of Beaurayn in Ponthieu, and for Thomas de Driffeld to receive the castles of Roche-sur-Yon, Dun-le-Roy, and Ynay *Westm.* R. iii p ii. 701 O vi 414 H iii p ii 78
May 26	The K accepts the renewal of the oath of Peter d'Alençon and the other hostages *Westm* R iii p. ii 702. O vi 414 H iii. p ii 78
May 26	Restitution of the temporalties to Thomas bp of Ferns, late archdeacon of Ferns *Westm* R iii p ii. 702

DATE	SUBJECT
1363. May 26	Gerard lord of Bontreshem, seneschal of Ponthieu, is authorized to take possession of Helicourt in Veyment, given to the K by Edward de Balliol K. of Scotland *Westm* R. iii p ii 702 O. vi 415 H iii p ii 78
May 27	Edward K of Scotland grants the town of Helicourt to the K of England *Whetlay near Doncaster* R iii p ii 702
May 27	The K orders Richard de Ravensere, keeper of the hanaper, to deliver the patent for the reversion of an annual rent of 10*l* issuing from the Haye of Willeye in the forest of Sherwood, granted to Edward de Balliol and William de Aldeburgh without the payment of the fee for the K.'s seal *Westm*. R iii p ii 703 O vi 416 H. iii p. ii. 79.
May 27	The K appoints the prince of Wales regent during his intended absence *Westm*. R iii. p ii 703
June 1.	Grant of 20*l* to John Paladyn, the K's physician *Westm*. R iii.p ii. 703 O vi 417. H. iii p ii 79
June 1	Licence to the abbot of Abingdon, the prior of St Frideswide's, and others, to assign messuages to the scholars of Canterbury Hall, Oxford *Westm* R iii p ii 703
June 14.	Warrant for the payment of 10 marks to Faukon, herald king of arms *Westm* R iii p ii. 704. O vi 417 H. iii p ii. 79
June 1	The several sheriffs are ordered to prohibit useless sports, and to encourage archery. *Westm* R iii p ii 704 O vi 417 H iii p ii. 79
June 4	Warrant for William de Walsyngham to arrest painters for the chapel of St Stephen's, within the palace of Westminster. *Westm*. R. iii p ii 704 O vi 417. H iii. p ii 79
June 4	The K. releases John Comyn, in the retinue of Elizabeth duchess of Clarence, from the payment of subsidy for his lands in Ireland *Westm* R iii p ii 704 O vi 418 H iii p ii 79
June 6.	The K. orders the mayor and aldermen of Calais to prevent evasions of the ordinance concerning the money of Calais *Westm* R iii p ii 704
June 7.	Licence to Andrew Destrer, of Bruges, queen Philippa's cithern-player, to export 25 cattle to Flanders free of duty *Westm* R iii p ii 704 O vi 418 H iii p ii 79
June 8	The K. orders the treasurer of Calais to deliver the engines for the defence of the city to the mayor and aldermen of Calais *Westm* R iii. p ii. 705
June 10.	Thomas de Brantyngham, treasurer of Calais, and Henry de Brisele, master of the mint, are appointed examiners of money at Calais *Westm* R iii p ii 705.
June 12	The K. orders the mayor and sheriffs of London to publish certain articles for preserving the peace in London. *Westm*. R iii p ii 705.
June 12	The K orders Gerald lord of Bontreshem, seneschal of Ponthieu, to complete the processes commenced by Simon abbot of Clugny, before the cession of Ponthieu to him *Westm*. R. iii p ii 705
June 13	Warrant for the payment of 100*l* to Goubert de Boyville, of Gascony, for the capture of the K of France *Westm* R iii p ii 706 O vi. 418. H. iii. p ii 79
June 14	Safe conducts for the count of Bren and the lord of Hangest *Westm* R iii p. ii 706 O vi 419 H iii p ii 80
June 17	Licence to Guy count of S Poule to visit our Lady of Walsingham *Westm* R. iii p ii 706 O vi 419 H iii. p ii 80.
June 20	Roger de Wyderyngton, late sheriff of Northumberland, is ordered to deliver Thomas del Hay, Scotch hostage, to Richard de Horsley, the present sheriff *Westm* R. iii p ii 706 O vi. 419 H iii p ii 80
June 20.	Warrant for the payment of 200*l* to Bartholomew de Burghersh, which the K. owes him for the count of Ventadour, his prisoner. *Westm*. R iii p. ii. 706 O vi 420 H iii p ii 80
June 20.	The K revokes the commission to John de Holand and John de Crophull to take possession of the temporalities of the see of Lincoln, now vacant, which commission is contrary to a grant of Edward II. to the dean and chapter *Westm* R iii p ii 706
June 23	Restitution of the temporalities to John de Bukyngham, bp. of Lincoln, late archdeacon of Northampton *Westm*. R iii p ii 707.
June 24	Commission to John Berholte and three others to arrest carpenters and other workmen for works at Windsor and Langley *Westm* R iii p ii 707
June 29	Pope Urban [V] desires credence for John de Cahrespino, canon of Narbonne *Avignon* R iii p ii 707 O vi. 420 H iii p ii 80

DATE	SUBJECT.
1363 July 14.	Restitution of the temporalities to John de Ewasham, bishop of Cloyne. *Rockingham.* R m p ii. 708
July 30	Urban [V] requests William Wilcham, archdeacon of Lincoln, to obtain a safe conduct for John de Cabrespino *Avignon.* R m p ii. 708 O vi. 420. H m p ii 80
Sept. 4.	Grant of an annuity of 100s. to Roger del Ewerie, the K.'s barber *Beskwood.* R m p ii 708
Sept 6	John K of France creates his fourth son Philip (who was wounded at the battle of Poictiers and taken prisoner) duke of Burgundy. *Germigniac-sur-Marne.* R m. p. ii. 708 O vi 421. H. m p ii 80.
Sept. 20	Prorogation of the leave of absence granted to William earl of Sutherland until Whit-suntide *Westm.* R m p ii 709 O vi. 423. H m p ii 81
Sept 21.	Ralph de Nevill is ordered to receive the earl of Sutherland's oath for his return *Westm.* R. m. p ii 709 O vi. 423. H. m p ii. 81.
Sept. 21.	The K. licenses John de Gabrespino to send bows and arrows to the pope *Westm.* R. m. p ii 709.
Oct 1	Protection for sir Nicholas de Loveyne and William son and heir of sir John de Pulteney. *Westm* R m p ii 709.
Oct. 6.	The sheriffs of London are ordered to pay John Braban, keeper of the mews at West-minster, for falcons bought by him for the K. *Westm* R m p ii 709
Oct. 8	The K forbids the exportation of herrings, cloth, and other merchandize, except to Gascony and Germany *Westm* R m p ii. 710
Oct 10.	Receipt of 10,000 "moutons" of gold from John K of France for the duchy of Bur-gundy. *Westm.* R. m p ii. 710. O vi. 423 H. m, p ii. 81
Oct. 10.	Commission to Thomas de Pykenham, Henry de Bruseleye, William Bisshop, and Roger Rotour to receive the above sum. *Westm.* R m p ii 711
Oct 10.	Protection for Reignaud lord of Maulevrier, French hostage. *Westm* R. m p ii 711. O vi 424 H m p ii 81.
Oct. 15.	Commissions to Thomas Plungeon and two others to arrest workmen to dig stone in the quarries at Willesford, Hellwell, and Careby, and to Simon Huet and another to carry it to Windsor Castle *Westm* R m p ii. 711.
Oct 20.	Exemplification of an article in the treaty of Bretigny confirming the collations to benefices during the war *Westm.* R. m. p ii. 711.
Oct 24.	The K orders Gerard lord of Bontreshem, seneschal, and Nicholas de Louthe, treasurer of Ponthieu, to attend to the complaint of the commonalty of Abbeville concerning a toll on grain *Westm* R m p ii 712
Oct 26.	The K orders them to reform customs at Abbeville, which are unjust and unprofitable. *Westm.* R m p ii 712
Oct 26	Grant to the commonalty of Abbeville of tolls on wine and beer to defray the expense of their fortifications *Westm.* R m. p ii 712
Oct. 27	Restitution of certain property in Abbeville to Baudewyn de Hallenghes. *Westm.* R. m p ii 712
Nov 5	Urban [V] desires the K to confirm the translation of P bp of Rathbog [Rathbocensis] to the see of Armagh *Viterbo* R. m p ii 713 O vi. 424. H m p ii 82.
Nov 6.	Licence to the burgesses of Arde to hold a fair for six days, commencing on the eve of S. Remigius. *Westm.* R. m p ii 713.
Nov. 6.	The K orders the mayor and aldermen of Calais to pay the customary rents to the abbot of Boulogne, the master of the charter house at S. Omer, and other religious persons. *Westm.* R m p ii 713.
Nov 12	Henry le Scrop, governor, and Thomas de Brantyngham, treasurer of Calais, are ordered to survey the men-at-arms and archers. *Westm* R m. p ii. 713.
Nov. 15.	The K. orders the chancellor and treasurer of Ireland to allow no one to act as examiner of weights and measures in Ireland without their consent. *Westm.* R m p ii 714
Nov 15.	The K orders the same persons to collect the revenues, and deliver them to two or three persons, to provide for the war *Westm* R m p. ii. 714.
Nov. 16.	Power for Thomas de Beverle, prior of S. John of Jerusalem in Ireland, chancellor of Ireland, to appoint justices. *Westm* R m p ii 714
Nov. 16	Richard White is appointed chief justice in Ireland. *Westm.* R. m. p. ii. 714.

DATE.	SUBJECT.
1363 Nov 16	Pardon of a fine imposed on the citizens of Dublin for the escape of Adam Trop, who revived after being hung, but who was re-hung at Kildare *Westm.* R III p II 714
Nov 17.	The K orders Lionel duke of Clarence, and the chancellor and treasurer of Ireland, to respect the privileges granted by the Kings of England to the city of Dublin. *Westm.* R. III p II 714
Nov 20.	The K orders Gerard lord of Bontresheim, seneschal, and Nicholas de Louthe, treasurer of Ponthieu, to inquire into the right of the lord of Bouberch to hunt in the forest of Cressy. *Westm.* R III p II 715 O VI 425. H III p II 82
Nov. 20.	Licence to the commonalty of Coventry to inclose the town with a wall. *Westm.* R. III. p II 715
Nov. 25	Safe conduct for sir Walter de Lesley, of Scotland, coming to England. *Westm.* R. III. p II 715 O VI 425 H III. p II 82
Nov 27	Negotiations for the union of the two crowns of England and Scotland, if K David died without heirs *Westm* R III p II 715 O. VI. 426 H III. p. II. 82
Dec. 1.	Nicholas de Drayton is appointed warden of the K's Hall at Cambridge, with 4d a day and eight marks a year for robes *Westm* R. III p II 716
Dec. 5	Safe conducts for Henry Kerre and 28 other Scots. *Westm* R III. p. II. 716 O VI 428. H. III. p. II 83
Dec 5	Safe conducts for sir William de Ramsay and seven other Scots coming to England. *Westm* R. III. p II. 717. O VI 428 H. III p II 83
Dec. 5.	Safe conducts for Alexander de Redwell, chaplain, and five other Scots, coming to study at Oxford *Westm* R III. p II. 717. O. VI. 429. H. III. p II 83.
Dec 5.	General safe conduct for Scotch scholars coming to study at the English universities. *Westm* R III p II 717 O VI 429 H III p II 83
Dec. 6.	Safe conducts for the earl of Patrik, William earl of Douglas, and the earl and countess of Sutherland to visit S. Thomas of Canterbury. *Westm* R. III p II 717 O VI. 429. H. III p II 84
Dec 6	Power for the prince of Wales to receive 60,000 crowns in gold from the K. of France *Westm.* R III. p II 718 O VI 430 H III p II 84.
Dec. 10.	Safe conduct for John K of France to come to England. *Westm* R III p II 718 O VI. 430. H. III. p II 84
Dec 13	Another commission to the prince of Wales to receive 60,000 crowns in gold from the French K *Windsor* R III p II 718 O VI 431 H III p II 84.
Dec. 20.	The K orders Henry Lescrop, governor, and Thomas de Brantyngham, treasurer of Calais, to compose the differences between the mayor and aldermen of Calais and the merchants. *Westm* R III p II. 719
1364. Jan. 18.	Safe conduct for Yvo Derian, secretary of John K of France *Westm.* R. III. p. II. 719. O VI. 432. H. III p II 84.
Jan. 24.	Protection for sir John Basset in the retinue of the prince of Wales. *Westm* R. III. p. II. 719.
Jan. 27	Robert de Naylyngherst and Walter de Wotton are appointed attorneys for sir John Burghcher, who is in Gascony. *Westm* R III p. II 719
Feb. 1.	Safe conduct for Wuldemer K. of Denmark to come to England. *Westm* R. III p. II. 719. O VI. 432. H III. p II. 85.
Feb 7	Safe conduct for Nersis abbot of the monastery of S George in "Armenia Minor," and James his fellow monk *Westm* R III p II 719. O VI 432 H III. p II. 85
Feb 8.	John Dabernoun, John de Kendale, and Robert Wysdom are appointed to provide forage and litter for the prince of Wales in Gascony *Westm* R. III p II 720
Feb 8	John Dabernoun, John Clerc, of Hampton, and Thomas FitzHenry are ordered to arrest ships for the conveyance of the prince's horses to Gascony *Westm* R. III p II. 720.
Feb 10.	John Maillart has the K's permission to receive in exchange the prebend of S Wolfran, Abbeville, from William de Ys, for the prebend of S Katharine at S Omer's Intimation thereof to the seneschal of Ponthieu *Westm.* R III. p II 720 O VI 433 H III. p II 85.
Feb 10.	Mandate for the restitution of the head of S Hugh to the cathedral of Lincoln from which it had been stolen *Westm* R III p II. 720 O VI 433. H III p II. 85
Feb 12.	Grant of the chapel of S. Nicholas, Cressy, to John Bassim, clerk, vacant by the death of Peter le Veel Intimation thereof to the seneschal of Ponthieu. *Westm.* R III p. I. 720. O. VI. 433 H III. p II 85.

DATE	SUBJECT
1364. Feb 12	Receipt of 107,000 crowns in gold from the K of France *The Tower of London* R. iii p ii 721 O vi 434 H iii p ii 85
Feb. 13.	Safe conduct for the earl of Marre to visit S Thomas of Canterbury , also for Thomas de Balhol, brother of the earl of Marre, and Adam de Lanark, bp of Galloway *Westm.* R. iii. p ii 721. O. vi 434 H iii p. ii 85
Feb 13	John Keppok is appointed chief baron of the Exchequer in Ireland, John de Uppyngham, and Thomas Quixhull, second and third barons, and Richard Whyte and Nicholas Lumbard are appointed justices , five other appointments to offices in the Exchequer *Westm* R. iii p ii 721
Feb 13	The K. orders Lionel duke of Clarence, his lieutenant in Ireland, to release from prison Henry de Leycestre *Westm* R. iii. p ii. 722.
Feb 14	The K orders sir Henry Lescrop, governor of Calais, to restore the inheritance of Ivoria, daughter of Symon de Oye *Westm* R iii p ii 722
Feb. 15.	The chancellor and treasury of Ireland are ordered to levy the subsidy for the expenses of the persons sent to the council in England. *Westm* R iii p. ii 722.
Feb. 16.	The mayors, aldermen, and inhabitants of Calais are ordered to assist Henry Lescrop and others in reforming the state and governance of the town *Westm* R iii p. ii 722
Feb. 16	Henry Lescrop, governor of Calais, Thomas de Brantyngham, treasurer, Adam Fraunceys, William de Haule, Adam de Bury, and John Pyel are appointed justices to survey the state and government of the town *Westm.* R iii p ii. 723.
Feb. 20.	Safe conduct for David de Bruys to visit our Lady of Walsingham *Westm.* R iii p ii 723 O vi 435 H iii p ii 86
[Feb 20]	Safe conduct for Margaret, wife of David de Bruys, to visit S Thomas of Canterbury R iii p ii 723 O vi. 435. H iii. p ii 86
Feb. 20.	Henry Lescrop is appointed warden of Calais and Guisnes castles *Westm* R iii. p ii. 723.
Feb 20	Commission to Henry le Scrop as governor of Mark, Calais, Sangate, Bolyns, Hammes, Wale, Oye, and Guisnes *Westm* R iii p ii. 724.
Feb 20.	Thomas de Kyngeston, late warden of Calais castle, is ordered to surrender the castle to Henry le Scrop. *Westm* R iii p ii 724
Feb 22.	The K forbids lending money for interest at Calais *Westm* R iii p ii 724
Feb 25	The K forbids the exportation of horses, falcons, arms, or worsted. *Westm.* R. iii p ii 724
Feb 29.	Collard Perdrix is appointed sergeant of the seneschal of Ponthieu *Westm* R iii. p ii 724.
March 1	The K. orders that all merchants who buy wool at Calais shall send five sous in weight of gold bullion to the mint, or the same value of silver *Westm* R iii p. ii 725
March 4.	The K orders the prince of Wales to put Nicholas de Lovayne in possession of the provostship of Bersac in Aquitain *Westm* R iii p ii 725
March 4.	Protection for sir Geoffrey de Cornewaille and three others in the retinue of Walter Huet going to Brittany *Westm* R iii p ii. 725.
March 5	Walter de Dalby, treasurer of Ireland, is ordered to pay 200*l* for the expenses of conveying the countess of March, daughter of the duke of Clarence, to England *Westm* R. iii p ii 725 O vi 435 H iii p ii 86
March 6.	Pope Urban's bull for the promotion of Thomas dean of London to the see of Rochester *Avignon* O vi 435 H iii p ii 86
	Memorandum that the bp. of Rochester took the oath of fealty to the K on Jan. 6, 1364-5. R iii p ii 726 O vi. 436. H iii p ii 86
March 6	The K orders sir William de Ciryce and Bernard Brocas, clerk, collectors of the revenues in Aquitain, to hear the complaint of sir Guychard Dangle, whose lands they have seized. *Westm* R iii p ii. 726
March 7	The K orders Gerard lord of Bautrssein, seneschal of Ponthieu, to restore any lands or goods belonging to the commonalty of Notelle in his hands, in consequence of the suit between them and Katherine d'Artoys, countess of Aubivalle *Westm.* R iii p ii 726
March 16.	The K informs the mayors and aldermen of Calais that the late order for merchants to send bullion to the mint did not apply to foreign merchandise *Westm* R iii p ii. 727.
March 28	Power for Thomas de Brantyngham, treasurer of Calais, Adam Fraunceys, and two others, to receive 10,000 "moutons" in gold from the K of France for the duchy of Burgundy *Westm.* R. iii. p. ii 727. O. vi. 437. H iii. p ii. 86

DATE	SUBJECT.
1364 March 28	Receipt for the above 10,000 "moutons" for the duchy of Burgundy *Westm* R. iii p ii 727. O vi 437 H iii p ii 87
March 29.	Protection for Hugh Curson, going to Gascony. *Westm* R. iii p ii. 727
March 30	Safe conduct for Dougal Petre, of Scotland, coming to study at Oxford. *Westm.* R. iii. p ii 727. O vi 437 H iii p ii 87
April 1.	Gauter de Barde, master of the mint at the Tower of London, is appointed master of the mint at Calais. *Westm* R iii p ii 727.
April 5	The K forbids the exportation of gold and silver and jewels. *Westm.* R. iii p ii 728
April 6	The K orders Gerard lord of Botreshem, seneschal, and Nichol de Louthe, receiver of Ponthieu, to determine the right of the lord of Bouberche to hunt in the forest of Cressy *Westm* R iii p ii 728 O vi 438 H iii. p ii 87
April 6	Restitution of the temporalities to John bp. of Bath and Walls, translated from Worcester *Westm* R iii p ii. 729
April 10.	William de Boys, William de Villiammon, and eight others, are appointed attorneys for sir Thomas de Uvedale *Westm* R iii p ii 729
April 11.	Protection for sir John de Delves, in the retinue of the prince of Wales in Gascony *Westm.* R iii p. ii. 729.
April 12.	Exemplification of the treaty between Robert lord Fiennes, constable of France, and sir John de Dalton, dated Ducoirre, 1 Dec 1359 *Westm* R iii p ii 729
April 12	Protection for William de Pontefract, in the retinue of the prince of Wales in Gascony *Westm.* R iii p ii. 730
April 12	Licence to Walter Huwet to take 40 lances and 100 bows to Brittany. *Westm* R. iii. p ii 731
April 12.	Protection for sir Richard Fyton and four others in the retinue of Walter Huwet in Brittany *Westm* R iii p. ii 731
April 13	Protection for William de Osmundeston, parson of Wisshawe, and five others in the retinue of the prince of Wales *Westm* R. iii p ii 731
April 15.	Protection for Antony de Roos, parson of Goldebourgh, and sir Thomas de Roos of Dowesby, in the retinue of the prince of Wales *Westm* R iii p ii 731
April 15	The K orders Richard la Vache, constable of the Tower of London, to repair the banks from Ware to Waltham, and thence to the Thames *Westm* R iii. p ii 731.
April 16	Grant of an annuity of 3,000 cr. to John de Meleun, count of Tankervill *Westm.* R iii p ii. 731 O vi 438 H iii p ii 87
April 16	Protection for sir Stephen de Cosyngton and four others *Westm* R iii. p ii 732.
April 18	Licence to the merchants of Droghcda and Waterford, to export wool and other merchandise to England, Gascony, or elsewhere. *Westm* R iii p ii 732
April 20.	Licence to the merchants of Lenne to export cloth to Calais and other ports to the north and east, excepting Flanders *Westm.* R iii p ii 732
April 23	The K forbids certain exactions made by the mayor of the staple at Calais from the merchants of Wales and Berwick-upon-Tweed *Westm* R iii p. ii. 732.
April 24	The K orders Walter de Dalby, receiver of wages for the war in Ireland, to pay 13s 4d a day to Lionel duke of Clarence, as his wages *Westm.* R iii. p ii 732 O. vi 439. H iii p ii 87.
April 28	Protection for sir Peter le Veel in the retinue of the prince of Wales in Gascony *Westm.* R. iii. p ii 733
May 2	Urban [V] releases the priory of Heverynglond, in the diocese of Norwich, from certain penances *Avignon.* R iii p ii 733 O vi 439 H iii p ii. 87.
May 4	Simon de Neuton is appointed warden of Helycourt Castle in Ponthieu. *Westm.* R. iii p ii. 733.
May 6.	Licence to James Dirkeson of Holland, importer of eels, to buy cloth to take to Holland, as taking money out of the kingdom is forbidden *Westm* R iii p ii 733.
May 7	Pope Urban's bull of protection for the priory of Heverynglond. *Avignon.* R. iii p ii 733 O. vi 440 H iii. p ii 87
May 7.	Pope Urban desires the prior of Butley to compel, on pain of excommunication, the restitution of rents and lands withheld from the priory of Heverynglond. *Avignon.* R iii p ii 733. O vi 440. H iii p ii 88.

DATE.	SUBJECT
1364 May 8	Testification of the transfer of a fee in the castellany of Mark by Thomas Dolsaly, merchant of London, to Philippot de Neuton *Westm* R. iii p ii 734
May 8.	Thomas Dautre, sergeant-at-arms, and John Polmound, bailiff of Southampton, are ordered to provide shipping for the conveyance of John de Delves and others to Gascony. *Westm* R. iii p ii 734
May 9.	Declaration of the mayor, recorder, and others of the corporation of London, as to what persons are entitled to the privileges granted to the city R iii p ii 734.
May 10	William Freman of Brackele is appointed receiver of forfeitures from merchants at Calais *Westm* R iii p ii 735
May 28	Protection for sir William de Felton and Roger de Watlyngton, of Hengham, in the retinue of the prince of Wales, and for Thomas de Rokwode, in Felton's retinue *Westm* R iii p ii 735.
May 28	Release of James de Flemyng, burgess of Paris, and John de Lenure and Piers de la Porte, burgesses of Chartres, French hostages *Westm* R iii p ii 735. O vi 441. H iii. p ii. 88.
May 28	Licence for Ralph Taillour of Southampton to export cloth to Gascony Similar licences for nine other merchants *Westm* R iii p ii 735.
May 30.	Protection for John Mautravers of Crowell in the retinue of the prince of Wales *Westm* R iii p. ii. 736.
June 1	Urban [V] writes in favour of Nicholas Hethe, canon of Lichfield, two of whose benefices are detained by English clerks *Avignon* R iii p ii 736 O. vi 441 H iii p ii 88
June 6	Giles be Kellesey, Richard atte Dyk, Robert Padegrys, and John Bullok are appointed surveyors of the tapestry manufacture in London. *Westm.* R iii. p ii 736.
June 8	Safe conduct for Robert de Maxwell, Thomas de Somervill, and William de Roos, all Scots, to visit S Thomas at Canterbury *Westm* R. iii p ii 736 O vi 441 H. iii p ii. 88
June 10.	The R releases William bp of Winchester and his tenants from murage, pontage, pavage, and other tolls. *Westm* R iii p ii 737.
June 12.	The K. orders Thomas de Brantyngham, treasurer of Calais, to repair Ouderwyk Castle. *Westm* R iii p ii 737
June 12	The K accepts the surrender of letters patent granting certain powers of jurisdiction to the university of Cambridge, and confirms the liberties and privileges enjoyed by them before the said grant *Westm* R iii p. ii. 737
June 12.	The collectors of Dartmouth are ordered to allow the exportation of cloth called "grey-bakkes" and "blankettes" to Gascony *Westm* R iii p ii 737.
June 12	Protection for Robert, son of sir Ralph de Nevill, in Gascony *Westm* R. iii p ii 738
June 14.	The K orders the guardian and chancellor of Ireland to compose the differences between the English who have come from England and the English born in Ireland. *Westm* R iii p ii. 738 O vi 442 H iii p ii 88.
June 25	Protection for sir Stephen de Cosyngton, his son William, and five others, in the retinue of the prince of Wales *Westm* R iii p ii 738
June 26	Urban [V.] writes to the K. in favour of Francis Johannini and other Florentine merchants who are detained in London *Avignon* R iii. p ii 738. O vi 442. H iii. p. ii 88
June 26	Pope Urban writes in favour of the above-mentioned merchants to William Wikeham, canon of Lincoln, the K's secretary *Avignon* R iii p ii 738. O vi 443 H. iii p ii. 89.
June 26	Nicholas de Lovayne is appointed seneschal of Ponthieu and Montreuil *Westm* R iii. p. ii 739
June 28	Restitution of the temporalities to William bp of Worcester, translated from Rochester *Westm* R. iii. p ii 739
June 28	Licence to John Gouch of London to send cloth and other goods to Calais Similar licence to William de la Roke *Westm* R iii p ii 739
June 28.	Licences to William Pernell of Harwich, and 12 other merchants, to take money out of England for the purchase of salt at La Baye in Brittany *Westm* R iii p ii 739
July 5	John de Haddon and three others are ordered to provide ships for the conveyance of the duke of Clarence to Ireland. *Westm* R. iii p ii 740

DATE	SUBJECT.
1364 July 6	Sir Nicholas de Louthe, receiver of Ponthieu, and three others, are appointed attorneys for Joan, daughter and heiress of Henry le Frank of Newenham *Westm* R. iii p. ii 740
July 6	Protection for John le Botiller, Geoffrey de Werberton, and Matthew de Rixton, and their workmen, employed in building a bridge over the Mersey *Westm* R. iii p. ii 740
July 7	Ralph Spigurnell is appointed admiral of the King's fleet. *Westm* R. iii p. ii. 741.
July 7	Ralph Spigurnell is appointed constable of Dover Castle and warden of the Cinque Ports *vice* Robert de Herle, deceased Intimation thereof to the barons and commonalties of the Cinque Ports. *Westm* R. iii p. ii 741.
July 8	Licence to John Piel and John Philipot of London, to export wheat, malt, and other victuals to Calais *Westm*. R. iii p. ii 741
July 12	The K. orders certain regulations to be enforced for the sale of fish in London *Westm* R. iii p. ii 741
July 15.	Regulations for the sale of cloth in London. *Westm* R. iii. p. ii 742
[July 15.]	Regulations for the sale of wine in London R. iii p. ii 742
July 16	The K. orders Nicholas de Lovayne, seneschal of Ponthieu, to try the actions for debt brought by Simon abbot of Clugny, *Westm* R. iii. p. i 743 O. vi. 443. H. iii p. ii. 89
July 18	Safe conducts for William bp of S Andrew's, Walter Wardlau, archdeacon of Lothian sir Robert de Erskyne, and Gilbert Armstrange, to come to England on the affairs of David de Bruys, the K.'s prisoner *Westm* R. iii p. ii 743 O. v 444 H iii p ii 89
July 18	Inspeximus and confirmation of a patent of Edward [I.] concerning the variances between the barons of the Cinque Ports and the men of Great Yarmouth, dated Westm 31 March, 33 Edw [I] *Westm* R. iii p. ii 743
July 20	Power for Simon bp of London, William earl of Salisbury, and Henry le Scrop, governor of Calais, to treat for a marriage between the K.'s son Edmund de Langley and Margaret duchess of Burgundy, daughter of the count of Flanders *Westm* R. iii p. ii 744 O. vi 444 H. iii. p. ii. 89
July 20	The K. orders Thomas de Brantyngham, treasurer of Calais, to pay the wages of the mayors and aldermen of Calais *Westm* R. iii. p. ii 745
July 20	Edmund Rose is appointed warden of Sandegate Castle near Calais. Intimation thereof to Henry le Scrop *Westm* R. iii p. ii. 745
July 20	The K. orders Walter de Leycestre, sergeant-at-arms, to take security from men-at-arms and archers about to embark from Portsmouth to Mousehole in co Cornwall, that they will go to Brittany. *Westm* R. iii p. ii 745
July 20	Release to John Wrothe, mayor of Calais, of the rent for his office for one year, *Westm* R. iii. p. ii 745.
July 21	Similar release for Adam de Bury, Roger Rotour, and 18 other aldermen *Westm* R. iii p. ii 745
Aug 2	Inspeximus and confirmation of the grants by the prince of Wales of the ferry of Saltash in co Cornwall, and an annuity of 20*l* to William Lenche, who lost an eye at the battle of Poictiers, dated London, 1 Oct 30 Edw III, and London, 29 Feb. 38 Edw III *Eltham*. R. iii p. ii. 746
Aug 8	Robert de Appelby and William de Spalding, are ordered to provide ships at Liverpool for the passage of the duke of Clarence to Ireland *Havering*. R. iii p. ii 746
Aug. 8.	Release of Lienart de Haugart, burgess of Amiens, and three other French hostages. *Haveryng* R. iii p. ii 747
Sept. 3.	Grant of the prebend of S Wolfran, Abbeville, to Fermin Barbery Intimation thereof to the seneschal of Ponthieu *Windsor* R. iii p. ii 747
Sept. 25.	Lionel duke of Clarence is appointed the K.'s lieutenant in Ireland. *Westm* R. iii p. ii 747
Sept. 26.	Protection for sir Richard de Totesham, in the retinue of the prince of Wales. R. iii p. ii 747.
Sept. 30	Urban [V] revokes the citation of Richard earl of Arundel and others, at the suit of the bp of Chichester, and sends the abbot of S Bavo, at Ghent, to settle the case *Avignon* R. iii p. ii 747. O. vi 445 H iii p ii 90
Sept. 30.	Licence to Flemish fishermen to take money out of the kingdom. *Westm* R. iii p. ii 748.

DATE	SUBJECT
1364 Sept 30	Licence to John Jouwy, of Bodmin, to export cloth from Cornwall to Gascony *Westm* R iii p ii 748.
Oct 2.	Licence to John de S Haude of Normandy to reside at Abbeville. *Canterbury.* R iii p ii 748
Oct 3	Adam de S Ives of London is appointed exchanger of money for two years *Westm* R iii p ii 748
Oct. 3	The sheriffs of London are ordered to proclaim the above-mentioned appointment, and the keepers of the mint at the Tower of London are ordered to provide him with a house there. *Westm.* R iii p ii. 749.
Oct 3	The K forbids the execution of the sentence against Savary de Vinoune, lord of Tours, while his appeal is pending *Canterbury* R iii p ii 749
Oct 10	Safe conduct and protection for the lord of Tours *Westm* R iii p ii 749
Oct 16.	Grant of tolls on wine and beer to the commonalty of Abbeville, for the expense of their fortifications *Westm* R iii p ii 750
Oct. 19.	Treaty of marriage between Edmund earl of Cambridge and Margaret duchess of Burgundy *Dover Castle* R iii p ii 750 O vi 445 H iii p ii 90
Oct 20	Safe conduct for the ambassadors of Albert duke of Bavaria, and the nobles and commonalties of Hainault *Dover Castle* R iii p ii 751 O vi 449. H iii p ii 91
Oct. 20	Licence to Peter Arnaud, of Mendie, merchant of Bayonne, to export corn from London to Gascony *Westm* R iii p ii 752
Oct. 24	Robert de Assheton is appointed chancellor of Ireland, *vice* Thomas de Burle, prior of S. John of Jerusalem in Ireland *Westm.* R iii p ii. 752
Oct. 24.	Power for the duke of Clarence, Robert de Assheton, and Thomas de Dale to examine charters granted by the K to cities and towns in Ireland *Westm* R iii. p ii 752
Oct 24	Licence to John de Troye, treasurer of Ireland, to retain three men-at-arms and six archers at the K's expense *Westm.* R. iii p. ii 752
Oct 28.	The collectors of the customs at Sandwich are ordered to pay the fee of Ralph Spigurnell, as warden of Dover Castle and the Cinque Ports *Westm* R iii p. ii 752.
Oct [(?) Sept 28	Ratification by Peter K of Castile of the treaty of 22 June 1362. *Calaehamb.* R. iii. p ii 753 O vi 450 H. iii p. ii 91
Oct. 30	Licence to Richard Bailiff, servant of the prince of Wales, to export herrings from Great Yarmouth *Westm* R iii p ii 753
Oct. 30	Protection for sir Thomas Okoure, in the retinue of the prince of Wales. R. iii. p ii 753
Nov. 3	Charles V, K of France, grants to John of Brittany, earl of Montfort, respite for the performance of his homage *Paris* R iii p ii 753 O. vi 450 H iii p ii 92
Nov. 8.	The K appoints the mayor and bailiffs of Coventry, Thomas de Nassyngton and two others, to assess the subsidy for the fortification of the town. *Westm.* R. iii p ii. 753.
Nov 4	Safe conducts for William de Cresswyll and Andrew de Ormiston, squires of the bp of S Andrew's, and for Maurice de Sotherland of Scotland *Westm* R iii p. ii 754 O vi 451. H iii p ii. 92
Nov. 5.	Protection for John de Beauchamp, in the retinue of Thomas de Beauchamp, earl of Warwick, in Gascony R. iii p ii 754
Nov 6	Safe conduct for David de Bruys to visit S Thomas of Canterbury *Westm.* R iii p ii 754 O vi 451 H. iii p ii. 92.
Nov. 6.	Safeguard and protection for the abbey of Savigny, in Brittany *Westm.* R. iii. p ii 754
Nov. 14.	The K requests the K of France to pay 1,500 cr to John de Melune, count of Tankarvill *Westm.* R iii p ii 754.
Nov 14	The K forbids sir Eustace d'Abelichecourt, sir Robert Scot, and sir Hugh de Calverle, to make war in France. Letters on the same subject to the prince of Wales, John Chaundos, and the K's other officers in France. *Westm.* R iii p ii 754
Nov 18	Licence to Baudewyn, Otto, and Matthew *de Garretis, merchants of Ast, to reside in* Ponthieu. *Westm.* R. iii p ii 755
Nov. 20.	The K desires the K. of France to compel Louis duke of Anjou, his brother, the counts of Grantpree and Brene, and the lords of Clere and Derval, to return to England as hostages; to send others in place of John d'Estamps and the lord of Hangest, who are dead, and to compel Charles d'Artoys to return to prison. *Westm.* R. iii. p. ii. 755. O. vi. 452. H. iii. p. ii. 92.

EE 2

DATE	SUBJECT.
1364. Nov 20	The K writes to Louis duke of Anjou and the other hostages to desire them to return *Westm* R III p II 756 O VI 453. H III. p II. 93
Nov 20	Declaration that Louis duke of Anjou has broken his oath by leaving England without licence *Westm* R III. p II 756 O VI 454 H III p II 93
[Nov 20]	Similar declaration as to the count of Grantpree and the lord of Derval and de Clere, the above-mentioned hostages. R III p. II 756 O. VI 454. H. III p II 93.
Nov. 20.	Letter on the same subject to the peers of France *Westm.* R III p II 757 O VI. 455. H III p II 93
Nov 20	Letter on the same subject to the mayor of S. Omer and the bailiff of Amiens. *Westm.* R III. p II 757 O VI 455 H. III p. II 93
Nov. 20.	Power for Walter de la Roge to demand the return of the hostages and of Charles d'Artoys *Westm* R III p II. 757. O VI 456 H III p II 93
Nov 28.	The K orders his officers to assist Richard atte Celer and John de Yestelee, who have a secret commission from the K *Westm* R III p II 757
Dec 6.	Safe conduct for Joan countess of Sutherland to come to England. *Westm* R III p II. 757 O VI 456 H III p II 94
Dec 7	Warrant for the custody of William de Wenlock, clerk, in the Tower of London. R. III. p II 758
Dec 12	The K licenses William earl of Sutherland, one of the hostages of David de Bruys, the K's prisoner, to remain in Scotland till Easter 1366 *Westm.* R III p. II 758. O VI 457 H III p II 94
Dec. 18	Pope Urban refuses the K's request for a dispensation for the marriage of his sons and daughters with persons within the third or fourth degree of consanguinity or affinity. *Avignon.* R III p II 758 O VI 457 H III p II 94
Dec 18.	Power for Henry le Scrop, governor of Calais and John de Branketre, treasurer of York, to treat with the count of Flanders for the alteration of the day fixed for the marriage of the earl of Cambridge and the duchess of Burgundy, *Windsor* R III p II 758 O VI. 457 H III. p II 95
Dec 27.	Philip duke of Orleans (son of the K of France) grants to Thomas, son of the K. of England, the castles of Chisoc, Melle, Chivray, and Villeneuve, and his other possessions in Poictou and Saintouge *London* R III p II 758 O VI 458 H III p II 95
Dec 28	Philip duke of Orleans informs the inhabitants of the above places of his grant *London.* R III p II 759 O VI 459 H III p II 95
Dec. 28. 1365.	Similar letter from the duke of Orleans to the counts of Tancarville, Dempmartin, and others *London* R III p II 759 O VI 460 H III p. II 95
Jan 12.	Grant to Nicholas de Roos, master of the K's scholars at Cambridge, of 4*d* a day and eight marks a year for his robes. *Westm.* R III p II 760
Jan 26.	Protection for sir Peter de Cusance, Peter, son of sir William de Cusance, and two others, in the retinue of the prince of Wales *Westm* R III p II 760
Jan 31	The K forbids the exportation of wool, fleeces, or hides. *Westm.* R III p II. 760
Feb. 6.	Restitution of the temporalities to Thomas bp of Rochester, late dean of London *Westm.* R III p II 760
Feb 7	Protection for sir Henry le Scrope *Westm* R III p II 760
Feb. 12	Release of Amand de Landas le Jeune, burgess of Douay, and 15 other French hostages. *Westm* R. III p II 761 O VI. 461. H III p II 96
Feb 20	Henry le Scrope is appointed governor and surveyor of Marke, Calais, Sandgate, &c· *Westm* R III. p. II 761
Feb. 20.	Confirmation by Edward prince of Wales of the marriage treaty between the earl of Cambridge and the duchess of Burgundy *Angoulême* R III. p. II. 761. O VI 461. H. III. p II 96
Feb 12.	Safe conducts for William bp. of S Andrew's and three others to come to England on the affairs of David the Bruys, the K's prisoner *Westm* R. III p I 761 O V 462 H. III p II 96
Feb. 13.	Safe conduct for Thomas earl of Marr, also for Thomas Baillol, brother of the earl of Marr, and Robert Catnesse, his squire *Westm*, *May* 26 R III p II 762 O VI 462. H III p II 96
Feb 26	The K orders the seneschal of Aquitain, the lord of Pomiers, and Stephen de Caseton, lord of Gordon, to hear the appeal of sir Arnald Savage, lieutenant of the seneschal. *Westm* R. III p. II 762.

DATE	SUBJECT
1365 Feb. 26.	John de Monemuthe and James Tykenesse are ordered to send 12 miners from the forest of Dean to the prince of Wales in Aquitain. Similar commission to Thomas Sergeaunt and Robert Cole *Westm* R m. p n. 762
April 2	John Dabernoun, and William de Spaldyng, sergeant-at-arms, are ordered to provide ships for the conveyance of troops to Aquitain *Westm* R m. p n 762
April 2.	Roger de Saham and two others are ordered to provide ships for the conveyance of beans and pease to Aquitain *Westm.* R. m p. ii 763
April 13.	Benedict Zacharie, merchant of London, is released from the customs payable by foreign merchants *Windsor* R m p n 763
May 3.	Protection for sir John de Branneestre, sir Edmund de Reynbam, sir Richard Walkfare, and 23 others, in the retinue of the prince of Wales. *Westm* R m p n 763
May 7	Warrant to Nicholas de Styvecle, Richard Alberd, and Robert Waryn to arrest William de Rameseye, late monk of Sautre Abbey. *Westm* R m p n. 763
May 11.	Giles Maynard is appointed to arrest workmen for Windsor Castle *Westm* R m. p ii 764
May 12.	The justices of the K's Bench are ordered to observe the statute concerning attorneys proctors, notaries, &c *Westm* R m p n 764
May 12	William de Spaldyng, sergeant-at-arms, William Leneh, and John Dabernoun are appointed to provide shipping for the transport of men and horses to Aquitain *Westm.* R m p ii 764
May 14	Safe conduct for the abbot of S Denis de Brouncurne, Peter Caumbrone, Gerard lord of Botresham, and the lord of Gomeniez, the ambassadors of Albert duke of Bavaria. *Westm.* R. m p n 764
May 16.	Safe conduct for William de Roos, of Scotland, scutifer of Godfrey de Roos. *Westm.* R. m p n. 765 O. vi 463 H m p n 96
May 16.	Protection for John Wetherherde, Thomas de Stathum, lord of Stopford, and 37 others, in the retinue of the prince of Wales *Westm.* R m p n 765
May 20.	Safe conduct for David de Bruys to visit the tomb of S Thomas of Canterbury *Westm* R m p n 765 O vi 463 H m p. n 96
May 20	Safe conducts for William bp of S Andrews, sir David Flemyng, and 16 others, to come to England on pilgrimages *Westm.* R m p n 765. O vi 463 H m p n. 96.
May 20.	The K orders Ralph Spigurnel, the K's admiral, or his lieutenant at the port of Great Yarmouth, to release from arrest a ship called "Le Seinte Maryshipp," of Aberdeen. *Westm.* R m p n 766 O vi 464 H. m p n 96.
May 20.	Negotiations for the prorogation of the truce with Scotland for 25 years, and for the ransom of David de Bruys *London* R m p n. 766 O. vi 464 H m p n. 97.
May 23.	Power for the prince of Wales to appoint judges in Aquitain. *Westm.* R. m. p. n. 766. O vi 465 H m p n 97.
May 24	Richard de Preston of London is appointed mayor of Calais. *Westm* R m p n 767
May 24.	The K. orders Nichol de Lovayne, seneschal of Ponthieu, to inquire into the alleged infractions of the K's rights by the mayor and échevins of Abbeville , to order the mayor and échevins to repair the bridge and the walls of the castle and the town. *Westm* R m p n 767
May 26.	The K writes again to the seneschal of Ponthieu concerning the right of the lord of Bouberehe to hunt in the forest of Cressy *Westm* R m. p n 767. O vi 466 H m p n 97
May 26.	John de Norffolk of S Edmund's is appointed to receive fines from merchants at Calais. *Westm* R m p n 768
May 28.	The K. orders the mayor and sheriffs of London to publish the regulations for the sale of sweet wines *Westm* R m p n. 768
May 30.	Release of Philip duke of Orleans (son of the K of France), a French hostage *Windsor.* R m p n 768 O vi 467 H m p n 98.
June 1	Ordinances for the government of the town of Calais. R m. p. n 768.
June 2	The K forbids the sheriffs of London to hear the suit of John Baret against William de Notyngham, clerk of the Chancery. *Westm* R m p n 769
June 9	The K orders Thomas abp of Dublin to allow the abp of Armagh to carry the cross in his province. Similar letter to the abp of Armagh *Westm* R. m. p ii 769 O vi. 467 H m p. ii 98.

DATE	SUBJECT
1365 June 12.	The several sheriffs are ordered to forbid useless games and to encourage archery. *Westm* R iii p ii 770 O vi. 468. H. iii. p ii. 98.
June 12.	Ratification by David K of Scotland of the prorogation of the truce with England for four years , ratified by the K of England, Windsor, 20 June *Edinburgh.* R ii p ii 770 O vi 470 H ii p ii 98
June 16	Release of John sire de Audresel, a French hostage. *Windsor.* R. iii p ii. 770. O v 470. H iii p ii. 93.
June 20.	Indenture between the K and Nichol Prill of Ludlow and John de Northbury, for the farm of the subsidy of cloth in Warwick, Leicester, Stafford, and Shropshire. Seven similar indentures in other counties of various dates *Westm.* R iii p ii 771
June 20	Release to the duke of Orleans for the "*amende*" due to the K in consequence of his suit with John de Stodeye, citizen of London. *Westm* R iii. p ii 772 O vi. 470 H. iii. p ii 99
June 26	Proclamation to be made in London ordering swordmakers and cutlers to mark their wares *Westm* R iii p ii 772
June 30	Philip duke of Orleans declares that he has been well treated while he was a hostage in England *London* R iii p ii 772 O. vi 471 H iii p ii 99
July 1	Thomas Kyng is appointed master of the mint at Calais *Westm* R iii p ii 772
July 12	Pardon for Joceus Dullard of Flanders for a robbery at Calais *Westm* R. iii. p ii 772
July 20	Receipt by Ingelbert count of Marke for 3,600 florins, being his annuity for nine years. *Wettere Castle* R iii p ii 773 O vi 472 H iii p ii 99
July 26	The K forbids the exchange of money at Calais except for trade *Windsor.* R. iii. p ii 773
July 27.	Engerrain sire de Coucy acknowledges that he has been well treated while he was a hostage in England *London* R iii p ii 773 O vi 472 H iii p ii 100
July 28	Promises of John count of Harecourt, a French hostage, whom the K has licensed to go to France, to return to England in a year *Windsor.* R iii. p. ii. 773 O vi 473 H iii p ii 100.
July 28	Loys de Harecourt, viscount of Chastelleraut, becomes security for the return of John count of Harecourt *Windsor* R iii p ii 774 O vi 474 H iii p ii 100
July 28.	Henry le Scrope is appointed governor of Mark, Calais, Sandegate, Colyns, Hammes, Wale, Hoye, and Guisnes. *Westm* R iii p ii 774
July 28	Henry le Scrop, governor of Calais, the mayors of Calais, and the K's officers in Ponthieu, are ordered to search persons coming from England for gold, silver, or papal bulls *Westm* R iii p ii 775 O vi 475 H iii p ii 101
Sept 17	Wenceslaus of Bohemia, duke of Luxembourg, Lorraine, and Brabant, appoints Gerart delle Heide, lord of Boutresham, Groudefroit de la Tbour, and Henry de Romagne, his commissioners in England *Brussels* R iii p ii 775 O vi 477 H iii p ii 102
Sept. 23	Thomas de Brantyngham, treasurer of Calais, is ordered to pay the wages of John Wrothe, warden of Hammes Castle. *Westm* R iii p ii 775
Oct 6	The sheriffs of London are ordered to pay John Braban, keeper of the mews at Westminster, for the falcons which he has bought for the K , the price of each sort is given *Westm* R iii p ii 776 O vi 477 H iii p ii 102
Oct. 12	Receipt for 15,000*l.* of the clerical subsidy granted to the K by Innocent VI *Westm* R. iii p ii 776
Oct 16	Safe conducts for sir Archibald de Donglas, sir Alexander de Lyndessay, and 17 other Scots, coming to England as pilgrims *Westm* R iii p ii 776 O vi 478 H iii. p ii 102
Oct. 18	Receipt for 500 marks from John de Bukyngham, bp of Lincoln, due from him when lieutenant of Brittany R iii p ii. 776
Oct 14.	The K grants to Helyas de Pomers 100*l* a year The prince of Wales is ordered to pay it *Westm* R iii p ii 777
Oct 22.	The K forbids the assessors of the subsidy for fortifying Coventry exacting payment from religious persons. *Westm* R iii p ii. 777.
Oct 24	The K sends sir Nichol de Tamworth and John Wyn to put down the companies who are plundering Burgundy, Nevers, and Rech *Westm* R iii p ii 777 O vi 479 H iii p ii 102
Oct. 27.	Nicholas de Tamworth is appointed warden of Hammes *Westm* R iii p ii 777

DATE	SUBJECT.
1365 Oct 29	John Knyvet is appointed chief justice of the K's Bench, *vice* Henry Grene , William de Fyncheden and William de Wychyngham, justices of the common bench , and Thomas de Lodelowe and Aymer de Shirlande, barons of the Exchequer *Westm* R m. p n 777
Nov 3.	John de Stok is appointed a baron of the Exchequer *Westm* R m p n 778
Nov 14	The mayor of London is ordered to examine the wine in cellars and taverns, and to do what is customary with putrid and bad wines *Westm.* R m p n 778
Nov. 18	Release until Easter of Maheu, lord of Roye, a French hostage. *Westm* R ni p n 778 O vi 479 H m p ii 102
Nov 22	The sheriff of Northumberland is ordered to repair the castle at Newcastle-upon-Tyne *Westm* R m. p. ii. 778
Nov 26	Licence to Ingerram sire de Coucy and his wife Isabella, the K's daughter, to go to France *Westm.* R m. p n 778
Dec 6	Safe conduct for Albert duke of Bavaria to come to England *Westm* R m. p n 779 O vi. 480 H ill p 102
Dec 6	John de Chaundos, viscount of S Sauveur, sir Hugh de Calverle, sir Nichol de Dagworth, and sir William de Elmham, are ordered to prevent English men at arms from entering Spain *Westm* R m p n 779 O vi 481 H m p n 103
Dec 6.	The K desires the K of France to compel the count "de Fuix" to do homage to him for his lands in Bearne *Westm.* R. m p n 779 O. vi 481 H m p ii 103.
Dec. 10	Power for Edward prince of Wales to receive 60,000 crowns in gold from the K of France *Windsor.* R m p n 780 O vi 482 H. m p n 103
Dec 10	The K forbids the sale of sweet wine *Westm* R m p n 780
Dec 17	The K orders the abp of York to convene the clergy of the archdeaconries of Richmond and Cleveland to consult concerning the new taxation of benfices The bps of Durham and Carlisle are ordered to convene the clergy of their dioceses for the same purpose. *Langley*
1366 Jan 12	R m p n 780 O vi 483 H m p n 104
	Safe conduct for Margaret, wife of David de Bruys, to visit the tomb of S. Thomas of Canterbury. *Westm* R m p n 781 O. vi. 484 H m p n. 104.
Jan. 15.	The K informs the mayor and bailiffs of Dartmouth that Spanish wines are not included in the recent prohibition of the sale of sweet wines *Westm* R m p n 781
Jan. 20	Charles K of France agrees to appoint commissioners to decide the dispute with the K. of England about the delivery of Belleville *Paris,* le " 20 jour de Janvier, l'an de la nativité nostre seigneur M CCC soixante & six, selon le stille de court de Rome " R m p. n. 781 O vi 485 H m p n 105
Jan. 22	Promise of Peter count of Alençon to remain in England as a hostage until the decision of the above mentioned matter *Wetsm* R m p n 782 O vi 486. H ni p n 105
Jan 22	Promise of Louis duke of Bourbon to return to England at the expiration of his leave of absence *Westm* R m p n 782 O v 488 H. m p n 106.
Jan. 22	John duke of Berry is security for the return of Louis duke of Bourbon and Berant, dauphin of Auvergne *London* R m p n 783 O vi 489 H m p n. 106.
Jan 22.	Repetition of the prohibition of the sale of sweet wines *Westm* R m p. n 783.
Jan 22.	Power for Ralph lord de Nevill, sir John de Nevill his son, John de Thorp, canon of London, and Aleyn de Struther, constable of Roxburgh Castle, to receive 6,000 marks from David de Bruys *Westm.* R. m p. n 784 O vi 490 H. m p. n 106
Jan 23	The mayor and sheriffs of London are ordered to prevent wine being sold without being gauged *Westm* R m p ii. 784
Jan 26	Receipt for 6,200 crowns from the K of France as a portion of his ransom *Westm* R m p n 784. O vi. 490 H m. p. n 106
Jan. 26.	Receipt for 93,800 crowns, another portion of the said K's ransom *Westm* R m p. n 784 O vi 491 H m p n 107
	Memorandum that the sum of 6,200 crowns was assigned as the fees of John le Meangre, *alias* Bouciquant, marshal of France, and William de Dormanc, chancellor of Normandy R. m p n 785 O vi 491 H m p n 107
Feb 1.	The K accepts the proposed plan for the decision of the dispute about Belleville, and will allow the duke of Berry and the count of Alençon to go to France until Easter 1368 *Westm.* R m p. n 785 O vi 492 H. m p n. 107
Feb. 3.	Receipt for 6,000 marks from David de Bruys as a portion of his ransom *Westm.* R. m p n 785 O vi 493 H m p n 108

DATE	SUBJECT
1366 Feb 5.	Safe conduct for John de Carrick, canon of Glasgow, and three others, bringing the money for the ransom above mentioned to Berwick *Westm* R III p. II. 786 O VI 493. H. III p II 108
Feb 6	Proclamation to be made by the several sheriffs that persons possessing 40*l* a year are to assume knighthood *Westm* R III p II 786 O VI 494 H III p II 108.
Feb 13.	The K promises the prince of Wales, that if he die abroad his executors shall hold his lands for four years for the payment of his debts. *Langley.* R. III p II 786
Feb. 18	Warrant for the payment of 100*l* to William de Wessefeld, for his expenses in prosecuting the murderers of John de Coupeland *Westm* R III. p II 786 O VI 494 H III p. II 108
Feb 21.	Guy count of S. Paul, a French hostage, promises to return at the expiration of his leave, his sons Waleram and Robert remaining as hostages for him. *Westm.* R. III p II 786. O VI 494 H III p II 108
Feb 21	Licence to Guy de Lucenburgh, count of S Paul, to leave England *Westm.* R III p II 787 O VI. 495 H III p II 108.
March 1.	Power for the prince of Wales to receive 60,000 crowns from the K of France, as a part of his ransom *Westm* R. III p II 787 O VI 496 H III p II 109.
March 18	Safe conducts for David de Bruys, his wife Margaret, and Patrick de Dunbarre, earl of March, to visit the tomb of S Thomas of Canterbury *Westm* R III. p II 787 O VI 497 H III p II 109
March 20	Safe conducts for Adam de Tynyngham, dean of Aberdeen, and 22 others, to come to England as pilgrims. *Westm* R III p II 788 O VI 497. H. III p II. 109.
March 20	Safe conduct for Sir Walter de Leslye of Scotland *Westm* R III p II 788. O VI 498 H III p II 109.
April 10	Grant of the freedom of the city of London to Walter de Bardes of Lombardy *Westm* R III p II. 788
April 17.	Release of Henry de Manda and James Carou, burgesses of Tournay, and two other French hostages *Westm* R III p II 788 O VI 498 H III p II. 109
April 19.	Notification that Thomas de Cleremes and Jaques Vytour, burgesses of Tournay, have taken the place of the above-mentioned hostages. *Westm* R III. p II 788. O. VI 498 H III p II 110.
May 8.	Revocation of the grant to Bernard lord of Lebret, of Puy Normand and the bastide of Ville Franche *Westm* R III. p II 789 O VI 499 H III p II 110
May 8.	The prince of Wales is ordered to publish the above-mentioned revocation *Westm* R III p II 789 O VI 500 H III p II 110
May 11	Prorogation until Michaelmas of the leave of absence granted to William earl of Sutherland, one of the hostages of David de Bruys, the K's prisoner *Westm* R III p II. 789 O VI 500 H III p II 110
May 12	The K orders the meetings of the county of Somerset and the assizes to be held at Ilchester *Westm* R. III p II 789
May 15	Safe conduct for Albert duke of Bavaria coming to the K relative to the heritage of Q Philippa. *Westm* R III p II 789 O VI 500 H III p II. 110
May 18.	Protection for Richard de Stafford and his son Richard, and for Thomas de Arderne *Westm* R III p II 790
May 20	The K of England desires the K of France to pay 3,000 gold royals to John de Melon, count of Tankervill *Hadley Castle* R III p II 790 O VI 501. H III. p. II. 111
June 3	The town of Chepyng Toriton in co Devon relieved from sending members to parliament, as the town had never elected members before the 24th of Edw III *Westm* R III. p II 790 O VI. 502 H III p II 111
June 6	Grant of a weekly market to the town of Crotoye in Ponthieu *Westm.* R III p II 790. O VI 502 H III p II 111
June 8.	The K orders the abp of Bourdeaux, the abbot of Sewe, and Arnaud de Claus, canon of Bourdeaux, to hear the appeal of Raymond de Mountant, lord of Mussidan, relative to Blaignac *Westm* R III. p II 791. O VI. 503 H III p II 111
June 8	John Dabernon, Thomas le Havener, and four others, are ordered to arrest ships for the conveyance of the men-at-arms and archers to Aquitain Similar order to the sheriff of Sussex *Westm* R III p II ¯91

DATE	SUBJECT
1366 June 13	Safe conduct for William duke of Juliers. *Westm* R iii p ii 791 O vi 504 H iii p. ii. 112
June 13.	Grant of an annuity of 1,000 marks to William duke of Juliers *Westm.* R iii. p. ii 792 O vi 504 H p iii ii 112.
June 13.	Licence to the duke of Juliers to pledge or sell the 9,000 marks due to him from the K *Westm* R. iii p ii. 792 O. vi 505 H. iii p ii 112
June 13.	Similar licence to the said duke to pledge his annuity. *Westm.* R. iii p ii 792. O vi 505 H iii p ii 112
June 13	Grant to the same duke of an annuity of 1,400l in compensation for his lands occupied by the K of France. *Westm* R iii. p ii 792 O vi. 505 H iii p ii 112.
June 13	The K. undertakes to pay the 9,000 marks to the aforesaid duke by yearly instalments of 1,000 marks *Westm* R. iii p ii. 793. O vi. 506 H. iii p ii. 112
June 13.	The K appoints Collarde de Beaucourt, bailiff of Abbeville, John Malicorne, and eight others, commissioners to decide the dispute about the delivery of Montreuil *Westm* R iii. p. ii 793
June 15.	The homage of William duke of Juliers to the K. of England. *London.* R iii p. ii 793 O vi 507 H iii p ii 113
June 15	The K. orders the customers of London and 11 other ports to allow the exportation of corn, malt, beer, and other victuals to Calais. *Westm* R iii p ii 793
June 15.	William duke of Juliers absolves the K from the debts due to the late marquis, his father *London* R iii. p ii. 794. O vi. 507 H iii. p ii 113
July 20.	William de Vikers is appointed coroner of the county of Roxburgh *Westm.* R. iii. p ii. 794. O vi 508 H iii p ii 113
June 20.	Richard de Preston of London is appointed mayor of Calais *Westm* R. iii p ii 794
June 21.	The K orders the mayor of London to assemble the aldermen, vintners, merchants, and others, for the purpose of regulating the sale of wine *Westm* R iii p. ii. 795.
June 23.	Licence to the merchants of the staple of Calais to elect the mayor and constables of the staple *Westm* R iii p ii 795
June 28.	Henry le Scrope is appointed governor of Mark, Calais, &c. *Westm.* R iii. p. ii 795,
June 28.	Warrant for the payment of 80 marks as a reward to the French esquire who brought the news of the delivery of the Q of France *Clarendon.* R iii p ii 795 O vi 508 H ii p ii. 113
July 1.	Warrant for the payment of 100l. to the lord of Caupeyne, of Gascony, for the ransom of the count of Tankerville, his prisoner *Westm.* R iii. p ii 796. O vi 508. H. iii p ii 113
July 12	Lease of the exchange of money in England to Adam de S. Ive of London *Westm.* R iii. p. ii. 796
July 12	The K forbids sir William de Cloptom, junior, Walter and Edmund de Cloptom, leaving England *Westm* R. iii p ii 796.
July 18	Payment of 40s to Peter de Troye, brother of Bernard de Troye, who captured John late K of France. R iii p ii 796 O vi 509 H iii p ii 113
July 20	John Chaundos and William de Seriz are appointed governors of the castles and lands granted by the duke of Orleans to Thomas of Woodstock, the K's son *Westm* R iii. p ii 796 O vi 509. H. iii p ii 113
July 22	The K forbids the exportation of corn except to Calais *Westm* R iii p ii. 797.
July 24	The K. forbids the sheriffs of London trying suits against the clerks of the chancery. *Westm* R iii p ii 797
July 30.	Power for Humfrey de Bohun, earl of Hereford, and sir Nicholas de Tamworth, to treat for a marriage between Lionel duke of Clarence and Violanta, daughter of Galeazzo lord of Milan, also for a marriage between Edmund earl of Cambridge and Violanta. *Westm.* R iii p ii 797 O vi 509. H iii p ii 114
July 30.	The sheriff of Nottingham and Derby, and John Foucher, are ordered to provide 100 archers for the service of the prince of Wales in Aquitain 14 similar commissions *Westm* R iii p. ii 797
Aug 1	Warrant for the payment of 5l to Peter de Troy and Pelegrin de Cause for their expenses in assisting the late Bernard de Troye in capturing John K of France at the battle of Poitiers *Westm* R iii p ii 798. O vi 510 H iii p ii 114

DATE	SUBJECT
1366. Aug. 1.	Pope Urban [V] has received sir Bartholomew de Burghersh, sir Richard de Stafforde, Thomas de Bukton, and John de Carleton, the K's ambassadors, and refers the K to them for his answer *Avignon* R iii p ii 798 O vi 510 H iii p ii. 114
Aug 14	Pope Urban [V] requests the K. to prorogue the leave of absence of Louis duke of Bourbon, a hostage *Avignon* R iii. p ii 798 O vi 510 H iii p ii 114
Aug 18.	Safe conducts for William bp of S. Andrew's, Walter de Wardelagh, archdeacon of Lothian, sir Robert de Erskyn, and Gilbert Armstrang, provost of S Andrew's, coming to England on the affairs of David de Bruys *Westm* R. iii p ii. 798. O vi 511 H iii p. ii 114
Aug 20	The K forbids the officers of the prince of Wales in Aquitain to execute the sentence against Bernard Pelegrini, who has appealed to the prince *Westm* R iii p ii 798 O. vi 511 H iii p ii 114
Sept 16.	William de Nessefeld and Walter de Ursewyk, constable of Richmond Castle, are appointed to provide 100 archers to accompany John duke of Lancaster to Gascony Three similar commissions *Havering* R iii p ii 799
✓ Sept. 23.	Letters obligatory of Peter K of Castile for 56,000 florins which the K of England has paid for him to the K of Navarre *Libourne* R iii p ii 799 O vi 512 H iii p ii. 115
✓ Sept. 23	Treaty between Edward prince of Wales, Peter K of Castile, and Charles K of Navarre, against Henry count of Trastemare, who has usurped the throne of Castile *Libourne* R iii p ii 800 O vi 514 H iii p ii 116
✓ Sept. 23	Peter K of Castile grants to Edward prince of Wales the castle of Vermeo [Bermeo], Vilbau [Bilbao], de la Queyte [Lequeytio], and the Castle de Ordialibus [Ordialus? or Aldeis]. *Libourne* R. iii p ii 802 O. vi 521 H iii p ii 118
✓ Sept 23	Peter K. of Castile informs the inhabitants of the above-mentioned places of his grant *Libourne* R iii p ii 804 O vi 524 H iii p ii 119
✓ Sept. 23	Peter K of Castile empowers John Chaundos, viscount of S Sauveur and constable of Aquitain, Thomas de Felton, seneschal of Aquitain, Roger lord de la Ware, and three others, to put the prince of Wales in possession of the above-mentioned places. *Libourne* R iii p ii 804 O vi 525. H iii. p ii 120
✓ Sept. 23	Peter K of Castile promises to perform the covenants in his grant *Libourne*. R iii p. ii 805 O vi 527 H iii p ii 121
✓ Sept 23	Peter K of Castile promises to pay the wages of the troops with which the prince of Wales assists him, giving his three daughters as hostages. *Libourne* R iii p. ii 805. O vi 528. H iii p ii 121
✓ Sept 23	Peter K of Castile grants to the K, the prince of Wales, and their successors, the right of fighting in the first battle against the infidels, or of having their banner there *Libourne* R iii p ii 807 O. vi. 531. H iii. p ii 122.
Oct 5	Licence to Daniel Wilhbart of Ghent to build a fortress in the lordship of Marke, near Calais *Westm* R iii p ii 807
Oct. 6.	Pope Urban [V] requests the K's assistance against the Saracens, who threaten Cyprus and Rhodes *Avignon*. R iii p ii 807 O vi 533 H iii. p ii. 123
Oct 10	The K orders the prince of Wales to make restitution for infractions of the peace with France, and to punish those who are in fault *Westm* R iii p ii 808
Oct 13	Safe conducts for William de Calabre, chaplain, sir John Graunt, William Lyndesay, and seven other Scots *Westm* R. iii p ii 808. O vi 534 H iii p ii 123
Oct 13	Safe conducts for John de Langton, John de Tourgayth, parson of Burnok, and seven other Scots, coming to study in the university of Oxford and elsewhere in England. *Westm* R iii p ii 809 O vi 534 H iii p ii 124
Oct. 16	William Bacoun, mayor of Southampton, and two others, are ordered to provide ships to convey Henry de Berkhampstede, marshal of the prince of Wales, to Gascony *Westm* R iii p. ii. 809.
✓ Oct 20	Protection for the prince of Wales and for sir John de Sulley, Humfrey de Stafford, and four others in his retinue *Westm* R iii p ii 809.
Oct 20	The K orders the bailiffs of Great Yarmouth to allow the barons of the Cinque Ports to keep the peace during the fair, according to the grant of Edward I *Westm* R iii p ii 809
Oct. 20	Commission to Andrew de Gildeford and John Hound, sergeants-at-arms, and John Herle, to provide ships for the passage of John duke of Lancaster to Gascony. *Westm* R iii. p. ii. 810

DATE.	SUBJECT.
1366 Oct 24	The K desires the prince of Wales to attend to the petition of Joan lady of Surgcretz, and to do her justice *Westm* R m. p. ıı 810 O. vı 535. H ııı. p. ıı 124
Oct 24	The K desires the prince of Wales to grant letters of pardon to the said lady and others, according to the peace of Bretigny *Westm* R ııı p ıı 811. O vı 537 H ııı p ıı́ 125
Oct 25.	The K orders the bailiffs of Beverley to issue a proclamation against the excessive price of wine *Westm* R ııı. p. n. 811
Oct 25	Walter de Barde is appointed master of the mint at Calais *Westm* R ııı p ıı 811.
Oct. 26.	Licence to John de Conceaulx and his wife Agnes of Abbeville to found a chapel in the church of S. Wolfran *Westm* R ııı p ıı 812
Nov 2	Protection to John duke of Lancaster and for sir John de Rocheford, and 21 others in his retinue going to Aquitain *Westm* R ııı. p. ıı 812
Nov. 3	Pardon to John de Valloilles of Abbeville for the homicide of Walter de Hastieux *Westm* R ııı p ıı 812.
Nov. 5	The K appoints the viscount of Pois, John de Boberche, the lord of Crezeques and Louc, and five others, to complete the purchase of certain lands which he has granted to sir Nichol de Lovayne *Westm*. R ııı p ıı 812
Nov. 5.	The K orders certain persons to execute the sentence in the case between the dean and chapter of S Severin, Bourdeaux, and Peter de Crayssano *Westm*. R. ııı p ıı 813 O vı. 538. H ııı p ıı 125
Nov 7	The K orders Nicholas de Lovayn, seneschal, and Nicholas de Louthe, receiver of Ponthieu, to garrison the castles of Crotoye, Arreynes, and Wahben. *Westm* R ııı p ıı 813.
Dec. 3.	Safe conduct for John de Cabrespino, nuncio of the pope *Westm* R. ııı p ıı 813 O vı 539 H ııı. p ıı 125
Dec 7.	Warrant for the payment of five marks a day to Thomas de Beauchamp, earl of Warwick, for his wages while in Flanders *Westm* R ııı p ıı 814 O vı 539 H ııı p ıı 125.
Dec 15	Bull of pope Urban for the translation of John bp of Bath and Wells to the see of Ely *Avignon* R. ııı p ıı 814 O. vı 539 H ııı p ıı 126
Dec 20	Power for Henry le Scrop, governor of Calais, and Nicholas de Lovaygne, seneschal of Ponthieu, to extend the leave of absence granted to the duke of Bourbon. Similar commissions to sir Thomas de Dovedale, sir Nicholas de Tamworth, sir John de Cobham, and Thomas de Bukton, clerk *Windsor* R ııı p ıı 814 O vı 540 H ııı p ıı 126
1367. Jan 18.	Obligation of Louis duke of Bourbon to return to England by the time agreed upon *Paris* R ııı p ıı 814 O vı 541 H ııı p ıı. 126.
Jan 18	John duke of Bern, son of the K. of France, becomes security for the duke of Bourbon *Paris*. R ııı p ıı. 816 O vı 544. H ııı p ıı 127
Jan 19	Louis duke of Bourbon swears to observe the above-mentioned obligation *Louvre* R ııı p. ıı 815 O vı 542 H ııı p ıı 127
Jan 19	John duke of Bern swears to perform his security. *Louvre*. R ıı p ıı. 816 O vı 548. H ııı p ıı. 128
Jan 19.	Galeazzo viscount of Milan offers his daughter Violanta in marriage with Lionel duke of Clarence *Pavia* R ııı p ıı 817 O vı . H ııı p ıı 128
Jan 21	Pope Urban [V] desires William de Wykham, archdeacon of Lincoln, the K's secretary, to recommend to the K Alexander de Nevyle, archdeacon of Cornwall. *Montpellier* R. ııı p ıı 317. O vı 548 H ııı p ıı 129
Jan 23	Beraut dauphin of Auvergne becomes security for the duke of Bourbon *Paris*. R ııı p ıı 817 O vı 549 H ııı p ıı. 129
Jan. 26	The K orders Henry del Strother, sheriff of Northumberland, and Alan del Strother, constable of Roxburgh Castle, to send to York the money received from David de Bruys *Westm* R ııı p ıı 818. O vı. 550. H ııı p ıı 130.
Feb 2	Receipt for 6,000 marks in part payment from David de Bruys. *Westm* R ıı p ıı 818 O vı 550 H ııı p ıı 130.
Feb 5.	Release of John de Ferrou, burgess of Troyes, and three other French hostages *Westm*. R ııı p ıı 818 O vı 550 H ııı p ıı 130
Feb. 8	The K forbids any person leaving the realm *Westm* R. ııı. p ıı 818
Feb 10	Licence to Guy count of S Paul to remain abroad until Michaelmas. *Westm* R ııı p ıı. 819 O. vı 551 H ııı p ıı 130

DATE	SUBJECT
1367 Feb 10	Exemplification of a patent of Charles K of France, when dauphin, ordering his officers to issue a proclamation for the payment of ransoms, dated Chartres, 10 May 1360. *Westm* R iii. p ii. 819
Feb 10	Humfrey de Bohun, earl of Hereford, and 17 others, having lands in Wales, are ordered to array their men *Westm* R iii p ii. 819.
Feb 10	Leave of absence for Reynaud lord of Mauleverer, a French hostage *Westm*. R. iii. p ii 820. O vi 551 H iii p ii 130
Feb 11	Letters obligatory of Reynaud lord of Mauleverer. *Westm* R. iii. p ii 820.
Feb 13	Protection for sir Thomas de Arden, in the retinue of the prince of Wales *Westm* R iii p ii 821
Feb 16	The treasurer and barons of the Exchequer are ordered to pay the annuity of 1,000 marks, granted to Ralph earl of Stafford, which had been assigned to him on the customs of London and S Botolph *Westm* R iii p ii 821
Feb 20	Obligation of Peter K of Castile to repay 5,000 florins, lent to him by the prince of Wales *Bayonne* R iii p ii 821 O vi 553 H iii p ii 131
Feb 20	The K orders the seneschal of Poictou and Saintonge to seize the lands alienated without licence by the viscount Daunay *Westm* R. iii p ii 821
Feb 20	Gerald FitzMorice, earl of Desmond, is appointed justiciary of Ireland. The prelates, nobles, and commons are ordered to obey him *Westm* R iii p ii 822
Feb 20	Thomas bp. of Lismore and Waterford is appointed chancellor of Ireland, *vice* Robert de Assheton *Westm* R iii p ii 822
Feb 20	Pardon for the K's subjects in Ireland of their debts due to the crown *Westm* R iii p ii 822
Feb 20	The K forbids the extortions of his officers in Ireland *Westm* R. iii p. ii. 822.
Feb 24.	The K. forbids the exportation of worsteds, grindstones, seacoal, and "felware," except to Calais. *Westm* R iii p ii 823
Feb. 25.	The K. forbids the exportation to Scotland of horses, arms, or victuals *Westm* R. iii p. ii 823.
March 20	Safe conducts for William earl of Sutherland, his wife Joan, and his son William de Murref *Westm* R iii p ii 823 O. vi 553 H iii p ii 131
April 1.	Letter in Spanish and Latin from the prince of Wales to Henry count of Trastamare, offering to mediate between him and the K. of Castile. *Navarreta in Castile* R. iii. p. ii 823 O vi
April 2	Henry count of Trastamare informs the prince of Wales, in Spanish and Latin, that he has been elected K of Castile in consequence of the misconduct of the late K Peter, and requests him to retreat from Castile. *Najara* R iii p ii 824 O vi 556 H iii p ii 132
July 5	Payment of 16*l* 13*s* 4*d* to Franskyn Forsset, valet of the prince of Wales, for conveying to the K the horse of Henry, bastard of Spain, [count of Trastamare,] taken at the battle of Najara in Spain, on April 3. R iii p ii 825 O vi 557 H iii. p ii 132.
Nov 22.	John duke of Lancaster grants 40*l* a year to Walter de Ursewyk, whom he had knighted at the battle of Najara* *Hertford* R iii p ii 825 O vi 557 H iii p ii 132
May 2	Confirmation by Peter K of Castile, of his promise to pay the expenses of the prince of Wales, and of his other grants *Burgos* Obligation for 1,000,000 gold pieces *Elgis near Burgos* 6 *May* R iii. p ii 825 O vi 559 H iii. p ii 133
May 26	Treaty of alliance by the K. of England and Louis count of Flanders R iii p ii 826 O vi. 560 H. iii. p. ii. 134.
May 13	Receipt for 100,000 crowns from the K of France, in part payment of his ransom *Westm* R. iii p ii 826 O vi 562 H iii p ii 134.
May 15.	The K consents to the prorogation of the term for the decision of the question about Belleville until July 22. *Westm* R iii p ii 826. O vi 562 H iii p ii 134.

---

* Here, in the original edition, vi 558 and in the Hague, iii p ii 133, is introduced K Richard the Second's confirmation (dated 28 May a° 4) of his father's grant (20th July in the 45th year of the reign of Edward III) to sir Thomas Cheyne of 1,483*l* 6s 8*d* "pur le Fynance" of sir Bertram de Gueselyn taken at the battle of Najara

Also the grant of John Shakel to K Richard II (dated 23rd Sept 7 Richard II) of his right and interest in the ransom of the count de Dene, who was taken prisoner at the battle of Najara

DATE	SUBJECT
1367. May 15.	Treaty of marriage between Lionel duke of Clarence, and Violanta, daughter of the lord of Milan. *Westm* R iii p. ii. 827 O vi. 564 H iii p. ii. 135
May 18	John de Hurst is appointed chancellor of the Exchequer in Ireland, and the treasurer and barons there are ordered to admit him to the office *Westm.* R. iii p ii 828
May 29.	Power for sir Henry Lescrope, governor, and Thomes de Brantyngham, receiver, of Calais and Guisnes, to take an oath for the K to the treaty with the count of Flanders. *Westm.* R. iii. p ii 928
June 1	Licence to William duke of Juliers to do homage to the K of France for the castles of Urson and Lucy *Westm* R iii p ii 828 O vi 566 H iii p ii 136
June 1	Licence to Henry de Halle, German merchant, to bring eight large horses from Flanders to England for sale *Westm* R iii p ii 829 O vi 566 H iii p ii. 136.
June 3.	Safe conduct for John lord Cobham going to the court of Rome for the K *Westm* R. iii p. ii 829 O vi 567 H. ii. p ii 136
June 16	Exemplification of the 9th and 10th articles of the peace of Bretigny concerning the K's possessions in France *Westm* R. iii p ii 829
June 20.	Grant of an annuity of 20 marks to Geoffrey Chaucer. *Queensborough Castle.* R. iii. p. ii. 829 O vi 567 H. iii. p. ii. 136.
June 28.	Henry le Scrope is appointed governor of Marke, Calais, &c *Westm.* R. iii p ii 829
July 2	Leave of absence until July 1 for Gerard lord of Boucherche, a French hostage. *Westm.* R iii p. ii. 830. O vi 567. H iii. p. ii 137
July 6.	Safe conduct for Albert duke of Bavaria coming to England *Westm* R iii p. ii 830 O vi 568 H iii. p ii. 137
July 6	Licence to Dyermyd to use the name Makmorghyth, and grant to him of an annuity of 80 marks *Westm* R iii p ii. 130.
July 8.	Leave of absence for Guy de Blois, lord of Beaumont, French hostage *Westm* R iii p. ii. 830 O vi. 568 H iii p ii 137
July 20.	Leave of absence for Charles lord of Montgomery, and Matheu lord of Roy, hostages. *Westm* R. iii p ii 830 O vi 568 H iii p ii 137
July 26.	Pope Urban [V] writes to the K against the intended invasion of Provence by the duke of Lancaster *Viterbo.* R iii p ii 830 O vi 569. H iii p ii 137
Sept. 4.	Treaty between the earl of Warwick and three others for England, and the bps of S Andrew and Glasgow, and six others, for Scotland, for keeping peace on the marches and the appointment of wardens *Roxburgh* R iii p ii 831 O vi 569 H iii p ii 137
Sept. 8	Warrant to the keeper of the peace and sheriff in Sussex, and to John Wyn, mayor of Chichester, and three others, to arrest those who resist the K's appointment of Robert de Derby to the precentorship of Chichester. *Westm* R. iii p ii 831 O vi 572 H iii p. ii. 138
Sept 15	The K orders sir Nicholas de Lovayne, seneschal of Ponthieu, to fortify the castles there *Westm.* R iii p ii 832
Sept 20.	Gilbert de Umframvill, earl of Anegos, Henry de Percy, father and son, Peter de Mauley, and four others, are appointed wardens of the West March *Westm* R iii p ii 832 O. vi 573. H iii p ii 139
Sept 20	Safe conduct for Thomas earl of Marr coming through England on a pilgrimage to the Holy Places. *Westm.* R iii. p ii 832 O vi 574 H. iii p ii 139
Oct 4	Power for Gerald FitzMaurice, earl of Desmond, justiciary of Ireland, to grant pardons, with the consent of the chancellor and treasurer *Westm.* R. iii p ii 833
Oct 4	Commission to the chancellor of Ireland, and Robert de Preston, chief justice of the Common Bench there, to examine the state of the Exchequer in Ireland. *Westm.* R. iii. p ii 833.
Oct. 12.	Restitution of the temporalties to William de Wykeham, bp of Winchester, late archdeacon of Lincoln. *Westm* R iii. p ii 833 O vi 574 H iii. p ii 139
Oct. 16.	Safe conduct for William earl of Douglas coming to England. *Westm.* R iii p ii. 833 O. vi 575. H iii. p ii. 139
Oct. 22.	Protection for the towns of Isledon, North and South Mimms, Uxbridge, and others, assigned for providing for the household of the duke of Clarence, when visiting the K. *Westm.* R. iii. p. ii. 833. O vi 575 H. iii. p. ii 140

DATE	SUBJECT
1367	
Oct. 22	John Keppok is appointed chief justice in Ireland *Westm* R iu p ii 884
Oct 22	Nicholas Lumbard is appointed second justice in Ireland. *Westm.* R iii. p ii 884.
Oct 26	Safe conducts for James de Douglas, son of sir John de Douglas, Thomas Erskyn, son of sir Robert de Erskin, and 11 other Scots, coming to England as pilgrims *Westm.* R. iii p ii 834. O vi 576 H iii p ii 140
Oct 28.	Safe conducts for Walter bp of Glasgow, sir Robert de Erskyn, and sir Walter de Lesley, Scotch ambassadors. *Westm.* R. iii p. ii. 834. O. vi 576. H. iii p ii 140.
Nov. 4	The K. desires Thomas de Dale to remain in Ireland *Westm* R iii. p ii 834
Nov 16	The K forbids his subjects to do damage to the territories of the K. of France. *Westm·* R iii p ii 834 O vi 577 H iii p ii 140.
[Nov 16]	The K sends a copy of the above-mentioned letter to the prince of Wales, and desires him to prevent injuries to France *Westm* R iii p ii 835 O vi 578. H iii p ii 141
[Nov 16]	The K orders sir Nichol de Tamworth to publish the above-mentioned letters *Westm* R iii p ii 835 O vi 579 H iii p ii 141
Nov. 16	The K. orders Henry Lescrop, governor of Calais, Nichol de Lovaigne, seneschal, Nichol de Louth, canon of Salisbury and receiver of Ponthieu, and Frenun de Cromont, to meet the French commissioners at Montreuil, for the decision of certain questions relating to Ponthieu *Westm* R iii p ii 836
Nov. 18	The K orders John Tracy, examiner of the forfeitures at Calais, to weigh the wool that is imported *Westm* R iii p ii 836
Nov 18	Receipt of 92,000 crowns from the K of France, in part payment *Westm* R. iii. p ii 936 O vi 579 H iii p ii 141
Nov 18.	The K orders the wardens of the passage at Dover to exact from merchants and burgesses of Calais 4s. 3d for each man and horse and 1s for each man *Westm.* R. iii. p ii. 836
Nov 18.	Licence to the merchants of the staple at Calais to export cloth for their own use, free of duty *Westm* R iii p ii 836
Nov 22.	Protection for sir Aubrey de Veer, in the retinue of the prince of Wales *Westm.* R iii p ii. 837
Dec 1	The K's letter to John count of Harecourt, desiring him to return to London, as his leave of absence has expired *Westm.* R iii p ii 837 O vi 580 H iii p ii 141
Dec. 1	The K desires sir Nicholas de Lovaigne, seneschal of Ponthieu, to present the above-mentioned letters to the count of Harecourt. *Westm* R. iii p ii 837. O vi 580 H iii p. ii 141.
Dec 1	The K informs the bailiff of Amiens of the death of Piers de Cokeray, burgess of Amiens, and requests him to send another hostage in his stead *Westm* R iii p. ii 837 O vi 580 H iii p ii. 142
Dec 6	Receipt for 10,000 marks from John duke of Brittany *Westm* R. iii p ii 887. O vi 581 H. iii. p ii 142.
Dec 7	Receipt of 10,000 crowns from Louis duke of Bourbon *Westm* R iii p ii 837. O vi 581 H iii. p. ii 142
Dec 8.	Licence to James, heir of William de Douglas of Degbemont, to take armour from London for a duel against Thomas de Erskyn *Westm* R iii p ii 838. O vi 582 H iii p ii 142
Dec 8	The K forbids the circulation of foreign money in England. *Westm.* R iii p ii 838
Dec 8.	The K orders the exchange of money in London to be held at Bucklersbury *Westm* R. iii p ii 839
Dec 20	Protection for the prince of Wales and for Sir Thomas Florak, in his retinue *Westm* R iii p ii 839
Dec 29	The K. orders Henry Lescrope, governor, and Thomas de Brantyngham, treasurer of Calais, and the mayor of the staple, to settle the disputes between the Lombard merchants and the brokers of the staple *Windsor* R. iii p ii. 839.
1368 Jan 4	Safe conducts for David de Bruys and his wife Margaret to visit the tomb of S. Thomas of Canterbury. *Windsor* R iii. p ii. 839. O vi 582 H iii p ii 142
Jan 5.	The K summons the count of Harecourt, his hostage, to return to England. *Westm* R iii p. ii 840. O. vi. 582. H iii. p. ii. 142.

DATE	SUBJECT
1368 Jan 5.	Licence to Thomas de Erskyn of Scotland to take armour from London for his duel [with James de Douglas]. *Windsor* R iii p ii 840 O vi 583 H iii p ii 143
Jan 20.	Safe conduct for Walter Byger, parson of Erroll, chamberlain of Scotland, to come to Berwick *Westm.* R iii p ii 840 O vi 583. H iii. p ii 143
Jan 22.	Safe conducts for William bp of S Andrew's, Walter bp of Glasgow, sir Hugh de Eglinton, and two others, to come to London *Westm* R iii p ii. 840 O. vi. 584 H iii p ii. 143
Jan 26	Safe conducts for sir Walter de Lesleye, William Mudy, and nine others, to come to England *Westm* R iii p ii 840. O. vi. 584. H iii p ii 143
Jan 26	The K. orders Gilbert de Umframvill, earl of Anegos, and Henry de Percy to keep the treaty with Scotland until Aug 1 *Westm* R iii p ii 841. O vi 584 H iii. p ii 143
Jan 26	John de Humbleton is appointed attorney in England for sir John Chaundos. *Westm* R iii p ii 841.
Jan 27	The K orders Henry Lescrop to summon the aldermen and burgesses of Calais and the wardens of the neighbouring castles to furnish them with victuals and stores. *Westm* R iii. p ii 841
Jan. 28.	Memorandum that John de Branketre delivered to Helmyng Leget the obligations of the duke of Bourbon for 40,000 crowns, of which 10,000 are paid. R. iii. p. ii. 841 O vi 585 H iii p ii 143
Feb. 2	Receipt for 6,000 marks from David de Bruys *Westm* R iii p. ii 841 O. vi. 585 H iii p ii 143
Feb 2.	Writs to 26 sheriffs to send arrows to London *Westm* R iii p ii 842.
Feb. 5	Protection for the French burgesses who are hostages in England *Westm* R. iii. p ii 842 O. vi 586 H iii. p ii 144.
Feb. 6.	Oath of William le Mercier, a French hostage *Westm* R. iii p ii 842 O. vi 586. H iii p ii 144
Feb. 10	Baldewin de Whiteneye and Richard de Hortesleye, are appointed attorneys for Robert de Whiteneye, who is in the retinue of the duke of Clarence going to Milan Similar letters for 26 others *Westm* R iii p ii 842 O vi 587 H iii p ii. 144
Feb 20.	Restitution of the temporalities from 29 April to John de Harewell, bp of Bath and Wells, who is with the prince of Wales *Westm.* R iii p. ii 843 O. vi. 587. H. iii. p. ii 144
Feb. 23.	Release of Henry de Leglise, burgess of Compiegne, and five other French hostages. *Westm* R iii p ii. 843 O. vi. 588. H iii p ii 144.
Feb. 23	Receipt of Symon de Bully and three others as French hostages. *Westm.* R iii p ii 843 O vi 588. H iii p ii 145.
Feb 28	Protection for sir Edward le Despenser and sir John de Daunteseye, in the retinue of the duke of Clarence *Westm.* R iii p. ii. 843.
March 1	Receipt of 100,000 florins from Galeazzo lord of Milan *Windsor.* R. iii. p. ii. 843. O. vi 589 H iii p ii 145.
March 3	Protection for John Holand and 13 others in the retinue of the duke of Clarence *Westm.* R iii p ii 844
March 13.	Robert de Assheton is appointed warden of Sandgate Castle near Calais. The governor of Calais is ordered to deliver the castle to him *Westm.* R iii p ii. 844.
March 20	William de Gunthorpe is appointed treasurer of Calais. *Westm* R iii p. ii 844
March 24.	The K orders the mayor and sheriffs of London to compel the gauging of all wine for sale in the city. *Westm* R. iii p ii. 844
March 26.	The K. orders the several sheriffs and his other officers to provide carriages for the prince of Wales, who is about to return to England. *Westm* R. iii p ii. 845 O. vi
April 20.	Grant of an annuity of 40*l* to Peter de Florence, physician to the K and Q. *Windsor.* R iii p ii 845 O vi 589 H iii p ii 145
May 4.	Protection for John and William Vueman and John Lietuyt of Delft, clockmakers, coming to England to exercise their trade *Westm.* R iii. p ii. 845 O. vi. 590. H iii p ii 145
May 7.	Safe conduct for Thomas earl of Marre coming to England. *Westm* R. iii p ii. 845 O. vi. 590. H. iii p ii 145.

DATE	SUBJECT
1368 May 10	Warrant for the payment of 173*l* 6*s* 8*d* for the expenses of the passage from Dover to Calais of the duke of Clarence, going to Milan with 457 men and 1,280 horses in his retinue. *Westm* R III p II 845 O. VI 590 H III p II 145
May 14	Inspeximus of the testament of sir Thomas de Uvedale, dated Nov 6, 1367. *Westm.* R III p II 846 O VI 591. H III p. II 146.
May 18.	The K. exempts the town of Toriton from sending members to parliament, because they had never sent members before the 21st year of his reign *Westm* R III. p II 846. O VI 593 H III p II 146
May 24	The K orders the warden and chamberlain of Berwick-upon-Tweed to allow the burgesses to use the lands and customs enjoyed by them in the time of K Alexander *Westm.* R. III p II 846 O VI 593 H III p II 146.
May 25	Thomas de Burele, friar of the hospital of S John of Jerusalem in Ireland, is appointed chancellor of Ireland *Westm* R III p II 847
May 25	Stephen bp of Limerick is appointed treasurer of the Exchequer in Ireland *Westm* R. III p II 847
May 26	John de Troye is appointed chancellor of the Exchequer in Ireland, *vice* John Hirst The treasurer and barons are ordered to admit him *Westm.* R III p II 847
June 28	Henry le Scrope is appointed governor of Marke, Calais, &c *Westm.* R III p II 847
June 29.	Licence to the abbot of Kelleshowe in Scotland to buy victuals in England *Westm* R III p II 847. O VI 594 H III p II 147.
July 28	The K orders Thomas de Roos of Hamelak, and 15 others, to prepare men for the defence of their lands in Ireland, and to attend the council at Westminster *Guildford* R III p II. 148 O V 595 H III p II. 147
Sept 18	Commissions to John Witegode and John Clerk of Southampton to provide ships for the conveyance of men-at-arms and archers to Aquitain. Two similar commissions *Westm* R III p II 848
Sept. 28	Letters to the same commissioners on the same subjects *Westm* R. III p II 849
>Oct 1.	Receipt by William duke of Juliers for 2,293 marks 8*s* 8*d* from the K *London* R III p II 849 O VI 596 H III p II 147
Oct. 11	Bull of pope Urban for the translation of William de Lenn, bp of Chichester, to the see of Worcester The oath of fealty was taken by the bishop, June 4, 1369 *Viterbo* R III p II 849 O VI 596-7. H III p II 148
Oct. 16	Safe conduct for Thomas earl of Marre who is going to Amiens *Westm* R III. p II 849 O VI 597 H III p. II. 148
Oct 28	Safe conduct for William duke of Juliers, who is leaving England *Westm.* R. III. p. II 850 O VI 598 H III p II 148
Oct. 30	Safe conducts for the counts of Tankarvill and Salesburgg, Sir William Dormantz, and James de Riche, dean of Paris *Westm* R III p II. 850 O VI 598 H. III p II 148
Nov. 1.	The K orders the justices, chancellor, and treasurer of Ireland to send ships to the port of Liverpool for the conveyance of men to Ireland *Westm.* R III. p. II 850
[Nov 1]	Similar letters to the mayors and bailiffs of Dublin, Drogheda, and Waterford R III p II 850
Nov 6.	Protection for the prince of Wales *Westm.* R III p II. 850.
Nov 12.	Licence to William de Hasthorp and John Cok, lieutenants of Walter Hewet, warden of Guernsey, Sark, and Alderney, to buy wine, cider, bows and arrows, in the western counties *Westm* R III p II 850
Nov. 20.	Treaty, offensive and defensive, between Charles K. of France and Henry K of Castile, the latter promising to assist the former against the K of England *Toledo.* Power of Charles K of France, to Francis de Perilionbus, viscount of Rode, and John lord of Rue, to treat with the K of Castile *Paris*, 19 *July* R III p II 850 O VI 598. H III. p II 148-9
Nov. 20.	Henry K of Castile promises to refer his dissensions with the K. of Arragon to the K. of France *Toledo* R III p II 152. O. VI 602 H III p II 150
Nov 24	The K exempts sir Robert de Insula from attendance at parliaments and councils, from serving on juries or assizes, from the holding of offices, the payment of subsidies, and military service. *Westm* R III. p II 852 O VI 603. H III. p II 150.
Nov 28	Power for Edward prince of Wales to receive the oath of fealty of John bp. of Bath and Wells, the prince's chancellor in Aquitain *Westm* R III. p II. 852 O VI 603 H III. p II. 150

DATE.	SUBJECT
1368 Nov 29.	Commission to sir William de Aldeburgh and Robert de Wykford, archdeacon of Winchester, to treat with pope Urban [V.] *Westm* R. iii. p. ii. 853. O vi 604 H. iii. p ii 151
Nov 29.	Commission to John Colpepii, William Appulderfelde, and the sheriff of Kent to send archers to Calais Two similar commissions *Westm* R iii p ii 853
Dec 1	The K orders the justiciary, chancellor, and treasurer of Ireland to convoke a parliament to treat concerning the ordinances made in England for the government in Ireland *Westm* R iii p. ii 853 O vi 605 H iii p ii 151
Dec 20	The sheriff of York, William de Wyndesore, and nine others are ordered to provide archers to be sent to Ireland Three similar commissions in the counties of Lancashire, Westmoreland, and Nottingham *Windsor* R iii p. ii 854
	The K has received the report of the Irish parliament held at Dublin on May 1, and orders all persons who have lands in Ireland to go thither. R iii p. ii 854.
1369 Jan 4.	Receipt of 1,928*l* 18*s* from John duke of Brittany *Westm* R iii p ii 855
Jan 10	Alliance between the K of England and Peter K of Aragon *Westm.* R iii p ii 855 O. vi. 606 H. iii p ii 151
Jan 12	Power for the abp of Bourdeaux, the bps of Bazas and Perigord, John Chaundos, constable, Thomas de Felton, seneschal of Aquitain, and seven others, to take the oath for the K of England to the above alliance *Westm* R. iii p ii 855. O vi 607. H iii p ii
Jan. 13.	Receipt for 6,000 marks from David de Bruys *Westm* R iii p ii 856 O vi 608 H iii p. ii. 152.
Jan 13	Commission to Peter de Maulay, warden, John de Bolton, chamberlain of Berwick, and the sheriff of Northumberand to send the money above mentioned to York The mayor and sheriff of York are ordered to forward it to London *Westm* R iii p ii 856 O vi 609 H iii p ii 152
Jan 15	Restitution of the temporalities to William abp of Canterbury, translated from Worcester in the room of Simon [de Langham], raised by the pope to a cardinalate *Westm.* R iii p ii 857 O vi 610 H iii p ii 153
Jan 16	Protection for John de Hastynges, earl of Pembroke, in the retinue of the prince of Wales, and of 15 persons in his retinue *Westm* R iii p ii 857
Jan. 16.	Protection for the same earl of Pembroke and 12 others *Westm* R iii p ii 857
Jan. 20.	Safe conduct for Walter de Bykere, chamberlain of Scotland, who is bringing the 6,000 marks to Berwick *Westm* R iii p ii 857 O vi 611 H iii p ii 153
Jan 23	Safe conduct for Firmin Grevette, coming to treat for the ransom of Peter Seny, of Amiens, prisoner of William la Zouche, also for Walter de Rus. *Westm.* R. iii p ii 858
Jan 23	Warrant to Guy de Briene to arrest ships to serve against the French *Westm.* R iii. p ii 858.
Jan 26	The K. orders William de Mulsho and John de Newenham, chamberlains of the Exchequer, John de Thorp, keeper of the mint at the Tower of London, and four others to test certain plate made for the earl of Salisbury. *Westm.* R iii p ii 858. O v 611 H iii. p ii 153
Feb. 2	Receipt for 6,000 marks from David de Bruys *Westm* R iii p ii 858 O vi 611 H iii. p ii 153
Feb. 6.	Receipt for 2,960 marks 5s from John duke of Brittany. *Westm.* R iii. p. ii 858 O vi 612 H iii p ii. 153
Feb 8.	Protection for sir John de Cherleton, lord of Powys, and 18 others, in the retinue of the prince of Wales *Westm* R iii p ii 859
Feb 10.	Grant by Edward prince of Wales of Talement sur Gonde to the Soudan de la Trau *Angouleme.* R iii p ii 859 O vi 612 H iii p ii 154.
Feb 12.	Release of Raoul Grosparmy and John le Flamenc, burgesses of Caen, French hostages. *Westm.* R iii p ii 859 O vi 612. H iii p ii 154.
Feb 12	Receipt of Robert de la Coulombe and Robert Panette as hostages in the place of the aforesaid Raoul Grosparmy and John le Flamenc *Westm* R iii p ii 859 O vi. 612. H iii p. ii 154
Feb. 15.	Restitution to sir John Wogan of his lands in Ireland, forfeited for absence, for which he has excused himself. *Westm* R iii p ii 859

F F

DATE	SUBJECT
1369 Feb. 16	Confirmation of the confirmation by the prince of Wales of grants by Kings Charles, Philip, and Louis of France to the abbey of S Maxentius in Poictou *Westm* R iii p ii 860.
Feb. 21	Licence to sir Nicholas Gernoun, who has lands in Ireland, to remain in England in the retinue of Matilda de Lancaster, mother of Elizabeth late countess of Ulster. *Westm* R iii p ii 861 O vi. 613 H iii. p. ii 154.
Feb 24.	Richard de Imworth, sergeant-at-arms, and Peter Rede are ordered to arrest ships from Faversham to Portsmouth, and the bailiffs of the said ports are ordered to assist them. Similar commission to Thomas Dautry and William Lynche, from Cornwall to Christchurch, and similar letters to the bailiffs of the ports *Westm* R iii p ii 861.
Feb 26.	Letters of attorney for John de Hastynges, earl of Pembroke, in the names of William bp of Winchester, sir Walter de Manny, and two others *Westm* R iii p ii 862.
Feb 28	Protection for sir Hamo de Felton, sir John de Nowers, and 41 others going to Aquitain in the retinue of Edmund earl of Cambridge *Westm* R iii p ii. 862.
March 9	Henry Leserope, governor of Calais, Robert de Assheton, Ralph de Ferrers, and William de Gonthorpe, treasurer of Calais, are ordered to put the castles at Calais, Guisnes, &c in a state of defence Similar commission to Nicholas de Loveyne, governor of Ponthien and three others *Westm* R iii p ii 862
March 10	Safe conducts for David de Bruys and six other persons coming to England. *Westm.* R iii p ii 862 O vi 613 H iii. p ii 154.
June 17	Safe conducts for John Gray, keeper of the rolls and register of Scotland, Adam de Tynyngham, dean of Aberdeen, and eight other Scots *Westm* R iii p ii 863 O vi 614 H iii p ii 154.
March 20	The K orders the mayor, aldermen, and sheriffs of London to array the men of the city and to punish workmen who refuse to work at the fixed wages Similar letters to the bp. of Durham, Ralph Spigurnel, constable of Dover Castle and warden of the Cinque Ports, and the mayors and bailiffs of Winchester and Southampton. *Windsor* R iii p ii. 863 O vi 614 H iii p ii 154
March 31.	Safe conduct for Hugh de Digorne, coming to England with money from the duke of Bourbon *Westm* R iii p ii 863 O vi 615 H iii. p ii 615
April 6.	Release of John de Durchie and Thomas de Varey, burgesses of Lyons, French hostages. *Westm* R iii p. ii 863 O vi 616 H iii p ii 155
April 6	Receipt of Louis de Fuer and John de Precy as hostages in the place of the above-named John and Thomas. *Westm* R iii p ii 864 O vi. 616. H iii p. ii. 155.
April 15	Commission to Richard Lescrop, Walter de Urswyk, and John de Seyville to provide 200 archers in Yorkshire to accompany the duke of Lancaster to Aquitain Similar commissions in Lancashire, Derby, and Stafford *Westm* R iii p ii 864
April 26.	Safe conduct for John Eustache, butler of the K. of France, to go to France. *Westm.* R. iii. p. ii. 864. O vi 616 H iii p ii 155.
April 26.	Safe conduct for a ship containing 50 pipes of wine sent by the K. of France as a present to the K. of England, but who, for certain reasons (not mentioned), sends them back *Westm* R iii p ii 864. O. vi 617 H iii. p ii 155
April 26.	The K. orders the mayor and sheriffs of London to issue a proclamation forbidding any insult or molestation to the French hostages. *Westm.* R. iii. p ii. 864. O. vi. 617. H iii p ii 155
May 3.	Roger Beler and Robert de Morton are ordered to select 100 archers in Yorkshire, Nottinghamshire, and Derbyshire *Westm* R iii p ii 865 O vi 617 H iii p ii 156
May 5	Stephen de Valence is appointed warden of Calais castle, *vice* John Tirel *Westm.* R iii p ii 865
May 7.	Sir Walter Huwet is appointed arrayer in the town of Southampton *Westm.* R. iii. p ii 865
May 7	Warrant to Thomas Moys, master of the ship called *Dieulagarde* to arrest 60 sailors Similar warrants to eight other masters of ships *Westm* R iii p ii 865.
May 8	Protection for Geoffrey de Walden, William de Herward, and 17 others in the retinue of Humfrey de Bohun, earl of Hereford *Westm.* R. iii p ii. 866
May 8.	Warrant to Walter Howet to arrest ships and sailors for the defence of the country. *Westm* R iii p ii. 866
May 9	The K. orders the mayor and bailiffs of Southampton to forbid the inhabitants to leave the town or send away their goods *Westm.* R. iii. p. ii 866.

DATE	SUBJECT
1369 May 10	Humfrey earl of Hereford is appointed the K s lieutenant and captain in Marke, Calais, and Guisnes Intimation thereof to the governor and treasurer *Westm* R iii p ii 866.
May 10.	The K orders the mayor and sheriffs of London to prevent all persons from molesting the merchants of Flanders and Lombardy *Westm* R iii p ii 867 O, vi 618. H iii p. ii 156
May 30	Protection for the earl of Hereford, and for John Braughyng and seven others in the retinue of the same Earl *Westm.* R. iii p. ii. 867.
May 15.	Thomas de Middleton and three others are commissioned to buy victuals in Ireland for the castles of the prince of Wales in North Wales *Westm* R. iii p ii 867 O vi 618 H iii p ii 156
May 16.	Licence to Thomas del Hay, a Scotch hostage, to go to Rome. *Westm.* R. iii. p. ii 867 O vi 619 H iii p ii 156
May 26	Safe conduct for John de Lyndowe, goldsmith to convey jewels sent by Q Philippa to the duchess of Holland *Westm* R iii p ii 868 O vi. 619 H iii p ii 156
May 28.	Commission to Simon atte Halle to buy 1,200 stones for the K.'s engines in Kent *Westm* R. iii. p. ii 868. O vi 619 H iii. p ii 156
May 29	The K orders the chancellor and chamberlain of Berwick and his other officers in Scotland to allow the inhabitants of Berwick to buy and sell according to the laws of K Alexander *Westm* R iii p ii 868 O vi 620 H iii. p ii 157
June 3.	Memorandum that in consequence of the breach of the peace by Charles K of France, the K of England resumes the title of K of France, and seals with this title were thereupon delivered to William bp of Winchester, the K's chancellor, and other officers. *Westm* R iii p. ii 868. O vi 621 H iii p ii 157
June 2.	Grant of the subsidy on cloth to the commonalty of Winchester for the repair of their walls *Westm* R iii p ii 869
June 5	The K forbids the burgesses of Shrewsbury leaving the town, and orders them to provide for its defence *Westm.* R iii p ii 869
June 8	Declaration of Henry K of Castile, explaining certain articles in his treaty with the K of France *Toledo* R. iii p ii 869 O vi 622. H. iii p ii 157
June 11.	Commission to John de Cobeham, Robert Bealknap, William de Horne and two others to fortify certain places on the coast of the isle of Thanet. *Westm* R. iii. p ii 870. O vi. 623 H iii p ii 158.
June 11	Licence to Godfrey de Roos of Scotland to bring 40 men-at-arms to the K.'s assistance Similar licence to Patrick Macolagh, of Scotland. *Westm* R iii p ii 870 O. vi 624 H. iii p ii 158
June 11.	Protection for sir John Montagne and 13 others in the retinue of John duke of Lancaster *Westm* R. iii. p. ii 870
June 11.	Protection for sir Roger de Trompyngton, John FitzWilliam, and 55 others, in the retinue of the duke of Lancaster *Westm* R iii p ii 871
June 12	Power for sir Richard de Stafford, John Shepeye, and Adam de Bury to treat with Louis count of Flanders, and the commonalties of Bruges, Ghent, and Ypres for the performance of the treaties between them and the K of England. *Westm* R. iii. p ii 871 O vi 624 H iii p ii 158.
June 12	John duke of Lancaster is appointed the K's lieutenant and captain of Marke, Guisnes, and Calais William de Gunthorp, treasurer of Calais, is ordered to assist him. *Westm.* R. ii. p. ii, 871.
June 12	Nicholas de Tamworth is appointed admiral from the Thames northwards. *Westm* R iii. p ii. 871
June 12	Grant of the castle and manor of Banelyngham in the lordship of Guisnes, forfeited by sir John de Banelyngham, to Adam de Bury, citizen of London Henry Lescrope is ordered to deliver them to him *Westm.* R. iii p. ii 872
June 12.	The inhabitants of Hereford and Winchester are forbidden to absent themselves from their respective towns *Westm* R iii. p ii. 872
June 14.	Protection for sir William de Botreaux, sir Walter Bluet, and nine others. *Westm.* R iii p ii 872
June 16.	Licence to Walter bp. of Glasgow to exercise his office within the K.'s dominions in Scotland *Westm.* R. iii. p. ii 872 O vi 624. H. iii p ii 158.

DATE.	SUBJECT
1369 June 17	Protection for William de Mothirby, Robert de Derby, and 27 others in the retinues of the duke of Lancaster, the earl of Hereford, and others *Westm* R iii p ii 873
June 18	Protection for Walter bp of Glasgow, and his men and tenants in the county of Roxburgh *Westm* R iii. p ii 873 O vi 625 H iii p ii 158
June 18	The K orders the truce for 14 years with Scotland to be published throughout England and Ireland. *Westm* R. iii p ii 873 O vi 625 H iii p ii 158
June 19	The K informs Edward prince of Wales of his intention to resume his claim to the crown of France, and that he will grant all lands in France, except those of the crown and of the church, to any persons who may conquer them *Westm* R iii p ii 874 O vi 626. H. iii p ii 159
June 27.	The prince of Wales grants the county of Bigorre to John de Greyly, captal de Bouch. *Angouleme* R iii p. ii. 874 O vi 627 H iii p ii 159
June 28.	Memorandum of the delivery of the K 's confirmation of the above grant to sir Arnald Savage R iii p ii 874 O vi 627 H iii p ii 159
July 2.	The K orders the men in the several counties of England to be arrayed in readiness for the war against France *Westm* R iii p ii 874 O vi 628 H iii p ii 159
July 3	The K forbids the prior of Spalding to pay his pension of 40*l* to the abbey of S. Nicholas Anjou Similar writs to the prior de Novoloco near Ancolm [of Newstead], and the abbots of Thornton and Rufford *Westm* R iii p. ii 975 O vi 629 H. iii. p ii 160
July 4	Louis duke of Bourbon becomes security for Berard dauphin of Auvergue, who owes the K. of England 12,000 gold nobles, for his realease *Souvigny* R iii p ii 875 O vi 629 H iii p ii 160.
July 6	The archbishops and bishops of England are ordered to array the ecclesiastics of their respective dioceses *Westm* R iii p ii 876 O vi. 631 H iii p ii 161
July 8	Writs to 16 sheriffs to provide arrows *Westm* R iii p ii 876
July 20.	The truce with Scotland for 14 years The Scotch treaty *Edinburgh* R iii. p ii. 877. O vi 632. H. iii p ii 161
Aug 15.	Almaric de S Amand is appointed captain and warden of Southampton, Waryn de l'Isle, of Portsmouth, and Roger de Elmerugge, of Porchester *Westm* R iii p ii 878 O vi 633 H iii p ii 162
Aug. 15.	The arrayers of Wiltshire, Bedfordshire, and four other counties are ordered to send their men to resist an expected invasion of the Isle of Wight by the French *Westm* R iii p ii 878 O vi. 634 H iii p ii 162
Aug 24.	Counterpart by the K of England of the truce with Scotland *Westm* R iii p ii 878 O. vi 635 H iii p. ii. 163
Aug 29	Safe conduct for sir Baldewin de Beaulo, Sauxcius Lupi, and two other ambassadors of Charles K of Navarre *Rotherhithe* R iii p ii 879 O vi 637 H iii p ii. 163
Aug. 29.	Warrant to John de Watlyngton, and David de Brettevill, sergeant-at-arms, to arrest William de Stoke, canon of Dunmow, suspected of coining false money *Rotherhithe.* R iii p ii 879 O vi 637. H iii p ii 163.
Sept 20	Indenture between the K of England and sir Piers de Mauley for the custody of Berwick-upon-Tweed *Westm* R iii p ii 879 O vi 638. H iii p ii 163.
Sept. 29.	Commission to the abbot of Titchfield, the prior of Southwick, Thomas del More, and five others, to ascertain whether Portsmouth, which has been burnt by the French, is able to pay the usual rent to the K *Langley* R iii p ii 880 O vi 638. H iii p ii. 164.
Oct 6	Safe conducts for Jurdan Daugen, valet of John Prescy and Louis de Foer, burgesses of Lyons, and also for Stephen Viners, valet of John de Vangeulay, burgess of Troye, French hostages *Westm* R iii p. ii 880
Oct 16	The K orders the abps of Canterbury and York to summon convocations for the purpose of granting a subsidy. *Westm* R iii p ii 880
Oct. 26	Ralph Spigurnell, constable of Dover Castle and warden of the Cinque Ports, is ordered to send two men from each port to consult about the state of the navy. Similar writs to the mayors and bailiffs of Plymouth and 29 other ports *Westm* R iii p ii 880. O vi 639-40. H. iii p ii 164.
Oct 27.	Writs to the sheriffs of London and Middlesex and 23 others to provide arrows *Westm.* R iii. p. ii. 881
Nov 26	Indenture by which John duke of Lancaster appoints Henry de Scrop, captain of Calais *Calais* R iii p. ii 881 O vi 640. H. iii p ii 164

DATE	SUBJECT
1369. Dec. 1	Indenture between the duke of Lancaster and John "sire de Gomenyz," whom he appoints captain of Arde *Calais* R iii p ii 882 O vi 641 H iii p ii 165.
Dec 6	Safe conduct for John Massiner, of France, prisoner of John Meysy. *Westm* R iii. p ii 882.
Dec 8	The mayor and bailiffs of Salisbury are ordered to find men and victuals for the ships of William Gys and others Three similar commissions *Westm* R iii p ii 882
Dec 10.	Safe conduct for Hugh Logerell, valet of the dauphin of Auvergne. *Westm.* R iii p ii. 882 O vi. 641 H iii p ii 165
Dec 24	The K orders the duke of Lancaster and 17 other lords to fortify their castles in Wales and array their men. *Langley* Similar letter to the prince of Wales *Westm* R iii. p ii 883 O vi 642 H. iii p ii 164.
Dec. 30	The K. of England writes in French to the lord of . . to inform him of the breaking of the peace by the K of France, and of the resumption of his title to the crown *The Tower of London* R iii p ii 883 O vi 643–5. H. iii p ii 166
	Similar letter in Latin to the abbot of *Westm* R iii p ii 884 O vi 645 H iii p ii 166
1370. Jan 1.	Commission for the appointment of judges of appeal in Aquitain, the names being left for insertion by the prince of Wales *The Tower of London* R iii p. ii 884 O vi 646. H iii. p ii 167
Jan 17	Commission to John Hankyn and Thomas de Stafford to arrest ships in the north and bring them to Winchelsea Five similar commissions. *Westm.* R iii p ii 885
Jan 18	Safe conduct for Walter de Bygar, chamberlain of David de Bruys, coming to England to pay money for him *Westm* R iii p ii 885 O vi 647 H. iii p ii. 167
Jan 20	Commission to William Beaufay to count and weigh the money received from David de Bruys *Westm* R iii p ii 885 O vi 647 H iii p. ii 167
Jan 20	Grants of annuities of 10 marks and smaller sums to Alice de Preston and eight other ladies of the late Q Philippa. *Westm.* R iii p ii 886 O. vi 648. H iii p ii 167.
Jan 26	Revocation of the pardon of William Clerk for the death of John son of Ralph Hunt. *Westm* R iii p ii. 886
Feb 2	Receipt for 4,000 marks from David de Bruys *Westm* R iii p ii 886. O vi 648 H iii p ii 167
Feb 13.	Licence to Thomas de Crickelade, squire of John earl of Pembroke, to go to Aquitain with 40 men-at-arms and 40 archers *Westm* R iii p ii 886
Feb 14	Release to William bp of Chichester, late provost of Wengham, for the revenues of the see from June 4 to June 9 *Westm* R iii p ii 886 O vi 649 H. iii. p. ii. 168
Feb. 14	The commissioners of array throughout England are ordered to have their men ready by Palm Sunday. *Westm* R. iii p ii 887
Feb. 15.	William de Skipwyth is appointed chief justice in Ireland *Westm* R iii p ii 887
Feb 17.	The K appoints William Brigge, John Scrope, and Roger Enyas to act for the executors of Lionel late duke of Clarence, in Ireland. *Westm.* R. iii. p ii 887 O vi 649. H. iii. p ii 168
Feb 18	Protection for John de Hastynges, earl of Pembroke, and 47 others in the retinue of the prince of Wales *Westm* R iii p ii 888
Feb 28	Safe conduct for David de Bruys to come to England *Westm.* R. iii. p ii. 888. O vi 651 H iii p ii 168
March 19	Restitution of the temporalities to William de Courteney, bp of Hereford late canon of York *Westm* R. iii p ii 889.
March 20	Licence to Simon bp of London to imprison Nicholas de Drayton, convicted of heresy *Westm* R iii. p ii 889. O vi 651 H iii p ii 169
March 22.	The sheriffs of Norfolk and Suffolk, Essex and Hertfordshire, and of Cambridgeshire and Huntingdonshire, are ordered to proclaim that victuals are to be sent for the supply of the fleet at Orewell. *Westm* R iii p ii 889 O vi 651 H iii p ii 169
April 12.	Safe conducts for William bp of S Andrew's, sir Robert de Erskyn, and John de Carryk, canon of Glasgow, ambassadors from David de Bruys *Westm* R iii p ii 889 O vi 652 H. iii. p ii 169.
April 20	Inspeximus and confirmation of the grant by the prince of Wales of the county of Bigorre to John de Grely, captal de Beuche, dated Angoulême, 27 June 1369. Intimation thereof to the inhabitants of Bigarre *Westm* R iii p ii 890

DATE	SUBJECT
1370 April 22	Letters of safe conduct for the doge and people of Venice *Westm* R iii. p. ii. 890 O vi 653 H iii p ii 169
May 6.	The several sheriffs are ordered to proclaim that all persons intending to serve in Normandy are to be at Southampton before July 1, to accompany Robert Knolles *Westm* R iii p ii 890 O vi 653 H iii p ii 169
May 10.	Commission to sir Hugh Cheyne, Thomas Beaupeny, and two others to arrest ships from Weymouth to Moushole, and bring them to Dartmouth 14 similar commissions for other parts of the coast *Westm* R iii p ii 890
May 12	John lord of Gumeny is appointed captain of Arde *Westm* R iii. p ii 891
May 12	Safe conduct for two ships conveying victuals and other goods to Robert de Knolles in Brittany *Westm* R iii p ii 892
May 18.	Power to sir John atte Wode and Robert de Wykford, archdeacon of Winchester, to treat with Wenceslaus duke of Brabant *Westm* R iii. p ii 892 O vi 654 H iii p ii 170.
May 30	Guy Bryane is appointed admiral from the Thames westwards, and John de Neville of Raby from the Thames northward. *Westm* R iii p ii 892
June 4	Respite to David de Bruys until June 24 for the annual payment of 4,000 marks due on Feb 2 *Westm* R iii p ii 892 O vi. 654 H iii p ii 170
June 4	Letters obligatory of David de Bruys for the 52,000 marks which he owes to the K *London.* R. iii p ii 893 O vi 655 H iii p ii 170
June 10	Commission for the appointment of justices in Aquitain, the names to be filled up by the prince of Wales *Westm.* R. iii p ii 893
June 13	The K assigns the loan of 2,000 marks from Thomas bp of Durham, to be repaid from the triennial tenth of the provinces of York and Durham *Westm* R iii p ii. 893 O vi 655 H iii p ii 170
June 16.	Safe conduct for Peter de Terturon, secretary of the K of Navarre, and for William Dordane. *Westm* R iii p ii 893 O vi 655 H iii p ii 170
June 17.	Obligation of 1,000*l.* of Florimond lord de la Sparre *London* R iii p ii. 893 O vi 656. H iii. p ii 170.
June 17	Acquittance of Florymond lord de la Sparre for the K's debts to his father *London* R iii. p ii. 894 O vi 656 H iii p ii 170
June 28	Memorandum that William bp of Winchester, chancellor, delivered to sir Arnald Savage the confirmation of the prince's grant of Bigorre to the captal de Buch. R iii p ii 894
July 1	Safe conduct for Pascalotus Ususmaris, ambassador of the duke of Genoa *Westm* R. iii. p ii 894. O vi 657. H iii p ii 171
July 1.	Power for John duke of Lancaster to receive the fealty of persons in Aquitain and elsewhere in France, and to punish felony and treason *Westm.* R iii p ii 894
July 1.	Sir Robert de Knolles, sir Aleyn de Buxhill, the K's chamberlain, sir Thomas de Granson, Sir John Bourcher are appointed the K's lieutenants in France *Westm* R iii. p ii 894
July 3	John Chidvok, Edmund Cheyne, sheriff of Dorset, John de Hale, and Thomas de Bridport are ordered to send 100 men-at-arms and 100 archers to go abroad with the earls of Warwick and Suffolk Two similar commissions. *Westm* R iii. p ii 895
July 5.	Exemplification of the fourteen years truce with Scotland. *Westm.* R iii p ii 895 O vi 657 H iii p ii 171
July 5.	Thomas bp of Carlisle, Gilbert de Umframvill, earl of Angus, Roger de Clifford, William Latymer, steward of the household, and sir Henry le Scrop are appointed wardens of the West March Henry le Percy, John le Nevill, Thomas bp of Durham, and three others are appointed wardens of the East March *Westm* R iii p ii 895 O vi. 657 H. iii. p ii. 171
July 6	John de Nevill and Guy de Bryene, admirals of the K's fleet, are ordered to provide ships to convey Robert de Knolles to France Similar commissions to Richard de Pembrugg, constable of Dover Castle and warden of the Cinque Ports, and to nine others *Westm* R iii p. ii. 896 O vi 658 H iii p ii 171
July 8	Inspeximus and ratification of a declaration by sir Robert Knolles that any towns or castles between the Seine and Loire given into his charge by the K shall have liberty to govern themselves Dated London, 1 July 1367 *Westm* R iii p ii 896

DATE	SUBJECT
1370. July 8.	Inspeximus and confirmation of the promise by sir Robert Knolles of a share in the profits of the expedition to Alayn de Buxhill, the K's chamberlain, sir Thomas de Grauntzoun, and sir John Bourch Dated London, 13 June, 1367 *Westm* R m. p n 897
July 8	Ralph de Ferrers is appointed admiral of the fleet for the transport of sir Robert Knolles *Westm.* R m p. n. 897.
July 8	Licence to John de Botheby, chancellor of Ireland, to retain six men-at-arms and 12 archers at the K's expense *Westm.* R m p n 897
July 10.	Exemplification of the engagement of sir Walter FitzWalter, John de Lisle of Wodyton, and 11 others about to serve in France with sir Robert Knolles. Dated Westm , 5 July, 1367. *Westm.* R m p n. 897
July 10.	John de Harlaston is appointed warden of Guisnes castle *vice* Ralph de Ferrers *Westm* R m p. n 898.
Aug. 4.	Confirmation of the treaty with the count and commonalties of Flanders. *Clarendon* R m p n 898. O vi 659 H m p n 172
Aug 6.	Release of William Maillart, burgess of Lisle, and Engerran Pylat, burgess of Douay, French hostages. *Clarendon* R. m. p n 898
Aug. 12	Safe conduct for the K of Navarre to pass through England *Clarendon* R m p ii 899 O vi 661. H m p n 172.
Aug 14	The K informs lord de Latymer and Roger de Beauchamp that he has concluded an abstinence of war with the K of Navarre *Clarendon* R m p n 899 O vi 662 H m. p n 172
Aug 14.	Restitution of the temporalities to Henry Dispenser, bp. of Norwich, late canon of Salisbury *Clarendon* R m p n 900.
Sept. 6.	Adam de Bury, of London, is appointed mayor of Calais *Westm* R. m p ii 900.
Sept 7	Richard de Preston, Richard Lyouns, and 10 others are appointed aldermen of Calais *Westm* R m. p n 900.
Sept. 14	Hugh de Courteney, earl of Devon, is ordered to array the men of the county, as an invasion by the French is expected Similar letter to the abbot of Quarre, Theobald Gorges, and two others in the Isle of Wight. *Havering* R. m p n 900 O, vi 662 H m. p n 173.
Sept 23	The K orders the mayor and bailiffs of Bristol, Walter de Frompton, and three others to array the men of Bristol *Westm.* R. m. p n, 901.
Sept. 14	Pope Urban [V] writes to the K in favour of the owners of certain Genoese ships laden with wool and cloth taken by the English *Avignon.* R m p n 901 O vi 663 H iii. p. n 173.
Oct 28	The K informs the sheriff of Kent and five others that the proclamation against forestallers does not apply to ecclesiastics *Westm.* R. m p n. 901
Nov 10	John duke of Lancaster, the prince of Wales, Walter de Manny lord of Merioneth, and 19 other lords are ordered to fortify their castles in Wales *Westm* R m. p n. 901. O vi 664 H m p n 173
Nov 12	The K commits the duchess of Brittany to the charge of Godfrey Folejambe with an annuity of 105*l*, payable from the rents of High Peak Castle. Isabella, widow of John Delves, is ordered to deliver the duchess to him, and the warden of the castle is ordered to pay the annuity *Westm* R. m p n 902 O vi 664 H iii. p n 174
Nov 12	The sheriffs of Kent, Southampton, Sussex, and seven other counties are ordered to array their men for the defence of the coast against the French *Westm.* R m p n 902 O vi 665 H m p. n 174.
Nov 17.	Safe conduct for John de Carryk, chancellor of David de Bruys and for Sir Duncan Walas of Scotland. *Westm.* R m. p ii. 902 O. vi 666 H. m. p ii 174
Nov 26	Alan de Buxhall is appointed captain of S Sauveur in Normandy, *vice* William Latymer. *Westm.* R m p ii. 903
Nov. 26.	The K desires him to order the men of war in the Cotentin to go elsewhere, as there is a truce with the K. of Navarre *Westm* R m p n. 903. O. vi. 666 H iii. p n. 174
Nov 26.	Commissions to Alan de Buxhill, lord Robert de Knolles, sir Thomas de Graunson, and sir John Burghchier to perform the treaty with the K of Navarre *Westm* R. m p. n. 903 O vi 667 H m p n 175.
Nov 28	Safe conduct for the K of Navarre to come to England *Westm.* R m p n 904 O vi. 668 H m p n 175

DATE	SUBJECT
1370 Nov 28	Commission to John lord de Neville, sir Guy de Brienne, the K.'s admirals, Peter de Lascy, canon of Dublin, keeper of the Privy Seal, and Thomas Juvenis to treat with the duke and commonalty of Genoa　*Westm*　R iii p ii 904　O. vi. 670　H iii p ii 176
Nov 29.	Release of Baldwin de Buloigne and Nicholas Dane, burgesses of S Omer, French hostages, on payment of 1,500 francs　*Westm.*　R iii. p ii 905
Dec. 1.	Release of George de Clere, French hostage, on payment of 400 marks.　*Westm*　R iii p. ii. 905　O vi. 671　H. iii p ii 176
Dec 1.	Safe conduct for Sancius Lupi de Uricio　*Westm*　R iii. p ii 905　O vi 671.　H iii p ii 176
Dec. 1.	Safe conducts for John de Telly, Guillerm des Trois Monts, abbot of S Mary *de Boto*, near Cherbourg, and for Peter de Tertre, secretary of the K of Navarre　*Westm.*　R iii p ii 905　O vi 672　H iii p ii 176
Dec 5	Safe conduct for Pascalotus Ususmaris, Genoese ambassador　*Westm*　R iii p ii 906　O vi 672　H iii p ii 177
Dec 6.	Dominicus de Campofregoso, duke of Genoa, desires restitution for ships belonging to Andrew Spinula and Obert Squartzafico, taken by Englishmen　*Genoa*　R iii p ii. 906　O vi 673　H iii. p ii. 177.
Dec 7	Dominicus Campofregoso, duke of Genoa, to Pasqualotus Ususmaris, on the business above mentioned.　*Genoa*　R iii p ii 906　O vi 673　H iii p ii 177
Dec 12.	The K orders the bailiffs of Lenn and Hull to search persons arriving from abroad for letters and papal bulls.　*Westm*　R iii p ii 907　O vi. 676.　H. iii p ii 178.
1371 Jan. 1	The K restores the ships taken from the merchants of Genoa.　*London*　R iii p ii 907　O vi 676　H iii p ii 178
Jan. 22.	The K of England informs the K. of Navarre that the prince of Wales will not agree to the treaty with him　*Westm*　R iii. p ii 907.　O vi 677　H iii p ii 178
	Inspeximus of a minute on the rolls of the chancery notifying the K's resumption of the title of K of France　R iii p ii 908
Jan. 26.	The K orders Simon bp. of London to reform the abuses in S Paul's Cathedral　*Westm*　R iii p ii 908　O vi. 678　H iii p ii 179
Jan 26	Commissions to John Haukyn, sergeant-at-arms, and James Lyouns to arrest ships and bring them to Lenn　*Westm*　R iii p ii 909.
Feb 3	The K orders proclamations to be made by the sheriff of Southampton and six others that all persons having tenements in the Isle of Wight are to go thither for its defence　*Westm*　R iii p ii 909
Feb. 3.	Confirmation of the treaty with Genoa　*Westm*　R iii p ii 909　O vi. 679.　H iii p ii 179
Feb. 6.	The K orders proclamation of the above treaty to be made.　*Westm*　R iii p ii 910　O vi 682　H iii p ii. 180
Feb 8	The K forbids corn or other victuals to be taken out of the Isle of Wight　*Westm*　R iii p ii 911
Feb 14	Writs to 21 sheriffs to send arrows to the Tower of London.　*Westm*　R iii p ii 911
Feb 24	Grant by Edward prince of Wales of the bailiwick of Marempne to the Sondan de la Trau, for his services at the siege of Montpaon　*Bordeaux*　R iii. p. ii 911.　O vi 683　H iii p ii 181
March 14	Memorandum of the delivery of the great seal to the K by William bp of Winchester, and of the delivery of the said seal to Sir Robert de Thorp, who is appointed the K.'s chancellor　*Westm*　R iii p ii 911　O vi 683　H iii p ii 181
March 18	Commission to Walter de Wodeburgh, sergeant-at-arms, to arrest ships in the Severn and bring them to Plymouth　*Westm*　R iii p ii 912
March 27.	The K desires the abps of Canterbury and York to summon convocations for the purpose of granting a subsidy　*Westm*　R iii p ii 912
March 28	Memorandum of the delivery of four seals to the K by William bp of Winchester, late chancellor.　*Westm*　R iii p ii 912　O vi 683　H iii p ii 181.
April 21	Grant of annuities of 25 marks to John de Claront, a Flemish knight, and Diederic Van Hessene, of Cleves　*Westm*　R iii p ii 912　O vi 684　H iii p ii 181.
April 21	Pope Gregory [XI.] commends to the K Howell bp elect of Bangor　*Avignon*　R iii p ii 912　O vi 684　H. iii. p ii 181

DATE	SUBJECT
1371 April 27.	Prorogation of the truce with Navarre until Michaelmas. *Westm* R iii p. ii 913. O vi 685 H iii p ii 182
April 27.	Confirmation by Louis count of Flanders of the treaty between him and the commonalties of Flanders and the K Dated 4 Aug, 44 Edw III *Ghent* R iii. p ii 913 O vi 686 H. iii. p ii 182
April 28	Release of John de Grey, of Codnore, from attendance at parliament and from serving on commissions of array, or of the peace *Westm* R iii p ii 914.
May 1	Nicholas de Tamworth is appointed captain of Calais. *Westm* R iii p ii 914.
May 8	The K. orders the treaty with Flanders to be published in Calais and in 26 ports of England *Henley* R. iii. p ii 914. O. vi. 687 H. iii p ii. 182
May 29.	Exemplification of the obligation of David de Bruys, dated 4 June 1370. *Westm* R iii p ii. 915. O. vi. 687 H iii p ii 182
May 12	Restitution of the temporalities to Alexander bp of Ossory, late canon of Ossory *Guildford.* R. iii p. ii, 915.
May 20	The K. appoints Bardet de Maleprilys, of Florence, master of the mint at Calais. *Westm.* R iii p. ii 915
May 24	The K orders John de Neville, admiral to the north of the Thames, to restore the vessel called *la Bone Huere*, belonging to merchants of Bruges Letters to Nicholas de Tamworth, captain, William de Gunthorp, treasurer of Calais, and Guy de Briène, admiral west of the Thames, for the restitution of other Flemish ships *Westm.* R. iii. p ii 917.
May 30 *	The K , having heard that French are preparing to invade England, commands John de Clynton to repair to his manor of Folkestone, in co Kent, with all his power, to defend those parts *Westm* R iii p ii. 942 O vi 688 H iii p ii 183
June 3	Alan de Buxhull is appointed captain of S. Sauveur in Normandy *Westm* R iii p ii 917.
June 4.	William Dareys is appointed warden of Oterwyk Castle, *vice* Godfrey de Roos *Westm* R iii p ii 918
June 4	Herman de Bosco is appointed warden of Oye Castle, *vice* William de Hoo *Westm.* R iii p ii 918.
June 12.	The K orders the several sheriffs to proclaim that no tax will be imposed on wool without the consent of parliament *Westm.* R iii p. ii 918
June 12.	Letter on the same subject to the customers of Hull and 11 other towns. *Westm* R iii p ii 918
June 14	Release to the burgesses of Portsmouth of their annual rent to the K , the town having been burnt. *Winchester* R. iii p ii. 918.
June 18.	The K forbids the circulation of Scotch or other foreign money in England *Winchester* R iii p ii 919.
June 20.	Safe conduct for John le Manner, a French hostage. *Winchester.* R iii. p. ii. 919. O vi. 688 H iii p ii 183
June 20.	The K orders the sheriffs of Northumberland and Yorkshire and the mayor of York to forward to London the 4,000 marks due from the late David de Bruys *Westm.* R iii p ii 919 O vi. 688 H iii p ii 183
June 26	The K of England acknowledges to have received 4,000 marks from Robert K. of Scotland *Westm* R iii p ii 919 O vi 689 H iii p ii 183.
July 1.	The K orders the commissioners of the peace in Wilts, Somerset, and Dorset, to arrest those who impugn the K's right of presentation to the prebend of Bere and Charminster *Westm.* R iii. p ii. 920 O vi 690 H iii p ii 183
July 1.	Power to sir Nicholas de Lovaign, Robert de Wykford, and Adam de Bury, mayor of Calais, to treat with the commonalties of Flanders for the redress of injuries *London.* R iii p. ii. 920. O vi 690 H. iii. p. ii 183.
July 1	Safe conduct for sir Nicholas de Lovaign and his colleagues *London* R iii p ii 920
July 14.	Safe conduct for Andrew Peyntour, coming to London to provide for the funeral of David de Bruys *Westm* R iii p ii 920 O vi 691 H iii p. ii 184.
Aug 7.	The K summons to his council at Westminster the bp of Waterford and Lismore, the dean of Dublin, Stephen Bray, and two others, to treat of Irish affairs *Westm* R iii. p ii 920
Aug 10	Commission to sir Nichol de Lovaigne, Nicholas de Tamworth, captain of Calais, John de Shepeye, and John Pyel, to treat with the ambassadors of Flanders at Calais *Westm* R iii p ii 921 O vi 691 H iii p ii 184
Aug 10	Adam de Bury is appointed mayor of Calais *Westm.* R iii p ii 921

* This instrument apparently belongs to 30 May 1372. See p 460, 30 May

DATE	SUBJECT
1371 Aug 26	The mayors and bailiffs of Hull and eight other ports are ordered to arrest Flemings and their goods *Westm* R. iii p ii 921
Aug 19	The K assigns the repayment of the loan of 2,000 marks from Thomas bp of Durham, on the triennial tenth in the provinces of York and Durham *Westm* R iii p ii 921 O vi 692 H iii p ii 184
Sept 6.	Grant to William Humfray, of Boole, of the fruits of the benefice of S Ewayn, in the Isle of Jersey, the bp of Coutances being the K.'s enemy. Similar grants of the benefices of S Helier and S Pierre to Roger de Walden and John Condit *Westm* R iii p. ii. 922. O vi 692 H iii. p ii 184
Sept 10	The K forbids William de Wyndesore to levy the sums for which he has extorted grants from the commonalty of Dublin *Westm* R iii p ii 922
[Sept 10]	Similar letter concerning grants made by the commonalty of Drogheda R iii p ii 922.
Sept 17	Commission of Dominicus de Campofregoso, duke of Genoa, and the council, to Conrad Catanei, to require from the K of England the performance of his obligations *Genoa* R iii p ii 922 O vi 693 H iii p ii 184
Sept 25	Gregory [XI] asks the K. to obtain from John de Greli, captal de Buet [Buch,] the release of his holiness's brother, Roger de Belloforti *Villeneuve* R iii p ii. 923 · O vi 695 H iii. p ii 185
Oct. 6.	Sir Ralph de Ferrers is appointed admiral north of the Thames and sir Robert de Assheton west of the Thames. *Westm.* R iii p. ii. 923
Oct. 10.	The K. writes to the treasurer and barons of the Exchequer in Ireland concerning the extortions of William de Wyndesore on the citizens of Dublin *Westm* R iii p ii. 924
Oct. 14	Safe conduct for John de Rednash and three other Genoese merchants *Westm.* R iii p. ii. 924 O vi 695. H iii p ii 185
Oct. 18.	Gregory [XI] recommends to the K Arnald Guarneru, canon of Chalons, whom he has appointed collector in England *Avignon* R iii p ii 924. O vi 696 H iii p ii 186
Oct. 20	The K rebukes William de Wyndesore, his lieutenant in Ireland, for his extortions *Westm* R iii. p ii 924
Oct. 25	William de Ufford, earl of Suffolk, William de Bardolf, of Wyrmegeye, and William de Morle, are ordered to protect the coast of Norfolk and Suffolk Henry Rose is appointed captain of Yarmouth *Westm* R iii p ii 925
Oct 27	Licence to Philip de Norton, vicar of S Giles beyond Cripplegate, to go to the court of Rome *Westm* R iii p ii 925
Oct 28	Treaty between Robert K of Scotland and Charles K of France *Edinburgh* R iii p ii 925 O vi. 698 H iii p ii 187
Nov 1.	Power for sir Robert de Novylle and Raulyn Barry, squire of the chamber, to treat with the duke of Brittany touching the delivery of Becherel *Westm.* R iii p ii 926 O vi 698 H iii p ii 187
Nov 4	Power for the same commissioners to treat for a perpetual alliance *Westm* R iii p ii 927 O vi 699 H iii p ii 187
[Nov 4]	Power for the same commissioners to deliver Becherel to the duke of Brittany *Westm* R iii p ii 927 O vi 701 H iii p ii 187
[Nov 4]	Power for the said commissioners to deliver Chisek, Melle, and Cynray to the duke of Brittany R iii p ii 928 O vi 701. H iii p ii 188
Nov. 5.	Safe conduct for John de Vinere, of France, servant of the lord of Roy *Westm* R. iii p ii 928 O vi. 702 H iii p. ii 188
Nov. 10	Grant of a messuage in Calais to John de Hastinges, earl of Pembroke *Westm* R. iii p ii 928
Nov 12.	The K commands William de Wyndesore, his lieutenant in Ireland, not to institute proceedings against the commonalties of Dublin, Drogheda, or other places, for resisting certain impositions extorted by him *Westm* R. iii p ii 928
Nov 13.	Gregory [XI] sends two cardinals to exhort the Kings of England and France to preserve peace *Avignon* R iii p ii 929 O vi 702 H iii p ii 188
Dec. 3	The K orders proclamation to be made at Bristol and 16 other ports that Portuguese merchants are to be allowed to trade in England *Westm* R iii. p. ii. 929. O vi 703 H iii p ii 188
Dec. 6	Safe conducts for Gancaleo Grande, master of the ship called " la Seinte Marie," and three other Portuguese ship masters *Westm* R iii p ii 929 O. vi 703. H iii. p ii 188.

DATE	SUBJECT
1371. Dec 6	William de Cranewell, steward of the prince of Wales, in Cornwall is ordered to release the above-mentioned ships from arrest. *Westm.* R iu p. u 929 O vi. 704. H. iii p u. 189.
Dec 8	The K orders the treasurer and barons of the Exchequer in Ireland to release John Frombold, mayor of Drogheda, arrested by command of William de Wyndesore *Westm* R iii p u 930
Dec 21	The K forbids the sale of ships to foreigners *Westm* R ui p. u 930
1372 Jan 21.	Pope Gregory [XI] expresses his pleasure that negotiations have been commenced for a peace between England and France *Avignon* R. iii. p n. 930 O v 704. H iii. p. u 189
Jan 23.	Protection for the cardinal of Beauvais, sent by the pope, to negociate the peace *Westm* R. iii p u. 930 O. vi. 705 H iii p u 189.
Jan 26	Declaration of the peace concluded between England and Genoa. *Westm.* R. iii. p u 931 O vi 706 H iii p u 189
Jan 30	Receipt by Corrad Catanei, Genoese ambassador, of 2,000 marks, in redress for the capture of the ship called *Le Beyard.* *London* R iii p u 931 O vi 707 H iii p u 190
Feb 2	The K. exempts the merchants of Bayonne from the tax of 3*d.* in the pound on their merchandise and goods *Westm.* R. iii p u 932
Feb 6	Power for sir Henry Lescrope, sir Hugh de Segrave, John Shepeye, Adam de Bury, and John Pyel to treat with the count and commonalty of Flanders *Westm* R iii p u. 932
Feb 7	Power for the cardinal of Canterbury and sir Henry Lescrope to grant safe conducts to the Flemish commissioners. *Westm* R iii p u 932.
Feb 7	Commission to Walter Haule, sergeant-at-arms, to arrest ships for the K's passage to France Seven similar commissions to other persons *Westm* R iii p u 933 O. vi 708 H iii p u 190.
Feb. 10.	The K substitutes Roger de Freton, dean of Chichester, for John de Shepeye in the commission for treating with Flanders *Westm* R iii p u. 933
Feb. 13.	Oath of fealty taken by Arnaud Garnier, papal receiver in England *Westm* R. iii p u 933 O. vi 709 H iii p u 191.
Feb. 16.	The K orders the abbot of S Maxentius, John Reynaut, and four others to hear the appeal of John Gyrard and Marie Lunelle, his wife. *Westm* R iii p u 934 O vi 710 H iii p u 191
Feb 19.	Power for Simon bp of London, sir Guy de Bryene, sir Roger Beauchamp, sir Arnald Savage, John de Appelby, dean of London, and John de Branketre, treasurer of York, to treat with the K of France *Westm* R iii p u. 934
Feb 20	Safe conduct for the French ambassadors coming to treat for peace *London.* Also for the bp of Laon, the dean of Paris, the lord of Chastillon, and Ingelram de Hedon *Westm.*, 3 *March* R. iii p u 935 O vi 711 H iii p u 191-2
Feb. 20.	Power for Simon bp of London, sir Guy de Bryenne, and sir Roger de Beauchamp, to grant safe conducts to Frenchmen *Westm* R iii p u 935.
Feb. 20.	Writ to the sheriffs of London to release from prison John Daummartyn, clerk of the cardinal de Agrifolio. *Westm* R iii p u 935 O vi. 710. H iii. p. u 191
Feb. 21	John duke of Brittany promises to maintain his alliance with the K of England *Vannes* R iii p u 935 O vi 712 H iii p u 192
Feb. 25.	Commission by the duke of Brittany to Thomas de Melburn to treat with the K of England *Aubrey* R iii p ii 936 O vi 712 H iii p u. 192
Feb. 25.	The duke of Brittany also empowers Thomas de Melburn to accept in his name the duchy of Richmond and the marches between Brittany and Pocitou *Aubrey.* R. iii. p u 936 O vi. 713 H. iii p u. 192
Feb. 26	The K. orders Thomas bp of Durham, Henry de Percy, Gilbert de Umframvill, earl of Angus, and three others to remain on the marches for their defence. *Westm* R iii p. u. 936 O vi 713 H iii p u 192.
Feb 26	The K. orders the bp of Durham and the sheriffs of Northumberland, Westmoreland, and Cumberland to forbid men-at-arms leaving the country *Westm* R. iii. p u 936. O vi 714 H. iii p u 192
Feb 26	The arrayers of the five northern counties are ordered to prepare their men for the defence of the realm against the Scots *Westm* R. iii p u 936.

DATE	SUBJECT
1372 March 3	Safe conduct for John Roche, of Zealand, going to Prussia for the K *Westm* R m p II 937 O vi. 714 H m p II 193
March 3.	Inspeximus and confirmation of the confirmation by the prince of Wales of a grant of Richard I to the commonalty of Bayonne, dated 16 Oct , 2 Ric. I. *Westm.* R. ih. p II 937.
March 7	Philip de Courtenay is appointed admiral west of the Thames, and William de Neville admiral north of the Thames *Westm* R m p II 937
March 24	Safe conduct for Peter van Campe, going to Flanders for the ransom of John Blome, prisoner of Robert Haulee *Westm* R m p. II. 938 O vi. 714 H m p II 193.
March 28.	The K orders the peace with Flanders to be proclaimed in London, Lenn, and other ports *Eltham* R m p II 938. O vi 715 H m p II 193
April 4	Commissions to Philip de Courtenay, the K.'s admiral to the west of the Thames, Walter de Haule, Thomas Fishacre, and the bailiffs of 16 seaports, to arrest ships for the K.'s passage *Westm* R m p II 938 O vi 715 H m p II 193
April 5.	Confirmation of the treaty with Flanders *Westm* R m p II 938. O vi 716 H m. p II 193
April 7.	Power for sir Hugh de Calverley, Reymund Guillaume de Puy, judge of Bourdeaux, and two others to treat with Peter K of Arragon *Westm* R m p II. 939
April 7	Licence to John Suerd, of York, to export Rhine wine to Prussia *Westm.* R. m p II 940. O vi 718 H m p II 194
April 12.	The K orders William de Latymer, constable of Dover Castle and warden of the Cinque Ports, to provide six ships of war *Westm.* R m p II 940
April 16	The K. appoints the abp of S Maxentius his chancellor in Aquitain *London* R m. p II 940
April 17	The K. appoints the abp of Bourdeaux, the bp of Poictiers, the abbots of S Severin and S Maxentius, Florimond lord de le Sparre, Berard de Lebret, and two others, judges of resort in Aquitain *Westm* R m p II 940 O. vi 719 H m p II 195
April 18.	The K orders his officers in Aquitain and elsewhere to assist Charles d'Artoys, count of Pesenatz, in making war on France *Westm* R m p II 941 O vi. 720 H m. p. II 195.
April 20	The K appoints John earl of Pembroke his lieutenant in Aquitain. *Westm* R m. p II. 941.
May 6	Roger de Beauchamp is appointed captain of Calais, *vice* Nicholas de Tamworth. *Westm.* R. m p II 941
May 6.	William de Risceby, junior, is appointed warden of Calais Castle Intimation thereof to Nicholas de Tamworth *Westm* R m p II 941
May 22	The K forbids the treasurer and barons of the Exchequer in Ireland exacting scutage from persons whose lands are in the possesssion of the rebels Similar letter to Milo de Courcy *Westm* R m p II 942
May 24	Safe conduct for William Guppill and Andrew Payntour to provide a stone for the tomb of David de Bruys *Westm* R m p II 942 O vi 721 H m p II 195
May 24	Licence to William de Patrington, John de Wulseleye, and Geoffrey Mason to go to Scotland to make the tomb of David de Bruys *Westm.* R m p II 942 O vi 721 H m p II 195
May 28	The K orders Robert de Assheton, justiciary of Ireland, to revoke, with the consent of parliament, certain customs imposed by William de Wyndesore. *Westm.* R. m p II. 942.
May 30	The K orders John de Clynton to go to his manor of Folkestone, as a French fleet is reported to be ready to invade the kingdom *Westm.* R m p. II 942 See p 457, 30 May
June 1	Power for John lord de Nevill to treat with John duke of Brittany *Westm* R m p II 943 O vi 721. H m p II 195
	Instructions to lord de Nevill relative to the above mentioned treaty R m p II 943 O vi 722. H m. p. II 196.
June 8	The K forbids the exportation of wine *Westm* R. m p I 943
June 8.	The K allows the exportation of corn to friendly countries *Westm* R m p II 943.
June 8	The K orders the sheriff of Hampshire to proclaim that all persons having lands in the Isle of Wight are to go thither for its defence. *Westm* R II p II. 944

DATE	SUBJECT
1372. June 9	The K. appoints the abbot of Quarre, Ralph de Wolverton, William de Ryngebourn, and Laurence de Lisle, wardens of the coast of the Isle of Wight. *Westm* R. iii. p. ii. 944. O. vi 723 H iii p ii 196
June 10.	Safe conduct for the lord of Ghistel, Philip Masinnies, Gossum le Wilde, the dean of Bruges, chancellor of Flanders, and 15 other Flemish commissioners *Westm* R iii. p. ii. 944
June 10	Power for sir Henry Lescrop and four others to treat with the above-named persons *Westm* R iii p ii 945.
June 11.	Power for John de Appelby, dean of London, and John de Thorp to treat with duke Albert of Bavaria *Westm* R iii p ii 945 O. vi. 724 H iii p n 196
June 12.	The K orders William la Zouche, Thomas West, William de Melton, and 10 others to go to their lands on the coast of Hampshire. *Westm* R. iii p ii, 945
June 12	The K. orders proclamation to be made in Hampshire for the defence of the coast, as the French are preparing to invade the country. *Westm* R. iii p ii. 946
June 12.	Similar proclamations to be made in Kent, the Isle of Wight, and 11 other counties. *Westm* R iii p ii 946.
June 13.	Commission to Peter Manlay, warden, and John de Bolton, chamberlain of Berwick, Aleyn del Strother, sheriff of Roxburgh, and the sheriff of Northumberland, to send the next instalment of the ransom of David de Bruys to York *Westm* R iii p ii 946. O. vi 724 H iii p ii 197.
June 15.	Power for John de Appelby, dean of London, and John de Thorp to surrender the K's right to lands in Holland through the late Q. Philippa *Westm* R. iii p ii 947 O vi 725. H iii p ii 197
June 16	The K orders the abps. of Canterbury and York to array the ecclesiastics of their provinces to resist the expected invasion of the French *Westm* R. iii. p ii. 947. O vi 726 H. iii p ii 197
June 18.	The K. orders the bailiffs of Canterbury and Rochester to have horses ready for the use of messengers coming to the K from abroad *Westm* R iii p ii 947 O vi 727 H. iii p. ii 197
June 18	The arrayers of all the counties, except Kent, Sussex, Southampton and Wilts, are ordered to array the men of their several counties, and to place beacons on the hills *Westm* R iii. p. ii. 947.
June 23	Obligation of Margaret widow of David Bruys for 500 marks lent by Adam Franceys and other merchants *Avignon* R iii p ii 948 O vi 727 H. iii p ii 198
June 23	Protection for John de Nevill, and for sir Henry Gramary, and 11 others in his retinue. *Westm* R iii p ii 948
June 25	John K of Castile, duke of Lancaster surrenders the earldom of Richmond to his father the K of England in exchange for certain lands. *London* R iii. p. ii 948 O vi 728 H iii p n 198
June 25.	The K grants to his son John duke of Lancaster, the manors of Tykhill, High Peak, Knaresborough, Gryngeley, Whetelay, Wighton, Ailesham, and several other places *Westm* R iii. p ii. 949 O vi. 729–31 H iii. p ii. 199.
June 26	Letters Patent for the delivery of the above-mentioned lands. *Westm* R. iii. p ii 950. O vi. 732 H iii. p ii 199.
June 26.	Notification to tenants of the lands referred to in the above-mentioned grant. *Westm* R iii p ii 950 O vi 733. H. iii p ii 200
[June 26].	Similar letters to the tenants of Tikhill and High Peak, &c. R. iii. p. ii. 951. O. vi. 734 H iii p ii 200
June 26.	Receipt of 4,000 marks from Robert K of Scotland *Westm* R iii p. ii. 951. O vi 734. H iii. p ii 200
June 27.	Safe conduct for the bp. of Carpentras, the viscount of Torrayne, and other papal nuncios who are about to leave England *Westm* R. iii p ii. 951. O. vi 734. H. iii p ii. 200,
June 29.	Memorandum of the death of Sir Robert de Thorp, the K's chancellor, at the house of the bp of Salisbury, in Fleet Street, London, and of the appointment of Sir John Knyvet as chancellor on July 5. R iii p ii 951. O. vi 735. H. iii. p ii 201.
July 10.	Agreement of the English and Flemish commissioners that the decision of claims for redress shall be deferred until Candlemas. *Calais.* R. iii p ii. 951. O. vi 735. H. iii. p ii 201

DATE	SUBJECT
1372 July 14	John duke of Lancaster empowers sir John de Stafford and two others to deliver the manor of S Botolph in co Lincoln and other appurtenances of the earldom of Richmond to the K his father *The Savoy* R iii p ii 952. O vi. 736 H iii. p ii. 201.
July 13.	Similar commission from John duke of Lancaster to John Wenteburg and Thomas Wilham to deliver the manor of Chesthunt in co Hertford to the K *The Savoy* R iii p ii 952 O vi 736 H iii p ii 201
July 15	Sir Stephen de Valence, Sir William Pympe, and John Colepepir are ordered to assist the wardens of the coast of Kent *Westm.* R iii p ii 952.
July 16	The duke of Lancaster desires the clergy, nobles, and others in the county of Richmond to assist the K's officers in respect to the grants above mentioned *The Savoy* R iii p ii 952 O vi 737 H iii p ii 202
July 16.	The K orders the abbot of S Augustine's, Canterbury, to repair to his lands in the Isle of Thanet in co Kent for the defence of the same. *Westm* R iii p ii. 953.
July 18	The K orders proclamations to be issued forbidding any molestation of Flemish merchants *Westm* R iii p ii 953 O vi 737 H iii p ii 202.
July 19	Treaty of alliance offensive and defensive between the K. of England and John duke of Brittany *Westm.* R iii p. ii. 953. O vi. 738. H iii. p ii 202
July 19.	Commission to Richard de Ravenser, archdeacon of Lincoln, to receive the earldom of Richmond in the K's name *Westm* R iii p ii 955
July 20.	Richard de Ravenser archdeacon of Lincoln is appointed attorney for the duke of Brittany in the earldom of Richmond. *Westm.* R. iii. p ii 955 O. vi. 742 H. iii. p i 203.
July 20.	Acquittance for the sums of money due from the duke of Brittany for Becherel and other places *Westm* R iii p ii 955
July 20	The K desires the inhabitants of the earldom of Richmond to obey the officers of the duke of Brittany *Westm* R iii p ii 956 O vi. 743. H. iii p ii 204
[July 20]	The K grants the marches between Poictou and Brittany to the duke of Brittany R iii p ii 956 O vi 743 H iii p ii 204
[July 20]	The K desires the inhabitants of the marches above mentioned to obey the duke of Brittany R iii p ii 956 O vi 744 H. iii p i 204.
July 20.	The K orders the bp of Exeter, Hugh de Courteney, earl of Devon, John de Cheverston, and six others, to array the men of Devon *Westm* R iii p ii 956
July 20	Protection for John Roos of Clynton and 14 others in the retinue of Thomas Kanne *Westm* R iii p ii 957.
July 21	Protection for John Meadow and 16 others in the retinue of Alan de Buxhull. *Westm* R iii p ii 957
July 21.	Adam de Bury is appointed mayor of Calais. *Westm.* R iii p ii 957
July 30.	Protection for sir Robert Corbet, junior, John de Shroveshury, and 11 others in the retinue of William de Ufford, earl of Suffolk *Westm* R. iii p ii. 957
Aug 4	Restitution of the temporalties to W abp of Canterbury, seized for the arrears of the subsidy Similar restitution to the apb of York and 15 bps *Westm* R iii p ii. 958
Aug 5	Memorandum of the delivery into the treasury by John de Brankette of letters concerning the duke of Brittany. R. iii. p. ii 958
Aug 8	Protection of sir Thomas de Cobbeham and 20 others in the retinue of Thomas de Beauchamp, earl of Warwick *Westm.* R iii. p ii. 958.
Aug 8	Notification of the K.'s covenants with the duke of Brittany *Westm* R iii p ii 958
Aug 11.	The K desires the prayers of the apbs and bps of England and Wales *Westm.* R iii p ii 960 O vi 745 H iii p. ii 204
Aug. 12	Safe conduct for sir James de Douglas, son of the earl of Douglas *Westm.* R. iii p ii 960 O vi 746. H. iii. p ii 205
Aug 14	The K. desires Edmund Rose, constable of Gurry Castle, Jersey, and Nicholas le Fevere to send information concerning the property of foreign religious houses *Westm* R iii p ii 960
Aug 20.	Walter deHaule, sergeant-at-arms, is ordered to arrest ships to convey John lord de Nevill and others to Brittany. *Sandwich* R iii. p. ii 961.
[Aug. 20].	Warrants to Thomas Havener, water bailiff in Cornwall, and to five others to arrest sailors R. iii. p. ii. 961.

DATE	SUBJECT
1372. Aug 23	The K. orders sir Richard atte Lees, sir John Normaund, and Richard Cheyne to go to their estates in the Isle of Sheppey, for the protection of the island. *Westm.* R iii p. ii 961 O vi 746 H iii. p ii 205
Aug 24.	The K orders the wardens of the coast of Kent to survey the Isle of Thanet, and to make provision for its defence *Preston* R. iii. p ii 961 O vi. 747 H iii p ii. 205.
Aug 28.	The abbot of S Augustine's, Canterbury, sir Thomas Chicche, Robert Bealknap, and two others are appointed arrayers in the Isle of Thanet Similar commission for the Isle of Sheppey *Preston* R. iii p ii. 961.
Aug 30	Memorandum of the delivery of the great seal by sir John Knyvet, chancellor, to the K, who gave him another seal for use during his absence *Sandwich* R iii p ii 962. O vi 747 H iii p ii 205
Aug 31.	Richard son of Edward prince of Wales is appointed regent during the K's absence *Sandwich* R. iii p ii. 962 O vi 748 H iii p ii 206
Aug 31	Specification of the powers granted to the regent, prince Richard *Sandwich* R iii p. ii 962 O vi 748 H iii p ii 206
Sept 3	The steward and marshal of the K's household are appointed to the same offices in the household of the regent, *teste custode.* *Wallingford* R iii p ii. 963. O vi. 749. H iii p ii. 206
Sept 14	Safe conduct for Bertrand de Chivanhac, and Ralph de Letranges, messengers of the bp of Carpentras, *teste custode* *Wallingford* R. iii. p. ii. 963 O vi 749 H iii p ii 206.
Oct 28	Protection for the marquis of Spinola and nine other Genoese merchants *Westm* R. iii. p ii 963 O vi 75C H iii p ii 206
Oct 29	Pardon for Aleyn de Buxhull for all faults in the performance of his commission as the K's lieutenant in France *Westm* R iii p ii 963
Nov 12.	Power for James Provan, John de Mari, of Genoa, and Geoffrey Chaucer, the K's squire, to treat with Dominicus de Campofregoso, duke of Genoa. *Westm* R iii p ii 964
Nov 22	Declaration by the duke of Brittany of his alliance with the K of England *Brest* R iii. p ii 964 O vi 750 H iii p ii. 206.
Nov 22	The K exempts the burgesses of Portsmouth from the payment of the subsidy granted at the last parliament *Westm* R iii p ii 965
Nov. 22	The K. appoints Peter de Campofregoso, brother of the duke of Genoa, captain of his galleys *Westm* R. iii p ii 965 O vi. 754 H. iii. p ii 208.
Nov 23	Sir James Pronan is appointed under captain of Peter de Campofregoso *Westm* R iii p ii 965 H iii p ii 208
Nov 27.	Commission of Fernando K. of Portugal to John Fernandi de Audeiro and Velasco Dominici to treat with the K of England and the prince of Wales *Ubuar* R iii p ii 966 O vi 754 H iii p. ii. 208.
Nov 12	Power to James Pronan, John de Mari, and Geoffrey Chaucer to treat with the duke of Genoa concerning the grant of a place on the English coast for Genoese merchants *Westm* R iii p ii 966 O vi. 755. H iii p ii. 209
Dec 12	Inspeximus of a petition presented to parliament by the burgesses of Calais concerning their privileges, and the answers hereto *Westm* R. iii. p. ii. 966.
Dec. 12	Commission to Simon, bp. of London, Edmund de Mortimer, earl of March, Guy de Briene, Roger de Beauchamp, captain of Calais, and William de Guuthorp, treasurer of Calais, to ascertain the advisability of granting the petition of the burgesses of Calais to allow them to try pleas according to their ancient laws *Westm.* R iii. p ii. 967
Dec 12	Declaration that the acquittances given to Robert K. of Scotland are valid although he is not named K. of Scotland. *Westm* R. iii. p. ii. 967 O vi 755. H. iii p ii 209.
Dec 12	Safe conduct for David, son of Robert, K of Scotland. *Westm* R iii. p ii 968 O. vi 756 H iii. p ii. 209.
Dec 16	Pope Gregory's dispensation to John Marshal, rector of Swepston, in the dioc of Lincoln, to hold another benefice. *Avignon* R. iii. p. ii 968. O vi 756 H iii p ii. 209.
Dec 19	Grant to the duke of Brittany of all the lands he may conquer in France *Westm.* R. iii. p ii 968. O vi 757 H. iii p ii. 209
[Dec 19]	The K promises that all Englishmen whom the duke receives into his service shall obey him. R. iii p. ii. 968. O. vi 758 H. iii. p. ii. 209.

DATE	SUBJECT
1372 Dec 21	Gregory [XI] refuses the K's request for the annexation of the Church of Hemyngburgh to the prior and chapter of Durham. *Avignon.* R. iii p ii 969. O vi. 759 H iii. p ii 210
1373 Jan 8	Safe conduct for Thomas earl of Marre, of Scotland *Westm* R. iii p ii 969 O vi 760 H iii p ii 210
Jan. 8	Safe conduct for the cardinal of Beauvais, whom the pope sends to England to negotiate a peace with France *Westm.* R. iii p ii. 969. O. vi. 760. H. iii p. ii. 210
Jan 8	Commission to Simon bp of London, Edmund earl of March, Richard de Stafford, and four others to treat for peace with the K of France *Westm.* R. iii. p ii 969 O vi 760 H iii p ii 210
Jan 8	Indenture by which Gregory Us de Meei, and Obert Gay of Genoa, engage to serve the K of England *Westm* R. iii. p ii. 970 O vi 762 H iii p ii. 211.
Jan 9	Oath taken by the above-mentioned commissioners *London* R iii p ii. 970 O vi 763 H iii p ii. 211
Feb 3	Safe conduct for sir Robert de Erskyn, sir Walter de Lessele, and four others of Scotland *Westm.* R iii p ii 970 O vii 1. H. iii. p iii 3
Feb 8	Indenture between the K and William de Montagu, earl of Salisbury, captain of the fleet *London* R iii p ii 971 O vii 2 H iii p iii 3
Feb 16	The K commands all his subjects to obey the earl of Salisbury as captain of the fleet. *Westm.* R. iii p ii 971 O. vii 2 H iii p iii 3
Feb. 14	Safe conduct for a servant of Berard del Bret, prisoner of William de Beauchamp, coming to England *Westm.* R iii p ii 971 O vii 2 H iii p iii 3
Feb. 16	Commission to sir Henry le Scrop, sir Ralph de Hastynges, and Roger de Fulthorp to treat with Scotch commissioners concerning the variances between Henry lord de Percy and William earl of Douglas *Westm* R iii p ii 971. O vii 2. H iii 3
Feb. 20	The K orders Benedict de Bodelsall, lieutenant of Philip de Courtenay, admiral in the west, to release from arrest a ship of Guetary, in the service of John K of Castile and duke of Lancaster *Westm* R iii p ii 971 O vii 3 H iii p iii 4
March 5	Licence to the inhabitants of Southwark to build a house near S Margaret's church for the court of the marshal of the K's household *Westm* R iii p ii 972
March 6	Sir Thomas de Felton is appointed seneschal of Aquitain *Westm* R iii p ii 972
March 7	Robert de Wykford is appointed constable of Bordeaux Intimation thereof to the K's officers and others in Saintonge and Aquitain *Westm.* R. iii p ii. 972
March 15	Power for Thomas de Felton, seneschal of Aquitain, Robert de Rous, mayor of Bourdeaux, and two others to negotiate an alliance with Peter K of Arragon. *Westm* R iii p ii 972 O vii. 4 H iii p iii. 4
March 15	Pardon to the commonalty of Bourdeaux for infractions of the regulations concerning the currency. *Westm.* R. iii. p ii 973 O vii 4 H iii p ii 4
April 1	The K annuls the revocation of the grant of Puy Norman and Villa Francqua to Berart de Lebret *Westm.* R iii p ii 973 O vii. 5 H iii p iii 4
April 4	Commission to Frederick de Tilneye, William de Spaigne, and William de Harcourt, of S Botulph's, to arrest 70 sailors, 15 armed men, and 15 archers Six similar commissions. *Westm.* R iii p ii 973
April 12.	Commission to Thomas de Felton, seneschal of Aquitain, and Robert de Wykford, constable of Bourdeaux, to take possession of the principality of Aquitain, which the prince of Wales has surrendered into the K.'s hands *Westm.* R iii p ii 974 O vii 6 H iii p. iii 5
April 12.	Power for Elias bp of Perigord, Robert de Wykford, and two others to hear appeals in Aquitain *Westm* R iii p ii 974. O vii 6 H iii p iii 5
April 22	The K orders his officers at Southampton and Plymouth to provide ships for the conveyance of sir William de Asthorpe, warden of Guernsey, Jersey, Sark and Alderney, and John Coke to the said islands. *Westm.* R. iii. p. ii. 974
April 28.	Commission to Walter de Haulee and John Polymond to provide sailors for the passage of John K of Castile and duke of Lancaster. *Westm* R iii p ii 975. O vii 7 H iii. p iii 5
April 28.	The sheriffs of Norfolk and Suffolk and Lincolnshire are ordered to prevent all persons leaving the kingdom *Westm* R iii p ii 975
May 7.	Commission to Roger de Beauchamp, captain of Calais, to redress infractions of the peace with Flanders *Westm.* R. iii p ii 975 O. vii 8. H iii p iii 5

DATE.	SUBJECT.
1373.	
May 7.	Roger de Beauchamp is appointed captain of Calais *Westm.* R. iii. p. ii. 975.
May 9.	Warrant to Thomas Fakenham, sergeant-at-arms, to arrest armed men, archers, and sailors. *Westm* R. iii. p ii 976.
May 10	H. bp. of Norwich, William de Ufford, earl of Suffolk, William de Morlee, and 11 others, are appointed wardens of the coast of Norfolk. Similar commissions for Suffolk and Devon. *Westm.* R. iii. p ii. 976.
May 11.	Licence to the bps of Winchester and London, the earl of Arundel, and eight others, to hold the lands of the K of Castile as his executors after his death *Westm.* R iii. p. ii 976 O. vii. 9 H. iii. p iii 6.
May 13.	Commissions to Thomas Clerc and John Elys to arrest sailors. *Westm.* R iii. p. ii 977.
May 20	Inquisition held at Drogheda before Robert de Assheton, justiciary of Ireland, and Robert de Preston, concerning the extortions in Meath of William de Wyndesore, the K's lieutenant in Ireland. R iii p ii. 977
May 31	Similar inquisition concerning the extortions of William de Wyndesore in Uriel. *Drogheda* R. iii. p ii. 978
May 27.	Another inquisition concerning the extortions of William de Wyndesore in Meath *Drogheda* R iii p ii 979
May 22	The K orders Roger de Beauchamp, captain of Calais, to forbid the soldiers in that and other towns in those parts going beyond the walls. *Westm.* R iii p ii. 980.
May 26.	Commission to Thomas bp of Durham, Thomas bp of Carlisle, Edmund de Mortimer, earl of March, and six others, to redress violations contrary to the peace with Scotland *Westm* R. iii p ii. 980 O. vii 9 H iii p iii 6
May 28.	Safe conduct for Andrew Peyntoui and two others, of Scotland, to buy black stones for the tomb of David de Bruys. *Westm.* R iii p ii 980. O vii 10. H. iii p. iii. 6.
May 28.	The K. appoints Walter de Haule, sergeant-at-arms, and Adam Blakemore, marshal of the duke of Brittany, to act as harbingers for the duke and the forces which the K. has sent to serve him *Westm* R iii p ii 981 O vii 10. H iii p iii 6.
June 1.	Power for William lord de Latymer and Thomas Juvenis, official of the court of Canterbury, to treat with Fernando K. of Portugal and his consort Eleanor. *Westm.* R iii. p ii 981 O. vii. 11 H iii. p. iii. 6.
June 6.	The K orders Peter Manlay, warden of Berwick-upon-Tweed, and three others, to send to York the 4,000 marks received from Robert K of Scotland *Westm* R iii p. ii. 981. O vii 12 H iii p iii 7
June 8.	John lord of Gumery is appointed captain of Arde *vice* Canovus Robertsart. *Westm.* R iii p ii 982
June 12.	The K appoints John K of Castile, duke of Lancaster, as his lieutenant and captain-general in France and Aquitain. *Westm.* R iii. p ii. 982 O vii. 13 H iii. p iii 7.
June 16.	The K desires the prayers of the clergy for the success of his war with France. *Westm.* R. iii. p. ii 983. O. vii. 15. H. iii. p iii 8
June 16.	Treaty of perpetual alliance between England and Portugal. *London.* R iii. p. ii. 983. O. vii. 15. H. iii p. iii. 8
June 16.	Portuguese counterpart of the above-mentioned treaty. *London.* R. iii. p. ii. 984 O. vii. 19. H. iii. p iii 10.
June 17.	Lease by the K of the gold and silver mines in Devon and Somerset to William de Notyngham, of Bisseye *Westm.* R iii p ii. 986. O. vii 22. H. iii p iii 11.
June 18.	The K orders Robert de Hales, prior of S John of Jerusalem in England, to array the brethren of the order. *Hadley.* R. iii. p ii 986.
June 20.	The K. orders Thomas Jolyf, John Lumbard, and John White, to arrest those persons who resist the K's right of presentation to the prebend of S James at Beverley. Four other commissions on the same subject. *Westm.* R. iii p. ii. 986. O. vii 24 H iii p. iii. 12.
June 23.	The mayor and sheriffs of London are ordered to issue a proclamation summoning men-at-arms and archers in the retinue of the duke of Lancaster and other lords to join them for their passage to France. *Westm.* R. iii. p ii 987.
June 24.	Writ to sir Thomas Moraunt, Richard Stokke, sheriff of Kent, and seven others, to arrest those who impugn the K's right to the presentation to the church of Orpyngton *Westm.* R iii p. ii. 987. O. vii. 26. H. iii. p. iii. 12

DATE	SUBJECT
1373 June 26	Receipt of 4,000 marks from Robert K of Scotland, in part payment for the ransom of David de Bruys *Westm* R iii p ii. 987. O vii. 26. H iii p iii. 12.
July 12.	The K orders William de Weston, his squire, and John Legg, his sergeant-at-arms, to convey the two sons of Charles de Bloys from Devizes to Nottingham *Westm* R iii. p ii 988. O vii 26 H. iii p iii 13
July 16	Sir John Beamond, Walter Hauley, lieutenant of Philip de Courteney, admiral in the west, are ordered to provide archers and sailors. Similar warrant to sir Richard Sergeaux and three others *Westm* R. iii p ii 988.
July 20	The K orders William bp of Winchester to array the clergy of his diocese, and send them to Southampton, for the protection of those parts. *Westm* R iii. p ii 988 O vii 27 H iii p. ii 13
July 20	The K. orders John de Montacute, Luke de Ponynges, and five others, to protect Southampton and the coast *Westm* R iii p ii. 988.
July 26	Safe conduct for John de Neyvyll of France, prisoner of William lord de Latymer, going to France to procure his ransom *Westm* R iii p ii 989 O vii 27 H iii. p iii 13
Aug 5	Sir John de Burele, Adam de Hertyngdon, and Adam de Bury are ordered to repair the castle of Oderwyk and the fortresses of Chauntereyn and Plank. *Woodstock* R. iii. p. ii 989.
Aug 5	Also to survey Calais, Arde, Guisnes, Mark, Sandgate, and Oye *Woodstock.* R iii. p. ii 989.
Aug 6	The K. orders the mayor and sheriffs of London to allow the moneyers of London to enjoy the privileges claimed by them, until the matter is decided *Westm* R iii. p. ii 989
Aug 8	Grant to Alice Perrers, lady of the late Q Philippa, of certain jewels and other goods of the Queen's *Woodstock* R iii p ii. 989 O vii. 28 H iii. p iii 13
Aug 16	The K. orders Philip de Courtenay, admiral, and sir Ralph de Ferrers, to take possession of the castle of Gurry in Jersey. *Westm.* R. iii p ii 990
Sept. 20.	The K appoints sir William de Wyndesore governor of Ireland. Intimation thereof to Robert de Assheton, late justiciary, and to the people of Ireland *Westm* R ii. p ii 990 O vii 28 H iii p iii 13
Sept 24	Pope Gregory [XI.] writes to the K in favour of William, master-general of the order of Sempryngham, who is molested by the bp of Lincoln. *Villeneuve.* R. iii p ii 990 O vii 29 H. iii p iii. 14
Oct 6	The K. orders the bridges in Oxfordshire to be repaired, as he is going thither to hawk. *Westm* R iii p ii. 990
Oct 8.	Commission to Simon Charwelton, clerk, and Walter de Eure, to arrest ships for the passage of William de Wyndesore to Ireland. *Westm.* R iii. p. ii. 991.
Oct. 15	Commission to Andrew de Tyndale, sergeant-at-arms, to seize captured ships and goods, which ought to belong to the K. *Westm* R. iii p ii. 991. O vii 29 H iii p. iii. 14
Oct. 18	The K forbids the prior of the Friars Preachers at Oxford admitting foreigners. *Westm.* R iii p ii 991
Oct. 20.	The K forbids the exportation of wine. *Westm* R iii p ii 991
Oct 22	Safe conduct for Thomas earl of Marre coming to England. *Westm.* R iii p ii 991. O. vii 30, H. iii p iii 14.
Oct. 26	The K. orders the prince of Wales and the earl of Pembroke to provide ships for the passage of William de Wyndesore to Ireland *Westm* R iii p. ii. 992.
Oct 26	Sir Thomas de Baunfeld is appointed warden of Calais Castle *Westm* R. ii p ii 992
Oct. 26.	Robert Salle is appointed warden of Marke Castle, *vice* William de Gunthorpe. *Westm.* R iii. p ii 992
Oct. 26.	John de Romeseye is appointed treasurer of Calais *Westm.* R iii. p. ii 992.
Oct 28	John de Beurle is appointed captain of Calais. *Westm.* R. iii p. ii. 992.
Oct. 30.	Sir John Bureley, captain of Calais, and John Geans, lord of Gomems, are appointed captains of the forces at Calais, Guisnes, and Marke *Westm.* R iii. p. ii 993
Nov 10	The chapter of York and the guardian of the spiritualities of the see are desired to convoke the clergy of the province. *Westm.* R. iii. p ii. 993 O. vii 30, H. iii. p iii 14
Nov 10	Elizabeth Chaundos, sister and heir of sir John de Chaundos, resigns to the K the barony of S. Sauveur and the other possessions in France of sir John Chaundos. *London.* R iii. p. ii 993 O. vii. 31, H. iii. p. iii. 14.

DATE.	SUBJECT
1373 Nov 20	Edmund Rose is appointed warden of Jersey and of Gurry Castle. *Westm.* R iii p ii 993
Nov 21	Parliamentary regulation for the measure of cloth, and that Scotch money shall be current at three-fourths of the value of English money *Westm* R. iii p ii 994
Nov. 26.	The K orders the above-mentioned ordinances to be proclaimed throughout England *Westm* R iii. p ii 994.
Nov 30	Grant of an annuity of 300 francs to Galeotus de Spinolis de Luthulo *Westm.* R iii p ii 994. O vii. 31. H iii p iii 14.
Dec. 8.	Safe conducts for Eleanor de Bruys, countess of Carrick, and sir James de Douglas, of Daweth, coming on a pilgrimage to Canterbury *Westm* R. iii p ii 994 O vii. 32 H iii. p iii, 15.
Dec. 10.	Grant to sir Nicholas Bonde of the lands forfeited by the lord de Lebret Intimation thereof to the seneschal of Gascony and the constable of Bourdeaux *Westm.* R iii p ii. 994 O. vii. 32 H iii p. iii 15.
Dec. 19	Restitution of the temporalities to Philip Torynton, bp of Cashel *Westm* R iii p ii. 995.
Dec 20	The K. orders the collection of the subsidy lately granted in Ireland. *Westm.* R iii p ii 995.
Dec. 21	The K orders William de Asthorpe to collect the revenues of Guernsey, Sark, Alderney, and Erme, the castle of Cornet and the tower of Beauregard in Guernsey *Westm* R iii p ii. 995
1374. Jan 1	The K informs pope Gregory of the election of Alexander de Nevill to the abprick of York. *Westm* R. iii p ii 995 O. vii. 33. H. iii p iii. 15.
Jan 8	The K. orders Edmund Rose to allow Thomas de Ryby to enjoy the benefice of S. Martin in Jersey *Westm* R iii p ii 996
Jan 28.	Warrant to Thomas Herytig, master of the vessel called "*la Alice*," to arrest 60 sailors in Kent Similar warrants to seven other masters of ships. *Westm.* R iii. p. ii, 996.
Jan. 28.	Grant of an annuity of 20*l* to John Fastolf, the K's squire *Westm* R. iii p ii 996
Feb 1	Commission to William de Asthorp, warden of Guernsey, Sark, and Alderney, Thomas de Appelby, Peter Gyon, Nicholas Saumareis, and Nicholas le Fever, to make inquisition concerning wards, marriages, forfeitures, &c. Similar commission for Jersey to Edmund Rose and Thomas Appelby. *Westm.* R. iii. p. ii. 996.
Feb 1.	The K forbids the bailiffs of Jersey hearing causes which do not pertain to them *Westm* R iii. p ii 997
Feb 2	The K orders all his officers abroad and in England to assist sir Nicholas de Dagworth, John Fastolf, and Thomas Durant, in certain secret business. *Westm.* R. iii p ii. 997 O vii. 33. H. iii. p. iii. 15.
Feb 3	Commission to John Daumarle, sheriff of Devon, and three others, to arrest sailors Similar commissions in Cornwall, Somerset, and Dorset. *Westm* R iii p ii 997
Feb 3	William Tank is appointed chief baron of the Exchequer. *Westm* R iii. p. ii. 997.
Feb 3	Hugh Fastolf of Great Yarmouth, and John Brice of Little Yarmouth, are appointed lieutenants of William Nevill, admiral north of the Thames *Westm.* R iii p ii 997
Feb 7.	The K. orders the mayors and bailiffs of Hull, Beverley, and seven other towns, to send barges with their crews to Sandwich by March 16 *Westm.* R iii. p ii 998
Feb. 10.	The K orders William de Wyndesore, governor of Ireland, to pay the wages of the men retained by Stephen bp. of Meath *Westm* R iii p ii. 998
Feb 10.	The K orders the mayors and bailiffs of Cork and Dublin to pay annuities of 40 marks to the bp of Meath, whom he retains as his councillor *Westm* R ii p ii 998
Feb. 10.	Grant of the custody of the manor of Cromelyn to the bp of Meath Intimation of the above to the treasurer of Dublin *Westm* R. iii. p ii 998
Feb. 14	Warrants for the arrest of crews for *la George de Bristoll, la Gracedieu de Bristoll,* and *la Seint Maricogge de Bruggewater Westm.* R iii p ii 999
March 6	The K desires the bishops and sheriffs of England to send information concerning benefices held by foreigners *Westm.* R. iii p ii 999
March 6.	The K orders the mayors and bailiffs of Dublin and Drogheda, and the sheriffs of Dublin, Meath, Uriel, and Kildare, to issue a proclamation for the payment of the subsidy. *Westm* R iii p ii 999
March 6	The K orders the constable of Bourdeaux to pay the wages of sir Thomas de Felton as seneschal of Aquitain *Westm* R. iii p ii 1000

DATE	SUBJECT
1374 March 11.	The K will send ambassadors to meet the papal nuncios either at Bruges or Calais. *Westm* R iii p ii 1000 O vii. 33 H iii p iii. 15.
March 17	Commission of Louis, son of the K of France, and brother of the K of France, and his lieutenant in Languedoc, duke of Anjou and Touraine, and count of Maine, to John de S Cervin, the marquis de Cardillac, and Migon de la Pomerade, to treat with the count of Foix *Thoule* R. iii. p ii 1000 O vii 34 H iu p iii 16
March 24.	Safe conduct for Margaret, widow of David de Bruys, coming to England. *Westm.* R iii. p. ii. 1001. O vii 35 H iii p iii. 16
March 24	The K orders the sheriff of Hampshire, the mayor and bailiffs of Southampton, and two others, to arrest sailors for the barge furnished by the said town Similar warrant for the barge furnished by the town of Salisbury *Westm* R. iii. p ii 1001
March 25	Protection for sir John, son of John de Burgh, warden of the castle of S Sauveur. *Westm* R iii p ii 1001.
April 12	The K forbids the taking of lampreys in the Thames before Michaelmas. *Westm.* R iii p ii 1001.
April 21	Protection for sir William, son of William Bruys. *Westm.* R. iii, p ii. 1001.
April 22.	Grant of a pitcher of wine daily to Geoffrey Chaucer, the K's esquire *Windsor* R. iii p ii 1001 O vii. 35 H. iii p iii 16
May 3.	The sheriff of Wiltshire, and the mayor and bailiffs of Salisbury, are ordered to arrest all papal bulls and letters prejudicial to the K *Westm* R. iii p ii 1001
May 4	Pope Gregory [XI] will send as nuncios to Bruges the bps. of Pampeluna and Seni- gaglia, and Giles Sancii Muñonis, provost of Valenciennes; and desires credence for Walter de Svulavoe, archdeacon of the East Riding. *Villeneuve* R iii p ii. 1002. O vii 36. H iii p iii 16
May 5.	Restitution of the temporalities to Thomas bp of Ely, late archdeacon of Taunton. *Westm* R iii p ii 1002 O vii 36. H iii p. iii. 16
May 12	Summons to John Godfrey, master of the barge of Bristol, and to 18 other masters of ships, to appear before the council *Westm.* R iii p ii 1002
May 16	Safe conduct for sir Henry de Douglas of Scotland going on a pilgrimage to Canterbury. *Westm* R iii p ii 1002 O. vii. 37. H iii p iii 17.
May 24.	Protection for the inhabitants of Guernsey, Jersey, Sark, and Alderney *Westm* R. iii p ii 1003
May 28.	Restitution to cardinal John bp of Sabina of the benefice of Abburbury, granted to William de Redenesse on a report of the cardinal's death. *Westm.* R. iii p ii 1003
June 6	Restitution of the temporalities to Alexander abp elect of York *Westm* R. iii p ii 1003 O vii 37. H iii p iii 17
June 6.	Thomas de Musgrave, warden of Berwick, and three others, are ordered to receive 4,000 marks from Robert K of Scotland *Westm* R iii p ii 1003 O vii 37 H. iii. p iii 17.
June 8.	Geoffrey Chaucer is appointed comptroller of the customs and subsidy on wool, hides, and fleeces in London. *Westm.* R. iii. p. ii. 1004. O. vii 38. H iii p iii 17
June 8	Protection for the K of Navarre and his eldest son Charles going to Cherbourg Castle *Westm* R iii p ii 1004. O vii 39 H iii. p. iii 17
June 8	Safe conduct for the barge of the K. of Navarre to come from Cherbourg to England *Westm* R iii p. ii. 1004.
June 8.	Safe conduct for Pilleus abp of Ravenna, papal nuncio. *Westm* R. iii p ii. 1004. O vii 39 H iii p iii 17
June 15	The K forbids the exaction of customs from the fishermen of Holkham, Wells, Blakeneye, and five other towns, for fish sold in England *Westm.* R iii. p ii. 1004
June 20	Safe conduct for John de Neyvill, prisoner of William lord of Latymere. *Westm.* R iii p ii 1005 O vii 39. H iii p iii. 17.
June 26	Receipt of 4,000 marks from Robert K. of Scotland. *Westm.* R. iii. p ii 1005 O vii 40. H. iii. p. iii 18.
June 26.	Safe conduct for Berengarius de Ferrariis, messenger of the cardinal of Albano. *Westm.* R iii p ii 1005.
July 5	Exemption from toll of the inhabitants of the K.'s manors of Modyngham and Woolwich. *Westm* R iii p ii 1005
July 9.	Pope Gregory [XI] writes to the K on behalf of the Alberti of Florence, two of whose ships have been captured by the English. R. iii. p. ii. 1005. O. vii. 40. H. iii. p. iii. 18.

DATE	SUBJECT
1374 July 12	The custody of the manor of Cheltenham, forfeited by the abbot of Fécamp, is committed to Simon de Burlee. *Westm.* R. iii. p. ii 1005
July 13.	Protection for Matilda countess of Oxford *Westm.* R. iii p ii 1006.
July 15	Safe conduct for Gerard Droem, agent of the cardinal of S Martial, going to Ireland *Westm.* R. iii. p ii. 1006 O. vii. 41 H. iii. p iii 18
July 17.	Commission to Andrew de Tyndale and John Staple, sergeants-at-arms, to arrest ships. Similar commissions to William de Nevill and Philip de Courtenay, admirals, the prince of Wales, the earl of Pembroke, and Margaret lady Segrave. R iii p ii. 1006.
July 20.	The K. orders the restitution of a ship of Catalonia, arrested at Southampton. *Westm* R. iii. p ii 1006.
July 24	The K. orders John de Bolton, chancellor and chamberlain of Berwick-upon-Tweed, to publish the statute concerning the circulation of Scotch money *Westm.* R. iii p. ii 1007 O vii 41 H iii. p. iii 18.
July 24.	Safe conduct for Arnald Garnern, papal nuncio about to return to the papal court. *Westm.* R. iii. p. ii. 1007.
July 26.	Commission to John bp of Bangor, John de Wiclif, S.T.P., John Guteri, dean of Segovia, and four others, to treat with the papal nuncios *London* R iii p ii 1007 O vii 41. H iii. p iii. 18.
Aug. 1	Restitution of the temporalities to William Andrews, bp of Achaden *Westm* R. iii. p. ii. 1007
Aug. 8	The K informs the tenants of the archbishopric of Canterbury of the appointment of Thomas Newe, parson of Godmersham, and five others, as custodians of the temporalities of the see. *Westm* R. iii p ii 1007. O. vii 42 H. iii p iii 18
Aug 9	Commission of the duke and council of Genoa to Eberto Gentilis and Raffo Grifroto, to demand from the K redress for violations of the peace *Genoa.* R iii p. ii. 1008 O. vii. 42. H iii. p. iii 19.
Aug. 12.	Attestation to the above commission by Andrew abp of Genoa. *Genoa* R iii p. ii 1008 O. vii 43. H. iii p. iii 19
Aug 12	Sir Thomas de Beauchamp is appointed captain of Guernsey, Sark, and Alderney *Westm* R iii p ii 1009.
Aug 20.	The K. desires the prayers of the clergy. *Westm* R iii p. ii. 1009. O. vii. 45 H. iii. p iii 20.
Aug 20	John de Harleston is appointed warden of Guisnes Castle. *Westm* R iii p ii 1009
Aug. 23.— Oct 23	Protection for Simon Dode, John Pensfold, sir Thomas Mordok, and 258 others, in the retinue of John duke of Brittany and earl of Richmond. *Westm.* R iii p ii. 1009.
Aug 26	Safe conduct for sir Alexander Steward and sir Walter Lesle of Scotland, coming to England *Westm* R iii. p. ii. 1011 O vii. 45. H. iii. p iii. 20.
Aug 29.	Commission to Thomas bp. of Carlisle, Hugh earl of Stafford, John lord Nevill, Thomas lord Roos, and four others, to meet the commissioners of the K. of Scotland, for the settlement of the disputes between Henry lord Percy and William earl of Douglas relative to the forest of Jeddeworth. *Westm.* R iii p. ii. 1011. O vii 45 H iii p iii 20
Aug. 31.— Dec 14	Protection for Richard Wynchedon, Philip Barry, and 155 others, in the retinue of Edmund earl of Cambridge *Westm* R. iii. p. ii 1012.
Sept. 14.	The K orders proclamation to be made in London, the Cinque Ports, and six other ports, forbidding any molestation of Portuguese merchants *Westm.* R. iii p ii 1013
Sept. 22.— Dec. 20.	Protection for Henry de Hopton, chaplain, Thomas Burford, and 94 others, in the retinue of Edmund earl of March *Westm.* R. iii. p ii. 1013.
Oct. 10.	Commission to Guy de Brien and Richard de Stafford to hear the petition of Thomas More, concerning the detention of a prisoner by Ralph Basset. *Westm.* R iii p. ii 1014 O vii. 46 H. iii. p. iii. 20
Oct. 10.	Robert Bealknapp is appointed chief justice of the Common Bench. *Westm* R iii. p. ii. 1015.
Oct 20.	Safe conducts for the abp of Ravenna, and Odio de Mirolio and Herman de Colonia, his servants *Westm* R. iii p ii 1015.
Oct. 21.	Restitution of the manor of Cobhambury and the other temporalities to Thomas de Brintone, bp of Rochester, late monk of Norwich *Westm.* R. iii p. ii 1015 O. vii. 46 H. iii p. ii. 20.

DATE.	SUBJECT
1374 Oct 23	Grant to the bp of Rochester of the revenues of the bishopric while vacant *Westm.* R iii p. ii 1015 O vii 47 H iii p. iii. 20.
Oct 24.	The K orders the treasurer and barons of the Exchequer to deliver two dies for the exchange at York to the abp *Westm.* R. iii p ii 1015 O. vii 47. H. iii p iii 21.
Oct 26.	Warrant to the sheriff of Derby to pay to John K of Castile, duke of Lancaster, the annuity of 20*l* enjoyed by Henry late duke of Lancaster *Westm.* R. iii p. ii. 1016 O. vii 48 H iii p iii 21
Oct. 26.	John lord of Gumerey is appointed captain of Arde *Westm.* R iii p. ii 1016
Oct 28	Safe conduct for Francisco Feraru, scribe of the K of Aragon, and Peter Martin, his servant, who are going to Aragon. *Westm.* R. iii p ii 1016. O vii. 48. H. iii p. iii. 21.
Oct. 30.	Protection for John duke of Brittany. *Westm.* R. iii p. ii 1016
Nov 2	The K forbids the exportation of wheat *Westm.* R iii p ii 1016
Nov 10	The K orders the captain of Calais and his other officers there to deliver to Geoffrey de Westwyk the revenues of the benefice of S. Mary in Calais, although the bp. of Terouenne, who is the K's enemy, has not admitted him. *Westm* R iii p ii 1016.
Nov. 18.	The K orders William le Latymere, constable of Dover Castle and warden of the Cinque Ports, to assist James Lyons, and John de Bentham, esquire of the duke of Brittany, in providing ships for the transport of Edmund earl of Cambridge *Westm* R iii p ii 1017.
Nov. 18	Commission to James Lyons and John de Bentham to provide ships *Westm.* R. iii p. ii. 1017 O vii 48 H iii p iii. 21
Nov 20.	Powers of jurisdiction committed to John de Beurley, captain of Calais *Westm* R. ii. p ii 1017
Nov. 20.	Safe conduct for Berard de la Bret, prisoner of sir Thomas de Felton. *Westm.* R. iii. p ii. 1017. O. vii 48. H iii p iii 21.
Nov 20	The K promises that the grant of a subsidy by the inhabitants of the liberty of Durham shall not be taken as a precedent *Westm* R. iii p ii 1018 O vii 49 H. iii p. iii. 21
Nov. 21 — Jan. 19.	Protection for Adam Basyng, John de Frome, and 67 others in the retinue of Edward le Despenser. *Westm* R iii. p ii 1018.
Nov 24.	Edmund earl of Cambridge and John duke of Brittany are appointed the K's lieutenants and captains general in France *Westm* R iii. p ii 1018. O. vii 49. H. iii p iii 21.
Nov. 28.	Roger de Fulthorp is appointed justice of the Common Bench. The other justices are ordered to admit him *Westm* R iii p ii 1019.
Nov 29	Safe conduct for sir Alexander Lyndeseye and sir James Lyndeseye. *Westm* R iii. p ii 1019 O vii 52 H. iii p iii 22
Dec. 10	The K orders Thomas Beauchamp, warden of Guernsey, Sark, and Alderney, Thomas de Appelby, and three others, to send information as to wards, marriages, forfeitures, and other dues of the crown in these islands *Westm* R. iii p ii 1019.
Dec 16	The K orders Hugh Tyrel, captain of Orrey Castle in Brittany, to deliver the castle to the duke of Brittany *Westm.* R. iii. p ii 1019. O vii 53 H. iii p. iii 22
Dec 16	Similar letter to the K's other captains in Brittany. *Westm.* R. iii. p. ii. 1020. O. vii. 53 H iii p iii. 22
Dec 16	The K permits all persons to come to Waterford to sell corn and other victuals. *Westm.* R iii p. ii. 1020.
Dec 23	The K orders Guy de Brien, Ralph de Ferrers, Richard de Imworth, sergeant-at-arms, and William Beaufoy and Thomas Durant, tellers of the Exchequer, to provide shipping for the men-at arms going to Brittany, and to pay their wages. *Westm.* R. iii. p. ii. 1020.
Dec 24	The K. orders John Deveros, captain of Brest Castle, to deliver it to the duke of Brittany *Westm.* R iii p ii. 1020. O vii 53. H iii p iii. 22.
Dec 26	The K orders the warden of the Isle of Wight to send all the sailors of the island to Southampton. *Westm.* R iii p ii. 1020.
Dec 29.	The K. orders proclamation to be made in London that men belonging to the retinues of the earl of Cambridge and the duke of Brittany are to join the above lords. *Westm.* R iii. p ii. 1021.
1375 Jan. 9.	Commission to John Joce and Thomas Bray to send 12 miners from the forest of Dean to serve Edward le Despenser in the K's service abroad *Westm.* R. iii p ii 1021
Jan. 8.	Power for John de Burlay, captain of Calais, John de Herlaston, captain of Guisnes, and John de Shepeye, to treat for peace with France, by the mediation of the papal nuncios. *Westm.* R iii p. ii. 1021. O. vii 53. H. iii p. iii. 22.

DATE.	SUBJECT
1375 Feb. 5.	Andreas Contareno, doge of Venice, desires a safe conduct for six merchant galleys about to be sent to Flanders. *Venice.* R. m. p. n. 1021 O vii. 54. H iii. p iii. 23
Feb. 8	The K orders the mayor and bailiffs of Bristol to prevent the exportation of Scotch money or foreign plate. *Westm.* R. iii p ii 1022.
Feb. 11.	Safe conduct for Walter de Lesley lord Ross, coming to England *Westm* R iii p. ii. 1022. O. vii 54 H. iii p iii. 23.
Feb. 11	Truce with France for Picardy and Artois until Easter *Bourbourg* R iii. p. ii. 1022 O vii 54 H iii p iii 23
Feb. 13.	The K orders William de Wyndesore, governor of Ireland, to publish the order concerning the circulation of Scotch money Similar letter to William de Montacute, earl of Salisbury, lord of Man *Westm* R iii p ii 1023
Feb 16	John de Beurley, captain of Calais, John lord of Gomereys, captain of Arde, and John de Harleston, captain of Guisnes, are appointed conservators of the truce. *Westm.* R. iii p. ii 1023. O vii 56 H iii p iii 24
Feb. 13	Pope Gregory [XI.] desires the K to release from arrest the goods of the prior of S John of Jerusalem in England *Avignon* R iii p ii 1024. O vii 56 H iii p iii 24.
Feb 16.	Licence to sir James Douglas of Scotland, son of the earl of Douglas, to buy wheat and malt in Lincolnshire and Norfolk. *Westm.* R iii p ii 1024 O vii. 58 H iii p. iii 25
Feb 17	The K orders Alan de Buxhull, constable of the Tower of London, to prepare a tower with necessary chambers and houses for the reception of the count of S Paul, prisoner of William de Latymere, the K.'s chamberlain *Westm* R iii p ii 1024.
Feb 20.	Power for John K of Castile and duke of Lancaster, Simon bp of London, William earl of Salisbury, John Cobham, and four others, to treat for peace with France. *Westm* R iii p ii 1024 O vii 58 H iii p iii 25
Feb. 21.	Power for the above-mentioned commissioners to make a truce R. iii. p. ii. 1025 O. vii 59. H. iii. p iii. 25.
Feb. 23.	The K orders William de Latymer, constable of Dover Castle and warden of the Cinque Ports, to allow Oberto Genulys and Raffo Griffioto, Genoese ambassadors, to take the goods they have recovered without payment of customs *Westm* R iii p. ii 1025 O vii 60 H iii p iii. 26
Feb. 24	The K orders Alan de Buxhull, constable of the Tower of London, to deliver up to William de Latymer a fit and proper tower, with the chambers, keys, &c, which he has prepared for the count of S. Paul, prisoner of the same William *Westm.* R iii p ii 1025. O vii 61 H. iii p iii 26.
Feb. 26.	Safe conduct for Henry de Manny, Anguerran de Hedyn, or two other French knights in the company of John earl of Pembroke. *Westm* R. iii p ii 1026.
Feb. 28	Power for J. bp. of Bangor, John de Shepeye, Simon de Multon, clerks, and John Pyel, citizen of London, to redress injuries to Flemings *Westm.* R iii p ii 1026.
March 1.	Letters of attorney for John K of Castile and duke of Lancaster, in the names of William bp. of Winchester and Richard earl of Arundel. Six other letters of attorney for the duke *Westm* R iii. p. ii 1026 O vii 61. H iii p. iii 26
March 1.	The K forbids the exportation of corn. *Westm.* R. iii p ii. 1026.
March 2.	Confirmation of the truce with France dated Feb 11 *Westm* R iii p ii. 1027.
March 3	Safe conduct for Philip duke of Burgundy, the bp. of Amiens, and John count of Tankervill, going to Flanders to treat for a peace with England *Westm.* R iii p ii 1027. O vii. 61 H iii. p iii 26
March 18.	Power for sir Thomas de Felton, seneschal of Aquitain, sir William de Elmham, and sir John de Multon, mayor of Bourdeaux, to treat with the K. of Navarre. *Westm.* R iii p. ii 1027. O vii 63 H iii p. iii 27.
March 24.	Power for sir Thomas de Felton, seneschal of Aquitain, Florymund lord de le Sparre, William Elmham, governor of Bayonne and seneschal of the Landes, and Raymund Gulhelmi de Puy to treat for an alliance with the count of Foix. *Westm* R iii.p ii 1027 O. vii. 63 H iii. p. iii. 27.
April 19,	Commission to the abp. of Bourdeaux, the abbot of S Croix Bordeaux, the dean of S Severin, and five others, to hear appeals in Aquitain *Westm.* R iii p ii 1028 O vii 64 H iii. p. iii 27
May 4.	Safe conduct for Walter de Bygar, chamberlain of Scotland, coming to Berwick *Westm.* R iii. p. ii. 1028. O vii 54. H. iii p iii. 27.

DATE	SUBJECT.
1375. May 8	The K. desires the prayers of the prelates of England for the success of the expedition of Edward earl of Cambridge and John duke of Brittany *Westm* R iii. p ii. 1028 O vii 64 H iii p iii 27
May 10.	Safe conduct for sir Robert de Heskyn of Scotland coming to London to speak with the prior of S John of Jerusalem in England *Westm* R iii p ii. 1028. O. vii 65 H iii iii 27.
May 16	The K orders William de Wyndesore, governor of Ireland, to appoint counsel for Hugh cardinal of S Martial *Westm* R iii. p ii 1028 O vii 65 H iii p iii. 27
May 30.	The K orders his officers to furnish horses to Helmyng Leget, and Edmund Tettesworth, sergeant-at-arms. Similar warrant for Thomas Stanes and two others. *Westm.* R iii. p ii 1029.
June 5.	Restitution of the temporalties to Simon abp. of Canterbury, late bp of London *Westm.* R iii p ii 1029 O vii. 66 H iii p iii 28
June 8.	Power to John K. of Castile, duke of Lancaster, to make a truce with France *Westm* R iii p ii 1029. O vii 66 H iii p. iii. 28.
June 19	Safe conduct for the countess of Douglas coming to Canterbury on a pilgrimage. *Westm* R iii. p ii 1030 O vii 80 H iii. p iii 33.
June 20	The K orders the officers of the city of Bourdeaux to take an oath annually to do justice *Westm* R. iii p ii 1030.
June 26	The K. orders sir Thomas de Felton, seneschal of Aquitain, William de Elmham, seneschal of the Landes, and Richard Rotour, constable of Bourdeaux, to desist from executing the sentence of sir Guy de Bran and Edmund de Mortimer, earl of March, marshal of England, against Robert de Wykford, late constable of Bourdeaux *Westm.* R iii p. ii 1030 O vii 67 H iii p iii 28
June 26	Receipt for 4,000 marks from Robert K of Scotland. *Westm* R iii p. ii. 1030. O vii 68. H iii p iii 28
June 27.	Truce with France for one year. *Bruges.* R iii p. ii. 1031. O. vii 68 H iii p. iii 29.
June 27.	French counterpart of the above-mentioned truce. *Bruges.* R. iii p. ii 1032. O vii 72. H iii p iii. 30.
June 27.	Supplementary articles of the truce. *Bruges.* R iii p ii 1033 O. vii 74 H. iii p iii 31
[June 27.]	Counterpart of the above articles R. iii p. ii 1034 O vii 77. H iii p iii 32
June 27.	The K. orders sir Matthew de Redeman and Thomas de Catherton to publish the above-mentioned truce in Brittany and S. Sauveur *Westm.* R. iii p ii 1034 O. vii 78 H iii p. iii 33
June 27.	Article for the delivery of S Sauveur by the English to the papal nuncios *Bruges* R iii p ii 1035. O vii 79 H iii p iii 33
June 29	The K orders the clergy, nobles, and commons of Ireland to consult with sir Nicholas Dagworth about the state of the island *Westm.* R. iii p ii. 1035.
July 6	Pope Gregory [XI] writes to the K. in favour of Hugo cardinal of S. Mary *in Porticu*, on whom pope Innocent VI conferred the archdeaconry of Meath, but the K. has granted it to Nicholas Runehy *Villeneuve* R iii. p ii. 1035 O. vii 80. H iii. p. iii. 33
July 15.	The K. orders the prince of Wales, William Latymer, constable of Dover Castle and warden of the Cinque Ports, and the several sheriffs, to publish the truce with France. *Westm.* R iii p ii 1036 O vii 80 H iii p iii 33
	Form of the proclamation of the truce R iii. p ii 1036 O. vii 82 H. iii p iii 34.
July 29	Sir Ralph de Sutton is appointed captain of Calais Castle. *Denham* R iii p. ii. 1036
Aug 10	Obligation for 12,000 francs to Ralph Basset of Drayton, from whom the K has bought his prisoner, Reyner Grymbaud, of Genoa *Yardley Hastings* Prom.se of John lord Nevill, seneschal, and four others, to procure the performance of the above obligation *Drayton Hastings* R iii p ii 1036 O vii 82 H iii p iii 34
Aug 24	Confirmation of the truce with France. *Rockingham* R iii. p ii 1037. O. vii 82 H iii p iii 34.
Aug 24	Confirmation of the supplementary articles *Rockingham* R. iii. p ii. 1037. O. vii 83 H iii p iii 34

DATE.	SUBJECT
1375. Sept 1.	Pope Gregory [XI] confirms all the K's presentations to benefices His bulls, deciding the suits of Richard de Ravensbere and other English clerks against Roman cardinals and others in favour of the former. Annulling the reservation of benefices in England. Remission of the first fruits to the holders of certain benefices No English person shall be cited to appear personally at Rome for three years He desires the abps and bps. of England to order the agents of Roman cardinals who have benefices in England to repair those churches which need it. *Villeneuve.* R iii. p ii 1037. O. vii. 83–87 H. iii. p. iii. 34–36.
Sept. 1.	The K forbids the exportation of wool, hides, or fleeces after Michaelmas *Rockingham.* R iii p ii 1039.
Sept 20.	Power for John K of Castile and duke of Lancaster, Simon abp. of Canterbury, Edmund earl of Cambridge, William de Montagu, earl of Salisbury, William lord de Latymer, and John lord Cobham to treat with Charles K of France. *Westm.* R. iii p. ii. 1039 O. vii. 88. H. iii. p. iii. 36.
Sept 23.	Power for the above-mentioned commissioners to prorogue the truce with France. Similar power for the duke of Lancaster. *Westm* R. iii p ii 1040 O vii 89 H iii p iii 37
Sept 23.	Safe conduct for Louis duke of Anjou, Philip duke of Burgundy, the bp. of Amiens, John count of Tankervill, and John count of Salebrugg, French ambassadors, to come to Flanders. *Westm.* R iii. p. ii 1040. O. vii. 89. H iii p iii 37
Sept 24	Safe conduct for Simon Swartyng, proconsul of Lubeck, and Hertewic Beteke, proconsul of Elvyng, coming as ambassadors to England *Westm.* R iii p ii. 1040. O. vii 20. H iii. p iii. 37.
Sept. 27.	Pope Gregory [XI] requests the K. to grant a safe conduct to the vicars of James abbot of Clugny. *Avignon.* R iii p ii.1040. O. vii 90 H iii p iii 37.
Oct. 3.	William Bonewe is appointed judge of appeals in Gascony *Westm* R. iii. p. ii. 1041. O vii 91. H iii p iii 37
Oct. 10.	The K appoints John K of Castile and duke of Lancaster his lieutenant for the negotiations with France *Westm* R. iii p ii 1041 O vii 91 H iii p iii 38
Oct. 15.	Pope Gregory repeats his request to the K. to release from arrest the property of the master of S John of Jerusalem. *Avignon* R iii p. ii. 1041. O vii. 92. H. iii. p iii 38.
Oct. 18.	Hugh de Calvyle is appointed captain of Calais. *Westm* R. iii. p ii 1042.
Oct 20.	Power for John K of Castile and duke of Lancaster, Simon abp of Canterbury, and William lord de Latymer to treat with the count of Flanders and the commonalties of Flanders and Friesland. Also separate powers for treating with Flanders and Friesland. *Westm.* R iii p ii 1042
Oct. 26.	The K. orders Richard Lyouns to deliver to Simon de Burgh 40l from the property of the cardinal of Genevere in England, in compensation for his detention by the subjects of the said cardinal Letter on the subject to the abp of York. *Westm* R iii p ii 1042. O. vii 93. H. iii. p. iii 39.
Oct. 28.	The K appoints sir Thomas Graunson and sir Thomas Fogges to demand the performance of the obligations of John de Chastiloun, count of Porteyn, and Ingelram earl of Bedford and lord of Coucy *Westm.* R iii. p ii 1043 O vii 94. H iii p iii 39.
Nov 6	William de Weston is appointed warden of Outherwyk Castle *Westm* R. iii p. ii 1043
Nov 27	Laurence de Allerthorp is appointed a baron of the Exchequer. The treasurer and barons are ordered to admit him *Westm.* R iii. p ii. 1043
Dec 2.	Restitution of the temporalities to William bp of London, translated from Hereford. *Hatton Grange* R iii. p ii 1043 O vii 95. H iii p iii 39.
Dec. 4.	Restitution of the temporalities to John bp. of Hereford, translated from Bangor *Hatton Grange* R. iii p ii 1044 O vii 96 H. iii. p iii. 39
Dec. 8.	Pope Gregory [XI] requests the K. to send aid against the Turks, to prevent their invasion of Romania *Avignon* R. iii. p ii 1044 O vii 96 H iii p iii 40.
Dec. 8	Pope Gregory [XI] to the K about the sequestration of the property of the priory of S John of Jerusalem in England *Avignon* R iii. p. ii 1044. O vii. 97 H iii p iii 40.
Dec 14	The K orders William Ilger, his escheator in Ireland, to resume lands leased at less than their value. *Westm* R iii p ii 1045
1376 Jan 2.	Commission to William Latymer, John de Cobham, the sheriff of Kent, and four others, to array the men of Kent, and to place beacons on the hills. Similar commissions for 18 other counties. *Westm.* R iii. p. ii 1045

DATE.	SUBJECT.
1376 Jan 4	Philip de Courteneye and William de Nevyll, the K.'s admirals, are ordered to provide ships at Hamel and Sandwich by March 1 *Westm* R. m p u 1046
Jan 16.	The K. forbids corn to be carried out of the counties of Warwick, Worcester, and Gloucester, on account of the scarcity. *Westm* R. ui p u 1047.
Jan 30.	Restitution of the temporalities to Robert, bp elect of Dublin, late archdeacon of Winchester *Westm* R. m p u 1047 O vn 98 H. m. p. m 40
Feb 16.	Maurice FitzThomas, earl of Kildare, is appointed justiciary of Ireland. *Westm* R. ui p u 1047.
Feb. 18.	Commission of Charles K of France to Louis duke of Anjou and Philip duke of Burgundy, to treat with the duke of Lancaster *Bois de Vincennes* R. m. p ii. 1047 O vn 99 H. m p u 41
March 5	Safe conducts for George de Dunbarre, earl of Marche, and James Douglas, coming to England *Westm.* R. m. p. u. 1048. O vn 100 H m. p m. 41.
March 12.	Prorogation of the truce with France until June 30 *Bruges* R. m p u 1048 O vn 100 H m. p m 41
March 12	French counterpart of the prorogation. *Bruges* R. iii. p. ii. 1048. O vn. 101. H m. p. m 41.
March 28.	Commission to sir Nicholas de Tamworth to put Southampton and the Isle of Wight in a state of defence *Westm* R m p u 1049
March 28	The commissioners of array in Norfolk and 12 other counties are ordered to make proclamation that persons having property on the coast are to go thither for its defence. *Westm.* R. m. p u 1049.
April 1.	Confirmation by the K of the prorogation of the truce with France. Confirmation by the K of France, dated 6 May *Westm* R m p u 1049 O vn 102 H. m p m 42.
April 24	The K. desires the abps of Canterbury and York to summon convocations of their clergy, for the purpose of granting a subsidy. *Westm* R m p u 1049
May 8	The mayor, bailiffs, and commonalty of Rye, are ordered to array the inhabitants and fortify the town *Westm* R m p u 1050
May 10	The K. forbids the sale of armour to any person leaving the kingdom *Westm* R m p. u 1050.
May 12.	Confirmation of the grant of an annuity of 1,200 florins to Robert de Nameur, dated Calais, July 1, 21 Edw III *Westm* R ui p u 1050 O vn. 103 H m. p m 42.
May 13.	The K orders his treasurer and chamberlains to pay 1,833*l* 6s 8d. to John de Harleston and Philip la Vache, from whom the K. has bought John lord de Poys and Walter Chastillon, their prisoners *Westm* R m. p u 1050 O vn 103 H m. p. ni. 42
May 18.	Pope Gregory asks the K.'s assistance in the execution of certain processes against Florentines for offences against the Church *Avignon* R in p. u 1050 O. vn. 103 H m p m 42.
May 21.	Power for John Harleston, captain of Guisnes, William de Eyrmyn, treasurer of Calais, and John Organ, of London, to receive the 40,000 francs due from the K of France for the surrender of S Sauveur *Westm* R m p u 1051 O vn 104 H m p u 42
May 24.	Exemption of Thomas bp. of Carlisle and his tenants of Horncastle from the payment of toll throughout the realm *Westm* R m. p. u 1051. O. vn. 105 H m p ni 43.
May 28.	The K orders Thomas de Felton, seneschal of Aquitain, the sondyke de Latrane, and William de Elmham, seneschal of Bayonne, to observe the truce with France and Castile *Westm* R m. p u 1051 O vn 105 H m p m 43
June 2.	Receipt for 40,000 francs from the K of France for S Sauveur *Westm.* R. m. p. u 1052 O vn 107 H m p m 44
June 3	The K. orders the mayor and sheriffs of London to arrest the goods of French men in retaliation for English merchandise arrested in France *Westm* R m p. u 1052 O vn. 108 H m p m. 44
June 3	The K forbids the mayor and bailiffs of Dover and Sandwich exacting tolls from the citizens of York, contrary to their privileges *Westm.* R. m p u 1053
June 6	Commission to Thomas Durant to count and weigh the 4,000 marks paid by Robert K. of Scotland *Westm* R m p u 1053 O vn 109 H m p m 44
June 6	Commission to Thomas de Musgrave, warden of Berwick-upon-Tweed, John de Boulton, chamberlain of Berwick, and two others, to receive the above money *Westm* R m. p. u. 1053 O vn. 109. H m p m 45

DATE	SUBJECT
1376 June 12.	Power for John bp of Hereford, John lord Cobham, sir Henry l'Scrop, and John Shepeye to treat for peace with France. *Westm* R. iii. p. ii 1053. O. vii. 110. H iii p iii 45
June 12.	Power for the same commissioners to grant safe conducts to French ambassadors *Westm* R iii p. ii. 1054 O vii 111 H iii. p. iii 45.
June 16	Writs to the mayor and sheriffs of London, and the bailiffs of Sandwich, Southampton, Weymouth, and Poole, for the arrest of French merchandise *Westm* R iii. p ii. 1054.
June 18.	The K orders the publication of the truce in London, Weymouth, Poole, Calais, and the Cinque Ports, and by the admirals *Westm* R iii p ii 1054 O vii 111 H iii p iii 45.
June 20.	Commission to W. bp. of London, Thomas bp of Ely, A bp. of S David's, and two others, to settle the dissensions in the university of Oxford *Westm.* R. iii. p ii 1055 O. vii 112 H iii p. iii 46
June 24.	Safe conduct for Giles Sancii, papal nuncio, coming to England. *Westm* R. iii p ii 1055 O. vii 113 H iii. p iii 46
June 26	Receipt of 4,000 marks from Robert K. of Scotland *Westm* R iii. p. ii. 1055. O vii 113 H iii. p iii 46.
June 28	William de Risceby is appointed warden of Oye Castle, *vice* Herman de Boys, deceased *Westm* R iii p ii 1055.
July 2.	The K orders Robert de Asheton, treasurer, and John de Ipre, seneschal of the household, to receive certain jewels pledged to Richard Lyons of London by John duke of Brittany, and to deliver them to the duchess of Brittany *Westm* R. iii p ii 1056 O. vii 113. H iii p iii 46
July 2	Pope Gregory [XI] desires credence for Pileus abp of Ravenna and Guillerme abp of Rouen. *Villeneuve* R. iii p. ii 1056 O vii. 115. H. iii. p. iii 47.
July 3.	Pope Gregory [XI] informs the K that he intends to transfer the court to Rome in the beginning of September *Villeneuve* R. iii p ii 1056 O vii 115 H iii p ii 47
July 16.	William de Ufford, earl of Suffolk, is appointed admiral north of the Thames, and William de Montacute, earl of Say [Salisbury], admiral west of the Thames R iii p ii 1057
July 17	Safe conduct for Charles K of Navarre going to Cherbourg *Westm.* R iii p ii 1057 O vii 116 H iii p iii 47.
July 18	Power for Hugh de Calvyle, captain, William Eyremyn, treasurer, and Ralph de Sutton, comptroller of Calais, to lease the K.'s houses and lands there *Westm* R iii p ii 1057.
July 18	Robert de Wykford, abp of Dublin, is appointed chancellor of Ireland, *vice* the prior of S John of Jerusalem in Ireland. *Westm* R iii p ii 1057
July 23.	Grant to the burgesses of Calais of the privilege of holding a staple, &c there Intimation thereof to the captain and treasurer of Calais *Westm* R iii p ii. 1057. O vii 117 H iii p iii 47
July 24.	Proclamation of the above to be made by the sheriffs of London, Essex, Norfolk, and Suffolk, and the constable of the Cinque Ports *Westm.* R iii p ii 1058 O vii 118 H iii. p. iii. 48
July 24	James le Botiller, earl of Ormond, is appointed justiciary of Ireland Intimation thereof to the late governor and people of Ireland *Westm* R iii p ii. 1058.
July 25	The K orders the justiciary and chancellor of Ireland to pay the expenses of persons coming to the parliament in England. *Westm* R iii p ii 1059
July 28.	Thomas de Felton, seneschal of Guyenne, William de Elmham, governor of Bayonne, the seneschal of the Landes, and the sondyk de la Trane, are ordered to observe the truce with France, and to redress injuries *Westm.* R. iii p ii 1059 O vii 118 H. iii. p. iii. 48.
Aug. 2	Power for J bp of Hereford, John lord Cobham, Henry le Scrop, and John Shepeye to receive 40,000 francs from the K of France *Westm.* R iii p ii 1059. O vii. 119. H iii p iii 48.
Aug. 2.	The K orders John de Harlaston, captain of Guisnes, and William de Ermyn, treasurer of Calais, to deliver the K.'s letters of acquittance for the above sum to the bp. of Hereford and his colleagues. *Westm* R iii. p. ii 1059 O. vii 120. H iii p iii. 49.
Aug 6.	Notification that the powers of granting pardon committed to the justiciary of Ireland, do not extend to prelates or nobles convicted of felony or treason *Westm* R iii p ii 1060.
Aug. 6	James de Boys is appointed chamberlain of the Exchequer in Ireland *Westm* R iii p ii 1060

DATE	SUBJECT
1376 Aug 6.	Licence to Alexander bp. of Ossory, treasurer of Ireland, to retain six men-at-arms and 12 archers. *Westm* R m. p. ii. 1060.
Aug. 6	John Tyrell is appointed justice in Ireland *Westm.* R m p n 1060
Aug 7	The K orders proclamation to be made by the sheriffs of Kent and Sussex that he has appointed conservators of the truce with France. *Westm.* R. m. p n 1060. O. vn 120. H m p m 49
Aug 8	Richard Plunket is appointed justice of the common bench in Ireland. *Westm* R m. p n 1060.
Aug 12	Safe conduct for Noffre de Rosse and Donatus Barbadour, Florentine ambassadors. *Westm.* R. m p. n 1061. O vn 121 H m p. m 42.
Aug 12	The K releases the commonalty of Cork from their rent of 86 marks, for the farm of their town and the hamlet of La Fayth beyond the walls of the city, the town having been much injured by the rebels *Westm* R m p n 1061.
Aug 12	Thomas Bache is appointed chancellor of the Exchequer in Ireland. The treasurer and barons are ordered to admit him *Westm* R m p. n 1061
Aug 12	Stephen Bray is appointed chief baron of the Exchequer of Ireland The treasurer and barons are ordered to admit him *Westm* R m p n 1061
Aug 12	John de Pembroke is appointed second baron of the Exchequer in Ireland. *Westm.* R m. p n 1061.
Aug 19	Obligation of Geralde de Tartays, lord of Puyan, and four others, for 1,000 marks for the purchase of the lord of Poys, a French prisoner, from the K *London.* R. m p n 1061. O vn 121 H m p m 499
Aug. 23	The K orders sir John Austyn and sir John Lakynghethe to guard Brest Castle, as the duke of Brittany has gone to Flanders without informing the K. Similar letters to John Cornewaile and Thomas Norreys, captains of the castles of Orray and S. Mathieu. *Pleshy.* R m p n 1062
Sept. 1	Sir Thomas de Beauchamp is appointed warden of Cornet Castle and Beauregard Tower in Guernsey *Westm* R m p n 1062
Oct. 15	Privileges granted to the burgesses of Calais *Havering* R. m p n 1062.
Oct. 24	The K orders John de Cobham, sir Stephen Valence, and three others, to examine the claim of the abp. of Canterbury that his tenants in certain lands in Kent are exempt from the expense of sending knights to parliament The sheriff of Kent is ordered to desist from distraining for such contributions till the claim is decided. *Westm* R m. p ii. 1063 O vn 122. H. m. p. m. 50.
Oct 28	Restitution of the temporalities to John bp of Bangor, late bp. of Cloyne. *Westm* R. m p n 1063 O vn 123 H m p m 50
Nov 4	The K orders the constable of Bourdeaux to pay the arrears of the pension due to the warden and friars of S. Macaire. *Westm* R m p n 1064 O vn 124. H. m p m 50
Nov 12	Grant of an annuity of 69l. 10s 6d to William Syward, the K's confessor. *Westm.* R m p n 1064 O vn. 124 H m p m 50
Nov 14	Nicholas de Drayton is appointed baron of the Exchequer. The treasurer and barons are ordered to admit him. *Havering* R m. p. n. 1064
Nov. 16.	The K orders John Cavendish and his fellow justices to proceed with the suit of the bp of Durham and Walter Tyrell, concerning a ferry over the Tweed. *Westm* R m p n 1064 O vn 125 H m p m 51
Nov. 18.	The K. orders the provost and scholars of "La Quenehalle," Oxford, to submit their dissensions to the decision of the abp of York Letter on the subject to the chancellor of the university and the mayor of the town *Westm* R. m p n. 1064. O. vn. 125. H m p m 51
Nov 20	The K orders the lands of Edward late prince of Wales to be delivered to Richard, his son and heir *Havering atte Bower.* R. m p n 1065. O vn. 126 H m p m 51.
Nov. 24.	Robert de Hales, prior of S John of Jerusalem in England, is appointed admiral west of the Thames, and Michael de la Pole, admiral north of the Thames *Westm* R m. p n. 1065 O vn 127 H m p m 52
Nov 26.	Walter Haule and John Legg are appointed deputies of the admirals The mayors and bailiffs of Ipswich, Colchester, and six other ports are ordered to prepare their barges. *Westm* R m p n 1066
Nov. 28	The K appoints Robert de Knolles and Thomas Moriaux conservators of the truce with France, in conjunction with sir William de Faryndon, John de Cornwaille, and John de Fastolf *Westm.* R. m. p. n. 1066.

DATE.	SUBJECT
1376 Dec 2.	Sir Thomas Fogg is appointed captain of Calais, *vice* sir Ralph de Sutton. *Westm.* R iii p. ii. 1056
Dec. 2.	The K orders the treasurer and barons of the Exchequer to pay the annuity of his son Thomas de Woodstock, constable of England, according to his grant dated 24 Aug. 1376. *Westm.* R. iii p. ii 1067 O. vii 128 H. iii. p iii. 52.
Dec 4	Warrant to the sheriff of Kent to pay to the princess of Wales the annuity of 30*l* granted to the prince and herself, 20 Nov 35 Edw III *Westm* R iii p ii 1067. O vii 129 H iii p iii 52.
Dec 7.	The K. orders sir Edward de Berkele to join Thomas de Felton and his colleagues in their negotiations with the count of Foix. *Westm.* R. iii p ii. 1067. O vii 130. H iii p. iii. 59
Dec. 12.	Treaty of the conservators of the truce between France and England, for the redress of injuries *Merquize* R iii p ii 1068 O vii 130 H iii p iii 53
Dec. 16.	The K. orders proclamation to be made throughout England and Ireland of the establishment of a staple at Calais. *Westm.* R. iii. p ii 1068
Dec. 18.	Power for Thomas de Felton, seneschal of Aquitain, John de Multon, mayor of Bourdeaux, and three others, to treat for alliance with *Charles K* of Navarre and with the count of Foix *Westm.* R iii p ii 1069 O vii 132 H iii p. iii 53.
1377 Jan 7	The K postpones the hearing of the charges of extortion against W bp of Winchester *Westm* R. iii. p. ii. 1069. O vii 132 H iii p iii 54
Jan. 8	Confirmation of the treaty made by the conservators of the truce with France. *Westm.* R iii p ii 1069. O. vii. 132 H iii p iii. 54
Jan 11.	Henry bp. of Worcester is appointed treasurer of the Exchequer, *vice* Robert de Assheton *Havering* R iii p. ii 1069.
Jan. 11	Adam bp. of S David's is appointed chancellor, *vice* John Knyvet. *Havering*, R. iii p ii 1069
Jan 11	Memorandum of the delivery of the seal to the bp of S David's R. iii. p. ii. 1069
Jan. 12.	Safe conduct for Charles K of Navarre. *Westm.* R. iii. p ii. 1069. O vii. 133. H iii p. iii 54.
Jan 13.	The K orders Walter Leicestre and John Ashewell, sergeants at-arms, to convey the sons of Charles de Blois from Nottingham to Devizes Warrants to Nicholas Dauhnchecourt, warden of Nottingham Castle, and Roger de Beauchamp, warden of Devizes Castle, to deliver and receive them. *Westm* R iii. p. ii. 1070. O vii 133 H iii p. iii. 54
Jan. 16.	The K orders the sheriff of Bedford to compel Giles Danbeneye and Fulk de Pembrugge, lords of the manor of Kempston, to contribute to the expense of sending knights to parliament *Westm* R. iii p. ii. 1070 O vii 134. H iii p. iii. 54.
Jan. 26.	Power for Richard prince of Wales to open parliament *Havering*. R. iii. p ii. 1070 O. vii 134 H iii. p iii 54
Jan. 30.	Safe conduct for John de Neyvill of France, prisoner of Guy Briene. *Westm* R iii. p. ii 1070. O vii. 134. H iii p iii 54.
Jan. 30.	The K orders the mayor and sheriffs of London to restore the goods of the Florentines which were seized, to protect them from the pope, and to allow the Florentines to reside in London as the K's servants Letter on the same subject to Hugh de Calvyley, captain of Calais *Westm* R iii p ii 1071 O vii 135. H. iii p iii 55
Feb. 8.	The K orders the wardens of Guernsey and Jersey to maintain his rights. , *Westm.* R iii. p. ii 1071
Feb. 13.	Warrants to Michael de la Pole and the prior of S John of Jerusalem, the K.'s admirals, to arrest ships and barges *Westm.* R iii. p. ii 1071
Feb 15.	Treaty between the K. and pope Gregory [XI], who promises to be more moderate in collating to English benefices ; to give benefices to those who could reside on them , to moderate the amount of the first-fruits ; and to grant fewer reversions and provisions. *Westm* R iii p. ii 1072 O. vii. 1136. H iii. p iii 55.
Feb. 18.	The K orders the mayors and bailiffs of Salisbury and Southampton to proclaim that parliament has removed the prohibition of the sale of sweet wines *Westm.* R. iii p. ii. 1072
Feb. 20.	Power for John bp. of Hereford, John lord Cobham, John Montacu, and John Shepeye to treat with the K of France *Westm.* R iii p. ii. 1073.

DATE	SUBJECT
1377 Feb 28	Grant to John K of Castile, duke of Lancaster, of jurisdictions and liberties in the county of Lancaster, similar to those enjoyed by the earl of Chester in Cheshire　*Westm.*　R m. p ii 1073　O vii 138　H iii p iii 56
March 2.	The K orders William de Montacute, earl of Salisbury, and 18 others, to go to their lands in the Isle of Wight, to defend it from invasion　*Westm*　R iii p ii 1073　O vii 139　H iii p iii 56
March 4	Confirmation of the grant of the manors of Gryngeley and Whetely by John duke of Lancaster to Katherine de Swynford　*Shene*　R iii p ii 1074.　O. vii. 140　H. iii p iii. 56
March 6	Grant to Richard Hereford, herald of arms, of the tenements in Calais lately belonging to lord FitzWalter　*Westm*　R iii p ii 1074
March 11	Powers for J bp of Hereford to treat with the count of Flanders and with the commonalties of Flanders　Similar powers to the bp and John de Shepeye　*Westm., April 11.*　R iii p ii. 1074　O vii. 140　H iii p iii. 57
March 12.	Safe conduct for Charles K of Navarre to come to Cherbourg in Normandy　Similar safe conduct, dated April 30　*Westm*　R iii p ii 1074　O vii 141.　H. iii p iii 57
March 12	The K. orders James de Botiller, earl of Ormond justiciary, and William Tany, prior of S John of Jerusalem in Ireland, chancellor of Ireland, to compel Gerard Droem, agent of the cardinal of S Martial, to account to the cardinal for the sums he has collected.　*Westm.*　R iii p ii 1074　O vii 141　H iii p iii 57
March 15	Grant of the custody of the temporalities of the see of Winchester to Richard prince of Wales　*Westm*　R iii p ii 1075　O vii. 142　H iii. p iii 57.
March 15	The K orders John K. of Castile and duke of Lancaster, and 22 other lords, to fortify their castles in Wales　*Westm*　R iii p ii. 1075　O vii 142　H. iii p iii 58
March 16	Proclamation to be made by the sheriffs of Kent and 14 other counties that persons having lands near the sea-coast are to go thither for the defence of the realm　*Westm*　R. iii p ii 1075
March 20	Warrant to the prior of S John of Jerusalem in England, admiral of the west, to arrest ships　*Westm*　R iii p ii 1076.
March 21	The K orders the aldermen and commonalty of London to elect a mayor, as he has released the late mayor from his office　*Shene*　R iii p ii 1076
March 26	Power for Adam bp of S David's, John bp of Hereford, William de Montague, earl of Salisbury, and six others, to treat with France　*Westm*　R. iii p ii 1076　O. vii 143　H iii p iii 58
April 30	Safe conduct for Charles K of Navarre to come to Cherbourg　*Westm.*　R. iii. p ii 1076.
May 1	The K. grants to the precentor and chapter of S David's the custody of the temporalties of the see during any vacancy　*Westm*　R. iii p ii 1076　O vii 144　H. iii. p iii 58
May 4	Warrant to Walter Haule, John Legg, sergeants-at-arms, and William Welles, master of the ship called *Grace Dieu*, to arrest 160 sailors　Four similar warrants　*Westm*　R iii. p iii. 1077.
May 4	William de Burstall, keeper of the rolls, Richard de Ravenser, and Thomas de Newenham, clerks of the chancery, are appointed keepers of the great seal during the absence abroad of Adam bp. of S. David's on the K.'s business　R. iii. p ii 1077
May 8	Henry de Percy, marshal of England, is commissioned to levy men and survey the castles at Calais, Guisnes, and elsewhere in Ponthieu　*Westm*　R iii p ii 1078
May 14	The K. orders Thomas bp of Exeter, the abbot of Buckfast, and six others, to go to their lands near Dartmouth, as the coast is threatened by a French fleet　Similar letters to the abbots of Tavistock and Buckland, and 11 others, to go their lands near Plymouth　*Westm*　R iii p ii 1078.　O. vii. 145　H. iii. p iii 58
May 27	Safe conduct for Guy de Roche, archdeacon and papal collector, and Guy la Bardonia, sergeant-at-arms of the pope, coming to pay the ransom of Roger de Beaufort and John de Roche, prisoners of the captal de Buch　*Westm*　R iii p ii. 1078　O vii 146.　H iii. p iii 59
May 30	The K releases the inhabitants of the Isle of Wight from the necessity of attendance at the sessions in Hampshire　Letters on the subject to the sheriff of Southampton, Hugh Tyrell, warden, and John Griffyth, constable of Carisbrook Castle　*Westm.*　R. iii. p ii 1078　O. vii 147.　H. iii p iii 59
June 6	Safe conduct for sir William de Ramsey, who is ill, and under the care of the prior of Bermondsey　*Westm.*　R iii p ii. 1079　O vii. 148　H iii p iii 59

DATE	SUBJECT.
1877. June 12	Licence to John K. of Castile and duke of Lancaster to coin money at Bayonne or elsewhere in the Landes. *Westm.* R. iii p ii 1079. O vii. 148 H iii p iii 60
June 18.	Restitution of the temporalities to the bp of Winchester, who has undertaken certain charges for the defence of the kingdom *Westm* R iii. p. ii 1079 O vii 149 H. iii p iii 60
June 18.	Warrant to the prince of Wales to deliver the temporalities to the said bishop *Westm* R. iii p ii. 1079. O. vii. 149.
	Testament of the K , Edward the Third, executors, John K of Castile and duke of Lancaster, John bp of Lincoln, Henry bp of Worcester, J bp of Hereford, William lord Latymer, sir John Knyvet, sir Robert de Assheton, sir Roger de Beauchamp, sir John de Ipre, and Nicholas de Careu. *Havering atte Bower*, 7 Oct 1376. R iii. p ii, 1080
June 21.	Memorandum that K Edward died at Shene on the Sunday next before the feast of S John the Baptist in the year 1377, in the 51st year of his reign O vii 151

END OF VOL. I.

The Index to this volume will be found at the end of Vol. II

CATALOGUE

OF

RECORD PUBLICATIONS

ON SALE

BY

Messrs. Longman & Co., London;
Messrs. James Parker & Co., Oxford and London;
Messrs. Macmillan & Co., Cambridge and London;
Messrs. A. & C. Black, Edinburgh;
and Mr. A. Thom, Dublin.

CONTENTS

CALENDARS OF STATE PAPERS, &c.

[IMPERIAL 8vo., cloth. *Price* 15s. each Volume or Part.]

As far back as the year 1800, a Committee of the House of Commons recommended that Indexes and Calendars should be made to the Public Records, and thirty-six years afterwards another Committee of the House of Commons reiterated that recommendation in more forcible words, but it was not until the incorporation of the State Paper Office with the Public Record Office that the present Master of the Rolls found himself in a position to take the necessary steps for carrying out the wishes of the House of Commons.

On 7 December 1855, he stated to the Lords of the Treasury that although " the Records, State Papers, and Documents in his charge constitute the most " complete and perfect series of their kind in the civilized world," and although "they are of the greatest value in a historical and constitutional " point of view, yet they are comparatively useless to the public, from the " want of proper Calendars and Indexes."

Acting upon the recommendations of the Committees of the House of Commons above referred to, he suggested to the Lords of the Treasury that to effect the object he had in view it would be necessary for him to employ a few persons fully qualified to perform the work which he contemplated.

Their Lordships assented to the necessity of having Calendars prepared and printed, and empowered the Master of the Rolls to take such steps as might be necessary for this purpose

The following Works have been already published under the direction of the Master of the Rolls :—

CALENDARIUM GENEALOGICUM ; for the Reigns of Henry III. and Edward I. *Edited by* CHARLES ROBERTS, Esq , Secretary of the Public Record Office. 2 Vols. 1865.
> This is a work of great value for elucidating the early history of our nobility and landed gentry

CALENDAR OF STATE PAPERS, DOMESTIC SERIES, OF THE REIGNS OF ED-
WARD VI., MARY, and ELIZABETH, preserved in Her Majesty's Public
Record Office. *Edited by* ROBERT LEMON, Esq., F.S.A. 1856–1865
    Vol. I.—1547–1580. | Vol. II.—1581–1590.

CALENDAR OF STATE PAPERS, DOMESTIC SERIES, OF THE REIGN OF ELIZA-
BETH (continued), preserved in Her Majesty's Public Record Office.
Edited by MARY ANNE EVERETT GREEN. 1867–1869.
    Vol. III.—1591–1594. | Vol. IV.—1595–1597.

    Of the above series, four volumes are published, extending from 1547 to 1597

CALENDAR OF STATE PAPERS, DOMESTIC SERIES, OF THE REIGN OF JAMES
I., preserved in Her Majesty's Public Record Office. *Edited by* MARY
ANNE EVERETT GREEN. 1857–1859.
    Vol. I.—1603–1610 | Vol. III.—1619–1623.
    Vol. II.—1611–1618. | Vol. IV —1623–1625, with Addenda.

    Mrs Everett Green has completed a Calendar of the Domestic State Papers
of the reign of James I in four volumes. The mass of historical matter thus
rendered accessible to investigation is large and important. It throws new light
on the Gunpowder plot, the rise and fall of Somerset, the particulars connected with the Overbury murder, the disgrace of Sir Edward Coke, and other
matters connected with the reign.

CALENDAR OF STATE PAPERS, DOMESTIC SERIES, OF THE REIGN OF
CHARLES I., preserved in Her Majesty's Public Record Office. *Edited
by* JOHN BRUCE, Esq., F S A. 1858–1869
    Vol I.—1625–1626. | Vol. VII.—1634–1635
    Vol II —1627–1628. | Vol VIII —1635
    Vol III.—1628–1629 | Vol IX —1635–1636.
    Vol. IV —1629–1631 | Vol X —1636–1637.
    Vol V.—1631–1633 | Vol. XI.—1637.
    Vol VI —1633–1634. | Vol. XII.—1637–1638

    This Calendar is in continuation of that of the Domestic State Papers of the
reign of James I, and will extend to the Restoration of Charles II. At present
it comprises the first fourteen years of the reign of Charles I, but is in active progress towards completion. It presents notices of a large number of original
documents of great value to all inquirers into the history of the period to which
it relates. Many of these documents have been hitherto unknown.

CALENDAR OF STATE PAPERS, DOMESTIC SERIES, OF THE REIGN OF
CHARLES II, preserved in Her Majesty's Public Record Office. *Edited
by* MARY ANNE EVERETT GREEN. 1860–1866
    Vol. I.—1660–1661. | Vol. V.—1665–1666.
    Vol II —1661–1662 | Vol VI.—1666–1667.
    Vol III —1663–1664 | Vol VII —1667.
    Vol IV.—1664–1665.

    Seven volumes, of the period between 1660 and 1667, have been published

CALENDAR OF STATE PAPERS relating to SCOTLAND, preserved in Her
Majesty's Public Record Office. *Edited by* MARKHAM JOHN THORPE
Esq., of St. Edmund Hall, Oxford. 1858
    Vol I, the Scottish Series, of the Reigns of Henry VIII.
Edward VI, Mary, and Elizabeth, 1509–1589.
    Vol II, the Scottish Series, of the Reign of Elizabeth, 1589–1603;
an Appendix to the Scottish Series, 1543–1592, and the State
Papers relating to Mary Queen of Scots during her Detention in
England, 1568–1587.

    The above two volumes of State Papers relate to Scotland, and embrace the
period between 1509 and 1603. In the second volume are notices of the State
Papers relating to Mary Queen of Scots

CALENDAR OF STATE PAPERS relating to IRELAND, preserved in Her Majesty's Public Record Office Edited by HANS CLAUDE HAMILTON, Esq , F.S A   1860–1867.

    Vol. I.—1509–1573 | Vol. II.—1574–1585.

> The above have been published under the editorship of Mr Hans Claude Hamilton , another volume is in progress.

CALENDAR OF STATE PAPERS, COLONIAL SERIES, preserved in Her Majesty's Public Record Office, and elsewhere. Edited by W. NOEL SAINSBURY, Esq. 1860–1862.

    Vol. I.—America and West Indies, 1574–1660.

    Vol. II.—East Indies, China, and Japan, 1513–1616.

> These volumes include an analysis of all Papers from the three great archives of the Public Record Office, the India Office, and the British Museum The third volume is in the press The regular series of the East India Papers in the Public Record Office are calendared to the year 1623 , those relating to the same subject in the Domestic Correspondence to 1625 , in the Foreign Correspondence to 1621 , the Court Minutes of the East India Company to 1621 , and the Original Correspondence in the India Office to 1621. Many undated Papers have been dated and arranged

CALENDAR OF LETTERS AND PAPERS, FOREIGN AND DOMESTIC, OF THE REIGN OF HENRY VIII., preserved in Her Majesty's Public Record Office, the British Museum, &c Edited by J S BREWER, M A., Professor of English Literature, King's College, London. 1862–1867.

    Vol. I.—1509–1514.

    Vol II (in Two Parts)—1515–1518.

    Vol III. (in Two Parts)—1519–1523

> These volumes contain summaries of all State Papers and Correspondence relating to the reign of Henry VIII , in the Public Record Office, of those formerly in the State Paper Office, in the British Museum, the Libraries of Oxford and Cambridge, and other Public Libraries , and of all letters that have appeared in print in the works of Burnet, Strype, and others Whatever authentic original material exists in England relative to the religious, political, parliamentary, or social history of the country during the reign of Henry VIII , whether despatches of ambassadors, or proceedings of the army, navy, treasury, or ordnance, or records of Parliament, appointments of officers, grants from the Crown, &c , will be found calendared in these volumes

CALENDAR OF STATE PAPERS, FOREIGN SERIES, OF THE REIGN OF EDWARD VI., preserved in Her Majesty's Public Record Office. 1547–1553 Edited by W. B. TURNBULL, Esq , of Lincoln's Inn, Barrister-at-Law, and Correspondant du Comité Impérial des Travaux Historiques et des Sociétés Savantes de France. 1861.

CALENDAR OF STATE PAPERS, FOREIGN SERIES, OF THE REIGN OF MARY, preserved in Her Majesty's Public Record Office. 1553–1558. Edited by W. B. TURNBULL, Esq., of Lincoln's Inn, Barrister-at-Law, and Correspondant du Comité Impérial des Travaux Historiques et des Sociétés Savantes de France 1861.

> The two preceding volumes exhibit the negotiations of the English ambassadors with the courts of the Emperor Charles V. of Germany, of Henry II of France, and of Philip II of Spain. The affairs of several of the minor continental states also find various incidental illustrations of much interest
> A valuable series of Papers descriptive of the circumstances which attended the loss of Calais merits a special notice , while the progress of the wars in the north of France, into which England was dragged by her union with Spain, is narrated at some length The domestic affairs of England are of course passed over in these volumes, which treat only of its relations with foreign powers

CALENDAR OF STATE PAPERS, FOREIGN SERIES, OF THE REIGN OF
ELIZABETH, preserved in Her Majesty's Public Record Office, &c
Edited by the Rev. JOSEPH STEVENSON, M A., of University College,
Durham. 1863–1869.

Vol. I.—1558–1559.	Vol. IV —1561–1562.
Vol. II.—1559–1560.	Vol V.—1562
Vol III.—1560–1561.	Vol. VI —1563.

These six volumes contain a calendar of the Foreign Correspondence of
Queen Elizabeth, from her accession in 1558, to 1563, of which the originals,
drafts, or contemporary copies, are deposited in the Public Record Office, &c
These documents are of the greatest value as exhibiting the position of England
at one of the most interesting periods of history, in regard to its relations with
France, Scotland, Spain, and Germany They are of especial importance as
illustrating not only the external but also the domestic affairs of France during
the period which immediately preceded the outbreak of the first great war of
religion under the Prince of Condé and the Duke of Guise

CALENDAR OF TREASURY PAPERS, preserved in Her Majesty's Public Record
Office. 1557–1696. *Edited by* JOSEPH REDINGTON, Esq 1868.

The Papers connected with the administration of the affairs of the Treasury,
from 1556–7 to 1696, comprising petitions, reports, and other documents relating to services rendered to the State, grants of money and pensions, appoint-
ments to offices, remissions of fines and duties, &c., are calendared in this
volume They illustrate civil and military events, financial and other matters,
the administration in Ireland and the Colonies, &c, and afford information
nowhere else recorded

CALENDAR OF THE CAREW PAPERS, preserved in Lambeth Library *Edited
by* J. S. BREWER, M A., Professor of English Literature, King's College,
London , and WILLIAM BULLEN, Esq. 1867–1869.

Vol I.—1515–1574.	Vol III —1589–1600
Vol. II.—1575–1588.	

The Carew Papers relating to Ireland deposited in the Lambeth Library are not
only unique in themselves, but are of great importance Three volumes of the
Calendar of these valuable Papers have been published, extending from 1515 to
1600, which cannot fail to be welcome to all students of Irish history Another
volume is in the press

CALENDAR OF LETTERS, DESPATCHES, AND STATE PAPERS, relating to the
Negotiations between England and Spain, preserved in the Archives
at Simancas, and elsewhere. *Edited by* G. A BERGENROTH. 1862–
1868

Vol. I.—Hen VII —1485–1509.
Vol II.—Hen. VIII —1509–1525.
Supplement to Vol I and Vol. II

Mr Bergenroth was engaged in compiling a Calendar of the Papers relating
to England preserved in the archives of Simancas in Spain, and the corresponding
portion removed from Simancas to Paris Mr Bergenroth also visited Madrid,
and examined the Papers there, bearing on the reign of Henry VIII The
first volume contains the Spanish Papers of the reign of Henry VII ; the
second volume, those of the first portion of the reign of Henry VIII. The
Supplement contains new information relating to the private life of Queen
Katharine of England , and to the projected marriage of Henry VII. with Queen
Juana, widow of King Philip of Castile, and mother of the Emperor Charles V.

CALENDAR OF STATE PAPERS AND MANUSCRIPTS, relating to ENGLISH AFFAIRS, preserved in the Archives of Venice, &c. *Edited by* RAWDON BROWN, Esq. 1864–1867.

    Vol. I —1202–1509.

    Vol. II —1509–1519

        Of the Papers in the Venetian archives, Mr Rawdon Brown has published two volumes of his Calendar, extending from 1202 to 1519, and has made considerable progress in the third volume Mr Brown's researches have brought to light a number of important documents relating to the various periods of English history, and his contributions to historical literature are of the most interesting and important character.

REPORT OF THE DEPUTY KEEPER OF THE PUBLIC RECORDS AND THE REV. J. S. BREWER TO THE MASTER OF THE ROLLS, upon the Carte and Carew Papers in the Bodleian and Lambeth Libraries. 1864. *Price* 2s. 6d.

REPORT OF THE DEPUTY KEEPER OF THE PUBLIC RECORDS TO THE MASTER OF THE ROLLS, upon the Documents in the Archives and Public Libraries of Venice. 1866 *Price* 2s. 6d.

SYLLABUS, IN ENGLISH, OF RYMER'S FŒDERA. *By* THOMAS DUFFUS HARDY, Esq., Deputy Keeper of the Public Records. Vol. I. — Will. I. — Edw III., 1066–1377. 1869

        The "Fœdera," or "Rymer's Fœdera," is a collection of miscellaneous documents illustrative of the History of Great Britain and Ireland, from the Norman Conquest to the reign of Charles II Several editions of the "Fœdera" have been published, and the present Syllabus was undertaken to make the contents of this great National Work more generally known

---

In the Press.

CALENDAR OF STATE PAPERS, COLONIAL SERIES, preserved in Her Majesty's Public Record Office, and elsewhere. *Edited by* W. NOEL SAINSBURY, Esq. Vol. III.—East Indies, China, and Japan, 1617, &c.

CALENDAR OF LETTERS AND PAPERS, FOREIGN AND DOMESTIC, OF THE REIGN OF HENRY VIII., preserved in Her Majesty's Public Record Office, the British Museum, &c. *Edited by* J. S. BREWER, M.A., Professor of English Literature, King's College, London. Vol IV.—1524, &c.

CALENDAR OF STATE PAPERS AND MANUSCRIPTS, relating to ENGLISH AFFAIRS, preserved in the Archives of Venice, &c. *Edited by* RAWDON BROWN, Esq Vol. III.—1520–1526.

CALENDAR OF STATE PAPERS, DOMESTIC SERIES, OF THE REIGN OF ELIZABETH (continued), preserved in Her Majesty's Public Record Office *Edited by* MARY ANNE EVERETT GREEN. Vol V.—1598–1601

CALENDAR OF THE CAREW PAPERS, preserved in Lambeth Library. *Edited by* J. S. BREWER, M.A , Professor of English Literature, King's College, London , and WILLIAM BULLEN, Esq. Vol. IV.—1601, &c

Calendar of State Papers, Foreign Series, of the Reign of Elizabeth, preserved in Her Majesty's Public Record Office. *Edited by* the Rev Joseph Stevenson, M.A., of University College, Durham Vol VII,—1564.

Syllabus, in English, of Rymer's Fœdera, with Index. Vol. II

In Progress.

Calendar of State Papers relating to Ireland, preserved in Her Majesty s Public Record Office *Edited by* Hans Claude Hamilton, Esq, F.S A. Vol. III—1586, &c.

Calendar of State Papers, Domestic Series, of the Reign of Charles I., preserved in Her Majesty's Public Record Office *Edited by* John Bruce, Esq., F S A. Vol XIII—1638.

Calendar of Letters, Despatches, and State Papers, relating to the Negotiations between England and Spain, preserved in the Archives at Simancas and elsewhere. *Edited by* Don Pascual de Gayangos. Hen. VIII

THE CHRONICLES AND MEMORIALS OF GREAT BRITAIN AND IRELAND DURING THE MIDDLE AGES.

[ROYAL 8vo., half-bound. *Price* 10*s*. each Volume or Part]

On 25 July 1822, the House of Commons presented an address to the Crown, stating that the editions of the works of our ancient historians were inconvenient and defective; that many of their writings still remained in manuscript, and, in some cases, in a single copy only. They added, " that an " uniform and convenient edition of the whole, published under His Majesty's " royal sanction, would be an undertaking honourable to His Majesty's reign, " and conducive to the advancement of historical and constitutional know- " ledge , that the House therefore humbly besought His Majesty, that He " would be graciously pleased to give such directions as His Majesty, in His " wisdom, might think fit, for the publication of a complete edition of the " ancient historians of this realm, and assured His Majesty that whatever " expense might be necessary for this purpose would be made good "

The Master of the Rolls, being very desirous that effect should be given to the resolution of the House of Commons, submitted to Her Majesty's Treasury in 1857 a plan for the publication of the ancient chronicles and memorials of the United Kingdom, and it was adopted accordingly In selecting these works, it was considered right, in the first instance, to give preference to those of which the manuscripts were unique, or the materials of which would help to fill up blanks in English history for which no satisfactory and authentic information hitherto existed in any accessible form. One great object the Master of the Rolls had in view was to form a *corpus historicum* within reasonable limits, and which should be as complete as possible. In a subject of so vast a range, it was important that the historical student should be able to select such volumes as conformed with his own peculiar tastes and studies, and not be put to the expense of purchasing the whole collection , an inconvenience inseparable from any other plan than that which has been in this instance adopted

Of the Chronicles and Memorials, the following volumes have been published. They embrace the period from the earliest time of British history down to the end of the reign of Henry VII.

1. THE CHRONICLE OF ENGLAND, by JOHN CAPGRAVE   *Edited by* the
Rev. F C. HINGESTON, M A , of Exeter College, Oxford.   1858

> Capgrave was prior of Lynn, in Norfolk, and provincial' of the order of the
> Friars Hermits of England shortly before the year 1464   His Chronicle extends
> from the creation of the world to the year 1417   As a record of the language
> spoken in Norfolk (being written in English), it is of considerable value

2. CHRONICON MONASTERII DE ABINGDON   Vols I and II.   *Edited by*
the Rev. JOSEPH STEVENSON, M A., of University College, Durham,
and Vicar of Leighton Buzzard.   1858.

> This Chronicle traces the history of the great Benedictine monastery of
> Abingdon in Berkshire, from its foundation by King Ina of Wessex, to the
> reign of Richard I , shortly after which period the present narrative was drawn
> up by an inmate of the establishment   The author had access to the title-deeds
> of the house , and incorporates into his history various charters of the Saxon
> kings, of great importance as illustrating not only the history of the locality
> but that of the kingdom   The work is printed for the first time

3. LIVES OF EDWARD THE CONFESSOR.   I —La Estoire de Seint Aedward
le Rei   II —Vita Beati Edvardi Regis et Confessoris.   III.—Vita
Æduuardi Regis qui apud Westmonasterium requiescit.   *Edited by*
HENRY RICHARDS LUARD, M A , Fellow and Assistant Tutor of Trinity
College, Cambridge   1858.

> The first is a poem in Norman French, containing 4,686 lines, addressed to
> Alianor, Queen of Henry III., and probably written in the year 1245, on the
> occasion of the restoration of the church of Westminster   Nothing is known
> of the author   The second is an anonymous poem, containing 536 lines, written
> between the years 1440 and 1450, by command of Henry VI , to whom it
> is dedicated   It does not throw any new light on the reign of Edward the
> Confessor, but is valuable as a specimen of the Latin poetry of the time   The
> third, also by an anonymous author, was apparently written for Queen Edith,
> between the years 1066 and 1074, during the pressure of the suffering brought
> on the Saxons by the Norman conquest.   It notices many facts not found in
> other writers, and some which differ considerably from the usual accounts

4. MONUMENTA FRANCISCANA ; scilicet, I.—Thomas de Eccleston de Ad-
ventu Fratrum Minorum in Angliam.   II —Adæ de Marisco Epistolæ.
III.—Registrum Fratrum Minorum Londoniæ.   *Edited by* J. S.
BREWER, M.A., Professor of English Literature, King's College,
London.   1858.

> This volume contains original materials for the history of the settlement of
> the order of Saint Francis in England, the letters of Adam de Marisco, and
> other papers connected with the foundation and diffusion of this great body   It
> has been the aim of the editor to collect whatever historical information could be
> found in this country, towards illustrating a period of the national history for
> which only scanty materials exist   None of these have been before printed

5 FASCICULI ZIZANIORUM MAGISTRI JOHANNIS WYCLIF CUM TRITICO.
Ascribed to THOMAS NETTER, of WALDEN, Provincial of the Carmelite
Order in England, and Confessor to King Henry the Fifth   *Edited by*
the Rev W. W SHIRLEY, M A., Tutor and late Fellow of Wadham
College, Oxford   1858.

> This work derives its principal value from being the only contemporaneous
> account of the rise of the Lollards.   When written, the disputes of the school-

men had been extended to the field of theology, and they appear both in the writings of Wycliff and in those of his adversaries. Wycliff's little bundles of tares are not less metaphysical than theological, and the conflict between Nominalists and Realists rages side by side with the conflict between the different interpreters of Scripture. The work gives a good idea of the controversies at the end of the 14th and the beginning of the 15th centuries.

6. THE BUIK OF THE CRONICLIS OF SCOTLAND; or, A Metrical Version of the History of Hector Boece; by WILLIAM STEWART. Vols. I., II, and III Edited by W. B. TURNBULL, Esq., of Lincoln's Inn, Barrister-at-Law 1858

This is a metrical translation of a Latin Prose Chronicle, and was written in the first half of the 16th century. The narrative begins with the earliest legends, and ends with the death of James I. of Scotland, and the "evil ending of the traitors that slew him." Strict accuracy of statement is not to be looked for in such a work as this; but the stories of the colonization of Spain, Ireland, and Scotland are interesting if not true; and the chronicle is valuable as a reflection of the manners, sentiments, and character of the age in which it was composed. The peculiarities of the Scottish dialect are well illustrated in this metrical version, and the student of language will find ample materials for comparison with the English dialects of the same period, and with modern lowland Scotch.

7. JOHANNIS CAPGRAVE LIBER DE ILLUSTRIBUS HENRICIS. Edited by the Rev F. C. HINGESTON, M A., of Exeter College, Oxford. 1858.

This work is dedicated to Henry VI of England, who appears to have been, in the author's estimation, the greatest of all the Henries. It is divided into three distinct parts, each having its own separate dedication. The first part relates only to the history of the Empire, and extends from the election of Henry I, the Fowler, to the end of the reign of the Emperor Henry VI. The second part is devoted to English history, and extends from the accession of Henry I in the year 1100, to the year 1446, which was the twenty-fourth year of the reign of King Henry VI. The third part contains the lives of illustrious men who have borne the name of Henry in various parts of the world.

Capgrave was born in 1393, in the reign of Richard II, and lived during the Wars of the Roses, for the history of which period his work is of some value.

8 HISTORIA MONASTERII S AUGUSTINI CANTUARIENSIS, by THOMAS OF ELMHAM, formerly Monk and Treasurer of that Foundation Edited by CHARLES HARDWICK, M A, Fellow of St. Catharine's Hall, and Christian Advocate in the University of Cambridge. 1858.

This history extends from the arrival of St Augustine in Kent until 1191. Prefixed is a chronology as far as 1418, which shows in outline what was to have been the character of the work when completed. The only copy known is in the possession of Trinity Hall, Cambridge. The author was connected with Norfolk, and most probably with Elmham, whence he derived his name.

9. EULOGIUM (HISTORIARUM SIVE TEMPORIS): Chronicon ab Orbe condito usque ad Annum Domini 1366; a Monacho quodam Malmesbiriensi exaratum. Vols. I., II., and III. Edited by F. S. HAYDON, Esq, B A. 1858–1863

This is a Latin Chronicle extending from the Creation to the latter part of the reign of Edward III, and written by a monk of the Abbey of Malmesbury, in Wiltshire, about the year 1367. A continuation, carrying the history of England down to the year 1413, was added in the former half of the fifteenth century by an author whose name is not known. The original Chronicle is divided into five books, and contains a history of the world generally, but more especially

12

of England to the year 1366   The continuation extends the history down to the coronation of Henry V   The Eulogium itself is chiefly valuable as containing a history, by a contemporary, of the period between 1356 and 1366   The notices of events appear to have been written very soon after their occurrence   Among other interesting matter, the Chronicle contains a diary of the Poitiers campaign, evidently furnished by some person who accompanied the army of the Black Prince   The continuation of the Chronicle is also the work of a contemporary, and gives a very interesting account of the reigns of Richard II and Henry IV   It is believed to be the earliest authority for the statement that the latter monarch died in the Jerusalem Chamber at Westminster

10. MEMORIALS OF HENRY THE SEVENTH   Bernardi Andreæ Tholosatis Vita Regis Henrici Septimi ; necnon alia quædam ad eundem Regem spectantia. *Edited by* JAMES GAIRDNER, Esq. 1858.

The contents of these volumes are—(1) a life of Henry VII, by his poet laureate and historiographer, Bernard André, of Toulouse, with some compositions in verse, of which he is supposed to have been the author ; (2) the journals of Roger Machado during certain embassies on which he was sent by Henry VII to Spain and Brittany, the first of which had reference to the marriage of the King's son, Arthur, with Catharine of Arragon, (3) two curious reports by envoys sent to Spain in the year 1505 touching the succession to the Crown of Castile, and a project of marriage between Henry VII. and the Queen of Naples , and (4) an account of Philip of Castile's reception in England in 1506. Other documents of interest in connexion with the period are given in an appendix.

11 MEMORIALS OF HENRY THE FIFTH. I.—Vita Henrici Quinti, Roberto Redmanno auctore   II —Versus Rhythmici in laudem Regis Henrici Quinti. III.—Elmhami Liber Metricus de Henrico V   *Edited by* CHARLES A. COLE, Esq. 1858

This volume contains three treatises which more or less illustrate the history of the reign of Henry V , viz   A Life by Robert Redman , a Metrical Chronicle by Thomas Elmham, prior of Lenton, a contemporary author , Versus Rhythmici, written apparently by a monk of Westminster Abbey, who was also a contemporary of Henry V   These works are printed for the first time

12. MUNIMENTA GILDHALLÆ LONDONIENSIS , Liber Albus, Liber Custumarum, et Liber Horn, in archivis Gildhallæ asservati. Vol. 1 , Liber Albus   Vol II (in Two Parts), Liber Custumarum   Vol III , Translation of the Anglo-Norman Passages in Liber Albus, Glossaries, Appendices, and Index. *Edited by* HENRY THOMAS RILEY, Esq., M.A., Barrister-at-Law. 1859–1862.

The manuscript of the *Liber Albus*, compiled by John Carpenter, Common Clerk of the City of London in the year 1419, a large folio volume, is preserved in the Record Room of the City of London   It gives an account of the laws, regulations, and institutions of that City in the twelfth, thirteenth, fourteenth, and early part of the fifteenth centuries
The *Liber Custumarum* was compiled probably by various hands in the early part of the fourteenth century during the reign of Edward II   The manuscript, a folio volume, is also preserved in the Record Room of the City of London, though some portion in its original state, borrowed from the City in the reign of Queen Elizabeth and never returned, forms part of the Cottonian MS Claudius D. II in the British Museum   It also gives an account of the laws, regulations, and institutions of the City of London in the twelfth, thirteenth, and early part of the fourteenth centuries

13. CHRONICA JOHANNIS DE OXENEDES. *Edited by* Sir HENRY ELLIS, K H. 1859.

Although this Chronicle tells of the arrival of Hengist and Horsa in England in the year 449, yet it substantially begins with the reign of King Alfred, and comes down to the year 1292, where it ends abruptly The history is particularly valuable for notices of events in the eastern portions of the kingdom, which are not to be elsewhere obtained, and some curious facts are mentioned relative to the floods in that part of England, which are confirmed in the Friesland Chronicle of Anthony Heinrich, pastor of the Island of Mohr

14. A COLLECTION OF POLITICAL POEMS AND SONGS RELATING TO ENGLISH HISTORY, FROM THE ACCESSION OF EDWARD III. TO THE REIGN OF HENRY VIII. Vols. I. and II. *Edited by* THOMAS WRIGHT, Esq., M.A. 1859-1861.

These Poems are perhaps the most interesting of all the historical writings of the period, though they cannot be relied on for accuracy of statement. They are various in character; some are upon religious subjects, some may be called satires, and some give no more than a court scandal, but as a whole they present a very fair picture of society, and of the relations of the different classes to one another The period comprised is in itself interesting, and brings us, through the decline of the feudal system, to the beginning of our modern history The songs in old English are of considerable value to the philologist

15 The "OPUS TERTIUM," "OPUS MINUS," &c, of ROGER BACON. *Edited by* J S BREWER, M A., Professor of English Literature, King's College, London. 1859.

This is the celebrated treatise—never before printed—so frequently referred to by the great philosopher in his works It contains the fullest details we possess of the life and labours of Roger Bacon also a fragment by the same author, supposed to be unique, the "*Compendium Studii Theologiæ*"

16 BARTHOLOMÆI DE COTTON, MONACHI NORWICENSIS, HISTORIA ANGLICANA, 449-1298: neenon ejusdem Liber de Archiepiscopis et Episcopis Angliæ *Edited by* HENRY RICHARDS LUARD, M A., Fellow and Assistant Tutor of Trinity College, Cambridge. 1859

The author, a monk of Norwich, has here given us a Chronicle of England from the arrival of the Saxons in 449 to the year 1298, in or about which year it appears that he died The latter portion of this history (the whole of the reign of Edward I more especially) is of great value, as the writer was contemporary with the events which he records An Appendix contains several illustrative documents connected with the previous narrative

17 BRUT Y TYWYSOGION; or, The Chronicle of the Princes of Wales. *Edited by* the Rev. JOHN WILLIAMS AB ITHEL, M A. 1860

This work, also known as "The Chronicle of the Princes of Wales," has been attributed to Caradoc of Llancarvan, who flourished about the middle of the twelfth century It is written in the ancient Welsh language, begins with the abdication and death of Caedwala at Rome, in the year 681, and continues the history down to the subjugation of Wales by Edward I, about the year 1282

18 A COLLECTION OF ROYAL AND HISTORICAL LETTERS DURING THE REIGN OF HENRY IV 1399-1404. *Edited by* the Rev. F. C. HINGESTON, M.A, of Exeter College, Oxford. 1860.

This volume, like all the others in the series containing a miscellaneous selection of letters, is valuable on account of the light it throws upon biographical history, and the familiar view it presents of characters, manners, and events The period requires much elucidation; to which it will materially contribute

19. THE REPRESSOR OF OVER MUCH BLAMING OF THE CLERGY. By REGINALD PECOCK, sometime Bishop of Chichester Vols. I. and II. *Edited by* CHURCHILL BABINGTON, B D, Fellow of St. John's College, Cambridge. 1860

The "Repressor" may be considered the earliest piece of good theological disquisition of which our English prose literature can boast The author was born

about the end of the fourteenth century, consecrated Bishop of St. Asaph in
the year 1444, and translated to the see of Chichester in 1450 While Bishop of
St Asaph, he zealously defended his brother prelates from the attacks of those
who censured the bishops for their neglect of duty He maintained that it was no
part of a bishop's functions to appear in the pulpit, and that his time might be
more profitably spent, and his dignity better maintained, in the performance of
works of a higher character Among those who thought differently were the
Lollards, and against their general doctrines the "Repressor" is directed Pecock
took up a position midway between that of the Roman Church and that of the
modern Anglican Church, but his work is interesting chiefly because it gives a
full account of the views of the Lollards and of the arguments by which they were
supported, and because it assists us to ascertain the state of feeling which ulti-
mately led to the Reformation Apart from religious matters, the light thrown upon
contemporaneous history is very small, but the "Repressor" has great value
for the philologist, as it tells us what were the characteristics of the language in
use among the cultivated Englishmen of the fifteenth century Pecock, though
an opponent of the Lollards, showed a certain spirit of toleration, for which he
received, towards the end of his life, the usual mediæval reward—persecution.

20. ANNALES CAMBRIÆ. *Edited by* the Rev JOHN WILLIAMS AB ITHEL,
M.A. 1860.

These annals, which are in Latin, commence in the year 447, and come down
to the year 1288 The earlier portion appears to be taken from an Irish Chronicle,
which was also used by Tigernach, and by the compiler of the Annals of Ulster
During its first century it contains scarcely anything relating to Britain, the
earliest direct concurrence with English history is relative to the mission of
Augustine Its notices throughout though brief, are valuable. The annals
were probably written at St Davids, by Blegewryd, Archdeacon of Llandaff,
the most learned man in his day in all Cymru

21. THE WORKS OF GIRALDUS CAMBRENSIS Vols I, II, and III. *Edited
by* J S. BREWER, M.A., Professor of English Literature, King's College,
London. Vols V and VI. *Edited by* the Rev JAMES F. DIMOCK,
M.A, Rector of Barnburgh, Yorkshire. 1861–1868.

The first three volumes contain the historical works of Gerald du Barry, who
lived in the reigns of Henry II, Richard I, and John, and attempted to re-
establish the independence of Wales by restoring the see of St Davids to its
ancient primacy His works are of a very miscellaneous nature, both in prose
and verse, and are remarkable chiefly for the racy and original anecdotes which
they contain relating to contemporaries He is the only Welsh writer of any
importance who has contributed so much to the mediæval literature of this
country, or assumed, in consequence of his nationality, so free and independent
a tone His frequent travels in Italy, in France, in Ireland, and in Wales, gave
him opportunities for observation which did not generally fall to the lot of mediæval
writers in the twelfth and thirteenth centuries, and of these observations Giraldus
has made due use. Only extracts from these treatises have been printed before,
and almost all of them are taken from unique manuscripts
The Topographia Hibernica (in Vol V.) is the result of Giraldus' two visits to
Ireland The first in the year 1183, the second in 1185–6, when he accompanied
Prince John into that country Curious as this treatise is, Mr Dimock is of
opinion that it ought not to be accepted as sober truthful history, for Giraldus
himself states that truth was not his main object, and that he compiled the work
for the purpose of sounding the praises of Henry the Second. Elsewhere, however, he declares that he had stated nothing in the Topographia of the truth of
which he was not well assured, either by his own eyesight or by the testimony,
with all diligence elicited, of the most trustworthy and authentic men in the
country, that though he did not put just the same full faith in their reports as
in what he had himself seen, yet, as they only related what they had themselves
seen, he could not but believe such credible witnesses A very interesting portion
of this treatise is devoted to the animals of Ireland. It shows that he was a very
accurate and acute observer, and his descriptions are given in a way that a
scientific naturalist of the present day could hardly improve upon. The Expug-
natio Hibernica was written about the year 1188, and may be regarded rather

as a great epic than a sober relation of acts occurring in his own days No one can peruse it without coming to the conclusion that it is rather a poetical fiction than a prosaic truthful history

Vol VI. contains the Itinerarium Kambriæ et Descriptio Kambriæ.

22 LETTERS AND PAPERS ILLUSTRATIVE OF THE WARS OF THE ENGLISH IN FRANCE DURING THE REIGN OF HENRY THE SIXTH, KING OF ENG- LAND. Vol I , and Vol II (in Two Parts) *Edited by* the Rev. JOSEPH STEVENSON, M A., of University College, Durham, and Vicar of Leighton Buzzard 1861–1864

> The letters and papers contained in these volumes are derived chiefly from originals or contemporary copies extant in the Bibliothèque Impérial, and the Depôt des Archives, in Paris They illustrate the line of policy adopted by John Duke of Bedford and his successors during their government of Normandy, and such other provinces of France as had been acquired by Henry V We may here trace, step by step, the gradual declension of the English power, until we are prepared to read of its final overthrow

23. THE ANGLO-SAXON CHRONICLE, ACCORDING TO THE SEVERAL ORIGINAL AUTHORITIES Vol. I., Original Texts Vol. II., Translation. *Edited and translated by* BENJAMIN THORPE, Esq , Member of the Royal Academy of Sciences at Munich, and of the Society of Netherlandish Literature at Leyden 1861

> This Chronicle, extending from the earliest history of Britain to the year 1154, is justly the boast of England , for no other nation can produce any history, written in its own vernacular, at all approaching it, either in antiquity, truthful- ness, or extent, the historical books of the Bible alone excepted There are at present six independent manuscripts of the Saxon Chronicle, ending in different years, and written in different parts of the country In the present edition, the text of each manuscript is printed in columns on the same page, so that the student may see at a glance the various changes which occur in orthography, whether arising from locality or age

24 LETTERS AND PAPERS ILLUSTRATIVE OF THE REIGNS OF RICHARD III AND HENRY VII Vols. I and II *Edited by* JAMES GAIRDNER, Esq 1861–1863.

> The Papers are derived from MSS in the Public Record Office, the British Museum, and other repositories The period to which they refer is unusually destitute of chronicles and other sources of historical information, so that the light obtained from these documents is of special importance The principal contents of the volumes are some diplomatic Papers of Richard III , correspon- dence between Henry VII. and Ferdinand and Isabella of Spain, documents relating to Edmund de la Pole, Earl of Suffolk , and a portion of the corre- spondence of James IV of Scotland

25 LETTERS OF BISHOP GROSSETESTE, illustrative of the Social Condition of his Time. *Edited by* HENRY RICHARDS LUARD, M A., Fellow and Assistant Tutor of Trinity College, Cambridge. 1861.

> The Letters of Robert Grosseteste (131 in number) are here collected from various sources, and a large portion of them is printed for the first time. They range in date from about 1210 to 1253, and relate to various matters connected not only with the political history of England during the reign of Henry III , but with its ecclesiastical condition. They refer especially to the diocese of Lincoln, of which Grosseteste was bishop

26. DESCRIPTIVE CATALOGUE OF MANUSCRIPTS RELATING TO THE HISTORY OF GREAT BRITAIN AND IRELAND Vol. I. (in Two Parts) , Anterior to the Norman Invasion Vol. II ; 1066–1200 *By* THOMAS DUFFUS HARDY, Esq., Deputy Keeper of the Public Records 1862–1865

> The object of this work is to publish notices of all known sources of British history, both printed and unprinted, in one continued sequence. The materials,

when historical (as distinguished from biographical), are arranged under the year in which the latest event is recorded in the chronicle or history, and not under the period in which its author, real or supposed, flourished. Biographies are enumerated under the year in which the person commemorated died, and not under the year in which the life was written. This arrangement has two advantages; the materials for any given period may be seen at a glance, and if the reader knows the time when an author wrote, and the number of years that had elapsed between the date of the events and the time the writer flourished, he will generally be enabled to form a fair estimate of the comparative value of the narrative itself. A brief analysis of each work has been added when deserving it, in which the original portions are distinguished from those which are mere compilations. When possible, the sources are indicated, from which such compilations have been derived. A biographical sketch of the author of each piece has been added, and a brief notice has also been given of such British authors as have written on historical subjects.

27. ROYAL AND OTHER HISTORICAL LETTERS ILLUSTRATIVE OF THE REIGN OF HENRY III. From the Originals in the Public Record Office. Vol I., 1216–1235. Vol II., 1236–1272. *Selected and edited by* the Rev. W W SHIRLEY, D D, Regius Professor in Ecclesiastical History, and Canon of Christ Church, Oxford. 1862–1866.

The letters contained in these volumes are derived chiefly from the ancient correspondence formerly in the Tower of London, and now in the Public Record Office. They illustrate the political history of England during the growth of its liberties, and throw considerable light upon the personal history of Simon de Montfort. The affairs of France form the subject of many of them, especially in regard to the province of Gascony. The entire collection consists of nearly 700 documents, the greater portion of which is printed for the first time.

28 CHRONICA MONASTERII S. ALBANI.—1. THOMÆ WALSINGHAM HISTORIA ANGLICANA, Vol I., 1272–1381. Vol. II., 1381–1422. 2. WILLELMI RISHANGER CHRONICA ET ANNALES, 1259–1307. 3. JOHANNIS DE TROKELOWE ET HENRICI DE BLANEFORDE CHRONICA ET ANNALES, 1259–1296, 1307–1324, 1392–1406. 4. GESTA ABBATUM MONASTERII S ALBANI, A THOMA WALSINGHAM, REGNANTE RICARDO SECUNDO, EJUSDEM ECCLESIÆ PRÆCENTORE, COMPILATA; Vol I., 793–1290. Vol II., 1290–1349. Vol. III, 1349–1411. *Edited by* HENRY THOMAS RILEY, Esq, M A, of Corpus Christi College, Cambridge, and of the Inner Temple, Barrister-at-Law. 1863–1869.

In the first two volumes is a history of England, from the death of Henry III to the death of Henry V, written by Thomas Walsingham, precentor of St Albans and prior of the cell of Wymundham, belonging to that abbey. Walsingham's work is printed from MS VII in the Arundel Collection in the College of Arms, London, a manuscript of the fifteenth century, collated with MS 13 E IX in the King's Library in the British Museum, and MS VII in the Parker Collection of Manuscripts at Corpus Christi College, Cambridge.
In the third volume is a Chronicle of English History, from 1259 to 1306, attributed to William Rishanger, monk of Saint Albans, who lived in the reign of Edward I, printed from the Cottonian Manuscript, Faustina B. IX (of the fourteenth century) in the British Museum, collated with MS 14 C VII (fols 219–231) in the King's Library, British Museum, and the Cottonian Manuscript Claudius E III, fols 306–331. Also an account of transactions attending the award of the kingdom of Scotland to John Baliol by King Edward I, 1291–1292, from MS Cotton. Claudius D VI, attributed to William Rishanger above mentioned, but on no sufficient ground. A short Chronicle of English History, from 1292 to 1300, by an unknown hand, from MS Cotton Claudius D. VI. A short Chronicle from 1297 to 1307, Willelmi Rishanger Gesta Edwardi Primi Regis Angliæ, from MS 14 C I in the Royal Library, and MS Cotton Claudius D. VI, with an addition of Annales Regum Angliæ, probably by the same hand. A fragment of a Chronicle of English History, 1299, 1300, from MS Cotton Claudius D VI. A fragment of a Chronicle of English History,

1295 to 1300, from MS Cotton Claudius D VL. and a fragment of a Chronicle
of English History, 1285 to 1307, from MS 14 C I. in the Royal Library

In the fourth volume is a Chronicle of English History, by an anonymous
writer, 1259 to 1296, from MS Cotton. Claudius D. VI Annals of King
Edward II, 1307 to 1323, by John de Trokelowe, a monk of St Albans, from
MS Cotton Claudius D. VI · A continuation of Trokelowe's Annals, 1323,
1324, by Henricus de Blaneforde, from MS Cotton Claudius D VI A
full Chronicle of English History, by an anonymous writer of St. Albans, 1392
to 1406, from MS VII in the Library of Corpus Christi College, Cambridge
and an account of the benefactors of St. Albans, written in the early part of
the fifteenth century, from MS. VI. in the same Library

The fifth, sixth, and seventh volumes (which form an entirely separate work),
contain a history of the Abbots of St. Albans, and of the fortunes and vicissitudes of the house, from 793 to 1411, mainly compiled by Thomas Walsingham,
Præcentor of the Abbey in the reign of Richard II, and transcribed from MS
Cotton Claudius E. IV, in the British Museum; with a brief Continuation of
the History, extracted from the closing pages of the Parker MS No VII, in the
Library of Corpus Christi College, Cambridge

29. CHRONICON ABBATIÆ EVESHAMENSIS, AUCTORIBUS DOMINICO PRIORE
EVESHAMIÆ ET THOMA DE MARLEBERGE ABBATE, A FUNDATIONE AD
ANNUM 1213, UNA CUM CONTINUATIONE AD ANNUM 1418. *Edited by*
the Rev. W. D. MACRAY, M.A, Bodleian Library, Oxford. 1863.

The Chronicle of Evesham illustrates the history of that important monastery
from its foundation by Egwin, about 690, to the year 1418 Its chief feature is
an autobiography, which makes us acquainted with the inner daily life of a
great abbey, such as but rarely has been recorded. Interspersed are many
notices of general, personal, and local history which will be read with much
interest. This work exists in a single MS, and is for the first time printed.

30. RICARDI DE CIRENCESTRIA SPECULUM HISTORIALE DE GESTIS REGUM
ANGLIÆ. Vol. I, 447-871. Vol. II., 872-1066. *Edited by* JOHN E. B.
MAYOR, M.A., Fellow of St. John's College, Cambridge. 1863-1869.

The compiler, Richard of Cirencester, was a monk of Westminster, 1355-
1400 In 1391 he obtained a licence to make a pilgrimage to Rome. His
history, in four books, extends from 447 to 1066 He announces his intention
of continuing it, but there is no evidence that he completed any more This
chronicle gives many charters in favour of Westminster Abbey, and a very full
account of the lives and miracles of the saints, especially of Edward the Confessor, whose reign occupies the fourth book A treatise on the Coronation, by
William of Sudbury, a monk of Westminster, fills book III c 3. It was on this
author that C J Bertram fathered his forgery, *De Situ Brittaniæ*, in 1747

31. YEAR BOOKS OF THE REIGN OF EDWARD THE FIRST. Years 20-21,
30-31, and 32-33 *Edited and translated by* ALFRED JOHN HORWOOD,
Esq, of the Middle Temple, Barrister-at-Law. 1863-1866.

The volumes known as the "Year Books" contain reports in Norman-French
of cases argued and decided in the Courts of Common Law. They may be considered to a great extent as the "lex non scripta" of England, and have been held
in the highest veneration by the ancient sages of the law, and were received by
them as the repositories of the first recorded judgments and dicta of the great
legal luminaries of past ages They are also worthy of the attention of the
general reader on account of the historical information and the notices of public
and private persons which they contain, as well as the light which they throw
on ancient manners and customs

32. NARRATIVES OF THE EXPULSION OF THE ENGLISH FROM NORMANDY;
1449-1450.—Robertus Blondelli de Reductione Normanniæ. Le Re-
couvrement de Normendie, par Berry, Hérault du Roy. Conferences
between the Ambassadors of France and England. *Edited, from MSS.*

II

in the Imperial Library at Paris, by the Rev. JOSEPH STEVENSON, M.A., of University College, Durham. 1863.

> This volume contains the narrative of an eye-witness who details with considerable power and minuteness the circumstances which attended the final expulsion of the English from Normandy in the year 1450. The history commences with the infringement of the truce by the capture of Fougères, and ends with the battle of Formigny and the embarkation of the Duke of Somerset. The whole period embraced is less than two years.

33. HISTORIA ET CARTULARIUM MONASTERII S PETRI GLOUCESTRIÆ. Vols. I., II., and III. *Edited by* W. H. HART, Esq., F.S.A., Membre correspondant de la Société des Antiquaires de Normandie. 1863–1867.

> This work consists of two parts, the History and the Cartulary of the Monastery of St. Peter, Gloucester The history furnishes an account of the monastery from its foundation, in the year 681, to the early part of the reign of Richard II, together with a calendar of donations and benefactions. It treats principally of the affairs of the monastery, but occasionally matters of general history are introduced Its authorship has generally been assigned to Walter Froucester, the twentieth abbot, but without any foundation.

34 ALEXANDRI NECKAM DE NATURIS RERUM LIBRI DUO ; with NECKAM'S POEM, DE LAUDIBUS DIVINÆ SAPIENTIÆ. *Edited by* THOMAS WRIGHT, Esq., M.A. 1863.

> Neckam was a man who devoted himself to science, such as it was in the twelfth century In the "De Naturis Rerum" are to be found what may be called the rudiments of many sciences mixed up with much error and ignorance Neckam was not thought infallible, even by his contemporaries, for Roger Bacon remarks of him, "this Alexander in many things wrote what was true and useful, " but he neither can nor ought by just title to be reckoned among authorities" Neckam, however, had sufficient independence of thought to differ from some of the schoolmen who in his time considered themselves the only judges of literature He had his own views in morals, and in giving us a glimpse of them, as well as of his other opinions, he throws much light upon the manners, customs, and general tone of thought prevalent in the twelfth century The poem entitled "De Laudibus Divinæ Sapientiæ" appears to be a metrical paraphrase or abridgment of the "De Naturis Rerum" It is written in the elegiac metre , and though there are many lines which violate classical rules, it is, as a whole, above the ordinary standard of mediæval Latin.

35. LEECHDOMS, WORTCUNNING, AND STARCRAFT OF EARLY ENGLAND ; being a Collection of Documents illustrating the History of Science in this Country before the Norman Conquest Vols. I , II., and III *Collected and edited by* the Rev. T. OSWALD COCKAYNE, M.A , of St. John's College, Cambridge 1864–1866.

> This work illustrates not only the history of science, but the history of superstition In addition to the information bearing directly upon the medical skill and medical faith of the times, there are many passages which incidentally throw light upon the general mode of life and ordinary diet. The volumes are interesting not only in their scientific, but also in their social aspect The manuscripts from which they have been printed are valuable to the Anglo-Saxon scholar for the illustrations they afford of Anglo-Saxon orthography

36. ANNALES MONASTICI Vol. I —Annales de Margan, 1066–1232 ; Annales de Theokesberia, 1066–1263 ; Annales de Burton, 1004–1263. Vol. II. —Annales Monasterii de Wintonia, 519–1277, Annales Monasterii de Waverleia, 1–1291. Vol. III. .—Annales Prioratus de Dunstaplia, 1–1297 , Annales Monasterii de Bermundeseia, 1042–1432. Vol IV. —Annales Monasterii de Oseneia, 1016–1347; Chronicon vulgo dictum Chronicon Thomæ Wykes, 1066–1289 ; Annales Prioratus de

Wigornia, 1–1377. Vol. V. —Index and Glossary. *Edited by* HENRY
RICHARDS LUARD, M A., Fellow and Assistant Tutor of Trinity
College, and Registrary of the University, Cambridge. 1864–1869.

> The present collection of Monastic Annals embraces all the more important
> chronicles compiled in religious houses in England during the thirteenth
> century These distinct works are ten in number The extreme period
> which they embrace ranges from the year 1 to 1432, although they refer more
> especially to the reigns of John, Henry III , and Edward I. Some of these narra-
> tives have already appeared in print, but others are printed for the first time.

37. MAGNA VITA S. HUGONIS EPISCOPI LINCOLNIENSIS From Manuscripts
in the Bodleian Library, Oxford, and the Imperial Library, Paris. *Edited
by* the Rev. JAMES F. DIMOCK, M A., Rector of Barnburgh, Yorkshire
1864.

> This work contains a number of very curious and interesting incidents, and
> being the work of a contemporary, is very valuable, not only as a truthful
> biography of a celebrated ecclesiastic, but as the work of a man, who, from per-
> sonal knowledge, gives notices of passing events, as well as of individuals who
> were then taking active part in public affairs The author, in all probability,
> was Adam Abbot of Evesham He was domestic chaplain and private confessor
> of Bishop Hugh, and in these capacities he was admitted to the closest intimacy
> Bishop Hugh was Prior of Witham for 11 years before he became Bishop of
> Lincoln His consecration took place on the 21st September 1186 , he died on
> the 16th of November 1200 , and was canonized in 1220

38 CHRONICLES AND MEMORIALS OF THE REIGN OF RICHARD THE FIRST.
Vol. I. —ITINERARIUM PEREGRINORUM ET GESTA REGIS RICARDI.
Vol. II. —EPISTOLÆ CANTUARIENSES , the Letters of the Prior and
Convent of Christ Church, Canterbury ; 1187 to 1199. *Edited by*
WILLIAM STUBBS, M.A., Vicar of Navestock, Essex, and Lambeth
Librarian. 1864–1865.

> The authorship of the Chronicle in Vol I , hitherto ascribed to Geoffrey
> Vinesauf, is now more correctly ascribed to Richard, Canon of the Holy Trinity
> of London The narrative extends from 1187 to 1199 , but its chief interest
> consists in the minute and authentic narrative which it furnishes of the exploits
> of Richard I , from his departure from England in December 1189 to his death
> in 1199 The author states in his prologue that he was an eye-witness of much
> that he records , and various incidental circumstances which occur in the course
> of the narrative confirm this assertion
> The letters in Vol II , written between 1187 and 1199, are of value as
> furnishing authentic materials for the history of the ecclesiastical condition of
> England during the reign of Richard I They had their origin in a dispute which
> arose from the attempts of Baldwin and Hubert, archbishops of Canterbury, to
> found a college of secular canons, a project which gave great umbrage to the
> monks of Canterbury, who saw in it a design to supplant them in their function
> of metropolitan chapter These letters are printed, for the first time, from a MS
> belonging to the archiepiscopal library at Lambeth

39. RECUEIL DES CRONIQUES ET ANCHIENNES ISTORIES DE LA GRANT BRE-
TAIGNE A PRESENT NOMME ENGLETERRE, par JEHAN DE WAURIN. Vol. I.
Albina to 688. Vol. II., 1399–1422 *Edited by* WILLIAM HARDY, Esq ,
F S.A 1864–1868.

40. A COLLECTION OF THE CHRONICLES AND ANCIENT HISTORIES OF GREAT
BRITAIN, NOW CALLED ENGLAND, by JOHN DE WAVRIN Albina to 688.
('Translation of the preceding Vol I) *Edited and translated by*
WILLIAM HARDY, Esq., F.S.A. 1864.

> This curious chronicle extends from the fabulous period of history down to the
> return of Edward IV to England in the year 1471, after the second deposition of

Henry VI The manuscript from which the text of the work is taken is preserved in the Imperial Library at Paris, and is believed to be the only complete and nearly contemporary copy in existence The work, as originally bound, was comprised in six volumes, since rebound in morocco in 12 volumes, folio maximo, vellum, and is illustrated with exquisite miniatures, vignettes, and initial letters It was written towards the end of the fifteenth century, having been expressly executed for Louis de Bruges, Seigneur de la Gruthuyse and Earl of Winchester, from whose cabinet it passed into the library of Louis XII at Blois

41. POLYCHRONICON RANULPHI HIGDEN, with Trevisa's Translation. Vols. I. and II. *Edited by* CHURCHILL BABINGTON, B D., Senior Fellow of St John's College, Cambridge. 1865–1869

This is one of the many mediæval chronicles which assume the character of a history of the world It begins with the creation, and is brought down to the author's own time, the reign of Edward III. Prefixed to the historical portion, is a chapter devoted to geography, in which is given a description of every known land To say that the Polychronicon was written in the fourteenth century is to say that it is not free from inaccuracies It has, however, a value apart from its intrinsic merits It enables us to form a very fair estimate of the knowledge of history and geography which well-informed readers of the fourteenth and fifteenth centuries possessed, for it was then the standard work on general history.

The two English translations, which are printed with the original Latin, afford interesting illustrations of the gradual change of our language, for one was made in the fourteenth century, the other in the fifteenth. The differences between Trevisa's version and that of the unknown writer are often considerable.

42. LE LIVERE DE REIS DE BRITTANIE E LE LIVERE DE REIS DE ENGLETERE. *Edited by* JOHN GLOVER, M.A, Vicar of Brading, Isle of Wight, formerly Librarian of Trinity College, Cambridge. 1865.

These two treatises, though they cannot rank as independent narratives, are nevertheless valuable as careful abstracts of previous historians, especially "Le Livere de Reis de Engletere." Some various readings are given which are interesting to the philologist as instances of semi-Saxonized French

It is supposed that Peter of Ickham must have been the author, but no certain conclusion on that point has been arrived at

43. CHRONICA MONASTERII DE MELSA, AB ANNO 1150 USQUE AD ANNUM 1406. Vols I, II, and III *Edited by* EDWARD AUGUSTUS BOND, Esq., Assistant Keeper of the Manuscripts, and Egerton Librarian, British Museum. 1866–1868.

The Abbey of Meaux was a Cistercian house, and the work of its abbot is both curious and valuable It is a faithful and often minute record of the establishment of a religious community, of its progress in forming an ample revenue, of its struggles to maintain its acquisitions, and of its relations to the governing institutions of the country In addition to the private affairs of the monastery, some light is thrown upon the public events of the time, which are however kept distinct, and appear at the end of the history of each abbot's administration The text has been printed from what is said to be the autograph of the original compiler, Thomas de Burton, the nineteenth abbot

44. MATTHÆI PARISIENSIS HISTORIA ANGLORUM, SIVE, UT VULGO DICITUR, HISTORIA MINOR. Vols. I., II., and III. 1067–1245 *Edited by* Sir FREDERIC MADDEN, K H , Keeper of the Department of Manuscripts, British Museum 1866–1869

The exact date at which this work was written is, according to the chronicler, 1250 The history is of considerable value as an illustration of the period during which the author lived, and contains a good summary of the events which followed the Conquest This minor chronicle is, however, based on another work (also written by Matthew Paris) giving fuller details, which has been called the 'Historia Major' The chronicle here published, nevertheless, gives some information not to be found in the greater history.

45. Liber Monasterii de Hyda : A Chronicle and Chartulary of
Hyde Abbey, Winchester, 455–1023. *Edited, from a Manuscript in
the Library of the Earl of Macclesfield, by* Edward Edwards, Esq.
1866.

> The "Book of Hyde" is a compilation from much earlier sources, which are
> usually indicated with considerable care and precision   In many cases, however,
> the Hyde chronicler appears to correct, to qualify, or to amplify—either from
> tradition or from sources of information not now discoverable—the statements
> which, in substance, he adopts   He also mentions, and frequently quotes from,
> writers whose works are either entirely lost or at present known only by fragments
>   There is to be found, in the "Book of Hyde," much information relating to the
> reign of King Alfred which is not known to exist elsewhere   The volume
> contains some curious specimens of Anglo-Saxon and Mediæval English

46 Chronicon Scotorum : A Chronicle of Irish Affairs, from the
Earliest Times to 1135 , with a Supplement, containing the Events
from 1141 to 1150. *Edited, with a Translation, by* William Maunsell
Hennessy, Esq., M.R.I.A. 1866.

> There is, in this volume, a legendary account of the peopling of Ireland and of
> the adventures which befell the various heroes who are said to have been con-
> nected with Irish history   The details are, however, very meagre both for this
> period and for the time when history becomes more authentic   The plan adopted
> in the chronicle gives the appearance of an accuracy to which the earlier portions
> of the work cannot have any claim   The succession of events is marked, year by
> year, from A M 1599 to A D. 1150.   The principal events narrated in the later
> portion of the work are the invasions of foreigners and the wars of the Irish
> among themselves   The text has been printed from a MS preserved in the
> library of Trinity College, Dublin, written partly in Latin, partly in Irish

47. The Chronicle of Pierre de Langtoft, in French Verse, from
the earliest Period to the Death of Edward I. Vols. I. and II.
Edited by Thomas Wright, Esq , M A. 1866–1868.

> It is probable that Pierre de Langtoft was a canon of Bridlington, in Yorkshire,
> and that he lived in the reign of Edward I., and during a portion of the reign of
> Edward II   This chronicle is divided into three parts , in the first is an
> abridgment of Geoffrey of Monmouth's "Historia Britonum," in the second, a
> history of the Anglo-Saxon and Norman kings, down to the death of Henry III ,
> and in the third a history of the reign of Edward I.   The principal object of the
> work was apparently to show the justice of Edward's Scottish wars   The
> language is singularly corrupt, and a curious specimen of the French of Yorkshire

48. The War of the Gaedhil with the Gaill, or, The Invasions of
Ireland by the Danes and other Norsemen. *Edited, with a
Translation, by* James Henthorn Todd, D.D., Senior Fellow of
Trinity College, and Regius Professor of Hebrew in the University,
Dublin. 1867.

> The work in its present form, in the editor's opinion, is a comparatively modern
> version of an undoubtedly ancient original.   That it was compiled from contem-
> porary materials has been proved by curious incidental evidence   It is stated in
> the account given of the battle of Clontarf that the full tide in Dublin Bay on the
> day of the battle (23 April 1014) coincided with sunrise , and that the returning
> tide in the evening aided considerably in the defeat of the Danes   The fact has
> been verified by astronomical calculations, and the inference is that the author of
> the chronicle, if not himself an eye-witness, must have derived his information
> from those who were eye-witnesses   The contents of the work are sufficiently
> described in its title.   The story is told after the manner of the Scandinavian
> Sagas, with poems and fragments of poems introduced into the prose narrative.

49. GESTA REGIS HENRICI SECUNDI BENEDICTI ABBATIS. THE CHRONICLE OF THE REIGNS OF HENRY II. AND RICHARD I, 1169–1192 ; known under the name of BENEDICT OF PETERBOROUGH Vols. I. and II. *Edited by* WILLIAM STUBBS, M.A., Regius Professor of Modern History, Oxford, and Lambeth Librarian. 1867.

> This chronicle of the reigns of Henry II and Richard I., known commonly under the name of Benedict of Peterborough, is one of the best existing specimens of a class of historical compositions of the first importance to the student.

50. MUNIMENTA ACADEMICA, OR, DOCUMENTS ILLUSTRATIVE OF ACADEMICAL LIFE AND STUDIES AT OXFORD (in Two Parts). *Edited by* the Rev. HENRY ANSTEY, M.A., Vicar of St. Wendron, Cornwall, and lately Vice-Principal of St. Mary Hall, Oxford. 1868.

> This work will supply materials for a History of Academical Life and Studies in the University of Oxford during the 13th, 14th, and 15th centuries.

51. CHRONICA MAGISTRI ROGERI DE HOUEDENE. Vols I. and II. *Edited by* WILLIAM STUBBS, M A, Regius Professor of Modern History, and Fellow of Oriel College, Oxford. 1868–1869.

> This work has long been justly celebrated, but not thoroughly understood until Mr Stubbs' edition The earlier portion, extending from 732 to 1148, appears to be a copy of a compilation made in Northumbria about 1161, to which Hoveden added little From 1148 to 1169—a very valuable portion of this work—the matter is derived from another source, to which Hoveden appears to have supplied little, and not always judiciously. From 1170 to 1192 is the portion which corresponds with the Chronicle known under the name of Benedict of Peterborough (*see* No 49); but it is not a copy, being sometimes an abridgment, at others a paraphrase, occasionally the two works entirely agree, showing that both writers had access to the same materials, but dealt with them differently From 1192 to 1201 may be said to be wholly Hoveden's work ; it is extremely valuable, and an authority of the first importance

In the Press.

A COLLECTION OF SAGAS AND OTHER HISTORICAL DOCUMENTS relating to the Settlements and Descents of the Northmen on the British Isles. *Edited by* GEORGE WEBBE DASENT, Esq., D.C L., Oxon.

OFFICIAL CORRESPONDENCE OF THOMAS BEKYNTON, SECRETARY TO HENRY VI , with other LETTERS and DOCUMENTS. *Edited by* the Rev. GEORGE WILLIAMS, B.D., Senior Fellow of King's College, Cambridge

ROLL OF THE PRIVY COUNCIL OF IRELAND, 16 RICHARD II. *Edited by* the Rev JAMES GRAVES, A.B , Treasurer of St. Canice, Ireland.

THE WORKS OF GIRALDUS CAMBRENSIS. Vol. IV. *Edited by* J. S. BREWER, M.A., Professor of English Literature, King's College, London. Vol. VII. *Edited by* the Rev. JAMES F. DIMOCK, M.A., Rector of Barnburgh, Yorkshire

CHRONICON RADULPHI ABBATIS COGGESHALENSIS MAJUS, and, CHRONICON TERRÆ SANCTÆ ET DE CAPTIS A SALADINO HIEROSOLYMIS. *Edited by* the Rev. JOSEPH STEVENSON, M.A., of University College, Durham.

ITER BRITANNIARUM . THE PORTION OF THE ANTONINE ITINERARY OF THE ROMAN EMPIRE RELATING TO GREAT BRITAIN. *Edited by* WILLIAM HENRY BLACK, Esq., F.S.A.

WILLELMI MALMESBIRIENSIS DE GESTIS PONTIFICUM ANGLORUM LIBRI V. *Edited, from William of Malmesbury's Autograph MS.*, by N. E. S. A. HAMILTON, Esq., of the Department of Manuscripts, British Museum.

YEAR BOOKS OF THE REIGN OF EDWARD THE FIRST. Years 21–22. *Edited and translated by* ALFRED JOHN HORWOOD, Esq , of the Middle Temple, Barrister-at-Law.

HISTORICAL AND MUNICIPAL DOCUMENTS IN THE ARCHIVES OF THE CITY OF DUBLIN, &c. *Edited by* JOHN T. GILBERT, Esq , M.R.I.A., Secretary of the Public Record Office of Ireland.

THE ANNALS OF LOCH CÉ. *Edited by* WILLIAM MAUNSELL HENNESSY, Esq., M.R.I.A.

CHRONICLE OF ROBERT OF BRUNNE. *Edited by* FREDERICK JAMES FURNIVALL, Esq , M.A , of Trinity Hall, Cambridge, Barrister-at-Law.

POLYCHRONICON RANULPHI HIGDEN, with Trevisa's Translation. Vol. III. *Edited by* the Rev. JOSEPH RAWSON LUMBY, M.A , of Magdalene College, Cambridge.

CHRONICA MONASTERII S ALBANI.—5. JOHANNIS AMUNDESHAM, MONACHI MONASTERII S. ALBANI, ANNALES. *Edited by* HENRY THOMAS RILEY, Esq., M.A., of Corpus Christi College, Cambridge ; and of the Inner Temple, Barrister-at-Law.

24

THE ANGLO-LATIN SATIRISTS OF THE TWELFTH CENTURY. *Edited by* THOMAS WRIGHT, Esq., M.A.

DESCRIPTIVE CATALOGUE OF MANUSCRIPTS RELATING TO THE HISTORY OF GREAT BRITAIN AND IRELAND. Vol. III.; 1201, &c *By* THOMAS DUFFUS HARDY, Esq , Deputy Keeper of the Public Records.

In Progress.

DOCUMENTS RELATING TO ENGLAND AND SCOTLAND, FROM THE NORTHERN REGISTERS *Edited by* the Rev JAMES RAINE, M.A , Canon of York, and late Fellow of the University, Durham.

LIBER NIGER ADMIRALITATIS *Edited by* Sir TRAVERS TWISS, D.C.L., Queen's Advocate-General

THE METRICAL CHRONICLE OF ROBERT OF GLOUCESTER. *Edited by* WILLIAM ALDIS WRIGHT, Esq., M.A., Librarian of Trinity College, Cambridge.

ORIGINAL LETTERS AND DOCUMENTS ILLUSTRATIVE OF GENERAL AND DOMESTIC HISTORY. *Edited by* the Rev. WILLIAM CAMPBELL, M.A

RECUEIL DES CRONIQUES ET ANCHIENNES ISTORIES DE LA GRANT BRETAIGNE A PRESENT NOMME ENGLETERRE, par JEHAN DE WAURIN Vol. III. *Edited by* WILLIAM HARDY, Esq., F.S.A.

CHRONICA MAGISTRI ROGERI DE HOUEDENE Vol III. *Edited by* WILLIAM STUBBS, M.A., Regius Professor of Modern History, and Fellow of Oriel College, Oxford.

LIVES OF ARCHBISHOP DUNSTAN. *Edited by* the Rev. JOHN RICHARD GREEN, M.A., Vicar of St. Philip's, Stepney, Middlesex.

PUBLICATIONS

OF

THE RECORD COMMISSIONERS, &c.

ROTULORUM ORIGINALIUM IN CURIÂ SCACCARII ABBREVIATIO. Henry III.
—Edward III. *Edited by* HENRY PLAYFORD, Esq 2 vols. folio
(1805—1810). *Price 25s.* boards, or 12s. 6d. each.

CALENDARIUM INQUISITIONUM POST MORTEM SIVE ESCAETARUM. Henry III.
—Richard III. *Edited by* JOHN CALEY and JOHN BAYLEY, Esqrs
Vols. 3 and 4, folio (1821—1828), boards . vol 3, *price 21s ;* vol 4,
price 24s.

LIBRORUM MANUSCRIPTORUM BIBLIOTHECÆ HARLEIANÆ CATALOGUS.
Vol. 4. *Edited by* the Rev. T. HARTWELL HORNE. Folio (1812),
boards. *Price 18s.*

ABBREVIATIO PLACITORUM. Richard I —Edward II. *Edited by* the Right
Hon. GEORGE ROSE and W. ILLINGWORTH, Esq. 1 vol. folio (1811),
boards. *Price 18s.*

LIBRI CENSUALIS vocati DOMESDAY-BOOK, INDICES. *Edited by* Sir HENRY
ELLIS. Folio (1816), boards, (Domesday-Book, vol. 3). *Price 21s.*

LIBRI CENSUALIS vocati DOMESDAY-BOOK, ADDITAMENTA EX CODIC. AN-
TIQUISS. *Edited by* Sir HENRY ELLIS Folio (1816), boards, (Domesday-Book, vol. 4). *Price 21s.*

STATUTES OF THE REALM. *Edited by* Sir T. E. TOMLINS, JOHN RAITHBY,
JOHN CALEY, and WM. ELLIOTT, Esqrs. Vols. 4 (in 2 parts), 7, 8, 9,
10, and 11, including 2 vols. of Indices, large folio (1819—1828)
Price 31s. 6d. each ; except the Alphabetical and Chronological Indices,
price 30s. each.

VALOR ECCLESIASTICUS, temp. Hen. VIII , Auctoritate Regia institutus.
Edited by JOHN CALEY, Esq., and the Rev. JOSEPH HUNTER. Vols.
3 to 6, folio (1817–1834), boards *Price 25s.* each
⁎ The Introduction, separately, 8vo., cloth. *Price 2s. 6d.*

ROTULI SCOTIÆ IN TURRI LONDINENSI ET IN DOMO CAPITULARI WEST-
MONASTERIENSI ASSERVATI. 19 Edward I.—Henry VIII *Edited by*
DAVID MACPHERSON, JOHN CALEY, and W. ILLINGWORTH, Esqrs., and
the Rev. T. HARTWELL HORNE. 2 vols. folio (1814—1819), boards.
Price 42s.

FŒDERA, CONVENTIONES, LITTERÆ, &c. ; or, RYMER'S FŒDERA, New
Edition Vol. 3, Parts 1 and 2, 1344—1377, folio (1825—1830) : Vol, 4,
1377—1383 (1869). *Edited by* JOHN CALEY and FRED. HOLBROOKE,
Esqrs. Vol. 3, *price 21s.* each Part ; vol. 4, *price 6s.*

DUCATUS LANCASTRIÆ CALENDARIUM INQUISITIONUM POST MORTEM, &c. Part 3, Calendar to the Pleadings, &c., Henry VII.—Ph. and Mary, and Calendar to the Pleadings, 1—13 Elizabeth. Part 4, Calendar to the Pleadings to end of Elizabeth (1827—1834.) *Edited by* R J. HARPER, JOHN CALEY, and WM. MINCHIN, Esqrs. Folio, boards, Part 3 (or Vol. 2), *price* 31s. 6d., and Part 4 (or Vol. 3), *price* 21s.

CALENDARS OF THE PROCEEDINGS IN CHANCERY, IN THE REIGN OF QUEEN ELIZABETH, to which are prefixed, Examples of earlier Proceedings in that Court from Richard II. to Elizabeth, from the Originals in the Tower. *Edited by* JOHN BAYLEY, Esq. Vols. 2 and 3 (1830—1832), folio, boards, *price* 21s. each.

PARLIAMENTARY WRITS AND WRITS OF MILITARY SUMMONS, together with the Records and Muniments relating to the Suit and Service due and performed to the King's High Court of Parliament and the Councils of the Realm. *Edited by* Sir FRANCIS PALGRAVE (1830—1834) Folio, boards, Vol. 2, Division 1, Edward II., *price* 21s., Vol. 2, Division 2, *price* 21s, Vol 2, Division 3, *price* 42s.

ROTULI LITTERARUM CLAUSARUM IN TURRI LONDINENSI ASSERVATI. 2 vols. folio (1833, 1844). Vol. 1, 1204—1224. Vol. 2, 1224—1227. *Edited by* THOMAS DUFFUS HARDY, Esq. *Price* 81s., cloth, or separately, Vol. 1, *price* 63s., Vol. 2, *price* 18s.

PROCEEDINGS AND ORDINANCES OF THE PRIVY COUNCIL OF ENGLAND. 10 Richard II.—33 Henry VIII. *Edited by* Sir NICHOLAS HARRIS NICOLAS 7 vols royal 8vo. (1834—1837), cloth. *Price* 98s, or separately, 14s each.

ROTULI LITTERARUM PATENTIUM IN TURRI LONDINENSI ASSERVATI 1201 —1216. *Edited by* THOMAS DUFFUS HARDY, Esq. 1 vol. folio (1835), cloth. *Price* 31s. 6d.

* The Introduction, separately, 8vo., cloth *Price* 9s.

ROTULI CURIÆ REGIS. Rolls and Records of the Court held before the King's Justiciars or Justices. 6 Richard I—1 John. *Edited by* Sir FRANCIS PALGRAVE 2 vols. royal 8vo. (1835), cloth. *Price* 28s.

ROTULI NORMANNIÆ IN TURRI LONDINENSI ASSERVATI. 1200—1205; also, 1417 to 1418 *Edited by* THOMAS DUFFUS HARDY, Esq. 1 vol. royal 8vo. (1835), cloth. *Price* 12s. 6d.

ROTULI DE OBLATIS ET FINIBUS IN TURRI LONDINENSI ASSERVATI, tempore Regis Johannis. *Edited by* THOMAS DUFFUS HARDY, Esq. 1 vol. royal 8vo. (1835), cloth. *Price* 18s.

EXCERPTA E ROTULIS FINIUM IN TURRI LONDINENSI ASSERVATIS. Henry III., 1216—1272. *Edited by* CHARLES ROBERTS, Esq. 2 vols. royal 8vo. (1835, 1836), cloth, *price* 32s., or separately, Vol. 1, *price* 14s.; Vol 2, *price* 18s.

FINES, SIVE PEDES FINIUM; SIVE FINALES CONCORDIÆ IN CURIA DOMINI REGIS. 7 Richard I.—16 John, 1195—1214. *Edited by* the Rev. JOSEPH HUNTER. In Counties. 2 vols. royal 8vo. (1835—1844), cloth, *price* 11s.; or separately, Vol. 1, *price* 8s. 6d; Vol. 2, *price* 2s. 6d.

ANCIENT KALENDARS AND INVENTORIES OF THE TREASURY OF HIS MAJESTY'S EXCHEQUER, together with Documents illustrating the History of that Repository. *Edited by* Sir FRANCIS PALGRAVE, 3 vols. royal 8vo. (1836), cloth. *Price 42s.*

DOCUMENTS AND RECORDS illustrating the History of Scotland, and the Transactions between the Crowns of Scotland and England; preserved in the Treasury of Her Majesty's Exchequer. *Edited by* Sir FRANCIS PALGRAVE. 1 vol. royal 8vo. (1837), cloth. *Price 18s.*

ROTULI CHARTARUM IN TURRI LONDINENSI ASSERVATI. 1199—1216. *Edited by* THOMAS DUFFUS HARDY, Esq. 1 vol. folio (1837), cloth. *Price 30s.*

REPORT OF THE PROCEEDINGS OF THE RECORD COMMISSIONERS, 1831—1837 1 vol. folio (1837), boards. *Price 8s.*

REGISTRUM vulgariter nuncupatum "The Record of Caernarvon," e codice MS. Harleiano, 696, descriptum. *Edited by* Sir HENRY ELLIS. 1 vol. folio (1838), cloth. *Price 31s. 6d.*

ANCIENT LAWS AND INSTITUTES OF ENGLAND; comprising Laws enacted under the Anglo-Saxon Kings, from Æthelbirht to Cnut, with an English Translation of the Saxon, the Laws called Edward the Confessor's; the Laws of William the Conqueror, and those ascribed to Henry the First; also, Monumenta Ecclesiastica Anglicana, from the 7th to the 10th century; and the Ancient Latin Version of the Anglo-Saxon Laws, with a compendious Glossary, &c. *Edited by* BENJAMIN THORPE, Esq. 1 vol. folio (1840), cloth. *Price 40s.* Or, 2 vols. royal 8vo cloth. *Price 30s.*

ANCIENT LAWS AND INSTITUTES OF WALES; comprising Laws supposed to be enacted by Howel the Good, modified by subsequent Regulations under the Native Princes, prior to the Conquest by Edward the First; and anomalous Laws, consisting principally of Institutions which, by the Statute of Ruddlan, were admitted to continue in force. With an English Translation of the Welsh Text. To which are added, a few Latin Transcripts, containing Digests of the Welsh Laws, principally of the Dimetian Code. With Indices and Glossary. *Edited by* ANEURIN OWEN, Esq. 1 vol. folio (1841), cloth *Price 44s.* Or, 2 vols. royal 8vo cloth. *Price 36s.*

ROTULI DE LIBERATE AC DE MISIS ET PRÆSTITIS, Regnante Johanne. *Edited by* THOMAS DUFFUS HARDY, Esq. 1 vol. royal 8vo (1844), cloth *Price 6s.*

THE GREAT ROLLS OF THE PIPE FOR THE SECOND, THIRD, AND FOURTH YEARS OF THE REIGN OF KING HENRY THE SECOND, 1155—1158. *Edited by* the Rev. JOSEPH HUNTER 1 vol. royal 8vo (1844), cloth. *Price 4s 6d.*

THE GREAT ROLL OF THE PIPE FOR THE FIRST YEAR OF THE REIGN OF KING RICHARD THE FIRST, 1189—1190. *Edited by* the Rev. JOSEPH HUNTER. 1 vol. royal 8vo. (1844), cloth. *Price 6s.*

DOCUMENTS ILLUSTRATIVE OF ENGLISH HISTORY in the 13th and 14th centuries, selected from the Records of the Department of the Queen's Remembrancer in the Exchequer. *Edited by* HENRY COLE, Esq. 1 vol. tcp. folio (1844), cloth. *Price 45s. 6d.*

MODUS TENENDI PARLIAMENTUM. An Ancient Treatise on the Mode of holding the Parliament in England. *Edited by* THOMAS DUFFUS HARDY, Esq. 1 vol. 8vo. (1846), cloth. *Price 2s 6d*

MONUMENTA HISTORICA BRITANNICA, or, Materials for the History of Britain from the earliest period. Vol. 1, extending to the Norman Conquest. Prepared, and illustrated with Notes, by the late HENRY PETRIE, Esq., F.S A , Keeper of the Records in the Tower of London, assisted by the Rev. JOHN SHARPE, Rector of Castle Eaton, Wilts Finally completed for publication, and with an Introduction, by THOMAS DUFFUS HARDY, Esq., Assistant Keeper of Records. (Printed by command of Her Majesty.) Folio (1848). *Price 42s.*

REGISTRUM MAGNI SIGILII REGUM SCOTORUM in Archivis Publicis asservatum 1306—1424 *Edited by* THOMAS THOMSON, Esq Folio (1814). *Price 15s.*

THE ACTS OF THE PARLIAMENTS OF SCOTLAND. 11 vols. folio (1814—1844). Vol. I. *Edited by* THOMAS THOMSON and COSMO INNES, Esqis. *Price 42s.* Also, Vols. 4, 7, 8, 9, 10, and 11 , *price 10s. 6d. each.*

THE ACTS OF THE LORDS AUDITORS OF CAUSES AND COMPLAINTS (ACTA DOMINORUM AUDITORUM). 1466—1494. *Edited by* THOMAS THOMSON, Esq Folio (1839) *Price 10s 6d*

THE ACTS OF THE LORDS OF COUNCIL IN CIVIL CAUSES (ACTA DOMINORUM CONCILII) 1478—1495 *Edited by* THOMAS THOMSON, Esq. Folio (1839). *Price 10s. 6d.*

ISSUE ROLL OF THOMAS DE BRANTINGHAM, Bishop of Exeter, Lord High Treasurer of England, containing Payments out of His Majesty's Revenue, 44 Edward III , 1370. *Edited by* FREDERICK DEVON, Esq. 1 vol. 4to. (1835), cloth. *Price 35s.* Or, royal 8vo. cloth. *Price 25s.*

ISSUES OF THE EXCHEQUER, containing similar matter to the above ; James I. , extracted from the Pell Records. *Edited by* FREDERICK DEVON, Esq. 1 vol. 4to (1836), cloth *Price 30s.* Or, royal 8vo. cloth. *Price 21s*

ISSUES OF THE EXCHEQUER, containing similar matter to the above; Henry III.—Henry VI. ; extracted from the Pell Records. *Edited by* FREDERICK DEVON, Esq. 1 vol. 4to. (1837), cloth *Price 40s.* Or, royal 8vo. cloth. *Price 30s.*

HANDBOOK TO THE PUBLIC RECORDS. *By* F. S THOMAS, Esq , Secretary of the Public Record Office. 1 vol. royal 8vo. (1853), cloth. *Price 12s.*

HISTORICAL NOTES RELATIVE TO THE HISTORY OF ENGLAND ; from the Accession of Henry VIII. to the Death of Queen Anne (1509—1714). Designed as a Book of instant Reference for ascertaining the Dates of Events mentioned in History and Manuscripts. The Name of every Person and Event mentioned in History within the above period is placed in Alphabetical and Chronological Order, and the Authority whence taken is given in each case, whether from Printed History or from Manuscripts. *By* F. S. THOMAS, Esq. 3 vols. 8vo. (1856), cloth. *Price 40s.*

STATE PAPERS, DURING THE REIGN OF HENRY THE EIGHTH : with Indices of Persons and Places. 11 vols., 4to. (1830—1852), cloth. *Price 5l. 15s. 6d.* , or separately, *price 10s 6d.* each.

Vol I.—Domestic Correspondence.
Vols. II. & III.—Correspondence relating to Ireland.
Vols. IV. & V.—Correspondence relating to Scotland
Vols. VI. to XI.—Correspondence between England and Foreign Courts.

WORKS PUBLISHED IN PHOTOZINCOGRAPHY.

DOMESDAY BOOK, or the GREAT SURVEY OF ENGLAND OF WILLIAM THE CONQUEROR, 1086, fac-simile of the part relating to each county, separately (with a few exceptions of double counties). Photozincographed, by Her Majesty's Command, at the Ordnance Survey Office, Southampton, Colonel SIR HENRY JAMES, R.E., F.R.S., &c., Director. 35 parts, imperial quarto and demy quarto (1861–1863) boards. *Price 4s. 6d.* to 1*l.* 1*s.* each part, according to size, or, bound in 2 vols., 18*l.*

This important and unique survey of the greater portion of England* is the oldest and most valuable record in the national archives It was commenced about the year 1084 and finished in 1086. Its compilation was determined upon at Gloucester by William the Conqueror, in council, in order that he might know what was due to him, in the way of tax, from his subjects, and that each at the same time might know what he had to pay It was compiled as much for their protection as for the benefit of the sovereign The nobility and people had been grievously distressed at the time by the king bringing over large numbers of French and Bretons, and quartering them on his subjects, "each accord-" ing to the measure of his land," for the purpose of resisting the invasion of Cnut, King of Denmark, which was apprehended. The commissioners appointed to make the survey were to inquire the name of each place, who held it in the time of King Edward the Confessor, the present possessor, how many hides were in the manor, how many ploughs were in demesne, how many homagers, how many villeins, how many cottars, how many serving men, how many free tenants, how many tenants in soccage, how much wood, meadow, and pasture; the number of mills and fish-ponds, what had been added or taken away from the place, what was the gross value in the time of Edward the Confessor, the present value, and how much each free man or soc-man had, and whether any advance could be made in the value Thus could be ascertained who held the estate in the time of King Edward, who then held it, its value in the time of the late king; and its value as it stood at the formation of the survey So minute was the survey, that the writer of the contemporary portion of the Saxon Chronicle records, with some asperity—"So very narrowly he caused it to be " traced out, that there was not a single hide, nor one virgate of land, nor even, " it is shame to tell, though it seemed to him no shame to do, an ox, nor a cow, " nor a swine was left, that was not set down."

Domesday Survey is in two parts or volumes The first, in folio, contains the counties of Bedford, Berks, Bucks, Cambridge, Chester and Lancaster, Cornwall, Derby, Devon, Dorset, Gloucester, Hants, Hereford, Herts, Huntingdon, Kent, Leicester and Rutland, Lincoln, Middlesex, Northampton, Nottingham, Oxford, Salop, Somerset, Stafford, Surrey, Sussex, Warwick, Wilts, Worcester, and York The second volume, in quarto, contains the counties of Essex, Norfolk, and Suffolk

Domesday Book was printed *verbatim et literatim* during the last century, in consequence of an address of the House of Lords to King George III in 1767 It was not, however, commenced until 1773, and was completed early in 1783 In 1860, Her Majesty's Government, with the concurrence of the Master of the Rolls, determined to apply the art of photozincography to the production of a fac-simile of Domesday Book, under the superintendence of Colonel Sir Henry James, R.E, director of the Ordnance Survey, Southampton The fac-simile was completed in 1863.

---

* For some reason left unexplained, many parts were left unsurveyed, Northumberland, Cumberland, Westmoreland, and Durham, are not described in the survey, nor does Lancashire appear under its proper name, but Furness, and the northern part of Lancashire, as well as the south of Westmoreland, with a part of Cumberland, are included within the West Riding of Yorkshire That part of Lancashire which lies between the Ribble and Mersey, and which at the time of the survey comprehended 688 manors, is joined to Cheshire Part of Rutland is described in the counties of Northampton and Lincoln.

FAC-SIMILES of NATIONAL MANUSCRIPTS, from WILLIAM THE CONQUEROR to QUEEN ANNE, selected under the direction of the Master of the Rolls, and Photozincographed, by Command of Her Majesty, by Colonel SIR HENRY JAMES, R E, Director of the Ordnance Survey. Price, each part, double foolscap folio, 1*l*. 1*s*.

Part I, with translations and notes (William the Conqueror to Henry VII), 1865.

Part II (Henry VIII. and Edward VI.), 1866.

Part III. (Mary and Elizabeth), 1867.

Part IV. (James I. to Anne), 1868.

The first Part extends from William the Conqueror to Henry VII, and contains autographs of the kings of England, as well as of many other illustrious personages famous in history, and some interesting charters, letters patent, and state papers The second Part, for the reigns of Henry VIII and Edward VI, consists principally of holograph letters and autographs of kings, princes, statesmen, and other persons of great historical interest, who lived during those reigns The third Part contains similar documents for the reigns of Mary and Elizabeth, including a signed bill of Lady Jane Grey The fourth Part concludes the series, and comprises a number of documents taken from the originals belonging to the Constable of the Tower of London, also several records illustrative of the Gunpowder Plot, and a woodcut containing portraits of Mary Queen of Scots and James VI, circulated by their adherents in England, 1580-3

Public Record Office,
July 1869.

Lightning Source UK Ltd.
Milton Keynes UK
UKHW020559210619

344772UK00003B/135/P